A GRAMMAR OF AKKADIAN

Second Edition

HARVARD SEMITIC MUSEUM PUBLICATIONS

Lawrence E. Stager, General Editor
Michael D. Coogan, Director of Publications

HARVARD SEMITIC STUDIES

Jo Ann Hackett and John Huehnergard, editors

Syriac Manuscripts: A Catalogue	Moshe H. Goshen-Gottstein
Introduction to Classical Ethiopic	Thomas O. Lambdin
The Songs of the Sabbath Sacrifice	Carol Newsom
Non-Canonical Psalms from Qumran: A Pseudepigraphic Collection	Eileen M. Schuller
An Exodus Scroll from Qumran	Judith E. Sanderson
You Shall Have No Other Gods	Jeffrey H. Tigay
Ugaritic Vocabulary in Syllabic Transcription	John Huehnergard
The Scholarship of William Foxwell Albright	Gus Van Beek
Features of the Eschatology of IV Ezra	Michael E. Stone
Studies in Neo-Aramaic	Wolfhart Heinrichs, Editor
Lingering over Words: Studies in Ancient Near Eastern Literature in Honor of William L. Moran	Tzvi Abusch, John Huehnergard, Piotr Steinkeller, Editors
A Grammar of the Palestinian Targum Fragments from the Cairo Genizah	Steven E. Fassberg
The Origins and Development of the Waw-Consecutive: Northwest Semitic Evidence from Ugaritic to Qumran	Mark S. Smith
Amurru Akkadian: A Linguistic Study, Volume I	Shlomo Izre'el
Amurru Akkadian: A Linguistic Study, Volume II	Shlomo Izre'el
The Installation of Baal's High Priestess at Emar	Daniel E. Fleming
The Development of the Arabic Scripts	Beatrice Gruendler
The Archaeology of Israelite Samaria: Early Iron Age through the Ninth Century BCE	Ron Tappy
A Grammar of Akkadian (2nd ed.)	John Huehnergard
Key to A Grammar of Akkadian *(2nd ed.)*	John Huehnergard
Akkadian Loanwords in Biblical Hebrew	Paul V. Mankowski
Adam in Myth and History: Ancient Israelite Perspectives on the Primal Human	Dexter E. Callender Jr.
West Semitic Vocabulary in the Akkadian Texts from Emar	Eugen J. Pentiuc
The Archaeology of Israelite Samaria, vol. II: The Eighth Century BCE	Ron E. Tappy
Leaves from an Epigrapher's Notebook: Collected Papers in Hebrew and West Semitic Palaeography and Epigraphy	Frank Moore Cross
Semitic Noun Patterns	Joshua Fox
Eighth-Century Iraqi Grammar: A Critical Exploration of pre-Ḫalīlian Arabic Linguistics	Rafael Talmon
Amarna Studies: Collected Essays	William L. Moran
Narrative Structure and Discourse Constellations: An Analysis of Clause Function in Biblical Hebrew Prose	Roy L. Heller
The Modal System of Old Babylonian	Eran Cohen
Studies in Semitic Grammaticalization	Aaron D. Rubin

A GRAMMAR OF AKKADIAN

Second Edition

by

John Huehnergard

EISENBRAUNS
Winona Lake, Indiana
2005

A GRAMMAR OF AKKADIAN

by

John Huehnergard

2nd edition, 2005

Printed in the United States of America

The Akkadian font used to print Akkadian signs in this work is available from
Linguist's Software, Inc., PO Box 580, Edmonds, WA 98020-0580 USA
(425) 775-1130 www.linguistsoftware.com

Library of Congress Cataloging-in-Publication Data

Huehnergard, John
A grammar of Akkadian / by John Huehnergard. — 2nd ed.
p. cm. — (Harvard Semitic studies ; no. 45)
Includes index.
ISBN 1-57506-922-9 (hardback : alk. paper)
1. Akkadian language—Grammar. I. Title. II. Series.
PJ3251.H84 2005
492′.182421—dc22

2005020386

The paper used in this publication meets the minimum requirements of the American National Standard for Information Sciences—Permanence of Paper for Printed Library Materials, ANSI Z39.48-1984.⊗™

for

William L. Moran

at seventy-five

the best teacher,
the dearest friend

Preface to the First Edition

Over the years since its earliest incarnation nearly two decades ago, the present textbook has had the benefit of input from many students and scholars of Akkadian, and it is a sincere pleasure to acknowledge here those individuals who gave so much of their time to improve it.

The first thanks must be to the many students who have used this book in its various pre-publication manifestations, in my own classes at Columbia, Johns Hopkins, and Harvard, and in the classes of other instructors at Arizona, Berkeley, Boston, Brandeis, Chicago, Emory, Harvard, Johns Hopkins, Michigan, North Carolina, SUNY, and elsewhere. For their many valuable suggestions for improving the volume and for their patience with the sometimes unclear explanations, nonsensical exercises, and bewildering typos of the earlier versions, these intrepid students have my heart-felt thanks.

Many individuals took the time to send me lists of corrections and suggestions. Of these Matthew W. Stolper and Daniel A. Foxvog must be singled out for their painstaking reading of earlier drafts and for the pages and pages of helpful criticism they gave. Others who provided lists of improvements are Esther Flueckiger-Hawker, Matthias Henze, Sara Chute Hsiang (and the rest of Prof. Anne D. Kilmer's class of 1993–94), Jan Jackson, Eugene C. McAfee, P. Kyle McCarter, Judith H. Newman, Neal H. Walls, Chris Woods, and Norman Yoffee. My thanks to these colleagues for saving me from many errors.

I am also grateful to a number of colleagues for taking the time to discuss, in person or in writing, issues in the presentation of Akkadian grammar in an introductory textbook: Walter R. Bodine, Steven W. Cole, Jerrold S. Cooper, W. Randall Garr, Brigitte Groneberg, Thomas O. Lambdin, Piotr Michalowski, William L. Moran, Jack M. Sasson, Daniel C. Snell, Piotr Steinkeller, Wheeler M. Thackston, Raymond Westbrook, Paul E. Zimansky, and the late Thorkild Jacobsen. None of these kind individuals should, of course, be held responsible for the final product.

Rachel Rockenmacher has my thanks for typing lessons of an earlier draft onto disk, and for doing much of the work of preparing the English–Akkadian word list.

Many aspects of the present textbook are modeled on Thomas O.

Lambdin's exemplary introductory grammars of Hebrew, Ethiopic, and Coptic. In addition, I have learned much and incorporated many ideas from the three earlier textbooks of Akkadian that have appeared in English: Richard Caplice, *Introduction to Akkadian* (3rd ed., 1988); David Marcus, *A Manual of Akkadian* (1978); Kaspar K. Riemschneider, *An Akkadian Grammar* (translated by T. Caldwell et al.; 3rd ed., 1977). I must also express my sincere admiration for the fundamental work on Akkadian grammar that Wolfram von Soden has carried out over the past sixty years; his reference grammar, his dictionary, his sign list, and his many articles have assured a secure basis for the study of Akkadian.

I owe a special debt of gratitude to Kathryn Slanski, who devoted several hundred hours to working on this book: drawing most of the cuneiform signs in the book, compiling much of the Akkadian–English glossary, and looking after many details in the preparation of the volume. Her reading of previous drafts and her use of them in teaching several introductory Akkadian classes at Harvard resulted in many improvements, as did our many hours of discussion on matters of grammar and formatting. Her steadfast friendship and her gentle humor have also helped me see this book to its completion. I acknowledge here a grant from Consortium for Language Teaching and Learning (New Haven, Ct.), which allowed me to remunerate Ms. Slanski for a part of the time she devoted to this project.

For permission to include copies of cuneiform texts I am grateful to Béatrice André-Salvini of the Musée du Louvre (Paris), to P. Pasquale Puca of Editrice Pontificio Istituto Biblico (Rome), to the Trustees of the British Museum (London), to Harrassowitz Verlag (Wiesbaden), and to Éditions Dalloz-Sirey (Paris).

As always I am profoundly indebted to Jo Ann Hackett, who has had to put up with this book from the beginning. Her unfailing encouragement and support, her willingness to discuss, at all hours, matters from the smallest detail of Akkadian grammar to the broadest problems of computer formatting, are an unending source of wonder to me.

This book is dedicated to Professor William L. Moran, my beloved mentor and friend, who taught me Akkadian, and so much more. For half my life now Bill has exemplified for me the true scholar: a person of perfect integrity and constant modesty, pursuing learning for the sheer joy of it.

Carlisle, Mass.
August 11, 1996

On the Second Edition

A few typographical errors and other problems were corrected in the second and third printings of this textbook. In the present version, considerably more revisions have been made. Again most of the changes are minor and cosmetic, although in a few instances I have made more substantial changes in the presentation of the grammar, and I have incorporated some of the findings of scholarship on Akkadian grammar in the past decade, and added references to research and learning tools that have appeared recently. The supplementary reading, Gilgameš tablet II, has been revised in accordance with Andrew George's magnificent new critical edition of the epic (2003). Despite the large number of revisions, the pagination of the first edition has been retained (with minor exceptions), so that copies of both editions may be used side-by-side in the classroom.

The Old Babylonian cuneiform signs in this edition have been scanned from three sign lists: Harper (1904) for the lapidary, and Ranke (1906) and Goetze (1947a) for the cursive. The Neo-Assyrian font is LaserAkkadian™ (for Macintosh) from Linguist's Software, Inc.

Once again it is my great pleasure to thank the many individuals who generously took the time to send corrections and other suggestions for improvement: Tzvi Abusch, Elitzur Bar-Asher, Karljürgen Feuerheim, Sergei Lyosov, Gianni Marchesi, Jennie Myers, Aaron Rubin, Gonzalo Rubio, Michael Seleznev, Brad Spencer, Matthew Tarazi, Benjamin Thomas, and Avi Winitzer. Among the reviewers of the first edition I am especially grateful for their remarks and suggestions to D. Charpin, W. Farber, B. Groneberg, N.J.C. Kouwenberg, E. Robson, M.P. Streck, and N. Wasserman. I am also grateful to Michael Coogan and Jim Eisenbraun for their wise advice and their patience in seeing this revision through to completion, and to Benjamin Studevent-Hickman, who provided corrections and improvements, and scanned and formatted the cuneiform texts and signs. Finally, my friend Michael Patrick O'Connor, who has used the book several times in his Akkadian classes at the Catholic University of America, in addition to reporting many typos, offered scores of thoughtful proposals for improving the pedagogical value of the work, many of which I was able to include in this edition; my sincere thanks to him for the many hours he devoted to making the book more useful.

Carlisle, Mass.
July, 2005

CONTENTS

Preface vi

Abbreviations xvii

Introduction

The Akkadian Language xxi
Dialects of Akkadian xxiii
Akkadian and Sumerian xxv
Old Babylonian xxvi
Text Genres xxvi
About This Book xxvii
Research Tools xxix
Selected Bibliography xxxii

1.1 The Sounds of Akkadian 1
1.2 Syllabification 3
1.3 Stress (Accent) 3
Exercises 4

2.1 Noun Declension 6
2.2 Prepositions 10
2.3 The Determinative Pronoun *ša* 10
2.4 Independent Personal Pronouns 11
2.5 Verbless Sentences 12
Exercises 12

3.1 The Semantic Root 15
3.2 Verb Morphology: Introductory Considerations 16
3.3 The G Infinitive: Form and Meaning 17
3.4 Verb Semantics: General Comments 18
3.5 The G Preterite: Form and Meaning 18
3.6 Word Order and Agreement in Verbal Clauses 19
Exercises 20

4.1 Vowel Syncope 24
4.2 The Attributive Adjective: Declension and Agreement 24
4.3 The G Verbal Adjective 25
4.4 The Substantivization of Adjectives 27
4.5 The Negative Adverb *ul(a)* 28
Exercises 28

5.1 Assimilation of *n* 32
5.2 Weak Verbs 32
5.3 The G Infinitive, Preterite, and Verbal Adjective: Verbs I–*n* 33
5.4 Sound Changes before the Feminine Marker *t* 33
5.5 Verbs with Two Accusatives 34
5.6 Prepositions with Verbs 35
Exercises 35

6.1 Vowel Changes due to Consonant Loss 38
6.2 Denominative Adjectives 40
6.3 Demonstrative Adjectives and Pronouns 41
Exercises 42

7.1 The Sound Change *i* › *e* 45
7.2 Vowel Harmony (*a* › *e*) 45
7.3 The G Infinitive, Preterite, and Verbal Adjective: Verbs III–weak 46
7.4 The Coordinators *-ma, u,* and *ū (lū)* 49
7.5 Asyndeton 51
Exercises 51

8.1 The G Infinitive, Preterite, and Verbal Adjective: Verbs I–ʾ (I–*a* and I–*e*); *alākum* 54
8.2 The Genitive Chain 55
8.3 The Bound Form of the Noun 57
Exercises 63

9.1 The G Infinitive, Preterite, and Verbal Adjective: Verbs II–weak 67
9.2 The Writing System 68
Exercises 74

10.1 The G Infinitive, Preterite, and Verbal Adjective: Verbs I–*w* 79
10.2 The Verb *babālum* 79
10.3 Pronominal Suffixes on Prepositions 79
10.4 Double-Duty Objects 80
Exercises 80

11.1 The Noun with Possessive Pronominal Suffixes 84
11.2 Apposition 91
11.3 The Quantifier *kalûm* 92
Exercises 92

12.1 The G Durative: Sound Verbs; Verbs I–*n*; Verbs III–weak 96
12.2 The Meaning of the Durative 98
12.3 Prepositional Phrases 99
12.4 Compound Noun Phrases 101
Exercises 102

13.1 The G Durative: Verbs I–ʾ (I–*a* and I–*e*); *alākum* 106
13.2 Logograms 107
13.3 Determinatives 111
13.4 Personal Names 112
13.5 Old Babylonian Contracts 113
Exercises 114

14.1 The G Durative: Verbs II–weak 121
14.2 Interrogative Words 122
14.3 Indefinite Pronouns and Indefinite Adjective 123
14.4 The Abstract Suffix -*ūt* 124
14.5 Verbal Hendiadys 125
Exercises 126

15.1 The G Durative: Verbs I–*w* 132
15.2 The Ventive 133
15.3 Indefinite or Unspecified Subject 135
15.4 Direct Speech 135
Exercises 137

16.1 The G Imperative 142
16.2 The Precative 144
16.3 Negative Commands and Wishes (Prohibitive and Vetitive) 146
16.4 The Use of Injunctive Forms to Express Purpose 147
Exercises 148

17.1 The G Perfect: Sound Verbs; Verbs I–*n*; Verbs III–weak 155
17.2 The Meaning of the Perfect 157
17.3 Conditional Sentences 159
17.4 The "Laws of Ḫammurapi" 160
Exercises 162

18.1 The G Perfect: Verbs I–ʾ (I–*a* and I–*e*); *alākum* 168
18.2 Object Pronominal Suffixes on the Verb 169
18.3 The Adverbial Use of the Accusative 172
18.4 Morphographemic Writings 173
Exercises 174

19.1 The G Perfect: Verbs II–weak; Verbs I–*w* 182
19.2 The Subordination Marker -*u* 183
19.3 Relative Clauses 185
Exercises 189

20.1 The G Participle 195
20.2 The Particularizing Suffix -*ān* 198
20.3 Irregular Masculine Plurals 198
20.4 Negation 199
Exercises 199

21.1 Summary of the G Stem 205
21.2 *E*–type Verbs 205
21.3 Doubly Weak Verbs 206
21.4 The Writing of ʾ 209
21.5 Topicalization by Preposing 211
Exercises 213

22.1 The Predicative Construction 219
22.2 Injunctions in Verbless Clauses 223
22.3 Omen Texts 224
Exercises 225

23.1 The Absolute Form of the Noun 234
23.2 Numbers 235
23.3 The Expression of the Vocative 242
Exercises 243

24.1 Derived Verbs 252
24.2 The D Stem: Sound Verbs; Verbs I–*n*; Verbs III–weak 253
24.3 The Meaning of the D Stem 256
24.4 Features of Late OB Texts 258
24.5 Old Babylonian Letters 260
Exercises 261

25.1 The D Stem: Verbs I–ʾ (I–*a* and I–*e*); Verbs I–*w* 270
25.2 The Independent Pronouns: Remaining Forms 272

25.3 The Independent Possessive Adjectives 273
Exercises 274

26.1 The Verbs *edûm* and *išûm* 282
26.2 Subordinate Clauses 283
Exercises 288

27.1 The Š Stem: Sound Verbs; Verbs I–*n*; Verbs III–weak 297
27.2 The Meaning of the Š Stem 299
27.3 The Expression of the Comparative and the Superlative 302
Exercises 302

28.1 The Š Stem: Verbs I–ʾ (I–*a* and I–*e*); Verbs I–*w* 309
28.2 The Terminative-adverbial Ending *-iš* 311
28.3 The Locative-adverbial Ending *-um* 312
28.4 Adverbs 313
Exercises 314

29.1 Verbs II–weak: the D and Š Stems 323
29.2 Non-coordinating *-ma* 325
29.3 The Particle *lū* 326
29.4 Old Babylonian Letters from Mari 326
Exercises 327

30.1 The Syntax of the Infinitive 337
30.2 Old Babylonian Literary Diction 346
30.3 Royal Inscriptions 348
Exercises 348

31.1 The N Stem: Sound Verbs; Verbs I–*n*; Verbs III–weak 358
31.2 The Meaning of the N Stem 361
31.3 The Genitive: Constructions and Functions 363
Exercises 365

32.1 The N Stem: Verbs I–ʾ (I–*a*, I–*e*); Verbs I–*w*; Verbs II–weak 377
32.2 Noun Patterns 378
32.3 Sumerian Loanwords 380
Exercises 381

33.1 The Gt Stem 390
33.2 The Transitive *parsāku* Construction 393
33.3 Akkadian Poetry 395
33.4 Old Babylonian Hymns and Prayers 397
Exercises 398

34.1 The Gtn Stem 409
34.2 The Partitive Use of *ina* 412
Exercises 412

35.1 The Dt Stem 422
35.2 The Dtn Stem 424
35.3 Interrogative Sentences 425
Exercises 425

36.1 The Št Stems 433
36.2 The Štn Stem 436
36.3 Oaths 436
Exercises 438

37.1 The Ntn Stem 450
37.2 The Irregular Verb *izuzzum* 450
Exercises 452

38.1 Quadriradical Verbs 460
38.2 Special Features of Geminate Verbs 461
38.3 Rare Stems: ŠD; Nt; R; others 462
38.4 Old Babylonian Myths and Epics 465
Exercises 466

Supplementary Reading: OB Gilgamesh, tablet II 475

Glossaries

Akkadian Words 485
Logograms 532
Determinatives 537
English–Akkadian Word List 538

Sign List 563

Alphabetical Cross-Index of Sign Values 575

Appendices

A. Systems of Dating 577
B. Measures 579
C. Historical Akkadian Phonology 586
D. Standard Babylonian 595
E. Assyrian Phonology and Morphology 599

Paradigms

1. Personal Pronouns: Independent Forms 606
2. Personal Pronouns: Suffixes on Nouns, Prepositions, Verbs 606
3. Personal Pronouns: Independent Possessive Adjectives 606

4a. Nouns and Adjectives: Basic Declension 607
4b. Nouns and Adjectives: Final-weak Forms 607
5. Adjectives: Attributive Forms 607
6. Nouns and Adjectives: Bound and Suffixal Forms 608

Sigla for the Derived Stems in the Main Dictionaries 610

7a. Sound Verbs: Stem Forms 611
7b. Sound Verbs: Finite Forms (G,N,D,Š) 612
7c. Sound Verbs: Non-Finite Forms (G,N,D,Š) 614
8a. Verbs I–*a* (I–$^{\supset}{}_{1-2}$) including *alākum*: Stem Forms 616
8b. Verbs I–*a* (I–$^{\supset}{}_{1-2}$) including *alākum*: Finite Forms (G) 617
9a. Verbs I–*e* (I–$^{\supset}{}_{3-4}$ and I–*y*): Stem Forms 618
9b. Verbs I–*e* (I–$^{\supset}{}_{3-4}$ and I–*y*): Finite Forms (G) 619
10a. Verbs I–*n*: Stem Forms 620
10b. Verbs I–*n*: Finite Forms (G) 621
11a. Verbs I–*w*: Stem Forms 622
11b. Verbs I–*w*: Finite Forms (G) 623
12a. Verbs II–weak: Stem Forms 624
12b. Verbs II–weak: Finite Forms (G,D) 625
13a. Verbs III–weak: Stem Forms 626
13b. Verbs III–weak: Finite Forms (G) 628
13c. Verbs III–weak: Non-Finite Forms (G) 629
13d. Verbs III–weak: Finite Forms (N) 630
13e. Verbs III–weak: Non-Finite Forms (N) 631
13f. Verbs III–weak: Finite Forms (D,Š) 632
13g. Verbs III–weak: Non-Finite Forms (D,Š) 633
14. Doubly Weak Verbs: Stem Forms 634
15. Quadriradical Verbs: Stem Forms 636
16. The Verb with the Ventive 637
17. The Verb with Object Suffixes 638

Index of Texts 639
Index of Grammatical Forms and Subjects 644

ABBREVIATIONS

I. Bibliographical

AbB	*Altbabylonische Briefe*; vol. 1,4,5,7 see Bibliography under Kraus; vol. 2,3,6 see under Frankena; vol. 8 see under Cagni; vol. 11 see under Stol; vol. 12 see under van Soldt
ABZ^4	R. Borger, *Assyrisch-Babylonische Zeichenliste*, 4th ed.
AfO	*Archiv für Orientforschung*
AHw	W. von Soden, *Akkadisches Handwörterbuch*
ANET	J. Pritchard, ed., *Ancient Near Eastern Texts*
ARM(T)	*Archives royales de Mari (Transcriptions)*; vol. 2 see Bibliography under Jean; vol. 4,10 see under Dossin; 26 see under Durand
AoF	*Altorientalische Forschungen*
ArOr	*Archiv Orientální*
AS^4	W. von Soden and W. Röllig, *Das akkadische Syllabar*, 4th ed.
AuOr	*Aula Orientalis*
BE	The Babylonian Expedition of the University of Pennsylvania, Series A: Cuneiform Texts; vol. 6/1 see Bibliography under Ranke
BIN	Babylonian Inscriptions in the Collection of J.B. Nies
BiOr	*Bibliotheca Orientalis*
BM	British Museum tablet number
CAD	*The Assyrian Dictionary of the University of Chicago*
CH	Code of Ḫammurapi; see Bibliography under Bergmann
CT	Cuneiform Texts from Babylonian Tablets in the British Museum; vol. 2,4,6,8 see Bibliography under Pinches; vol. 29 see under King; vol. 43 see under Figulla; vol. 52 see under Walker
Edzard, *Tell ed-Dēr*	see Edzard 1970a in Bibliography
FM	Fitzwilliam Museum (Cambridge) tablet number
GAG	W. von Soden, *Grundriss der akkadischen Grammatik*
HKL	R. Borger, *Handbuch der Keilschriftliteratur*
IOS	*Israel Oriental Studies*
Iraq	*Iraq* (journal of the British School of Archaeology in Iraq)
JCS	*Journal of Cuneiform Studies*
JEOL	*Jaarbericht Ex Oriente Lux*
JESHO	*Journal of the Economic and Social History of the Orient*

Jeyes, *OB Extisp.*	see Jeyes 1989 in Bibliography
JNES	*Journal of Near Eastern Studies*
LAA	E. Reiner, *A Linguistic Analysis of Akkadian*
LIH	L.W. King, *The Letters and Inscriptions of Ḫammurabi*
MAH	Museum of Art and History (Geneva) tablet number
MEA[6]	R. Labat and F. Malbran-Labat, *Manuel d'épigraphie akkadienne*, 6th ed.
Meissner, *BAP*	see Meissner 1893 in Bibliography
NABU	*Nouvelles assyriologiques brèves et utilitaires*
OECT	Oxford Editions of Cuneiform Texts; vol. 3 see under Driver
OLZ	*Orientalistische Literaturzeitung*
Or.	*Orientalia (Nova series)*
OrAnt	*Oriens Antiquus*
PBS	Publications of the Babylonian Section of the Museum of the University of Pennsylvania; vol. 7 see Bibliography under Ungnad; vol. 8/2 see under Chiera
RA	*Revue d'assyriologie et d'archéologie orientale*
RGTC	*Répertoire géographique des textes cunéiformes*
RIME	Royal Inscriptions of Mesopotamia, Early Periods; vol. 4 see Bibliography under Frayne
RLA	*Reallexikon der Assyriologie*
RSO	*Rivista degli studi orientali*
Scheil, *SFS*	see Scheil 1902 in Bibliography
Schorr, *VAB* 5	see Schorr 1913 in Bibliography
SEL	*Studi epigrafici e linguistici*
StOr	Studia Orientalia (Helsinki)
Szlechter, *Tablettes*	see Szlechter 1958 in Bibliography
Szlechter, *TJA*	see Szlechter 1963 in Bibliography
TCL	Textes cunéiformes du Louvre; vol. 1,7 see Bibliography under Thureau-Dangin
TIM	Texts in the Iraq Museum; vol. 2 see Bibliography under van Dijk; vol. 7 see Edzard 1970b
TLB	Tabulae cuneiformes a F.M.Th. de Liagre Böhl collectae; vol. 4 see Frankena 1965 in Bibliography

UCP	University of California Publications in Semitic Philology; vol. 9/4 see Bibliography under Lutz
UET	Ur Excavations, Texts; vol. 6/2 see Bibliography under Gadd–Kramer
UF	*Ugarit-Forschungen*
UMM	University Museum of Manchester tablet number
Ungnad, *Babylonische Briefe*	see Ungnad 1914 in Bibliography
VAB	Vorderasiatische Bibliothek; vol. 5 see Bibliography under Schorr; vol. 6 see Ungnad 1914
VAS	Vorderasiatische Schriftdenkmäler der Königlichen Museen zu Berlin; vol. 7,8 see Ungnad 1909 in Bibliography; vol. 16 see under Schroeder
Waterman, *Bus.Doc.*	see Waterman 1916 in Bibliography
WO	*Die Welt des Orients*
WZKM	*Wiener Zeitschrift für die Kunde des Morgenlandes*
YOS	Yale Oriental Series; vol. 10 see Goetze 1947a in Bibliography
ZA	*Zeitschrift für Assyriologie und vorderasiatische Archäologie*

II. Other Abbreviations and Conventions

abs.	absolute
acc(.)	accusative
adj.	adjective, adjectival
adv.	adverb(ial)
Akk.	Akkadian
App.	Appendix
bnd.	bound (form)
c	common (gender)
C	(any) consonant
ca.	circa (about)
cf.	compare
conj.	conjunction
dat.	dative
denom.	denominative
det.	determinative
DN	divine name
du(.)	dual
Dur.	Durative
esp.	especially
ext.	extispicy
f(.), fem.	feminine
fp	feminine plural
fs	feminine singular
gen(.)	genitive
GN	geographical name
Im(p)v.	Imperative
indef.	indefinite
Inf(in).	Infinitive
interrog.	interrogative
intr.	intransitive
LB	Late Babylonian
lex.	lexical
log.	logogram, logographic
lw.	loanword
m(.)	masculine
MA	Middle Assyrian
masc.	masculine
MB	Middle Babylonian
MN	month name
mp	masculine plural
ms	masculine singular
n.	noun

NA	Neo-Assyrian
NB	Neo-Babylonian
neg.	negation, negative
nom(.)	nominative
OA	Old Assyrian
OAkk	Old Akkadian
OB	Old Babylonian
obl(.)	oblique (case)
obv.	obverse
p(.)	page; plural
Parad.	Paradigm
pass.	passive
Perf.	Perfect
pl.	plural
PN	personal name
Prec.	Precative
prep.	preposition
Pret.	Preterite
Proh(ib).	Prohibitive
pron.	pronoun
Ptcpl.	Participle
r.	reverse
rel.	relative (pron., adj.)
rev.	reverse
RN	royal name
s(.)	singular
SB	Standard Babylonian
sf.	suffix(al)
sg.	singular
s.o.	someone
s.th.	something
suff.	suffix(al)
Sum.	Sumerian
syl.	syllable, syllabic
tr.	transitive
V	(any) vowel
v., vbl.	verb
Vent.	Ventive
Vet.	Vetitive
x	illegible sign
1	first person
2	second person
3	third person
›	becomes, goes to
‹	develops, comes from
*	reconstructed/unattested form
**	ungrammatical form

INTRODUCTION

The Akkadian Language

Akkadian is the language of the Assyrians and Babylonians of ancient Mesopotamia, that is, the region 'between the rivers', the Euphrates and the Tigris (roughly the area of modern Iraq). The name 'Akkadian' is a translation of the ancient speakers' term for their language, *Akkadûm*, which derives from Akkad(e), the name of the still-undiscovered town built about 2300 BCE by king Sargon as his capital. (In both ancient and modern times Akkadian has also been called 'Assyrian' and 'Babylonian', terms that are now generally restricted to the main geographical dialects, which are discussed below.)

Akkadian is the earliest-attested member of the Semitic family of languages. Other Semitic languages include Arabic, Aramaic, Ethiopic, and Hebrew. As the following chart illustrates, Akkadian and Eblaite, the recently-discovered language of the ancient Syrian city of Ebla, comprise East Semitic, while all other members of the family comprise West Semitic.

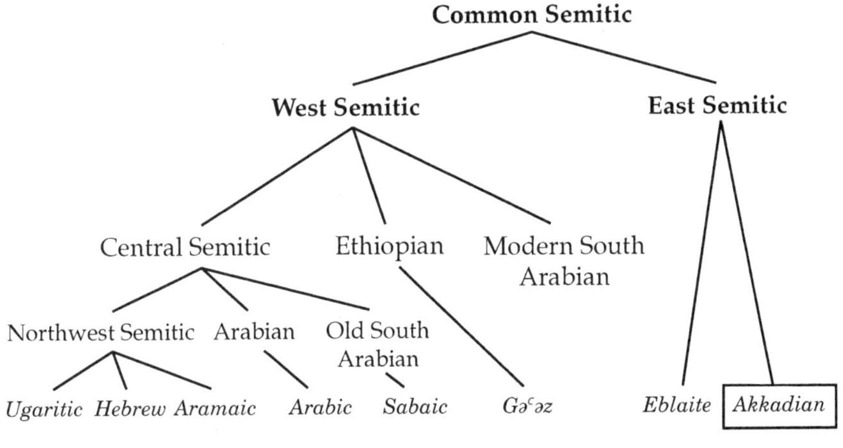

It is not certain when speakers of Akkadian or its linguistic predecessor(s) first arrived in Mesopotamia. The first written evidence of the language is found in names in texts from the 26th century BCE, while connected texts begin to appear in the 24th century. It is also not known when Akkadian ceased to be a spoken language — probably during the mid-first millennium BCE, having been replaced over a number of centuries by Aramaic — but it continued to be used as a written medium of literature and scholarship until the first century CE.

After the demise of Akkadian both the language and its complicated writing system were forgotten for over a millennium and a half. In the 17th century European travelers to the Middle East began to bring home a few clay artifacts with unusual wedge-shaped writing. Attempts at decipherment were aided in the 19th century by the publication of a long trilingual inscription, Akkadian–Old Persian–Elamite. After the simpler Old Persian script was decoded it became possible to tackle the Akkadian version successfully; the Akkadian script was deciphered and the basic elements of the grammar were established by the 1850's. In the past 150 years much scholarship has been devoted to the publication of texts, to the further elucidation of the grammar, and to the preparation of dictionaries. Today the Akkadian language may be said to be well — but by no means completely — understood.

Because Mesopotamian scribes were exceedingly prolific and because they usually wrote on the virtually indestructible medium of clay, vast numbers of the ancient documents have been preserved to posterity. The number of Akkadian texts extant has not been counted, but it is certainly in the hundreds of thousands, and many new texts are discovered in archaeological excavations every year. While many texts have received scholarly publication over the last century and a half, many other texts remain unpublished, awaiting interested scholars in museums around the world.

As was just noted, Akkadian texts were usually written on clay, a material found in great abundance in Mesopotamia. Moist clay was molded into a rectangular tablet and the writing was impressed into the clay with a stylus made of reed. The size of tablets varied from about an inch square to some 18 inches along a side; the most common shape was a rectangle that was longer than it was wide. The reed stylus made wedge-shaped, i.e., **cuneiform**, impressions in the clay. Because the writing system is very cumbersome, modern publications, including this textbook, present elements of Akkadian grammar in transcription; and because the writing system is unquestionably the most difficult aspect of learning Akkadian, it is not introduced here until Lesson 9, by which time the student will have acquired some familiarity with Akkadian forms and structures. (It is worth remembering that ancient

Mesopotamian students were fluent in Akkadian — it was their native tongue — before they began to tackle the writing system.)

Dialects of Akkadian

All languages change over time. English texts of a few centuries ago, such as the writings of Shakespeare, contain spellings, words, phrases, and grammar that are sometimes unfamiliar; the 14th-century writings of Chaucer are more difficult to understand still; and Old English, of the 8th–10th centuries, must be studied almost as a foreign language to be understood by modern speakers of English. When we consider that the recorded history of Akkadian is over twice as long as that of English, we should not be surprised to witness the development of significant chronological variations in Akkadian as well. Further, geographical variations are also evidenced in the texts, particularly between those of Assyria in the north and Babylonia in the south (see further below), but also in many smaller dialect regions. Although these developments arose continuously, so that neat divisions cannot be drawn in actuality, scholars refer nevertheless for the sake of convenience to the following sub-phases, or dialects, of Akkadian, which correspond roughly to periods in Mesopotamian political history (common abbreviations for the dialects are given in parentheses):

Old Akkadian (OAkk), mid-3rd to beginning of 2nd millennium

Old Assyrian (OA)	2000–1500	Old Babylonian (OB)
Middle Assyrian (MA)	1500–1000	Middle Babylonian (MB)
Neo-Assyrian (NA)	1000–600	Neo-Babylonian (NB)
	600–100 CE	Late Babylonian (LB)

These may be reviewed briefly in turn.

The earliest Akkadian texts, to about the beginning of the second millennium, are referred to collectively as **Old Akkadian**. These include documents dating to the reigns of Sargon, Naram-Sin, and other kings of Akkad and the few Akkadian texts from the Ur III period. There are Old Akkadian letters, legal texts, economic dockets, royal inscriptions, and a few literary texts (such as a love incantation).

In the second and first millennia, two major geographical dialects are attested, **Assyrian** in northern Mesopotamia and **Babylonian** in the south. Linguistically these are distinguished by a number of phonological, morphological, and lexical differences. (This textbook presents the grammar of [Old] Babylonian; see Appendix E for major features of Assyrian.) The Assyrian and Babylonian scripts also developed somewhat independently of one another.

Old Assyrian is known from some 15,000 letters and legal and economic documents dating from the mid-20th to the mid-18th century, most of which have been found in Cappodocia (eastern Turkey) at the site of Kanesh (modern Kültepe), although other sites in Anatolia and Assyria have also produced a few similar texts. Most of these documents concern the business activities of Assyrian merchant houses and their trade with outposts in Anatolia.

Middle Assyrian is sparsely attested, although it is known from a variety of genres, including letters, legal and economic texts, and inscriptions of the kings of the nation and early empire of Assyria. There is also a set of harem decrees and, of great interest, 14 tablets containing the Middle Assyrian laws, discovered in the city of Asshur.

Neo-Assyrian is the spoken language of first-millennium Assyria, attested until the downfall of the empire late in the seventh century. There are a great many letters and administrative texts. Many royal inscriptions and scholarly writings are also attested; as in all periods, literary texts exhibit a considerable amount of linguistic influence from the more prestigious Babylonian dialect.

Old Babylonian is the Akkadian of southern Mesopotamia during the period of the first dynasty of Babylon. It is the dialect covered in the present textbook, and is described in detail further below.

Middle Babylonian is the language of texts from the period of the Kassite domination of Babylonia, after the fall of Hammurapi's dynasty to the Hittites in 1595. Like Middle Assyrian, Middle Babylonian is less well represented than the dialects that precede and follow it. It is known from letters, legal texts, economic texts, a few royal inscriptions, and inscribed boundary stones (*kudurru*s).

Already during the Kassite period Old Babylonian had come to be regarded as the classical period of Akkadian language and literature, and scribes in both Babylonia and Assyria attempted to duplicate it in a purely literary (i.e., unspoken) dialect that Assyriologists call **Standard Babylonian** (SB). The scribes' efforts to reproduce the classical language usually had mixed results, as their own language patterns frequently intruded. Standard Babylonian is the dialect in which such important works as *Enūma eliš* and the later, longer version of Gilgamesh are written, indeed, all of the literary texts of the late second and the first millennia, as well as many royal inscriptions. The grammatical features of Standard Babylonian are presented in Appendix D.

Beginning in the Old Babylonian period, but especially in the second half of the second millennium, Akkadian, particularly in its Babylonian form, was used as an international *lingua franca;* Akkadian texts have been found in a great many sites outside Mesopotamia, including Ugarit (Ras Shamra) and Emar (Tell Meskeneh) in modern Syria, Hattusas (modern Boğazköy, the capital of the Hittite empire) and Alalah (Tell Açana) in Turkey, and el-Amarna in Egypt, to name a few. The language of these texts, which was often written by non-native speakers, is termed **Peripheral Akkadian**; the texts vary considerably in their fidelity to the grammar of native Mesopotamian Akkadian and frequently betray the influence of the scribes' own languages.

Neo-Babylonian is the spoken language of southern Mesopotamia until the end of the Assyrian empire, after which the term **Late Babylonian** is used for the final period of texts written in Akkadian. These dialects are attested in large numbers of letters and administrative documents. For literary and monumental texts, Standard Babylonian (see above) was employed.

Akkadian and Sumerian

Akkadian was not the first language to be given written form in Mesopotamia. History's earliest writing appeared in southern Mesopotamia, near the end of the fourth millennium; the language for which this first writing was invented was Sumerian, which was not genetically related to the Semitic languages, or indeed to any other known language. Speakers of Sumerian and speakers of Akkadian coexisted in southern Babylonia for centuries, and the two languages naturally had a significant impact on each other. Thus, many features of Akkadian grammar, from its phonology to its syntax, reflect Sumerian influence, and many Akkadian words are loans from Sumerian. (Conversely many original Akkadian words were borrowed into Sumerian.) And the writing system originally devised for Sumerian was taken over to write the very different Akkadian as well.

Sumerian died out as a spoken language long before Akkadian; the date of its demise is much debated, however, placed variously between the mid-third and the early second millennium. Even after it ceased to be spoken, Sumerian remained a language of learning and scholarship, like Latin in medieval Europe.

Old Babylonian

It is customary to begin the study of Akkadian with Old Babylonian. Old Babylonian Akkadian was spoken and written in southern Mesopotamia during the first half of the second millennium BCE. Several tens of thousands of documents are attested from the first dynasty of Babylon, from the Isin and Larsa dynasties and from other cities in Babylonia (such as Kish, Nippur, Sippar, Umma, Ur, and Uruk), from sites in the Diyala region, and from farther afield, such as the city of Susa in Elam and the city of Mari in Syria some 250 miles up the Euphrates from Babylon (see Lesson 29.4).

There are several reasons to choose Old Babylonian as the entry to Akkadian language study. Although there was naturally some dialectal diversity among the wide geographical range of texts, on the whole the Old Babylonian corpus presents a remarkably uniform grammar. Moreover, many texts, especially those of the royal court, were carefully written in a clear and relatively simplified system of signs that is considerably easier to learn than, for example, the more cumbersome sign set used later to write Standard Babylonian. The grammar of Old Babylonian exhibits both a consistency and a number of significant features that were lost in later dialects, including Standard Babylonian; it is therefore easier to move from a familiarity with Old Babylonian to the later dialects than it is to work one's way back in time. The Old Babylonian period is also the time in which Akkadian literature began to blossom, in such stunning works as the Epic of Gilgamesh. Indeed, the Old Babylonian literary dialect (see Lesson 30.2) was considered the classical form of Akkadian for the rest of Mesopotamian history, and was the model for the later literary dialect of Standard Babylonian.

Text Genres

An extremely diverse variety of genres has been preserved, nearly all of which are represented in Old Babylonian documents. In addition to the myths and epics such as Gilgamesh, mentioned just above, there are other literary genres, such as hymns and prayers. Still other intellectual works include a wide range of scholarly texts, among which are lexical texts (encyclopedic lists of words, often with their Sumerian counterparts), grammatical texts, medical texts, and mathematical texts. Texts written for public display include many royal inscriptions and documents like the famous "code" of laws of Hammurapi (the longest single Old Babylonian document).

Equally important are the many documents that inform us of matters of everyday life. There are thousands of letters, from kings to their viziers, from men and women to their business partners, and from schoolchildren to their parents. Much greater in number still are the legal contracts and economic documents that record marriages, adoptions, sales, rentals, leases, loans, guarantees, and the proceedings of lawsuits. Finally, there are the many omen texts, records of attempts to foretell the future, from which we learn both what was seen as normal and what was considered unusual.

About this Book

The present textbook is a graded introduction that covers the grammar and writing system of Old Babylonian Akkadian in 38 lessons. It is primarily intended to be used under the supervision of an instructor in a college class, but it is also meant to be sufficiently clear, thorough, and self-contained to be used profitably by an individual in independent study. The 38 lessons require the better part of a full academic year to cover adequately, but at the end of the lessons the student will be familiar with all the main and most of the minor points of Old Babylonian grammar and script, will already have read quite a few texts, and will be ready to move on to additional Old Babylonian texts and to begin the study of Standard Babylonian texts (with the aid of Appendix D).

In each lesson two or three points of grammar are covered. The grammar sections are followed by ten to fifteen vocabulary items to be learned and, beginning in Lesson 9, by about ten cuneiform signs that are also to be memorized. (It should be noted here that the English glosses given in the vocabularies are for the most part based on those of the *Chicago Assyrian Dictionary*, about which see the next section. See above on the rationale for delaying presentation of the writing system until Lesson 9.) The vocabulary items (and signs) are followed in turn by a series of exercises that are intended to drill the points of grammar covered in the lesson, to review new and old vocabulary (and signs), and to present samples of Akkadian texts.

One of the first exercises in each lesson consists of words, phrases, or short sentences to "write in Akkadian." There is some feeling that it is unrealistic to ask students to "compose" in a dead language. Without the repeated need to reproduce forms accurately, however, a student's knowledge of a language remains passive rather than active, and an active knowledge is essential for full understanding of the details of grammar, for attention to the fine points and nuances of a sentence or text, and for awareness of unusual or even improper constructions on the part of the scribe. Students are therefore encouraged to write vocabulary, signs, and paradigms on flash cards and to learn not only to recognize forms but also to reproduce them.

Other exercises ask the student to translate Akkadian phrases and sentences. In the earliest lessons, these have of necessity been invented, although they are modeled on phrases and sentences found in actual texts. As early as is practical, authentic sentences from Old Babylonian texts are given, either reproduced verbatim or adapted slightly to accommodate the grammar and vocabulary that have been introduced to that point.

Beginning in Lesson 13, thus, by about the mid-point of the first semester, actual Old Babylonian texts are reproduced as part of the exercises. The texts introduced in Lesson 13 are contracts; laws from Hammurapi's "code" are introduced in Lesson 17, omen texts in Lesson 22, letters in Lesson 24, Mari letters in Lesson 29, royal inscriptions in Lesson 30, hymns and prayers in Lesson 33. In the presentation of real texts it has of course been necessary to provide glosses and explanatory notes for words and features that have not yet been covered in the grammar sections and vocabularies. The presentation of a significant number of texts in a wide range of genres is intended both to hold students' interest and to introduce them to the rich variety of textual material preserved to us in Akkadian.

In deciding how many exercises to include in this textbook it seemed preferable to err on the side of overabundance. Quite simply, there are too many, especially if one wants to complete the book within a single academic year. Thus, both instructors and independent students should choose a **selection** of the exercises and texts to work through, sometimes only half of them, particularly in the later lessons; this, at least, has proven to be a successful strategy with forerunners of this textbook to teach Akkadian. Nevertheless it has not seemed unreasonable to provide additional texts and exercises for students who have more time available to them or who want additional practice.

A *Key* to most of the exercises is published separately.

Research Tools

Akkadian and Sumerian texts offer the modern reader extraordinary views of one of humanity's earliest literate societies. But the languages of the texts are obscure, and the script in which they are written is very difficult to read, both in its complexity and in its (usual) presentation as a series of hard-to-make-out impressions in tablets of not-quite-flat clay. The most fundamental task of the Assyriologist is to make these texts accessible to a wider audience.

The full publication of a text, either in a journal article or as one of many texts in a monograph, involves a number of steps. Although photographs of tablets are frequently very useful, they generally do not capture the full three-dimensional effect of the impressed signs; further, tablets are often inscribed around their sides and on their edges as well as on their faces, and these peripheral parts of a tablet are difficult to photograph adequately. It is therefore the common practice for the Assyriologist to produce a hand drawing of a text in ink; this is called an "**autograph copy**" or simply an "autograph" or a "copy." A sign-by-sign rendering in Latin script, called a **transliteration**, is then produced, along with a translation. For the interpretation of individual signs a **sign list** is consulted. For the interpretation of individual words, of course, one consults one of the standard **dictionaries**; and for larger philological and linguistic matters there are the standard reference and dialect **grammars**. A brief review of these standard Assyriological tools, with their customary abbreviations, follows.

Sign Lists. Three modern sign lists are in common use. R. Labat's *Manuel d'épigraphie akkadienne* (6th ed. by F. Malbran-Labat, 1988; *MEA*^{6}) presents the chronological development of the forms of individual signs through all the various dialects, their phonological values, and their usage as logograms (see Lesson 13), all in an "at-a-glance" format. R. Borger's *Mesopotamisches Zeichenlexikon* (2003; *MZ*) is a comprehensive reference work. W. von Soden and W. Röllig's *Das akkadische Syllabar* (4th ed., 1991; *AS*^{4}) does not give the history of sign shapes or their logographic values, but it is the authoritative reference for phonetic sign values in Akkadian.

A very useful tool for learning signs is Daniel C. Snell's *A Workbook of Cuneiform Signs* (1979). W. Schramm's *Akkadische Logogramme* (2003) lists logograms alphabetically with their Akkadian equivalents. L.-J. Bord and R. Mugnaioni's *L'écriture cunéiforme* (2002), gives lists of sign forms by period, including a list of Old Babylonian signs.

Dictionaries. There are two excellent reference dictionaries of Akkadian. W. von Soden's three-volume *Akkadisches Handwörterbuch* (1965–81; *AHw*) lists many occurrences for each word, but usually without extensive citation of the context and usually without translation of passages. Useful features are the clear layout of the verb entries, the inclusion of Semitic cognates, and the listing of roots at the beginning of each "letter." *The Assyrian Dictionary of the University of Chicago*, less formally known as the *Chicago Assyrian Dictionary* (*CAD*), is produced by an editorial board of noted Assyriologists. It is an encyclopedic reference work in which each volume is devoted to words beginning with one of the Akkadian phonemes; several of the volumes are in two or even three parts. The first volume to appear was Ḫ, in 1956; the latest, R, was published in 1999; thus far, 17 of 21 volumes have appeared (P, T, Ṭ, and U remain to be published). In *CAD* many occurrences of each word are cited, often with their full context and a translation; comparative Semitic data are not given. The inexpensive *Concise Dictionary of Akkadian*, edited by J. Black, A. George, and N. Postgate (1999; *CDA*), is a thoroughly reliable one-volume work (updated at www.trin.cam.ac.uk/cda_archive/). (Also to be noted are K. Hecker's *Rückläufiges Wörterbuch des Akkadischen* [1990], a "reverse dictionary" that is very useful for working with damaged texts in which the beginnings of words are broken away, and T. Kämmerer and D. Schwiderski's *Deutsch–Akkadisches Wörterbuch* [1998], in which one may find out the Akkadian word for something by looking up its German equivalent.)

Grammars. The standard reference grammar of Akkadian is W. von Soden's *Grundriss der akkadischen Grammatik* (3rd ed., with W. R. Mayer, 1995; *GAG*); the presentation of the grammar in the present textbook follows that of von Soden's *GAG* in most details, particularly in the few minor points over which there is some disagreement or uncertainty among Assyriologists. Another fine reference grammar, though less complete than *GAG*, is A. Ungnad's *Grammatik des Akkadischen*, 5th ed. by L. Matouš (1969), which has been translated into English by H. Hoffner, Jr. as *Akkadian Grammar* (1992). There are also a number of linguistically-oriented grammars of Akkadian: I. J. Gelb, *Sequential Reconstruction of Proto-Akkadian* (1969); G. Buccellati, *A Structural Grammar of Babylonian* (1996). E. Reiner's *A Linguistic Analysis of Akkadian* (1966) and B. Groneberg's *Syntax, Morphologie und Stil der jungbabylonischen "hymnischen" Literatur* (2 volumes; 1987) are excellent linguistic descriptions of Standard Babylonian.

Reference grammars of many of the individual dialects, both Mesopotamian and peripheral, also exist. The following list is not intended to be comprehensive.

Adler, H.-P. *Das Akkadische des Königs Tušratta von Mitanni* (1976).

Aro, J. *Studien zur mittelbabylonischen Grammatik* (1955); *Glossar zu den mittelbabylonischen Briefen* (1957).

Berkooz, M. *The Nuzi Dialect of Akkadian* (1937).

Finet, A. *L'Accadien des lettres de Mari* (1956).

Gelb, I.J. *Old Akkadian Writing and Grammar*, 2nd ed. (1961); *Glossary of Old Akkadian* (1957).

Hämeen-Anttila, J. *A Sketch of Neo-Assyrian Grammar* (2000).

Hasselbach, R. *Sargonic Akkadian: A Historical and Comparative Study of the Syllabic Texts* (2005).

Hecker, K. *Grammatik der Kültepe-Texte* (1968).

Huehnergard, J. *The Akkadian of Ugarit* (1989).

Izre'el, Sh. *Amurru Akkadian: A Linguistic Study* (2 volumes; 1991).

Labat, R. *L'Akkadien de Boghaz-Köi* (1932).

Luukko, M. *Grammatical Variation in Neo-Assyrian* (2004).

Mayer, W. *Untersuchungen zur Grammatik des Mittelassyrischen* (1971).

Meyer, L. de. *L'Accadien des contrats de Suse* (1962).

Seminara, Stefano. *L'accadico di Emar* (1998).

Soden, W. von. Der hymnisch-epische Dialekt des Akkadischen. *Zeitschrift für Assyriologie* 40 (1931) 163–227; 41 (1933) 90–183.

Soldt, W.H. van. *Studies in the Akkadian of Ugarit: Dating and Grammar* (1991).

Stein, P. *Die mittel- und neubabylonischen Königsinschriften bis zum Ende der Assyrerherrschaft: Grammatische Untersuchungen* (2000).

Streck, M. P. *Zahl und Zeit: Grammatik der Numeralia und des Verbalsystems im Spätbabylonischen* (1995).

Vaan, J.M.C.T. de. *«Ich bin eine Schwertklinge des Königs»: Die Sprache des Bēl-ibni* (1995).

Wilhelm, G. *Untersuchungen zum Ḫurro-Akkadischen von Nuzi* (1970).

Bibliographies. The field of Assyriology is very fortunate to have R. Borger's three-volume *Handbuch der Keilschriftliteratur* (1967–75; *HKL*), in which all Akkadian and Sumerian texts published in journals and monographs through the end of 1973 are listed under the names of publishing scholars, with detailed cross-references to all subsequent discussion of individual texts; the third volume of *HKL* organizes the texts by content. Updates of *HKL*, i.e., texts and discussions of texts published since 1973, appear in the "Register Assyriologie" of the periodical *Archiv für Orientforschung*. Notice should also be taken of the annual "Keilschriftbibliographie" in the journal *Orientalia*.

Journals. Several scholarly journals are devoted to the field of Assyriology:

Archiv für Orientforschung (*AfO*)
Journal of Cuneiform Studies (*JCS*)
Nouvelles assyriologiques brèves et utilitaires (*NABU*)
Revue d'assyriologie et d'archéologie orientale (*RA*)
Zeitschrift für Assyriologie und vorderasiatische Archäologie (*ZA*)

Other journals at least partly concerned with Assyriology are:

Altorientalische Forschungen (*AoF*)
Archiv Orientální (*ArOr*)
Aula Orientalis (*AuOr*)
Bibliotheca Orientalis (*BiOr*)
Iraq
Journal of Near Eastern Studies (*JNES*)
Journal of the American Oriental Society (*JAOS*)
Journal of the Ancient Near Eastern Society of Columbia University (*JANES*)
Journal of the Economic and Social History of the Orient (*JESHO*)
Oriens Antiquus (*OrAnt*)
Orientalia (*Or.*)
Orientalistische Literaturzeitung (*OLZ*)
Rivista degli studi orientali (*RSO*)
Studi epigrafici e linguistici (*SEL*)
Sumer
Syria (revue d'art oriental et d'archéologie)
Welt des Orients (*WO*)

Other Reference Works. An encyclopedic work covering all aspects of Assyriology is the *Reallexikon der Assyriologie* (begun by E. Ebeling et al.; most recently edited by D. Edzard); the first two volumes of *RLA* appeared in 1932 and 1938, after which publication ceased for two decades, resuming in 1957; as of 2004, nine large volumes, and half of a tenth, covering topics beginning (in German) with A through P, have been published.

Akkadian (and Sumerian) personal names are treated in the now-outdated but still-indispensable work of J. Stamm, *Die akkadische Namengebung* (1939); see also Stol 1991 in the Bibliography below.

Geographical names (towns, cities, regions, lands, rivers) are collected in the several volumes of *Répertoire géographique des textes cunéiformes* (*RGTC*; 1974–; for the Old Babylonian period: volume 3, by B. Groneberg).

Selected Bibliography

It was noted in the preceding section that the grammar of Akkadian as presented in this textbook follows in the main the outlines of W. von Soden's *GAG*. During the preparation of the textbook the second, 1969, edition of *GAG* was consulted (the third edition having appeared too late to be used). But in addition to *GAG* numerous other articles and monographs devoted to issues of Akkadian grammar were also consulted, especially studies published after 1969. A few of those are specifically cited within the text; the findings of most, however, are incorporated into the presentation of the grammar silently. For the record, and for reference, there follows a list of those works consulted. The list also contains full references for the Akkadian texts reproduced in the Lessons.

Aro, Jussi. 1961. *Die akkadischen Infinitivkonstruktionen*. StOr 26; Helsinki.

——. 1963. Präpositionale Verbindungen als Bestimmungen des Nomens im Akkadischen. *Or.* 32 395–406.

Bergmann, E. 1953. *Codex Ḫammurabi. Textus primigenius*. 3rd ed. Rome.

Black, Jeremy A. 1984. *Sumerian Grammar in Babylonian Theory*. Rome.

Bottéro, J. 1973. La lexicographie accadienne. Pp. 25–60 in P. Fronzaroli, ed., *Studies on Semitic Lexicography*. Florence.

Buccellati, Giorgio. 1968. An Interpretation of the Stative as a Nominal Sentence. *JNES* 21 1–12.

——. 1972. On the Use of Akkadian Infinitive after "ša" or Construct State. *Journal of Semitic Studies* 17 1–29.

——. 1976a. On the Akkadian "Attributive" Genitive. *Afroasiatic Linguistics* 3 19–27.

——. 1976b. The Case against the Alleged Akkadian Plural Morpheme *-ānū*. *Afroasiatic Linguistics* 3 28–30.

——. 1988. The State of the "Stative." Pp. 153–89 in Yoël L. Arbeitman, ed., *Fucus: A Semitic/Afrasian Gathering in Remembrance of Albert Ehrman*. Amsterdam/New York.

——. 1990. On Poetry — Theirs and Ours. Pp. 105–34 in T. Abusch, et al., edd. *Lingering over Words: Studies in Ancient Near Eastern Literature in Honor of William L. Moran*. Atlanta.

Cagni, L. 1980. *Altbabylonische Briefe*, vol. 8: *Briefe aus dem Iraq Museum (TIM II)*. Leiden.

Cavigneaux, Antoine. 1989. Le nom akkadien du grain. *NABU* 1989, no. 52.

Charpin, Dominique. 1986. *Le Clergé d'Ur au siècle d'Hammurabi*. Geneva/Paris.

Chiera, Edward. 1922. *Old Babylonian Contracts*. PBS 8/2. Philadelphia.

Cohen, Eran. 2001 Focus Marking in Old Babylonian. *WZKM* 91 85–104.

——. 2003/4. Paronomastic Infinitive in Old Babylonian. *JEOL* 38 105–12.

——. 2005. *The Modal System of Old Babylonian*. Winona Lake.

Deutscher, Guy. 2000. *Syntactic Change in Akkadian: The Evolution of Sentential Complementation*. Oxford.

Dijk, J.J.A. van. 1965. *Cuneiform Texts. Old Babylonian Letters and Related Material*. TIM 2. Wiesbaden.

Dossin, Georges. 1951. *Correspondance de Šamši-Addu et de ses fils (suite)*. ARMT 4. Paris.

——. 1978. *Correspondance féminine*. ARMT 10. Paris.

Driver, G.R. 1924. *Letters of the First Babylonian Dynasty*. OECT 3. Oxford.

Durand, Jean-Marie. 1988. *Archives épistolaires de Mari I*. ARM 26. 2 volumes. Paris.

Edzard, Dietz Otto. 1965. Die Stämme des altbabylonischen Verbums in ihrem Oppositionssystem. Pp. 111–20 in H. Güterbock and T. Jacobsen, edd., *Studies ... B. Landsberger*. Chicago.

——. 1970a. *Altbabylonische Rechts- und Wirtschaftsurkunden aus Tell ed-Dēr im Iraq Museum, Baghdad*. Munich.

——. 1970b. *Cuneiform Texts. Altbabylonische Rechts- und Wirtschaftsurkunden aus Tell ed-Dēr bei Sippar*. TIM 7. Wiesbaden.

——. 1973. Die Modi beim älteren akkadischen Verbum. *Or*. 42 (Festschrift I.J. Gelb) 121–41.

——. 1977. Der gegenwärtige Stand der Akkadistik (1975) und ihre Aufgaben. Pp. 47–51 in W. Voigt, ed., *XIX. Deutscher Orientalistentag, Vorträge*. Wiesbaden.

——. 1980. Keilschrift. *RLA* 5 544–68.

——. 1982. Zu den akkadischen Nominalformen *parsat-*, *pirsat-*, und *pursat-*. *ZA* 72 68–88.

——. 1996. *Die Iterativstämme beim akkadischen Verbum: Die Frage ihrer Entstehung; ihre Funktion; ihre Verbreitung*. Munich.

Farber, Walter. 1982. Altbabylonische Adverbialbildungen auf *-āni*. Pp. 39–47 in *Zikir Šumim* (Festschrift F. Kraus).

Ferry, David. 1990. Prayer to the Gods of the Night. P. 171 in T. Abusch, et al., edd. *Lingering over Words: Studies in Ancient Near Eastern Literature in Honor of William L. Moran*. Atlanta.

Figulla, Hugo Heinrich. 1963. *Cuneiform Texts ... in the British Museum*, vol. 43: *Old Babylonian Letters*. London.

Foster, Benjamin R. 2005. *Before the Muses*. 2 volumes. 3rd ed. Bethesda, Md.

Frankena, R. 1965. *Altbabylonische Briefe*. TLB 4. Leiden.

——. 1966. *Altbabylonische Briefe*, vol. 2: *Briefe aus dem British Museum (LIH und CT 2–33)*. Leiden.

——. 1968. *Altbabylonische Briefe*, vol. 3: *Briefe aus der Leidener Sammlung (TLB IV)*. Leiden.

——. 1974. *Altbabylonische Briefe*, vol. 6: *Briefe aus dem Berliner Museum*. Leiden.

Frayne, Douglas R. 1990. *Old Babylonian Period*. Royal Inscriptions of Mesopotamia, Early Periods, vol. 4. Toronto.

Gadd, C.J. 1963. Two Sketches from the Life at Ur. *Iraq* 25 177–88.

Gadd, C.J. and S.N. Kramer. 1966. *Literary and Religious Texts, Second Part.* UET 6/2. London.
Gelb, Ignace J. 1955. Notes on von Soden's Grammar of Akkadian. *BiOr* 12 93–111.
——. 1961. WA = aw, iw, uw in cuneiform writing. *JNES* 20 194–96.
——. 1970. A Note on Morphophonemics. Pp. 73–77 in D. Cohen, ed., *Mélanges Marcel Cohen*. The Hague.
——. 1973. [Review of *GAG Ergänzungsheft*]. *BiOr* 30 249–53.
George, A.R. 2003. *The Babylonian Gilgamesh Epic: Introduction, Critical Edition and Cuneiform Texts*. 2 volumes. Oxford.
Glassner, Jean-Jacques. 2000. ŠU+BAR dans les textes divinatoires paléo-babyloniens. *NABU* 2000, no. 67.
Goetze, Albrecht. 1936. The t-form of the Old Babylonian Verb. *JAOS* 56 297–334.
——. 1942. The So-called Intensive of the Semitic Languages. *JAOS* 62 1–8.
——. 1945. The Akkadian Dialects of the Old-Babylonian Mathematical Texts. Pp. 146–51 in O. Neugebauer and A. Sachs, edd., *Mathematical Cuneiform Texts*. New Haven.
——. 1946a. Number idioms in Old Babylonian. *JNES* 5 185–202.
——. 1946b. Sequence of two short syllables in Akkadian. *Or.* 15 233–38.
——. 1946c. The Akkadian Masculine Plural in *-ānū/ī* and its Semitic Background. *Language* 22 121–30.
——. 1947a. *Old Babylonian Omen Texts*. YOS 10. New Haven.
——. 1947b. Short or Long *a*? (Notes on Some Akkadian Words). *Or.* 16 235–50.
——. 1947c. The Akkadian Passive. *JCS* 1 50–59.
——. 1958. The Sibilants of Old Babylonian. *RA* 52 137–49.
Greenstein, Edward L. 1986. The Phonology of Akkadian Syllable Structure. *Afroasiatic Linguistics* 9 1–71.
Groneberg, Brigitte. 1978–79. Terminativ- und Lokativadverbialis in altbabylonischen literarischen Texten. *AfO* 26 15–29.
——. 1980. Zu den "gebrochenen Schreibungen." *JCS* 32 151–67.
——. 1989a. Reduplication of Consonants and "R"-Stems. *RA* 83 27–34.
——. 1989b. Dimtu. *NABU* 1989, no. 73.
Haayer, G. 1986. Languages in Contact: The Case of Akkadian and Sumerian. Pp. 71–84 in H.L.J. Vanstiphout, et al., edd. *Scripta signa vocis: Studies about Scripts, Scriptures, Scribes and Languages in the Near East, presented to J.H. Hospers*. Groningen.
Harper, Robert Francis. 1904. *The Code of Ḫammurabi King of Babylon about 2250 B.C.* Chicago/London.
Hecker, Karl. 1974. *Untersuchungen zur akkadischen Epik*. Neukirchen.
——. 2000. *i* oder *ī* im Status constructus? *AoF* 27 260–68.
Heidel, Alexander. 1949. *The System of the Quadriliteral Verb in Akkadian*. Chicago.
Hirsch, Hans. 1969. Zur Frage der *t*-Formen in den keilschriftlichen Gesetzestexten. Pp. 119–31 in *Lišān mitḫurti* (Festschrift W. von Soden). Neukirchen.

——. 1975. Akkadische Grammatik — Erörterungen und Fragen. *Or.* 44 245–322.

Huehnergard, John. 1986. On Verbless Clauses in Akkadian. *ZA* 76 218–49.

——. 1987a. "Stative," Predicative, Pseudo-Verb. *JNES* 46 215–32.

——. 1987b. Three Notes on Akkadian Morphology. Pp. 181–93 in D. Golomb, ed., *Working With No Data: Semitic and Egyptian Studies Presented to Thomas O. Lambdin*. Winona Lake, Ind.

——. 2002. *izuzzum* and *itūlum*. Pp. 161–85 in Tzvi Abusch, ed., *Riches Hidden in Secret Places: Ancient Near Eastern Studies in Memory of Thorkild Jacobsen*. Winona Lake, Ind.

——. 2003. Akkadian *ḫ* and West Semitic **ḥ*. Pp. 102–19 in Leonid Kogan, ed., *Studia Semitica.* Orientalia: Papers of the Oriental Institute, 3 (Alexander Militarev volume). Moscow: Russian State University for the Humanities.

—— and Christopher Woods. 2004. Akkadian and Eblaite. Pp. 218–87 in Roger D. Woodard, ed., *The Cambridge Encyclopedia of the World's Ancient Languages*. Cambridge.

Izre'el, Shlomo. 1991. On the Person Prefixes of the Akkadian Verb. *JANES* 20 35–56.

—— and Eran Cohen. 2004. *Literary Old Babylonian*. Munich.

Jacobsen, Thorkild. 1960. *Ittallak niāti. JNES* 19 101–16.

——. 1963. The Akkadian Ablative Accusative. *JNES* 22 18–29.

Jean, Charles-François. 1950. *Lettres diverse.* ARMT 2. Paris.

Jeyes, Ulla. 1989. *Old Babylonian Extispicy: Omen Texts in the British Museum*. Istanbul.

Kaplan, Golda H. 2002. *Use of Aspect-Tense Verbal Forms in Akkadian Texts of the Hammurapi Period (1792–1750 B.C.)*. Munich.

Khan, Geoffrey A. 1988. *Studies in Semitic Syntax*. Oxford.

Kienast, Burkhardt. 1957. Verbalformen mit Reduplikation im Akkadischen. *Or.* 26 44–50.

——. 1961. Weiteres zum R-Stamm des Akkadischen. *JCS* 15 59–61.

——. 1962. Das System der zweiradikaligen Verben im Akkadischen. *ZA* 55 138–55.

King, Leonard W. 1898–1900 *The Letters and Inscriptions of Ḫammurabi, King of Babylon*. 3 volumes. London.

——. 1910. *Cuneiform Texts ... in the British Museum*, vol. 29. London.

Knudsen, Ebbe Egede. 1980. Stress in Akkadian. *JCS* 32 3–16.

——. 1986. Innovation in the Akkadian Present. Pp. 231–39 in Tryggve Kronholm and Eva Riad, edd. *On the Dignity of Man: Oriental and Classical Studies in Honor of Frithiof Rundgren* (= *Orientalia Suecana* 33–35). Uppsala.

Kobayashi, Yoshitaka. 1975. Graphemic Analysis of Old Babylonian Letters from South Babylonia. PhD diss., UCLA.

Kogan, Leonid. 2001. **ġ* in Akkadian. *UF* 33 263–98.

Kouwenberg, N.J.C. 1997. *Gemination in the Akkadian Verb.* Assen.

——. 2001. The Interchange of *e* and *a* in Old Babylonian. Pp. 225–49 in W.H. van Soldt et al., eds., *Veenhof Anniversary Volume: Studies Presented to Klaas R. Veenhof on the Occasion of His Sixty-fifth Birthday*. Leiden.

——. 2002. Ventive, Dative and Allative in Old Babylonian. *ZA* 92 200–40.

Kraus, F. R. 1957. Eine Besonderheit der älteren akkadischen Orthographie. *RSO* 32 103–8.

——. 1964. *Altbabylonische Briefe*, vol. 1: *Briefe aus dem British Museum (CT 43 und 44)*. Leiden.

——. 1968. *Altbabylonische Briefe*, vol. 4: *Briefe aus dem Archive des Šamaš-Ḫāzir in Paris und Oxford (TCL 7 und OECT 3)*. Leiden.

——. 1972. *Altbabylonische Briefe*, vol. 5: *Briefe aus dem Istanbuler Museum*. Leiden.

——. 1973. Ein altbabylonischer '*i*-Modus'? Pp. 253–65 in M.A. Beek, et al., edd., *Symbolae Biblicae et Mesopotamicae F.M.T. de Liagre Böhl Dedicatae*. Leiden.

——. 1976. Der akkadische Vokativ. Pp. 293–97 in B. Eichler, ed., *Kramer Anniversary Volume*. Neukirchen.

——. 1977. *Altbabylonische Briefe*, vol. 7: *Briefe aus dem British Museum (CT 52)*. Leiden.

——. 1984. *Nominalsätze in altbabylonischen Briefen und der Stativ*. Amsterdam.

——. 1987. *Sonderformen akkadischer Parataxe: die Koppelungen*. Amsterdam.

Leichty, Erle. 1970. *The Omen Series Šumma Izbu*. Locust Valley, N.Y.

Lieberman, Stephen J. 1977. *The Sumerian Loanwords in Old-Babylonian Akkadian*. Volume 1: Prolegomena and Evidence. Missoula, Mt.

Livingstone, Alasdair. 1990. *Šērtu*, «ring», *šeršerratu*, «chain». *NABU* 1990, no. 87.

Loesov, Sergey. 2004. T-Perfect in Old Babylonian: The Debate and a Thesis. *Babel und Bibel* 1 83–181.

Lutz, Henry Frederick. 1929. *Old Babylonian Letters*. UCP 9/4. Berkeley.

Macelaru, Adrian. 2003. Coding Location, Motion and Direction in Old Babylonian Akkadian. Pp. 189-210 in Erin Shay and Uwe Seibert, eds., *Motion, Direction and Location in Languages*. Amersterdam.

Malbran-Labat, Florence. 1979–84. L'expression du serment en akkadien. *Comptes rendus du groupe linguistique d'études chamito-sémitiques* 24–28 233–38.

——. 1991. Le "passif" en akkadien. Pp. 977–90 in A.S. Kaye, ed., *Semitic Studies ... W. Leslau*, vol. 2. Wiesbaden.

Maloney, John Frederick. 1982. The T-Perfect in the Akkadian of Old-Babylonian Letters, with a Supplement on Verbal Usage in the Code of Hammurapi and the Laws of Eshnunna. Ph.D. diss., Harvard U.

Marchesi, Gianni. 2002. On the Divine Name ^{d}BA.Ú. *Or.* 71 161–72.

Mayer, Werner R. 1989. Die Verwendung der Negation im Akkadischen zur Bildung von Indefinit- bzw. Totalitätsausdrücken. *Or.* 58 145–70.

——. 1995. Zum Terminativ-Advervialis im Akkadischen: Die Modaladverbien auf *-iš*. *Or.* 64 161–86.

Meissner, Bruno. 1893. *Beiträge zum altbabylonischen Privatrecht.* Leipzig.

Metzler, Kai Alexander. 2002. *Tempora in altbabylonischen literarischen Texten*. Münster.

Moran, William L. 1993. UET 6 402: Persuasion in the Plain Style. *JANES* 22 (Festschrift Yohanan Muffs) 113–20.

Nougayrol, Jean. 1948–51a La détermination et l'indétermination du nom en accadien. *Comptes rendus du groupe linguistique d'études chamito-sémitiques* 5 73-76, 78.

——. 1948–51b. La phrase dite nominale en accadien. *Comptes rendus du groupe linguistique d'études chamito-sémitiques* 5 22–24.

Oppenheim, A. Leo. 1933. Die Rolle der T-Formen im Codex Ḫammurapi. *WZKM* 40 181–220.

——. 1935. Die mittels T-Infixes gebildeten Aktionsarten des Altbabylonsichen. *WZKM* 42 1–30.

——. 1960. A Caesarian Section in the Second Millennium B.C. *Journal of the History of Medicine and Allied Sciences* 15 292–94.

Pardee, Dennis and Robert M. Whiting. 1987. Aspects of Epistolary Verbal Usage in Ugaritic and Akkadian. *Bulletin of the School of Oriental and African Studies* 50 1–31.

Patterson, Richard Duane. 1970. Old Babylonian Parataxis as Exhibited in the Royal Letters of the Middle Old Babylonian Period and in the Code of Hammurapi. PhD diss., UCLA.

Pedersén, Olof. 1989. Some Morphological Aspects of Sumerian and Akkadian Linguistic Areas. Pp. 429–38 in Hermann Behrens et al., edd. *Dumu-E$_2$-Dub-Ba-A: Studies in Honor of Åke W. Sjöberg*. Philadelphia.

Pinches, Theophilus Goldridge. 1896. *Cuneiform Texts ... in the British Museum,* 2. London.

——. 1898a. *Cuneiform Texts ... in the British Museum,* 4. London.

——. 1898b. *Cuneiform Texts ... in the British Museum,* 6. London.

——. 1899. *Cuneiform Texts ... in the British Museum,* 8. London.

Poebel, Arno. 1939. *Studies in Akkadian Grammar*. Chicago.

Powell, Marvin A. 1979. Notes on Akkadian Numbers and Number Syntax. *JSS* 24 13–18.

——. 1987–90. Metrologie. *RLA* 7 457–517.

——. 1991. Epistemology and Sumerian Agriculture: The Strange Case of Sesame and Linseed. *AuOr* 9 (Festschrift M. Civil) 155–64.

Pritchard, James B., ed. 1969. *Ancient Near Eastern Texts Relating to the Old Testament*. 3rd ed. Princeton.

Rainey, Anson F. 1976. Enclitic *-ma* and the Logical Predicate in Old Babylonian. *IOS* 6 51–58.

Ranke, Hermann. 1906. *Babylonian Legal and Business Documents from the Time of the First Dynasty of Babylon, chiefly from Sippar.* BE 6/1. Philadelphia.

Ravn, O.E. 1941. *The So-Called Relative Clauses in Accadian or the Accadian Particle* ša. Copenhagen.

——. 1949. Babylonian Permansive and Status Indeterminatus. *ArOr* 17 300–6.

Reiner, Erica. 1964. The Phonological Interpretation of a Sub-System in the Akkadian Syllabary. Pp. 167–80 in *Studies Presented to A. Leo Oppenheim*. Chicago.

——. 1970. Akkadian. Pp. 274–303 in T.A. Sebeok, ed., *Current Trends in Linguistics*, vol. 6. The Hague.

——. 1973a. How we Read Cuneiform Texts. *JCS* 25 3–58.

——. 1973b. New Cases of Morphophonemic Spellings. *Or.* 42 (Festschrift I.J. Gelb) 35–38.

——. 1984. *Damqam-īnim* Revisited. *Studia Orientalia Memoriae Jussi Aro dedicata*. StOr 55 177–82.

Röllig, W. 1987. Überblick über die akkadische Literatur. *RLA* 7 48–66.

Römer, W.H.Ph. 1966. Studien zu altbabylonischen hymnisch-epischen Texten (2). Ein Lied über die Jugendjahre der Götter Sîn und Išum (CT 15, 5-6). *JAOS* 86 138–47.

Roth, Martha T. 1995. *Law Collections from Mesopotamia and Asia Minor*. Atlanta.

Rowton, M.B. 1962. The Use of the Permansive in Classic Babylonian. *JNES* 21 233–303.

Sallaberger, Walther. 1999. *"Wenn Du mein Bruder bist, ..." Interaktion und Textgestaltung in altbabylonischen Alltagsbriefen*. Groningen.

Scheil, Vincent. 1902. *Une saison de fouilles à Sippar*. Cairo.

Schorr, M. 1913. *Urkunden des altbabylonischen Zivil- und Prozessrechts*. Vorderasiatische Bibliothek, 5. Leipzig.

Schroeder, Otto. 1917. *Altbabylonische Briefe*. VAS 16. Leipzig.

Soden, Wolfram von. 1936. Schwer zugängliche russische Veröffentlichungen altbabylonischer Texte. *ZA* 43 305–9.

——. 1948. Vokalfärbungen im Akkadischen. *JCS* 2 291–303.

——. 1950. Verbalformen mit doppeltem t-Infix im Akkadischen. *Or.* 19 385–96.

——. 1960. Status Rectus-Formen vor dem Genitiv im Akkadischen und die sogenannte uneigentliche Annexion im Arabischen. *JNES* 19 163–71.

——. 1961. Die Zahlen 20–90 im Semitischen und der Status absolutus. *WZKM* 57 24–28.

——. 1965. Das akkadische *t*-Perfect in Haupt- und Nebensätzen und sumerische Verbalformen mit den Präfixen *ba-*, *imma-*, und *u-*. Pp. 103–10 in *Studies ... Landsberger*. Chicago.

——. 1973a. Der akkadische Subordinativ-Subjunktiv. *ZA* 63 56–58.

——. 1973b. Iterativa im Akkadischen und Hethitischen. Pp. 311–19 in *Festschrift Heinrich Otten*.

——. 1983. Zu den semitischen und akkadischen Kardinalzahlen und ihrer Konstruktion. *ZA* 73 82–91.

——. 1991. Tempus und Modus im älteren Semitischen. Pp. 463–93 in H.-P. Müller, ed., *Babylonien und Israel: Historische, religiöse und sprachliche Beziehungen*. Darmstadt.

Soldt, W.H. van. 1990. *Altbabylonische Briefe*, vol. 12: *Letters in the British Museum*. Leiden.

Stol, Marten. 1986. *Altbabylonische Briefe*, vol. 11: *Letters from Collections in Philadelphia, Chciago and Berkeley*. Leiden.

——. 1991. Old Babylonian Personal Names. *SEL* 8 191–212.

Streck, Michael P. 2002. Die Nominalformen *maPRaS(t)*, *maPRāS* und *maPRiS(t)* im Akkadischen. Pp. 223–57 in Norbert Nebes, ed., *Neue Beiträge zur Semitistik*. Wiesbaden.

——. 2003. *Die akkadischen Verbalstämme mit* ta-*Infix*. Münster.

Szlechter, Emile. 1958. *Tablettes juridiques de la Ire Dynastie de Babylone*. 2 volumes. Paris.

——. 1963. *Tablettes juridiques et administratives de la IIIe Dynastie d'Ur et de la Ire Dynastie de Babylone*. 2 volumes. Paris.

Thureau-Dangin, François. 1910. *Lettres et contrats de l'époque de la première dynastie babylonienne*. TCL 1. Paris.

——. 1924. *Lettres de Ḫammurapi à Šamaš-ḫâṣir*. TCL 7. Paris.

——. 1925. Un hymne à Ištar de la haute époque babylonienne. *RA* 22 169–77.

Ungnad, Arthur. 1909. *Altbabylonische Urkunden*. VAS 7, 8. Leipzig.

——. 1914. *Babylonische Briefe aus der Zeit der Ḫammurapi-Dynastie*. Vorderasiatische Bibliothek, 6. Leipzig.

——. 1915. *Babylonian Letters of the Ḫammurapi Period*. PBS 7. Philadelphia.

Vanstiphout, Herman. 1989. The Akkadian word for grain and *Laḫar and Ašnan*, ll. 189–90. *NABU* 1989, no. 98.

Walker, C.B.F. 1976. *Cuneiform Texts ... in the British Museum*, vol. 52: *Old Babylonian Letters*. London.

Wasserman, Nathan. 2003. *Style and Form in Old Babylonian Literary Texts*. Leiden.

Waterman, Leroy. 1916. *Business Documents of the Ḫammurapi Period from the British Museum*. London.

Westenholz, Aage. 1991. The Phoneme /o/ in Akkadian. *ZA* 81 10–19.

Westenholz, Joan Goodnick. 1971. Some Aspects of Old Babylonian Syntax as Found in the Letters of the Period. Ph.D. diss., U. of Chicago.

Whiting, R.M., Jr. 1981. The R Stem(s) in Akkadian. *Or.* 50 1–39.

Wilcke, Claus. 1984. CT 45, 119: Ein Fall legaler Bigamie mit *nadītum* und *šugītum*. *ZA* 74 170–80.

Winitzer, Abraham. 2003. UD-*gunû* as *manzānu* / *naplastu* in *TIM* 9 79. *NABU* 2003, no. 94.

LESSON ONE

1.1 The Sounds of Akkadian

Since there have been no native speakers of Akkadian for some two millennia, it is impossible to determine exactly how the language was pronounced. The pronunciation used by scholars is merely an educated guess, based largely on comparisons with languages related to Akkadian, such as Arabic, Amharic, and Hebrew.

(a) Vowels

There are four short vowels, *a, e, i, u,* and four corresponding long vowels. Long vowels are marked either with a macron, *ā, ē, ī, ū,* or with a circumflex, *â, ê, î, û,* depending on the origin of the length (see §6.1). The vowels may be pronounced as follows:

SHORT VOWELS		LONG VOWELS	
a	as in sw*a*p	*ā, â*	as in f*a*ther
e	as in p*e*t	*ē, ê*	as in r*ei*n
i	as in p*i*t	*ī, î*	as in mar*i*ne
u	as in p*u*t	*ū, û*	as in r*u*le

The distinction between short *a* and long *ā/â* is basically one of duration.

It is crucial to know the length of a vowel, since a difference in length may mark a significant difference in meaning between otherwise identical words, as in

mutum 'husband'	vs.	*mūtum* 'death'
dannatum 'fortress'	vs.	*dannātum* 'fortresses'
bêlum 'to rule'	vs.	*belûm* 'to be extinguished'

(b) Consonants

Most of these are pronounced like their English equivalents:

b	as in *b*et	*m*	as in *m*et	*š*	as *sh* in *sh*ot
d	as in *d*ot	*n*	as in *n*ot	*t*	as in *t*ot
g	as in *g*et	*p*	as in *p*ot	*w*	as in *w*et
k	as in *k*id	*r*	as in *r*ot	*y*	as in Ma*y*an
l	as in *l*ot	*s*	as in *s*et	*z*	as in *z*oo

Note that *w* does not occur before other consonants (except itself, as in *nuwwurum* 'to brighten') or at the end of words. The consonant *y* occurs between vowels (singly, as in *elīya* 'against me', or doubly, as in *dayyānum* 'judge'), and at the beginning of a few words (as in *yûm* 'mine'); many scholars prefer to transcribe *j* rather than *y*, and the phoneme is counted as *j* for alphabetization in the modern dictionaries.

Five consonants require special comment:

The phonemes ***q***, ***ṣ***, and ***ṭ*** are usually referred to as "emphatic" consonants. The ancient pronunciation of these is not known, and most modern students of Akkadian pronounce *q* like *k*, *ṣ* as *ts* in fi*ts*, and *ṭ* like *t*.

The sounds corresponding to Akkadian *q*, *ṣ*, *ṭ* in the modern Semitic languages of Ethiopia and South Arabia are glottalized, that is, pronounced like *k*, *s*, and *t* with accompanying glottal closure and sharp ejection of air (*q* = [kʾ]; *ṣ* = [sʾ]; *ṭ* = [tʾ]). In Arabic the phonemes corresponding to the Akkadian emphatics are pronounced as follows: *q* is articulated farther back than *k* (at the uvula); *ṣ* and *ṭ* resemble *s* and *t*, respectively, but with a simultaneous constricting of the throat (pharyngealization).

Consider the following table (note: "voiced" consonants are pronounced with resonance of the vocal cords, "voiceless" without):

Voiced	Voiceless	Emphatic
b	*p*	
d	*t*	*ṭ*
g	*k*	*q*
z	*s*	*ṣ*

One of the several difficulties with the Akkadian writing system is its frequent failure to distinguish voiced, voiceless, and emphatic consonants that have otherwise identical articulation. Thus, for example, the same sign is used to write both *za* and *ṣa*; another sign is used to write any of *ag*, *ak*, or *aq*. This problem will be considered in detail under "The Writing System," §9.2.

The phoneme ***ḫ*** should be pronounced like *ch* in German *ach* and Scottish *loch*. The student should be sure to include the "hook" when writing this consonant.

The remaining consonant, transcribed ʾ (or, conveniently, as a single close-quote mark: '), is referred to as "aleph" (after the corresponding Hebrew consonant). It is the glottal stop or catch, the sound heard between *n* and *i* in 'an iceman' when one wishes to distinguish carefully that phrase from 'a nice man', or the sound heard in some pronunciations of 'bottle' as [bɔʾl]. Like *w* and *y*, ʾ is of limited distribution: it occurs only between vowels, either singly or doubled (as in *naʾādum* 'to heed', *šitaʾʾal* 'interrogate!'), and, rarely, at the end of a syllable (e.g., *naʾdum* 'attentive'; see §21.4). In modern Akkadian dictionaries, ʾ is ignored in alphabetization.

All consonants may occur doubled, as in *wuššurum* 'to release', *libbum* 'heart'. Doubled consonants should be held longer (cf. [nn] in 'meanness' or 'penknife'; [dd] in 'bad day'; [tt] in 'hot tub').

Alphabetization in modern Akkadian dictionaries is as follows:

a, b, d, e, g, ḫ, i, j(y), k, l, m, n, p, q, r, s, ṣ, š, t, ṭ, u, w, z.

As noted above, words containing ʾ are listed as though the ʾ were not present.

1.2 Syllabification

The cuneiform writing system, as adapted for Akkadian (see below, §9.2), was based on the syllabification of the language; that is, to "spell" a given word, the scribe thought in terms of the constituent syllables of that word. It is therefore important that the student be able to determine the syllables that make up Akkadian words. There are three essential rules:

(a) Every syllable has one, and only one, vowel.

(b) With two exceptions, no syllable may begin with a vowel. The exceptions are: the beginning of a word; the second of two successive vowels (note: some scholars prefer to write ʾ between any two vowels in a word: e.g., *kiʾam* rather than our *kiam*).

(c) No syllable may begin or end with two consonants.

Some examples:

balāṭī: *ba / lā / ṭī*	*īteneppuš*: *ī / te / nep / puš*	*kiam*: *ki / am* (or,
elûm: *e / lûm*	*narkabtum*: *nar / kab / tum*	*kiʾam*: *ki / ʾam*)
ṣabat: *ṣa / bat*	*epištašu*: *e / piš / ta / šu*	

1.3 Stress (Accent)

For any Akkadian word, the position of the stress is completely predictable, according to the rules given below. To determine which syllable bears the stress in any given word, it is convenient to consider syllables as being of three different types:

(a) Light: ending in a short vowel: e.g., *-a*, *-ba*.
(b) Heavy: ending in a long vowel marked with a macron, or in a short vowel plus a consonant: e.g., *-ā*, *-bā*, *-ak*, *-bak*.
(c) Ultraheavy: ending in a long vowel marked with a circumflex, or in any long vowel plus a consonant: e.g., *-â*, *-bâ*, *-āk*, *-bāk*, *-âk*, *-bâk*.

The syllable bearing the stress may be determined for any given word by applying the following rules, in order:

(a) If the last syllable is ultraheavy, it bears the stress, as in

ibnû: *ib / nû*; *idūk*: *i / dūk*.

(b) Otherwise, stress falls on the last non-final heavy or ultraheavy syllable, as in

iparras: *i / par / ras*; *tēteneppušā*: *tē / te / nep / pu / šā*;
nidittum: *ni / dit / tum*; *itâršum*: *i / târ / šum*;
idūkū: *i / dū / kū*; *napištašunu*: *na / piš / ta / šu / nu*.

(c) Words that contain no non-final heavy or ultraheavy syllables have the stress on the first syllable:

zikarum: *zi / ka / rum*; *ilū*: *i / lū*.
šunu: *šu / nu*;

EXERCISES

A. VOCABULARY 1.

Nouns:

abum 'father'.
ālum 'town, city'.
amtum 'female slave, womanservant'.
bēlum 'lord, master, owner'.
ḫurāṣum 'gold'.
iltum 'goddess'.
ilum 'god'.
kaspum 'silver'.
mārtum 'daughter'.
mārum 'son'.
qaqqadum 'head, top; person; principal (amount)'.
ṣābum 'gang, army, troop(s); worker, soldier'.
šarratum 'queen'.
šarrum 'king'.
wardum 'male slave, manservant'.

Conjunction:

u 'and'.

B. How is *š* pronounced? *q*? *ḫ*? *ṣ*? *ṭ*? the vowels? Pronounce the vocabulary words aloud.

C. Which Akkadian consonants are voiced? voiceless? emphatic?

D. Divide the nouns in the vocabulary into syllables, and mark the syllable with the stress: e.g., *abum*: *a̲/bum*.

E. For additional practice, divide the following words into syllables, and mark the syllable with the stress:

1. *mušallimum*	5. *tabnianni*	9. *tabnû*	13. *paris*
2. *išāl*	6. *niqīaš*	10. *iššiakkum*	14. *išmeānim*
3. *idin*	7. *epēšum*	11. *rēdûm*	15. *pete*
4. *iddinūniššum*	8. *kullumum*	12. *iqbi*	16. *šūṣû*

LESSON TWO

2.1 Noun Declension

(a) Paradigms

Study the following paradigms of the masculine words *ilum* 'god' and *šarrum* 'king' and the feminine words *iltum* 'goddess', *šarratum* 'queen' and *nārum* 'river':

		MASCULINE		FEMININE		
SINGULAR	nominative	*ilum*	*šarrum*	*iltum*	*šarratum*	*nārum*
	genitive	*ilim*	*šarrim*	*iltim*	*šarratim*	*nārim*
	accusative	*ilam*	*šarram*	*iltam*	*šarratam*	*nāram*
DUAL	nominative	*ilān*	*šarrān*	*iltān*	*šarratān*	*nārān*
	gen.–acc.	*ilīn*	*šarrīn*	*iltīn*	*šarratīn*	*nārīn*
PLURAL	nominative	*ilū*	*šarrū*	*ilātum*	*šarrātum*	*nārātum*
	gen.–acc.	*ilī*	*šarrī*	*ilātim*	*šarrātim*	*nārātim*

(b) Definiteness

Akkadian has neither a definite nor an indefinite article; thus, e.g., according to the context in which it occurs, *šarrum* may be rendered 'king', 'a king', or 'the king'.

(c) Base and Endings

It is convenient to consider the noun (and the adjective; see §4.2–4) as consisting of a base, which conveys the meaning, plus an ending or endings, which signify gender, number, and case.

(d) Case

Akkadian nouns and adjectives have three cases:

Nominative (nom.):	for the subject of the sentence, and the nominal predicate of some verbless sentences (see §2.5 below);
Genitive (gen.):	to indicate possession and other noun–noun modification, and after prepositions (cf. §31.3);
Accusative (acc.):	for the direct object of the verb, and in several adverbial expressions (see §18.3).

The cases are expressed by specific endings.

On all **singular nouns**, the case-endings are:

nom.:	*-um*	as in	*ilum*	*šarrum*	*iltum*	*šarratum*	*nārum*
gen.:	*-im*	as in	*ilim*	*šarrim*	*iltim*	*šarratim*	*nārim*
acc.:	*-am*	as in	*ilam*	*šarram*	*iltam*	*šarratam*	*nāram*

The final *-m*, which also appears on feminine plurals, on masculine plural adjectives, and on some verb forms, is called "mimation."

(e) Gender

Akkadian has two genders, **masculine** and **feminine**. As is to be expected, nouns signifying male animate beings are masculine and nouns signifying female animate beings are feminine. For other nouns, there is usually no apparent semantic factor that determines their gender.

Masculine singular nouns have no special formal marker:

ilum 'god', *šarrum* 'king', *mārum* 'son', *ālum* 'city', *kaspum* 'silver'.

Many nouns that are masculine in the singular are always or sometimes construed as feminine in the plural; see the next section.

Most **feminine singular nouns** have *-t* or *-at* after the base, *-t* if the base ends in a single consonant or in a vowel, *-at* if the base ends in two consonants:

with *-t*: *iltum* 'goddess', *mārtum* 'daughter', *qibītum* 'utterance';
with *-at*: *šarratum* 'queen', *warkatum* 'back'.

Some nouns without *-t* or *-at* are also feminine, however; these include both animate and non-animate nouns, such as

ummum 'mother', *enzum* 'she goat', *nārum* 'river', and most paired parts of the body, such as *īnum* 'eye', *šēpum* 'foot'.

All nouns that are feminine in the singular, including those without the ending *-(a)t*, remain grammatically feminine in the plural.

Still other nouns without *-t* or *-at* are of **variable gender**, that is, they sometimes take masculine modifiers, sometimes feminine; e.g.,

abnum 'stone', *gerrum* 'way', *ṭuppum* 'tablet', *ugārum* 'open field'.

Such nouns also usually exhibit variable gender in the plural.

A few nouns with *t* before the case-ending are masculine, the *t* being part of the base rather than the fem. marker:

bītum 'house', *liptum* 'handiwork'.

In the vocabularies, nouns with *t-* before the case-ending are to be taken as feminine (e.g., *iltum, šarratum, mātum* 'country') and other nouns as masculine, except as otherwise noted.

(f) Number

There are three categories of number: **singular**, **dual**, and **plural**. The dual and the plural both distinguish only two cases, each having a common form for the genitive and accusative (gen.–acc., sometimes referred to as the oblique case).

The **dual** case-endings are:

nom.	*-ān*
gen.–acc.	*-īn*

(The final *-n* is called "nunation.") These endings replace the sg. endings, following the base and the fem. sg. marker *-(a)t* if it is present:

	MASCULINE		FEMININE		
nom.	*ilān*	*šarrān*	*iltān*	*šarratān*	*nārān*
gen.–acc.	*ilīn*	*šarrīn*	*iltīn*	*šarratīn*	*nārīn*

The dual usually indicates precisely **two** of something. In OB, the use of the dual is generally confined to natural pairs of objects (that is, it is not normally used with words like 'god', 'king', 'goddess', 'queen', 'river', as the examples above might suggest); thus, where English has, for example, simply 'my eyes', Akkadian normally has 'my two eyes'. The dual also occurs on a small number of nouns with the same meaning as the singular, e.g.,

išdum and *išdān* 'foundation' (dual originally 'buttocks');
qablum and *qablān* 'middle, waist, hips';
rēšum and *rēšān* 'top'.

Adjectives, verbs, and pronouns do not have dual forms in OB, and so nouns that are dual in form have plural agreement. Most nouns that occur in the dual in OB are feminine in the singular, and dual forms of these take feminine plural adjectives and verbs. Dual forms of nouns that are masculine in the singular may also take feminine plural adjectives and verbs, or, less often, masculine plural.

In the **plural**, the declensional endings of the masculine and the feminine differ from one another.

Masculine plurals replace the sg. case-endings with:

nom.	*-ū*	as in	*ilū* 'gods'	*šarrū* 'kings'	*wardū* 'slaves'
gen.–acc.	*-ī*		*ilī*	*šarrī*	*wardī*

Feminine plurals, like sg. nouns, end in *-m*:

nom.	*-ātum*	as in	*ilātum* 'goddesses'	*šarrātum* 'queens'
gen.–acc.	*-ātim*		*ilātim*	*šarrātim*

Note that the fem. pl. endings replace both the sg. case-endings **and** the sg. fem. marker: *šarratum*, pl. *šarrātum*; *iltum*, pl. *ilātum*; *amtum*, pl. *amātum*.

As noted earlier, all nouns that are feminine in the singular, including those without the ending *-(a)t*, have *-ātum*, *-ātim* in the plural; e.g.,

nārum 'river', pl. *nārātum*;
ummum 'mother', pl. *ummātum*.

Many nouns that are masculine in the singular become feminine in the plural, such as

dīnum 'legal decision', pl. *dīnātum*;
igārum 'wall', pl. *igārātum*.

Other nouns that are masculine in the singular exhibit both masculine and feminine plurals, e.g.,

kunukkum 'seal', pl. *kunukkū* or *kunukkātum*;
naškapum 'granary', pl. *naškapū* or *naškapātum*.

Nouns that are of variable gender in the singular usually exhibit both masculine and feminine plural forms:

abnum 'stone', pl. *abnū* or *abnātum*;
ṭuppum 'tablet', pl. *ṭuppū* or *ṭuppātum*.

It should be noted that in the plural, it is the ending that effectively determines the gender of the form: all plurals ending in

-ātum / *-ātim* are grammatically feminine plural, and all but one or two plurals ending in *-ū* / *-ī* are grammatically masculine plural.

In the lesson vocabularies, it should be assumed that masculine nouns have masculine plurals and that feminine nouns have feminine plurals, unless there is a note to the contrary.

For designating groups of animate beings of both sexes, the masculine plural usually serves as the common plural:

ilū 'gods (and goddesses)'; *ilātum* is only 'goddesses';
mārū 'sons' or 'children'; *mārātum* is only 'daughters'.

Some words occur only as plurals, e.g.,

namrirrū 'divine luminosity';
šīpātum 'wool'.

In some instances the singular and the plural have the same meaning:

dibbatum and *dibbātum* 'agreement, discussion';
uzzum and *uzzātum* 'anger';
zīmum and *zīmū* 'appearance, looks';
sg. *emūqum*, dual *emūqān*, pl. *emūqū* and *emūqātum*, all 'strength'.

Some nouns are singular in form but may denote groups or collections of people or things. Such **collectives**, as they are called, may be construed with either singular or plural modifiers and verbs; e.g.,

ṣābum 'worker, soldier'; as collective, 'gang, workers, troop(s), army' (construed as masc. sg. or pl.).

2.2 Prepositions

Most Akkadian prepositions are two-syllable words ending in a short vowel, such as

ana 'to, for, at' *ina* 'in, among, with, by, from'
ištu 'from, out of' *itti* 'with, in the company of'.

Nouns following prepositions are always in the **genitive** case:

ana iltim 'to the goddess' *ina šarrī* 'among the kings'
ištu ālim 'from the town' *itti bēlim* 'with the lord'.

2.3 The Determinative Pronoun *ša*

The determinative pronoun *ša* literally means 'the one of', as in

ša Bābilim 'the one of Babylon, he of Babylon'.

Usually, *ša* occurs in apposition to a preceding noun, and may be translated simply 'of' (apposition is considered in detail in §11.2):

> *šarrum ša Bābilim* '(the) king of Babylon' (lit.: 'the king, the one of B.').

Nouns after *ša* are in the **genitive**:

> *šarrum ša ālim* 'the king of the city';
> *itti wardim ša šarratim* 'with the servant of the queen, with the queen's servant';
> *ḫurāṣum ša ilātim* 'the goddesses' gold'.

2.4 Independent Personal Pronouns

Akkadian personal pronouns have distinct masculine and feminine forms not only for the third person singular ('he', 'she'), but also for the third person plural and for the second person singular and plural (so that there are four forms for 'you'). To refer to a group of people or objects in which both sexes or genders are present, the masculine forms are used. The first person forms ('I', 'we') are common for both genders. (A dual pronoun existed for the third person [common gender] in the oldest stages of Akkadian, but fell out of use very early in OB.)

In this and subsequent sections concerning both pronouns and verbs, person, gender, and number will be referred to, for example, as 3ms (i.e., third person, masculine, singular), 2fp (second person, feminine, plural), 1cs (first person, common gender, singular).

The nominative forms of the independent personal pronouns are:

1cs	*anāku* 'I'	1cp	*nīnu* 'we'
2ms	*atta* 'you (ms)'	2mp	*attunu* 'you (mp)'
2fs	*atti* 'you (fs)'	2fp	*attina* 'you (fp)'
3ms	*šū* 'he, it (m)'	3mp	*šunu* 'they (m)'
3fs	*šī* 'she, it (f)'	3fp	*šina* 'they (f)'

These pronouns are used as subjects of verbless clauses (see the next section; other uses are discussed in §3.5).

When more than one person is expressed, the Akkadian order is the reverse of the English:

> *anāku u atti* 'you and I' (lit. 'I and you');
> *anāku u wardum* 'the servant and I' (lit. 'I and the servant');
> *atta u šī* 'she and you' (lit. 'you and she').

2.5 Verbless Clauses

Akkadian has no verb 'to be'. Such clauses are expressed simply by juxtaposing the subject and the predicate, and are called verbless (or nominal) clauses.

If the subject of a verbless clause is a noun, it stands at the beginning of the clause; if the subject is a pronoun, it stands at the end. The tense in such clauses can be determined only from the surrounding context. Some examples:

Ḫammurapi šarrum ša Bābilim 'Hammurapi is/was (the) king of Babylon.'
amātum ina ālim 'The womenservants are/were/will be in the town.'
mārtum ša šarrim atti 'You are the king's daughter.'
ina ālim nīnu 'We are/were/will be in the town.'

Clauses of the type Adverb (phrase) — Noun (phrase) also occur, but infrequently; most of these are existential clauses: e.g.,

ina libbim ša ālim nārum 'In the center of town (there) is a river' or 'There is a river in the center of town' (vs. *nārum ina libbim ša ālim* 'The river is in the center of town').

Verbless clauses may also express simple possession when *ša* and a following genitive constitute the predicate:

bītum ša iltim 'The house is the goddess's, belongs to the goddess.'
kaspum u ḫurāṣum ša ālim 'The silver and gold belong to the town.'
wardū ša bēlim 'The slaves belong to the lord, are the lord's.'
ša ilim šū 'It is the god's, belongs to the god.'

EXERCISES

A. VOCABULARY 2.

Nouns (note: nouns with *t-* before the case-ending are fem., others masc., except as indicated):

aššatum 'wife'.
bītum (masc.; pl. fem. *bītātum*) 'house, estate, household'.
emūqum (dual *emūqān*; pl. masc. *emūqū* and fem. *emūqātum*) 'strength, power, force, ability; armed forces; value'; also used in the dual and pl. with the same meanings.

īnum (fem.) 'eye; spring'.
išdum (dual *išdān* [often = sg.]; pl. *išdātum*) 'base, foundation, bottom; lower extremities; administration, organization (of a government)'.
libbum 'heart; mind, thought, wish; inside, center, midst'.
mutum (masc.) 'husband, man'.
nārum (fem.) 'river, canal'.
šīpātum (always pl.) 'wool'.
ṭuppum (masc. and fem.; pl. *ṭuppū* and *ṭuppātum*; Sum. lw.) '(clay) tablet, document, letter'.
ummum (fem.) 'mother'.
uznum (fem.) 'ear; wisdom, understanding'.

Prepositions:

ana 'to, toward, unto, for'; temporally, 'for, (with)in'.
ina 'in, into, at, among; with (things), by means of, by; from, from within (a place, with verbs of motion and of taking, seizing; see §5.6)'; temporally, 'in, on, at the time of'.
ištu 'from, out of, away from (a place)'; temporally, 'since'.
itti 'with (persons, deities), in the company of, from (a person, with verbs of taking, receiving; see §5.6)'.

Other:

ša 'the one of; of'.

B. Divide the vocabulary words into syllables, and mark the syllable with the stress.

C. Give the plural (nominative) of the following:

1. *amtum*	5. *bēlum*	9. *mārum*	13. *emūqum*	17. *bītum*
2. *wardum*	6. *aššatum*	10. *ilum*	14. *nārum*	18. *šarrum*
3. *ummum*	7. *mutum*	11. *iltum*	15. *ṭuppum*	
4. *mārtum*	8. *išdum*	12. *šarratum*	16. *ṣābum*	

D. For what is the accusative case used?

E. Write in Akkadian (remember to use the dual where appropriate):

1. from the town
2. in the center of the house
3. with the menservants of the queen

4. the lord's eyes
5. the one of strength
6. among the wives of the husbands
7. the head of the lord
8. the silver and gold of the king's son
9. the one of the town
10. with eyes and ears
11. by the power of the gods
12. out of the house
13. (he received it) from the slave
14. with the king's wool
15. the foundation of the city
16. among the daughters' tablets

F. Translate the following sentences:

1. *Ninḫursag* (a goddess) *šarratum ša ilātim; šarratum ša ilātim šī.*
2. *amātum ša bēlim anāku u attina.*
3. *bēlum ša ālim anāku.*
4. *amātum ina nārim; ina nārim šina.*
5. *ṭuppum ša mārim ša bēlim; ša mārim ša bēlim šū.*
6. *ilū ina libbim ša ālim; ina libbim ša ālim šunu.*
7. *wardū ša šarratim nīnu.*
8. *emūqū ša šarrim ina ālim.*
9. *mutum u aššatum ina bītim itti mārī u mārātim; ina bītim šunu.*
10. *šīpātum ša wardim.*
11. *emūqān ša šarrim išdān ša ālim.*

G. Write in Akkadian:

1. You are the mother of the gods.
2. The gold was in the house; it was in the house.
3. You are the sons of the female slaves; you are the daughters of the male slaves.
4. The army of the king was in the river.
5. You are the father of the womanservant.
6. The principal of the silver belongs to the mother.
7. The goddess was in the midst of the army.
8. The wife's wool is in the house.

LESSON THREE

3.1 The Semantic Root

In the Semitic languages, including Akkadian (see above, page xxi), most nouns, adjectives, and verbs consist of a sequence of consonants plus an internal vowel pattern; other modifications include affixes (prefixes, suffixes, infixes) and consonant doubling. Study the following words, which share the consonantal base *k–ṣ–r*:

		VOWEL PATTERN	AFFIXES, ETC.
kaṣārum	'to bind'	$R_1aR_2\bar{a}R_3$	suffix *-um* (case-ending)
kuṣur	'bind!'	$R_1uR_2uR_3$	none
kuṣṣurum	'well tied'	$R_1uR_2R_2uR_3$	doubling of R_2; suffix *-um* (case-ending)
makṣarum	'bundle'	$R_1R_2aR_3$	prefix *ma-* and suffix *-um* (case-ending)

These words are all clearly related in meaning; they all have to do with 'binding'. The sequence of consonants *k–ṣ–r* is called the **root** of these words (and of others containing the same sequence and having related meanings). The consonants *k*, *ṣ*, and *r* are referred to as the **radicals** of the root (hence R_1, R_2, and R_3). As a further example, note the following words, which have the root *d–n–n* (hence, R_2 and R_3 are the same), and have to do with 'strength':

		VOWEL PATTERN	AFFIXES, ETC.
danānum	'to grow strong'	$R_1aR_2\bar{a}R_3$	suffix *-um* (case-ending)
idnin	'it grew strong'	$R_1R_2iR_3$	prefix *i-*
dunnum	'strength'	$R_1uR_2R_3$	suffix *-um* (case-ending)
tadnintum	'strengthening'	$R_1R_2iR_3$	pref. *ta-*; suffixes *-t* (fem.) and *-um* (case-ending)

The vowel patterns and the affixes give the words their precise meanings; they also provide morphological information: e.g., the pattern $R_1aR_2\bar{a}R_3$*(-um)* is the basic Infinitive of the verb (as in *kaṣārum*, *danānum*); $R_1uR_2uR_3$ is one of the patterns of the Imperative (*kuṣur*).

Because the use of *R_1–R_2–R_3* is cumbersome, Assyriologists have adopted one root as paradigmatic, namely, ***p–r–s***, which has to do with 'separating, deciding', where ***p*** stands for *R_1*, ***r*** for *R_2*, and ***s*** for *R_3*. Thus, the basic Infinitive, as in *kaṣārum* and *danānum* above, is said to be "of the pattern *parās*" or to be a "*parās* form" (the case-ending may be omitted in the discussion of patterns); the patterns of the other nouns given above are as follows:

WORD	PATTERN	WORD	PATTERN
kuṣṣurum	*purrus*	*dunnum*	*purs*
makṣarum	*mapras*	*tadnintum*	*taprist*

In this grammar, we will usually follow the tradition of using *p–r–s* as the paradigmatic root, although there will be occasions on which *R_1–R_2–R_3* will be more convenient.

Not all roots have three radicals; many have only two, and some have four and even five. In such cases, obviously, the paradigmatic root *p–r–s* is not useful. For roots with two radicals, therefore, we will use ***p–s*** or *R_1–R_2*; e.g.,

WORD	PATTERN	WORD	PATTERN
mutum	*pus* or *R_1uR_2*	*nārum*	*pās* or *$R_1āR_2$*

(See also the next paragraph, however.) For four-radical roots, the paradigm will be either ***p–r–s–d*** (or *R_1–R_2–R_3–R_4*) or ***p–s–p–s*** (or *R_1–R_2–R_1–R_2*); five-radical roots are very rare.

From comparison with other Semitic languages, it is known that, very early in its history, Akkadian merged five consonants that it had inherited from Proto-Semitic; these are transcribed *ʾ*, *h*, *ḥ*, *ʿ*, *ǵ* by students of Semitic philology, although Assyriologists often refer to them as ʾ$_1$, ʾ$_2$, ʾ$_3$, ʾ$_4$, ʾ$_5$, respectively. (ʾ$_5$, Semitic *ǵ*, merged with *ḫ* is some instances; Kogan 2001.) The phonemes *w* and *y* also merged with these in some instances; in such cases, they are referred to as ʾ$_6$ and ʾ$_7$, respectively. The loss of ʾ$_{1-5}$ in most phonological positions, and of ʾ$_{6-7}$ in some positions, resulted in various further sound changes, including vowel lengthening and vowel contraction, and changes of vowel quality, changes that are taken up in LESSON 6. The word *abum* 'father', for example, was originally **ʾabum*, and so it is in effect of the pattern *pas*; *nārum* 'river' was originally **nahrum*, and so may be said to be either *pās* or *pars* (see above); similarly *ālum* 'city', originally **ʾahlum*, may be said to be either *pās* or *pars*, and *bēlum*, originally **baʿlum*, either *pēs* or *pars*.

3.2 Verb Morphology: Introductory Considerations

Akkadian verbs present to the beginning student a bewildering array of forms. There are three nominal or non-finite forms (Infinitive,

Participle, Verbal Adjective). Finite forms, that is, forms that are inflected for person, gender, and number, include indicative "tenses" (Preterite, Durative, Perfect) as well as injunctive forms (Imperative, Precative). Besides sound roots, there are several weak root types, in which one or more of the radicals is subject to phonological change. Finally, most roots occur in several stems or conjugations, each with its own semantic range. Not surprisingly, then, much of the grammar presented in this text will concern verbal morphology.

Up to LESSON 23, only the basic stem or conjugation will be considered; it is called the **G Stem**, after German *Grundstamm* ('basic stem'). It has been thought best to introduce the G stem of weak root types before the other conjugations of the sound roots, since many of the most common verbs in the language have weak roots.

As will be seen from the descriptions that follow in this and subsequent lessons, the term "tense" for the Preterite, Durative, and Perfect is inadequate. None of these forms is limited to a single time value, and all involve certain aspectual notions such as (non-)duration of action and present relevance of action.

3.3 The G Infinitive: Form and Meaning

The Infinitive is a **declinable noun** (masc. sg.; plural forms of infinitives do not occur); in the G stem, it has the pattern ***parās***: e.g., *šakānum* 'to place, install'; *maḫārum* 'to receive'; *šarāqum* 'to steal'.

Infinitives often follow prepositions (thus, in the genitive case); in such instances, the prepositions frequently have special nuances (e.g., *ana* 'in order to'; *ina* 'when, while, by'), and the Infinitive is often best translated by the English gerund:

> *wardum ina šarāqim ša ḫurāṣim imqut* 'The slave fell (*imqut*) while/when stealing the gold (lit.: in the stealing of the gold).'
>
> *šarrum ana ālim ana šakānim ša ilim ikšud* 'The king arrived (*ikšud*) at the city to install the god (lit.: for the installing of the god).'

The use of the Infinitive will be treated in greater detail in a later lesson (§30.1).

Verbs are listed under their Infinitives in modern Akkadian dictionaries, as they were by ancient scribes in their lexical texts.

3.4 Verb Semantics: General Comments

Most verbs may be assigned to one of three semantic categories:

(1) Active-transitive verbs: these are verbs that take a direct object, such as *šakānum* 'to place', *šarāqum* 'to steal', *maḫāṣum* 'to strike', *ṭarādum* 'to send'.

(2) Active-intransitive verbs: here belong especially verbs of motion, such as *naḫāsum* 'to recede', *wašābum* 'to sit down, dwell', *maqātum* 'to fall', *ḫalāqum* 'to escape, perish', and a few other verbs, such as *balāṭum* 'to live'.

(3) Stative or adjectival verbs: these mean 'to be X' or 'to become X', where "X" is an adjective, as in *damāqum* 'to be/become good, improve', *marāṣum* 'to be/get sick', *rapāšum* 'to be/become wide', *warāqum* 'to be/turn yellow'.

A few verbs belong to two of these categories: e.g., *kašādum* 'to reach (+ direct object)' and 'to arrive (intransitive)'; *palāḫum* 'to fear (+ direct object)' and 'to be afraid (intransitive)'.

The significance of these semantic categories for a thorough understanding of the verbal system will become apparent over the course of the next few lessons.

3.5 The G Preterite: Form and Meaning

The base of the G Preterite is $\boldsymbol{R_1R_2VR_3}$, where *V* is one of the short vowels. This vowel, which is called the **theme vowel** (or, stem vowel), is unpredictable and must be learned for each root. Prefixes and suffixes are added to the base to indicate person, gender, and number (as is traditional in Semitic grammar, verbal paradigms proceed from the third person to the first):

3cs	*i-*		3mp	*i-*	*-ū*
			3fp	*i-*	*-ā*
2ms	*ta-*		2cp	*ta-*	*-ā*
2fs	*ta-*	*-ī*			
1cs	*a-*		1cp	*ni-*	

Note that there is a common form for the third person singular, for the second person plural, as well as for both singular and plural first person forms. Below are the G Preterites of *šakānum* (theme vowel *u*) 'to place', *šarāqum* (*i*) 'to steal', and *ṣabātum* (*a*) 'to seize':

3cs	*iškun* 'she/he/it placed'	*išriq* 'she/he/it stole'	*iṣbat* 'she/he/it seized'
2ms	*taškun* 'you (ms) placed'	*tašriq* 'you (ms) stole'	*taṣbat* 'you (ms) seized'
2fs	*taškunī* 'you (fs) placed'	*tašriqī* 'you (fs) stole'	*taṣbatī* 'you (fs) seized'
1cs	*aškun* 'I placed'	*ašriq* 'I stole'	*aṣbat* 'I seized'
3mp	*iškunū* 'they (m) placed'	*išriqū* 'they (m) stole'	*iṣbatū* 'they (m) seized'
3fp	*iškunā* 'they (f) placed'	*išriqā* 'they (f) stole'	*iṣbatā* 'they (f) seized'
2cp	*taškunā* 'you (pl) placed'	*tašriqā* 'you (pl) stole'	*taṣbatā* 'you (pl) seized'
1cp	*niškun* 'we placed'	*nišriq* 'we stole'	*niṣbat* 'we seized'

The Preterite denotes an action seen by the speaker/writer as occurring or having occurred at a single point in time (hence "punctual"). It is therefore usually best translated as a **simple past tense**: *aškun* 'I placed'. (In temporal clauses, it may on occasion be rendered by the pluperfect: '(when/after) I had placed'.)

The pronominal subject ('I', 'you', etc.) is always included in the verb form. The independent nominative pronouns (§2.4) may be used for two reasons:

(a) For emphasis: *atta tašriq* 'It was you (ms) who stole.'

(b) When the subject involves different persons: *anāku u atta niṣbat* 'You and I (we) seized.'

Note that the independent pronouns stand at the beginning of verbal clauses (see the next section), rather than at the end as they do when subjects of verbless clauses (§2.5).

3.6 Word Order and Agreement in Verbal Clauses

In verbal clauses in prose texts, the normal order of constituents is:

Subject—Direct Object—Adjunct—Verb.

"Adjuncts" are adverbs and prepositional phrases (including indirect objects). Naturally, all of these elements need not be present in any given clause. While the order of constituents may be rearranged in a variety of ways, usually to emphasize one element of the clause over the others (e.g., by placing the direct object before the subject), the **verb** is always the **last word** in its clause. Since there is no punctuation in the writing, this is an essential key in determining where one clause ends and the next begins. Occasionally, the direct object may be left unexpressed, where English would have a pronoun; thus, in certain contexts, *wardum išriq* may mean 'The servant stole it'. But Akkadian too normally has a pronoun here (§18.2). As in English, conjunctions always precede all other constituents in a clause, as do certain sentence-modifying adverbs and prepositional phrases (such as 'moreover', 'at that time'). Some examples of verbal sentences:

amtum kaspam iṣbat ina bītim iškun 'The woman slave seized the silver; she put (it) in the house';

ḫurāṣam ša šarrim tašriqā 'You (pl) stole the king's gold';

bēlum abam ša šarratim ina ālim iṣbat 'The lord seized the queen's father in the town.'

Verbs must agree with their subjects in person, gender, and number: e.g.,

ilātum ḫurāṣam ša šarrim iṣbatā 'The goddesses seized the king's gold';

wardū šīpātim ina bītim iškunū 'The menservants put the wool in the house.'

As was noted in §2.1(f), subjects that are dual in form are normally construed as feminine plural, even when the noun in the dual is masculine when singular:

šarrān iškunā (only rarely *šarrān iškunū*) 'The two kings placed';

šarratān iškunā 'The two queens placed'.

Compound subjects ('X and Y', 'X, Y, and Z') take plural verbs; if any of the elements is masculine, the verb is masculine plural:

mārum u mārtum imqutū 'The son and the daughter fell';

amtum wardum u mārātum imqutū 'The female slave, the male slave, and the daughters fell';

aššatum u mārātum imqutā 'The wife and the daughters fell'.

Collective nouns may be construed as singular or plural:

ṣābum ālam iṣbat / iṣbatū 'The troop seized the town.'

EXERCISES

A. VOCABULARY 3.

Verbs:

damāqum (Preterite *idmiq*) 'to become good, better, improve, prosper'.

danānum (*idnin*) 'to become strong'.

ḫalāqum (*iḫliq*) 'to disappear, go missing, get lost; to escape; to perish'.
kašādum (*ikšud*) 'to arrive (at a place: *ana* or acc.); to reach, achieve; to conquer, defeat'.
maḫāṣum (*imḫaṣ*) 'to strike, hit, smite, wound, kill'.
maqātum (*imqut*) 'to fall, fall down, collapse; to arrive (said of news, etc.), happen; to fall upon, attack (with *ana*, *eli*)'.
marāṣum (*imraṣ*) 'to become sick, fall ill; to be(come) painful; to become troublesome, difficult (to, for someone: *eli*, *ana*)'; with *libbum* as subject: 'to become annoyed' (e.g., *libbum ša šarrim imraṣ* 'the king became annoyed').
rapāšum (*irpiš*) 'to become wide, broad'.
ṣabātum (*iṣbat*) 'to seize, take hold of, arrest, capture'.
šakānum (*iškun*) 'to place, set, put; to establish, install, appoint, assign, impose'.
šarāqum (*išriq*) 'to steal'.

Nouns (reminder: nouns with *t*- are fem., others masc.):

awīlum 'human being, person; grown man; free man; boss'.
mātum (fem.; pl. *mātātum*) 'country (political unit), native land; land, open country'.
qātum (fem.) 'hand; care, charge, responsibility'; *ina qātim ša* 'from (a person, with verbs of receiving, taking, seizing, etc.); in the charge of, under the authority of (a person); through the agency of (a person)'; *qātam ṣabātum* 'to help' (e.g., *qātam ša wardim aṣbat* 'I helped the slave'); *qātam šakānum* 'to begin' (+ *ana* + Infin.: 'to do', as in *qātam ana šarāqim ša kaspim iškunū* 'they began to steal the silver'; + *ana* + noun: 'begin work on', as in *qātam ana bītim aškun* 'I began work on the house'); the plural form *qātātum* means 'guarantee, security, pledge'.
šarrāqum 'thief' (cf. *šarāqum* above).

Preposition:

eli 'on, upon, over, above, towards, against, beyond, more than'.

B. Divide the vocabulary words into syllables, and note the syllable that bears the stress.

C. 1. What are the radicals (i.e., what is the root) of each of the verbs in the vocabulary?

2. Give the verb in the vocabulary to which each of the following nouns and adjectives is related (i.e., the verb with which each shares its root). Note the pattern of each (using either *p–r–s* or R_1–R_2–R_3).

   Example: *mitḫuṣum* is related to *maḫāṣum* (root *m–ḫ–ṣ*), of the pattern *pitrus* (or $R_1itR_2uR_3$ [infix *-t-*]).

miqtum	*kāšidum*	*šarrāqum*	*šaknum*
naṣbutum	*dummuqum*	*damqiš*	*tadnintum*
murappišum	*šaḫluqtum*	*maškanum*	*ritpāšum*
ḫulqum	*šuṣbutum*	*murṣum*	*šikānum*

D. Give the full Preterite conjugation, with meanings, of *ḫalāqum*, *kašādum*, and *maḫāṣum*.

E. Write in Akkadian:

1. he escaped
2. I conquered
3. you (ms) stole
4. it became wide
5. they (m) improved
6. we got sick
7. she seized
8. you (pl) placed
9. they (f) struck
10. you (fs) became strong
11. you (mp) and I fell

F. Translate the following sentences:

1. *ḫurāṣum u kaspum ša wardī iḫliqū.*
2. *amtam ša šarratim taṣbat.*
3. *qaqqadam ša mārim ša šarrāqim ina emūqim tamḫaṣī.*
4. *ṣābum ina libbim ša mātim.*
5. *ilum īnīn ša mutim imḫaṣ.*
6. *šīpātim ina bītim ša ummim išriqū.*
7. *ilū šarram eli mātim iškunū.*
8. *itti mārātim ša awīlim atta.*
9. *ṣābum ša šarrim idninū; ana libbim ša mātim ištu nārim ikšudū.*
10. *bītum ša awīlim idmiq.*
11. *abum u ummum uznīn u qātīn ša mārim imḫaṣū.*
12. *nārātum ša mātātim irpišā.*
13. *aššatum u mārū ša bēlim imraṣū; bītum ša bēlim iḫliq.*
14. *iltum išdīn ša ālim ina qātim ša šarrim iškun.*
15. *išdum ša ālim ina qātim ša ilī.*

16. *šarrāqum ina ḫalāqim ištu mātim imraṣ.*
17. *ṭuppātim ina qātim ša šarrāqim aṣbat.*
18. *qātam ana maḫāṣim ša wardim iškun.*
19. *libbum ša šarratim eli awīlim imraṣ.*
20. *qātam ana bītim ša ilim aškun.*

G. Write in Akkadian:

1. The owners of the house became strong; they prospered.
2. She placed (her) hands on (her) daughter's ears.
3. We caught the thief stealing (lit.: in stealing).
4. I was in the city.
5. The army of the lord fell upon the land to conquer the land.
6. You (pl) helped the womanservant.

LESSON FOUR

4.1 Vowel Syncope

In §1.3, a light syllable was defined as one that ends in a short vowel. Akkadian phonology does not tolerate sequences of two or more light syllables in a word, except in a number of instances that are described below. When two or more light syllables would appear successively, the vowel of the last one is omitted (syncopated). As an example, consider the word *napištum* 'life, throat', which may be broken down into *napiš-* (base), *-t-* (fem. marker), *-um* (case-ending). The plural of *napištum* will have the elements *napiš+āt+um*. But a form ****napišātum** (** indicates an unattested or impossible form) would begin with two light syllables; thus, syncope of the second vowel takes place, and the form is *napšātum*. Further examples appear in §4.3 below.

Exceptions to the rule of vowel syncope occur:

(a) regularly at the end of a word, where two successive light syllables are permitted, as in *iškunu* '(who) placed', *ina* 'in';

(b) regularly before a vowel, as in *rabiam* 'great (acc.)', *biniā* 'build (pl)!';

(c) frequently before *r*, as in *zikarum* 'male', *šikarum* 'beer', *labirum* 'old', *nakirum* 'hostile'; byforms with syncope, such as *nakrum*, also occur;

(d) occasionally before *l*, as in *akalum* 'food', *ubilū* 'they (m) brought'; byforms with syncope often occur: *aklum*;

(e) when certain pronominal suffixes are added, as in *ṭuppašunu* 'their tablet' (see §11.1);

(f) in some Sumerian loanwords, such as *nuḫatimmum* 'cook', *gabaraḫḫum* 'rebellion'.

4.2 The Attributive Adjective: Declension and Agreement

Adjectives may be attributive, as in 'the mighty king', or predicative, as in 'the king is mighty'. The latter are taken up in §22.1. Attributive adjectives, like nouns, are declined; they agree with the nouns they modify in case, number, and gender. The endings are the same as those on nouns, except for the masc. pl. Thus, in the sg., the case-endings are nom. *-um*, gen. *-im*, acc. *-am*. The fem. sg. has *-t-* after the base (before the case-ending) if the base ends in one consonant, *-at-* if it ends in two (cf. the nouns *mārtum*, *šarratum*). The fem. pl. endings, as on nouns, are nom. *-ātum*, gen.-acc. *-ātim*. As noted above, the only distinction between the declension of attributive adjectives and that of nouns lies in the masc. pl.: whereas nouns have nom. *-ū*, gen.-acc. *-ī*, adjectives have nom. *-ūtum*, gen.-acc. *-ūtim* for the masc. pl. Below are the full declensions of *ṭābum* (base *ṭāb-*) 'pleasant' and *dannum* (base *dann-*) 'strong':

		MASCULINE	FEMININE	MASCULINE	FEMININE
SINGULAR	nom.	*ṭābum*	*ṭābtum*	*dannum*	*dannatum*
	gen.	*ṭābim*	*ṭābtim*	*dannim*	*dannatim*
	acc.	*ṭābam*	*ṭābtam*	*dannam*	*dannatam*
PLURAL	nom.	*ṭābūtum*	*ṭābātum*	*dannūtum*	*dannātum*
	gen.-acc.	*ṭābūtim*	*ṭābātim*	*dannūtim*	*dannātim*

The attributive adjective follows the noun it modifies, as in

šarrū dannūtum 'strong kings';
ina qātim dannatim 'with a strong arm'.

An adjective may modify more than one noun; it appears in the plural:

abum u mārum dannūtum 'the strong father and son';
ummum u mārtum dannātum 'the strong mother and daughter';

an adjective modifying a compound antecedent of mixed gender is masc. pl.:

abum u ummum dannūtum 'the strong father and mother'.

Adjectives do not have dual forms; dual nouns are modified by plural adjectives (normally feminine pl.; see §2.1(f)):

īnān ṭābātum 'pleasant eyes'.

4.3 The G Verbal Adjective

Associated with verbal roots, in all stems (see §3.2), is a form referred to as the Verbal Adjective. Most Akkadian adjectives belong to this category (for other types of adjectives, see §§6.2, 6.3, 25.3).

(a) Form

The Verbal Adjective in the sound verb has the pattern *parVs*, where *V* is one of the short vowels. For most verbs, this second vowel is *i*; only a few stative/adjectival verbs have *a* or *u* (see below); examples are *ṣabit-* 'seized'; *damiq-* 'good'; *rapaš-* 'wide'; *zapur-* 'malicious'. Because of the vowel syncope rule (§4.1 above), however, the distinctive second vowel of such bases disappears when case-endings are added in the masc. sg. and in all pl. forms. Thus, the vowel appears only in the fem. sg. forms.

		MASCULINE	FEMININE
SINGULAR	nom.	*damqum*	*damiqtum*
	gen.	*damqim*	*damiqtim*
	acc.	*damqam*	*damiqtam*
PLURAL	nom.	*damqūtum*	*damqātum*
	gen.-acc.	*damqūtim*	*damqātim*

Similarly:

ms	*rapšum*	fs	*rapaštum*	ms	*zaprum*	fs	*zapurtum*
mp	*rapšūtum*	fp	*rapšātum*	mp	*zaprūtum*	fp	*zaprātum*

These adjectives, like all others, are listed in dictionaries, and in the vocabularies of this textbook, by their masc. sg. forms (e.g., *damqum*). As noted above, the second vowel of active roots (both transitive and intransitive) is almost invariably *i*; for adjective/stative roots, however, the vowel is unpredictable. For such roots, the student must be careful to learn either the base (*damiq-*, *rapaš-*) or the fem. sg. (*damiqtum*, *rapaštum*) as well; note that the vowel is not necessarily the same as the theme-vowel of the Preterite: *idmiq* 'became good' and *damiq-* 'good', but *imraṣ* 'became sick' and *maruṣ* 'sick', *irpiš* 'became wide' and *rapaš-* 'wide'.

Verbal Adjectives of adjectival verbs in which R_2 and R_3 are the same, such as *danānum* 'to become strong', have *pass-* as their base, as in ms *dannum*, fs *dannatum*. Active verbs of this type have regular bases: thus, e.g., the Verbal Adj. of *šakākum* 'to harrow' is ms *šakkum*, fs *šakiktum*.

(b) Meaning

The Verbal Adjective describes the condition or state resulting from the action of the verb from which it is derived. The basic meaning of any such adjective is determined by the semantic nature of its root (see §3.4); in particular:

(1) Active-transitive roots have **passive** Verbal Adjectives, as in *maḫṣum* 'struck, smitten', *ṣabtum* 'seized, captive', *šaknum* 'placed, installed', *šarqum* 'stolen';

(2) Active-intransitive roots have **resultative** Verbal Adjectives, as in *ḫalqum* 'escaped, missing, lost', *maqtum* 'fallen, collapsed, in ruins';

(3) Stative/adjectival roots have simple **descriptive** Verbal Adjectives, as in *damqum* 'good', *dannum* 'strong', *marṣum* 'sick', *rapšum* 'wide'.

Although it is clear that Verbal Adjectives could be formed at will for any verbal root, semantics and the fortuitousness of discovery have meant that Verbal Adjectives are in fact not attested in texts for all roots. Further, some Verbal Adjectives that do occur are not yet attested attributively, but only in predicative use, in a construction to be treated in a later lesson (§22.1).

In the lesson vocabularies, Verbal Adjectives will usually be given in the entries of new verbs, though not in the case of all active-transitive verbs, since for those roots the form and meaning of the Verbal Adjective, if attested, are generally predictable. (Even when not specifically cited in the vocabularies, however, such forms may nevertheless appear in the exercises and readings.) Finally, it should be noted that for stative/adjectival roots, the Verbal Adjective is often of greater frequency than finite forms like the Preterite. (Rarely, finite forms are not yet attested at all; in such cases, the Adjective will be listed separately, without a corresponding Infinitive.)

4.4 The Substantivization of Adjectives

Any adjective may be used as a noun, meaning 'one (person or thing) who/that is X', where "X" is the quality described by the adjective. Adjectives used as nouns are said to be **substantivized**. Examples:

ṣabtum 'seized, captive (m); a captive, a prisoner';
dannūtum 'strong (pl); strong men, the strong ones';
ḫaliqtum 'escaped, missing (f); an escaped/missing woman'.

As indicated by the example *dannūtum*, the masc. plural of substantivized adjectives normally retains the adjectival endings *-ūtum* / *-ūtim*; occasionally, however, the noun pl. endings occur, as in:

nakirum 'hostile, inimical; enemy'; pl. *nakirūtum* when used as an attributive adjective (*šarrū nakirūtum* 'enemy kings'), *nakirū* when substantivized as 'enemies'.

The feminine singular of an adjective may be used as an abstract noun, indicating the quality descibed by the adjective:

damqum 'good'; *damiqtum* 'good (f); good(ness), favor, luck; fame';
zaprum 'malicious, false'; *zapurtum* 'malicious, false (f); malice, falsehood'.

Sometimes the meaning of the substantivized feminine form is more concrete:

dannum 'strong, hard (m)'; *dannatum* 'strong, hard (f); hard times; fortress'.

4.5 The Negative Adverb *ul(a)*

The predicate of a main clause is negated with an adverb that usually has the form *ul*; a less common byform is *ula*. This stands immediately before the verb in verbal clauses, before the head of the predicate in verbless clauses. Examples:

ḫurāṣam ina bītim ul aṣbat 'I did not seize the gold from the house.'
Išme-Dagan ula šarrum ša Bābilim 'Ishme-Dagan is not king of Babylon.'
ul šarrum ša Bābilim šū 'He is not king of Babylon.'

EXERCISES

A. VOCABULARY 4.

Verbs:

balāṭum (Preterite *iblut̩*) 'to live, be alive, be healthy; to get well, recover'; the Infinitive is used as a noun, 'life'; Verbal Adj. *balṭum* (base *baliṭ-* [fem. sg. see §5.4]) 'alive, healthy, safe'.

gamārum (*igmur*) 'to bring to an end; to annihilate; to use up; to settle; to encompass, control; to finish (doing: *ina* + Infinitive); to come to an end'; Verbal Adj. *gamrum* (*gamir-*) 'finished, settled; complete, entire, full (may follow another adj.: *šamnum ṭābum gamrum* 'the entire (amount of) fine oil')'.

kanākum (*iknuk*) 'to seal; to place under seal'; Verbal Adj. *kankum* (*kanik-*) 'sealed, under seal'.

maḫārum (*imḫur*) 'to accept, receive (from someone: *itti* or *ina qātim ša*); to approach, meet, confront'; *īnam ša X maḫārum* 'to please X' (e.g., *īnam ša šarrim tamḫur* 'you (ms) pleased the king'); Verbal Adj. *maḫrum* (*maḫir-*) 'received'.
šalāmum (*išlim*) 'to become whole, sound, well, uninjured, safe; to recover; to arrive safely; to succeed, prosper; to be completed'; Verbal Adj. *šalmum* (*šalim-*) 'whole, sound, well, safe, in good condition, intact, complete, favorable'.

Nouns:

aḫum 'brother'.
alpum 'ox, bull'.
eṭlum (pl. like an adjective: *eṭlūtum*) 'young man, youth'.
kakkum 'weapon'.
napištum (pl. *napšātum*) 'life, vigor, good health; person; personnel; self; throat'.
šamnum 'oil, fat'.
šikarum 'beer, intoxicating liquid'.

Adjectives:

damqum (base *damiq-*; Verbal Adj. of *damāqum*) 'good, of good quality; beautiful; favorable; expert'; fem. *damiqtum* 'good(ness), favor, luck; fame'.
dannum (*dann-*; Verbal Adj. of *danānum*) 'strong, solid; mighty, powerful; fortified; fierce, savage; severe, difficult; urgent'; substantivized fem. *dannatum* 'famine, hard times; fortress'.
ḫalqum (*ḫaliq-*; Verbal Adj. of *ḫalāqum*) 'escaped; missing, lost'.
kašdum (*kašid-* [fem. sg. see §5.4]; Verbal Adj. of *kašādum*) 'successful, achieved; conquered; having arrived, available'.
maqtum (*maqit-*; Verbal Adj. of *maqātum*) 'fallen, collapsed, in ruins'.
marṣum (*maruṣ-* [fem. sg. see §5.4]; Verbal Adj. of *marāṣum*) 'sick, ill; diseased, painful; difficult'; substantivized fem. *maruštum* (pl. *marṣātum*) 'difficulty, hardship, trouble, duress'.
nakarum, *nakirum*, and *nakrum* (base *nakar-* or *nakir-*; Verbal Adj. of *nakārum*, Vocab. 21) 'hostile, inimical; foreign'; substantivized (pl. *nak(a/i)rū*), 'enemy, foe'.
rapšum (*rapaš-*; Verbal Adj. of *rapāšum*) 'wide, broad'; *uznum rapaštum* 'great intelligence, understanding'.

ṣabtum (*ṣabit-*; Verbal Adj. of *ṣabātum*) 'seized; deposited; captive, prisoner'.
šaknum (*šakin-* [fem. sg. see §§5.1, 5.4]; Verbal Adj. of *šakānum*) 'placed, lying, situated, located, present; established, appointed; endowed, provided'; substantivized, 'governor'.
šarqum (*šariq-*; Verbal Adj. of *šarāqum*) 'stolen'.
ṭābum (*ṭāb-*; Verbal Adj. of *ṭiābum*, Vocab. 9) 'pleasant, pleasing (to: *eli*), sweet, fine, good'.

Adverb:

ul, less often *ula* 'not'.

B. To which verbs are the following words related?

1. *šiknum*	4. *muqqutum*	7. *šumḫurtum*	10. *tamḫīṣum*
2. *ḫaliqtum*	5. *kanīkum*	8. *gamriš*	11. *bulṭum*
3. *ṣābitānum*	6. *tašlamtum*	9. *rapaštum*	12. *kašdum*

C. Give the plurals of the following words:

1. *napištum* 2. *rapaštum* 3. *zapurtum* 4. *šariqtum*.

D. Give the full Preterite, with meanings, of *balāṭum*, *ṣabātum*, and *šalāmum*.

E. Decline in full (sg. and pl.) and translate the phrases *wardum ḫalqum* and *amtum ḫaliqtum*.

F. Write in Akkadian:

1. strong weapons
2. fine beer
3. diseased eyes
4. a lord of great intelligence
5. among the good daughters
6. missing oxen
7. against the mighty youth
8. with fine oil
9. with the sick brother
10. fallen houses
11. hostile kings
12. stolen wool
13. sealed tablets
14. against the foreign country
15. for captive husbands
16. foundations in ruins
17. with the healthy son
18. mighty strength
19. in the wide river
20. with the entire heart
21. received silver
22. successful attacks (*tībū*)

G. Translate the following sentences:

1. *amraṣ; inanna* ('now') *napištam akšud, ablut̩, adnin.*
2. *ilū napištam ša et̩lim dannim imh̬aṣū.*
3. *šīpātum ina bītim ša awīlim ih̬liqā; ah̬um ša awīlim šarrāqam ina kašādim ša dannatim iṣbat.*
4. *ṣābam nakiram ina kakkī dannūtim nigmur.*
5. *šamnam t̩ābam u alpī šalmūtim itti šarrāqim ul amh̬ur.*
6. *abum ša šarratim ul ina bītim ša iltim.*
7. *amātum ina qātim ša bēlim ih̬liqā.*
8. *t̩uppī itti aššatim ša awīlim nimh̬ur; t̩uppī niknuk.*
9. *ṣābum ša šarrim dannātim ša nakrī ikšudū.*
10. *wardū ālam ana gamārim ša išdim ša bītim ikšudū.*
11. *šarrum dannum ṣabtūtim ina kakkī ul imh̬aṣ.*
12. *damiqtum ša ilī ana ah̬im ša et̩lim imqut.*
13. *šikaram t̩ābam ina qātim ša šarrāqim taṣbatā.*
14. *alpū ša awīlim īnam ša bēlim imh̬urū.*
15. *wardū marṣūtum ištu dannatim ana nārim rapaštim ih̬liqū.*
16. *ina kanākim ša t̩uppī ul nigmur.*
17. *qātam ana bītim maqtim aškun.*

H. Write in Akkadian:

1. They are the youth's mother's oxen.
2. The king imposed (a tribute of) silver and gold on the conquered town.
3. The sick man put fine oil on (his) head.
4. The mothers of the youths reached the center of the fortified city.
5. You (fs) placed the entire (amount of) silver under seal.
6. The lords of the city approached the king of the land.
7. Foreign youths stole the governor's beer (and) used (it) up.
8. Famine fell upon the land; we became sick.

LESSON FIVE

5.1 Assimilation of *n*

The consonant *n* nearly always assimilates completely to a following consonant; the following consonant is then doubled (i.e., $nC_1 > C_1C_1$). As examples, consider the Verbal Adjectives *šaknum* with base *šakin-* 'placed' and *qatnum* with base *qatan-* 'thin, fine'. In the feminine singular of these adjectives, the final *n* of the base assimilates to the *t* of the feminine; the plural forms are not affected by this sound change, since the final *n* precedes a vowel in those forms:

> *šaknum*, fem. sg. *šakittum* (‹ *šakintum*); mp *šaknūtum*; fp *šaknātum;*
> *qatnum*, fem. sg. *qatattum* (‹ *qatantum*); mp *qatnūtum*; fp *qatnātum.*

Another set of examples of this sound change is offered by nouns of the pattern *pirist*, such as *miḫirtum* 'copy' (for details on noun patterns, see §32.2); *pirist* nouns from roots whose third radical is *n* show assimilation of *n* before the fem. *t* in the sg., and syncope of the second *i* of the pattern (§4.1) in the pl.:

> *libittum* (‹ *libintum*), pl. *libnātum* (‹ *libinātum*) 'brick';
> *nidittum* (‹ *nidintum*), pl. *nidnātum* (‹ *nidinātum*) 'gift, present'.

Still another example of the assimilation of *n* appears in the common noun *šattum*, originally **šantum*, 'year', the pl. of which is *šanātum.*

The assimilation of *n* is also found in verbs whose first radical is *n*, for which see §5.3 below.

Exceptions to the assimilation of *n* regularly occur in Verbal Adjectives of roots whose second radical is *n*, such as *kankum* 'sealed' and *enšum* 'weak', and in certain loanwords from Sumerian, such as *entum* 'high priestess'. (There are also sporadic exceptions in forms like those cited above, such as *qatantum* for expected *qatattum, nidintum* for expected *nidittum;* some of these may be dialectal variations, but most probably reflect morphographemic writings, a subject to be taken up in a later lesson [§18.4].)

5.2 Weak Verbs

Weak verbs are those with roots containing one or more radicals susceptible to phonological changes under certain conditions. Such verbs will be designated by a Roman numeral, indicating the radical affected, followed by the "weak" consonant in question. For example, I–*n* denotes verbs with first radical *n* (see the next section), while II–*w* denotes verbs with second radical *w*. The consonants that give rise to weak verbs are *n*, ʾ (or *ø*, since ʾ simply disappears in many environments), *w*, and *y*. In certain instances, we will refer to verbs more broadly as II–weak or III-weak; these designations indicate that the second or third radical, respectively, is ʾ, *w*, or *y*, since these often behave similarly.

5.3 The G Infinitive, Preterite, and Verbal Adjective: Verbs I–*n*

In the G Preterite of verbs I–*n*, the first radical *n* is always followed by another consonant, and therefore always assimilates, as illustrated by the following paradigms of *nadānum* (Preterite theme vowel *i*) 'to give' and *naqārum* (Preterite *u*) 'to tear down':

	nadānum	*naqārum*
3cs	*iddin*	*iqqur*
2ms	*taddin*	*taqqur*
2fs	*taddinī*	*taqqurī*
1cs	*addin*	*aqqur*
3mp	*iddinū*	*iqqurū*
3fp	*iddinā*	*iqqurā*
2cp	*taddinā*	*taqqurā*
1cp	*niddin*	*niqqur*

The G Infinitive and Verbal Adjective of verbs I–*n* are regular, since the initial *n* is always followed by a vowel in such forms: *naqārum*, *naqir-*.

5.4 Sound Changes before the Feminine Marker *t*

A number of consonants undergo some modification when they appear immediately before the marker *t* of the feminine singular. We have just seen above in §5.1 that *n* as third radical assimilates completely to the fem. sg. *t* in Verbal Adjectives and in the noun pattern *pirist* as in,

šaknum, fem. *šakittum*; *qatnum*, fem. *qatattum*;
nidittum (‹ *nidintum*) 'gift, present'.

The consonants *d* and *ṭ* also assimilate completely to the *t* of the fem. sg.; e.g.,

in Verbal Adjectives; the plural forms are regular: *kašdum*, fem. *kašittum* (mp *kašdūtum*, fp *kašdātum*); *paqdum* 'entrusted', fem. *paqittum* (mp *paqdūtum*, fp *paqdātum*); *mādum* 'much', fem. *māttum* (mp *mādūtum*, fp *mādātum*); *balṭum*, fem. *balittum* (mp *balṭūtum*, fp *balṭātum*);

in *pirist* nouns: *kišittum* (< **kišidtum*; pl. *kišdātum*) 'conquest, acquisition'; *piqittum* (< **piqidtum*; pl. *piqdātum*) 'delivery; inspection'.

Exceptions to these changes are rare.

The consonants *s*, *ṣ*, and *z* normally become *š* before the fem. sg. *t*:

in Verbal Adjectives; the plural forms are regular: *parsum* 'separated', fem. *parištum* (mp *parsūtum*, fp *parsātum*); *maḫṣum*, fem. *maḫištum* (mp *maḫṣūtum*, fp *maḫṣātum*); *marṣum*, fem. *maruštum* (mp *marṣūtum*, fp *marṣātum*);

in *pirist* forms: *pirištum* (root *p–r–s*) 'secret'.

As with the assimilation of *n*, occasional exceptions, in which *s*, *ṣ*, and *z* appear before the fem. *t* unchanged, are attested.

5.5 Verbs With Two Accusatives

Some Akkadian verbs may govern two direct objects, both in the accusative case, where English verbs have only one, the other object (from the Akkadian point of view) being rendered by a prepositional phrase. (A rare English verb that takes two objects is 'to envy', as in 'I envy him his knack with languages'.) Two main types of verbs with double accusative may be distinguished, according to their English equivalents. In one, the first accusative (usually a person, less often a thing) is translated as a direct object and the second requires the preposition 'with', as in 'to provide/satisfy/anoint/burn/clothe/touch/punish/surround someone/something with something'. Examples are *paqādum* (Pret. *ipqid*), which may mean 'to provide someone with something'; *pašāšum* (*ipšuš*) 'to anoint someone with something':

amtam šikaram tapqid 'you (ms) provided the female slave with beer';

qaqqadam ša šarrim šamnam ipšušū 'they (m) anointed the king's head with oil'.

In the second type, one accusative, a thing, is rendered as a direct object and the other, a person, is translated with the preposition 'from', as in 'to receive/request/claim/take away something from someone':

awīlam eqlam abqur 'I claimed (*baqārum*) the field from the man'.

Usually the second object in this type is a pronoun suffixed to the verb; object suffixes are covered in §18.2, but an example may be cited here:

kaspam amḫuršu 'I received silver from him' (-*šu* = 'him', acc.).

Frequently, one of the objects is replaced by a prepositional phrase (as is normally the case in English):

šikaram ana amtim tapqid;
qaqqadam ša šarrim ina šamnim ipšušū;
eqlam itti awīlim abqur.

Since only certain verbs take two direct objects, the student should not use this double-accusative construction in the English-to-Akkadian exercises unless it is explicitly noted for the verb in question in the Vocabulary in which it is introduced.

5.6 Prepositions with Verbs

The range of meaning of certain Akkadian prepositions and prepositional phrases requires comment. In particular, it will have been noted that the preposition *ina* is primarily locative and instrumental in meaning ('in; with, by'), yet may in some situations mean 'from', as in

amtum ina bītim iḫliq 'the slave escaped from the house'.

This phenomenon has a simple explanation: the preposition *ina* denotes the location of its object before the action of the verb ('escaped from within, from being in the house'; the slave was in the house before her escape). A similar explanation underlies the use of *itti* and *ina qātim ša* for 'from' with verbs of taking, receiving, and seizing:

kaspam itti awīlim amḫur 'I received the silver from the man' ('from with the man'; the silver was 'with the man' before 'I received' it);
ḫurāṣam ina qātim ša šarrāqim niṣbat 'we seized the gold from the thief' (the gold was 'in the hand of the thief' before 'we seized').

EXERCISES

A. VOCABULARY 5.

Verbs:

nadānum (*iddin*) 'to give, grant; to hand over, deliver, transfer; to

set, assign; to allow'; *ana kaspim nadānum* 'to sell'.
naqārum (*iqqur*) 'to tear down, destroy'.
nasāḫum (*issuḫ*) trans.: 'to remove, tear out, expel, reject, deport, transfer'; intrans.: 'to move on, remove oneself; to pass (of time)'; *qātam ša X nasāḫum* 'to keep X away, keep the claim of X away' (e.g., *dayyānū qātam ša eṭlim issuḫū* 'the judges kept (the claim of) the youth away'); Verbal Adj. *nasḫum* (*nasiḫ-*) 'uprooted, removed (from office)'.
naṣārum (*iṣṣur*) 'to watch (over), protect, guard; to keep'; Verbal Adj. *naṣrum* (*naṣir-*) 'watched, protected, guarded, under guard'.
paqādum (*ipqid*) 'to hand over, entrust, assign (something: acc.; to someone: *ana*); to supply (someone with something: double acc.), deliver; to take care of, look after; to inspect, muster'; *paqdum* (*paqid-*; fem. *paqittum*) 'delivered, assigned'.
pašāšum (*ipšuš*) 'to anoint, rub, smear (someone: acc.; with something: acc. or *ina*)'; Verbal Adj. *paššum* (*pašiš-*) 'anointed'.
qatānum (*iqtin*) 'to become thin, narrow, fine'; Verbal Adj. *qatnum* (*qatan-*; fem. *qatattum*) 'thin, narrow; fine (of wool, textiles)'.
rakābum (*irkab*) 'to mount; to ride; to board'.

Nouns:

ḫarrānum (fem.) 'road, path, way; journey; military expedition or campaign; caravan'; *ḫarrānam ṣabātum* 'to take to the road, undertake a campaign'.
kalbum 'dog'.
kišādum (pl. *kišādātum*) 'neck, throat; bank (of a river, canal, etc.)'.
narkabtum '(war-) chariot' (cf. *rakābum* above).
šēpum (fem.) 'foot'.

Adjective:

mādum (fem. *māttum* [*mattum* in the dictionaries]; mp *mādūtum*, fp *mādātum*; Verbal Adj. of *miādum*, lesson 9) 'much'; pl.: 'many'.

Preposition:

kīma 'like, as, according to, instead of'.

B. Give the full Preterite, with meanings, of *nasāḫum* and *naṣārum*.

C. Write in Akkadian:

1. from the conquered fortress
2. with the living womanservant
3. the feet and ears of the smitten daughter
4. on the eyes of the sick wife
5. a woman prisoner
6. a narrow road
7. complete sealed tablets
8. like the strong goddess
9. the anointed goddess
10. many campaigns and many weapons
11. the lives of the enemy youths
12. in the stolen chariots
13. like torn down houses
14. much hardship
15. lords removed (from office)
16. many chariots of good quality
17. much beer

D. Translate:

1. *šarrum qaqqadam u kišādam ša ilim šamnam ṭābam ipšuš.*
2. *maruštum ana šarrim u ana ṣābim ina ḫarrānim imqut.*
3. *aḫum ša šarratim narkabtam damiqtam ana ālim irkab.*
4. *išdum ša bītim iqtin; bītum imqut.*
5. *alpī šalmūtim ana ummim ša awīlim ul taddinā.*
6. *qātam eli kišādim qatnim ša kalbim aškun.*
7. *ṭuppātim kankātim ina qātim ša šarrāqim ina emūqīn niṣbat.*
8. *maruštum bēlam imḫur.*
9. *šarrum bēlam ḫurāṣam u šikaram mādūtim ipqid.*
10. *bēlū ša mātim šarram issuḫū; abam ša šarratim iškunū.*
11. *wardam ṣabtam ana mārim ša awīlim ana naṣārim apqid; šū wardam ul iṣṣur; wardum iḫliq.*
12. *mutam ša amtim šīpātim qatnātim tapqidī; mutum šīpātim ana kaspim iddin.*
13. *ālam u dannātim ša nakarim ula niqqur.*
14. *anāku kīma libbim ša ilī nakram ina mātim assuḫ.*
15. *ilum napištam ša awīlim iṣṣur.*
16. *šēpum ša kalbim imraṣ.*
17. *ilū šēpam ša šarrim eli kišādim ša nakrūtim iškunū.*
18. *šarrum ṣābam damqam ipqid; ḫarrānam iṣbatū.*

LESSON SIX

6.1 Vowel Changes due to Consonant Loss

It was noted in §3.1 (p. 16) that Akkadian lost a number of consonants known from other Semitic languages. Five Proto-Semitic consonants, called *aleph*s by Assyriologists, merged in Akkadian into a single consonant, ʾ; this Akkadian ʾ was in turn lost in most phonological environments. The five Proto-Semitic consonants in question are:

ʾ = ʾ$_1$	*ḥ* = ʾ$_3$	*ǵ* = ʾ$_5$
h = ʾ$_2$	ʿ = ʾ$_4$	

The development of Semitic *ǵ* = ʾ$_5$, which was rare, is complex: sometimes it was lost, sometimes it appeared as *ḫ*, and sometimes as ʾ.

The consonants *w* and *y* were also lost whenever they stood immediately before another consonant; in such cases, they too may be referred to as *aleph*s:

w = ʾ$_6$ *y* = ʾ$_7$

The loss of ʾ$_{1\text{–}7}$ resulted in several other phonological changes, which are described in the following paragraphs.

(a) If the consonant that dropped out stood at the beginning or end of a word, no further change occurred:

*ʾ*abum* › *abum* 'father';	**imla*ʾ › *imla* 'he filled';
**halākum* › *alākum* 'to go';	**puttuḥ* › *puttu* 'is opened';
**yūmum* › *ūmum* 'day';	**zakuw* › *zaku* 'is clear'.

Note that *w* was not lost word-initially: *wardum* 'male slave', *wašābum* 'to dwell'.

(b) The loss of one of ʾ$_{1\text{–}7}$ that stood directly before or after another consonant caused the lengthening of the immediately preceding vowel (marked in transcription with a macron): e.g.,

**nahrum* › *nārum* 'river';	**mar*ʾ*um* › *mārum* 'son';
**šuyšur* › *šūšur* 'is straightened';	**ḫudwum* › *ḫūdum* 'joy';
**zakuwtum* › *zakūtum* 'clear' (fs);	**tib*ʿ*um* › *tībum* 'attack'.

(The Old Babylonian developments of Proto-Semitic **aw* and **ay* were *ū* and *ī* respectively, as in *mūtum* ‹ **mawtum* 'death' and *bītum* ‹ **baytum* 'house'.)

(c) When any of ʾ$_{1-7}$ stood between two vowels, its loss left those vowels contiguous, as in **kalāʾum* › **kalāum*; **ibniyū* › **ibniū*; **ḫaduwim* › **ḫaduim*. In Old Babylonian, most pairs of contiguous vowels contract to one vowel, which is marked in transcription with a circumflex. Contiguous vowels contract according to the following rules:

(1) Sequences of long or short *e* or *i* followed by long or short *a* remain uncontracted:

rabiam 'great (ms, acc.)'; *ilqeā* 'they (f) took';

an original long *ē* or *ī* that remains as the first vowel in most such sequences is shortened (i.e., a long vowel does not usually occur immediately before another vowel):

kī+am › *kiam* 'thus'; *maḫrī+ātum* › *maḫriātum* 'former (fp)'.

Note that the presence of the *i* or *e* in some examples, such as *rabiam* 'great (acc.)', constitutes an exception to the rule of vowel syncope, as already noted in §4.1.

(2) A long *ā* or *ē* followed by long or short *i* contracts to *ê*:

banā+im › *banêm* 'to build (gen.)';
šemē+im › *šemêm* 'to hear (gen.)';
purussā+ī › *purussê* 'decisions (gen.-acc.)'.

Note that only long *ā* and *ē* are affected by this rule; short *a* and *e* are affected by rule (3).

(3) In all other sequences of contiguous vowels, the vowels contract to a long vowel, marked in transcription with a circumflex, that is the quality of the original second vowel; some examples:

imla+ā › *imlâ* 'they (f) filled'	*banā+am* › *banâm* 'to build (acc.)'
rabi+im › *rabîm* 'great (ms, gen.)'	*rabi+um* › *rabûm* 'great (ms, nom.)'
ibni+ū › *ibnû* 'they (m) built'	*tamla+ī* › *tamlî* 'you (fs) filled'
zaku+im › *zakîm* 'clear (ms, gen.)'	*zaku+ūtum* › *zakûtum* 'clear (mp)'
telqe+ī › *telqî* 'you (fs) took'	*leqē+um* › *leqûm* 'to take (nom.)'

There are some instances in which intervocalic ʾ was not lost, namely,

in certain forms of verbs II-weak (see §29.1) and of doubly-weak verbs (§21.3), where ʾ is morphologically significant;
in certain pronominal forms (see §6.3 below);
in some Sumerian loanwords.

The features outlined in the preceding paragraphs are illustrated more fully in the following paradigms:

(1) The base of the demonstrative adjective meaning 'this, these' was originally **hanniy-* (for the demonstratives in general, see §6.3 below);

with the loss of the initial *h* and the base-final *y*, the declension of this word is:

		MASCULINE	FEMININE
SING.	nom.	*annûm* (‹ **hanniyum*)	*annītum* (‹ **hanniytum*)
	gen.	*annîm* (‹ **hanniyim*)	*annītim* (‹ **hanniytim*)
	acc.	*anniam* (‹ **hanniyam*)	*annītam* (‹ **hanniytam*)
PLUR.	nom.	*annûtum* (‹ **hanniyūtum*)	*anniātum* (‹ **hanniyātum*)
	g.-a.	*annûtim* (‹ **hanniyūtim*)	*anniātim* (‹ **hanniyātim*)

(2) The noun 'decision' was originally **purussāʾum*; its declension is:

SING.	nom.	*purussûm* (‹ **purussāʾum*)
	gen.	*purussêm* (‹ **purussāʾim*)
	acc.	*purussâm* (‹ **purussāʾam*)
PLUR.	nom.	*purussû* (‹ **purussāʾū*)
	g.-a.	*purussê* (‹ **purussāʾī*)

ʾ$_3$ (**ḥ*) and ʾ$_4$ (**ʿ*) had a further effect on the vocalism of the language before they were lost: they caused nearby short *a* and long *ā* to become, respectively, short *e* and long *ē*; e.g.,

**ḥaqlum* › **ḥeqlum* › *eqlum* 'field'; **zarʿum* › **zerʿum* › *zērum* 'seed'
**baʿlum* › **beʿlum* › *bēlum* 'lord'; **ḥimārum* › *imērum* 'donkey'.

The standard grammars of Akkadian state that ʾ$_5$ (**ǵ*) also caused the change of *a* to *e*; but there are few clear examples of this, and so we will refer to ʾ$_{3\text{–}4}$ as causing the change *a* › *e* (rather than the traditional ʾ$_{3\text{–}5}$).

6.2 Denominative Adjectives

The ending *-ī* is added to the base of many nouns, including proper nouns, to form adjectives that denote 'pertaining to, related to X', where "X" is the base noun: e.g.,

maḫrûm (base *maḫrī-*) 'former, earlier, previous, first', from *maḫrum* 'front, front side';
elûm (base *elī-*) 'upper', from *elum* 'top, upper part';
šaplûm (base *šaplī-*) 'lower', from *šaplum* 'bottom, underside';

Denominative adjectives formed by the addition of *-ī* to place names are referred to as gentilic adjectives:

Akkadûm (base *Akkadī-*) 'Akkadian', from *Akkade* 'Akkad'.

Denominative adjectives are declined like *annûm* in the preceding section:

		MASCULINE	FEMININE
SING.	nom.	*maḫrûm*	*maḫrītum*
	gen.	*maḫrîm*	*maḫrītim*
	acc.	*maḫriam*	*maḫrītam*
PLUR.	nom.	*maḫrûtum*	*maḫriātum*
	g.-a.	*maḫrûtim*	*maḫriātim*

6.3 Demonstrative Adjectives and Pronouns

The most common near demonstrative adjective in Old Babylonian is *annûm* (base *anni-*; for the complete declension see §6.1 above), which is best translated 'this, these'.

> *kaspam anniam ina qātim ša maruštim amḫur* 'I received this silver from the sick woman';
>
> *šīpātim ana amātim anniātim niddin* 'We gave wool to these female slaves'.

annûm follows other adjectives:

> *šamnam ṭābam anniam aṣṣur* 'I protected this fine oil'.

The fem. sg. *annītum* may also be used as a neuter demonstrative pronoun, 'this (thing, matter, etc.)'.

The most common forms for 'that, those' are the third person independent personal pronouns. In the declension of these forms, the gen. and acc. have the same form, and there is a special dative case that is used immediately after *ana*. Alternative forms listed below for the sing. gen.-acc. and dative reflect dialectal variation within Old Babylonian.

	MASCULINE SINGULAR	FEMININE SINGULAR
nom.	*šū*	*šī*
gen.-acc.	*šuāti, šuātu, šâti, šâtu*	*šuāti, šâti, šiāti*
dative	*šuāšim, šâšim, šâšum*	*šuāšim, šâšim, šiāšim*
	MASCULINE PLURAL	FEMININE PLURAL
nom.	*šunu*	*šina*
gen.-acc.	*šunūti*	*šināti*
dative	*šunūšim*	[*šināšim* unattested]

This pronoun is called the **anaphoric pronoun**, since it always refers to something already mentioned or known. Thus, while it may be translated 'that, those', it is sometimes better rendered 'the aforementioned' or 'said' or even 'this, these'. When used attributively, the forms follow and agree with the noun they modify:

> *amtum šī aššatum ša wardim ḫalqim* 'That womanservant is the wife of the missing manservant';
>
> *alpam šuātu ana eṭlim iddin* 'He gave said ox to the youth';
>
> *šīpātum qatnātum ana bītātim šināti* 'The fine wool is for the aforementioned estates'.

Another demonstrative is *ullûm* (base *ulli-*; declined like *annûm*), meaning 'that, those' and 'distant'. It occurs infrequently in OB texts.

EXERCISES

A. VOCABULARY 6.

Verbs:

nasākum (Preterite *issuk*) 'to throw (off, down), hurl, shoot (*ana*: to, into); to pile up (grain)'.

naṭālum (*iṭṭul*) 'to see, look, look at, observe; to consider; to face'.

parāsum (*iprus*) 'to divide, separate (out), select; to decide (a legal case); to keep away (enemy, demons, etc.)'; Verbal Adj. *parsum* (*paris-*) 'divided, separated, separate'.

šaṭārum (*išṭur*) 'to inscribe, write, write down, enter, register (something in an account, list, etc.); to assign (something to someone, someone to a task, duty)'; Verbal Adj. *šaṭrum* (*šaṭir-*) 'inscribed; registered; assigned'.

ṭarādum (*iṭrud*) 'to send, dispatch (person); to drive away'; Verbal Adj. *ṭardum* (*ṭarid-*) 'expelled, banished, exile(d)'.

Nouns:

dayyānum 'judge'.

ekallum (fem.; Sum. lw.) '(royal) palace'.

kussûm (fem.; base *kussi-*) 'chair, seat; throne'; *kussiam ṣabātum* 'to take the throne' (referring to both regular succession and usurpation).

purussûm (base *purussā-*) 'legal decision, case' (cf. *parāsum*).

rubātum (fem. of *rubûm* below; pl. *rubâtum* [< *rubā+ātum*]) 'princess'.
rubûm (base *rubā-*) 'prince, ruler'.
šadûm (base *šadu-*) 'mountain, mountain region'.

Adjectives:

annûm (base *anni-*) 'this, these'.
maḫrûm (*maḫrī-*) 'first; former, earlier, previous'.
šaplûm (*šaplī-*) 'lower'.
šū, šī, šunu, šina (anaphoric pronoun) 'that, those, the aforementioned, said, this, these'.

B. Decline in full (ms, fs, mp, fp) the adjectives *parsum* and *ṭardum*.

C. Decline in full (sing. and pl.) the following phrases:

1. this princess
2. previous decision
3. lower mountain
4. this prince
5. former seat

D. Write in Akkadian:

1. the aforementioned palaces
2. to the feet of that judge
3. upon that road
4. like the governor of said land
5. the neck of that dog
6. to that captive enemy
7. the aforementioned weapon
8. that lower river
9. for that life
10. out of those houses
11. with those inscribed tablets

E. Translate:

1. *īnān ša dayyānim ul iṭṭulā.*
2. *ilū išdīn ša kussîm ša šarrim šuātu issuḫū; bēlum nakarum kussiam iṣbat.*
3. *alpam ana aḫim ša rubêm apqid; alpum šū imraṣ-ma imūt* (*-ma imūt* 'and died'); *rubûm alpam šuātu ana kalbī issuk.*
4. *rubûm qaqqadam ša iltim šamnam ṭābam ipšuš.*
5. *ina šaṭārim ša ṣābim ul nigmur.*
6. *bēlū ša mātim purussâm ša mutim iprusū; aššatam ina bītim parsim iškunū.*
7. *ḫarrānam rapaštam šâti ul nikšud.*
8. *ṣābum nakirum ekallātim ša šarrim iqqur; ekallātim*

maqtātim šināti ul niṭṭul.

9. *rubâtum ša ālim šuāti šikaram mādam ana nārim issukā.*
10. *rubûm bītam šâtu ana qātim ša dayyānim išṭur u iknuk.*
11. *ul mārū ša aššatim maḫrītim ša rubêm attunu.*
12. *dayyānū narkabtam ištu kišādim ša nārim annītim ana šadîm irkabū.*
13. *šarrāqī u nakirī ištu mātim ina qātim dannatim taṭrud.*
14. *ṣābam damqam ina eṭlūtim ša ālim annîm aprus.*
15. *wardū šunu ina qātim ša ummim ša šarrim.*
16. *bēlū wardī šunūti ana bītim ša awīlim marṣim iṭrudū.*
17. *ṭuppam maḫriam ša purussêm annîm anāku ul ašṭur; atti tašṭurī.*
18. *mārtum maruštum iblut.*

LESSON SEVEN

7.1 The Sound Change *i* > *e*

The vowels *i* and *ī* were apparently pronounced as *e* and *ē*, respectively, when they occurred before the consonants *r* and *ḫ*. This sound change is not consistently indicated in the writing system, however, so that byforms are freqently attested, as in

> *laberum* and *labirum* (and fem. *labertum* and *labirtum*) 'old';
> *meḫrum* and *miḫrum* 'copy, reply'.

In some cases the writing system simply does not adequately distinguish the vowels *i* and *e* (see §9.2), so that it is not clear whether we should transcribe, for example,

> *nakirum* or *nakerum* for 'enemy'.

In this textbook, transcriptions with both *i* and *e* will appear for these forms, as they do in actual texts and in Assyriological publications.

The third person and the 1cp verbal prefixes may also be affected by this phonological process. This occurs infrequently, however, and is not detectable in the writing system in Preterite forms, where *ir-* and *er-* are written the same, as are *iḫ-* and *eḫ-*. In the form called the Durative (§12.1), however, note

> *irakkab*, less often *erakkab*, 'he mounts';
> *iḫalliqā*, less often *eḫalliqā*, 'they (f) escape'.

7.2 Vowel Harmony (*a* > *e*)

In Old Babylonian, *a*-vowels and *e*-vowels are incompatible in the same word, with certain notable exceptions considered below. Whenever there is an *e* or *ē* in a word, an expected *a* or *ā* in most instances becomes *e* or *ē* as well. For example,

> the plural of the noun *bēltum* 'lady' (the fem. of *bēlum*) is *bēlētum* < *bēlātum*;
> the 2ms of the verb 'to hear', originally _*tašma_^{c}, becomes first _*tašme_^{c} (see §6.1, end), then *tašme* (§6.1(b)), and finally *tešme*, the form usually attested in OB texts.

Many forms show a change of *a* (or *ā*) to *e* (or *ē*) even when the culprit *e*-vowel no longer appears because of subsequent vowel contraction;

note, for example:

> *telqî* 'you (fs) took' (< **telqeī* < **talqeī* < **talqeḥī* < **talqaḥī*);
> *leqûm* 'to take' (Infinitive; < **leqēum* < **laqēum* < **laqēḥum* < **laqāḥum*).

Exceptions to vowel harmony, i.e., instances in which *a* and *ā* do not become *e* and *ē*, are the following:

(a) *a* in the accusative sg. ending *-am*, as in *bēlam*;
(b) *ā* of the dual nom. ending *-ān*, as in *šēpān*;
(c) *-ā* of 3fp and 2cp verbs: *tēpušā* (< **teḥpušā*) 'you (pl.) made';
(d) *a* as a linking vowel immediately before possessive pronominal suffixes (§11.1), as in *têrtašu* 'his instruction';
(e) *a* and *ā* in pronominal suffixes (§§11.1, 18.2), as in *bēlka* 'your (ms) lord'; *ēzibšināti* 'I left them (f)';
(f) *a* of the Ventive ending *-am* (§15.2): *tērubam* 'you (ms) came in';
(g) *ê* that results from the contraction of *ā+ī̆* (§6.1(c2)) does not cause *a*-vowels to change: *banêm* < **banāim* < **banāyim* 'to build (Infinitive, gen.)'; note: the mark ¯̆ over a vowel indicates that the vowel may be long or short (called an "anceps vowel");
(h) *e* that results from *i* by the phenomenon described above in §7.1 does not normally cause *a*-vowels to change; note, e.g., *nakerum* and *laberum* 'old'; a notable exception to the exception, however, is *ṣeḫrum* 'small, young', the base of which is *ṣeḫer-*, from earlier *ṣaḫer-* < *ṣaḫir-* (fs *ṣeḫertum*; fp *ṣeḫrētum*);
(i) the change of *a* to *e* before a *following* *e* or *ē* does not always occur in some verb forms; thus, we find both *ešme* and, less often, *ašme* (see above) for 'I heard'.

Other phonological conditions also gave rise to *e*-vowels, apparently sporadically. One such condition was the presence of both a preceding ʾ$_1$ (the Proto-Semitic ʾ) and a following sonorant (*l*, *m*, *n*, *r*), as in

> *erṣetum* < **ʾarṣatum* 'earth' (the second *e* is due to vowel harmony);
> *enšum* < **ʾanšum* 'weak';
> *šumēlum* < **šumʾālum* 'left (side)'.

7.3 The G Infinitive, Preterite, and Verbal Adjective: Verbs III–weak

Verbs III–weak are verbs in which the third radical was one of the consonants that dropped out of the language (see §6.1). The forms of these verbs present very little difficulty once the rules of vowel contraction and vowel harmony have been learned.

Forms that would have ended with the third radical, such as the 3cs (cf. *iprus*), end simply with the theme-vowel, as in

ibni 'she built' (< _*ibniy_; i.e., root originally _*b–n–y_);
tamla 'you (ms) filled' (< _*tamlaʾ_; root originally _*m–l–ʾ_);
nilqe 'we took' (< _*nilqeḫ_ < _*nilqaḫ_; root originally _*l–q–ḫ_).

Forms in which the third radical would have occurred before a consonant, such as the fem. sg. of the Verbal Adjective, have a long vowel before that consonant:

šemītum 'heard (fs, nom.)' (< _*šami_^{c}_tum_);
zakūtum 'clear (fs, nom.)' (< _*zakuwtum_).

In forms with a **vocalic ending**, that is, an ending that begins with a vowel, such as the 3mp (cf. _iprus-ū_) or the Infinitive (_parās-um_), vowel contraction takes place according to the rules outlined in §6.1(c):

ibnû 'they (m) built' (< _*ibniū_ < _*ibniyū_);
tamlâ 'you (pl) filled' (< _*tamlaā_ < _*tamlaʾā_);
ilqeā 'they (f) took' (< _*ilqeḫā_ < _*ilqaḫā_);
banûm 'to build' (Infinitive, nom.; < _*banāum_ < _*banāyum_);
zakîm 'clear (ms, gen.)' (< _*zakuim_ < _*zakuwim_).

(a) Infinitive

The Infinitives of verbs III–weak, originally of the pattern _parās_ as in sound verbs, have bases ending in _-ā_ (_-ē_ in verbs III–_e_), and thus are declined like the noun _purussûm_ given in §6.1 (end); as examples, note _banûm_ (< _*banāum_ < _*banāyum_) 'to build' and _leqûm_ 'to take' (< _*leqēum_ < _*laqēum_ < _*laqēḫum_ < _*laqāḫum_):

nom.	_banûm_	_leqûm_
gen.	_banêm_	_leqêm_
acc.	_banâm_	_leqēam_

(b) Preterite

In general, the Preterite theme vowels of these verbs were determined by the (now lost) third radical:

roots originally III–_y_ have the theme-vowel _i_, as in _ibni_ 'he built', and may be referred to as Verbs III-_i_;
roots originally III–_w_ have _u_, as in _iḫdu_ 'she rejoiced' (< _iḫduw_, root originally _*ḫ–d–w_), and thus may be called verbs III-_u_;
verbs originally III–ʾ$_{1\text{-}2}$ (i.e., III–_*ʾ_ and III–_*h_) have _a_, as in _imla_ 'he filled' (< _*imlaʾ_), and may be called verbs III–_a_;
verbs originally III–ʾ$_{3\text{-}4}$ (III–_*ḥ_; III–_*_^{c}) have _e_, as in _ilqe_ 'she took' (< _*ilqeḫ_ < _*ilqaḫ_), and may be referred to as verbs III–_e_.

In verbs III–_e_, the _a_ in the 1cs and second person prefixes usually becomes _e_ in accordance with the vowel harmony rule outlined in the preceding section; exceptions, with *a*, are common in the 1cs, rare in the second person forms.

	banûm (III–*i*) 'to build'	*hadûm* (III–*u*) 'to rejoice'	*malûm* (III–*a*) 'to fill'	*leqûm* (III–*e*) 'to take'
3cs	*ibni*	*iḫdu*	*imla*	*ilqe*
2ms	*tabni*	*taḫdu*	*tamla*	*telqe* / *talqe*
2fs	*tabnî*	*taḫdî*	*tamlî*	*telqî* / *talqî*
1cs	*abni*	*aḫdu*	*amla*	*elqe* / *alqe*
3mp	*ibnû*	*iḫdû*	*imlû*	*ilqû*
3fp	*ibniā*	*iḫdâ*	*imlâ*	*ilqeā*
2cp	*tabniā*	*taḫdâ*	*tamlâ*	*telqeā* / *talqeā*
1cp	*nibni*	*niḫdu*	*nimla*	*nilqe*

(c) Verbal Adjective

The second vowel of the base of the Verbal Adjective, as in sound verbs, is usually *i*, as in

> *bani-* (‹ **baniy-*) 'well-formed'; *ḫadi-* (‹ **ḫadiw-*) 'happy'; *mali-* (‹ **maliʾ-*) 'filled, full'.

For a few (but not most) stative verbs, the theme-vowel is not *i*, as in

> *zaku-* 'clear' (‹ **zakuw-*).

In verbs III–*e*, the original *a* of the first syllable usually becomes *e*:

> *leqi-* 'taken' (less often *laqi-*; ‹ **laqiḥ-*).

Note that, because of their respective vowel contractions, the nom. ms form of a III-weak Verbal Adjective is identical to the nom. form of the Infinitive: *banûm* (Verbal Adj. ‹ **baniyum*; Infinitive ‹ **banāyum*). Other forms of the declension differ for most verbs, however.

Below is the full declension of three Verbal Adj.s of roots III-weak; note the long theme-vowel in the fem. sg. (*rabītum* ‹ **rabiytum*, etc.).

		rabûm (*rabi-*) 'great'	*šemûm* (*šemi-*) 'heard'	*zakûm* (*zaku-*) 'clear'
MASC. SG.	nom.	*rabûm*	*šemûm* / *šamûm*	*zakûm*
	gen.	*rabîm*	*šemîm* / *šamîm*	*zakîm*
	acc.	*rabiam*	*šemiam* / *šamiam*	*zakâm*
FEM. SG.	nom.	*rabītum*	*šemītum* / *šamītum*	*zakūtum*
	gen.	*rabītim*	*šemītim* / *šamītim*	*zakūtim*
	acc.	*rabītam*	*šemītam* / *šamītam*	*zakūtam*

MASC. PL.	nom.	*rabûtum*	*šemûtum / šamûtum*	*zakûtum*
	gen.-acc.	*rabûtim*	*šemûtim / šamûtim*	*zakûtim*
FEM. PL.	nom.	*rabiātum*	*šemiātum / šamiātum*	*zakâtum*
	gen.-acc.	*rabiātim*	*šemiātim / šamiātim*	*zakâtim*

7.4 The Coordinators *-ma, u,* and *ū (lū)*

The conjunction *u* is an independent word that may be used to connect both noun phrases, as in *abum u ummum* 'father and mother', and sentences.

The enclitic particle *-ma* is a coordinating conjunction that may be attached to the end of any finite verb form (or other predicate). Any final short vowel is lengthened when *-ma* is added; as a result, stress invariably falls on the syllable before *-ma*:

> *ibni* 'he built', but *ibnī-ma* 'he built and ...';
> *iṣbat* 'she seized', but *iṣbat-ma* 'she seized and ...'
> *taṣbatā* 'you (pl) seized', but *taṣbatā-ma* 'you seized and ...'

Note that a word-final *n* normally assimilates to *-ma* (§5.1):

> *iddim-ma* (‹ *iddin-ma*) 'she gave and ...';
> *aškum-ma* (‹ *aškun-ma*) 'I placed and ...'

In a similar vein, the consonants *b* and, very rarely, *p* are also assimilated to a following *-ma*:

> *irkam-ma* (‹ *irkab-ma*) 'he rode and ...'

These assimilations are frequently not indicated in the writing system; i.e., we find written both *iddim-ma* and *iddin-ma,* both *irkam-ma* and *irkab-ma.* See further §18.4.

Both *-ma* and *u* are used for 'and' to create compound sentences. They occur in different environments, however, and have different semantic connotations.

(a) *u* is used only when the verbs in both clauses are the same mood (i.e., indicative or injunctive), whereas *-ma* has no such restriction.

(b) Clauses connected with *u* bear equal semantic or thought stress, and are reversible; that is, the clauses could be reversed without altering their essential meaning or relationship to each other. When clauses are connected with *-ma,* the main thought stress, the emphasis, lies with the last clause. Further, clauses connected with *-ma* may not be reversed without changing the meaning.

(c) Clauses connected with *-ma* are logically related in some way. The first clause normally presents the conditions that result in the action of the second clause. The first clause may be said to be "logically subordinate" to the second; that is, the first clause, although formally a main clause, is often best thought of as an unmarked (apart from *-ma*) subordinate clause, subordinate to the clause following *-ma*. Several interpretations are often possible:

ilū šarram ul iškunū-ma mātum iḫliq
'The gods did not install a king, **and so** (or **and then**) the land perished.'
'**Because/When/If** the gods did not install a king, the land perished.'
'The gods **not having installed** a king, the land perished.'

With *u*, no such dependent relationship is implied:

bītam iṣṣurū u kaspam itti šarrim imḫurū
'They (m) kept the house and (also) they received silver from the king.'

As the last example suggests, *u* as a conjunction between clauses may often be rendered 'and also, moreover, furthermore, additionally, as well'.

(d) There is no Akkadian word meaning 'but'. Rather, both *u* and *-ma* may be translated 'but' in certain instances, particularly when one of the two clauses connected by them contains a negative, as in

dayyānum ana šadîm ikšud-ma ṣābam nakram ul iṭṭul 'The judge arrived at the mountain, but did not see the enemy troop.'

(e) Clauses are in rare instances connected by *-ma u*. Such clauses contain the same mood, are irreversible, and the emphasis or thought stress is on the first clause. *-ma u* is best translated 'and also' or 'and then':

mutum ana aššatim kaspam iddim-ma u mimmê ša bītim ša abim ana aššatim ušallim 'The husband gave silver to (his) wife and also restored (*ušallim*) to (his) wife the property (*mimmê*) of (her) father's house'.

(f) The conjunction 'or' is expressed in Akkadian by *ū* or by *ū lū*. The word *ū* is indistinguishable from *u* 'and' in the writing system, so that the presence of the former is frequently uncertain unless it is followed by *lū*. There are several patterns of coordination possible with *ū (lū)*; for example, '(either) he gave or he took' may be expressed by any of the following (see also Vocab. 16 and §29.3):

iddin ū ilqe | *lū iddin ū lū ilqe*
iddin ū lū ilqe | *ū lū iddin ū lū ilqe*

Clauses connected with *ū (lū)* have the same verbal mood, and, because of the nature of the conjunction, are reversible.

7.5 Asyndeton

Clauses may also follow one another without a coordinator. When a semantic relationship exists between two clauses that are not formally connected (i.e., that are not joined by a conjunction), they are said to be asyndetically joined (or, joined with asyndeton). Essentially, each of the coordinators discussed above in §7.4 may be deleted; the use of asyndeton lends distinctiveness, emphasis, or urgency to the clauses so joined:

šarrum wardam iṭrud wardum ul ikšud 'The king sent a slave, (but) the slave did not arrive.'

EXERCISES

A. VOCABULARY 7.

Verbs:

banûm (Preterite *ibni*) 'to build, rebuild, construct, create'; Verbal Adj. *banûm* (*bani-*) 'well-made, well-formed; fine'.

ḫadûm (*iḫdu*) 'to rejoice, be happy (at, in something: *ina* or *ana*)'; Verbal Adj. *ḫadûm* (*ḫadi-*) 'happy, joyful, rejoicing'.

leqûm (*ilqe*) 'to take (in one's hand), accept, receive, obtain (from: *itti*), take along, take away; to take (a wife), marry'.

malûm (*imla*) 'to become full of, fill with' (+ acc.; e.g., *eqlum mê imla* 'the field filled with water, became full of water'); rarely: 'to fill' (something: acc.; with something: a second acc., as in *bēlum bītam šīpātim qatnātim imla* 'the owner filled the house with fine wool'); Verbal Adj. *malûm* (*mali-*) 'filled, full'.

rabûm (*irbi*) 'to become large, great; to grow (up), increase'; Verbal Adj. *rabûm* (*rabi-*) 'big, large; great, important; mature'.

šemûm (*išme*) 'to hear; to listen; to listen to, obey'; Verbal Adj. *šemûm* (*šemi-*) 'heard; having heard, informed, aware; obedient'.

zakûm (*izku*) 'to become clean, clear; to become free (of claims, obligations)'; Verbal Adj. *zakûm* (*zaku-*) 'clear; clean(ed), pure; free (of claims)'.

Nouns:

bēltum (pl. *bēlētum*) 'lady; mistress, (female) owner'.
eqlum (pl. *eqlētum*) 'plot of land, field; area, region'.
mû (always pl.; gen.-acc. *mê*) 'water, liquid'.
narûm (base *naru-* / *narā-*; Sum. lw.) 'stela'.
qīštum (pl. *qīšātum*) 'gift; fee; votive offering'.
ṣibittum (fem.) 'prison, imprisonment' (cf. *ṣabātum*).
ṭēmum (pl. *ṭēmū* and *ṭēmētum*) 'information, news, report; command; mind, attitude, intention, decision'; *ṭēmam ṣabātum* 'to take action (concerning: *ana*)'; *ṭēmam šakānum* 'to give a report, information (to someone: *itti* [or *maḫar*, Vocab. 12])'.

Adjective:

ṣeḫrum (base *ṣeḫer-*; Verbal Adj. of *ṣeḫērum*, §21.2) 'small, young'; as a noun: 'child'.

Conjunction:

-ma 'and (then)' (see §7.4).

B. Give the full Preterite of *rabûm*, *zakûm*, and *šemûm*.

C. Decline in full (sg. and pl.) the following phrases:

1. clear field
2. great lady
3. well-formed stela
4. previous command
5. small throne
6. this gift
7. joyful prince
8. full chariot

D. Translate:

1. *eqlētum ša bēlētim mê mādūtim imlâ.*
2. *rubātum ṭēmam itti eṭlūtim iškum-ma ana šadî irkab.*
3. *ina emūqātim ša qātīn išdīn ša ekallim annītim abnī-ma ṣābam damqam apqid-ma ina ekallim aškun.*
4. *aḫum ša rubêm qīštam itti bēltim ilqe ana mārim ša rubêm iddin.*
5. *ṭēmam šuāti nišmē-ma niḫdu.*

6. *nakrum narâm šaṭram ša šarrim issuk-ma iqqur.*
7. *mû ištu nārim šaplītim ana ālim ikšudū.*
8. *ṭuppam ša bēltim ešmē-ma ana ṭuppim šuāti ṭēmam aṣbat.*
9. *qātān ša ilī šunūti mātātim ibniā.*
10. *amātum anniātum ina kašādim ana ālim iḫdâ.*
11. *libbum ša šarrim dannim irbī-ma kakkam ina qātim ilqē-ma nakram imḫaṣ.*
12. *alpū marṣūtum išlimū.*
13. *īnān ša ṣeḫrim irbiā-ma imraṣā.*
14. *bēlū ša ālim purussâm ša awīlim iprusū-ma ina purussêm šuāti eqlum ša awīlim izku.*
15. *šarrum nakirūtim ina ṣibittim iškum-ma ṣibittum imla.*
16. *ṭuppātim anniātim ul taṭṭul-ma wardam šuāti ul taṭrud.*
17. *ḫurāṣam gamram itti mārtim ul alqe.*

LESSON EIGHT

8.1 The G Infinitive, Preterite, and Verbal Adjective: Verbs I–ʾ (I–*a* and I–*e*); *alākum*

The verbs presented in this section are those in which the first radical was ʾ, *h*, *ḥ*, ʿ, *ǵ*, or *y* (i.e., $ʾ_{1\text{-}5}$ or $ʾ_7$; *not*, however, *w*, for which see §10.1). The Infinitives, Preterites, and Verbal Adjectives of these verbs exhibit the developments brought about by the loss of those consonants, already covered in §6.1 and §7.2. Specifically,

(a) In the **Infinitive** and **Verbal Adjective**, since the weak initial radical appeared at the beginning of the form (cf. *parāsum* and *parsum*), no lengthening of the following vowel took place:

> *amārum* 'to see' (‹ **ʾamārum*); *alākum* 'to go' (‹ **halākum*);
> *arkum* 'long' (‹ **ʾarkum*); *arītum* 'pregnant' (‹ **hariytum*).

(b) In the **Preterite**, on the other hand, since the weak initial radical stood before another consonant (cf. *iprus*), the vowel of the prefix was always lengthened:

> *īzib* 'he left' (‹ **iʿzib*); *tāmurī* 'you (fs) saw' (‹ **taʾmurī*).

(c) Roots in which the first radical was $ʾ_{3\text{-}4}$ (i.e., *ḥ*, ʿ) also exhibit the change of original *a*-vowels to *e*-vowels, with the regular exceptions of the acc. ending *-am* in the Infinitive and Verbal Adj., and the *-ā* of the 3fp and 2cp in the Preterite:

> *epēšum* 'to do' (‹ **ḥapāšum*; acc. *epēšam*);
> *epšum* 'done' (‹ **ḥapšum*; acc. *epšam*);
> *ēpuš* 'I did' (‹ **aḥpuš*); *tēpušā* 'you (pl) did' (‹ **taḥpušā*); note that forms with *ā* in the prefix, such as ***āpuš* and ***tāpušā*, do not occur.

Verbs in which the first radical was *y*, such as *ešērum* 'to become straight' and *eṣērum* 'to draw', have merged with verbs I–$ʾ_{3\text{-}4}$ in nearly all forms, and will accordingly be presented with the latter, usually without further comment, throughout this textbook.

(d) We may refer to verbs in which the first radical was $ʾ_{1\text{-}2}$ (e.g., *amārum* 'to see') as verbs **I–*a***, and to those in which the first radical was $ʾ_{3\text{-}4}$ or *y* as **I–*e***. The few roots originally I–$ʾ_5$ either have initial *ḫ* or follow the I–*a* (I–$ʾ_{1\text{-}2}$) type or, rarely, the I–*e* (I–$ʾ_{3\text{-}4}$) type.

(e) Below are presented the Preterites and Verbal Adjectives of the I–*a* verbs *amārum* (Preterite *īmur*) 'to see' and *arākum* (*īrik*) 'to become long' and the I–*e* verbs *epēšum* (*īpuš*) 'to do' and *ezēbum* (*īzib*) 'to leave':

	amārum	*arākum*	*epēšum*	*ezēbum*
		PRETERITE		
3cs	*īmur*	*īrik*	*īpuš*	*īzib*
2ms	*tāmur*	*tārik*	*tēpuš*	*tēzib*
2fs	*tāmurī*	*tārikī*	*tēpušī*	*tēzibī*
1cs	*āmur*	*ārik*	*ēpuš*	*ēzib*
3mp	*īmurū*	*īrikū*	*īpušū*	*īzibū*
3fp	*īmurā*	*īrikā*	*īpušā*	*īzibā*
2cp	*tāmurā*	*tārikā*	*tēpušā*	*tēzibā*
1cp	*nīmur*	*nīrik*	*nīpuš*	*nīzib*
		VERBAL ADJECTIVE		
ms	*amrum*	*arkum*	*epšum*	*ezbum*
fs	*amirtum*	*ariktum*	*epištum*	*ezibtum*
mp	*amrūtum*	*arkūtum*	*epšūtum*	*ezbūtum*
fp	*amrātum*	*arkātum*	*epšētum*	*ezbētum*

(f) The very common verb ***alākum*** 'to go' (‹ **halākum*) has an irregular G Preterite: the second radical *l* is doubled (as in verbs I–*n*), while the prefix-vowel remains short. The theme-vowel of the G Preterite is *i*:

3cs	*illik*	3mp	*illikū*
2ms	*tallik*	3fp	*illikā*
2fs	*tallikī*	2cp	*tallikā*
1cs	*allik*	1cp	*nillik*

8.2 The Genitive Chain

The construction that we have learned for expressing a genitival relationship ('X of Y') is

governing noun (also called the nomen regens) + *ša* + governed noun (genitive; also called the nomen rectum), as in

bēlum ša bītim 'the owner of the house'.

There is, however, a more common construction for expressing a genitival relationship, namely, the simple juxtaposition of the governing and governed nouns (in that order); such a construction is called a **genitive chain** (or **construct chain**). When it is used, the governing noun, i.e., the first noun in the chain, normally appears without any case-ending (i.e., without *-um*/*-im*/*-am*, and thus the same for all cases; as will be seen below, masc. pl. and dual nouns do retain their case-endings). A word of this type is said to be in the **bound form** (or **construct form**; also referred to in some grammars as the status constructus); the regular form with a case-ending may be called the **free form** or **unbound form** (also called the status rectus). The governed noun, as in the construction with *ša*, is in the genitive. Some examples:

> *bēl bītim* 'the owner of the house';
> *ana šarrat mātim* 'for the queen of the land';
> *qaqqad awīlim tamḫaṣ* 'you (ms) struck the man's head';
> *bītāt eṭlim* 'the youth's houses'.

The removal of the case-ending, however, causes phonological changes to occur in many types of nouns, and these changes must be memorized for each noun type (see §8.3, below).

A genitive chain constitutes an inseparable unit; the governed noun (i.e., the genitive) must follow the governing noun immediately. Thus, an adjective modifying the governing noun follows the entire chain; the adjective must have the appropriate case-ending, even though the noun it modifies may be endingless:

> *mār šarrim ṣeḫram amḫaṣ* 'I struck the king's young son';
> *itti bēlēt ālim rabiātim* 'with the great ladies of the city'.

Since the genitive must follow its governing noun immediately, it is normally not possible for two or more genitive nouns to be dependent on one bound form, except when the genitives form a natural or logical group in the speaker's mind, as in

> *bēl šamê u erṣetim* 'lord of heaven (*šamû*, pl.) and earth (*erṣetum*)'.

It is never possible for more than one bound form to govern a single genitive. Thus, to express, for example, 'the man's hand and foot', *ša* must be used:

> *qātum u šēpum ša bēlim* (not the incorrect ***qāt u šēp bēlim*).

Chains containing more than two elements may occur; all but the last element appear in the bound form; e.g.,

> *bīt mār šarrim* 'the king's son's house'.

Infinitives often appear in the bound form; they may govern a following

(a) objective genitive, i.e., a noun that would be the direct object if the verb were finite, as in

ana paqād ṣābim ikšud 'he arrived to inspect the troop' (lit.: 'for the inspecting of the troop'); or

(b) subjective genitive, as in

ina maqāt bītim 'while the house was collapsing' (lit.: 'in/during the collapsing of the house').

Adjectives may also appear in the bound form; the following genitive noun qualifies or limits the adjective in some way:

bēlum rapaš uznim 'an intelligent lord' (lit.: 'a lord wide of ear'; for the bound form of *rapšum*, see the next section).

8.3 The Bound Form of the Noun

As was noted in the preceding section, the bound form is distinguished from the free form in most instances by the absence of the case-endings *-um* / *-im* / *-am*. The loss of these endings often must also result in other phonological changes in the shape of the noun. This is the case particularly when the base ends in two consonants, as in *libb-* and *kalb-*; it will be recalled that syllables, and thus words, may not end in two consonants (see §1.2).

The following paragraphs present the rules for producing the bound form of all nouns and adjectives in the language; a chart summarizing the rules concludes the section.

(a) Masculine plural nouns. The bound forms are the same as the free (unbound) forms. Masc. pl. bound forms and dual bound forms (next paragraph) are the only bound forms that are always declined:

bēlū mātim 'the lords of the land';
ana mārī šarrim 'for the king's sons';
kalbī awīlim amḫaṣ 'I struck the man's dogs'.

(b) Duals. The final *n* of the free form is dropped in the bound form; no other changes occur. These bound forms, like those of masc. pl. nouns, are therefore declined:

īnā eṭlim ul iṭṭulā 'the youth's eyes did not see';
ana uznī marṣim 'for the sick man's ears';
qātī rubātim tamḫaṣī 'you (fs) struck the hands of the princess'.

(c) All others, namely, **singular nouns**, **feminine plural nouns**, and **all adjectives.** The bound forms are derived by removing the case-endings *-Vm*. The shape of the bound form depends on two features:

(a) the ending of the noun or adjective base, i.e., whether the base (the form without the case-ending) ends in one consonant (e.g., *awīl-*), two consonants (*libb-*), or a vowel (*rubā-*);

(b) the number of syllables in the base, whether one or more.

(c 1) Bases ending in a single consonant. For these the bound form is either simply the base or, for one-syllable bases, sometimes the base with a final *-i* (for all 3 cases; i.e., this *-i* is unrelated to the genitive marker).

(c 1 i) Bases ending in a single consonant, more than one syllable. The bound form is simply the base:

awīl ālim 'the man of the city';
ḫarrān šarrim 'the king's road';
qaqqad awīlim 'the man's head'.

Here belong all **feminine plural** forms and all **plural adjectives**:

nārāt mātim 'the rivers of the land';
ina eqlēt šarrim 'among the royal fields';
itti amāt bēlim 'with the master's womenservants';
dannūt ālim 'the mighty ones (m) of the city';
marṣāt bītim 'the sick women in (lit.: of) the house',

and the **G Infinitive** (except of verbs III–weak), examples of which appear in §8.2 above.

We may also list here the masc. sg. bound forms of **G Verbal Adjectives** (except for verbs III–weak [§7.3] and verbs II–weak [§9.1]). Although these forms exhibit two consonants before the case-ending in the masc. sg. free form, their bases are of the form *parVs*; the masc. sg. bound form of these adjectives is thus simply the base (for the bound forms of the plurals of these, see immediately above; for the fem. sg. bound form, see below, c 2 v):

damiq ilī 'the good one (m) of the gods';
qatan kišādim 'one (m) with a thin neck' (lit.: 'the thin one of [i.e., with respect to] neck');
maruṣ bītim 'the sick man in (lit.: of) the house'.

(c 1 ii) Bases ending in a single consonant, one syllable. The bound form in all cases is either simply the base or the base plus *-i*:

qāt rubêm imraṣ or *qāti rubêm imraṣ* 'the prince's hand hurt';
itti bēl mātim or *itti bēli mātim* 'with the lord of the land'.

The bound forms of ***abum*** and ***aḫum*** always end in *-i*:

abi wardim imqut 'the slave's father fell';
aḫi šarrim ṣeḫram tamḫaṣ 'you (ms) struck the king's young brother'.

(c 2) Bases ending in two consonants. The unacceptable cluster of consonants at the end of a form is usually resolved in one of three ways:

(a) addition of a final *-i* (e.g., *libb-* → *libbi*);
(b) insertion of a vowel between the two consonants (e.g., *kalb-* → *kalab*);
(c) simplification of a doubled consonant (e.g., *ekall-* → *ekal*).

In particular:

(c 2 i) Bases ending in a doubled consonant, one syllable. The bound form ends in *-i*:

ummi šarrim ina ekallim 'the king's mother is in the palace';
ana libbi ālim nikšud 'we arrived at the center of town';
ṭuppi dayyānī amḫur 'I received the judges' tablet'.

A small number of nouns of this type have alternative bound forms, in which the final doubled consonant is simplified, and no *-i* is added; of the nouns encountered thus far in the vocabularies, only *šarrum* and *kakkum* exhibit this feature:

šar mātim or *šarri mātim* 'the king of the land';
kak eṭlim or *kakki eṭlim* 'the youth's weapon'.

(c 2 ii) Bases ending in a doubled consonant, more than one syllable.

If the base ends in *-tt-*, the bound form ends in *-tti*:

ṣibitti ālim irpiš 'the city prison expanded';
lemutti ilim iṭṭul 'she saw the god's evil intention (*lemuttum*)'.

If the base ends in any doubled consonant except *-tt-*, the doubling is simplified in the bound form:

ekal šarrim 'the king's palace';
kunuk dayyānim 'the judge's seal (*kunukkum*)'.

(c 2 iii) Bases ending in two different consonants, one syllable, without feminine *-t*. These are nouns of the type *pVrs*, where *V* is any short vowel. The bound forms of these have the shape *pVrVs*, in which a copy of the vowel that appears between R_1 and R_2 is also inserted between R_2 and R_3, as in

kalab awīlim 'the man's dog';
alap mutim 'the husband's ox';
eqel bēltim 'the lady's field';
išid bītim 'the base of the house';
uzun rubêm 'the prince's ear'.

(c 2 iv) Bases ending in consonant + feminine *-t*, one syllable. There are two unpredictable possibilities for the bound form; any given noun usually exhibits only one of these possibilities, which must therefore be learned for each such noun:

(a) Addition of *-i* to the base (cf. nouns like *libbum* and *ṣibittum*, above):

qīšti bēltim amḫur 'I received the lady's gift'; note also, e.g., *têrtum* 'order', bound form *têrti*.

(b) Insertion of *a* before the final *-t*, as in

mārat šarrim 'the king's daughter'; similarly for *amtum* (*amat*); *iltum* (*ilat*); note also, e.g., *šubtum* 'dwelling', bound form *šubat*.

The inserted *a* becomes *e* in words with *e* or *ē*:

bēlet bītim 'the mistress of the estate'.

(c 2 v) Bases ending in consonant + feminine-*t*, more than one syllable. As with one-syllable bases, there are two possibilities, but in this case they are predictable:

(a) For most words of this type, the bound form before other nouns has a final *-i*:

napišti mātim 'the life of the land';
narkabti šarrim 'the king's chariot'.

The fem. of Verbal Adjectives (except of verbs III–weak and II–weak) have bound forms of this type:

marušti rubātim 'the misfortune of the princess';
damiqti šarrim 'a favor (i.e., good thing) of the king'.

(b) Exceptions are fem. Participles (§20.1), with *a* inserted before the *-t*:

māḫirtum (G Participle), bound form *māḫirat*;
mušamḫirtum (Š Participle; see §27.1), bound form *mušamḫirat*.

The inserted *a* becomes *e* in words with *e* or *ē*:

ēpištum (Participle of *epēšum* 'to do'), bound form *ēpišet*.

Note: Bases of more than one syllable that end in two consonants, in which the second of those consonants is not the feminine *-t*, do not normally occur.

(c 3) Bases ending in a vowel. Most of these nouns and adjectives have their simple bases as bound forms: e.g.,

kussi šarrim 'the king's throne'.

There are, however, a number of additional forms to be noted:

(a) Words with bases ending in short *-a* or *-u* may have bound forms in *-i*; e.g., from *šadûm* 'mountain', base *šadu-*:

šadi ilī 'mountain of the gods'.

(b) Words with bases ending in a single consonant and a short vowel may have alternative bound forms without the final vowel:

rab beside *rabi* 'great one of'; *šad* beside *šadi*; note also, e.g., *nāši* and *nāš*, bound forms of *nāšûm* (base *nāši-*) 'bearer' (Participle of *našûm* 'to bear'), and, like this word, all Participles of verbs III–weak (§20.1).

(c) Words with bases ending in long *-ā* normally exhibit bound forms ending in *-ê*, although less commonly byforms in *-i* and in *-ā* also occur (some final vowel always appears on these forms):

purussê (less often *purussi* and *purussā*) *bēlim* 'the lord's decision';

rubê (less often *rubi* and *rubā*) *mātim* 'the prince of the country'.

Here belong also the G Infinitives of verbs III–weak:

banê bītim 'the building of the house';
leqê kaspim 'the taking of the silver'.

* * *

Given below for reference are the bound forms of the nouns and adjectives that have appeared in the vocabularies of the first seven lessons. In the vocabularies of this and subsequent lessons, the bound form will be given for each new noun and adjective introduced.

abum: *abi*
aḫum: *aḫi*
alpum: *alap*
ālum: *āl(i)*
amtum: *amat*
aššatum: *aššat*
awīlum: *awīl*
bēltum: *bēlet*
bēlum: *bēl(i)*
bītum: *bīt(i)*
damiqtum: *damiqti*
damqum: *damiq*
dannatum: *dannat*
dannum: *dan(ni)*
dayyānum: *dayyān*
ekallum: *ekal*
emūqum: *emūq*
eqlum: *eqel*
eṭlum: *eṭel*
ḫalqum: *ḫaliq*
ḫarrānum: *ḫarrān*

Summary Table of the Bound Form of the Noun and Adjective

base ending	no. of syll. in base	free form	bound form	comments
masc. pl.-*ū*	any	*mārū*	*mārū*	free and bound forms are
-*ī*	any	*mārī*	*mārī*	identical
dual -*ān*	any	*uznān*	*uznā*	final -*n*
-*īn*	any	*uznīn*	*uznī*	lost
1 consonant	2	*awīlum*	*awīl*	
		šarrātum	*šarrāt*	includes fem. pl. nouns
		damqūtum	*damqūt*	and all plural
		damqātum	*damqāt*	adjectives
	2	*damqum*	*damiq*	Vbl. Adjectives, masc. sg.
		marṣum	*maruṣ*	bound form = base
		rapšum	*rapaš*	
	1	*bēlum*	*bēl(i)*	final -*i* optional
		abum	*abi*	*abi* and *aḫi* always in -*i*
		aḫum	*aḫi*	
doubled consonant	1	*libbum*	*libbi*	
	2	*ṣibittum*	*ṣibitti*	2-syl. base in -*tt*-
		ekallum	*ekal*	all 2-syl. bases except in -*tt*-
2 different consonants, $C_2 \neq$ fem. *t*	1	*kalbum*	*kalab*	*pVrs*
		eqlum	*eqel*	
		išdum	*išid*	nouns
		uznum	*uzun*	
consonant + fem. *t*	1	*qīštum*	*qīšti*	*qīšti* and *mārat* are unpredictable variants; *bēlet* is *e*-vowel variant of *mārat*
		mārtum	*mārat*	
		bēltum	*bēlet*	
	2	*napištum*	*napišti*	most
		māḫirtum	*māḫirat*	feminine Participles
vowel -*CCi*	any	*kussûm*	*kussi*	
vowel -*VCi*	any	*rabûm*	*rab(i)*	final -*i* is optional
vowel -*ā*	any	*rubûm*	*rubê*	less often, *rubi* or *rubā*
vowel other	any	*šadûm*	*šad(V)*	i.e., *šadi* or *šad*

ḫurāṣum: *ḫurāṣ*
iltum: *ilat*
ilum: *il(i)*
īnum: *īn(i)*
išdum: *išid*
kakkum: *kak(ki)*
kalbum: *kalab*
kaspum: *kasap*
kišādum: *kišād*
kussûm: *kussi*
libbum: *libbi*
mādum: *mād(i)*
maqtum: *maqit*
marṣum: *maruṣ*
mārtum: *mārat*
mārum: *mār(i)*
maruštum: *marušti*
mātum: *māt(i)*
mû: *mû, mê*
mutum: *mut(i)*
nakrum: *nakir, nakar*
napištum: *napišti*
narkabtum: *narkabti*
narûm: *naru, nari, nar*
nārum: *nār(i)*
purussûm: *purussê, purussi, purussā*
qaqqadum: *qaqqad*
qatnum: *qatan*
qātum: *qāt(i)*
qīštum: *qīšti*
rapšum: *rapaš*
rubātum: *rubāt*
rubûm: *rubê, rubi, rubā*
ṣabtum: *ṣabit*
ṣābum: *ṣāb(i)*
ṣeḫrum: *ṣeḫer*
ṣibittum: *ṣibitti*
šadûm: *šadi, šad*
šaknum: *šakin*
šamnum: *šaman*
šarqum: *šariq*
šarrāqum: *šarrāq*
šarratum: *šarrat*
šarrum: *šar(ri)*
šēpum: *šēp(i)*
šikarum: *šikar*
šīpātum: *šīpāt*
ṭābum: *ṭāb(i)*
ṭēmum: *ṭēm(i)*
ṭuppum: *ṭuppi*
ummum: *ummi*
uznum: *uzun*
wardum: *warad*

EXERCISES

A. VOCABULARY 8.

Verbs:

aḫāzum (Preterite *īḫuz*) 'to seize, hold, take; to take (a wife), marry; to learn'.

alākum (*illik*) 'to go, walk, move, act'; *alākam epēšum* 'to travel'; *ḫarrānam alākum* 'to travel, undertake a military campaign; to do/perform corvée service'.

amārum (*īmur*) 'to see, look at, observe; to find, discover, experience; to read (a tablet, etc.)'; Verbal Adj. *amrum* (*amir-*) 'seen, checked'.

arākum (*īrik*) 'to become long, last long; to be delayed'; Verbal Adj. *arkum* (*arik-*) 'long'.

epēšum (*īpuš*) 'to do (something: acc.; to someone: acc. or *ana*); to act (according to: *kīma*), be active; to make, build, construct; to treat (someone: acc.; like: *kīma*; for [e.g., a wound]: acc.)';

alākam epēšum 'to travel'; *kakkī epēšum* 'to fight, do battle, make war'; Verbal Adj. *epšum* (*epiš-*) 'built, cultivated, worked'; substantivized fem. *epištum* (*epišti*; pl. *epšētum*) 'work; construction; act, activity, achievement'; *epšēt qātim* 'handiwork'; *eqel epšētim* 'a field worked/prepared (for something; lit.: a field of [plowing, etc.] activities)'.

erēbum (*īrub*) 'to enter, arrive, invade' (normally with *ana*: e.g., *ana bītim ērub* 'I entered the house').

ešērum (*īšir*) 'to become straight; to move straight toward, charge (with *ana*); to prosper'; Verbal Adj. irregularly *išarum* (base *išar-*) 'regular, normal; correct, fair, just; in good condition; prosperous'.

ezēbum (*īzib*) 'to leave, leave behind, abandon; to neglect; to leave (something: acc.; with someone: *ana*), entrust; to divorce; to make out (a legal document)'.

Nouns:

akalum, aklum (bound form *akal*) 'bread, food'.

awātum (*awāt*; pl. *awâtum* [‹ *awā* + *ātum*]) 'word, message, command; matter, affair, thing'; *awātam / awâtim amārum* 'to investigate/look into a matter/case/situation'.

dīnum (*dīn(i)*; pl. *dīnātum*) 'legal decision, verdict; legal case, lawsuit'.

epištum see above under *epēšum*.

puḫrum (*puḫur*; pl. *puḫrātum*) 'gathering, assembly, (council) meeting; totality'.

qarrādum (*qarrād*) 'warrior, hero'.

šumum (*šum(i)*; pl. *šumū* and *šumātum*) 'name; fame, reputation; line (of a tablet); meaning'.

ūmum (*ūm(i)*; pl. *ūmū* and *ūmātum*) 'day, daytime'.

B. Give the full Preterite, with meanings, of *aḫāzum, alākum, erēbum,* and *ešērum.*

C. Write in Akkadian, using bound forms wherever possible:

1. the warrior's lawsuit
2. lives (that are) long of day
3. by the activity of the assembly
4. the man's gift
5. the name of the inscribed stela
6. the food of the city

7. the prison of the palace
8. the palace of the king of the land
9. the field of the lady of the house
10. the throne of the prince of the city
11. from the mountain of the enemy
12. against this enemy of the judges
13. in order to (*ana*) see the river
14. like the words of that report
15. the neck of the princess's dog
16. in the center of the great fortress
17. the hands and feet of the husband
18. with the governor of the land
19. the silver of the queen's father
20. the goddess of this small house
21. the ears of the husband's ox
22. with the youth's weapon
23. the army's beer
24. the good daughter of the thief
25. the slave's brother
26. the brother's slave
27. fine palace oil
28. the aforementioned palace wool
29. the son's chariot
30. the sons' many chariots
31. the sick (people) of the lower mountain region
32. the hardship of the master's womanservant
33. the wife's mother's tablet
34. on the roads of the land
35. handiwork of the gods
36. with river water
37. the mighty strength of the king
38. the youths of the army
39. the previous decisions of the assembly
40. on (*ina*) hearing these words

D. Give the bound form of the following words:

1. *almattum* 'widow'
2. *ašlum* 'rope'
3. *bābum* 'gate'
4. *abullum* 'city gate'
5. *bašītum* 'property'
6. *ḫulqum* 'missing property'
7. *imērum* 'donkey'
8. *kiṣrum* 'knot'
9. *qabûm* 'to speak'
10. *mānaḫtum* 'toil'

E. Translate:

1. *ina kašād abim niḫdu.*
2. *qātā ilim rabîm awīlam ibniā.*

3. *nār ālim mê ul imla.*
4. *mārū bēlim aššātim īḫuzū-ma bītātim rabiātim īpušū.*
5. *akalum ša bēlī u bēlētim idmiq u akalum ša wardī u amātim ul idmiq.*
6. *wardū awât qarrādim damqātim išmû-ma ana dannatim šuāti īrubū.*
7. *šikar ekallim ṭābam itti rubêm nilqē-ma ana maruštim niddin.*
8. *ina dīnim šuāti azkū-ma ṭuppam kankam amḫur.*
9. *dayyānum šū ana šadîm alākam īpuš-ma awât aḫi šarratim īmur.*
10. *kīma ṭēm šarrim ul tēpušī-ma amtam ḫaliqtam ana ālim ul taṭrudī.*
11. *šamnam ana pašāš qaqqad ilim kīma qīštim ana bīt ilim addim-ma ana warad bīt ilim apqid.*
12. *šarrum nakrum dayyānī ālim issuḫ u narâm šaṭram ša šarrim maḫrîm ina nārim issuk.*
13. *kasap bēlim mādam ina mātim nakartim ēzim-ma ana āli bēlim ul allik.*
14. *ṣāb šarrim ḫarrānam illikū; ana ṣāb nakrim ina dannat nakrim īšerū-ma kakkī īpušū-ma ṣābam šuāti ikšudū.*
15. *akalam u mê ṭābūtim ul elqē-ma amraṣ-ma ul ēšer.*
16. *mātum ina emūqī šarrim rabîm īšir-ma mātam ul nīzib.*
17. *ūmū marṣim īrikū-ma ibluṭ-ma ana bīt ilim īrum-ma iḫdu.*
18. *šar mātim awīlum išarum.*

LESSON NINE

9.1 The G Infinitive, Preterite, and Verbal Adjective: Verbs II–weak

Verbs II–weak originally had as their second radical *w*, *y*, or one of the five *aleph*s that were lost in Akkadian.

(a) Infinitive

The G Infinitives of II–weak roots are a result of vowel contraction:

Verbs II–*w*:	*kânum* (‹ **kuānum* ‹ **kawānum*) 'to become firm';
Verbs II–*y*:	*qiāšum* (‹ **qayāšum*) 'to bestow';
Verbs II–ʾ$_{1-2}$:	*šâmum* (‹ **šaʾāmum*) 'to buy';
Verbs II–ʾ$_{3-4}$:	*nêrum* (‹ **neʾērum* ‹ **naḥārum*, much less often *nârum*, without *a* › *e*), 'to slay'.

Note that the Infinitives of verbs II–*w* and verbs II–ʾ$_{1-2}$ (and sometimes verbs II–ʾ$_{3-4}$) have the same form, while those of verbs II–*y* and (usually) verbs II–ʾ$_{3-4}$ are distinct. (Note: roots originally II–ʾ$_5$ are rare.)

(b) Preterite

These have a long vowel in their bases in lieu of the weak second radical; the nature of the vowel depends on the original second radical:

Verbs II–*w*:	*ū*, as in *ikūn* 'he became firm' (*kânum*);
Verbs II–*y*:	*ī*, as in *iqīš* 'he bestowed' (*qiāšum*);
Verbs II–ʾ$_{1-2}$:	*ā*, as in *išām* 'he bought' (*šâmum*);
Verbs II–ʾ$_{3-4}$:	*ē*, as in *inēr* (less often *ā*, as in *inār*) 'he slew' (*nêrum*).

The affixes that mark person are the same as in the sound verb, except that in roots II–ʾ$_{3-4}$, the *a* of the 1cs and second person prefixes (but not -*ā* in the 3fp and 2cp) becomes *e* when the base has *ē* (i.e., usually *tenēr*, less often *tanār*):

	II–*w*	II–*y*	II–ʾ$_{1-2}$	II–ʾ$_{3-4}$
	kânum	*qiāšum*	*šâmum*	*nêrum* / *nârum*
3cs	*ikūn*	*iqīš*	*išām*	*inēr* / *inār*
2ms	*takūn*	*taqīš*	*tašām*	*tenēr* / *tanār*
2fs	*takūnī*	*taqīšī*	*tašāmī*	*tenērī* / *tanārī*
1cs	*akūn*	*aqīš*	*ašām*	*enēr* / *anār*

3mp	*ikūnū*	*iqīšū*	*išāmū*	*inērū / inārū*
3fp	*ikūnā*	*iqīšā*	*išāmā*	*inērā / inārā*
2cp	*takūnā*	*taqīšā*	*tašāmā*	*tenērā / tanārā*
1cp	*nikūn*	*niqīš*	*nišām*	*ninēr / ninār*

(c) Verbal Adjective

II–*w*, II–*y*: most have the pattern *pīs* (cf. the *i*-vowel of *paris*), as in

kīnum 'true', from II–*w kânum* 'to become firm';
mītum 'dead', from II–*w mâtum* 'to die';
qīšum 'bestowed', from II–*y qiāšum* 'to bestow'.

a few stative roots have the pattern *pās* (cf. *rapaš*), as in

ṭābum 'fine', from II–*y ṭiābum* 'to become fine';
mādum 'much', from II–*y miādum* 'to become much'.

II–ʾ1–2: usually *pās*, as in

šāmum 'bought', from *šâmum* 'to buy';

II–ʾ3–4: usually *pēs*, as in

ṭēnum 'ground', from *ṭênum* 'to grind'.

9.2 The Writing System

Akkadian was written with a system of symbols called **cuneiform** signs ('cuneiform' = 'wedge-shaped'; note *santakkum* 'triangle, wedge'; *tikip santakkim* 'cuneiform sign'). These signs were most often pressed into moist clay tablets with a stylus that was tapered and cut at the end, so that it left a small triangle in the clay. (Less often, texts were written on stone, metal, and wax.) An individual sign may consist of one wedge (e.g.,  AŠ), or a few ( BE;  HU), or many wedges ( IN). There are five types of wedges:

In modern lists of cuneiform signs (see the Introduction above, p. xxix), signs are arranged in the order presented above (i.e., signs beginning with the first type of wedge, , are placed before those beginning with the second type, , and so on; within types, signs beginning with one of the wedges, such as , are listed before signs beginning with two, such as , etc.; see the Sign List, pp. 563–74).

With the exception of the few signs that represent simple vowels (e.g.,  A), the signs with which Akkadian words are written do not represent individual phonemes (sounds), but rather sequences of two or more phonemes (e.g.,  MA;  ŠUM). Thus, an Akkadian "alphabet" does not exist.

An individual sign may represent several different things:

(a) a **syllable** or **part of a syllable** in an Akkadian word;
(b) a whole **word**;
(c) a **determinative** (classifier) for a following or preceding word.

As an example, consider the sign :

(a) it may represent a syllable (e.g., *iṣ*), as in the spelling *iṣ-ba-at* for *iṣbat* 'she seized', or part of a syllable, as in the word spelled *ki-iṣ-rum* for *kiṣrum* 'knot';
(b) or it may represent, by itself, the word *iṣum* 'wood, tree' (§13.2);
(c) or, as a determinative, it may precede any of the many words for (types of) wood or trees, merely signifying the type of material of which the item denoted by the following word is made (§13.3).

For the time being, we will be concerned only with signs that represent syllables or parts of syllables; they are referred to as **syllabograms**. There are four types of syllabograms, namely, signs that represent

(a) Simple vowels, i.e., *V* signs: e.g., *a*, *e*, etc.
(b) A consonant followed by a vowel, i.e., *CV* signs: e.g., *ba*, *te*, etc. Not all of the possible combinations of a consonant plus a vowel are represented by their own unique sign. In particular, for only four of the consonants (*b*, *m*, *š*, *t*) are there separate signs for both the *e* and *i* vowels; for all others, one sign serves for both *Ce* and *Ci* (thus, e.g., *ke* and *ki* are written with the same sign). Further, one sign, , serves for both *bu* and *pu*. One sign, , is used for *wa*, *we*, *wi*, and *wu*. The IA sign, , may be used to represent the consonant *y* plus any vowel. The emphatic consonants are very poorly represented: normally the sign for either the voiced or the voiceless counterpart plus a vowel is used for an emphatic plus that vowel (e.g., the sign serves for both *da* and *ṭa*).
(c) A vowel followed by a consonant, i.e., *VC* signs: e.g., *aš*, *un*, etc. In this group, only *l*, *n*, and *š* have separate signs for both *e* and *i* vowels (thus, e.g., is used to write both *em* and *im*). Further, none of these signs distinguishes voiced, voiceless, or emphatic consonants; thus, e.g., one sign alone, , is used for *ed*, *et*, *eṭ*, *id*, *it*, and *iṭ*. Finally, the consonant *ḫ* preceded by any vowel is written with only one sign (i.e., may be *aḫ*, *eḫ*, *iḫ*, or *uḫ*).
(d) A consonant plus a vowel plus a consonant, i.e., *CVC* signs. These are not common in OB. Usually, they represent a sequence *CVm* (especially at the end of spellings of nouns in the free form), although *CVl*, *CVr*, and others (e.g., *maḫ*) also occur. These are even more ambiguous than *CV*s and *VC*s in their lack of distinction of *e* and *i*, and of voiced, voiceless, and emphatic consonants.

Signs that represent more than one sequence of sounds (e.g.,  for *da* and *ṭa*) are said to be **polyphonous**. Many signs represent several sequences that are not phonologically related; e.g., the sign  may represent both *aš* and *rum*; the sign  may represent *ud*, *ut*, and *uṭ*, but also *tam* (and, in later dialects, also *par*, *pir*, *laḫ*, *liḫ*, *ḫiš*). These possibilities are referred to as the **values** of the sign in question. In this grammar, values of signs are written in lower case italics; the most common value will also appear in small capital letters to refer generally to a sign, without reference to any particular value of the sign: e.g., UD refers to the sign , which has the values *ud*, *ut*, *uṭ*, and *tam* (the value written in small capitals may also be called the name of the sign:  is "the UD-sign").

Not infrequently, there are several signs with the same phonological value, i.e., that are pronounced the same; e.g., the signs , , , and  may all be pronounced "*sa*." To distinguish these signs when they are transliterated into Roman characters, diacritical marks and subscript numbers are used, usually according to the frequency of their occurrence in the later literary dialect called Standard Babylonian:

> the most common sign for a certain pronunciation receives no mark;
> the second most frequent has an acute accent (´) on the vowel;
> the third has a grave accent (`) on the vowel;
> thereafter, subscript numbers are used.

The four signs written above, then, are transliterated, respectively, *sa* (called "*sa*–one"), *sá* ("*sa*–two"), *sà* ("*sa*–three"), *sa*$_4$ ("*sa*–four"). These signs are said to be **homophonous**. Often two or more homophonous signs interchange freely in the writing of a particular sound sequence, such as  *ur* and  *úr*, both of which are common in OB for /*ur*/. In a small number of cases, homophones have separate spheres of use; for example,  *ù* is used with rare exception in OB to write the conjunctions *u* 'and' and *ū* 'or' but is not often used otherwise, whereas  *ú* is the sign used to write most other instances of /*u*/, as in *ú-zu-un* for *uzun* 'ear of ...'.

No single dialect of Akkadian, and no single area in which Akkadian was written, used all of the signs that are known. Thus, for example, in Standard Babylonian and other dialects, there is an individual sign explicitly for the sound sequence /*qi*/. In Old Babylonian, however, to write /*qi*/, the scribes used the same sign that they used to write /*ki*/. Since the later dialect has a separate QI sign, the KI sign with the value /*qi*/ is transliterated *qí*. It is essential to remember the diacritical mark when transliterating a sign, since, for example, *qí* is as different in shape from *qi* as it is from *ba*.

Akkadian scribes always "spelled" words following the syllabification of the language. Thus, for example, the word *išarum* may be written *i-ša-rum* or *i-ša-ru-um* (see below), but never ***iš-ar-um* (** indicates an impossible form). It is a general rule of cuneiform orthography that the sequence *(C)VC-V(C)* never occurs within a word (except to indicate the presence of the consonant ʾ after another consonant; see below, §21.4). When a syllable both begins and ends with a consonant, it may be written with a *CVC* sign, if there is one in use, as in *i-ša-rum*, above; more often, however, and necessarily when there is no appropriate *CVC* sign, such syllables are written with **two** signs, a *CV* sign followed by a *VC* sign containing the appropriate consonants and vowel, as in *i-ša-ru-um*, above, or *ka-as-pu-um* for *kaspum*.

Long vowels transcribed with a **macron** are usually written no differently than short vowels; i.e., they are not normally marked as long in the script; e.g.,

ṣa-bu-um for *ṣābum*; *a-ma-tum* for *amātum*;
ḫu-ra-ṣú-um for *ḫurāṣum*; *i-nu-um* for *īnum*.

Occasionally, however, in the middle of a word an extra vowel-sign may be written; e.g., the word *kīn* will usually be written *ki-in*, but occasionally a scribe will write *ki-i-in* instead. There is no difference in the pronunciation of these two writings. Extra vowel signs do not usually occur for these long vowels at the beginning or end of a word; exceptions are some monosyllabic forms; e.g.,

āl 'town of ...' (bound form) may be written *a-al*;
šū 'he, that', *šī* 'she, that', and *kī* 'how' are usually written *šu-ú*, *ši-i*, and *ki-i* (to avoid confusion with pronominal suffixes; see §§11.1, 18.2);
lā 'not' is written *la* or *la-a*; *lū* 'indeed' is written *lu* or *lu-ú*.

Short vowels are almost never written with an extra vowel-sign; again, exceptions are monosyllabic forms such as the negative adverb *ul*, which is normally written *ú-ul* in OB.

Long vowels transcribed with a **circumflex**, at the end of a word, will almost invariably be written with an extra vowel sign; e.g.,

im-la-a for *imlâ*.

When not at the end of a word, these ultraheavy vowels may or may not be written with an extra vowel-sign; e.g.,

either *ra-bi-im* or *ra-bi-i-im* for *rabîm*;
either *ib-nu-ma* or *ib-nu-ú-ma* for *ibnû-ma*.

When **two vowels** occur **in sequence**, the second is written with a *V* sign if it constitutes a complete syllable, as in

ra-bi-a-tum for *rabiātum* 'great (fp)';
iš-me-a-ma for *išmeā-ma* 'they (f) heard and ...'.

If the second of two vowels in sequence begins a syllable that ends in a consonant, the syllable may simply be indicated by a *VC* sign; more often, however, an extra *V* sign occurs to introduce the second vowel:

ra-bi-a-am, less often *ra-bi-am*, for *rabiam* 'great (ms, acc.)'.

Note that writings like *-a-am* in the last example do not necessarily indicate long vowels.

Double consonants may or may not be indicated in the script. There is no rule; only the whim of the scribe prevails. Thus, for example, the word *ikaššassi* may be written any of the following ways:

i-ka-ša-si, i-ka-aš-ša-si, i-ka-ša-as-si, i-ka-aš-ša-as-si.

A consonant written double in the script always indicates that a double consonant is to be transcribed and pronounced.

The sound sequence /*ayyV*/, where *V* is any vowel, is often indicated by the double writing of the A sign, as in *da-a-a-nu-um* for *dayyānum* 'judge'.

Akkadian is written from left to right. There is no special word divider, and, often, not even any extra space between words. Words may not be divided at the end of a line, and prepositions rarely appear at the end of a line.

A sign-by-sign rendering of a cuneiform word or text is called a **transliteration**. Signs in the same word are connected by hyphens:

qá-ra-dum na-ra-am i-pu-uš.

A word or text put in the form that represents our closest approximation to the actual pronunciation, with all long vowels properly marked, and all doubled consonants indicated, is a **normalization** or **transcription**; e.g., for the above transliteration, the normalization would be:

qarrādum narâm īpuš 'the warrior made a stela'.

Notice that in a transliteration, vowel length (macrons and circumflexes) is not indicated, while in a normalization, the diacritics (acute, grave, subscripts) that distinguish homophonous signs are not written.

The cuneiform writing system, which the Akkadians borrowed from the Sumerians, underwent a significant evolution during its long period of use. The KA sign, for example, was originally a picture of a head with the mouth area hatched (KA means 'mouth' in Sumerian): ; this was current about 3000 BCE. Over time, the pictograms began to be drawn with a wedge-shaped stylus; about 2500 BCE, KA appeared as . Different styles of writing also emerged, which depended on the material being inscribed: a formal, lapidary style for important inscriptions on stone; a cursive style for texts on clay tablets. The difference between the two may be compared to the modern difference between typeset and handwritten forms. In the OB period, the lapidary KA was 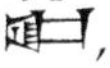, its cursive counterpart 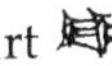 or  (cursive forms of signs may vary considerably from one scribe to another, and even within individual texts). The evolution of the shapes of the signs continued throughout the time cuneiform was written. In the first millennium BCE, a relatively simple style, that of the scribes of the courts of the Neo-Assyrian kings, was used to copy the great epics and myths written in the literary Standard Babylonian dialect. In Neo-Assyrian script, KA appears as .

In the subsequent lessons of this textbook, cuneiform signs will be presented in three varieties: OB lapidary, OB cursive (often two or three examples), and Neo-Assyrian. The OB lapidary is a beautiful script in which is written the famous "Code of Ḫammurapi," laws of which will be introduced beginning in Lesson 17; the majority of OB texts, however, such as the letters, contracts, and omens that will also be read in subsequent lessons, are written in cursive signs, and it is these that the student should learn both to recognize and to draw. The Neo-Assyrian forms of the signs are included because modern sign lists are arranged according to those forms and because some students may wish to learn from the start the signs in which the great literary texts of the later Standard Babylonian dialect are written. The student will learn approximately 150 signs during the course of this grammar; they are presented about ten at a time in the following lessons. Pages 563–74 present a list of all the signs encountered in this text, in the order in which they appear in the standard sign lists; an alphabetical index of the sign values follows the Sign List (pp. 575–76).

There are a number of conventions used by Assyriologists in transliterating texts:

Square brackets, [ ], indicate that the text is broken at the point in question, a common occurrence in clay tablets. When the identity of the missing signs can be determined with relative certainty, usually based on parallel or similar texts, the signs are written inside the square brackets; e.g., the transliteration *a-na e-ka-al-l*[*im i-r*]*u-ub* 'he entered the palace'

indicates that the first five signs and the last sign are present, the beginning of the sign *lim* and the end of the sign *ru* are visible, while the sign *i* is missing entirely. Half brackets, ⸢ ⸣, are sometimes used to indicate partially damaged signs; e.g., *a-*⸢*na e-ka*⸣*-al-lim* indicates that the NA, E, and KA signs are all partly damaged.

Angle brackets, ‹ ›, enclose scribal omissions: e.g., *a-na e-ka-al-lim i-*‹*ru*›*-ub* indicates that, although the text is not broken, the expected sign *ru* has been erroneously omitted by the scribe.

Either double angle brackets, « », or braces, { }, enclose scribal plusses; thus, *a-na e-ka-al-lim i-ru-*«*ru*»*-ub* (or *i-ru-*{*ru*}*-ub*) indicates that the scribe mistakenly repeated *ru*.

An *x* is used to indicate a sign whose reading is unclear; in *a-na x x i-ru-ub* 'he entered ...' the transliteration indicates that there are two signs between *a-na* and *i-ru-ub*, but that the reading of neither is clear. A question mark may be used to indicate that a possible reading is uncertain, as in *a-na bi(?)-tim(?)* (or *bi*$^{?}$*-tim*$^{?}$) *i-ru-ub*.

An exclamation point indicates a scribal error that the modern scholar has changed to the correct reading; the incorrect sign should follow in parentheses: e.g., *a-na!*(UD) *e-ka-al-lim i-ru-ub* signifies that the scribe mistakenly wrote UD (𒌓) for the expected NA (𒈾). An exclamation point in parentheses, or a raised exclamation point ($^{!}$), means *sic!*, i.e., that the modern reader believes a form to be incorrect, but has left it stand in transliteration: e.g., *a-na e-ka-al-lum(!)* (or *e-ka-al-lum*$^{!}$) *i-ru-ub*, where the scribe has written the nominative for 'palace' instead of the expected genitive.

EXERCISES

A. VOCABULARY 9.

Verbs:

agārum (Preterite *īgur*) 'to hire, rent'; Verbal Adj. *agrum* (*agir-*) 'hired, rented', as noun (pl. *agrū*), 'hireling'.

enēšum (*īniš*) 'to be(come) weak, impoverished'; Verbal Adj. *enšum* (*eniš-*) 'weak, powerless'.

kânum (*ikūn*) 'to be(come) true, just, honest, correct; to be(come) firm, fixed, secure; to endure, last'; Verbal Adj. *kīnum* (*kīn-*; fem. *kīttum*; fp *kīnātum*) 'true, just; honest, loyal; normal, regular, correct; proper, legitimate; firm, fixed'; substantivized fem. *kīttum* (bound form *kītti*) 'truth, justice; honesty, loyalty; normal situation, correctness' [given as *kittum* in the dictionaries].

miādum (*imīd*) 'to increase, be(come) much, abundant, numerous, plentiful'; Verbal Adj. *mādum* see Vocab. 5.
nêrum / *nârum* (*inēr* / *inār*) 'to slay, kill; to strike, destroy, defeat'.
qiāšum (*iqīš*) 'to give, bestow, grant'; Verbal Adj. *qīšum* (*qīš-*) 'bestowed, granted' (substantivized fem. *qīštum* 'gift', Vocab. 7).
šâmum (*a*) 'to buy, purchase (from someone: *itti* or *ina qāt*)'; Verbal Adj. *šāmum* (*šām-*) 'purchased, bought'.
šatûm (*išti*) 'to drink'.
târum (*itūr*) 'to return (intrans.), go/come back, turn back; to turn into, become (+ *ana*)'.
ṭiābum (*iṭīb*) 'to become pleasant, pleasing (to: *eli*), sweet, good; to become satisfied'; Verbal Adj. *ṭābum* see Vocab. 4.

Nouns:

kīttum see above under *kânum*.
kunukkum (*kunuk*; pl. *kunukkū* and *kunukkātum*) 'seal, cylinder seal; seal impression; sealed tablet, document'.
ummānum (fem.; *ummān*) 'army, gang, crowd'.

B. Learn the following signs:

OB Lapid.	OB Cursive	NA	values
			*aš*, *rum*
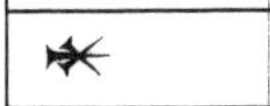	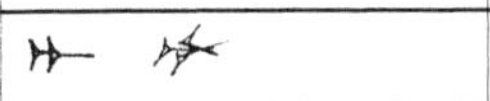	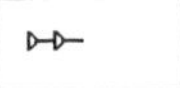	*ḫal*
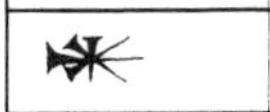	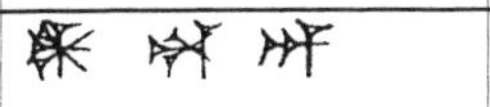	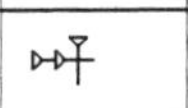	*an*
	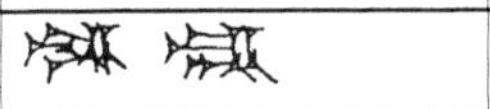	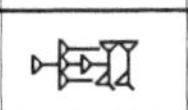	*maḫ*
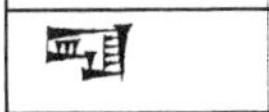	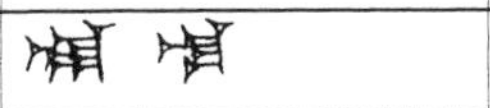	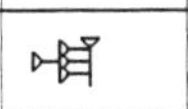	*la*
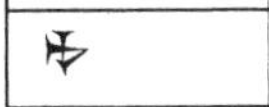	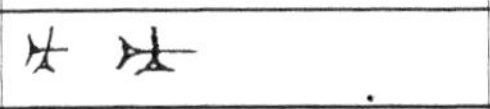		*nu*
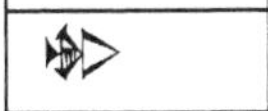	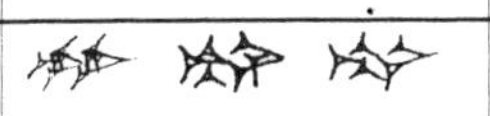		*dim*, *tim*, *ṭim**
	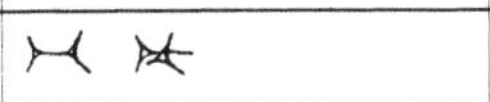	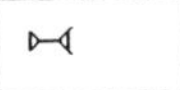	*be*, *bad* / *t* / *ṭ***, *til*
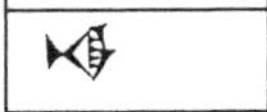	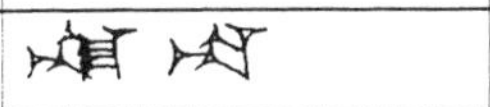		*na*
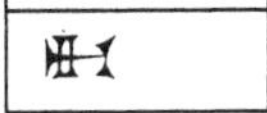		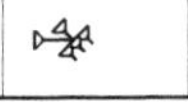	*mu*

*Most *CiC* signs may also have the value *CeC*, so that the DIM sign is *tim* and *tem*, *dim* and *dem*, *ṭim* and *ṭem*; normally, only the *CiC* value will be given.

**I.e., *bad*, *bat*, and *baṭ*.

C. Write the following words in cuneiform and in transliteration:

1. *anna* 3. *mutim* 5. *nālā* 7. *ašlātim*
2. *maḫlaš* 4. *naḫal* 6. *nubattim* 8. *bērum*

D. Give the full Preterites of the following verbs:

1. *agārum* 4. *miādum* 6. *šatûm*
2. *enēšum* 5. *šâlum* (II–ʾ$_{1-2}$) 'to ask' 7. *târum*
3. *bêlum* 'to rule'

E. Write in (normalized) Akkadian; use bound forms where applicable:

1. the truth of the word
2. the seal of the warrior
3. the hireling of the prince
4. the fields of the assembly of the town
5. the weak of the land
6. the name of the prisoner
7. the day of the lawsuit
8. the gifts of the mistress of the throne
9. the king's army
10. a full prison
11. small seals
12. a stolen stela
13. pure water

F. Normalize and translate:

1. *ag-ra-am šu-a-ti a-na ga-ma-ar ba-ne-e bi-tim a-gu-úr-ma i-na ba-ne-e bi-tim ú-ul ig-mu-úr.*
2. *i-na ú-mi-im ša-ti en-šu-ut ma-ti-im id-ni-nu ù a-na-ku e-ni-iš-ma ú-ul e-še-er.*
3. *al-pa-am ni-ša-am-ma im-ra-aṣ-ma al-pa-am mar-ṣa-am šu-a-ti a-na be-el al-pí-im maḫ-ri-i-im ni-di-in.*
4. *eq-la-am ep-ša-am a-na a-ša-at wa-ar-di-im ta-qí-ši.*
5. *ša-ru-um ka-ki it-ti na-ki-ri-im i-pu-uš-ma na-ki-ra-am i-né-er.*
6. *am-tum ša-am-tum iḫ-li-iq-ma a-na bi-it be-li-im ú-ul i-tu-úr.*
7. *i-ši-id ku-us-sí ša-ri-im i-ku-um-ma ú-ma-at ša-ri-im i-ri-ka.*
8. *a-wi-lum šu-ú bi-tam ù eq-lam i-ša-am-ma i-ni-iš.*
9. *da-a-a-nu a-na pu-ḫu-ur a-li-im il-li-ku-ma ḫu-ra-ṣa-am ma-da-am ù ši-pa-tim qá-at-na-tim a-na ru-ba-tim i-qí-šu.*
10. *um-ma-nu-um na-ka-ar-tum šar-ra-am ra-bi-a-am ù ma-ri šar-ri-im i-na e-ka-li-im i-na-ar.*
11. *e-mu-qá um-ma-an na-ak-ri-im i-ni-ša-ma um-ma-nu-um ši-i im-qú-ut.*
12. *ni-nu i-na ma-at na-ak-ri-im ú-ul ni-ku-un a-na ma-tim an-ni-*

tim ni-tu-ur-ma a-na da-na-tim ni-ru-ub.

13. *qá-ar-ra-dum ku-nu-uk da-a-a-ni-im i-ḫu-uz-ma is-sú-uk.*
14. *i-na ki-ti-im ši-ka-ar e-ka-al-li-im ú-ul ni-iš-ti ù a-ka-al a-li-im ú-ul ni-ḫu-uz.*
15. *da-a-a-nu-um ṭu-pa-am i-zi-ma a-na-ku ù at-ta a-wa-at ṭu-pí-im ki-na-tim ni-mu-úr.*
16. *mu-ú na-ri-im ša-ap-li-tim i-mi-du-ma na-ru-um ir-pí-iš-ma mu-ú e-li ki-ša-ad na-ri-im il-li-ku.*
17. *šar-ru-um ṭe*$_4$*-ma-am it-ti eṭ-lu-ti-im iš-ku-um-ma na-ar-ka-ba-ti-im a-na ša-di-im an-ni-i-im ir-ka-bu.*
18. *i-na ep-še-tim i-ša-ra-tim ša ru-be-em šu-a-ti na-pí-iš-ti ma-tim i-ṭi-ib-ma ma-tum iḫ-du.*

G. Transliterate, normalize, and translate:

1. 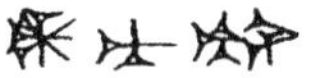

2. 

LESSON TEN

10.1 The G Infinitive, Preterite, and Verbal Adjective: Verbs I–*w*

(a) The **Infinitives** of verbs with first radical *w* present no difficulties; some examples:

warāqum 'to be/turn yellow';	*watārum* 'to be surpassing';
walādum 'to bear';	*waṣābum* 'to add to, enlarge';
warādum 'to descend';	*wašābum* 'to sit, dwell'.

(b) There are two **Preterite** conjugations of verbs I–*w* in the G stem, one for stative/adjectival verbs (as in the first row of examples), one for active verbs (either transitive or intransitive, as in the second and third rows of examples above; see §3.4).

(i) The finite G forms of stative verbs I–*w* are conjugated as in verbs I–*e* (i.e., verbs I–$ʾ_{3-5}$ and I–*y*; see §8.1). The theme-vowel is invariably *i*. Thus, for the G Preterite of *watārum* 'to be surpassing' we find:

3cs	*ītir*	3mp	*ītirū*
		3fp	*ītirā*
2ms	*tētir*	2cp	*tētirā*
2fs	*tētirī*		
1cs	*ētir*	1cp	*nītir*

(ii) Active verbs I–*w* also all have *i* as their theme-vowel in the G Preterite. The **prefix** of these verbs, however, always contains ***u*** rather than the usual *i* or *a*. Here is the G Preterite of *wašābum* 'to sit, dwell':

3cs	*ušib*	3mp	*ušbū*
		3fp	*ušbā*
2ms	*tušib*	2cp	*tušbā*
2fs	*tušbī*		
1cs	*ušib*	1cp	*nušib*

Note that the 3cs and the 1cs forms are the same. Note also that when a vocalic ending (i.e., an ending beginning with a vowel) is added, the theme-vowel *i* is lost due to syncope (§4.1).

(c) **Verbal Adjectives** of roots I–*w* are unremarkable:

warqum (*waruq-*) 'yellow, green';
watrum (*watar-*) 'additional, excessive';
waldum (*walid-*) 'born';
wašbum (*wašib-*) 'seated; in residence'.

10.2 The Verb *babālum*

The forms of the very common verb *w–b–l* 'to carry' require comment. The expected Infinitive *wabālum* and Verbal Adj. *wablum* are normally replaced in OB texts by *babālum* and *bablum* (*babil-*), respectively, with assimilation of the first radical to the second. The Preterite of this verb is essentially regular, but the third radical *l* occasionally prevents the syncope of the theme-vowel when a vocalic ending is added (§4.1(d)), so that byforms are attested:

3cs	*ubil*	3mp	*ublū* or *ubilū*
		3fp	*ublā* or *ubilā*
2ms	*tubil*	2cp	*tublā* or *tubilā*
2fs	*tublī* or *tubilī*		
1cs	*ubil*	1cp	*nubil*

10.3 Pronominal Suffixes on Prepositions

The pronominal objects of a few Akkadian prepositions take the form of suffixes attached directly to the preposition. The suffixes have the following forms:

1cs	*-ya*	1cp	*-ni*
2ms	*-ka*	2mp	*-kunu*
2fs	*-ki*	2fp	*-kina*
3ms	*-šu*	3mp	*-šunu*
3fs	*-ša*	3fp	*-šina*

Two prepositions that take pronominal suffixes have been encountered thus far, *eli* and *itti*; in both, the final vowel is lengthened:

1cs	*elīya* 'on me'	*ittīya* 'with me'
2ms	*elīka* 'on you (ms)'	*ittīka* 'with you (ms)'
2fs	*elīki* 'on you (fs)'	*ittīki* 'with you (fs)'
3ms	*elīšu* 'on him'	*ittīšu* 'with him'
3fs	*elīša* 'on her'	*ittīša* 'with her'

1cp	*elīni* 'on us'	*ittīni* 'with us'
2mp	*elīkunu* 'on you (mp)'	*ittīkunu* 'with you (mp)'
2fp	*elīkina* 'on you (fp)'	*ittīkina* 'with you (fp)'
3mp	*elīšunu* 'on them (m)'	*ittīšunu* 'with them (m)'
3fp	*elīšina* 'on them (f)'	*ittīšina* 'with them (f)'

Note that the vowel *a* in the pronominal suffixes is not affected by the incompatibility of *e* and *a* (§7.2(e)) when attached to *elī-*.

Most other prepositions are followed by a genitive (or dative, after *ana*) form of the pronoun. The third person forms are the same as those of the anaphoric pronoun, presented in §6.3; e.g.,

kīma šuāti 'like him'; *ana šināšim* 'for them (f)'.

The forms of the other persons will be given in a later lesson (§25.2).

10.4 Double-Duty Objects

As in English, a word that is the direct object of two verbs need not be repeated in the second clause; this is especially true if the second verb may then follow the first immediately (usually, but not necessarily, with the conjunction *-ma*):

wardam šuāti iṣbatū-ma imḫaṣū 'they seized and struck that slave'.

The verbs may, however, also be separated by a short phrase:

bītam ašām-ma ana agrim addin 'I purchased and gave the hireling a house'.

In both examples, the deleted object may also be resumed by a pronominal object suffix, as in English ('they seized that slave and struck him'; 'I purchased a house and gave it to the hireling'). Object suffixes are presented in a later lesson (§18.2).

EXERCISES

A. VOCABULARY 10.

Verbs:

akālum (Preterite *īkul*) 'to eat, consume; to use, have the use of (a field, etc.); to take for oneself'.

babālum (from *wabālum*; Preterite *ubil* [pl. *ublū* or *ubilū*]) 'to bear, carry, transport, convey'; Verbal Adj. *bablum* (*babil-*) 'carried, transported' (rare).

edēšum (*īdiš*) 'to be/become new'; Verbal Adj. *eššum* (< **edšum*; fem. *eššetum*, rarely *edištum*) 'new, fresh'.

labārum (*ilbir*) 'to become old, last, endure'; Verbal Adj. *labirum* (*labir-*) 'old, ancient, remote (in time); original, traditional'.

mâtum (*imūt*) 'to die'; Verbal Adj. *mītum* (*mīt-*; fem. *mīttum*) 'dead'.

šiābum (*išīb*) 'to become/grow old, gray'; Verbal Adj. *šībum* (*šīb-*) 'gray, gray-haired, old'; as noun (bound form *šīb(i)*; pl. *šībū* and *šībūtum*) 'old man, elder; witness'.

wašābum (*ušib*) 'to sit down; to sit, be sitting, seated; to stay, remain (somewhere), reside, dwell'; Verbal Adj. *wašbum* (*wašib-*) 'seated; resident, in residence'.

watārum (*ītir*) 'to be/become exceeding, surpassing; to exceed, surpass'; Verbal Adj. *watrum* (*watar-*) 'additional, in excess, superfluous; foremost, pre-eminent, excellent'; substantivized fem. *watartum* (bound form *watarti*) 'excess, surplus, extra'.

Nouns:

karānum (bound form *karān*) 'grapes; grapevine; vineyard; wine'.

nišū (always masc. pl. in form, but takes **fem.** pl. verbs and adjectives) 'people'.

šattum (bound form *šatti*; pl. *šanātum*) 'year'.

Adjective:

lemnum (*lemun-*; fem. *lemuttum*; fp *lemnētum*; Verbal Adj. of a rare verb *lemēnum* [cf. §21.2]) 'evil, bad, malevolent'; substantivized fem. *lemuttum* (bound form *lemutti*) 'evil, wickedness; evil intentions; misfortune, danger'.

B. Learn the following signs:

OB Lapid.	OB Cursive	NA	values
			*ti*, *ṭì*
			*ḫu*
		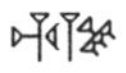	*nam*

𒂗	𒂊𒉌	𒂗	en
𒊑	𒊑	𒊑	ri, re, tal, ṭal
𒍣	𒍣 𒍣	𒍣	zi, ze, sí, sé, ṣí, ṣé
𒄀	𒄀	𒄀	gi, ge
𒀝	𒀝 𒀝 𒀝	𒀝	ag/k/q
𒅅	𒅅 𒅅 𒅅	𒅅	ig/k/q, eg/k/q

C. Write the following words in cuneiform and in transliteration:

   1. *annam*   4. *tillatim*   7. *ṣēnam*   10. *muḫḫūtim*
   2. *gere*   5. *bennū*   8. *zīmū*   11. *ṭīdim*
   3. *sebe*   6. *ḫallatī*   9. *egrum*

D. Give the full Preterites of the following verbs:

   1. *mâtum*   4. *warādum* 'to descend'
   2. *šiābum*   5. *warāqum* 'to be/turn yellow'
   3. *akālum*

E. Write in normalized Akkadian:

   1. with us   8. against them (m)
   2. against you (ms)   9. like them (f)
   3. like them (m)   10. on you (mp)
   4. on him   11. for her
   5. with you (fp)   12. against them (f)
   6. like him   13. I received silver from you (fs).
   7. with me and with her

F. Normalize and translate:

   1. ṭe-ma-am it-ti am-tim aš-ku-um-ma a-na ma-ra-at ša-ar-ra-tim aṭ-ru-ud.
   2. qá-ra-dum šu-ú i-na bi-tim ú-ši-ib ḫa-ra-nam it-ti-ni ú-ul il-li-ik.
   3. i-na di-nim eq-la-am za-ka-am an-ni-a-am am-ḫu-úr-ma a-ku-ul be-el eq-li-im maḫ-ru-ú-um im-ra-aṣ-ma ú-ul iš-li-im-ma i-mu-ut.
   4. ši-bu-um ma-ar-ṣú-um a-na wa-ar-di ḫal-qú-tim me-e ṭa-bu-tim a-na ša-te-e-em ù ak-lam a-na a-ka-lim i-qí-iš.

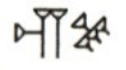

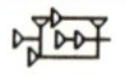

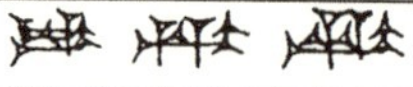

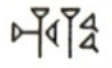

5. *eṭ-la-am šu-a-ti il-qú-ma a-na bi-it i-li-im ub-lu.*
6. *šar-ra-am ma-ru šar-ri-im i-na e-kal-lim i-né-ru.*
7. *ṭe*$_4$*-ma-am a-na wa-tar-ti bi-tim šu-a-ti ta-aṣ-ba-ta-ma ka-ra-an bi-tim a-na be-el bi-tim ta-di-na.*
8. *i-na ša-ti-im ša-a-ti ni-šu ma-tim bi-it i-lim la-be-ra-am i-qú-ra-ma bi-tam eš-ša-am ib-ni-a.*
9. *ma-ar da-a-a-nim ṣé-eḫ-rum be-el-tam i-ḫu-uz-ma ni-šu iḫ-da-a.*
10. *a-na ma-tim it-ti um-ma-nim ni-tu-ur-ma i-na a-lim nu-ši-ib.*
11. *il-tum ra-bi-tum le-mu-tam i-na ma-tim ip-ru-ús.*
12. *a-wa-at ši-bu-tim ki-na-tim eš-me-ma en-ša-am šu-a-ti ú-ul am-ḫa-aṣ.*
13. *a-ka-lum i-na eq-le-tim i-te-er-ma ni-šu ma-dam i-ku-la.*
14. *da-na-tum ši-i a-na ša-na-tim ma-da-tim il-bi-ir-ma i-na ša-at-tim an-ni-tim im-qú-ut.*
15. *ag-ra-am a-na na-ṣa-ar ku-nu-uk a-wi-lim ta-gu-ri-ma šu-ú ku-nu-ka-am iš-ri-iq.*
16. *al-pu ma-du-tum ša ru-be-em i-mu-tu al-pí mi-tu-tim it-ti-ni ú-ul i-ša-am.*
17. *ḫu-ra-ṣú-um wa-at-ru-um a-na e-ka-al-li-im i-ru-um-ma ḫu-ra-ṣú-um i-mi-id-ma li-ib-bi šar-ri-im i-ṭi-ib.*

G. Transliterate, normalize, and translate:

1. 

2. 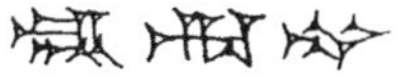

3. 

4. 

LESSON ELEVEN

11.1 The Noun with Possessive Pronominal Suffixes

In the last lesson it was seen that the pronominal objects of some prepositions take the form of suffixes (§10.3). The same set of suffixes, with an additional form for the 1cs, is also attached to nouns to indicate possession, as in

mārūki wardīya imḫaṣū 'your (fs) sons hit my slaves';

bēlni ḫurāṣam ana qarrādīšu iddin 'our lord gave gold to his warriors'.

Nouns with suffixes may be modified by adjectives; this includes the demonstrative adjectives, which in English must be rendered, e.g., 'this x of (yours, hers, etc.)'; e.g.,

emūqšu dannum 'his mighty strength';

ṭēmki annûm 'this report of yours (fs)';

ana wardīya šunūti 'for those servants of mine'.

Nouns with suffixes may also be modified by another noun, but *ša* must be used to express the genitive relationship:

eli kussīka ša ḫurāṣim 'on your throne of gold'.

As already noted, the forms of the possessive suffixes are the same as those learned in the last lesson, except that the 1cs suffix has two forms, the distribution of which is discussed at the end of this section:

1cs	*-ī, -ya*	1cp	*-ni*
2ms	*-ka*	2mp	*-kunu*
2fs	*-ki*	2fp	*-kina*
3ms	*-šu*	3mp	*-šunu*
3fs	*-ša*	3fp	*-šina*

Again, *a* in these suffixes does not become *e* when they are attached to words with *e* (§7.2(e)):

bēlkina 'your (fp) lord'; *bēlētūya* 'my ladies'; *ṭēmša* 'her report'.

In general, as indicated by forms like *bēlni* 'our lord' and *ṭēmša* 'her report', the possessive suffixes are added to the **bound form** of the noun. In some types of bases, however, the bound form undergoes certain modifications before suffixes; the various noun types will therefore be covered in detail in the following paragraphs. (The form of the noun with pronominal suffixes is referred to in some Akkadian grammars as the status pronominalis.)

(a) Plural Forms

Masculine Plural Nouns. Suffixes are attached directly (remember that the bound form and the free form are identical in masculine plural nouns):

mārūki 'your (fs) sons'; *ana rubêni* 'for our princes';
kunukkūša 'her seals'; *itti dayyānīkunu* 'with your (mp) judges';
ilūšunu 'their (m) gods'; *mutīšina āmur* 'I saw their husbands'.

Feminine Plural Nouns. The unbound form, minus its mimation and with its case-vowel lengthened, serves as the presuffixal base:

qīšātūšu 'his gifts'; *kīma napšātīkina* 'like your (fp) lives';
narkabātūka 'your (ms) chariots'; *ina puḫrātīkunu* 'in your (mp) assemblies';
epšētūša 'her deeds'; *awâtīni išmû* 'they (m) heard our words'.

(Note: Some Assyriologists consider the vowel before the suffixes on feminine plurals to be short: *qīšātušu, napšātikina*, etc.)

Plural Adjectives. These take suffixes only when substantivized (§4.4); they behave like fem. pl. nouns, i.e., the long case-vowel of masc. pl. nouns is added to the bound form before the suffixes:

rabûtūni 'our nobles'; *ina mītūtīšunu* 'among their (m) dead';
šarqātūšu 'his stolen items'; *watrātīšu ašām* 'I bought his extras' (referring, e.g., to *narkabātum* 'chariots').

(Note: Again, some Assyriologists consider the vowel before the suffixes on these forms to be short: *rabûtuni, mītūtišunu*, etc.)

(b) Dual Forms

The suffixes are added directly to the bound form of the dual (i.e., to the case-vowel after the final *-n* of the free form has been dropped):

īnāki 'your (fs) eyes'; *ina qātīšina* 'in their (f) hands';
emūqāšu 'his strength'; *išdīšu abni* 'I built its (m) foundation'.

(c) Singular Forms

Most singular nouns have at least two forms before the possessive suffixes, depending on case: for the majority of nouns, the genitive is distinguished from a common nominative–accusative form; a few nouns distinguish all three cases before suffixes.

Genitive. The genitive of **all** sg. nouns before the suffixes is the **free** form without mimation and with the case-vowel lengthened to *-ī-*:

ina kašādīki 'on your (fs) arrival';
ana amtīša 'for her womanservant';
šar mātīšunu 'the king of their (m) land'.

Thus, in many instances, the gen. sg. with a suffix is identical in form to the gen.–acc. pl. with a suffix; only context can resolve the ambiguity:

eli mārīka 'against your son/sons';
kīma dayyānīni 'like our judge/judges'.

(Note: Here too, some Assyriologists believe that the sg. genitive case-vowel remains short before suffixes: *ina kašādiki, ana amtika, šar mātišunu,* etc. In this view, the sg. and pl. forms are therefore not identical.)

Nominative and Accusative. A review of §8.3 will show that, apart from some nouns with bases ending in a vowel, the singular bound form ends either in a consonant or in *i*. For most nouns, the bound form serves as a common nominative–accusative pre-suffixal base, albeit with an important modification when the bound form ends in *-i*.

(i) Bound form ending in a consonant. Suffixes are normally added directly to the bound form without any further change; it bears repeating that the following forms are both nominative and accusative:

kalabša 'her dog';	*išidka* 'your (ms) foundation';
eqelšina 'their (f) field';	*puḫuršunu* 'their (m) assembly';
šarratni 'our queen';	*šikarka* 'your (ms) beer';
māratni 'our daughter';	*ilatki* 'your (fs) goddess';
alākšu 'his going';	*epēška* 'your (ms) doing';
nakeršu 'his enemy';	*ṣabitkunu* 'your (mp) prisoner (m)'.

It will be recalled that *n* assimilates to a following consonant (§5.1). This applies to *n* before pronominal suffixes as well, although often forms are written as though the *n* did not assimilate (a morphographemic writing; see §18.4):

uzušša 'her ear', written *ú-zu-(uš)-ša* or *ú-zu-un-ša;*
nadāššina 'their (f) giving', written *na-da-(aš)-ši-na* or *na-da-an-ši-na.*

Another important sound change involving the pronominal suffixes occurs whenever a third-person suffix follows directly a base ending in a dental (*d*, *t*, *ṭ*) or a sibilant (*s*, *ṣ*, *š*, *z*): the two sounds change to ***ss***. Some examples:

qaqqassa (‹ **qaqqadša*) 'her head';
bēlessunu (‹ **bēletšunu*) 'their (m) lady';
balāssina (‹ **balāṭšina*) 'their (f) life';
parāssu (‹ **parāššu*) 'his deciding';
ḫurāssa (‹ **ḫurāṣša*) 'her gold';
epēssu (‹ **epēššu*) 'his doing';
aḫāssa (‹ **aḫāzša*) 'her grasping'.

Two noun types with bound forms ending in a consonant are exceptions to the general rule, having instead presuffixal forms in *-a-* like the nouns in (ii) below. One type consists of nouns the bases of which have more than one syllable and end in a doubled consonant, such as *ekallum* 'palace' and *kunukkum* 'seal'; while in the bound form of these the doubled consonant is simplified, before suffixes the doubling is retained:

ekal šarrim 'the king's palace', but *ekallašu* 'his palace';
kunuk aššatim 'the wife's seal', but *kunukkaša* 'her seal'.

The second type are feminine Participles (§20.1):

free form *pāristum*, bound form *pārisat*, but before suffixes *pārista-*.

(ii) Bound form ending in -i. The final *-i* is replaced by an unaccented **short *-a-*** before the suffixes, as in these nom. and acc. forms:

ṭuppaša 'her tablet';
maruštašu 'his difficulty';
qīštaka 'your (ms) gift';
libbaki 'your (fs) heart';
ummani 'our mother';
ṣibittašu 'its (m) prison'.

When the suffixes of the second and third person pl. are added, vowel syncope does not take place, even though the resulting form contains three short syllables in succession (see §4.1(e)):

šarrašunu 'their (m) king'; *napištakina* 'your (fp) life';

This presuffixal *-a-* does not undergo vowel harmony (§7.2(d)):

epištaša 'her deed'; *lemuttaka* 'your (ms) wickedness'.

A number of noun types constitute **exceptions** to this pattern:

The nouns *abum* 'father' and *aḫum* 'brother' exhibit a full triptotic declension before pronominal suffixes, with long case-vowels:

nom.	*abūšu*	*aḫūki*
gen.	*abīšu*	*aḫīki*
acc.	*abāšu*	*aḫāki*

Nouns with one-syllable bases ending in a single consonant, such as *ilum* 'god' and *bēlum* 'lord', have two possible bound forms, with and without a final *-i*: *il* or *ili*, *bēl* or *bēli*. They likewise exhibit two sets of forms with suffixes, one set like those of the nouns in (i) above, the other (which is the less common) like those of *abum* and *aḫum*:

nom.	*ilša* or *ilūša*	*bēlni* or *bēlūni*
gen.	*ilīša*	*bēlīni*
acc.	*ilša* or *ilāša*	*bēlni* or *bēlāni*

Note that nom. forms like *ilūša* and *bēlūni* (as well as the gen. forms *ilīša* and *bēlīni*; see above) may be sg. or pl.: 'her god/gods', 'our lord/lords'. (Note: Again, some Assyriologists consider the case-vowel, when it is present before suffixes in these examples, to be short. In this view, the sg. and pl. forms are therefore not identical.)

Nouns and adjectives with **bases** ending in *-i*, such as *kussûm* 'throne' and *rabûm* 'great', usually have presuffixal forms in *-ī* for all three cases:

nom.-gen.-acc. *kussīka* 'your (ms) throne', *rabīšu* 'his great one (m)'.

Rarely, these words exhibit a three-case declension before suffixes like those in the following paragraph.

(iii) Bound form ending in a vowel other than -i. The pronominal suffixes are added to the base plus the appropriate case-ending (with the normal rules of vowel contraction), e.g.:

	šadûm (*šadu-*)	*rubûm* (*rubā-*)	*banûm* (*banā-*)	*leqûm* (*leqē-*)
nom.	*šadûšu*	*rubûni*	*banûšunu*	*leqûša*
gen.	*šadîšu*	*rubêni*	*banêšunu*	*leqêša*
acc.	*šadâšu*	*rubâni*	*banâšunu*	*leqēaša*
	'his mountain'	'our prince'	'their (m) building'	'her taking'

(d) First Person Singular Suffix

As was noted at the beginning of this section, the 1cs suffix has two forms, the distribution of which depends on the number and case of the noun or adjective to which it is attached. The forms are:

(i) ***-ī***, attached directly to the base (the free form without its case-ending), on all singular nouns and adjectives in the nom. and acc.:

mārtī 'my daughter';	*awātī* 'my word';
abī 'my father';	*aḫī* 'my brother';
epēšī 'my doing';	*libbī* 'my heart'.

Note that some forms may be identical with the gen.-acc. pl.:

ilī 'my god' (nom. or acc.) or 'gods' (gen.-acc.).

When the base ends in a vowel, normal vowel contraction takes place:

kussî 'my throne'; *rabî* 'my great one (m)';
šadî 'my mountain'; *rubê* 'my prince';
banê 'my building' *leqê* 'my taking'.

(ii) ***-ya***, otherwise, including after the case-vowel of sg. nouns and adjectives in the gen. (as before the other suffixes, the short case-vowels of the sg., the fem. pl., and pl. adjectives are lengthened):

ana mārtīya 'to my daughter'; *kīma awātīya* 'like my word';
itti abīya 'with my father'; *ina libbīya* 'in my heart';
eli kussīya 'on my throne'; *ina šemêya* 'in my hearing';
īnāya 'my eyes' (nom.); *īnīya* 'my eyes' (gen.-acc.);
mārūya 'my sons' (nom.); *mārīya* 'my sons' (gen.-acc.);
mārātūya 'my daughters' (nom.); *mārātīya* 'my daughters' (gen.-acc.);
rabûtūya 'my nobles (i.e., great ones)' (nom.); *rabûtīya* 'my nobles (i.e., great ones)' (gen.-acc.);
epšētūya 'my deeds' (nom.); *epšētīya* 'my deeds' (gen.-acc.).

The form *-ya* is usually written with the IA sign:

ki-ma a-wa-ti-ia; i-na še-me-(e)-ia; i-na-ia; etc.

After *-ū-* (i.e., after nominative plural nouns and adjectives), however, *-ya* is more often written with the A sign, although writings with IA are also common (especially in texts from the northern OB area):

ma-ru-a; ep-še-tu-a; etc.; less often *ma-ru-ia; ep-še-tu-ia;* etc.

Summary of the Bound and Suffixal Forms of the Noun

A. Plural

		free form	bound form	suffixal form
Masc. Pl. Nouns	nom.	*mārū*	*mārū*	*mārūka*
	gen.-acc.	*mārī*	*mārī*	*mārīka*
Fem. Pl. Nouns/Adj.s	nom.	*mārātum*	*mārāt*	*mārātūka*
	gen.-acc.	*mārātim*		*mārātīka*
Masc. Pl. Adj.s	nom.	*damqūtum*	*damqūt*	*damqūtūka*
	gen.-acc.	*damqūtim*		*damqūtīka*

B. Dual

		free form	bound form	suffixal form
	nom.	*uznān*	*uznā*	*uznāka*
	gen.-acc.	*uznīn*	*uznī*	*uznīka*

C. Singular

1. base in -*VC*

a. 2-syllable	nom.	*awīlum*		*awīlka*
	acc.	*awīlam*	*awīl*	"
	gen.	*awīlim*		*awīlīka*
	nom.	*nakrum*		*nakerka*
	acc.	*nakram*	*naker*	"
	gen.	*nakrim*		*nakrīka*
b. 1-syllable	nom.	*bēlum*		*bēl(ū)ka*
	acc.	*bēlam*	*bēl(i)*	*bēl(ā)ka*
	gen.	*bēlim*		*bēlīka*
c. *abum, aḫum*	nom.	*abum*		*abūka*
	acc.	*abam*	*abi*	*abāka*
	gen.	*abim*		*abīka*

2. base in -C_1C_1

a. 1-syllable	nom.	*libbum*		*libbaka*
	acc.	*libbam*	*libbi*	"
	gen.	*libbim*		*libbīka*
b. 2-syllable, *-tt*	nom.	*ṣibittum*		*ṣibittaka*
	acc.	*ṣibittam*	*ṣibitti*	"
	gen.	*ṣibittim*		*ṣibittīka*
c. 2-syllable, other	nom.	*ekallum*		*ekallaka*
	acc.	*ekallam*	*ekal*	"
	gen.	*ekallim*		*ekallīka*

3. base in -C_1C_2, $C_2 \neq t$, i.e., *pVrs*

	nom.	*puḫrum*		*puḫurka*
	acc.	*puḫram*	*puḫur*	"
	gen.	*puḫrim*		*puḫrīka*

4. base in -*Ct* (fem.)

a. 2-syllable

i. most 2-syll. nouns in -*Ct*	nom.	*napištum*		*napištaka*
	acc.	*napištam*	*napišti*	"
	gen.	*napištim*		*napištīka*

		free form	bound form	suffixal form
ii. fem. Participles	nom.	*māḫirtum*		*māḫirtaka*
	acc.	*māḫirtam*	*māḫirat*	"
	gen.	*māḫirtim*		*māḫirtīka*

b. 1-syllable

i.	nom.	*qīštum*		*qīštaka*
	acc.	*qīštam*	*qīšti*	"
	gen.	*qīštim*		*qīštīka*
ii.	nom.	*mārtum*		*māratka*
	acc.	*mārtam*	*mārat*	"
	gen.	*mārtim*		*mārtīka*

5. base in -*V*

a. -*CCi*	nom.	*kussûm*		
	acc.	*kussiam*	*kussi*	*kussīka*
	gen.	*kussîm*		
b. -*Ci*	nom.	*rabûm*		
	acc.	*rabiam*	*rab(i)*	*rabīka*
	gen.	*rabîm*		
c. -*ā*	nom.	*rubûm*	*rubê* /	*rubûka*
	acc.	*rubâm*	*rubi* /	*rubâka*
	gen.	*rubêm*	*rubā*	*rubêka*
d. other vowels	nom.	*šadûm*		*šadûka*
	acc.	*šadâm*	*šad(i)*	*šadâka*
	gen.	*šadîm*		*šadîka*

11.2 Apposition

When two or more substantives or phrases in a clause refer to the same thing, they are said to be in apposition. In Akkadian, words in apposition are in the same case: e.g.,

ana šēpī šarrim bēlīya amqut 'At the feet of the king, my lord, I fell';
awīlam šuāti abāka iṣbatū 'They seized that man, your father';
Enlil bēlum rabûm nakram ina mātim iṭrud '(The god) Enlil, the great lord, drove the enemy from the land'.

Sometimes the order of appositional elements differs from the usual English order, especially when an independent personal pronoun or a pronominal suffix is involved:

bēlī atta nakrī ilī tenēr 'You, my lord, slew the enemies of the gods';
dayyānum aḫī aššatam īḫuz 'My brother the judge got married'.

11.3 The Quantifier *kalûm*

The word *kalûm* 'entirety, whole', which always occurs in the singular, is the most common means of expressing 'all (of)' and 'every' in Old Babylonian. It may be used in the bound form (*kala*, rarely *kali* or *kal*) before another noun; e.g.,

kala ilī 'all the gods';
kala mātim 'the whole/entire land, all the land'.

Much more commonly, however, *kalûm* occurs **after** the noun it modifies; in these instances, it is in apposition to the previous noun (hence, in the same case), and has a third person pronominal suffix, the gender and number of which correspond to those of the antecedent noun:

šarrū kalûšunu ina mātātīšunu ušbū 'All the kings (lit.: the kings, all of them) remained in their lands' (note that the verb is m. pl., agreeing with the antecedent noun rather than with the sg. *kalûšunu*);
māt nakrīya kalâša akšud 'I conquered all of my enemy's land';
mê ana amātīšu kalîšina niddin 'We gave water to all his women-servants'.

kalûm may also be used without an expressed antecedent:

ana kalîšunu 'for all of them (m)'.

EXERCISES

A. VOCABULARY 11.

Verbs:

kaṣārum (Preterite *ikṣur*) 'to tie, bind, join (together), put together, form; to compile, collect; to organize, arrange'; Verbal Adj. *kaṣrum* (*kaṣir-*) 'joined, organized'.
nakāsum (*ikkis*) 'to cut off, cut down'; Verbal Adj. *naksum* (*nakis-*) 'cut (off, down), felled'.
paḫārum (*ipḫur*) 'to gather, assemble (intrans.), come together'.

rašûm (*irši*) 'to receive, obtain, get, acquire, gain'.
ṭeḫûm (*iṭḫe*) 'to go near, draw near, approach (+ *ana*)'.
walādum (*ulid*) 'to give birth, bear; to beget'; Verbal Adj. *waldum* (*walid-*) 'born'.

Nouns:

iṣum (bound form *iṣi*) 'tree; wood, lumber, timber'.
nēmettum (*nēmetti*; with suf. *nēmetta-*) 'complaint; tax, tribute; support, staff, crutch'; *nēmettam rašûm* 'to have cause for complaint'.
sinništum (*sinništi*; suf. *sinništa-*) 'woman; female'.
ṣuḫārum (*ṣuḫār*) '(male) child, adolescent; male servant, employee'; fem. *ṣuḫārtum* (*ṣuḫārti*; suf. *ṣuḫārta-*) '(female) child, young woman; female servant, employee' (cf. *ṣeḫrum*).

Pronoun:

kalûm (bound form *kala* [rarely *kali* or *kal*]; with suf. *kalû/î/â-*) 'entirety, whole, all' (see §11.3).

Adverb:

adīni 'until now'; usually with negative: '(not) yet'.

B. Learn the following signs:

OB Lapid.	OB Cursive	NA	values
	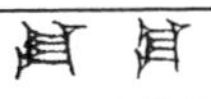		*šu*
			*gur*
			*si, se*
			*ru*
	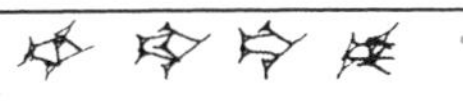		*ub/p*
		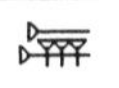	*sa*
	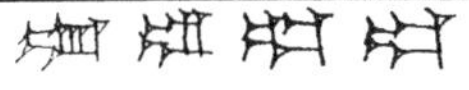		*um*
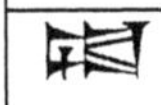			*ad/t/ṭ*
	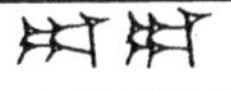	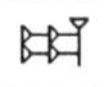	*ab/p*
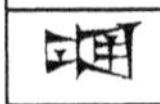	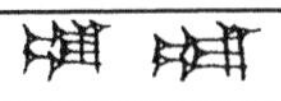	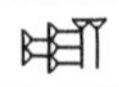	*ṣi, ṣe, zí, zé*

C. Write the following words in cuneiform and in transliteration:

1. *mugur*	4. *sadrum*	7. *tallašu*	10. *abnam*
2. *saphum*	5. *ṣerrētim*	8. *ḫubtim*	11. *šuḫurrum*
3. *zērum*	6. *šugītim*	9. *sekrum*	12. *šubtim*

D. Give the full Preterites, with meanings, of *ṭeḫûm* and *walādum*.

E. Write in normalized Akkadian (nominative unless otherwise noted):

1. its (f) evil
2. my witnesses
3. your (mp) vineyard
4. their (f) well-made seals
5. his army of force
6. its (m) becoming new
7. the excess of their (m) cultivated field
8. for all of their (f) dead (mp)
9. the women of their (m) land
10. his thin neck
11. your (ms) difficulty and my difficulty
12. our king and his queen
13. this (female) employee of hers
14. their (m) cutting down
15. the long days of his years
16. my just judge
17. their (m) great assembly
18. my true word
19. my true words
20. I accepted their decision.
21. my father and his brother
22. your (fs) good deed
23. your (fs) good deeds
24. her painful hand
25. his wide ear
26. his wide ears
27. your (fp) hireling and my hireling
28. her husband
29. in that sealed tablet of mine
30. with all of your (mp) new chariots
31. your (fs) complete report
32. on your (ms) throne
33. our healthy oxen
34. with my fine oil and beer
35. her life of hardship
36. your (mp) stolen silver
37. its (m) collapsed foundation
38. his missing slave (f)
39. their (f) additional tax
40. my son and my daughters
41. my inscribed stela
42. your (fs) joyful people
43. like your (ms) guarded prisoner
44. his entire town
45. in her separate house
46. out of its (m) pure water
47. my acquiring
48. his banished enemy
49. our prince and his wife
50. their (f) lower road

F. Normalize and translate:

1. *ṣa-ab šar-ri-im i-ṣa-am ma-da-am ik-ki-sú-ma i-ṣa-am na-ak-sa-am a-na e-ka-li-šu ub-lu.*
2. *ni-šu i-na pu-úḫ-ri-im ip-ḫu-ra-ma ka-sa-ap-ši-na ù ḫu-ra-sí-na a-na qá-ra-di-im da-nim ip-qí-da.*
3. *i-na di-nim ša-a-tu wa-ar-di ù a-ma-tim ar-ši-ma a-di-ni a-na bi-ti-ia ú-ul i-ru-bu.*
4. *si-in-ni-iš-tum ši-i ma-ri ma-du-tim a-na mu-ti-ša ú-li-id-ma ka-lu-šu-nu i-ši-ru.*
5. *šar-ru-um um-ma-nam ra-bi-tam ik-ṣú-ur-ṃa a-na ma-tim na-ka-ar-tim iṭ-ḫe-ma ka-ak-ki i-pu-uš-ma be-el-ša na-ke-er-šu is-su-uḫ.*
6. *a-bu-šu-nu ù um-ma-šu-nu a-na a-li-šu-nu maḫ-ri-im i-tu-ru-ma i-na a-li-im šu-a-tu uš-bu-ma i-ši-bu-ma i-mu-tu.*
7. *da-a-a-nu ka-as-pí ka-la-šu ki-ma ne-me-ti-ia il-qú-ú-ma a-di-ni ši-pa-tim ú-ul a-ša-am.*
8. *a-bi a-ma-sú a-na i-li-šu a-na ba-la-ṭi-šu i-qí-iš.*
9. *i-na ṭe-ḫe-e a-ḫi-ša ṣé-eḫ-ri-im i-na-ša me-e im-la-a-ma a-ḫa-ša ú-ul iṭ-ṭú-ul.*
10. *i-lum le-em-nu-um a-na ṣú-ḫa-ri-im šu-a-tu i-na ḫa-ra-nim i-ši-ir-ma ṣú-ḫa-ru-um i-lam ú-ul i-mu-úr.*
11. *i-ṣa-am ka-la-šu ša be-li-ku-nu ta-ak-ṣú-ra i-na ki-tim e-pí-iš-tum an-ni-tum i-in be-li-ku-nu im-ḫu-ur.*
12. *si-in-ni-iš-tam ša-ti mu-us-sà i-zi-im-ma a-na bi-it a-bi-ša i-tu-ur.*
13. *ka-al-bu-um an-nu-um ša be-li-ki ú-ul ka-la-ab-ki šu-ú.*
14. *i-na ša-at-tim šu-a-ti šar-ra-qú-um šu-ú e-qé-el-ni wa-at-ra-am i-ku-ul-ma ka-as-pa-am ne-me-et-ta-ni it-ti-šu ú-ul ni-im-ḫu-ur.*
15. *i-na pa-ḫa-ar ni-ši i-lu iḫ-du-ú.*

G. Transliterate, normalize, and translate:

1. 

4. 

2. 

5. 

3. 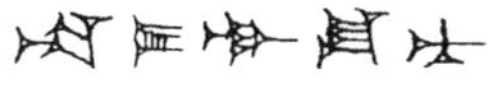

LESSON TWELVE

12.1 The G Durative: Sound Verbs; Verbs I–*n*; Verbs III–weak

(a) Sound Verbs

Study the following paradigms:

	šakānum	*ṣabātum*	*šarāqum*	*maqātum*
3cs	*išakkan*	*iṣabbat*	*išarriq*	*imaqqut*
2ms	*tašakkan*	*taṣabbat*	*tašarriq*	*tamaqqut*
2fs	*tašakkanī*	*taṣabbatī*	*tašarriqī*	*tamaqqutī*
1cs	*ašakkan*	*aṣabbat*	*ašarriq*	*amaqqut*
3mp	*išakkanū*	*iṣabbatū*	*išarriqū*	*imaqqutū*
3fp	*išakkanā*	*iṣabbatā*	*išarriqā*	*imaqqutā*
2cp	*tašakkanā*	*taṣabbatā*	*tašarriqā*	*tamaqqutā*
1cp	*nišakkan*	*niṣabbat*	*nišarriq*	*nimaqqut*

The prefixes and suffixes that mark person, gender, and number are the same as those of the G Preterite.

The base of the G Durative for sound verbs is $R_1aR_2R_2VR_3$ (i.e., *parrVs*). The **second radical** in all Duratives (except verbs II–weak; see §14.1) is always **doubled** (even though the doubling may not be indicated in the script; see above, p. 71). In sound verbs (and in verbs I–*n* and verbs III–weak, except III–*e*), the vowel between the first and second radicals is *a* (› *e* in verbs III–*e*). Between the second and third radicals there is a **theme-vowel**. Sound verbs with *i* as the theme-vowel in the Preterite also have *i* in the Durative; verbs with *a* in the Preterite have *a* likewise in the Durative. Verbs with *u* in the Preterite, however, have either *u* or *a* as the theme-vowel in the Durative, and this must be learned for each such verb. The majority of verbs with *u* in the Preterite have *a* in the Durative. The Durative forms of the sound verbs encountered thus far in the vocabularies are presented in the following chart:

Durative	Preterite	Durative Forms of Sound Verbs
a	*a*	*imaḫḫaṣ, imarraṣ, irakkab, iṣabbat*
i	*i*	*idammiq, idannin, iḫalliq, ilabbir, ipaqqid, iqattin, irappiš, išallim, išarriq*
u	*u*	*iballuṭ, imaqqut, ipaḫḫur*
a	*u*	*igammar, ikannak, ikaṣṣar, ikaššad, imaḫḫar, iparras, ipaššaš, išakkan, išaṭṭar, iṭarrad*

It follows from the foregoing discussion that sound verbs occur in the G in four **vowel classes**. Thus, *maḫāṣum, marāṣum, rakābum*, and *ṣabātum* are referred to as *a*-class verbs (or as *a–a* verbs, listing the theme-vowel of both the Durative and the Preterite); *damāqum, danānum, šarāqum*, etc., are *i*-class verbs (or *i–i* verbs); *balāṭum, maqātum*, and *paḫārum* are *u*-class verbs (or *u–u* verbs). The other verbs encountered thus far, such as *gamārum, kanākum, šakānum*, are referred to as *a–u* verbs (i.e., with the vowel of the Durative before that of the Preterite; in the *CAD*, the forms are cited in full, but in the opposite order, as in *gamārum*: *igmur–igammar*; other terms for this type are Ablaut and vowel-change verbs). Beginning with the vocabulary of this lesson, verbs will be listed only by the Infinitive, followed by the vowel-class in parentheses. Thus, the entry "*saḫāpum* (*a–u*)" indicates that the Durative is *isaḫḫap*, the Preterite *isḫup*; the entry "*kanāšum* (*u*)" indicates that the Durative is *ikannuš*, the Preterite *iknuš*.

(b) Verbs I–*n*

These verbs offer no difficulties in the Durative, since the *n* is always followed by the vowel *a*. They occur in the same vowel classes as the sound verb, except that no I–*n* verbs of the *a*-class are attested:

i:	*inaddin, inakkis*
u:	*inassuk*
a–u:	*inaqqar, inassaḫ, inaṣṣar, inaṭṭal*

(c) Verbs III–weak

As in the Preterite, the base of these verbs ends in the theme-vowel. For **all** verbs III–weak, the theme-vowel of the G Durative is the **same** as that of the G Preterite. In verbs III–*e* (thus, *e*-class), both the *a* between R_1 and R_2 and the *a* of the prefixes of the second person forms and the 1cs form usually, but not invariably, become *e*; in the second person and 1cs forms, either both of these *a*-vowels change, or neither does, so that, for example, both *teleqqe* and *talaqqe* occur for the 2ms, but ***taleqqe* and ***telaqqe* do not.

	banûm	*ḫadûm*	*malûm*	*leqûm*
3cs	*ibanni*	*iḫaddu*	*imalla*	*ileqqe / ilaqqe*
2ms	*tabanni*	*taḫaddu*	*tamalla*	*teleqqe / talaqqe*
2fs	*tabannî*	*taḫaddî*	*tamallî*	*teleqqî / talaqqî*
1cs	*abanni*	*aḫaddu*	*amalla*	*eleqqe / alaqqe*
3mp	*ibannû*	*iḫaddû*	*imallû*	*ileqqû / ilaqqû*
3fp	*ibanniā*	*iḫaddâ*	*imallâ*	*ileqqeā / ilaqqeā*
2cp	*tabanniā*	*taḫaddâ*	*tamallâ*	*teleqqeā / talaqqeā*
1cp	*nibanni*	*niḫaddu*	*nimalla*	*nileqqe / nilaqqe*

The 3cs Duratives of the other III–weak verbs so far presented are:

irabbi (*rabûm*), *irašši* (*rašûm*), *išatti* (*šatûm*), *išemme / išamme* (*šemûm*), *iṭeḫḫe / iṭaḫḫe* (*ṭeḫûm*), *izakku* (*zakûm*).

12.2 The Meaning of the Durative

The Durative describes action that takes place over a period of time (duration; thus, non-punctual or imperfective), or action that has not yet taken place. Thus, it may be translated by a wide range of tenses and nuances. The various types of action that the Durative denotes may be categorized roughly as follows:

(a) Simple future:

warassa ana kaspim inaddin 'she will sell her slave'.

(b) Present tense:

ṭuppašu ikannak 'he is sealing his tablet'.

(c) Durative/Circumstantial:

inaddin 'he was giving, he is giving, he will be giving';

note that the tense may only be determined from the context. Circumstantial clauses may be expressed by a verb in the Durative followed by *-ma* and a subsequent verb (which may also be a Durative) that establishes the tense:

šikaram išattī-ma bītum imqut 'he was drinking beer, and the house collapsed', or 'as he was drinking beer, the house collapsed', or 'he was drinking beer when the house collapsed';
bītī tanaṣṣar-ma ana nārim arakkab 'while you (ms) guard my house, I will ride to the river'.

(d) Habitual (or customary):

inaddin 'he used to give (or, would give), he gives, he will give (customarily, or as a habit)'.

Again, the tense must be gained from the context.

(e) Modal, including potential action and probable action:

inaddin 'he may/might/could/can/should/would give'.

For the most part, which of these English translation values best reflects a Durative verb in any given context must be determined on the basis of the surrounding context.

The Durative, like the Preterite, is negated with *ul(a)* in main clauses:

bītam eššam ul nibanni 'we will not build a new house';
ilam ina šamnim ula tapaššašā 'you (pl) do not anoint the god with oil'.

In most Assyriological works, the form called the Durative in this textbook is referred to as the **Present** or **Present-Future**.

12.3 Prepositional Phrases

Very frequently, the prepositions *ana* and *ina* occur with the bound form of a noun in a prepositional phrase. While these expressions may be translated literally, a more idiomatic rendering is often preferable. The following list presents some of the most common prepositional phrases that occur in OB texts, arranged alphabetically by noun:

(a) *birītum* 'interval, intervening space':

ina birīt 'between, among'; before a suffix, a byform *bīrī-* is used; e.g.,

ina birīt eṭlūtim 'among the young men';
ina bīrīšunu 'among them (m)'.

(b) *libbum* 'heart, center, midst':

ana libbi 'to the center of, into':

iṣam ana libbi ālim ubilū 'they (m) carried the wood into the town'.

ina libbi 'in the midst of, inside, within, among, out of, from':

šarrum ina libbi ālim ušib 'the king remained within the city';
ina libbi 3 ūmī ikaššad 'it will arrive within 3 days';
ina libbīkunu 'among you (mp)'.

(c) *maḫrum* 'front (part)':

    ana maḫar, with suffixes *ana maḫrī-*, 'to, toward, before':

        ṭēmī ana maḫar bēlīya ašpur 'I sent (*ašpur*) my report to my lord';
        ṣuḫāram šuāti ana maḫrīya taṭrudī 'you (fs) sent that servant to me'.

        In southern OB texts and OB texts from Mari (§29.4), *ana maḫar* is usually replaced by *ana ṣēr* (see below, h).

    ina maḫar, with suffixes *ina maḫrī-*, 'in front of, in the presence of, with (a person), (from) before, away from'; it is very common for *ina* to be omitted in this phrase, so that we usually find *maḫar* + noun, *maḫrī-* + suffix:

        (ina) maḫar bēlīya aḫdu 'I rejoiced in my lord's presence';
        ṭuppātim (ina) maḫrīni telqe 'you (ms) took the tablets away from us';
        ana 10 ūmī maḫrīkunu anāku 'I will be with you (mp) in ten days'.

(d) *muḫḫum* 'skull, top (part)':

    ana muḫḫi 'toward, into the care of' is rare in OB.

    ina muḫḫi 'on, upon, over, to the debit of' (essentially a synonym of *eli*):

        mû ina muḫḫi kišād nārim illikū 'water flowed over the river bank';
        kaspum šū ina muḫḫīka 'you owe that silver' (lit.: 'that silver is upon you/to your debit').

(e) *pānum* 'front (part)':

    ana pān(i) 'at the disposal of, for the benefit of, for, on account of; opposite; before the arrival of, (rarely) toward':

        wardī ana pāni aḫīya aškun 'I placed servants at my brother's disposal';
        ana ālim ana pān ṣuḫārtim allik 'I came to town for the servant' (*ana pānīša* 'for her').

    ina pān(i) (in southern OB) 'in view of, in the presence of, in front of, (temporally) just before':

        ina pāni ṣāb nakrim 'in the presence of the enemy force';
        ina pānīšu 'in front of it (m)'.

(f) *pûm* 'mouth; utterance; opening':

    ana pī and *ša pī* may both mean 'according to, in accordance with':

        ana pī ṭuppi bēlīni nīpuš 'we acted according to our lord's tablet'.

(g) *qātum* 'hand; power, authority; care, charge, responsibility':

ina qāt(i) 'in the possession of, from (the possession of, with verbs of taking); in the care/custody of, in the jurisdiction of, by/under the authority of, through the agency of (a person)':

kaspam šuāti ina qātīka tanaṣṣar 'you (ms) will keep that silver in your custody';
ina qāti ekallim šū 'it (m) is the responsibility of the palace'.

ana qāt(i) 'into the possession, custody of' is rare in OB.

Note also *ša qāt(i)*, which has the same meanings as *ina qāt(i)*:

awīlum šū ul ša qātīya 'that man is not under my jurisdiction';
kaspum ša qāt dayyānim īter 'the silver (that is) in the judge's possession increased'.

(h) *ṣērum* 'back, back country':

ana ṣēr (rarely, with assimilation, *aṣ-ṣēr*) 'to, toward, against, in addition to, on account of' (replaces *ana maḫar* in southern and Mari OB texts):

ana ṣēr abīya allik 'I went to my father'.

ina ṣēr 'upon, on top of' occurs only in poetry in OB.

12.4 Compound Noun Phrases

The noun phrase *mār(i) šiprim* 'messenger' means literally 'son of a message', with *mār(i)* a bound form governing the genitive noun *šiprim* 'message'. Normally the plural of this expression, 'messengers', is made as one would expect, namely, with the pluralization of the governing first word: *mārū šiprim* (gen.–acc. *mārī šiprim*). Occasionally, however, the phrase is construed as a morphological unit, and the marker of plurality appears at the end, after the second element; the marker is always the gen.–acc., regardless of the case of the expression:

mār šiprī ana ālim ikšudū 'the messengers arrived in the town'.

Other examples:

bēl ḫubullīšu aššassu ul iṣabbatū 'his creditors may not seize his wife' (*ḫubullum* 'debt');
iṣam ana šikir maqqarī īmurū 'they (m) found wood for chisel handles' (*šikrum* 'handle'; *maqqarum* 'chisel').

Note that examples with pronominal suffixes may be ambiguous:

mār šiprīšu ul āmur 'I did not see his messenger/messengers'.

EXERCISES

A. VOCABULARY 12.

Verbs:

ḫepûm (*e*) 'to smash, destroy, wreck; to break, invalidate (a tablet, document); to split, divide'; Verbal Adj. *ḫepûm* (*ḫepi-*) 'smashed, broken, split'.

kanāšum (*u*) 'to bow down, submit'; Verbal Adj. *kanšum* (*kaniš-*) 'submissive, subjected'.

pašāḫum (*a*; less often also *i*) 'to refresh oneself; to calm down, become appeased, content'.

saḫāpum (*a–u*) 'to cover, spread over, overwhelm'.

Nouns:

birītum (bound form *birīt*) 'interval, intervening space'; *ina birīt* (before suffix *ina bīrī-*) 'between, among'.

ḫubullum (*ḫubul*; with suff. *ḫubulla-*) 'obligation, debt with interest'; *bēl ḫubullim* (with suff. *bēl ḫubullī-*; pl. *bēlū ḫubullim* or *bēl ḫubullī*) 'creditor'.

maḫrum (*maḫar*) 'front (part, side)'; *(ina) maḫar* (prep.; with suff. *(ina) maḫrī-*) 'in front of, in the presence of, with (a person), (from) before, away from' (note *maḫar X šakānum* 'to inform X', as in *awâtīšu maḫrīni iškun* 'he informed us of his affairs'); *ana maḫar* (with suff. *ana maḫrī-* [northern OB; for southern and Mari, see *ṣērum*]) 'to, toward, into the presence of, before (a person)' (cf. *maḫārum*, *maḫrûm*).

muḫḫum (*muḫḫi*) 'skull, top (part, side)'; *ina muḫḫi* 'on, onto, upon, on top of, over; to the debit of'.

pānum (*pān(i)*; pl. *pānū*) 'front (side, part)'; pl. *pānū* (occasionally also sg.) 'face'; *ana pān(i)* 'at the disposal of, for the benefit of, for, on account of; opposite; before the arrival of, (rarely) toward'; *ina pān(i)* 'in the presence of, in front of, before; in view of, because of; just before (temporal)'; *pānam rašûm* 'to become clear, plain'; *pān(i)/pānī X ṣabātum* 'to lead X' (e.g., *pān ṣābīya aṣbat* 'I led my army'; *pānam/pānī šakānum* 'to proceed; to intend, decide (to do: *ana* + Infin.: *pānīšu ana epēš bītim iškun* 'he intended to build a house')'; *pānī X babālum* 'to favor; to forgive X' (e.g., *šarrum pānīya ul ubil* 'the king did not favor/forgive me').

pûm (gen. *pîm*, acc. *piam* and *pâm*; bound form *pī*; with suff. *pī-* in all cases; pl. *pâtum*) 'mouth; word(s); utterance, speech, command; opening'; *piam epēšum* to work/open one's mouth'; *piam šakānum* 'to issue commands'; *ana pī* and *ša pī* 'according to, in accordance with'; *ana pîm* 'obediently'; *ina pîm* can mean 'orally'.

ṣērum (*ṣēr(i)*) 'back (part, side); hinterland, back country; steppeland'; *ana ṣēr* (rarely with assimilation: *aṣ-ṣēr* [southern OB and Mari; for northern OB, see *maḫrum*]) 'in the direction of, to, toward, against; in addition to'.

šiprum (*šipir*; pl. *šiprū* and *šiprātum, šiprētum* [with an irregular shift of *ā* to *ē*]) 'sending, mission; message; work, labor, task; activity, action'; *mār šiprim* (with suff. *mār šiprīšu*, etc.; pl. *mārū šiprim* or *mār šiprī*) 'messenger'; *šipram epēšum* 'to do (assigned) work; to work (something: acc.; e.g., *eqlam šipram īpuš* 'he worked [i.e., plowed] the field')'.

B. Learn the following signs:

OB Lapid.	OB Cursive	NA	values
		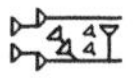	*ug/k/q**
	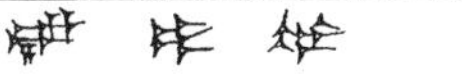	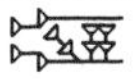	*as/ṣ/z**
			*du*
			*uš, ús/ṣ/z*
			*úr*
			*tum, dum, ṭum*
	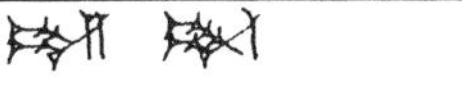	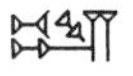	*il*
			*iš, ís/ṣ/z, mil*
			*bi, bé, pí, pé*
		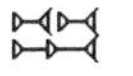	*kum*

*UG and AZ are usually identical; occasionally they are distinguished by the addition of  (the UD sign) for UG and  (ZA) for AZ.

C. Write the following words in cuneiform and in transliteration:

1. *dūkšu*
2. *urḫum*
3. *šumgur*
4. *gimil*
5. *sikkum*
6. *nadrum*
7. *rupšum*
8. *peṣītum*
9. *mušḫuššum*
10. *sassatum*

D. Give the full Durative conjugation, with meanings, of *ḫepûm*, *kanāšum*, *malûm*, *nakāsum*, and *saḫāpum*.

E. Write in normalized Akkadian:

1. you (fs) will issue commands
2. within them (m)
3. they (m) used to throw down
4. she will decide to build
5. according to their (f) witnesses
6. you (pl) are growing up
7. I will lead them (m)
8. they (m) used to collect
9. upon you (mp)
10. you (pl) will ride
11. we were falling
12. it is broadening
13. in the presence of that woman
14. they (f) were looking
15. you (pl) may hit
16. toward the governor
17. it will fill
18. toward the army
19. you (fs) will become annoyed
20. I will decide
21. in view of this matter
22. they (m) will tear down
23. you (ms) will recover
24. under the jurisdiction of the judges
25. they (f) will take
26. we would reach
27. between them (m)
28. we are bringing to an end
29. you (ms) were writing
30. I will arrive safely
31. your (fp) messengers
32. we may hear
33. we rejoice
34. you (pl) will seal
35. I am becoming strong
36. she will send
37. he becomes free
38. they (f) will meet
39. he is removing
40. it will improve
41. I will be guarding
42. for the benefit of that employee (m)
43. you (fs) should entrust
44. between these vineyards
45. they (m) will drink
46. we will anoint
47. our creditors
48. I will cut off
49. they (f) may disappear
50. it is becoming thin
51. they (m) would gather
52. you (fs) will acquire
53. they (m) were becoming calm

F. Normalize and translate:

1. *i-lum ra-bu-um pí-šu i-pu-uš-ma a-wa-ti-šu ka-la-ši-na ni-iš-me.*
2. *ṭú-pa-tim la-bi-ra-tim te-ḫe-pé-ma eš-še-tim ta-ša-ṭa-ar.*
3. *i-na e-pé-ši-im an-ni-im be-li pa-ni-ia ú-la ú-bi-il-ma li-ib-bi im-ra-aṣ.*
4. *ṣú-ḫa-ra-tu-ni eq-lam šu-a-ti ši-ip-ra-am a-di-ni ú-ul i-pu-ša ù a-na bi-it a-bi-ši-na i-tu-ra.*
5. *mu-ú i-na na-ri-im i-mi-du-ma eq-le-ti-ia ra-ap-ša-tim is-ḫu-pu.*
6. *na-re-e ḫe-pu-tim ša na-ak-ri-ia i-na a-li-šu a-mu-úr.*
7. *ka-as-pa-am ma-da-am a-na be-el ḫu-bu-ul-li-ka ta-na-ad-din-ma ṭú-up-pí ḫu-bu-ul-li-ka i-ḫe-ep-pu-ú.*
8. *i-na e-pí-iš-tim an-ni-tim li-ib-bi il-tim i-pa-aš-ša-aḫ.*
9. *a-wa-at di-nim šu-a-ti ma-ḫar da-a-a-nim i-ga-ma-ru ma-ar ši-ip-ri-šu-nu a-na ṣé-er be-li-šu-nu i-ṭa-ar-ra-du.*
10. *i-lum lem-nu-um ni-ši bi-tim ša-a-ti is-ḫu-up-ma i-mu-ta.*
11. *i-na ša-at-tim an-ni-tim i-ṣa-am na-ak-sa-am wa-ta-ar-ta-ni ki-ma né-me-ti-ni a-na e-ka-al-lim ni-id-din.*
12. *na-ak-ri ka-an-šu-um a-na maḫ-ri-ia il-li-ik-ma a-na še-pí-ia im-qú-ut.*
13. *si-in-ni-ša-tum ši-na it-ti mu-ti-ši-na i-na a-li-ni uš-ba-ma ma-ri ù ma-ra-tim ma-du-tim ul-da-ma na-ap-ša-tu-ši-na i-ṭi-ba.*
14. *ni-šu ma-ta-tim ka-li-ši-na i-na pa-ni-ia i-ka-nu-ša.*
15. *a-ḫi a-wa-tam an-ni-tam maḫ-ri-ia iš-ku-un qá-as-sú a-na e-pé-eš bi-ti-šu i-ša-ka-an.*

G. Transliterate, normalize and translate:

1. 
2. 
3. 
4. 
5. 
6. 
7. 
8. 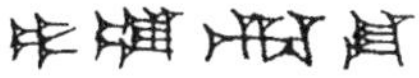

LESSON THIRTEEN

13.1 The G Durative: Verbs I–ʾ (I–*a* and I–*e*); *alākum*

If the first consonant of these verbs, the *aleph*, were a regular consonant, the G Durative would have the following shape, e.g., from *amārum* (an *a–u* verb): ***iʾammar* (cf. *išakkan*). A consistently applied rule with verbs I–ʾ, however, is that, if the *aleph* would appear between two vowels, both the *aleph* and the following vowel are lost. Thus, the G Durative 3cs of *amārum* is *immar*; the Durative 3cs of *arākum*, an *i*-class verb, is *irrik*.

As expected, in verbs in which the first radical was $ʾ_{3-4}$ or *y* (i.e., verbs I–*e*), all *a*-vowels, except those in endings, become *e*. The vowel class of *epēšum* is *e–u* (originally *a–u*) or, in late OB texts, also *u*; *ezēbum* is an *i*-class verb, and *erēbum* is *u*-class.

	amārum	*arākum*	*epēšum*	*ezēbum*	*erēbum*
3cs	*immar*	*irrik*	*ippeš* / *ippuš*	*izzib*	*irrub*
2ms	*tammar*	*tarrik*	*teppeš* / *teppuš*	*tezzib*	*terrub*
2fs	*tammarī*	*tarrikī*	*teppešī* / *teppušī*	*tezzibī*	*terrubī*
1cs	*ammar*	*arrik*	*eppeš* / *eppuš*	*ezzib*	*errub*
3mp	*immarū*	*irrikū*	*ippešū* / *ippušū*	*izzibū*	*irrubū*
3fp	*immarā*	*irrikā*	*ippešā* / *ippušā*	*izzibā*	*irrubā*
2cp	*tammarā*	*tarrikā*	*teppešā* / *teppušā*	*tezzibā*	*terrubā*
1cp	*nimmar*	*nirrik*	*nippeš* / *nippuš*	*nizzib*	*nirrub*

The vowel classes of the verbs I–ʾ introduced thus far are:

a–u *agārum, aḫāzum, akālum, amārum;*

e–u *epēšum;*

i *arākum, edēšum, enēšum, ešērum, ezēbum;*

u *erēbum* (also *epēšum* occasionally in late texts).

The irregular verb *alākum* is considered below.

The Durative forms of verbs I–ʾ that begin with a vowel (i.e., the 1cs and the third person forms) are written in two different fashions in OB. The 3cs form *immar*, for example, may be written

i-ma-ar (i.e., with the doubling not indicated)
or *i-im-ma-ar* (with both doubling and an extra initial vowel sign).

Similarly, 1cs *eppeš* appears as

e-pé-eš or *e-ep-pé-eš*.

Expected writings of the type *im-ma-ar* and *ep-pé-eš* are not normally found. Note that in verbs with the same theme vowel in both the Preterite and the Durative, the shorter writing of the Durative of these forms will be identical to the writing of the Preterite: e.g.,

a-ri-ik for 1cs Durative *arrik* or Preterite *ārik;*
i-ni-iš for 3cs Durative *inniš* or Preterite *īniš;*
e-ru-ub for 1cs Durative *errub* or Preterite *ērub*.

Such ambiguity is also present with writings of the other persons of verbs I–ʾ in which the theme vowels of the Durative and Preterite are the same, whenever the doubling of the Durative is not indicated:

te-zi-bi for 2fs Durative *tezzibī* or Preterite *tēzibī;*
ni-ši-ir for 1cp Durative *niššir* or Preterite *nīšir*.

The tense intended to be read in these cases can only be determined from the surrounding context.

alākum. The G Durative resembles that of other verbs I–*a*; the theme-vowel is *a*, so that *alākum* is an *a–i* verb (a rare vowel class):

3cs	*illak*	3mp	*illakū*
		3fp	*illakā*
2ms	*tallak*	2cp	*tallakā*
2fp	*tallakī*		
1cs	*allak*	1cp	*nillak*

As with other verbs I–*a*, the Durative forms beginning with a vowel are normally written, e.g., either *i-la-ak* or *i-il-la-ak*, but not *il-la-ak*. (Preterite forms, on the contrary, are normally written, e.g., *il-li-ik*, occasionally *i-li-ik*, but not *i-il-li-ik*.)

13.2 Logograms

Logograms are signs that represent whole words rather than syllables or part-syllables. In transliterations of Akkadian texts, they are given in Roman (non-italicized) capital letters, according to their **Sumerian**, rather than their Akkadian pronunciation: e.g.,

𒉣 NUN (= *rubûm*) 'prince';

i.e., the sign 𒉣 represents the Sumerian word n u n 'prince', which is equivalent to Akkadian *rubûm*. Logograms do not differ in their physical shape from syllabograms; in other words, there is nothing special about the shape or appearance of a given sign to distinguish it as a logogram rather than a syllabogram. In fact, many signs are used with both functions: e.g.,

> 𒂗 has a syllabic value *en* and a logographic value EN (= *bēlum*) 'lord'.

The logographic transliteration is often different from the syllabic one, however:

> 𒁍 is syllabic *bu, pu*, and also logographic GÍD (= *arkum*) 'long'.

Further, as is the case with syllabic values for many signs, not a few signs have more than one logographic value: e.g.,

> 𒀭 *an*, and also AN (= *šamû*) 'sky' and DINGIR (= *ilum*) 'god'.

In rare instances, a single logographic value (i.e., one Sumerian word) is equivalent to more than one Akkadian word:

> 𒆳 KUR for both *mātum* 'country' and *šadûm* 'mountain'.

Many signs with logographic values have no syllabic values in OB; e.g.,

> 𒇽 LÚ (= *awīlum*) 'person'.

The values of many logograms are polysyllabic; in this textbook, all homophonic multi-syllable values are indicated with subscript numbers (i.e., even the second and third such values), as are the fourth and higher numbers of monosyllabic values, rather than with a diacritic accent over the vowel of one of the syllables: e.g., 𒊩𒆳 GEME$_2$, rather than GÉME. Some sign-lists do use the accent marks, in a somewhat confusing fashion, for the second through fifth signs with the same value: e.g., ÚMUN for UMUN$_2$, ÙMUN for UMUN$_3$, UMÚN for UMUN$_4$, UMÙN for UMUN$_5$.

In some instances, a combination of signs is used to represent an Akkadian word logographically. Such combinations are called **compound logograms**; in transliteration, the individual components that represent a single Akkadian word are separated by a period:

> 𒌉𒊩 DUMU.MUNUS (= *mārtum*) 'daughter' consists of 𒌉 DUMU (= *mārum*) 'son' and 𒊩 MUNUS (= *sinništum*) 'woman';
>
> 𒂍𒃲 É.GAL (= *ekallum*) 'palace' consists of 𒂍 É (= *bītum*) 'house' and 𒃲 GAL (= *rabûm*) 'large'.

Not infrequently, the connection between the meaning of the compound logogram and the meanings of the constituent signs is not apparent:

> 𒀀𒊮 A.ŠÀ (= *eqlum*) 'field' is made up of 𒀀 A (= *mû*) 'water' and 𒊮 ŠÀ (= *libbum*) 'heart'.

The sign 𒈨𒌍 MEŠ, which means 'they are' in Sumerian, may be written after logograms to express plurality: e.g.,

𒀭𒈨𒌍 𒃲𒈨𒌍 DINGIR.MEŠ GAL.MEŠ (= *ilū rabûtum*) 'great gods';

𒀫𒈨𒌍 A.ŠÀ.MEŠ (= *eqlētum*) 'fields'.

Also common as a mark of plurality after logograms is 𒄭𒀀 ḪI.A (formerly also transliterated ḪÁ); unlike MEŠ, ḪI.A does not appear with logograms denoting human beings (or gods):

𒄞 GUD (= *alpum*) 'ox', pl. 𒄞𒄭𒀀 GUD.ḪI.A (= *alpū*) 'oxen'.

Some Assyriologists prefer to indicate these plural markers in transliteration as determinatives (e.g., A.ŠÀ^meš; GUD^hi.a); see §13.3, below. Still another means of expressing plurality is the repetition of a logogram; usually, this denotes totality: e.g.,

𒂗 𒆳𒆳 EN KUR.KUR (= *bēl mātātim*) 'master of (all) the lands'.

To clarify the intended value or meaning of a logogram, especially of one with more than one possible reading in Akkadian, a logogram is occasionally followed by one or more syllabograms, which give the pronunciation of the last part of the word; syllabograms used in this way are called **phonetic complements**:

𒀭𒌑 AN-*ú* for *šamû* 'sky', but

𒀭𒈝 DINGIR-*lum* for *ilum* 'god'.

Similarly, the sign 𒆳 KUR, as noted above, represents both *mātum* and *šadûm*; to indicate which Akkadian word is intended, a phonetic complement may be added: e.g.,

𒀹𒈾 𒆳𒁴 *i-na* KUR-*tim* (= *ina mātim*) 'in the country', but

𒀹𒈾 𒆳𒄿𒅎 *i-na* KUR-*i-im* (= *ina šadîm*) 'in the mountain'.

In other instances, a phonetic complement may simply clarify the case of the noun represented by a logogram:

𒀫𒌝 A.ŠÀ-*um* or 𒀫𒈝 A.ŠÀ-*lum* for nom. *eqlum* 'field' (the writings A.ŠÀ-*um* and A.ŠÀ-*lum* both indicate the appropriate case-ending; the second also reflects the last consonant of the base).

Possessive pronominal suffixes are nearly always indicated by syllabograms:

𒂍𒋢 É-*sú* (= *bīssu*) 'his house';

𒂍𒈨𒌍 𒌉𒅀 É.MEŠ DUMU-*ia* (= *bītāt mārīya*) 'my son's houses'.

The 1cs allomorph -*ī* is usually indicated after a logogram not by the sign I, but rather by a *Ci* sign, in which *C* is the final consonant of the stem of the Akkadian word: e.g.,

𒈗𒊑 LUGAL-*ri* for *šarrī* 'my king';

𒂗𒇷 EN-*lí* for *bēlī* 'my lord'.

The frequency of logograms depends to a great extent on the genre of the text in question. In OB, letters (§24.5), omen texts (§22.3), the laws of Ḫammurapi (§17.4), and literary texts (§33.3, §35.4) have relatively few logograms, and those are normally used only for nouns and adjectives (and even then, only for a few frequently occurring words). In legal contracts (introduced later in this lesson, §13.5), logograms are of greater frequency, essentially because of the more formulaic nature of such documents; economic texts are still more formulaic, and are often written entirely with logograms. Nevertheless, the fact that a logogram existed for a given Akkadian word did not necessarily mean that it would always or even commonly be used; the scribe always had the option of "spelling" the word syllabically.

A transliteration of a series of signs in which logograms appear may be given in several ways. As noted above, logograms are normally given in Roman capitals. (In another convention, they are given in letter-spaced lower case Roman letters, e.g., d u m u l u g a l, rather than DUMU LUGAL for *mār šarrim* 'son of the king'.) A normalization of the logogram may accompany the logographic value, however. In such renderings, the logographic writing is given in parentheses after the normalization; phonetic complements are written either on the line, separated from the logographic transliteration by a hyphen, or above the line, immediately after the logogram. The following will serve to illustrate these points:

𒌉 𒈗 𒀀𒈾 𒂍𒃲𒅆 𒄿𒊒𒌒

DUMU LUGAL *a-na* É.GAL-*lim i-ru-ub*

or *mār*(DUMU) *šarrim*(LUGAL) *a-na ekallim*(É.GAL-*lim* or É.GAL^{lim}) *i-ru-ub*.

In the exercises that involve transliteration in this textbook, the first method will be used for logograms that the student has learned (i.e., no normalization will be given); for logograms that have not been encountered, the second method will be employed.

In the normalization of a transliteration that includes logograms (including the normalization and translation exercises accompanying each lesson), the grammatically correct Akkadian form must be supplied for each logogram. The sentence of the foregoing paragraph, then, must be normalized *mār šarrim ana ekallim īrub* 'the king's son entered the palace'.

Another example:

DINGIR.MEŠ GAL.MEŠ KUR-*tam i-na qá-at* DUMU-*ka iš-ku-nu*, i.e,
ilū rabûtum mātam ina qāt mārīka iškunū 'the great gods placed the land in your son's hand'.

Assyriologists use two additional symbols, + and x, to indicate individual components that constitute a single logographic value. The plus-sign, +, indicates that the constituents appear one after the other, as in

 ZABAR (ud+ka+bar) *siparrum* 'bronze'.

(The + sign is also used to indicate ligatures of syllabograms: e.g., *i+na* indicates that the two signs are written together as if they are a single sign.) The multiplication sign, x, indicates that the second sign is written inside the first, as in

 EME (ka x me) *lišānum* 'tongue, language'.

13.3 Determinatives

Some signs, again physically indistinguishable from syllable signs, are used as graphic indicators of the class of objects to which the item denoted by a given noun belongs; they are called determinatives. Determinatives may be used to denote the material out of which an object is made or that a given noun denotes a proper name, a female, a city, a country, a river, a kind of animal (e.g., a fish, a bird), a part of the body, a profession, a month name, etc.

Most determinatives stand before the nouns they classify, although a few follow their nouns. They are represented in transliteration according to their Sumerian pronunciation (as with logograms), with lower case Roman letters (usually in smaller type), written as superscripts, i.e., **above** the line. All determinatives also occur as logograms, but not all logograms occur as determinatives; in fact, the number of determinatives is quite small, about two dozen. (A list of the most common determinatives is given on page 537.) Again, some signs may be used to write either a syllable (or part-syllable), a logogram, or a determinative: e.g.,

 = syllabogram *is / ṣ / z, es / ṣ / z*, but also
logogram GIŠ (= *iṣum*) 'wood', and
determinative ^{giš} before words for objects made of wood, as in 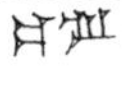 ^{giš}MÁ or in ^{giš}*e-le-ep-pu-um*, both for *eleppum* 'boat'.

Other signs are used only as logograms or determinatives: e.g.,

𒀯 = logogram NA₄ (= *abnum*) 'stone', and determinative ⁿᵃ⁴ before words for objects made of stone or for kinds of stone: 𒀯𒍕𒋾 ⁿᵃ⁴ZA.GÌN (= *uqnûm*) 'lapis lazuli'.

Some names of cities are both preceded by 𒌷 ᵘʳᵘ (URU = *ālum* 'city') and followed by 𒆠 ᵏⁱ (KI = *erṣetum* 'land, district'): e.g.,

𒌷𒁇𒋛𒉺𒆠 ᵘʳᵘ*bar-sí-pa*ᵏⁱ, i.e., *Barsippa* '(the city of) Borsippa'.

Note that determinatives are optional; they are very frequent with certain words and names, but they are not a necessary part of the writing of any word.

Exceptions to the practice of transliterating determinatives with their Sumerian value are the following frequently occurring determinatives:

𒀭 ᵈ (for ᵈⁱⁿᵍⁱʳ), before divine names, as in 𒀭𒂗𒇸 ᵈEN.LÍL (*Enlil* or *Ellil*) 'Enlil' (an important god);

𒁹 ᴵ or ᴾ or ᵐ, before personal names: 𒁹𒄩𒄠𒈬𒊏𒉿 ᴵ*ḫa-am-mu-ra-pí* (*Ḫammurapi*) 'Hammurapi';

𒊩 ᶠ or ᵐⁱ, before women's names: 𒊩𒅆𒅁𒌅 ᶠ*ši-ib-tu* (*Šibtu*) 'Shibtu'.

Since determinatives are graphic devices only, without phonological value (i.e., they were not pronounced), they need not be indicated in normalization. As an illustration, consider the following sentence:

ᴵ*ḫa-am-mu-ra-pí* LUGAL KÁ.DINGIR.RAᵏⁱ ᵍⁱˢMÁ *ir-ka-ab*, i.e., *Ḫammurapi šar Bābilim eleppam irkab* 'Hammurapi, king of Babylon, boarded the ship.'

13.4 Personal Names

Akkadian personal names (PNs) have several forms.

(a) Single nouns or adjectives: e.g., *Aḫum* 'Brother'.

(b) Genitive chains, in which the second element is normally a divine name, such as *Awīl-Marduk* 'Man-of-Marduk'; *Warad-Sîn* 'Slave-of-Sîn'; note also *Warad-ilīšu* 'Slave-of-his-god'; *Warassa* 'Her-slave'.

(c) Sentences, which also usually have a divine name or *ilum* as one of the elements. The sentences may be

(1) Verbless: e.g., *Sîn-šar-ilī* 'Sîn-is-king-of-the-gods'; *Marduk-abūšu* 'Marduk-is-his-father'; *Itti-Sîn-dīnī* 'My-judgment-is-with-Sîn'; *Šamaš-rabi* 'Šamaš-is-great' (for the predicate adjective *rabi*, see §22.1).

(2) Verbal; the verb is usually Preterite or an injunctive form called the Precative (preformative *li-* for 'may/let ...'; see §16.2): *Iddin-Sîn* 'Sîn-has-given(-a-son)'; *Aḫam-arši* 'I-acquired-a-brother'; *Šamaš-liwwer* 'May-Šamaš-shine' (*nawārum* 'to shine').

(d) Abbreviations of longer constructions, often with hypocoristic endings such as *-(i)ya*, *-(y)atum*.

Usually, PNs, even those ending in *-um*, are indeclinable: e.g., *ana Aḫum* 'for Aḫum' (vs. *ana aḫim* 'for the brother'); there are many exceptions, however.

Not all names in OB texts are Akkadian. Most non-Akkadian names are either Sumerian (e.g., ^{d}NANNA-IBILA-MA.AN.SUM = *Nanna-ibila-mansum* 'Nanna-has-given-me-an-heir') or Amorite (e.g., *Ḫammurapi*, better *ʿammu-rapiʾ* 'The-(divine) kinsman-is-a-healer'). Less often, Hurrian, Elamite, and other names also occur.

Personal names may be preceded by the sign 𒁹, transliterated ^{I}, ^{m}, or ^{p}); this determinative occurs more frequently when a name stands at the beginning of a line. Women's names may instead be preceded by the sign 𒊩, transliterated ^{f} or ^{mí}; as with men's names, however, no determinative is necessary.

13.5 Old Babylonian Contracts

With this lesson begins the presentation in the exercises of actual Old Babylonian texts in transliteration. The first type of text to be presented is the contract. The thousands of OB contracts record a wide range of legal transactions and other activities, including, inter alia: marriage, divorce, and adoption; manumission of slaves; loans of silver, grain, and other commodities; guarantees of surety; purchases of houses, fields, animals, children, and slaves; exchanges of property; rentals, leases, and hires; and proceedings of and decisions of lawsuits.

The main topic of a contract — the person being adopted, the house being sold, etc. — is usually the first item mentioned, even though this frequently results in a reversal of the normal word order, when the topic is the direct object of the verb. Further, in purchases and similar transactions, the original owners, from whom the item is purchased, may precede the buyers. Thus, the first sentence in a contract may have the order Object – *itti* X – Subject – Verb:

eqlam itti PN$_1$ PN$_2$ *išām* 'PN$_2$ bought a field from PN$_1$'.

A contract normally concludes with a list of witnesses of the transaction. These are listed after the logogram IGI for *maḫar* 'before, in the presence of' (§12.3(c)). Following the witnesses there is often a date, in which a year-name is written in Sumerian (e.g., 'Year Ḫammurapi became king'); in some instances the month and day are also given. The Old Babylonian and other systems of recording dates are discussed below in Appendix A (pp. 577–78).

Many contracts were enclosed in clay envelopes, on which much or all of the text may be repeated, sometimes verbatim, sometimes with minor discrepancies. The existence of such envelopes frequently allows the complete reading of otherwise broken texts.

Contracts present a number of difficulties to the beginning student. Chief among these is that many formulaic terms are written in Sumerian; some of these will be introduced gradually in the next several lessons, while those that have not been introduced will be given in normalized Akkadian form when they occur in the contracts in the exercises. Another difficulty is the frequent presence of numbers and of units of measurement that are best presented only in a later lesson (see §23.2). When such numbers and units occur in our texts, we will usually either omit them altogether or replace them with an "x", as in

x *eqlam* PN_1 *išām* for 'PN_1 bought a field of x dimensions';

in other instances, numbers, which are invariably written with logograms (i.e., '1', '2', rather than 'one', 'two', etc.) will appear as such in our transliterations, and the student should refrain from normalizing them until they have been formally introduced in lesson 23.

EXERCISES

A. VOCABULARY 13.

Verbs:

ragāmum (*u* and *a–u*; i.e., Durative *iraggum* or *iraggam*) 'to shout; to call, summon, demand; to complain (against), sue (someone: *ana*; for/concerning: *ana* or *aššum*)'; *rugummûm* (base *rugummā-*) 'lawsuit; penalty, fine awarded/assessed in a lawsuit'.

tamûm (*a*) 'to swear, take an oath (by someone: acc. or *ina*)'.

zâzum (Preterite *izūz*) 'to divide, separate' (intrans.); 'to divide, divide into shares (trans.), distribute (to/among: *ana*); to share, take a share (of: *ina*)'; Verbal Adj. *zīzum* 'divided; sharing'.

Nouns:

bābtum (bound form *bābti*; pl. *bābātum*) 'city quarter, neighborhood, district; goods/merchandise outstanding; loss, deficit'.
ebūrum (*ebūr*) 'harvest(-time); crop; summer'.
nīšum (*nīš(i)*; log. MU) 'life'; *nīš X tamûm* 'to swear by (the life of) X' (e.g., *nīš šarrim nitma* 'we swore by the life of the king').
rēšum (*rēš(i)*; dual *rēšān* [often = sg.]; log. SAG) 'top; head; chief, principal; beginning; slave'.
šamšum (*šamaš*; log. UTU) 'sun'; see also *Šamaš*, below.
šamû (always pl.; base *šamā-* [gen.-acc. *šamê*]; log. AN) 'sky, heaven'.
tappûm (base *tappā-*; Sum. lw.) 'business associate, partner'; *tappûtum* (*tappût*) 'partnership, association; position of helper, partner'; *tappût X alākum* 'to assist X, lend X a hand, come to the aid of X' (e.g., *tappût aḫīya illikū* 'they assisted my brother'; *tappûssu allik* 'I assisted him'); *tappûtam epēšum* 'to do/ enter into business together'.
ûm (gen. *îm* or *êm*, acc. *âm*; bound form *ê*; with suff. nom. *û*-, gen. *î*-/*ê*-, acc. *â*-; with 1cs suff., nom.-acc. *ê*, gen. *êya*; Sum. lw.?; always written with log. ŠE, e.g., acc. ŠE-*am* or ŠE-*a*-*am* for *âm*; also written either ŠE.UM or ŠE.IM, regardless of case) 'barley, grain' Note: until recently this very common word was read in Akkadian as *šeum* (bound form *šê*), and so it appears in both dictionaries and all text publications up through 1989 (Cavigneaux 1989), and many since then; *šeum* may in fact be the more correct (or more common) reading.

Preposition:

adi 'up to, as far as, until'.

Proper Names:

Sîn (Sum. lw.; log. written ^{d}EN.ZU, read ^{d}ZUEN) 'Sin', the moon god.
Šamaš (log. ^{d}UTU) 'Shamash', the sun god; cf. *šamšum* above.

Idiom:

aḫum aḫam 'one (subject) ... the other (object)' (e.g., *aḫum aḫam immar* 'one sees the other'; *aḫum ana aḫim* 'one (subject) ... to the other' (e.g., *aḫum ana aḫim ul iraggam* 'one will not lay claim against the other').

the other' (e.g., *aḫum ana aḫim ul iraggam* 'one will not lay claim against the other').

B. Learn the following signs:

OB Lapid.	OB Cursive	NA	values
			 *an* (lesson 9); AN = *šamû*; DINGIR = *ilum*; determinative d (for dingir) before divine names; ligature of d and EN in divine names such as dEN.ZU
	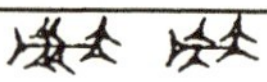		*mu* (lesson 9); MU = *nīšum, šattum, šumum*
	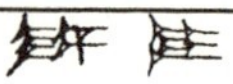		DUMU = *mārum*; also in DUMU.MUNUS (below)
	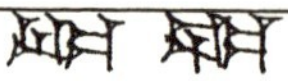		SAG = *rēšum*; in SAG.DU = *qaqqadum*; also in SAG.ÌR and SAG.GEME2 (below)
			É = *bītum*
			ÌR (also read ARAD) = *wardum*; SAG.ÌR (or SAG.ARAD) also = *wardum*
			*ud/t/ṭ, tam*; UD (also read U4) = *ūmum**; UTU = *šamšum*, and UTU in dUTU = *Šamaš*; BABBAR in KUG.BABBAR (below)
			*še*; ŠE = *ûm*
			*ki, ke, qí, qé*; KI = *itti*; determinative ki *after* geographical names

			KUG (also read KÙ) in KUG. BABBAR = *kaspu* and KUG.SIG$_{17}$ (SIG$_{17}$ = GI; this log. is also read GUŠKIN) = *ḫurāṣum*
			'1' (see §23.2); determinative ^{I} or ^{m} or ^{P} before personal names
		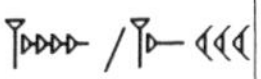	MEŠ or ^{meš} plural marker
	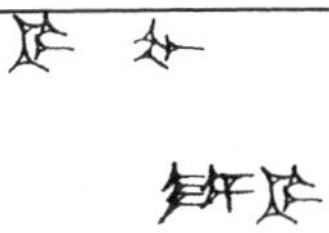		MUNUS (also read MÍ) = *sinništum*; DUMU.MUNUS = *mārtum*; determinative ^{f} or ^{mí} (or ^{sal}) before women's names and occupations
	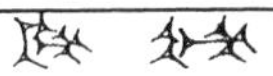		GEME$_2$ = *amtum*; SAG.GEME$_2$ also = *amtum*

**ūmum* 'day' is usually written, e.g., UD-*mu-um*, gen. UD-*mi-im*, bound form UD-*um* (for *ūm*); many Assyriologists prefer to assign the syllabic value u_4 to the sign UD in such writings, thus, u_4-*mu-um*, u_4-*um*, etc.

C. Write the following words in cuneiform and in transliteration; use logograms where appropriate to write 1–4:

1. *amassa*
2. *šum mārim*
3. *kasap qaqqadīšu*
4. *ḫurāṣī*
5. *išruk*
6. *qerub*
7. *azbil*
8. *šumūt*
9. *šebērum*
10. *milkum*
11. *šuknuš*
12. *durrusī*

D. Give the full Durative conjugations of *aḫāzum*, *erēbum*, *enēšum*, and *tamûm*:

E. Write in normalized Akkadian:

1. We will not assist those young men.
2. I was becoming weak.
3. You (ms) will marry her employee (f).
4. They (m) will collect your (mp) tax before the harvest.
5. We will eat the grain.
6. You (fs) will not see the thief's dog.
7. All the gods are gathering in the sky.

8. They (f) will swear by the life of the prince.
9. You (ms) will not open your mouth.
10. The chief of the partners will prosper.
11. at your (fp) disposal
12. between these new chariots
13. They (m) will bow down before you (ms).
14. upon them (m)

F. Normalize and translate:

1. ŠE-*um i-na eq-le-tim i-te-er-ma ni-šu ba-ab-tim an-ni-tim* ŠE-*am wa-at-ra-am a-na* KUG.BABBAR *i-na-di-na*.
2. DUMU *ši-ip-ri-ia i-na qá-at be-el ḫu-bu-ul-li-ia e-zi-im-ma šu-ú ši-ip-ri i-pé-eš*.
3. *i-na* UD-*mi-im šu-a-ti i-na-ni* UTU *ú-ul i-ṭú-la*.
4. *a-na-ku ù aš-ša-ti i-na pa-ni ru-gu-me-em ša-a-ti ú-ul ni-pa-aš-ša-aḫ*.
5. *a-na ma-ḫa-ar be-el-ti-ia eṭ-ḫe-ma i-in-ša ú-ul am-ḫu-ur-ma pa-ni-ia ú-ul ú-bi-il*.
6. *al-pí ša-al-mu-tim a-ag-ga-ar-ma eq-li ši-ip-ra-am e-ep-pé-eš*.
7. UD.MEŠ *ma-ar-ṣí-im ú-ul i-ir-ri-ku-ma ú-ul i-ba-al-lu-uṭ*.
8. *ag-ru i-ṣa-am ma-da-am ik-ki-sú-ma a-na pí-i ṭe-em be-li-šu-nu i-ṣa-am šu-a-ti a-na da-an-na-tim ub-lu*.
9. *ta-ap-pé-e* KUG.SIG$_{17}$ *ma-da-am ir-ši-ma ṭú-up-pí ta-pu-ti-ni ka-an-kam iḫ-pé-ma* KUG.SIG$_{17}$ *a-di-ni ú-ul ni-zu-uz*.
10. *da-an-na-tum ma-tam ša-a-ti is-ḫu-up-ma ni-šu ma-da-tum i-mu-ta-ma* MUNUS.MEŠ DUMU.MEŠ *ú-ul ul-da*.

G. Contracts. Normalize and translate the following texts; following each text are normalizations of personal names and glosses of words not given thus far in the vocabularies. The first text is also furnished with a full normalization and a translation as an illustration.

1. Formation of a partnership (*CT* 2 28 = Schorr, *VAB* 5 no. 172):

[1] ^{I}*e-ri-ib-*^{d}EN.ZU [2] *ù nu-úr-*^{d}UTU [3] *tap-pu-tam i-pu-šu-ma* [4] *a-na* É ^{d}UTU *i-ru-bu-ma* [5] *ṭe*$_4$*-em-šu-nu i-pu-šu-ma* [6] KUG.BABBAR-*am ba-ab-tam* SAG.GEME$_2$ *ù* SAG.ÌR [7] *ša ḫa-ra-nim ù li-bi a-li-im* [8] *mi-it-ḫa-ri-iš i-zu-zu* [9] *a-wa-ti-*[*šu*]*-nu ig-mu-ru-ma* [10] *a-na* KUG. BABBAR «KUG.BABBAR-*am*» SAG.ÌR [11] *ù* SAG.GEME$_2$ *ù ba-ab-tim* [12] *ša ḫa-ra-nim ù li-bi a-li-im* [13] *iš-tu pé-e a-di* KUG.SIG$_{17}$ [14] *a-ḫu-um a-na a-ḫi-im* [15] *ú-ul i-ra-ga-am* [16] MU ^{d}UTU ... [17] *ù ḫa-am-mu* (!MI)*-ra-pí*(! AM) *itmû*(IN.PÀD. DÈ.MEŠ) [18–34] Witnesses.

PNs: *Erīb-Sîn; Nūr-Šamaš.*
[8]*mitḫāriš* 'equally'.
[10] KUG.BABBAR-*am* after the first KUG.BABBAR is a scribal error.
[13] *pûm* b (often pl. *pû;* base *pā-*) 'chaff'; *ištu pê adi ḫurāṣim* 'from chaff to gold', i.e., 'everything'.

Erīb-Sîn u Nūr-Šamaš tappûtam īpušū-ma	Erib-Sin and Nur-Shamash entered into a partnership;
ana bīt Šamaš īrubū-ma	they entered the Shamash temple
ṭēmšunu īpušū-ma	and carried out their intention:
kaspam bābtam amtam u wardam ša ḫarrānim u libbi ālim mitḫāriš izūzū.	they divided equally the silver, outstanding goods, (and) female and male slaves of (both) business trip(s) and within the city.
Awâtīšunu igmurū-ma	They completed their dealings,
ana kaspim wardim u amtim u bābtim ša ḫarrānim u libbi ālim ištu pê adi ḫurāṣim aḫum ana aḫim ul iraggam.	and one will not lay claim against the other for the silver, male or female slave(s), or outstanding merchandise of (either) business trip(s) or within the city, from chaff to gold.
Nīš Šamaš ... u Ḫammurapi itmû.	They took an oath by the life of Shamash ... and Hammurapi.

2. Lawsuit over a piece of property (*CT* 6 42a = Schorr, *VAB* 5 no. 274, adapted):

[1] *eq-la-am* [2] KI *a-li-kum* [3] DUMU *ar-wu-um* [4] [I]*ta-ku-ma-tum* [5] DUMU.MUNUS *a-mu-ru-um* [6] *ù ra-ba-tum um-ma-ša* [7] *i-ša-ma* [8] [I]*a-li-kum* DUMU *ar-wu-um* [9] [I]*sú-mu-ra-me-e* [10] *ù ma-ru-šu ka-lu-šu-nu* [11] *a-na ta-ku-ma-tim* [12] *ir-gu-mu-ma* [13] *da-ia-nu i-na* É [d]UTU [14] *ru-gu-me-šu-nu i-sú-ḫu.* Oath. Names of judges. *di-in* É [d]UTU. Witnesses.

PNs: *Ālikum; Arwûm; Takūm-mātum* (f); *Amurrûm; Rabbatum* (f); *Sumu-ramê.*

3. Loan of silver for payment of a ransom (*CT* 6 40c = Schorr, *VAB* 5 no. 52, adapted):

[1] x KUG.BABBAR [2] *eš-re-tum* KI [d]UTU [3] [I]*ki-šu-šu-ú* [4] *il-qé* [5] *a-na*

Anum(AN)*-a-bi* ^{6} *a-na ip-ṭe*$_4$*-ri-šu* ^{7} *i-di-in* ^{8} *i-na* UD *ebūrim*(BURU$_{14}$) ŠE-*am* ^{9} *a-na* ^{d}UTU ^{10} *i-na-di-in* $^{11-16}$ Witnesses. $^{17-18}$ Date.

PNs: *Kišūšû; Anum-abī.*

^{2} *ešrētum* (always pl.) 'tithe' (here nom. for expected acc.).

^{6} *ipṭerū* (always pl.) 'ransom'.

H. Transliterate, normalize, and translate:

1. 

2. 

3. 

4. 

5. 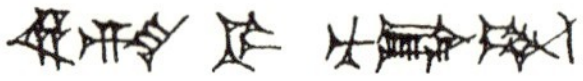

6. 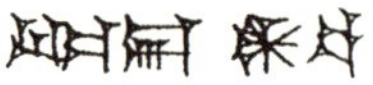

7. 

LESSON FOURTEEN

14.1 The G Durative: Verbs II–weak

Consider the G Durative paradigms of the four types of verbs II–weak presented in §9.1:

	II–*w*	II–*y*	II–ʾ$_{1–2}$	II–ʾ$_{3–4}$
	kânum	*qiāšum*	*šâmum*	*nêrum / nârum*
3cs	*ikân*	*iqīaš*	*išâm*	*inêr / inâr*
2ms	*takân*	*taqīaš*	*tašâm*	*tenêr / tanâr*
2fs	*takunnī*	*taqiššī*	*tašammī*	*tenerrī / tanarrī*
1cs	*akân*	*aqīaš*	*ašâm*	*enêr / anâr*
3mp	*ikunnū*	*iqiššū*	*išammū*	*inerrū / inarrū*
3fp	*ikunnā*	*iqiššā*	*išammā*	*inerrā / inarrā*
2cp	*takunnā*	*taqiššā*	*tašammā*	*tenerrā / tanarrā*
1cp	*nikân*	*niqīaš*	*nišâm*	*ninêr / ninâr*

The form of the base of the G Durative for these verbs depends on whether there is a vocalic ending (2fs; second and third persons plural). When there is no vocalic ending, the forms are those resulting from vowel and consonant reduction:

> *ikân* ‹ *ikūan* ‹ **ikawwan* (with **aw* › *ū* as elsewhere in Akkadian);
>
> *iqīaš* ‹ **iqayyaš* (with **ay* › *ī* as elsewhere; *īa* does not contract in OB; note that the *-ī-* is marked long as in the Preterite *iqīš*, whereas in the Infinitive *qiāšum* the *-i-* is marked short and the *-ā-* long);
>
> *išâm* ‹ **išaam* ‹ **išaʾʾam*;
>
> *inêr* ‹ **ineer* ‹ **ineḫḫer* ‹ **inaḫḫar* (forms with *a*, *inâr*, are uncommon).

In verbs II–ʾ, the forms without endings are distinguished from the corresponding Preterite forms in normalization by means of the circumflex vs. the macron, as in Durative *išâm*, *inêr* vs. Preterite *išām*, *inēr*. In the writing, however, the Durative and Preterite are generally identical, both written *i-ša-am* and *i-ne-er*, respectively (the Durative occasionally appears as *i-ša-a-am*, *i-ne-e-er*).

When a vocalic ending does follow, the base of each type has a **short vowel**, the short version of the long vowel of the Preterite, and a

doubled *final* radical. Note that if the doubling is not explicitly indicated in the script, such forms will be distinguishable from the corresponding Preterites only by context: e.g.,

i-qí-šu may be Preterite *iqīšū* or Durative *iqiššū*.

In terms of vowel classes,

verbs	II–*w*,	such as	*ikân–ikūn*,	may be called	*a–u*	(also, Verbs II–*u*);
	II–*y*,		*iqīaš–iqīš*		*a–i*	(also, Verbs II–*i*);
	II–ʾ$_{1-2}$		*išâm–išām*		*a*	(also, Verbs II–*a*);
	II–ʾ$_{3-4}$		*inêr–inēr*		*e*	(also, Verbs II–*e*).

14.2 Interrogative Words

Each of the following is declinable for case.

(a) The personal interrogative pronoun is *mannum* (gen. *mannim*, acc. *mannam*) 'who?' There is no special feminine form or plural:

mannum ana bītim īrub 'Who entered the house?'
mannam tāmurā 'Whom did you (pl) see?'
ana mannim kaspam tanaddinī 'To whom will you (fs) give the silver?'
mār mannim atta 'Whose son are you?'

Note that the interrogative normally stands as close as possible to the beginning of the sentence.

(b) The impersonal interrogative pronoun 'what?' occurs in two forms, *mīnum* (base *mīn-*; gen. *mīnim*, acc. *mīnam*) and *minûm* (base *mina-*; gen. *minîm*, acc. *minâm*). Again, no feminine or plural forms occur, and the form stands at or near the beginning of the sentence:

mīnum ina eqlim 'What is in the field?'
minâm tēpuš 'What did you (ms) do?'

Note the common phrase *ana mīnim*, often contracted to *am-mīnim* 'why?' (literally: 'for what?'):

am-mīnim ana ālīšu tallikī? 'Why did you (fs) go to his town?'

(c) The interrogative adjective *ayyum* 'which?' agrees with the noun it modifies in case, number, and gender. The base of this form is *ayy-* (thus, sg. gen. *ayyim*, acc. *ayyam*; mp *ayyūtum*; fp *ayyātum*), but the fem. sg. is irregularly *ayyītum*. When used attributively, *ayyum* may precede or follow its noun:

ana ayyim ṣuḫārim âm tapqid 'To which servant did you (ms) supply grain?'

ilū ayyūtum ištu šamê ikšudū 'Which gods arrived from the sky?'
narkabti šarrim ayyītam irakkab 'Which royal chariot will he ride?'

(In predicate use, which is rare, *ayyum* stands first:

ayyūtum ana bēlīya 'Which are my lord's?')

(d) In sentences in which an interrogative word, such as the three discussed in the previous paragraphs, occurs, the negative adverb *ul* is replaced by another adverb, *lā* (written *la-a* or simply *la*):

am-mīnim mārkunu ana maḫrīšu lā taṭrudā 'Why did you (mp) not send your son to him?'

14.3 Indefinite Pronouns and Indefinite Adjective

In general, these are formed by reduplication of the bases of the interrogative words discussed in the preceding section, or by adding the particle *-ma* to their bases.

(a) The personal indefinite pronoun is *mamman* (< **manman*), occasionally shortened to *mamma* 'anyone, someone', with a negative 'no one'; the form is indeclinable:

mamman ul illik 'No one went';
mamma ul āmur 'I did not see anyone/I saw no one';
šamnam ana mamman addin 'I gave oil to someone'.

mamman may also be used in apposition after a noun; in such cases, it should be translated 'any', with a negative 'not any, no':

ḫurāṣam ana ṣuḫārtim mamman ul niddin 'We did not give the gold to any female servant'.

(The phrase *mamman ša*, i.e., the indefinite pronoun followed by the determinative-relative pronoun, means 'anyone who, whoever'; see §19.3(b), end.)

(b) From *mīnum* is formed the impersonal indefinite pronoun *mimma* 'anything, something, all' and, with a negative, 'nothing'; like *mamman*, *mimma* is indeclinable:

mimma ul nīmur 'We did not see anything/We saw nothing';
mimma ana šarrim anaddin 'I will give something to the king'.

mimma may occur in apposition before or after a noun, as in

eqlam mimma (or *mimma eqlam*) *ula imaḫḫar* 'she may not receive any field',

or as a bound form before a genitive, as in

mimma eqlim 'all (i.e., anything of) the field'.

In apposition, *mimma* occurs in the common expression *mimma šumšu* 'anything at all, everything' (literally, 'whatever its name'). Finally, *mimma* may be used adverbially, with a negative, meaning '(not) at all, (not) in any way, in (no) way':

mimma ul niḫdu 'We did not rejoice at all'.

(The phrase *mimma ša* means 'anything that, whatever'; see §19.3(b), end.)

(c) The adjectival *ayyumma* 'whichever, any, some' is based on *ayyum* and is declined like the latter with *-ma* attached:

ana ālim ayyimma 'toward some/any town';
amtam ayyītamma ša qātīya aṭarrad 'I will send whichever slave (f) is at my disposal'.

ayyumma may also occur independently, meaning 'someone':

ayyumma imât 'Someone will die'.

14.4 The Abstract Suffix *-ūt*

The suffix *-ūt* may be added to the base of many nouns and adjectives to form abstract nouns. It corresponds to the English endings '-ness, -ship, -hood, -ity, -ery'. Although the ending *-ūt* is formally identical to the masc. pl. ending of adjectives, nouns formed with it are grammatically feminine singular:

bēlūtam rabītam teppeš 'you (ms) exercise great lordship';

The bound form corresponds to other polysyllabic nouns ending in a single consonant:

bēlūt ilim annîm 'the lordship of this god';
bēlūssu 'his lordship'.

The feminine marker *-(a)t* is normally dropped when *-ūt* is added:

aššūtum 'wifehood'; *sinnišūtum* 'womanhood'.

For reference, the most common nouns ending in *-ūt* that are derived from the vocabulary to this point are listed here:

abbūtum (with *-bb-*) 'father's legal status; fatherly attitude';
aḫḫūtum (with *-ḫḫ-*) 'brotherhood, brotherliness; status of brother';
aššūtum 'marriage; status of wife';
awīlūtum 'humanity, human species, people; someone, anyone; soldier, worker, status of *awīlum*';
bēlūtum 'lordship, dominion, rule; position of owner'; *bēlūtam epēšum* 'to exercise lordship';
dannūtum 'strength, power, violence' (late, also 'fortress');

ilūtum 'divinity, divine nature, divine power';
mārūtum 'sonship; status of son (natural or adopted)';
mutūtum 'position of a husband';
nišūtum 'family, relatives';
qarrādūtum 'ability in battle, heroism' (rare in OB);
rabûtum 'greatness';
rēšūtum 'slavery; service';
rubûtum 'principality; dominion';
šarrūtum 'kingship; dominion; majesty'; *šarrūtam epēšum* 'to exercise kingship';
šībūtum '(old) age; testimony; witness';
tappûtum 'partnership, association; position of helper, partner' (see Vocab. 13);
wardūtum 'slavery; position of slave'.

14.5 Verbal Hendiadys

Verbal hendiadys is the use of two verbs, co-ordinated either with *-ma* or asyndetically (i.e., without a conjunction), in which the first verb qualifies or restricts the meaning of the second. A literal translation of such a contruction may be quite awkward, and it is often preferable to render the first verb adverbially in English. Perhaps the most common verb to appear in this type of construction is *târum* 'to return'; in hendiadys, *târum* also means 'to do (something) again', in which 'something' is conveyed by the second verb: e.g.,

atūr-ma wardam ana bēlīya aṭrud 'I sent the slave to my lord again';
dayyānum šū ul itâr-ma itti dayyānī ina dīnim ul uššab 'that judge will no longer sit in judgment with the judges' (*uššab* = *wašābum* G Durative, §15.1).

Note also *gamārum*, which may mean 'to do something completely', and *kanākum* 'to give/take/send something under seal':

eqlam anniam šipram igammar-ma ippeš 'he will work this field completely';
kaspam ana bēlīya aknuk-ma addin 'I gave the silver to my lord under seal'.

Also frequent in hendiadys is the verb *sadārum* 'to occur/do regularly':

isaddar-ma kaspam ana bēlīšu inaddin 'he will regularly give silver to his lord'.

From the examples given above it may be seen that complements (objects, prepositional phrases) may appear either before both verbs or between them. The subject normally precedes both verbs, as in the second example above (*dayyānum šū* ...), but occasionally follows the first, as in

ul iturrū-ma mārūšu ul iraggamū 'his sons will not contest again'.

EXERCISES

A. VOCABULARY 14.

Verbs:

apālum (*a–u*) 'to answer, respond; to satisfy a demand or claim; to pay (something: acc.; to someone: acc. or *ana*)'.

dâkum (*a–u*) 'to kill, execute; to defeat'.

diānum (*a–i*) 'to judge, give a judgment (*dīnum*); to start a lawsuit, go to court' (cf. *dayyānum, dīnum*).

emēdum (*i*) 'to lean against, touch, cling to; to reach, stand near/by; to place or lean (something against something: double acc.); to load, impose (taxes, punishment, etc.: acc.; on someone: acc.)'.

qabûm (*i*) 'to say, tell, speak; to command, order; to give orders'; Infin. as noun: 'utterance, saying, command, speech'; *qabâm šakānum* 'to promise, give a pledge'.

sadārum (*a–u*) 'to arrange, put in order; to enter (something into an account)'; in hendiadys: 'to occur/do regularly'; Verbal Adj. *sadrum* (*sadir-*) 'in a row; regular, continual'.

Nouns:

bābum (bound form *bāb*; pl. *bābū* and *bābātum*; log. KÁ) 'opening, door, gate; city quarter'.

bēlūtum (*bēlūt*) 'lordship, dominion, rule; position of power; status of owner'; *bēlūtam epēšum* 'to rule, exercise authority'.

itûm (base *itā-*; bound form *itê* and *itā*; log. ÚS.SA.DU) 'border, neighbor, neighboring field, plot'; the bound form *itā* is used as a preposition (also with log. ÚS.SA.DU), 'bordering on, beside'.

kirûm (base *kiri-*; pl. *kiriātum*; Sum. lw.) 'garden, orchard'.

mārūtum (*mārūt*) 'sonship; status of son (natural or adopted)'; *ana mārūtim leqûm* 'to adopt'.

šērtum (*šēret*) 'penalty, punishment'; *šērtam emēdum* 'to impose a penalty, punishment' (on someone: acc.).

warkītum (*warkīt*; pl. *warkiātum* often = sg.) 'future, later time, time afterward'; *ina warkītim / warkiātim* 'in (the) future, later on, afterward'; *ana / ina warkīt / warkiāt ūmim / ūmī* 'in future'.

Pronouns:

ayyum (fem. irregularly *ayyītum*) 'which?'.

ayyumma (fem. *ayyītumma*) 'whichever, any, some'.

mamman (occasionally also *mamma*) 'anyone, someone', with a negative 'no one'.

mannum 'who?'.

mimma 'anything, something, all', with a negative 'nothing'; *mimma šumšu* 'anything at all, everything'.

mīnum (base *mīn-*) and *minûm* (*mina-*) 'what?'; *ana mīnim* and *am-mīnim* 'why?'.

Preposition:

aššum (with suff. *aššumīya, aššumīka,* etc.) 'concerning, because of, on account of, for the sake of'.

Adverb:

lā (written *la-a* and *la*) 'not' (with interrogative pronouns; see §20.4).

Place Name:

Bābilim (log. KÁ.DINGIR.RA^{ki}) 'Babylon'.

B. Learn the following signs:

OB Lapid.	OB Cursive	NA	values
		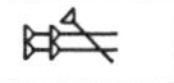	*šum*
	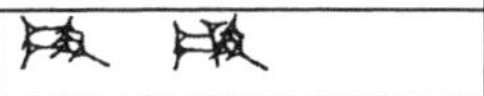		*am*
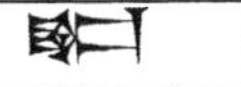	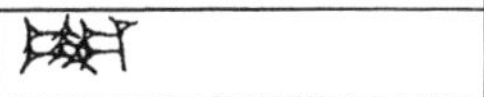	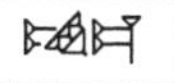	*ne, bí, bil, pil, ṭè*
			*bíl, píl*
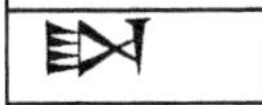	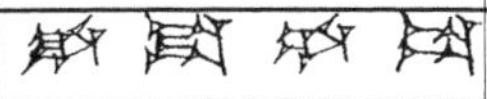		*ša**
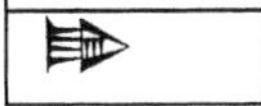	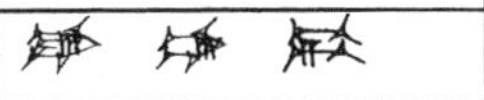		*ga, qá*

	*ta*, *ṭá**
	*tar*, *ṭar*; KUD in DI.KUD (below)
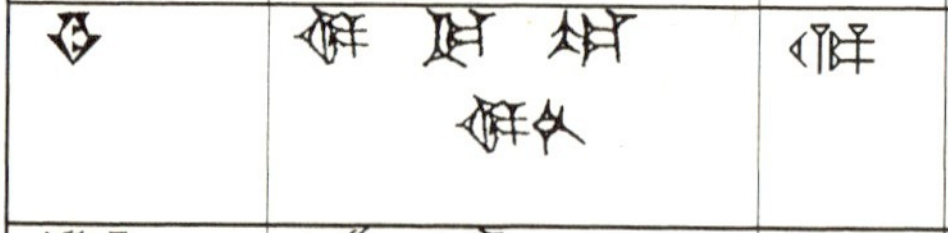	*di*, *de*, *ṭi*, *ṭe*; DI = *dīnum*; DI.KUD = *dayyānum*
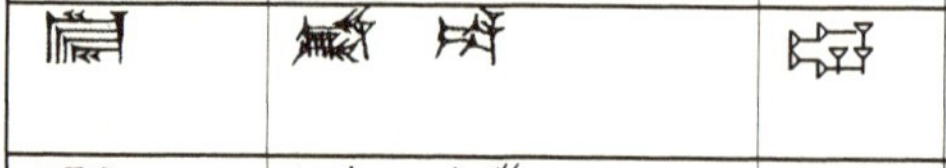	KÁ = *bābum*; KÁ.DINGIR.RA[ki] = *Bābilim*
	LUGAL = *šarrum*

*ŠA and TA are indistinguishable in some OB texts.

C. Write the following words in cuneiform and in transliteration; use logograms where appropriate to write 10–12:

1. *qibīšum*	4. *ṭēmum*	7. *tadūk*	10. *dayyānū Bābilim*
2. *pilšum*	5. *nutār*	8. *mušēpišum*	11. *wardū ša Šamaš*
3. *taptaṭar*	6. *nēšum*	9. *qadum*	12. *kasap amāt šarrim*

D. Write in normalized Akkadian:

1. you (pl) will execute
2. his heart will become satisfied
3. they (m) will die
4. you (ms) will grow old
5. we will divide
6. they (m) will become firm
7. I will bestow
8. you (fs) will buy
9. you (fs) bought
10. she will return
11. she returned
12. they (f) will return
13. they (f) returned
14. it will become plentiful
15. you (pl) will slay
16. you (pl) slew
17. I will judge
18. they (m) will judge
19. they (m) will become pleasant
20. they (f) will become numerous
21. we will die
22. it will endure
23. I will answer
24. you (fs) will abandon
25. you (pl) will lean
26. it will become new
27. I will become weak
28. you (fs) will prosper

E. Normalize and translate:

1. *ma-an-nu-um di-ni ù di-in-ki i-di-a-an.*

2. *a-na ṣé-er a-wi-lim al-li-ik-ma i-na pa-ni-šu aq-bi-ma šu-ú qá-bé-e i-pu-ul.*
3. *qá-ra-du-um šu-ú* KUG.BABBAR *ma-da-am ki-ma ne-me-tim e-li-ni i-mi-id-ma ne-me-ta-am šu-a-ti ú-ul ni-pa-al.*
4. *ni-šu a-lim a-ka-lam it-ti* LUGAL *im-ḫu-ra-ma i-na wa-ar-ki-a-at* UD-*mi i-sa-ad-da-ra-ma i-na e-bu-rim* ŠE-*am ša-am-na-am ù* KUG.SIG$_{17}$ *a-na* LUGAL *i-na-ad-di-na.*
5. *be-el um-ma-ni-im a-na da-a-ak na-ak-ri-im qá-ba-šu iš-ku-un.*
6. *am-mi-nim ṭup-pa-tum sa-ad-ra-tum a-na ma-ḫa-ar a-bi-ia la-a i-il-la-ka.*
7. *eq-lam ki-ri-a-am ù ka-ra-nam i-ta* KÁ É ^{d}UTU *ni-ša-am-ma al-pa-am ni-ga-ar-ma eq-lam ši-ip-ra-am ni-pé-eš.*
8. *ma-am-ma-an ṣé-eḫ-ra-am an-ni-a-am a-na ma-ru-tim ú-ul i-le-eq-qé-ma i-ma-ar-ra-aṣ-ma i-ma-at.*
9. *a-ii-i-tam ma-tam* LUGAL *a-na* DUMU-*šu a-na e-pé-eš be-lu-tim i-qí-a-aš.*
10. *i-na re-eš* MU *an-ni-tim a-a-ú-um-ma i-na ni-ši e-ka-al-li-im* LUGAL *i-du-uk-ma i-na mu-uḫ-ḫi ku-us-sí-šu ú-ši-ib.*
11. KUG.BABBAR *ḫa-al-qá-am ú-ul a-mu-ur mi-na-a-am e-ep-pé-eš ù ma-an-nu-um ta-ap-pu-ti i-il-la-ak.*
12. *mi-im-ma šu-um-šu ša bi-ti-šu-nu i-na ba-ab-ti-ni ú-ul ni-mu-ur.*
13. *ma-tum a-na* LUGAL *šu-a-ti ik-nu-uš-ma i-na be-lu-ti-šu ip-ša-aḫ-ma le-mu-tum mi-im-ma e-li-ša ú-ul im-qú-ut.*
14. *i-na wa-ar-ki-a-at* UD-*mi-im ma-am-ma-an mi-im-ma i-na qá-ti-ka ú-ul i-le-qé.*

F. Contracts. Normalize and translate the following texts:

1. A lawsuit over a house (*CT* 8 24b = Schorr, VAB 5, no. 267).

^{1} *aš-šum ...* É *ki-di-im* ^{2} ^{I}*ni-ši-i-ni-šu* DUMU.MUNUS *a-bu-na-nu-um* ^{3} *a-na e-ri-iš-ti-*^{d}*a-a* ^{4} DUMU.MUNUS ^{d}EN.ZU-*e-ri-iš ir-gu-um-ma* ^{5} DI.KUD.MEŠ LUGAL *ik-šu-da-ma* ^{6} DI.KUD.MEŠ *a-wa-ti-ši-na i-mu-ru-ma* ^{7} *še-er-tam* ^{I}*ni-ši-i-ni-šu* ^{8}*i-mi-du* ^{9}*ú-ul i-ta-ar-ma* ^{10} ^{I}*ni-ši-i-ni-šu* DUMU.MUNUS *a-bu-na-nu-um* ^{11} *a-na e-ri-iš-ti-*^{d}*a-a* ^{12} DUMU.MUNUS ^{d}EN.ZU-*e-ri-iš* ^{13}*ú-ul i-ra-gu-um* ^{14}MU ^{d}UTU ^{d}*a-a ... ù sa-am-su-i-lu-na* LUGAL *itmâ*(IN.PÀD.DÈ.MEŠ) $^{17–26}$ Witnesses. $^{27–28}$ Date.

PNs: *Nīši-īnīšu; Abunānum; Erišti-Ayya* (^{d}*a-a* = *Ayya*, consort of *Šamaš*); *Sîn-ēriš; Samsu-iluna.*

^{1} *kīdum* 'open country'.

2. A lawsuit over property (*CT* 2 50 = Schorr, *VAB* 5, no. 290).

^{1} *a-na eqlim*(A.ŠÀ) É SAG.GEME$_{2}$ SAG.ÌR ^{2} *ù kirîm*(^{giš}KIRI$_{6}$) ... ^{3} *i-ta bi-zi-za-na* ^{4} *ù iš-ka-ri-im ša* ^{d}UTU ^{5} ^{I}*be-le-sú-nu ù na-ap-sa-nu-um* ^{6} *ù ma-ta-tum* DUMU.MUNUS *i-ṣí-da-re-e* ^{7} *a-na ma-ia-tum ù su-mu-ra-aḫ* ^{8} DUMU.MEŠ *a-za-li-ia* ^{9} *ir-gu-mu-ú-ma* ^{10} DI.KUD.MEŠ *i-na* É ^{d}UTU ^{11}*ru-gu-mé-šu-nu i-sú-ḫu* ^{12} *ú-ul i-tu-ru-ma* ^{13} *a-na wa-ar-ki-at* UD-*mi* ^{14} *a-na eqlim*(A.ŠÀ) É SAG.GEME$_{2}$ SAG.ÌR ^{15} *ù kirîm* (^{giš}KIRI$_{6}$) ^{16} *ša ma-ia-tum ù su-mu-ra-aḫ* ^{17} ^{I}*be-le-sú-nu* ^{I}*na-ap-sa-nu-um* ^{18} *ù ma-ta-tum* DUMU.MUNUS *i-ṣí-da-re-e* ^{19} *iš-tu zi-ka-ri-im* ^{20} *a-di sí-ni-iš-tim*(! TUM) ^{21} DUMU.MEŠ *a-mur-ru-um* ^{22} *a-na ma-ia-tum ù su-mu-ra-aḫ* ^{23} *ú-ul e-ra-ga-mu* ^{24} *di-in* É ^{d}UTU *i-na* É.BABBAR ^{25} MU ^{d}UTU ^{d}*a-a* ... ^{26} *ù ṣa-bi-um it-ma* (! for *it-mu-ú*) $^{27-30}$ 5 names ^{31} DI.KUD.MEŠ $^{32-37}$ Witnesses. $^{38-39}$ Date.

PNs: *Bizīzāna; Bēlessunu; Napsānum; Mātātum; Iṣi-darê; Mayyatum; Sumu-rāḫ; Azalīya; Amurrûm; Ṣabium* (king).

^{4} *iškarum* 'work assignment; supplies; delivery items; field on which assigned work is to be done'.

^{19} *zikarum* 'male, man'.

^{24} É.BABBAR = *Ebabbar* the temple of Shamash in the city of Sippar; line 24 constitutes a summary label of the tablet.

3. Loan of silver for formation of business partnership (Szlechter, *Tablettes* 125 MAH 16.351).

^{1} *x* KUG.BABBAR ... ^{2} KI *qí-i-šu*(?)-*a* ... ^{3} ^{I}*ik-kà-ki-na* ... ^{4} *ù* ÌR-*ku-bi* ... ^{5} *a-na tappûtim*(TAB.PA) ... ^{6} *ilqû*(ŠU.BA.AN.TI.MEŠ) ^{7} *i-ša-am-mu i-na-ad-di-nu* ^{8} *um-mi-a-an-šu-*[*nu*] ^{9} *i-ip-pa-lu-ú-*[*ma*] ^{10} *ne-me-la i-zu-uz-*[*zu*] ...

PNs: *Qīšūʾa; Ikkā-kīnā; Warad-Kūbi.*

^{8} *ummiānum* 'artisan; scholar, expert; money lender'.

^{10} *ne-me-la* for *nēmelam; nēmelum* 'gain, profit'.

4. Delivery of a slave (*VAS* 8 123–24 = Schorr, *VAB* 5, no. 70, adapted).

^{1} *maḫar*(IGI) *li-bu-ra-am* ^{2} *maḫar* ŠEŠ-BA.TUK ^{3} *maḫar* ÌR-*sà* ^{4} *maḫar pa-lu-uḫ-ri-gim-šu* ^{5} *ma-aḫ-ri-šu-nu* ^{6} *i-na* KÁ *ga-gi-im* ^{7} ^{I}*la-ma-sí* ^{8} DUMU.MUNUS *a-ḫu-ši-na* ^{9} *am-tam a-na* ^{d}UTU-*ṣu-lu-lí* ^{10} *ip-qí-id* ^{11} *am-tum i-ma-at* ^{12} *i-ḫa-li-iq-ma* ^{13} *ša la-ma-sí* ^{14} *ú-ul a-wa-sà* ^{15} Date.

PNs: *Libūram; Šeš-batuk* (= Akk. *Aḫam-arši*); *Warassa; Paluḫ-rigimšu; Lamassī; Aḫūšina; Šamaš-ṣulūlī.*

[6] *gagûm* (base *gagi-*) 'cloister'.

[13–14] Note the word order of this clause: lit., 'of PN, it is not her affair' for 'it is not PN's affair'.

G. Transliterate, normalize, and translate:

1. 

2. 

3. 

4. 

5. 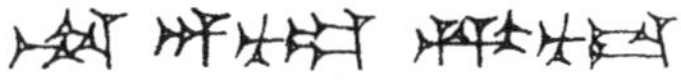

LESSON FIFTEEN

15.1 The G Durative: Verbs I–*w*

As in the Preterite (§10.1(b)), stative/adjectival verbs must be distinguished from active verbs.

(a) Stative verbs are all *i*-class, and, as in the Preterite, the Durative resembles that of verbs I–*e* (for which see §13.1); e.g., for *watārum*:

3cs	*ittir*	3mp	*ittirū*
		3fp	*ittirā*
2ms	*tettir*	2cp	*tettirā*
2fs	*tettirī*		
1cs	*ettir*	1cp	*nittir*

(b) Active verbs I–*w* are all *a–i* verbs (except those that are also III–weak; see §21.3(g)). The prefix always contains a short *u* (cf. the Preterite), the only vestige of the initial *w* of the root; the second radical is doubled, as usual in Durative forms; e.g., for *wašābum*:

3cs	*uššab*	3mp	*uššabū*
		3fp	*uššabā*
2ms	*tuššab*	2cp	*tuššabā*
2fs	*tuššabī*		
1cs	*uššab*	1cp	*nuššab*

Note that, as in the Preterite, the 3cs and 1cs forms are identical. Durative forms beginning with a vowel occur in three variant spellings, the expected writing *uš-ša-ab*, but also *ú-ša-ab* (without the doubling indicated) and *ú-uš-ša-ab* (with both doubling indicated and an extra initial vowel-sign; cf. writings of the Durative of verbs I–ʾ of the type *i-ḫa-az* and *i-iḫ-ḫa-az*).

The Durative of *babālum* 'to carry' is regular, e.g., 3cs/1cs *ubbal*, 2ms *tubbal*, 3fp *ubbalā*, etc.

15.2 The Ventive

The Ventive is a morpheme that may be added to any finite verb. It has three allomorphs, which occur as follows:

-am on the 3cs, 2ms, 1cs, and 1cp: e.g.,
imqut 'she fell', with Ventive *imqutam;*
takaššad 'you (ms) will arrive', with Ventive *takaššadam;*
allik 'I went', with Ventive *allikam;*
nibni 'we built', with Ventive *nibniam;*

-m on the 2fs:
tallakī 'you (fs) will go', with Ventive *tallakīm;*
telqî 'you (fs) took', with Ventive *telqîm;*

-nim on the 3mp, 3fp, and 2cp:
ibannû 'they (m) will build', with Ventive *ibannûnim;*
illikā 'they (f) went', with Ventive *illikānim;*
telqeā 'you (pl) took', with Ventive *telqeānim.*

The ending *-am* is subject to the regular rules of vowel contraction (§6.1) when it occurs with verbs III–weak:

abanni 'I will build', with Ventive *abanniam;*
imla 'it became full', with Ventive *imlâm;*
niḫaddu 'we rejoice', with Ventive *niḫaddâm;*
tešme 'you (ms) heard', with Ventive *tešmeam.*

Note that forms that already have endings, such as *ibnû* 'they (m) built' and *taḫdî* 'you (fs) rejoiced', take the Ventive with no further alteration: *ibnûnim; taḫdîm.*

Further, the addition of *-am* affects the Preterite forms of active verbs I–*w* and the Durative forms of verbs II–weak in the same way as the addition of *-ū, -ā, -ī*:

ušib 'he sat', with Ventive *ušbam;*
nubil 'we carried', with Ventive *nubilam* or *nublam;*
atâr 'I will return', with Ventive *aturram;*
tenêr 'you (ms) will slay', with Ventive *tenerram.*

Note in the last example and in others given above that the *a* of *-am* does not become *e* when there is an *e*-vowel elsewhere in the word; another example:

eppeš 'I will do', with Ventive *eppešam.*

The Ventive is essentially a directional element that denotes motion or activity in the direction of, or to a point near, the speaker (or a person being addressed, when the speaker places herself in the location of the person addressed; see further below). The Ventive appears most commonly on verbs of motion. Akkadian verbs of motion do not convey a lexical distinction between motion away from the speaker and motion to the speaker, English 'go' vs. 'come'. Thus, for example, *ana bītim erēbum* means 'to enter a house'; the absence or presence of the Ventive morpheme specifies whether the speaker is outside or inside the house:

ana bītim īrub 'he went into the house'
vs. *ana bītim īrubam* 'he came into the house'
(both may also be translated 'he entered the house').

Further examples:

ana dannatim atâr 'I will go back to the fortress' (speaker not in fortress)
vs. *ana dannatim aturram* 'I will come back to the fortress' (speaker in fortress)
(both may also be translated 'I will return to the fortress').

ištu ālim turdā 'you (pl) went down from the town' (speaker in the town) (*warādum* 'to descend')
vs. *ištu ālim turdānim* 'you (pl) came down from the town' (speaker below the town)
(both may also be translated 'you descended from the town').

ana bābti aḫīni nillik 'we went to our brother's district'
vs. *ana bābti aḫīni nillikam* 'we came to our brother's district'.

The Ventive often occurs when the second person is involved, i.e., when a person is being addressed, because the speaker may place himself in the location of the latter; contrast

ana āl bēlīya akaššad 'I will arrive at my lord's city'

when speaking/writing to a third party, but

ana āl bēlīya akaššadam (same translation)

when speaking/writing to the lord himself. Similarly,

wardūya kaspī ana Bābilim ublū 'my slaves carried my silver to Babylon',

whereas *ublūnim* (i.e., with the Ventive) in the same sentence would imply that either the person speaking/writing or the person being addressed was in Babylon:

wardūya kaspī ana Bābilim ublūnim 'my slaves brought my silver (here/there) to Babylon'.

Connected with the use of the Ventive to indicate motion in the direction of the speaker/writer is its use as the 1cs dative suffix:

taddinam 'you (ms) gave to me';
iṭarradūnim 'they (m) will send (here) to me';
tēpušīm 'you (fs) acted for me'.

For dative pronominal suffixes for the other persons, see §18.2.

When two verbs are connected with the enclitic conjunction *-ma*, and the second verb has the Ventive, the first will also often have it, with no change of nuance perceptible to the modern reader: e.g.,

ṭuppašu iknukam-ma ina qāt ṣuḫārīšu išpuram 'He sealed his tablet and sent (it) here with his servant' (*šapārum* 'to send').

Not infrequently, the particular lexical or contextual nuance of a given occurrence of the Ventive is difficult to ascertain; this is especially true in poetry.

15.3 Indefinite or Unspecified Subject

To express an indefinite or unspecified subject (i.e., English 'one', or the indefinite 'they' or 'people'; French *on*; German *man*), Akkadian uses the 3mp form of the verb. As an example, consider

dīnam iprusū lit. 'they decided the case';

if the context does not include anyone to whom 'they' obviously refers, the clause may be rendered

'one decided the case'.

In more idiomatic English, such expressions are normally passivized:

'the case was decided'.

Another example:

(If a man stole silver,) *qāssu inakkisū* 'his hand will be cut off' (lit. 'they will cut off his hand').

15.4 Direct Speech

Since the writing system does not involve the use of any punctuation marks, the presence of quoted speech can be a difficult feature in Akkadian texts. Sometimes there is no overt indication of a direct quotation at all, and its presence must be inferred from surrounding context. More often, however, some signal of the presence of direct speech does appear. Sometimes a verb of speaking, telling, writing, approaching, informing, or the like occurs after a quotation:

> DUMU *a-na a-bi-šu ú-ul a-bi at-ta i-qá-bi-ma a-bu-um* DUMU-*šu a-na* KUG.BABBAR *i-na-di-in = mārum ana abīšu "ul abī atta" iqabbī-ma abum māršu ana kaspim inaddin* 'If the son says to his father, "You are not my father," the father may sell his son.'

In some instances, especially in letters (§24.5), direct quotations are introduced with a formula like the following:

> PN *kiam iqbiam umma šū-ma* lit. 'PN spoke thus to me, he (said) as follows',
>
> *kiam tašpurānim umma attunū-ma* lit. 'you (pl) wrote to me thus, you (said) as follows',

in which there appear the adverbs *kiam* 'thus, in this manner' and *umma* 'as follows', the latter of which is used only to introduce direct speech; the formula is completed with the particle *-ma*, which is attached to a noun or pronoun referring to the speaker/writer, and which should not be translated. Not infrequently, a quote is introduced simply by *umma* followed by the person being quoted, in the nominative, plus *-ma*:

> *umma awīlum-ma* 'the man (said) as follows';
> *umma Sîn-nāṣir-ma* 'Sîn-nāṣir (said) as follows'.

Occasionally, the quote is followed by an inclusio, such as

> *kiam iqbiam* 'thus he said to me';
> *kiam tašpurīm* 'thus you (fs) wrote to me'.

Sometimes direct speech is indicated by another means, namely, the addition of the particle *-mi* to a word at or near the beginning of each clause of the quotation (sometimes to more than one, or even to every, word in a clause). Like the particle *-ma* (§7.4), *-mi* causes an immediately preceding short vowel to become long. An example:

> *awīlum-mi ulā-mi imḫuranni* ' "the man did not approach me" ' (*-anni* on the verb = 'me').

EXERCISES

A. VOCABULARY 15.

Verbs:

madādum (*a–u*) 'to measure (out), pay (in a measured amount)'.
šapārum (*a–u*) 'to send (someone, e.g., a messenger); to send word, send a message, report; to write; to command, give orders; to administer, govern'; rarely, 'to convey (goods)' (cf. *šiprum*).
warādum (*urrad – urid*) 'to descend, go/come down'.
waṣābum (*uṣṣab – uṣib*) 'to add (to), increase, enlarge; to pay as interest' (cf. *ṣibtum* below).

Nouns:

abullum (fem.; bound form *abul*; suff. *abulla-*; pl. *abullātum*; log. ABUL [formerly read KÁ.GAL]) 'city gate, entrance gate'.
eleppum (fem.; *elep*; suff. *eleppa-*; pl. *eleppētum*; log. $^{(giš)}$MÁ) 'ship, boat'.
erṣetum (*erṣet*; pl. *erṣētum*; log. KI) 'the earth; land, district, area; ground, earth; the nether world'.
ṣibtum (*ṣibat*; pl. *ṣibātum*; log. MÁŠ) 'interest' (cf. *waṣābum* above).

Adjectives:

elûm (base *elī-*; fem. *elītum*) 'upper'.
pānûm (base *pānī-*; fem. *pānītum*) 'earlier, former, previous; earliest, first' (cf. *pānum*).

Adverbs:

kiam 'thus, in this manner'.
umma 'as follows' (introducing direct quotations).

Particle:

-mi indicates that the clause of the word to which it is suffixed is part of a direct quotation.

Divine Name:

Enlil (or *Ellil*; log. ^{d}EN.LÍL) 'Enlil', one of the heads of the Mesopotamian pantheon.

B. Learn the following signs:

OB Lapid.	OB Cursive	NA	values
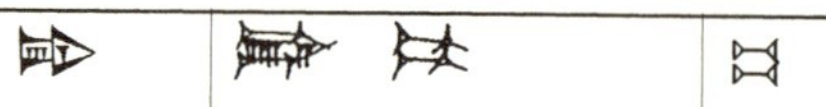			*bi, bé, pí, pé* (lesson 12); . BI denotes Sum. 'its' (m. and f., non-personal referent), i.e., Akk. *-šu* and *-ša*, e.g., KÁ.BI = *bābša* 'its (the palace's [f.]) gate'; MÁŠ.BI = *ṣibassu* 'its (the grain's [m.]) interest'
			MÁŠ = *ṣibtum*
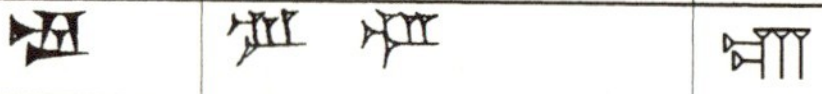			MÁ (also ^{giš}MÁ) = *eleppum*
			*e*
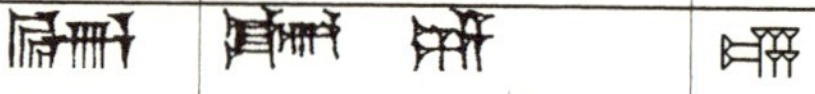			*un*; UN (also read UKU3) = *nišū*; KALAM = *mātum*
			*kal, dan, tan*
			*pa*
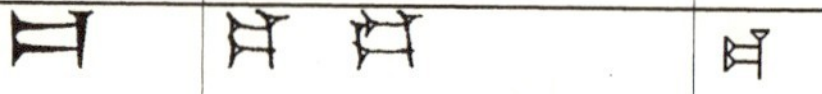			*is/ṣ/z, es/ṣ/z*; GIŠ = *iṣum*; ^{giš} before objects of wood and names of trees
			*mar*
			*ú*
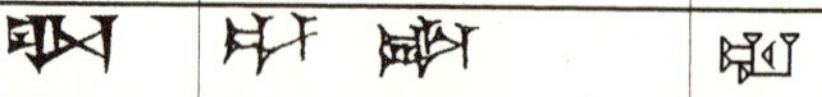			*al*
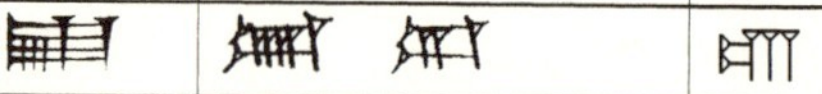			LÍL in ^{d}EN.LÍL = *Enlil*
			*gal, qal, kál*; GAL = *rabûm*; É.GAL = *ekallum*; ká+gal, read ABUL (or KÁ.GAL) = *abullum*

C. Write the following words in cuneiform and in transliteration; use logograms where appropriate to write 1–5:

1. *ṣibat Šamaš*
2. *šar mātim*
3. *elep dayyānim*
4. *abul Bābilim*
5. *bīt Enlil*
6. *ubil*
7. *ugallab*
8. *padû*
9. *tammar*
10. *ukāl*
11. *nêrum*
12. *edēšum*
13. *išḫun*
14. *paqādum*
15. *šalmūtum*
16. *šaṭār narîšu*

D. Write in normalized Akkadian:

1. I will carry
2. he will pay (as interest)
3. I gave birth
4. you will give birth
5. it will become pleasant for me
6. you (pl) will bring to me
7. they (m) will exceed
8. we came down
9. you (fs) will judge
10. you (fs) gave
11. I sat down
12. they (m) will kill
13. they (f) endured
14. they (f) will endure
15. you (pl) will dwell

E. Add the Ventive to the following verbs, and then translate:

1. *tašpur*
2. *taqīaš*
3. *nikaššad*
4. *tulladī*
5. *ippalū*
6. *tēmidā*
7. *ubil*
8. *iḫalliqū*
9. *iḫdu*
10. *tanaddinī*
11. *ileqqe*
12. *taṣṣurā*
13. *tazūz*
14. *idâk*
15. *nušib*
16. *tašâm*
17. *imallâ*
18. *išme*
19. *taturrī*
20. *tapḫurā*
21. *iṭeḫḫe*
22. *turid*
23. *tērub*
24. *iṭarradū*
25. *ibnû*
26. *idmiqā*
27. *tamqutī*

F. Normalize and translate:

1. *i-lu ka-lu-šu-nu iš-tu ša-me-e a-na er-ṣe-tim ur-ra-du-nim-ma i-na pu-úḫ-ri-im i-pa-aḫ-ḫu-ru-ma pu-ru-us-se-e* KALAM *i-pa-ar-ra-sú.*
2. *a-ḫu-ni maḫ-ri-ni ki-a-am iš-ku-un um-ma šu-ú-ma mu-tum šu-ú ši-pa-tim qá-at-na-tim a-na aš-ša-ti-šu i-sa-da-ar-ma i-pa-qí-id.*
3. *i-na ṭú-pí-ka pa-ni-i-im ki-a-am ta-aš-pu-ra-am um-ma at-ta-a-ma i-na* gišMÁ-*ia ar-ka-am-ma iš-tu na-ri-im ša-ap-li-tim a-di na-ri-im e-li-tim al-li-ik.*

4. *ši-ka-ru-um a-na ša-te-e-em ù* ŠE *a-na a-ka-lim a-na ṣé-ri-ia a-di-ni ú-ul il-li-ku-nim am-mi-nim at-ti ma-am-ma-an la-a ta-ša-pa-ri-im i-na ki-it-tim a-ma-ra-aṣ-ma a-ma-a-at.*
5. *sí-in-ni-iš-tum ši-i a-na ša-ak-ni-im aš-šum ki-ri-im* ÚS.SA.DU *ka-ra-an ru-ba-tim ir-gu-um-ma da-a-a-nu a-na pí-i a-wa-at ši-bu-ti-šu ru-gu-um-ma-ša is-sú-ḫu-ma še-er-tam sí-in-ni-iš-tam i-mi-du ù ni-iš* ^{d}UTU *it-ma.*
6. *a-na mi-ni-im* DUMU.MEŠ *ši-ip-ri-ni iš-tu er-ṣe-tim e-li-tim a-di-ni la ur-du-nim.*
7. *i-na uz-ni-ia šar-ra-tam eš-me um-ma ši-i-ma* LUGAL *i-ša-rum mu-ti ka-ak-ki it-ti na-ak-ri-im i-ip-pé-eš-ma qá-aq-qá-ad na-ak-ri-im i-ma-aḫ-ḫa-aṣ i-na ep-še-tim an-ni-a-tim i-ši-id be-lu-ti-šu ù šu-um-šu ra-bi-a-am i-ša-ak-ka-an ki-a-am iq-bi-a-am.*
8. *ṭú-up-pí i-na ku-nu-ki-ia a-ka-an-na-kam-ma a-na be-lí-ia i-na qá-at tap-pé-e-ia a-ša-ap-pa-ra-am.*
9. *a-a-ú-um i-lum le-mu-ut-tam ù ma-ru-uš-tam an-ni-a-tim e-li-ia iš-ku-un.*
10. *wa-ta-ar-ti ša-am-nim ki-ma ṣi-ib-tim a-na a-wi-lim a-ma-da-ad-ma a-na-ad-din.*
11. *i-na* UD-*mi-im ša-a-ti ma-an-num i-da-ni-im-ma ma-an-num i-ni-iš.*
12. *mi-na-am a-na maḫ-ri-ia ta-ša-pa-ra-nim ù mi-na-am a-na maḫ-ri-ku-nu a-ša-pa-ra-am.*

G. Contracts. Normalize and translate the following texts:

1. A loan of barley (*TIM* 7 23 = Edzard, *Tell ed-Dēr* no. 23).

[1] x ŠE *ḫubullim*(UR$_5$.RA) [2] MÁŠ ŠE y ŠE *ú-ṣa-ab* [3] KI *Anum*(AN)-*pi$_4$-ša* [4] ^{I}*šu-ì-lí-šu* [5] DUMU *i-bi-*^{d}EN.ZU [6] *ilqe*(ŠU.BA.AN.TI) [7] *a-na e-bu-ri-im* [8] *i-na ma-aš-ka-nim* [9] ŠE-*am* MÁŠ.BI [10] *i-ma-da-ad* [11] *maḫar* (IGI) *i-túr-rum* DINGIR-*šu-a-bu-šu* [12] DUMU.ME(Š) *ì-lí-ub-lam* [13] *maḫar*(IGI) ^{d}EN.ZU-*e-mu-qí* DUMU *pí-ṣa-ia*

PNs: *Anum-pīša; Šū-ilīšu; Ibbi-Sîn; Iturrum; Ilšu-abūšu; Ilī-ublam; Sîn-emūqī; Pīṣāya.*

[1] *ê ḫubullim* 'interest-bearing (loan of) barley'.

[2] This line, grammatically, is a parenthetical insertion: ([1–6]) 'x interest-bearing barley—(as) the interest of the barley he will add y barley (more)—Š s. I. received from A.'

[8] *maškanum* 'threshing floor'.

2. Adoption (*VAS* 8 127 = Schorr, *VAB* 5, no. 8, adapted).

^{1} ^{Id}UTU-*a-pí-li* ^{2} KI *ša-ḫa-ma-tim* ^{3} ^{I}DUMU.MUNUS-*eš*$_4$-*tár ma-a*[*r-ti-ša*] ^{4} *ù ta-ri-bu-um ma-ri-*[*ša*] ^{5} ^{d}*bu-né-né-a-bi* ^{6} *ù ḫu-šu-tum* ... ^{7} *aššassu*(DAM.A.NI) ... ^{8} *a-na ma-ru-ti-im il-qú-ú* ^{9} *ù i-na ma-ri* ^{d}*bu-né-né-a-bi* ^{10} *ù ḫu-šu-tum* ^{11} ^{d}UTU-*a-pí-li* ^{12} *a-ḫu-šu-nu ra-bu-um* ^{13} *šum-ma a-na wa-ar-ki-a-at* ^{14} UD-*mi* ^{Id}UTU-*a-pí-li* ^{15} *a-na* ^{d}*bu-né-né-a-bi* ^{16} *ù ḫu-šu-tum* ^{17} *ú-ul a-bi at-ta* ^{18} *ú-ul um-mi at-ti* ^{19} *i-qá-bi* ^{20} ... ^{21} *a-na* KU[G.BABBAR] *i-na-di-nu-šu* ^{22} *ù šum-ma* ^{d}*bu-né-né-a-bi* ^{23} *ù ḫu-šu-*[*tum a-na* ^{d}]UTU-*a-pí-li* ^{24} *ma-ri-šu-nu ú-ul ma-ru-ni* ^{25} *at-ta i-qá-bu-ú* ^{26} *i-na bi-tim* ^{27} *i-te-lu-ú* ... $^{28–29}$ ... $^{30–36}$ Witnesses. ^{37} Date.

PNs: *Šamaš-āpilī*; *Šaḫamatum*; *Mārat-Ištar*; *Tarībum*; *Bunene-abī*; *Ḫuššūtum*.

^{13} *šumma* 'if' (see §17.3).

^{21} *-šu* 'him'.

$^{26–27}$ *ina* ... *ītellû* 'they will forfeit ... .

3. Receipt of silver for grain purchase (Szlechter, *TJA* 41 UMM G4).

^{1} x KUG.BABBAR ^{2} *a-na šâm*(ŠÁM) ŠE-*e* ^{3} KI ^{d}EN.ZU-*be-el-ap-lim* ... ^{4} *a-na qá-bé-e* ^{d}*za-ba*$_4$-*ba*$_4$-DINGIR DUMU *ib-ni-*^{d}*Adad*(IŠKUR) ^{5} ^{Id}*Nabû*(AG)-*ma-lik* DUMU ^{d}*Marduk*(AMAR.UTU)-*mu-ba-lí-iṭ* ^{6} *ù* ^{d}EN.ZU-*aḫam*(ŠEŠ)-*i-din-nam* DUMU *be-lí-ia* ^{7} *ilqû*(ŠU.BA.AN.TI) ^{8} [*i*]-*na ma-ḫir* ŠE-*e-šu-nu* ^{9} [ŠE]-*am imaddadū*(Ì.ÁG.E) $^{10–12}$ Witnesses. $^{13–16}$ Date.

PNs: *Sîn-bēl-aplim*; *Zababa-ilum*; *Ibni-Adad*; *Nabû-malik*; *Marduk-muballiṭ*; *Sîn-aḫam-iddinam*; *Bēlīya*.

^{2} ŠE-*e* for ŠE-*e-em* (see §24.4(a)).

^{4} *qabûm* here 'authorization'.

^{8} *maḫīrum* 'current/going price, rate'.

H. Transliterate, normalize, and translate:

1. 

2. 

3. 

4. 

LESSON SIXTEEN

16.1 The G Imperative

The Imperative is the form used for commands; it occurs only in the second person. With some modifications in the various weak root types (and in the derived stems), the form of the Imperative is essentially the Preterite without a prefix. Thus, the theme vowel of the Imperative is always that of the Preterite. The usual second person endings, *-ī* for the fem. sg., *-ā* for the common pl., also occur on the Imperative.

(a) Sound Verbs. Without its prefix, the base of the Preterite of sound verbs begins with two consonants. Since that situation is not tolerated in Akkadian, a vowel is inserted between the first two radicals; for all but a very few roots (listed below), the vowel inserted is the same as the Preterite theme-vowel. Because of the vowel syncope rule (§4.1), when the fem. sg. ending *-ī*, the pl. ending *-ā*, and the Ventive ending *-am* are added, the theme-vowel between R_2 and R_3 drops out. In the following paradigm, forms with the Ventive are given in parentheses.

	šakānum (a–u)	*paqādum (i)*	*ṣabātum (a)*
ms	*šukun (šuknam)*	*piqid (piqdam)*	*ṣabat (ṣabtam)*
fs	*šuknī (šuknīm)*	*piqdī (piqdīm)*	*ṣabtī (ṣabtīm)*
cp	*šuknā (šuknānim)*	*piqdā (piqdānim)*	*ṣabtā (ṣabtānim)*

As the forms given here indicate, the fs and cp undergo no further changes when the Ventive is added, and this is true for all verb types. Hence, for the weak root types presented in the following paragraphs, only the ms will be presented with its corresponding Ventive form (in parentheses); for the Ventive on the fs, add *-m*, on the cp, add *-nim*, as with the Preterite and Durative.

The only sound verbs in which the vowel inserted between R_1 and R_2 differs from the theme-vowel are five *a*-class verbs:

lamādum 'to learn';
palāḫum 'to fear, worship';
pašāḫum 'to refresh oneself';
rakābum 'to ride, mount';
takālum 'to trust'.

In these verbs the vowel inserted between R_1 and R_2 is *i*: e.g., ms *rikab* (with Ventive *rikbam*), fs *rikbī*, cp *rikbā*.

(b) Verbs III–Weak. These offer few difficulties; the usual rules of vowel contraction are applied.

	banûm (i)	*ḫadûm (u)*	*malûm (a)*	*šemûm (e)*
ms	*bini (biniam)*	*ḫudu (ḫudâm)*	*mili (milâm)*	*šeme (šemeam)*
fs	*binî*	*ḫudî*	*milî*	*šemî*
cp	*biniā*	*ḫudâ*	*milâ*	*šemeā*

Notes: All verbs III–*a*, like the five exceptional sound verbs of the *a*-class listed above, have *i* between R_1 and R_2. Verbs III–*e* also occur with *i* between R_1 and R_2: *šime (šimeam), šimî, šimeā.* With the addition of *-ma*, the final vowel of the ms forms is lengthened: *binī-ma, ḫudū-ma, milā-ma, šemē-ma / šimē-ma.*

(c) Verbs I–*n*. The initial radical *n* does not appear in the G Imperatives of these verbs; forms begin with the copy of the theme-vowel (i.e., from *naqārum*, we find *uqur* ‹ **nuqur*, from *nadānum* we find *idin* ‹ **nidin*). Exceptions to the loss of the *n* are verbs that are also II–weak, such as *nêrum* (see e, below).

	naqārum (a–u)	*nadānum (i)*
ms	*uqur (uqram)*	*idin (idnam)*
fs	*uqrī*	*idnī*
cp	*uqrā*	*idnā*

(d) Verbs I–ʾ. The Imperatives of all verbs I–*a* begin with a short *a*, regardless of the theme-vowel; this applies to *alākum* as well. Verbs I–*e*, as expected, begin with *e* rather than *a*.

	aḫāzum (a–u)	*alākum (a–i)*	*epēšum (e–u)*	*ezēbum (i)*
ms	*aḫuz (aḫzam)*	*alik (alkam)*	*epuš (epšam)*	*ezib (ezbam)*
fs	*aḫzī*	*alkī*	*epšī*	*ezbī*
cp	*aḫzā*	*alkā*	*epšā*	*ezbā*

(e) Verbs II–weak. The Imperative of these verbs is in all instances simply the prefixless base of the Preterite, with no further modifications.

	târum (a–u)	*qiāšum (a–i)*	*šâmum (a)*	*nêrum (e)*
ms	*tūr (tūram)*	*qīš (qīšam)*	*šām (šāmam)*	*nēr (nēram)*
fs	*tūrī*	*qīšī*	*šāmī*	*nērī*
cp	*tūrā*	*qīšā*	*šāmā*	*nērā*

(f) Verbs I-*w*. For adjectival verbs I–*w*, such as *watārum*, no Imperatives are attested.

For active verbs I–*w*, as for verbs II–weak, above, the Imperative is the prefixless base of the Preterite. The Imperative of *babālum* is formed like those of other verbs I–*w*.

	wašābum (*a–i*)	*babālum* (*a–i*)
ms	*šib* (*šibam*)	*bil* (*bilam*)
fs	*šibī*	*bilī*
cp	*šibā*	*bilā*

For *wašābum* there also exists an alternate Imperative, with prefix *t-*: *tišab* (*tišbam*), fs **tišbī* (thus far unattested), cp *tišbā* or *tašbā*.

(g) Syntax of the Imperative. Like all other verbs, the Imperative stands at the end of its clause:

ina ālim šibī 'stay (fs) in the town';
aklam mādam u šikaram ṭābam ana ummānātīkunu idnā 'give (mp) much food and good beer to your troops';
šamnam leqeam-ma ana maḫrīya bilam 'obtain (ms) the oil and bring (it) to me'.

The Imperative is never used with a negative adverb. To express a negative command, i.e., to negate the Imperative, the Prohibitive is used (below, §16.3(a)).

16.2 The Precative

The Precative expresses either a wish or an indirect command (see further below); it occurs in the third and first persons (sg. and pl.), but not in the second person. Thus, with the Imperative, it forms a suppletive injunctive (command) paradigm.

The forms of the Precative, like those of the Imperative, are based on the Preterite. Third person forms and the 1cs form are marked by a prefix beginning with *l-* that replaces the prefix of the Preterite; the 1cp is marked by a preposed particle. As the examples will illustrate, the following rules apply to **all** the verbs in the language, including verbs I–*w* (also the derived stems, such as the D and Š, in which the prefix of the Preterite is *u-*; §§24.2, 27.1, etc.):

all 3rd person forms: the prefix *li-* replaces the *i-* or *u-* of the Preterite:
liškun 'let him/her place'; *lišbā* 'let them (f) dwell';

1cs, the prefix *lu-* replaces the *a-* or *u-* of the Preterite:
luškun 'let me place'; *lušib* 'let me dwell';

1cp: the Preterite is preceded by an unattached short *i*:
i niškun 'let us place'; *i nušib* 'let us dwell'.

In verbs I–ʾ and stative verbs I–*w*, in which the prefix vowel of the Preterite is long (because of the loss of the initial consonant), the vowel of the prefix in the Precative is likewise long: e.g.,

1cs *lūḫuz* 'let me seize'; *lūpuš* 'let me do';
3cs *līkul* 'let her/him eat'; 3mp *līterū* 'let them (m) increase'.

For reference, the G Precative of one of each verb type is given below.

	Sound	III–weak	I–*n*	I–*a*	I–*e*	II–weak	I–*w* (active)
	šakānum	*banûm*	*nadānum*	*aḫāzum*	*epēšum*	*târum*	*wašābum*
3cs	*liškun*	*libni*	*liddin*	*līḫuz*	*līpuš*	*litūr*	*lišib*
1cs	*luškun*	*lubni*	*luddin*	*lūḫuz*	*lūpuš*	*lutūr*	*lušib*
3mp	*liškunū*	*libnû*	*liddinū*	*līḫuzū*	*līpušū*	*litūrū*	*lišbū*
3fp	*liškunā*	*libniā*	*liddinā*	*līḫuzā*	*līpušā*	*litūrā*	*lišbā*
1cp	*i niškun*	*i nibni*	*i niddin*	*i nīḫuz*	*i nīpuš*	*i nitūr*	*i nušib*

The Ventive morpheme may be added to any Precative: e.g.,

lulqeam 'may I take (here)'; *i nitūram* 'may we come back';
lirdam 'may she come down'; *liddinūnim* 'may they (m) give to me'.

As stated above, the Precative expresses:

(a) a wish:

lillik 'may he go, would that he would go';
lukšud 'may I arrive, I would/I'd like to arrive, I wish to arrive';
i nīmur 'may we see, we would/we'd like to see';

(b) an indirect command:

lillik 'let him go, he should/ought to/must go';
lukšud 'let me arrive, I should/ought to/must arrive';
i nīmur 'let us see, let's see, we should/ought to/must see'.

Which of these nuances is intended for any given form must be determined from the context. The 1cs Precative is particularly common in questions: e.g.,

am-mīnim ana bīt abīya lullik 'Why should I go to my father's house?'
mīnam lūpuš 'What should I do/am I to do?'

The Precative also figures in the protases of unmarked conditional sentences (i.e., 'let/should x happen' = 'if x happens'; see §17.3), as in

> *kaspum līter limṭī-ma ul atâr-ma ul araggam* 'whether the silver increases or decreases, I will not contest again' (lit., 'let the silver increase, let it decrease, and ...'; *maṭûm* 'to decrease').

The Precative does not occur with a negative adverb; rather, a negative wish or indirect command is expressed with either the Vetitive or the Prohibitive (see the next section).

16.3 Negative Commands and Wishes

It was pointed out in the two foregoing sections that neither the Imperative nor the Precative may be used with a negative; instead, there are two distinct forms used to express negative commands and wishes: the Prohibitive and the Vetitive.

(a) The Prohibitive for all verbs consists of the negative adverb *lā* followed immediately by the Durative. It is used to express negative commands and prohibitions. Some examples:

> *lā tašappar* 'do not send, you may not send (ms)';
> *lā uššabū* 'they (m) may not/shall not stay';
> *lā terrubī* 'do not enter, you may not enter (fs)'.

It is important to note the very distinct meanings of *ul* and *lā* with the Durative in main clauses:

> *ul taturram* 'you (ms) do/will not come back, are/were not coming back';
> but *lā taturram* 'do not come back, you may not come back (ms)'.

(b) The Vetitive is formed by prefixing *ayy-* or *ē-* to the Preterite; the former occurs before vowels, the latter before consonants: e.g., for *šakānum*:

3cs	*ayy-iškun*	3mp	*ayy-iškunū*
		3fp	*ayy-iškunā*
2ms	*ē-taškun*	2cp	*ē-taškunā*
2fs	*ē-taškunī*		
1cs	*ayy-aškun*	1cp	*ē-niškun*

The allomorph *ayy-* may be indicated in the script by *a-*, *a-a-*, or *a*-IA; e.g., *ayy-iškun* may be written in any of the following ways:

> *a-iš-ku-un*, *a-a-iš-ku-un*, *a-ii*(IA)*-iš-ku-un*.

The Vetitive expresses a negative wish; it is therefore less forceful than the Prohibitive. Some examples:

ē-tamḫurā 'may you (pl) not receive, you should not receive';
ayy-itūrūnim 'may they (m) not come back, they should not come back';
ayy-amūt 'may I not die, I do not wish to die';
ē-nīmur 'may we not see, we do not wish to see'.

The Vetitive is found rather infrequently, and is occasionally replaced by the Prohibitive.

16.4 The Use of Injunctive Forms to Express Purpose

In a sequence of two or more clauses in which the first verb is an injunctive form, i.e., an Imperative, a Precative, a Prohibitive, or a Vetitive, and the following verb or verbs are also injunctive forms, and the verbs are connected either by *-ma* or, less often, asyndetically (§§7.4–7.5), the second and following clauses are often to be translated as purpose clauses (i.e., 'so that', 'in order that', 'that'). Some examples:

kaspam šuāti piqdam-ma ekallam lūpul-ma bītī lā iṣabbatū 'Provide (ms) me with the aforementioned silver, (so) that I may pay the palace, and/(so) that my estate not be seized';
bēlī âm ana wardīšu liddim-ma līkulū 'May my lord give grain to his menservants, (so) that they may eat';
mārī ṭurdam ittīšu ludbub 'Send my son here, that I may speak with him' (*dabābum* [*u*] 'to speak');
mimma lā takallâ-ma bītni i nibni 'Do not withhold (pl) anything, so that we may build our house' (*kalûm* [*a*] 'to withhold').

Especially common in letters is the imperative of *šapārum* followed by a precative, with the meaning 'give order that ... may happen':

šupur wardī šunūti ana ekallim liṭrudūnim 'Give (ms) order that those servants be sent here to the palace'.

Even the sequence {Precative(±*-ma*)+Imperative} may connote purpose:

warkatam liprusū-ma ṭēmam ṣabat 'They (m) should investigate the case so that you (ms) may take action' (*warkatum* see Vocabulary of this lesson).

When a verb in the second or following clause is the Prohibitive or the Vetitive, a translation involving 'lest' is often appropriate:

mê idnam-ma lā amât 'Give (ms) me water, lest I die';
ana mātim šuāti lā tallak-ma nakrum napištaka lā inakkis 'Do not go (ms) to that land, lest the enemy kill you' (lit., 'cut off your life').

EXERCISES

A. VOCABULARY 16.

Verbs:

etēqum (*i*) 'to pass along, pass by, advance, elapse; to pass through, across; to exceed, transgress; to avoid'.

palāḫum (*a*; Impv. irregular: *pilaḫ*) 'to fear, be afraid (of: acc.); to worship, respect, revere'; Verbal Adj. *palḫum* (*paliḫ-*) 'feared, fearsome; timid, reverential'.

petûm (*e*) 'to open' (transitive); Verbal Adj. *petûm* (*peti-*; fem. *petītum*) 'open'.

redûm (*e*) 'to escort, conduct, lead, guide; to drive (animals, ships, wagons), follow; to lay claim to; to move along'.

šaqālum (*a–u*) 'to weigh out (silver, etc.), pay'; Verbal Adj. *šaqlum* (*šaqil-*) 'weighed (out)'.

takālum (*a*; Impv. irregular: *tikal*) 'to trust (someone/something: + *ana*)'; Verbal Adj. *taklum* (*takil-*) 'trustworthy, true, reliable'.

tebûm (*e*) 'to arise, rise up, stand up; to occur, happen, appear on the scene; to set out'; Verbal Adj. *tebûm* (*tebi-*; fem. *tebītum*) 'standing, erect; under way; rebellious'.

Nouns:

ilkum (*ilik*; pl. *ilkū* and *ilkātum*) 'work or service performed, usually on a field, garden, for the state (king) by someone holding the land in tenure from the state; part of the yield of the land, i.e., payment; the land itself; the holder of the land'; *ilkam alākum* 'to perform such service, work such land' (cf. *alākum*).

šarrūtum (*šarrūt*; log. LUGAL(*-ru*)- [e.g., LUGAL(*-ru*)*-tam* = *šarrūtam*]) 'kingship; dominion; majesty'; *šarrūtam epēšum* 'to exercise kingship, rule as king'.

têrtum (*têrti*; with suf. *têrta-*; pl. *têrētum*) 'direction, instruction, order, command, commission; extispicy (examination of entrails), extispicy omen, oracle, omen report/diagnosis'; *têrtam* / *têrētim epēšum* 'to perform extispicy'.

warkatum (*warkat*; pl. *warkātum*) 'rear, back (part, side; of a building, person, animal); estate, inheritance; circumstances (of a legal case)'; *warkatAam parāsum* 'to investigate the circumstances of a case'.

Adjective:

šanûm (*šani-*; fem. *šanītum*) 'second; other, another; different' (see also §23.3(c)); as noun: 'another person, someone else'.

Conjunctions:

ū, lū, ū lū (*ū* written *ù*, like *u* 'and') 'or, either ... or' (see §7.4(f)):

(a) to connect nouns and noun phrases: *ḫurāṣum ū kaspum, ḫurāṣum ū lū kaspum* both for 'gold or silver'; *lū ḫurāṣum lū kaspum (ū) lū šīpātum* 'gold, silver, or wool';

(b) to connect clauses: *šib ū alik, šib ū lū alik, (ū) lū šib ū lū alik* all for '(either) stay or go'.

Divine Name:

Marduk (log. ^{d}AMAR.UTU) 'Marduk', chief god of Babylon.

B. Learn the following signs:

OB Lapid.	OB Cursive	NA	values
			*en* (lesson 10); EN = *bēlum*
			*ba**
		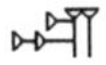	*zu, sú, ṣú*
		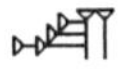	*su*
	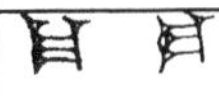		*ku, qú;** TUKUL, ^{giš}TUKUL = *kakkum*
			*ma**
			*gi₄, ge₄*
			*i*
		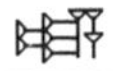	*ia, ie, ii, iu*
		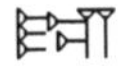	*ra*
			*gàr, qar*

			*ás / ṣ / z, áš*
	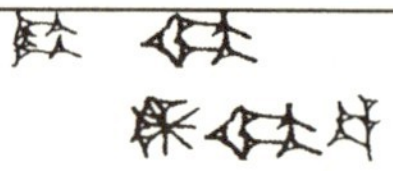		*ṣur;* AMAR, in ^{d}AMAR.UTU = *Marduk*

*Later forms of KU and MA are difficult to distinguish; in general, KU is somewhat narrower than MA. BA properly has the lowest horizontal at an angle; often, however, it is easily confused with MA and KU.

Note also ŠU.BA.AN.TI (also ŠU.BA.TI) = *ilqe*; ŠU.BA.(AN.)TI.(M)EŠ = *ilqû*.

C. Write the following words in cuneiform and in transliteration; use logograms where appropriate to write 12–15:

1. *imaggar*
2. *Igigi*
3. *nārātum*
4. *iṣbatā*
5. *rapaštam*
6. *qarrādum*
7. *ētiqam*
8. *izuzzum*
9. *marrātim*
10. *parāsum*
11. *alqû*
12. *māssu*
13. *ṣibat Marduk*
14. *eleppētīya*
15. *bēlam uṣur*

D. Write in normalized Akkadian:

1. open (ms) the door that I may enter
2. pay your (mp) entire tax
3. may they (m) judge your (fp) case so that you may pass through
4. let me pass by
5. do not (fs) seal your tablet
6. come down (pl)
7. may they (f) not accept your (mp) additional oil
8. protect (pl) the life of my exiled daughters
9. let us inspect our army
10. they (m) may not anoint
11. do (ms) not fall lest you die
12. come back (fs) that we may see your face
13. do not swear (fs) by the life of the king
14. sit down here (pl)
15. drink (ms) the fine beer
16. take (ms) a wife
17. he should board the full boat
18. open (fs) your mouth and let me hear your speech
19. may they (m) drive the healthy oxen
20. come here (fs)
21. do not (pl) slay the young ones (m)
22. eat (pl) much food that you may recover
23. cut down (ms) this tree lest it fall on our house
24. do not approach (pl)
25. enter (fs) to me
26. trust (fs) the good goddess
27. arise (pl)
28. may no one arrive here
29. take (ms) (to) the road
30. make (pl) war

31. bestow (fs) a great gift on (= to) me that I may rejoice
32. may we not die
33. look (pl) at my face and rejoice
34. may I not see this evil, that my god may favor me
35. build (ms) a narrow gate
36. let me write my just words
37. break (ms) the seal for me
38. strike (fs) the head of my subjected enemy
39. give (ms) me water
40. they (f) may not purchase anything at all
41. let's escape
42. fear (ms) the gods
43. may his days become long and prosper
44. it must not become old
45. pile up (pl) the grain on the ground
46. may the upper canal not widen
47. may the weak princess recover, that she may bear a son
48. add (ms) a field regularly
49. refresh yourself (ms)
50. destroy (pl) their (f) prison

E. Normalize and translate:

1. *am-mi-nim di-in ṣú-ḫa-ar-ti-ia la i-di-nu wa-ar-ka-as-sà pu-ru-ús-ma di-iš-ša di-in.*
2. *a-ḫi ṣe-eḫ-ru-um i-na ḫa-ra-an* LUGAL *a-wi-lum ša-nu-um i-li-ik-šu la i-la-ak.*
3. ABUL *pé-te-a-nim-ma a-na a-li-im lu-ru-um-ma na-ak-ri na-pí-iš-ti la i-na-ak-ki-is.*
4. *i-li* ÌR-*sú pa-al-ḫa-am li-ir-de-ma ma-ru-uš-tum mi-im-ma a-im-qú-tam.*
5. *eṭ-la-am a-a-am a-na ma-ru-tim e-le-eq-qé-ma šu-ú il-ki i-il-la-kam.*
6. *ni-šu ra-ap-ša-tum ka-lu-ši-na be-lu-ut* ^{d}AMAR.UTU DINGIR GAL *li-ip-la-ḫa.*
7. *mi-nam i-na pa-ni ši-bu-tim ta-qá-bi-i mi-im-ma le-em-na-am e-ta-aq-bi-i.*
8. *wa-ar-ka-at si-ni-iš-tim šu-a-ti ša* DUMU.MUNUS.MEŠ-*ša ú-ul ša mu-ti-ša ši-i.*
9. *a-wi-lum šu-ú* GEME$_2$ *ḫa-li-iq-tam i-na ṣe-ri-im iṣ-bat-ma a-na be-li-ša ir-de be-el* GEME$_2$ *ša-ti* KUG.BABBAR *a-na a-wi-lim li-id-di-in.*
10. *ù lu eq-li li-tu-ra-am ù lu eq-lam ša-ni-a-am ki-ma eq-li-ia li-di-nu-nim.*
11. *a-na-ku ù a-ḫi tap-pu-tam i ni-pu-uš.*

12. *a-na qá-bé-e ma-nim ṭe-em te-er-tim šu-a-ti a-na ma-aḫ-ri-ia la ta-aš-pu-ra-am.*
13. *wa-ar-ka-at* É-*ia la-be-ri-im li-im-qú-ut-ma* É *eš-ša-am e-pé-eš.*
14. DUMU.MEŠ *eq-le-tim za-ka-tim ša a-bi-šu-nu mi-tim li-im-du-du-ma li-zu-zu.*
15. ŠE *ša-aq-la-am i-na qá-at* ÌR-*ka ta-ak-li-im ku-uṣ-ri-im-ma šu-up-ri-im.*
16. LUGAL *im-ḫu-ru-ma um-ma šu-nu-ma mi-im-ma ša-ar-qá-am ša* EN *i-na qá-ti-ni li-iṣ-ba-tu-ma še-er-tam dan-na-tam li-mi-du-ni-a-ti* (*-niāti* = 'us').
17. *a-ḫi a-bi-ki i-na a-ma-ar ṭú-pi-ki an-ni-im li-it-be-am-ma a-na a-li-ni li-il-li-kam.*

F. Contracts:

1. Adoption (*VAS* 8 73 = Schorr, *VAB* 5, no. 9, adapted).

^{1} ^{I}*a-ḫu-wa-qar* ^{2} DUMU *ša-at-*^{d}*Adad*(IŠKUR) ^{3} KI *ša-at-*^{d}*Adad* (IŠKUR) *um-mi-šu* ^{4} ^{I}*ṣillī*(MI-*lí*)-^{d}*Adad*(IŠKUR) DUMU *e-ri-ib-*^{d}EN.ZU ^{5} *a-na ma-ru-ti-šu* ^{6} *il-qé* ^{7} *ù ma-ri ša-nu-tim ṣillī*(MI-*lí*)-^{d}*Adad* (IŠKUR) ^{8} *li-ir-ši-i-ma* ^{9} ^{I}*a-ḫu-wa-qar a-ḫu-um* GAL ^{10} ^{I}*a-ḫu-wa-qar a-na ṣillī*(MI-*lí*)-^{d}*Adad*(IŠKUR) ^{11} *a-bi-šu ú-ul a-bi* ^{12} *at-ta i-qa-bi-ma* ^{13} ... ^{14} ^{I}*a-ḫu-wa-qar a-na* KUG.BABBAR *i-na-di-in* ^{15} *ù ṣillī*(MI-*lí*)-^{d}*Adad*(IŠKUR) *a-bu-šu* ^{16} *a-na a-ḫu-wa-qar* ^{17} *ma-ri-šu ú-ul ma-ri* ^{18} *at-ta i-qa-bi-ma* ^{19} *i-na* É ... ^{20} *it-ta-aṣ-ṣí.*

PNs: *Aḫu-waqar; Šāt-Adad; Ṣillī-Adad; Erīb-Sîn.*
^{20} *ina ... ittaṣṣi* 'he will forfeit ...'.

2. Lease of a roof (Szlechter, *Tablettes* 68 MAH 16.643).

^{1} [1 *r*]*u-ug-ba-am* ^{2} KI *nu-nu-ri-ša-at* ^{3} ^{Id}*Nanna*(ŠEŠ.KI)*-tum* ^{4} *a-na šattīšu*(MU.1.KAM-*šu*) ^{5} *i-gu-ur* ^{6} *ki-iṣ-ri* ^{7} x KUG.BABBAR ^{8} [*išaq*]*qal* ([Ì.L]AL.E) $^{9–10}$ Witnesses. $^{11–14}$ Date.

PNs: *Nunu-rīšat; Nannatum.*
^{1} *rugbum* 'roof'.
^{4} *ana šattīšu* lit. 'for his year' = 'for one year'.
^{6} *kiṣrū* (pl) 'payment'.

3. Loan of silver, slaves to a father by a daughter (Pinches, *CT* 8 42b = Schorr, *VAB* 5, no. 41, lines 1–13 [lines 14–20 witnesses, 21 date]).

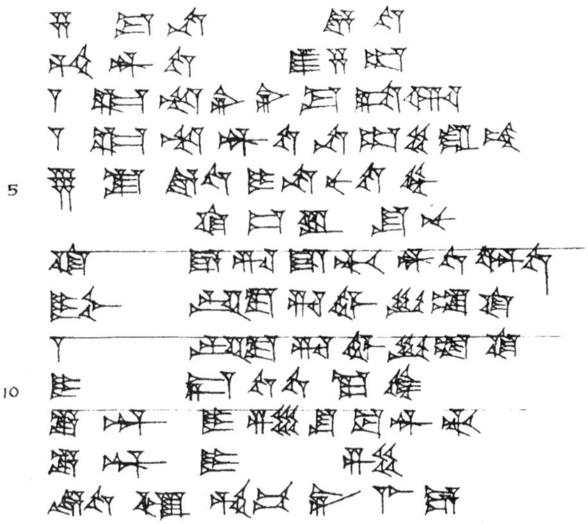

Signs not yet introduced, in the order in which they appear:

4; also *za, ṣa, sà*;

ì-lí;

ar;

8 GÍN;

KAM;

ME;

im, em;

ŠEŠ;

UNUG

lu;

mur;

ITI;

ù;

LAL

Notes:

PNs: *Ilī-maṭar*; *Šamaš-napšeram*; *Erišti-Šamaš*(f); *Sîn-rīm-Ur*; *Ebabbar-lūmur*.

[1] 4 MA.NA; read 4 *manā kaspam* '4 minas of silver' (see §23.2(b2)).

[2] Line 2 is a parenthetical sentence.

[5] 8 GÍN; read 8 *šiqil kaspum* '8 shekels of silver'; *i-na* MU.1.KAM (MU poorly formed) = *ina* 1 *šattim*.

[6] *kiṣrū* (pl.) 'payment'. Lines 5–6 are a parenthetical verbless sentence.

[7] SAL(MUNUS).ME = LUKUR = *nadītum* a type of priestess (see Vocab. 20).

[9] ŠEŠ.UNUG^{ki} = URI$_2^{ki}$ = *Ur* 'Ur'.

[10] UD.UD = BABBAR$_2$; É.BABBAR$_{(2)}$ = temple of Šamaš in Sippar.

[11] ITI = *warḫum* 'month'; ^{d}DUMU.ZI = *Dumuzi* (god and month name).

[13] Ì.LAL.E = *išaqqal*.

G. Transliterate, normalize, and translate:

1. 

2. 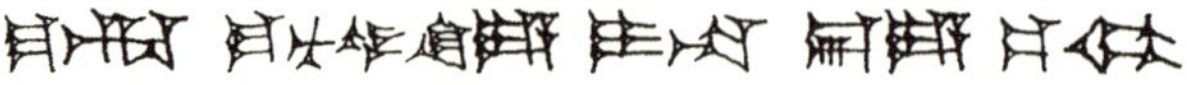

3. 

LESSON SEVENTEEN

17.1 The G Perfect: Sound Verbs; Verbs I–*n*; Verbs III–weak

The Perfect is a finite form of the verb, inflected with the same affixes for person, gender, and number as the Preterite and the Durative.

(a) Sound Verbs. The base of the G Perfect is $R_1taR_2VR_3$ (i.e., *ptarVs*). The predominant feature of the Perfect is an **infixed *-ta-*** immediately after the first consonant. The vowel between R_2 and R_3 is the **theme-vowel of the Durative**. When a vocalic suffix (pl *-ū*, *-ā*, 2fs *-ī*, the Ventive *-am*, Subordination marker *-u* [§19.2]) is added, the theme-vowel between R_2 and R_3 drops out in accordance with §4.1

	šakānum (*a–u*)	*šarāqum* (*i*)	*maqātum* (*u*)
3cs	*ištakan*	*ištariq*	*imtaqut*
2ms	*taštakan*	*taštariq*	*tamtaqut*
2fs	*taštaknī*	*taštarqī*	*tamtaqtī*
1cs	*aštakan*	*aštariq*	*amtaqut*
3mp	*ištaknū*	*ištarqū*	*imtaqtū*
3fp	*ištaknā*	*ištarqā*	*imtaqtā*
2cp	*taštaknā*	*taštarqā*	*tamtaqtā*
1cp	*ništakan*	*ništariq*	*nimtaqut*

3cs forms with the Ventive: *ištaknam, ištarqam, imtaqtam.*

When the first radical of the root is *d, ṭ, s, ṣ,* or *z* (but not *š*), the infixed *-t-* of the Perfect is assimilated completely to that consonant throughout the paradigm. Consider the following 3cs forms:

iddamiq (*damāqum*); *iṣṣabat* (*ṣabātum*);
iṭṭarad (*ṭarādum*); *izzaku* (*zakûm*);
issaḫap (*saḫāpum*); but *ištakan* (*šakānum*).

The writing of certain forms from these roots (and also from roots with first radical *t*, such as *takālum*) may ambiguously represent either Perfects or Duratives, if no doubling is indicated in the script; e.g.,

i-ṭa-ra-ad may be Durative *iṭarrad* or Perfect *iṭṭarad;*
ta-ṣa-bat may be Durative *taṣabbat* or Perfect *taṣṣabat.*

Only Perfect forms exhibit vowel syncope, however:

i-ṭa-ra-du may only be Durative *iṭarradū*, while *i-ṭa-ar-du* may only be Perfect *iṭṭardū*;

ta-ṣa-ba-ti may only be Durative *taṣabbatī*, while *ta-ṣa-ab-ti* may only be Perfect *taṣṣabtī*.

In forms with first radical *g*, the infixed *-t-* of the Perfect usually becomes *-d-*:

3cs *igdamar*; 2fs *tagdamrī*; etc.

(b) Verbs I–*n*. The initial radical *n* assimilates to the infixed *-t-*:

	naqārum (*a–u*)	*nadānum* (*i*)
3cs	*ittaqar*	*ittadin*
2ms	*tattaqar*	*tattadin*
2fs	*tattaqrī*	*tattadnī*
1cs	*attaqar*	*attadin*
3mp	*ittaqrū*	*ittadnū*
3fp	*ittaqrā*	*ittadnā*
2cp	*tattaqrā*	*tattadnā*
1cp	*nittaqar*	*nittadin*

3cs forms with the Ventive: *ittaqram*, *ittadnam*.

(c) Verbs III–weak. Again, these resemble sound verbs, but without a final radical. With the addition of endings, the theme-vowel is subject to the normal rules of vowel contraction (rather than syncope, as in sound verbs). In verbs III–*e*, both the *-a-* after the infixed *-t-* and the *-a-* of the prefixes become *e*:

	banûm (*i*)	*ḫadûm* (*u*)	*malûm* (*a*)	*leqûm* (*e*)
3cs	*ibtani*	*iḫtadu*	*imtala*	*ilteqe*
2ms	*tabtani*	*taḫtadu*	*tamtala*	*telteqe*
2fs	*tabtanî*	*taḫtadî*	*tamtalî*	*telteqî*
1cs	*abtani*	*aḫtadu*	*amtala*	*elteqe*
3mp	*ibtanû*	*iḫtadû*	*imtalû*	*ilteqû*
3fp	*ibtaniā*	*iḫtadâ*	*imtalâ*	*ilteqeā*
2cp	*tabtaniā*	*taḫtadâ*	*tamtalâ*	*telteqeā*
1cp	*nibtani*	*niḫtadu*	*nimtala*	*nilteqe*

3cs forms with the Ventive: *ibtaniam*, *iḫtadâm*, *imtalâm*, *ilteqeam*.

17.2 The Meaning of the Perfect

As a tense, the Perfect often corresponds roughly to the English present perfect, as in

aštakan 'I have placed'.

As with the Durative, however, a discussion of the use or meaning of the Perfect cannot be confined to tense alone; other important nuances are also involved. Further, the Perfect has slightly different uses in different genres of texts. In general, it may be said that, in main clauses, the Perfect denotes the central event in a sequence of events, the event on which the action in subsequent clauses is based.

Old Babylonian laws, exemplified by the "Laws of Hammurapi" (see below, §17.4), usually consist of two sets of clauses, of which the first set, called the protasis, presents the circumstances of a given case, most often with verbs in the Preterite and/or Perfect. The protasis almost always begins with *šumma* 'if', and is thus a conditional clause (see the next section). If the protasis consists of one clause, the verb may be either Preterite or Perfect: e.g.,

šumma awīlum makkūr ilim ... išriq 'If a man stole property (*makkūrum*) belonging to (lit.: of) a god ...' (Law §6);

but *šumma awīlum mār awīlim ṣeḫram ištariq* 'If a man kidnapped (lit.: stole) the young son of a(nother) man ...' (Law §14).

If, however, the protasis consists of a sequence of more than one clause, most often only the verb of the last clause (sometimes of the last two) is Perfect, while the verb(s) of the foregoing clause(s) is (are) Preterite. The last verb is Perfect because it indicates the critical event, the event upon which the judgment in the second set of clauses (the apodosis) is based: e.g.,

šumma awīlum alpam īgur-ma ilum imḫassū(< *imḫaṣ-šu*)*-ma imtūt* 'If a man rented an ox and a god struck it (*-šu*), and it has died (*imtūt*, Perfect of *mâtum*), (the man who rented the ox will swear an oath and be set free)'.

The Perfect does not normally occur in relative clauses (see §19.3).

In OB letters (see §24.5), the Perfect again has a focusing nuance; it indicates the crucial event, the main point, of the letter. Because of this assertive or emphatic nuance, it does not often occur in questions, in relative clauses (similarly in the Laws), or after a negative (unlike the Laws). Further, as the central statement of the letter, the Perfect is not usually followed by *-ma*. Instead, the next main clause verb (if there is one), is almost always an injunctive form (i.e., Imperative, Precative, Prohibitive, Vetitive). These points are illustrated by the following sequence of clauses:

> *Ṭēm šiprātim ... ul tašpuram. Nabi-Sîn ana Bābilim īliam-ma ṭēmka ... ul tašpuram. Inanna Nabi-Sîn ana maḫrīka aṭṭardam: ittīšu ana eqlim rid-ma ... ina ṭuppīka ... šupram.*
>
> 'You (ms) have not sent me a report of the work ... Nabi-Sîn has come up (*īliam*, a Preterite) to Babylon, but you have (still) not sent me your ... report. I have now (*inanna*) sent Nabi-Sîn to you: go down to the field with him, and ... (another Imperative) ... write me ... in your tablet.' (*Altbabylonische Briefe* 1 102:5–16)

In this text, the Perfect *aṭṭardam* presents the main point of the letter, the sending of Nabi-Sîn to the addressee. The clause with *aṭṭardam* begins with the adverb *inanna* 'now'; this adverb, or another, *anumma* 'now, herewith, hereby', or both (*inanna anumma*), often (but not necessarily) accompany the Perfect, to emphasize the immediacy, the current relevance, of the event. This use of the Perfect, in which the verb may denote the actual performance of the action it describes, is variously termed by grammarians the "announcement Perfect" or "epistolary Perfect." (Some scholars prefer, in such cases, to translate the Perfect into English by the present rather than by the present perfect; in the example above: 'I now send Nabi-Sîn ...'.)

In letters, since the Perfect does not normally occur after a negative, but is replaced by the Preterite, the latter is often to be translated by the English present perfect in such cases:

> *amatka ḫaliqtam ul nīmur* 'we have not seen/did not see your (ms) escaped womanservant'.

The choice of the English tense, of course, will depend on the context.

The Perfect is uncommon in OB contracts. A majority of the few attested main clause examples occur in direct quotes. As in other genres, the Perfect in contracts may be said to convey the central point of a section of text, but unlike the case with letters, it is not necessarily followed by an injunctive form:

> *inanna umma šū-ma x âm ana* PN ... *amtadad âm ul anaddinakkum* 'Now (*inanna*) thus he (said): "I have paid x grain to PN ...; I will not give grain to you (*-akkum*)"' (Schorr, *VAB* 5 273:37–39).

In subordinate clauses (especially temporal clauses), the Perfect usually emphasizes the anteriority of the action to that of the main clause; thus, it acts like the future perfect in English. See further §26.2.

17.3 Conditional Sentences

A conditional sentence consists of two parts, a **protasis** ('if ...') and an **apodosis** ('then ...'), each of which consists of one or more verbal or verbless clauses. A conditional sentence may be unmarked (i.e., have no explicit word for 'if') or, more commonly, marked with *šumma* 'if'.

(a) Unmarked conditions consist simply of two or more clauses connected with *-ma* (see §7.4(c)). In many OB examples, the tense in both the protasis and the apodosis is the Durative: e.g.,

> *kasapka ana Bābilim ul tubbalam-ma âm ul anaddin* 'Should you (ms) not/If you do not bring your silver to Babylon, I would/will not give (you) grain';
>
> *nakrum ana mātīni irrum-ma alpīni iṣabbat-ma napištašu ninakkis* 'Should/If the enemy enter(s) our land and (try/tries to) seize our oxen, we will kill him (cut off his life)'.

In other examples, the protasis has instead the Preterite, as in

> *mamman ul taškum-ma šīpātim išarriqū* 'Should you not appoint someone, the wool will be stolen',

or the Precative (see §16.2, end), which often has concessive force ('though, even if'):

> *mārī šanûtim liršû-ma* PN *aḫūšunu rabûm* 'Even if they (the adoptive parents) acquire other children, PN will be their older brother'.

(b) More frequent are conditional sentences in which the protasis begins with *šumma* 'if'. In such sentences, there is no conjunction between the protasis and the apodosis, and no word for 'then'. The negative adverb in protases beginning with *šumma* is *lā* (in apodoses, it is *ul*, unless a negative command is called for).

The apodosis in most OB examples normally either contains a form indicating present or future time (i.e., Durative, Imperative, Precative, Prohibitive, or Vetitive) or is a verbless clause (including the Predicative construction, for which see §22.1).

In the protasis, on the other hand, the action is normally represented as having already taken place. (Thus, a conditional sentence with *šumma* is literally of the form: 'Given that/If a person did/has done X, one will do/does Y'.) Like the apodosis, the protasis may involve a verbless clause or clauses; in verbal clauses, the tense may be Preterite, Perfect, or Durative. For the distinction between the Preterite and the Perfect, see the preceding section. The Durative in a protasis expresses either habitual activity, as in

šumma eqlam ikkal 'if he uses the field (generally)',

or intent, wish, or obligation, as in

šumma kaspam inaddin 'if he wishes/intends to give the silver'.

The following additional examples will further illustrate the conditional sentence:

šumma kaspum ina qātīka alkam-ma idnam 'If the silver is in your possession, come and give (it) to me';
šumma awīlum kaspam išriq/ištariq qāssu inakkisū 'If a man stole silver, his hand will be cut off';
šumma awīlum alpam iggar idūšu x ûm 'If a man wishes to hire an ox, its hiring-fee (*idum*) is x grain'.

17.4 The "Laws of Hammurapi"

Hammurapi, the sixth and most illustrious of a line of Amorite kings in Babylon, ruled ca. 1792–1750 BCE. Near the end of his reign, after he had conquered most of Mesopotamia, he ordered that a collection of laws be inscribed and set up in a public place. The most important monument on which these laws are preserved is a large (2.25 m. high) stela of polished black diorite, which was placed on display in the temple of Shamash (the sun god) in the city of Sippar. When the neighboring Elamites invaded Babylonia in the mid-twelfth century BCE, they removed the stela to their capital in Susa. In the late nineteenth century CE, Susa was excavated by a French expedition, which discovered the monument and removed it to the Louvre in their capital. The inscription on the stela is the longest OB document extant. It consists of three parts: a prologue, in poetic style (see §30.2), describing the gods' naming Hammurapi "to proclaim equity in the land, to destroy the wicked and the evil, that the strong not oppress the weak"; a collection of 282 laws, dealing with many aspects of society (see below); a long epilogue, also in poetic language, which includes curses and blessings upon those who would destroy the stela or refurbish it properly.

The laws are case-laws, typical not only of Mesopotamia but of many ancient Near Eastern cultures. (In Mesopotamia, the format has antecedents in earlier Sumerian laws.) Each law presents a legal situation in the form of a conditional sentence: 'If such and such (has) occurred, this and that will/should be done'. Not infrequently, the situation presented in one law is an elaboration or variation of that given in the previous law: e.g., Law §3 deals with perjury in a capital case, Law §4 with perjury in a case involving commodities. The laws appear to be arranged by topics, but the precise topics or categories that governed the arrangement remain debated by scholars. To give the reader some idea of the contents, a broad overview of the topics covered may be presented. (Note: the numbering of the laws or paragraphs, although it follows the text of the stela, is modern.)

§§1–5	Trials (perjury; corrupt judges).
§§6–14	Theft, robbery of property (including slaves; kidnapping).
§§15–65 (and fragments)	Land and land tenure.
(fragments and) §§100–126	Commerce (merchants; financial transactions; debt; safe keeping).
§§127–194	The family (women; marriage; concubines; inheritance; adoption).
§§195–214	Assault.
§§215–277	Professional fees and responsibilities; rates of hire.
§§278–282	Slaves.

Since shortly after its discovery, the collection of laws inscribed on Hammurapi's stela has been referred to as the "Code of Hammurapi." Although they do not strictly constitute a code, but rather merely a collection, we will follow the custom of referring to the laws by the abbreviation CH.

Duplicates of some of the laws, and laws that are missing where the stela was damaged in antiquity, are preserved on numerous fragmentary clay tablets. Fragments of at least one other diorite stela were also found at Susa, and it has often been suggested that copies of the stela were set up in other cities. It should also be noted that other collections of laws have been found in Mesopotamian sites; some of these collections, both in Sumerian and in Akkadian, predate that of Hammurapi.

A few laws from CH will be given in the exercises to each of the subsequent lessons, most in transliteration but a few in the lapidary cuneiform of the stela. Most of the laws will be given unchanged from the original. Thus, they will not be presented in the order in which they occur on the stela; rather, the student will read laws for which sufficient grammar and vocabulary have been covered to allow a minimum of notes and glosses.

A recent presentation and discussion of CH may be found in Roth 1995: 71–142.

EXERCISES

A. VOCABULARY 17.

Verbs:

kalûm (*a*) 'to detain, delay, keep in custody; to prevent, hinder (someone, something: acc.; from doing: *ana* or *ina* + Infin.); to refrain (from doing: *ana* + Infin.); to withhold, hold back (something: acc.; from someone: *ana*/dat. or *ina*)'.

paṭārum (*a–u*) trans.: 'to loosen, untie, remove, strip; to free, ransom, redeem; to end'; intrans.: 'to break camp; to withdraw, go away, disperse, desert, avoid'.

Note also *iddâk* (N stem of *dâkum* [see §32.1], Durative 3cs) 'he/she will be executed'.

Nouns:

aḫum b (bound form *aḫ* [usually written *a-aḫ*] or *aḫi*; pl. rare) 'arm; side, flank; bank (of a river, canal), shore, edge; half, first half'; note also the relative adjective *aḫûm* (base *aḫī-*; fem. *aḫītum*) 'strange, foreign; hostile; unusual, additional'.

lētum (*lēt(i)*; pl. rare) 'cheek; side, vicinity, nearby region'.

mišlum (*mišil*; log. MAŠ) 'half; middle'.

pīḫatum (also *pāḫatum*; bound form *pīḫat, pāḫat*) 'responsibility, obligation, duty'; *ana pī/āḫatim šakānum* 'to assign to a task'; *bēl pī/āḫatim* 'deputy, delegate; commissioner'.

rittum (*ritti*; suff. *ritta-*; dual *rittān*) 'hand; possibility'.

ṣimdatum (*ṣimdat*; pl. *ṣimdātum*) 'royal decree; (specific) royal regulation' (also *ṣimdat šarrim*).

šīmum (*šīm(i)*; pl. *šīmū* and *šīmātum*; log. ŠÁM) 'purchase; price; article purchased' (cf. *šâmum*).

Adverbs:

anumma 'now, hereby, herewith'.

inanna 'now'; *(ina) kīma inanna* 'right now'.

Preposition:

warki (with suf. *warkīšu*, etc.) locally 'behind, in back of'; temporally: 'after, after the departure of, after the death of'.

Conjunction:

šumma 'if'.

B. Learn the following signs:

OB Lapid.	OB Cursive	NA	values
			*maš**; MAŠ = *mišlum;*
			*bar, pár**
			DUB = *ṭuppum***
	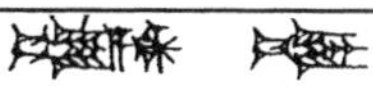	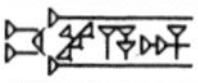	ŠÁM = *šīmum*
			GUD (or GU$_4$) = *alpum*
			*da, ṭa*
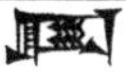	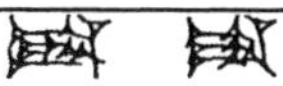	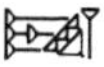	*id/t/ṭ, ed/t/ṭ*
			*ni, né, ì* (in *ì-lí* for *ilī;* rare otherwise); *lí* (only in *ì-lí* for *ilī, be-lí* for *bēlī,* and a few other archaic spellings); .NI denotes Sum. 'his', 'her', i.e., Akk. *-šu, -ša* (for personal/divine referent), e.g., DUMU.NI = *māršu* 'his son' or *mārša* 'her son'; Ì = *šamnum;* in Ì.GIŠ, also = *šamnum*
			*ir, er*
	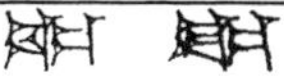		*ka*
			ERIN$_2$ (or ERIM) = *ṣābum; ummānum*
			*ši, še*$_{20}$*, lim;* IGI = *īnum; maḫrum* (and bound form *maḫar* 'before', before names of witnesses), *maḫrûm; pānum, pānū, pānûm; šībum*

*Distinct signs in the early period, MAŠ and BAR coalesced in later scripts, such as the Neo-Assyrian.

**In OB cursive, forms of DUB are often indistinguishable from forms of UM.

C. Write the following words in cuneiform and in transliteration; use logograms where appropriate in 14–15:

1. *unammaš*
2. *nimmar*
3. *eṭṭettum*
4. *kabātum*
5. *gerrum*
6. *maškum*
7. *irrū*
8. *kasûm*
9. *ulabbar*
10. *nišappar*
11. *ikūn*
12. *marṣum*
13. *nimaggar*
14. *īn alpīšu*
15. *šīpāt bēlīya*

D. Write in normalized Akkadian:

1. I have ransomed your (ms) missing female slave.
2. You (fs) have torn down the old door.
3. We have adopted our female employee.
4. They (m) have trusted that goddess.
5. You (pl) have set out for the lower country.
6. He has anointed the sick prince.
7. They (f) have drunk the fine beer.
8. You (ms) have sent the youths to me.
9. You (fs) have acquired much gold.
10. The gods have gathered in heaven.
11. They (m) have removed the judge for the queen's sake.
12. I have approached (Ventive) the bank of the upper river.
13. They (f) have seized your (fs) deputy and have struck his cheek.
14. The chief of the captives has fallen at the feet of the governor.
15. I have placed (Ventive) my chariot at your (ms) disposal.
16. They (m) have held the other woman in prison according to the royal decree.
17. We have not heard the dogs.
18. The wide fields have filled with water.
19. If a man made out a tablet and has sealed (it), no one may open (it).
20. The people have feared your name.
21. My eyes have observed the sun.
22. They (m) have settled their lawsuit in their neighborhood.

E. Normalize and translate:

1. *a-wi-lum šu-ú* GUD.MEŠ-*ia i-gur-ma i-na-an-na* GUD.MEŠ-*a šu-nu iḫ-ta-al-qú a-wi-lum šu-ú* ŠÁM GUD.MEŠ-*ia li-di-nam ù lu* GUD.MEŠ *ša-nu-ú-tim ki-ma* GUD.MEŠ-*ia li-ša-ma-am.*
2. *šum-ma mu-tum aš-ša-sú i-iz-zi-ib a-na* IGI LUGAL *i-il-la-ak-ma wa-ar-ka-sú i-pár-ra-sú.*

3. *wa-ar-ki um-mi-ni* MAŠ KUG.BABBAR-*ša a-na a-ḫi-ni ṣé-eḫ-ri-im a-na pí-i te-er-ti-ša ni-qí-iš.*
4. ERIN$_2$.MEŠ-*ka ka-la-ši-na a-na ṣe-ri-ia re-de-a-am-ma ḫa-ra-nam i ni-iṣ-bat-ma na-ak-ra-am ù* ERIN$_2$-*šu i ni-né-er.*
5. ^{d}EN.LÍL *i-na pu-ḫu-úr* DINGIR.MEŠ *be-lu-ut* KALAM.MEŠ *a-na* ^{d}AMAR.UTU *id-di-in ù be-lu-ut* AN-*e a-na* ^{d}UTU *id-di-in.*
6. *a-wi-lum a-ḫu-um i-te-bé-ma i-na ku-sí* LUGAL-*tim uš-ša-ab.*
7. *it-ti ṣú-ḫa-ri-ia ri-da-nim-ma ta-pu-tam it-ti-ia ep-ša.*
8. *eq-le-tim a-na me-e ni-zi-ma a-a-um-ma eq-le-tim ši-ip-ra-am ú-ul i-pé-eš.*
9. *a-nu-um-ma ṭe*$_4$*-em il-ki-im šu-a-ti a-na be-lí-ia aš-tap-ra-am be-lí* ŠE-*a-am mi-im-ma a-na* ÌR-*šu la i-ka-al-la-am* ŠE-*a-am šu-up-ra-am-ma la a-ma-a-at.*
10. LUGAL *da-an-nu-um né-me-tam ra-bi-tam e-li ni-ši ši-na-ti iš-ku-un am-mi-nim né-me-ta-ši-na a-na* É.GAL *la ub-la-nim.*
11. *am-mi-nim ri-it-ta-ki e-li a-aḫ* DUMU.MUNUS-*ki ta-aš-ku-ni.*
12. ERIN$_2$.MEŠ-*ia lu-up-qí-id-ma a-na ma-ḫa-aṣ na-ak-ri-ia li-li-ku.*
13. *a-ḫu-ú-tum iš-tu ma-tim le-mu-ut-tim ik-šu-du-nim-ma a-na* KI-*ti-ka i-ti-qú-nim i-na-an-na a-ḫu-ú-tum šu-nu* DUMU *ši-ip-ri-ia i-na* KI-*ti-ka iṣ-ṣa-ab-tu* DUMU *ši-ip-ri-ia i-na qá-ti-šu-nu pu-uṭ-ra-am-ma li-tu-ra-am.*
14. *i-na* MU *šu-a-ti aš-ša-ti maḫ-ri-tum* DUMU *ul-dam.*
15. *be-el-ti pa-ni-tum ki-a-am iq-bi-am um-ma ši-i-ma i-na-an-na i-ṣa-am dam-qá-am i-na li-ib-bi ša-di-i a-na* ^{giš}MÁ.MEŠ-*ia am-ra-a-ma ik-sa* ^{giš}MÁ.MEŠ-*ia ši-na-ti bi-ni-a-nim-ma a-na maḫ-ri-ia re-de-a-nim.*
16. *ša pí-i* DUB-*pí-im an-ni-im ki-ri-a-am* ÚS.SA.DU *ki-ša-ad na-ri-im mu-du-ud-ma a-na* DUB-*pí-ka ṣi-ib.*

F. CH. Normalize and translate the following laws:

§195 *šum-ma* DUMU *a-ba-šu im-ta-ḫa-aṣ ritta*(KIŠIB.LÁ)-*šu i-na-ak-ki-su.*

§205 *šum-ma* ÌR *a-wi-lim le-e-et* DUMU *a-wi-lim im-ta-ḫa-aṣ ú-zu-un-šu i-na-ak-ki-su.*

§247 *šum-ma a-wi-lum* GUD *i-gur-ma* IGI-*šu úḫ-tap-‹pí›-id* KUG.BABBAR *mi-ši-il* ŠÁM-*šu a-na be-el* GUD *i-na-ad-di-in.*

uḫtappid 'he has blinded'.

§14. Transliterate, normalize, and translate:

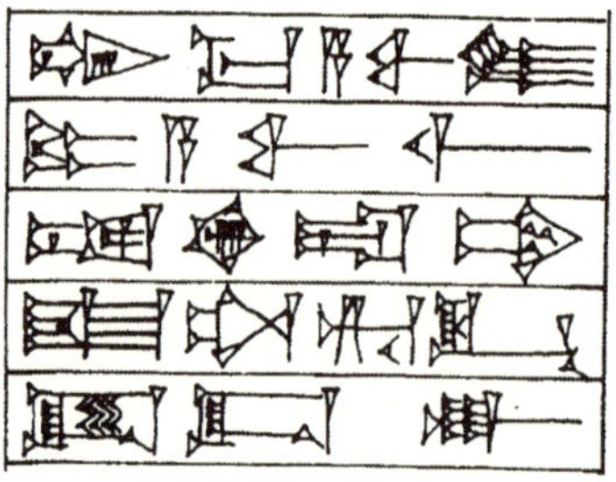

Signs not yet introduced, in the order in which they appear:

 *a;*

 *wi;*

 *lum;*

 *eḫ*

G. Contracts:

1. Marriage contract (Meissner, *BAP* no. 90 = Schorr, *VAB* 5, no. 2, adapted)

1 ^{I}*ba-aš-tum* ... 3 DUMU.MUNUS *ú-ṣí-bi-tum* 4 ^{I}*ri-mu-um* DUMU *ša-am-ḫa-tum* 5 *a-na aš-šu-tim ù mu-tu-tim* 6 *i-ḫu-uz* ... 11 [*šum*]-*ma* ^{I}*ba-aš-tum* 12 [*a-na*] *ri-mu-um* 13 [*mu-t*]*i-ša ú-ul mu-ti* 14 [*at-t*]*a iq-ta-bi* 15 [^{I}*ba-aš*]-*tum a-na na-ri-im* 16 *i-na-ad-du-ú* 17 [*šu*]*m-ma ri-mu-um* 18 [*a-n*]*a ba-aš-tum aš-ša-ti-šu* 19 *ú-ul aš-ša-ti at-ti* 20 *iq-ta-bi* x KUG.BABBAR 21 *i-ša-qal* 22 MU ^{d}UTU *ù* ^{I}*sa-am-su-i-lu-na* 23 *it-mu-ú* 24–29 Witnesses.

PNs: *Bāštum; Uṣi-bītum; Rīmum; Šamḫatum; Samsu-iluna* (king).
5 *aššūtum, mutūtum* cf. §14.4.
16 *nadûm* (*i*) 'to throw'.

2. Hire of a harvester (Szlechter, *Tablettes* 110 MAH 16.148).

1 1 GÍN KUG.BABBAR 2 *a-na ēṣidim*(ERIN$_2$.ŠE.KIN.KUD) 3 KI *ì-lí-i-qí-ša-am muʾir*(GAL.UKKIN.NA) ERIN$_2$ KÁ É.GAL 4 ^{Id}EN.ZU-*šar-ì-lí* DUMU *še$_{20}$-le-bu-um* 5 ŠU.BA.AN.TI 6 *ana ūm ebūrim*(UD.BURU$_{14}$.ŠÈ) *i-na eqlim*(A.ŠÀ) *pí-ḫa-at* 7 ^{I}*uṣ-ri-ia iššiakkim*(ENSI$_2$) 8 *ēṣidum*(ERIN$_2$. ŠE.KIN.KUD) *i-la-ak* 9 *ú-ul i-la-ak-ma* 10 *ki-ma ṣi-im-da-at šar-ri.* 11–14 Witnesses. 15–17 Date.

PNs: *Ilī-iqīšam; Sîn-šar-ilī; Šēlebum; Uṣriya.*
1 1 GÍN KUG.BABBAR = 1 *šiqil kaspam* '1 shekel of silver', the object of the verb in line 5 (see §23.2(b,2)).
2 *ēṣidum* (log. ERIN$_2$.ŠE.KIN.KUD [kud = tar]) 'harvester'.
3 *muʾirrum* (log. GAL.UKKIN.NA) 'director'; *ṣāb bāb ekallim* 'palace work force'.
7 *iššiakkum* (log. ENSI$_2$ [written pa+te+si]) 'farmer'.

[8, 9] *alākum* here may be rendered 'to work'.
[10] '(The penalty will be) according to ...'.

H. Transliterate, normalize, and translate:

1. 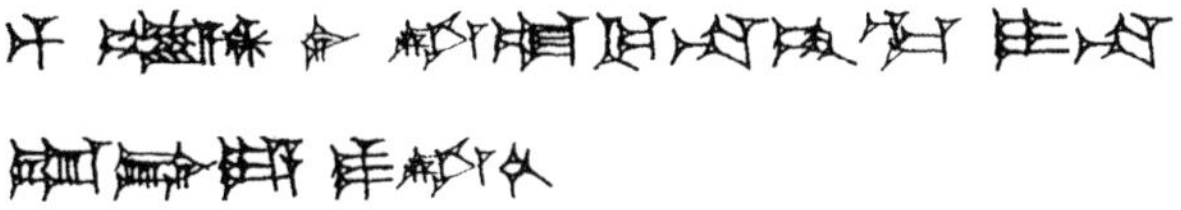

2. 

LESSON EIGHTEEN

18.1 The G Perfect: Verbs I–ʾ (I–*a* and I–*e*); *alākum*

Since the initial radical stood before another consonant (the infixed *-t-*), its loss resulted in the lengthening of the vowel of the prefix, as in the Preterite.

	amārum (*a–u*)	*arākum* (*i*)	*epēšum* (*e* / *u–u*)	*ezēbum* (*i*)	*erēbum* (*u*)
3cs	*ītamar*	*ītarik*	*ītepeš* / *ītepuš*	*ītezib*	*īterub*
2ms	*tātamar*	*tātarik*	*tētepeš* / *tētepuš*	*tētezib*	*tēterub*
2fs	*tātamrī*	*tātarkī*	*tētepšī*	*tētezbī*	*tēterbī*
1cs	*ātamar*	*ātarik*	*ētepeš* / *ētepuš*	*ētezib*	*ēterub*
3mp	*ītamrū*	*ītarkū*	*ītepšū*	*ītezbū*	*īterbū*
3fp	*ītamrā*	*ītarkā*	*ītepšā*	*ītezbā*	*īterbā*
2cp	*tātamrā*	*tātarkā*	*tētepšā*	*tētezbā*	*tēterbā*
1cp	*nītamar*	*nītarik*	*nītepeš* / *nītepuš*	*nītezib*	*nīterub*

Note also the following 3cs forms with the Ventive: *ītaḫzam, ītarkam, ītepšam, ītezbam, īterbam.*

alākum. As in the Preterite, *alākum* behaves like a verb I–*n* in the Perfect. The theme-vowel of the Perfect, as with all G verbs, is that of the Durative.

3cs	*ittalak*	3mp	*ittalkū*
		3fp	*ittalkā*
2ms	*tattalak*	2cp	*tattalkā*
2fs	*tattalkī*		
1cs	*attalak*	1cp	*nittalak*

With the Ventive, 3cs *ittalkam.*

18.2 Object Pronominal Suffixes on the Verb

Just as genitive personal pronouns occur as suffixes attached to nouns and prepositions, so object pronouns are suffixed to finite verb forms. There are two sets of these:

accusative suffixes, which denote the direct object of the verb;
dative suffixes, which denote the indirect object.

	Accusative	Dative
1cs	*-anni / -nni / -ninni*	*-am / -m / -nim*
2ms	*-ka*	*-kum*
2fs	*-ki*	*-kim*
3ms	*-šu*	*-šum*
3fs	*-ši*	*-šim*
1cp	*-niāti*	*-niāšim*
2mp	*-kunūti*	*-kunūšim*
2fp	*-kināti*	*-kināšim*
3mp	*-šunūti*	*-šunūšim*
3fp	*-šināti*	*-šināšim*

For the **accusative** suffixes, note the following particulars:

1cs: the form of this suffix is the Ventive morpheme plus *-ni*, with the *-m* of the Ventive assimilated to the *-n-* of the suffix: e.g., *iṣbatanni* 'she seized me'; *taṣbatīnni* 'you (fs) seized me'; *iṣbatūninni* 'they (m) seized me'; *taṣbatāninni* 'you (pl) seized me';

3fs: the form is *-ši*, as opposed to the genitive *-ša* on nouns;

1cp: *-āti* is added to the genitive *-ni*: *ina bītīni īmurūniāti* 'they (m) saw us in our house';

2,3 p: the suffixes are those of the set attached to nouns, with the addition of *-ti* and the lengthening of the preceding vowel: *ina bītīšunu nīmuršunūti* 'we saw them (m) in their house'.

The **dative** forms all end in *m* (a feature that is undoubtedly related to the Ventive morpheme):

1cs: for the 1cs dative, the Ventive form alone is used; see §15.2;

the other singular forms simply add *-m* to the accusative forms, with the notable exception, however, of the 2ms:

2ms: *-kum* (not ***-kam*);

the plural forms end in *-šim* in place of the *-ti* of the accusative forms.

When any of the suffixes, except the 1cs forms, is added directly to a form of a III–weak verb ending in a short vowel, that vowel is lengthened:

iklāšu 'she detained him'; *nileqqēšunūti* 'we will take them (m)';
qibīšim 'speak (ms) to her'; *luḫdūšim* 'let me rejoice for her'.

As is true of the genitive suffixes on nouns, *a*-vowels in the object suffixes are not subject to the vowel-harmony rule (i.e., do not change to *e*; see §7.2(e)):

> *eštemēka* 'I have heard you (ms)';
> *eppeškinâšim* 'I will act for you (fp)'.

The third person forms of both sets of suffixes are subject to the same changes as their genitive counterparts: final *d, t, ṭ, s, ṣ, z, š*, plus the *-š-* of the suffix change to *-ss-*, as in

aḫḫassi 'I will marry her';	*nimḫassunūti* 'we struck them (m)';
piqissu 'inspect (ms) it (m)';	*imqussum* 'it happened (fell) to him';
ikkissu 'he cut it (m) off';	*lūpussinâšim* 'let me act for them (f)'.

Both sets of suffixes follow all verbal morphemes, namely, 2fs *-ī*, pl *-ū, -ā*; the Ventive (see the next paragraph); the subordination marker *-u* (see §19.2); and the subject pronoun suffixes of the predicative construction (see §22.1). The suffixes precede the conjunction *-ma*, which, it will be recalled (§7.4), causes a preceding short vowel to be lengthened. Some examples:

> *ana mārīka taddiššū-ma ittīka imḫurūšu* 'You (ms) gave it (m) to your sons, and they accepted it from you';
> *āmurkinātī-ma aḫdu* 'I rejoiced when I saw you (fp)'.

Both sets of suffixes may follow the Ventive (with the exception of the 1cs dative, which **is** the Ventive; the 1cs accusative, as already noted, always includes the Ventive). The final *-m* of the Ventive is always assimilated to the first consonant of the suffix:

> *ublūniššu* 'they (m) brought him here (or: to me)';
> *ṣuḫārī aṭṭardakkum* 'I have sent you (ms) my servant';
> *tereddeāniššunūti* 'you (pl) will conduct them (m) here (or: to me)';
> *alkīnniāšim* 'come (fs) to us'.

The **dative case**, and, therefore, the dative suffixes, usually indicates the person or thing to which an action is directed, or for which an action is done; thus, it often corresponds to the use of the preposition *ana*; e.g.,

> *ana bēlīya allakam* 'I will come to my lord'; *allakakkum* 'I will come to you';
> *annītam ana mārīni nītepeš* 'we have done this for our sons'; *annītam nītepessunūšim* 'we have done this for them'.

A verb may have both a dative and an accusative suffix; when this occurs, the dative precedes the accusative, and the final *-m* of the dative suffix, like that of the Ventive, is assimilated to the following consonant. The Ventive may also appear, preceding both suffixes, as expected, so that the order is Verb–Ventive–Dative–Accusative:

aṭrudakkuššu 'I sent him to you (ms)'.

Occasionally in such instances, the singular accusative suffixes lose their vowel, and the resulting final doubled consonant is simplified: *aṭrudakkuš*.

A dative or accusative suffix is occasionally added to a verb redundantly from the English point of view, when the noun to which it refers is also present in the clause. **Resumptive pronouns**, as these are called, serve a number of discourse functions. In the following example the dative object stands at some distance from the verb; the resumptive pronoun makes the clause easier to grasp.

šumma awīlum ana aššatīšu eqlam kiriam bītam ū bīšam išrukšim 'if a man gave (*šarākum*) his wife a field, orchard, house, or moveable item of property (*bīšum*), ...' (CH Law §150).

While resumptive pronouns are more common when the nominal object is separated from the verb by a phrase or two, as in the preceding example, they are also found in shorter clauses. In the latter, the pronouns serve other functions: to announce a new topic (or the main topic, e.g., of a letter) or some other shift in a narrative (to a different subject, scene, or mood); to highlight a previously secondary topic; or to signal the end of a section of discourse. In the laws of Hammurapi sequences of laws often begin with a formulaic *šumma awīlum*; if *awīlum* is the direct object and accordingly appears in the accusative, it may retain its position after *šumma* and may be (but need not be) resumed by an object suffix, as in

šumma awīlam e'iltum iṣbassu 'if a financial obligation (*e'iltum*) "seized" a man, ...' (CH Law §117); note that the direct object here precedes the subject, deviating from normal word order.

As the two examples cited here illustrate, resumptive pronouns are frequently not represented in English translation.

It has already been noted (§§3.6, 10.4), that a pronominal direct object may be omitted. This deletion is particularly common when the same object is governed by two (or more) successive verbs, and is also possible in English. (The phenomenon is more common in Akkadian than in English, however.) An example:

wardum akalam išriq-ma īkul 'The male slave stole the food and ate (it)', or 'The male slave stole and ate the food'.

The nominal (or non-finite) forms of the verb, namely, the Infinitive (§3.3), the Verbal Adjective (§4.3), and the Participle (§20.1), take the genitive suffixes that are attached to nouns. With the Infinitive, a suffix may be subjective or objective, as is true of a genitive noun after an Infinitive (§8.2, end; further, §30.1); e.g.,

ana amārīša 'to see her' or 'for her to see'.

18.3 The Adverbial Use of the Accusative

The accusative case may be used adverbially, with a wide range of functions. In principle, any preposition (except probably *ana*) may be deleted, and the noun then put in the accusative, if the relationship of that noun to the rest of the sentence (particularly the verb) is clear without the preposition. There are, however, restrictions on the adverbial use of the accusative that are not yet well understood; thus, the student should learn to recognize the adverbial accusative, but should refrain from using it when constructing sentences in Akkadian. Among the uses of the adverbial accusative, the following may be noted:

(a) The accusative of **place**:

šarrāqam abullam iṣbatū 'the thief was seized (lit.: they seized the thief) at the city gate';

ṭuppaka Bābilim kunuk-ma šupram 'seal (ms) your tablet in Babylon (acc.) and send (it) to me';

māssunu uššabū 'they (m) will live in their land';

note also *maḫar* for *ina maḫar* 'before' (§12.3(c)).

(b) The **ablative** accusative, replacing *itti* (cf. §5.5):

qīšātīšunu lā teleqqēšunūti 'do not accept (ms) their (m) gifts from them (acc.)';

kaspam ašqul-ma ula imḫurūninni 'I paid the silver, but they (m) did not accept (it) from me (acc.)'.

(c) The accusative of **time**; this may indicate

(1) duration of time ("time how long"):

šalāš šanātim ina ālīni ušbū 'they (m) remained in our town (for) three (*šalāš*) years';

(2) the time when an action took/takes place; this usage is equivalent to *ina* with the noun in the genitive:

šattam šuāti (or *ina šattim šuāti*) *nakrum ana mātim īrub* '(in) that year, the enemy invaded the land'.

(d) The accusative of **respect**, **manner**, or **means**:

rīqūssu illak 'he will go empty-handed', lit.: 'in his emptiness' (_rīqūtum_ 'emptiness', acc.);

ḫamuttam alkam 'come (ms) quickly' (_ḫamuttum_ 'haste', acc.).

It was noted in the discussion of the indefinite pronouns (§14.3) that _mimma_ may be used adverbially:

mimma libbaka lā imarraṣ 'do not be (ms) upset in any way' (lit.: 'your heart must not become upset in any way').

18.4 Morphographemic Writings

In several lessons we have noted that certain sound changes are not always reflected in writing; the following are representative:

qá-ta-(at)-tum and _qá-ta-an-tum_ for expected _qatattum_ < _*qatantum_ 'thin', the fem. of _qatnum_, with assimilation of _n_ (§§5.1, 5.4);

similarly _ú-zu-(uš)-ša_ and _ú-zu-un-ša_ for expected _uzušša_ < _*uzunša_ 'her ear', with assimilation of _n_ (§11.1);

_ir-ka-(am)-ma_ and _ir-ka-ab-ma_ for expected _irkam-ma_ < _irkab_ + _-ma_ 'he rode and ...', with assimilation of _b_ to _m_ (§7.4).

Since sound changes normally take place without exception, that is, always produce the same form or pronunciation, the pairs of writings just cited must be considered variant spellings of a single form. The writings in which the sound change is reflected are **phonetic**, that is, they represent the actual pronunciations of the forms; the writings in which the sound change is not reflected are **morphographemic**, that is, they show the constituent morphemes of the forms more clearly. (As examples of morphographemic writings in English spelling we may cite spellings of plural words with the letter _s_ even when the plural marker is pronounced [z], as in _dogs_ for [dɔgz].)

A number of other morphographemic writings occurring in Akkadian texts may be noted here:

A stem-final dental or sibilant and the _-š-_ of third person pronominal suffixes become _-ss-_, as in _qāssa_ 'her hand', _aṭrussu_ 'I sent him'; _tapqissunūšim_ 'you (ms) entrusted to them (m)' (§§11.1, 18.2). In Old Babylonian, this change is usually reflected in writing (i.e., in phonetic spellings); occasionally, however, and more commonly in later dialects, writings that are partly morphographemic show a stem-final dental, although the suffix is always written with _-s-_: _qá-at-sà_, _aṭ-ru-ud-su_, _ta-ap-qí-id-sú-nu-ši-im_.

The Ventive morpheme may simply be "tacked on" the end of a verb, in violation of the otherwise regular spelling of words according to their syllabification; for example, while *išpuram* 'he sent to me' is usually written *iš-pu-ra-am*, as expected, it is occasionally written *iš-pur-am*; similarly, for *išpuranni* 'he sent me' both *iš-pu-ra-an-ni* and, less often, *iš-pur-an-ni* occur. In other examples, in order to avoid the use of a *VC* sign after another *VC* or a *CVC* sign (as in *iš-pur-am*) scribes wrote a *CV* sign that repeated the final consonant of the verb, so that a false doubling appears, as in *iš-pur-ra-am*, again for *išpuram* (or *iš-pur-ra-an-ni* for *išpuranni*); a very common example of this phenomenon, especially in PNs, is the writing *i-din-nam* for *iddinam* 'he gave to me'.

EXERCISES

A. VOCABULARY 18.

Verbs:

baqārum (*a–u*) 'to claim, lay claim to; to contest, bring suit (against someone: acc.; for something: acc. or *aššum* or *ana*)'; note *baqrū* (usually pl.) 'legal claims'; *baqrī rašûm* 'to incur legal claims'.

kabātum (*i*) 'to be(come) heavy, fat; to be(come) important, honored; to be(come) difficult, painful'; Verbal Adj. *kabtum* (*kabit-*) 'heavy, fat; difficult, painful; important, serious, honored'.

nasāqum (*a–u*) 'to choose, select'; Verbal Adj. *nasqum* (*nasiq-*) 'selected, chosen, choice, precious'.

palāšum (*a–u*) 'to pierce, break through, into'; note *pilšum* (*piliš*; pl. *pilšū*) 'breach, hole'.

riābum (*a–i*) 'to replace, give back'.

šarākum (*a–u*) 'to give, bestow'; note *širiktum* 'gift, dowry'.

zaqāpum (*a–u*) 'to erect, set up; to plant (a garden), prepare (a garden, field) for planting'.

Nouns:

asûm (gen. *asîm* or *asêm*, acc. *asâm* or *asiam*; bound form *asi*?; pl. *asû*; log. A.ZU; Sum. lw.) 'physician'.

makkūrum (*makkūr*; log. NÍG.GA) 'property, assets, valuables, goods'.

muškēnum (*muškēn*; pl. *muškēnū*; log. MAŠ.GAG.EN or MAŠ.EN.GAG) 'dependent, poor person, serf, commoner'.

simmum (*simmi*; suf. *simma-*) 'wound; (skin) disease, carbuncle'.

šīmtum (*šīmat* or *šīmti*; pl. *šīmātum*) 'what is established, fixed, decreed (by the gods), fate, destiny'; a euphemism for death, as in *ana šīmtim alākum* 'to die' (lit.: 'to go to one's fate').

terḫatum (*terḫat*) 'bride-price'.

zīttum (*zītti*; sf. *zītta-*; pl. *zīzātu*; substantivized fem. Verbal Adj. of *zâzum*, with irregular assimilation in sg. [given as *zittum* in the dictionaries]; log. ḪA.LA) 'share (of an inheritance); inheritance'.

Adverb:

mitḫāriš 'equally, to the same extent, each one; everywhere'.

B. Learn the following signs:

OB Lapid.	OB Cursive	NA	values
			*ad/t/ṭ* (lesson 11); AD = *abum*
	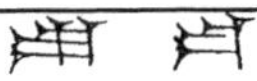		URU = *ālum*
			*tab, tap*; TAB in TAB.BA = *tappûm*
			DÙ = *banûm, epēšum*; GAG in MAŠ.GAG.EN or MAŠ.EN.GAG = *muškēnum*
	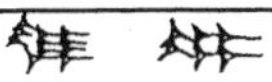	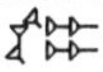	*lum, núm*
	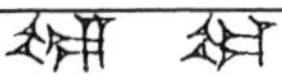	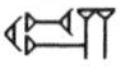	*lam*
	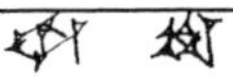		*te, ṭe₄*
			*kar*
			ŠÀ (or ŠAG₄) = *libbum*; A.ŠÀ (below)
			*a*; A in A.MEŠ = *mû*; A.BA = *abum*; . A.NI = .NI (lesson 17); A.ŠÀ = *eqlum*; A.ZU = *asûm*
			*ḫa*; ḪA.LA = *zīttum*

	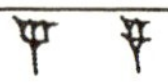		NÍG (or NÌ) (Sumerian for 'thing', frequent as a formative in compound words), in NÍG.GA = *makkūrum*
			LAL (or LÁ) = *šaqālum*, in Ì.LAL.E = *išaqqal*

C. Write the following words in cuneiform and in transliteration; use logograms where appropriate in 3–14:

1. *unakkar*	6. *zītti abīka*	11. *īn muškēnim*	16. *apālum*
2. *ištappar*	7. *makkūr ilim*	12. *ṣibat kaspim*	17. *irtede*
3. *šamaššu*	8. *mišil šīmim*	13. *ina libbi ṭuppim*	18. *ṭēḫam*
4. *tappûya*	9. *alpū ālīka*	14. *kakkū ṣābim*	19. *eṭlam*
5. *bīt asîm*	10. *mû eqlim*	15. *iṭrudakkušši*	20. *dannum*

D. Write in normalized Akkadian:

1. I will pierce it (m)
2. you (pl) have laid claim to them (m)
3. do not withhold (pl) it (f) from me
4. may she not bestow upon (= dat.) you (fs)
5. choose (ms) them (m)
6. you (ms) will replace it (f)
7. he has married her
8. we have abandoned them (f)
9. fear (ms) them (m)!
10. this has happened to me
11. they (f) have entered to you (ms) (i.e., before you; dat.)
12. weigh (ms) out the wool for her
13. let them (m) remove it (f)
14. I will trust you (fs)
15. you (fs) have come to us
16. I opened the city gate for you (mp)
17. I have seen you (fp)
18. do not lead (pl) them (m) to me
19. may they (m) not kill me
20. it has become long
21. you (pl) have passed me by
22. they (f) have complained against you (ms)
23. you (pl) have prospered
24. they (m) judged them (m)
25. I have acted for them (fp)
26. he has imposed a penalty on her
27. it has improved for me
28. we have hired you (ms)
29. you (pl) have weakened
30. she has not eaten
31. it has become new
32. I have paid it (m) to you (ms)
33. he will kill me
34. it has become (too) heavy for him
35. she has planted

E. Normalize and translate:

1. *da-a-a-nu wa-ar-ka-at* MAŠ.GAG.EN *šu-a-ti ip-ru-su-ma* MAŠ. GAG.EN *ba-aq-ri ir-ta-ši i-na-an-na šu-ú ù ma-ru-šu ba-aq-ri ki-ma ṣí-im-da-at* LUGAL *li-pu-lu.*
2. *ru-bu-um i-na ḫa-ar-ra-nim i-ma-ra-aṣ-ma i-ma-at.*
3. *i-na-an-na* DUB.MEŠ-*ka ša* GUD.MEŠ-*ka ša qá-ti-ia as-sa-dar-ma aš-tap-ra-kum.*
4. *a-di-ni ṣú-ḫa-ar-ta-ka ú-ul aṭ-ru-da-ak-kum a-nu-um-ma aṭ-ṭar-da-ak-ku-uš-ši* ŠÀ-*ka mi-im-ma la-a i-ma-ar-ra-aṣ.*
5. EN *pa-nu-ú-um ša* A.ŠÀ *an-ni-im i-na pa-ni il-ki-im* A.ŠÀ-*šu i-zi-ma ša-ni-a-am a-na e-pé-eš ši-pi-ir* A.ŠÀ *an-ni-im aš-ta-ṭar.*
6. UD-*ma-am ša-a-tu* LUGAL *pi-a-am iš-ku-nam-ma pa-ni ṣa-bi-im ṣe-eḫ-ri-im aṣ-bat-ma šar-ra-qí i-na bi-ri-it* KÁ.DINGIR.RA[ki] *ù* URU-*ni a-aḫ na-ri-im ni-iṣ-bat-sú-nu-ti-ma te-er-ḫa-tam ša-ri-iq-tam i-na qá-ti-šu-nu ú-ul ni-mu-úr.*
7. *a-ḫi e-pí-iš-tam le-mu-tam an-ni-tam a-a-i-pu-ša-an-ni.*
8. DUMU.MEŠ A.BA *ki-ma e-mu-uq zi-it-ti-šu* ŠE Ì.GIŠ *ù ši-pa-tim a-na a-ḫi-šu-nu ṣé-eḫ-ri-im i-na-ad-di-nu mi-ši-il ka-ra-nim ú-ul i-na-ad-di-nu-šum.*
9. MU *šu-a-ti* LUGAL *it-ti* ERIN$_2$-*šu a-na* URU *a-ḫi-i-im i-it-ti-iq-ma pí-il-ša-am i-na* ABUL URU *i-pa-al-la-aš.*
10. *ta-pé-e iš-pur-ra-am um-ma šu-ú-ma a-na* ŠE-*em šu-a-ti be-el pí-ḫa-tim šu-ku-un-ma ma-ru-uš-ti la i-mi-a-ad ù um-ma-nam ap-la-an-ni-ma iš-da-am ma-aq-tam lu-pu-uš um-ma-nam ú-ul ta-ap-pa-la-an-ni-ma pí-ḫa-tam šu-a-ti i-na mu-úḫ-hi-ka i-ša-ak-ka-nu.*
11. A.ZU *ša le-tim ša-ap-li-tim* KUG.BABBAR *ù ṣí-ba-at-sú a-na be-el ḫu-bu-li-šu* (§12.4) *li-di-in* KUG.BABBAR *ù ṣí-ba-at-sú ú-ul i-ma-ḫa-ru-šu-ma id-da-ak.*
12. *i-na te-re-e-tim ša-al-ma-a-tim ù i-na qá-bé-e* [d]EN.LÍL *be-lí-šu šar-ra-ni i-ša-rum a-na e-pé-eš ka-ak-ki it-ti na-ak-ri-ni pa-ni-šu iš-ku-un-ma ma-ta-tum na-ka-ra-tum ka-lu-ši-na ik-nu-ša-šum-ma na-ra-am ša* LUGAL-*ru-ti-šu ra-bi-tim ib-ni.*

F. CH:

§21 *šum-ma a-wi-lum bi-tam ip-lu-uš i-na pa-ni pí-il-ši-im šu-a-ti i-du-uk-ku-šu-ma i-ḫa-al-la-lu-šu.*

ḫalālum (*a–u*) 'to hang, suspend' (transitive).

§60 *šum-ma a-wi-lum* A.ŠÀ *a-na kirîm*(^{giš}KIRI$_6$) *za-qá-pí-im a-na nukaribbim*(NU.^{giš}KIRI$_6$) *id-di-in nukaribbum*(NU.^{giš}KIRI$_6$) *kiriam* (^{giš}KIRI$_6$) *iz-qú-up* 4 *šanātim*(MU.4.KAM) *kiriam*(KIRI$_6$) *ú-ra-ab-ba i-na ḫa-mu-uš-tim ša-at-tim be-el kirîm*(^{giš}KIRI$_6$) *ù nukaribbum*(NU. ^{giš}KIRI$_6$) *mi-it-ḫa-ri-iš i-zu-zu be-el kirîm*(^{giš}KIRI$_6$) ḪA.LA-*šu i-na-sà-aq-ma i-le-qé.*

nukaribbum (*nukarib*; pl. *nukaribbātum*; NU.KIRI$_6$; Sum. lw.) 'gardener'.

MU.4.KAM: KAM is a determinative that frequently appears after numerals in logographic expressions (§23.2(d)).

urabba 'he will raise, tend'.

ḫamšum (*ḫamuš-*) 'fifth'.

§167 *šum-ma a-wi-lum aš-ša-tam i-ḫu-uz-ma* DUMU.MEŠ *ú-li-súm* MUNUS *ši-i a-na ši-im-tim it-ta-la-ak wa-ar-ki-ša* MUNUS *ša-ni-tam i-ta-ḫa-az-ma* DUMU.MEŠ *it-ta-la-ad wa-ar-ka«-nu-um» a-bu-um a-na ši-im-tim it-ta-al-ku* DUMU.MEŠ *a-na um-ma-tim ú-ul i-zu-uz-zu še-ri-ik-ti um-ma-ti-šu-nu i-le-qú-ma* NÍG.GA É A.BA *mi-it-ḫa-ri-iš i-zu-uz-zu.*

ittalad = *walādum* Perfect 3cs.

warka abum ... ittalku 'after the father has gone ...'.

ana X zâzum 'to divide, share according to X'.

§183 *šum-ma a-bu-um a-na* DUMU.MUNUS-*šu šu-gi$_4$-tim še-ri-ik-tam iš-ru-uk-ši-im a-na mu-tim id-di-iš-ši ku-nu-uk-kam iš-ṭur-ši-im wa-ar-ka a-bu-um a-na ši-im-tim it-ta-al-ku i-na* NÍG.GA É A.BA *ú-ul i-za-az.*

šugītum (*šugīt*; log. (MUNUS.)ŠU.GI$_4$; Sum. lw.) 'junior wife'.

warka abum ... ittalku 'after the father has gone ...'.

§§218–220 §218 *šum-ma* A.ZU *a-wi-lam sí-im-ma-am kab-tam i-na karzil*(GÍR.NI) *siparrim*(ZABAR) *i-pu-uš-ma a-wi-lam uš-ta-mi-it ù lu na-kap*!(ID)-*ti a-wi-lim i-na karzil*(GÍR.NI) *siparrim*(ZABAR) *ip-te-ma i-in a-wi-lim úḫ-tap-pí-id ritta*(KIŠIB)-*šu i-na-ki-su* §219 *šum-ma* A.ZU *sí-ma-am kab-tam* ÌR MAŠ.EN.GAG *i-na karzil*(GÍR.NI) *siparrim*(ZABAR) *i-pu-uš-ma uš-ta-mi-it* ÌR *ki-ma* ÌR *i-ri-ab* §220 *šum-ma na-kap-ta-šu i-na karzil*(GÍR.NI) *siparrim* (ZABAR) *ip-te-ma i-in-šu úḫ-tap-‹pí›-id*!(DA) KUG.BABBAR *mi-ši-il* ŠÁM-*šu i-ša-qal.*

karzillum (*karzil*; log. GÍR.NI; Sum. lw.) 'physician's lancet'.

siparrum (log. ZABAR; Sum. lw.) 'bronze'.

uštamīt 'he has killed'.

nakkaptum (*nakkapti*; suf. *nakkapta-*; pl. *nakkapātum*) 'temple (of the head)'.

uḫtappid 'he has blinded'.

§246:

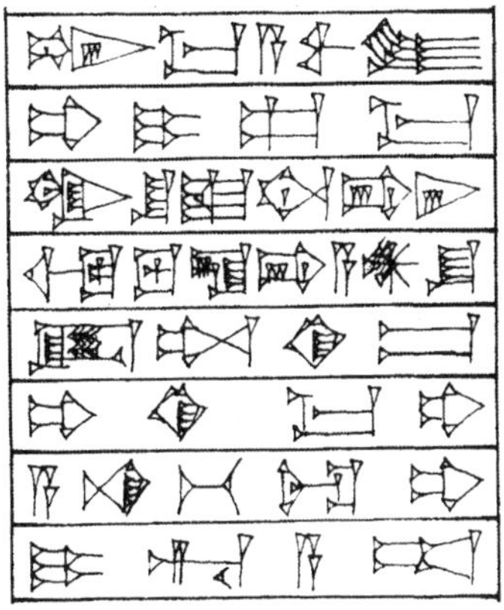

Signs not yet introduced, in the order in which they appear:

 *wi;*

 GÌR = *šēpum;*

 *ù;*

 *lu;*

 *el.*

išteber 'he has broken'.
labiānum 'tendon of the neck'.

G. Contracts:

1. Hire of a slave (Chiera, *PBS* 8/2 no. 188, adapted).

^{1} 1 GEME$_2$ *ma-du-mu-uq-bé-el-[tim]* ^{2} KI *erišti*(NIN!(GEME$_2$)-*ti*)-^{d}UTU ^{3} DUMU_.MUNUS› *šu-pí-ša* ^{4} $^{[I]}$*li-pí-it-eš$_4$-tár* ... ^{6} *a-na* GEME$_2$ *i-gu-ur-ši* ^{7} *i-di* GEME$_2$.MEŠ ^{8} x ŠE ... ^{10} *imaddad*(Ì.ÁG.E). $^{11–15}$ Witnesses. $^{16–17}$ Date.

PNs: *Mād-dumuq-bēltim; Erišti-Šamaš; Šū-pīša; Lipit-Eštar.*
^{7} *idū* (pl.) 'payment'.

2. Lawsuit over a garden (Meissner, *BAP* no. 43 = Schorr, *VAB* 5, no. 259, adapted).

^{1} *kiriam*(^{giš}KIRI$_6$) *ša* ^{d}EN.ZU-*ma-gir* ^{2} ^{I}DUMU-^{d}*Amurrim*(MAR.TU) *a-na* KUG.BABBAR *i-ša-am* ^{3} ^{I}*Anum*(AN)-*ba-ni a-na ṣi-im-da-at šar-ri*!(UŠ)-*im aš-šum kirîm*(^{giš}KIRI$_6$) *ša-a-ti* ^{4} *ib-qú-«ru»-ur-ma a-na* DI.KUD.MEŠ ^{5} *il-li-ku-ma* DI.KUD.MEŠ ^{6}*a-na* KÁ ^{d}*nin-mar*^{ki} *iṭ-ru-du-šu-nu-ti-ma* ^{7} *a-na* DI.KUD.MEŠ *ša* KÁ ^{d}*nin-mar*^{ki} ^{8} ^{I}*Anum*(AN)-*ba-ni i-na* KÁ ^{d}*nin-mar*^{ki} ^{9} *ki-a-am iq-bi um-ma šu-ú-ma* ^{10} DUMU ^{d}EN.ZU-*ma-gir a-na-ku* ^{11} *a-na ma-ru-tim il-qé-a-an-ni* ^{12} *ku-nu-uk-ki ú-ul iḫ-pu-ú* ^{13} *ki-a-am iq-bi-šu-nu-ši-im-ma* ^{14} *kiriam*(^{giš}KIRI$_6$) *ù* É *a-na Anum*(AN)-*ba-ni* ^{15}*ú-bi-ir-ru* ^{16}*i-tu-ur* ^{Id}EN.ZU-*mu-ba-lí-iṭ* ^{17} *kiriam* (^{giš}KIRI$_6$) *Anum*(AN)-*ba-ni ib-qú-ur-ma* ^{18} *a-na* DI.KUD.MEŠ *il-li-ku-ma* ^{19} DI.KUD.MEŠ *a-na «a-na» a-lim* ^{20} *ù ši-bu-tim iṭ-ru-du-šu-nu-ti-*

ma ... 25 *ši-bu-tum pa-nu-tum ša* DUMU-^{d}*Amurrim*(MAR.TU) 26 *i-na* KÁ ^{d}*nin-mar*^{ki} 27 *Anum*(AN)-*ba-ni ma-ru-um a-na-ku* 28 *it-ma iq-bu-ú-ma* 29 *kiriam*(^{giš}KIRI$_6$) *ù* É *a-na Anum*(AN)-*ba-ni ú-bi-ru* 30 ^{Id}EN.ZU-*mu-ba-lí-iṭ la i-ta-ar-ma* 31 *la i-ba-qá-ar* 32 MU ^{d}UTU ^{d}AMAR.UTU 33 *ù ḫa-am-mu-ra-pí* LUGAL *itma*(IN.PÀD). 34–43 Witnesses.

PNs: *Sîn-magir*; *Mār-Amurrim*; *Anum-bānî*; *Sîn-muballiṭ*.

7 *Ninmar* a goddess; the determinative ^{ki} accompanies the genitive chain *bāb Ninmar*.

15, 29 *ubirrū* 'they confirmed, certified'.

3. Adoption of a slave (Ungnad, *VAS* 8, no. 4–5 = Schorr, *VAB* 5, no. 32, lines 1–25 [lines 26–30 oath, 31–49 witnesses]).

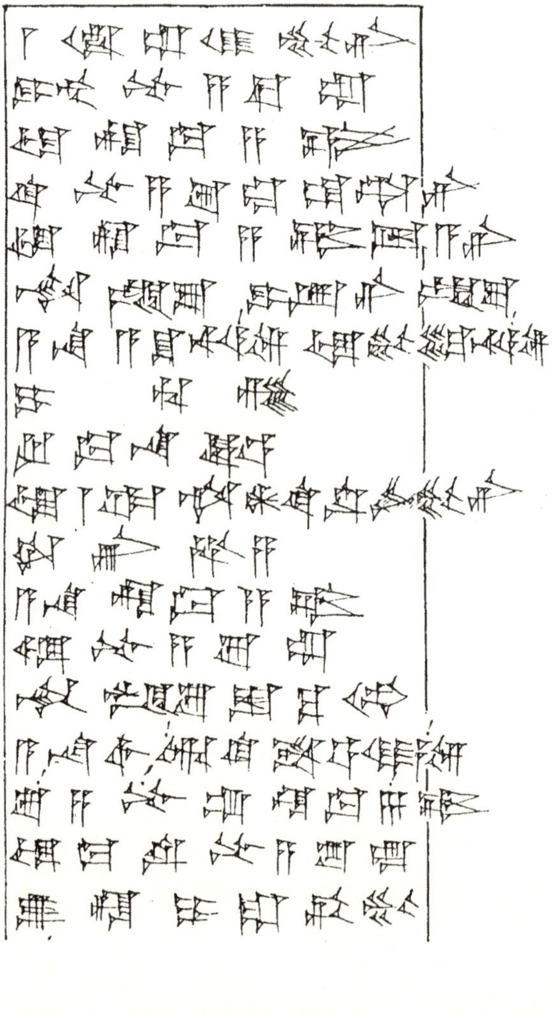

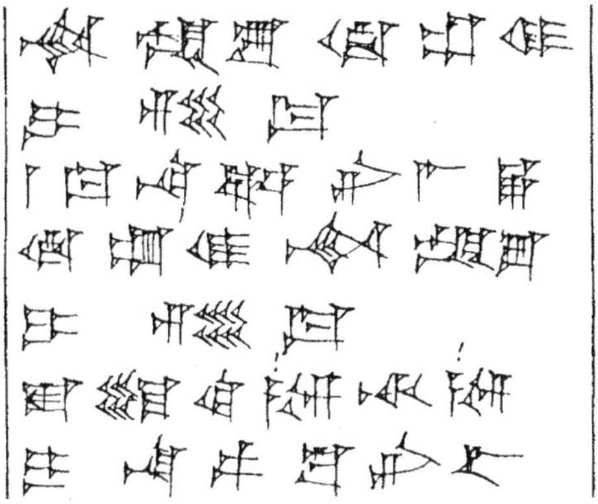

Signs not yet introduced, and signs with anomalous forms:

 *eš$_4$-tár;*	 *ù;*	 *tu;*	 *wa;*
 *mi;*	 AMA;	 $^{2}/_{3}$;	 *ar.*
 *bu, pu;*	 *ib, ip;*	 1;	
 *za, ṣa, sà;*	 *im, em;*	 *ul;*	

Notes:

PNs: *Eštar-ummī; Buzāzum; Lamassatum; Warad-Sîn; Ibni-Sîn; Kišub-lugal.*

[1, 10] The phrase PN *šumšu / šumša,* literally 'PN his/her name', is used of slaves and means 'PN by name' or 'a certain PN'.

[4] AD.TA.NI = AD(.A).NI.

[5] AMA = *ummum.*

[7] Cf. §14.4, and the contract G.1 (1line 5) given in Lesson 17 (p. 166).

[9] $^{2}/_{3}$ MA.NA; read $^{2}/_{3}$ *mana kaspam* '$^{2}/_{3}$ mina of silver'.

[10] RU with the value ŠUB in the PN *Kišub-lugal.*

[16] The order of the signs is curiously incorrect, for the PN *Buzāzum.*

[21] 1 MA.NA; read 1 *mana kaspam* '1 mina of silver'.

[24] *dimtum* (*dimat;* pl. *dimātum*) 'tower; fortified area, settlement; district'.

[25] *napāṣum* (*a–u*) 'to hurl, dash down; to kick, strike; to smash, crush, demolish; to clear (accounts)'; the meaning of *ištu dimtim napāṣum* is debated, either 'to hurl (someone) from a tower' or 'to throw (someone) out of (her husband's) settlement/district'.

LESSON NINETEEN

19.1 The G Perfect: Verbs II–weak; Verbs I–*w*

(a) Verbs II–weak. Unlike the Perfect of other verb types covered thus far, that of verbs II–weak appears to be based on the Preterite: the forms of the II–weak Perfect are simply those of the Preterite with the *-t-* inserted after the initial radical; since the medial theme-vowel is always long, no reduction takes place when vocalic suffixes are added:

	kânum (*a–u*)	*qiāšum* (*a–i*)	*šâmum* (*a*)	*nêrum* (*e*)
3cs	*iktūn*	*iqtīš*	*ištām*	*ittēr*
2ms	*taktūn*	*taqtīš*	*taštām*	*tettēr*
2fs	*taktūnī*	*taqtīšī*	*taštāmī*	*tettērī*
1cs	*aktūn*	*aqtīš*	*aštām*	*ettēr*
3mp	*iktūnū*	*iqtīšū*	*ištāmū*	*ittērū*
3fp	*iktūnā*	*iqtīšā*	*ištāmā*	*ittērā*
2cp	*taktūnā*	*taqtīšā*	*taštāmā*	*tettērā*
1cp	*niktūn*	*niqtīš*	*ništām*	*nittēr*

(b) Verbs I–*w*. Adjectival verbs are conjugated in the Perfect either like verbs I–*e*, as expected, or like verbs I–*a*, i.e., without the change *a* › *e*. Thus, for *watārum*:

3cs	*ītetir* / *ītatir*	3mp	*ītetrū* / *ītatrū*
		3fp	*ītetrā* / *ītatrā*
2ms	*tētetir* / *tātatir*	2cp	*tētetrā* / *tātatrā*
2fs	*tētetrī* / *tātatrī*		
1cs	*ētetir* / *ātatir*	1cp	*nītetir* / *nītatir*

Active verbs I–*w* in the Perfect do not have as their prefix vowel *u-*, *tu-*, *nu-*, as might be expected from the Preterite and Durative forms, but rather *i-*, *ta-*, etc., like Perfects of other root types. Further, the *-t-* is doubled, as in *alākum* (§18.1); thus, these forms resemble those of verbs I–*n* in the Perfect. The theme-vowel, as in the Durative, is *a*. Thus, for *wašābum*:

3cs	*ittašab*	3mp	*ittašbū*
		3fp	*ittašbā*
2ms	*tattašab*	2cp	*tattašbā*
2fs	*tattašbī*		
1cs	*attašab*	1cp	*nittašab*

The verb *babālum* exhibits two Perfect conjugations, one like that of other active verbs I–*w* and one with a single -*t*-:

3cs	*ittabal* / *itbal*	3mp	*ittablū* / *itbalū*
		3fp	*ittablā* / *itbalā*
2ms	*tattabal* / *tatbal*	2cp	*tattablā* / *tatbalā*
2fs	*tattablī* / *tatbalī*		
1cs	*attabal* / *atbal*	1cp	*nittabal* / *nitbal*

19.2 The Subordination Marker *-u*

The subordination marker -*u* is a verbal morpheme the occurrence of which is entirely predictable: it is attached to every finite verb that occurs in a subordinate (i.e., dependent) clause, provided that the verb has no other verbal ending, namely, 2fs -*ī*, pl -*ū*, -*ā*; the Ventive morpheme. Verbs that have one of these endings do not exhibit an overt marker in subordinate clauses (or, we may say that the marker of subordination on such verbs is -*ø*).

The addition of -*u* affects the Perfect and certain weak verb types in the same way as the addition of any other vocalic ending:

in the Perfect, the theme-vowel between R_2 and R_3 drops out;
in verbs III–weak, vowel contraction takes place;
the Preterite forms of active verbs I–*w* lose their theme vowel;
the Durative forms of verbs II–weak have a short theme-vowel and a doubled final radical.

For reference, below are presented paradigms, without and with the subordination marker, of the Preterite, Durative, and Perfect of a sound verb (*šakānum*), the Preterite forms of a verb III–weak (*banûm*) and an active verb I–*w* (*wašābum*), and the Durative of a verb II–weak (*kânum*).

	PRETERITE		DURATIVE		PERFECT	
3cs	*iškun*	*iškunu*	*išakkan*	*išakkanu*	*ištakan*	*ištaknu*
2ms	*taškun*	*taškunu*	*tašakkan*	*tašakkanu*	*taštakan*	*taštaknu*
2fs	*taškunī*	*taškunī*	*tašakkanī*	*tašakkanī*	*taštaknī*	*taštaknī*
1cs	*aškun*	*aškunu*	*ašakkan*	*ašakkanu*	*aštakan*	*aštaknu*

	PRETERITE		DURATIVE		PERFECT	
3mp	*iškunū*	*iškunū*	*išakkanū*	*išakkanū*	*ištaknū*	*ištaknū*
3fp	*iškunā*	*iškunā*	*išakkanā*	*išakkanā*	*ištaknā*	*ištaknā*
2cp	*taškunā*	*taškunā*	*tašakkanā*	*tašakkanā*	*taštaknā*	*taštaknā*
1cp	*niškun*	*niškunu*	*nišakkan*	*nišakkanu*	*ništakan*	*ništaknu*

	banûm PRETERITE		*wašābum* PRETERITE		*kânum* DURATIVE	
3cs	*ibni*	*ibnû*	*ušib*	*ušbu*	*ikân*	*ikunnu*
2ms	*tabni*	*tabnû*	*tušib*	*tušbu*	*takân*	*takunnu*
2fs	*tabnî*	*tabnî*	*tušbī*	*tušbī*	*takunnī*	*takunnī*
1cs	*abni*	*abnû*	*ušib*	*ušbu*	*akân*	*akunnu*
3mp	*ibnû*	*ibnû*	*ušbū*	*ušbū*	*ikunnū*	*ikunnū*
3fp	*ibniā*	*ibniā*	*ušbā*	*ušbā*	*ikunnā*	*ikunnā*
2cp	*tabniā*	*tabniā*	*tušbā*	*tušbā*	*takunnā*	*takunnā*
1cp	*nibni*	*nibnû*	*nušib*	*nušbu*	*nikân*	*nikunnu*

The subordination marker precedes both object pronominal suffixes (§18.2) and the enclitic conjunction *-ma*. The appearance of either a pronominal suffix or *-ma* causes the lengthening of the marker to *-ū-*; e.g.,

(ša) aškunu '(which) I placed';
but *(ša) aškunūšim* '(which) I placed for her';
(ša) aškunū-ma '(which) I placed and ...'.

Note that in cuneiform and in transliteration, the 3cs with the subordination marker will be identical in appearance to the 3mp, for any given verb, such as *iš-ku-nu*. In normalized transcription, the 3cs with the subordination marker and the 3mp are identical only for verbs III–weak (e.g., *ibnû*). The addition of a pronominal suffix or *-ma*, however, causes the forms to be identical for all verbs in normalized transcription as well: *(ša) iškunūšim* 'which he/she/they (m) placed for her'.

As noted above, the subordination marker does not appear on any verb that has the Ventive morpheme.

The subordination marker appears, with the above-mentioned restrictions, on all verbs in subordinate clauses. The latter are discussed in the next section, and in §26.2. Note that verbs in protases of conditional sentences (§17.3) do **not** have the subordination marker.

Note: In most Akkadian grammars, the subordination marker is called the **subjunctive marker**, and verbs with the marker are said to be "in the subjunctive."

19.3 Relative Clauses

Relative clauses constitute the most frequent type of subordinate clause. For English 'who, whose, whom, which, that', Akkadian uses only the determinative-relative *ša*, which is indeclinable in OB and later dialects. As in main clauses, the verb is always final in relative clauses.

The negative adverb in all subordinate clauses is *lā* (see §20.4). The Perfect (§17.2) is not normally found in relative clauses.

(a) *ša* may occur without an antecedent noun, in which case it must be translated 'the one(s) who(m), he/she/they who(m), who(m)-ever, that/those which/that, what', and the like. The entire clause that begins with *ša* is syntactically equivalent to a noun or noun phrase, and thus may occupy any position in the sentence that a noun may occupy. Thus, the clause may occur:

(1) as subject:

ša šarrum ina ṣibittim ikallû imât 'He/She/The one whom the king holds in prison will die' or 'Whomever ... will die';

(2) as direct object:

ša ittīni lā illakam nizzib 'We will abandon him/her/the one who will not come with us' or '... whoever will not come';

(3) after a preposition:

ana ša tašpuram ṭēmam aṣbat 'I took action concerning what/ that which you (ms) wrote me'.

(b) Much more often, *ša* occurs in apposition to an antecedent noun; it follows the antecedent noun, and any adjectives modifying it, directly:

šarrāqam ṣeḫram ša ina eqlīni niṣbatu nidūk 'We killed the young thief whom we had seized in our field';

kaspam ana mārim ša uldu inaddin 'She may give the silver to the son whom she bore';

aššum ṭēmim damqim ša imqutam luqbiakkim 'I must speak to you (fs) about the favorable report that came to me'.

Because it follows the antecedent noun directly, *ša* may not in these instances be preceded by a preposition (or by itself with the meaning 'of'), unlike English relative pronouns; instead, the preposition follows *ša* (not necessarily immediately), and governs a resumptive third person pronoun, which has the same gender and number as the antecedent noun. Thus a sentence like

'The slave with whom I went to town has escaped'

is rendered as follows in Akkadian:

wardum ša ana ālim ittīšu alliku iḫtaliq (lit., 'the servant who, I went to town with him, has escaped').

Where *ana* plus a resumptive pronoun would be expected, a dative suffix normally occurs:

tappâšunu ša kasapšunu iddinūšum ul īmurū 'They (m) did not find their partner, to whom they had given their silver' (lit., '... their partner who, they had given their silver to him').

Where English has 'whose' or 'of whom/which', Akkadian has a resumptive suffix on the appropriate noun:

ṣeḫram ša abūšu ištu ḫarrān šarrim lā itūru ana mārūtim elqe 'I adopted the child whose father did not return from the royal campaign' (lit., '... the child who, his father did not return');

mannum awīlum ša ṭuppaka ana maḫrīšu tašpuru 'Who is the man to (the presence of) whom you sent your tablet?' (lit., '... the man who, you sent your tablet to his presence').

Be sure the following additional examples are clear:

wardū kalûšunu ša bītum elīšunu imqutu imūtū 'All the slaves on whom the house collapsed died';

awīlum ša bītam eššam ēpušūšum kaspam ul iddinam 'The man for whom I built a new house has not paid me';

bēlam ša alapšu âm īkulu ṣabtā 'Arrest (pl) the owner whose ox ate the grain'.

When *ša* represents the direct object of the verb in its own clause, it may optionally be resumed by a suffix on the verb (the suffix should not be translated); e.g.,

am-mīnim šarrāqam ša ina bītīšunu iṣbatūšu (or simply *iṣbatū*) *lā idūkū* 'Why did they (m) not execute the thief whom they seized in their house?'

The indefinite pronouns (§14.3) may be used in conjunction with *ša* to form indefinite relative pronouns meaning 'anyone who(m), who(m)ever, anything that/which, whatever':

mamman ša awâtīya lā išemmû 'whoever does not heed my words';

ina mimma ša iddinūnikkim 'of (lit.: in) whatever they (m) gave you (fs)'.

(c) Relative clauses need not be verbal; verbless clauses may also be governed by *ša*:

> *nakram ša ina ṣērim ul nipallaḫ* 'We do not fear the enemy who is in the open country';
>
> *mārka awīlam ša kīma šuāti imḫaṣ* 'Your (ms) son struck a man of equal rank' (lit., 'a man who is/was like him').

As in English, Akkadian nouns may be modified by prepositional phrases, as in the following examples:

> *ḫarrānum ištu Bābilim adi ālīni* 'the road from Babylon to our city';
>
> *iṣum ana eleppētim* 'wood for ships'.

More commonly, however, the prepositional phrase is preceded by *ša*, so that the noun is modified by a verbless relative clause, as in

> *sinništum ša ina bītim* 'the woman in the house' (lit., 'the woman who (is) in the house');
>
> *eqlum ša warki ekallim* 'the field (that is) behind the palace'.

When the prepositional phrases *ina libbi, ina maḫar/maḫrī-*, and *ina muḫḫi* (§12.3) occur immediately after *ša, ina* is often deleted; e.g.,

> *qarrādum ina libbi ālim ušib* 'The warrior remained within the city' but *qarrādum ša libbi ālim ušbu* 'the warrior who remained within the city';
>
> *kaspum šū ina muḫḫīka* 'You (ms) owe that silver' (lit., 'That silver is upon you'), but *kaspam ša muḫḫīka apul* 'Pay the silver that you owe'.

In the constructions that result from the deletion of the preposition after *ša*, the noun that follows *ša* is, in effect, an adverbial accusative (§18.3).

(d) It is not uncommon for more than one clause to be dependent on *ša*; normally, the clauses are connected by *-ma* (less often, asyndetically; see §7.5):

> *alpam ša tašāmū-ma ana abīni taṭrudu* (or *taṭrudūšu*) *ul āmur* 'I have not seen the ox that you (ms) bought and sent to our father' (note the optional resumptive suffix);
>
> *nišū ina kašād qarrādim ša nakram inērū-ma ilū šarrūtam iqīšūšum iḫdâ* 'The people rejoiced at the arrival of the hero on whom, when he had defeated the enemy, the gods bestowed the kingship'.

(e) As in English, it is possible for the relative pronoun to be deleted in Akkadian. It will be recalled that when *ša* is deleted from a genitive construction, the governing noun appears in the bound form:

bītum ša abīya or *bīt abīya* 'the house of my father'.

Likewise, when *ša* is deleted from a relative clause, the antecedent noun appears in the bound form. Consider the following examples:

bītum ša ēpušu imqut or *bīt ēpušu imqut* 'The house I built collapsed';
awātam ša šarrum iqbû ul ešme or *awāt šarrum iqbû ul ešme* 'I did not hear the word the king said';
wardam ša iḫliqu liṣbatū or *warad iḫliqu liṣbatū* 'The slave who escaped must be caught'.

As can be seen from the examples, the deletion of *ša* normally occurs only when the relative clause is quite short. No examples of the deletion of *ša* are attested when the relative clause is verbless. While this construction is not as common as the use of *ša*, it is by no means rare. Note that it can be identified by the appearance of a form other than a genitive after the bound form. (The case of a noun after a bound form, such as the nominative *šarrum* in the second example above, will of course be obscured if it is written logographically.)

ša may also be omitted after the indefinite pronouns; in such cases, the pronouns are used by themselves as indefinite relatives, i.e., *mamma(n)* 'who(m)ever', *mimma* 'whatever'.

(f) Another word that is used as a relative pronoun is *mala* (in southern and Mari OB, *mali*; also *mal*) 'as much/many as, however much, everything that, everyone who, whoever, whatever'. Like *ša*, it follows the noun to which it refers:

âm mala ērišūki idnīm 'Give (fs) me as much grain as (however much grain, whatever grain) I requested of you' (*erēšum* 'to ask someone for something, request something of someone');
ṣābum mala ittīka illaku lillikam 'Let as many troops as are (lit.: go) with you (ms) come here'.

Without an antecedent:

mali ina mātīšu eppešu tešemme 'You (ms) will hear whatever I do in his country'.

Occasionally, *ša* follows *mal(a/i)*:

ṭēmam mal ša ištu mātim šuāti imaqqutakkunūšim šuprānim 'Send me whatever news (as much news as) comes to you (mp) from that country'.

EXERCISES

A. VOCABULARY 19.

Verbs:

erēšum (*i*) 'to ask, request (something: acc.; from someone: acc. or *itti*), desire, wish'.
pašārum (*a–u*) 'to loosen, release, set free, dissolve; to sell; to explain, clarify; to report, reveal (a dream)'.
râmum (*a*) 'to love, care for'.
zakārum (also *saqārum*) (*a–u*) 'to declare, mention; to speak, address; to name, invoke'; *nīš X zakārum* 'to swear by X' (lit.: 'to invoke the life of X').
Note also *utār* (*târum* D stem Durative 3cs [see §29.1]) 'he/she will give back, send back, put back, return, restore', 3mp *utarrū*.

Nouns:

bašītum (*bašīt*), *bīšum* (*bīš(i)*), *bušûm* (*buši*; pl. *bušû*), *būšum* (*būš(i)*; pl. *būšū*) 'moveable property, valuables, goods; stock, what's on hand'.
idum (fem. and masc.; bound form *idi*, rarely *id*; dual *idān*; pl. *idū* and *idātum*; log. Á) 'arm; side, edge; strength; goal, purpose'; in sg. and in masc. pl. (log. also Á.BI): 'wages, hire, rent'; *idi* (preposition; with suf. *idī-*), *ina idi, ana idi* (prep. phrases) 'near, next to, beside, on the side of, with'.
immerum (*immer*; pl. *immerū* or *immerātum*; log. UDU) 'sheep, ram'.
kanīkum (*kanīk*; pl. *kanīkātum*) 'sealed document' (cf. *kanākum*).
maḫīrum (*maḫīr*; pl. *maḫīrū* and *maḫīrātum*) 'market place; business activity; rate; purchase price' (cf. *maḫārum*).
šamallûm (*šamallê*; base *šamallā-*; Sum. lw.) 'trading agent; assistant; apprentice'.
tamkārum (*tamkār*; pl. *tamkārū*; log. DAM.GÀR) 'merchant, trader'.
warḫum (*waraḫ*; pl. *warḫū*; log. ITI/ITU) 'month; new moon'.

Preposition:

mala (also *mali, mal*) 'according to, as much as, as large as, to the same amount/degree as'; also a conjunction: 'as much/many as;

everyone/everything that, whoever, whatever' (§19.3(f)); *mimma mala* (= *mimma ša*) 'anything that/which, whatever'.

B. Learn the following signs:

OB Lapid.	OB Cursive	NA	values
	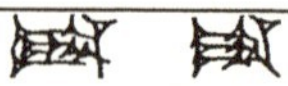	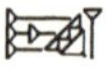	*id/t/ṭ, ed/t/ṭ* (lesson 17); Á = *idum* (also, Á.BI = *idum*)
		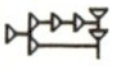	ITI (or ITU) = *warḫum*
			*bu, pu*
		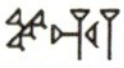	*us/ṣ/z*
			*li, le*
			*tu, ṭú*
	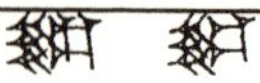		*šar*; KIRI$_6$ (usually ^{giš}KIRI$_6$)=*kirûm*
			*in*
			SÍG = *šīpātum*
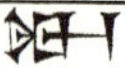	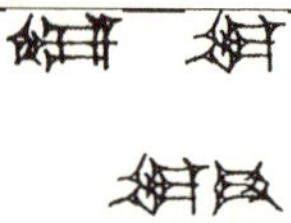		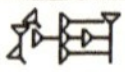 *dam, ṭam*; DAM = *aššatum, mutum*; DAM. GÀR = *tamkārum*
			*lu*; UDU = *immerum*

C. Write the following words in cuneiform and in transliteration; use logograms where appropriate in 1–8:

1. *eqel abi asîm*
2. *libbi warḫim*
3. *makkūr tappêya*
4. *kiri tamkārim*
5. *zītti aššatim*
6. *immerātūki*
7. *šīpāt ālim*
8. *idū alpīša*
9. *luštur*
10. *būdam*
11. *ūtaššar*
12. *qūlam*
13. *anaddin*
14. *līḫuz-ma līter*
15. *kartappum*
16. *ḫālum*

D. Write in normalized Akkadian:

1. we have loved them (m)
2. you (pl) have judged him
3. the commoners have died
4. I have replaced them (m)
5. he has defeated us
6. you have born to him

7. we have brought them (f) here
8. the trading agents have come back
9. they (f) have become surpassing
10. we have purchased it (m)
11. I have granted them (f)
12. you (fs) have executed her
13. it has come down to you (fs)
14. they (m) became fixed
15. we have divided it (m) equally
16. you (fs) have sat down
17. his heart has become satisfied with the going rate
18. I have herewith paid as interest
19. they (f) have become numerous
20. they (m) have grown old
21. the legal claims that you (ms) incurred
22. in the month that you (fs) mentioned
23. the gift that you (ms) will select for her
24. as far as the breach that is next to the city gate
25. the deputy whose cheek you (ms) struck
26. the excess that I will remove
27. for the prince who will become important and strong
28. the royal decree concerning which we rejoiced
29. the upper country, which dwelled obediently
30. the merchant for whom you (pl) will collect the oil
31. like the thief whom they seized and detained
32. the fortress that had become old and (that) the enemy overwhelmed
33. the warrior who did not recover but went to his fate
34. the judge whose legal decision I did not accept
35. up to the great river, to the bank of which we rode
36. the youth whom he asked for her bride-price
37. the commoner whom I assisted
38. as much food as we will purchase
39. the word of truth that she has spoken
40. the god whose name we have invoked

E. Normalize and translate:

1. TAB.BA-*e* ŠÁM ^{giš}MÁ-*ia ša i-gu-ru-ma iḫ-li-qú li-iš-qú-lam.*
2. *a-na eṭ-li-im ša* UDU.MEŠ-*ia ù* SÍG-*ia tu-ub-lu-šum lu-uq-bi.*
3. *aš-šum ṭe*$_4$*-em* TAB.BA.MEŠ-*ia aš-pu-ra-ku-nu-šim ma-la ša i-ip-pa-lu-ku-nu-ti ṭe*$_4$*-ma-am šu-up-ra-nim.*
4. *šar-ra-aq* NÍG.GA É ^{d}UTU *iš-ri-qú* KÁ É-*ti-šu iṣ-ba-tu-ma ri-it-ta-šu ik-ki-su a-ḫi* DUMU *ši-ip-ri-ia šu-ú.*

5. UD-*ma-am šu-a-ti a-wi-lum ša* ^{giš}KIRI$_6$-*ni i-ka-lu im-ra-aṣ-ma i-mu-ut.*
6. MU *šu-a-ti na-ak-ru ša e-li-šu-nu i-na ṣé-ri-im ni-im-qú-tu-ma it-ti-šu-nu ka-ak-ki ni-pu-šu i-na pa-ni ka-ak-ki-ni da-nu-tim ip-ṭú-ru.*
7. *si-ni-iš-tum ša* DUMU-*ša i-na ṣí-bi-tim im-ta-aḫ-ra-an-ni i-na-an-na ù lu di-in* DUMU-*ša pu-ru-ús ù lu* DUMU-*ša pu-ṭú-ur.*
8. *tap-pu-ú-ia at-tu-nu am-mi-nim* A.ŠÀ *ma-la pí-i ka-ni-ki-ia la ta-na-di-na-nim.*
9. *šum-ma a-wi-lum pa-ni-šu a-na e-ze-eb aš-ša-ti-šu iš-ta-kan si-in-ni-iš-tum ši-i a-na* É *a-bi-ša i-ta-ar ù* DUMU.MEŠ-*ša ka-lu-šu-nu ša a-na mu-ti-ša ul-du it-ti-ša uš-ša-bu.*
10. A.ŠÀ *šu-ú ša* Á ^{giš}KIRI$_6$-*ia ú-ul a-na pa-ša-ri-im.*
11. DAM.GÀR *šu-ú* MAŠ É-*šu ù bi-ši-šu a-na ṣé-eḫ-ri-im ša a-na ma-ru-tim il-qú-ú iš-ru-uk i-na pa-ni ši-bu-tim* DUB *iš-ṭú-úr-ma i-zi-ib-šum i-na-an-na ma-am-ma-an ṣé-eḫ-ra-am šu-a-ti la i-ba-qar.*
12. DUMU-*ka a-na-ku am-mi-nim ki-ma* DUMU.MEŠ-*ka ša-nu-tim la-a ta-ra-am-ma-an-ni.*

F. CH. Normalize and translate the following laws:

§104 *šum-ma* DAM.GÀR *a-na šamallêm*(ŠAMAN$_2$.LÁ) ŠE SÍG Ì.GIŠ *ù mi-im-ma bi-ša-am a-na pa-ša-ri-im id-di-in šamallûm*(ŠAMAN$_2$.LÁ) KUG.BABBAR *i-sa-ad-dar-ma a-na* DAM.GÀR *ú-ta-ar šamallûm* (ŠAMAN$_2$.LÁ) *ka-ni-ik* KUG.BABBAR *ša a-na* DAM.GÀR *i-na-ad-di-nu i-le-qé.*

§119 *šum-ma a-wi-lam e-ʾì-il-tum iṣ-ba-sú-ma* GEME$_2$-*sú ša* DUMU. MEŠ *ul-du-šum a-na* KUG.BABBAR *it-ta-din* KUG.BABBAR DAM.GÀR *iš-qú-lu be-el* GEME$_2$ *i-ša-qal-ma* GEME$_2$-*s*[*ú*] *i-pa-ṭár.*
eʾiltum '(financial) liability, obligation'.

§150 *šum-ma a-wi-lum a-na aš-ša-ti-šu* A.ŠÀ ^{giš}KIRI$_6$ É *ù bi-ša-am iš-ru-uk-šim ku-nu-uk-kam i-zi-ib-ši-im wa-ar-ki mu-ti-ša* DUMU. MEŠ-*ša ú-ul i-ba-qá-ru-ši um-mu-um wa-ar-ka-sà a-na* DUMU-*ša ša i-ra-am-mu i-na-ad-di-in a-na a-ḫi-im ú-ul i-na-ad-di-in.*

§249 *šum-ma a-wi-lum* GUD *i-gur-ma i-lum im-ḫa-sú-ma im-tu-ut a-wi-lum ša* GUD *i-gu-ru ni-iš i-lim i-za-kar-ma ú-ta-aš-šar.*
ūtaššar 'he will be released'.

§6:

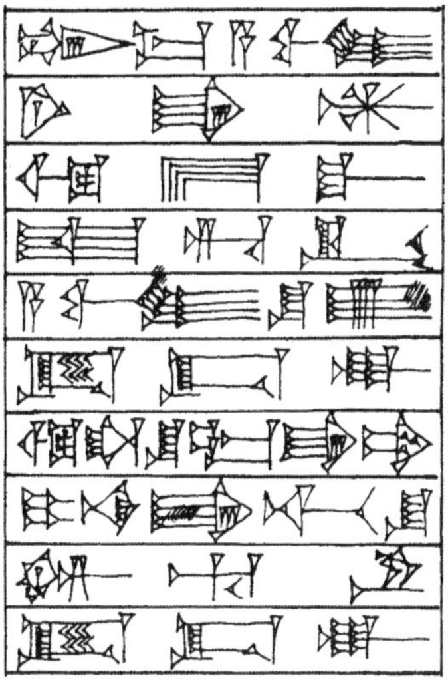

Signs not yet introduced, in the order in which they appear:

 *wi;*

 *ù;*

 *im.*

šurqum 'theft, stolen property' (cf. *šarāqum*).

G. Contracts. Normalize and translate the following texts:

1. Record of the hire of an ox (Szlechter, *TJA* 26 UMM H10).

[1] 1 GUD MU.3 [2] *ša it-ti* ^{d}EN.ZU-*na-di-in-šu-mi* [3] DUMU *e-tel-pi*$_4$-^{d}AMAR.UTU *šangêm*(SANGA) [4] *a-na niqi*(SISKUR) *na-ab-ri-i* [5] ^{I}*i-din-*^{d}AMAR.UTU ^{lú}*rēdûm*(ÚS) [6] DUMU ^{d}*za-ba*$_4$-*ba*$_4$-*na-ṣi-ir* [7] *il-qú-ú* [8] *a-na warḫim ešrim* (ITI.10.KAM) [9] 1 GUD MU.3 [10] *a-na* ^{d}EN.ZU-*na-di-in-šu-mi* [11] DUMU *e-tel-pi*$_4$-^{d}AMAR.UTU *šangêm*(SANGA) [12] *i-na-ad-di-in*. [13–18] Witnesses. [19–22] Date.

PNs: *Sîn-nādin-šumi; Etel-pī-Marduk; Iddin-Marduk; Zababa-nāṣir.*

[1–7] constitute an incomplete sentence that serves as a label: '1 ox ... that PN ... received'.

[1] GUD MU.3 = *alap 3 šanātim.*

[3] *šangûm* (base *šangā-*; log. SANGA; Sum. lw.) 'temple administrator'.

[4] *niqûm* (base *niqi-*; log. SISKUR) 'offering, sacrifice'; *nabrûm / nabrû* (usually pl.) the name of a festival.

[5] ^{lú}*rēdûm* (*rēdi-*; log. ÚS) a type of soldier (see Vocab. 20).

[8] *ana warḫim ešrim* 'in the tenth month'.

2. A loan of wool (*CT* 8 36a = Schorr, *VAB* 5, no. 54).

^{1} x SÍG *ša* É.GAL ^{2} ŠÁM y KUG.BABBAR ^{3} *ša* DINGIR-*šu-ib-ni* ... ^{4} *i-na* É.GAL *im-ḫu-ru* ^{5} ... ^{6} KI DINGIR-*šu-ib-ni* ... ^{7} ^{I}*ta-ri-bu-um* DUMU *i-bi-*^{d}UTU ^{8} ^{I}*ip-qú-*^{d}*ma-mu*(!) ^{9} ^{I}*be-lí-ia-tum* DUMU.MEŠ DINGIR-*šu-ib-ni* ^{10} *ù ku-ub-bu-rum* ^{11} ŠU.BA.AN.TI.I.MEŠ ^{12} UD-*um* É.GAL KUG. BABBAR *i-ri-*[*šu*] ^{13} É.GAL KUG.BABBAR *i-ip-pá-lu.* ^{14} Witness. $^{15–17}$ Date.

PNs: *Ilšu-ibni; Tarībum; Ibbi-Šamaš; Ipqu-Mama; Bēlīyātum; Kubburum.*

^{12} *ūm* + subordinate verb: see §19.3(e); 'on the day (that) x happens' = 'when x happens' (see also §26.2).

3. A loan of silver (Edzard, *TIM* 7 4 = idem, *Tell ed-Dēr* no. 4, lines 1–9 [10–13 witnesses]).

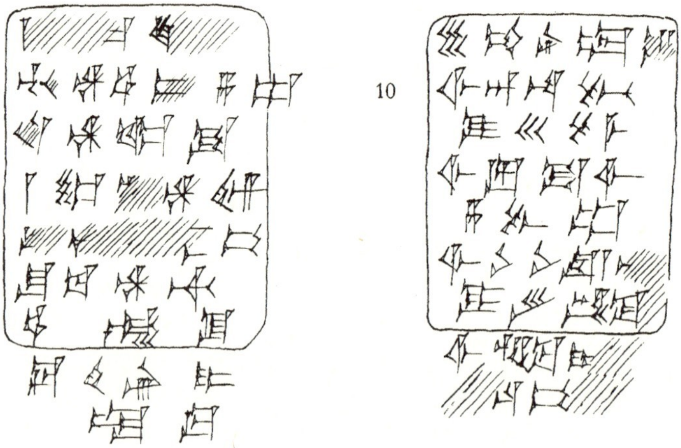

Notes:

PNs: *Annum-pīša; Šarma-Adad; Adad-rabi.*

^{1} ⌜1⌝ [GÍ]N KUG.[BABBAR] = *1 šiqil kaspam* '1 shekel of silver' (acc.).

^{2} Fourth and fifth signs: ⌜*ú*⌝-*ṣa-*. Line 2 is a parenthetical insertion; see comment on Edzard, *Tell ed-Dēr* no. 23:2, above, in Lesson 15, p. 140.

^{3} First sign: ⌜KI⌝; the PN is *Annum*(AN)-*pi₄*(KA)-*ša*.

^{4} Third sign: ⌜*ma*⌝; thereafter ^{d}IŠKUR(the IM sign) = *Adad* (the storm-god).

^{5} Read ⌜DUMU ^{d}⌝[IŠKUR-*r*]*a-bi*.

^{7} UD.BURU₁₄.ŠÈ(the KU sign) = *ana ūm ebūrim*.

^{8} Second sign: *ḫi*.

^{9} Last three signs: Ì.ÁG.⌜E⌝ = *imaddad*.

LESSON TWENTY

20.1 The G Participle

(a) Form. The Participle is an adjective of the pattern *pāris*. As an adjective, it is declinable, and has fem. and pl. forms:

	SINGULAR			PLURAL	
	MASC.	FEM.		MASC.	FEM.
nom.	*pārisum*	*pāristum*	nom.	*pārisūtum*	*pārisātum*
gen.	*pārisim*	*pāristim*	gen.-acc.	*pārisūtim*	*pārisātim*
acc.	*pārisam*	*pāristam*			

When used as a noun, the masc. pl. may have the plural endings found on nouns, i.e., nom. *pārisū*, gen.-acc. *pārisī*. The bound forms are all straightforward, except for the fem. sg., which is *pārisat* before nouns, but *pārista-* before pronominal suffixes (see §§8.3(c 2v a); 11.1(c 1)).

The Participles of **verbs I–*n*** and **verbs I–*w*** are completely regular: e.g., *nādinum*, *wāšibum*. As is also true of its Infinitive (see §9.2), the Participle of *babālum* is always written with initial *b* instead of *w* (except in Mari OB), thus, *bābilum*.

Verbs I–ʾ (including *alākum*) offer no difficulties. The initial ʾ has been lost with no further changes in verbs I–*a*: *āḫizum*, *ālikum*. In verbs I–*e*, as usual, *a*-vowels become *e*: ms *ēribum*, *ēribtum* (bound form *ēribet*, but with suffix *ēribta-*), mp *ēribūtum*, fp *ēribētum*.

For verbs **III–weak**, the loss of R_3 results in the base *pāri-* for III–*a* / *i* / *u*, and *pēri-* for III–*e* (note *manûm* (*u*) 'to count'):

		banûm (*i*)	*manûm* (*u*)	*kalûm* (*a*)	*šemûm* (*e*)
ms	nom.	*bānûm*	*mānûm*	*kālûm*	*šēmûm*
	gen.	*bānîm*	*mānîm*	*kālîm*	*šēmîm*
	acc.	*bāniam*	*māniam*	*kāliam*	*šēmiam*
fs	nom.	*bānītum*	*mānītum*	*kālītum*	*šēmītum*
mp	nom.	*bānûtum*	*mānûtum*	*kālûtum*	*šēmûtum*
fp	nom.	*bāniātum*	*māniātum*	*kāliātum*	*šēmiātum*

Note that *ā* does not become *ē* in *šēmiātum* (fp), contrary to expectation.

The bound forms of the ms follow the pattern of other words whose bases end in *i*: e.g., *bāni* or *bān*; with suff. *bānīšu* for all cases (see §§8.3 (c 3), 11.1(c 2)). Like Participles of other verb types, the fs bound form before nouns usually has *a* inserted before the *t*: *bāniat* (as opposed to *rabīt* from *rabītum*); likewise usually *a* even in verbs III–*e*: *šēmiat* (but note also *re-di-*IT for *rēdīt* or *rēdiet*, from *rēdûm*); before a suffix the *a* drops out: *bānītka* (nom.–acc.), *bānītīka* (gen.) 'your (ms) maker (fs)'.

Verbs II–weak have Participles that follow the pattern of the sound verb, with ʾ representing R_2: e.g., *dāʾikum*, *šāʾimum*, *nēʾirum* (for the writing of ʾ, see §21.4). A few verbs II–weak of the *a–u* and *a–i* classes also have irregular Participles of the form *mupīs*: e.g. *mudīkum* (from *dâkum*, alongside *dāʾikum*).

(b) Meaning and Use. The G Participle is active in voice; Participles of stative verbs, such as *watārum* or *marāṣum*, do not occur. When used to modify a noun, the Participle corresponds to English adjectives ending in '-ing' or relative clauses of the type 'who/that does/did X':

> *kakkum māḫiṣum* 'a smiting weapon, a weapon that smites'.

The Participle may **not** be used to express the English progressive tenses: 'the king is going' will always be *šarrum illak* (Durative), never *šarrum ālikum*; the latter means 'a going/walking king, a king who goes'.

The Participle often occurs as a bound form before a genitive. With active-transitive verbs, the following genitive is normally what would be the direct object if the verb were finite:

> *šarrum māḫiṣ mātim nakartim* 'the king who smites the enemy land' (cf. *šarrum mātam nakartam imaḫḫaṣ* 'the king smites the foreign land');
>
> *bēlet ilī bāniat nišī* (gen.) 'the mistress of the gods who creates the people' (cf. *bēlet ilī nišī* (acc.) *ibanni* 'the mistress of the gods creates the people').

Pronominal suffixes on Participles are those added to nouns (cf. §18.2, end):

> *ummī wālittī* (‹ **wālid-t-ī*; cf. §5.4) 'my mother who bore me' (cf. *ummī uldannī* 'my mother bore me').

With active intransitive verbs, especially verbs of motion, the genitive after a Participle may express what would be a prepositional phrase with a finite verb:

> *ilum ālik pānīya* 'the god who goes before me' (cf. *ilum ina pānīya illak* 'the god goes before me');

bēltum ēribet bīt ilim 'the lady who enters the temple' (cf. *bēltum ana bīt ilim irrub* 'the lady enters the temple');

ṣābum wāšib maḫar šarrim 'the army dwelling/that dwells before the king' (cf. *ṣābum ina maḫar šarrim uššab* 'the army dwells before the king').

A Participle modifying a plural noun, when the former stands in the bound form before another noun, may be singular; the reason for this is not clear (but cf. perhaps phrases such as *bēl ḫubullīšu* 'his creditors', cited in §12.4): e.g.,

ilū wāšib ālim annîm 'the gods dwelling/who dwell in this town'.

The Participle is very frequently substantivized (see §4.4), with the meaning '(the) one who/that does/did X':

pāris purussê 'one (masc.) who makes decisions';
wāšibūt ālim 'city-dwellers';
nādinum 'the one who gives/gave, the seller (masc.)';
wālidūtum 'parents' (lit., 'those who begot');
pāqidum 'inspector'.

As can be seen from these examples, the substantivized Participle often denotes an agent noun or a noun of occupation. Further examples:

ālikum 'traveler, messenger (masc.)';
šāpirum 'overseer, governor, prefect';
bānûm and *bānītum* 'creator (masc. and fem.)';
sābītum 'innkeeper (fem.)' (from *sabûm* 'to brew beer').

It is important that the distinction in meaning between the two adjectives derivable from most active roots, the Verbal Adjective and the Participle, be clear, particularly since certain forms of the two, such as the ms bound form, appear the same in cuneiform and in transliteration (e.g., *pa-ri-is* for *paris* and *pāris*). For transitive roots, the Verbal Adjective is passive in meaning, while the Participle is active:

ṣabtum 'captured, captive, prisoner' vs. *ṣābitum* 'captor';
maḫṣum 'smitten' vs. *māḫiṣum* 'smiting';
epištum 'done (f), deed' vs. *ēpištum* 'doer, worker (f)'.

For active-intransitive roots, the distinction between the two forms is one of aspect: the Verbal Adjective is perfective while the Participle is imperfective, as in

wašbum 'having sat down, seated' vs. *wāšibum* 'sitting (down)'.

As with English 'seated' vs. 'sitting', some semantic overlap between *wašbum* and *wāšibum* may be assumed.

20.2 The Particularizing Suffix *-ān*

The morpheme *-ān*, which occurs immediately before the case-ending on nominal forms, serves to indicate a specific or particular member of the class or object denoted by the word to which it is attached. It is often best translated 'the X in question' or 'that X':

šarrāqānum 'the thief in question, that (particular) thief';
nādinānum 'the seller in question, that (particular) seller';
māḫirānum 'he who received (something) in that (particular) instance'.

Sometimes a word with *-ān* acquires its own individual meaning:

rabiānum 'mayor' (a specific great man);
šulmānum 'greeting-gift' (cf. *šulmum* 'well-being, greeting').

With plurals, *-ān* may denote a particular group:

ilū 'the gods' (i.e., the pantheon in general), but *ilānū* '(a certain group of) gods' (usually the active group of high gods);
šarrū 'kings' (in general), but *šarrānū* '(a particular group or number of individual) kings'.

In later dialects (post-OB), these forms become the normal plurals of *ilum* and *šarrum*. In some instances, the original function of *-ān* on plurals seems to have been lost; thus, for example, both *šiprū* and *šiprānū* (as well as *šiprētum*) occur as plurals of *šiprum*, with no apparent difference in meaning. See also the next section.

20.3 Irregular Masculine Plurals

(a) In the plurals of *abum*, *aḫum*, and *iṣum*, the consonant before the endings *-ū* / *-ī* is doubled; this is also true of the fem. counterpart of *aḫum*, *aḫātum* 'sister':

abbū 'fathers, ancestors'; *iṣṣū* 'trees, woods';
aḫḫū 'brothers'; *aḫḫātum* 'sisters'.

The forms *aḫḫū* and *aḫḫātum* are often written with an extra A sign at the beginning, i.e., *a-aḫ-ḫu*, *a-aḫ-ḫa-tum*.

(b) The nouns *awīlum* and *ṣuḫārum* have the following pl. forms:

nom.	*awīlû*	*ṣuḫārû*
gen.-acc.	*awīlê*	*ṣuḫārê*

The endings *-û*, *-ê* are contractions of *-āʾū* and *-āʾī*, respectively.

(c) The pl. of *ālum* 'town' always has the suffix *-ān*; the pl. markers may be either the usual *-ū*, *-ī* or those found on *awīlum*, *ṣuḫārum*:

nom. *ālānū* or *ālānû*; gen.-acc. *ālānī* or *ālānê*.

20.4 Negation

The two negative adverbs encountered in OB, *ul* and *lā*, have clearly defined, and mutually exclusive, ranges of use.

ul, introduced in §4.5, is spelled *ú-ul* in OB; the less common byform *ula* appears especially in early OB texts (another, extremely rare, byform is *uli*). *ul(a)* is used to negate main-clause assertions; these may be verbal ('you did not go') or verbless ('he is not in the city'). It also negates interrogative sentences in which no interrogative pronoun or adverb occurs (these are taken up in §36.3; examples: verbal 'did you not go?'; verbless 'is he not in the city?').

lā (written both *la-a* and *la*) is used in all other situations:

(a) in all subordinate clauses (§§19.3, 26.2) and in protases (but not apodoses) of conditional sentences with *šumma* (§17.3(b));

(b) in negative injunctions, specifically, in the Prohibitive (*lā* + Durative; §16.3) and in negative injunctive verbless clauses (such as *lā ina ālim šū* 'may he not be in the city'; see §22.2);

(c) after interrogative pronouns and adverbs (§14.2);

(d) to negate individual nouns and adjectives: e.g.,

> *lā epištam tēpuš* 'you (ms) did a non-deed';
> *eqlam šuāti ina lā mê īzibū* 'they abandoned that field for lack of water (lit.: with/due to no water)';
> *ṭēmum lā damqum imqutam* 'an unfavorable report reached me';
> *alaktum lā išartum* 'unjust conduct (*alaktum*)'.

It is often appropriate to translate *ša lā* ('of no ...') as 'without'; similarly, a bound form before *lā*:

> *eqlum ša lā mê* 'a field without water';
> *kasap lā kanīkim* 'silver without a sealed document'.

EXERCISES

A. VOCABULARY 20.

Verbs:

šadādum (*a–u*) 'to pull, draw, drag, tow, haul, convey; to bear; to stretch; to pull, tear out, off; to measure, survey (a field)'; Verbal

Adj. *šaddum* (*šadid-*) 'taut; elongated'; Participle *šādidum* 'boat-hauler'.
šapākum (*a–u*) 'to heap up, pile up, store; to pour'.

Nouns:

agûm (base *agā-*; log. AGA; Sum. lw.) 'crown, tiara'.
aḫātum (*aḫāt*; pl. *aḫḫātum*; log. NIN) 'sister'.
aplum (*apil*; log. IBILA [dumu+uš]) 'heir, (oldest) son'; *aplūtum* (*aplūt*; log. also IBILA) 'position of heir; inheritance, estate'.
gagûm (base *gagi-*; Sum. lw.; log. GÁ.GI.A and GÁ.GI4.A) part of the temple area, in which the *nadītum* women (see below) lived.
imērum (*imēr*; pl. *imērū*; log. ANŠE) '(male) donkey'.
nadītum (*nadīt*; pl. *nadiātum*) 'fallow, bare land'; (log. LUKUR [munus+me]) a woman dedicated to a god and not permitted to have children; the *nadītum* usually lived in a *gagûm*.
rēdûm (base *rēdi-*; pl. *rēdû*; Participle of *redûm*; log. AGA.ÚS) 'foot-soldier, attendant'; the fem. Participle *rēdītum* (*rēdīt* or *rēdiet*) denotes '(legitimate) claimant, heir (fem.)'.
šāpirum (*šāpir*; Participle of *šapārum*) 'overseer; governor, prefect'; *šāpir mātim* 'governor'.
wardūtum (*wardūt*) 'slavery; position of slave'.

B. Learn the following signs:

OB Lapid.	OB Cursive	NA	values
	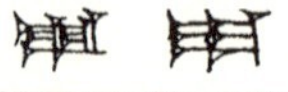		AGA = *agûm*; AGA.ÚS = *rēdûm*
	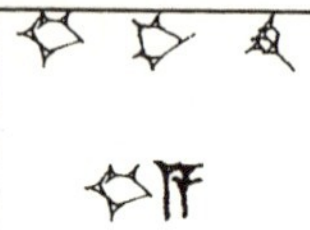		*ḫi*, *ḫe*; *ṭà*; DÙG (also read DU10) = *ṭābum*; ḪI in ḪI.A (also read ḪÁ; or as a determinative ḫi.a or ḫá) plural marker (not used with persons or deities; see p. 109)
		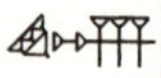	*aḫ*, *eḫ*, *iḫ*, *uḫ*
			*kam*, *qám*
		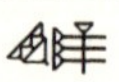	*ḫar*, *ḫur*, *mur*
	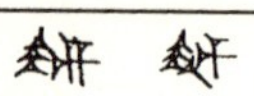	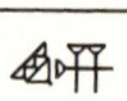	*im*, *em*

	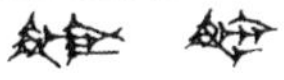		ANŠE = *imērum*
	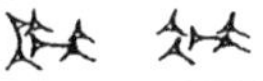		*gu*
			*zum, ṣum, súm; ṣu*
	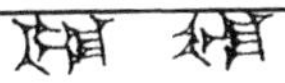	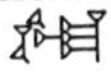	*nin;* NIN = *aḫātum, bēltum**
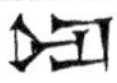	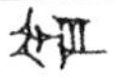	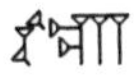	*el, il*$_5$

*Originally the logograms for *aḫātum* and *bēltum* were distinct; the old logogram for *aḫātum* is read NIN$_9$.

C. Write the following words in cuneiform and in transliteration; use logograms where appropriate in 1–6:

1. *waraḫ iḫliqu*
2. *libbum ṭābum*
3. *rēdû mātim*
4. *agā ilim*
5. *aḫāt tamkārim*
6. *idū imērī āguru*
7. *ina maḫīrim*
8. *išarrakam*
9. *elteqe*
10. *iqtin*
11. *līpussu*
12. *ṭurdīm*
13. *lūmur*
14. *imaḫḫar*
15. *maḫāṣum*

D. Write in normalized Akkadian, using Participles when possible:

1. with the one (m) who hires him
2. the woman who does this
3. the particular one (m) who seizes
4. the receiver (f) of the beer
5. a conquering weapon
6. a rider (m)
7. the brothers who protect the sisters
8. cutters (m) of trees
9. one (f) who hears the words of Enlil
10. the god who created me
11. the god who goes before me
12. the servants (m) who dwell in that town
13. the opener (m) of the gate
14. the god who loves you (fs)
15. the coming (lit.: entering) year
16. the inspector of the sealed documents
17. the overseer of the foot-soldiers
18. the claimant (m) in question

E. Normalize and translate.

1. *a-nu-um-ma* ANŠE *na-as-qá-am a-na qí-iš-ti-ki at-ta-ad-na-ki-im i-na-an-na qí-ša-tim ma-da-tim a-na maḫ-ri-ia šu-up-ri.*
2. *i-na la ša-di-di-im* ^{giš}MÁ *ša na-di-it* ^{d}UTU *i-gu-ru a-na ṣe-ri-ša ú-ul il-li-ik.*
3. DINGIR.MEŠ GAL.MEŠ AGA *be-lu-tim i-qí-šu-nim.*

4. *a-su-um* A.ŠÀ *la-bi-ra-am ša ša-ma-lu-um i-ri-šu-šu iš-du-ud-ma ki-ma zi-it-ti ša-ma-le-em iš-ru-uk-šum.*
5. *ša-pí-ri iš-pu-ra-am um-ma šu-ma ša pí-il-ša-am i-na bi-tim eš-ši-im ip-lu-šu-ma* NÍG.GA *iš-ri-qú ṣa-ba-at i-na-an-na a-wi-le-e šu-nu-ti aṣ-ṣa-bat-ma še-er-tam ka-bi-it-tam e-te-mi-sú-nu-ti.*
6. *a-ḫu-um ša na-pí-iš-ta-šu ki-ma na-pí-iš-ti-ia a-ra-mu at-ta.*
7. *am-ra-aṣ-ma pí-i e-pu-uš-ma i-la-at ša-me-e be-el-ti az-ku-ur-ma um-ma a-na-ku-ma a-a-mu-ut lu-uš-li-im-ma i-na-ia ša-am-ša-am li-iṭ-ṭú-la-ma uz-na-ia qá-ba-a-ki li-iš-me-a.*
8. *ša-am-nam a-na qá-qá-ad mar-ṣí-im šu-pu-uk-ma li-ib-lu-uṭ.*
9. *a-la-nu-ú na-ak-ru-tum ṣa-ab-tu-ti-šu-nu a-na* KUG.SIG$_{17}$ *ma-di-im i-pa-ša-ru.*
10. IBILA LUGAL *a-na pa-ni ka-ša-ad a-bi-šu a-na ši-im-ti-šu it-ta-lak.*
11. *ṣú-ḫa-ru-ú šu-nu me-e za-ku-tim li-iš-tu-ú-ma la i-mu-ut-tu.*
12. ŠE *ša i-na* É *a-ḫa-ti-ia aš-pu-ku mi-it-ḫa-ri-iš ni-za-az.*
13. *a-a-um-ma bi-ša-am ša ru-ba-a-tim la na-ṭi-la-tim ma-la iḫ-li-qú i-ri-ib-ši-na-ši-im.*

F. CH. Normalize and translate the following laws:

§278 *šum-ma a-wi-lum* ÌR GEME$_2$ *i-ša-am-ma* ITU-*šu la im-la-ma bé-en-ni e-li-šu im-ta-qú-ut a-na na-di-na-ni-šu ú-ta-ar-ma ša-a-a-ma-nu-um* KUG.BABBAR *iš-qú-lu i-le-qé.*

waraḫšu imla 'one (lit., his) month elapsed (lit., was fulfilled)'.

bennum (often pl. *bennū*) a type of epilepsy; here, pl. gen.-acc. *bennī* incorrectly for sg. nom. *bennum.*

šayyāmānum 'the buyer in question' (cf. *šâmum*).

§279 *šum-ma a-wi-lum* ÌR GEME$_2$ *i-ša-am-ma ba-aq-ri ir-ta-ši na-di-na-an-šu ba-aq-ri i-ip-pa-al.*

§175:

Signs not yet introduced, in the order in which they appear:

 *ù;*  *wi, wa;* 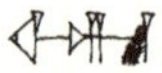 *ar;*  *ul.*

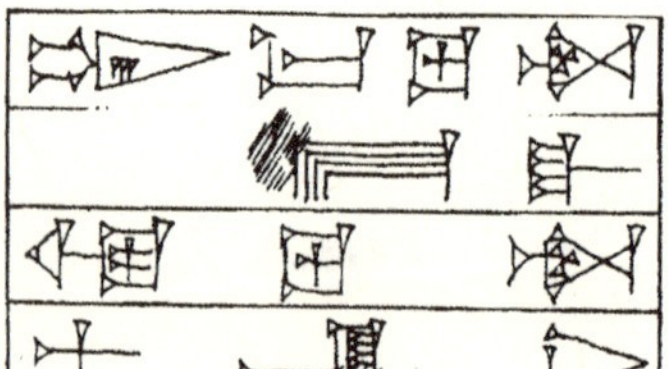

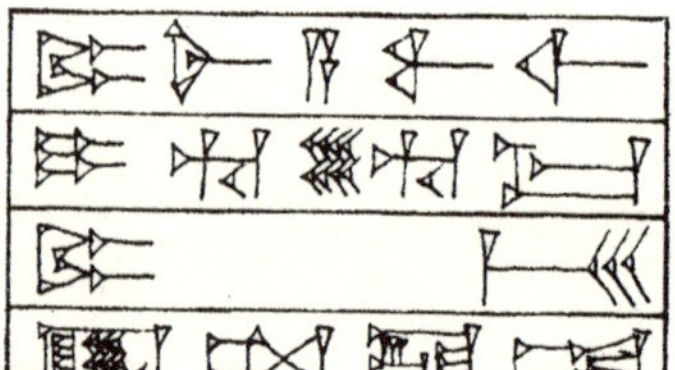

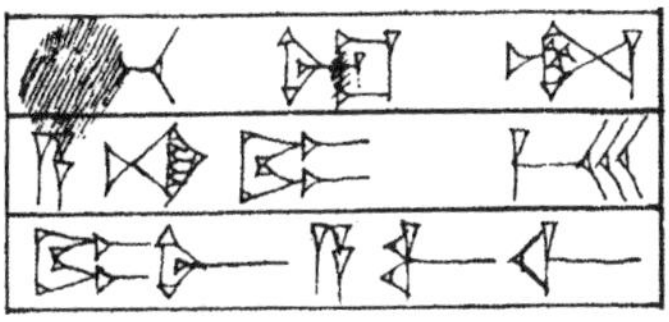
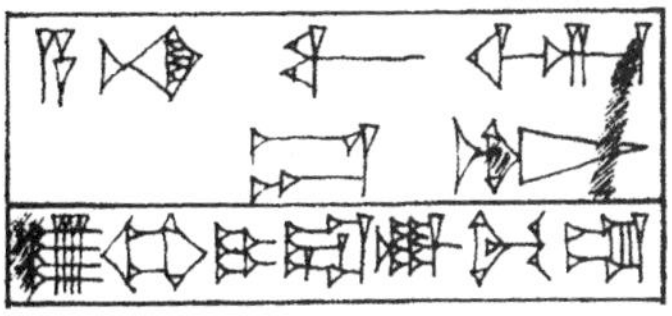

G. Contracts:

1. Inheritance of property by a *nadītum* (*CT* 2 41 = Schorr, *VAB* 5, no. 19, adapted).

^{1}*[ap-lu-ut] ša-at-*^{d}*a-a* LUKUR ^{d}UTU ^{2}DUMU.MUNUS ^{d}UTU-DINGIR ^{3} ^{I}*a-ma-at-*^{d}*ma-mu* LUKUR ^{d}UTU ^{4} DUMU.MUNUS *ša-ì-lí-šu* ^{5} *re-di-it wa-ar-ka-ti-ša* ^{6} A.ŠÀ *i-na ga-mi-na-nu-um* ^{7} *i-ta* A.ŠÀ ^{d}*i-ba-nu-um-qá-sú* ^{8} *ù i-ta* A.ŠÀ *a-ḫu-ni* DUMU *a-ab-ba* ^{9} x *bītam epšam*(É.DÙ.A) *i-na ga-gi-im* ^{10} Á É *mu-ḫa-ad-di-tum* DUMU.MUNUS *ab-di-im* ^{11} *mi-im-ma an-ni-im* ^{12} *ša-at-*^{d}*a-a* LUKUR ^{d}UTU *um-ma-ša* ^{13} *a-na a-ma-at-*^{d}*ma-mu* DUMU.MUNUS *ša-ì-lí-šu* ^{14} *id-di-in* ^{15} A.ŠÀ ^{16} *i-na ga-mi-na-nu-um* ^{17} *i-ta* A.ŠÀ ^{d}EN.ZU-*re-me-ni* ^{18} *ù i-ta* A.ŠÀ *na-bi-*^{d}UTU ^{19} A.ŠÀ *i-na qá-ab-lu-um* ^{20} *i-ta* A.ŠÀ *be-el-šu-nu* ^{22} 1 SAG.GEME$_2$ ^{23} *mi-im-ma an-ni-im ša-ì-lí-šu a-bu-ša* ^{24} *ù ša-mu-uḫ-tum um-ma-ša* ^{25} *a-na a-ma-at-*^{d}*ma-mu ma-ar-ti-šu-nu id-di-nu* ^{26} *i-na aḫ-ḫi-ša a-na ša i-ra-mu* ^{27} *ap-lu-sà i-na-di-in.*

PNs: *Šât-Ayya; Šamaš-ilum; Amat-Mamu; Ša-ilīšu; Ibānum-qāssu; Aḫūni; Abba; Muḫaddītum; Abdum; Sîn-rēmēnī; Nabi-Šamaš; Bēlšunu; Šamuḫtum.*

$^{1-2}$ an incomplete sentence that serves as a label or title of the document.

$^{3-5}$ comprise a verbless sentence, 'Amat-Mamu ... is the *re-di-it wa-ar-ka-ti-ša*'.

$^{6-10}$ a list of property, in apposition to *mimma annîm* in line 11.

^{6} *Gamīnānum* a place name.

^{9} *bītum epšum* 'built-on property'.

$^{15-22}$ another list of property, in apposition to *mimma annîm* in line 23.

^{19} *Qablum* a place name.

^{27} *inaddin* 'she may give'.

2. Adoption, as legitimate son, of the son of a slavewoman (Pinches, *CT* 8 37d = Schorr, *VAB* 5, no. 12, lines 1–17 [18–24 witnesses, 25 date]).

Signs not yet introduced:

 *za, ṣa, sà;*  *ul;*  *ar;*  PÀD.

 5;  *wa;*  *mi;*

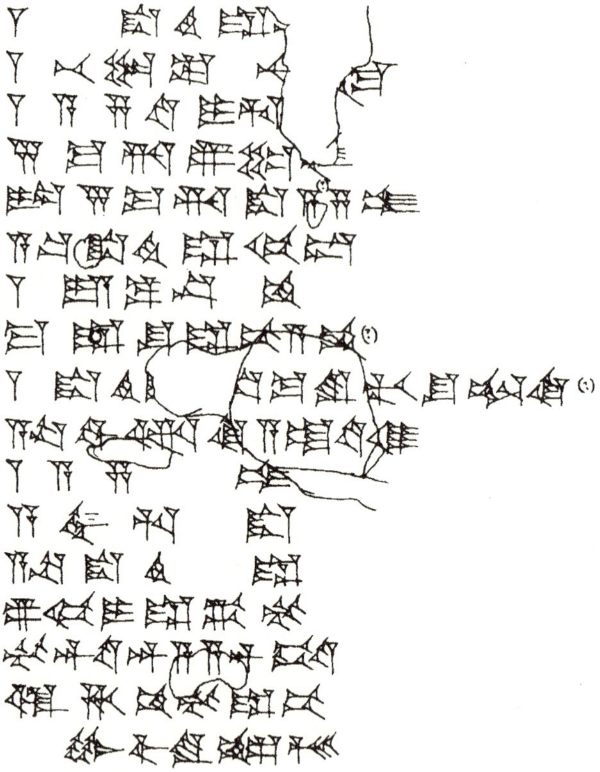

Notes:

PNs: *Šaḫira; Bēlessunu; Asatum; Iakūnum.*

[1] The patronymic (DUMU ...) is lost in the break.

[2] Before the break is *nu;* in the break and after it is *ù.*

[3] Restore *i-ḫu-*[*uz*], here 'took (as wife)' (both Bēlessunu and Asatum).

[4] The second-last sign, TU, is a mistake for LI; the last sign, partly broken, is ZUM. The subject of the verb is Asatum.

[6] The second sign, UD, is a mistake for *na.*

[9] Restore ^{I}*ša-ḫi-*[*ra a-n*]*a* ...

[11] Understand *ù* between ^{I}*a-sà-tum* and *a-aḫ-ḫu-ša.*

[15] ^{d}*a-a* = *Ayya* the consort of Šamaš.

[17] NE here = DÈ; IN.PÀD.DÈ.MEŠ = *itmû.*

LESSON TWENTY-ONE

21.1 Summary of the Verb in the G Stem

The student has now encountered all of the forms associated with the verb in the G stem. These are:

(a) Three indicative "tenses": Durative, Preterite, and Perfect;
(b) Four injunctive forms: Imperative, Precative, Prohibitive, and Vetitive;
(c) Three non-finite or nominal forms: the Infinitive, the Participle, and the Verbal Adjective.
(d) Two morphemes that may occur with any finite verb: the Ventive and the Subordination Marker.

All verbs in the language, in theory at least, occur in each of these forms. Thus far, the G-stem (basic stem) has been presented for triradical sound verbs and for all verb types with one radical subject to phonological change (weak verbs). Following the standard descriptive grammar of Akkadian, W. von Soden's *Grundri_ der akkadischen Grammatik,* we may present verbs in paradigms consisting of "principal parts," arranged in the following order: Infinitive, Durative, Perfect, Preterite, Imperative, Participle, Verbal Adjective (and its base). (Von Soden prefers a slightly different order of presentation.) The finite forms are given in the 3cs (ms for the Imperative), the non-finite forms in the ms. Thus, the G-stem of *parāsum* appears as follows:

parāsum iparras iptaras iprus purus pārisum parsum (paris)

(The Precative and Vetitive are based on the Preterite, the Prohibitive on the Durative.) Paradigms of this type are given for all verb types, in all stems, beginning on page 611.

21.2 *E*-type Verbs

In certain OB dialects, a small group of sound verbs exhibit forms with *e*-vowels in nearly every instance in which normal verbs have *a*-vowels, except the usual endings. These verbs usually have a liquid (*l*, *r*) or nasal (*m*, *n*) as their second or third radical; most have *e* as their theme-vowel. Many of these verbs also exhibit "regular" forms with the expected *a* rather than *e* (and with theme-vowel *i*). Some examples:

šebērum 'to break': *tešebber* (also *tašabbir*) 'you (ms) will break'; *šebram* (*šabram*) 'broken (ms acc.)';

qerēbum 'to approach': *iqterbū* (also *iqtarbū*) 'they (m) have approached'; *qerbētum* (*qarbātum*) 'near (fp nom.)';

ṣeḫērum 'to diminish': *iṣeḫḫerā* (also *iṣaḫḫirā*) 'they (f) diminish';

lemēnum 'to become evil, angry': *eltemnakkim* (also *altamnakkim*) 'I have become angry with you (fs)'.

21.3 Doubly Weak Verbs

The roots of some verbs, many of them among the most common verbs in the language, contain not one but two radicals subject to phonological change: e.g.,

nadûm 'to lay down' (I–*n* and III–weak);
elûm 'to go up' (I–*e* and III–weak);
wârum 'to advance' (I–*w* and II–weak).

In general, it may be said that, if the two weak radicals are the first and third, the phonological changes and peculiarities of each, as described in the previous lessons, will occur. If, however, the middle radical is one of the usually weak consonants, it is most often treated like a strong (regular) radical. In the following paragraphs, the G-stem forms of one or two examples of each doubly weak root type are given in paradigms of the type discussed above in §21.1.

(a) I–*n* and II–ʾ. Most often, the ʾ is a strong (unaltered) radical, as in *naʾādum* (*i*) 'to pay attention, heed'; other roots, however, behave like normal roots II–ʾ, as in *nêrum* (*e*; also *nârum*, see §9.1) 'to slay'.

Infinitive	*naʾādum*	*nêrum* (*nârum*)
Durative	*inaʾʾid*	*inêr* (*inâr*), pl. *inerrū* (*inarrū*)
Perfect	*ittaʾid*	*ittēr* (*ittār*)
Preterite	*iʾʾid*	*inēr* (*inār*)
Imperative	*iʾid*	*nēr* (sic; not ***ēr*) (*nār*)
Participle	*nāʾidum*	**nēʾirum* (**nāʾirum*)
Verbal Adj.	*naʾdum* (*naʾid*)	*nērum* (*nēr*) (*nārum*, *nār*)

(b) I–*n* and II–*w* or II–*y*. A middle *w* behaves like a regular consonant in some roots, such as *nawārum* (*i*) 'to shine', but like a weak consonant in others, such as *nâḫum* (*a–u*) 'to rest'. Verbs I–*n* and II–*y* are conjugated like other verbs II–*y*, as in *niālum* (*a–i*) 'to lie down'.

Infinitive	*nawārum*	*nâḫum*	*niālum*
Durative	*inawwir*	*inâḫ*, pl. *inuḫḫū*	*inīal*, pl. *inillū*
Perfect	*ittawir*	*ittūḫ*	*ittīl*
Preterite	*iwwir*	*inūḫ*	*inīl*
Imperative	**iwir*	**nūḫ*	**nīl*
Participle	**nāwirum*	—	—
Verbal Adj.	*nawirum*	*nēḫum* (*nēḫ*)	*nīlum* (*nīl*)

(c) I–*n* and III–weak. Both weak radicals undergo the usual changes; examples: *nadûm* (*i*) 'to put, lay down'; *nesûm* (*e*) 'to become far away'.

Infinitive	*nadûm*	*nesûm*
Durative	*inaddi*	*inesse*
Perfect	*ittadi*	*ittese*
Preterite	*iddi*	*isse*
Imperative	*idi*	**ise*
Participle	*nādûm*	—
Verbal Adj.	*nadûm* (*nadi*)	*nesûm* (*nesi*)

(d) I–ʾ and II–weak. In this small group, the middle radical is a strong ʾ in *eʾēlum* (*i*) 'to bind', but the first ʾ is preserved between vowels in *êrum* (*e*) 'to awaken'.

Infinitive	*eʾēlum*	*êrum*
Durative	*iʾʾil*	*iʾêr*?
Perfect	?	?
Preterite	*īʾil*?	*iʾēr*
Imperative	*eʾil*	*ēr*?
Participle	—	—
Verbal Adj.	*eʾlum* (*eʾil*)	*ērum* (*ēr*)

(e) I–ʾ and III–weak. Both R_1 and R_3 undergo the usual changes; all of these verbs are III–*i* and most are I–*e*, like *elûm* 'to go up', but note also *arûm* (Durative *irri*, 2fs *tarrî*) 'to conceive, become pregnant'.

Infinitive	*elûm*
Durative	*illi*, *telli*, etc. (rarely also *talli*)
Perfect	*īteli*, *tēteli*, etc. (rarely also *tātali*)
Preterite	*īli*, *tēli*, etc. (rarely also *tāli*)

Imperative	*eli*, fs *elî*, cp *eliā* (rarely also *ali*, etc.)
Participle	*ēlûm*
Verbal Adj.	*elûm* (*eli*)

(f) I–*w* and II–weak. For the most part, the *w* (R_1) remains strong (though sometimes lost) and R_2 behaves as in other verbs II–weak; cf. *wârum* (*a–i*) 'to advance'; **wiāṣum* (*a–i*) 'to become (too) little'.

Infinitive	**wiārum* / *wârum*	**wiāṣum*
Durative	**iwīar* / *i(w)âr*, pl. *i(w)irrū*	**iwīaṣ*, pl. *iwiṣṣū*
Perfect	?	?
Preterite	*iwīr*	*iwīṣ*
Imperative	(*iʾir*)	—
Participle	—	—
Verbal Adj.	?	(*w*)*īṣum* ((*w*)*īṣ*)

(g) I–*w* and III–weak. These exhibit the features of both verbs I–*w* and verbs III–weak. The theme-vowel is the same for both Durative and Preterite, as in other verbs III–weak, and unlike other verbs I–*w* (which are *a–i* verbs); the majority are III–*i*, like *waṣûm* (*i*) 'to go out, forth', but note also *watûm* (*a*) 'to find' and *warûm* (*u*) 'to lead'.

Infinitive	*waṣûm*	*watûm*	*warûm*
Durative	*uṣṣi, tuṣṣi*	*utta, tutta*	*urru, turru*
Perfect	*ittaṣi, tattaṣi*	*ittata, tattata*	*ittaru, tattaru*
Preterite	*uṣi, tuṣi*	*uta, tuta*	*uru, turu*
Imperative	*ṣi*, fs *ṣî*, cp *ṣiā*	*ta*, fs *tî*, cp *tâ*	*ru*, fs *rî*, cp *râ*
Participle	*wāṣûm*	*wātûm*	*wārûm*
Verbal Adj.	*waṣûm* (*waṣi*)	*watûm* (*wati*)	*warûm* (*wari*)

(h) II–ʾ and III–weak. Usually the middle ʾ remains as a regular consonant, although forms with contraction also occur; in non-finite forms ʾ is sometimes replaced by *y* (written with IA; see §21.4, below). In most forms of these verbs, expected *a*-vowels become *e*; the theme-vowel usually vacillates between *i* and *e*; e.g., *leʾûm* 'to be able':

Infinitive	*leʾûm* or *leyûm*, gen. *leʾêm* or *leyêm* or *lêm*		
Durative	*ileʾʾi, teleʾʾi* and *ilê* / *ilî, telê* / *telî*	Imperative	?
Perfect	*ilteʾi, telteʾi* and *iltê, teltê*	Participle	*lēʾûm* / *lēyûm*
Preterite	(*ilʾe, telʾe*) usually *ilē, telē*	Verbal Adj.	**leʾûm* (*leʾi*)

Durative *ilê* is found in northern OB texts, *ilî* in southern texts (and CH).

(i) II–*w* and III–weak. The *w* behaves like a regular consonant, e.g., in *lawûm* (*i*) 'to go around'.

Infinitive	*lawûm*		
Durative	*ilawwi*	Imperative	*liwi*
Perfect	*iltawi*	Participle	*lāwûm*
Preterite	*ilwi*	Verbal Adj.	*lawûm* (*lawi*)

(j) II–*w* or II–*y* and III–ʾ (as opposed to III–*w* / *y* as in the preceding). These are generally conjugated like other verbs II–*w* / *y*, with or without the final ʾ indicated.

bâʾum (*a*) 'to walk along': Durative *ibâ(ʾ)*, Preterite *ibā(ʾ)*.

(k) Trebly weak verbs. There are a few trebly weak verbs:

ewûm 'to become': Durative *iwwi*, Perfect *ītewi*, Preterite *īwi*;
nawûm 'to be abandoned, in ruins': Durative *inawwi*, Verbal Adj. *nawûm* (*nawi*);
awûm (III–*u*) 'to speak' (not in the G-stem in OB).

In these, as the forms indicate, the middle radical *w* is a strong consonant. Still another trebly weak verb, however, is inflected like other verbs II–weak:

nêʾum 'to turn around': Durative *inêʾ*, Preterite *inēʾ*.

21.4 The Writing of ʾ

In Middle Babylonian and later texts, there is a specific sign with the values *V*ʾ and ʾ*V*, i.e., the glottal stop ʾ preceded or followed by any vowel; this sign, Aʾ (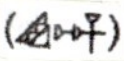), originated as a graphic differentiation of AḪ. In texts of the Old Babylonian period, however, a specific sign for the representation of ʾ was not in use, and so other means were employed to indicate the glottal stop in those words in which it occurred.

The least ambiguous representation of ʾ in OB writing is the use of *ḫ*-signs: for syllable-closing ʾ, the sign AḪ may be used; for syllable-initial ʾ, one finds ḪA, ḪI, and ḪU. Some Assyriologists assign special values to these signs when they are used to indicate ʾ, a convention that will be followed in this textbook:

AḪ = *aḫ*, *eḫ*, *iḫ*, *uḫ*, but also, in OB, *a*ʾ, *e*ʾ, *i*ʾ, *u*ʾ (these values are assigned to the special Aʾ sign in later texts);
ḪA = *ḫa*, but also ʾa_4;
ḪI = *ḫi*, *ḫe*, but also ʾ*ì*;
ḪU = *ḫu*, but also ʾu_5.

Other Assyriologists prefer simply to transliterate these signs with their *ḫ*-values, sometimes using Roman capital letters to indicate that the actual phonetic value is not the usual one. Some examples:

> *i-na-aʾ-ʾì-id* or *i-na-*AḪ-ḪI-*id* for *inaʾʾid* 'she will heed';
> *i-ʾì-id* or *i-*ḪI-*id* for *iʾid* 'heed! (ms)';
> *na-ʾa*$_4$*-du-um* or *na-*ḪA-*du-um* for *naʾādum* 'to heed';
> *na-aʾ-du-um* or *na-*AḪ-*du-um* for *naʾdum* 'pious';
> *nu-uʾ-ʾu*$_5$*-du-um* or *nu-*UḪ-ḪU-*du-um* 'to instruct' (§29.1);
> *še-er-ʾa*$_4$*-num* or *še-er-*ḪA-*num* for *šerʾānum* 'band, vein, tendon';
> *e-ʾì-il-tum* or *e-*ḪI-*il-tum* for *eʾiltum* '(financial) obligation';
> *i-ʾa*$_4$*-al-la-lu-šu* or *i-*ḪA-*al-la-lu-šu* for *iʾallalūšu* 'they (m) will hang him' (CH §21).

Examples like the last, which is the Durative of the verb *alālum* 'to hang' (*a–u*), with a strong ʾ, are exceptions to the usual conjugation of verbs I–ʾ, probably the result of inter-dialectal mixing.

The most common indication of ʾ is simply the writing of an appropriate vowel sign, as in

> *le-ú-um* for *leʾûm* 'to be able' (or Participle *lēʾûm*);
> *it-ta-i-id* for *ittaʾid* 'he has heeded';
> *ša-i-mu-um* for *šāʾimum* 'the one (m) who purchases';
> *še-er-a-num* for *šerʾānum* 'band, vein, tendon'.

Note that a broken writing, i.e., *VC-V(C)*, as in the last example, regularly indicates the presence of ʾ (otherwise, the sequence *VC-V(C)* appears only in certain morphographemic writings; see §18.4). Writings like the first three examples, it will be noted, are the same as writings for two vowels in sequence, as described on p. 71, such as

> *ra-bi-a-am* for *rabiam* 'great (ms, acc.)';
> *ra-bi-a-tum* for *rabiātum* 'great (fp)';
> *ki-a-am* for *kiam* 'thus'.
> *qí-a-šu-um* for *qiāšum* 'to give'.

Whether such writings are to be normalized with or without ʾ depends on a number of factors. It is partly a matter of whether the ʾ is represented as a strong consonant by other means in other writings of the form (e.g., the use of *ḫ*-signs as in *it-ta-*ḪI-*id* for *ittaʾid*; see above), or in writings of other forms of the same root (e.g., the broken writing in *il-e* for *ilʾe* 'he was able'). It is also in part simply a matter of convention; as was noted in §1.2(b), some Assyriologists prefer to transliterate ʾ between *any* two vowels, thus, *rabiʾam, rabiʾātum, kiʾam, qiʾāšum*. In the normalizations in this textbook, the sequences *ia* and *ea* (with long or short *a*) are generally not separated by ʾ, whereas other sequences of two vowels are transliterated *VʾV* (apart from most sequences involving the same vowels; see below).

In some instances, especially in non-finite forms of roots that are both II–ʾ and III–weak, expected ʾ is written with the IA sign, apparently indicating the pronunciation of intervocalic ʾ as a glide, *y*: e.g.,

LUGAL *le-iu-um* for *šarrum lēyûm* 'able king' in the Prologue to CH; contrast *šar-ru-um le-ú-um* for *šarrum lēʾûm* with the same meaning in the Epilogue to CH;

a-na re-ie-em for *ana reyêm* 'in order to tend' (*reʾûm* 'to tend', conjugated like *leʾûm*) in a royal inscription of king Samsu-iluna (Ḫammurapi's successor); contrast *a-na re-em* for *ana reʾêm* or *ana rêm* with the same meaning in CH §265.

Double ʾʾ, which appears only in forms of II–weak verbs and their derivatives, may also be indicated by a vowel sign, as in

i-na-i-id for *inaʾʾid* 'she will heed';
i-na-i-du for *inaʾʾidū* 'they (m) will heed'.

A special difficulty is presented by cases in which vowels of the same quality appear on either side of ʾ or ʾʾ, and *ḫ*-signs are not used. Thus, for example, is the Infinitive *na-a-dum* to be interpreted as *naʾādum* or as *nâdum* (cf. *ša-a-mu-um* for *šâmum* 'to buy')? The former is preferred by most Assyriologists because other forms of this verb frequently have a strong ʾ indicated (whereas other forms of *šâmum* do not). Similarly, writings such as *i*-LI-*i* for the Durative of *leʾûm* 'to be able' may represent either *ileʾʾi*, with strong medial ʾʾ, or *ilî*, with loss of ʾʾ and vowel contraction; since the Preterite occurs as both *il-e* for *ilʾe* and *i-le* for *ilē*, i.e., both with and without ʾ preserved, the Durative writing is ambiguous. A similar difficulty obtains in writings in which ʾ is expected before another consonant, and yet is not indicated by AḪ; e.g., the Verbal Adj. written *na-a-dum* or *na-dum* may be normalized *naʾdum* or *nādum* (with loss of ʾ and compensatory lengthening).

21.5 Topicalization by Preposing

Topicalization is the announcement or emphasis of the topic of a sentence, when the speaker/writer wishes the hearer/reader to focus on a part of the sentence other than the grammatical predicate (i.e., other than the verb in verbal sentences). One means of topicalization in most languages is by intonation or stress (e.g., '*I* saw you there' or 'I saw you *there*'). Presumably, intonation was one means of emphasis in Akkadian, but this type of emphasis is not reflected in the written language. There are two means of topicalizing in Akkadian that are discernible, however: the addition of *-ma* to a word, for which see §29.2; and preposing. In **preposing** (also called "extraposition"), a noun or noun phrase that is the topic of its clause, or that needs emphasis, is dissociated from its clause, and placed at the beginning of the clause, in the **nominative** case. Clauses of this kind thus appear to have two subjects; in fact, however, the first nom. noun (phrase) is not part of the grammar of the clause, and is therefore sometimes termed the **nominative absolute** (also referred to as "casus pendens" [Latin for "hanging case"] or "suspended subject"). The noun or noun phrase that is topicalized in this way is always replaced in its clause by an appropriate pronoun suffix. Some examples:

šarrum māršu imraṣ '(As for) the king — his son fell ill.'

sinništum šī aḫūka iḫḫassi '(As for) that woman — your (ms) brother will marry her.'

ṣuḫārû ša taṭrudīm âm attadiššunūšim '(As for) the servants you (fs) sent me — I have given them grain.'

As the translations indicate, the most convenient representation of preposing in Akkadian is preposing in English: 'As for X ...'. Preposing in Akkadian, however, does not always connote the same emphasis as it does in English; often it is simply a means of announcing the topic of the sentence. Further, the phrase 'as for X' is somewhat stilted in English. Thus, it is often best to translate such sentences by reinserting the preposed noun (phrase) into its original position in the clause. The above sentences, then, could be rendered:

'The king's son fell ill.'

'Your brother will marry that woman.'

'I have given grain to the servants you sent me.'

Like resumptive pronouns (§18.2, p. 168), preposing serves several discourse functions, including easing comprehension in a complicated sentence, highlighting a topic, announcing a new topic, or marking the end of a section of discourse. The frequency of preposing varies from genre to genre: it is common in the protases of laws and of omens (§22.3), less so in contracts and letters (§24.5).

EXERCISES

A. VOCABULARY 21.

Verbs:

elûm (*i*) 'to go up, ascend'; with Ventive: 'to come up, emerge, appear'; Verbal Adj. *elûm* (*eli-*; fem. *elītum*) 'high, tall, exalted'.

lawûm (*i*) 'to go around, circle, encircle; to surround, besiege'; Verbal Adj. *lawûm* (*lawi-*) 'encircled, surrounded'.

leʾûm (*i*) 'to be able' (to do: + acc. Infin.; e.g., *epēš(am ša) bītim eleʾʾi* 'I am able to build the house'); 'to become expert, a master; to overpower (someone), win (a legal case)'; Participle *lēʾûm* (fem. *lēʾītum*) 'able, capable, expert'.

naʾādum (*i*) 'to pay attention, heed (someone: *ana*/dat.); to be concerned, worried (about: *ana*/dat.)'; in hendiadys: 'to do (something) carefully'; Verbal Adj. *naʾdum* (*naʾid-*) and *nādum* (*nād-*) 'attentive, pious; careful'.

nadûm (*i*) 'to throw (down), set (down), lay (down), pour (something into something); to neglect, abandon, ignore; to knock out (e.g., a tooth); to lay a criminal charge (against: *eli*)'; *aḫam nadûm* 'to be negligent (lit.: to let down one's arm)'; *ša libbim nadûm* 'to have a miscarriage'; Verbal Adj. *nadûm* (*nadi-*; fem. *nadītum*) 'abandoned; fallow; laid, lying, situated'; substantivized fem. *nadītum* see Vocab. 20.

nakārum (*i*) 'to become different, strange; to become hostile, engage in hostilities; to change (intrans.); to deny, dispute (something: acc.; to/with someone: acc.)'; Verbal Adj. *nakarum*, *nakirum*, *nakrum* see Vocab. 4.

našûm (*i*) 'to lift (up), raise; to carry, bear, support; to transport, deliver; to take, accept, receive (from: *ina qāt*); to remove'; *īnīn našûm* 'to look up'; *īnīn ana X našûm* 'to look at X, covet X'.

qerēbum (*e* or *i*) 'to draw near, approach' (+ *ana*/dat.); Verbal Adj. *qerbum* (*qerub-*) 'near, at hand, close by'; as noun: 'relative'.

waṣûm (*i*) 'to go out, go forth, depart, leave, escape; to protrude, grow'; with Ventive: 'to come forth, out, emerge, appear'; Verbal Adj. *waṣûm* (*waṣi-*) 'gone (forth), outside; protruding'.

Nouns:

dūrum (*dūr(i)*; pl. *dūrānū*; log. BÀD) 'wall'.

kiṣrum (*kiṣir*; pl. *kiṣrū*) 'knot; joint (of the body or a plant); constriction, concentration; lump; band, contingent (of soldiers); payment (for rent, services, etc.; often pl.); region, section'; *kiṣir libbim* 'anger'; *kiṣir šadîm* 'bedrock' (cf. *kaṣārum*).

meḫrum (*meḫer*; pl. *meḫrū* and *meḫrētum*) 'copy (of a document), list; answer, reply; equivalent, fellow, person of the same rank; weir' (cf. *maḫārum*).

šībūtum (*šībūt*) '(old) age; testimony, witness' (cf. *šiābum*).

šinnum (fem.; *šinni*; sf. *šinna-*; dual *šinnān*; log. ZÚ [= the KA sign]) 'tooth'; for 'teeth' the dual (i.e., two rows) is used.

B. Learn the following signs:

OB Lapid.	OB Cursive	NA	values
			LÚ = *awīlum*; determinative [lú] before men's occupations
	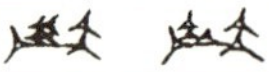		ŠEŠ = *aḫum*
			BÀD = *dūrum*
			*wa, we, wi, wu*; *pi, pe* (in southern OB texts)
		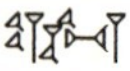	*úḫ*
			*u* (rare)
			*ul*
	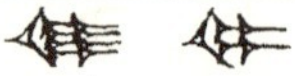		*mi, mé; ṣíl*
		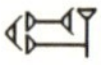	*nim, num*
			*eš, ìš*
	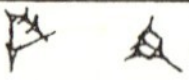		*din*

Note also the additional values of AḪ, ḪA, ḪI, ḪU given above in §21.4.

C. Write the following words in cuneiform and in transliteration; use logograms where appropriate in 1–5:

1. *immer awīlim* 3. *idi dūrim* 5. *aḫāt rēdîm* 7. *inaʾʾidūnim*
2. *imēr aḫīya* 4. *agûšu* 6. *inaddin* 8. *ul imḫur*

9. *idin*
10. *naʾādum*
11. *puḫrum*
12. *tešmî*
13. *elteʾi*
14. *waṣûm*
15. *laʾbum*
16. *šarkam*
17. *warādam*
18. *līgurānim*

D. Write in normalized Akkadian:

1. I have come up.
2. Go forth (fs) from the house of the prefect!
3. We will approach their (m) district.
4. Whose valuables did they (m) covet?
5. Throw (ms) them (m) from the top of the wall!
6. I am able to go up the mountain.
7. May the heir heed his father.
8. You (pl) have encircled the entire land.
9. They (f) have drawn near.
10. Survey (pl) the fallow fields!
11. What did the pious prince heap up?
12. The message has gone forth.
13. You (fs) approached me.
14. The reply to (lit.: of) my tablet has not yet come forth to me.
15. I am not able to drink the beer.
16. Put down (ms) the new seal.
17. They will surround us.
18. Go up (pl) with her gift.
19. The princess will come near.
20. I besieged it (m).
21. You (pl) have emerged (lit.: come up) from your slavery.
22. The evil one (m) has overpowered him.
23. You (ms) have become negligent concerning my mother.
24. Go out (ms) by the gate.
25. We have come out of the house.

E. Normalize and translate:

1. *šum-ma* DUB-*pu-um ša-nu-um ša pu-ru-sé-em an-ni-im i-li-a-am* DUB-*pa-am šu-a-ti i-ḫe-ep-pu-ú*.
2. *wa-ši-ib bi-tim ki-iṣ-ra-am ga-am-ra-am a-na ma-ḫi-ir i-la-ku a-na be-el bi-tim ù ne-me-ta-šu wa-ta-ar-tam a-na* É.GAL *li-is-du-ur-ma li-id-di-in*.
3. *ša-ak-nu-um me-ḫe-er ka-ni-ki-ia ka-an-ki-im i-ri-ša-an-ni*.
4. LUKUR *la ba-li-tum iš-tu* GÁ.GI$_4$.A *a-di* UD-*um ru-gu-um-me-em la-a ú-uṣ-ṣí*.
5. ÌR *la-a ta-ak-lum ša šu-um be-lí-šu la-a iz-ku-ru le-et-sú am-ḫa-aṣ-ma ši-in-na-šu ú-ṣí-a-nim*.
6. *ni-šu ḫa-di-a-tum ša i-na pa-ni* LUGAL *ip-ḫu-ra-ma a-wa-ti-šu na-as-qá-tim iš-me-a li-ib-ba-ši-na ip-ša-aḫ*.

7. *i-na-an-na ṣú-ḫa-ru-ú ša a-na pa-ni-ia ta-aš-ku-nu a-na al-pí ša e-zi-bu-šu-nu-ti li-i*^{ʾ}*-*^{ʾ}*ì-du-šu-nu-ši-im-ma ba-aq-ri a-a-ir-šu-ú.*
8. *i-na-an-na ma-tum an-ni-tum id-da-ni-in-ma it-ti-ni it-ta-ki-ir ki-iṣ-ri-ka ku-ṣu-ur-ma it-ti-ša ka-ak-ki e-pu-uš.*
9. *aš-ša-tum maḫ-ri-tum te-er-ḫa-tam ù še-ri-ik-tam a-na ma-ri-ša ša i-ra-am-mu i-šar-ra-ak a-na a-ḫi-i-im la-a i-pa-aš-šar-ši-na-ti.*
10. *na-še-e ma-ru-uš-tim an-ni-tim ša ì-lí e-li-ia i-mi-du ú-ul e-le-i.*

F. CH:

§3 *šum-ma a-wi-lum i-na di-nim a-na ši-bu-ut sà-ar-ra-tim ú-ṣí-a-am-ma a-wa-at iq-bu-ú la uk-ti-in šum-ma di-nu-um šu-ú di-in na-pí-iš-tim a-wi-lum šu-ú id-da-ak.*

sarrum (adj.; fem. sg. irregular: *sartum*) 'false'.
uktīn 'he has proved'.

§106 *šum-ma šamallûm*(ŠAMAN$_2$.LÁ) KUG.BABBAR *it-ti* DAM.GÀR *il-qé-ma* DAM.GÀR-*šu it-ta-ki-ir* DAM.GÀR *šu-ú i-na ma-ḫar i-lim ù ši-bi i-na* KUG.BABBAR *le-qé-em šamallâm*(ŠAMAN$_2$.LÁ) *ú-ka-an-ma šamallûm*(ŠAMAN$_2$.LÁ) KUG.BABBAR *ma-la il-qú-ú adi*(A.RÁ) 3-*šu a-na* DAM.GÀR *i-na-ad-di-in.*

ina kaspim leqêm ... ukān 'he will convict ... of taking the silver'.
adi 3-šu 'three-fold' (see §23.2(f)).

§200:

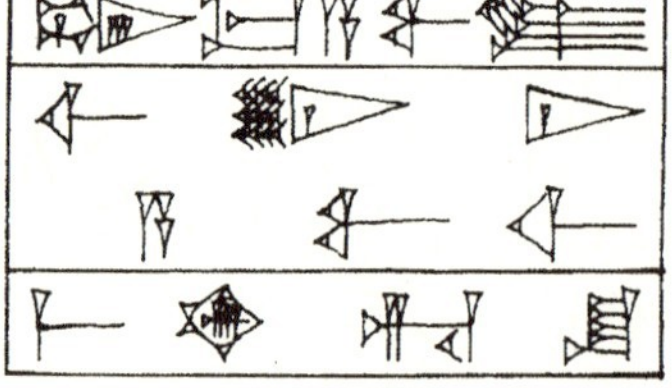

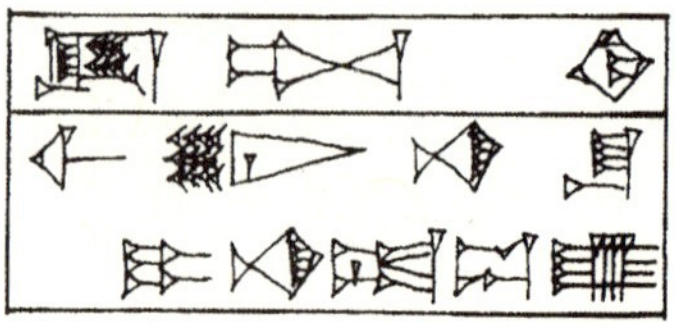

 *me.*

G. Contracts:

1. Marriage to a main and a secondary wife (*CT* 2 44 = Schorr, *VAB* 5, no. 4).

^{1} ^{I}*ta-ra-am-*SAG-ÍL ^{2} *ù il-ta-ni* ^{3} DUMU.MUNUS ^{d}EN.ZU-*a-bu-šu* ^{4} ^{I}ÌR-^{d}UTU *a-na aš-šu-tim* ^{5} *ù mu-tu-tim i-ḫu-sí-na-ti* ^{6} ^{I}*ta-ra-am-*SAG-ÍL ^{7} *ù il-ta-ni* ^{8} *a-na* ÌR-^{d}UTU *mu-ti-ši-na* ^{9} *ú-ul mu-ti at-ta* ^{10} *i-*

qá-ab-bi-ma iš-tu dimtim(AN.ZAG.GAR^{ki}) [11] *i-na-du-ni-ši-na-ti* [12] *ù* ^{I}ÌR-^{d}UTU *a-na ta-ra-am*-SAG-ÍL [13] *ù il-ta-ni aš-ša-ti-šu* [14] *ú-ul aš-ša-ti at-ti* [15] *i-qá-bi-ma i-na bi-tim* [16] *... i-te-li* [17] *ù il-ta-ni* [18] *še*$_{20}$*-pí ta-ra-am*-SAG-ÍL [19] *i-me-sí-i* [20] *kussī*(^{giš}GU.ZA)*-ša a-na* É *i-li-ša* [21] *i-na-ši ze-ni ta-ra-am*-SAG-ÍL [22] ^{I}*il-ta-ni i-ze-né ...* [24] *ku-nu-ki-ša ú-ul i-pé-te ...* [26–35] Witnesses.

PNs: *Tarām-Sagil; Iltani; Sîn-abūšu; Warad-Šamaš.*
[10] *dimtum* (log. AN.ZA.GÀR; the writing here is unique) 'tower'.
[16] *ina X ītelli* 'he will forfeit X'.
[19] *mesûm* (*e* or *i*) 'to wash'; here with extra final vowel-sign.
[21] *zenûm* (*e*) 'to hate'.

2. Sale of oil (Szlechter, *TJA* p. 42 UMM H 32)

[1] *x* Ì.GIŠ ... [3] KI *šum-šu-nu ...* [4] *a-na qá-bé-e ba-aš-ti-il-a-bi* [5] ^{I}*in-bu-ša* DUMU *ba-zi-ia* [6] ŠU.BA.AN.TI [7] *ūm ebūrim*(UD.BURU$_{14}$.ŠÈ) [8] *a-na na-ši ka-ni-ki-šu* [9] *y* ŠE ... [10] *imaddad*(Ì.ÁG.E) [11–13] Witnesses. [14–16] Date.

PNs: *Šumšunu; Bāšti-il*ʾ*abi; Inbūša; Baziya.*

3. Lease of a house (Chiera, *PBS* 8/2, no. 186).

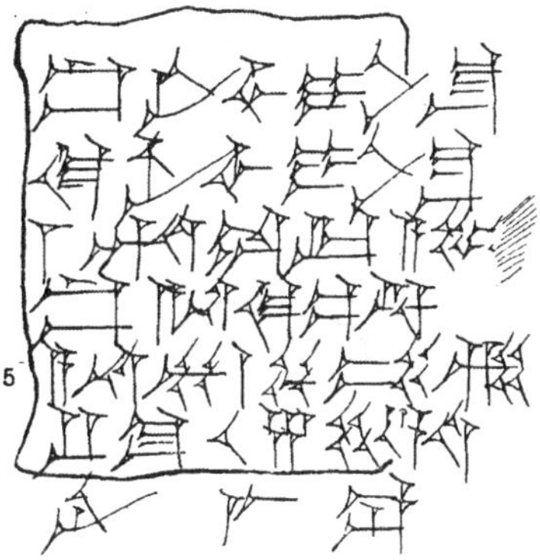

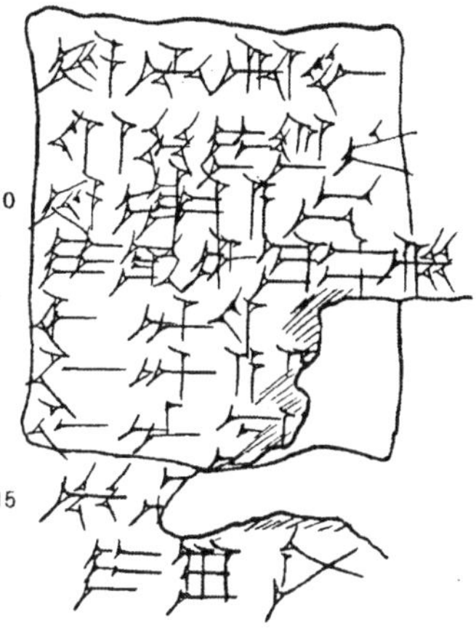

Signs not yet introduced:

 *ur*;  1/3 GÍN;  15;  EZEN.

Notes:

PNs: *Nīši-īnīšu; Šamaš-dūr-āli.*
[5] *a-na* MU.1.KAM = *ana 1 šattim; ušēṣi* 'he rented, leased'.

[6] ŠE as a unit of measurement = *uṭṭetum* 'grain'; this line reads $^{1}/_{3}$ GÍN 15 ŠE KUG.BABBAR = *$^{1}/_{3}$ šiqil 15 uṭṭet kaspam* '$^{1}/_{3}$ shekel, 15 grains of silver' (see §23.2(b,2)).

[8,10] *Tirum* month name.

[9] UD.1.KAM read *ūmam maḫriam* '(on) the first day' (of the month of Tirum).

[10] EZEN = *isinnum* 'festival', also to write the city of *Isin*; *Isin-abi* month name.

[12] Probably nothing followed ^{d}UTU.

[13] Probably nothing followed ^{d}*a-a* (the goddess *Ayya*, consort of Shamash).

[14] Restore ^{d}*ma-[ma]*, the goddess *Mama*.

[15–16] These lines give the date: MU *s[a-am-su]-i-lu-ni*, presumably for 'year Samsu-iluna (became king)', i.e., Samsu-iluna year 1 = ca. 1749 BCE.

LESSON TWENTY-TWO

22.1 The Predicative Construction

Adjectives may be used attributively, as in 'the wide river', and predicatively, as in 'the river is wide'. As we have seen (§4.2), an attributive adjective in Akkadian follows the noun it modifies and agrees with it in gender, number, and case. Adjectives that serve as the predicate of their clause normally appear in an entirely different syntactic construction. This predicative construction is comprised of two elements:

(1) the base of the adjective;
(2) an enclitic (i.e., suffixed) pronoun that serves as the subject.

The two elements of a predicative construction constitute a verbless predication in which the predicate precedes its pronominal subject, as we have seen to be the case in other verbless clauses (see §2.5); for example, compare the following two clauses:

ina ālim anāku 'I am/was/will be in the town' (lit., 'in the town–I');
dannāku 'I am/was/will be strong' (lit., 'strong–I').

The difference between these two clauses is that when the predicate is an adjective (or an unmodified noun; see below), the predicative construction with its enclitic form of the pronoun is used. Below are the forms of the enclitic subject pronouns, and the complete paradigm of the predicative construction with the adjective *marṣum* 'sick':

1cs	*-āku*	as in	*marṣāku*	'I am/was/will be sick'
2ms	*-āta*	as in	*marṣāta*	'you (ms) are/were/will be sick'
2fs	*-āti*	as in	*marṣāti*	'you (fs) are/were/will be sick'
3ms	*-ø*	as in	*maruṣ*	'he is/was/will be sick'
3fs	*-at*	as in	*marṣat*	'she is/was/will be sick'
1cp	*-ānu*	as in	*marṣānu*	'we are/were/will be sick'
2mp	*-ātunu*	as in	*marṣātunu*	'you (mp) are/were/will be sick'
2fp	*-ātina*	as in	*marṣātina*	'you (fp) are/were/will be sick'
3mp	*-ū*	as in	*marṣū*	'they (m) are/were/will be sick'
3fp	*-ā*	as in	*marṣā*	'they (f) are/were/will be sick'

Note also the following rare byforms: 2ms *-āti* and *-āt*, 2fs *-āt*, and 1cs *-āk*.

As can be seen from the example above, the form of the pronoun in the first and second persons is reminiscent of the independent personal pronouns; in the third person plural (and dual), the pronoun elements are the same as the corresponding endings on finite verbs; for the third fem. sg. the enclitic pronoun is *-at*, while for the third masc. sg. it is *-ø*, i.e., no ending appears after the adjective base. Note that the addition of the pronominal elements causes the expected syncope of the theme-vowel in the Verbal Adjective, so that the full adjective base appears only with the 3ms subject.

The predicative form that results from the combination of adjective base and enclitic pronoun is subject to the usual rules of vowel contraction. Vowel harmony affects only *a*-vowels that are *non-final*; further, vowel harmony does not usually affect the pronominal elements after adjectives of roots III–*e*. When the base of the adjective ends in a double consonant, as in *dann-* 'strong', the doubling is simplified in the predicative form with 3ms subject: *dan* 'he is/was/will be strong'. Additional paradigms of predicative forms will illustrate these points; note *ezbum* 'abandoned', *rabûm* 'great', *šemûm* 'heard', *dannum* 'strong':

1cs	*ezbēku*	*rabiāku*	*šemiāku*	*dannāku*
2ms	*ezbēta*	*rabiāta*	*šemiāta*	*dannāta*
2fs	*ezbēti*	*rabiāti*	*šemiāti*	*dannāti*
3ms	*ezib*	*rabi*	*šemi*	*dan*
3fs	*ezbet*	*rabiat*	*šemiat*	*dannat*
1cp	*ezbēnu*	*rabiānu*	*šemiānu*	*dannānu*
2mp	*ezbētunu*	*rabiātunu*	*šemiātunu*	*dannātunu*
2fp	*ezbētina*	*rabiātina*	*šemiātina*	*dannātina*
3mp	*ezbū*	*rabû*	*šemû*	*dannū*
3fp	*ezbā*	*rabiā*	*šemiā*	*dannā*

Like the root of the verb *danānum* 'to be strong', the verb *madādum* 'to measure' has a root in which R_2 and R_3 are the same. But whereas *danānum* is a stative verb, and so has a Verbal Adj. with base *dann-*, *madādum* is active, and so the base of its Verbal Adj. is *madid-* (see §4.3(a), end); thus the predicative form with 3ms subject is *madid* 'it (m) is/was/will be measured'. (Predicative forms with other subjects resemble those of *dann-*, e.g., with 3fs: *maddat*; with 3mp: *maddū*.)

When a noun is the subject of a clause with an adjectival predicate, that noun is resumed by the appropriate third person enclitic pronoun in the predicative construction:

ilatni ina mātīšunu palḫat 'our goddess is/was feared/fearsome in their (m) land';

qarrādū šarrim ana māt nakrim tebû 'the king's warriors are/were under way to the enemy's land';
ṭuppātūšunu ḫepiā 'their (m) tablets are/were broken';
bābum peti (i.e., *peti-ø*) 'the door is/was open'.

As these examples show, the predicative form stands at the end of its clause. Occasionally, an independent pronoun also occurs before a predicative form, usually to focus attention on the pronoun subject:

anāku ul wašbāku 'I myself was not around' (lit.: 'resident');
atta ana mārūtim nadnāta 'it is you who were given up for adoption'.

It is important that the distinction in meaning between the predicative form of a Verbal Adjective and the finite tenses of the same verb be clear, especially when active-intransitive verbs and adjectival/stative verbs are involved. The tenses (Preterite, Durative, and Perfect) all denote the **process** of a verbal root; the predicative construction, as its name implies, predicates the **condition** or **state** that is the result of the action of the verb. Some examples:

uššab 'he is/was (in the process of) sitting down', *ušib* 'he sat down, became seated', but *wašib* 'he is/was seated, sitting';
amraṣ 'I got sick, fell ill', but *marṣāku* 'I am/was sick';
iḫliq 'she escaped, got lost', but *ḫalqat* 'she is/was escaped, lost';
imaqqut 'it is/was collapsing' (or, 'will collapse'), but *maqit* 'it (m) is in ruins (collapsed)';
idmiqā 'they (f) became good, they improved', but *damqā* 'they are/were good';
īter 'it became excessive', but *watar* 'it is/was excessive';
tadannin 'you (ms) are/were growing strong, growing in strength', but *dannāta* 'you are/were strong';
itebbû 'they (m) are/were setting out, (in the process) of standing up', but *tebû* 'they are/were under way, standing'.

In a subordinate clause, a predicative form with 3ms subject is marked with *-u*, but other persons are unchanged; e.g.,

ṣuḫārum ša ana Bābilim ṭardu imūt 'the servant who was sent to Babylon died';
amtam ša ina bītīki wašbat ul āmur 'I have not seen the female slave who is living in your (fs) house'.

Predicative forms with 3ms subject and with third person plural subject may occur with the Ventive morpheme, as in the following examples:

dayyānū tebûnim 'the judges are on their way here';
awâtum kašdānim 'the news (lit., 'words') has arrived here'.

Predicative forms may also be accompanied by dative suffixes:

bītum šū nadiššim 'that house is/was given to her';
mār šiprim ša ṭardūkum / ṭardakkum 'the messenger who is/was sent to you (ms)';
amtum ša ṭardassum 'the female slave who is/was sent to him';
iltum wašbatkum 'the goddess is present for you (ms)'.

In most Assyriological works, including the standard grammars and dictionaries, the predicative construction with a Verbal Adjective base is referred to as the **Stative**, a term reserved in this textbook to describe the semantic characteristics of certain verbal root types, such as *danānum* 'be(come) strong'. In the modern Akkadian dictionaries, further, the predicative forms of Verbal Adjectives are usually listed not under the Verbal Adjective itself but rather under the Infinitive of the verb (although there is some inconsistency in this regard).

While the vast majority of examples of the predicative construction involve Verbal Adjectives, the construction may also be used in verbless clauses in which the predicate is a noun. The enclitic pronouns are added directly to the noun base; even the feminine ending *-(a)t* does not appear before the pronouns (or, is replaced by them):

PN_1 *ana* PN_2 *aššat; ana* PN_3 *amat* 'PN_1 is wife to PN_2; she is servant to PN_3';
sinnišānu 'we are women';
mārāku kallāku ḫīrāku u abrakkāku 'I am daughter, bride (*kallatum*), spouse (*ḫīrtum*), and steward (*ab(a)rakkum*)'.

The same rules of vowel harmony, vowel contraction, and simplification of double consonants apply to predicative forms with noun bases as were seen to apply to those with adjective bases:

ina šamê bēlēti 'you are mistress in heaven';
rubâku 'I am/was prince';
šar 'he is/was king'.

The predicative construction with a noun base occurs only in a very restricted environment. Specifically, it may occur only if the predicate noun is not followed by any modifiers, viz., an adjective, a genitive noun, a possessive (genitive) pronominal suffix, a relative clause, the particle *-ma* when it is not a coordinator (§29.2). When a modifying word or phrase follows, the noun appears in its regular or bound form, and the subject, if it is a pronoun, is an independent nominative pronoun

(§2.4). Even when no modifier follows the predicate noun, the use of the predicative construction is not required, but merely optional. Study the following sets of examples:

Ḫammurapi šarrum dannum 'Hammurapi is a mighty king'
Ḫammurapi šar Bābilim 'Hammurapi is/was king of Babylon';
Ḫammurapi šarrani 'Hammurapi is/was our king';
Ḫammurapi šar(rum ša) nipallaḫu 'Hammurapi is/was the king we revere';
Ḫammurapi šarrum or *Ḫammurapi šar* 'Hammurapi is/was (the) king'

šarrum dannum atta 'you (ms) are a mighty king'
šar Bābilim atta 'you (ms) are king of Babylon'
šarrani atta 'you (ms) are our king'
šar(rum ša) nipallaḫu atta 'you are/were the king we revere'
šarrum atta or *šarrāta* 'you (ms) are (the) king'

The distinction in meaning between *Ḫammurapi šarrum* and *Ḫammurapi šar* is one of markedness; the former may mean 'Hammurapi is king', but also, in some contexts, 'king Hammurapi'; the latter is specifically marked as a predication. Similarly, *šarrum atta* may mean 'you (ms) are (the) king' or 'you, O king', whereas *šarrāta* is only 'you are (the) king'.

22.2 Injunctions in Verbless Clauses

To express positive injunctions in verbless clauses, i.e., to express 'may/let ... be', the particle *lū* is used:

Adad lū bēl dīnīka 'may Adad (storm-god) be your (ms) adversary' (*bēl dīnim* 'adversary');
abūšu lū atta 'be (ms) his father';
lū dannātunu 'be (mp) strong';
lū ṭardū 'may they/let them (m) be on their way' (lit., 'sent');
lū awīlāta or *lū awīlum atta* 'be (ms) a man'.

The negative of *lū* in such expressions is *lā*; note that the use of *lā* instead of *ul* is all that marks verbless clauses as negative injunctions rather than negative statements (just as with *lā* vs. *ul* before Durative verbs; see §16.3(a)):

kaspum ul nadin 'the silver is/was not given';
kaspum lā nadin 'the silver may/must not be given'.

ul enšēta 'you (ms) are not weak';
lā enšēta 'do (ms) not be weak, you may/must not be weak'.

22.3 Omen Texts

The ancient Mesopotamians believed that the future could be foretold. A given natural phenomenon that had been observed to be followed by a certain event was deemed to be predictive; i.e., that phenomenon would *always* be followed by, or associated with, the same event. Because the ability to predict the future was obviously very advantageous, the Mesopotamians did not simply wait for predictive phenomena; they actively solicited them. A wide range of phenomena were considered portentive; among the most frequently consulted by the diviners were the internal organs of slaughtered animals (usually sheep or goats), especially the arrangement, characteristics, and distinctive features of the liver, gall bladder, and lungs. The general term for this kind of divination is extispicy (examination of the exta); the examination of the liver in particular is called hepatoscopy. Other phenomena observed were the flights of birds; the behavior of other animals, including insects; patterns of smoke in the air and of oil on water; strange births of animals; and dreams.

Because so many different kinds of phenomena were deemed ominous, and the possible variations within each type of phenomenon virtually infinite, it was necessary for the diviners to write down individual omens. These were then assembled into collections of omens, called series, some of them quite large, to be learned and consulted by the diviners. Omen texts constitute a distinctly Akkadian genre; although there are references to the practice of divination in Sumerian texts, the earliest recorded omens stem from the OB period, and are in Akkadian. The genre continues to the end of the time during which Akkadian was written. After economic or administrative documents, omen texts form the largest genre of cuneiform texts.

Formally, individual omens are conditional sentences. The protasis presents the observation of a certain phenomenon, while the apodosis indicates the event that is expected as a result of the observation (frequently in a very curt, sometimes enigmatic phrase). The tenses used are those indicated for conditional sentences in general (see §17.3(b)), although it should be noted that verbless clauses, including many predicative forms, abound. Another grammatical point of note is orthographic: there are frequent, and unexplained, writings of final short vowels with an extra vowel sign, as in *qá-as-sú-ú* for *qāssu* 'his hand'. Some examples from *YOS* 10:

šumma marrātum šittā — dikšum 'If the gall-bladders (*martum*) are two (*šittā*) — a wound (*dikšum*)' (31 x 45–47);

šumma marrātum šalāš — dikšān šinā itebbûšum 'If the gall-bladders are three — two (*šinā*) wounds will happen to him' (31 x 48–52);

šumma martum ina qablīša naksat — gillatum ina mātim ibašši 'If the gall-bladder is cut in its middle (*qablum*) — there will be (*ibašši*) crime (*gillatum*) in the land' (31 v 31–36);

šumma izbum kīma libittim — mā[tam d]annatum iṣabbat-ma kurrum imaqqut 'If a deformed foetus (*izbum*) is like a brick (*libittum*) — duress will seize the land, and the *kur*-measure will fall' (56:8–9);

šumma ina birīt martim šīlum šakin — šarram ina pānī pilšim idukkūšu 'If a depression (*šīlum*) is situated in the middle of the gall-bladder — they will kill the king in front of a breach' (31 i 41–46).

Note that in the last two protases the usual order of subject and object is reversed, a common occurrence in these texts.

Extremely frequent in omen protases is the device of topicalizing by preposing (§21.5); e.g.,

šumma martum pānūša ana šumēlim šaknū 'if the "face" of the gall-bladder is located on the left' (lit.: 'if the gall-bladder — its "face" is located ...') (31 ii 42–45).

In their attempts to make the omen lists as complete as possible, the diviners often followed one symptom with its antithesis, or another closely related symptom: e.g., 'If the two dark marks of the left side ride up against one another — you will acquire a partner and defeat your enemy. If the two dark marks of the right side ride up against one another — your enemy will acquire a partner and defeat you' (11 v 3–8). Sometimes the desire for completeness resulted in protases involving rather unlikely phenomena: e.g., 'If the gall-bladders are seven — the king of the universe' (31 xiii 19–21).

EXERCISES

A. VOCABULARY 22.

Verbs:

maṣûm (*i*) 'to be equal to; to amount to, be sufficient for'; *mala libbim maṣûm* 'to have full discretion, do what one wants' (e.g., *mala libbīšu imaṣṣi* 'he may do what he wants'); Verbal Adj. *maṣûm* (*maṣi-*) 'sufficient, enough', in predicative use, *maṣi* 'is sufficient, enough; amounts to'; *kī maṣi* 'how much(?)'; *mala maṣû* 'as far as it extends, as much as there is'.

saḫārum (*u*) 'to go/walk around, surround, circle, curve; to turn, turn around, turn back, rotate, twist (intrans.); to seek, look for, turn to (someone)'.

šebērum (*e* or *i*) 'to break (trans.)'; Verbal Adj. *šebrum* (*šebir-*) 'broken'.

tabālum (*a*) 'to take away, carry off, away; to take for oneself, take along' (cf. *wabālum*).

Nouns:

amūtum (fem.; pl. rare) '(sheep's) liver; (liver) omen'.

bāʾerum (*bāʾer*; Participle of *bârum* 'to fish'; log. (lú)ŠU.ḪA) 'fisherman'; also, a class of soldier.

imittum a (fem. and, often in omens, masc.; *imitti*; fem. of rare adj. *imnum* 'right'; log. ZAG) 'right (side), right hand'.

imittum b (*imitti*; dual *imittān*; log. ZAG) 'shoulder of an animal' (cf. *emēdum*).

martum (fem., rarely masc. in omens; originally *marratum*, the fem. of a Verbal Adj. *marrum* 'bitter'; pl. *marrātum*; log. ZÉ) 'gall bladder; bile, gall'.

maṣṣarum (*maṣṣar*; pl. *maṣṣarū*) 'watchman; watch; garrison'; *maṣṣarūtum* (*maṣṣarūt*) 'safe-keeping, custody' (cf. *naṣārum*).

pūḫum (*pūḫ(i)*; pl. *pūḫū* and *pūḫātum*) 'substitute, replacement'; often in apposition to a preceding noun (e.g., *eqlam pūḫam idnam* 'give me a replacement field, a field as replacement').

riksum (*rikis*; pl. *riksātum* [often = sg.]) 'band; contract, agreement, treaty'; *riksam/riksātim šakānum* 'to establish an agreement, make out a contract'.

šumēlum (*šumēl*; log. GÙB) 'left (side), left hand'.

Preposition:

balum (with suffix *balukka*, *balušsu*, etc.) 'without, without the knowledge/consent of; apart from'; *ina balum* = *balum*.

Proper Name:

Adad (log. IŠKUR [the IM sign]) 'Adad' (storm god).

Note also the following terms referring to parts/areas of the liver:

bāb ekallim ('palace gate') the umbilical fissure.
kakkum ('weapon') a distinctive (and portentive) mark on the liver.
naplaštum (pl. *naplasātum*; cf. §5.4) 'flap, lobe'.
padānum ('path') near the *naplaštum*.
šēpum ('foot') like the *kakkum*, a distinctive mark.

B. Learn the following signs:

OB Lapid. / OB Cursive / NA	values
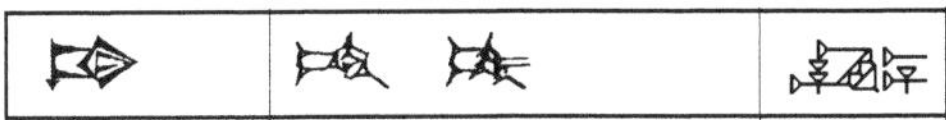	*dur, ṭur, túr*
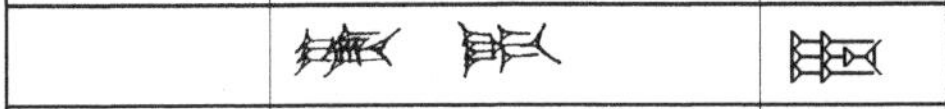	ZAG = *imittum* (a and b)
	*gir, kir, qir*
	*bur, pur*
	*ar*
	*ù* (in *u* 'and', *ū* 'or'; rare otherwise)
	*me, mì*; munus+me = LUKUR = *nadītum*
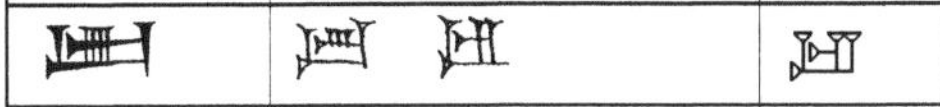	*ib/p, eb/p*
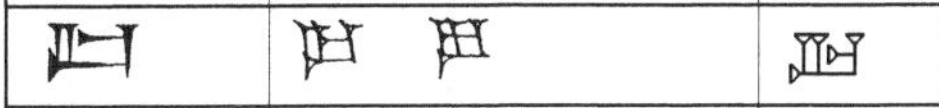	*ur, lig/k/q, taš*
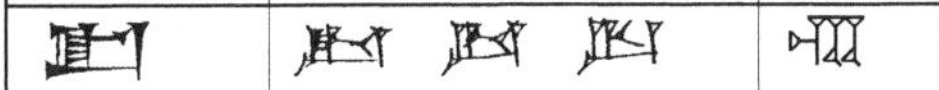	*kab/p*; GÙB = *šumēlum*
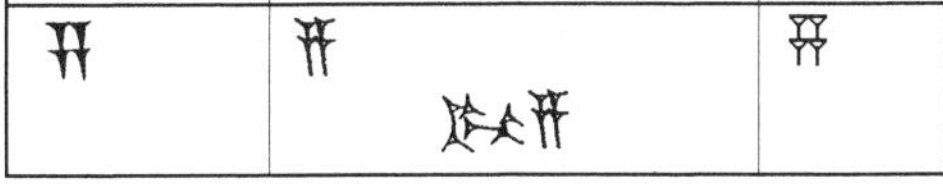	*ṣa, za, sà*; (giš)GU.ZA = *kussûm*

Note also the following three logograms used in various omen texts for *šumma*:  DIŠ;  BE;  MAŠ.

C. Write the following words in cuneiform and in transliteration; use logograms where appropriate in 1–6:

1. *kussi aḫīkunu*
2. *rēš martim*
3. *dūr ālim*
4. *aḫāt awīlim kabtim*
5. *imittum u šumēlum*
6. *warkat rēdîm*
7. *ikkir*
8. *am-mīnim luddin*
9. *urṣam šebram*
10. *ešmē-ma allik*
11. *lušpur*
12. *ul tašṭur*
13. *aturram*
14. *ṭuḫdam*
15. *eʾiltum*

D. Write in normalized Akkadian:

1. Our fields filled with water; our fields were full of water.
2. May his name ascend; may his name be exalted.
3. They (f) are resident in these towns; they will live in these towns.
4. The lower rivers will become wide; they are wide.
5. May you (ms) not become ill; you were not ill.
6. She is dead; she has died.
7. The army of the enemy is approaching us; it is near (Ventive).
8. You (fs) became well; you were well.
9. The wall became old; it was old.
10. Among the people you are father; you are the father of the people.
11. You are mistress in heaven; you are their (f) mistress.
12. You are women; you are the women who entered the vineyard.
13. May warriors be assembled; let them assemble.
14. Our cities have fallen; they are in ruins (i.e., having fallen).
15. I have mentioned the words that are written in my stela.
16. You (mp) were abandoned in the mountains.
17. You are the son who was born to her; I am the daughter who was born to her.
18. Be (ms) strong; do not be weak.
19. This is the chariot that was towed to the judge.
20. I was detained by force.
21. We are princes; we are fearsome princes.
22. He is not my apprentice.
23. My teeth are broken.
24. I am a youth.
25. The queen's head was anointed with fine oil.
26. He is seized by his neck like a dog.
27. I am careful; I will not be negligent.
28. It (m) is turned to the left.
29. Its (m) shoulder is surrounded.

E. Normalize and translate:

1. URU-*ka šu-ú it-ti-ka i-na-ak-ki-ir-ma a-na* LUGAL *ša it-ti-i-ka na-ak-ru i-sa-ḫu-ur-ma i-na* ^{giš}TUKUL-*ki ta-da-ak-šu-ma* URU *šu-a-ti ta-la-wi-i-ma* BÀD-*šu ta-na-aq-qa-ar ù i-ši-id* ^{giš}GU.ZA LUGAL-*ti-šu ta-na-sa-aḫ*.
2. *te-re-tu-ia ša ep-ša-nim ú-ul i-ša-ra te-re-tum ši-na le-em-na i-na ši-bu-ti-ia* É-*ti ú-ul i-iš-še-er*.

3. *ki-ma ki-it-tim ša* ^{d}UTU *ù* ^{d}AMAR.UTU *ra-i-im-ka iš-ru-ku-ni-ik-kum* ŠE-*am ša ma-aḫ-ri-ka mu-du-ud-ma šu-pu-uk.*
4. *mu-ut a-ḫa-ti-ia i-li-ik-šu ú-ul ša-li-im ṣí-ib-tam wa-tar-tam ki-ma ṣi-im-da-at* LUGAL *la te-em-mi-is-sú.*
5. *a-wi-lam ta-ak-lam ša na-aʾ-du-ú-ma ta-ta-ka-lu-šum i-na ma-tim šu-a-ti pu-ḫi ša-pí-ri-im šu-ku-un.*
6. LUKUR *ša i-na* GÁ.GI$_4$.A *wa-aš-ba-at ki-a-am iq-bi-a-am um-ma ši-i-ma i-na-an-na* UDU.ḪI.A *im-ti-da-ma na-ša-a-ši-na ú-ul e-le-i ma-am-ma-an šu-up-ra-am-ma tap-pu-ti li-il-lik.*
7. *šum-ma mar-tum wa-ṣi-a-at* AGA *iš-tu ma-tim uṣ-ṣi.*
8. KUG.BABBAR *ša ni-it-ba-lu a-na* ŠÁM ^{giš}KIRI$_6$ *ša-ni-im ú-ul i-ma-aṣ-ṣí.*
9. *su-ḫu-ur-ma ši-pa-tim qá-at-na-tim ša-ma-am-ma le-qé-a-am.*
10. *le-et* ^{lú}ŠU.ḪA *am-ḫa-aṣ-ma ri-it-ta-šu eš-be-er-ma a-na ma-aṣ-ṣa-ri ap-qí-sú.*
11. *ba-lum be-el pí-ḫa-tim me-ḫe-er ku-nu-ki-ia i-pu-šu e-pí-iš-ta-šu-nu an-ni-tum ú-ul da-am-qá-at.*

F. CH:

§26 *šum-ma lu* AGA.ÚS *ù lu* ŠU.ḪA *ša a-na ḫar-ra-an šar-ri-im a-la-ak-šu qá-bu-ú la il-li-ik ù lu* ^{lú}*agram*(ḪUN.GÁ) *i-gur-ma pu-úḫ-šu iṭ-ṭa-ra-ad lu* AGA.ÚS *ù lu* ŠU.ḪA *šu-ú id-da-ak mu-na-ag-ge-er-šu* É-*sú i-tab-ba-al.*

munaggerum 'denouncer'.

§33 *šum-ma lu* PA.PA *ù lu-ú laputtûm*(NU.BANDA$_5$) ERIN$_2$ *ni-is-ḫa-tim ir-ta-ši ù lu a-na ḫarrān*(KASKAL) *šar-ri-im* ^{lú}*agram*(ḪUN. GÁ) *pu-ḫa-am im-ḫu-ur-ma ir-te-de lu* PA.PA *ù lu laputtûm*(NU. BANDA$_5$) *šu-ú id-da-ak.*

PA.PA 'captain' (or the like); reading uncertain, perhaps *ša ḫaṭṭātim* (lit. 'the one of the scepters'; *ḫaṭṭum* 'scepter') or UGULA.GIDRU = *wakil ḫaṭṭim* (lit. 'overseer of the scepter').

laputtûm (Sum. lw.) 'lieutenant' (or the like).

nisḫum (or *nisiḫtum*; pl. *nisḫātum*) 'removal' (cf. *nasāḫum*); *ṣāb nisḫātim rašûm* uncertain, perhaps 'to have deserters' or 'to acquire conscripts'.

§7:

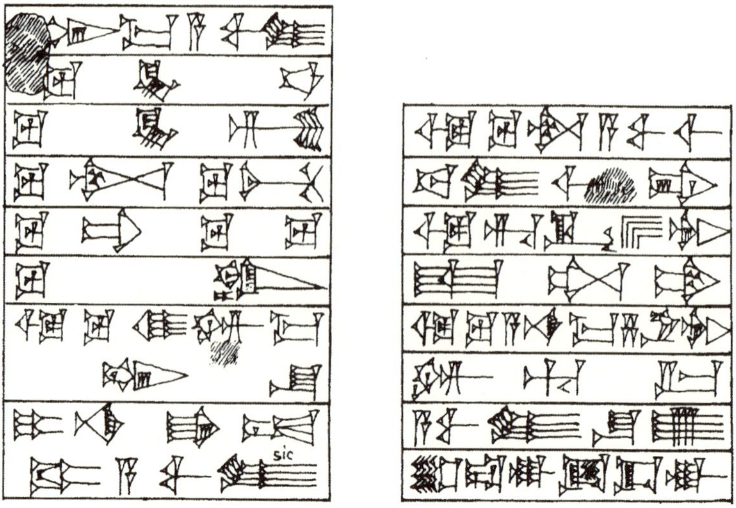

§128:

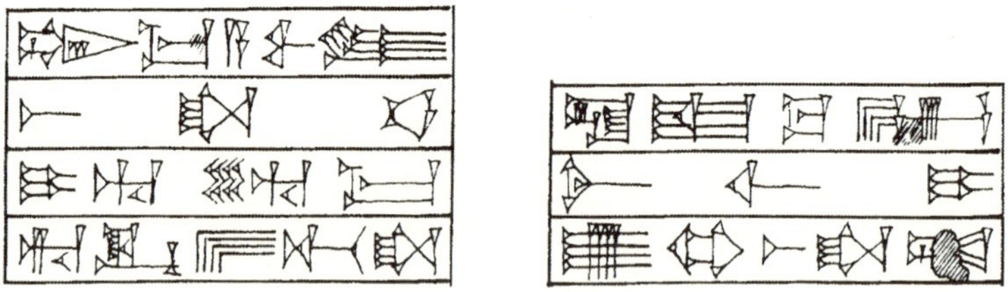

G. Omens from *YOS* 10:

1. DIŠ ^gišTUKUL *i-mi-tim i-na re-eš mar-tim ša-ki-im-ma mar-tam ir-de* ^gišTUKUL *qú-li-im.* (9:13–14)

   qūlum 'silence, stillness'.

2. DIŠ ŠÀ *ki-ma iš-ki im-me-ri-im a-mu-ut ma-ni-iš-ti-šu ša e-ka-lu-šu* [*i*]*-du-ku-šu.* (9:21–23)

   iškum 'testicle'.

   Maništū/*īšu* king of Akkad, ca. 2269–55 (son and second successor of Sargon).

   ekallûm (*ekallī-*; denominative adj. of *ekallum*) 'palace official'.

3. MAŠ *i-mi-ti li-bi qé-e* [*ṣú-bu*]*-ut ki-ṣí-ir li-bi* DINGIR-*lim a-na a-wi-lim* [*ú-ul pa*]-*ṭe*$_4$-*er*. (42 i 54–55)
   li-bi (first occurrence) for *libbim* (see §24.4).
   qê ṣubbut 'is held by filaments'.
4. 31 ii 1–12:

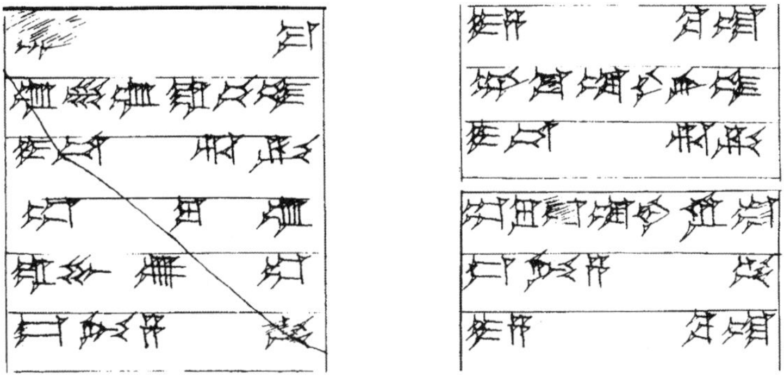

   The second sign in lines 1, 8 is *ma*; the third sign in lines 7, 12 is *ba*.
   ummum here is an unidentified part of the gall-bladder.
5. 31 v 37–39:

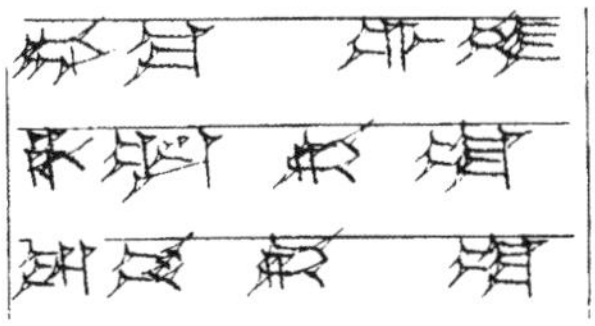

6. 31 x 21–25:

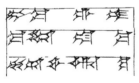

   Line 3, last sign: *qú*.
   warāqum (*i*) 'to become yellow, pale'; Verbal Adj. *warqum* (*waruq-*).
   rādum 'cloudburst, downpour'.
7. 31 xi 22–25:

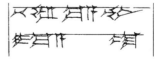

   Line 1 has only four signs; in the middle is a scribal erasure, not a sign.
   The meaning of *ṣabtum* here is uncertain; 'held (in place)'?

H. Contracts:

1. Purchase of a woman as a concubine (*CT* 8 22b = Schorr, *VAB* 5, no. 77, adapted).

^{1} ^{I} ^{d}UTU-*nu-ri* DUMU.MUNUS *i-bi-ša-a-an* ^{2} KI *i-bi-*^{d}*ša-a-an a-bi-ša* ^{3} ^{I} ^{d}*bu-né-né-a-bi* ^{4} *ù be-le-sú-nu i-ša-mu-ši* ^{5} *a-na* ^{d}*bu-né-né-a-bi a-ša-at* ^{6} *a-na be-le-sú-nu a-ma-at* ^{7} ^{d}UTU-*nu-ri a-na be-le-sú-nu* ^{8} *be-el-ti-ša ú-ul be-el-ti at-ti* ^{9} *i-qá-bi-ma* ^{10} *a-na* KUG.BABBAR *i-na-ad-di-iš-ši* ^{11} *ana šīmīša gamrim* (ŠÁM.TIL.LA.BI.ŠÈ) *x* KUG.BABBAR ^{12} *iš-qú-lu* ... ^{14} *awāssa*(INIM.BI) *gamrat*(AL.TIL) ^{15} ŠÀ.NI *ṭāb*(AL.DÙG) ^{16} *ana warkiāt ūmim* (UD.KÚR.ŠÈ) LÚ LÚ.RA ^{17} *lā ibaqqar*(INIM.NU. GÁ.GÁ.A) ^{18} MU ^{d}UTU ^{d}AMAR.UTU ^{19} *ù ḫa-am-mu-ra-pí itmû*(IN. PÀD.DÈ.MEŠ). $^{20–26}$ Witnesses. $^{27–28}$ Date.

PNs: *Šamaš-nūrī; Ibbi-Ša(ḫ)an; Bunene-abī; Bēlessunu.*

$^{14–15}$ Common quitclaim clauses: 'its (the property's, thus, usually *awāssu*) transaction is settled; his (the seller's) heart is satisfied'.

^{16} The Sumerian postposition RA = the Akkadian preposition *ana*.

2. Rental of a field (Ungnad, *VAS* 8 62 = Schorr, *VAB* 5, no. 130).

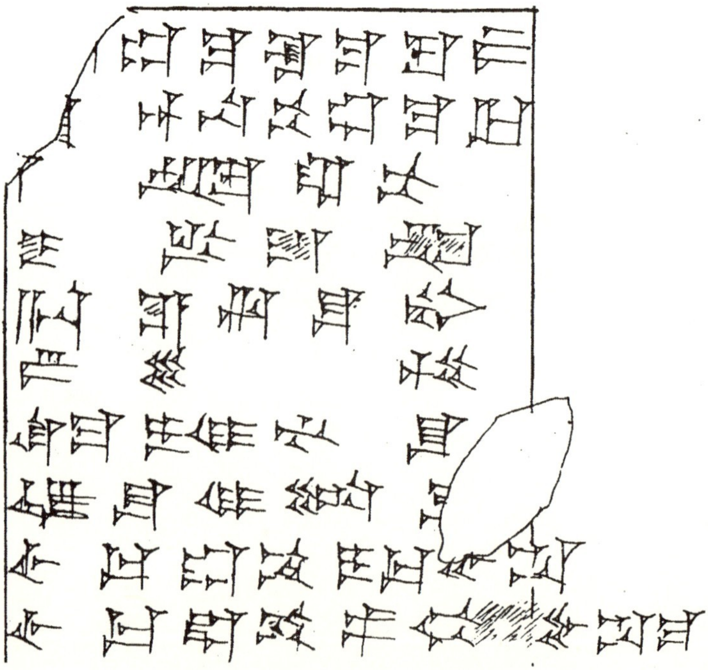

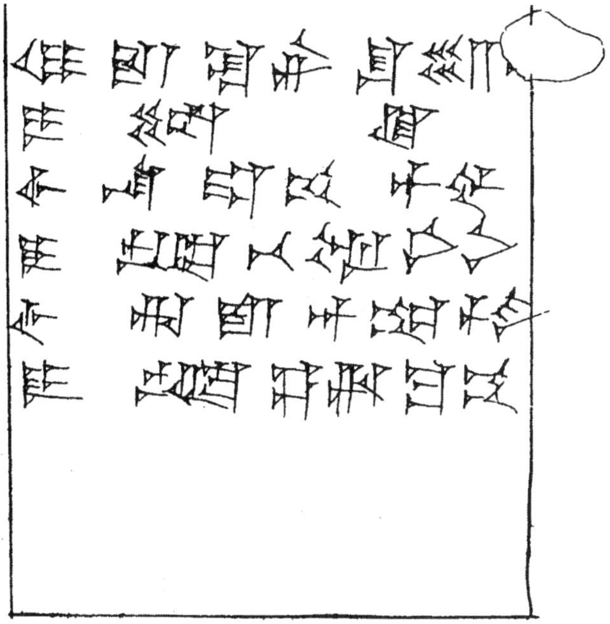

PNs: *Nabium-mālik; Sîn-rabi; Igmil-Sîn; Narām-Adad; Sîn-bēl-ilī; Rīš-Girra; Sîn-erībam.*

[1] Restore the beginning as [A.ŠÀ]-*um*; here nominative for expected acc.

[2] Restore the beginning as [K]I.

[4] ⸢DUMU⸣ *ig*-⸢*mil*-^{d}EN.ZU⸣.

[5] The first sign is a poorly written *a*; *errēšūtum* 'tenancy (of a field)'.

[6] *ušēṣi* (§28.1) 'he rented'.

[7–8] These lines refer to neighboring tenants. The last sign in [8] is -*š*[*u*].

[9] The second last sign is ⸢*pu*⸣.

[10] Between *ul* and *pu* restore [*i*].

[11] *mišlānū* (pl.) 'half share' (cf. *mišlum*; here in apposition to *ûm*). The last three signs in the line are ŠE-*a*-*a*[*m*].

[15] BIL.GI is read GIBIL (cf. EN.ZU for ZUEN) = *Girra* (fire god).

LESSON TWENTY-THREE

23.1 The Absolute Form of the Noun

The absolute form is an indeclinable form of the noun and adjective. The form has no case-ending: for most noun and adjective types, the absolute form resembles the predicative form, 3ms; for nouns with feminine *-(a)t*, the absolute form usually resembles the predicative form, 3fs, rarely 3ms. Some examples:

eṭel 'youth'	*šanat* 'year'
šar 'king'	*bēlet* 'lady'
um 'mother'	*têret* 'omen'
ṣeḫer 'small'	*napšat* 'life'
rabi 'large'	but *sinniš* 'woman, female'
dan 'strong'	

A few instances of an absolute form of the fem. pl., in *-ā*, are known; no examples of the masc. pl. are extant. The paucity of plural forms is undoubtedly connected with the function of the absolute form.

The use of the absolute form is not fully understood; the following may be noted, however:

(a) It is employed in expressions of mass and quantity; in these, both the number and the unit of measurement appear in the absolute form. (See the next section.)

(b) It may be used for the vocative (see §23.3, below):
bēlet 'lady!' *šar* 'king!'

(c) It may be used to indicate that a substantive is expressly singular:
šanat 'a single year' *uṭṭet* 'a single grain (of wheat, silver)' (*uṭṭetum* 'grain, wheat')

(d) The cardinal numbers usually occur in the absolute form, the numbers 'one' and 'two' almost invariably so. (See the next section.)

(e) Several fixed expressions, usually adverbial in nature, employ the absolute form, for reasons that are unclear:
ṣeḫer rabi 'small (and) great';
zikar sinniš 'male (and) female' (*zikarum* 'male');
lā šanān 'without equal' (*šanānum* 'to rival, equal').

(The absolute form is called the status absolutus in some grammars. In origin it is probably an embedded predicative form: *ṣeḫer rabi* 'being small, being great'.)

23.2 Numbers

(a) The Cardinal Numbers

In English it is common to write numbers logographically, as in '23' rather than 'twenty-three'. This is almost invariably the case in Akkadian texts, to the extent that the pronunciation and construction of the Akkadian numbers are not fully understood.

The numbers from 'one' to 'nineteen' have masc. and fem. forms; numbers up to 'ten' (except 'two') occur in both absolute and, less often, free forms.

			WITH MASC. NOUN		WITH FEM. NOUN	
	LOG.	Sumerian	Absolute	Free	Absolute	Free
1	𒁹	DIŠ	*ištēn*	*(ištēnum)*	*išteat, ištēt*	*(ištētum)*
2	𒈫	MIN	*šinā*	—	*šittā*	—
3	𒐈	EŠ5	*šalāšat*	*šalāštum*	*šalāš*	*šalāšum*
4	𒐉	LIMMU	*erbet(ti)*	*erbettum*	*erbe / erba*	*erbûm*
5	𒐊	IÁ	*ḫamšat*	*ḫamištum*	*ḫamiš*	*ḫamšum*
6	𒐋	ÀŠ	*šeššet*	*šedištum*	*šediš*[?]	*šeššum*
7	𒐌	IMIN	*sebet(ti)*	*sebettum*	*sebe*	*sebûm*
8	𒐍	USSU	*samānat*	*samāntum*	*samāne*	*samānûm*
9	𒐎	ILIMMU	*tišīt*	*tišītum*	*tiše*	*tišûm*
10	𒌋	U	*eš(e)ret*	*ešertum*	*ešer*	*eš(e)rum*
11	𒌋𒁹		*ištēššeret*		*ištēššer*	
12	𒌋𒈫		*šinšeret*		*šinšer*	
13	𒌋𒐈		*šalāššeret*		*šalāššer*	
14	𒌋𒐉		*erbēšeret*		*erbēšer*	
15	𒌋𒐊		*ḫamiššeret*		*ḫamiššer*	
16	𒌋𒐋		*šeššeret*[?]		*šeššer*[?]	
17	𒌋𒐌		*sebēšeret*		*sebēšer*	
18	𒌋𒐍		*samāššeret*		*samāššer*	
19	𒌋𒐎		*tišēšeret*		*tišēšer*	

The tens from 'twenty' to 'fifty' have the following forms:

	LOG.	Sumerian	WITH MASC./FEM. NOUN
20		NIŠ	*ešrā*
30		UŠU3	*šalāšā*
40	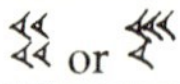	NIMIN	*erbeā / erbâ*
50		NINNU	*ḫamšā*

'Twenty' to 'fifty' look like nom. dual forms without the final *-n*, 'twenty' of 'ten' and 'thirty', 'forty', and 'fifty' of 'three', 'four', and 'five'. These forms are normally indeclinable (although obl. *ešrē* occurs at Mari). For 'sixty' to 'ninety', see further below.

As the logograms accompanying the tables above indicate, units are indicated by vertical wedges, tens by angle wedges. (There is no 'zero'.) In compound numbers, higher order components precede lower (i.e., tens precede ones):

	LOG.	WITH MASC. NOUN	WITH FEM. NOUN
32		(*šalāšā (u) šinā*??)	(*šalāšā (u) šittā*??)
59		(*ḫamšā (u) tišīt(um)*??)	(*ḫamšā (u) tiše / ûm*??)

(The pronunciation of such numbers is unknown.)

The speakers of Akkadian inherited from the Sumerians a sexagesimal (i.e., base 60) system of counting, in addition to the decimal system. Higher numbers in the sexagesimal system are:

			WITH MASC./FEM. NOUN	
	LOG.	Sumerian	Absolute	Free
60		GÍŠ	*šūš(i)*	*šūšum*
600	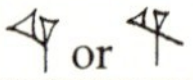	GÍŠ-U	*nēr*	*nērum*
3600		ŠÁR	*šār*	*šārum*

The cuneiform and Sumerian for '600' represent 60ī10. The sign for '3600' is distinct in OB script, but falls together with ḪI in Neo-Assyrian script (). These elements may occur in compound numbers. Again, higher orders precede lower, so that '70' is written  (i.e., 60+10), as opposed to  for '11' (i.e., 10 +1). The pronunciations of 'seventy' and 'eighty' are unknown; 'ninety' is *tišeā*.

70		(i.e., 60+10)
80		(i.e., 60+20)
90		(i.e., 60+30)
120		(i.e., 2ī60, *šinā šūši*)
150		(i.e., 2ī60+30)
599		(i.e., 9ī60+5ī10+9)
5000		(i.e., 3600+2ī600+3ī60+2ī10)

Higher numbers in the decimal system are *meatum* (fem.; usually abs. *meat*; pl. *meātum*) 'hundred' and *līmum* 'thousand':

	Absolute	Free	Writing
100	*meat*	*(meatum)*	ME (), less often *me-at*
1000	*līm(i)*	*līmum*	LIM (, i.e., 10ī100), *li-im*, or simply LI

These elements also appear in compound numbers; e.g.,

300	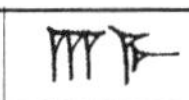	*šalāš meāt* (the pl. of *meat*)
3000		*šalāšat līm(i)*
3333	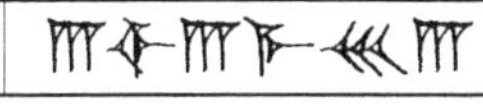	

The word for 'both', not surprisingly, occurs as a dual:

masc.:	nom.	*kilallān* (in southern and Mari OB, *kilallūn*)
	gen.-acc.	*kilallīn*
fem.	nom.	*kilattān*
	gen.-acc.	*kilattīn*

These forms may be used independently or in apposition to a preceding noun, which is normally plural (dual with natural pairs); verbs are likewise plural:

kilallūn illakū 'both (m) will go';
kilattīn ṭurdam 'send (ms) both (female slaves) to me';
šumma ina kilallīn ištēn ana šīmtim ittalak 'if one of the two (brothers) dies';
bēlū kilallān izuzzū 'both owners will divide';
alpī kilallīn šām 'buy (ms) both oxen';
birīt īnīn kilattīn 'between both eyes'.

The forms for 'both' may also occur with suffixes:

kilallāšunu (or *kilallūšunu*) *tamkāram ippalū* 'both of them (m) will pay the merchant';
kilallūkunu lā tallakā 'neither of you (m) may go';
ekallū šunu kilallūšunu ša PN 'both of those palaces belong to PN';
kilallīšunu ana mê inaddû 'they (m) will throw them both (m) into the water';
šarrum eleppam ana kilallīni ittadnanniāšim 'the king has given the boat to both of us'.

(b) Construction of the Cardinal Numbers

(1) With No Unit of Measurement

Normally in OB, when no unit of measurement is involved, the absolute form of the number precedes the item counted; the item counted appears in the appropriate case of the free form, usually in the plural, viz.,

NUMBER (absolute) + ITEM COUNTED (free form, pl., case from context)

Rarely, the singular occurs after numbers; after 'two' usually pl., rarely dual or sg.; after 'one', of course, always sg.

The gender of the numbers 'one' and 'two' is the same as that of the item counted; but the gender of the numbers 'three' to 'nineteen' is the *opposite* of that of the item counted (as elsewhere in Semitic; this phenomenon is referrred to as "chiastic concord"). Some examples:

ištēn wardum imūt 'one male slave died';
ištēt amtum imūt 'one female slave died';
šinā wardī nīmur 'we saw two male slaves';
šittā amātim nīmur 'we saw two female slaves';
šalāšat eṭlūtum illikū 'three young men went';
šalāš sinnišātum illikā 'three women went';
ḫamšat alpī ašām 'I bought five oxen';
ḫamiš eleppētim abni 'I built five boats';
ana ešret ūmī 'for ten days';
ešer šanātim 'in ten years' (adverbial acc.);
šalāššeret tamkārū īlûnim 'thirteen merchants came up';
šalāššer immerātim ana kaspim niddin 'we sold thirteen sheep'.

The cardinal numbers rarely follow the noun, perhaps to connote emphasis. In such instances, the number most often appears in the free form with the appropriate case ending:

šadî sebettam nīmur 'we saw *seven* mountains'.

When *ištēn / išteat* 'one' follows its noun, the meaning is 'single' or 'each'; the absolute form is used (the free forms *ištēnum, ištētum* are rare):

kīma aplim ištēn 'like a single/individual heir';
ana amtim išteat 'for each slave'.

(2) With a Unit of Measurement Expressed

When a unit of measurement appears, the following construction is used:

NUMBER	+	MEASUREMENT	+	ITEM MEASURED
absolute; gender from measurement		absolute form		free form; sing.; case from context

Thus, to express, for instance, 'I gave him seven grains of silver', as in the first example below, the Akkadian has literally 'I gave him seven grain silver'.

sebe uṭṭet kaspam addiššum 'I gave him seven grains (*uṭṭetum*) of silver' (note *sebe* with fem. *uṭṭetum*; acc. sg. *kaspam* as the direct object of the verb);
ḫamšat kur ûm iḫtaliq 'five kor (*kurrum*, about 300 liters) of barley have disappeared' (note *ḫamšat* with masc. *kurrum*; nom. sg. *ûm* as the subject of the verb);
ina libbi šalāšat šiqil ḫurāṣim ša elīka 'out of the three shekels (*šiqlum*) of gold that you owe (lit., that is against you)' (note *šalāšat* with masc. *šiqlum*; gen. *ḫurāṣim* after bound form *libbi*).

(c) The Ordinal Numbers

Like the cardinal numbers, the ordinals are usually written with logograms, the same signs as for the cardinals. Since they are adjectives, they have both masc. and fem. forms, and these always agree with the gender of the modified noun (vs. the chiastic concord of the cardinals '3' and higher). Apart from the words for 'first', the ordinals, though adjectives, normally *precede* their noun (following the noun rarely, perhaps for emphasis).

Several terms for 'first' occur. Based on the same root as *ištēn* 'one' is the relative adjective *ištīʾum* (an archaic form, without vowel contraction; see §30.2), but this is found only rarely, in poetry. The usual terms are the relative adjectives *pānûm* and *maḫrûm*, both of which also mean 'former, earlier, previous'. As noted above, these follow their noun. The cardinal forms *ištēn*, fem. *išteat*, are also occasionally used for 'first'.

'Second' (also 'next') is *šanûm* (f. *šanītum*), which like other ordinals precedes the modified noun; *after* a noun, *šanûm* means 'other, another' (Vocab. 16).

The base of the ordinals from 'third' to 'tenth' is *parus* (*perus* in roots in which *a* › *e*; other bases are attested in other dialects).

	MASCULINE	FEMININE
'first'	*pānûm* *maḫrûm* *(ištīʾum* *ištēn*	*pānītum* *maḫrītum* *ištītum)* *išteat*
'second'	*šanûm*	*šanītum*
'third'	*šalšum*	*šaluštum*
'fourth'	*rebûm*	*rebūtum*
'fifth'	*ḫamšum*	*ḫamuštum*
'sixth'	*šeššum*	*šeduštum*
'seventh'	*sebûm*	*sebūtum*
'eighth'	*samnum*	*samuntum*
'ninth'	*tešûm*	*tešūtum*
'tenth'	*ešrum*	*ešurtum*

The ordinals above 'tenth' are denominative adjectives of the corresponding cardinals; e.g.,

'eleventh'	*ištēššerûm*	*ištēššerītum*
'thirteenth'	*šalāššerûm*	*šalāššerītum*

The form *ešrûm* (‹ *ešrā+ī+um*) occurs for 'twentieth (day of the month)'. It is possible that after 'twentieth', the cardinal numbers served as ordinals as well.

(d) Expressions of Time

In cuneiform, certain expressions involving numbers, especially with words denoting periods of time (*ūmum, warḫum, šattum*), are written entirely logographically. The normal order of the number and the noun in the spoken language is reversed in the script, and the sign KAM, which indicates numerals in Sumerian, follows; the word modified by the number is written singly (i.e., without MEŠ). Examples:

UD.5.KAM *i-ti-qu* for *ḫamšat ūmū ītiqū* 'five days passed';

iš-tu MU.3.KAM for *ištu šalāš šanātim* 'for three years' (or, 'since three years ago');

ITI.2.KAM *ik-lu-šu* for *šinā warḫī iklûšu* 'they held him (for) two months (adverbial acc.)'.

Writings of the type MU.x.KAM are unfortunately ambiguous, however, since they are also employed when the ordinal number is intended, as in the following examples:

UD.5.KAM *i-ti-iq* for *ḫamšum ūmum ītiq* 'the fifth day passed';
i-na MU.3.KAM for *ina šaluštim šattim* 'in the third year';
ITI.2.KAM *al-li-ik-šum* for *šaniam warḫam allikšum* 'I went to him (on) the second month (adverbial acc.)'.

Which of these two possibilities is intended in such writings must be determined according to context.

(e) Fractions

Most fractions with numerator '1' may be expressed logographically as IGI.x.GÁL (GÁL is the IG sign). Some common fractions, such as $^1/_2$, are written with specific signs; in some instances, such as $^1/_3$ and $^1/_6$, both special signs and the formula IGI.x.GÁL occur. The OB Akkadian terms for the fractions with numerator '1' either are the same as the ordinals, thus with base *parus* to $^1/_{10}$ (see under (c), above; cf. English 'third' and 'one-third'), or have base *paris* or *pur(u)s*. Some fractions have fem. forms (i.e., with *-(a)t*), others masc. forms (without *-(a)t*), while some exhibit both; since most are simply written logographically, differences in meaning between these are usually unclear.

Forms are presented in the table below by increasing denominator; note the forms for $^2/_3$ and $^5/_6$.

$^1/_2$		MAŠ	*mišlum* (bound form and absolute *mišil*), less often *muttatum* or *bāmtum* (*bāmat*)
$^1/_3$		ŠUŠANA	rarely for *šuššān* (i.e., 'two-sixths', dual of *šuššum* 'one-sixth'); usually to be read *šaluš(tum)* (see next)
		IGI.3.GÁL	*šaluš* (bound/abs., especially in divisions of land and crop shares, as in 'he leased the field *ana šaluš* for a one-third share') and *šaluštum* (bound *šalušti*, abs. *šalšat*; lessoften in the same contexts, and the normal form otherwise, as in *šalušti šamnim* 'one-third of the oil')
$^2/_3$		ŠANABI	*šinip(ûm)*, usually fem. *šinipiāt(um)*
		—	*šittān*, obl. *šittīn* (written syllabically)
$^1/_4$		IGI.4.GÁL	*rabiat*, *rebiat*, *ra/ebât* (bound/abs. forms of unattested **ra/ebītum*)
$^1/_5$		IGI.5.GÁL	*ḫamuštum* (and bound *ḫamušti*, abs. *ḫamšat*); also *ḫumuš*

$^1/_6$	 	ŠUŠ IGI.6.GÁL	*šuduš* (bound/abs. form of rare *šuššum*) or *šeššat* same as preceding
$^5/_6$		KINGUSILA	*parasrab* (also *parab*)
$^1/_7$		IGI.7.GÁL	*sebītum, sebiatum,* bound/abs. form *sebiat*
$^1/_8$		IGI.8.GÁL	*samnat* (bound/abs. form of unattested **samuntum*)
$^1/_9$		IGI.9.GÁL	*tešât* (‹ *tešiat,* bound/abs. form of unattested **tešītum*)
$^1/_{10}$		IGI.10.GÁL	*ešret* (bound/abs. form of unattested **ešir-tum*); note also *ešrētum* (always pl.) 'tithe'
$^1/_{12}$	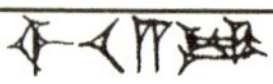	IGI.12.GÁL	*šinšerûm*
$^1/_{13}$		IGI.13.GÁL	*šalāššerītum,* bound form *šalāššeriat*

The syntax of the fractions is not well understood, since expressions are not normally written syllabically; it is likely, however, that they usually occurred as bound forms with a following genitive, as in

rebiat šikarim ašti 'I drank one-fourth of the beer.'

(f) Multiplicatives

To express 'x times', 'x-fold', the ending *-īšu* (*-šu* for 'one time') is added to the base of the cardinal number; e.g.,

ištīššu 'once, one time';
šinîšu 'twice, two times, twofold';
šalāšīšu 'thrice, three times, threefold';
erbîšu 'four times, fourfold';
šalāššerīšu 'thirteen times'.

These forms are often preceded by the preposition *adi* 'up to, as far as', with no apparent difference in meaning:

adi ḫamšīšu 'five times, fivefold'.

23.3 The Expression of the Vocative

The vocative may be expressed by the free form of the noun in the nominative or by the absolute form. More commonly, however, the 1cs suffix is attached:

bēltī '(O) my lady!', less often *bēltum* or *bēlet* '(O) lady!'.

EXERCISES

A. VOCABULARY 23.

Verb:

bašûm (i) 'to exist; to be present, available; to happen'; Dur. 3cs *ibašši* 'there is/are' may occur with pl. subjects (cf. *bīšum*, etc.); Verbal Adj. *bašûm* (*baši-*) 'on hand, available, present' (listed in the dictionaries as a Participle, *bāšûm*); substantivized fem. *bašītum* see Vocab. 19.

Nouns:

išātum (*išāt*; log. IZI [the NE sign]) 'fire'.

izbum (*izib*) 'malformed newborn human or animal' (cf. *ezēbum*).

kurrum (absolute form *kur*; log. GUR; Sum. lw.) 'kor' (unit of dry measure, = 30 *sūtum* = ca. 300 litres; see Appendix B.5); note: *ḫamšat kur ûm* for 'five kor of barley' is usually written 5 ŠE. GUR (i.e., with ŠE and GUR reversed); numbers of GUR from 'one' to 'nine' are written with horizontal wedges (𒀸, 𒐀, 𒐁, ...; see Appendix B.5).

manûm (base *manā-*; absolute form *manā*; log. MA.NA) 'mina' (60 *šiqlum*, about 500 grams; see Appendix B.1).

pagrum (*pagar*; pl. *pagrū*) 'body, corpse; self' (often as a reflexive pronoun; e.g., *pagarka uṣur* 'guard yourself').

qablum (*qabal*; dual *qablān* [often = sg.]; log. MURUB$_4$) 'hip, waist; middle'.

sūtum (*sūt*; absolute *sât*$^{?}$; pl. *sâtum*; log. BÁN, etc. [see B.]) 'seah' (unit of dry measure, about 10 litres; see Appendix B.5).

šiqlum (*šiqil*; log. GÍN) 'shekel' ($^{1}/_{60}$ *manûm*, about 8 grams; see Appendix B.1; cf. *šaqālum*).

šūt-rēšim (*šūt* is an archaic masc. pl. of *ša*; lit. 'those at the head'; with suffix *šūt-rēšīšu*) 'court officials, courtiers, commanders'.

ṭupšarrum (*ṭupšar*; pl. *ṭupšarrū*; log. DUB.SAR [SAR = the *šar* sign]; Sum. lw.) 'scribe' (cf. *ṭuppum*).

ubānum (fem.; *ubān*; pl. *ubānātum*; log. ŠU.SI) 'finger, toe'; a unit of length (about 1.67 cm.; see Appendix B.2); part of the liver ('processus pyramidalis'); *ubān šēpim* 'toe'.

Learn to recognize the signs and words for the numbers 1–10, 60, 100, 600, 1000, 3600, and 'both', and the signs for the fractions.

B. Learn the following signs:

OB Lapid.	OB Cursive	NA	values
		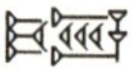	MURUB4 = *qablum*
			GÍN = *šiqlum*
			BÁN = *sūtum*
			2 BÁN (or BÁNMIN) = *2 sâtum*
			3 BÁN (BÁNEŠ) = *3 sâtum*
			4 BÁN (BÁNLIMMU) = *4 sâtum*
			5 BÁN (or BÁNIA) = *5 sâtum*

Signs for numerals and fractions will also appear in the exercises.

C. Write the following in normalized Akkadian (nominative unless otherwise specified), in transliteration, and in cuneiform; use logograms where possible:

1. the middle of the gall-bladder
2. seven shekels of gold
3. twenty gates
4. the fourth knot
5. one-seventh of the beer
6. nineteen 'fishermen'
7. the seventh body
8. eight able warriors
9. the sixth goddess
10. the left side of the captive's (m) head
11. six hundred tablets
12. nine persons
13. I broke both tablets.
14. the eighth princess
15. the second report
16. another report
17. I bought three kor of barley.
18. She will take five-sixths.
19. ten gifts
20. Carry (fs) one-fifth of the food.
21. half of the assembly
22. between two trees
23. one-third of the debt
24. forty minas of silver
25. twelve attentive courtiers
26. for three months
27. seven "fingers"
28. The fire consumed one new house.
29. both of us (m) have turned
30. one-tenth of the tax
31. five partners
32. three seahs of barley
33. bordering three orchards
34. the first city gate
35. Adad received two-thirds.
36. the fifth breach

37. the right side of the throne
38. the third share
39. the eleventh physician
40. Three copies were present.
41. I rode.
42. You (ms) sent a message.
43. The scribe ransomed.
44. It became hostile.
45. I have seized.
46. one-fourth of the excess
47. thirty witnesses
48. for six days
49. in the fourth year
50. a single (wr. syllab.) report

D. Normalize and translate:

1. *šum-ma* AGA.ÚS *ša ma-aṣ-ṣa-ru-ut ka-ni-ki šar-ra-tim pa-aq-da-as-sú-um pu-úḫ-šu i-gur wa-ar-ka-as-sú lu-ú pár-sà-at.*
2. *aš-ša-tum* DUMU *ša mu-us-sà pa-nu-um a-na ma-ru-tim il-qú-ú la i-ba-qar-šu i-na di-nim la i-ra-gu-um-šum.*
3. *a-na* KALAM.MEŠ *ši-na-ti te-el-li-ma* ^{giš}TUKUL.MEŠ *na-ak-ri-ka ma-la ma-ṣú-ú te-še-eb-bé-er.*
4. *a-na* BÀD *la-be-ri-im ša* URU *šu-a-ti e-li-ma ni-šu* URU *it-ti-ia ik-ke-ra-ma e-re-ba-am ú-ul e-le.*
5. *a-nu-um-ma* ŠU.ḪA *šu-ú* ANŠE *an-ni-a-am ba-lum ri-ik-sa-tim a-na* 5 GÍN KUG.BABBAR *ù* 2 BÁN ŠE *it-ta-ad-nam.*
6. *ša-ma-lu-um* 10 GÍN KUG.BABBAR *ša i-na qá-ti* DAM.GÀR *im-ḫu-ru a-na a-ḫa-ti-šu iš-ru-uk.*
7. *i-na di-in ša-ar-ru-um i-di-nu ma-ma-an ú-ul i-ra-gu-um.*
8. ITI.6.KAM*šar-ra-qá-am ša pí-il-ša-am i-na* É-*ia ip-lu-šu-ma* NÍG. GA-*ri ḫal-qá-am i-na qá-ti-šu iṣ-ba-tu i-na ṣí-bi-tim ik-lu-šu.*
9. *ṣú-ḫa-re-e šu-nu-ti ka-la-šu-nu be-le-sú-nu a-na* 1 MA.NA KUG. BABBAR *ip-ta-ṭár-šu-nu-ti.*
10. *a-na* ^{d}EN.LÍL *ta-ta-kal-ma ru-bu-um a-a-ú-um* ^{giš}GU.ZA LUGAL-*ti-ka i-ṣa-ab-bat ù ma-nu-um le-mu-tam i-ip-pé-eš-ka.*
11. *wa-ar-ki a-bi-im* DUMU.MEŠ *um-ma-šu-nu aš-šum pu-ru-sé-em an-ni-im la i-ba-aq-qá-ru ù um-mu-um ba-aq-ri ša-nu-tim ú-ul i-ra-aš-ši.*
12. *i-na-an-na* LUGAL *šu-ut-re-ši-šu a-na maḫ-ri-ka iṭ-ṭa-ra-ad it-ti-šu-nu a-na a-aḫ na-ri-im e-li-tim ri-id-ma ni-iš* DINGIR *zu-ku-ur.*

E. CH. Normalize and translate the following laws:

§133–133b §133 *šum-ma a-wi-lum iš-ša-li-il-ma i-na* É-*šu ša a-ka-lim* [*i*]-*ba-aš-ši* [*aš*]-*ša-sú* [É-*sú i*]-*ṣa-*[*ab-ba-a*]*t* [*ù pa-gàr-š*]*a* [*i-na-aṣ-ṣa-a*]*r* [*a-na* É *ša-ni-i*]*m* [*ú-ul i-ir-r*]*u-ub* §133b *š*[*um-m*]*a* MUNUS *ši-i [pa]-gàr-ša la iṣ-ṣur-ma a-na* É *ša-ni-im i-te-ru-ub* MUNUS *šu-a-ti ú-ka-an-nu-ši-ma a-na me-e i-na-ad-du-ú-ši.*

iššalil 'has been carried off (as booty)'.

ša akālim 'something to eat'.

ukannūši 'they will convict her'.

§200–201 (§200, cf. Lesson 21, F: *šumma awīlum šinni awīlim meḫrīšu ittadi, šinnašu inaddû*) §201 *šum-ma ši-in-ni*(!GAG) MAŠ. EN.GAG *it-ta-di* ŠUŠANA MA.NA KUG.BABBAR *i-ša-qal.*

§273 *šum-ma a-wi-lum* ^{lú}*agram*(ḪUN.GÁ) *i-gur iš-tu re-eš ša-at-tim a-di ḫa-am-ši-im* ITI-*im* 6 *uṭṭet*(ŠE) KUG.BABBAR *i-na* UD.1. KAM *i-na-ad-di-in iš-tu še*$_{20}$*-ši-im* ITI-*im a-di ta-aq-ti-it*(!DA) *ša-at-tim* 5 *uṭṭet*(ŠE) KUG.BABBAR *i-na* UD.1.KAM *i-na-ad-di-in.*

uṭṭetum 'barleycorn; grain' (.05 gram).

taqtītum 'end'.

§277 *šum-ma a-wi-lum* ^{giš}MÁ.60.GUR *i-gur i-na* UD.1.KAM IGI.6. GÁL KUG.BABBAR Á-*ša i-na-ad-di-in.*

^{giš}MÁ.60.GUR reading uncertain, perhaps *elep šūš kurrī*.

§59:

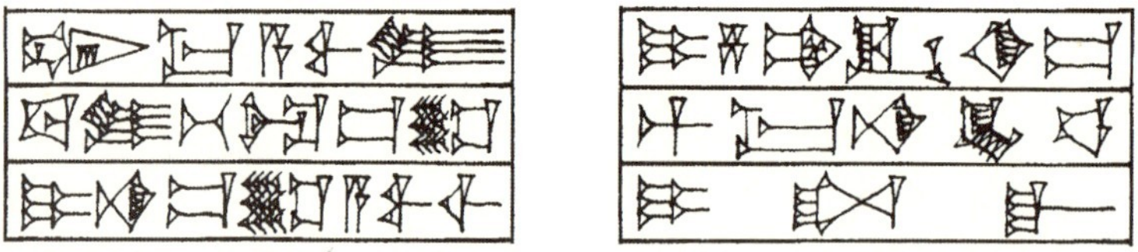

§204:

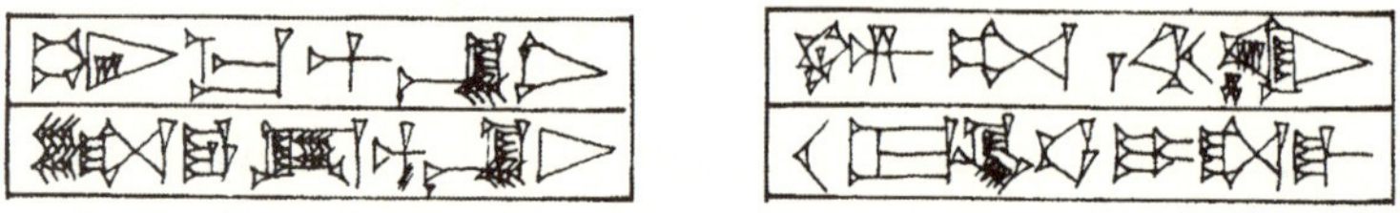

In the last line, the second sign is a defective writing of GÍN.

§§268–269:

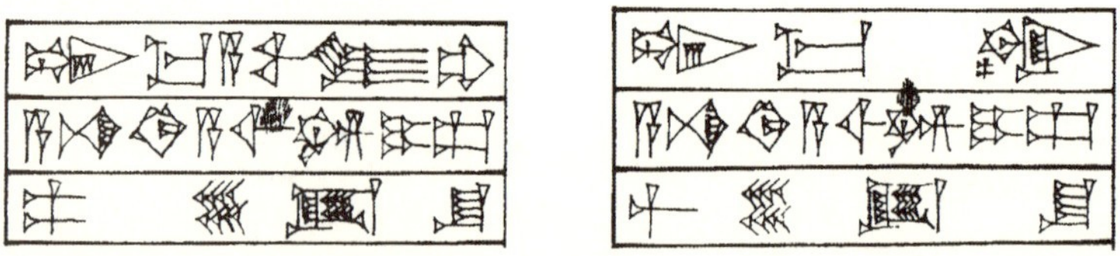

diāšum (*i*) 'to trample, thresh'.

Omens from *YOS* 10:

1. *šum-ma [i-na a-mu-tim] 4 na-ap-la-sà-[tu]m šar-ru-ú ḫa-am-me-e ki-ib-ra-at ma-a-tim i-te-bu-ú-nim an-nu-ú-um i-ma-qú-tam an-nu-ú-um i-te-bé.* (11 ii 3–6)
   ḫammû 'rebels'; *šar ḫammê* 'usurper king'.
   kibrum (pl. *kibrātum*) 'edge, bank'; pl. 'region, periphery'.
   annûm ... *annûm* 'one ... the other'.

2. *šum-ma na-ap-la-aš-tum a-na pa-da-nim iq-te-er-ba-am tu-ru-ku-tum a-na šar-ri-im i-qé-er-re-bu-nim-ma a-wi-il*$_5$*-šu-‹nu›* É.GAL-*la-am i-be-el.* (11 ii 14–17)
   Turukkûm (relative/gentilic adj.) 'inhabitant of Turukkum'.
   bêlum (*e*) 'to rule'.

3. *šum-ma i-na li-ib-bi na-[aṣ]-ra-ap-tim pa-da-ṇum šar-ru-um ma-as-sú a-na pi-i-šu uš-ša-ab.* (11 iv 16–18)
   naṣraptum 'depression'; for the word order of the protasis, see §2.5.

4. *[šum-m]a mar-tum [l]i-ib-ba-ša li-pi-a-am ma-li* ^{giš}TUKUL *šar-ru-ki-in.* (31 i 1–4).
   lipûm (*lipi-*) 'fat'.
   Šarru(m)-kīn 'Sargon' (king of Akkad, ca. 2334–2279).

5. *šum-ma mar-tum is-ḫu-ur-ma ú-ba-na-am il-ta-we-e šar-ru-um ma-ta-am na-ka-ar-[ta]-am i-[ṣa]-ab-ba-a[t].* (31 ii 24–30)
   il-ta-we-e for *iltawi.*

6. *šum-[m]a mar-tum is-ḫu-ur-ma mu-úḫ-ḫa-am ša ú-ba-ni-im il-ta-wi šar-ru-um* SUKKAL.MAḪ-*šu i-na-as-sà-aḫ.* (31 ii 31–37)
   SUKKAL.MAḪ = *sukkalmaḫḫum* a high court official ('chief minister').

7. *šum-ma mar-tum it-bé-e-ma mu-úḫ-ḫi ú-ba-ni-im iṣ-ṣa-ba-at šar-ru-um a-la-am na-ak-ra-am qá-as-sú-ú i-ka-aš-ša-ad.* (31 viii 30–37)

8. DIŠ *iz-bu-um er-ru-šu i-na mu-uḫ-ḫi-šu ša-ak-nu bi-ša-am ša ma-tim ša-a-ti [ma]-tum [ša]-ni-tum i-ta-ab-ba-al.* (56 i 31–33)
   errū (pl.) 'intestines'.

9. DIŠ *iz-bu-um uẓ-na-šu i-ni-šu ik-ta-⸢at⸣-ma a-wi-lum i-ḫa-al-li-iq.* (56 ii 23–24)
   katāmum (*a–u*) 'to cover'.

10. 31 ii 13–15:

šarrū ḫammê see above under no. 1.

11. 31 ii 42–47:

Line 5: the first sign is DINGIR; the last sign is *im*.

šabāsum (*u*) 'to become angry, annoyed' (with someone: *eli*); Verbal Adj. *šabsum* (*šabus-*) 'angry, annoyed'.

12. 31 iv 19–24:

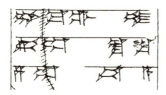

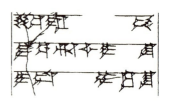

13. 31 iv 45–50:

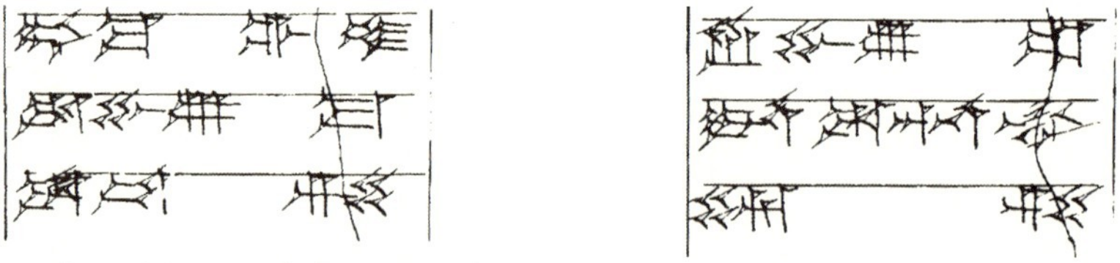

ṭebûm (*u*) 'to sink, become submerged'.

14. 31 ix 28–35:

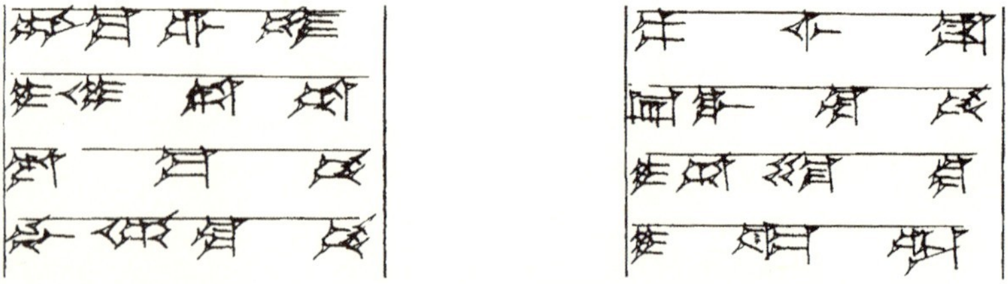

damum 'blood'.

bullûm (*bullu-*) adjective, meaning unknown.

15. 31 xi 43–47:

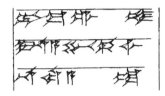

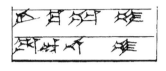

nikurtum / *nukurtum* 'hostility, war'.

16. 56 ii 35–39:

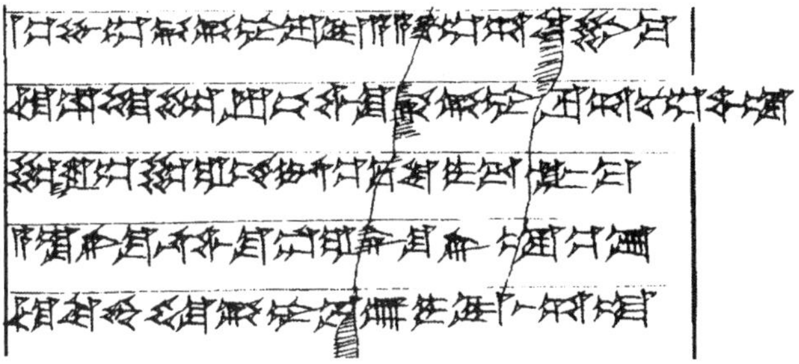

Line 1: the sign in the first crack is *nu*, in the second is *ki*.

Line 2: the sign in the first crack is *qá*; the PI sign has both the value *pi* and the value *wa* here.

kayyānum 'normal' (cf. *kânum*).

nawûm (*nawā-*) 'steppeland; area around a town'.

ṭeḫḫûm (*ṭeḫḫē-*) 'neighboring area or region'.

G. Contracts. Normalize and translate the following texts:

1. Lease of a field for cultivation (Szlechter, *Tablettes* p. 82, MAH 15.880)

[1] A.ŠÀ *ma-la qá-as-sú i-ka-aš-ša-du* [2] *ugāram*(A.GÀR) [*š*]*a* DÙG-*ba-a-tum* [3] *šu-ṣú-ut a-wi-il-*^{d}EN.ZU [4] KI *a-wi-il-*^{d}EN.ZU [5] DUMU DUMU-*er-ṣe-tim* [6] ^{I}*gi-mil-lum* [7] DUMU ÌR-*eššešim*(ÈŠ.ÈŠ) [8] A.ŠÀ *a-na er-re-šu-tim* [9] *a-na* MU.1.KAM [10] *ú-še-*[*ṣí*] [11] *ana ūm ebūrim*(UD.BURU$_{14}$.ŠÈ) [12] *ši-it-ti-in er-re-šu* [13] *ša-lu-uš be-el* A.ŠÀ. [14–18] Witnesses. [19–22] Date.

PNs: *Ṭābātum*; *Awīl-Sîn*; *Mār-erṣetim*; *Gimillum*; *Warad-eššešim*.

[2] *ugārum* (*ugār*; pl. *ugārû*, *ugārātum*; log. A.GÀR; Sum. lw.?) 'open field, meadow, arable land'.

[3] *šūṣūtum* 'leasehold estate'.

[8] *errēšūtum* 'tenancy (of a field)'.

[10] *ušēṣi* 'he leased'.

12 For *errēšum* (see §24.4); *errēšum* 'tenant farmer, cultivator'.
12–13 In both of these lines the verb *ileqqe* is to be understood.

2. Concerning delivery of sheep for offering (Pinches, *CT* 4 31b = Schorr, *VAB* 5, no. 66).

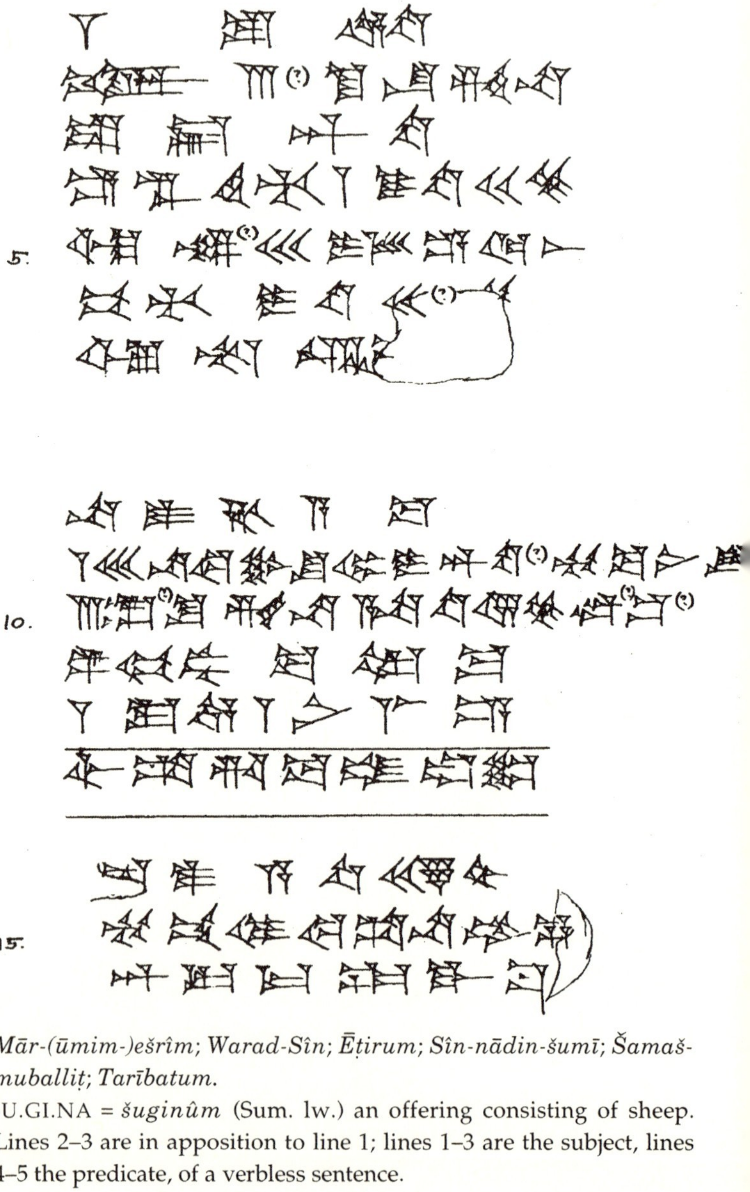

PNs: *Mār-(ūmim-)ešrîm; Warad-Sîn; Ēṭirum; Sîn-nādin-šumī; Šamaš-muballiṭ; Tarībatum.*

2 ^{udu}ŠU.GI.NA = *šuginûm* (Sum. lw.) an offering consisting of sheep. Lines 2–3 are in apposition to line 1; lines 1–3 are the subject, lines 4–5 the predicate, of a verbless sentence.

4 *esiḫtum / isiḫtum* (*e / isiḫti*) 'assignment, duty'. The last sign is KÁM, an alternative to KAM in logographic expressions of time (§23.2(d)), which also appears in line 10; the regular KAM appears in line 14.

5 Read after *ù* ÌR-^{d}30; the same man's name is written ÌR-^{d}EN.Z[U] in line 7. Many of the most important god names have alternate logographic writings that are numbers; 30 is the moon god *Sîn*.

6 The first sign is *qá*.

6–8 *qātam nasāḫum* here means 'to withdraw a claim'; *na-ás-ḫa-a* is either f. pl. agreeing with *qātāt*, which also occurs in this expression, rather than the written *qāti*; or an archaic dual form, due to the two persons; or an error for *na-as-ḫa-at*.

10 After KÁM (see note to line 4) read ‹*ub*›-*ba!-lam!*.

12 The first four signs are to be read 1 GÍN KUG.BABBAR!(1).

14 The first sign is ⸢ITU⸣. The ÁŠ sign has the value ZÍZ in the month name ZÍZ.A, read *Šabāṭum* (the eleventh month, Jan.–Feb.).

15–16 Years of a king's reign in the First Dynasty of Babylon were each referred to by a significant event of that year, written in Sumerian (and often abbreviated); see Appendix A. This is the beginning of Ammiditana's 27th year date formula, MU *am-mi-di-ta-na* LUGAL.E ^{d}URAŠ (the IB sign) UR.SAG (= *qarrādum*) GAL.LA (= GAL) 'Year King Ammiditana (dedicated a great weapon of gold ...) to Uraš the great warrior'. *Uraš* is a grain god.

LESSON TWENTY-FOUR

24.1 Derived Verbs

The verb forms encountered thus far all belong to the G, or basic, stem; they consist of the simple or basic root plus an inflectional pattern for each finite and non-finite form. But other verbs may be formed, or derived, from these same roots by the use of special prefixes, infixes, or other characteristic features. These derived verbs (or derived stems) are most conveniently referred to by letters that signify the essential characteristic of each. (Some scholars and reference works, notably the *CAD*, use a system of numerical notation to refer to the verb stems; these are given below in square brackets.) The most common verb stems are the following:

G	basic (German *Grundstamm*; a few scholars write B for basic) [I/1]
D	doubled middle radical [II/1]
Š	prefixed *š* [III/1]
N	prefixed *n* [IV/1]
Gt, Dt, Št	infixed *t* [I/2, II/2, III/2, respectively]
Gtn, Dtn, Štn, Ntn	infixed *tan* [I/3, II/3, III/3, IV/3, respectively]

All of these stems are inflected for the same finite and non-finite forms (e.g., Preterite, Imperative, Participle) as the G stem. Each stem has a characteristic range of meanings or functions; the forms and meanings of each will be presented in the remaining lessons. It should be noted that most roots occur in more than one stem, but very few are found in all the possible stems.

In modern Akkadian dictionaries, derived verbs are listed under the G-stem entry, usually with a special sub-section for each stem. Some roots do not occur in the G; these are generally listed under the Infinitive of the most frequently attested stem: e.g.,

naprušum (N Infinitive, root *p-r-š*) 'to fly';
kullumum (D Infinitive, root *k-l-m*) 'to show'.

24.2 The D Stem: Sound Verbs; Verbs I–*n*; Verbs III–weak

(a) Sound Verbs

The D stem, for all verb types except verbs II–weak, is characterized by a **doubled middle radical** in **all** of its forms. (This doubling will not, of course, always be indicated in the script.) The "principal parts" (cf. §21.1) of *parāsum* in the D are:

Infinitive:	*purrusum*	Imperative:	*purris*
Durative:	*uparras*	Participle:	*muparrisum*
Perfect:	*uptarris*	Verbal Adj.:	*purrusum* (*purrus*)
Preterite:	*uparris*		

All D verbs, regardless of their vowel-class in the G, are *a–i* verbs. This difference in vowels between R_2 and R_3 is the only feature that distinguishes the Durative (*uparr***a***s*) and the Preterite (*uparr***i***s*). Note that the Perfect has the vowel of the Preterite in the D, rather than that of the Durative as in the G. The prefixes that mark person in the **Durative**, **Perfect**, and **Preterite** all have *u*, rather than the *i* and *a* of G verbs. Note that the 3cs and 1cs forms are identical.

	Durative	Preterite	Perfect
3cs	*uparras*	*uparris*	*uptarris*
2ms	*tuparras*	*tuparris*	*tuptarris*
2fs	*tuparrasī*	*tuparrisī*	*tuptarrisī*
1cs	*uparras*	*uparris*	*uptarris*
3mp	*uparrasū*	*uparrisū*	*uptarrisū*
3fp	*uparrasā*	*uparrisā*	*uptarrisā*
2cp	*tuparrasā*	*tuparrisā*	*tuptarrisā*
1cp	*nuparras*	*nuparris*	*nuptarris*

The *-t-* of the Perfect undergoes the same changes as in the G (cf. §17.1); e.g., *uṣṣabbit, ussaḫḫer, ugdammer* (the last two also with *i* › *e*; §7.1).

The **Precative** has the same prefixes, attached to the base of the Preterite, as in the G (except in the 1cp, with *i nu-* in the D, vs. G *i ni-*).

3cs	*liparris*	3mp	*liparrisū*
		3fp	*liparrisā*
1cs	*luparris*	1cp	*i nuparris*

The **Imperative**, as expected, has the "theme-vowel" of the Preterite (*i*) between R_2 and R_3; between the first two radicals, however, the vowel is *u*, not *a* as in the Preterite:

ms	*purris*	cp	*purrisā*
fs	*purrisī*		

The forms of the negative commands are completely predictable: **Vetitive** 3cs *ayy-uparris*, 2ms *ē-tuparris* (i.e., *ayy-* / *ē-* plus Preterite); **Prohibitive** 3cs *lā uparras* (i.e., *lā* plus Durative).

The **Participles** of all stems other than the G have prefix *mu-*, and *i* between R_2 and R_3. The characteristic feature of the D Participle is of course the doubled middle radical:

ms	*muparrisum*	mp	*muparrisūtum*
fs	*muparristum*	fp	*muparrisātum*

The bound form of the fs is *muparrisat*, with suffix *muparristaka* (cf. the G *pāristum*, bound form *pārisat*, suff. *pāristaka*, §§8.3(c 2v), 11.1(c 1), 20.1).

In each of the derived stems, the **Infinitive** and the **Verbal Adjective** are identical in form; all have *u* between R_2 and R_3. Note that the vowel between R_2 and R_3 is the only difference in the D between the base of the Imperative, *purris-*, and the base of the Verbal Adj. (and Infin.), *purrus-*.

In *e*-type verbs (§21.2), *a*-vowels again usually (though not always) become *e*; e.g.,

D Durative *uqerreb* (but also *uqarrab*);
D Preterite *uqerrib* (but also *uqarrib*).

It is important to note that for many such verbs, the Durative and the Preterite will be written identically, as in

ú-qe-er-RI-IB for Durative *uqerreb* and Preterite *uqerrib*.

(b) Verbs I–*n*

These offer little difficulty. The only form in which assimilation of *n* takes place is the Perfect; all other forms correspond to those of the sound verb.

Infinitive:	*nukkurum*	Imperative:	*nukker*
Durative:	*unakkar*	Participle:	*munakkerum*
Perfect:	*uttakker*	Verbal Adj.:	*nukkurum* (*nukkur*)
Preterite:	*unakker*		

(c) Verbs III–weak

Since there are no distinctive vowel-classes, most of these verbs fall together into one paradigm, as sound verbs do. In verbs III–*e* (i.e., those whose third radical was ʾ$_{3\text{–}4}$ [*ḥ*, ʿ]), however, *a*-vowels, with the usual exceptions, most often become *e*. Below are the D stem "principal parts" of the four types of G verbs III–weak:

	banûm (*i*)	*malûm* (*a*)	*ḫadûm* (*u*)	*ṭeḫûm* (*e*)
Infinitive:	*bunnûm*	*mullûm*	*ḫuddûm*	*ṭuḫḫûm*
Durative:	*ubanna*	*umalla*	*uḫadda*	*uṭeḫḫe* / *uṭaḫḫa*
Perfect:	*ubtanni*	*umtalli*	*uḫtaddi*	*uṭṭeḫḫi* / *uṭṭaḫḫi*
Preterite:	*ubanni*	*umalli*	*uḫaddi*	*uṭeḫḫi* / *uṭaḫḫi*
Imperative:	*bunni*	*mulli*	*ḫuddi*	*ṭuḫḫi*
Participle:	*mubannûm*	*mumallûm*	*muḫaddûm*	*muṭeḫḫûm* / *muṭaḫḫûm*
Verbal Adj.:	*bunnûm*	*mullûm*	*ḫuddûm*	*ṭuḫḫûm*
(V. Adj. base:	*bunnu*	*mullu*	*ḫuddu*	*ṭuḫḫu*)

As in the case of *uqerrib* / *uqerreb* cited above at the end of (a), writings of the D Durative and Preterite of verbs III–*e* may be identical:

ú-ṭe-eḫ-ḪI for Durative *uṭeḫḫe* and Preterite *uṭeḫḫi*.

Vowel contraction takes place as usual, as the Durative and Preterite paradigms of *mullûm* illustrate:

	Durative	Preterite
3cs	*umalla*	*umalli*
2ms	*tumalla*	*tumalli*
2fs	*tumallî*	*tumallî*
1cs	*umalla*	*umalli*
3mp	*umallû*	*umallû*
3fp	*umallâ*	*umalliā*
2cp	*tumallâ*	*tumalliā*
1cp	*numalla*	*numalli*

Note that because of vowel contraction the Durative and Preterite forms are identical in the 2fs and 3mp.

The base of the Participle ends in *-i* (cf. *muparrisum*). For reference, the forms of the Participle of *mullûm* are:

ms	*mumallûm* (bound *mumalli*)	mp	*mumallûtum*
fs	*mumallītum* (bound *mumalliat*)	fp	*mumalliātum*

The bases of the Infinitive and Verbal Adjective end in *-u* (cf. *purrusum*). Thus, they have the following forms:

Infin. / attributive Verbal Adj., ms:	nom.	*mullûm*
	gen.	*mullîm*
	acc.	*mullâm*
attributive Verbal Adj.,	fs:	*mullūtum*
	mp:	*mullûtum*
	fp:	*mullâtum*
predicate Verbal Adj., subject	3ms:	*mullu*
	3fs:	*mullât*
	3mp:	*mullû*
	etc.	

24.3 The Meaning of the D Stem

(a) **Factitive** of verbs that are adjectival in the G stem; thus, if a G verb means 'to be(come) X', where X is an adjective, the D means 'to make (something) X'; e.g.,

> *damāqum* 'to be(come) good, improve' (intransitive), *dummuqum* 'to make good, improve' (transitive);
> *rapāšum* 'to be(come) wide', *ruppušum* 'to widen (something)'.

Be certain the following sentences are clear:

> *mātum irpiš* 'the land became wide';
> *mātam urappiš* 'I/she/he widened the land';
> *mātum rapšat* 'the land is/was wide';
> *mātum ruppušat* 'the land is/was widened/made wide'.

(b) **Causative** of some verbs that are active-intransitive in the G: e.g.,

> *ḫalāqum* 'to disappear, perish', *ḫulluqum* 'to cause to perish, destroy'.

Sometimes this is merely a transitivizing effect in English:

> *nišū ipaḫḫurā* 'the people will gather' (intrans.),
> but *nišī upaḫḫar* 'I will gather the people'.

(c) **Pluralic**, denoting activity on a plurality of objects, or by a plurality of subjects (rare); e.g.,

> *ālšu anaqqar* 'I will tear down his city', but
> but *ālānīšunu unaqqar* 'I will tear down their (m) cities';

šēpīya iššiq 'he kissed my feet',
but *šēpīya unaššiqū* 'they (m) kissed my feet'.

(d) **Denominative**, i.e., derived from a noun, as in

ruggubum 'to roof over', from *rugbum* 'roof'.

(e) **Lexical**; i.e., the basic form of the verb is D stem, the root not occurring in the G, as in

kullumum 'to show', *wuššurum* 'to release'.

(f) Many active-transitive verbs occur in both the G and the D with no perceptible difference in nuance. In the lesson vocabularies, this will be noted by an "equals" sign; e.g.,

petûm G 'to open'; *puttûm* D = G.

(g) Not all verbs occur in the D. In the vocabularies of this and subsequent lessons, the D of a verb will be given only if it is of relatively frequent occurrence. Its meaning should be learned together with that of the G. Below are listed the frequently-found D stems of sound verbs, verbs I–*n*, and verbs III–weak encountered thus far; they are arranged in semantic groups. Their meanings, especially those that are not predictable, should be learned.

(a) factitive:

dummuqum 'to make good, pleasing; to improve; to treat kindly (with acc. or *ana*/dative)'.
dunnunum 'to strengthen, fortify, reinforce; to speak severely'; in hendiadys: 'to do something forcefully'.
ḫuddûm 'to make happy'.
kubbutum 'to honor, show respect to; to aggravate, make difficult'.
lubburum 'to make last, prolong (the life of)'.
rubbûm 'to make large, great; to raise (offspring), raise (in rank)'.
ruppušum 'to widen, broaden'.
šullumum 'to keep whole, well, safe; to heal (trans.); to preserve, take care of; to conduct or deliver safely; to make good, replace in full; to complete'.
zukkûm 'to cleanse, clear, winnow; to free, release'.

(b) causative:

bulluṭum 'to keep (someone) alive, healthy, safe; to heal (trans.)'.
ḫulluqum 'to make disappear, let escape, destroy'.

kunnušum 'to bend; to make submissive'.
muṣṣûm 'to make reach, release'.
nukkurum 'to change, alter (trans.); to move, remove'.
puḫḫurum 'to gather, collect, assemble (trans.)'.
puššuḫum 'to pacify, soothe, calm'.
qurrubum 'to bring/send near; to present, offer'.
suḫḫurum 'to turn around, aside, divert; to turn away, back, send away, back, repel, expel'.
tukkulum 'to cause to trust; to encourage; to make trustworthy'.
tummûm 'to make swear, adjure, bind by oath'.
ṭuḫḫûm 'to bring near'.

(c) = G:

ḫuppûm	*nukkusum*	*purrusum*	*suddurum*
kuṣṣurum	*nussuḫum*	*puššurum*	*suḫḫupum*
muddudum	*nussuqum*	*puṭṭurum*	*ṣubbutum*
muḫḫuṣum	*puqqudum*	*puttûm*	*šubburum*

(d) other:

gummurum = G; also, 'to pay in full'.
kuššudum 'to pursue, chase (away), exile; to approach; to conquer'.
muḫḫurum 'to approach; to make accept'.
mullûm 'to fill (something: acc.; with something: acc.); to pay or deliver in full; to assign'.
ruddûm 'to add to, contribute to' (i.e., 'to make follow').

24.4 Features of Late OB Texts

The spoken OB dialect (or, better, cluster of dialects), like all languages, was constantly changing during its history. Although written language tends to be more conservative than its spoken counterpart (cf. English spelling), some changes, especially phonological ones, begin to appear in later OB texts. Because the spelling habits of the scribes were deeply ingrained, however, the later forms do not usually appear consistently; rather, it is quite common for the later, spoken forms to occur in texts, sometimes sporadically, sometimes overwhelmingly, alongside older, learned forms. Below are three phonological developments that appear in later OB texts.

(a) Mimation, the final *m* that appears on all singular and on fem. pl. nouns, on all adjectives, on the forms of the Ventive morpheme (*-am*, *-m*,

-nim), and on the dative pronouns was lost, probably quite early in the OB period. Compare the following pairs of classical and late OB forms:

> *šarrum* ~ *šarru* 'king' (nom.);
> *šarrātim* ~ *šarrāti* 'queens' (gen.-acc.);
> *tašpuram* ~ *tašpura* 'you (ms) sent to me';
> *išpurūnim* ~ *išpurūni* 'they (m) sent to me';
> *ašpurakkum* ~ *ašpurakku* 'I sent (Ventive) to you (ms)'.

Because of this change, several formal distinctions are lost:

(1) The 2fs, 3ms, and 3fs dative pronouns (classical *-kim*, *-šum*, *-šim*), when at the end of a verb, become identical to their accusative counterparts (i.e., *-ki*, *-šu*, *-ši*, respectively; but note 2ms dative *-ku* vs. acc. *-ka*).

(2) The Ventive no longer appears formally on the 2fs verb (i.e., *tašpurī* 'you sent' or 'you sent to me'), although it is still clearly marked on all other forms.

(3) Because the writing system does not normally distinguish short and long vowels, the nom. and gen. of masc. sg. nouns are written the same as their pl. counterparts; likewise, certain verb forms are written identically:

> *ka-al-bu* for nom. *kalbu* 'dog' or *kalbū* 'dogs';
> *ka-al-bi* for gen. *kalbi* or *kalbī* (but note that the acc. sg. *ka-al-ba* remains distinct from the acc. pl. *ka-al-bi*).
> *iš-pu-ra* can be 3fp *išpurā* 'they (f) sent' or 3cs with Ventive *išpura* 'she/he sent to me'; similarly *ta-aš-pu-ra* for 2cp *tašpurā* or 2ms *tašpura*.

The loss of mimation occurred only if the *m* was word-final; thus, if the conjunction *-ma* or any other ending or suffix followed, *m* was retained, or assimilated, as earlier:

> *tašpura*, but *tašpuram-ma* and *tašpuraššu*;
> *ašpurakki*, but *ašpurakkim-ma*.

(b) The sequences *ia* and *ea* (and *iā*, *īa*, *eā*) contracted to *â*; e.g.,

> *rabiam* › *rabâ* 'great (ms, acc.)'; *qiāšum* › *qâšu* 'to bestow';
> *rabiātum* › *rabâtu* 'great (fp, nom.)'; *aqīaš* › *aqâš* 'I will bestow';
> *iqbiam* › *iqbâ* 'she said to me'; *šemeam* › *šemâ* 'listen (ms) to me';
> *taqabbiā* › *taqabbâ* 'you (pl) say'; *šemeā* › *šemâ* 'listen (pl)'.

(c) Rarely, initial *w* was lost and intervocalic *w* was written as *m*; these developments are normal in later dialects of Akk.:

> *wardum* › *ardu* 'male slave'; *awātum* › *amātu* 'word';
> *waṣiam* › *aṣâ* 'it (m) is protruding'; *awīlum* › *amīlu* 'man'.

24.5 Old Babylonian Letters

There are several thousand OB letters. They are perhaps the most difficult genre of text to understand, since most often a certain amount of background information, assumed by the correspondents, is unavailable to the modern reader. Much of the content can often only be surmised. Further, apart from the standardized formulae of greetings (see below), the language of letters is more colloquial than that of other genres. They are therefore of considerable linguistic interest because their language is closer to the spoken Akkadian of the writers; but for the same reason they often present idioms and turns of phrase of uncertain meaning.

The OB letter format involves several standardized formulae (see Sallaberger 1999). The letters were actually dictated to a scribe, and were in turn read aloud by another scribe to the addressee. Thus, the introductory greeting-formula is as follows:

> *ana* PN$_1$ *qibī-ma umma* PN$_2$-*ma* 'Speak to PN$_1$ (the addressee); thus (says) PN$_2$ (the sender): ...'.

In this formula, *qibi* (usually written *qí-bí-ma*, with NE = *bí* as the second sign) is the ms Imperative of *qabûm*; *umma* is an adverb meaning 'thus', which is followed by a direct quotation. The reasons for the occurrence of *-ma* after *qibi* and the sender are not known. The introduction may be embellished:

> *ana abīya ša Marduk uballaṭūšu qibī-ma umma Sîn-nāṣir mārūkā-ma* 'Speak to my father whom Marduk keeps well (*bulluṭum*, D Durative); thus (says) Sîn-nāṣir your son: ...'

Following the opening formula, wishes for the well-being of the addressee may be expressed; the most common of these, in its simplest form, is

> DN *liballiṭka* 'May DN keep you well'.

This too may be embellished, as in

> *Šamaš u Marduk aššumīya dāriš ūmī liballiṭūka* 'May Shamash and Marduk keep you well for my sake forever (*dāriš ūmī*)'.

There are no strict rules governing the introduction of the subject matter of the letter. Sometimes, topicalization by preposing (§21.5) is used, often, but not necessarily, with *aššum* or *ana*:

> *aššum eqlim ša tašpuram* 'Concerning the field about which you (ms) wrote to me: ...';
> *ana amtim ša taṭrudīm* 'As to the slave (f) whom you (fs) sent me: ...';
> PN$_1$ *ṣuḫārum aḫi* PN$_2$ '(Concerning) the servant PN$_1$, brother of PN$_2$: ...'.

A difficult feature of letters is the frequent occurrence of direct quotations within the body of the letter; review of §15.4 is encouraged. Also characteristic of letters is the common use of the Perfect to indicate the main point of the letter; see §17.2.

The letters incorporated into the exercises will, for the most part, be cited according to the most recent and comprehensive edition of OB letters from Mesopotamian sites: *Altbabylonische Briefe* (abbreviated *AbB*), series edited by F. R. Kraus.

EXERCISES

A. VOCABULARY 24.

Verbs:

ḫiārum G (*a–i*) 'to choose a mate'; Verbal Adj., fem. *ḫīrtum* (*ḫīrti*; sf. *ḫīrta-*; pl. *ḫīrātum*) 'wife (of equal status with the husband)'; Participle *ḫāʾirum* / *ḫāwirum* '(first) husband'.

kullumum D (not in G) 'to show, reveal (something to someone: double acc.); to produce (a person, document)'.

lamādum G (*a*; Imperative irregular: *limad*) 'to learn, study; to become aware of, informed of; to understand; to know sexually'; *lummudum* D 'to inform, teach'.

manûm G (*u*) 'to count; to include; to hand over, deliver'; Verbal Adj. *manûm* (*mani-*) 'counted, included, delivered' (cf. *manûm* 'mina').

Nouns:

appum (*appi*; dual *appān*; pl. *appātum*) 'nose; tip, end, edge'.

bulṭum (*buluṭ*) 'life, health' (cf. *balāṭum*).

dārum (*dār(i)*) 'perpetuity', rare except in the adverb *dāriš* (see §28.2) and the adverbial phrase *dāriš ūmī* both meaning 'forever'; Adj. *dārûm* (*dārī-*) 'perpetual, lasting, everlasting'; note also the substantivized fem. pl. *dāriātum* 'perpetuity, eternity', and *ana dāriātim* 'forever'.

eṣemtum (*eṣemti*; pl. *eṣmētum*; log. GÌR.PAD.DU) 'bone'.

lišānum (fem., rarely masc.; *lišān*; pl. *lišānātum*, rarely *lišānū*; log. EME) 'tongue; language, speech'.

šulmum (*šulum*) 'well-being, health; wish for well-being, greeting' (cf. *šalāmum*).

tību m (*tīb(i)*) 'rise, uprising, attack, onslaught'; *tībum kašdum* 'successful attack' (cf. *tebûm*).

B. Learn the following signs:

OB Lapid.	OB Cursive	NA	values
			EME (ka • me) = *lišānum*
			KÚR (also ^{lú}KÚR or LÚ.KÚR) = *nakrum*
	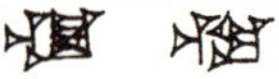	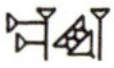	*dar*, *tár*, *ṭár*
			*tir*
		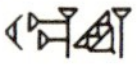	*eš₄-tár* or EŠ₄.TÁR or IŠTAR, the writing of the goddess *Ištar* (better, *Eštar*) in PNs
			GÌR = *šēpum*; see also next
	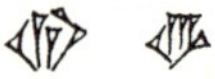		PAD, in GÌR.PAD.DU = *eṣemtum*

C. Write the following words in cuneiform and in transliteration; use logograms where possible:

1. *bīt Sîn*
2. *nakeršu*
3. *dūr ālīni*
4. *tasaddar*
5. *awīlû*
6. ^{I}*Mār-Ištar*
7. *šēp kussîm*
8. *lišān mātim*
9. *šittā sât ûm*
10. *rebīt terḫatim*
11. *šaman bāʾerim*
12. *imitti martim*
13. *qabal eṣemtīša*
14. *šumēl immerim*
15. *ḫamšat šiqil ḫurāṣum*

D. Write in normalized Akkadian:

1. it (f) is clean
2. it will become clean
3. I will cleanse it (f)
4. it (f) is cleansed
5. keep (ms) her alive
6. you (ms) will fill them (m) both
7. the fire is brought near
8. one who makes his goddess happy
9. I have assembled (Vent.) them (m)
10. may they (m) treat us kindly
11. they (f) have come forth
12. may they (m) not be negligent

13. the slave whom you (ms) let escape
14. I have surrounded it (m)
15. show (pl) me the wall
16. I was not able to carry off the bride-price
17. the god who causes you (fs) to trust
18. be (fs) informed of the attack
19. the people were made submissive
20. count (pl) them (m)
21. a widened canal (river)
22. she adjured the scribe forcefully
23. we have diverted him
24. they (m) presented (Vent.) them (m)
25. he may not alter it (m)
26. you (ms) have come up
27. they (m) will prolong his life
28. I must calm him
29. he has honored his courtiers
30. I will inform them (f)

E. Normalize and translate the following late OB forms; then rewrite them as they would appear in earlier texts.

1. *ta-ab-na-ni*
2. *il-qá-a*
3. *ar-da maḫ-ra-a a-ra-a-ab*
4. *a-wa-ti-ia na-ás-qá-ti še-ma-a*
5. *ṭe$_4$-mu ša ta-aš-pu-ra*
6. *a-na šar-ra-ti ra-bi-ti*
7. *a-na šar-ra-ti ra-ba-ti*
8. *le-mu-tu im-qú-ta-ma aš-ta-ap-ra-ku*

F. Normalize and translate:

1. AGA.ÚS.MEŠ *ù* ŠU.ḪA.MEŠ *le-ú-tum iš-tu* KI *qé-ru-ub-tim ur-ra-du-nim-ma* ERIN$_2$.MEŠ *a-ḫu-tim ša iš-tu ša-di-i i-ti-qú i-né-ru.*
2. *wa-ar-ki ḫa-wi-ri-ia ru-ba-tum ku-nu-ka* SÍG *ù* 6 ŠE GUR *a-na še-ri-ik-tim iš-ru-ka.*
3. *šum-ma ap-pi li-ša-an ka-al-bi-im na-ki-is bi-it a-wi-lim i-ma-qú-ut-ma ú-ul i-ba-an-ni-šu.*
4. *ma-am-ma-an le-e-et a-ḫa-ti-ia im-ḫa-aṣ-ma ši-ni-ša id-di i-na-an-na šum-ma ta-ra-ma-ni te-er-ta šu-ku-um-ma a-wi-lam šu-a-ti ṣú-bi-it-ma i-na ṣí-bi-ti i-di-šu ù me-ḫe-er* DUB-*pí-ia šu-up-ra.*
5. *mu-úḫ-ḫi qar-ra-di-im ù qá-ab-la-šu ma-ar-ṣú ù ú-ba-na-at ri-it-ti-šu ša šu-me-lim še-eb-ra.*

G. CH:

§190 *šum-ma a-wi-lum ṣe-eḫ-ra-am ša a-na ma-ru-ti-šu il-qú-šu-ma ú-ra-ab-bu-šu it-ti* DUMU.MEŠ-*šu la im-ta-nu-šu tar-bi-tum ši-i a-na* É *a-bi-šu i-ta-ar.*

tarbītum (*tarbīt*) 'offspring; adopted child' (cf. *rabûm* a).

§192 *šum-ma* DUMU *gerseqqêm*(GÌR.SÌ.GA) *ù lu* DUMU *sekretim* (^{mí}ZI.IK.RU.UM) *a-na a-bi-im mu-ra-bi-šu ù um-mi-im mu-ra-bi-ti-šu ú-ul a-bi at-ta ú-ul um-mi at-ti iq-ta-bi* EME–*šu i-na-ak-ki-su.*

gerseqqûm (base *gerseqqā;* log. GÌR.SÌ.GA; Sum. lw.) 'an attendant, domestic (attached to the palace or a temple)'.

sekretum (*sekret;* pl. *sekrētum;* pseudo-log. ^{mí}ZI.IK.RUM/RU.UM) 'a (cloistered?) woman of high status'.

§215–217 §215 *šum-ma* A.ZU *a-wi-lam sí-im-ma-am kab-tam i-na karzil*(GÍR.NI) *siparrim*(ZABAR) *i-pu-uš-ma a-wi-lam ub-ta-al-li-iṭ ù lu na-kap-ti a-wi-lim i-na karzil*(GÍR.NI) *siparrim*(ZABAR) *ip-te-ma i-in a-wi-lim ub-ta-al-li-iṭ* 10 GÍN KUG.BABBAR *i-le-qé* §216 *šum-ma* DUMU MAŠ.EN.GAG 5 GÍN KUG.BABBAR *i-le-qé* §217 *šum-ma* ÌR *a-wi-lim be-el* ÌR *a-na* A.ZU 2 GÍN KUG.BABBAR *i-na-ad-di-in.*

karzillum (*karzil;* log. GÍR.NI; Sum. lw.) 'physician's lancet'.

siparrum (log. ZABAR; Sum. lw.) 'bronze'.

nakkaptum (*nakkapti;* pl. *nakkapātum*) 'temple (of the head)'.

§221 *šum-ma* A.ZU GÌR.PAD.DU *a-wi-lim še-bé-er-tam uš-ta-li-im ù lu še-er-ʾa*$_4$*-nam mar-ṣa-am ub-ta-al-li-iṭ be-el si*$_{20}$(ṢI)*-im-mi-im a-na* A.ZU 5 GÍN KUG.BABBAR *i-na-ad-di-in.*

šerʾānum (*šerʾān*) 'band, strip; vein, artery, tendon, sinew'.

§122:

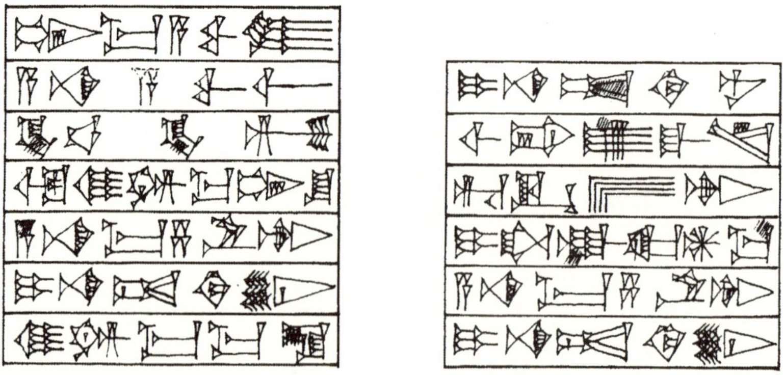

§138:

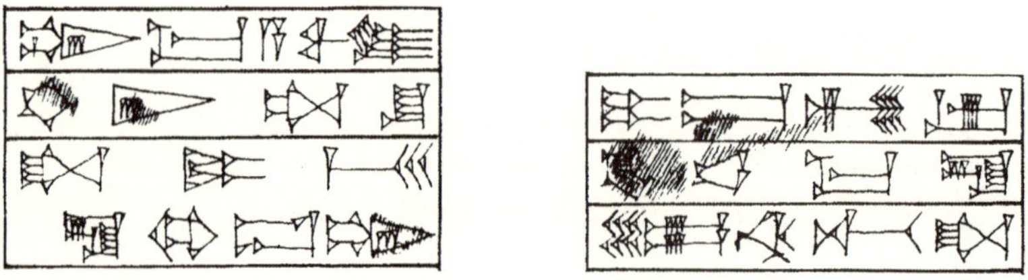

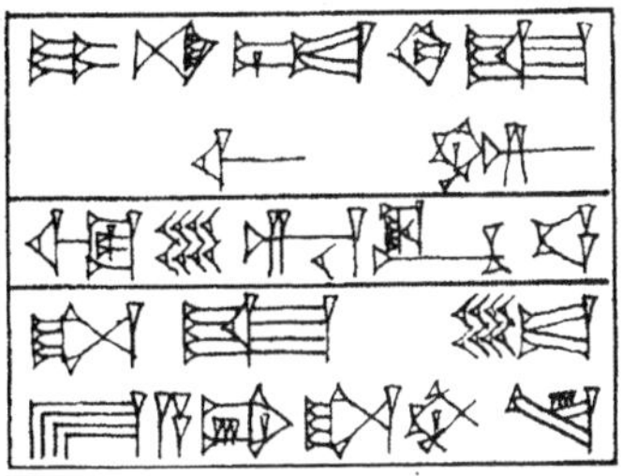

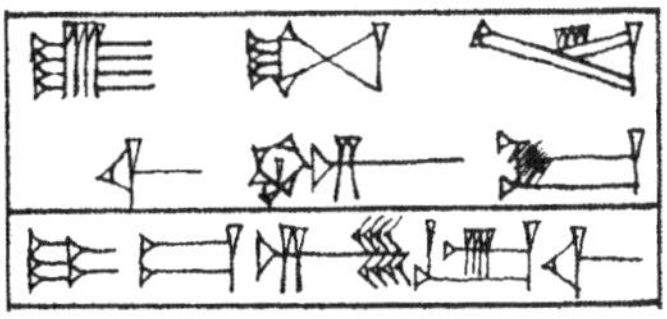

§196–199:

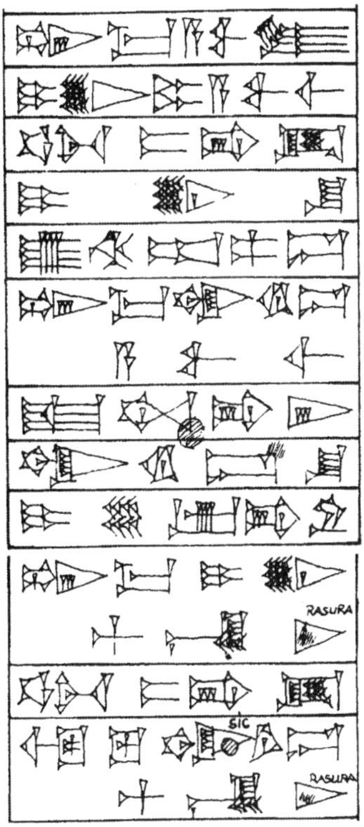

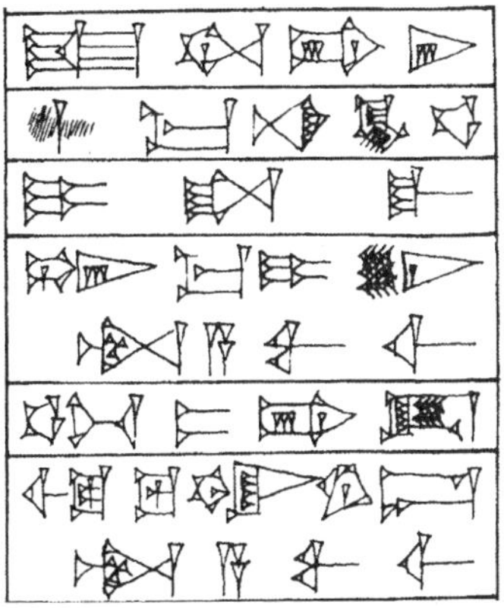

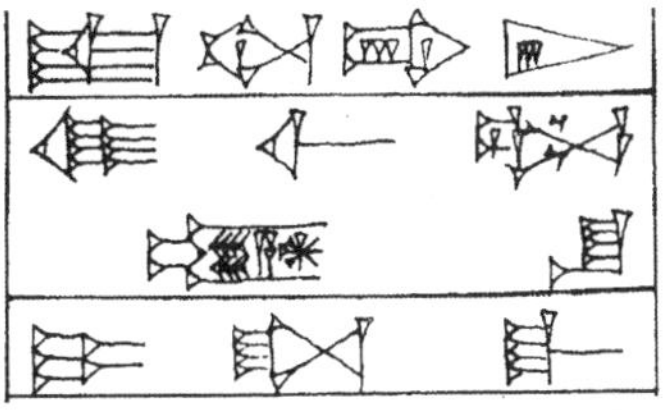

ḫuppudum D 'to blind'.

Omens from *YOS* 10:

1. *šum-ma pa-da-nu ši-na a-li-ik ḫa-ar-ra-*[*ni*]*m ḫa-ra-an-šu* [*i*]-*ka-aš-ša-ad.* (11 i 3–4)
   ālik ḫarrānim 'expeditionary force'.
2. *šum-ma pa-da-nu-um a-di ša-la-ši-i-šu pu-ru-us a-li-ik ḫa-ar-*

ra-nim ḫa-ar-ra-nu-um a-na ḫa-ar-ra-nim i-na-di-šu UD-*mu-šu i-ri-iq-qú.* (11 i 14–17)

riāqum G (*a–i*) 'to become empty, idle, unoccupied, useless'.

3. *šum-ma ma-aṣ-ra-aḫ mar-tim ku-un-nu-uš šar-ru-um na!*(ŠA)-*ak-ru-um a-na šar-ri-im i-ka-nu-uš.* (11 v 1–2)

maṣraḫum 'cystic duct'(?).

4. 31 ii 48–55:

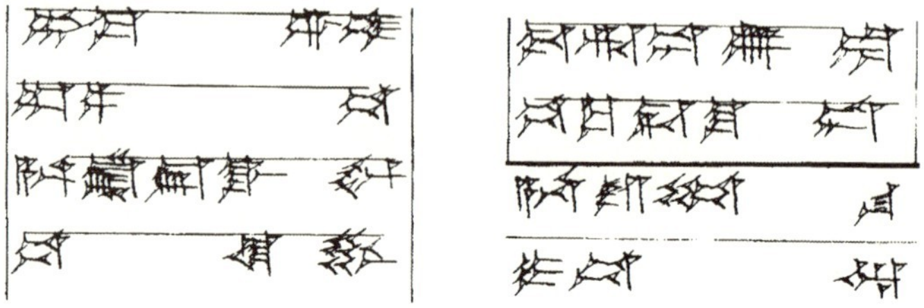

For *ṭa-ri-* read *ṭa-ar!-*.

5. 56 ii 11–13:

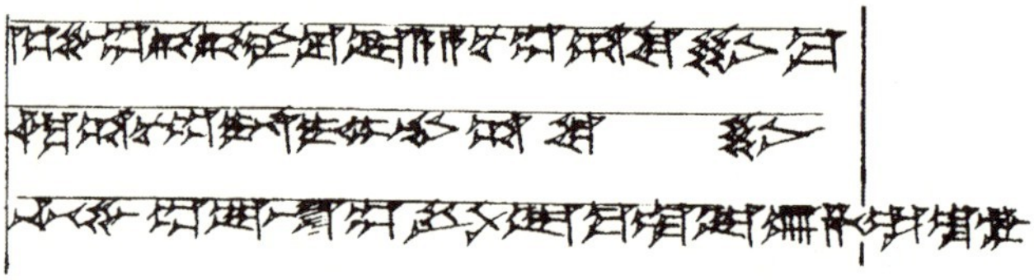

kayyānum 'normal'.

I. Contract:

1. Naming a niece as heir (*CT* 2 35 = Schorr, *VAB* 5, no. 13A).

[1] *ana aplūt* (IBILA.ŠÈ) *tab-ni-eš$_4$-tár* [2] DUMU.MUNUS *na-bi-*^{d}EN.ZU [3] *be-le-sú-nu* [4] DUMU.MUNUS *nu-úr-ì-lí-šu* [5] *a-ḫi-ša a-di tab-ni-eš$_4$-tár* [6] *ba-al-ṭà-at* [7] *be-le-sú-nu tab-ni-eš$_4$-tár* [8] *i-pa-la-aḫ ú-ka-ba-sí* [9] *šum-ma pa-al-ḫi-ša* [10] É *ša ga-gi-im* [11] *ù bu-še-ša* [12] *ma-la i-ba-šu-ú* [13] *i-na ga-gi-im* [14] *ša be-le-sú-nu* [15] MU ^{d}UTU ^{Id}AMAR.UTU [16] *ù su-mu-la*-DINGIR [17] *ša pí* DUB *a-ni-im* [18] *ú-na-ka-ru.* [19–34] Witnesses.

PNs: *Tabni-Eštar*; *Nabi-Sîn*; *Bēlessunu*; *Nūr-ilīšu*; *Sumu-la-il* (king of Babylon, ca. 1880–45).

[1–2] These lines constitute a label: 'Concering the estate of PN'.

[5] *-ša* refers to Tabni-Eshtar; *adi* here 'as long as' (§26.2).

[9] This line is garbled; what is expected is *šumma iplaḫši.*

[11] For expected nom. *bušûša.*

[13] *ina gagîm* was added as an afterthought; it must go with *mala ibaššû.*

[15–18] 'The oath ... is (upon/against) whoever ...' The ^{I} before ^{d}AMAR.UTU is unusual.

J. Letters:

1. Scheil, *SFS*, p. 131 = Kraus, *AbB* 5 225. This first letter is furnished with a full normalization and a translation as an illustration.

[1] *a-na bi-bi-ia* [2] *qí-bí-ma* [3] *um-ma gi-mil-*^{d}AMAR.UTU-*ma* [4] ^{d}UTU *ù* ^{d}AMAR.UTU *aš-šu-mi-ia* [5] *da-ri-iš* UD-*mi li-ba-al-li-ṭú-ki* [6] *a-na šu-ul-mi-ki* [7] *aš-pu-ra-am* [8] *šu-lum-ki šu-up-ri-im* [9] *a-na* KÁ.DINGIR. RA^{ki} [10] *al-lik-kam-ma* [11] *ú-ul a-mu-ur-ki* [12] *ma-di-iš az-zi-iq* [13] *ṭe-em a-la-ki-ki* [14] *šu-up-ri-im-ma* [15] *lu-uḫ-du* ... [18] *aš-šum-mi-ia da-ri-iš* [19] UD-*mi* [20] *lu ba-al-ṭa-a-ti.*

PNs: *Bibiya* (fem.); *Gimil-Marduk.*
[10] *al-lik-kam* and [18] *aš-šum-mi-ia* see §18.4.
[12] *mādiš azziq* 'I became very upset'.

Ana Bibiya qibī-ma; umma Gimil-Marduk-ma.	Speak to Bibiya; thus (speaks) Gimil-Marduk.
Šamaš u Marduk aššumīya dāriš ūmī liballiṭūki.	May Shamash and Marduk keep you alive forever for my sake.
Ana šulmīki ašpuram; šulumki šuprīm.	I wrote concerning your well-being; send me (news about) your well-being.
Ana Bābilim allikam-ma, ul āmurki; mādiš azziq.	I came to Babylon, but did not see you; I became very upset.
Ṭēm alākīki šuprīm-ma, luḫdu. ...	Send me news of your traveling, that I may rejoice ...
Aššumīya dāriš ūmī lū balṭāti.	Be well forever for my sake.

2. Van Soldt, *AbB* 12 10 (BM 97170, copy not yet published).

[1] *a-na* ^{d}*na-bi-um-at-pa-lam* [2] *qí-bí-ma* [3] *um-ma be-la-nu-um-ma* [4] ^{d}UTU *ù* ^{d}AMAR.UTU *li-ba-al-li-ṭú-ka* [5] *lu-ú ba-al-ṭa-ta* [6] *lu-ú* [*š*]*a-al-ma-ta* [7] *a-na šu-u*[*l-m*]*i-ia ta-aš-pur-ra-a*[*m*] [8] *ša-a*[*l*]*-ma-ku* [9] *ša-la-am-ka a-na da-ri-a-tim* [10] ^{d}AMAR.UTU *li-iq-bi* [11] *iš-tu i-na-an-na* UD.2.KAM [12] *a-na-ku a-na Sippar*(UD.KIB.NUN)^{ki} [13] *a-al-la-kam* [14] *aš-šum ṣú-ḫa-re-e* [15] *ša ta-aš-pur-am* [16] *a-na* DUMU-^{d}UTU [17] *aš-tap-ra-am* [18] *i-na-ad-di-na-ak-kum.*

PNs: *Nabium-atpalam; Bēlānum; Mār-Šamaš.*
[7, 15] *ta-aš-pur(-ra)-am* see §18.4.

3. Van Soldt, *AbB* 12 128 (BM 97653, copy not yet published).

^{1} *a-na* ^{d}EN.ZU-*e-ri-ba-am* ^{2} *qí-bí-ma* ^{3} *um-ma ta-ri-ba-tum* ^{4} $^{1}/_{2}$ GÍN KUG.BABBAR ^{5} *a-na bu-ra-tum* ^{6} *i-di-in.*

PNs: *Sîn-erībam; Tarībatum; Būratum.*

4. *CT* 52 30 = Kraus, *AbB* 7 30.

^{1} *a-na i-bi-*^{d}EN.ZU *ša* ^{d}AMAR.UTU *ú-ba-al-la-ṭú* ^{2} *qí-bí-ma* ^{3} *u[m-m]a a-at-ta-a-ma* ^{4} ^{d}UTU *ù* ^{d}AMAR.UTU *aš-šu-mi-ia* ^{5} *li-ba-al-li-ṭú-ka* ^{6} *a-nu-um-ma* ^{I}*ta-ri-ba-tum* ^{7} *a-ṭar-da-kum* 1 GÍN KUG.BABBAR ^{8} *it-ti a-ḫi-ka* ^{9} *am-ra-a[m]-ma* ^{10} *šu-bi-lam* ^{11} *i-na an-ni-tim at-ḫu-‹ut›-ka [l]u-mur.*

PNs: *Ibbi-Sîn; Attâ; Tarībatum.*

^{10} *šūbilam* 'have (ms) sent to me' (Imperative).

^{11} *atḫûtum* 'brotherly attitude, relationship, partnership' (cf. *aḫum*).

5. *TIM* 2 11 = Cagni, *AbB* 8 11.

^{1} *[a]-na* ^{d}UTU-*ma-gir* ^{2} *qí-bí-ma* ^{3} *um-ma* ^{d}EN.ZU-*mu-ba-lí-iṭ-ma* ^{4} ^{d}UTU *li-ba-al-li-iṭ-ka* ^{5} *aš-šum ṭe-e-em ig-mil-*^{d}EN.ZU DUMU *ku-uk-ši-k[a-d]a* ^{6} *ša ta-aš-pu-ra-am* ^{7} *a-na ig-mil-*^{d}EN.ZU *ki-a-am šu-pu-ur-[ma]* ^{8} *um-ma at-ta-a-ma* ^{9} DUB-*pa-am a-na ṣe-er bé-e-lí-ia* ^{10} *uš-ta-bi-il* ^{11} *ṭe-e-em bé-e-lí i-ša-ap-pa-ra-am* ^{12} *a-ša-pa-ra-ak-kum.*

PNs: *Šamaš-magir; Sîn-muballiṭ; Igmil-Sîn; Kukšikada.*

^{10} *uštābil* 'I have had sent'.

6. King, *LIH* 1 2 = Frankena, *AbB* 2 2.

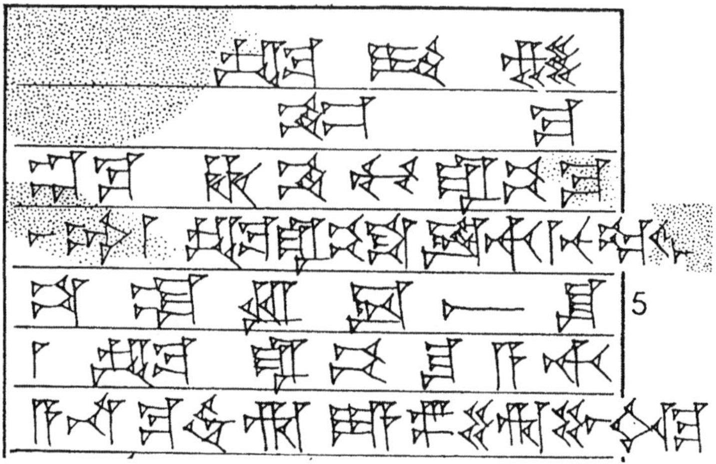

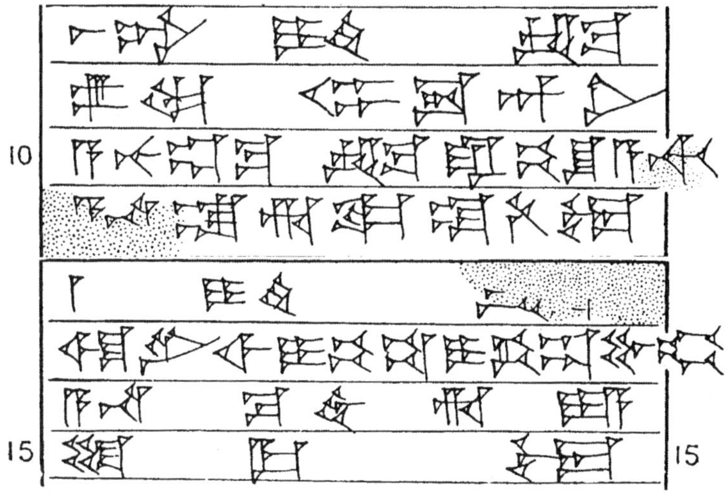

PNs: *Sîn-iddinam; Ḫammurapi; Sîn-rabi; Nūr-Eštar; Iddin-Sîn.*

1 At the beginning restore [*a-na*].

2 At the beginning restore [*qí*].

4 At the end restore *eš*$_4$-*t*[*ár*].

7 *ušēribūnim* 'they (m) brought in'.

LESSON TWENTY-FIVE

25.1 The D Stem: Verbs I–ʾ (I–*a* and I–*e*); Verbs I–*w*

(a) Verbs I–ʾ

Three basic rules have been seen to operate concerning the loss of the initial radical ʾ in these verbs (see §§8.1, 13.1):

(1) At the beginning of a form, ʾ is lost with no further changes, as in the G Infinitive (e.g., *arākum* < **ʾarākum*); in the D, this applies to the forms of the Imperative, the Infinitive, and the Verbal Adjective:

Imperative: *urrik* < **ʾurrik;*
Infinitive and Verbal Adjective: *urrukum* < **ʾurrukum.*

(2) Before a consonant, the loss of ʾ caused the lengthening of the preceding vowel (e.g., G Preterite *īrik* < **iʾrik*); in the D, the Perfect reflects this change:

Perfect: *ūtarrik* < **uʾtarrik.*

(3) Between vowels, both ʾ and the vowel following it are lost (e.g., G Durative *irrik* < **iʾarrik*); in the D, this is also the case with the Durative, Preterite, and Participle:

Durative: *urrak* < **uʾarrak;* Participle: *murrikum* < **muʾarrikum*
Preterite: *urrik* < **uʾarrik;*

In verbs I–*e*, as expected, *a*–vowels become *e*, as in *ūteppiš*, the D Perfect of *epēšum;* an important exception to this rule, however, is the Durative, where *a* between R_2 and R_3 remains unchanged: *uppaš*.

The D forms of *arākum*, *epēšum*, and *elûm* (also III–*i*);

Infinitive:	*urrukum*	*uppušum*	*ullûm*
Durative:	*urrak*	*uppaš*	*ulla*
Perfect:	*ūtarrik*	*ūteppiš*	*ūtelli*
Preterite:	*urrik*	*uppiš*	*ulli*
Imperative:	*urrik*	*uppiš*	*ulli*
Participle:	*murrikum*	*muppišum*	*mullûm*
Verbal Adj.:	*urrukum*	*uppušum*	*ullûm*
(V. Adj. base:	*urruk*	*uppuš*	*ullu*)
(V. Adj. + 3fs:	*urrukat*	*uppušet*	*ullât*)

Note that the Preterite and Imperative forms are the same. It will be recalled that G Durative forms of verbs I–ʾ that begin with a vowel, such as *irrik*, may be written either *i-ri-ik* or *i-ir-ri-ik*, i.e., always with an initial *V*-sign. The same feature is characteristic of D Durative and Preterite forms; thus,

> D Durative *urrak* is written *ú-ur-ra-ak* or *ú-ra-ak* (not *ur-ra-ak*);
> D Preterite *urrik* is written *ú-ur-ri-ik* or *ú-ri-ik* (not *ur-ri-ik*).
> (The Imperative, however, even though pronounced the same as the Preterite, is written *ur-ri-ik* or *ú-ri-ik*, but not *ú-ur-ri-ik*.)

As in the G, verbs originally I–*y* are conjugated like verbs I–*e* in the D.

(b) Verbs I–*w*

All verbs I–*w*, whether active or adjectival, are conjugated alike in the D stem. Only two points require comment:

(1) In the Perfect, the sequence *uw-* became *ū-* before the *t*, thus *ūtatter* (‹ **uwtattir*).

(2) When *w* stood at the beginning of a form, it was often (though not always) dropped.

The forms of *watārum* in the D (with *i* › *e* before *r*):

Infinitive:	*(w)utturum*	Imperative:	*(w)utter*
Durative:	*uwattar*	Participle:	*muwatterum*
Perfect:	*ūtatter*	Vbl. Adj.:	*(w)utturum*
Preterite:	*uwatter*	(V. Adj. base:	*(w)uttur*)

(c) D Stems of verbs I–ʾ and verbs I–*w* encountered thus far:

uddušum 'to renew, restore'.
uḫḫuzum 'to mount, set, overlay (something: acc.; in/with a precious material: acc.)'.
ullûm 'to raise, elevate, extol'.
ummudum 'to lean, push, rest, set (something) on, against (something)'.
unnušum 'to make weak, weaken (trans.)'.
uppušum = G (not common in OB).
urrukum 'to lengthen, extend, prolong; to delay.
(w)ulludum 'to bear, beget (many offspring; i.e., pluralic)'.
(w)uṣṣubum = G (not common in OB).
(w)utturum 'to augment, increase (trans.)'.

25.2 The Independent Pronouns: Remaining Forms

In §2.4, the nominative forms of the independent personal pronouns were presented. In this section are given the corresponding forms for the oblique cases. The third person forms have already been presented in §6.3 as the demonstrative 'that, those'. The other persons, too, have a common gen.-acc. form and a special dative form used after *ana*. The nom. forms are given again below for comparison. Parentheses enclose rare forms; square brackets denote as yet unattested forms.

	NOM.	GEN.-ACC.	DATIVE
1cs	*anāku*	*yâti*	*yâšim, ayyâšim*
2ms	*atta*	*kâta*, (*kâti*)	*kâšim, kâšum*
2fs	*atti*	*kâti*	*kâšim*
3ms	*šū*	*šuāti, šuātu, šât*^{u}/*i*	*šuāšim, šâšim, šâšum*
3fs	*šī*	*šuāti, šâti*, (*šiāti*)	*šuāšim, šâšim*, (*šiāšim*)
1cp	*nīnu*	*niāti*	*niāšim*
2mp	*attunu*	*kunūti*	*kunūšim*
2fp	*attina*	[*kināti*]	[*kināšim*]
3mp	*šunu*	*šunūti*	*šunūšim*
3fp	*šina*	*šināti*	[*šināšim*]

Note that the forms (other than nom.) are based on the pronominal suffixes. The gen.-acc. forms end in *-ti*, the dative in *-šim*. The final *-m* of the dative forms is occasionally omitted in later OB texts (cf. §24.4). The plural gen.-acc. and dative forms are the same as the corresponding acc. and dative suffixes (§18.2).

The first person singular forms are written in a variety of fashions:

gen.-acc. as *ia-(a-)ti, i-ia-(a-)ti*;
dative as *ia-ši-im, ia-a-ši-im, i-ia-ši-im, a-ia-ši-im*.

The gen.-acc. forms occur under several conditions:

(a) in apposition after a noun in the gen. or acc.:

ina maḫar abīya kâta 'before you, my father';
bēlī kâta ul āmur 'I have not seen you, my lord';

(b) in tandem with a noun in the gen. or acc.:

ša yâti u tamkārim 'of the merchant and me';
mātka u kâta uḫallaq 'I will destroy you (ms) and your land';

(c) after *ša* (see also b, above), and after prepositions (other than *ana*) that do not take suffixes (viz., *adi, ina, ištu, kīma, mala,* and others; see §10.3, end):

> *kīma kunūti* 'like you (mp)';
> *ša lā kâta* 'except you (ms)' (cf. §20.4d).

(d) as direct object, for emphasis, usually with a suffix on the verb as well:

> *am-mīnim niāti ṣeḫrūtim tuḫallaqniāti* 'why do you (ms) destroy us children?';
> *kâti ašapparki* 'I will send you (fs)'.

(e) *kâta / kâti* often occurs as subject with *anāku* in OB letters:

> *anāku u kâta nillik* 'you (ms) and I went'.

The dative forms are usually, though not always, preceded by *ana*:

> *ana kâšim taklāku* 'I trust *you* (fs)' (emphasis);
> *šeššet šiqil kaspam (ana) yâšim iddinam* 'To me she gave six shekels of silver'.

Occasionally, the gen.-acc. form replaces the expected dative after *ana*, especially when the pronoun is in apposition to a noun: e.g.,

> *ana bēlīya kâta* 'to you, my lord'.

25.3 The Independent Possessive Adjectives

These are a set of adjectives that appear most commonly as predicates of verbless clauses (as in 'the house is mine'); they are also used in place of (sometimes in addition to) the genitive pronominal suffixes, to emphasize possession. The forms are based on the masculine forms of the genitive suffixes. Since they are adjectives, they agree in case, gender, and number with the modified noun; they do not agree with the gender of the "possessor" (thus, e.g., 'his' and 'her(s)' are not distinguished). Essentially, the markers of gender and number are those of other adjectives: none for ms; *-at-* for fs; *-ūt-* for mp; *-āt-* for fp. There are two unusual tendencies, however: the *-t-* that occurs in all forms but ms is often written double; many forms, except in the ms, have nunation (final *n*) rather than mimation (final *m*). Below are listed for reference most of the attested forms. Only the ms forms have been declined; the others offer no difficulties in this regard (fs nom. *-um / n,* gen. *-im / n,* acc. *-am / n;* pl. nom. *-um / n,* gen.-acc. *-im / n*).

	MASC. SG.	FEM. SG.	MASC. PL.	FEM. PL.
1s	*yûm(yaʾum) / yêm / yâm*	*yattu*^{m} / *n*	*yaʾūt(t)u*^{m} / *n*, *yût(t)u*^{m} / *n*	*yât(t)u*^{m} / *n*
2s	*kûm / kêm / kâm*	*kattu*^{m} / *n*	*kûttu*^{m} / *n*	*kâttu*^{m} / *n*
3s	*šûm / šêm / šuʾam(šâm)*	*šattu*^{m} / *n*	*šûttu*^{m} / *n*	—
1p	*nûm / nîm / nâm(niam)*	*niattu*^{m} / *n*	*nûttu*^{m} / *n*	—
2p	*kunûm*	—	—	—
3p	*šunûm / šunîm / šuniam*	—	—	—

Examples of possessive adjectives as predicates:

bītum šū yûm (*iu-ú-um*) 'that house is mine';
šattam kûm nûm 'this year (adv. acc.) yours (scil. grain) is ours';
eleppum šī ul kattum 'that boat is not yours';
ṣuḫārû yûtun (*iu-ú-tu-un*) 'the servants are mine';
ḫiblēt PN *ul yâttun* (*ia-a-at-tu-un*) 'PN's wrongs (for *ḫiblāt*, pl. of *ḫibiltum*) are not mine (i.e., my responsibility)'.

These forms may also modify a noun attributively, to provide more emphasis than the suffix pronoun, which is normally (but not always) omitted, or to negate possession:

kaspam yâm u kaspam kâm ul inaddinam 'He will not give me my silver or your silver';
ana wardim lā šêm 'to a slave (that is) not hers/his'.

Occasionally, there is no antecedent noun:

lā šuniam ibqurū 'They (m) laid claim to what is not theirs'.

EXERCISES

A. VOCABULARY 25.

Verbs:

ebēbum G (*i*) 'to become clean'; Verbal Adj. *ebbum* (*ebb-*; fem. *ebbetum*) 'clean, pure, holy; shining, polished; trustworthy'; *ubbubum* D 'to clean, purify; to clear (of claims), clear oneself'.
erēšum b G (*i*) 'to (plow and) seed, plant, cultivate (a field)'; note *errēšum* (*errēš*; pl. *errēšū*) 'cultivator, tenant farmer'.

esērum a G (*i*) 'to enclose, shut in'; *ussurum* D 'to enclose, take captive'.
esērum b G (*i*) 'to press (someone: acc.; for payment, silver: acc.), put under pressure, collect'; *šērtam esērum* 'to impose a penalty, punishment'; *ussurum* D = G.
gerûm G (*e*) 'to be hostile; to start a lawsuit (intrans.), sue (trans.)'; *gurrûm* D = G.
lapātum G (*a–u*) 'to touch; to strike; to apply, smear (someone or something); to assign (workers to a task)'; *lupputum* D 'to touch, smear; to tarry, delay'.
sanāqum G (*i*) 'to arrive at, reach; to approach with a claim, proceed against (+ *ana*/dat.); to check, control, supervise; to question'; *sunnuqum* D 'to check, inspect; to control; to question'.
(w)uššurum D (not in G) 'to release, set free'.

Nouns:

lītum (also *littum*; bound form *līt(i), litti*; log. ÁB [but in OB, ÁB usually = *arḫum* 'cow']) 'cow'; pl. *liātum* (log. ÁB.GUD.ḪI.A) 'cattle, bovines (of both sexes)'.
našpakum (*našpak*; pl. *našpakātum*; log. (É.)Ì.DUB) 'storage area for barley, dates, etc.; granary, silo'; also (with log. (giš)MÁ.Ì. DUB) 'cargo boat' (cf. *šapākum*).
qibītum (*qibīt*; pl. *qibiātum*) 'word, utterance, instruction, order, command' (cf. *qabûm*).
šubtum (*šubat*; pl. *šubātum*) 'dwelling, residence' (cf. *wašābum*).
ummiānum (*ummiān*; pl. *ummiānū*; log. UM.MI.A) 'artisan; scholar, expert; money lender'.
zērum (*zēr(i)*; pl. *zērū*; log. NUMUN and ŠE.NUMUN) 'seed; (male) descendants, progeny, offspring'.
zikarum (also *zikrum*; bound form *zikar*; pl. *zikarū*) 'male; man'.

Idiom:

ša qāt(i) (log. NÍG.ŠU) 'in the charge of, under the authority of' (written syllabically before a pron. suff., NÍG.ŠU before PN's: *ṣābum ša qá-ti-ia* 'the work-force in my charge'; *awīlû* NÍG.ŠU I*gi-mil-lum* 'the men in G.'s charge').

Also, the pronominal forms given in §§25.2, 25.3.

B. Learn the following signs:

OB Lapid.	OB Cursive	NA	values
	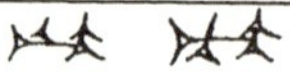		NUMUN = *zērum*; ŠE.NUMUN also = *zērum*
			*kán*; IKU = *ikûm* a surface measure (ca. 3600 $m.^2$; see App. B.3)
	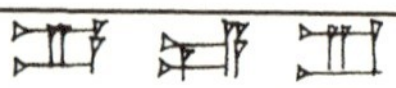		*dag/k/q, tág/k/q*
			ÁB = *lītum* (rarely); ÁB.GUD.ḪI.A = *liātum*
		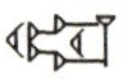	(*gul* not in OB), *kúl, qúl*
	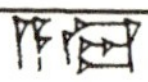	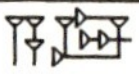	ÍD (also read I_7) = *nārum*; íd determinative before names of rivers
	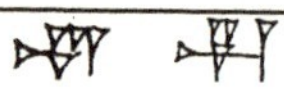		INANNA = *Ištar*

C. Write the following words in cuneiform and in transliteration; use logograms where possible:

1. *agê Ištar*
2. *tukultī*
3. *išakkan*
4. *eṣemti imittim*
5. *liāt ummiānim*
6. *nār nakrim*
7. *našpak zērim*
8. *lišānum nakirtum*
9. *utakkil*

D. Write in normalized Akkadian:

1. we will augment it (m)
2. I have renewed it (f)
3. prolong (pl) his life!
4. they (m) were released
5. she bore him many sons
6. it (m) is overlaid with fine gold
7. let me lean my arm on him
8. the people extolled you, my lord
9. they (f) have increased it (m)
10. it (f) is pure; it (f) is purified
11. you (fs) will mount the (statue of the) god with silver
12. do not (fs) weaken them (m)
13. we have elevated them (m)
14. they (f) have not released him
15. the prince who raises the tops (dual) of the temple
16. let me extol the name of the goddess who bore (D) them (m) all
17. I am not able to turn my neck
18. like us
19. like you (mp) and like me
20. for you (fs)

E. Normalize and translate the following sentences, many of which are adapted from letters:

1. PN ÌR LUKUR ^{d}UTU *a-na mi-nim ta-ak-la ú-ul* DUMU *a-wi-lim šu-ú* ÌR LUKUR ^{d}UTU *wu-uš-še-er-ma* LUKUR ^{d}UTU *šar-ra-am la i-ma-ḫa-ar a-na a-wi-lim ú-ul wa-li-id um-ma-šu* GEME$_2$ LUKUR ^{d}UTU *a-na mi-nim a-na re-di-i ta-aš-ṭú-úr-šu.*
2. PN *ša* A.ŠÀ-*šu a-na* PN$_2$ *im-qú-tu ki-a-am iq-bi-kum um-ma šu-ú-ma ù lu i-ia-ti it-ti* A.ŠÀ *a-na* PN$_2$ *li-id-di-nu-ni-in-ni ù lu pu-úḫ* A.ŠÀ-*ia li-id-di-nu-nim.*
3. *ka-ta ù a-ḫa-ka ma-an-nu-um ú-wa-še-er-ku-nu-ti-ma i-na* É *a-bi-ni ta-at-ta-aš-ba-ma i-li-ik-ni tu-úḫ-ta-li-qá šu-mi ì-lí-ku-nu ù mu-ta-ki-li-ku-nu ša ka-ta ù a-ḫa-ka a-na* É *a-bi-ni ir-du-ú li-iḫ-li-iq.*
4. *lu-ú ša-al-ma-ta šu-lum-ka šu-up-ra-am aš-šum* A.ŠÀ *ša i-di* É-*ka* MAŠ A.ŠÀ *ia-ši-im ù* MAŠ A.ŠÀ *a-na ka-šum ù aš-šum* ŠE-*em ke-em ša aš-pu-ra-ak-kum* ŠE-*am a-na ma-am-ma-an la ta-na-din.*
5. *šum-ma lu-up-pu-ta-tu-nu* DUMU *ši-ip-ri-ku-nu ṭú-ur-da-nim-ma ṣú-ḫa-ar-ku-nu li-il-qé.*
6. ^{d}IŠKUR *ša šu-um-šu ul-lu-ú* NUMUN *šar-ru-tim ša le-em-nim ša-tu li-di-in-ma li-ḫa-li-iq.*
7. *i-na ma-ri* PN *zi-ka-ri-im ù si-in-ni-iš-tim ma-am-ma-an la i-ge-er-re-a-an-ni ù ma-am-ma-an* KUG.BABBAR *la i-is-si-ra-an-ni.*
8. *i-na qí-bi-it* LUGAL *zi-ka-ra-am a-a-am-ma i-na* URU *ša-tu i-du-ku.*
9. *a-ḫa-ti ki-a-am ú-la-am-mi-da-an-ni um-ma ši-ma i-na-an-na* É-*ti ḫu-ul-lu-uq mi-nu-um šu-ub-ti.*
10. *um-mi-a-an-ni ul i-mu-ut bu-ul-ṭa-am ik-šu-ud i-na-an-na* ÁB.GUD.ḪI.A-*ni ša nu-ka-al-li-mu-ka ù* ŠE *ša i-na* É.Ì.DUB *ni-iš-pu-ku i-te-er-ša-an-ni-a-ti.*
11. *na-ak-ru i-na ti-bi-im šu-a-ti* GÌR.PAD.DU.MEŠ *ša ḫi-ir-ti-ia iš-bé-ru ù* DUMU.MEŠ-*ni ú-sí-ru-ma i-na ṣa-ab-tu-ti-šu-nu im-nu-ma šu-ba-at-ni iq-qú-ru.*

F. CH. Normalize and translate the following laws:

§1 *šum-ma a-wi-lum a-wi-lam ú-ub-bi-ir-ma ne-er-tam e-li-šu id-di-ma la uk-ti-in-šu mu-ub-bi-ir-šu id-da-ak.*

ubburum D (G *abārum* rare) 'to accuse'.
nērtum 'murder'; here, '(a charge of) murder' (cf. *nêrum*).
uktīn 'he has convicted'.

§47 *šum-ma er-re-šum aš-šum i-na ša-at-tim maḫ-ri-tim ma-na-ḫa-ti-šu la il-qú-ú* A.ŠÀ *e-*RI*-ša-am iq-ta-bi be-el* A.ŠÀ *ú-ul ú-up-pa-as er-re-su-ma* A.ŠÀ*-šu i-ir-ri-iš-ma i-na ebūrim*(BURU$_{14}$) *ki-ma ri-ik-sa-ti-šu* ŠE *i-le-qé.*

eqlam erēšam iqtabi 'has said he would plow the field (again)', or *"eqlam errišam" iqtabi* 'has said "I will plow the field (again)"'.

er-re-su-ma = *errēssū-ma* 'that very tenant farmer of his'.

mānaḫtum (*mānaḫti*; sf. *mānaḫta-*) 'toil, weariness; maintenance, upkeep, improvements'; here, probably '(the wages of) his labors'.

epēsum G 'to object' (rare); *uppusum* D = G (rare).

§121 *šum-ma a-wi-lum i-na* É *a-wi-lim* ŠE *iš-pu-uk i-na ša-na-at a-na* 1 ŠE.GUR.E *ḫamšat qa âm* (5 SILA$_{3}$ ŠE) Á *na-aš-pa-ki-im i-na-ad-di-in.*

ŠE GUR.E = ŠE.GUR.

qûm (base *qa-*; log. SILA$_{3}$) = .1 *sūtum* (ca. 1'liter').

Á here = *idū* 'rent'.

§226 *šum-ma gallābum*(ŠU.I) *ba-lum be-el* ÌR *ab-bu-ti* ÌR *la še-e-em ú-gal-li-ib ritti*(KIŠIB.LÁ) *gallābim*(ŠU.I) *šu-a-ti i-na-ak-ki-su.*

gallābum (*gallāb*; log. ŠU.I) 'barber'; *gullubum* D (not in G) 'to shave'.

abbuttum (*abbutti*) 'characteristic hairstyle of slaves'.

§254 *šum-ma* (*a-wi-lum*, from §253) *aldâm*(AL.DÙ.A*-am*) *il-qé-ma* ÁB.GUD.ḪI.A *ú-te-en-ni!*(GAG)*-išta-*[*aš*]*-na* ŠE *ša im-ḫu!*(RI)*-ru i-ri-ab.*

aldûm (base *aldu-*; log. AL.DÙ(.A); Sum. lw.) 'store of barley'.

tašna (adverb) 'double, doubly'.

§2

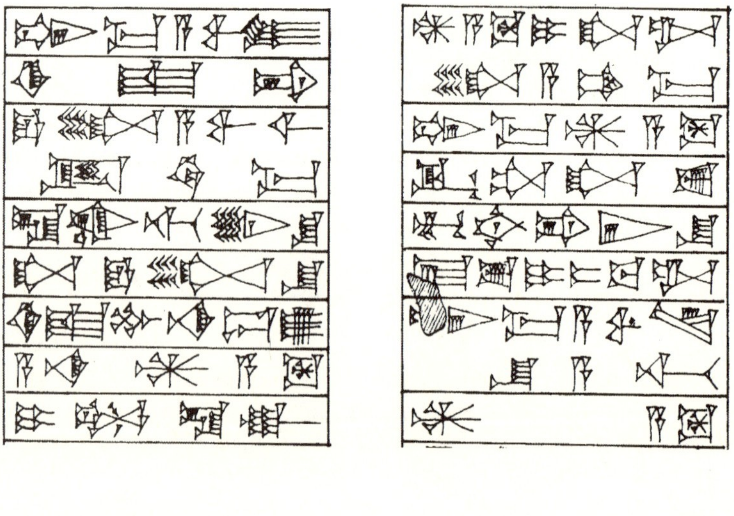

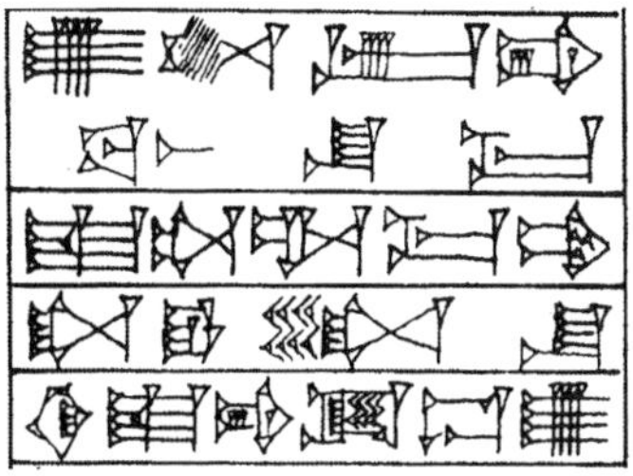

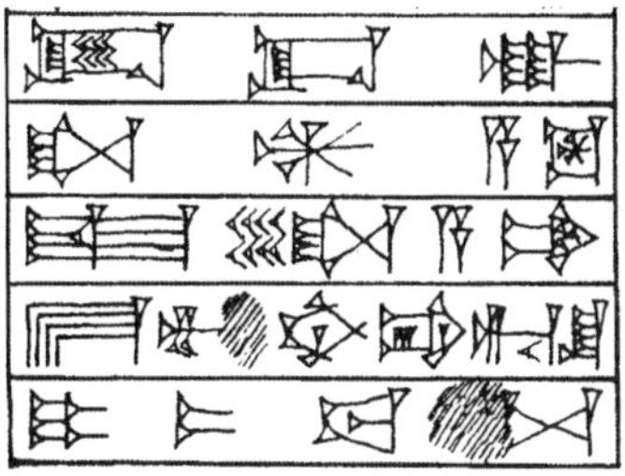

kišpū (always pl.) 'witchcraft, sorcery'.
uktīn 'he has convicted'.
dÍD = *Id* the River-god.
šalûm (*i*) 'to dive, plunge into (+ acc.)'.
ubburum D cf. Law §1 above.

G. Omens from *YOS* 10:

1. *šum-ma ši-rum i-na šu-me-el ú-ba-nim ki-i-ma* ⸢*ṭú*⸣*-li-mi-im ša-ki-in ma-at na-ak-ri-im tu-sà-na-aq a-ša-ar iš-te-en tu-pá-ḫa-ar-ši.* (11 ii 24–26)
   šīrum (*šīr(i)*) '(piece of) flesh'.
   ṭulīmum 'spleen'.
   ašar ištēn 'in one place'.

2. DIŠ KÁ É.GAL *sú-un-nu-uq i-*[*n*]*a* gišTUKUL LÚ.KÚR ⸢*um-ma-nam ú-sà-ar* UD⸣*-ma-am re-qá-a-am šà-tam-mu* É.GAL*-am ú-sà-na-qú.* (24:29)
   rēqum 'far, distant'; *ūmam rēqam, ina ūmim rēqim* 'some time'.
   šatammum (*šatam*; Sum. lw.) 'clerk, administrator'.

3. DIŠ UDU *i-na* ŠÀ *li-ša-ni-šu ši-rum na-pi-iḫ-ma a-na «i-na» i-mi-tim ù šu-me-lim* [*k*]*a-pi-iṣ a-a-ú-um-ma a-na* LUGAL *i-te-bé-ma ú-sà-ar-šu-ma* [*i-da-ak*]*-šu.* (47:9)
   šīrum (*šīr(i)*) 'flesh'.
   napāḫum G (*a–u*) 'to blow (something); to light (a fire, stove); to become visible, shine, light up'; Verbal Adj. *napḫum* (*napiḫ-*) 'kindled, burning, shining; swollen, bloated'.
   kapāṣum G (*i*) 'to bend, curl, droop'.

4. DIŠ *iz-bu-um ši-in-na-šu wa-ṣa-a* LUGAL UD.[MEŠ*-šu*] *ga-am-ru i-na* gišGU.ZA*-šu ša-nu-um uš-*[*ša*]*-ab.* (56 i 34–35)

5. 11 ii 20–23:

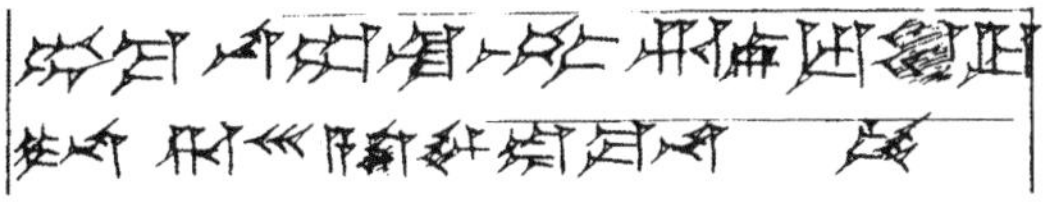

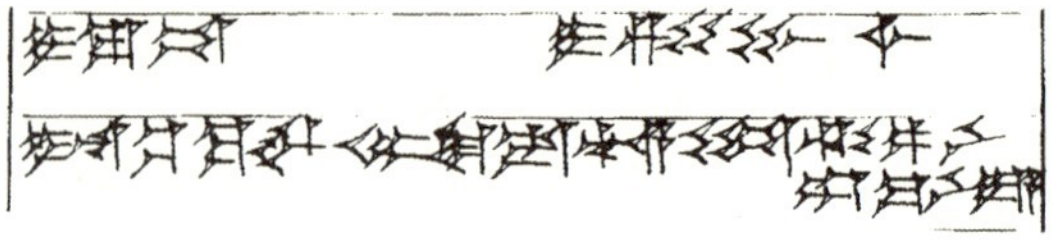

rēš eqlim 'destination'.
miqittum 'downfall' (cf. *maqātum*).

H. Contract. Normalize and translate the following text:

1. Dissolution of a partnership (Meissner, *BAP* 78 = Schorr, *VAB* 5, no. 171).

[1] ^{I}*ṣi-lí-*^{d}INANNA [2] *ù i-ri-ba-am-*^{d}EN.ZU [3] *tap-pu-ta-am i-pu-šu-ú* [4] *a-na ta-az-ki-tim* [5] *da-a-a-ni ik-šu-du-ú-ma* [6] *a-na* É ^{d}UTU *i-ru-bu-ú-ma* [7] *i-na* É ^{d}UTU *um-mì-a-nam* [8] *i-pu-lu-ú-ma* [9] 1 ÌR *lu-uš-ta-mar-*^{d}UTU [10] 1 GEME$_2$ *li-iš-li-ma-am* [11] ḪA.LA *i-ri-ba-am-*^{d}EN.ZU [12] 1 ÌR *ib-ši-na-*DINGIR [13] 1 GEME$_2$ ^{d}GEŠTIN.AN.NA-*la-ma-sí* [14] ḪA.LA *ṣi-lí-*^{d}INANNA [15] *zi-i-zu-ú* [16] *i-na* É ^{d}UTU *ù* ^{d}EN.ZU [17] *iz-ku-ru a-ḫu-um a-na a-ḫi-im* [18] *ú-ub-bi-bu-ú* [19] *a-ḫu-um a-ḫa-am* [20] *la i-tu-ru la i-ge-er-ru-ú* [21] *e-li mi-im-ma ša a-ḫu-um* [22] *a-na a-ḫi-im ir-gu-mu-ú* [23] *mi-im-ma ú-ul i-šu-ú* [24–26] Oath. [27–32] Witnesses. [33–36] Date.

PNs: *Ṣillī-Ištar; Irībam-Sîn; Luštamar-Šamaš; Lišlimam; Ibši-(i)na-ilim; Geštinanna-lamassī.*

[3] *i-pu-šu-ú* here and often in this text, final *-ū* on 3mp verbs is indicated with an extra vowel sign.

[4] *tazkītum* 'purification, cleansing; release, dissolution' (cf. *zakûm*).

[9–11] and [12–14] each constitute a verbless clause.

[15] *zīzū* here, 'they have made the division'.

[17] *zakārum* here, elliptically without *nīš*, 'to swear'.

[18] The verbs here and in lines 20, 22, 23 are plural according to the sense, even though the grammatical subject *aḫum* is singular: 'they cleared one another', etc.

[21–23] *eli ... mimma ul īšû* 'they have no claim to ...'.

I. Letters:

1. *VAS* 7 196 = Frankena, *AbB* 6 213.

[1] *a-na a-wi-lim ša* ^{d}AMAR.UTU *ú-ba-al-la-ṭ[ú-š]u* [2] *qí-bí-ma* [3] *um-ma* ^{d}NANNA-IBILA-MA.AN.SUM-*ma* [4] ^{d}UTU *ù* ^{d}AMAR.UTU *da-ri-iš* UD-*mi* [5] *a-ḫi ka-ta li-ba-li-ṭú-ka* [6] *lu ša-al-ma-ta* [7] *aš-šum* 1, 2 BÁN 5 SILA$_3$ *ša ma-aḫ-ri-ka* [8] *e-zi-bu* [9] 1 BÁN 5 SILA$_3$ ŠE *ru-ud-di-ma* [10] 1, 4 BÁN ŠE *mu-ul-li-ma* [11] *a-na ša-al-lu-rum i-di-in* [12] *a-na* ŠE.NUMUN *ḫa-ši-iḫ* [13] *la ta-ka-la-šu* [14] *ar-ḫi-iš i-di-in-šu* [15] *i-dam la tu-šar-ša-am-ma* [16] *la ta-ša-pa-ra-am.*

PNs: *Nanna-ibila-mansum*; *Šallurum*.

[7] A measure of dry volume/capacity: 1 (NIGIDA = *pānum*) + 2 BÁN (= *sūtum*, absolute *sât*$^{?}$) + 5 SILA3 (= *qûm*, absolute *qa*). The *qûm* is about 1 liter; the *sūtum* (Vocab. 23) is 10 *qûm*; the *pānum* is 6 *sūtum* or 60 *qûm*; thus, the amount is 85 *qûm* (of grain). The amount to be added in line 9 is 15 *qûm*, giving the 100 *qûm* in line 10. It is often difficult to be certain how to normalize expressions of measurement, since they are almost invariably written logographically; in line 7, perhaps *ištēn pān šittā sât ḫamšat qa*, with gen. *êm* understood. See Appendix B.5.

[12] *ḫašiḫ* 'he is in need (of: *ana*)'.

[14] *arḫiš* 'quickly'.

[15] *idam lā tušaršâm* 'do not raise objections'.

2. Figulla, *CT* 43 76 = Kraus, *AbB* 1 76.

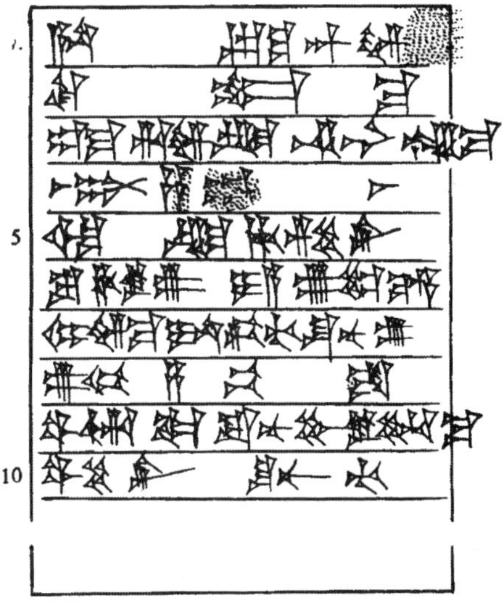

PNs: *Ipqu-Adad*; *Rīm-Sîn-Enḫalmaḫ*; *Ṣabrum*; *Sîn-ḫāzir*.

[4] Fourth sign: ⸢*ab*⸣.

[7] The extra *-ú* sign for the suffix *-šunu* is unusual.

LESSON TWENTY-SIX

26.1 The Verbs *edûm* and *išûm*

The verbs *edûm* 'to know' and *išûm* 'to have' share several peculiarities in the G stem: they are found only in the Preterite, Infinitive, and, for *edûm* only, the Participle; the prefixes of the Preterite forms are irregular in that they have *i* in the first and second person, rather than *a* (or *e* ‹ *a*); though formally Preterite, the finite forms have no specific tense value. (Since these verbs have no Verbal Adjectives, there is no predicative construction; instead the Preterite form is used.) *edûm* (Infinitive also *idûm*) is a III–*e* verb; *išûm* is III–*u*.

3cs	*īde*	*īšu*	3mp	*īdû*	*īšû*
2ms	*tīde*	*tīšu*	3fp	[*īdeā*]	*īšâ*
2fs	[*tīdî*]	[*tīšî*]	2cp	*tīdeā*	[*tīšâ*]
1cs	*īde*	*īšu*	1cp	*nīde*	*nīšu*

Note that the 3cs and 1cs forms are identical:

īde 'he/she knows, I know';
īšu 'he/she has, I have'.

These verbs do not have formal Imperative and Precative forms. Instead, injunctions are expressed by the Preterite preceded by *lū*:

lū tīde 'know, may you (ms) know';
abī lū īde 'may my father know, my father should know';
ṭēmam šupram-ma lū īde 'send (ms) me a report, that I may know';
lū īšu 'may I/he/she have, let me/him/her have'.

The G Participle of *edûm* is irregular, with a prefixed *mu-*:

ms	*mūdûm* (bound form *mūde*)	mp	*mūdûtum*
fs	*mūdētum* (bound form *mūdeat*)	fp	*mūdeātum*

An example:

šībum mūde bīšīya 'a witness who knows my property'.

The verb *išûm* has no Participle.

The verb *edûm* also occurs in the D stem, where the root is I–*w*:

(w)uddûm (Pret. *uweddi*) 'to mark; to make known, reveal, inform; to recognize, identify, assign'.

26.2 Subordinate Clauses

It is convenient to group Akkadian subordinate clauses into three main types: relative clauses (§19.3), temporal clauses, and others. All of these have in common that they are dependent on a main clause, are introduced by a subordinating conjunction (which may be deleted in some relative clauses), and have verbs marked by the subordination marker *-u* when no other verbal ending appears (§19.2).

(a) Temporal Clauses

The following are the most common temporal conjunctions in Old Babylonian; most of them, it will be noted, also occur as prepositions.

inūma (in poetry, also *inu*) 'when, as soon as, after, at the time that, while'. Action either before or simultaneous with that of the main clause.

ūm Same range of meaning and use as *inūma*.

ina 'as long as, while'. Action simultaneous with that of the main clause. With rare exception used only in certain legal expressions, before predicative Verbal Adjectives and forms of *edûm*:

ina balṭu u šalmu 'while he was in good and sound health';
ina lā īdû 'without my/his/her/their(m) knowing; unknowingly' (lit., 'while I/he/she/they(m) was/were not aware').

ištu 'after, as soon as, since'. Action always before that of the main clause. Also used causally: 'since, because'; see (b), below.

kīma (in poetry, also *kī*) 'as soon as, when'. Action immediately before that of the main clause. Also used non-temporally: 'that; as'; see (b), below.

warka/*warki* 'after'. In OB, only in expressions involving death.

adi (rarely also *qadum*) 'until, as long as, while'.

adi (...) *lā* 'before'.

lāma 'before'.

Temporal clauses normally precede the main clause, but may, if short, be imbedded in the main clause (like an adverb); e.g.,

ṣuḫ̮ārī inūma ittalkam ṭurdam 'Send (ms) me my servant as soon as he has arrived.'

Clauses with *adi* occasionally follow the main clause (examples below).

More than one temporal clause may be dependent on a single main clause: e.g.,

warka abum imtūtu inūma aḫḫū izuzzū qīšti abum iddinūkum teleqqe 'After (our) father has died, when the (other) brothers take shares, you (ms) may take the gift (your) father gave you.'

The tenses of the verbs of both the temporal clauses and the main clauses follow certain relatively well-established patterns, summarized in the following chart, and then described in detail with examples.

	Main Clause Action in	Main Clause Action in
	Past;	**Present or Future;**
	Tense of Temporal Clause:	Tense of Temporal Clause:
(1) *inūma, ūm, ištu,*	Preterite	Perfect: explicit anteriority
kīma, warki, adi		Durative: unmarked
(2) *adi ... lā*	—	Preterite: explicit anteriority
		Durative: unmarked
(3) *lāma*	Durative	Preterite: real, immediate
		Durative: potential, indefinite

(1) *inūma, ūm, ištu, kīma, warka / i, adi* (for *adi lā,* see (2)):

When the main clause describes action in the **past** (i.e., verb in Preterite or Perfect [rarely also past Durative], or verbless clause), the temporal clause, if verbal, has the Preterite: e.g.,

inūma / ištu / kīma âm tašāmu tallikam 'When/After/As soon as you (ms) (had) bought the grain, you came here';

mārum šū warki abūšu imūtu irgum 'That son brought suit after his father (had) died';

adi ašpurakkim taklîšināti 'You (fs) held them (f) until I wrote to you'.

[With a past Durative in the main clause, note, e.g.,

šumma awīlum ṣeḫram ana mārūtim ilqe inūma ilqûšu abāšu ... iḫīaṭ 'if a man adopted a youngster (and) after he adopted him he would look for (*ḫiāṭum*) his (true) father' (CH §186).]

When the main clause describes action in the **present or future** (verb in Durative, Imperative, Precative, or Prohibitive, or a verbless clause), the temporal clause, if verbal, contains either the Perfect or the Durative. The Perfect, here used like the English future perfect, marks specifically the anteriority of the action in the temporal clause vis-à-vis that of the main clause:

inūma / ištu / kīma âm taštāmu alkam / tallakam 'When/As soon as/ Immediately after you (ms) have bought the grain, come/you will come here'.

The Durative is used when no such specific marking is intended, or when the actions of the two clauses are roughly simultaneous:

inūma / ištu / kīma âm tašammu alkam / tallakam 'When/After you (ms) buy the grain, come/you will come here'.

The Durative is not as yet attested in a clause with *warka / i* nor the Perfect in a clause with *adi*:

mārum šū warki abūšu imtūtu lā iraggum 'That son may not bring suit after his father has died';

kilîšināti adi ašapparakkim 'Hold (fs) them (f) until I write to you'.

When the action of the main clause is present or future, and a clause with *ištu* or *kīma* contains the Preterite, the force of the subordinate clause is probably always causal rather than temporal (see (b), below): e.g.,

ištu / kīma âm tašāmu allakakkum 'Since/Because you (ms) (have) bought grain, I will come to you'.

Regardless of the "tense" of the main clause, *inūma, ištu,* and *adi* may also govern verbless clauses: e.g.,

ša ištu ṣeḫrēku lā āmuru ātamar 'I have seen what I had not seen since I was young';

inūma ina ālim wašbu iparrasū 'It will be decided while he is resident in town';

adi balṭānu ina bītīni wašbāti 'You (fs) may live in our house as long as we are alive';

inūma ana ālim ḫarrāššu âm addiššum 'When his travel was to the city, I gave him grain'.

Verbless clauses are not attested after *ūm* or *kīma*.

(2) *adi ... lā*:

Adi ... lā (with *lā*, as expected, always directly before the verb) is used **only** when the main clause describes action in the **present or future**. The verb of the temporal clause may be Preterite or Durative. The Preterite marks anteriority (cf. the Perfect with *inūma*, etc., above):

adi abī lā illikam ul atâr 'I will not return before my father has come'.

The Durative is used when no such marking is intended:

adi lā nimmarūši ul niṭarrassunūti 'We will not send them (m) before we see her'.

(3) *lāma*:

When the action of the main clause is **past** tense, this conjunction is followed by the Durative, as in

lāma allakam eqlam ipšurū 'They (m) sold the field before I came'.

When the main clause action is **present or future**, the verb after *lāma* may be Durative or Preterite. The Preterite (or, very rarely, the Perfect) indicates that the action is seen as certain and immediate:

lāma ipšurūšu alkīm 'Come (fs) before they sell/have sold it'.

The Durative indicates that the action of the temporal clause is seen as only possible, or of indefinite time:

lāma ālam šuāti ikaššadu šuprānim 'Write (pl) me before he can reach that town'.

(b) Other Subordinate Clauses

In general, no firm rules exist for the use of tenses in subordinate clauses other than temporal ones; the tenses for the most part have the same range as in main clauses, with the important exception that the Perfect does not occur (except very rarely as a future perfect, with present or future action in the main clause). Below are the remaining common subordinating conjuctions of OB, and their meanings, with one or two examples of each. The clauses they govern either precede the main clause, or, if short, may be inserted into the main clause.

ana ša 'because (of the fact that)':

ana ša bēlī udammaqam-ma alpam ušabbalam 15 šiqil kaspam ana bēlīya kâta ušabbalam 'Because my lord will be kind and dispatch (*wabālum*, Š Dur.) an ox to me, I will dispatch to you, my lord, the 15 shekels of silver.'

ana ša is rare as a conjunction; most often it simply means 'to the one who/which':

ana ša bēlī iṭrudam šamnam addin 'I gave the oil to him/the one whom my lord sent to me'.

ašar (bound form of *ašrum* 'place') 'where(ver)':

ṣuḫāram ašar bēlī iqabbû aṭarrad 'I will send the servant wherever my lord commands.'

Rarely, *ašar* also means 'what' and 'when'.

aššum 'because':

aššum marṣākū-ma lā alliku aḫī aṭrud 'Because I was sick and (could) not go, I sent my brother.'

Rarely, *aššum* also means 'so that'; this is especially the case in the letters from Mari (§29.4).

ēma, rarely *ēm*, 'where(ever)':

ēma eleppašunu kalât-ma mūṣâm lā īšû tappûssunu alkī 'Wherever their (m) boat is detained and has no exit (*mūṣûm*), assist (fs) them.'

ištu 'because, since':

ištu bēlī eqlī lā iddinam bēlī kaspam mala šīm eqlīya liddinam 'Since my lord did not give me my field, may my lord give me silver equivalent to the value of my field.'

ištu is rare as a conjunction except in temporal clauses; see (a).

kīma has a number of meanings in addition to its use as a temporal conjunction (see above, under (a)):

'that, the fact that' (with verbs of speaking, perceiving, knowing, showing, etc., in the main clause):

šāpirum kīma immerī nēmettaka ana ekallim lā tublam ulammidanni 'The prefect informed me that you (ms) had not brought the sheep, your tax, to the palace';

'as, according as' (also *ana kīma*, *ak-kīma*):

kīma ina ṭuppi ekallim šaṭru apulšu 'Pay (ms) him as (according to what) is written in the palace record';

ana kīma bēlī išpuram eppeš 'I will do according as my lord wrote me';

kīma also occasionally means 'because' and 'so that':

kīma ana abīya ašapparu 'because I am writing to my father';

kīma šumi bīt abi lā azakkaru tētepšannī 'you (ms) have treated me so that I cannot mention the name of (my) household';

note also *kīma ša* 'as if':

kīma ša abī ištēn mana kaspam iddinam aḫaddu 'I rejoice as if my father had given me a *mina* of silver';

kīma ša bēl lemuttīka anāku 'as if I were your (ms) adversary (lit: lord of evil)'.

kīma sometimes appears immediately before the predicate of its clause, rather than at the beginning:

eqlum kīma zīttī ul īde 'he did not know that the field is my share'.

EXERCISES

A. VOCABULARY 26.

Verbs:

edûm / *idûm* G (Preterite *īde*; see §26.1) 'to know, be experienced, familiar with'; *(w)uddûm* D 'to mark, assign; to make known, reveal, inform; to recognize, identify'.

elēlum G (*i*) 'to become pure, clean, free (of debt)'; Verbal Adj. *ellum* (*ell-*; fem. *elletum*) 'clean, pure, holy, free'; *ullulum* D 'to purify, keep pure; to declare innocent, free (of debt); to consecrate (to a god)'.

išûm G (Preterite *īšu*; see §26.1) 'to have, own'; *X Y eli Z īšu* 'Z owes Y to X' (e.g., *tamkārum šinā šiqil kaspam eli aḫīya īšu* 'my brother owes two shekels of silver to the merchant'); *ṣibit ṭēmim išûm* 'to take action'.

zêrum G (*e*) 'to dislike, hate; to reject; to avoid'.

Nouns:

andurārum (*andurār*) 'freedom, manumission (of slaves); remission (of debts)'.

ašrum (*ašar*; pl. *ašrū* and *ašrātum*) 'place, locale, setting'; *ašar ištēn* '(in) one place'; for *ašar* as a conjunction, see below.

kallatum (*kallat*; pl. *kallātum*; log. É.GI$_4$/GI.A) 'daughter-in-law, bride'.

ṣītum (*ṣīt*; pl. *ṣiātum*) 'rise, rising (of sun), east; emergence, birth, origin; produce, product; lease; expenditure, loss; departure'; *ṣīt pîm* 'utterance, command'; pl. *ṣiātum* (also *ūm ṣiātim*) 'distant time (past or future)'; *ṣīt šamšim* 'sunrise, east' (cf. *waṣûm*).

šammum (*šammi*; pl. *šammū* [often = sg.]; log. Ú) 'plant, grass; herb, drug; hay, fodder'.

Conjunctions that are also used as prepositions:

adi 'until, as long as, while'; *adi* ... *lā* 'before'.
aššum 'because'; rarely 'so that' (esp. Mari).
ēma (rarely *ēm*) 'where(ever)' (as prep.: 'in/at every place/time of').
ina 'as long as, while' (usually in legal expressions, before predicative Verbal Adjectives and forms of *edûm*).
ištu 'after, as soon as, since'; rarely causal 'because, since'.

kīma 'as soon as, when; that, the fact that; as, according as (also *ana kīma, ak-kīma*)'; rarely 'because; so that'; *kīma ša* 'as if'.
lāma 'before' (cf. *lā; lāma* as prep. 'before (temporal)').
warka, warki 'after' (in OB only in expressions involving death).

Other Conjunctions:

ana ša (rare) 'because (of the fact that)'.
ašar 'where(ever)'; rarely 'when, what'.
inūma (poetic/archaizing *inu*) 'when, as soon as, after, at the time that, while'.
ūm (also *ina ūm*) 'when, as soon as, after, at the time that, while'.

B. Learn the following signs:

OB Lapid. / OB Cursive / NA	values
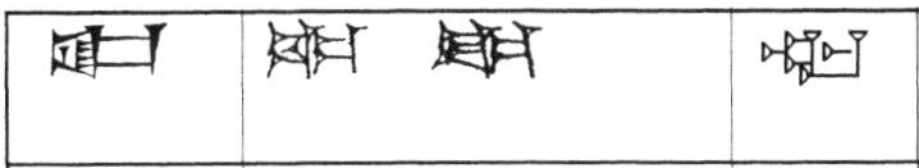	*ka* (lesson 17); KA = *pûm*
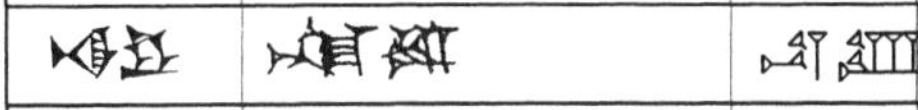	NA.RU = *narûm*
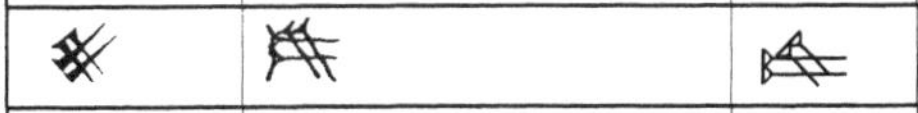	KASKAL = *ḫarrānum*
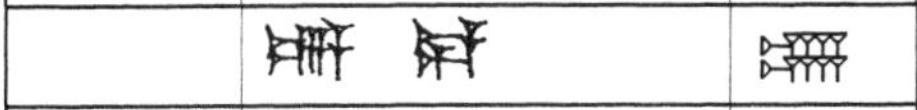	*nir*
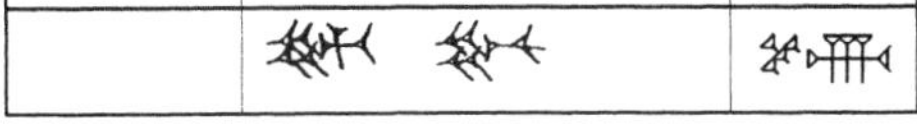	*ṣir, zìr*

C. Write the following words in cuneiform and in transliteration; use logograms where possible:

1. *šēp narîya*
2. *qabal martim*
3. *Ištar linēršu*
4. *utirrū*
5. *uktaṣṣir*
6. *pī nārim*
7. *zēr šammim līter*
8. *liāt kallatim*
9. *ḫarrān šarrim*

D. Write in normalized Akkadian:

1. When you (ms) rode to the city wall, what did you hear?
2. You will not marry her before you bestow the bride-price.
3. When that youth grows up he will subjugate the entire land.
4. As soon as my witness is released I will adjure him.
5. I did not knowingly alter your (ms) stela.
6. Present (pl) him to me when he has come up.
7. He was not able to pay his money lender.
8. She bore many male children (lit., many males).

E. Normalize and translate:

1. *ki-ma ti-du-ú e-bu-ru-um qé-ru-ub it-ti ṣú-ḫa-ri-ia al-kam-ma wa-ar-ka-at a-bi-ni i ni-zu-uz.*
2. *a-na re-eš* ITI *ši-ip-ra-am šu-a-ti i-ga-am-ma-ru.*
3. *šum-ma né-me-ta-ni* 1 MA.NA KUG.BABBAR *i-ma-aṣ-ṣí a-na* DI.KUD.MEŠ *i ni-il-li-ik-ma ki-ma qí-bi-ti-šu-nu i ni-pu-uš.*
4. *am-mi-nim pu-ru-sà-am ša* A.ZU *la tu-ga-me-ra-am-ma la ta-aš-pu-ra-am.*
5. *a-nu-um-ma* DUB-*pí i-na qá-at a-ḫi-ia ki-ma aq-bu-kum aš-tap-ra-ak-kum ku-nu-uk-ki-šu ša-al-mu-tim a-ḫi ku-ul-li-im-ma wu-uš-še-er-šu-ma li-is-ni-qá-am.*
6. *ki-ma eṭ-lum šu-ú la ṣe-eḫ-ru-ú-ma ra-bu-ú lu-ú ti-de ki-ma a-wi-le-e aḫ-ḫi-šu* A.ŠÀ-*lam ù ka-ra-nam a-pu-ul-šu ki-ma ta-ta-ap-lu-šu me-ḫe-er* DUB-*pí-ia šu-up-ra-am.*
7. *i-nu-ma* DUMU-*ka* KUG.BABBAR *a-na a-wi-lim id-di-nu i-na ma-aḫ-ri-ia id-di-in ù a-na-ku a-wa-tim i-de šum-ma a-na* É DINGIR-*lim i-ša-ap-pa-ru-ni-in-ni a-pa-lam ú-ul e-le-i at-ta ki-ma te-le-ú e-pu-uš šum-ma i-na* ŠE-*em ša ta-ša-mu* KUG.BABBAR *ti-šu ku-un-ka-aš-šu-ma a-na i-ia-ši-im id-nam-ma it-ti* KUG. BABBAR-*im ie-e-em lu-um-nu-šu.*
8. *am-mi-nim ki-ma ša um-ma-an na-ak-ri-im i-ṭe*$_4$*-eḫ-ḫu-kum ta-pa-al-la-aḫ.*
9. *iš-tu i-na* URU *wa-aš-ba-ku ma-ma-an ú-ul ú-ta-mi-a-ni.*
10. *ki-ma aš-pu-ra-ak-kum* ÁB.GUD.ḪI.A *a-ṭa-ar-ra-da-ak-kum a-aḫ-ka la ta-na-ad-di ṭe*$_4$*-ma-am ga-am-ra-am šu-up-ra-am-ma* ÁB.GUD.ḪI.A *lu-uṭ-ru-da-ak-kum.*
11. *ki-ma* DUB-*pí ta-am-ma-ru* ^{giš}MÁ *pu-uṭ-ra-am-ma li-iṣ-ba-ta-ni ù a-di pa-ni-ia ta-am-ma-ru* UDU.ḪI.A *la ta-pa-šar.*
12. *iš-tu al-li-kam i-na* URU *šu-a-ti a-na-ku e-li a-a-i-im-ma* ŠE-*a-am ú-ul i-šu iš-tu i-na-an-na* UD.5.KAM ÌR-*di* ŠE-*a-am ub-ba-la-ak-kum li-ib-ba-ka mi-im-ma la i-ma-ra-aṣ ù ṭe*$_4$*-em* PN *id-nam a-mu-ur-šu-ma ṭe*$_4$*-ma-šu šu-up-ra-am ki-ma ta-ta-am-ru-ú-šu ki-a-am qí-bi-šum um-ma at-ta-a-ma be-el-ka ṭe*$_4$*-em-ka li-il-ma-ad.*
13. *ni-i-nu* É *an-ni-a-am la-ma be-el-ni ur-ra-dam iš-tu* MU.20.KAM *ni-iṣ-ba-at i-na-an-na* LÚ.MEŠ *a-ḫu-ú-tum* É-*ni ib-ta-aq-ru-ni-a-ti be-el-ni wa-ar-ka-at-ni li-ip-ru-us.*
14. *ki-ma a-na* URU *as-ni-qú* UD.4.KAM *ú-la-pí-it-ma tap-pé-e aṭ-ṭar-dam* ^{giš}KIRI$_6$ *ku-ul-li-im-šu.*

15. *iš-tu* A.ZU GÌR.PAD.DU *ru-bé-e-em iš-bé-ru* EME-*šu ik-ki-su.*
16. *zi-ka-rum šu-ú i-na pu-ḫur* URU *li-it-ma-a-ma i-nu-ma i-tam-mu-ú ṭe-ma-am šu-up-ra-am-ma pu-ru-sà-am lu-ú i-de a-aḫ-ka la ta-na-ad-di.*

F. CH. Normalize and translate the following laws:

§102 *šum-ma* DAM.GÀR *a-na šamallêm*(ŠAMAN2.LÁ) KUG.BABBAR *a-na ta-ad-mi-iq-tim it-ta-di-in-ma a-šar il-li-ku bi-ti-iq-tam i-ta-mar qá-qá-ad* KUG.BABBAR *a-na* DAM.GÀR *ú-ta-ar.*

tadmiqtum (*tadmiqti*) 'interest-free advance (for a business trip)' (cf. *damāqum*).
bitiqtum (*bitiqti*) 'deficit, loss'.

§114–115 §114 *šum-ma a-wi-lum e-li a-wi-lim* ŠE *ù* KUG.BABBAR *la i-šu-ma ni-pu-sú it-te-pé a-na ni-pu-tim iš-ti-a-at* 1/3 MA.NA KUG. BABBAR *i-ša-qal* §115 *šum-ma a-wi-lum e-li a-wi-lim* ŠE *ù* KUG. BABBAR *i-šu-ma ni-pu-sú ip-pé-ma ni-pu-tum i-na* É *ne-pí-ša i-na ši-ma-ti-ša im-tu-ut di-nu-um šu-ú ru-gu-um-ma-am ú-ul i-šu.*

nepûm G (*e*) 'to distrain, take as pledge, distress'; *nipûtum* (fem.) 'person or animal taken as pledge or distress'.

§170–171 §170 *šum-ma a-wi-lum ḫi-ir-ta-šu* DUMU.MEŠ *ú-li-súm ù* GEME2-*sú* DUMU.MEŠ *ú-li-súm a-bu-um i-na bu-ul-ṭì-šu a-na* DUMU.MEŠ *ša* GEME2 *ul-du-šum* DUMU.MEŠ-*ú-a iq-ta-bi it-ti* DUMU.MEŠ *ḫi-ir-tim im-ta-nu-šu-nu-ti wa-ar-ka a-bu-um a-na ši-im-tim it-ta-al-ku i-na* NÍG.GA É A.BA DUMU.MEŠ *ḫi-ir-tim ù* DUMU. MEŠ GEME2 *mi-it-ḫa-ri-iš i-zu-uz-zu* IBILA DUMU *ḫi-ir-tim i-na zi-it-tim i-na-sà-aq-ma i-le-qé* §171 *ù šum-ma a-bu-um i-na bu-ul-ṭì-šu a-na* DUMU.MEŠ *ša* GEME2 *ul-du-šum* DUMU.MEŠ-*ú-a la iq-ta-bi wa-ar-ka a-bu-um a-na ši-im-tim it-ta-al-ku i-na* NÍG.GA É A.BA DUMU.MEŠ GEME2 *it-ti* DUMU.MEŠ *ḫi-ir-tim ú-ul i-zu-uz-zu an-du-ra-ar* GEME2 *ù* DUMU.MEŠ-*ša iš-ša!*(TA)-*ak-ka-an* DUMU.MEŠ *ḫi-ir-tim a-na* DUMU.MEŠ GEME2 *a-na wa-ar-du-tim ú-ul i-ra-ag-gu-mu ḫi-ir-tum še-ri-ik-ta-ša ù nu-du-na-am ša mu-sà id-di-nu-ši-im i-na* DUB-*pí-im iš-ṭú-ru-ši-im i-le-qé-ma i-na šu-ba-at mu-ti-ša uš-ša-ab a-di ba-al-ṭa-at i-ik-ka-al a-na* KUG.BABBAR *ú-ul i-na-ad-di-in wa-ar-ka-sà ša* DUMU.MEŠ-*ša-ma.*

iššakkan 'it will be established'.
nudunnûm (base *nudunnā-*) 'gift, dowry' (cf. *nadānum*).
ša mārīšā-ma 'belongs to her children only' (cf. §29.2).

§182–184: §182 *šum-ma a-bu-um a-na* DUMU.MUNUS-*šu* LUKUR ^{d}AMAR.UTU *ša* KÁ!(É).DINGIR.RA^{ki} *še-ri-ik-tam la iš-ru-uk-ši-im ku-nu-kam la iš-ṭur-ši-im wa-ar-ka a-bu-um a-na ši-im-tim it-ta-al-ku i-na* NÍG.GA É A.BA IGI.3.GÁL IBILA-*ša it-ti aḫ-ḫi-ša i-za-az-ma il-kam ú-ul i-il-la-ak* LUKUR ^{d}AMAR.UTU *wa-ar-ka-sà e-ma e-li-ša ṭa-bu i-na-ad-di-in* §183 *šum-ma a-bu-um a-na* DUMU.MUNUS-*šu šu-gi*$_4$*-tim še-ri-ik-tam iš-ru-uk-ši-im a-na mu-tim id-di-iš-ši ku-nu-uk-kam iš-ṭur-ši-im wa-ar-ka a-bu-um a-na ši-im-tim it-ta-al-ku i-na* NÍG.GA É A.BA *ú-ul i-za-az* §184 *šum-ma a-wi-lum a-na* DUMU.MUNUS-*šu šu-gi*$_4$*-tim še-ri-ik-tam la iš-ru-uk-šim a-na mu-tim la id-di-iš-ši wa-ar-ka a-bu-um a-na ši-im-tim it-ta-al-ku aḫ-ḫu-ša ki-ma e-mu-uq* É A.BA *še-ri-ik-tam i-šar-ra-ku-ši-im-ma a-na mu-tim i-na-ad-di-nu-ši.*

šugītum (*šugīt*; log. ^{mí}ŠU.GI$_4$; Sum. lw.) a junior wife.

§193 *šum-ma* DUMU *gerseqqêm*(GÌR.SÌ.GA) *ù lu* DUMU *sekretim* (^{mí}ZI.IK.RU.UM) É *a-bi-šu ú-we-ed-di-ma a-ba-am mu-ra-bi-šu ù um-ma-am mu-ra-bi-sú i-zé-er-ma a-na* É *a-bi-šu it-ta-la-ak i-in-šu i-na-sà-ḫu.*

gerseqqûm (base *gerseqqā*; log. GÌR.SÌ.GA; Sum. lw.) 'an attendant, domestic (attached to the palace or a temple)'.

sekretum (*sekret*; pl. *sekrētum*; pseudo-log. ^{mí}ZI.IK.RUM/RU.UM) ' a (cloistered?) woman of high status'.

§282 *šum-ma* ÌR *a-na be-lí-šu ú-ul be-lí at-ta iq-ta-bi ki-ma* ÌR-*sú ú-ka-an-šu-ma be-el-šu ú-zu-un-šu i-na-ak-ki-is.*

ukān 'he will convict/prove'; *kīma warassu* 'that (he is) his slave'.

§180:

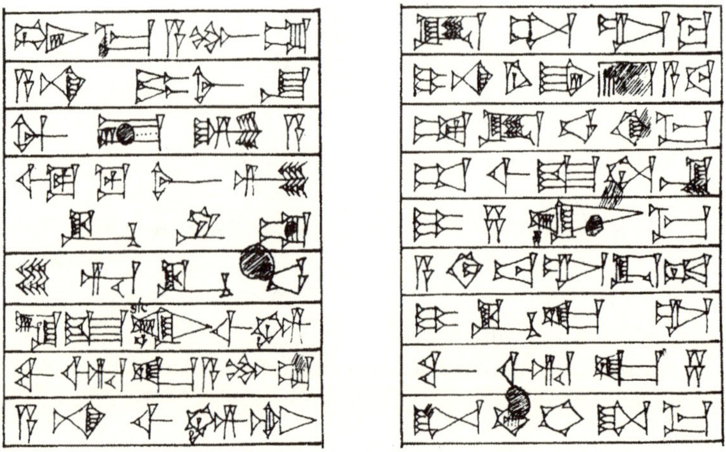

^{mí}ZI.IK.RUM/RU.UM pseudo-logogram for *sekretum* (*sekret*; pl. *sekrētum*) 'a (cloistered?) woman of high status'.

Note the scribal omission in line 6: *la iš-‹ru›-uk-ši-im ša aḫḫīšā-ma* 'belongs to her brothers only' (cf. §29.2).

§280:

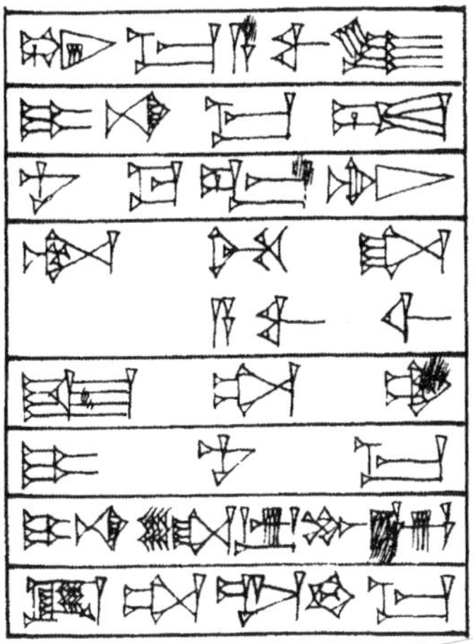

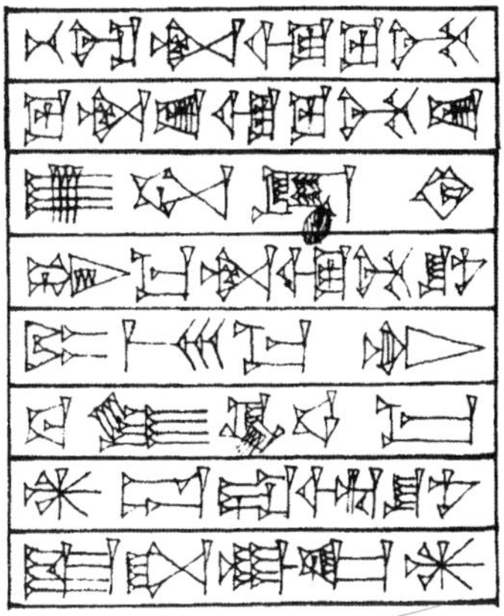

nukurtum (also *nikurtum*; bound form *nu/ikurti*; sf. *nu/ikurta-*; pl. *nukurātum*) 'war; hostility, enmity' (cf. *nakārum*).

ina libbu for *ina libbi* (see §28.3).

The *-ma* on *ittalkam-ma* is an error that should be deleted.

balum kaspim-ma 'without any silver' (see §29.2).

iššakkan 'it will be established'.

G. Omens from *YOS* 10:

1. *šum-ma ú-ba-an ḫa-ši-im ša-ap-li-tum a-na šu-me-lim iš-ḫi-iṭ-ma* [*a-na?*] *ṣe-er ḫa-ši-im šu-me-lam a-na pa-ni-ša i-šu-ú šar-ru-um er-ṣé-tam la ša-tam qá-at-sú i-ka-ša-ad*. (4:1–8)

   šaḫāṭum G (*i*) 'to jump (up), leap; to attack; to twitch'.
   ḫašûm (*ḫaša-*) 'lung(s), entrails'.

2. *šum-ma mar-tum la-ri-a-*[*am*] *i-šu-ú aš-ša-at šar-ri-im zi-ka-ra-am ul-la-ad*. (11 v 12–13)

   larûm (*lari-*) 'branch, fork'.

3. 31 iii 6–12:

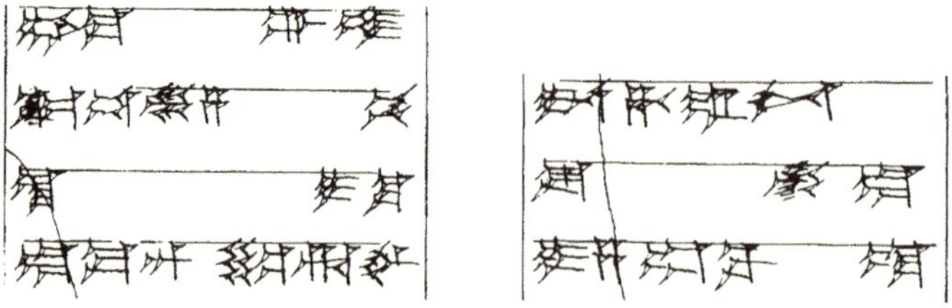

mūṣûm (*mūṣā-*) 'exit' (cf. *waṣûm*).
ṣūmum (*ṣūm(i)*) 'thirst'.

4. 31 iv 7–11:

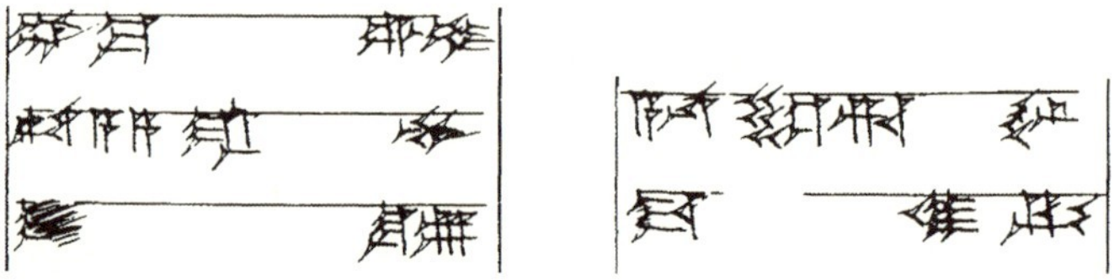

tayyartum 'return; pardon'; here, 'coiling'? (cf. *târum*).

H. Contract.

1. Adoption and manumission of a slave (*CT* 8 48a = Schorr, *VAB* 5, no. 27).

1 ^{Id}*kal-kal-mu-ba-lí-iṭ* 2 DUMU ^{d}*a-a-damqat*(SA_6.GA«.MEŠ») 3 ^{Id}*a-a-damqat*(SA_6.GA) LUKUR ^{d}UTU 4 DUMU.MUNUS DINGIR-*šu-i-bi-šu* 5 *um-ma-šu ú-li-il-šu* 6 *a-na ṣí-it ša-am-ši* 7 *pa-ni-šu iš-ku-un* 8 ^{Id}*kal-kal-mu-ba-lí-iṭ* 9 *a-di ba-al-ṭà-at* 10 *i-ta-na-aš-ši-ši-ma* 11 *ina warkīt ūmim* (UD.KÚR.ŠÈ) *ma-am-ma-*[*an*] 12 *mi-im-ma e-li* ^{Id}*kal-kal-mu-ba-lí-iṭ* 13 *ú-ul i-šu-ú* 14 *ul-lu-ul* 15 DUMU.MEŠ DINGIR-*šu-i-bi-šu* 16 *ù* DUMU.MEŠ *bur-nu-nu* 17 *ma-am-ma-an ú-ul i-ra-ga-am-šum* 18 M U ^{d}U T U ^{d}*a-a* ^{d}A M A R.U T U 19 *ù ḫa-am-mu-ra-pí* 20 *itmû*(IN.PÀD.DÈ. MEŠ). 21–36 Witnesses. 37 Date.

PNs: *Kalkal-muballiṭ; Ayya-damqat; Ilšu-ibbīšu; Būr-Nunu.*
10 *ittanaššīši* 'will support her'.

I. Letters:

1. *OECT* 3 35 = Kraus, *AbB* 4 113

1 *a-na* ^{d}UTU-*ḫa-zi-ir* 2 *qí-bí-ma* 3 *um-ma* LÚ-^{d}NIN.URTA-*ma* 4 ^{d}UTU *li-ba-al-li-iṭ-ka* 5 *aš-šum* A.ŠÀ *ša* DUMU.MEŠ *i-lu-ni* 6 *a-wi-lu-ú na-pi-iš-ta-am* 7 *ú-ul i-šu-*[*ú*] 8 *ki-ma ta-ad-‹di›-nu-šu-nu-ši-im*

9 *ma-am-ma-an la ú-na-ka-ar-šu-nu-ti* 10 *i-na qí-bi-it be-el-ia* 11 *aš-pu-ra-ak-kum.*

PNs: *Šamaš-ḫāzir; Lu-Ninurta; Iluni.*

6 *napištum* here, 'livelihood'.

10 *be-el-ia* for expected *be-lí-ia.*

2. Van Soldt, *AbB* 12 84 (copy not yet published).

1 *a-na* PA.PA *ša* ^{d}AMAR.UTU *ú-ba-al-la-ṭú-š[u]* 2 *qí-bí-ma* 3 *um-ma* ^{d}EN.ZU-*mu-ša-lim-ma* 4 ^{d}UTU *li-ba-al-li-iṭ-ka* 5 *lu ša-al-ma-ta* 6 10 GÍN KUG.BABBAR *da-qá-ti ib-ni-*^{d}*Amurrum*(MAR.TU) *wakil* (UGULA) *Amurrîm*(MAR.TU) 7 *mu-ḫu-ur-ma* 8 *ša* 10 GÍN KUG. BABBAR *šu-a-ti* 9 *ú lu ma-aḫ-ri-ka* 10 *ú lu i-na a-lim e-ma i-ba-aš-š[u]-ú* 11 *ša-a-am* 12 *ṭe*$_4$*-ma-am šu-up-ra-am-ma* 13 *i-na Sippar*(UD. KIB.NUN)^{ki} *a-na pu-úḫ-ḫi lu-ud-di-in-ma* 14 *pu-úḫ-šu* 15 *i-na* KÁ. DINGIR.RA^{ki} 16 *lu-ul-qé.*

PNs: *Sîn-mušallim; Ibni-Amurrum.*

1 PA.PA see note to CH §33 on p. 229.

6 *da-qá-ti* unclear; perhaps bound form *daqqat* (with final *-i* in sandhi with following PN), meaning 'the small remainder of'(?).

7 *waklum* (*wakil*; log. UGULA [the PA sign]) 'overseer'; MAR.TU = *Amurrûm* 'Amorite'; the *wakil Amurrîm* is a high military officer.

8 *ša* 10 GÍN KUG.BABBAR *šu-a-ti* is probably to be construed as the direct object of *šâm* in l. 11: 'buy something worth (lit., that of) said ten shekels of silver'.

9 *maḫrīka* here, 'where you are'.

13 *pu-úḫ-ḫi* for *pūḫi(m).*

3. King, *LIH* 1 45 = Kraus, *AbB* 5 135.

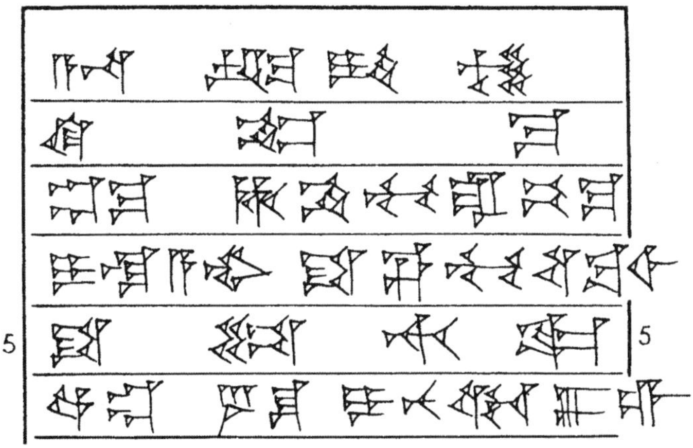

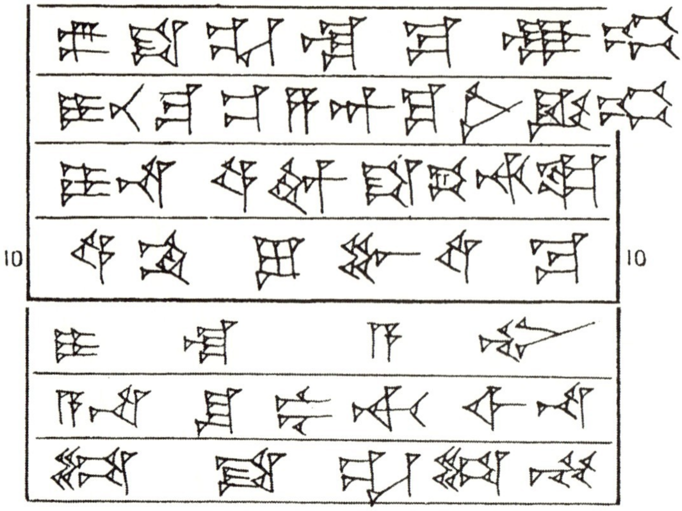

PNs: *Sîn-iddinam; Ḫammu-rapi; Inūḫ-samar.*

[4] *Emutbalum* a region east of the Tigris River.

[5] *lētum* here, 'authority'.

[8] Here and in line 13 (but not in line 7) *ṣābum* is construed as plural.

LESSON TWENTY-SEVEN

27.1 The Š Stem: Sound Verbs; Verbs I-*n*; Verbs III-weak

(a) Sound Verbs

The Š stem is characterized by a prefix *š*, which precedes the root consonants in all forms. The "principal parts" are as follows:

Infinitive:	*šuprusum*	Imperative:	*šupris*
Durative:	*ušapras*	Participle:	*mušaprisum*
Perfect:	*uštapris*	Verbal Adj.:	*šuprusum* (*šuprus*)
Preterite:	*ušapris*		

Note the following observations:

(1) R_2 follows R_1 immediately in all forms.

(2) A vowel always separates the *š* and R_1, *u* if *š* begins the form, *a* otherwise.

(3) Each form has the same vowel configuration as the corresponding D form: e.g.,

Durative: D $uR_1aR_2R_2aR_3$, Š $ušaR_1R_2aR_3$.

Thus, in the Š, as in the D, no special vowel-classes exist — the Durative of all Š verbs has *a* between R_2 and R_3, while the Perfect, Preterite, and Imperative have *i*; the prefixes of the Š Durative, Perfect, and Preterite have *u*, as do the D forms; the Imperative has *i* between R_2 and R_3, while the Infinitive and Verbal Adjective have *u*.

(4) The *t* of the Perfect follows the *š* immediately.

(b) Verbs I–*n*

Since R_1 always comes immediately before R_2 in the Š stem, the *n* is assimilated in all forms.

(c) Verbs III–weak

As in the D, verbs that in the G are III–*i*, III–*a*, and III–*u* are conjugated alike in the Š; in verbs III–*e*, *a*-vowels usually (though not always) become *e*. Again, the usual rules of vowel contraction apply.

(d) Paradigms

Paradigms of the Š stems of *parāsum, nadānum, banûm,* and *šemûm* follow.

Infinitive

nom.	*šuprusum*	*šuddunum*	*šubnûm*	*šušmûm*
gen.	*šuprusim*	*šuddunim*	*šubnîm*	*šušmîm*
acc.	*šuprusam*	*šuddunam*	*šubnâm*	*šušmâm*

Durative

3cs	*ušapras*	*ušaddan*	*ušabna*	*ušešme / ušašma*
2ms	*tušapras*	*tušaddan*	*tušabna*	*tušešme / tušašma*
2fs	*tušaprasī*	*tušaddanī*	*tušabnî*	*tušešmî / tušašmî*
1cs	*ušapras*	*ušaddan*	*ušabna*	*ušešme / ušašma*
3mp	*ušaprasū*	*ušaddanū*	*ušabnû*	*ušešmû / ušašmû*
3fp	*ušaprasā*	*ušaddanā*	*ušabnâ*	*ušešmeā / ušašmâ*
2cp	*tušaprasā*	*tušaddanā*	*tušabnâ*	*tušešmeā / tušašmâ*
1cp	*nušapras*	*nušaddan*	*nušabna*	*nušešme / nušašma*

Preterite

3cs	*ušapris*	*ušaddin*	*ušabni*	*ušešmi / ušašmi*
2ms	*tušapris*	*tušaddin*	*tušabni*	*tušešmi / tušašmi*
2fs	*tušaprisī*	*tušaddinī*	*tušabnî*	*tušešmî / tušašmî*
1cs	*ušapris*	*ušaddin*	*ušabni*	*ušešmi / ušašmi*
3mp	*ušaprisū*	*ušaddinū*	*ušabnû*	*ušešmû / ušašmû*
3fp	*ušaprisā*	*ušaddinā*	*ušabniā*	*ušešmiā / ušašmiā*
2cp	*tušaprisā*	*tušaddinā*	*tušabniā*	*tušešmiā / tušašmiā*
1cp	*nušapris*	*nušaddin*	*nušabni*	*nušešmi / nušašmi*

Perfect

3cs	*uštapris*	*uštaddin*	*uštabni*	*uštešmi / uštašmi*
etc.				

Precative

3cs	*lišapris*	*lišaddin*	*lišabni*	*lišešmi / lišašmi*
1cs	*lušapris*	*lušaddin*	*lušabni*	*lušešmi / lušašmi*
3mp	*lišaprisū*	*lišaddinū*	*lišabnû*	*lišešmû / lišašmû*
3fp	*lišaprisā*	*lišaddinā*	*lišabniā*	*lišešmiā / lišašmiā*
1cp	*i nušapris*	*i nušaddin*	*i nušabni*	*i nušešmi / i nušašmi*

Imperative

ms	*šupris*	*šuddin*	*šubni*	*šušmi*
fs	*šuprisī*	*šuddinī*	*šubnî*	*šušmî*
cp	*šuprisā*	*šuddinā*	*šubniā*	*šušmiā*

Participle

ms	*mušaprisum*	*mušaddinum*	*mušabnûm*	*muš*^{e}/$_{a}$*šmûm*
(bound	*mušapris*	*mušaddin*	*mušabni*	*muš*^{e}/$_{a}$*šmi*)
fs	*mušapristum*	*mušaddittum*	*mušabnītum*	*muš*^{e}/$_{a}$*šmītum*
(bound	*mušaprisat*	*mušaddinat*	*mušabniat*	*muš*^{e}/$_{a}$*šmiat*)
mp	*mušaprisūtum*	*mušaddinūtum*	*mušabnûtum*	*muš*^{e}/$_{a}$*šmûtum*
fp	*mušaprisātum*	*mušaddinātum*	*mušabniātum*	*muš*^{e}/$_{a}$*šmiātum*

Verbal Adjective

nom. ms	*šuprusum*	*šuddunum*	*šubnûm*	*šušmûm*
+3ms	*šuprus*	*šuddun*	*šubnu*	*šušmu*
+3fs	*šuprusat*	*šuddunat*	*šubnât*	*šušmât*
+2ms	*šuprusāta*	*šuddunāta*	*šubnâta*	*šušmâta*
etc.				

27.2 The Meaning of the Š Stem

Š verbs are essentially causatives of their G counterparts.

(a) For a few adjectival verbs, it is the Š rather than the D that serves as the factitive stem: e.g.,

šumruṣum 'to make sick, cause trouble'.

(b) The most frequent use of the Š is as a causative of active-intransitive verbs: e.g.,

šumqutum 'to cause to fall, to fell';
šuknušum 'to make submissive, to subjugate';
šutbûm 'to cause to stand up, to set aside, remove'.

With many verbs of motion, the Š means 'to send', 'to lead', or 'to take' (with the Ventive, 'to bring') an object in the direction denoted by the G, as in

šūrubum (*erēbum*) 'to send/lead/take/bring in';
šūṣûm (*waṣûm*) 'to send/lead/take/bring out';
šūlûm (*elûm*) 'to send/lead/take/bring up';
šūrudum (*warādum*) 'to send/lead/take/bring down'.

(c) Š forms of active-transitive verbs may be doubly transitive, i.e., they may take two accusative objects, one of the action of the (G) verb, which normally (but not always) comes first, and one of the causing: e.g.,

> *awâtīki aḫḫīya ušešmi* 'I made my brothers hear your (fs) words';
> *ṣuḫāram ṭuppam* (or *ṭuppam ṣuḫāram*) *uštābilakkum* 'I have had a servant take (*wabālum*, Š Perfect) the tablet to you (ms)';
> *âm šuāti šumḫerāšu* 'hand over (pl) that grain to him' (lit., 'cause him to receive that grain');
> *nēmettam muškēnam ušaddin* 'I collected the tax from the commoner' (lit., 'I caused the commoner to give the tax').

It is more common, however, for the object of the causing to be omitted; when this happens, the verbal notion is rendered passive in English:

> *awâtīki ušešmi* 'I caused your words to be heard' (lit., 'I caused (someone) to hear');
> *ṭuppam uštābil* 'I have had the tablet carried' (or, 'I have dispatched the tablet'; lit., 'I have caused (someone) to carry');
> *âm šumḫerā* 'hand over the grain' (i.e., 'cause the grain to be received'; lit., 'cause (someone) to receive');
> *nēmettam ušaddin* 'I collected the tax' (i.e., 'I caused the tax to be given'; lit., 'I caused (someone) to give the tax').

It is also possible for the first object to be omitted; if so, the verbal notion becomes intransitive:

> *aḫḫīya ušešmi* 'I made my brothers listen/pay attention'.

(d) A few verbs occur only in the Š stem (and related stems; see §36.1–2): e.g.,

> *šutlumum* 'to give, lend';
> *šuklulum* 'to complete'.

(e) Many verbs occur in both the D and the Š stems, in addition to the G. In a few cases, the meanings of the D and Š are difficult to differentiate:

> *kunnušum* and *šuknušum* 'to subjugate';
> *(w)utturum* 'to augment', *šūturum* 'to increase, surpass'.

Sometimes the meanings overlap only partly:

> *šumlûm* 'to fill, make full', *mullûm* 'to fill, make full', but also, 'deliver in full, assign';
> *šurbûm* 'to make great, increase', *rubbûm* 'to make great, raise (offspring)'.

Often, however, the meanings of the D and the Š are quite distinct:

nakārum 'to become hostile, to change (intransitive)', *nukkurum* 'to change (trans.)', *šukkurum* 'to cause to rebel, cause enmity';

redûm 'to guide, conduct', *ruddûm* 'to add to', *šurdûm* 'to cause to conduct, cause to flow'.

The same is true, of course, when the D and G have the same nuances:

ṣabātum and *ṣubbutum* 'to seize', *šuṣbutum* 'to cause to seize'.

(f) Closely related to the causative nuance of the Š is its occasional use to denote permission: e.g.,

ilū eṭlam ālšu ušakšidū 'The gods allowed the youth to reach his town'.

Such renderings must be derived from context.

(g) The causative meaning of the Š stem is predictable in most instances, and for the majority of verbs, it offers no special translation problems. In some cases, however, less obvious nuances have developed. These are listed below for the strong verbs, verbs I–*n*, and verbs III–weak encountered thus far.

šubšûm 'to make appear, produce, create'.
šuknušum 'to subjugate, make submissive' (=D).
šulputum 'to cause to touch (rare); to defeat, destroy; to desecrate, defile'.
šumḫurum 'to make accept, to offer; to hand over'.
šumqutum 'to cause to fall, fell, strike down, overthrow, defeat'.
šumruṣum 'to make sick, unhappy, worried; to cause trouble, difficulty'.
šumṣûm 'to make suffice'; *mala libbi X šumṣûm* 'to give X full discretion'.
šuddunum (*nadānum*) 'to cause to give, hand over, sell; to collect (taxes, etc.)'; Participle *mušaddinum* 'collector (of taxes, etc.)'.
šuddûm (*nadûm*) 'to cause to throw, drop, abandon; to let (a field) go fallow; to reduce to ruins'.
šukkurum (*nakārum*) 'to cause to rebel, cause enmity'.
šussukum (*nasākum*) 'to remove, reject, annul'.
šupšuḫum 'to quiet, calm, pacify, appease'.
šurbûm 'to make great, increase'.
šurdûm 'to cause to bring, conduct; to cause to flow'.
šurkubum 'to cause to mount; to load (a ship, wagon, etc.)'.
šuršûm 'to cause to acquire, provide (someone with something: double acc.)'; note *pānam šuršûm* 'to make clear, explicit (a report, tablet, matter)'; *idam šuršûm* 'to raise objections'.
šusḫurum 'to cause to turn, cause to seek; to place around, surround (something with something: double acc.)'.
šušmûm 'to cause (someone) to hear (something), inform, cause to pay attention'.
šutbûm 'to cause to arise; to set aside, remove'.

27.3 The Expression of the Comparative and the Superlative

There are no distinct forms of the adjective for the comparative or the superlative; the simple adjective (or its predicative form) is used.

In comparisons, 'than' is expressed by the preposition *eli*, as in

eli kala ilātim dannat 'she is stronger than all the (other) goddesses';
eli kakkabī šamê mādā 'they (f) are more numerous than the stars (*kakkabum*) of the sky';
awīlam ša elīšu rabû imḫaṣ 'he struck a man who is greater (in rank) than he';
ṣuḫāram elīya irammū 'they (m) love the servant more than me'.

The superlative (English 'X-est, most X') is usually expressed by the bound form of the adjective: e.g.,

Ištar rabīt ilātim 'Ištar is the greatest of the goddesses'.

The Š Verbal Adjective of adjectival verbs, called the Elative, can correspond to the English superlative, or to 'very X', as in

šurbûm 'very great, greatest';
šūturum (from *watārum*) 'most surpassing, pre-eminent'.

EXERCISES

A. VOCABULARY 27.

Verbs:

egûm G (*i* or *u*) 'to be careless, negligent (concerning: *ana* or *aššum*)'.
enûm G (*i*) 'to change, invert, revoke'.
rakāsum G (*a–u*) 'to bind, tie (on), wrap up; to put on, equip oneself with; to attack'; *rukkusum* D = G; 'to contract (with someone)' (cf. *riksum*).
reʾûm G (*i*; conjugated like *leʾûm*, see §21.3(h)) 'to tend, pasture (flocks); to graze (said of sheep)'; Participle *rēʾûm* (log. SIPA(D)) 'shepherd'.
tarāṣum G (*a–u*) 'to reach out, stretch out, extend, set up' (all trans.); *šutruṣum* Š = G.

Nouns:

entum (log. NIN.DINGIR(.RA); Sum. lw.) 'high priestess'.

migrum (*migir*; pl. *migrātum*) 'favorite, person endowed with favor (of the gods or the king)'.

narāmum (*narām*) 'beloved one, favorite' (may be used in apposition after a noun: e.g., *ana šarrim narāmīša* 'for her beloved king', lit. 'for the king, her beloved one') (cf. *râmum*).

ṣēnum (fem.), usually pl. *ṣēnū* (**fem.**! pl.), both normally written with log. U$_8$.UDU.ḪI.A (all of which is also read USDUḪA) 'sheep; sheep and goats; flock (of sheep and goats)'.

šamaššammum (often pl. *šamaššammū*; log. ŠE.GIŠ.Ì [also ŠE.Ì.GIŠ at Mari]) an oil-producing plant and its seed, probably 'sesame' (or, 'flax; linseed').

tarbaṣum (*tarbaṣ*; pl. *tarbaṣātum*) 'cattle-pen, stable, fold'.

Divine name:

Anum (log. AN, AN-*num*; Sum. lw.) sky god, head of the pantheon.

B. Learn the following signs:

OB Lapid.	OB Cursive	NA	values
			SIPAD = *rēʾûm*
			U$_8$ (or U S$_5$) in U$_8$.UDU.ḪI.A (also read USDUḪA) = *ṣēnū* (or, less often, *ṣēnum*)

C. Write the following words in cuneiform and in transliteration; use logograms where possible:

1. *šammi ḫarrānim*
2. *qibīt Ištar ṣīrtum*
3. *šamaššammū entim*
4. *eṣemti rēʾîm*
5. *kīma pī narîya*
6. *ṣēnū ša Anim*
7. *kallat rēʾîm*
8. *nērtum*
9. *terḫatum*

D. Write in normalized Akkadian:

1. I will have him detained.
2. because you (ms) had the troop surround the city
3. Cause (fs) them (m) to invoke the life of the god.
4. I had a breach made in the lower wall.
5. He has caused the people to hear his many deeds.
6. You (ms) will make them (m) hostile.
7. the capable one, who makes evil submit

8. They (m) have not yet allowed us to reach our dwellings.
9. Enlil, who makes my lordship great
10. Because you (ms) stole (moveable) property (that is) not yours, we will have your nose and your tongue cut off.
11. You (pl) will not let me take anything.
12. He will allow his wife (of equal status) to receive food during (i.e., in) her life.
13. wherever the sesame is collected (caused to be given)
14. You (ms) will overlay the new chariot with gold.
15. He has augmented it (m).

E. Normalize and translate:

1. GIŠ *ma-la ma-ṣú-ú a-na be-el-ti-ia e-le-ep-pa-am uš-ta-ar-ki-ib.*
2. ^{d}IŠKUR DINGIR GAL NUMUN LUGAL *ša* É *ša-tu ú-ša-al-pa-tu li-ḫa-li-iq.*
3. *da-a-a-nam ša di-in-šu i-nu-ú* LUGAL *ú-še-et-bi-šu.*
4. *a-di a-al-la-ka-am mi-im-ma la ta-ra-ga-am ša-pí-rum* ŠE.GIŠ.Ì *ú-ul ip-qí-dam a-na pa-ni-ia ṭe-ma-am ṣa-ba-at-ma* KUG. BABBAR ŠE.GIŠ.Ì-*ia šu-uš-qí-il-šu ši-ma-am a-ša-ma-am-ma a-la-ka-ak-kum.*
5. *e-em* ^{d}UTU *i-qá-bi-an-ni-a-ši-im i ni-il-li-ik.*
6. *a-na ša ma-aḫ-ri-šu-nu al-li-kam-ma* KUG.BABBAR-*pí ú-ša-ad-di-nu-šu-nu-ti i-ta-ap-lu-ni-ni.*
7. *aš-šum a-na* É *a-ḫi-ka a-la-kam ta-aš-ku-nam ṭe$_4$-mi ú-ul aš-pu-ra-ak-kum-ma aš-šu-mi-ka i-mé-ra-am ú-ul a-ša-am ù i-mé-ru iš-tu li-bi ma-tim i-lu-nim-ma i-na* É *a-ḫi-ia šu-nu la-ma i-mé-ri id-di-nu al-kam-ma ša-am.*
8. SIPAD *ša ta-aš-pu-ra-am* IGI.4.GÁL KUG.BABBAR *nu-uš-ta-am-ḫe-er.*
9. *ú-um ma-ru-um šu-ú li-bi a-bi-šu uš-ta-am-ri-ṣú a-bu-šu i-na ap-lu-ti-šu i-na-sà-aḫ-šu.*
10. *i-na* URU *an-ni-im* 1 GÍN KUG.BABBAR *mi-ma ú-ul šu-ud-du-un.*
11. *šum-ma* UDU GÌR-*šu it-ru-uṣ le-mu-ut-tum ti-bu-um ka-aš-du-um i-na ma-tim i-ba-aš-ši.*

F. CH. Normalize and translate the following laws:

§52 *šum-ma er-re-šum i-na* A.ŠÀ ŠE-*am ù lu* ŠE.GIŠ.Ì *la uš-tab-ši ri-ik-sa-ti-šu ú-ul* [*i*]-*in-ni.*

§127 *šum-ma a-wi-lum e-li* NIN.DINGIR *ù aš-ša-at a-wi-lim ú-ba-nam ú-ša-at-ri-iṣ-ma la uk-ti-in a-wi-lam šu-a-ti ma-ḫar da-a-a-ni i-na-*AD-DU-*ú-šu ù mu-ut-ta-sú ú-gal-la-bu.*

uktīn 'he has convicted'.

*i-na-*AD-DU-*ú-šu* is probably to be read *i-na-aṭ-ṭù-ú-šu* (DU = *ṭù* rarely in OB); *naṭûm* G (*u*) 'to hit, beat'.

muttatum (*muttat*) 'half'; here, 'half (of one's hair)'.

gullubum D (not in G) 'to shave (off)'.

§194 *šum-ma a-wi-lum* DUMU-*šu a-na mu-še-ni-iq-tim id-di-in-ma* DUMU *šu-ú i-n[a] qá-at mu-še-ni-iq-tim im-tu-ut mu-še-ni-iq-tum ba-lum a-bi-šu ù um-mi-šu* DUMU *ša-ni-a-am-ma ir-ta-ka-ás ú-ka-an-nu-ši-ma aš-šum ba-lum a-bi-[š]u ù um-mi-š[u]* DUMU *ša-ni-a-am ir-ku-[s]u tulâ*(UBUR)*-ša i-na-ak-ki-su.*

mušēniqtum (Š Participle, *enēqum* 'to suck') 'wet-nurse'.

šaniam-ma -ma denotes a certain emphasis (§29.2).

irtakas means either 'has attached (to her breast)' (i.e., 'is nursing') or 'has contracted (to nurse)'.

ukannū 'they will convict'.

tulûm (*tulā-*; log. UBUR) 'breast'.

§267 *šum-ma* SIPAD *i-gu!*(GEME$_2$)*-ma i-na tarbaṣim*(TÙR) BI-ZA-*tam uš-tab-ši* SIPAD *ḫi-ṭi-it* BI-ZA-*tim ša i-na tarbaṣim*(TÙR) *ú-ša-ab-šu-ú* ÁB.GUD.ḪI.A *ù* U$_8$.UDU.ḪI.A *ú-ša-lam-ma a-na be-lí-šu-nu i-na-ad-di-in.*

pissātum (*pissāt*) 'lameness?'.

ḫiṭītum (*ḫiṭīt*) 'damage, negligence, fault, crime'.

§179:

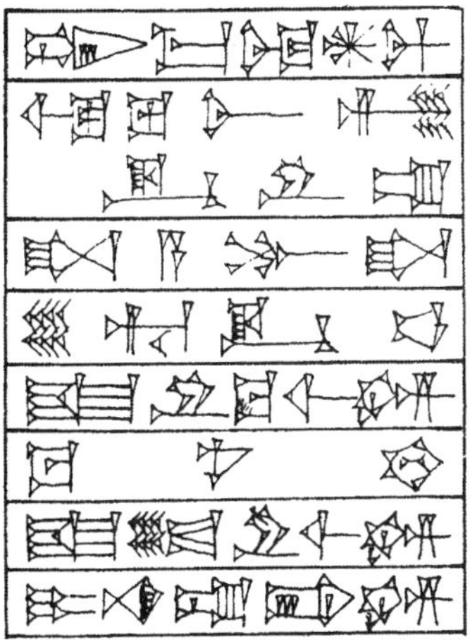

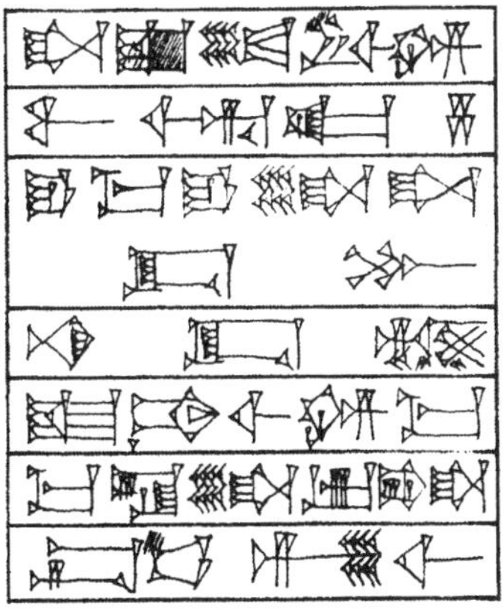

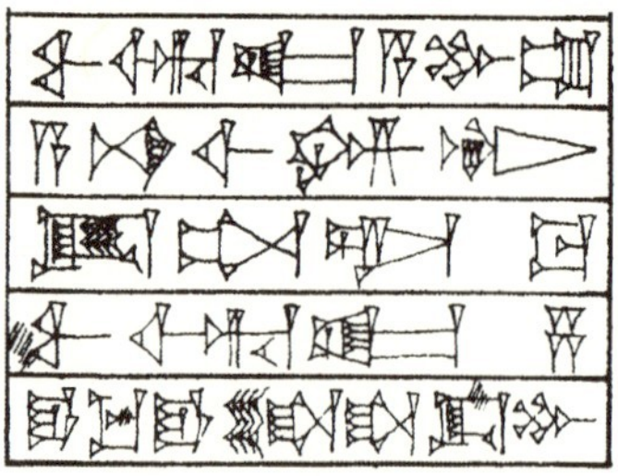

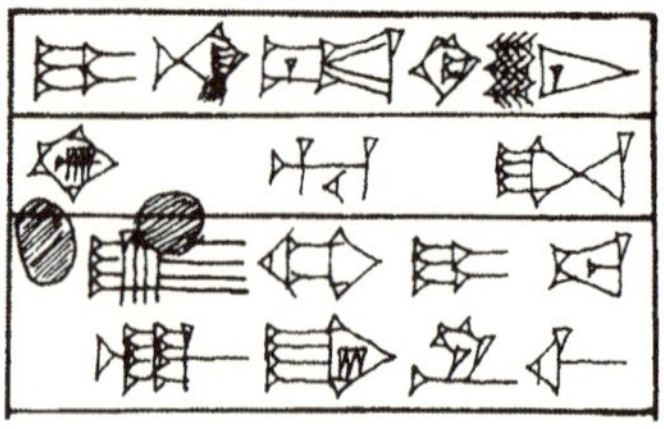

^{mí}ZI.IK.RUM/RU.UM pseudo-log. for *sekretum* (*sekret;* pl. *sekrētum*) 'a (cloistered?) woman of high status'.

warkassa ... nadānam išṭuršim 'he wrote for her to give her inheritance ...'.

G. Omens from *YOS* 10:

1. DIŠ *šēpum*(AŠ) *wa-[a]r-[k]a-sà pa-[ṭ]e*$_4$*-er še*$_{20}$*-ep i-ru-ba-ak-kum tu-ša-ad-da.* (44:19)

   šēpum with log. AŠ (in protasis) only when referring to part of the liver; in the apodosis, *šēpum* has the meaning '(military) expedition'.

   warkatum is curiously construed as masc. here; *paṭrat* is expected.

2. DIŠ *iz-bu-um i-n[a m]u-uḫ-ḫi-šu z[i]-iḫ-ḫu-um ša-ki-in* LÚ.KÚR *ma-tam ú-ša-am-qá-a[t] a-na mu-uš-ke-nim bi-is-sú ú ú-né-ti-š[u]* É.GAL *i-re-de-e.* (56 i 18–20)

   ziḫḫum (*ziḫḫi*) 'cyst, scar'.

   unūtum (pl. irreg. *uniātum/unêtum*) 'utensils, furnishings, property'.

3. [DIŠ] *iz-bu-um qá-qá-as-su ka-a-a-nu-um ša-ki-in-ma* [*ù*] *ša-nu-um ṣe-eḫ-ru-um i-na šu-me-lim ša-ki-in* [*ma*]*-at* LÚ.KÚR*-ka tu-ša-am-qá-at.* (56 iii 21–23)

   kayyānum 'normal' (cf. *kânum*).

4. 26 i 8:

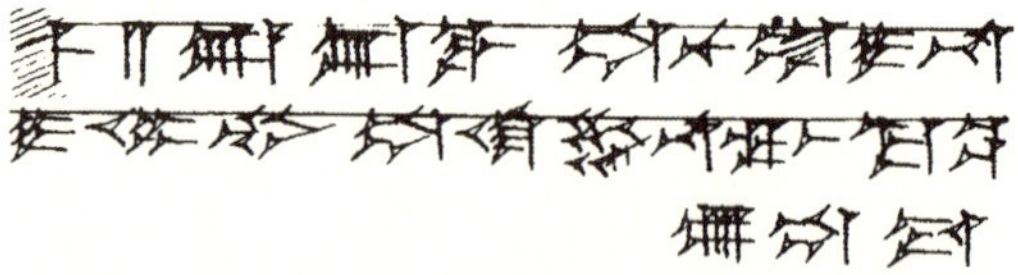

The protasis has two clauses: 'If there are two ... (and) the second is located ...'.

H. Contract:

1. Surety for an abductor (*VAS* 8 26 = Schorr, *VAB* 5, no. 64).

^{1} $^{2}/_{3}$ MA.NA KUG.BABBAR ^{2} *ša nu-úr-*^{d}UTU DUMU *Sîn*(30)*-še-me* ^{3} *e-li* AN-*ga-mil* ^{4} *ù be-le-sú-nu* DAM.A.NI *ir-šu-ú* ^{5} ^{I}*i-din-é-a* DUMU *ri-iš-*DINGIR ^{6} *a-na Malgîm*(SIG$_4$)^{ki} ^{I}*be-le-sú-nu* ^{7} *ú-se-pí-ši-i-ma* ^{8} ^{I}*nu-úr-*^{d}UTU *i-na* KÁ.DINGIR.RA^{ki} ^{9} ^{I}*i-din-é-a aš-šum be-le-sú-nu* ^{10} DAM AN-*ga-mil* ^{11} *ú-se-ep-pu-ú* ^{12} *iṣ-ba-at-sú* ^{13} ^{I}*Sîn*(30)*-i-qí-ša-am* DUMU *ḫa-ni-ia* ^{14} *qá-ta-at i-din-é-a* ^{15} *ki-iš-ša-at be-le-sú-nu* ^{16} *a-na* $^{1}/_{3}$ MA. NA 4 GÍN KUG.BABBAR ^{17} *a-na* ITI.1.KAM *il-qé!*(LI)*-e-ma* ^{18} *a-na* UD-*um ḫa-da-ni-šu* ^{19} ^{I}*i-din-é-a a-wi-il-tam* ^{20} *ú-ul ir-de-a-am-ma* ^{21} $^{1}/_{3}$ MA.NA 4 GÍN KUG.BABBAR ^{22} *a-na nu-úr-*^{d}UTU ^{23} *Sîn*(30)*-i-qí-ša-am uš-ta-aš-qí-il.* $^{24–28}$ Witnesses. $^{29–30}$ Date.

PNs: *Nūr-Šamaš; Sîn-šeme; Anum-gamil; Bēlessunu; Iddin-Ea; Rīš-ilim; Sîn-iqīšam; Ḫaniya.*

$^{1–4}$ These lines constitute an incomplete sentence, a heading of the text.

^{2}For 30 as a writing of *Sîn*, see the last note on p. 250.

^{6} *Malgûm* (rare log. SIG$_4$) a place name.

^{7} *suppûm* D (G *sepûm* rare) 'to abduct, remove by force' (rare).

^{14} *qātātum* (pl. of *qātum*) 'surety, guarantee'; *qātātim leqûm* 'to go surety, to guarantee'.

^{15} *kiššātum* (always pl.) 'debt-servitude'.

^{16} *adānum* (also *ḫadānum*) 'appointed time'.

^{19} *awīltum* (fem. of *awīlum*) 'woman, lady', here referring to Bēlessunu.

I. Letters:

1. *TCL* 7 13 = Kraus, *AbB* 4 13.

^{1} *a-na* ^{d}UTU-*ḫa-zi-ir* ^{2} *qí-bí-ma* ^{3} *um-ma ḫa-am-mu-ra-pí-ma* ^{4} ^{I}*a-píl-*^{d}UTU *utullum*(Ú.DÚL) ^{5} *ki-a-am ma-aḫ-ri-ia iš-ku-un* ^{6} *um-ma šu-ma* ^{7} *būr*(BÙR.IKU) ^{giš}KIRI$_6$ *ša* KA ÍD *la-la-ti-tim* ^{8} *ša be-lí a-na* SIPAD.MEŠ *ša qá-ti-ia* ^{9} *id-di-nam* ^{10} ^{I}*ar-wu-ú-um il-te-qé* ^{11} *ki-a-am ma-aḫ-ri-ia iš-ku-un* ^{12} ^{giš}KIRI$_6$ *šu-a-ti* ^{13} *a-na ar-wu-ú-um* ^{14} *ma-an-nu-um id-di-in* ^{15} *ṭe*$_4$*-em* ^{giš}KIRI$_6$ *šu-a-ti ga-am-ra-am* ^{16} *pa-nam šu-ur-ši-a-am-ma* ^{17} *šu-up-ra-am.*

PNs: *Šamaš-ḫāzir; Ḫammurapi; Apil-Šamaš; Arwûm.*

^{4} *utullum* (*utul*; log. Ú.DÚL; Sum. lw.) 'chief shepherd'.

^{7} *būrum* (*būr(i)*; log. BÙR(.IKU); Sum. lw.) a measure of area (about 6.5 hectares). *Lalatum* a place name.

2. Figulla, *CT* 43 96 = Kraus, *AbB* 1 96.

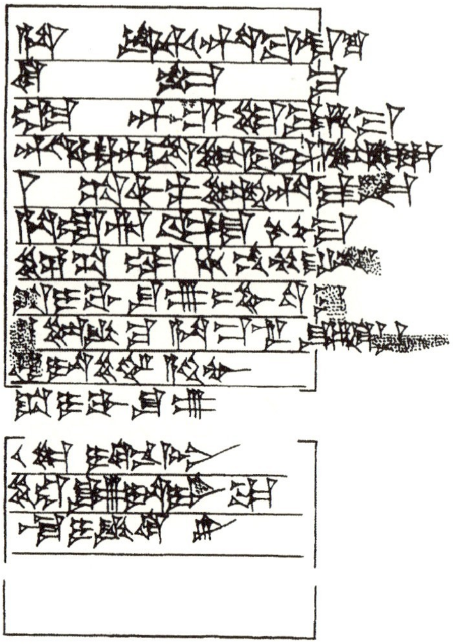

PNs: *Itti-Šamaš-balāssu*; *Amurrum-magir*; *Šalim-paliḫ-Šamaš*.

4 dMAR.TU = the god *Amurrum*. This crowded line reads dUTU *ù* dMAR.TU *li-ba-al-li-ṭú-ka*.

5 The last two signs, indicating Šalim-paliḫ-Šamaš's occupation, are unclear.

7 Last two signs: *-píki*; *Dūr-Ḫammurapi* is a place name.

8 First sign: *ša*; last sign: *sú*.

9 First sign: *a*; last four signs: *šu-ur-ki-*⌈*ib*⌉.

10 First sign: *ù*. *aḫītum* (*aḫīt*; substantivized fem. of *aḫûm*) 'additional payment; misfortune; secrecy'; pl. also 'outskirts, outlying regions; dependents'; here in apposition to ŠE-*im*.

12 First signs: 10 ŠE.GUR.

13 Second last sign: *ni*.

14 *waqārum* G (*i*) 'to become precious'.

LESSON TWENTY-EIGHT

28.1 The Š Stem: Verbs I–ʾ (I–*a* and I–*e*); Verbs I–*w*

(a) Verbs I–ʾ

It will be remembered that, in the Š of the strong verb, R_1 immediately precedes R_2 in all forms. In verbs I–ʾ, the loss of ʾ has, as expected, caused the lengthening of the preceding vowel, in all forms but one. The aberrant form is the Durative, in which, exceptionally, the vowel remains short, while R_2 is doubled (probably by analogy with the G Durative *iḫḫaz*). In verbs I–*e*, the usual change of *a*-vowels to *e* takes place. Below are the Š forms of *aḫāzum*, *epēšum*, and *elûm* (also III–weak):

Infinitive:	*šūḫuzum*	*šūpušum*	*šūlûm*
Durative:	*ušaḫḫaz*	*ušeppeš*	*ušelle*
Perfect:	*uštāḫiz*	*uštēpiš*	*uštēli*
Preterite:	*ušāḫiz*	*ušēpiš*	*ušēli*
Imperative:	*šūḫiz*	*šūpiš*	*šūli*
Participle:	*mušāḫizum*	*mušēpišum*	*mušēlûm*
Verbal Adj.:	*šūḫuzum*	*šūpušum*	*šūlûm*
(V. Adj. base:	*šūḫuz*	*šūpuš*	*šūlu*)

(b) Verbs I–*w*

These are conjugated like verbs I–ʾ in the Š. Most follow the pattern of verbs I–*a*, but a few have the change of *a*-vowels to *e* that is characteristic of Verbs I–*e*. In a very small group, including *waṣûm*, forms of both types occur; of these the forms with *a* › *e* predominate. As in the D, there is no distinction between active and adjectival verbs I–*w*. Here are the Š forms of *babālum* (*a*-type), *wašābum* (*e*-type) and *waṣûm* (also III–weak; usually *e*-type, also *a*-type):

Infinitive:	*šūbulum*	*šūšubum*	*šūṣûm*
Durative:	*ušabbal*	*ušeššeb*	*ušeṣṣe* (*ušaṣṣa*)
Perfect:	*uštābil*	*uštēšib*	*uštēṣi* (*uštāṣi*)
Preterite:	*ušābil*	*ušēšib*	*ušēṣi* (*ušāṣi*)
Imperative:	*šūbil*	*šūšib*	*šūṣi*

Participle:	*mušābilum*	*mušēšibum*	*mušēṣûm* (*mušāṣûm*)
Verbal Adj.:	*šūbulum*	*šūšubum*	*šūṣûm*
(V. Adj. base:	*šūbul*	*šūšub*	*šūṣu*)

Conjugated like *babālum* (*a*-type) are *walādum* and *watārum*.
Conjugated like *wašābum* (*e*-type) is *warādum*.

In OB poetry (§§33.3–4, 35.4), the Š Preterite and Participle of *wašābum* occasionally have *ū* rather than *ē*: *ušūšib, mušūšibum*. (Š Preterite and Participle forms with *ū* are also attested in poetry for *wapûm* G (*i*) 'to appear', Š 'to make manifest', and for *ešērum* (I–*e*; originally I–*y*) G (*i*) 'to go straight, prosper', Š 'to proceed, cause to go straight'.)

(c) Š stems of verbs I–ʾ and verbs I–*w* encountered thus far:

Verbs I–*a*

šūḫuzum 'to cause to hold, cause to marry; to obtain (a wife for someone); to teach, instruct, to incite'; *dīnam šūḫuzum* 'to grant a legal case, hearing to someone'.

šūkulum 'to cause, give to eat, to feed'.

šūlukum (rare) 'to cause to go; to fit'.

šūrukum (rare) 'to lengthen, prolong'.

Verbs I–*e*

šūdûm (*edûm*) 'to make known, announce, proclaim (something: acc.; to someone: acc. or *ana*/dat.)'.

šūlûm 'to cause to go up, send/lead/take/bring up; to raise, make emerge/appear; to summon/produce a witness (or document); to remove, oust'.

šūpušum 'to cause to do/make/build; to have (something) built; to direct work'.

šūrubum 'to cause to enter, send/lead/take/bring in'.

šūrušum (rare) 'to cause to (be) cultivate(d), put under cultivation'.

šūšurum 'to move straight toward; to set straight, set on the proper course, make prosper'.

šūtuqum 'to cause to move on/proceed/pass; to send on; to allow to elapse'.

šūzubum 'to cause to leave; to have (a document) made out; to save (persons, cities)'.

Verbs I–*w*

šūbulum (*a*-type) 'to cause to carry/bring; to send, dispatch (something; lit., to have something brought)'.

šūludum (rare) (*a*-type) 'to cause to bear'.

šūrudum (*e*-type) 'to send/lead/take/bring down'.

šūṣûm (*e*-type, rarely *a*-type) 'to cause to go/come out/forth, to send/lead/take/bring out; to make leave, send away, evict, expel; to remove (from a house, container), release; to let escape; to obtain, produce; to rent, hire'.

šūšubum (*e*-type) 'to cause to sit down/stay/dwell; to install (officers, etc.), to garrison (soldiers); to settle, resettle (people)'.

šūturum (*a*-type) 'to cause to increase/surpass, to enlarge'; Verbal Adj. *šūturum* 'pre-eminent, surpassing'.

28.2 The Terminative-adverbial Ending *-iš*

In this and the following section are presented two nominal endings, *-iš* and *-um*, both of which are adverbial in nature. These endings occur on singular noun (and adjective) stems, replacing the usual case-endings. (Examples on plural nouns are rare.)

The ending *-iš* corresponds semantically to the preposition *ana* plus the genitive. It occurs on nouns and on adjectives.

On nouns, *-iš* is no longer a productive morpheme by the OB period; its occurrence is restricted to a relatively small group of nouns, and, apart from a few frozen expressions, almost exclusively to poetry and some personal names, such as

> *Iliš-tikal* 'trust (ms)-in-god' (cf. the name *Ana-ilīya-atkal*).

On an Infinitive, *-iš* denotes purpose:

> *amāriš* '(in order) to see' (cf. *ana amārim*).

Apart from Infinitives, nouns with *-iš* most often occur as bound forms before following genitive nouns or with pronominal suffixes, as in

> *dāriš ūmī* 'forever' (lit.: 'for perpetuity of days');
> *akliška liṭṭul* 'let him look at your (ms) food'.

Note that *-šš-* remains unchanged when third person suffixes are added:

> *qātiššu* 'to his hand'.

Nouns with *-iš* plus a pron. suf. are often semantically equivalent to forms with locative *-um* plus a pron. suf.; see the next section, end.

Much more commonly, in both prose and poetry, *-iš* is added to ms adjective bases, from which are formed adverbs:

> *mādiš* 'much, greatly'; *lemniš* 'badly, wickedly';
> *damqiš* 'well'; *kīniš* 'truly'.

With vocalic stems, regular vowel contraction takes place:

> *rabîš* 'greatly'; *ḫadîš* 'joyfully'.

The ending *-išam* is an adverbial suffix that usually has distributive force:

ūmišam 'daily'; *warḫišam* 'monthly'.

28.3 The Locative-adverbial Ending *-um*

The ending *-um* is semantically equivalent to the preposition *ina* plus the genitive. When used without a following genitive, it has the same form as the nominative sg. case-ending: e.g.,

šanûm warḫum 'in the second month';
išteat sūtum 'for one seah'.

The final *m* is lost in later OB (see §24.4).

A form with the locative ending may occur as a bound form before a following noun; usually the final *m* is missing:

libbu ālim 'in the center of town' (contrast the bound form of nominative *libbum*, as in *libbi ālim* 'the center of town');
x kaspam libbu kaspīki idnī 'give (fs) x silver out of your silver'.

Before pronominal suffixes, the locative ending remains and the *m* is assimilated to the following consonant (cf. the *m* of the Ventive); the ending with the 1cs suffix, *-uyya*, is normally written *-Cu-a* (perhaps pronounced *-ūʾa*).

libbuššu 'in its (m) midst';
libbukki 'in your (fs) mind';
libbuyya (written *li-ib-bu-a*) 'within me'.

Occasionally, a noun with the locative-adverbial ending is preceded, redundantly, by the preposition *ina* (or, more rarely, by *ana*), as in

ina bītum 'in the house' (equivalent to both *ina bītim*, with the genitive, and the locative *bītum* alone);

ina libbu ālim 'in the center of town'.

In OB prose, apart from a few expressions involving time or measurement, such as the examples in the first paragraph above, the use of the locative-adverbial ending is largely restricted to a few frozen adverbial (or prepositional) forms, such as *libbu(m)* 'within'. In several forms, *-um* is preceded by the morpheme *-ān* (cf. §20.2), as in

šaplānum 'underneath, below' (from *šaplum* 'underside');
elēnum 'above, beyond' (cf. *elûm* 'upper')
qerbēnum 'inside' (*qerbum* 'inner part').

The Infinitive occasionally occurs with the locative-adverbial ending, often with *-ma*, to add emphasis to a finite verb:

tabālum tatbal 'you (ms) did indeed carry off';
šūpušum-ma lišēpišū 'they (m) must certainly direct the building'.

In poetry, use of the locative-adverbial is somewhat less restricted. Further, it sometimes has the instrumental nuance of *ina*: e.g.,

qibītušša 'by her command'.

When followed by pronominal suffixes, especially third person suffixes, the endings *-um* and *-iš* tend to become indistinguishable in meaning:

šēpuššu or *šēpiššu* 'at/to his foot'.

28.4 Adverbs

Most adverbs can be associated with nominal or pronominal bases. There are a number of endings from which adverbs are formed; the following paragraphs list the most common of these for reference.

(a) *-am*, often simply *-a* (cf. 24.4(a)), i.e., the accusative case, used adverbially (§18.3); examples:

ūmam 'today, for a day';	*pāna* 'before, earlier';
šanītam 'secondly, moreover';	*inanna* (<**ina annâ*) 'now';
imittam 'on the right';	*kiam* 'thus'.

(b) *-iš*, the terminative-adverbial ending (§28.2, above):

ašariš 'there' (cf. *ašrum*);	*šapliš* 'below' (*šaplum* 'underside');
mādiš 'much, greatly';	*annîš* 'hither';
rabîš 'greatly';	*êš* (< *ayyiš*) 'whither?'.

Note also the ending *-išam*:

ūmišam 'daily';	*ullîšam* 'thither';
warḫišam 'monthly';	*ayyîšam-ma* 'anywhere'.

(c) *-um*/*-u*, the locative-adverbial ending (§28.3, above):

apputtum 'please';	*ayyānum* 'where?' (cf. *ayyum*);
warkānum 'afterward, later';	*annânum* 'here' (cf. *annûm*);
elēnum 'above, in addition';	*ullânum* (*-ma*) 'already, from there' (*ullûm* 'that' [§6.3, end]).

(d) *-i*:

mati 'when?';	*ali* 'where?';
matīma 'ever';	*kī* 'how?'.

(e) *-ø*, i.e., the absolute form (§23.1):

zamar 'quickly, suddenly';	*pīqat* 'perhaps'.

Other adverbs are compounds of two or more elements:

annīkiam 'here';	*ullīkiam* 'there';
ayyīkiam 'where?';	*am-mīnim* (or *ana mīnim*) 'why?';
inūmīšūma (*ina*+*ūmī*+-*šu*+-*ma*) 'at that time, then';	*malmališ* / *mammališ* (*mal*+*mal*+-*iš*) 'likewise, to the same degree'.

Some sentence-modifying adverbs naturally stand first in their sentence, as in English:

> *šanītam aḫī warassu iṭrudakkum* 'Moreover, my brother sent you (ms) his slave'.

The normal position of most adverbs, however, is after the subject and object, i.e., directly before the verb:

> *aḫī warassu ašariš iṭrudakkum* 'My brother sent his slave there to you'.

It should be noted, however, that Akkadian word order, except for the position of the verb at the end, is not rigid, and many variations occur.

EXERCISES

A. VOCABULARY 28.

Verbs:

ekēmum G (*i*) 'to take away (something from someone: double acc.), deprive (someone of something: double acc.); to conquer, annex; to take away, snatch away; to absorb'; Verbal Adj. *ekmum* (*ekim-*) 'taken away', etc.; also, 'stunted, atrophied' (in extispicy).

esēḫum G (*i*) 'to assign'; *isiḫtum* (*isiḫti*) 'assignment, task, duty; material assigned'.

Nouns:

abnum (masc. and fem.; *aban*; pl. *abnū* and *abnātum*; log. NA4) 'stone; rock, pebble; precious stone; stone weight'.

kibsum (*kibis*) 'track, path; tracks, steps, traces; behavior'.

kīdum (*kīd(i)*; pl. *kīdū* and *kīdātum*) 'outside (region), open country'; *ana kīdim* '(to the) outside'; *ina kīdim* 'outside'.

pāṭum (*pāṭ(i)*; pl. *pāṭū*) 'boundary, border; district, territory'.
pītum (masc.; *pīt(i)*) 'opening, breach' (cf. *petûm*).
rabiānum (*rabiān*; pl. *rabiānū*) 'mayor' (cf. *rabûm*).
wēdum (*wēd-*) 'single, individual, solitary, alone'; *wēdûm* (*wēdī-*) 'unique; important, notable'.

Adverbs:

arḫiš 'quickly'.
elēnum 'above, upstream; beyond, besides, in addition'; as Preposition (with suf. *elēnukka*, etc.) 'above; beside, in addition to, apart from' (cf. *elûm*).
šaplānum 'below, underneath'; as Preposition (with suf. *šaplānukka*, etc.) 'below, under' (cf. *šaplûm*).
ullânum '(from) there'; as Preposition (with suf. *ullânukka*, etc.) 'apart from, other than'; note also *ullânum-ma* 'already'.

B. Learn the following signs:

OB Lapid.	OB Cursive	NA	values
			*du, ṭù* (lesson 12); RÁ in A.RÁ = *adi*
		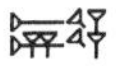	NA$_4$ = *abnum*; determ. ^{na_4} before words for stones, minerals
		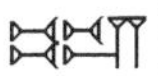	*šim*
			*kur, qúr, mad/t/ṭ*; KUR = *mātum, šadûm*; det. ^{kur} before names of countries, mountains

C. Write the following words in cuneiform and in transliteration; use logograms where possible:

1. *abnāt ḫarrānim*
2. *adi šalāšīšu*
3. *pī rēʾîm*
4. *mātāt šarrim*
5. *šamaššammū*
6. *ṣēnī entim addiššim*
7. *šammi šadîm*
8. *naru nakrim aqqur*

D. Write in normalized Akkadian:

1. According to your (ms) command, I have dispatched the sesame and the stones.
2. May the shepherd feed the flocks and the cattle that are present in the fold.
3. I greatly reinforced the foundations (dual) of these walls.
4. They (m) caused the evil thief who had carried off the beer and the oil for (lit., of) anointing the god to enter before the prince.
5. The high-priestess proclaimed to the wide people that the queen, her sister, had born a male (child), and they all rejoiced.
6. The judge may not change the verdict he has given (lit., judged).
7. Why did you (fs) oust him from (*ina*) his vineyard?
8. I will cause it (m) to move on.
9. I am the king who is pre-eminent among kings.
10. You (pl) may not rent these fields.
11. The gifts were sent down.
12. I had an extispicy performed.
13. Settle (ms) them (f) here quickly; do not tarry.

E. Normalize and translate:

1. *ki-i-ma ti-du-ú ni-šu ra-bi-a-an* URU *pa-ṭi-ka it-ta-as-ḫa-ma a-na ki-di-im uš-te-ṣí-a-šu.*
2. *i-nu-ma* ŠU.ḪA *qá-as-sú ú-ša-at-ri-ṣú-ma le-e-ti im-ḫa-ṣú ši-in-ni id-di i-na-an-na* GÌR.PAD.DU Á-*šu i-na qá-ab-li-ša eš-te-bé-er.*
3. *ša ba-aq-ri ma-aḫ-ru-tim* IGI.3.GÁL GÍN KUG.BABBAR *iš-te-a-at su-tu-um ša a-na* É.GAL *la ú-ma-al-lu-ú ú-ša-aš-qá-lu-šu.*
4. *ma-la* ŠÀ-*ša i-ma-ṣí-ma e-ma* ŠÀ-*ša ṭa-bu ka-ra-nam i-na-din.*
5. *aš-šum di-nam ú-ša-ḫi-zu-ka-ma di-ni la te-eš-mu-ú-ma te-gu-ú ki-i-ma* DUB-*pí an-ni-a-am ta-ta-am-ru a-na* KÁ.DINGIR.RA^{ki} *a-na ma-aḫ-ri-ia al-ka-am-ma ar-ḫi-iš si-in-qá-am.*
6. *šum-ma iz-bu-um ul-la-num-ma* SÍG *na-ši* (*naši* 'has') UD.MEŠ LUGAL *ga-am-ru na-ke-er-ka um-ma-an-ka i-na* ^{giš}TUKUL-*ki ú-ša-am-qá-at.*
7. A.ŠÀ *an-ni-a-am ma-la ma-ṣú-ú a-na e-pé-ši-im ù wa-ša-bi-im* PN KI PN$_2$ EN A.ŠÀ *a-na qa-bé-e* PN$_3$ *ú-še-ṣí.*

F. CH:

§15 *šum-ma a-wi-lum lu* ÌR É.GAL *lu* GEME$_2$ É.GAL *lu* ÌR MAŠ.EN. GAG *lu* GEME$_2$ MAŠ.EN.GAG ABUL *uš-te-ṣí id-da-ak.*

§§55–56 §55 *šum-ma a-wi-lum a-tap-pa-šu a-na ši-qí-tim ip-te a-aḫ-šu id-di-ma* A.ŠÀ *i-te-šu me-e uš-ta-bíl* ŠE *ki-ma i-te-šu i-ma-ad-da-ad* §56 *šum-ma a-wi-lum me-e ip-te-ma ep-še-tim ša* A.ŠÀ *i-te-šu me-e uš-ta-bíl ana būrim* (BÙR^{iku}.E) 10 ŠE.GUR *i-ma-ad-da-ad.*

atappum (fem.) '(small) branch or off-take of a canal'.

šiqītum (*šiqīt*) 'watering; irrigation'.

būrum (*būri*; log. BÙR; Sum. lw.) a surface measure (ca. 6.48 ha.).

§112 *šum-ma a-wi-lum i-na ḫar-ra-nim wa-ši-ib-ma* KUG.BABBAR KUG.SIG$_{17}$ NA$_4$ *ù bi-iš qá-ti-šu a-na a-wi-lim id-di-in-ma a-na ši-bu-ul-tim ú-ša-bíl-šu a-wi-lum šu-ú mi-im-ma ša šu-bu-lu a-šar šu-bu-lu la id-⸢di⸣-in-ma it-ba-al be-el ši-bu-ul-tim a-wi-lam šu-a-ti i-na mi-im-ma ša šu-bu-lu-ma la id-di-nu ú-ka-an-«nu»-šu-ma a-wi-lum šu-ú* A.RÁ 5-*šu mi-im-ma ša in-na-ad-nu-šum a-na be-el ši-bu-ul-tim i-na-ad-di-in.*

šībultum (*šībulti*) 'consignment, goods for transport' (cf. *babālum* Š).

ina ... ukāššu 'he will convict him concerning ...'.

ša innadnūšum 'which was given to him'.

§154 *šum-ma a-wi-lum* DUMU.MUNUS-*sú il-ta-ma-ad a-wi-lam šu-a-ti* URU *ú-še-eṣ-ṣú-ú-šu.*

§238 *šum-ma malāḫum*(MÁ.LAḪ$_5$) ^{giš}MÁ *a-wi-lim ú-ṭe$_4$-eb-bi-ma uš-te-li-a-aš-ši* KUG.BABBAR *mi-ši-il* ŠÁM-*ša i-na-ad-di-in.*

malāḫum (*malāḫ*; log. MÁ.LAḪ$_5$ [laḫ$_5$ = du+du]) 'sailor'.

ṭebûm G (*u*) 'to sink' (intrans.); *ṭubbûm* D 'to sink' (trans.).

§251 *šum-ma* GUD *a-wi-lim na-ak-ka-p[í-ma] ki-ma na-ak-ka-pu-ú ba-ab-ta-šu ú-še-di-šum-ma qar-ni-šu la ú-šar-ri-im* GUD *la ú-sa-an-ni-iq-ma* GUD *šu-ú* DUMU *a-wi-lim i[k-k]i-ip-ma u[š-ta]-mi-it* $^1/_2$ [MA].NA KUG.BABBAR *i-[na]-ad-di-in.*

nakāpum G (*i*) 'to gore, butt'; *nukkupum* D = G; *nakkāpûm* (denominative adj.; base *nakkāpī-*) 'prone to goring'.

qarnum (*qaran*) 'horn'.

šarāmum G (*a–u*) 'to beat out, cut out'; *šurrumum* D 'to cut off, trim'.

uštamīt 'it has killed'.

§§151–152:

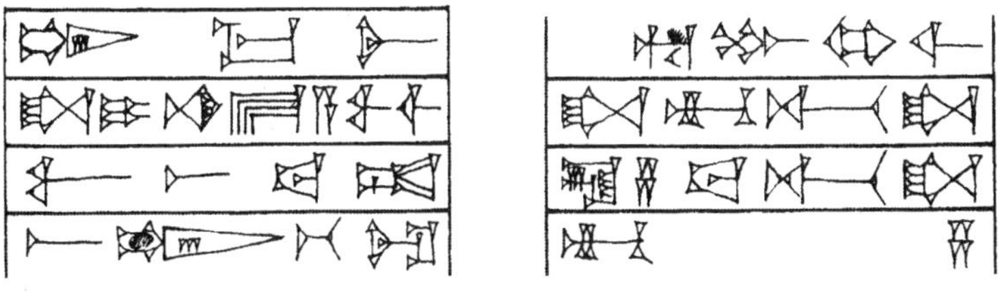

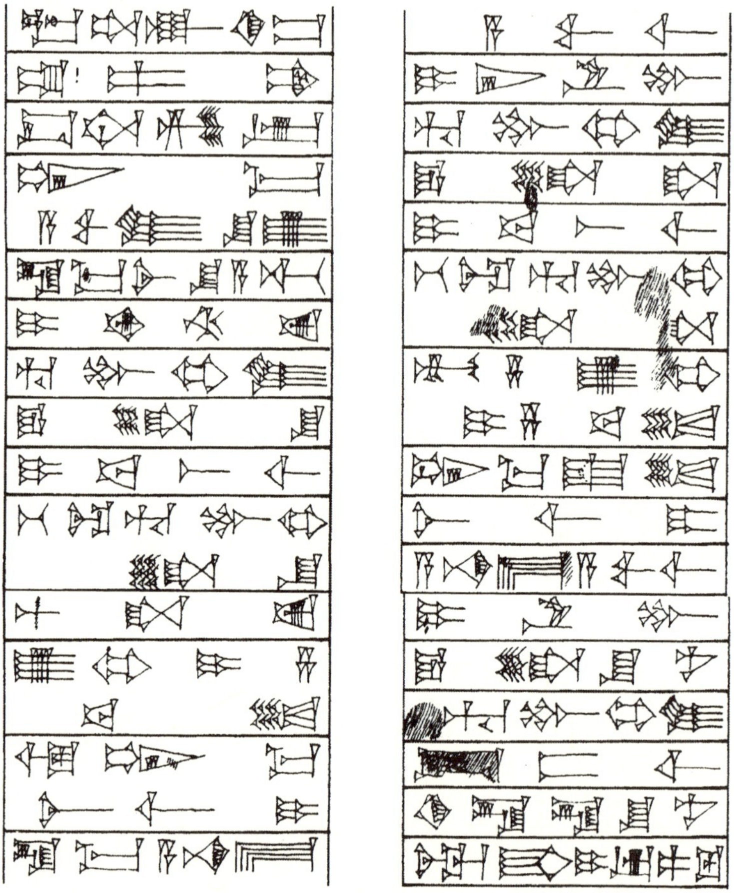

aššum ... lā ṣabātīša 'so that ... may not seize her'.
ittabši 'has come about'.
kilallān see §23.2(a), end.

G. Omens from *YOS* 10:

1. DIŠ *i-na re-eš ú-ba-nim né-ke-em-tum i-na li-ib-bi né-ke-em-tim* LÚ.KÚR-*rum qè-er-bi-iš i-ki-im-ka.* (6:3–6)
   nēkemtum 'loss; atrophied part of the exta' (cf. *ekēmum*).
   qerbiš 'in close combat(?)' (rare; cf. *qerēbum*).
2. *šum-ma a-mu-tum* KÁ É.GAL-*im mar-tam ú-ba-nam!*(NIM) *i-šu ù na-aṣ-ra-ap-ti i-mi-it-tim na-ap-la-aš-tam ik-šu-da-am ù ṣi-ib-tum a-na ka-ak-ki-im i-tu-ur na-ap-la-aš-tam iṭ-ṭú-ul i-na*

ta-ḫa-zi-im na-ak-ru-um um-ma-nam ú-ḫa-ap-pa-ra-am ti-bu-um ra-bu-um um-ma-na-am i-ka-aš-ša-da-am. (11 iii 3–12)

naṣraptum (*naṣrapti*) 'crucible; part of a sheep's liver'.
ṣibtum here, a part of the liver.
tāḫāzum 'battle' (cf. *aḫāzum*).
ḫapārum G 'surround'(?); *ḫuppurum* D = G?

3. *šum-ma mar-tum mu-*[*š*]*a a-na ki-di-im ḫa-al-ṣú ra-bi-a-na i-na a-li-šu ú-še*$_{20}$*-ṣú-ú-šu.* (31 x 34–39)
   ḫalāṣum G (*a–u*) 'to press, squeeze out'.
4. *šum-ma mar-tum ki-ma zi-ib-ba-at ḫu-mu-uṣ-ṣí-ri-im da-an-na-at na-ak-ru-um ša-al-la-ta-am ú-še*$_{20}$*-eṣ-ṣé.* (31 xi 30–36)
   zibbatum (*zibbat*) 'tail'.
   ḫumuṣṣīrum 'mouse'.
   šallatum 'plunder, booty, captives'.
5. DIŠ *iz-bu-um ul-la-nu-um-ma i-mi-ta-šu ša i-mi-ti na-as-ḫa-at a-*[*al*] *pa-ṭi-i-ka* LÚ.KÚR *i-ṣa-ba-at.* (56 i 10–11)
6. 11 i 1–2:

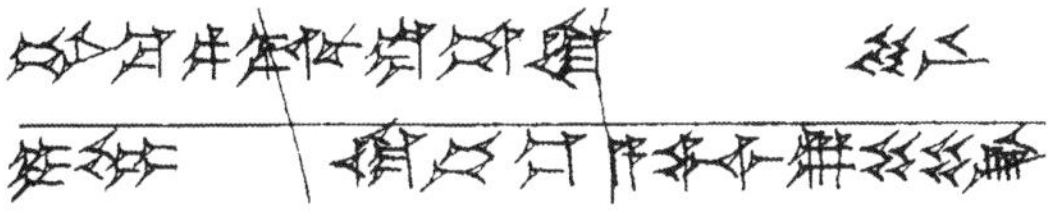

7. 11 ii 33 – iii 2:

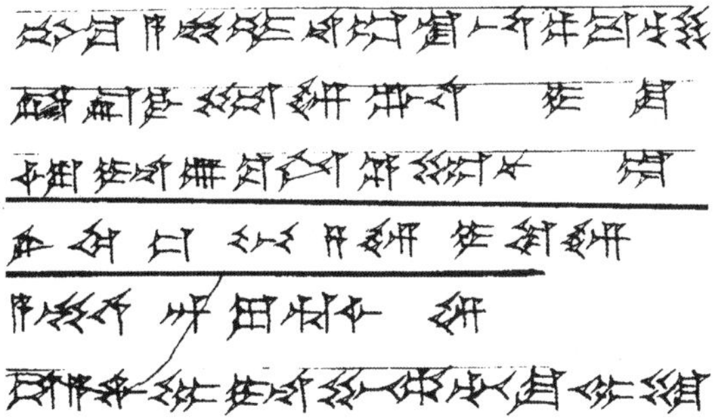

   nīdum (*nīd(i)*) 'lowering, base' (cf. *nadûm*); *nīdi kussîm* a part of the liver.
   Luḫuššum a name of Nergal, the god of pestilence and disease.
   ša here must be translated 'by which' or 'which means'.
8. 31 i 32–40:

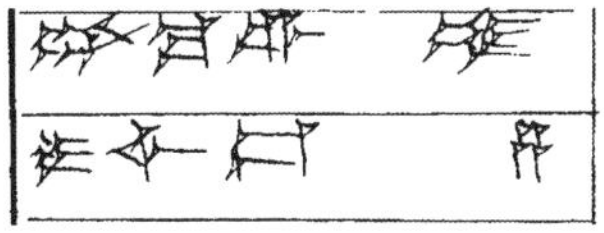

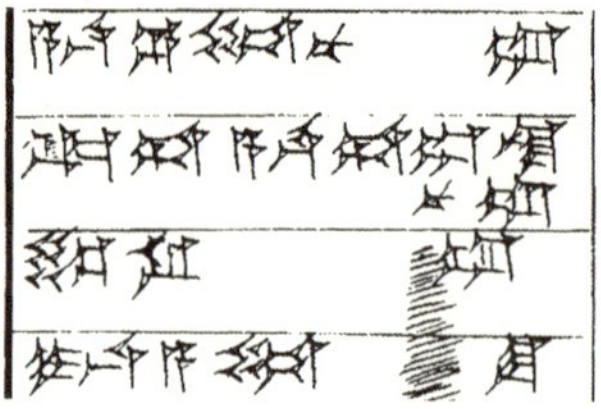

H. Contracts:

1. Loan of silver (*TIM* 7 15 = Edzard, *Tell ed-Dēr* no. 15).

^{1} 6 $^{5}/_{6}$ MA.NA 3 GÍN KUG.BABBAR ^{2} KI *a-wi-il*-DINGIR ^{3} ^{d}EN.ZU-*Illat*(ILLAT[KASKAL+KUR]) ^{4} *i-túr-ki-nu-um* ^{5} DINGIR-*šu-ba-ni* ^{6} AN-KA-*ša* ^{7} ITI *bi-bu-lum* ^{8} ŠU.BA.AN.TI.EŠ ^{9} ITI *li-is-mi-im* ^{10} *i-ša-qa-lu* ^{11} *ú-še-te-qú-ma* ^{12} 1 $^{1}/_{3}$ MA.NA KUG.BABBAR ^{13} *i-ša-qa-lu.*

PNs: *Awīl-ilim; Sîn-illat; Itūr-kīnum; Ilšu-bāni; Annum-pīša.*

^{7} *Bibbulum* month name ('flooding').

^{9} *Lismum* month name ('footrace').

2. Lease of a field (*TIM* 7 32 = Edzard, *Tell ed-Dēr* no. 32).

^{1} 6 IKU A.ŠÀ *kankallam*(KI.KAL) ^{2} *i-*[*n*]*a ta-aš-ku-un-eš*$_4$*-t*[*ár*] ^{3} *i-*[*t*]*a i-d*[*in*]-^{d}E[N.ZU] ^{4} *ù i-ta d*[*a-m*]*i-iq-ti*$^{?}$ ^{5} KI DINGIR-*šu-ba-*[*ni*] ^{6} ^{Id}UTU-*i-d*[*in-nam*] ^{7} DUMU AN-KA-*ša* ^{8} A.ŠÀ *a-na* MU.4.KAM ^{9} *ú-še-ṣí* ^{10} MU.4.KAM A.[Š]À ^{11} *i-*[*p*]*é-te-*[*ma*] *i-k*[*a-al*] ^{12} MU.[5.KAM *a-na biltim*(GUN)] *i-i*[*r-ru-ub*] ^{13} MU ⌜*x*⌝ [(broken)] $^{14–17}$ Witnesses.

PNs: *Iddin-Sîn; Damiqtī; Ilšu-bāni; Šamaš-iddinam; Annum-pīša.*

^{1} *ikûm* (*iku-*; log. IKU; Sum. lw.) a surface measurement (ca. 3600 m^2); *kankallum* (*kankal*; log. KI.KAL; Sum. lw.) 'unbroken, hard soil'; 6 IKU A.ŠÀ KI.KAL = *šeššet iku eqlam kankallam* 'a six-*iku* unplowed field'.

^{2} *Taškun-Eštar* place name.

^{12} *biltum* 'tribute; rent'; *ana biltim irrub* 'it (the field) will become liable for rent payment'.

I. Letters:

1. *TCL* 7 19 = Kraus, *AbB* 4 19.

^{1} [*a-na*] ^{d}UTU-*ḫa-zi-ir* ^{2} [*q*]*í-bí-ma* ^{3} *um-ma ḫa-am-mu-ra-pí-ma* ^{4} *aš-šum ša ta-aš-pu-ra-am um-ma at-ta-ma* ^{5} *pí-tum ša* [*b*]*i-na-a*^{ki} [*i*]*t-te-es-ke-er* ^{6} *mu-ú a-na* ^{íd}EDIN.NA [*g*]*u-um-mu-ru* ^{7} *be-lí a-na gi-mil-*^{d}AMAR.UTU ^{8}*ù im-gur-*AKŠAK^{ki} ^{9}*li-iš-pur-am-ma* ^{10}ERIN$_2$*-am ap-ši-ta-šu-nu li-iš-ku-nu-ma* ^{11}*pí-tam šu-a-ti li-da-an-ni-*[*n*] ^{12}*ù er-ṣe-et ma-tim ša qá-ti-šu-nu* ^{13} *li-še-ri-šu* ^{14} *ša ta-aš-pu-ra-am* ^{15} *a-na* *gi-mil-*^{d}AMAR.UTU ^{16} *ù im-gur-*AKŠAK^{ki} ^{17} *ú-da-an-ni-nam-ma aš-tap-ra-am* ^{18} ERIN$_2$*-am ap-ši-ta-šu-nu i-ša-ak-ka-nu-ma* ^{19} *[pí-tam š]a bi-na-a*^{ki} *ú-da-an-na-nu* ^{20} *ù er-ṣe-tam ša ma-tim* ^{21} *ša i-ša-ap-pa-ru* ^{22} *ú-še-er-re-šu.*

PNs: *Šamaš-ḫāzir; Gimil-Marduk; Imgur-Akšak.*

^{4} *ša* here is the determinative-relative without an antecedent: *aššum ša tašpuram* 'concerning what (or, that which) you wrote to me'.

^{5} *Binâ* place name; *ittesker* 'has become stopped up' (here, 'silted up').

^{6} ^{íd}EDIN.NA = *Edena* a canal.

^{10} *apšitûm (apšitā-*; Sum. lw.) 'agreed portion, number agreed upon'; here, in apposition to *ṣābum.*

^{17} *udannin* here in hendiadys with *aštapram*: 'I wrote forcefully'.

^{21} *šapārum* here 'to oversee'.

2. King, *LIH* 2 77 = Kraus, *AbB* 5 136.

^{1} *a-na* ^{d}EN.ZU*-i-din-nam* ^{2} *qí-bí-ma* ^{3} *um-ma ḫa-am-mu-ra-pí-ma* ^{4} ^{lú}*sēkirī*(A.IGI.DU$_8$.MEŠ) ^{5} *ša a-na ši-ip-ri-im e-pé-ši-im* ^{6} *es-ḫu-n[i-i]k-kum* ^{7} *mi-im-ma š[i-i]p-ra-am* ^{8} *la tu-še-ep-pe-es-sú-nu-ti* ^{9} *šu-pu-šu-um-ma li-še-pí-šu* ^{10} *ù i-na* SAG NÍG.GA ^{11} *ša* ^{lú}*mu-še-pí-ši-šu-nu* ^{12} *ú-sú-uḫ-šu-nu-ti.*

PN: *Sîn-iddinam.*

^{4} *sekērum* G (*e*) 'to close, dam up, block'; Participle *sēkirum* (log. $^{(lú)}$A.IGI.DU$_8$) 'canal worker'. At issue in lines 4–12 is who is to direct the work in question.

^{5} *ana šiprim epēšim* 'to do the work' (see §30.1).

^{10} NÍG.GA here is probably to be read *namkūrum*, a near-synonym of *makkūrum* (from the same root). The editors of the *CAD* read NÍG.GA in OB texts as *makkūrum* except in the compound SAG NÍG.GA, which is read *rēš namkūrim* 'available assets, stock', here probably 'list of available workers'.

3. *CT* 43 14 = Kraus, *AbB* 1 14.

^{1} *a-na a-wi-le-e* ^{2} *ša* ^{d}AMAR.UTU *ú-ba-al-la-ṭú-šu-nu-ti* ^{3} *qí-bí-ma* ^{4} *um-ma wakil*(UGULA) DAM.GÀR.MEŠ *ù* DI.KUD.MEŠ*-ma* ^{5} ^{d}UTU *ù* ^{d}AMAR.UTU *[d]a-ri-iš* UD*-mi* ^{6} *li-ba-al-li-ṭú-ku-nu-ti* ^{7} *aš-šum ap-lu-ut* LUKUR ^{d}UTU ^{8} *ša na-ra-am-ì-lí-šu* ^{9} *a-ḫi i-bi-*^{d}UTU ^{10} *il-qú-ú-ma* ^{11} *Dūrû*(LÚ.BÀD^{ki}.MEŠ) ^{12} *it-ti i-bi-*^{d}UTU ^{13} *i-di-nu* ^{14} *a-wa-ti-šu-nu* ^{15} *ni-mu-ur-ma* ^{16} *a-na pí-i* DUB*-pa-a-tim ša ap-lu-ti* ^{17} *[š]a i-bi-*^{d}UTU *na-šu-ú* ^{18} *di-nam a-na i-bi-*^{d}UTU *ni-ig-mu-ur* ^{19} *ù aš-šum Dūrû*(LÚ.BÀD^{ki}.MEŠ) ^{20} *a-na la a-wa-ti-šu-nu* ^{21} *i-di-nu* ^{22} *a-na pí-i* DUB*-pí ṣi-im-da-tim* ^{23} *ki-ma ša la šu-ni-a-am* ^{24} *ib-qú-ru* ^{25} *še-er-*

tam [26] *i-si-ru-šu-nu-ši-im* [27] *ù a-na la ta-ri-im-ma* [28] *la ba-qá-ri-im* [29] *ka-ni-kam nu-še-zi-ib-šu-nu-ti* [30] *ka-ni-kam šu-a-ti ši-me-a.*

PNs: *Narām-ilīšu; Ibbi-Šamaš.*

[4] *waklum* (*wakil;* log. UGULA [the PA sign]) 'overseer'.

[10] *Dūrum* (log. BÀD^{ki}) a place name; *Dūrûm* (*Dūrī-;* log. LÚ.BÀD^{ki}) 'inhabitant of Dūrum'.

[17] *ša* PN *našû* 'which PN has' (§33.2).

[20] *ana lā awātīšunu* 'concerning (what is) not their affair'.

4. Thureau-Dangin, *TCL* 7 30 = Kraus, *AbB* 4 30.

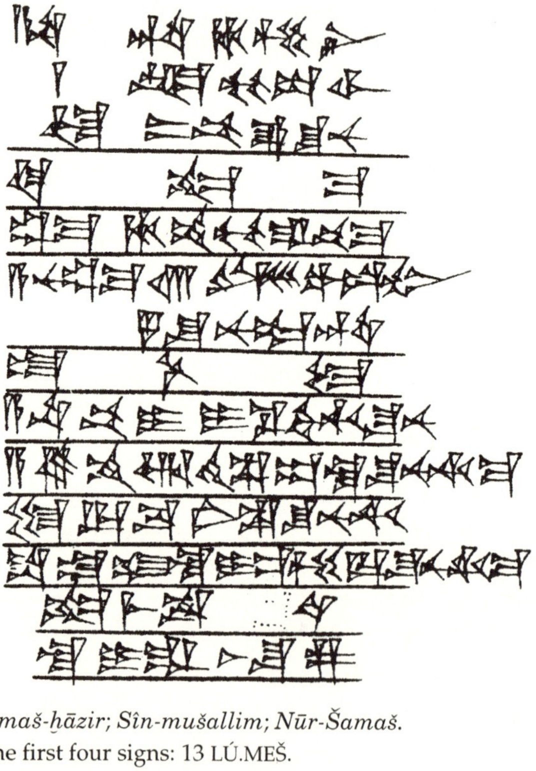

PNs: *Šamaš-ḫāzir; Sîn-mušallim; Nūr-Šamaš.*

[6] After the first four signs: 13 LÚ.MEŠ.

[12] *ezēbum* here, 'to pass (someone) by'.

LESSON TWENTY-NINE

29.1 Verbs II–Weak: the D and Š Stems

In the D and Š stems, verbs II–weak must be considered in two distinct groups:

(1) those whose middle radical was *w* or *y*;
(2) those whose middle radical was one of the five alephs (ʾ, *h*, *ḥ*, ᶜ, *ǵ*) that were lost (as noted in §6.1, *ǵ* was lost only sporadically).

(a) Verbs II–*w* and II–*y*

Verbs originally II–*w* are *a–u* (or II–*u*) in the G (e.g., *târum*, *mâtum*); those originally II–*y* are *a–i* (or II–*i*) in the G (e.g., *qiāšum*). These two types are conjugated alike in both the D and the Š stems. As is true in the sound verb, there are no special vowel-classes: the Durative is characterized by an *a*-vowel before R_3, while the Preterite, Perfect, Imperative, and Participle have an *i*-vowel and the Infinitive and Verbal Adjective have an *u*-vowel. In both stems, in any form that ends with the third radical (discounting pronominal suffixes and *-ma*), the preceding vowel is long, marked with a macron; in forms in which the third radical is followed by a vowel (including the Ventive *-am* and the subordination marker *-u*), the third radical is doubled and the preceding vowel is short (cf. the G Durative *iqīaš* ~ *iqiššū*, *itâr* ~ *iturrū*; but in the D and Š, this applies to all forms). In the paradigms below plural forms are also given, for comparison and reference; the verbs in the paradigms are *kânum* (*a–u*; i.e., II–*w*) G 'to be firm', D 'to make firm'; *mâtum* (*a–u*) G 'to die', Š 'to put to death'.

	D Stem	Š Stem
Infinitive:	*kunnum*	*šumuttum*
(Bound form:	*kunni*, suf. *kunnašu*	*šumūt*, suf. *šumuttašu*)
Durative:	*ukān*, 3mp *ukannū*	*ušmāt*, 3mp *ušmattū*
Perfect:	*uktīn*, 3mp *uktinnū*	*uštamīt*, 3mp *uštamittū*
Preterite:	*ukīn*, 3mp *ukinnū*	*ušmīt*, 3mp *ušmittū*
Imperative:	*kīn*, cp *kinnā*	*šumīt*, cp *šumittā*
Participle:	*mukinnum*	*mušmittum*
(Bound form:	*mukīn*, suf. *mukinnašu*	*mušmīt*, suf. *mušmittašu*)

Vbl. Adj.:	*kunnum*	*šumuttum*
(V. Adj.+3ms:	*kūn*, +3mp: *kunnū*	*šumūt*, +3mp: *šumuttū*)

Note that in the Š stem Durative, Preterite, and Participle, the *a*-vowel between the *š* and R_1 (*ušapras, ušapris, mušaprisum*) has been lost through syncope.

(b) Verbs II–ʾ

These are poorly attested in the D and Š stems. Verbs that are II-*a* in the G (thus, from II–ʾ$_{1-2}$) tend to be conjugated in the D with the middle ʾ as a strong consonant; contraction may take place (with the vowel then marked by a circumflex), however, especially when the vowels before and after the ʾ are the same, less frequently otherwise. These verbs are so rare in the Š that a full paradigm cannot be given.

Verbs that are II–*e* in the G (i.e., II–ʾ$_{3-4}$) are either treated like verbs II–*w*/*y*, but with *e*-vowels where the latter have *a*, or conjugated like verbs II–*a* (without *a* › *e*), as is the originally II–*g* (II–ʾ$_5$) verb *buʾʾûm* (also III–weak) D 'to look for, search' (not in G).

In addition to *buʾʾûm*, the verbs in the paradigms below are *wârum* (II–*a*) G 'to advance', D 'to send'; *rêqum* (II–*e*) G 'to be distant', D 'to keep far away'; *nêšum* (II–*e*) G 'to live', Š 'to keep alive'.

	D	Stem		Š Stem
Infinitive:	*wuʾʾurum* / *wûrum*	*buʾʾûm*	*ruqqum*	*šunuššum*
(Bound form:	*wuʾʾur* / *wûr*	*buʾʾu*	*ruqqi*	*šunūš*)
Durative:	*uwaʾʾar* / *uwâr*	*ubaʾʾa* / *ubâ*	*urēq*,	*ušnēš*
(3mp:	*uwaʾʾarū* / *uwarrū*	*ubaʾʾû*	*ureqqū*	*ušneššū*)
Perfect:	*ūtaʾʾer*	*ubtaʾʾi*	*urtīq*	?
Preterite:	*uwaʾʾer*(/ *uwêr*)	*ubaʾʾi*	*urīq*	*ušnīš*
(3mp:	*uwaʾʾerū*(/ *uwerrū*)	*ubaʾʾû*	*uriqqū*	*ušniššū*)
Imperative:	*wuʾʾer*	*buʾʾi*	*rīq*	?
Participle:	*muwaʾʾerum*	*mubaʾʾûm*	*muriqqum*	*mušniššum*
(Bound form:	*muwaʾʾer*	*mubaʾʾi*	*murīq*	*mušnīš*)
Vbl. Adj.:	*wuʾʾurum* / *wûrum*	*buʾʾûm*	*ruqqum*	?
(V.Adj.+3ms:	*wuʾʾur* / *wûr*	*buʾʾu*	*rūq*	?)

(c) D and Š stems of verbs II–weak encountered thus far:

dâkum: Š *šudukkum* 'to have (someone) killed' (rare).

kânum: D *kunnum* 'to establish as true, confirm, convict (of doing: *ina* + Infin.); to set (up), fix, establish, assign; to maintain'.

mâtum: Š *šumuttum* 'to put to death, to cause the death of'.

miādum: Š *šumuddum* 'to make much, increase, enlarge, make numerous'; in hendiadys, 'to do (something) much, a lot'.

naʾādum: D *nuʾʾudum* 'to ask to pay attention, alert, instruct'.
târum: D *turrum* 'to return (trans.), restore, give/take/send/put/ pay back; to turn (something: acc.; into something else: *ana*); to take captive in war'.
ṭiābum: D *ṭubbum* 'to make pleasant, sweet, good; to please, satisfy'; Š *šuṭubbum* = D (much less common than D).
zâzum: D *zuzzum* 'to divide, distribute' (rare).

29.2 Non-coordinating *-ma*

In verbal clauses, the enclitic particle *-ma* may occur on parts of speech other than the verb. In such instances, *-ma* is not a conjunction, but rather an emphasizing particle, marking the word to which it is attached as the logical predicate of its clause. (The predicate may be defined as the focus or new information of the clause. In a verbal clause, the true, or grammatical, predicate is the verb; when no other part of speech is emphasized, the verb is also the logical predicate; but when the focus or emphasis lies with an element other than the verb, that element is the logical predicate.) In English, a logical predicate other than the verb may be topicalized in a cleft sentence pattern (see below).

The following sentence will illustrate this predicating function of *-ma*, and the English equivalent. Given the sentence

> *šarrum mārī ina kakkīšu imḫaṣ* 'The king struck my son with his weapon',

any of the first three elements may be made the logical predicate by the addition to it of *-ma*:

> *šarrum-ma mārī ina kakkīšu imḫaṣ* 'It was the king who struck my son with his weapon';
> *šarrum mārī-ma ina kakkīšu imḫaṣ* 'It was my son whom the king struck with his weapon';
> *šarrum mārī ina kakkīšū-ma imḫaṣ* 'It was with his weapon that the king struck my son'.

In many instances, of course, translation by means of a cleft sentence is awkward. Other means may be used, but the emphatic force of the *-ma* should be indicated. Sometimes, for example, it has a limiting nuance:

> *iṣam warqam-ma šūbilam* 'Send (ms) me only green (*warqum*) wood';
> *šībum u ṣeḫrum lā innammar; eṭlam dannam-ma ṭurdam* 'Let no old man or child show up (*innammar*); send (ms) me only strong youth(s)'.

29.3 The Particle *lū*

This particle has three uses, two of which have already been encountered.

(a) To denote alternatives, with or without *ū* 'or' (§7.4(f)):

šumma awīlum lū wardam lū amtam išriq 'if a man stole either a male or a female slave';

(ū) lū bītī idnam (ū) lū bītam eššam idnam 'either give (ms) me my house or give me a new house'.

(b) To express injunctions in verbless clauses (§22.2):

abūšu lū atta 'be (ms) his father';

lū awīlāta 'be (ms) a man';

Adad lū bēl dīnīka 'may Adad be your adversary (*bēl dīnim*)'.

The negative of *lū* in such cases is *lā*.

(c) As an asseverative particle, meaning 'indeed, certainly, verily'. In expressions of oaths (§36.3), *lū* occurs in this usage before all tenses. Apart from oaths, *lū* in asseverative use normally appears only before the Preterite, and with rare exception only in royal inscriptions (§30.3), as in

lū ēpuš 'I verily built'.

29.4 Old Babylonian Letters from Mari

The site of Mari, situated on the Euphrates River about 250 miles upstream from Babylon, and thus well outside ancient Mesopotamia proper, was the seat of an important Amorite kingdom during the late nineteenth and early eighteenth centuries BCE. It was destroyed by Hammurapi in 1761 BCE. The French excavators at Mari (modern Tell Hariri in southeastern Syria) under the direction of A. Parrot and his successors, have, since the 1930's, unearthed over 20,000 OB tablets, of which some 5,000 are letters. The letters are for the most part written in style and grammar very close to those of contemporary Mesopotamian letters. There are, however, a few important differences to be noted.

(a) A few of the signs used at Mari are rare or unknown in Mesopotamian Texts: e.g., QA, used more often than GA for /qa/.

(b) The normally uncontracted vowel sequences *ia, iā, ea,* and *eā* all contract in the Mari dialect to *ê*: e.g.,

iqbêm 'he said to me';

išpurannêšim 'he sent to us'.

(c) There are occasional instances of non-Akkadian meanings of words and uses of forms, which reflect the underlying Northwest Semitic speech of the natives of Mari. These will be indicated with the glosses in the readings.

Mari texts are published in two companion series of volumes, *Archives Royales de Mari* (abbreviated *ARM*) for the cuneiform copies and *Archives Royales de Mari, transcrites et traduites* (abbreviated *ARMT*) for the transliterations and translations; some twenty-five volumes of these have appeared to date.

EXERCISES

A. VOCABULARY 29.

Verbs:

bârum G (*a–u*) 'to be firm, in good repair; to become proved' (rare in OB apart from PNs); *burrum* D 'to establish, ascertain (the true legal situation), prove, certify, explain, indicate'.

kullum D (root *k–w–l*; not in G) 'to hold, contain, have, maintain'; *rēšam kullum* 'to wait for, take care of, be ready for, at the disposal of' (e.g., *ṭuppaka rēšī likīl* 'let your (ms) tablet be ready for me, at my disposal'; *rēš awâtīša kīl* 'take (ms) care of her affairs'; note also, frequent in letters, DN *rēška ana damiqtim likīl* and DN *rēš damiqtīka likīl* 'may DN treat you (the addressee) well, provide you with good things'); Participle *mukillum* in *mukīl bābim* 'doorkeeper, guard', *mukīl rēšim* 'attendant, spirit; a feature on the exta'.

raḫāṣum G (*i*) 'to flood (trans.), inundate'.

riāqum G (*a–i*) 'to be empty, idle'; Verbal Adj. *rīqum* (*rīq-*) 'empty; idle'; *ruqqum* D and *šuruqqum* Š 'to empty; to leave idle'; note also *rīqūtum* (*rīqūt*) 'emptiness; idleness'; *rīqūt-* (with suf., e.g., *rīqūssu*; adv. acc., see §18.3(d)) 'empty-handed'.

šuklulum Š (not in G) 'to complete, finish, accomplish, bring to an end'.

warāqum G (*i*) 'to become yellow, green; to turn pale'; Verbal Adj. *warqum* (*waruq-*) 'yellow, green; fresh (of plants)'; *(w)urruqum* D factitive.

wârum G (root originally *w*–ʾ–*r* [see D], but G Dur. **iwīar*/*iwâr*, pl. *iwirrū*; Pret. *iwīr* [see §21.3(f)]) 'to advance against, attack'; *wuʾʾurum* D 'to send (a person, message); to command, order (to do: acc. Infin. or *ana*/*aššum* + Infin.)' (cf. *têrtum*).

Nouns:

bārûm (base *bāri-*; log. (lú)MÁŠ.ŠU.GÍD.GÍD [gíd = the BU sign]) 'diviner, haruspex'.
biltum (*bilat*; pl. *bilātum*; log. GUN/GÚ.UN) 'load, weight; tribute, rent'; *nāš(i) biltim* 'tenant (of a field owned by the state)' (cf. *babālum*).
emum (with suf. *emū*/*ī*/*ā*-, like *abum* and *aḫum*) 'father-in-law (wife's father)'; *bīt emim* (rare) 'wedding'.
itinnum (log. ŠITIM; Sum. lw.?) 'house builder'.
qištum (*qišti*; pl. *qišātum*; log. GIŠ.TIR) 'forest, grove'.

Adjective:

warkûm (*warkī-*; fem. *warkītum*) 'later, future' (cf. *warki*).

Adverbs:

magal 'very (much), greatly, exceedingly'.
warka (also *ina warka*) 'afterwards; behind, in the rear'.

B. Learn the following signs:

OB Lapid.	OB Cursive	NA	values
		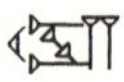	ŠITIM = *itinnum*
			GÚ = *kišādum*;
		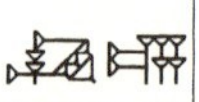	GUN (or GÚ.UN) = *biltum*
	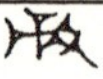		MÁŠ in MÁŠ.ŠU.GÍD.GÍD = *bārûm*

C. Write the following words in cuneiform and in transliteration; use logograms where possible:

1. *ḫamiš bilat kaspum*
2. *adi ḫarrān Anim*
3. *bārûm ana šīmtim illik*
4. *abnāt qištim*
5. *kallat itinnim*
6. *ul ibqur*
7. *ṣēnū bārîm*
8. *uterrū*
9. *ušmāt*

D. Write in normalized Akkadian:

1. Return (ms) it (ms) to me.
2. It (f) is fixed.
3. They (m) will put you (ms) to death.
4. the house that you (ms) are holding
5. She has had his father-in-law executed.
6. They (f) have returned the son.
7. It has turned pale.
8. one (ms) who returns truth
9. Do not (ms) increase (the number of) your fortresses.
10. Verily I accomplished it (f).
11. I instructed him.
12. My words pleased her heart greatly.
13. They (m) will prove it (m).
14. Why do you (pl) leave my oxen idle?
15. I ordered the going of the troop.

E. Normalize and translate:

1. *ki-ma ra-bi-a-num ú-wa-e-ra-an-ni* ^{giš}MÁ *ša* MÁŠ.ŠU.GÍD.GÍD *uš-ri-iq-ma* GUN-*sà a-na ṣe-ri-šu ú-ša-bi-il.*
2. *am-mi-nim aš-šum* SAG.ÌR *šu-a-ti a-wa-a-tim tu-uš-mi-da-am-ma ta-aš-pur-ra-am.*
3. *aš-šum* 10 ŠE.GUR *ša be-lí i-na* URU *ša-a-ti ú-ki-in-nam uz-na-ia ki-ma* ^{d}AMAR.UTU *a-na be-lí-ia ka-ta i-ba-aš-ši-a be-lí li-iq-bi-a-am e-ma be-lí* 10 ŠE.GUR *ú-ki-in-nu a-ša-ap-pa-ak-šu.*
4. *i-na* ŠÁM *an-ni-im li-ib-ba-šu ṭú-ub.*
5. *i-na* ^{giš}TUKUL *ša* DINGIR ŠE *ma-la i-na* A.ŠÀ ŠITIM *li-bi-ir-ru-ma* ŠITIM *mi-ši-il-šu li-il-qé.*
6. *šum-ma i-na re-eš mar-tim* ^{giš}TUKUL *ša-ki-in* ^{d}IŠKUR *um-ma-an-ka i-na ḫa-ra-nim i-ra-ḫi-iṣ.*
7. 1 ^{giš}*na-ar-kab-tam šu-uk-lu-ul-tam a-na e-mi-ia uš-ta-bi-il.*

F. CH:

§§27–29§27 *šum-ma lu* AGA.ÚS *ù lu* ŠU.ḪA *ša i-na dan-na-at šar-ri-im tu-úr-*⌜*ru*⌝ *wa-ar-[k]i-šu* A.ŠÀ-*šu ù* ^{giš}KIRI$_6$-*šu a-na ša-ni-im id-di-nu-ma i-li-ik-šu it-ta-la-ak šum-ma i[t]-tu-ra-am-ma* URU-*šu ik-ta-áš-dam* A.ŠÀ-*šu ù* ^{giš}KIRI$_6$-*šu ú-ta-ar-ru-šum-ma šu-ma i-li-ik-šu i-il-la-ak.* §28 *šum-ma lu* AGA.ÚS *ù lu-ú* ŠU.ḪA *ša i-na dan-na-at šar-ri-im tu-ú[r]-ru* DUMU-*šu il-kam a-la-kam i-le-i* A.ŠÀ *ù* ^{giš}KIRI$_6$ *in-na-ad-di-iš-šum-ma i-li-i[k a]-bi-šu i-il-[la-a]k.* §29 *šum-ma* DUMU-*šu ṣe-ḫe-er-[m]a i-li-ik a-bi-šu a-la-kam la i-le-i ša-lu-*

uš-ti A.ŠÀ *ù* ^{giš}KIRI$_6$ *a-na um-mi-šu in-na-a*[*d*]*-di-in-ma um-ma-šu ú-ra-ab-ba-šu.*

dannatum here, 'military service'.

innaddin 'it will be given'.

§§30–31 §30 *šum-ma lu* AGA.ÚS *ù lu* ŠU.ḪA A.ŠÀ-*šu* ^{giš}KIRI$_6$-*šu ù* É-*sú i-na pa-ni il-ki-im id-di-ma ud-da-ap-pí-ir ša-nu-um wa-ar-ki-šu* A.ŠÀ-*šu* ^{giš}KIRI$_6$-*šu ù* É-*sú iṣ-ba-at-ma* MU.3.KAM *i-li-ik-šu it-ta-la-ak šum-ma it-tu-ra-am-ma* A.ŠÀ-*šu* ^{giš}KIRI$_6$-*šu ù* É-*sú i-ir-ri-iš ú-ul in-na-ad-di-iš-šum ša iṣ-ṣa-ab-tu-ma i-li-ik-šu it-ta-al-ku šu-ma i-il-la-ak.* §31 *šum-ma ša-at-tam iš-ti-a-at-ma ud-da-ap-pí-ir-ma it-tu-ra-am* A.ŠÀ-*šu* ^{giš}KIRI$_6$-*šu ù* É-*sú in-na-ad-di-iš-šum-ma šu-ma i-li-ik-šu i-il-la-ak.*

duppurum D (not in G) 'to go away, absent oneself'.

innaddiššum 'it will be given to him'.

§44 *šum-ma a-wi-lum* A.ŠÀ *kankallim*(KI.KAL) *a-na* MU.3.KAM *a-na te-ep-ti-tim ú-še-ṣi-ma a-aḫ-šu id-di-ma* A.ŠÀ *la ip-te-te i-na re-bu-tim ša-at-tim* A.ŠÀ *ma-a-a-ri i-ma-aḫ-ḫa-aṣ i-mar-ra-ar ù i-ša-ak-ka-ak-ma a-na be-el* A.ŠÀ *ú-ta-ar ù ana būrim*(BÙR^{iku}.E) 10 ŠE. GUR *i-ma-a*[*d-d*]*a-ad.*

kankallum (*kankal;* log. KI.KAL; Sum. lw.) 'hard soil'.

teptītum (*teptīt*) 'opening; cultivation' (cf. *petûm*).

mayyarum (*mayyar*) 'plow'; *eqlam mayyarī maḫāṣum* 'to plow'.

marārum G (*a–u*) 'to hoe, break up soil'.

šakākum G (*a–u*) 'to harrow'.

būrum (*būri;* log. BÙR; Sum. lw.) a surface measure (ca. 6.48 ha.).

§45 *šum-ma a-wi-lum* A.ŠÀ-*šu a-na* GUN *a-na er-re-ši-im id-di-in-ma ù* GUN A.ŠÀ-*šu im-ta-ḫa-ar wa-ar-ka* A.ŠÀ ^{d}IŠKUR *ir-ta-ḫi-iṣ ù lu bi-ib-bu-lum it-ba-al bi-ti-iq-tum ša er-re-ši-im-ma.*

bibbulum / bubbulum 'flood' (cf. *wabālum*).

bitiqtum (*bitiqti*) 'loss' (cf. *batāqum*).

§R/75e *šum-ma a-wi-lum* ŠE-*am ù* KUG.BABBAR-*am it-ti* DAM.G[ÀR *i*]*l-qé-e-ma* ŠE-*am ù* KUG.BABBAR-*am a-na tu-ur-ri-im la i-šu*«*-ú*» *bi-ša-am-ma i-šu mi-im-ma ša i-na qá-ti-šu i-ba-aš-šu-ú ma-ḫar ši-bi ki-ma ub-ba-lu a-na* DAM.GÀR-*šu i-na-ad-di-in* DAM. GÀR *ú-ul ú-pa-as i-ma-ḫa-ar.*

epēsum G 'to object'; *uppusum* D = G (both rare).

§153 *šum-ma aš-ša-at a-wi-lim aš-šum zi-ka-ri-im ša-ni-im mu-sà uš-di-ik* MUNUS *šu-a-ti i-na ga-ši-ši-im i-ša-ak-ka-nu-ši.*

gašīšum (*gašīš*) 'impaling stake'.

§§224–225 §224 *šum-ma* A.ZU GUD *ù lu* ANŠE *lu* GUD *ù lu* ANŠE *si*$_{20}$*-im-ma-am kab-tam i-pu-uš-ma ub-ta-al-li-iṭ be-el* GUD *ù lu* ANŠE IGI.6.GÁL KUG.BABBAR *a-na* A.ZU Á-*šu i-na-ad-di-in.* §225 *šum-ma* GUD *ù lu* ANŠE *sí-im-ma-am kab-tam i-pu-uš-ma uš-ta-mi-it* IGI.4(? 5?).GÁL ŠÁM-*šu a-na be-el* GUD *ù lu* ANŠE *i-na-ad-di-in.*

§§228–229 §228 *šum-ma* ŠITIM É *a-na a-wi-lim i-pu-uš-ma ú-ša-ak-li-il-šum a-na* 1 *mūšar*(SAR) É 2 GÍN KUG.BABBAR *a-na qí-iš-ti-šu i-na-ad-di-iš-šum.* §229 *šum-ma* ŠITIM *a-na a-wi-lim* É *i-pu-uš-ma ši-pí-ir-šu la ú-dan-ni-in-ma* É *i-pu-šu im-qú!*(LU)*-ut-ma be-el* É *uš-ta-mi-it* ŠITIM *šu-ú id-da-ak.*

mūšarum (log. SAR) a surface measure (ca. 36 m.^{2}).

§§245 *šum-ma a-wi-lum* GUD *i-gur-ma i-na me-gu-tim ù lu i-na ma-ḫa-ṣí-im uš-ta-mi-it* GUD *ki-ma* GUD *a-na be-el* GUD *i-ri-a-ab.*

mēgûtum 'negligence' (cf. *egûm*).

§§162–163:

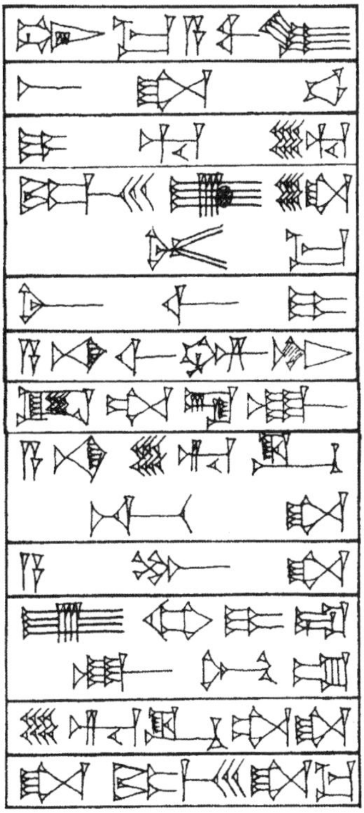

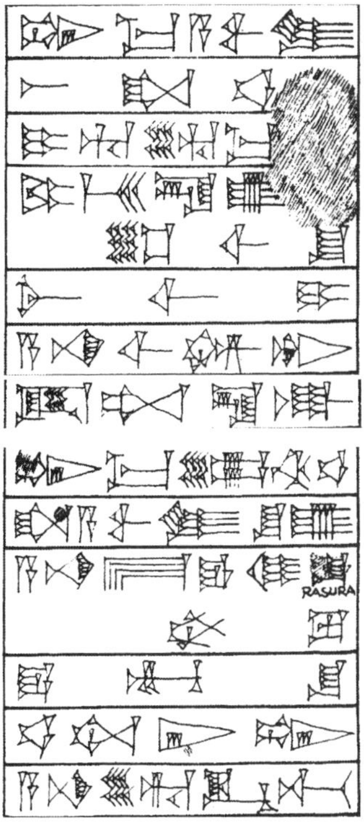

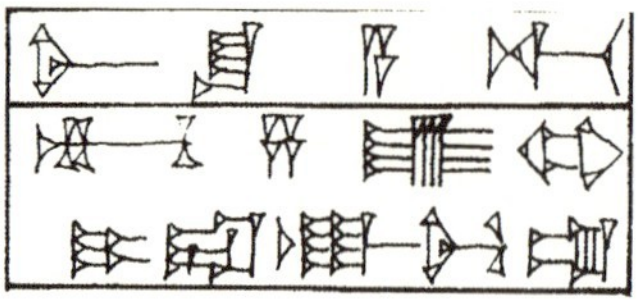
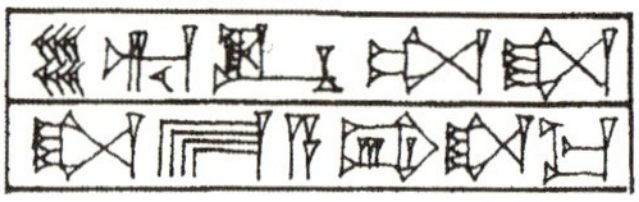

§§173–174 (cf. §§170–171, in Lesson 26):

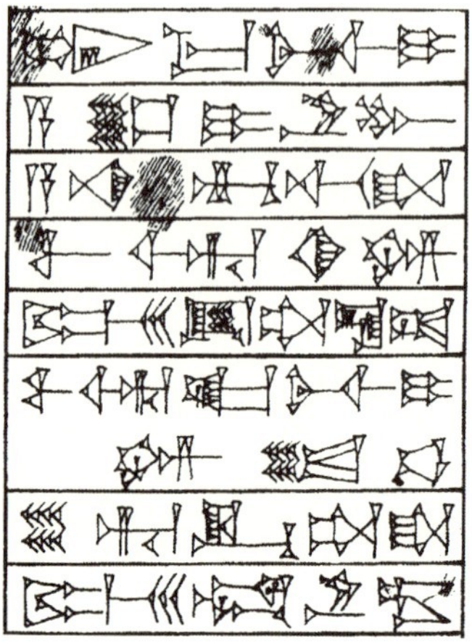
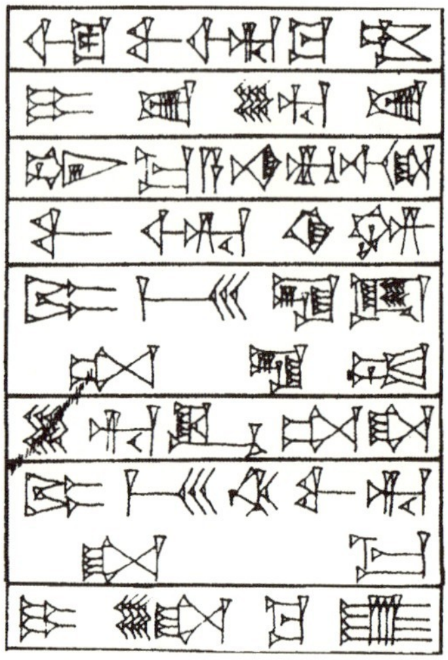

G. Omens from *YOS* 10:

1. [DIŠ *i-na* KÁ É].GAL *ù re-eš mar-tim qú-ú-um ṣa-bi-it ra-ki-ib i-me-ri* LÚ.KÚR *ú-ta-ar*. (25:25)
   qûm (base *qā-*) 'thread, filament'.
2. DIŠ [giš]TUKUL *i-mi-tim ki-ma sí-ik-ka-tim iz-zi-iz ka-ab-tum ša li-ib-bi be-li-šu-ú ú-ṭa-ab-bu ib-ba-aš-ši*. (46 iv 30–31)
   sikkatum (*sikkat*; pl. *sikkātum*) 'peg'.
   izziz 'it stands' (§37.2).
   ibbašši 'will appear' (§31.2(4)).
3. 31 v 13–17:

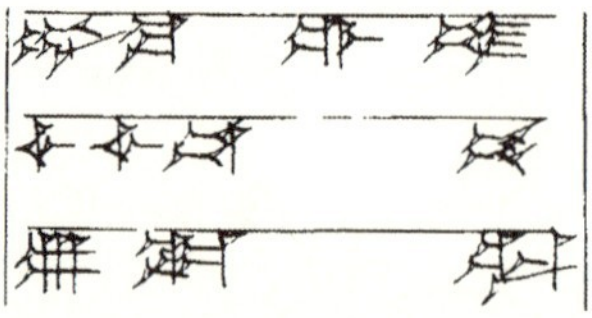
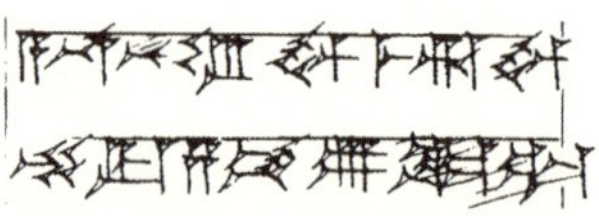

šišītum 'membrane'; *murṣum* 'disease, illness' (cf. *marāṣum*).

4. 51 ii 27–28:

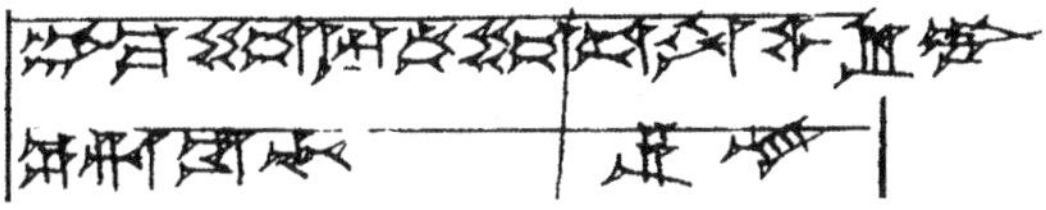

erištum (*erisšti*) 'desire, wish, request' (cf. *erēšum*).

H. Contracts:

1. Bequest to an adopted daughter (*CT* 8 5a = Schorr, *VAB* 5, no. 18).

^{1} *x* A.ŠÀ ... ^{2} *i-ta* PN ^{3} *ù i-ta* PN$_2$ ... ^{7} *y* É *i-na* GÁ.GI.A^{ki} ^{8} Á É PN$_3$ ^{9} 1 SAG.GEME$_2$ PN$_4$ ^{10} *bu-šu-ša wa-ar-ka-sà* ^{11} *iš-tu pé-e a-di* KUG.SIG$_{17}$-*ma*$^{?}$ *ša* ^{12} ^{I}*mu-na-wi-ir-tum* LUKUR ^{d}UTU DUMU.MUNUS ^{d}NANNA-MA.AN.SUM ^{13} *a-na ipqu*(SIG)-*ì-lí-ša* DUMU.MUNUS PN$_6$ ^{14} *ma-ri-ša id-di-nu* ^{15} *a-di mu-na-wi-ir-*[*tum*] *ba-al-ṭ*[*à-at*] ^{16} A.‹ŠÀ› É GEME$_2$ *qá-sà-ma ú-ka-*[*al*] ^{17} [*iš*]-*tu i-lu-ša iq-te-ru-*[*ši*] ^{18} *ša* [*ipqu*(SIG)-*ì-lí-šá*]-*ma*. $^{19–34}$ Witnesses. $^{35–36}$ Date.

PNs: *Munawwirtum; Nanna-mansum; Ipqu-ilīša.*

^{11} *pûm* b 'chaff'; *ištu pê adi ḫurāṣim* 'from chaff to gold', i.e., 'everything'. At the end of line 11 *ša* introduces the predicate: 'field ... house ... slave (lines 1–11) (are) what (*ša*) M. ... gave (line 14)'.

^{14} Note *mārum* here refering to the woman Ipqu-ilīša, thus, 'child'.

^{17} *qerûm* (*e*) 'to summon, invite'; the phrase in this line is a euphemism for dying.

2. Loan of barley (Szlechter, *TJA* 20–21 UMM H42).

^{1} 1 ŠE.GUR ^{2} [KI] *be-le-tum* ^{3} DUMU.MUNUS ^{d}*za-ba$_4$-ba$_4$-na-ṣi-ir* ^{4} ^{I}*pa-as-sà-lum* ^{5} ŠU.BA.AN.TI ^{6} *ana ūm ebūrim* (UD-*um* BURU$_{14}$.ŠÈ) ^{7} [*a*]-*na* É.Ì.DUB ^{8} [*il-q*]*ú-ú* ŠE-*am ú-ta-a-ar* $^{9-10}$ Witnesses. $^{11–13}$ Date.

PNs: *Bēletum; Zababa-nāṣir; Passalum.*

$^{7–8}$ *našpak ilqû* 'the granary he borrowed (from)'.

I. Letters:

1. King, *LIH* 2 72 = Frankena, *AbB* 2 56.

^{1} *a-na* ^{d}EN.ZU-[*i-din-na*]*m* ^{2}*qí-bí-*[*m*]*a* ^{3}*um-ma ḫa-am-mu-ra-pí-ma* ^{4} *kušabkī*(^{giš}AB.BA.ḪI.A) *a-na ši-ki-ir ma-aq-qá-ri* ^{5} *a-na qá-at qurqurrī*(TIBIRA.MEŠ) ^{6} *i-na* BÀD-TIBIRA^{ki} ^{7} *ù e-ma i-ba-aš-šu-ú* ^{8} *li-mu-ru-ni-ik-kum-ma* ^{9} 7200 *kušabkī*(^{giš}AB.BA.ḪI.A) *ši-ḫu-tim* ... ^{12} *li-ik-ki-su-ni-ik-kum-ma* ... ^{14} *i-na* MÁ.Ì.DUB *i-ta-ad-d*[*i-a-am-ma* ... ^{16}*a-na* KÁ.DINGI[R.RA^{ki}] ^{17}*li-ib-lu-nim* ^{18}*i-na kušabkī*(^{giš}AB.BA.ḪI.A) ^{19} *ša i-na-ak-ki-su* ^{20} GIŠ *ša i-na* GIŠ.TIR-*šu mi-tu* ^{21} *la i-na-ak-ki-su*

^{22} GIŠ *wa-ar-qá-am-ma li-ik-ki-su* ^{23} *ar-ḫi-iš kušabkī*(^{giš}AB.BA. ḪI.A) *šu-nu-ti* ^{24} *li-ib-lu-nim-ma* ^{25} *qurqurrū*(TIBIRA.MEŠ) *la i-ri-iq-qú.*

^{4} *kušabkum* (log. (A.)AB.BA) a thorn tree; *šikrum* (*šikir*) 'handle'; *maqqarum* (*maqqar*) 'chisel'; for the construction, see §12.4.

^{5} *qurqurrum* (log. TIBIRA) 'wood- or metal-worker'.

^{6} *Bad-tibira* (Tell Madāʾin) a city in the south, near Uruk.

^{9} *šīḫum* (Verbal Adj. of *šiāḫum* 'to grow') 'tall, high, full-grown'.

^{14} *itaddi* (Gtn imperative, ms, of *nadûm*; §34.1) 'put (them)'.

2. *VAS* 7 202 = Ungnad, *Babylonische Briefe* no. 259, lines 1–19.

^{1} *a-na a-wi-lim* ^{2} *qí-bí-ma* ^{3} *um-ma ib-ni-*^{d}*Amurrum*(MAR.TU)-*ma* ^{4} ^{d}UTU *ù* ^{d}AMAR.UTU *da-ri-iš* UD-*mi* ^{5} *li-ba-al-li-ṭú-ka* ^{6} *lu ša-al-ma-ta lu ba-al-ṭa-ta* ^{7} DINGIR *na-ṣi-ir-ka re-eš-ka a-na da-mi-iq-tim* ^{8} *li-ki-il* ^{9} *a-na šu-ul-mi-ka aš-pu-ra-am* ^{10} *šu-lum-ka ma-ḫar* ^{d}UTU *ù* ^{d}AMAR.UTU ^{11} *lu da-ri* ^{12} ^{I}*qí-iš-*^{d}*Amurrim*(MAR.TU) DUMU-*ka* ^{13} *ki-a-am iš-pu-ra-am um-ma šu-ú-ma* ^{14} É.Ì.DUB *i-na né-re-eb* KÁ *i-din-eš*$_4$*-tár* ^{15} *pa-ti-iḫ-ma* ŠE-*ú-um le-qí* ^{16} SAG.GEME$_2$ *ú-us-sí-ir-ma* ^{17} *um-ma* SAG.GEME$_2$-*ma* ^{18} *x* ŠE *ši-ni-šu* ^{19} ... *il-qé.*

PNs: *Ibni-Amurrum; Qīš-Amurrim; Iddin-Eštar.*

^{14} *nērebum* (*nēreb*) 'entrance; mountain pass' (cf. *erēbum*); *patāḫum* G (*a–u*) 'to break through, break into'.

3. *ARM* 10 90.

^{1} *a-na be-lí-[ia]* ^{2} *qí-bí-[m]a* ^{3} *um-ma* ^{f}*ad-ra-ka-*⌜*tum*⌝ ^{4} GEME$_2$-*ka-a-ma aš-šum* KUG.BABBAR ^{5} *ša i-din-*^{d}EN.ZU *ir-gu-ma-am-ma* ^{6} *be-lí di-nam ú-ša-ḫi-zu-né-ti* ^{7} *ak-šu-dam-ma* LÚ.MEŠ *mu-du-ú* ^{8} *a-wa-tim ša i-na re-eš mu-ut-bi-si-*⌜*ir*⌝ ^{9} *iz-zi-zu ú-ul wa-aš-bu* ^{10} *it-ti su-mu-ṭa-bi* ^{11} *il*$_5$*-li-ku ù a-di-ni a-wa-tam* ^{12} *ú-ul ás-ni-iq* ^{13} *i-na-an-na be-lí* ^{14} *aš-šum* KUG.BABBAR *ša-a-tu* ^{15} *iš-pu-ra-am-m[a]* ^{16} *a-na na-aš-pa-ar-ti be-lí-ia* ^{17} *ap-la-aḫ-ma* 6 GÍN KUG.BABBAR ^{18} *ki-iš*$_7$(AB)-*da-at* DUMU.MEŠ-*ia ša it-ti-ia* ^{19} *wa-aš-bu aš-qú-ul* ⌜*ša*⌝-*pí-il*$_5$*-tum* ^{20} 4 GÍN KUG.BABBAR *li-li-kam-ma* ^{21} *it-ti* DUMU.MEŠ *mu-ut-bi-si-ir li-ìs*(AB)-*ni-iq* ^{22} *ša-ni-tam aš-šum* É-*ia e-li-ia-a* ^{23} ^{I}*i-din-an-nu qa-qa-dam ir-ši-ma* ^{24} *ù i-na* É-*ia ú-še-ṣú-ni-ne-ma* ^{25} *ša-a-tu ú-še-ri-bu-šu* ^{26} ⌜*šum*⌝-*ma li-ib-bi be-lí-ia li-ib-bi* ^{27} *a-na ma-ra-ṣí-im be-lí la i-na-di-in* ^{28} É-*ti li-te-er-ru-nim* ^{29} *ù šum-ma a-bi ù um-mì* ^{30} A.ŠÀ *ù* $^{giš.ki}$KIRI$_6$ *ú-ul in-ḫi-lu-ni-in-ni* ^{32} *it-ti be-lí-ia-ma* ^{33} ⌜*e*⌝-*ri-iš be-lí li-ša-ḫi-iz-ma* ^{35} A.ŠÀ *ù* $^{giš.ki}$KIRI$_6$ ^{36} *li-wa-aš-ši-ru-nim* ^{37} *be-lí* ⌜*x x x*⌝ (rest of this line, the last, illegible).

PNs: *Adrakatum; Iddin-Sîn; Mut-bisir; Sumu-ṭābu(m); Iddin-Annu.*

$^{8–9}$ *ina rēš* PN *izzizzū* 'they are in the service of PN'.

12 *sanāqum* in this text means 'to investigate, go into (a matter)'.

16 *našpartum* (*našparti*) 'letter, message, instructions' (cf. *šapārum*).

18 *kišittum* (*kišitti*; pl. *kišdātum*) 'conquest; boot; seizure'; pl. 'assets, acquisition' (cf. *kašādum*).

19–20 *šapiltum* (*šapilti*) 'remainder, amount outstanding'; *šapiltum x kaspum* here is a complete verbless clause; *lillikam-ma* at the end of line 20 begins a new clause, with Iddin-Sîn as subject.

22–23 *eli X qaqqadam rašûm* unclear, 'to get the better of X'?; the reason for the extra vowel sign in *e-li-ia-a* is uncertain.

24 In *ú-še-ṣú-ni-ne-ma*, *-ni-ne* is for expected *-ninni*.

26 *šumma libbi X* 'if X is willing, if it pleases X'.

29 *u šumma* in Mari texts may mean 'even if, although'; note the following *ul* for expected *lā* (after *šumma*), an error found occasionally in Mari letters.

30 $^{giš.ki}$KIRI$_6$ an unusual writing of *kirûm.naḫālum* (*i*; a rare verb, found only in Mari texts, probably a Northwest Semitic word; note the unusual lack of assimilation in *inḫilū*) 'to hand over (property)'.

34 *šūḫuzum* here, 'to instruct'.

4. Dossin, *ARM* 10 80:1–24 (text republished by Durand as *ARM* 26/1 197).

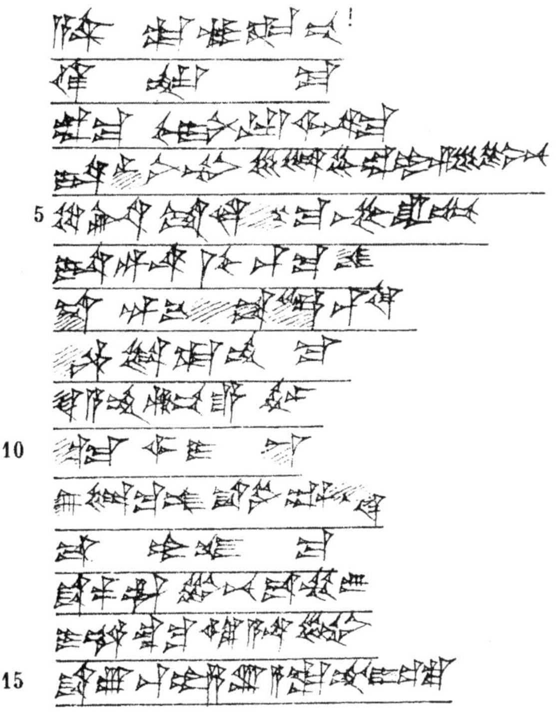

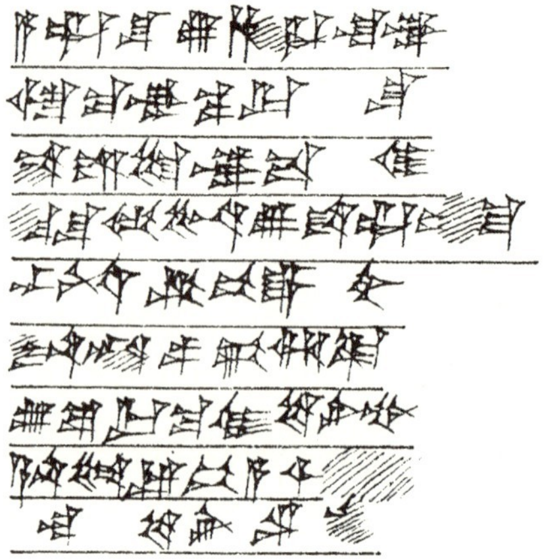

PNs: *Kakkabī; Inibšina; Šēlebum.*

4 Third sign: *pa. ina pānītim* 'previously'. *assinnnum* a member of the cult personnel (usually of Ištar).

5 Sixth sign: *nam.*

6 *qammatum* a very rare word, referring to a woman associated with the cult who wore a certain type of hair style.

7 *ša* ^{d}*d*[*a-gan*] *ša ter-qa*^{ki}. *Dagan* god of grain, an important deity in the Mari region; *Terqa* (modern Tell ᶜAšāra) a city on the Euphrates above Mari.

8 First sign: *il.*

10 First sign: *um*; last sign: *ma.*

11 *salīmātum* (always pl.) 'ally; alliance, partnership'. After LÚ, read *èš*(AB)-⸢*nun*⸣-*n*[*a*]^{ki}. *Ešnunna* (modern Tell Asmar), an important city east of the Tigris.

12 *dāṣtum* 'deception'.

13 *šapal* Preposition 'under, beneath' (cf. *šaplûm*). IN.NU.DA = *tibnum* (*tibin*) 'straw'.

14 *šētum* 'net'.

15 *qaṣārum* = *kaṣārum* (Northwest Semitic influence, preserving the original *q* of the root, which dissimilated to *k* in Akkadian); *kamāsum* G (*i*) 'to gather, collect'.

18 *aqdamū* (pl.) a rare word, presumably Northwest Semitic, meaning something like 'ancient times'.

19 First sign: *la.* Note that *šulput* lacks the expected subordination marker. Last two signs: *p*[*a-a*]*t.*

23 At the end, after *a-lim*, restore $^{[ki]}$.

24 Last sign: *ub.*

LESSON THIRTY

30.1 The Syntax of the Infinitive

(a) Introduction

The Infinitive is a verbal noun, always masculine singular, that corresponds in English not only to the infinitive, but also to the gerund, as in

kašādum '(to) arrive, (the) arriving'.

Moreover, English usage often requires that the Akkadian Infinitive be rendered by other de-verbal nouns, such as 'arrival' for *kašādum* or 'life' for *balāṭum*. Such renderings must be decided on the basis of the surrounding context in each example.

The Infinitive behaves both nominally (i.e., as a noun) and verbally. As a noun, it has the properties of all other nouns in the language, viz., it may

(1) occur in any case, nominative, accusative, or genitive (the latter after a preposition or after a bound form or *ša*); see below under (b) – (e); note that plural forms of infinitives do not occur;

(2) take the adverbial endings *-iš* and *-um*; see under (f);

(3) occur in the bound form before a genitive noun or pronoun; see under (g);

(4) be modified by an adjective (masc. sg.); this is not common, except for the demonstrative adjective *annûm*, as in

epēšum annûm 'this action' (lit., 'this doing');

(5) be modified by *ša* plus a genitive noun or by *ša* plus a relative clause; neither of these constructions is very common, but note the following examples:

ša plus genitive noun: *kaspam ša maḫārim ša aḫīya šūbilā* 'send (pl) the silver that my brother is to receive' (lit., 'the silver of the receiving of my brother'; for *ša* before the Infinitive see below under (e));

ša plus a relative clause: *epēšum ša tēpušu ul damiq* 'the action that you (ms) took is not appropriate' (lit., 'the doing that you did...').

Since the Infinitive is also verbal, it may have a subject or object (or both), either of which may be a noun or a pronoun. The Infinitive is also verbal in that it may govern adverbs and prepositional phrases. The constructions of the Infinitive with subject, object, and adverbial complements are discussed below under (g) and (h).

Although it is part of the verbal paradigm, the Infinitive, as just noted, is formally a noun, and so it does not express any tense, or take the Ventive or the subordination marker. The Infinitive is negated with *lā*; examples are given below in (d), (e), and (g2).

As is true of the English gerund, the Akkadian Infinitive of a transitive verb is essentially voiceless; thus, for example, in

ṭarād dayyānim 'the sending of the judge',

it is not clear without further context whether the judge did the sending (active voice, the judge as subject), or was sent (passive voice, the judge as object). Fortunately, the context usually resolves this ambiguity; examples appear under (g), below.

(b) Nominative Infinitive

The Infinitive in the nominative case is the subject of its clause. Such clauses are usually verbless or have a form of *bašûm* as predicate:

erēšum qerub 'planting is near';
epēšum ul damiq 'the action (lit., the doing) is not good';
šūpušum kûm 'directing (the work) is up to you' (lit., 'causing to do is yours');
paḫār ṣābim ul ibašši 'the assembling of the troop is not at hand'.

(c) Accusative Infinitive

The Infinitive in the accusative case is the direct object complement of a verb. Among the large number of verbs that may take the Infinitive in the accusative are

leʾûm 'to be able';	*šemûm* 'to hear about';
nadānum 'to allow';	*qabûm* 'to order, command';
šapārum 'to write, order';	*lamādum* 'to learn (how to do)'.

Some examples:

apālam teleʾʾî 'you (fs) can answer';
erēbam ul iddiššim 'he did not allow her to enter' (lit, 'entering he did not give to her');
ana bārîm nadānam ašpurakkum 'I wrote to you (ms) to give to the diviner' (for the prepositional phrase *ana bārîm* see under (h) below);

alāk bēlīya nakrum išemme 'the enemy will hear about my lord's travelling';
aššum alpim ša šâmam aqbûkum 'concerning the ox that I commanded you (ms) to buy' (lit., 'that I commanded to you the buying');

For additional examples, see below under (g) and (h). Some of these may also be constructed with *ana* or *ina* plus the Infinitive in the genitive; see the next section.

(d) Genitive Infinitive after a Preposition

The Infinitive may be governed by a wide range of prepositions. The most common of these by far are *ana* and *ina*.

ana usually expresses purpose or result, 'for the doing, (in order) to do':

ana kunnim ṭurdaššu 'send (ms) him here to verify (it)';
eqlum ana ṣabātim ibašši 'there is a field to be taken into possession';
ana târim pānīya aškun 'I decided (lit., I set my face) to return';
ana wašābim lā tanaddinīšum 'do not (fs) allow him to remain' (cf. the example with an acc. Infinitive under (c) above).

ina is usually equivalent to a temporal clause, 'when/while/upon doing'; occasionally, it denotes means or instrument, 'by/through doing'; it is also used instead of the acc. Infinitive as the complement of many verbs, such as those involving completing/finishing/establishing:

ina sanāqim imūt 'he died upon arriving/when he arrived';
ṣābum ina alākim lupput 'the troop was delayed in coming';
ištu šipir nārim ina ḫerêm tagdamru 'when you (ms) have finished the canal work, digging (it) out' (lit., 'in digging'; *ḫerûm* 'to dig');
ina šarāqim ukannūšu 'he will be convicted of stealing'.

kīma may be used temporally, 'as soon as, immediately upon', or to express purpose:

kīma šemêm ana ṣēr bēlīya allakam 'immediately upon hearing, I will come to my lord';
kīma lā ragāmim epuš 'act (ms) so that there be no legal contest' (lit., 'act according to not contesting').

adi 'until':

adi târīya ina bītim šibā 'stay (pl) in the house until my return' (for the pronominal suffix, see under (g), below).

aššum 'concerning, for the purpose of':

aššum elêm aštaprakkum 'I have written to you (ms) about coming up'.

Other prepositions that may govern Infinitives are *ašar* 'in/to the place of' (Mari only), *balum* 'without', *ištu* 'when, after', *lāma* 'before' (Mari):

ašar epēšim eppeš 'I will act where necessary' (lit., 'in the place of acting');
balum šâlīya illikam 'he came without asking me (or: without my asking)' (*šâlum* 'to ask'; for the pronominal suffix, see under (g));
ana ālīni ištu apālim nitūr 'we returned to our town after paying';
lāma alākīya annītam epšā 'do (pl) this before my coming'.

(e) Genitive Infinitive after a Bound Form or *ša*

The Infinitive is very frequent after a bound form or *ša*, as in

ūm erēšim qerub 'the day of planting is near';
bītum ša epēšim 'a house to build/to be built' (lit., 'a house of building').

Note: *ša* must be used if the noun before the Infinitive would be the direct object of a finite form of the verb, as in the second example above, which corresponds to *bītam ippeš* 'he will build a house'; exceptions occur when the Infinitive is negated (with *lā*), as in

ašar lā amārim 'a place that cannot be found' (lit., 'a place of not finding'; cf. *ašram immar* 'he will find the place').

Otherwise, viz., when the noun does not represent the direct object, either *ša* or the bound form of the noun may be used, as in the first example above, and in

bīt erēbim or *bītum ša erēbim* 'a house to enter/be entered' (lit., 'a house of entering'; cf. *ana bītim irrub* 'he enters the house').

The Infinitive after a bound form or *ša* has a range of meanings. It may denote command, wish, or potential (e.g., 'of doing, for (the purpose of) doing' or 'what/which must/should be done, is needed/necessary/appropriate to do/for doing/to be done, can be done').

Note that these nuances correspond to those of the finite injunctive forms (Precative, Imperative, Prohibitive, Vetitive). Unlike other finite verbs, injunctive forms may not appear in relative clauses; the Infinitives in the following examples may be thought of as substitutes for injunctives in relative clauses. In other words, whereas the verb in *bītam īpuš* 'he built a house' may be nominalized (i.e., turned into a relative clause as modifier) as *bītum ša īpušu* or *bīt īpušu* 'the house (that) he built', *bītam līpuš* 'let him/may he build a house' may be nominalized as *bītum ša epēšim* 'a house that he must/should/could build' or 'a house that must/should/could be built'.

šumma mārum arnam kabtam ša ina aplūtim nasāḫim lā ublam 'if the son has not committed (*babālum*) a serious offense (*arnum*) so that he must be removed from the inheritance' (lit., 'a serious offense of removing from the inheritance'; cf. *ina aplūtim lissuḫšu* 'he must remove him from the inheritance'; for the prepositional phrase *ina aplūtim* before the Infinitive, see (h) below);

akalšina ša adi Bābilim kašādim šurkib 'load (ms) food for them (f) to get/that they may get as far as Babylon' (lit., 'load their food of arriving as far as B.'; cf. *adi B. likšudā* 'may they get as far as B.'; for the phrase *adi Bābilim* before the Infinitive, see (h) below);

ṭuppi lā ragāmim anniam ušēzibūši 'they (m) made her make out this tablet of no (future) legal contest' (or 'this tablet according to which she may not contest'; cf. *lā iraggam* 'she may not contest'; note the adjective *anniam* modifying the acc. bound form *ṭuppi*).

ṣeḫram ša šapārim tīšu 'you (ms) have a youngster who could be sent/ whom you could send' (lit., 'a youngster of sending').

Another use of the Infinitive after *ša* or a bound form is to express a generic activity. In most such examples the Infinitive is negated and follows a bound form; often the negative may be translated 'without' (cf. §20.4(d)). Examples:

erṣet lā târim 'the land of no return/without return' (or 'from which one does not return'; a phrase denoting the underworld);

qabal lā maḫārim 'battle (*qablum*) that cannot be opposed' (or 'without opposition').

The Infinitive after *ša* may be from the same root as the finite verb:

ṣābī ša ṭarādim abī liṭrud 'may my father send the troops that are to be sent/can be sent' (or 'send the/whatever troops he can' or 'send the available troops'; lit., 'the troops of sending');

ṣēnī ša paqādim piqdanni 'provide (ms) me with the sheep that can be provided/that you can provide' (or 'the available sheep'; lit., 'the sheep of providing').

Frequently *ša* has no antecedent, and must be translated 'what, that which is to be ...' or 'enough to ...':

šumma šarrāqānum ša nadānim lā īšu 'if that thief does not have what is to be/must be given' (or 'anything/enough to give');

šumma ina bītīša ša akālim ibašši 'if there is in her house enough/ something to eat';

ša epēšim eppeš 'I am doing what can be done/is to be done'.

(f) The Infinitive with Locative *-um* and Terminative *-iš*

The Infinitive with the Locative-adverbial ending *-um*, often with *-ma*, is used in OB only to add emphasis to a finite verb of the same root:

tabālum tatbal 'you (ms) certainly took away';

ṭēmkunu šapārum-ma ul tašapparānim 'you (pl) do not send me your report'.

The Terminative-adverbial ending *-iš* occurs on Infinitives only in literary texts in OB (see §30.2, below); it is used in place of *ana* plus the gen. Infinitive, to express purpose:

amāriš palḫat 'she is afraid to look'.

(g) The Infinitive with Subjects and Objects

Since they function as verbs, Infinitives may be construed with subjects and objects. Two basic constructions occur.

(1) The Infinitive, as a Bound Form, ***before*** *its Subject or Object*

In one construction the Infinitive is a bound form before a genitive noun or pronominal suffix, which expresses the subject or the object of the Infinitive. This construction must be used when the subject or object is a pronoun (the genitive pronominal suffixes — those attached to nouns — are used), and it is also common when the subject or object is a noun.

With Infinitives of intransitive verbs, the genitive noun or pronominal suffix is always the subject of the Infinitive: e.g.,

elê ṣābim ul ibašši 'the going up of the troop will not take place';
elûšu qerub 'his going up is near';
alāk bēlīya iqbûnim 'I was told about my lord's coming';
ṭēm alākīki šuprīm 'send (fs) me news of your coming';
ḫalāq nišīšu liškunū 'May they (the gods) decree that his people perish' (lit., 'decree the perishing of his people').

When the Infinitive is that of a transitive verb, the following genitive may be either the subject or the object of the Infinitive (as in *ṭarād dayyānim* 'the sending of the judge'; see under (a)).

Examples of transitive Infinitives with subject genitives:

âm ana maḫārim ša PN *mudud* 'measure (ms) grain for PN to receive' (lit., 'for the receiving of PN');
âm ša leqêka itbalū 'they (m) carried off the grain that you (ms) were to take' (lit., 'the grain of your taking').

Examples of Infinitives with object genitives:

paṭārī qerub 'my release is near' (i.e., 'the releasing of me is near');
abūšu nadāššu iqbiam 'his father commanded me to give it (ms)' (lit., 'commanded to me the giving of it');
suḫḫur kišādīya ul eleʾʾi 'I am unable to turn my neck' (lit., 'the turning of my neck');
ṣābam ana naṣār ālim ušērib 'I sent in the troop to protect (for the protection of) the town';

ana parās warkatīša ina ālim wašib 'he is staying in town to investigate her case';
bēlni ana šūlîni išpuram 'our lord wrote to have us brought up' (Š Infin. of *elûm*).

*(2) The Infinitive **after** its Subject or Object*

The Infinitive may also, like a finite verb, follow its subject or object, which is then in the appropriate case. This construction is not used when the subject or object is a pronoun.

With a nominative Infinitive, this construction is rare; an example is

ašar igisûm ina MN_1 *ana Bābilim sanāqum qabû, ina* MN_2 *ana Bābilim lisniqam* 'wherever the arrival of the *igisûm*-tax in Babylon in $month_1$ was ordered, let it (now) arrive in Babylon in $month_2$'.

Examples with an accusative Infinitive:

eqlam wuššuram ašpurakkim 'I wrote to you (fs) to release the field';
bītam lā šâmam iqbûšum 'they (m) told him not to buy the house'.

Note: only an object (and/or adverbial complement; see (h)) may precede an accusative Infinitive; a subject follows the bound form of the accusative Infinitive (construction (1) above), as in *alāk bēlīya ešme* 'I heard about my lord's going'.

When the Infinitive follows a bound form or *ša*, a direct object that precedes the Infinitive follows the bound form or *ša*, and thus, like the Infinitive, is in the genitive case:

ūm kaspim šaqālim iktašdanni 'the day for (of) weighing out the silver has reached me (i.e., has arrived)';
aššum ṭēm šikarim nadānim ša tašpuram 'concerning the report of giving out the beer, which you (ms) sent me';
ša êm apālim epšā 'do (pl) what is necessary to pay for the grain'.

As is true of the accusative Infinitive, the subject of an Infinitive after a bound form or *ša* always follows the bound form of the Infinitive (construction (1)).

When the Infinitive follows a preposition, a noun subject or object may either precede or follow the preposition. When it precedes the preposition, it is in the appropriate case:

with a subject:

mû ina maqātim âm litēr 'when the water(-level) falls he must return the grain';

with an object:

ṭuppī anniam ina amārim alkam 'on seeing this tablet of mine, come (ms) here'.

Note the following rare example, from the prologue of CH, with both noun subject and noun object:

dannum enšam ana lā ḫabālim 'so that (*ana*) the strong not oppress (*ḫabālum*) the weak'.

Usually, if both subject and object are expressed, the subject is a pronoun:

kunukkī anniam ina amārīki 'when you (fs) see (on your seeing) this seal of mine';

šumma šamnum mê ina nadêka iṭbu 'if the oil, when you (ms) added water, sank' (lit., 'if the oil, in your putting water, sank (*ṭebûm*)').

When the subject or object noun follows the preposition, it is in the genitive, like the Infinitive:

with an object:

ana kaspim naṣārim lā teggu 'do not (ms) be negligent about protecting the silver';

awīlam šuāti ina êm leqêm ukannūšu 'that man will be convicted of (*ina*) taking the grain';

ana wardīka šūlîm illik 'he went to fetch (bring up) your (ms) slave';

with a subject (examples not common):

aḫūki ana ṣābim alākim ana ṣērīšu išpuram 'your (fs) brother wrote me for the troop to go to him'.

(In some instances, the subject remains in the nominative:

kīma awīlû šunu lā naparkîm 'so that (*kīma*) those men not leave' (*naparkûm*, see §38.1).)

Thus, when the Infinitive is governed by a preposition, three constructions are possible;

'he went to buy the house'

may be rendered in any of the following ways:

bound form plus genitive	*ana šâm bītim illik*
subject or object before the preposition	*bītam ana šâmim illik*
subject or object between the preposition and the Infinitive	*ana bītim šâmim illik*

(h) The Infinitive with Adverbial Complements

In addition to being construed with subjects and object, Infinitives, as verbs, may also govern adverbial complements, i.e., adverbs and prepositional phrases; these may precede or follow the Infinitive.

Certain tendencies are observable in the placement of adverbial complements before or after the Infinitive:

> when the Infinitive has no subject or object, or when it has a pronominal subject or object, adverbial complements usually precede the Infinitive, except when it is nominative;
>
> when the Infinitive has a noun subject or object, adverbial complements tend to be placed immediately after the subject or object.

Nominative Infinitive (see (b) above):

> *wašāb aḫīka ina ālim šuāti ul damiq* 'it is not good for your (ms) brother to live in that town' (lit., 'the living of your brother in that town is not good').

Accusative Infinitive (see (c) above):

> *ana* GN *erēbam ul ele*ʾʾ*i* 'I am unable to enter GN';
> *ana* PN *nadānam ašpurakkim* 'I wrote to you (fs) to give (it) to PN';
> *alāk wardīša ana* GN *aqbi* 'I ordered her slave to travel to GN'.

Infinitive dependent on a preposition (see (d) above); the adverbial complement governed by the Infinitive may appear

> before the preposition that governs the Infinitive:
>
> > *ana ālim ina erēbim imūt* 'he died upon entering the town';
> > *ana bītim ina erēbīya luddin* 'I would give (it) when I enter the house' (lit., 'upon my entering').
> > *ana ḫarrānim ana waṣêm pānīya aškun* 'I decided to go out to the road';
>
> between the preposition that governs the Infinitive and the Infinitive:
>
> > *aššum ana ālim elêm aštaprakkum* 'I have written to you (ms) concerning coming up to the town';
>
> after the Infinitive:
>
> > *ina elê šarrim ana Bābilim aqabbīšum* 'when the king goes up to Babylon, I will speak to him';
> > *ana ṭarād ṣuḫārim ana libbi mātim pānam iškunū* 'they (m) decided to send the servant to the center of the land'.

Infinitive after *ša* or a bound form (see (e) above):

> *arnum kabtum ša ina aplūtim nasāḫim* 'a serious offense (*arnum*) so that he must be removed from the inheritance' (lit., 'a serious offense of removing from the inheritance');
> *akalšina ša adi Bābilim kašādim šurkib* 'load (ms) food for them (f) to get/that they may get as far as Babylon' (lit., 'load their food of arriving as far as B.').

30.2 OB Literary Diction

OB literary texts, which include royal inscriptions, myths, epics, hymns, prayers, laments, and incantations, exhibit in common a set of features that distinguish them from texts such as contracts, laws, letters, and omens. Some of these features are due to a tendency of the scribes to archaize, i.e., to make the texts appear to be older, and, presumably, more august. None of the features listed below is found consistently in literary works, even in individual texts; usually, they alternate with the everyday-speech forms found in non-literary texts. (Some of the features are also occasionally attested in non-literary texts of certain OB dialects.)

(a) Vowel contraction is sometimes not carried out, especially at the end of verbs III–weak: e.g.,

ib-ni-ù, i.e., *ibniū* 'they (m) built' (for *ibnû*);
ša ... *ú-ma-al-li-ù*, i.e., *ša* ... *umalliu* 'which ... he handed over' (for *umallû*).

(b) Vowel-harmony, by which *a*-vowels become *e* (§7.2), occasionally does not occur:

epšātūšu 'his deeds' (for *epšētūšu*).

(c) The prepositions *ina*, *ana*, and *eli* may lose their final vowel. The short forms *in* and, less often, *an* are found in OB royal inscriptions. Otherwise, *in* and *an* are proclitic, with regular assimilation of the *n* to the first consonant of the following word; the *l* of *el* is also sometimes assimilated. The resultant doubling is usually not indicated in the writing, however, so that the prepositions appear as *i*- and *a*- (and *e*- for *el*). When *in* and *an* occur before words beginning with vowels, the *n* may be written as part of the following word. Examples:

in šarrī (in royal inscriptions) 'among the kings';
i-li-bi-ša for *il-libbīša* 'within it (f)';
i-ni-li for *in ilī* 'among the gods';
a-pa-ni-ia for *ap-pānīya* 'toward me';
el kala ilātim 'more than all the goddesses';
e-ni-ši-i for *en-nišī* 'above the people';
elni 'above us'.

(d) The bound form of the sg. and the fem. pl. before a noun may end in *-u*, regardless of case; gen. forms ending in *-i* also occur:

nom. *nabiu Anim* 'the one called (*nabûm* 'to call', V. Adj.) by An';
acc. *naḫbalu tiāmtim* 'the net of the sea';
gen. *mušarbi zikru Bābilim* 'the one who makes great (Š Ptcpl.) the

name (*zikrum*, gen.) of Babylon';
gen. *ana šīmātu awīlūtim* 'to humanity's fate (pl. of *šīmtum*)';
gen. *ana siqri eṭlim* 'at the young man's speech (*siqrum*)'.

The bound form before a suffix in the nom. and acc. may have a short *a*, even with nouns whose bound forms in prose end in a consonant:

nom. *rigmašu* 'his voice (*rigmum*)' (for *rigimšu*);
nom. *zamāraša* 'her song (*zamārum*)' (for *zamārša*).

(e) The genitive pronominal suffixes of the 2nd and 3rd persons may appear without their final vowels, especially on nouns in the nom. and acc., less often on gen. nouns. Of the singular forms, this is quite common with 3fs *-ša*, less so with the 3ms *-šu*, 2ms *-ka*, and 2fs *-ki*; the sing. short forms normally follow the appropriate case-vowel:

nom. *libbuš* 'her heart' (for *libbaša*);
acc. *awātak* 'your (ms) word' (for *awātka*).

Examples of shortened pl. suffixes:

gen. *šubātīšin* 'of their (f) dwellings' (for *šubātīšina*);
nom. *migrašun* 'their (m) favorite' (for *migiršunu*; for *-a-*, see (d));
with term.-adv. *-iš*, *puḫriššun* 'in their (m) assembly'.

The accusative suffixes (on verbs) are only rarely shortened (e.g., *-šunūt* for *-šunūti*, *-kunūt* for *-kunūti*).

(f) Some polysyllabic feminine nouns have alternative bound forms:

napšat nišī 'the life of the people' (in prose usually *napišti*);
napšassu 'his life' (in prose usually *napištašu*).

(g) The locative- and terminative-adverbial endings (§28.2–3) occur more frequently than in prose.

(h) The prefix of 3fs verbs is rarely *ta-* (or *te-*, *tu-*) rather than *i-* (or *u-*); such forms thus have the same shape as the 2ms:

tattadin 'she has given'; *tušatlim* 'she granted' (Š *šutlumum*).

(i) A rare conjugational stem occurs, viz., the ŠD, which is not encountered in prose. The forms, which have both a prefixed *š* and doubling of the middle radical, are given in §38.3; the meaning of the stem is the same as that of the corresponding D or Š:

ušrabbi 'he made great' (= *urabbi*, *ušarbi*).

(j) Main clauses may be negated with *lā* rather than *ul*:

balāṭam ša tasaḫḫuru lā tutta 'the life you (ms) seek you will not find' (*watûm* (*a*) 'to find').

(k) Word order is freer in literary texts. In particular, in some poetic genres (see §33.3), verbs need not occur at the end of their clause (although they do in royal inscriptions, for which see the next section).

inūma ilū ibnû awīlūtam	'When the gods made humanity,
mūtam iškunū ana awīlūtim	death they decreed for humanity;
balāṭam ina qātīšunu iṣṣabtū	life they kept in their possession.'

30.3 OB Royal Inscriptions

Royal inscriptions are usually dedicatory texts addressed to a deity or deities for whom the king has rendered a service, such as the rebuilding or repairing of a temple, or the making of an offering. Often the individual sentences or clauses are very long, since they contain extended series of epithets (of both the deities and the king). Otherwise, however, they offer few problems, and serve as a convenient introduction to literary diction.

EXERCISES

A. VOCABULARY 30.

Verbs:

bêlum G (*e*) 'to rule, have authority, power over' (cf. *bēl(t)um*).

magārum G (*a–u*) 'to be agreeable, agree (to do: *ana* + Infin.); to agree with, comply with, consent to (someone or something: acc.); to grant, permit; to find acceptance'.

nabûm G (*i*) 'to name; to invoke, call, summon, appoint; to decree, proclaim'; Verbal Adj. *nabûm* (*nabi-*) 'called, named'.

Nouns:

almattum (*almatti*; pl. *almanātum*; log. NU.MU.SU) 'widow'.

arnum (*aran*; pl. *arnū*) 'crime, offense, wrongdoing, guilt; punishment'.

ḫegallum (*ḫegal*; log. ḪÉ.GÁL [gál = the IG sign]; Sum. lw.) 'abundance; abundant yield'.

kibrum (*kibir*; pl. *kibrātum*) 'edge, rim, bank, shore'; pl. *kibrātum* 'regions, edge'; *kibrātum arbaʾum* 'the four regions (of the world)' (with an archaic writing of 'four'), i.e., 'the whole world'.

kūṣum (also *kuṣṣum*; bound form *kūṣ(i), kuṣṣi*) 'cold; winter'.

maškanum (*maškan*; pl. *maškanū, maškanātum*; log. KISLAḪ [= KI+UD]) 'threshing floor; empty lot; location, site' (cf. *šakānum*).

nāqidum (*nāqid*; log. NA.GADA) 'shepherd'.

parakkum (*parak*; log. BARAG; Sum. lw.) 'throne-dais; sanctuary'.

sūqum (*sūq(i)*; pl. *sūqātum, sūqānū*; log. SILA [= the TAR sign]) 'street'.

unūtum (pl. irregular *uniātum* and *unêtum*) 'utensils, furnishings, property'.

Idioms:

ša lā (used as Preposition) 'without' (e.g., *eqlum ša lā mê* 'a field without water').

šumma ... šumma 'whether ... or'.

B. Learn the following signs:

OB Lapid.	OB Cursive	NA	values
			BARAG = *parakkum*
			ḪÉ in ḪÉ.GÁL = *ḫegallum*
			GADA in NA.GADA= *nāqidum*

C. Write the following words in cuneiform and in transliteration; use logograms where possible:

1. *bilat ḫegallim*
2. *šammi qištim*
3. *almatti bārîm*
4. *parak Anim*
5. *ṣēnū nāqidim*
6. *sūqātum u ḫarrānātum*
7. *maškan itinnim*

D. Write in normalized Akkadian:

1. The king commanded me to go.
2. I am unable to kill him.
3. May the house builder finish building the house.
4. I decided to invoke him.
5. Agree (pl) to hold the load.
6. I wrote you (fs) concerning the arrival of my father-in-law and the flooding of my fields.
7. while hearing his words

E. Normalize and translate:

1. *a-na la e-re-eb ṣa-bi-im a-na a-lim am-gu-ur-šu-nu-ti.*
2. ^{lú}MÁŠ.ŠU.GÍD.GÍD *i-na ú-ni-a-at* NU.MU.SU *ša-ra-qí-im bu-ur.*
3. ^{lú}NA.GADA.MEŠ *aš-šum* U$_{8}$.UDU.ḪI.A *ši-na-ti šu-lu-mi-im ú-wa-e-er-šu-nu-ti.*
4. *be-lí* É-*tam na-da-nam ú-ša-ḫi-sú-nu-ti-ma* É-*tam ú-ul id-di-nu.*
5. *ak-lam mi-im-ma a-na da-an-na-tim a-na šu-ru-bi-im ú-ul ad-di-in-šum.*
6. *be-lí a-wa-tam li-iš-pu-ra-am-ma ša qá-bé-e be-lí-ia lu-pu-uš.*
7. *i-na-an-na a-bi* PN *li-iṭ-ru-dam-ma ša šu-ul-lu-um ma-a-tim i ni-pu-uš ù aš-šum* ÌR.MEŠ *ša ma-ḫar a-bi-ia wa-aš-bu a-bi li-iṭ-ru-da-aš-šu-nu-ti ù ṣa-ba-am ša ṭa-ra-di-im a-bi li-iṭ-ru-ud.*
8. *aš-šum* GIŠ.ḪI.A *ša be-lí a-na* PN *a-na tu-ur-ri-im iš-pu-ra-am* GIŠ.ḪI.A *šu-nu-ti ú-te-er-šum-ma mi-im-ma ú-ul iq-bi a-na* GIŠ.ḪI.A-*šu ḫa-du-um-ma ḫa-di.*
9. IGI.3.GÁL GÍN KUG.BABBAR *e-li* PN *i-šu bu-ul-ṭa-am i-na ka-ša-di-im* PN KUG.BABBAR *i-ip-pa-la-an-ni.*
10. A.ŠÀ *ša-a-tu aš-šum ḫu-bu-ul-li a-pa-li-im a-na be-el ḫu-bu-ul-li-ia ad-di-in.*

F. CH:

§8 *šum-ma a-wi-lum lu* GUD *lu* UDU *lu* ANŠE *lu šaḫâm*(ŠAḪ) *ù lu* ^{giš}MÁ *iš-ri-iq šum-ma ša i-lim šum-ma ša* É.GAL A.RÁ 30-*šu i-na-ad-di-in šum-ma ša* MAŠ.EN.GAG A.RÁ 10-*šu i-ri-a-ab šum-ma šar-ra-qá-nu-um ša na-da-nim la i-šu id-da-ak.*

šaḫûm (*šaḫa-*; log. ŠAḪ; Sum. lw.) 'pig'.
30-*šu* normalize *šalāšā'īšu*? (uncertain).

§113 *šum-ma a-wi-lum e-li a-wi-lim* ŠE *ù* KUG.BABBAR *i-šu-ma i-na ba-lum be-el* ŠE *i-na na-aš-pa-ki-im ù lu i-na ma-aš-ka-nim* ŠE *il-te-qé a-wi-lam šu-a-ti i-na ba-lum be-el* ŠE *i-na na-aš-pa-ki-im ù lu i-na* KISLAḪ *i-na* ŠE *le-qé-em ú-ka-an-nu-šu-ma* ŠE *ma-la il-qú-ú ú-ta-ar ù i-na mi-im-ma šum-šu ma-la id-di-nu i-te-el-li.*

ina X ītelli 'he will forfeit X'.

§144 *šum-ma a-wi-lum* LUKUR *i-ḫu-uz-ma* LUKUR *ši-i* GEME$_{2}$ *a-na mu-ti-ša id-di-in-ma* DUMU.MEŠ *uš-tab-ši a-wi-lum šu-ú a-na* ^{mí}*šu-gi$_{4}$-tim a-ḫa-zi-im pa-ni-šu iš-ta-ka-an a-wi-lam šu-a-ti ú-ul i-ma-ag-ga-ru-šu* ^{mí}*šu-gi$_{4}$-tam ú-ul i-iḫ-ḫa-az.*

šugītum (*šugīt*; log. ^{mí}ŠU.GI$_{4}$; Sum. lw.) a second wife (to a *nadītum*).

§177 *šum-ma* NU.MU.SU *ša* DUMU.MEŠ-*ša ṣe-eḫ-ḫe-ru a-na* É *ša-ni-im e-re-bi-im pa-ni-ša iš-ta-ka-an ba-lum da-a-a-ni ú-ul i-ir-ru-ub i-nu-ma a-na* É *ša-ni-im i-ir-ru-bu da-a-a-nu wa-ar-ka-at* É *mu-ti-ša pa-ni-im i-pár-ra-su-ma* É *ša mu-ti-ša pa-ni-im a-na mu-ti-ša wa-ar-ki-im ù* MUNUS *šu-a-ti i-pa-aq-qí-du-ma* DUB-*pa-am ú-še-ez-ze-bu-šu-nu-ti* É *i-na-ṣa-ru ù ṣe-eḫ-ḫe-ru-tim ú-ra-ab-bu-ú ú-ni-a-tim a-na* KUG.BABBAR *ú-ul i-na-ad-di-nu ša-a-a-ma-nu-um ša ú-nu-ut* DUMU.MEŠ NU.MU.SU *i-ša-am-mu i-na* KUG.BABBAR-*šu i-te-el-li* NÍG.GA *a-na be-lí-šu i-ta-ar.*

ṣeḫḫerum (*ṣeḫḫer-*) 'very small' (cf. *ṣeḫrum*).

šayyāmānum (*šayyāmān*) 'buyer' (cf. *šâmum*).

ina kaspīšu ītelli 'he will forfeit his silver'.

§§207–208 (§206 reads, in part, *šumma awīlum awīlam imtaḫaṣ* ...) §207 *šum-ma i-na ma-ḫa-ṣí-šu im-tu-ut i-tam-ma-ma šum-ma* DUMU *a-wi-lim* 1/2 MA.NA KUG.BABBAR *i-ša-qal.* §208 *šum-ma* DUMU MAŠ.EN.GAG 1/3 MA.NA KUG.BABBAR *i-ša-qal.*

§§209–211 §209 *šum-ma a-wi-lum* DUMU.MUNUS *a-wi-lim im-ḫa-aṣ-ma ša li-ib-bi-ša uš-ta-di-ši* 10 GÍN KUG.BABBAR *a-na ša li-ib-bi-ša i-ša-qal.* §210 *šum-ma* MUNUS *ši-i im-tu-ut* DUMU.MUNUS-*sú i-du-uk-ku.* §211 *šum-ma* DUMU.MUNUS MAŠ.EN.GAG *i-na ma-ḫa-ṣí-im ša li-ib-bi-ša uš-ta-ad-di-ši* 5 GÍN KUG.BABBAR *i-ša-qal.*

ša libbim 'foetus'; *ša libbim nadûm* 'to have a miscarriage'.

§250 *šum-ma* GUD *sú*(? *su*?)-*qá-am i-na a-la-ki-šu a-wi-lam ik-ki-ip-ma uš-ta-mi-it di-nu-um šu-ú ru-gu-um-ma-am ú-ul i-šu.*

nakāpum G (*i*) 'to gore, butt'; *nukkupum* D = G.

§42:

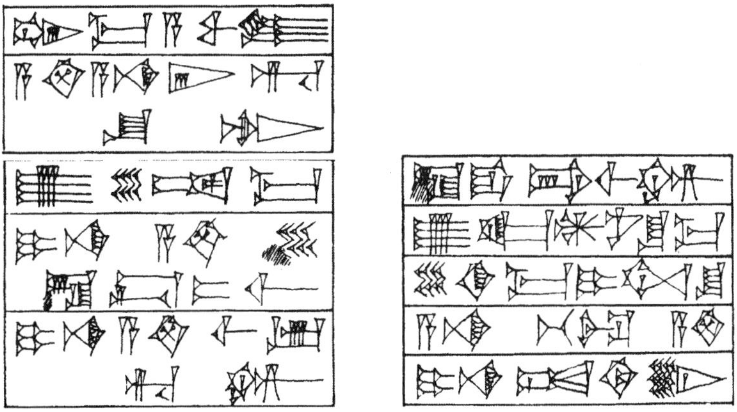

§168:

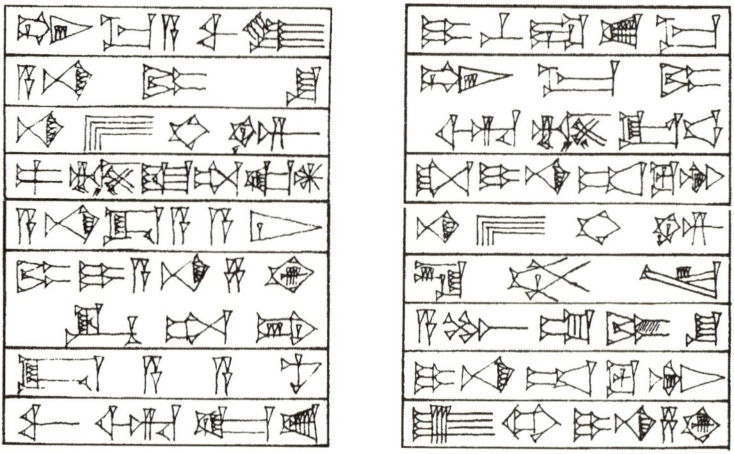

§261:

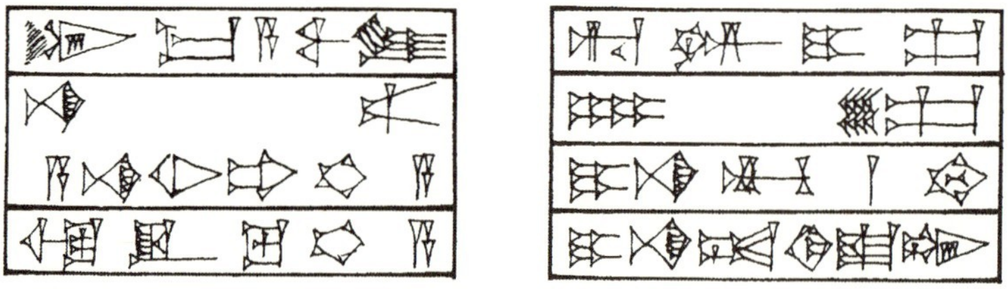

G. Omens from *YOS* 10:

1. BE *naplaštum*(IGI.BAR) *ki-ma* KASKAL *šar-ru-um ka-ab-tu-ti-šu i-da-ak-ma bi-ša-šu-nu ú*(sic) *ma-ku-ur-šu-nu a-na bi-ta-at i-la-ni i-za-az*. (14:8–9)

2. DIŠ *naplaštum*(IGI.BAR) *a-na* ^{giš}TUKUL *i-tu-ur-ma ni-ra-am i-ṭù-ul ti-bi le-mu-ut-tim a-na bi-*[*tim*] *i-te-*[*bé*]. (17:27)
   nīrum 'yoke; a part of the liver'.

3. *šumma*(AŠ) KÁ É.GAL *ma-aš-ka-an-šu i-zi-im-ma i-na šumēlim* (Á.GÙB) *ša-ki-in ma-tam la ka-tam q*[*á-at-ka*] *i-ka-ša-*⌜*ad*⌝ *šumma*(AŠ) KÁ É.GAL *ma-aš-ka-an-šu i-zi-im-ma i-na imittim* (Á.ZI) *ša-ki-in er-ṣe-et-ka* LÚ.KÚR *i-*⌜*ta-ba*⌝*-al šumma*(AŠ) KÁ É. GAL *i-na ma-aš-ka-ni-šu la i-ba-aš-ši-ma i-na wa-ar-ka-at a-mu-tim ša-ki-in ma-at* LÚ.KÚR *bi-il-tam i-na-aš-ši-a-ku*. (23: 5–7)

4. *šumma*(AŠ) KÁ É.GAL *ka-a-a-nu-um ka-a-a-nu-um i-na imittim* (Á.ZI) *ša-ki-in ka-ab-tu ki-ma be-li-šu i-ma-aṣ-ṣi* (23:9)
   kayyānum 'normal' (cf. *kânum*); *kayyānum kayyānum* 'completely normal'.
5. *šum-ma i-na ‹i-›ši-id mar-tim pi-iṭ-ru-um ša-ki-im-ma a-na zu-um-ri-ša ṭù-uḫ-ḫu a-wi-lum i-na la la-ma-di-šu ma-ru-uš-tum i-ma-aq-qú-ta-aš-šum.* (31 xii 27–35)
   piṭrum (*piṭir*) 'fissure, cleft' (cf. *paṭārum*).
   zumrum (*zumur*) 'body'.
6. [DIŠ *ṭ*]*ù-li-mu-um ša-ar-ta-am la-ḫi-im ma-a*[*r a*]*l-ma-tim ku-us-sí-a-am* ⸢*i-ṣa-ba*⸣*-at.* (41:30)
   ṭulīmum (*ṭulīm*) 'spleen'.
   šārtam (*šārat*) 'hair'.
   laḫmum (Verbal Adj. of *laḫāmum*, no finite G forms attested) 'hairy'; *šārtam laḫim* 'is covered with hair'.
7. MAŠ *i-na mu-*[*uḫ*]*-ḫi ni-ri* gišTUKUL *ši-na i-mi-tam ù šu-me-lam ša-ak-nu qá-ra-du i-a-ú-tu-un ù ša* LÚ.KÚR *iš-*[*t*]*e-*[*n*]*i-iš i-ma-qú-tu.* (42 iv 21–23)
   nīrum 'yoke; a part of the liver'.
   ištēniš 'together, as one' (cf. *ištēn*).
8. DIŠ 7 *šēpētum*(? AŠ) *ra-bu-um kab-tu-um a-na ma-ti-ka i-ṭe-ḫe-ak-kum.* (44:69)
9. [DIŠ] *na-ap-la-aš-tum re-eš*$_{15}$(IŠ)*-sa ra-pa-aš* DINGIR *re-eš a-wi-lim i-na-aš-ši.* (J. Nougayrol, *RA* 44 1950 23ff.:5–6)
   rēšam našûm 'to honor, exalt'.
10. 21:4:

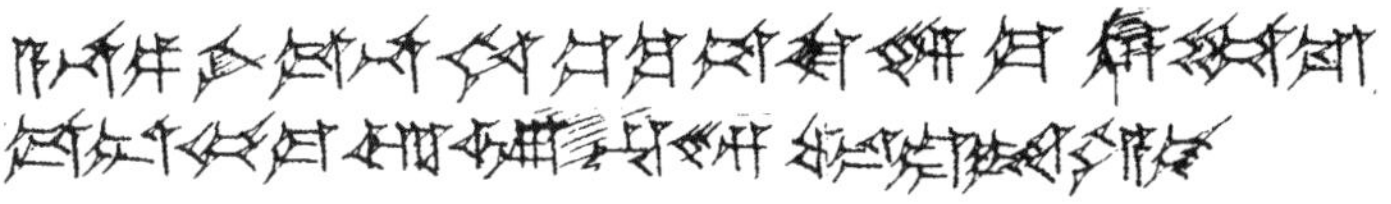

Damaged DIŠ to left of left margin.
danānum, here a part of the liver.
eliš (adverb) 'above, up(ward)' (cf. *elûm*).
Fourth last sign: *ṭe!*.

11. 24:30:

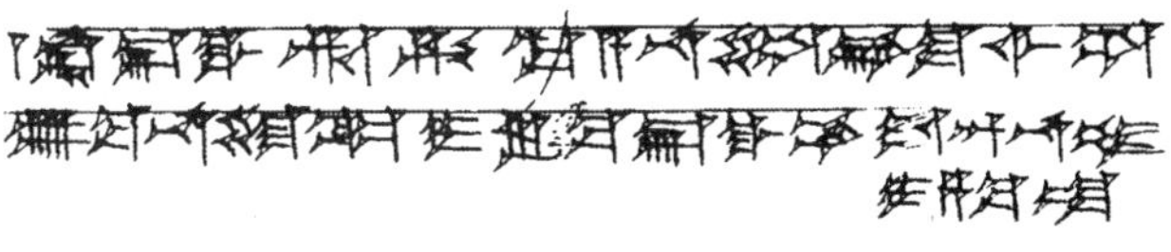

In *ú-ba-na-tu-ka*, *-ka* 'your' is addressed to the diviner.

H. Contracts:

1. Rental of a house (Szlechter, *Tablettes* 64 MAH 15.958, ll. 1–11).

[1] É *kankallim*(KI.KAL) *ma-la ma-ṣú-ú* [2] ÚS.SA.DU ^{d}EN.ZU-*ba-ni* ... [3] *ù* ÚS.SA.DU ^{d}IŠKUR-*ba-ni* ... [4] É ^{d}AMAR.UTU-*ku-un-da-rum* [5] KI ^{d}AMAR.UTU-*ku-un-da-rum* [6] *bēl bītim* (LUGAL.É.E.KE$_4$) [7] ^{I}*ku-dan-na* [8] *a-na e-pé-ši-im ù wa-ša-bi-im* [9] *a-na* MU.3.KAM *ušēṣi*(ÍB.TA.È.A) [10] *a-na qá-bé-e* ÌR-*ì-lí-šu* [11] *ù a-pil-*^{d}*Amurrim*(MAR.TU).

PNs: *Sîn-bānî; Adad-bānî; Marduk-kūn-dārum; Kūdanna; Warad-ilīšu; Apil-Amurrim.*

[1] *kankallum* (*kankal*; log. KI.KAL; Sum. lw.) 'unbroken, hard soil'.

[6] The writing LUGAL.É.E/A.KE$_4$, found in Sumerian contracts for 'owner of the house', is also common in OB contracts, where, however, it represents *bēl bītim*, even though LUGAL normally = *šarrum*.

2. Payment of a sheep (Szlechter, *Tablettes* 121–22 MAH 16.482).

[1] 1 UDU [2] ŠÁM $^1/_6$(ŠUŠ) GÍN KUG.BABBAR [3] *ša* ^{d}EN.ZU-*i-din-nam sirāšûm*(LÚ.ŠIM) [4] DUMU *e-ṭi-rum* [5] *a-na* ÌR-*ku-bi* DUMU-*ši*[*prim*] (K[IN]) [6] DUMU *u-bar-rum* [7] *a-na ši-ip-ri e-pé-ši-im* [8] *ki-ma i-di-šu* [9] *id-di-nu-šu* [10–12] (broken). [13–14] Witnesses. [15–17] Date.

PNs: *Sîn-iddinam; Ēṭirum; Warad-Kūbi; Ubarrum.*

[3] *sirāšûm* (*sirāši-*; log. ŠIM(also ŠIM•GAR, ŠIM+GAR); Sum. lw.?) 'brewer'.

3. Apprenticeship as musician (Szlechter, *TJA* 151 UMM G40, ll. 1–6 [ll. 7–10 Date]).

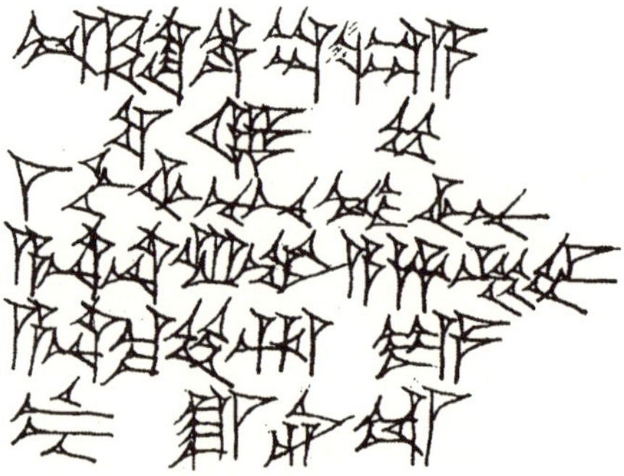

PN: *Šinunūtum.*

[1] ITI AB.È.A (È = UD+DU) = *Ṭebētum* (log. also AB(.BA.È)) the tenth month (Dec.-Jan.).

[3] After the name read IGI.NU.[TUK] = *lā nāṭilum.*

[4] *nārum* b (*nār(i)*) 'musician'; *nārūtum* 'musician's craft'; *aḫāzum*, here 'to learn' (cf. Š 'to teach').

[5] Note the first person form; the owner of the tablet is not identified.

[6] For the shortened suffix, see §30.2(e).

I. Letters:

1. *CT* 29 6a = Frankena, *AbB* 2 129.

1 *a-na* LÚ-^{d}BA.Ú 2 *qí-bí-ma* 3 *um-ma a-ḫu-um-ma* 4 *aš-šum i-pí-ir* 5 ^{I}*ia-ta-ra-tim* 6 *na-da-ni-im* 7 *lu aš-pu-ra-kum* 8 *a-na mi-ni-im* 9 *la ta-di-in* 10 *i-pí-ir* 11 ^{I}*ia-ta-ra-tim* 12 *i-[n]a ma-[t]i ta-na-di-i[n]* 13 *i-[d]i-in* 14 *šum-ma la [t]a-di-in* 15 *a-[š]a-pa-ra-am-ma* 16 *i-pí-ir* 17 *[š]a-ti-ša* 18 *i-na bi-ti-ka* 19 *ta-na-di-in* 20 *ša-n[i]-tam* 21 *am-ta-am* 22 *ša it-ti* 23 $^{[I]}$*be-la-a* 24 *a-na ia-ta-ra-tim* 25 *i-di-in.*

PNs: *Lu-Bau*; *Aḫum*; *Iataratum*; *Bēlâ*.

4 *iprum* (*ipir*; pl. *iprū*) 'barley ration, food allowance'.

12 *mati* (also *ina mati*) 'when?'.

2. *PBS* 7 99 = Stol, *AbB* 11 99.

1 *a-na a-wi-lim* 2 *[q]í-bí-ma* 3 *um-ma* ^{d}IŠKUR-MA.AN.SUM-*ma* 4 ^{d}UTU *ù* ^{d}AMAR.UTU *da-ri-iš* UD-*mi* 5 *li-ba-al-li-ṭú-ka* 6 *lu ša-al-ma-ta lu ba-al-ṭa-ta* 7 DINGIR *n[a]-ṣi-ir-ka re-eš-ka a-na da-mi-iq-tim* 8 *li-ki-il* 9 *a-na šu-ul-mi-ka aš-pu-ra-am* 10 *šu-l[um]-ka ma-ḫar* ^{d}UTU *ù* ^{d}AMAR.UTU 11 *lu da-ri* 12 *aš-šum* ŠE.GIŠ.Ì *na-sa-ḫi-im* 13 *i-[n]a qí-bi-it a-wi-lim be-lí-ia* 14 *ù* DINGIR-*šu-ba-ni a-ḫi-ka* 15 *iššiakkū* (ENSI$_2$.MEŠ) *i[l]-li-ku-nim* 16 *ki-ma ra-[bu-t]i-ka* 17 10 ERIN$_2$.MEŠ *[š]a [q]á-t[i-k]a* 18 *a-na* UD.1.KAM 19 *tap-pu-tam li-il-li-ku.*

PNs: *Iškur-mansum*; *Ilšu-bāni*.

15 *iššiakkum* (*iššiak*; log. ENSI$_2$; Sum. lw.) 'farmer; land agent'.

16 *rabûtum* 'high status, high position'.

3. *ARM* 2 105.

1 *a-na be-lí-ia* 2 *qí-bí-ma* 3 *um-ma ia-qí-im*-^{d}IŠKUR 4 ÌR-*ka-a-ma* 5 [UD]-*um* DUB-*pí an-né-em a-na ṣe-er be-lí-ia* 6 *ú-ša-bi-lam* LÚ.MEŠ *ša ba-za-ḫa-tim* 7 *ka-ša-ad ṣú-ra-ḫa-am-mu* 8 *ú-ba-ar-ru-nim um-ma-a-mi* 9 ^{I}*ṣú-ra-ḫa-am-mu* 10 *a-na ḫu-uḫ-ri-i*^{ki} 11 *ik-ta-aš-dam* 12 ^{I}*be-el-šu-nu* 13 *ù ia-aw*(PI)-*ṣí-ìl*(DINGIR) *ša be-lí-ia* 14 *a-li-ik i-di-šu it-ti-šu-ma i-la-ku-nim* 15 *ù* 1 ME *ṣa-bu-um it-ti-šu* 16 *i-la-kam ka-ša-as-sú ú-ba-ar-ru-nim-ma* 17 *[qa-tam] a-na [q]a-tim a-na ṣe-er* 18 *[be-lí-ia] aš-pu-ra-am.*

PNs: *Iaqim-Addu*; *Ṣūra-Ḫammu*; *Bēlšunu*; *Iawṣi-Il*.

3 ^{d}IŠKUR is read *Addu* in Mari names.

6 *baz(a)ḫatum* (Northwest Semitic word) 'military outpost'.

7 *ummāmi* (common in Mari letters) = *umma*.

9 *Ḫuḫrû* a place name.

12–13 PN *u* PN *ša bēlīya* 'PN and PN, (subjects) of my lord'.

17 *qātum ana qātim* (also *qāta(q)qāti*) a Mari idiom, 'immediately'.

J. A Royal Inscription of Ḫammurapi: the building of a sanctuary for Marduk in Borsippa (copy in King, *LIH* 2 94 = Frayne, *RIME* 4, pp. 354–55).

Note: the entire text consists of a single sentence.

6 Last sign: ÍL (= *našûm*); É.SAG.ÍL = *Esagil*, Marduk's temple in Babylon.

7 É.ZI.DA = *Ezida*, Marduk's temple in Borsippa (cf. line 33).

12 Read [*še*]-*mu*, for *šēmû*, despite the lack of a final vowel sign; note the vowel contraction in this form, vs. *nabiu* in l. 10.

13 Nothing missing at the beginning.

14 Restore [*mi*] at the beginning.

24 *ì-nu*, for *inu*, archaic or archaizing for *inūma*.

25 Last sign: SIG (= *enšum, qatnum*), here with the rare value *šì*.

28 *ṣerretum* (*ṣerret*; pl. *ṣerrētum*) 'nose-rope, halter, lead-rope'.

33 *Barsipa* 'Borsippa' (modern Birs Nimrud), a city 25 km. south of Babylon.

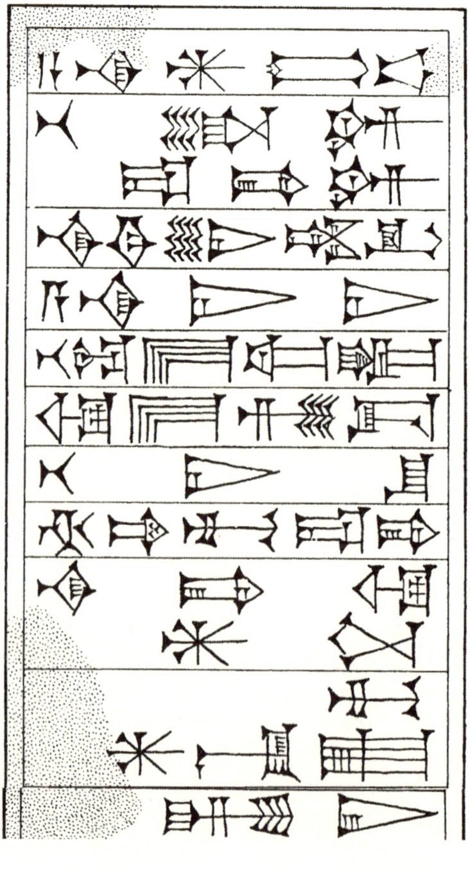

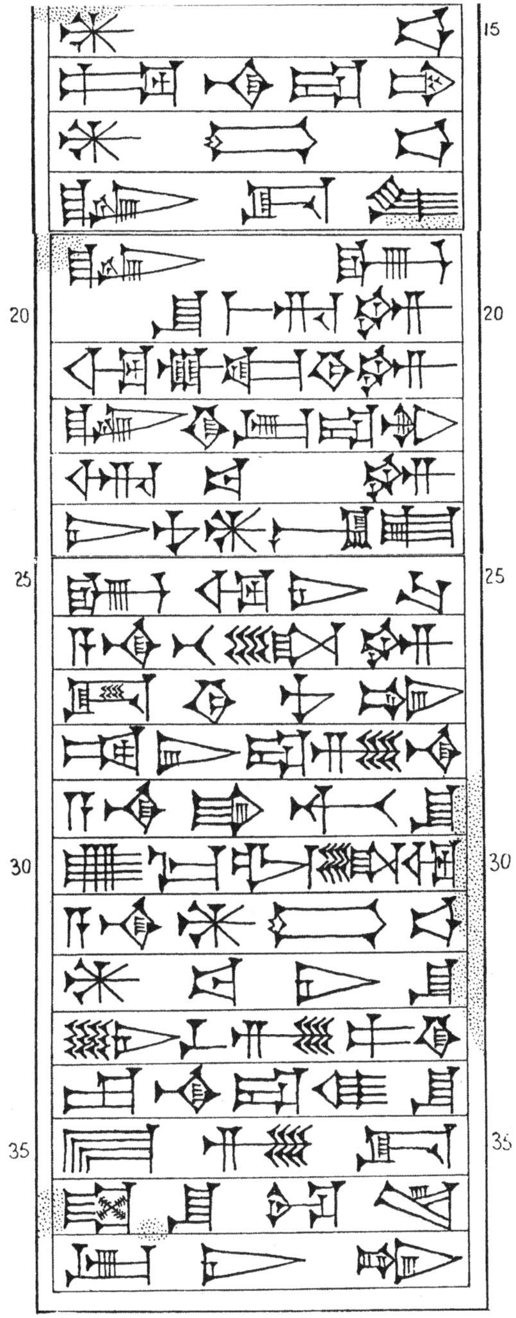

15
20
20
25
25
30
30
35
35

LESSON THIRTY-ONE

31.1 The N Stem: Sound Verbs; Verbs I–*n*; Verbs III–weak

As its name implies, this stem is characterized by an *n* before the root. In forms that have prefixes (Durative, Perfect, Preterite, Participle), this *n* stands before another consonant and is therefore assimilated. The other forms begin with *na-* (*ne-* in verbs with *e*).

(a) Sound Verbs

G theme:	*a–u* class	*a* class	*u* class	*i* class
Infinitive:	*naprusum*	*naṣbutum*	*nasḫurum*	*napqudum*
Durative:	*ipparras*	*iṣṣabbat*	*issaḫḫar*	*ippaqqid*
Perfect:	*ittapras*	*ittaṣbat*	*ittasḫar*	*ittapqid*
Preterite:	*ipparis*	*iṣṣabit*	*issaḫer*	*ippaqid*
Pret. 3mp:	*ipparsū*	*iṣṣabtū*	*issaḫrū*	*ippaqdū*
Imperative:	*napris*	*naṣbit*	*nasḫer*	*napqid*
Participle:	*mupparsum*	*muṣṣabtum*	*mussaḫrum*	*muppaqdum*
bound form:	*mupparis*	*muṣṣabit*	*mussaḫer*	*muppaqid*
Verbal Adj.:	*naprusum*	*naṣbutum*	*nasḫurum*	*napqudum*
V. Adj. base:	*naprus*	*naṣbut*	*nasḫur*	*napqud*

Note particularly the following features:

(1) The N Stem, unlike the D and Š, is based on the G stem. Thus, the personal prefixes of the Durative, Perfect, and Preterite are *i-*, *ta-*, *a-*, *ni-* as in the G (as opposed to *u-*, *tu-*, etc., in the D and Š).

(2) Further, the vowel class of an N verb depends in part on that of the corresponding G verb. If the G verb is *a–u*, *a*, or *u* class, the N is *a–i* class (as in the D and Š); if the G verb is *i*, the N also has *i* in both Durative and Preterite. Note that this means the N Preterite (and thus the Imperative as well) has *i* in all cases. In the N, the vowel of the Perfect is the same as that of the Durative, as in the G (and unlike in the D and Š), as in Dur. *ipparras*, Perf. *ittapras*. (*E*-type verbs may, as expected, exhibit *e* for *a*, as in Durative *iššebber*. An exception to the patterning of theme-vowels as presented here is the N of *epēšum*, which in addition to forms with the expected *e–i* pattern exhibits Durative, Preterite, and Perfect forms with theme-vowel *u*; see §32.1. Other exceptions occur in later dialects.)

(3) When vocalic suffixes are added to the Preterite, syncope occurs:

3cs *ipparis*, with Ventive *ipparsam*; 3mp *ipparsū*, etc.

(4) The base, and thus the ms bound form, of the Participle is *mupparis-*; the fs is *mupparistum* (bound form *mupparsat*).

(5) In the Infinitive and Verbal Adjective, the vowel between R_2 and R_3 is *u*, as in all the derived stems.

(6) Some confusion with the G stem is possible if doubling is not indicated in the script: e.g.,

i-pa-qí-id may be G Dur. *ipaqqid*, N Dur. *ippaqqid*, or N Pret. *ippaqid*.

(b) Verbs I–*n*

These present no difficulties in the Durative, Preterite, or Participle. In the Perfect, however, the *n* of the root is **not** assimilated. In the remaining forms (Imperative, Infinitive, Verbal Adjective), assimilation of the *n* of the root is apparently optional.

G theme:	*a–u*, *a*, or *u* class	*i* class
Infinitive:	*naqqurum* / *nanqurum*	*naddunum* / *nandunum*
Durative:	*innaqqar*	*innaddin*
Perfect:	*ittanqar*	*ittandin*
Preterite:	*innaqer*	*innadin*
Imperative:	*naqqer* / *nanqer*	*naddin* / *nandin*
Participle:	*munnaqrum*	*munnadnum*
Verbal Adj.:	*naqqurum* / *nanqurum*	*naddunum* / *nandunum*
V. Adj. base:	*naqqur* / *nanqur*	*naddun* / *nandun*

(c) Verbs III–weak

The vowel of the Durative and Perfect is that of the corresponding G, but the Preterite (and thus the Imperative) normally has *i*. Otherwise the forms require no further comment.

G theme:	*i*	*a*	*u*	*e*
Infinitive:	*nabnûm*	*naklûm*	*namnûm*	*nešmûm* / *našmûm*
Durative:	*ibbanni*	*ikkalla*	*immannu*	*iššemme* / *iššamme*
Perfect:	*ittabni*	*ittakla*	*ittamnu*	*ittešme* / *ittašme*
Preterite:	*ibbani*	*ikkali*	*immani*	*iššemi* / *iššami*
Imperative:	*nabni*	*nakli*	*namni*	*nešmi* / *našmi*
Participle:	*mubbanûm*	*mukkalûm*	*mummanûm*	*mušš*^{e}/*amûm*
bound form:	*mubbani*	*mukkali*	*mummani*	*muššemi* / *muššami*
Verbal Adj.:	*nabnûm*	*naklûm*	*namnûm*	*nešmûm* / *našmûm*
V. Adj. base:	*nabni*	*nakli(?)*	*namni(?)*	*nešmi* / *našmi(?)*

(d) Below are full paradigms of the N stems of *parāsum* (*a–u*), *nadānum* (*i*), *kalûm* (*a*), and *šemûm* (*e*).

Durative

3cs	*ipparras*	*innaddin*	*ikkalla*	*iššemme / iššamme*
2ms	*tapparras*	*tannaddin*	*takkalla*	*teššemme / taššamme*
2fs	*tapparrasī*	*tannaddinī*	*takkallî*	*teššemmî / taššammî*
1cs	*apparras*	*annaddin*	*akkalla*	*eššemme / aššamme*
3mp	*ipparrasū*	*innaddinū*	*ikkallû*	*iššemmû / iššammû*
3fp	*ipparrasā*	*innaddinā*	*ikkallâ*	*iššemmeā / iššammeā*
2cp	*tapparrasā*	*tannaddinā*	*takkallâ*	*teššemmeā / taššammeā*
1cp	*nipparras*	*ninnaddin*	*nikkalla*	*niššemme / niššamme*

Perfect

3cs	*ittapras*	*ittandin*	*ittakla*	*ittešme / ittašme*
2ms	*tattapras*	*tattandin*	*tattakla*	*tettešme / tattašme*
2fs	*tattaprasī*	*tattandinī*	*tattaklî*	*tettešmî / tattašmî*
1cs	*attapras*	*attandin*	*attakla*	*ettešme / attašme*
3mp	*ittaprasū*	*ittandinū*	*ittaklû*	*ittešmû / ittašmû*
3fp	*ittaprasā*	*ittandinā*	*ittaklâ*	*ittešmeā / ittašmeā*
2cp	*tattaprasā*	*tattandinā*	*tattaklâ*	*tettešmeā / tattašmeā*
1cp	*nittapras*	*nittandin*	*nittakla*	*nittešme / nittašme*

Preterite

3cs	*ipparis*	*innadin*	*ikkali*	*iššemi / iššami*
2ms	*tapparis*	*tannadin*	*takkali*	*teššemi / taššami*
2fs	*tapparsī*	*tannadnī*	*takkalî*	*teššemî / taššamî*
1cs	*apparis*	*annadin*	*akkali*	*eššemi / aššami*
3mp	*ipparsū*	*innadnū*	*ikkalû*	*iššemû / iššamû*
3fp	*ipparsā*	*innadnā*	*ikkaliā*	*iššemiā / iššamiā*
2cp	*tapparsā*	*tannadnā*	*takkaliā*	*teššemiā / taššamiā*
1cp	*nipparis*	*ninnadin*	*nikkali*	*niššemi / niššami*

Precative

3cs	*lipparis*	*linnadin*	*likkali*	*liššemi / liššami*
1cs	*lupparis*	*lunnadin*	*lukkali*	*luššemi / luššami*
3mp	*lipparsū*	*linnadnū*	*likkalû*	*liššemû / liššamû*
3fp	*lipparsā*	*linnadnā*	*likkaliā*	*liššemiā / liššamiā*
1cp	*i nipparis*	*i ninnadin*	*i nikkali*	*i niššemi / i niššami*

Imperative

ms	*napris*	*naddin* / *nandin*	*nakli*	*nešmi* / *našmi*
fs	*naprisī*	*naddinī* / *nandinī*	*naklî*	*nešmî* / *našmî*
cp	*naprisā*	*naddinā* / *nandinā*	*nakliā*	*nešmiā* / *našmiā*

Participle

ms	*mupparsum*	*munnadnum*	*mukkalûm*	*mušš*^{e}/$_{a}$*mûm*
(bound	*mupparis*	*munnadin*	*mukkali*	*mušš*^{e}/$_{a}$*mi*)
fs	*mupparistum*	*munnadittum*	*mukkalītum*	*mušš*^{e}/$_{a}$*mītum*
(bound	*mupparsat*	*munnadnat*	*mukkaliat*	*mušš*^{e}/$_{a}$*miat*)
mp	*mupparsūtum*	*munnadnūtum*	*mukkalûtum*	*mušš*^{e}/$_{a}$*mûtum*
fp	*mupparsātum*	*munnadnātum*	*mukkaliātum*	*mušš*^{e}/$_{a}$*miātum*

Verbal Adjective

nom.ms	*naprusum*	*naddunum* / *nandunum*	*naklûm*	*nešmûm* / *našmûm*
+3ms	*naprus*	*naddun* / *nandun*	*nakli(?)*	*nešmi* / *našmi(?)*
+3fs	*naprusat*	*naddunat* / *nandunat*	*nakliat(?)*	*nešmiat* / *našmiat(?)*

31.2 The Meaning of the N Stem

(1) **Passive** of active-transitive G verbs: e.g.,

> *iṣṣabbat* 'he will be seized';
> *ittaškanū* 'they (m) have been placed';
> *ṭuppum iššebir* 'the tablet was broken'.

Note that the agent of a passive verb ('broken **by** someone') is not usually expressed in Akkadian.

N forms of *šapārum* and *qabûm* (and similar verbs) sometimes appear without a subject expressed but with a complement expressed by *ana* or a dative suffix; a smooth translation may require making the complement the subject in English:

> *ana awīlê šunūti aššum alākim ittašpar* 'those men have been commanded to go' (lit., 'it has been commanded to those men to go');
> *aššum pūḫ eqlīya apālīya iqqabīkunūšim* 'you (mp) were ordered to pay me my substitute field' (lit., 'it was ordered to you to pay').

(2) **Middle**. Middle verbs in English look like active transitive verbs, but take no object, as in 'the gate opened' (middle) vs. 'she opened the gate' (active transitive; the subject of a middle verb is the object of a corresponding transitive verb); compare

> *bābam ipte* 'she opened the gate'
> and *bābum ippeti* 'the gate opened' (or 'the gate was opened');

ṭuppam išebber 'he will break the tablet'
and *ṭuppum iššebber* 'the tablet will break' (or 'will be broken').

There is a significant difference in meaning between finite N forms and predicative forms of the G Verbal Adjective. It may be said that the finite N forms of transitive G verbs turn G Verbal Adjectives into passive or middle action verbs ('is/was broken' → 'gets/got broken, breaks/ broke'): a finite N form connotes a process, an action (albeit passive), whereas a predicative G Verbal Adj. connotes only the condition or state resulting from the action of the G verb. Compare

narûm šaṭer 'the stela is/was inscribed',
but *narûm iššaṭṭar* 'the stela will be/is being inscribed',
narûm iššaṭer 'the stela was inscribed'.

In the first example the construction in English is the verb 'to be' followed by an adjective, while in the second and third the verb in English is the passive 'to be inscribed', which describes an action. Another set of examples:

bābum peti 'the gate is/was open',
but *bābum ippette* 'the gate is being/will be opened' or 'the gate is opening/will open',
bābum ippeti 'the gate was opened' or 'the gate opened'.

(3) Rarely, the N is **reflexive**, as in

nasḫurum 'to turn (oneself)'.

(4) The N stem of *bašûm* means 'to come into existence, appear, become available'.

N forms of other stative verbs are rare; those that do occur function in part like N forms of active verbs, providing fientive (action) counterparts to the G Verbal Adj. (see (2)), as in

šumšu immassik 'his name will become bad'; cf. *maskum* 'bad', Verbal Adj. of a verb *masākum* that does not otherwise occur in the G.

Such forms are labeled "ingressive" in some grammars; they have essentially the same meanings as finite G forms (see §22.1, p. 221).

(5) A few verbs occur lexically in the N stem, i.e., have the N rather than the G as their basic form. Others occur very rarely in the G, but normally in the N. The Š stem is used as the causative of such verbs, as expected.

naprušum N (not in G)'to fly'; *šuprušum* Š 'to cause to fly, to rout';
palāsum G (*a–u*) 'to see' (rare); *naplusum* N 'to see, look at'.

31.3 The Genitive: Constructions and Functions

(a) Constructions

The two major means of subordinating one noun to another were presented early in this textbook:

(1) The governing noun in the bound form (cf. §8.3): *mār šarrim*.

(2) The use of the determinative pronoun *ša* in apposition after the governing noun (§2.3): *mārum ša šarrim*. This construction may occur in any situation in which the bound form is used. There are, however, certain situations in which it is preferred, or in which it must be used:

(i) when there is more than one governing noun:
mārum u mārtum ša šarrim 'the son and daughter of the king';

(ii) when there is more than one governed noun:
eqlum ša dayyānim u aḫīšu 'the field of the judge and his brother'
(unless the governed nouns are seen as a unit by the writer: *bēl šamê u erṣetim* 'lord of heaven and earth');

(iii) to clarify which noun an adjective modifies:
ina bītim ṣeḫrim ša mārim 'in the small house of the son',
vs., e.g.,
ina bīt mārim ṣeḫrim in which *ṣeḫrum* could modify either *bītum* or *mārum*;

There are three other constructions to express a genitive relationship, none of which occurs frequently.

(3) *ša* plus genitive noun before the governing noun; *ša* in this construction must usually be translated 'worth, equivalent to':

ša šinā šiqil kaspim šamnam šūbilam 'send (ms) me oil worth two shekels of silver'.

This construction also occurs in poetry as a stylistic variant of the more common first two constructions.

(4) The addition of a 3rd person pronoun to the governing noun, a rare construction denoting marked determination of the governing noun; it is also rarely used when there is more than one governing noun. The suffix agrees in gender and number with the governed noun(s):

aḫūša ša šarratim 'the (very) brother of the queen';
ana maḫīrātīšunu ša kaspīšu u ṣibtīšu 'at the (very) value(s) of his silver and its interest'.
baqrūšunu u rugummûšunu ša mārī 'the children's claims and suits'.

(5) In poetry only (with very few exceptions), probably for stylistic reasons, the previous construction occasionally occurs with the governing and governed nouns reversed in order:

ša šarratim aḫūša 'the queen's brother';
ša nišī bēlūšina 'the people's rulers'.

(b) Functions

The function or purpose of a noun (or pronoun) in the genitive dependent on another noun is to delimit, specify, or explain that noun more precisely in some way. Usually, the genitive relationship may be translated 'of', and most Akkadian examples correspond to English usage: e.g., to express

possession: *bēl bītim* 'the owner of the house';

content: *karpat karānim* 'a jug (*karpatum*) of wine'; *ṭēm eqlim* 'the report of/about the field';

material: *kakki ḫurāṣim* 'a weapon of gold'.

Akkadian uses the genitive more frequently than does English, for example, to specify the material out of which something is made, or the nature, quality, or condition of something. In these and other instances, English normally prefers an adjective to a genitive noun; ***kakki ḫurāṣim***, for example, may also be rendered 'a gold(en) weapon'. Other examples:

šībūt sarrātim 'false testimony' ('testimony of falsehoods');
dayyān kīttim 'a just judge' ('a judge of justice').

A genitive of respect is sometimes found after a bound form adjective (cf. English 'swift of foot', 'hard of hearing'); examples are

bēlum rapaš uznim 'an intelligent lord' (lit., 'a lord wide of ear'; note the poetic *Ištar rapšat uznim* 'the intelligent Ištar');
ṣalmāt qaqqadim 'the black-headed ones' (lit., 'the black (*ṣalmum*) ones (fp, referring to *nišū*) with respect to the head', a common designation for the people of Sumer and Akkad);
saniq pīšu '(someone) whose speech is verified' (lit., 'one proven with regard to his speech');
ṭuppum kanik Bābilim 'a tablet sealed in Babylon'.

In a very rare variation of this construction, found in literary texts, the adjective is not in the bound form but in the free form acc., regardless of its syntactic case:

rapšam uznim instead of *rapaš uznim*.

EXERCISES

A. VOCABULARY 31.

Verbs:

belûm G (*e*) 'to go out, be extinguished'; *bullûm* D 'to put out, extinguish (fire), destroy'.

ḫabātum G (*a–u*) 'to rob, plunder'; *naḫbutum* N passive; note also *ḫabbātum* (*ḫabbāt*) 'robber'; *ḫubtum* (*ḫubut*) 'robbery'.

magārum G (*a–u*) see Lesson 30; *namgurum* N 'to come to an agreement, agree'.

maṭûm G (*i*) 'to diminish (intrans.), decrease, become small, few, missing, poor (in size or quality)'; Verbal Adj. *maṭûm* (*maṭi-*) 'small, cheap, low, humble'; *piam maṭiam šakānum* 'to speak humbly'; *muṭṭûm* D 'to diminish (in quantity or quality; trans.), cause a decrease'; *šumṭûm* Š 'to diminish, belittle, treat badly'.

napāḫum G (*a–u*) 'to blow, blow on (something); to light (a fire, stove); to become visible, shine, light up'; Verbal Adj. *napḫum* (*napiḫ-*) 'kindled, burning, shining; swollen, bloated'; *nanpuḫum* N 'to be kindled, break out' (of a fire).

palāsum G (*a–u*) 'to see' (rare); *naplusum* N 'to see, look at'.

sapāḫum G (*a–u*) 'to scatter, disperse, squander; to confound'; *suppuḫum* D = G; *naspuḫum* N passive.

sarārum G (*a–u*) 'to be(come) false; to cheat'; Verbal Adj. *sarrum* (*sarr-*; fs irregular *sartum*) 'false, criminal; liar'; *surrurum* D 'to make false claims, claim falsely, contest'; note also substantivized fem. sg. *sartum* (pl. *sarrātum*) 'lie, falsehood, treachery; misdeed, criminal act'.

Nouns:

kārum (*kār*; log. KAR; Sum. lw.) 'embankment, quay (wall); harbor district, harbor; merchant community'.

mimmû (base *mimmā-*; no mimation; gen. *mimmê*, acc. *mimmâ*) 'something; all of; property' (cf. *mimma*).

nikkassum (*nikkas*; pl. *nikkassū* [often = sg.]; log. NÍG.KAS$_7$; Sum. lw.) 'accounting, account (record)'.

numātum (*numāt*) 'household property, utensils, furnishings'.

ramānum (*ramān*) 'self, oneself; (one's) own; alone'; normally with a pron. suff., as a reflexive or intensive pronoun (e.g., *ramāššu ipaṭṭar* 'he will ransom himself'; *ramāššu illik* 'he himself went'); *ana ramānī-* 'for oneself'; *ina ramānī-* 'by oneself, of one's own accord, alone'; after a bound form: '(one's) own' (e.g., *ina ṭēm ramānīki* 'according to your (fs) own judgment').

suluppum (pl. *suluppū*; log. ZÚ.LUM(.MA) [ZÚ = ka]; Sum. lw.) 'date(s)'.

sūnum (*sūn(i)*) 'lap, crotch'.

šangûm (*šangā-*; log. SANGA; Sum. lw.) 'temple administrator'.

ugārum (*ugār*; pl. *ugārû*, *ugārātum*; log. A.GÀR; Sum. lw.?) 'open field, meadow, arable land'.

Place name:

Sippar (log. ZIMBIR^{ki} [ud.kib.nun^{ki}]) an important city about 60 km. north of Babylon (modern Abu Habba).

B. Learn the following signs:

OB Lapid.	OB Cursive	NA	values
	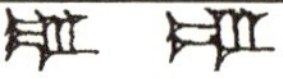		SANGA = *šangûm*; KAS$_7$ (or ŠID) in NÍG.KAS$_7$ (also read NÍG.ŠID) = *nikkassum*
			NUN = *rubûm*
			kib in ud.kib.nun^{ki} = ZIMBIR^{ki} = *Sippar*

C. Write the following words in cuneiform and in transliteration; use logograms where possible:

1. *nikkas nāqidim*
2. *bilat parakkī*
3. *mû ḫegallim*
4. *almatti itinnim*
5. *šangê Šamaš*
6. *kār nārim*
7. *sūq Sippar*
8. *adi maškan rubêm*
9. *ugārum u qištum*
10. *šittā bilat suluppum*

D. Write in normalized Akkadian:

1. The stone was weighed.
2. in your (ms) looking at the people
3. The temple administrator has been sent.
4. Your (ms) father-in-law will be conducted here.
5. Be turned (fs) to(ward) me!
6. The cattle were counted.
7. His utterance was not heard.

8. The judges have not been protected.
9. The sesame became available.
10. The cattle-pen was built.
11. The dates will be taken.
12. Your (ms) army has been cut off.
13. Her dwelling was surrounded.
14. The heir will be removed.
15. Be heard (pl)!
16. an opening (becoming open) gate
17. to become finished
18. May his name not be inscribed here.
19. His bones will be broken.
20. Be thrown down (ms)!
21. They (m) have come to an agreement.
22. The mayor got robbed.
23. A fire broke out in the harbor district.
24. May her name be invoked.
25. Her household property will be scattered.
26. My arable land has been inundated.
27. The foundation will loosen.

E. CH:

§§22–24 §22 *šum-ma a-wi-lum ḫu-ub-tam iḫ-bu-ut-ma it-ta-aṣ-ba-at a-wi-lum šu-ú id-da-ak.* §23 *šum-ma ḫa-ab-ba-tum la it-ta-aṣ-ba-at a-wi-lum ḫa-ab-tum mi-im-ma-šu ḫal-qá-am ma-ḫa-ar i-lim ú-ba-ar-ma* URU *ù ra-bi-a-nu-um ša i-na er-ṣe-ti-šu-nu ù pa-ṭi-šu-nu ḫu-ub-tum iḫ-ḫa-ab-tu mi-im-ma-šu ḫal-qá-am i-ri-a-ab-bu-šum.* §24 *šum-ma na-pí-iš-tum* URU *ù ra-bi-a-nu-um* 1 MA.NA KUG.BABBAR *a-na ni-ši-šu i-ša-qá-lu.*

i-ri-a-ab-bu-šum for *iribbūšum,* a morphographemic writing (i.e., the paradigmatic singular *irīab,* followed by the *-bu* sign to indicate the plural *iribbū*; see §18.4).

§25 *šum-ma i-na* É *a-wi-lim i-ša-tum in-na-pí-iḫ-ma a-wi-lum ša a-na bu-ul-li-im il-li-ku a-na nu-ma-at be-el* É *i-in-šu iš-ši-ma nu-ma-at be-el* É *il-te-qé*(!DI) *a-wi-lum šu-ú a-na i-ša-tim šu-a-ti in-na-ad-di.*

§32 [*š*]*um-ma lu* AGA.ÚS *ù lu* ŠU.ḪA *ša i-na ḫar-ra-an šar-ri-im tu-úr-ru* DAM.GÀR *ip-ṭú-ra-aš-šu-ma* URU-*šu uš-ta-ak-ši-da-aš-šu šum-ma i-na bi-ti-šu ša pa-ṭa-ri-im i-ba-aš-ši šu-ma ra-ma-an-šu i-pa-aṭ-ṭa-ar šum-ma i-na bi-ti-šu ša pa-ṭa-ri-šu la i-ba-aš-ši i-na* É DINGIR URU-*šu ip-pa-aṭ-ṭár šum-ma i-na* É DINGIR URU-*šu ša pa-ṭa-ri-šu la i-ba-aš-ši* É.GAL *i-pa-aṭ-ṭa-ar*(! RI)-*šu* A.ŠÀ-*šu* ^{giš}KIRI$_6$-*šu ù* É-*sú a-na ip-ṭe*$_4$*-ri-šu ú-ul in-na-ad-di-in.*

ipṭerū (always pl.) 'ransom (price)' (cf. *paṭārum*).

§49 *šum-ma a-wi-lum* KUG.BABBAR *it-ti* DAM.GÀR *il-qé-ma* A.ŠÀ *ep-še-tim ša* ŠE *ù lu* ŠE.GIŠ.Ì *a-na* DAM.GÀR *id-di-in* A.ŠÀ *e-ri-iš-ma* ŠE *ù lu-ú* ŠE.GIŠ.Ì *ša ib-ba-aš-šu-ú e-si-ip ta-ba-al iq-bi-šum šum-ma er-re-šum i-na* A.ŠÀ ŠE *ù lu* ŠE.GIŠ.Ì *uš-tab-ši i-na ebūrim* ($BURU_{14}$) ŠE *ù* ŠE.GIŠ.Ì *ša i-na* A.ŠÀ *ib-ba-aš-šu-ú be-el* A.ŠÀ-*ma i-le-qé-ma* ŠE *ša* KUG.BABBAR-*šu ù ṣi-ba-sú ša it-ti* DAM.GÀR *il-qú-ú ù ma-na-ḫa-at e-re-ši-im a-na* DAM.GÀR *i-na-ad-di-in.*

The words after *iddin* and before *iqbīšum* comprise a direct quotation.

esēpum G (*i*) 'to collect, gather up'.

mānaḫtum (*mānaḫti*; pl. *mānaḫātum*) 'toil, weariness; maintenance, upkeep, improvements'.

§§53–54 §53 *šum-m[a a-w]i-lum a-n[a* KAR A.ŠÀ]-*šu du-u[n-nu-n]im a-aḫ-šu i[d-di-m]a* KAR [A.ŠÀ-*šu*] *la ú-da[n-ni-in-ma] i-na* KA[R-*šu*] *pí-tum it-t[e-ep-te]* ⌜*ù*⌝ A.GÀR *me-e uš-ta-bíl a-wi-lum ša i-na* KAR-*šu pí-tum ip-pé-tu-ú* ŠE *ša ú-ḫal-li-qú i-ri-a-ab.* §54 *šum-ma* ŠE *ri-a-ba-am la i-le-i šu-a-ti ù bi-ša-šu a-na* KUG.BABBAR *i-na-ad-di-nu-ma* DUMU.A.GÀR.MEŠ *ša* ŠE-*šu-nu mu-ú ub-lu i-zu-uz-zu.*

DUMU.A.GÀR.MEŠ unclear; *mārū ugārim*?

§66 *šum-ma a-wi-lum* KUG.BABBAR *it-ti* DAM.GÀR *il-qé-ma* DAM.GÀR-*šu i-si-ir-šu-ma mi-im-ma ša na-da-nim la i-ba-aš-ši-šum* $KIRI_6$-*šu iš-tu tar-ki-ib-tim a-na* DAM.GÀR *id-di-in-ma suluppī*(ZÚ.LUM) *ma-la i-na* $KIRI_6$ *ib-ba-aš-šu-ú a-na* KUG.BABBAR-*ka ta-ba-al iq-bi-šum* DAM.GÀR *šu-ú ú-ul im-ma-gàr suluppī*(ZÚ.LUM) *ša i-na* $KIRI_6$ *ib-ba-aš-šu-ú be-el* $KIRI_6$-*ma i-le-qé-ma* KUG.BABBAR *ù* MÁŠ-*sú ša pī*(KA) DUB-*pí-šu* DAM.GÀR *i-ip-pa-al-ma suluppī*(ZÚ.LUM) *wa-at-ru-tim ša i-na* $KIRI_6$ *ib-ba-aš-šu-ú be-el* $KIRI_6$-*ma i-l[e-eq-qé].*

tarkibtum 'date-palm pollination'.

The words after *iddim-ma* and before *iqbīšum* are a direct quotation.

§105 *šum-ma šamallûm*($ŠAMAN_2$.LÁ) *i-te-gi-ma ka-ni-ik* KUG.BABBAR *ša a-na* DAM.GÀR *id-di-nu la il-te-qé* KUG.BABBAR *la ka-ni-ki-im a-na ni-ik-ka-as-sí-im ú-ul iš-ša-ak-ka-an.*

§109 *šum-ma sābītum*(MÍ.KURUN.NA) *sà-ar-ru-tum i-na* É-*ša it-tar-ka-sú-ma sà-ar-ru-tim šu-nu-ti la iṣ-ṣa-ab-tam-ma a-na* É.GAL *la ir-de-a-am sābītum*(MÍ.KURUN.NA) *ši-i id-da-ak.*

sābûm, fem. *sābītum* (log. LÚ/MÍ.KURUN.NA) 'innkeeper, beer merchant'.

narkusum N (*rakāsum*) rare, here 'to conspire'.

§§117–118 §117 *šum-ma a-wi-lam e-ʾì-il-tum iṣ-ba-sú-ma* DAM-*sú* DUMU-*šu ù* DUMU.MUNUS-*sú a-na* KUG.BABBAR *id-di-in ù lu a-na ki-iš-ša-a-tim it-ta-an-di-in* MU.3.KAM É *ša-a-a-ma-ni-šu-nu ù ka-ši-ši-šu-nu i-ip-pé-šu i-na re-bu-tim ša-at-tim an-du-ra-ar-šu-nu iš-ša-ak-ka-an.* §118 *šum-ma* ÌR *ù lu* GEME$_2$ *a-na ki-iš-ša-tim it-ta-an-di-in* DAM.GÀR *ú-še-te-eq a-na* KUG.BABBAR *i-na-ad-din ú-ul ib-ba-qar.*

eʾiltum '(financial) liability, obligation'.

kašāšum G (*a–u*) 'to exact services for a debt'; *kiššātum* (pl.) 'debt servitude'.

šayyāmānum (*šayyāmān*) 'buyer' (cf. *šâmum*).

§141 *šum-ma aš-ša-at a-wi-lim ša i-na* É *a-wi-lim wa-aš-ba-at a-na wa-ṣe-em pa-ni-ša iš-ta-ka-an-ma sí-ki-il-tam i-sà-ak-ki-il* É-*sà ú-sà-ap-pa-ah̬ mu-sà ú-ša-am-ṭa ú-ka-an-nu-ši-ma šum-ma mu-sà e-zé-eb-ša iq-ta-bi i-iz-zi-ib-ši h̬a-ra-an-ša ú-zu-ub-bu-ša mi-im-ma ú-ul in-na-ad-di-iš-ši-im šum-ma mu-sà la e-zé-eb-ša iq-ta-bi mu-sà* MUNUS *ša-ni-tam i-ih̬-h̬a-az* MUNUS *ši-i ki-ma* GEME$_2$ *i-na* É *mu-ti-ša uš-ša-ab.*

sakālum G (*i*) 'to acquire illegally'; *sikiltum* (*sikilti*) 'acquisition(s), property'.

uzubbûm (*uzubbā-*) 'divorce, divorce-payment' (cf. *ezēbum*).

§202 *šum-ma a-wi-lum le-e-et a-wi-lim ša e-li-šu ra-bu-ú im-ta-h̬a-aṣ i-na pu-úh̬-ri-im i-na qinnāz*(^{kuš}USAN$_3$) GUD 1 *šu-ši im-mah̬-h̬a-aṣ.*

qinnāzum (*qinnāz*; log. ^{kuš}USAN$_3$ [^{kuš}, the SU sign, before words for objects of leather]) 'whip'.

šūši see §23.2(a).

§§17–19:

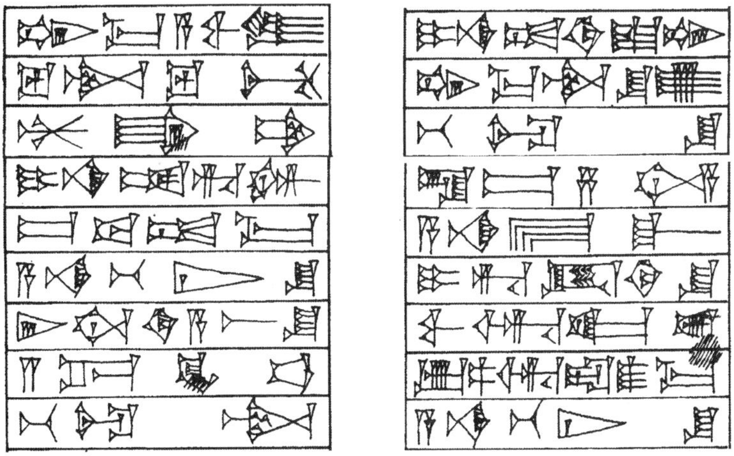

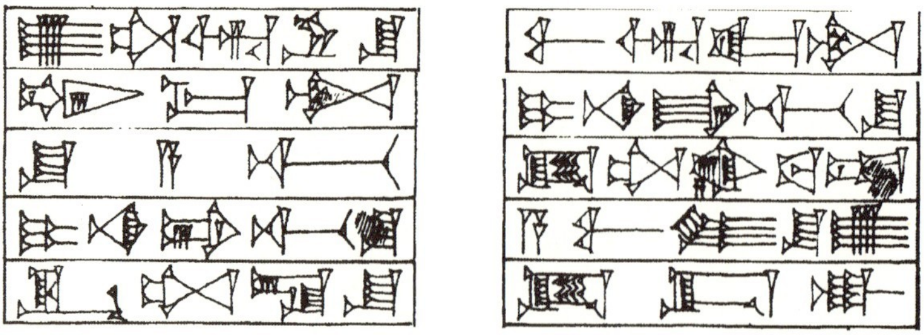

§265:

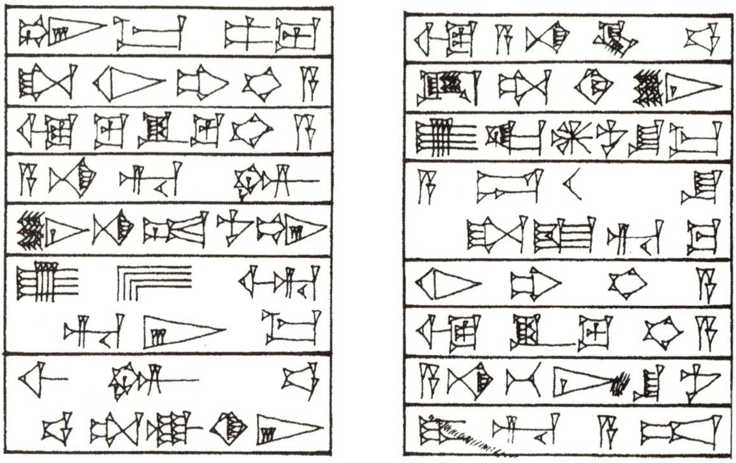

šimtum (*šimat* and *šimti*) 'mark, brand; color(ing)'.

F. Omens from *YOS* 10:

1. DIŠ *naplaštum*(IGI.BAR) *ki-ma na-al-ba-tim-ma ù ši-lum i-na* ŠÀ-*ša* URU[ki] LUGAL *i-la-wi iṣ-ṣa-ba-at-ma in-na-qá-ar.* (9:4–6)
   nalbattum (*nalbatti*; pl. *nalbanātum*) 'brick-mold'.
   šīlum 'hole'.
2. *šum-ma* 4 *na-ap-la-sà-tum qá-ab-lum i-na li-ib-*[*bi*] *ma-ti i*[*b-ba-aš-ši*]. (11 ii 1–2)
   qablum b (*qabal*) 'battle, warfare'.
3. DIŠ *iz-bu-um mu-uš-ti-nam la i-šu mi-lum i-na na-ri-im i-pa-ra-sà-am zi-nu i-na ša-me-e iš-ša-aq-qá-lu.* (56 i 23–25)
   muštinnum 'urethra'.
   mīlum (*mīl(i)*) '(seasonal) flood (of rivers)'.
   zinnum (*zinni*; pl. *zinnū* [often = sg.]) 'rain'.
   šaqālum b G (*a–u*) 'take (away), remove' (rare).

4. DIŠ *iz-bu-um pa-ni barbarim*(UR.BAR.RA) *ša-ki-in mu-ta-nu da-an-nu-tum ib-ba-aš-šu-ú-ma a-ḫu-um a-na bi-it a-ḫi-im ú-ul i-ru-ub.* (56 iii 3–5)
   barbarum (log. UR.BAR.RA) 'wolf'.
   mūtānū (always pl.) 'plague, epidemic' (cf. *mâtum*).
5. 31 viii 11–17:

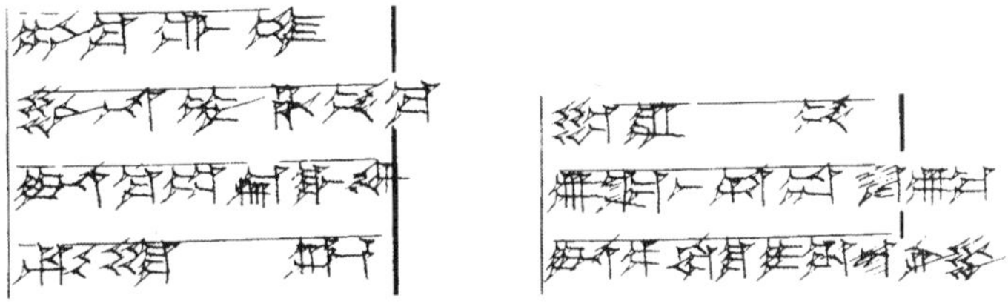

6. 31 xii 14–19:

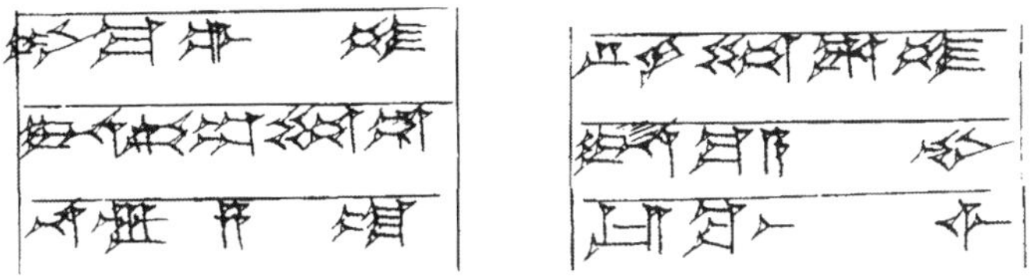

   gilittum 'fright, terror'.

G. Contract:

1. Exchange of houses (Szlechter, *TJA* 53–54 UMM H57).

[1] *x bītum epšum* (É.DÙ.A) [2] *ṭēḫi*(DA) É LÚ-DINGIR [3] *ù ṭēḫi*(DA) É *ì-lí-ù-*^{d}UTU [4] SAG.BI *rebītum*(SILA.DAGAL.LA) [5] SAG.BI *šanûm*(2.KAM.MA) É *kiš*^{ki}*-a-bi* [6]*pu-úḫ y bītim epšim* (É.DÙ.A) [7] *ša* ^{f}*da-an-e-re-es-sà* NIN.DINGIR ^{d}*za-ba*$_4$*-ba*$_4$ [8] DUMU.MUNUS *ma-ni-um* [9] *ù ip-*[*qú*?]-^{d}*èr-ra* SIPAD *laḫrātim*(U$_8$.ḪI.A) [10] *ša a-na* É.METE(!BU).UR.SAG *ša* ^{d}*za-ba*$_4$*-ba*$_4$ [11] *il-le-qú-ú* [12] *i-na qá-bé-*[*e*] *šar-ri-im* [13] ^{Id}*za-ba*$_4$*-ba*$_4$*-m*[*u-b*]*a-lí-iṭ ra-bi-a-an kiš*^{ki} [14] ^{I}*mu-na-wi-rum šakkanakkum*(GÌR.NITA$_2$) [15] ^{I}*mu-na-wi-rum nāgirum* [16]*ù ši-bu-ut kiš*^{ki} [17]*id-di-nu-šu-nu-ši-im.* [18–32] Witnesses. [33–35] Date.

PNs: *Awīl-ilim; Ilī-u-Šamaš; Kiš-abī; Dan-erēssa; Manium; Ipqu-Erra; Zababa-muballiṭ; Munawwirum.*

[2] *ṭēḫum* (*ṭēḫ(i)*; log. DA) 'proximity, what adjoins'; bound form as a preposition in OB contracts, DA É PN = *ṭēḫi bīt* PN 'adjoining the house of PN'.

[4] *rēšum* here 'front(age)'; *rebītum* (*rebīt*) '(town) square, plaza'.

[9] *laḫrum* (*laḫar*; pl. *laḫrātum*?; log. U$_8$) 'ewe'.

^{10} *Emeteursag*, temple of Zababa.

^{13} *Kiš*, an important and very ancient city some 10 km. to the east of Babylon.

^{14} *šakkanakkum* (*šakkanak*; log. GÌR.NITA2 [NITA2 = ÌR]) '(military) governor'.

^{15} *nāgirum*(*nāgir*; log. NIMGIR) 'herald'.

2. Szlechter, *TJA* 102–3 FM 31.

^{1} *x* GUR ZÚ.LUM ^{2} *šu-ku-un-ne* ^{giš}KIRI$_6$ ^{3} ^{I}*ta-ri-bu-um* ^{4} *ša a-na ì-lí-i-din-nam* ^{5} *iš-ša-ak-nu* ^{6} ITI *waraḫsamnam* ^{7} ZÚ.LUM *imaddad*(Ì. ÁG.E) $^{8-10}$ Witnesses. $^{11-15}$ Date.

PNs: *Tarībum; Ilī-iddinam.*

^{2} *šukunnûm* (*šukunnā-*) 'estimated yield' (cf. *šakānum*); *ana šukunnêm šakānum* 'to fix an estimate'.

^{6} *Waraḫsamnum*($^{(giš)}$APIN.DU$_8$.A) the eighth month (Oct.-Nov.).

H. Letters.

1. King, *LIH* 1 56 = Frankena, *AbB* 2 54

^{1} *a-na* ^{d}AMAR.UTU-*mu-ša-lim* ^{2} ^{Id}EN.ZU-*i-din-nam* ^{3} *ù a-wi-[i]l-*^{d}EN.ZU ^{4} *qí-bí-ma* ^{5} *um-ma am-mi-di-ta-na-ma* ^{6} LÚ.MEŠ *šu-ut pí-ḫa-a-tim ša i-na* ŠÀ.GA^{ki} *wa-aš-bu* ^{7} *ki-a-am iš-pu-ru-nim um-ma šu-nu-ma* ^{8} *x* ŠE.GUR ^{9} *a-na kurummat*(ŠUKU) ERIN$_2$ *bi-ir-ti* ŠÀ.GA^{ki} *ù a-ḫi-a-tim* ^{10} *ša* ITI *kislīmim*(GAN.GAN.È) ^{11} *iḫ-ḫa-aš-še-eḫ* ^{12} *ki-a-am iš-pu-ru-nim* ^{13} *a-na* LÚ.MEŠ *šu-ut pí-ḫa-a-tim ša i-na* ŠÀ.GA^{ki} *wa-aš-bu* ^{14} *aš-šum i-nu-ma ta-ša-ap-pa-ra-šu-nu-⌜ši-im⌝* ^{15} $^{lú.meš}$*ba-ab-bi-li a-na ma-aḫ-ri-ku-n[u ša-pa-ri-im]* ^{16} *it-ta-aš-pa-[ar]* ^{17} *šu-up-ra* $^{lú.meš}$*ba-[ab-bi-li]* ^{18}*a-nama-aḫ-ri-ku-nu l[i-iš-pu-ru-nim]-ma* ^{19} *i-na* ŠE-*em ša q[á-ti-ku-nu]* ^{20} *x* [ŠE.GUR] ^{21} *a-na kurummat* (ŠUKU) ERIN$_2$ *bi-ir-ti* ŠÀ.GA^{ki} *[ù a-ḫi-a-tim]* ^{22} *ša* ITI *kislīmim*(GAN. GAN.È) *šu-um-ḫi-ra-š[u-nu-ti]* ^{23} MÁŠ.ŠU.GÍD.GÍD.MEŠ *ša ma-aḫ-ri-k[u-nu]* ^{24} *wa-ar-ka-tam li-ip-ru-s[u-ma]* ^{25} *i-na* ^{uzu}*te-re-e-tim ša-al-ma-a-t[im]* ^{26} ŠE-*am šu-a-ti* ^{27} *a-na* ŠÀ.GA^{ki} *šu-bi-la.*

PNs: *Marduk-mušallim; Sîn-iddinam; Awīl-Sîn; Ammī-ditāna* (king of Babylon, ca. 1683–47);

^{6} *šūt* is an archaic, frozen pl. of *ša*, 'those of' (cf. *šūt-rēšim*); *awīlû šūt pīḫatim* 'the men responsible, the officials'.

^{7} *Šaga* a place name.

^{9} *kurummatum* (*kurummat*; log. ŠUKU) 'food allowance'; *birtum* (*birti*; pl. *bir(ān)ātum*) 'citadel, castle, fort'.

10 *Kislīmum* (log. GAN.GAN.È) the ninth month (Nov.–Dec.).

11 *ḫašāḫum* G (*i*) 'to desire; to require, need'; *nuḫšuḫum* N passive.

14–15 *aššum* governs the Infinitive *šapārim*; *inūma tašapparāšunūšim* is an intrusive temporal clause: 'concerning, when you write to them, the sending to you of bearers'; *babbilum* (*babbil*; pl. *babbilū*) 'bearer; tenant farmer' (cf. *babālum*).

25 UZU = *šīrum* 'flesh'; ^{uzu} determinative before parts of the body.

2. King, *LIH* 1 14 = Frankena, *AbB* 2 14.

1 [*a-na* ^{d}EN.ZU-*i-din-nam*] 2 [*qí-bí*]-*ma* 3 [*um-m*]*a* *ḫ*[*a*]-*am-mu-ra-pí-ma* 4 *ša-at-tum di-ri-ga-am i-šu* 5 *wa-ar-ḫu-um ša i-ir-ru-ba-am* 6 ITI *elūlum-šanûm*(KIN.^{d}INANNA.2.KAM.MA) *li-iš-ša-ṭe*$_{4}$*-er* 7 *ù a-šar igisûm*(IGI.SÁ) *i-na* ITI [*tašrīt*]*im*([DU$_{6}$.K]UG) UD.25.KAM 8 *a-na* KÁ.DINGIR.[RA^{ki}] 9 *sà-na-qum iq-*[*qá-bu*]*-ú* 10 *i-na* ITI *elūlim-šanîm* (KIN.^{d}INANNA.2.KAM.MA) UD.25.KAM 11 *a-na* KÁ.DINGIR. RA^{ki} 12 *li-is-ni-qá-am*.

PNs: *Sîn-iddinam*.

4 *šattum* here, '(this) year'; *dirigûm* (-*ā*; Sum. d i r i g (a)) 'intercalary month'; attested only here.

5 *ša irrubam* 'that is coming up' (i.e., 'next month').

6 *Elūnum* / *Elūlum* (later *Ulūlum*; log. KIN.^{d}INANNA) sixth month (Aug.–Sept.); here, *Elūlum-šanûm* 'second-Elūlum', a new month to be inserted into the calender of the year at issue, between the sixth and seventh months.

7 *igisûm* (-*ā*; IGI.SÁ; Sum. lw.) 'an annual tax (collected from merchants, priests); gift, offering'; *Tašrītum* (log. DU$_{6}$.KUG) the seventh month (Sept.–Oct.); for the construction in ll. 7–9, see §30.1(g 2, first example).

3. Schroeder, *VAS* 16 32 = Ungnad, *Babylonische Briefe* 116.

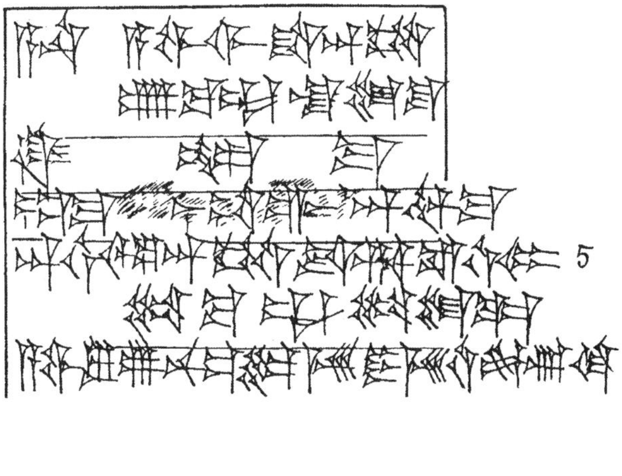

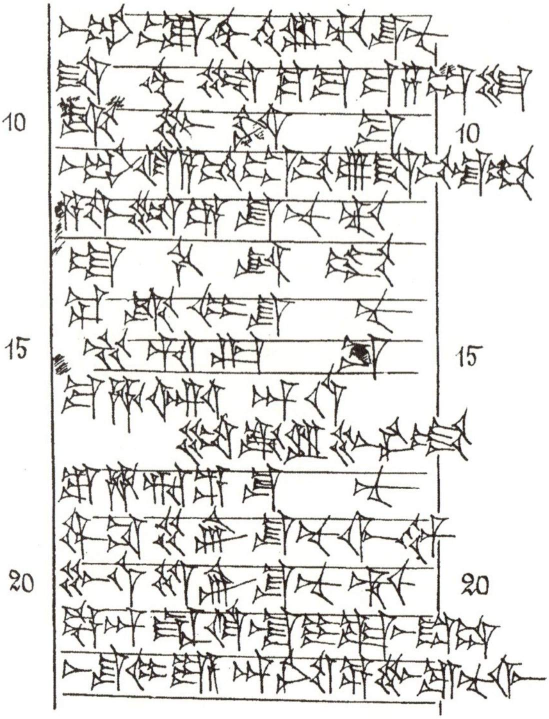

PN: *Aštamar-Adad.*

[7] NU.^{giš}KIRI$_6$ = *nukaribbum* (*nukarib*; pl. *nukaribbātum*) 'gardener'.

[8] *ṣeḫḫerum* (adj.) 'small'; substantivized pl. 'retainers, servants' (cf. *ṣeḫrum*).

[11] *aššum kiam* 'for this reason, therefore'.

[14] *sikmū* (always pl.) 'payment (for catching a fugitive)'.

[15] Last sign: *ma*.

[17] *karābum* G (*a–u*) 'to bless (someone: acc.), invoke blessings (on someone: *ana*/dat.); to praise'.

I. A Royal Inscription of Ḫammurapi: commemoration of laying the wall in Sippar (PBS 7 133 = Frayne, *RIME* 4, p. 334–36, lines 1–45; for 46–81, see Lesson 32).

[1] *i-nu* ^{d}UTU [2] *be-lum ra-bi-um* [3] *ša ša-ma-i ù er-ṣe-tim* [4] LUGAL *ša* DINGIR.DINGIR [5] *ḫa-am-mu-ra-pí* [6] *ru-ba-am mi-gir-šu ia-ti* [7] *in pa-ni-šu nam-ru-tim* [8] *ḫa-di-iš* [9] *ip-pa-al-sa*$_6$*-ni* [10] *šar-ru-tam da-rí-tám* [11] *palê*(BALA) UD-*mi ar-ku-tim* [12] *iš-ru-kam* [13] *išid*(SUḪUŠ) KALAM [14] *ša a-na be-li-im* [15] *i-din-na-am* [16] *ù-ki-in-nam* [17] *ni-šì* ZIMBIR^{ki} [18] *ù* KÁ.DINGIR.RA^{ki} [19] *šu-ba-at ne-eḫ-ti-im* [20] *šu-šu-ba-am*

[21] *in pí-šu el-li-im* [22] *ša la na-ka-ar iq-bi-ù* [23] BÀD ZIMBIR^{ki} [24] *e-pé-ša-am* [25] *re-ši-šu ul-la-a-am* [26] *ra-bi-iš* [27] *lu ‹ú›-we-er-ra-an-ni* [28] *i-nu-u*$_4$*-mi-šu* [29] *ḫa-am-mu-ra-pí* [30] LUGAL *da-núm* [31] LUGAL KÁ.DINGIR. RA^{ki} [32] *na-aʾ-du-um še-mu* ^{d}UTU [33] *na-ra-am* ^{d}*a-a* [34] *mu-ṭi-ib li-ib-bi* [35] ^{d}AMAR.UTU *be-li-šu a-na-ku* [36] *in e-mu-qí-in ṣi-ra-tim* [38] *ša* ^{d}UTU *id-din-na-am* [39] *in ti-bu-ut* [40] *um-ma-an ma-ti-ia* [41] *uš-ši* BÀD ZIMBIR^{ki} [42] *in e-pé-ri* [43] *ki-ma šadîm*(SA.DÚ-*im*) *ra-bi-im* [44] *re-še*$_{20}$*-sú-nu lu ú-ul-li* [45] BÀD *ṣīram*(MAḪ) *lu e-pu-uš.*

[1] *inu* poetic variant of *inūma.*

[7] *nawārum / namāru* G (*i*) 'to shine, be bright'; Verbal Adj. *nawirum / namrum* (*nawir / namir*) 'shining, bright, brilliant'.

[11] *palûm* (*palā-*; log. BALA; Sum. lw.) 'reign'.

[14] *bêlum* G (*e*) 'to rule' (cf. *bēlum*).

[19] *nēḫtum* 'peace, security'; *šubat nēḫtim šūšubum* 'to let (someone) dwell in security'.

[22] See §23.1(e).

[28] *inūmīšu* (Adverb) 'at that time, then', used in royal inscriptions as a correllative of *inu*: 'when ..., at that time ...'.

[33] *Ayya* is the consort of Šamaš.

[35] *anāku* is in apposition to *Ḫammurapi* of line 29 and the epithets that follow: 'I, Ḫammurapi, mighty king, ...'

[36] *ṣīrum* (*ṣīr-*; Vbl. Adj. of a rare verb *ṣiārum*; log. MAḪ) 'august, outstanding, first-rank, excellent'.

[39] *tibûtum* (*tibût*) 'rising, raising; muster, levy; attack' (cf. *tebûm*).

[41] *uššum*, usually pl. *uššū*, 'foundation'.

[42] *eperum, eprum* (*eper*; often pl. *ep(e)rū*) 'dust, (loose) earth'.

[43] SA.DÚ (or SA.TU) is a common pseudo-logogram for *šadûm.*

[44] *rēštum* (bound form usually *rēšti*, here *rēšet*; pl. *rēšētum*) 'beginning; peak; the best quality (of oil, dates, sheep); instalment (on a loan)' (cf. *rēšum*).

LESSON THIRTY-TWO

32.1 The N Stem: Verbs I–ʾ; Verbs I–*w*; Verbs II–Weak

(a) Verbs I–ʾ

In all N forms of these verbs, the initial radical ʾ is replaced by an *n*, which is **not** assimilated to a following radical. Thus, the forms look like N forms of verbs I–*n*. In verbs I–*e*, of course, *a*-vowels become *e*. Below are the N forms of *aḫāzum* (*a–u*), *ezēbum* (*i*), *epēšum* (*e–u*), and *enûm* (also III–*i*); note that finite N forms of *epēšum* may have either the expected theme-vowels (*e–i*) or *u* between R_2 and R_3.

Infinitive:	*nanḫuzum*	*nenzubum*	*nenpušum*	*nennûm*
Durative:	*innaḫḫaz*	*innezzib*	*inneppeš* / *inneppuš*	*innenni*
Perfect:	*ittanḫaz*	*ittenzib*	*ittenpeš* / *ittenpuš*	*ittenni*
Preterite:	*innaḫiz*	*innezib*	*innepiš* / *innepuš*	*inneni*
Imperative:	*nanḫiz*	*nenzib*	*nenpiš* / *nenpuš*	*nenni*
Participle:	*munnaḫzum*	*munnezbum*	*munnepšum*	*munnenûm*
Verbal Adj.:	*nanḫuzum*	*nenzubum*	*nenpušum*	*nennûm*
V. Adj. base:	*nanḫuz*	*nenzub*	*nenpuš*	*nennu*

In a very small group of verb I–ʾ, the ʾ is preserved as a strong (regular) consonant throughout the N paradigm: e.g., *adārum* G (*a–u*) 'to fear'; *naʾdurum* N 'to be feared': Durative *iʾʾaddar*, Perfect *ittaʾdar*, Preterite *iʾʾader*, etc.

As usual, verbs originally I–*y* (see §8.1(c)) have forms corresponding to *e*-class verbs I–ʾ: e.g., Durative *innezziḫ* 'he girds himself' (*ezēḫum* (I–*y*; *i*) 'to gird'); but forms without prefixes, such as the Verbal Adjective, have a long vowel rather than *n* before R_2: *nēzuḫat* 'she is girded' (vs., e.g., *nenpušum*).

(b) Verbs I–*w*

As far as N forms of these are attested, they are regular; thus, the *w* is doubled (*-ww-*) in the Durative and Preterite, the only forms known. The forms of *babālum* have *-bb-* rather than *-ww-*.

Durative:	*iwwallad*	*ibbabbal*
Preterite:	*iwwalid*	*ibbabil*

Occasionally, especially in later texts, *-ww-* is replaced by *-ʾʾ-*; thus, Durative *iʾʾallad*, Preterite *iʾʾalid*.

(c) Verbs II–Weak

These are poorly attested in the N paradigm. The Durative and Preterite forms resemble their G counterparts, but with doubling of the first radical (‹ nR_1).

Durative:	*iddâk*	*iqqīaš*	*iššâm*	*innêr*
3mp:	*iddukkū*	*iqqiššū*	*iššammū*	*innerrū*
Preterite:	[*iddīk* / *iddūk*?]	*iqqīš*	*iššām*	*innēr*
3mp:	[*iddīkū* / *iddūkū*?]	*iqqīšū*	*iššāmū*	*innērū*

No Preterite forms of Verbs II–*w* are attested. Note that the Preterite forms of verbs II–*a* and II–*e* have the theme-vowel of the G verb, rather than *i* like the N Preterites of other verb types.

32.2 Noun Patterns

All native Akkadian nouns and adjectives (i.e., those that are not loans from other languages) may be described in terms of their root and a pattern (using R_1, R_2, R_3, etc., or the paradigmatic root *p–r–s*; cf. §3.1). Thus, e.g., *kalbum* is a *pars* noun of the root *k–l–b*, *šeriktum* a *pirist* noun (or *piris* plus fem. *t*; with *e* ‹ *i*) of the root *š–r–k*; *bēlum* a *pars* noun of the root *b–*$^{\text{ʾ}}{}_4$*–l* (or *b–*^{c}*–l*, with ^{c} › ø). Most noun patterns are not classifiable with regard to meaning, but a few of them are, at least to some extent, and these are listed below, with examples. (Note: paradigmatic verbal noun patterns such as *pāris* [the G Participle], *šuprus* [the Š Infinitive and Verbal Adj.], are not included in the list.)

pirs nouns may frequently be associated with a passive nuance: e.g.,

šiprum 'message, task' (something sent, assigned; cf. *šapārum*);
izbum 'malformed foetus' (something abandoned; cf. *ezēbum*);
šiqlum originally 'weight' (cf. *šaqālum*);
pilšum 'breach' (cf. *palāšum*);
kiṣrum 'knot, constriction, payment' (cf. *kaṣārum*).

The feminine counterpart of *pirs* is ***pirist***:

isiḫtum 'assignment' (cf. *eseḫum*);
šeriktum 'gift' (cf. *šarākum*);
ṣibittum 'prison, imprisonment' (cf. *ṣabātum*);
qibītum 'speech' (cf. *qabûm*).

For roots II–weak and, usually, for roots III–weak, the pattern is ***pīs***. For many roots I–*w*, the pattern is ***R_2iR_3t***, i.e., a feminine noun without the initial *w*. Examples:

dīnum 'decision, judgment' (cf. *diānum*);
šīmum 'price, purchase' (cf. *šâmum*);
pītum 'opening' (cf. *petûm*);
ṣibtum 'interest' (cf. *waṣābum*);
biltum 'load, burden, tribute' (something carried; cf. *babālum*);
ṣītum 'coming forth, produce' (cf. *waṣûm*).

purs nouns (***pūs*** for roots II– and III–weak) are often abstracts of adjectival roots; the feminine counterpart is *purust*:

šulmum 'well-being' (cf. *šalāmum*);
rupšum 'width' (cf. *rapāšum*);
murṣum 'sickness' (cf. *marāṣum*);
ṭūbum 'goodness, satisfaction'; fem. pl. *ṭūbātum* 'gladness, voluntariness, friendly relations' (cf. *ṭiābum*);
ḫūdum 'joy' (cf. *ḫadûm*);
puluḫtum 'fear' (cf. *palāḫum*);
nukurtum 'hostility, war' (cf. *nakārum*).

parVst, i.e., the feminine of Verbal Adjectives, is often used substantively, denoting an instance of the adjectival nuance, or its abstract:

damiqtum 'good luck, favor' (cf. *damāqum*);
lemuttum 'evil' (cf. *lemēnum*);
maruštum 'difficulty' (cf. *marāṣum*).

From roots II–weak, the form is *pV̄st*:

qīštum 'gift' (cf. *qiāšum*);
ṭābtum 'kindness' (cf. *ṭiābum*).

parrās nouns denote occupations or habitual activities:

dayyānum 'judge' (cf. *diānum*);
šarrāqum 'thief' (cf. *šarāqum*);
errēšum 'cultivator, tenant farmer' (cf. *erēšum* 'to cultivate').

purussāʾ forms denote systematic, often legal, activities:

purussûm 'legal decision' (cf. *parāsum*);
rugummûm 'legal claim' (cf. *ragāmum*);
uzubbûm 'divorce(-payment)' (cf. *ezēbum*).

ipris is a less common variant of *pirs*; certain *ipris* nouns occur only as plurals:

ipṭerū (always pl.) 'ransom' (cf. *paṭārum*);
imṭû (always pl.) 'depletion, losses' (cf. *maṭûm*).

mapras(t) nouns denote place, instrument, or time, although they cannot be more precisely categorized. Some examples:

maškanum 'threshing floor, lot, location' (cf. *šakānum*);
maṣṣarum 'watch, garrison' (cf. *naṣārum*);
mūṣûm 'exit, opening' (< **mawṣaʾum*; cf. *waṣûm*);
mērešum 'cultivated land' (cf. *erēšum* 'to cultivate').

When the root contains one of the labial consonants *b*, *m*, or *p*, the *m* of the prefix is replaced by *n*:

narkabtum 'chariot' (cf. *rakābum*);
narāmum 'beloved' (cf. *râmum*);
našpakum 'storage area' (cf. *šapākum*);
nēmettum 'tribute, tax' (cf. *emēdum*).

taprās nouns are associated with the Gt stem (§33.1):

tamḫārum 'battle' (*mitḫurum* 'to oppose one another', Gt of *maḫārum*);
tāḫāzum 'battle, combat' (cf. *aḫāzum*).

taprīs and ***taprist*** nouns are associated with the D stem:

talmīdum 'student' (cf. *lummudum* 'to teach');
tarbītum 'offspring' (cf. *rubbûm* 'to rear');
tēliltum 'purification' (cf. *ullulum* 'to purify');
têrtum 'command, order' (< **tawʾertum*; cf. *wuʾʾurum* 'to commission').

32.3 Sumerian Loanwords

In addition to its lexical base inherited from common Semitic, Akkadian has a large number of loanwords from Sumerian. Nearly all such loans are nouns, although other parts of speech, such as the interjection *gana* 'come (on)!', are also sporadically attested.

The forms borrowed may be either discrete words or compounds in Sumerian:

agûm 'crown', Sum. a g a ;
pišannum 'basket, box', Sum. p i s a n ;
ekallum 'palace', Sum. é . g a l 'large (g a l) house (é)';
ṭupšarrum 'scribe', Sum. d u b . s a r (d u b 'tablet'; s a r 'to write').

Sumerian words ending in a vowel were usually borrowed into Akkadian as nouns with bases ending in a vowel; Sumerian final /a/ normally results in an Akkadian base in *-ā*:

kirûm (base *kiri-*) 'garden', Sum. k i r i_6 ;
tappûm (base *tappā-*) 'partner', Sum. t a b . b a (note also the Akkadian abstract *tappûtum*).

Sumerian words ending in a consonant usually appear in Akkadian with the final consonant doubled; less often, the vowel before the final consonant is lengthened instead. Examples:

kurrum 'kor measure', Sum. g u r;
parakkum 'sanctuary', Sum. b a r a g;
see also *ekallum, pišannum, ṭupšarrum,* above;
kārum 'embankment, harbor', Sum. k a r.

Sumerian had a number of phonemes not found in Akkadian, such as the nasal velar /g̃/ (English [ng]), as in s a g̃ (g̃) a = Akkadian *šangûm* 'temple administrator'; words containing such phonemes may have byforms in Akkadian, as in

ḫegallum or *ḫengallum* 'abundance', Sum. ḫ é . g̃ á l 'let there be'.

It will also be noted that Sumerian consonants transliterated as voiced (e.g., /b/, /g/) may appear in Akkadian as the voiceless counterpart (*p, k,* respectively), as in *ekallum, kurrum, parakkum,* etc. Other differences are the result of sound changes, especially vowel harmony, that operated in Sumerian after Akkadian had borrowed certain words:

siparrum 'bronze', Sum. z a b a r, earlier z i b a r.

Certain nouns that appear, on the basis of their logograms, to be Sumerian loans into Akkadian, are in fact Akkadian loans into Sumerian, with the Sumerian form serving in turn as a logographic writing in Akkadian:

manûm 'mina' (cf. *manûm* 'to count') → Sum. m a . n a;
tamkārum 'merchant' (cf. *makārum* 'to do business' [rare], *makkūrum* 'property') → Sum. d a m . g a r a$_3$.

EXERCISES

A. VOCABULARY 32.

Verbs:

amārum G see Lesson 8; *nanmurum* N 'to be seen, found, inspected; to appear, occur; to meet (see one another)'.

dabābum G (*u*) 'to speak, talk, tell; to discuss; to plead (in court); to complain, protest'; Infinitive as noun: 'speech, statement; plea, lawsuit; rumor'; *dubbubum* D 'to complain (to), entreat, bother'.

dekûm G (*e*) 'to move, remove; to arouse, raise, mobilize, call up (soldiers, officials)'.

emēdum G (*i*) see Lesson 14; *nenmudum* N 'to be joined, come together, meet; to join forces'.
ḫerûm G (*e*) 'to dig'.
naʾbutum N (not in G in OB; Infin. also *nābutum*; Dur. *innabbit*, Pret. *innabit* or *innābit* [pl. *innabtū* or *innābitū*], Perf. *ittabit* or *ittābit*) 'to flee'.
šalālum G (*a–u*) 'to plunder, loot; to take as booty; to take captive'; *našlulum* N 'to be plundered; to be taken captive, as booty'.
šâlum G (*a*) 'to ask, inquire, question (someone: acc.; about: acc. or *aššum* or *ana*)'.

Nouns:

iṣṣūrum (masc. and fem.; *iṣṣūr*; pl. *iṣṣūrū* and *iṣṣūrātum*; log. MUŠEN [= the ḪU sign]) 'bird'.
mūdûtum (*mūdût*) 'knowledge, information' (cf. *edûm*).
šīrum (*šīr(i)*) 'flesh, meat'; *ana šīr X ṭiābum* 'to be(come) pleasing to X' (e.g., *epištī ana šīr ilīya iṭīb* 'my deed pleased/was pleasing to my god').

Adverb:

warkānum (also *warkānum-ma*) 'afterward, later' (cf. *warki*).

Prepositions:

ezib and *ezub* 'apart from, besides' (cf. *ezēbum*).
qadum 'together with; inclusive of, including'.

B. Write in normalized Akkadian:

1. they (m) will join forces
2. we will flee
3. birds were purchased
4. it was plundered
5. he will be executed
6. it has been done
7. they (f) will be removed
8. they (f) will be bestowed
9. they (m) have been hired
10. it was brought here
11. when he was born
12. they (f) will be changed

C. Normalize and translate:

1. PN *a-ḫa-at* PN_2 KI PN_3 *a-bi-ši-na* PN_4 *a-na aš-šu-tim i-ḫu-sí* PN ^{giš}GU.ZA *a-ḫa-ti-ša a-na* É ^{d}AMAR.UTU *i-na-aš-ši* DUMU.MEŠ *ma-la wa-al-du ù i-wa-la-du* DUMU.MEŠ-*ši-na-ma*.
2. *a-na* ^{d}EN.ZU-*i-din-nam qí-bí-ma um-ma ḫa-am-mu-ra-pí-ma* PN *ki-a-am iq-bi-a-am um-ma šu-ma* $ERIN_2$ MÁ.Ì.DUB *ša be-lí i-si-ḫa-am a-di-ni ú-ul id-di-nu-nim-ma* MÁ.Ì.DUB *ú-ul e-pu-uš ki-a-*

am iq-bi-a-am am-mi-nim ERIN$_2$ MÁ.Ì.DUB *a-na* PN *la in-na-di-in-ma* MÁ.Ì.DUB *la in-ne-pu-uš* UD-*um* DUB-*pí an-ni-a-am ta-am-ma-ru* ERIN$_2$ MÁ.Ì.DUB PN *a-pu-ul-ma* MÁ.Ì.DUB *ša qá-ti-šu li-pu-uš ar-ḫi-iš* ERIN$_2$ MÁ.Ì.DUB *ú-ul ta-ap-pa-al-šu-ma pí-ḫa-tum ši-i i-na mu-úḫ-ḫi-ka iš-ša-ak-ka-an* (adapted from *AbB* 2 59).

3. *aš-šum* SÍG *qá-at-na-tim ša te-ri-ša-an-ni i-na-an-na* KUG.BABBAR SÍG *ši-na-ti iš-ša-qí-il-ma* SÍG *iš-ša-ma.*
4. *am-mi-nim* [lú]ŠU.ḪA.MEŠ *ša ma-aḫ-ri-ka uš-ša-bu-ma ri-qú am-mi-nim ki-a-am la ta-aš-pu-ra-am um-ma at-ta-a-ma* KASKAL *in-ne-ep-pé-eš.*
5. *i-na-an-na a-na* LUGAL *ma-tim ša-a-ti aš-šum it-ti-šu ne-en-mu-di-im aš-ta-pa-ar.*
6. *i-na wa-ṣé-e-ni wa-ar-ka-at nu-ma-ti-ni i-ša-lu-ni-a-ti.*
7. MUŠEN.ḪI.A *i-na* A.GÀR *it-ta-an-ma-ra.*

D. CH:

§5 *šum-ma da-a-a-nu-um di-nam i-di-in pu-ru-sà-am ip-ru-ús ku-nu-uk-kam ú-še-zi-ib wa-ar-ka-nu-um-ma di-in-šu i-te-ni da-a-a-nam šu-a-ti i-na di-in i-di-nu e-ne-em ú-ka-an-nu-šu-ma ru-gu-um-ma-am ša i-na di-nim šu-a-ti ib-ba-aš-šu-ú* A.RÁ 12-*šu i-na-ad-di-in ù i-na pu-úḫ-ri-im i-na* [giš]GU.ZA *da-a-a-nu-ti-šu ú-še-et-bu-ú-šu-ma ú-ul i-ta-ar-ma it-ti da-a-a-ni i-na di-nim ú-ul uš-ša*(!TA)*-ab.*

§§9–12 §9 *šum-ma a-wi-lum ša mi-im-mu-šu ḫal-qú mi-im-ma-šu ḫal-qá-am i-na qá-ti a-wi-lim iṣ-ṣa-ba-at a-wi-lum ša ḫu-ul-qum i-na qá-ti-šu ṣa-ab-tu na-di-na-nu-um-mi id-di-nam ma-ḫar ši-bi-mi a-ša-am iq-ta-bi ù be-el ḫu-ul-qí-im ši-bi mu-de ḫu-ul-qí-ia-mi lu-ub-lam iq-ta-bi ša-a-a-ma-nu-um na-di-in id-di-nu-šum ù ši-bi ša i-na maḫ-ri-šu-nu i-ša-mu it-ba-lam ù be-el ḫu-ul-qí-im ši-bi mu-de ḫu-ul-qí-šu it-ba-lam da-a-a-nu a-wa-a-ti-šu-nu i-im-ma-ru-ma ši-bu ša maḫ-ri-šu-nu ši-mu-um iš-ša-mu ù ši-bu mu-de ḫu-ul-qí-im mu-du-sú-nu ma-ḫar i-lim i-qá-ab-bu-ma na-di-na-nu-um šar-ra-aq id-da-ak be-el ḫu-ul-qí-im ḫu-lu-uq-šu i-le-qé ša-a-a-ma-nu-um i-na bi-it na-di-na-nim* KUG.BABBAR *iš-qú-lu i-le-qé.* §10 *šum-ma ša-a-a-ma-nu-um na-di-in id-di-nu-šum ù ši-bi ša i-na maḫ-ri-šu-nu i-ša-mu la it-ba-lam be-el ḫu-ul-qí-im-ma ši-bi mu-de ḫu-ul-qí-šu it-ba-lam ša-a-a-ma-nu-um šar-ra-aq id-da-ak be-el ḫu-ul-qí-im ḫu-lu-uq-šu i-le-qé.* §11 *šum-ma be-el ḫu-ul-qí-im ši-bi mu-de ḫu-ul-qí-šu la it-ba-lam sà-ar tu-uš-ša-am-ma id-ke id-da-ak.* §12 *šum-ma na-di-na-nu-um a-na ši-im-tim it-ta-la-ak ša-a-a-ma-nu-um i-na bi-it na-di-na-nim ru-gu-um-me-e di-nim šu-a-ti* A.RÁ 5-*šu i-le-qé*.

tuššum 'slander'.

§58 *šum-ma iš-tu* U$_8$.UDU.ḪI.A *i-na* A.GÀR *i-te-li-a-nim ka-an-nu ga-ma-ar-tim i-na* ABUL *it-ta-aḫ-la-lu* SIPA U$_8$.UDU.ḪI.A *a-na* A.ŠÀ *id-di-ma* A.ŠÀ U$_8$.UDU.ḪI.A *uš-ta-ki-il* SIPA A.ŠÀ *ú-ša-ki-lu i-na-ṣa-ar-ma i-na ebūrim*(BURU$_{14}$) *ana būrim* (BÙR^{iku}.E) 60 ŠE.GUR *a-na be-el* A.ŠÀ *i-ma-ad-da-ad*.

kannum (pl. *kannū*) 'fetter, band'; *gamartum* 'totality; completion' (cf. *gamārum*); *kannū gamartim* uncertain, but perhaps 'pennants (indicating) termination (of pasturing)'.

ḫalālum G (*a–u*) 'to hang, suspend'.

būrum (*būri*; log. BÙR; Sum. lw.) a surface measure (ca. 6.48 ha.).

§§61–62 §61 *šum-ma nukaribbum*(NU.^{giš}KIRI$_6$) A.ŠÀ *i-na za-qá-pí-im la ig-mur-ma ni-di-tam i-zi-ib ni-di-tam a-na li-ib-bi* ḪA.LA-*šu i-ša-ka-nu-šum*. §62 *šum-ma* A.ŠÀ *ša in-na-ad-nu-šum a-na* KIRI$_6$ *la iz-qú-up šum-ma abšinnum*(AB.SÍN) GUN A.ŠÀ *ša ša-na-tim ša in-na-du-ú nukaribbum*(NU.^{giš}KIRI$_6$) *a-na be-el* A.ŠÀ *ki-ma i-te-šu i-ma-ad-da-ad ù* A.ŠÀ *ši-ip-ra-am i-ip-pé-eš-ma a-na be-el* A.ŠÀ *ú-ta-a-ar*.

nukaribbum (*nukarib*; log. NU.$^{(giš)}$KIRI$_6$; Sum. lw.) 'gardener'.

nidītum (*nidīt*) 'uncultivated plot/land' (cf. *nadûm*).

ana libbi here, 'toward, as'.

abšinnum (*abšin*; log. AB.SÍN; Sum. lw.) 'furrow; cultivated field'.

§137 *šum-ma a-wi-lum a-na* ^{mí}*šu-gi$_4$-tim ša* DUMU.MEŠ *ul-du-šum ù lu* LUKUR *ša* DUMU.MEŠ *ú-šar-šu-šu e-zé-bi-im pa-ni-šu iš-ta-ka-an a-na* MUNUS *šu-a-ti še-ri-ik-ta-ša ú-ta-ar-ru-ši-im ù mu-ut-ta-at* A.ŠÀ KIRI$_6$ *ù bi-ši-im i-na-ad-di-nu-ši-im-ma* DUMU.MEŠ-*ša ú-ra-ab-ba iš-tu* DUMU.MEŠ-*ša úr-ta-ab-bu-ú i-na mi-im-ma ša a-na* DUMU.MEŠ-*ša in-na-ad-nu zí-it-tam ki-ma ap-lim iš-te-en i-na-ad-di-nu-ši-im-ma mu-tu li-ib-bi-ša i-iḫ-ḫa-as-sí*.

šugītum (*šugīt*; log. ^{mí}ŠU.GI$_4$; Sum. lw.) a junior wife.

muttatum (*muttat*) 'half'.

mutu unusual bound form of *mutum* (cf. §30.2(d)).

§159 *šum-ma a-wi-lum ša a-na* É *e-mi-šu bi-ib-lam ú-ša-bi-lu ter-ḫa-tam id-di-nu a-na* MUNUS *ša-ni-tim up-ta-al-li-is-ma a-na e-mi-šu* DUMU.MUNUS-*ka ú-ul a-ḫa-az iq-ta-bi a-bi* DUMU.MUNUS *mi-im-ma ša ib-ba-ab-lu-šum i-tab-ba-al*.

biblum (*bibil*) 'marriage-gift' (cf. *babālum*).

uptallis 'he has become distracted/attracted' (cf. *naplusum*).

§176 (For §175 see lesson 20) *šum-ma* ÌR É.GAL *ù lu* ÌR MAŠ.EN.GAG DUMU.MUNUS *a-wi-lim i-ḫu-uz-ma i-nu-ma i-ḫu-zu-ši qá-du-um še-ri-ik-tim ša* É *a-bi-ša a-na* É ÌR É.GAL *ù lu* ÌR MAŠ.EN. GAG *i-ru-ub-ma iš-tu in-ne-em-du* É *i-pu-šu bi-ša-am ir-šu-ú wa-ar-ka-nu-um-ma lu* ÌR É.GAL *ù lu* ÌR MAŠ.EN.GAG *a-na ši-im-tim it-ta-la-ak* DUMU.MUNUS *a-wi-lim še-ri-ik-ta-ša i-le-qé ù mi-im-ma ša mu-sà ù ši-i iš-tu in-ne-em-du ir-šu-ú a-na ši-ni-šu i-zu-uz-zu-ma mi-iš-lam be-el* ÌR *i-le-qé mi-iš-lam* DUMU.MUNUS *a-wi-lim a-na* DUMU.MEŠ-*ša i-le-qé.*

§§188–189 §188 *šum-ma* DUMU UM.MI.A DUMU *a-na tar-bi-tim il-qé-ma ši-pí-ir qá-ti-šu uš-ta-ḫi-sú ú-ul ib-ba-qar.* §189 *šum-ma ši-pí-ir qá-ti-šu la uš-ta-ḫi-sú tar-bi-tum ši-i a-na* É *a-bi-šu i-ta-ar.*

tarbītum (*tarbīt*) 'raising, upbringing; foster child, a child brought up' (cf. *rabûm*, D).

§§134–136:

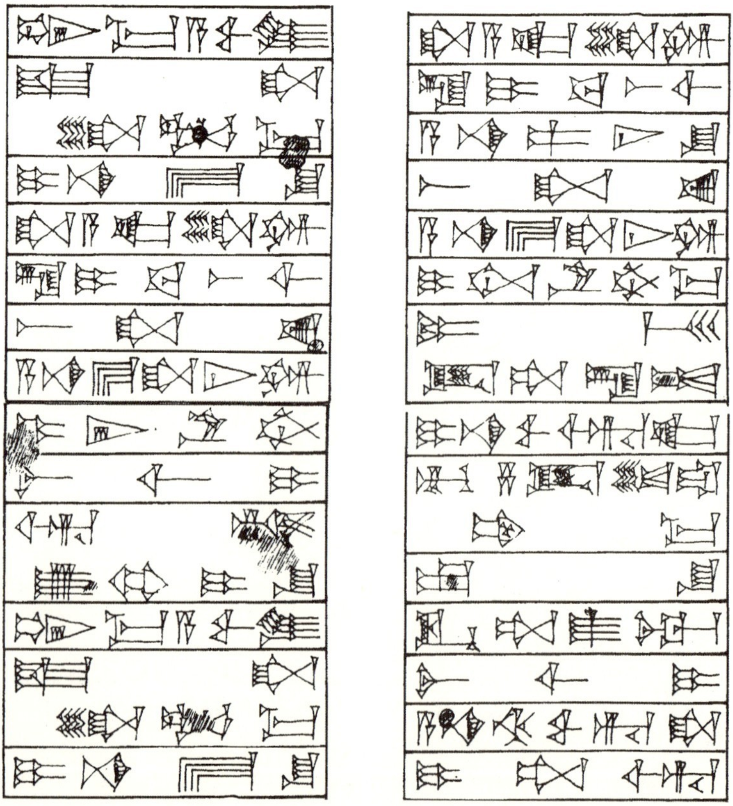

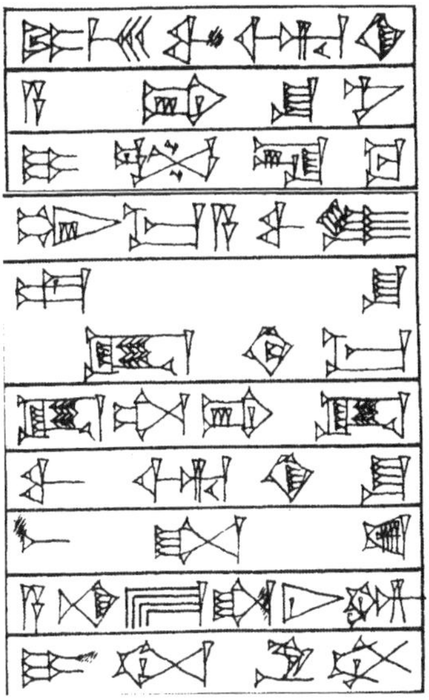

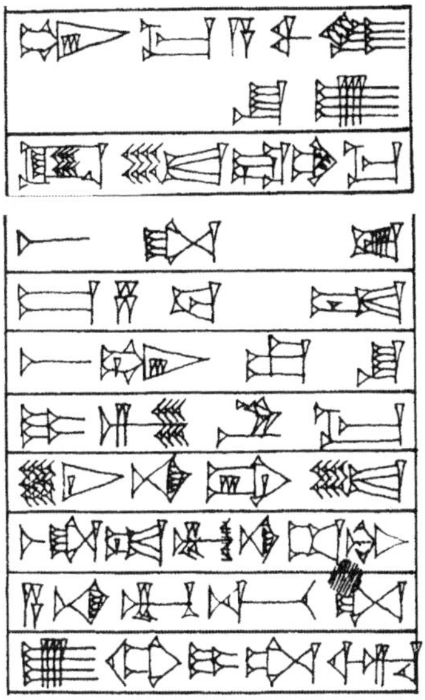

E. Omens from *YOS* 10:

1. *šum-ma* 2 *na-ap-la-sà-tum ṣe-el-lu-ši-na ni-in-m*[*u-du*] *su-un-qum i-na ma-a-tim i*[*b-b*]*a-aš-ši.* (11 iv 21–23)
   ṣēlum (less often *ṣellum*; pl. *ṣēlū* / *ṣellū*) 'rib; side'.
   ni-in-mu-du for *nenmudū.*
   sunqum 'famine'.

2. *šum-ma mar-tum na-as-ḫa-at-ma* [*i-n*]*a* KÁ É.GAL-*im* [*x-x*]-*a-at* [*nu*]-*ku-úr-tu-um iš-ša-ak-ka-an.* (31 i 12–17)
   nukurtum (*nukurti*; pl. *nukurātum*; also *nikurtum*) 'war, hostility' (cf. *nakārum*).

3. DIŠ *ubān*(SI) MUŠEN *imittam*(ZI) *ù* GÙB *na-we-er at-ta ù* LÚ.KÚR *ta-an-na-ma-ra.* (53:8)
   iṣṣūrum here a part of the liver.
   nawārum G (*i*; see §21.3(b)) 'to shine, become bright, clear'; Verbal Adj. *nawerum* (*nawer-*) 'shining, bright, clear'.

4. DIŠ *iz-bu-um pa-ni nēšim*(UR.MAḪ) *ša-ki-in* LUGAL [*d*]*a-an-nu-um ib-ba-aš-ši-ma ma-tam ša-ti ú-na-aš.* (56 i 26–27)
   nēšum (log. UR.MAḪ) 'lion'.

5. DIŠ *iz-bu-um ki-ma barbarim*(UR.BAR.RA) *bi-bu-um i-na ma-tim ib-ba-*[*aš*]-*ši.* (56 i 6–7)
   barbarum (log. UR.BAR.RA) 'wolf'.
   bibbum 'plague'.

6. DIŠ *iz-bu-um i-na i-ir-ti-šu pe-t*[*i*]*-i-ma ù da-al-tum ša š*[*i-x*]-⌜*x*⌝ *ša-ak-na-at-*[*m*]*a ip-pe-et-te ù i-‹né›-di-il ma-tum ši-i in-na-an-di* [*ḫ*]*a-ra-na-tu-ša ip-pe-ḫe-a.* (56 ii 1–4)
   irtum (*irat*) 'chest'.
   daltum (*dalat;* pl. *dalātum*) 'door, door-leaf'.
   edēlum G (*i*) 'to close, lock' (trans.).
   peḫûm G (*e*) 'to close, shut' (trans.).
7. 12:4–5:

   qinnatum (*qinnat*) 'anus, buttock(s).'
8. 31 iii 45–54:

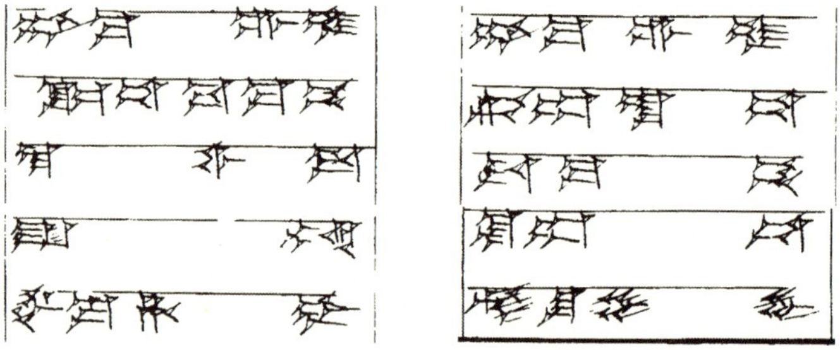

   damum (*dam(i);* pl. *damū*) 'blood'.
   line 48: SUKKAL.MAḪ = *sukkalmaḫḫum* (*sukkalmaḫ;* Sum. lw.) a high court official ('chief minister').

F. Contracts:

1. A husband's gift to his wife of a slave woman (*VAS* 8 15 = Schorr, *VAB* 5, no. 205).

^{1} 1 SAG.GEME$_{2}$ *mu-ti-ba-aš-ti* MU.NI ^{2} ^{Id}EN.ZU-*pí-la-aḫ* ^{3} *a-na ša-ad-da-šu* DAM.A.NI ^{4}*i-qí-i-iš* ^{5}DUMU.MEŠ ^{d}EN.ZU-*pí-la-aḫ* ^{6}*ú-ul i-ra-ag-ga-mu-ši-im* ^{7} *iš-tu* UD-*um* DUB-[*pu*]-*um* ^{8} *in-né-ez-bu* ^{9} ‹DUMU.MEŠ› *ma-la mu-ti-ba-aš-ti* ^{10} *ul-la-du* ^{11} *ša ša-ad-da-šu-ma* ^{12} ^{I}*sà-*«BI»*-ni-iq-pí-ša* ^{13} DUMU.MUNUS *ša-ad-da-šu.* $^{14–26}$Witnesses. ^{27} Date.
PNs: *Mutī-bāštī; Sîn-pilaḫ; Šaddašu; Saniq-pīša.*

2. Receipt for silver (*VAS* 8 37 = Schorr, *VAB* 5, no. 239).

^{1} $^{5}/_{6}$ MA.NA KUG.BABBAR ^{2} ŠÀ 1 MA.NA KUG.BABBAR ^{3} *ša* KI *im-lik-*^{d}EN.ZU ^{4} *a-na* 50 ^{lú}*agrī*(ḪUN.GÁ) ^{5} *in-na-ad-nu* ^{6} *ša a-na* KASKAL

LUGAL 7 *in-na-ag-ru* 8 *e-zu-ub tibût*(ZI.GA) 9 ⌜ERIN$_2$!?⌝ *i-din-é-a* 10 *ù eš*$_4$*-tár-i-na-ia* «*x*» 11–12 Date.

PNs: *Imlik-Sîn; Iddin-Ea; Ištar-īnāya.*

2 ŠÀ = bound form *libbi* (acc.) or *libbu* (locative), here as a preposition, 'in, from, belonging to'.

8 *tibûtum* (*tibût;* log. ZI(.GA)) 'rising, raising; muster, levy; attack' (cf. *tebûm*).

G. Letters:

1. *CT* 29 7a = Frankena, *AbB* 2 131.

1 *a-na* [*t*]*a-ri-bu-u*[*m*] 2 *qí-bí-ma* 3 *um-ma i-din-ia-tum-ma* 4 ^{d}UTU *li-ba-al-li-iṭ-ka* 5 ^{Id}ŠUL.PA.È*-ba-ni* DUMU.É.DUB.BA.A 6 *ki-a-am ú-lam-mi-id* 7 *um-ma šu-ú-ma* 8 *bi-it* A.BA *ú-ul i-šu-ú-ma* 9 *a-na bi-it* ^{f}*sé-ek-re-tim* 10 *a-na ma-ru-tim e*(!I)*-ru-ub* 11 *bi-it a-na ma-ru-tim e-ru-bu* 12 *a-na ṣí-it* É.GAL *uš-te-ṣú-ú* 13 [DUB]*-pí be-lí-ia a-na bi-tim na-da-nim* 14 [*i*]*l-li-ka-ak-ku-nu-ši-*[*i*]*m-*[*m*]*a* 15 *am-mi-ni la in-na-pí-il-ma* 16 *ú-da-ab-ba-ab* 17 *ù lu-ú bi-it a-na ma-ru-tim* 18 *i-ru-bu li-te-er-ru-šum* 19 *ù lu-ú bi-tam ma-a-li bi-tim* 20 *i-di-iš-šum-ma* 21 *la ú-da-a*[*b-b*]*a-ab.*

PNs: *Tarībum; Iddin-yatum; Šulpae-bāni.*

5 DUMU.É.DUB.BA.A = *mār bīt ṭuppim* 'military scribe' (originally, 'student' or 'graduate').

9 *sekretum* (pl. *sekrētum*) a woman of high status.

2. *TCL* 7 26 = Kraus, *AbB* 4 26, lines 1–10.

1 *a-na* ^{d}AMAR.UTU*-na-ṣi-ir* 2 *ù* ^{d}UTU*-ḫa-zi-ir* 3 *qí-bí-ma* 4 *um-ma ḫa-am-mu-ra-pí-ma* 5 *a-nu-um-ma* DUB*-pí i-si-iḫ-ti* ^{giš}KIRI$_6$.ḪI.A 6 *ša a-na* ŠANDANA.MEŠ 7 *iz-zu-uz-*[*z*]*a* 8 [*u*]*š-ta-bi-la-ak-ku-nu-ši-im* 9 [*a-na p*]*í-i* DUB*-pa-a-tim ši-na-ti* 10 [^{giš}KIRI$_6$.ḪI].A *zu-za-šu-nu-ši-im.*

PNs: *Marduk-nāṣir; Šamaš-ḫāzir.*

6 ŠANDANA (GAL + NI) = *šandanakkum* (*šandanak;* pl. *šandanakkātum;* Sum. lw.) 'administrator of date orchards'.

3. *VAS* 7 201 = Ungnad, *Babylonische Briefe* 258.

1 *a-na a-wi-lim* 2 *qí-bí-ma* 3 *um-ma ip-qú-ša-la-ma* 4 ^{d}UTU *ù* ^{d}AMAR.UTU *da-ri-iš* UD*-mi* 5 *li-ba-al-li-ṭú-ka* 6 *lu ša-al-ma-ta lu ba-al-ṭa-ta* 7 DINGIR *na-ṣi-ir-ka re-eš da-mi-iq-ti-ka* 8 *li-ki-il* 9 *a-na šu-ul-mi-ka aš-pu-ra-am* 10 *šu-lum-ka ma-ḫar* ^{d}UTU *ù* ^{d}AMAR.UTU *lu da-ri* 11 2 *maškī*(KUŠ.ḪI.A) *a-na pa-ra-*⌜*ás*⌝ ‹*wa*›*-ar-ka-tim* 12 *uš-ta-bi-la-ku* 13 *a-ḫi at-ta ki-ma ra-bu-ti-ka* 14 *wa-ar-ka-tam pu-ru-ús*

[15] *tu-uk-ki-il-ma* [16] ÁB.GUD.ḪI.A *da-an-na-a-tim* [17] *li-is-sú-ḫa-nim* *rēḫet*(ÍB.TAG$_4$) ÁB.GUD.ḪI.A-*ia* *šu-a-tu*$_4$(TUM) [19] *ša i-na ma-aḫ-ri-ka in-ne-ez-zi-ba* [20] *a-di a-ša-ap-pa-ra-am-ma* [21] *i-le-eq-qú-nim* [22] *a-ḫi at-ta ni-di a-ḫi-im* [23] *la ta-ra-aš-ši-ši-na-ši-im* [24] *a-na ša aš-pu-ra-ak-kum* [25] *la tu-uš-ta-ʾa*$_4$ [26] *šum-ma* ÁB.GUD.ḪI.A *da-an-na-⸢tum⸣* [27] *mi-it-ḫa-ri-iš a-la-kam* [28] *a-di ma-aḫ-ri-ia i-la-a* [29] *wa-ar-ka-tam tu-uk-ki-il* [30] *pu-ru-ús-ma* [31] *mi-it-ḫa-ri-iš-ma li-is-sú-ḫa-nim.*

PN: *Ipqu-Šala.*

[11] *maškum* (*mašak*; pl. *maškū*; log. KUŠ [the SU sign]) 'skin; hide'.

[15] *tukkulum* here and in line 29 is unclear, but apparently functioning in hendiadys with *parāsum*: 'investigate carefully'?

[17] *nasāḫum* here, 'to transfer'; *rēḫtum* (bound form *rēḫet* or *rēḫti*; pl. *rēḫētum*; log. ÍB.TAG$_4$) 'rest, remainder'.

[18] *nīdum* (*nīd(i)*) 'lowering, dropping'; *nīdi aḫim* 'negligence, laxity, procrastination'; *nīdi aḫim rašûm* 'to procrastinate, be negligent, lax' (cf. *aḫam nadûm*).

[25] *lā tušta*ʾʾ*a* 'do not be idle' (see §36.1).

[28] *i-la-a* from *leʾûm.*

H. Royal Inscription of Ḫammurapi: commemoration of laying the wall in Sippar, continued (PBS 7 133 = Frayne, *RIME* 4, p. 334–36, lines 46–81; for lines 1–45, see Lesson 31).

[46] *ša iš-tu* UD-*um ṣi-a-tim* [47] *šar-ru in* LUGAL-*rí* [48] *ma-na-ma la i-pu-šu* [49] *a-na* ^{d}UTU *be-li-ia* [50] *ra-bi-iš lu e-pu-ús-súm* [51] BÀD *šu-ú* [52] *in qí-bi-it* ^{d}UTU [53] *ḫa-am-mu-ra-pí* [54] *ma-ḫi-ri a-ir-ši* [55] *šum-šu* [56] *in palê*(BALA)-*ia dam-qí-im* [57] *ša* ^{d}UTU *ib-bi-ù* [58] ZIMBIR^{ki} [59] URU^{ki} *ṣi-a-tim ša* ^{d}UTU [60] ERIN$_2$-*šu in tupšikkim* (^{giš}DUSU) [61] *a-na* ^{d}UTU *lu as-sú-úḫ* [62] ÍD-*šu lu eḫ-re* [63] *a-na er-ṣe-ti-šu* [64] *me-e da-ru-tim* [65] *lu aš-ku-un* [66] *nu-uḫ-ša-am ù* ḪÉ.GÁL [67] *lu ú-kam-me-er* [68] *a-na ni-ši* ZIMBIR^{ki} [69] *ri-iš-tam lu aš-ku-un* [70] *a-na ba-la-ṭì-ia* [71] *lu i-ka-ar-ra-ba* [72] *ša a-na šīr*(SU) ^{d}UTU *be-li-ia* [73] *ù* ^{d}*a-a be-el-ti-ia* [74] *ṭa-a-bu lu e-pu-uš* [75] *šu-mi dam-qá-am* [76] UD-*mi-šam* [77] *ki-ma* DINGIR *za-ka-ra-am* [78] *ša a-na da-ar* [79] *la im-ma-aš-šu-ú* [80] *in pí-i ni-ši* [81] *lu aš-ku-un.*

[46] *ša ištu ūm ṣiātim šarrū ... lā īpušū ...* 'That which/What from ancient times kings ... had not done, ...'.

[48] *manāma* 'any(one), whoever', with negative 'no (one), none'.

[56] *palûm* (*palā-*; log. BALA; Sum. lw.) 'reign'.

[60] *tupšikkum* (*tupšik*; log. ^{gi}DUSU, ^{giš}DUSU) 'work, corvée duty'.

[66] *nuḫšum* (*nuḫuš*) 'abundance, prosperity'.

[67] *kamārum* G (*a–u*) 'to heap up, pile up'; *kummurum* D = G.

[69] *rīštum* (often pl. *rīšātum*) 'joy, rejoicing'.

[71] *karābum* G (*a–u*) 'to bless, invoke blessings; to praise'.

[78] The absolute form (cf. §23.1(e)) of *dārum*, always in the phrase *ana dār* 'forever', is confined to literary texts.

[79] *mašûm* G (*i*) 'to forget'; *namšûm* N passive.

LESSON THIRTY-THREE

33.1 The Gt Stem

(a) Form

(1) Sound Verbs

Infinitive:	*pitrusum*		
Durative:	*iptarras*	Imperative:	*pitras*
Perfect:	*iptatras*	Participle:	*muptarsum*
Preterite:	*iptaras*	Verbal Adj.:	*pitrusum*
Pret. 3mp:	*iptarsū*	V. Adj. base:	*pitrus*

The Gt stem has an **infixed *-t-*** between R_1 and R_2.

Durative, Perfect, and **Preterite.** The prefixes are those of the G stem. The theme-vowel between R_2 and R_3 in all three forms (and in the Imperative) is that of the corresponding G Durative. The Gt Preterite for all verb types is identical in form to the corresponding G Perfect; thus, vowel syncope occurs when a vocalic ending is added: *iptarsam, iptarsū*. Whether a form is Gt Preterite or G Perfect can be determined only from context; it should be noted, however, that Gt forms are relatively rare. The Durative differs from the Preterite only in that, as usual, it has a doubled middle radical. The Perfect has two infixed *-t-*s.

The base (and bound form) of the **Participle** is *muptaris*; thus, the fem. sg. form is *muptaristum*.

The *-t-* of the Gt stem undergoes the same changes as the *-t-* of the Perfect: it is assimilated to a preceding *d, ṭ, s, ṣ,* or *z*, as in

> Durative *iṣṣabbat* (note that confusion with the N Durative is possible with this form).

In the forms without prefixes (Infinitive, Imperative, and Verbal Adj.), these consonants and the *-t-* undergo metathesis; thus, e.g.,

Infinitive:	*tiṣbutum*		
Durative:	*iṣṣabbat*	Imperative:	*tiṣbat*
Perfect:	*iṣṣatbat*	Participle:	*muṣṣabtum*
Preterite:	*iṣṣabat*	Verbal Adj.:	*tiṣbutum*
Pret. 3mp:	*iṣṣabtū*	V. Adj. base:	*tiṣbut*

The *-t-* is also assimilated when *d, ṭ, s, ṣ, z,* or even *š* is the middle radical and follows the *-t-* immediately, in the Infinitive, Imperative, and Verbal Adj.: e.g.,

> *ḫissas* 'consider (ms)!' (Imperative, ‹ **ḫitsas*; from *ḫasāsum* (*a–u*));
> *iṣṣar* 'guard yourself (ms)!' (Imperative, ‹ **(n)itṣar*; from *naṣārum*);
> *piššušum* 'to anoint oneself' (Infinitive, ‹ **pitšušum*).

After *g*, *-t-* becomes *-d-*, as in Perfect forms: e.g.,

> Preterite *igderû* 'they (m) sued one another' (*gerûm*).

(2) Verbs I–*n*. In forms with prefixes, the *n* is assimilated to the following infix. In the remaining forms, in which *n* should stand first, it is omitted.

Infinitive:	*itqurum*		
Durative:	*ittaqqar*	Imperative:	*itqar*
Perfect:	*ittatqar*	Participle:	*muttaqrum*
Preterite:	*ittaqar*	Verbal Adj.:	*itqurum*
Pret. 3mp:	*ittaqrū*	V. Adj. base:	*itqur*

(3) Verbs III–weak. These offer no difficulties; note the III–*e* forms:

Infinitive:	*šitmûm*		
Durative:	*ištemme*	Imperative:	*šitme*
Perfect:	*ištetme*	Participle:	*muštemûm*
Preterite:	*išteme*	Verbal Adj.:	*šitmûm*
Pret. 3mp:	*ištemû*	V. Adj. base:	*šitmu*

(4) Verbs I–ʾ. In forms with prefixes, the loss of ʾ immediately before the *-t-* infix has resulted in the lengthening of the preceding vowel. The remaining forms begin with *a* (or *e*) rather than the *i* expected from the sound verb. The Gt of *alākum*, as might be expected, is irregular, an extra *-t-* replacing the long vowel of other I–ʾ verbs (cf. the G Perfect *ittalak*).

	I–*a*	I–*e*, III–weak		*alākum*
Infinitive:	*atḫuzum*		*etlûm*	*atlukum*
Durative:	*ītaḫḫaz*		*ītelli*	*ittallak*
Perfect:	*ītatḫaz*		*ītetli*	*ittatlak*
Preterite:	*ītaḫaz*		*īteli*	*ittalak*
Imperative:	*atḫaz*		*etli*	*atlak*
Participle:	*mūtaḫzum*		*mūtelûm*	—
Verbal Adj.:	*atḫuzum*		*etlûm*	—
V. Adj. base:	*atḫuz*		*etlu*	—

(5) Verbs I–*w*. Apart from the Durative and Preterite of *waṣûm*, these are poorly attested in the Gt. With the exception of the Imperative, the forms resemble the Gt of verbs I–*n* (cf. the G Perfect of verbs I–*w*). Some of the forms, especially the Imperative, may belong rather to derivative roots, such as *tarādum* and *taṣûm* (cf. *babālum* and *tabālum*).

	I–*w*	I–*w*, II–*ṣ*, III–weak
Infinitive:	*itrudum*	*iṣṣûm*?
Durative:	*ittarrad*	*ittaṣṣi*
Perfect:	*ittatrad*	[*ittaṣṣi*]
Preterite:	*ittarad*	*ittaṣi*
Imperative:	*tarad*?	*taṣi*?
Participle:	*muttardum*	*muttaṣûm*
Verbal Adj.:	*itrudum*	*iṣṣûm*?
V. Adj. base:	*itrud*	*iṣṣu*?

(6) Verbs II–weak. The Gt stem for these verbs is not well attested, apart from a few notable exceptions. The forms of *kânum*, given below, represent a composite of attested forms of Verbs II–*u* (II–*w*). As representative of Verbs II–*i* (II–*y*) is presented the Gt of *niālum* G 'to lie down', which is also I–*n*; the Gt has the same meaning, but also, 'to lie with someone (sexually)'.

	II–*u*(*w*)	II–*i*(*y*)	II–*a*(ʾ)
G:	*kânum*	*niālum*	*šâlum*
Infinitive:	*kitūnum*	*itūlum* / *utūlum*	*šitūlum*
Durative:	[*iktân*?]	[*ittīal*]	*ištâl*
3mp:	[*iktunnū*]	*ittillū*	*ištallū*
Perfect:	[*iktatūn*]	*ittatīl*	*ištatāl*
3mp:	[*iktatūnū*]	*ittatīlū*	*ištatālū*
Preterite:	*iktūn*	*ittīl*	*ištāl*
3mp:	*iktūnū*	*ittīlū*	*ištālū*
Imperative:	[*kitūn*]	*itīl*	*šitāl*
mp:	[*kitūnā*]	*itīlā*	*šitālā*
Participle:	*muktīnum*	*muttīlum*	*muštālum*
Verbal Adj.:	*kitūnum*	[*itūlum*]	*šitūlum*
V. Adj. base:	*kitūn*	[*itūl*]	*šitūl*

Note: The Gt Infinitive of *niālum* has a byform, *utūlum*, the result of irregular vowel harmony. The Gt stem of this verb is listed separately in the dictionaries.

(b) Meaning

The Gt is a rare stem that occurs for only a relatively small percentage of Akkadian verbal roots. Further, among the roots in which the Gt is found, the number of attestations is usually not large, with a few important exceptions. Thus, the basic meaning of the stem remains rather elusive; it seems, in fact, to be lexical, i.e., unpredictable, for each root, although a few general nuances can be observed, as indicated below. The examples given here should be learned.

(1) **Reciprocal:**

mitgurum 'to agree (with one another), come to an agreement';
mithurum 'to meet/face/confront/oppose one another, to correspond (to one another), be of equal size';
mithuṣum 'to fight, go to war' (i.e., 'to strike one another)';
iṭṭulum (*naṭālum*) 'to look at/face/point toward one another';
ritkubum 'to mate; to lie upon/against one another';
tiṣbutum 'to grasp one another, quarrel; to join/connect with one another'; Verbal Adj. *tiṣbutum* 'connected, joined, engaged'.

(2) **Separative**. This nuance is attested with a small group of verbs of motion, such as

atlukum 'to go away, move on, be off';
etlûm 'to move off, away'; *ina X etlûm* 'to forfeit X';
iṣṣûm (*waṣûm*) 'to depart'.

(3) **Reflexive**. This nuance is rare, but note

piššušum 'to anoint oneself';
šitūlum 'to ponder, deliberate, reflect'; also reciprocal, 'to consult, take counsel; to question'.

(4) **Other**. Some Gt verbs do not fall under any of the above:

itʾudum (*naʾādum*) 'to heed, watch carefully';
tizkurum / *tisqurum* 'to speak' (used like the G in literary texts).

33.2 The Transitive *parsāku* Construction

It has been seen that all verbal roots have a Verbal Adjective (§4.3), the meaning of which is determined by the semantic nature of the root: passive for transitive verbs, resultative for active intransitive verbs, and descriptive for stative verbs. The Verbal Adjective may occur attributively, with markers of gender, number, and case to agree with the modified noun (§4.2), or as a predicate, with an enclitic subject pronoun suffixed to the base of the adjective (§22.1).

Transitive verbs may exhibit a second construction that is identical in form to the predicative Verbal Adjective construction (i.e., *parsāku, parsāta, parsāti, paris, parsat,* etc.), yet transitive rather than passive, as in

> *šīmam maḫrātunu* 'you (mp) are in receipt of the purchase price';
> *mišil mana kaspam kaliāku* 'I have half a mina of silver in reserve';
> *ṭuppaka našû* 'they (m) have your (ms) tablet in their possession'.

Although such transitive constructions are identical in appearance to the predicative Verbal Adjective construction, the base of these forms is not the Verbal Adjective. In fact, the base *paris-* of the transitive forms has no independent existence, and does not occur attributively (with case endings, etc.); the transitive forms occur only with the suffixed subject pronoun (*parsāku, paris-ø,* etc.), as predicates of their clauses. What the transitive *parsāku* forms do share with the predicative Verbal Adjectives is the predication of a condition or state rather than a process (i.e., of 'being' rather than 'becoming'). Just as in

> *ušib* 'I sat down = became seated' vs. *wašbāku* 'I am/was seated',

an analogous relationship obtains between transitive *parsāku* forms and the Preterite, Durative, and Perfect forms that correspond to them:

> *amḫur* 'I received' vs. transitive *maḫrāku* 'I am in receipt of'.

Compare the following sets of examples:

> *bītam iṣbat* 'she took possession of the house';
> *bītam iṣabbat* 'she will take possession of the house';
> *bītam iṣṣabat* 'she has taken possession of the house';
> but *bītam ṣabtat* 'she is/was in possession of (i.e., owns) the house'.

> *aššatam īḫuz* 'he took a wife, got married';
> *aššatam iḫḫaz* 'he will take/is taking a wife, he will get/is getting married';
> *aššatam ītaḫaz* 'he has taken a wife, has gotten married';
> but *aššatam aḫiz* 'he has/had a wife, he is/was married'.

While examples of the transitive *parsāku* construction are attested with many transitive verbs, it is common only with a relatively small group of verbs that for the most part denote holding, grasping, or seizing, especially the following (see the examples given above):

> *aḫāzum*: *aḫiz* 'he has, is in possession of';
> *leqûm*: *leqi* 'he is in receipt of, has';
> *maḫārum*: *maḫir* 'he is in receipt of, has';
> *našûm*: *naši* 'he has in his possession, carries, bears responsibility for';
> *ṣabātum*: *ṣabit* 'he is in possession of, has, owns, is occupied/busy with'.

Although transitive *parsāku* forms are indistinguishable in form from predicate Verbal Adjectives, there is seldom any ambiguity as to which of the forms is intended in any given context: simply put, if there is a direct object present, a *parsāku* form is the transitive variety; otherwise, a *parsāku* form is the familiar predicate Verbal Adjective (cf. English, where the absence or presence of a direct object may mark a verb as middle or transitive: 'he turned' vs. 'he turned the page'):

bītum ṣabit 'the house is/was owned (is/was held in possession)';
bītam ṣabit 'he owns/owned (is/was in possession of) the house'.

šīpātum maḫrā 'the wool is/was received';
šīpātim maḫrā 'they (f) are in receipt of the wool'.

In grammars of Akkadian in which the predicate Verbal Adjectives are called "statives", transitive *parsāku* forms are termed **active statives**.

33.3 Akkadian Poetry

The principles of composition of Akkadian poetry are still not fully understood. What is presented here relies heavily on Buccellati 1990. Examples are from the OB version of Gilgamesh, tablet II (Pennsylvania tablet; see the Supplementary Reading beginning on p. 475).

Poetic lines (verses) regularly end in a trochee, that is, a stressed syllable followed by an unstressed syllable:

tammaršū-ma taḫaddu átta 'you will see him and rejoice;
eṭlūtum unaššaqū šēpíšu the young men will kiss his feet' (i 20–21).

Exceptions to this convention are

(a) words in which the final syllable is ultraheavy as the result of vowel contraction; these ultraheavy vowels may be considered to contain a virtual trochee; thus, e.g., in the following example, *šadû* is thought of and used as though [šadúŭ];

ina ṣēri iwwalid-ma urabbīšu šadú 'he was born on the steppe, and the hill-country raised him' (i 18–19);

(b) proper names.

Apart from the requirement of a trochee at the end of a line, Akkadian poetry is based not on patterns of word stress or length of syllables or number of syllables (unlike, for example, Greek, Latin, or much English poetry), but rather on syntactic stress units. The building blocks of the system are, in increasing order of size:

Word: Words may be classified as metrical or non-metrical; non-metrical words are prepositions, particles (including negative adverbs), *ša*, and coordinating conjunctions, while all other words are metrical.

Foot: A foot has one major stress (accent). Feet may be simple or complex; a simple foot has one metrical word and any number of non-metrical words. Each of the following constitutes a simple foot; note that the number of syllables may vary considerably:

> *šī* 'she' (ii 30);
> *ummī* 'my mother' (i 3);
> *ina birīt eṭlūtim* 'among the young men' (i 5);
> *teddiraššū-ma* 'you (ms) will embrace him' (i 22).

A complex foot has two metrical words and any number of non-metrical words. The most common constituents of a complex foot are a bound form and its genitive (as in the first example below), but other combinations are also possible, such as a noun and adjective, a verb and its object (second example), a subject and its verb. Any of these combinations, including a genitive chain, may, depending on the requirements of the poetic context, constitute two simple feet rather than one complex foot.

> *kakkabū šamāʾī* 'the stars of the sky' (i 6);
> *pâša īpušam-ma* 'opened her mouth' (ii 9).

Colon: Cola may contain one or two feet. Odd cola contain one simple foot:

> *inaṭṭal* 'he looks' (iii 4);
> *u ippallas* 'he sees' (iii 5); other examples appear below.

Even cola contain two feet, one of which is normally simple and the other of which may be simple or complex; in the examples below, the symbol ‿ joins the two constituents of complex cola:

simple – simple:

> *Uruk‿mātum* 'the land of Uruk' (i 10);
> *kīma muti‿ibašši* 'he becomes like a groom' (iii 27);

simple – complex:

> *ibbašûnim-ma‿kakkabū šamāʾī* 'the stars of the sky appeared' (i 6);

complex – simple:

> *aššāt šīmātim‿iraḫḫi* 'he mates with lawful wives' (iv 24).

Verse: A verse (or poetic line) usually consists either of two even cola or of three odd cola; other possibilities occur much less often.

two even cola:

> *Uruk‿mātum* *paḫer‿elīšu* 'the land of Uruk was gathered over it' (i 10);
> *iššī-ma‿īnīšu* *ītamar‿awīlam* 'he looked up, and saw a man' (iv 2–3);
> *eṭlum‿pīšu īpušam-ma* *issaqqaram‿ana Enkidu* 'the young man opened his mouth to speak to Enkidu' (iv 12–13);

three odd cola:

akalam iškunū maḫaršu 'food was placed before him' (iii 3);
iptēq-ma inaṭṭal u ippallas 'he squinted? to look and see' (iii 4–5);
šikaram ana šatêm lā lummud 'he was not used to drinking beer' (iii 8–9).

other: note the following verse of even – odd – even cola:

šamḫākū-ma‿attanallak ina birīt eṭlūtim ibbašûnim-ma ‿kakkabū šamāʾī 'as I walked around grandly? among the young men, the stars of the sky appeared' (i 4–6).

Larger Units: Verses usually constitute elements in larger poetic units; two verses (poetic lines) comprise a **couplet**; three comprise a **tercet**. Less commonly a single verse (line) may stand alone (called a monostich). Still larger units, **stanzas**, are more difficult to identify.

A poetic text is usually written on a tablet such that a line of text does not contain more than one verse (poetic line) or parts of more than one verse. Thus, the beginning of a verse corresponds to the beginning of a line of text; verses may take up one or two (less often three) lines of a tablet. (See the examples cited above.)

Finally, it is important to note that normal Akkadian word order is not always (or even frequently) followed in poetic texts. In fact, poets often varied the word order deliberately, to create certain effects:

šamnam iptašaš-ma awīliš iwwi
ilbaš libšam kīma muti ibašši

'he anointed himself with oil, becoming human,
he put on a garment, becoming like a groom' (iii 24–27).

In this couplet, the first verse is Object–Verb : Adjunct–Verb, while the second is Verb–Object : Adjunct–Verb.

33.4 OB Hymns and Prayers

Several types of literary texts sharing similar structure and content may be considered under the general rubric of hymns and prayers. Hymns are essentially texts in which a deity is praised by an anonymous devotee. (One OB hymn, a beautiful literary work praising Ištar, is presented in the exercises of this and the following two lessons.) Prayers include a lovely work addressed to the 'gods of the night' by a diviner (Lesson 38, exercises), laments and penitential psalms, and petitions to gods (see Lesson 36, exercises). Similar to these are incantations against demons, diseases, and the like.

EXERCISES

A. VOCABULARY 33.

Verbs:

atwûm Gt (G not used in OB) (*u*) 'to speak; to discuss' (cf. *awātum*).
gamālum G (*i*) 'to treat kindly, please; to come to an agreement; to spare, save'.
kamāsum a G (*i*) 'to gather, collect, assemble, bring in, complete'; *kummusum* D = G.
kamāsum b G (*i*) 'to squat, bend down, kneel'; *šukmusum* Š caus.
kasûm G (*u* or *i*) 'to bind, arrest, imprison; to join, tie, bond together'; *kussûm* D = G.
labāšum G (*a*) 'to put on clothing, clothe oneself, get dressed'; Verbal Adj. *labšum* (*labiš*-) 'clothed (in), wearing'; *litbušum* Gt 'to put on, wear'; *lubbušum* D 'to clothe, provide with clothing'.
nazāqum G (*i*) 'to worry, be upset'; *šuzzuqum* Š 'to cause worry, upset'.
niālum G (*i*; also *nâlum*, *a*) 'to lie down'; *itūlum* / *utūlum* Gt 'to lie down, lie (with someone: *itti*)'; *ina sūn(i) X niālum* / *itūlum* 'to have intercourse with X'.
qalûm G (*i*) 'to burn (down), roast, refine'.
ṣeḫērum G (*i*) 'to become small, few, decrease'; Verbal Adj. *ṣeḫrum* see Vocab. 7; *ṣuḫḫurum* D 'to make small(er), reduce'.

Nouns:

ḫīṭum (*ḫīṭ(i)*) 'fault, damage; offense, crime; negligence'.
šaptum (*šapat*; du. *šaptān*; pl. *šapātum*) 'lip; utterance; edge, rim'.
zibbatum (*zibbat*; dual *zibbān*; pl. *zibbātum*; log. KUN) 'tail; rear part'.

Adverb:

pāna 'before, earlier, previously' (cf. *pānum*).

B. Learn the following sign:

OB Lapid.	OB Cursive	NA	value
	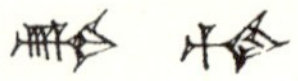	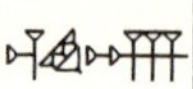	KUN = *zibbatum*

C. Write the following words in cuneiform and in transliteration; use logograms where possible:

1. *zibbat alpim*
2. *nikkas šangêm*
3. *suluppū rubêm*
4. *ugār almattim*
5. *kār Sippar*
6. *maškan nāqidim*

D. Write in normalized Akkadian:

1. we agreed with one another
2. go away (pl)!
3. oil for the self-anointing of my father
4. they (m) will watch carefully
5. why do you (pl) fight (strike each other)?
6. they (f) are connected
7. I deliberated
8. they (m) opposed each other
9. they (f) discussed (*atwûm*)
10. he has lain with her
11. you (pl) will quarrel
12. you (fs) forfeit your house

E. CH:

§§35–37§35 *šum-ma a-wi-lum* ÁB.GUD(! BI).ḪI.A *ù* U$_8$.UDU.ḪI.A *ša šar-ru-um a-na* AGA.ÚS *id-di-nu i-na qá-ti* AGA.ÚS *iš-ta-am i-na* KUG.BABBAR-*šu i-te-el-li.* §36 A.ŠÀ-*um* KIRI$_6$ *ù* É *ša* AGA.ÚS ŠU.ḪA *ù na-ši bi-il-tim a-na* KUG.BABBAR *ú-ul i-na-ad-di-in.* §37 *šum-ma a-wi-lum* A.ŠÀ KIRI$_6$ *ù* É *ša* AGA.ÚS ŠU.ḪA *ù na-ši* GUN *iš-ta-am* DUB-*pa-šu iḫ-ḫe-ep-pé ù i-na* KUG.BABBAR-*šu i-te-el-li* A.ŠÀ KIRI$_6$ *ù* É *a-na be-lí-šu i-ta-ar.*

nāši biltim 'tenant (of a field owned by the state)'.

§57 *šum-ma* SIPAD *a-na ša-am-mi* U$_8$.UDU.ḪI.A *šu-ku-lim it-ti be-el* A.ŠÀ *la im-ta-gàr-ma ba-lum be-el* A.ŠÀ A.ŠÀ U$_8$.UDU.ḪI.A *uš-ta-ki-il be-el* A.ŠÀ A.ŠÀ-*šu i-iṣ-ṣi-id* SIPA *ša i-na ba-lum be-el* A.ŠÀ U$_8$.UDU.ḪI.A *ú-ša-ki-lu e-le-nu-um-ma ana būrim* (BÙR^{iku}.E) 20 ŠE.GUR *a-na be-el* A.ŠÀ *i-na-ad-di-in.*

eṣēdum G (*i*) 'to harvest, reap'.

būrum (*būri*; log. BÙR; Sum. lw.) a surface measure (ca. 6.48 ha.).

§64 *šum-ma a-wi-lum* ^{giš}KIRI$_6$-*šu a-na nukaribbim*(NU.^{giš}KIRI$_6$) *a-na ru-ku-bi-im id-di-in nukaribbum*(NU.^{giš}KIRI$_6$) *a-di* ^{giš}KIRI$_6$ *ṣa-ab-tu i-na bi-la-at* KIRI$_6$ *ši-it-ti-in a-na be-el* KIRI$_6$ *i-na-ad-di-in ša-lu-uš-tam šu-ú i-le-qé.*

rukkubum D 'to pollinate'.

nukaribbum (pl. *nukaribbātum*; log. NU.^{giš}KIRI$_6$; Sum. lw.) 'gardener'.

§116 *šum-ma ni-pu-tum i-na* É *ne-pí-ša i-na ma-ḫa-ṣí-im ù lu i-na uš-šu-ši-im im-tu-ut be-el ni-pu-tim* DAM.GÀR-*šu ú-ka-an-ma šum-ma* DUMU *a-wi-lim* DUMU-*šu i-du-uk-ku šum-ma* ÌR *a-wi-lim* 1/3 MA.NA KUG.BABBAR *i-ša-qal ù i-na mi-im-ma šum-šu ma-la id-di-nu i-te-el-li.*

nepûm G (*e*) 'to distrain, take as pledge, distress'; *nipûtum* (fem.) 'person or animal taken as pledge or distress'.

ašāšum G (*u*) 'to become disturbed, worried'; *uššušum* D 'to cause distress, mistreat'.

§§129–132 §129 *šum-ma aš-ša-at a-wi-lim it-ti zi-ka-ri-im ša-ni-im i-na i-tu-lim it-ta-aṣ-bat i-ka-sú-šu-nu-ti-ma a-na me-e i-na-ad-du-ú-šu-nu-ti šum-ma be-el aš-ša-tim aš-ša-sú ú-ba-la-aṭ ù šar-ru-um* ÌR-*sú ú-ba-la-aṭ.* §130 *šum-ma a-wi-lum aš-ša-at a-wi-lim ša zi-ka-ra-am la i-du-ú-ma i-na* É *a-bi-ša wa-aš-ba-at ú-kab-bil-ši-ma i-na su-ni-ša it-ta-ti-il-ma iṣ-ṣa-ab-tu-šu a-wi-lum šu-ú id-da-ak* MUNUS *ši-i ú-ta-aš-šar.* §131 *šum-ma aš-ša-at a-wi-lim mu-sà ú-ub-bi-ir-ši-ma it-ti zi-ka-ri-im ša-ni-im i-na ú-tu-lim la iṣ-ṣa-bi-it ni-iš i-lim i-za-kar-ma a-na* É-*ša i-ta-ar.* §132 *šum-ma aš-ša-at a-wi-lim aš-šum zi-ka-ri-im ša-ni-im ú-ba-nu-um e-li-ša it-ta-ri-iṣ-ma it-ti zi-ka-ri-im ša-ni-im i-na ú-tu-lim la it-ta-aṣ-ba-at a-na mu-ti-ša* dÍD *i-ša-al-li.*

kubbulum D (*kabālum* G rare) 'to hinder, immobilize'.

ūtaššar 'will be released' (see §35.1).

ubburum D (G *abārum* rare) 'to accuse'.

dÍD = *Id* the River-god.

šalûm (*i*) 'to dive, plunge into (+ acc.)'.

§§142–143 §142 *šum-ma* MUNUS *mu-sà i-ze-er-ma ú-ul ta-aḫ-ḫa-za-an-ni iq-ta-bi wa-ar-ka-sà i-na ba-ab-ti-ša ip-pa-ar-ra-ás-ma šum-ma na-aṣ-ra-at-ma ḫi-ṭi-tam la i-šu ù mu-sa$_6$ wa-ṣí-ma ma-ga-al ú-ša-am-ṭa-ši* MUNUS *ši-i ar-nam ú-ul i-šu še-ri-ik-ta-ša i-le-qé-ma a-na* É *a-bi-ša it-ta-al-la-ak.* §143 *šum-ma la na-aṣ-ra-at-ma wa-ṣí-a-at bi-sà ú-sà-ap-pa-aḫ mu-sà ú-ša-am-ṭa* MUNUS *šu-a-ti a-na me-e i-na-ad-du-ú-ši.*

ḫiṭītum (*ḫiṭīt*) 'damage, negligence, fault, crime' (cf. *ḫīṭum*).

§§155–157 §155 *šum-ma a-wi-lum a-na* DUMU-*šu* É.GI$_4$.A *i-ḫi-ir-ma* DUMU-*šu il-ma-sí šu-ú wa-ar-ka-nu-um-ma i-na sú-ni-ša it-ta-ti-il-ma iṣ-ṣa-ab-tu-šu a-wi-lam šu-a-ti i-ka-sú-šu-ma a-na me-e i-na-ad-du-ú-šu*(!ŠI). §156 *šum-ma a-wi-lum a-na* DUMU-*šu* É.GI$_4$.A *i-ḫi-ir-ma* DUMU-*šu la il-ma-sí-ma šu-ú i-na sú-ni-ša it-ta-ti-il* 1/2 MA.NA KUG.BABBAR *i-ša-qal-ši-im-ma ù mi-im-ma ša iš-tu* É *a-bi-ša ub-lam ú-ša-lam-ši-im-ma mu-tu li-ib-bi-ša i-iḫ-ḫa-as-sí.* §157 *šum-ma a-wi-lum wa-ar-ki a-bi-šu i-na sú-un um-mi-šu it-ta-ti-il ki-la-li-šu-nu i-qal-lu-ú-šu-nu-ti.*

mutu unusual bound form (nom.) of *mutum* (cf. §30.2).

§§165–166:

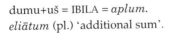

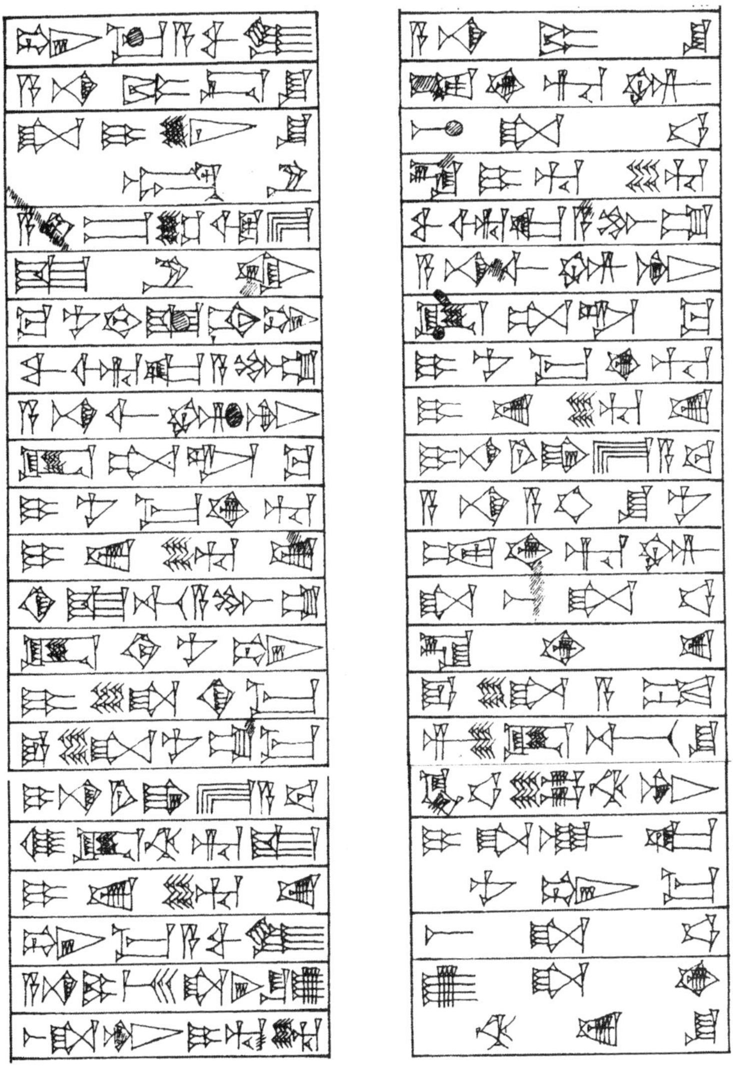

dumu+uš = IBILA = *aplum.*
eliātum (pl.) 'additional sum'.

F. Omens from *YOS* 10:

1. BE *i-na iš-di naplaštim*(IGI.BAR) ^{giš}TUKUL 2 *i-mi-tam ù šu-me-lam i-ta-aṭ-*[*lu*] *a-na šar-ri-im a-a-i-ma a-na sa-li-mi-im ta-ša-*[*pa-ar-ma*] *sa-li-im-šu te-le-qé-e-šu.* (15:17–19)
   salīmum (*salīm*) 'peace, concord'.
2. [DIŠ ^{giš}]TUKUL *ša-ki-in-*[*ma ṣ*]*i-it re-ši-im iṭ-ṭù-ul ù pi-iṭ-ru a-na pa-ni-šu pa-ṭi-ir* [*ma*]*-ri ši-ip-ri ma-aḫ-ru-ú-um bu-su-ra-at ḫa-de-e-em na-ši-kum.* (25:28)
   ṣīt rēšim, lit., 'loss of a slave', here part of the *bāb ekallim.*
   piṭrum (*piṭir*) 'fissure, split'.
   bussurtum (bound form irregularly *bussurat*) '(good) news, message'.
3. *šum-ma mar-tum ù ú-ba-nu-um ši-it-nu-na-a pu-uḫ-ru-um ú-la im-ta-ga-ar.* (31 x 41-44)
   šanānum G (*a–u*) 'to become equal, match, rival'; *šitnunum* Gt 'to equal one another, rival, compete with one another'.
4. MAŠ *i-na ṣe-er bi-ri-tim ka-ak-kum ši-na it-ta-aṭ-lu šar-ra-nu i-na pu-*⌈*úḫ-ri*⌉*-im in-na-am-ma-ru.* (33 ii 28–30)
   birītum here, 'border (region of the liver)'; note *kakkum* (sg.) *šinā* for 'two weapons'.
5. DIŠ ^{giš}TUKUL *i-mi-tim* 3 *it-ta-aṭ-lu-ú šar-ra-am i-na li-ib-bi* É.GAL-*šu ú-sà-ru-ú-šu*$^{!}$*-ma i-du-uk-ku-šu ša-nu-um šum-šu* MÁŠ.ŠU.GÍD.GÍD *a-ša-ar i-la-ku i-ma-qú-ut.* (46 iv 19-22)
   šumum here, 'meaning, interpretation' (of the omen); *šanûm šumšu* 'another interpretation of it'.
6. DIŠ 9 *še*$_{20}$*-e-tum at-ta ù na-ke-er-ka ta-aṣ-ṣa-ab-ba-ta-a-ma a-ḫu-um a-ḫ*[*a-a*]*m ú-ša-am-qá-at.* (50:8)
   šētum meaning uncertain.
7. DIŠ *iz-bu-um qá-qá-as-sú a-na ḫa-al-*⌈*li*⌉*-šu ka-mi-is-ma it-ti zi-ib-ba-ti-šu ti*$^{!}$*-iṣ-bu-ut a-wi-lum ṣe-ḫe-er bi-ti-šu ù ú-né-ti-šu i-na-šu i-ma-ra.* (56 ii 31–34)
   ḫallum 'crotch'; *ḫallān* (dual) 'hind legs'.
8. BE *re-*[*eš*] ⌈ŠÀ⌉ *qá-a sa-ḫe-er ni-iš* DINGIR LUGAL(*šarram*) *ṣa-bi-it.* (Jeyes, *Old Babylonian Extispicy* no. 14:31, p. 157)
   qûm (*qā-*) 'thread, string, filament'.
9. 23:8:

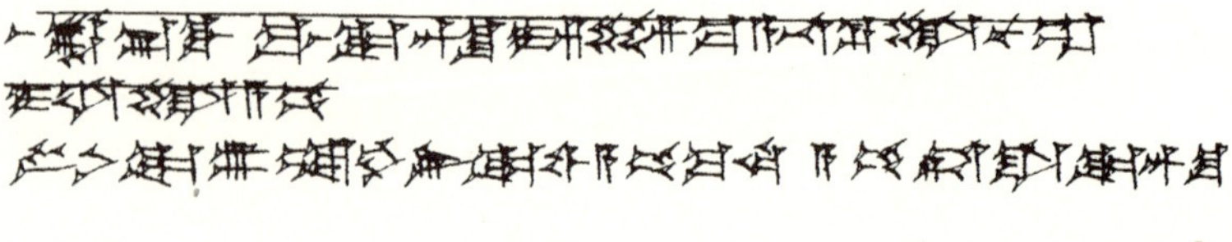

10. 31 viii 7-10:

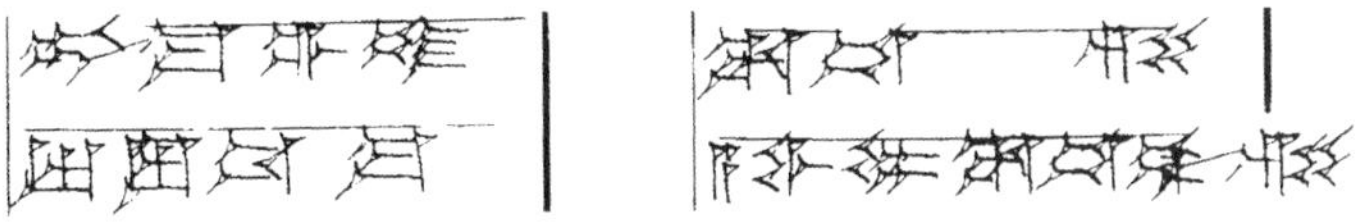

G. Contracts:

1. Hire of a tenant farmer (Chiera, *PBS* 8/2, no. 196).

[1] {I}*gi-mil-lum* DUMU *ap-pa-li* [2] KI *ra-ma-ni-šu* [3] {I}*i-na*-É.SAG.ÍL-NUMUN DUMU ÌR-*ì-lí-šu* [4] *a-na ikkarūtim*(ENGAR-*ru-tim*) [5] *a-di pa-ṭa-ar e-re-ši-im* [6] *i-gur-ma* [7] Á ITU.1.KAM.MA [8] 1 GÍN KUG.BABBAR Ì.LAL.E ... [14] GUD.ḪI.A *ú-ra-aq-ma* [15] KUG.BABBAR *i-ni-tim i-ša-qá-al* [16] *i-na* ITU.3.KAM *qá-tam i-ṣa-bat* [17] [GUD.ḪI.A] *i-na-pu-uš i-na-sà-aḫ* [18] *i-na-ad-di it-ta-al-la-ak* [19] *i-na* Á-*šu i-te-el-li* [20] *i-na* ŠÀ Á-*šu* 1 GÍN KUG.BABBAR *ma-ḫi-ir*. [21] Witness. [22–24] Date.

PNs: *Gimillum; Appalu(m); Ina-Esagil-zērum; Warad-ilīšu.*

[2] *itti ramānīšu*, lit. 'from himself'; i.e., he is a free agent.

[4] *ikkarum* (*ikkar*; pl. *ikkarū*; log. ENGAR; Sum. lw.) 'farmer, farm laborer, plowman'; *ikkarūtum* 'agricultural work, plowing'.

[7] KAM.MA= KAM.

[15] *inītum* (*inīt*; pl. *iniātum*) 'services or rate of hire of an ox (team)'.

[17] *napāšum* G (*u*) 'to breathe freely, to relax'.

[17–18] These lines constitute the protasis of an unmarked conditional sentence; *nasāḫum* and *nadûm*, missing their objects, must be understood elliptically: 'moves on, drops (the work)'.

2. Marriage contract (Chiera, *PBS* 8/2, no. 252).

[1] 2 *ṣubātū*(TÚG.ḪI.A) *ša la-ab-ša-at* [2] 2 {túg}*paršīgātum*(BAR.SI.ḪI.A) ‹*ša*› *ap-ra-at* [3] 1 {giš}*eršum*(NÁ) [4] 3 {giš}GU.ZA.ḪI.A [5] 1 {dug}*šiqqatum* (ŠAGAN) *ša* 4 *qa*(SILA₃) Ì.GIŠ *ma-li-a-at* [6] 1 {gi}*pišannum* (PISAN) *ga-ar-ru ša* 4 BÁN(!) *akalam*(NINDA) *ma-lu-ú* [7] *mi-im-ma an-ni-im* [8] *ša a-ta-na-aḫ-ì-lí a-bu-ša* DUMU *ṣíl-lí*-{d}UTU [9] *a-na* {f}*ṣi-ḫar-ṭì-lu-uk* {f}*e-gi-tim* [10] DUMU.MUNUS.A.NI *id-di-nu-ma* [11] *a-na* É *zi-me-er*-{d}UTU [12] *a-na* ÌR-{d}*ul-maš-ši-tum* DUMU-*šu* [14] *ú-še-ri-bu* [14] 5 GÍN KUG.BABBAR *te-er-ḫa-as-sà* [15] *i-na qá-ti zi-me-er*-{d}UTU [16] {I}*a-ta-na-aḫ-ì-lí a-bu-ša ma-ḫi-ir* [17] *li-ib-ba-šu ṭa-ab* [18] {If}*ṣi-ḫar-ṭì-lu-uk* [19] *a-na* ÌR-{d}*ul-maš-ši-tum mu-ti-ša* [20] *ú-ul mu-*[*ti at-ta*] [21] *i-q*[*á-bi-ma a-na* KUG.BABBAR *i-na-di-i*]*š-ši-i* [22] *ù* [ÌR-{d}*ul-maš-ši-tum*] [23] *a-na* [{f}*ṣi-ḫar-ṭì-lu-uk aš-ša-ti-šu*] [24] *ú-ul* [*aš-ša-ti at-ti*] [25] *i-*[*qá-bi-ma*] [26] 2/3 MA.NA [KUG.BABBAR *i-ša-qá-al* [27] MU {d}UTU {d}AMAR.UTU [*ù am-mi-ṣa-du-qá*] LUGAL [28] *itmû*(IN.PÀD.DÈ.[EŠ]). [29–39] Witnesses. [40–44] Date.

PNs: *Ātanaḫ-ilī; Ṣillī-Šamaš; Ṣiḫar-ṭilluk; Zimer-Šamaš; Warad-Ulmaššītum.*

1–6 These lines list the bride's dowry.

1 *ṣubātum* (*ṣubāt*; pl. *ṣubātū*; log. TÚG) 'garment' (note also determinative túg before items of clothing).

2 *paršīgum* (pl. *paršīgātum*; log. (túg)BAR.SI; Sum. lw.) 'headdress; cap'; *apārum* G (*i*) 'to cover the head, provide with a headdress'; Verbal Adj. *aprum* (*apir-*) 'with covered head, wearing on the head'.

3 *eršum* (fem.; log. (giš)NÁ) 'bed'.

5 *šiqqatum* (log. (dug)ŠAGAN) 'basin' (the determinative dug appears before words denoting vessels); *qûm* (absolute *qa*; log. SILA3) a capacity measure (ca. 1 liter).

6 *pišannum* (pl. *pišannū* and *pišannātum*; log. PISAN; Sum. lw.) 'basket'; *garārum* G (*u*) 'to turn, roll'; Verbal Adj. *garrum* (*garir-*) 'round, bulging'.

9 f*egītum* meaning uncertain; cf. *egûm*?

H. Letters:

1. *CT* 43 92 = Kraus, *AbB* 1 92.

1 *a-na* GEME2-*ka-la-tim* 2 *qí-bí-ma* 3 *um-ma* dUTU-*mu-še-zi-ib-ma* 4 dUTU *ù* dAMAR.UTU *li-ba-al-li-ṭú-ki* 5 *aš-šum* A.ŠÀ-*im ša at-ti* 6 *ù na-ra-am-ta-ni ti-iṣ-bu-ta-ti-na* 7 *a-na* DUMU-ZIMBIRki DUB-*pí ù* DUB-*pí* TAB.BA-*tum* 8 *ú-da-ni-nam-ma uš-ta-bi-lam* 9 *a-di a-la-kam* A.ŠÀ-*am ú-ul i-zu-za-ki-na-ši-im* 10 *i-na a-la-ki-ia* 11 *a-na* DI.KUD ‹.MEŠ› ZIMBIRki 12 *ú-ṭa-ḫa-ki-na-ti-ma* 13 *a-wa-ti-ki-na i-ma-ru-ú-ma* 14 É.GAL *i-ka-ša-du-ma* 15 *ḫi-bi-il-ta-ki ú-ga-ma-ra-ki-im* 16 *ap-lu-tum ṣe-ḫe-er-tum ù ra-bi-tum* 17 *i-na* ZIMBIRki *ú-ul i-ba-aš-ši.*

PNs: *Amat-Kallatim; Šamaš-mušēzib; Narāmtani; Mār-Sippar; Tappatum.*

15 *ḫibiltum* 'damage, wrong' (cf. *ḫubullum*).

16 *aplūtum ṣeḫertum u rabītum* institution of the younger and older heir.

2. *OECT* 3 54 = Kraus, *AbB* 4 132.

1 *a-na* dUTU-*ḫa-zi-ir* 3 *qí-bí-ma* 3 *um-ma* dEN.ZU-*i-din-nam-ma* 4 dUTU ù dAMAR.UTU *li-ba-al-li-ṭú-ka* 5 IdUTU-*ḫa-zi-ir* 6 *ki-a-am ú-lam-mi-da-an-ni* 7 *um-ma šu-ma* 8 *pa-na i-nu-ma a-na* AGA.ÚS-*ka* 9 *a-al-la-ku* 10 BÙR.2iku A.ŠÀ *ṣa-ab-ta-a-ku* 11 *i-na-an-na aš-šum a-na* GUN 12 [*il-qú*]-*ni-in-ni* 13 A.ŠÀ-*i* I*wa-ar-di-ia* 14 *ib-ta-aq-ra-an-ni* 15 *ki-a-am iq-bi-a-am* 16 *a-nu-um-ma* dUTU-*ḫa-zi-ir* 17 *aṭ-ṭar-dam* 18 A.ŠÀ *ša aš-šum-mi-šu ú-lam-mi-da-an-ni* 19 *na-di-iš-šu-um* 20 *ga-na ṭe4-ma-am šu-up-ra-am.*

PNs: *Šamaš-ḫāzir; Sîn-iddinam; Wardīya.*

5 *Šamaš-ḫāzir* here is not the same man as the addressee.

10 BÙR.2^{iku} A.ŠÀ = *šinā būr eqlum* 'a field of 2 *būr*' (= ca. 13 ha.).

20 *gana* (Sumerian g a n . a 'come!') 'come (on)!'.

3. *VAS* 16 9 = Frankena, *AbB* 6 9.

1 *a-na na-bi-ì-lí-šu* 2 *qí-bí-ma* 3 *um-ma* ^{d}EN.ZU-*be-el*-IBILA-*ma* 4 ^{d}UTU *ù* ^{d}AMAR.UTU *li-ba-li-ṭú-ka* 5 *i-na ši-tu-ul-ti ku-li-zu* 6 *iš-ta-lu-ma ig-mi-lu* 7 GUD.ḪI.A *ša-la-‹am›-šu-nu ṭà-ab* 8 *ú ḫi-ṭam ú-ul i-šu-ú* 9 *a-na* KA *su-qí-im ta-qú-ul-ma* 10 *an-ni-a-am ta-aš-pu-ra-am* 11 GUD.ḪI.A *ḫi-ṭam ‹ú›-ul i-šu-ú* 12 *mi-im-ma la ta-na-zi-iq* 13 GUD.ḪI.A *ka-la-šu-nu* 14 *a-na-ku-ma ú-ša-la-am* 15 *a-na a-wa-tim an-ni-tim* 16 *la ta-na-zi-iq* 17 GUD.ḪI.A *ša-al-mu ḫi-ṭam* 18 *ú-ul i-šu-ú* 19 *ù mé-re-ša-am er-ri-iš* 20 *mé-ḫe-er* DUB-*pí-im* 21 *uš-ta-bi-la-kum* 22 *mi-im-ma la ta-na-zi-iq* 23 *aš-šum ta-aš-pu-ra-am* 24 *um-ma at-ta-ma a-na* GUD.ḪI.A 25 *i-in-ka la ta-na-ši* 26 *aq-bi-ma* 27 *gi-im-lum* 28 *ti-iṣ-bu-ut-ma* 29 *a-na ga-ma-lim* 30 *ú-ul i-ba-aš-ši.*

PNs: *Nabi-ilīšu; Sîn-bēl-aplim.*

5 *šitultum* (*šitulti*) 'advice, counsel, consideration, deliberation' (cf. *šâlum*); *kullizum* (*kulliz*; pl. *kullizū*) 'ox-driver'.

8 *ú* for *ù*.

9 *qâlum* G (*u*) 'to heed, pay attention to'.

19 *mērešum* 'cultivated land, cultivation' (cf. *erēšum* b).

27 *gimlum* 'reserve ox' (very rare word).

4. *ARM* 4 22.

1 *a-na ia-ás-ma-aḫ*-[^{d}IŠKUR] 2 *qí-bí-m*[*a*] 3 *um-ma iš-me-*^{d}*da-gan* 4 *a-ḫu-ka-a-ma* 5 *aš-šum ṭe*$_4$*-em* LÚ‹.MEŠ› *tu-ru-ki-im* 6 *ša ta-aš-pu-ra-am* 7 *ṭe*$_4$*-em-šu-nu it-ta-na-ki-ir* 8 *i-na ki-a-am a-di i-na-an-na*! 9 *ta-ki-it-t*[*am*] 10 *ú-ul a-ša-ap-p*[*a-ra-kum*] 11 ‹*be-el*› *a-wa-ti-šu*-[*nu*] 12 *ša a-na sa-li-m*[*i-im*] 13 *ṣa-ab-t*[*u*] 14 *it-ta-at-la*-[*ak*/*ku*] 15 ^{I}*ia-an-ta-ki*-[*im*] 16 ^{I}LÚ-^{d}NIN.SU.AN.NA 17 ^{I}*wa-te-er-na-nam* 18 *ù* LÚ.MEŠ *ra-ab-bu-tim-ma* 19 *i-ḫa-ku-ú ù ki-a-am iš-pu-ru-nim* 20 *um-ma-mi iš-tu li-ṭì an-nu-tim* 21 *la ta-na-di-nam* 22 *ur-ra-am ú-lu ul-li-ti-iš* 23 *a-šar at-lu-ki-im ni-it-ta-la-ak* 24 *aš-ra-nu-um li-iš-pu*-[*ru*] 25 *ù a-šar at-lu-ki-im* 26 [*li*]-*it-ta-al*-[*ku*] 27 [*x x x*] *lu i*-[*de*] 28 [*i-na ḫ*]*a-al-ṣí*-[*im*] 29 [*š*]*a* [*w*]*a-aš-ba-at ṭe*$_4$*-em-ka lu ṣa-bi-it.*

PNs: *Iasmaḫ-Addu* (*Addu* rather than *Adad* at Mari); *Išme-Dagan; Iantakim; Lu-Ninsuanna; Water-Nanum.*

5 *Turukkum* a place name.

7 *ittanakkir* 'keeps changing' (see §34.1).
8 *ina kiam* 'therefore, thus'.
9 *takīttum* (*takītti*) 'confirmation' (cf. *kânum* D).
11 *bēl awātim* 'adversary (in court), litigant' (here sg. or pl.; cf. §12.4).
12 *salīmum* (*salīm*) 'peace, concord'.
18 *rabbûm* (*rabbi-*) 'very great; noble' (cf. *rabûm*).
19 *ḫakûm* G (Northwest Semitic word) 'to await' (only here).
20 *līṭum* (*līṭ(i)*; pl. *līṭū*) 'hostage, (person taken as a) pledge'.
22 *urram* (Adverb) 'tomorrow'; *ullītiš* (Adverb) 'the day after tomorrow'.
23 For *ašar* see §30.1(d), end.
24 *ašrānum* (Adverb) 'there' (cf. *ašrum*).
28–29 *ḫalṣum* 'fortification; fortress'; *wašbāt* 'you dwell' (see p. 219, end).

I. A hymn to Ištar (Thureau-Dangin, *RA* 22 169–77; English translation in Foster 2005, 1.68–71). The hymn is comprised of fourteen four-line stanzas (separated by a ruled line), plus a three-line entreaty on behalf of king Ammī-ditāna at the end; the first five stanzas (lines 1–20) are given below, the next five in Lesson 34, and the remainder in Lesson 35.

1. *[i]l-ta-am zu-um-ra-a ra-šu-ub-ti i-la-tim*
2. *li-it-ta-i-id be-le-et ni-ši ra-bi-it i-gi-gi*
3. *eš$_4$-⌜tár⌝ zu-um-ra ra-šu-ub-ti i-la-tim li-it-ta-i-id*
4. *be-le-et i-ši-i ra-bi-it i-gi-gi*

1 *zamārum* G (*a–u*) 'to sing, sing of, about'
rašābum G only in Verbal Adj. *rašbum* (*rašub-*) 'commanding respect, awe-inspiring, imposing, awesome'; see §27.3.
2 *littaʾʾid* 'let her be praised'; *nâdum* G (*a*) 'to praise, extol'; *nuʾʾudum* b D = G; this form is the passive Dt (see §35.1).
Igigi a name for the great gods.
4 *iššum* (pl. *iššū*) 'woman' (rare word).

5. *ša-at me-le-ṣi-im ru-à-ma-am la-ab-ša-at*
6. *za-aʾ-na-at in-bi mé-qí-a-am ù ku-uz-ba-am*
7. *eš$_4$-tár me-le-ṣi-im ru-à-ma-am la-ab-ša-at*
8. *za-aʾ-na-at in-bi mé-qí-a-am ù ku-uz-ba-am*

5 *šāt* an archaic feminine sg. of the determinative-relative *ša* 'the one of, the one who' (cf. the pl. *šūt* in *šūt-rēšim*).
mēleṣum 'joy?'.
ruʾāmum (*ruʾām*) 'charm, love' (cf. *râmum*). This form is the first of many in this text with PI (usually *wa*, etc.) with the value *à*.
6 *zaʾānum* G only in Verbal Adj. *zaʾnum* (*zaʾin-*) 'overlaid, covered, decorated, endowed (with: acc.)'; *zuʾʾunum* D 'to overlay, cover, decorate'.

inbum (*inib*; pl. *inbū* [often = sg.]) 'fruit, fruit tree; (sexual) attractiveness'.

mēqûm (*mēqi-*) 'cosmetics' (rare word).

kuzbum (*kuzub*) 'luxuriance, abundance; (sexual) attractiveness, sexual vigor'; also as euphemism for sexual parts.

9. [*ša*]*-ap-ti-in du-uš-šu-pa-at ba-la-ṭú-um pí-i-ša*
10. *si-im-ti-iš-ša i-ḫa-an-ni-i-ma ṣi-ḫa-tum*
11. *šar-ḫa-at i-ri-mu ra-mu-ú re-šu-uš-ša*
12. *ba-ni-à-a ši-im-ta-à-ša bi-it-ra-a-ma i-na-ša ši-it-a-ra*

9 *duššupum* (*duššup-*; Adj.) 'sweet'.

10 *simtum* (*simat*; pl. *simātum*) 'what is fitting, suitable, worthy, necessary (e.g., *bītum simat ilūtīšu* 'a temple befitting his divinity'); characteristic(s), features; proper appearance, behavior'.

ḫanāmum G (*i*) 'to bloom' (rare).

ṣīḫtum (*ṣīḫti*; pl. *ṣīḫātum*) 'smile, laughter'; *ṭuppum ṣīḫtum* 'fraud(ulent tablet)'.

11 *šarāḫum* G only in Verbal Adj. *šarḫum* (*šaruḫ-*) 'proud, splendid, magnificent'; *šurruḫum* D 'to make proud', etc.

i-ri-mu uncertain; either *irimmum* (pl. *irimmū*) 'bead' or *īrimum* / *irīmum* (pl. *-ū* [= sg.]) 'loveliness' (cf. *râmum*; Westenholz and Westenholz 1977: 205–7).

ramûm G (*i*) 'to throw, cast, scatter; to live, reside'.

12 *banûm* b G (*i*) 'to become good, beautiful'; Verbal Adj. *banûm* (*bani-*) 'good, beautiful'; *bunnûm* D factitive.

šimtum (bound form *šimti* or *šimat*; dual *šimtān*; pl. *šimātum*) 'color, mark, marking'.

barāmum G 'to be multicolored', only in Verbal Adj. *barmum* (*barum-*) 'multicolored, speckled, variegated'; *bitrumum* Gt only in Verbal Adj. *bitrumum* = *barmum*; *burrumum* D 'to color, weave in colors'; note *bitrāmum* (*bitrām-*; Adj.) 'brightly colored, multicolored' (*pitrās* is an adjectival pattern connoting abundance of a quality; see also the next entry).

šitʾārum (*šitʾār-*; Adj.) 'brilliant, iridescent (of eyes)'.

13. *il₅-tu-um iš-ta-à-ša i-ba-aš-ši mi-íl-ku-um*
14. *ši-ma-at mi-im-ma-mi qá-ti-iš-ša ta-am-ḫa-at*
15. *na-ap-la-su-uš-ša ba-ni bu-a-ru-ú*
16. *ba-aš-tum ma-aš-ra-ḫu la-ma-as-su-um še-e-du-um*

13 *išti* (with suffix *ištī-* or *ištā-*; in OB in literary texts only) 'with (a person, deity)' (synonym of *itti*).

milkum (*milik*) 'counsel, advice; intelligence; mood'.

14 *mimmāmu(m)* 'everything' (rare; cf. *mimma*).
tamāḫum G (*a–u*) 'to grasp, hold'.

15 *naplasum* (*naplas*) 'glance, look' (cf. *naplusum*).
buʾārum 'cheerfulness; prosperity'; here sg. despite the spelling.

16 *bāštum* (*bāšti*) 'dignity, pride; good looks'.
mašraḫū (always pl.) 'splendor' (rare).
lamassum (fem.) 'protective spirit'; *šēdum* is also a protective spirit; these represent good fortune, health.

17. *ta-ar-ta-am*(!MI) *te-eš-me-e ri-tu-ú-mi ṭú-ú-bi*
18. *ù mi-it-gu-ra-am te-be-el ši-i-ma*
19. *ar-da-at ta-at-ta-ab um-ma ta-ra-aš-ši*
20. *i-za-ak-ka-ar-ši i-ni-ši i-na-ab-bi šu-um-ša*

17 *ritūmum* Gt (rare) 'to love (= G?), love one another'; Infin. in pl. 'mutual love'?.
tešmûm (*tešmē-*; pl. *tešmû*) '(favorable) hearing; understanding; agreement' (cf. *šemûm*).
ṭūbum (*ṭūb(i)*; pl. *ṭūbū*) 'good, goodness; friendliness' (cf. *ṭiābum*).

18 *bêlum* G (*e*) 'to rule'.

19 *wardatum* (*wardat*; pl. *wardātum*) 'young woman' (cf. *wardum*).
ta-at-ta-ab is obscure; what is expected is 'the young woman whom she (Ištar) ... acquires (in Ištar) a mother' or 'the young woman who ...'; perhaps *ta-at-ta-ab-‹lu›* 'who was taken away'.

20 *i-ni-ši* for *in-nišī* or, less likely, *in-iššī* (cf. line 4).

LESSON THIRTY-FOUR

34.1 The Gtn Stem

(a) Form

From each of the major stems (i.e., G, D, Š, N) is derived a stem characterized by an infixed *-tan-* between R_1 and R_2 (called Gtn, Dtn, Štn, Ntn, respectively). In each of these stems, the *n* of this morpheme appears only in the Durative form. All forms of all verb types (except II–weak) have a doubled middle radical. Below are the forms of the Gtn stem for the various verb types.

(1) Sound Verbs

Infinitive:	*pitarrusum*	Imperative:	*pitarras*
Durative:	*iptanarras*	Participle:	*muptarrisum*
Perfect:	*iptatarras*	Verbal Adj.:	*pitarrusum*
Preterite:	*iptarras*	V. Adj. base:	*pitarrus*

The personal prefixes are those of the G (and Gt and N).

The theme-vowel for all finite forms is that of the corresponding G Durative; thus,

iptanarras, imtanaḫḫaṣ, iptanaqqid, imtanaqqut.

The Gtn Preterite for any verb is formally identical to the corresponding Gt Durative.

The *-t-* of the infix, as expected, is assimilated to a preceding *d, ṭ, s, ṣ, z;* after *g*, the *-t-* becomes *d*. Examples:

issanaḫḫur, iṣṣanabbat, iṭṭanarrad, izzanakkar;
igdanammar.

(2) Verbs I–*n*. As in the Gt, the *n* of the root is assimilated in forms with prefixes (i.e., when the *n* appears immediately before the *-t-* of the infix), and lost entirely in the forms in which it would stand first.

Infinitive:	*itaddunum*	Imperative:	*itaddin*
Durative:	*ittanaddin*	Participle:	*muttaddinum*
Perfect:	*ittataddin*	Verbal Adj.:	*itaddunum*
Preterite:	*ittaddin*	V. Adj. base:	*itaddun*

(3) Verbs III–weak. As usual, these offer no problems; presented here is the Gtn paradigm of *banûm*; in verbs III–*e*, of course, *a* › *e*.

Infinitive:	*bitannûm*	Imperative:	*bitanni*
Durative:	*ibtananni*	Participle:	*mubtannûm*
Perfect:	*ibtatanni*	Verbal Adj.:	*bitannûm*
Preterite:	*ibtanni*	V. Adj. base:	*bitannu*

(4) Verbs I–ʾ. As in the Gt, forms with prefixes have a lengthened vowel before the infix to compensenate for the loss of the ʾ, while the remaining forms begin with *a* (or *e*); the Gtn of *alākum*, like its Gt, has *-tt-* rather than a lengthened vowel in forms with prefixes.

	I–*a*	I–*e*	I–*e*, III–weak	*alākum*
Infinitive:	*ataḫḫuzum*	*eteppušum*	*etellûm*	*atallukum*
Durative:	*ītanaḫḫaz*	*īteneppeš*	*ītenelli*	*ittanallak*
Perfect:	*ītataḫḫaz*	*īteteppeš*	*ītetelli*	*ittatallak*
Preterite:	*ītaḫḫaz*	*īteppeš*	*ītelli*	*ittallak*
Imperative:	*ataḫḫaz*	*eteppeš*	*etelli*	*atallak*
Participle:	*mūtaḫḫizum*	*mūteppišum*	*mūtellûm*	*muttallikum*
Verbal Adj.:	*ataḫḫuzum*	*eteppušum*	*etellûm*	*atallukum*
V. Adj. base:	*ataḫḫuz*	*eteppuš*	*etellu*	*atalluk*

(5) Verbs I–*w*. As in the Gt, Gtn forms of verbs I–*w* resemble those of verbs I–*n* (i.e., with assimilation of *w* to the *-t-* of the infix in forms with prefixes, and with loss of initial *w* in the other forms).

	I–*w*	I–*w*, III–weak
Infinitive:	*itabbulum*	*itaṣṣûm*
Durative:	*ittanabbal*	*ittanaṣṣi*
Perfect:	*ittatabbal*	*ittataṣṣi*
Preterite	*ittabbal*	*ittaṣṣi*
Imperative:	*itabbal*	*itaṣṣi*
Participle	*muttabbilum*	*muttaṣṣûm*
Verbal Adj.:	*itabbulum*	*itaṣṣûm*
V. Adj. base:	*itabbul*	*itaṣṣu*

(5) Verbs II–weak. Verbs originally II–*w* and II–*y* are poorly attested in the Gtn; finite forms with vocalic suffixes exhibit the familiar doubling of the final radical (cf. G *ikân* ~ *ikunnū*), while the Infinitive and Verbal Adj. have *-yy-* for the middle radical. In most forms of verbs that were originally II–ʾ, the middle ʾ is treated as a strong consonant (although it may not be indicated in the writing, as in *ši-ta-ú-lum* for Infinitive *šitaʾʾulum*); in some forms, if the vowel on either side of the -ʾʾ- is the same, there may be contraction (writings may be ambiguous, as in *iš-ta-na-(a-)al* for Durative *ištanaʾʾal* or *ištanâl*). Below are the attested Gtn forms of verbs II–*w* (e.g., *kânum*), II–*y* (*qiāšum*), II–ʾ(*a*) (*šâlum*) and a verb II–weak and III–weak, *šeʾûm* 'to seek' (G like *leʾûm*; see §21.3(h)) that often occurs in the Gtn with the same meaning.

Infinitive:	*kitayyunum*	*qitayyušum*	*šitaʾʾulum*	*šiteʾʾûm*
Durative:	*iktanân*	*iqtanīaš*	*ištanaʾʾal* / *ištanâl*	*išteneʾʾi* / *ištenê*
3mp:	*iktanunnū*	*iqtaniššū*	*ištanaʾʾalū* / *ištanallū*[?]	*išteneʾʾû*
Perfect:	?	?	?	?
Preterite	*iktūn*[?]	*iqtīš*	*ištaʾʾal*	*išteʾʾi*
3mp:	*iktunnū*	*iqtiššū*	*ištaʾʾalū*	*išteʾʾû*
Imperative:	?	?	*šitaʾʾal*	*šiteʾʾi* / *šiteʾʾe*
Participle	?	?	*muštaʾʾilum*	*mušteʾʾûm*
Verbal Adj.:	[*kitayyunum*]	[*qitayyušum*]	[*šitaʾʾulum*]	[*šiteʾʾûm*]
V. Adj. base:	[*kitayyun*]	[*qitayyuš*]	[*šitaʾʾul*]	[*šiteʾʾu*]

(b) Meaning

The Gtn and other -*tan*- stems have an iterative force; they express repeated, habitual, or continuous action. Gtn forms are extremely frequent, and it is likely that they could be formed at will from any G verb. Some examples:

> *aštanapparakkim* 'I keep writing to you (fs)';
> *teštemme* 'you (ms) heard over and over, constantly';
> *ištatakkan* 'she has placed repeatedly';
> *mitaqqutum* 'to fall again and again'.

In certain instances, they may have a distributive force:

> *limtaḫḫarū* 'they (m) should each receive'.

Some examples of the -*tan*- stems denote the continuation or repetition of an activity until the desired effect is produced:

> *šuteṣṣī-ma šamaššammī šūbilam* 'produce (*waṣûm* Štn) and dispatch the sesame to me' (*AbB* 10 204:12–13);
> *šeʾûm* G 'to seek, search, look for'; *šiteʾʾûm* Gtn, lit., 'to look, search repeatedly' (i.e., until something is found).

Verbs of motion in the Gtn, in addition to the iterative force, may have an ambulatory nuance:

> *atallukum* 'to be in motion, walk about, run around; to live, act'.

The Gtn of adjectival verbs may be augmentative, as in

irtabbi 'he grew ever greater, grew greater and greater';
iṣṣeneḫḫer 'it gets smaller and smaller' (*ṣeḫērum* 'to become small').

Certain other Gtn verbs may sometimes require a translation differing somewhat from the usual G meaning:

atappulum (*apālum*) 'to answer, pay repeatedly'; also 'to be responsible for, answer for';
itabbulum (*babālum*) 'to carry repeatedly'; also 'to manage, direct, organize';
itaššûm (*našûm*) 'to bear continuously'; also, 'to support, take care of, provide for (someone)'.

34.2 The Partitive Use of *ina*

The preposition *ina* may be used partitively, that is, with the meaning 'out of', as in

ina êm ša ina qātīkunu ibaššû âm ana bīt Šamaš idnā 'give (mp) grain to the Šamaš temple out of the grain at your disposal'.

In some instances, *ina* must be rendered 'any of, some of'. Such a phrase occasionally functions as the subject or object of its clause, as in the following examples:

ina aḫḫīša illakūnim-ma iraggumū, šunū-ma ippalū '(should) any of her brothers come and sue, it is they who will pay';
ina eqlim kirîm u bītim ul inaddiššum 'he will not give him any of the field, orchard, or house'.

EXERCISES

A. VOCABULARY 34.

Verbs:

ṣiārum G, rare apart from Verbal Adj. *ṣīrum* (*ṣīr-*) 'august, outstanding, first-rank, excellent'.
šeʾûm G (*i* or *e*; conjugated like *leʾûm*, see §21.3(h)) 'to seek, search, look for'; *šiteʾʾûm* Gtn frequently used instead of G.
wapûm G (*i*) 'to appear, become visible'; *šūpûm* Š 'to proclaim

(someone's fame), announce, promulgate (a decree)'; Verbal Adj. *šūpûm* (*šūpu-*) 'proclaimed, illustrious, splendid'.

Nouns:

adānum (also *adannum*; bound form *adān*, *adanni*; pl. *adānātum*, *adannātum*) 'a specified period of time; a specific date'.

ereqqum (fem.; *ereq*, with suf. *ereqqa-*; pl. *ereqqētum*; log. $^{(giš)}$MAR.GÍD.DA) 'wagon, cart'.

irtum (bound form *irti* and *irat*; log. GABA) 'chest, breast'; *mār(at) irtim* (log. DUMU(.MUNUS) GABA) 'suckling baby'.

nūnum (*nūn(i)*; log. KU$_6$ [= the ḪA sign]) 'fish'.

parṣum (*paraṣ*; pl. *parṣū*) 'office; cultic custom, rite'.

sukkallum or *šukkallum* (*s* / *šukkal*; log. SUKKAL; Sum. lw.) 'minister, vizier'.

šakkanakkum (log. GÌR.NITA(Ḫ)$_2$ [nita(ḫ)$_2$ = ÌR; GÌR.NITA(Ḫ)$_2$ perhaps to be read ŠAKKANA$_6$]; Sum. lw.?) 'governor' (cf. *šakānum*).

tāḫāzum (*tāḫāz*; pl. *tāḫāzātum*) 'battle'; *tāḫāzam epēšum* 'to do battle, make war, fight' (cf. *aḫāzum*).

waklum (*wakil* [originally a Verbal Adj.]; pl. *waklū*, *waklūtum*; log. UGULA [= the PA sign]) 'overseer, inspector, foreman'.

zikrum / *siqrum* (*zikir* / *siqir*; pl. *zikrū* / *siqrū*) 'utterance, words; mention; (divine or royal) command, order; name, fame' (cf. *zakārum* / *saqārum*).

Adjective:

etellum (bound form *etel*; fem. *etelletum*) 'princely, sovereign, supreme'; this word often appears substantivized, masc. 'prince', fem. 'princess'.

Idiom:

šumma(n) lā 'except for'.

B. Learn the following signs:

OB Lapid.	OB Cursive	NA	values
		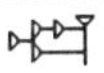	ÌR = *wardum* (lesson 13); NITA(Ḫ)$_2$ = *zikarum*; in GÌR.NITA(Ḫ)$_2$ = *šakkanakkum*
			GABA = *irtum*
			SUKKAL = *s* / *šukkallum*

C. Write the following words in cuneiform and in transliteration; use logograms where possible:

1. *irat šangêm*
2. *zibbat nūnim*
3. *nikkas suluppī*
4. *wakil itinnī*
5. *ugār Sippar*
6. *ereq šakkanakkim*
7. *šukkallum u rubûm*

D. Write in normalized Akkadian:

1. may they (m) constantly kneel
2. invoke (ms) again and again!
3. he keeps talking
4. you (pl) always get upset
5. they (f) have gone out repeatedly
6. while not always agreeing
7. we have entered again and again
8. I go up constantly
9. I will not keep scattering
10. I keep looking
11. keep (ms) asking him!
12. they (m) walk about
13. they (m) have repeatedly robbed us
14. I carried repeatedly
15. in order to give continually
16. I lay down here repeatedly
17. we keep hearing
18. you (fs) have kept requesting
19. it (f) is constantly in position (*šaknum*)
20. he will be continually responsible

E. CH:

§13 (For §§9–12 see lesson 32.) *šum-ma a-wi-lum šu-ú ši-bu-šu la qer-bu da-a-a-nu a-da-nam a-na* ITI.6.KAM *i-ša-ak-ka-nu-šum-ma šum-ma i-na* ITI.6.KAM *ši-bi-šu la ir-de-a-am a-wi-lum šu-ú sà-ar a-ra-an di-nim šu-a-ti it-ta-na-aš-ši.*

§125 *šum-ma a-wi-lum mi-im-ma-šu a-na ma-ṣa-ru-tim id-di-in-ma a-šar id-di-nu ù lu i-na pí-il-ši-im ù lu i-na na-ba-al-ka-at-tim mi-im-mu-šu it-ti mi-im-me-e be-el* É *iḫ-ta-li-iq be-el* É *ša i-gu-ma mi-im-ma ša a-na ma-ṣa-ru-tim id-di-nu-šum-ma ú-ḫal-li-qú ú-ša-lam-ma a-na be-el* NÍG.GA *i-ri-a-ab be-el* É *mi-im-ma-šu ḫal-qá-am iš-te-ne-i-ma* [*it*]-*ti šar-ra-*⌜*qá*⌝-*ni-šu i-le-qé.*

nabalkattum (*nabalkatti*; pl. *nabalkatātum*) 'crossing, scaling (of wall), burglary; retreat; rebellion, revolt'.

§§148–149 §148 *šum-ma a-wi-lum aš-ša-tam i-ḫu-uz-ma la-aʾ-bu-um iṣ-ṣa-ba-as-sí a-na ša-ni-tim a-ḫa-zi-im pa-ni-šu iš-ta-ka-an* *i-iḫ-ḫa-az aš-ša-sú ša la-a*ʾ*-bu-um iṣ-ba-tu ú-ul i-iz-zi-ib-ši i-na* É *i-pu-šu uš-ša-am-ma a-di ba-al-ṭa-at it-ta-na-aš-ši-ši.* §149 *šum-ma* MUNUS *ši-i i-na* É *mu-ti-ša wa-ša-ba-am la im-ta-gàr še-ri-ik-ta-ša ša iš-tu* É *a-bi-ša ub-lam ú-*[*š*]*a-lam-šim-ma it-ta-al-la-ak.*

*la*ʾ*bum* 'a skin disease'.

§191 *šum-ma a-wi-lum ṣe-eḫ-ra-am ša a-na ma-ru-ti-šu il-qú-šu-ma ú-ra-ab-bu-ú-šu* É-*sú*(! BA) *i-pu-uš wa-ar-ka* DUMU.MEŠ *ir-ta-ši-ma a-na tar-bi-tim na-sa-ḫi-im pa-nam iš-ta-ka-an* DUMU *šu-ú ri-qú-sú ú-ul it-ta-al-la-ak a-bu-um mu-ra-bi-šu i-na* NÍG.GA-*šu* IGI.3. GÁL IBILA-*šu i-na-ad-di-iš-šum-ma it-ta-la-ak i-na* A.ŠÀ KIRI$_6$ *ù* É *ú-ul i-na-ad-di-iš-šum.*

tarbītum (*tarbīt*) 'raising, upbringing; foster child, a child brought up' (cf. *rabûm*, D).

§§255–256 (For §254 see lesson 25) §255 *šum-ma* ÁB.GUD.ḪI.A *a-wi-lim a-na ig-ri-im it-ta-di-in ù lu* ŠE.NUMUN *iš-ri-iq-ma i-na* A.ŠÀ *la uš-tab-ši a-wi-lam šu-a-ti ú-ka-an-nu-šu-ma i-na ebūrim*(BURU$_{14}$) *ana būrim* (BÙR^{iku}.E) 60 ŠE.GUR *i-ma-ad-da-ad.* §256 *šum-ma pí-ḫa-sú a-pa-lam la i-le-i i-na* A.ŠÀ *šu-a-ti i-na* ÁB.GUD.ḪI.A *im-ta-na-aš-ša-ru-šu.*

igrum (*igir*; pl. *igrū*) 'hire, rent; wages' (cf. *agārum*).

būrum (*būri*; log. BÙR; Sum. lw.) a surface measure (ca. 6.48 ha.).

mašārum G (*a–u*) 'to drag (over the ground)'.

§4 (see §3 on p. 216):

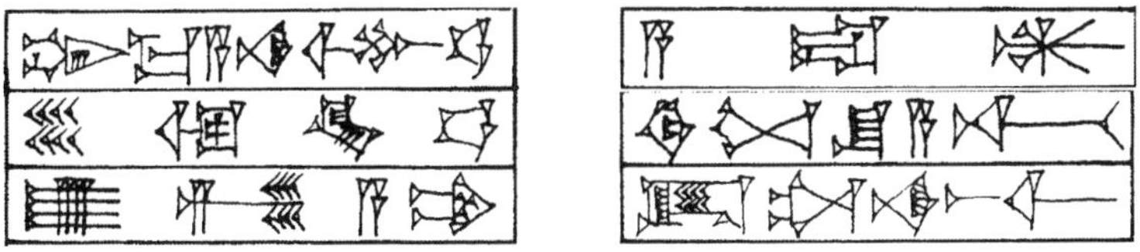

§271:

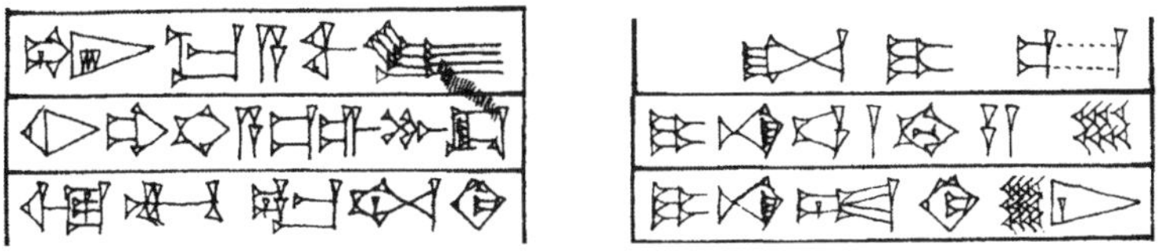

The numeral 3 after *i-na* UD.1.KAM denotes 3 *pānum* / *parsiktum* (about 180 litres); see Appendix B.5, pages 584–85.

F. Omens from *YOS* 10:

1. *šum-ma šu-me-el ú-ba-nim pu-ṣa-am i-ta-da-*[*at*] *ti-bu-ut er-bi-im.* (11 iii 25-26).
   pūṣum (*pūṣ(i)*) 'white; white fleck(s), spot(s)'.
   tibûtum (*tibût*) 'rising, raising; attack, invasion' (cf. *tebûm*).
   erbûm (base *erbi-*) 'locust(s)'.
2. DIŠ KÁ.É.GAL 2-*ma ri-it-ku-bu-ú* SUKKAL ^{giš}GU.ZA *be-li-šu iš-te-né-e.* (24:2)
3. *šum-ma* [*mar-tum*] *še-er-ʾa*$_4$-[*ni*] *ud-du-ḫa-*[*at*] *um-ma-*[*nu-u*]*m i-na ta-ḫa-zi-im im-ta-na-aq-qú-ut.* (31 iv 39-44)
   šerʾānum 'tendon, vein'.
   edēḫum G only in Verbal Adj. *edḫum* (*ediḫ-*) 'covered with patches or a network'; *udduḫum* D 'to cover completely with (patches, etc.)'.
4. [DIŠ *ṭù-li-mu-u*]*m ši-ir-ši-ri sa-mu-tim ma-li wa-ši-ib ma-*⸢*aḫ*⸣*-ri-ka-a* [*ka-ar*]*-ṣí-ka i-ta-na-ka-al.* (41:55–56)
   ṭulīmum (*ṭulīm*) 'spleen'.
   šeršerrum (pl. *šeršerrū*) 'chain; ring'.
   sāmum (*sām-*) 'red'.
   karṣum (*karaṣ*; pl. *karṣū*) 'calumny'; *karṣī X akālum* 'to calumniate'.
5. 36 iv 10–11:

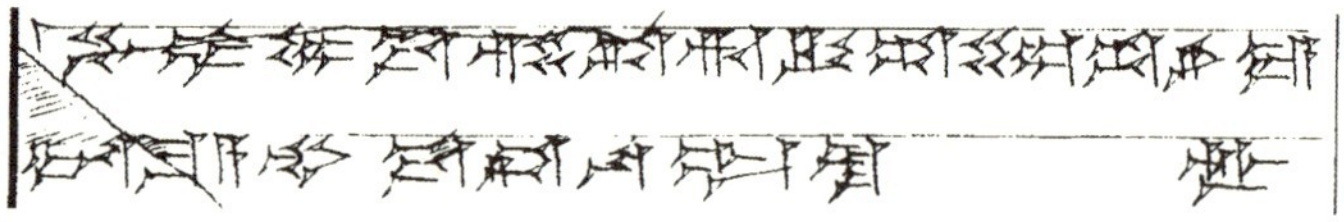

   puglum 'radish'; here, a part of the liver.
   Á.ZI = *imittum.*
   tarākum (*a–u*) 'to beat, pound'; V.Adj. *tarkum* (*tarik-*) 'pounded; dark'.
   ša lišānim 'informer'.
6. 51 iv 15–18:

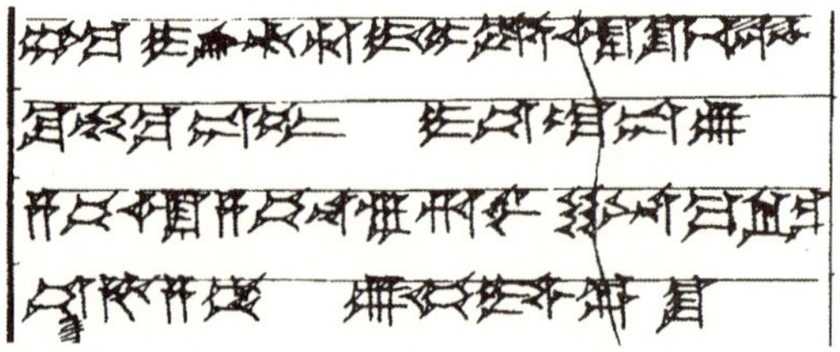

   iṣṣūrum here, part of the liver.
   At the end of the first line, read *šu-me-lam*!.
   sūmum (*sūm(i)*; pl. *sūmū*) 'redness, red spot' (cf. *sāmum* above in no. 4).
   i-pe-e-šu for *ippešū.*

G. Contracts:

1. Adoption of a child (Szlechter, *Tablettes* 3–4 MAH 15951).

^{1} *ṣú*(! SU)-*ḫa-ru-um ši-li-ip re-mi-im* ^{2} ^{I}DUMU‹-*eš*$_4$-*tár* DUMU› *at-ka-al-ši-im mīttim*(UG$_7$ [= BE]) ^{3} *itti*(TA) ^{d}UTU-*na-ṣir* [ŠEŠ] *ummīšu* (AMA.A.NI) ^{4} *ù ta-ri-iš-ma-tim* DAM(!NIN).A.NI ^{5} ^{I}*ipqu*(SIG)-*ìl-tum* DUMU *Sîn*(30)-*ma-gir* ^{6} *a-na ma-ru-tim il-qé* ^{7} 1 GÍN KUG.BABBAR *ù te-ni-iq* MU.2.KAM ^{8} *ipram*(ŠE.BA) *piššatam*(Ì.BA) *lubūšam*(SÍG.BA) ^{I}*ipqu*(SIG)-*ìl-tum* ^{9} *a-na* ^{d}UTU-*na-ṣir ù ta-ri-iš-ma-tim* ^{10} *id-di-in ma-aḫ-ru* [ŠÀ-*ba-š*]*u-nu ṭà-ab* ^{11} ^{Id}UTU-*na-ṣir ù ta-ri-iš-*[*ma-tum*] ^{12} *ú-ul i-tu-ru-ma* ^{13} *a-na* ^{I}*ipqu*(SIG)-*ìl-tum ú-ul i-ra-ga-mu* ^{14} 10 *ma-ri li-ir-ši-ma* ^{15} ⸢^{I}⸣DUMU-*eš*$_4$-*tár-ma a-píl-šu ra-bu-um* ^{16} MU ^{d}UTU ^{d}*a-a* ^{d}AMAR.UTU *ù ḫa-am-mu-ra-pí* ^{17} *itmû*(IN.PÀD.DÈ.MEŠ). $^{18–22}$ Witnesses. $^{23–24}$ Date.

PNs: *Mār-Eštar*; *Atkalšim*; *Šamaš-nāṣir*; *Tarīš-mātum*; *Ipqu-iltum*; *Sîn-magir*.

^{1} *šilpum* (*šilip*) 'a pulling out; something pulled out' (*šalāpum* 'to pull out, extricate'); *rēmum* (*rēm(i)*) 'womb; pity'; *šilip rēmim*, lit. 'something pulled from the womb', probably refers to a child born through caesarian section (Oppenheim 1960).

^{7} *tēnīqum* (*tēnīq*) 'suckling baby; wet-nursing expenses'.

^{8} *iprum* (*ipir*; log. ŠE.BA) 'barley ration'; *piššatum* (*piššat*; log. Ì.BA) 'oil ration'; *lubūšum* (*lubūš*; log. SÍG.BA) 'clothing, attire, wardrobe; clothing allowance' (cf. *labāšum*).

2. Adoption of a slave as daughter (*BE* 6/1 96 = Schorr, *VAB* 5, no. 29).

^{1} ^{If}*su-ur-ra-tum qá-du* DUMU.MUNUS GABA ^{2} DUMU.MUNUS *erišti*(NIN-*ti*)-^{d}*a-a* LUKUR ^{d}UTU ^{3} *ša erišti*(NIN-*ti*)-^{d}*a-a* LUKUR ^{d}UTU *um-ma-ša* ^{4} *ú-da-am-mi-qú-ši-ma* ^{5} *a-na ma-ru-ti-ša iš-ku-nu-ši* ^{6} [*ù*] *erišti*(NIN-*ti*)-^{d}*a-a* LUKUR ^{d}UTU DUMU.MUNUS *šar-rum*-^{d}IŠKUR ^{7} [*ú*]-*ul-li-il-ši* ^{8} [*pa-ni*]-*ša a-na ṣīt šamšim*(^{d}UTU.È.A) *iš-ku-un* ^{9} [*a-di*] *erišti*(NIN-*ti*)-^{d}*a-a* LUKUR ^{d}UTU *um-ma-ša* ^{10} *ba-al-ṭa-at* ^{11} *it-ta-na-aš-ši-ši* ^{12} *iš-tu erišti*(NIN-*ti*)-^{d}*a-a* LUKUR ^{d}UTU *um-ma-ša* ^{13} *i-lu-ša iq-te-ru-ši* ^{14} *el-le-et ša ra-ma-ni-ša ši-i* ^{15} *ma-la li-ib-bi-ša ma-ṣi-a-at* ^{16} *ana warkiāt ūmī*(UD.KÚR.ŠÈ) *i-na* DUMU.MEŠ *erišti*(NIN-*ti*)-^{d}*a-a* LUKUR ^{d}UTU ^{17} DUMU.MUNUS *šar-rum*-^{d}IŠKUR ^{18} *ù* DUMU.MEŠ *ka-lu-mu-um a-ḫi-ša* ^{19} NITA$_2$ *ù* MUNUS *ša ib-šu-ú* ^{20} *ù ib-ba-aš-šu-ú* ^{21} *a-na* ^{f}*su-ur-ra-tum qá-du* DU[MU GABA] ^{22} [DUMU.MUNUS] *erišti*(NIN-*ti*)-^{d}*a-a* LUKUR ^{d}UTU ^{23} [*ma-am-ma-an la i*]-*ra-ag-ga-mu*. $^{24–27}$ [Witnesses.] $^{28–33}$ Date.

PNs: *Surratum; Erišti-Ayya; Šarrum-Adad.*

$^{1-5}$ These constitute a single sentence: 'PN with a suckling baby is the daughter of PN$_2$, who ...'; *ana mārūtim šakānum* = *ana mārūtim leqûm.*

^{13} *qerûm* G (*i*) 'to summon, invite'; the idiom here is a euphemism for dying.

3. Marriage of a slave (*CT* 6 37a = Schorr, *VAB* 5, no. 35).

^{1} ^{I}DUMU-KI DUMU *a-ia-ti-ia* ^{2} ^{I}*at-kal-a-na-be-el-ti a-ma-sà*$^{!}$ ^{3} *a-na aš-šu-tim ù mu-tu-tim* ^{4} *i-ḫu-uz at-kal-a-na-be-el-ti* ^{5} *a-na a-ia-ti-ia be-el-ti-ša* ^{6} *ú-ul be-el-ti at-ti* ^{7} *i-qá-ab-bi-ma* ^{8} *ú-ga-la-ab-ši a-na* KUG.BABBAR ^{9} [*i-n*]*a-di-iš* ^{10} *mi-im-ma ša a-ia-ti-ia* ^{11} *ir-šu-ú ù i-ra-šu-ú* ^{12} *ša* DUMU-KI-*ma* ^{13} *a-di ba-al-ṭà-at ki-la-la-an* ^{14} *i-ta-na-šu-ú.* $^{15-21}$ Witnesses.

PNs: *Mār-erṣetim; Ayyatīya; Atkal-ana-bēlti(m).*

^{8} *gullubum* D (not in G) 'to shave'.

^{9} *i-na-di-iš* cf. §30.2(e); more likely, read *i-na-di-iš-‹ši›*.

H. Letters:

1. King, *LIH* 1 24 = Frankena, *AbB* 2 24.

^{1} *a-na* ^{d}EN.ZU-*i-din-nam* ^{2} *qí-bí-ma* ^{3} *um-ma ḫa-am-mu-ra-pí-ma* ^{4} ^{I}DINGIR-*šu-*⌜*i-bi*⌝ DAM.[GÀ]R [UGUL]A NAM.5 ^{5} *ki-a-am ú-*[*l*]*am-m*[*i-da-a*]*n-ni* ^{6} *um-ma šu-ú-*[*m*]*a* ^{7} 30 ŠE.GUR *a-*[*n*]*a* ^{d}EN.ZU-*ma-gir* GÌR.NITA$_2$ ^{8} *ad-di-im-ma* ^{9} DUB-*pa-šu na-ši-a-ku-ma* ^{10} [*i*]*š-*[*tu*] MU.3.KAM *e-te-ne-er-ri-is-su-ma* ^{11} [ŠE-*a*]*m ú-ul i-na-ad-di-nam* ^{12} [*ki-a*]*-am ú-lam-mi-da-an-ni* ^{13} DUB-*pa-šu a-mu-ur-ma* ^{14} ŠE-*am ù* MÁŠ.BI ^{15} ^{Id}EN.ZU-*ma-gir li-ša-ad-di-nu-ma* ^{16} *a-na* DINGIR-*šu-i-bi i-di-in.*

PNs: *Sîn-iddinam; Ilšu-ibbi; Sîn-magir.*

^{4} NAM in Sumerian serves to form abstracts (e.g., NAM.LUGAL = *šarrū-tum* 'kingship'); NAM.5 = *ḫamištum*$^{?}$ 'group/gang of five'.

2. King, *LIH* 2 80 = Frankena, *AbB* 2 62.

^{1} *a-na* ^{d}E[N.ZU]-*i-*[*din-nam*] ^{2} KA[R] ZIMB[IR^{ki}] ^{3} *ù* DI.KUD.MEŠ ZIMBI[R^{ki}] ^{4} *qí-bí-ma* ^{5} *um-ma sa-am-su-i-lu-na-m*[*a*] ^{6} *ki-ma a-na* A.GÀR *ra-bi-*[*i*]*-i*[*m*] ^{7} *ù* A.GÀR *ša-am-ka-nim* ^{8} MÁ.ḪI.A ŠU.ḪA.MEŠ ^{9} *it-ta-na-ar-ra-d*[*a-ma*] ^{10} KU$_6$.ḪI.A *i-ba-ar-r*[*u*] ^{11} *iq-bu-*[*nim*] ^{12} 1 *lāsimam*(LÚ.KAS$_4$.E) ^{13} *aṭ-ṭar-da*[*m*] ^{14} *ki-ma is-sà-an-qá-a*[*k-kum*] ^{15} MÁ.ḪI.A ŠU.ḪA.M[EŠ] ^{16} *ša i-na* A.GÀR *ra-bi-i-im* ^{17} *ù* [A.GÀR] *š*[*a-a*]*m-ka-nim* ^{18} [KU$_6$.ḪI.A *i-ba-ar-ru*] (lacuna of about 3 lines) rev. $^{1'}$ *ù* *la i-ta-ar-ma* $^{2'}$ MÁ.ḪI.A ŠU.ḪA.MEŠ $^{3'}$ ⸢*a-na*⸣ A.GÀR *ra-bi-i-im* $^{4'}$ ⸢*ù*⸣ A.GÀR *ša-am-ka-[nim]* $^{5'}$ *[l]a ur-ra-ad.*

PNs: *Sîn-iddinam; Samsu-iluna* (Ḫammurapi's son and successor).

^{6} *kīma* here 'that'.

^{7} *Šamkānum* a place name.

^{8} The *bāʾerū* are actual fishermen here.

^{9} *bârum* G (*a*) 'to catch (fish, etc.)' (cf. *bāʾerum*).

^{12} *lāsimum* (pl. *lāsimū*; log. LÚ.KAŠ$_4$(.E)) 'courier, express messenger'.

rev. $^{1',5'}$ Sg. verbs for expected fem. pl.

3. *OECT* 3 1 = Kraus, *AbB* 4 79.

^{1} *a-na* ^{d}UTU-*ḫa-zi-ir* ^{2} *qí-bí-ma* ^{3} *um-ma ḫa-am-mu-ra-pí-ma* ^{4} ^{I}*ì-lí-ip-pa-al-sà-am* SIPAD ^{5} *ki-a-am ú-lam-mi-da-an-ni um-ma šu-ma* ^{6} BÙR.3^{iku} A.ŠÀ *ša i-na ka-ni-ik be-lí-ia* ^{7} *ka-an-kam* ^{8} *iš-tu* MU.4. KAM ^{I}*e-tel-pí*-^{d}AMAR.UTU *i-ki-ma-an-ni-ma* ^{9} ŠE-*šu il-te-ne-eq-qé* ^{10} *ù* ^{d}EN.ZU-*i-din-nam ú-lam-mi-id-ma* ^{11} *ú-ul ú-te-er-ru-nim* ^{12} *ki-a-am ú-lam-mi-da-an-ni* ^{13} *a-na* ^{d}EN.ZU-*i-din-nam aš-tap-ra-am* ^{14} *šum-ma ki-ma ì-lí-ip-pa-al-sà-am šu-ú* ^{15} *iq-bu-ú* ^{16} BÙR.3^{iku} A.ŠÀ *ša i-na* É.GAL ^{17} *ka-an-ku-šum* ^{18} ^{I}*e-tel-pí*-^{d}AMAR.UTU *iš-tu* MU.4.KAM *il-qé-e-ma* ^{19} *i-ik-ka-al* ^{20} *e-li-ša a-wa-tum ma-ru-uš-tum* ^{21} *ú-ul i-ba-aš-ši* ^{22} *wa-ar-ka-at a-wa-tim šu-a-ti* ^{23} *dam-qí-iš pu-ur-sa-ma* ^{24} A.ŠÀ-*am ša pí-i ka-ni-ki-im* ^{25} *ša i-na* É.GAL *ik-ka-an-ku-šum* ^{26} *a-na ì-lí-ip-pa-al-sà-am te-er-[r]a* ^{27} *ù* ŠE-*am ša iš-tu* MU.4.KAM ^{28} *i-na* A.ŠÀ *šu-a-ti e-tel-pí*-^{d}AMAR.UTU ^{29} *il-te-eq-qú-ú* ^{30} *i-na* ^{giš}TUKUL *ša* DINGIR *bi-ir-ra-ma* ^{31} *a-na ì-lí-ip-pa-al-sà-am* SIPA ^{32} *id-na* ^{33} *ù ṭe*$_4$-*em di-nim šu-a-ti* ^{34} *šu-up-ra-nim.*

PNs: *Šamaš-ḫāzir; Ilī-ippalsam; Etel-pī-Marduk.*

^{6} BÙR.3^{iku} A.ŠÀ = *šalāšat būr eqlam* 'a field of 3 *būr*' (ca. 20 ha.).

^{9} ŠE-*šu* 'its (the field's) grain'.

^{20} *e-li-ša* elliptical for *eli awātim annītim*: 'there is no grievous thing beyond this (thing)', i.e., 'there is nothing more grievous than this'.

^{30} *kakkum ša ilim* a standard with a divine symbol.

I. Hymn to Ištar, stanzas 6–10 (lines 21–40; see Lesson 33, exercise I).

21. *a-iu-um na-ar-bi-à-aš i-ša-an-na-an ma-an-nu-um*
22. *ga-aš-ru ṣi-i-ru šu-ú-pu-ú pa-ar-ṣú-ú-ša*
23. *eš*$_4$-*tár na-ar-bi-à-aš i-ša-an-na-an ma-an-nu-um*
24. *ga-aš-ru ṣi-i-ru šu-ú-pu-ú pa-ar-ṣú-ú-ša*

^{21} *narbûm* (*narbi-*; acc. with suffix here *narbiaš* for prose *narbīša*) 'greatness' (cf. *rabûm*).

šanānum G (*a–u*) 'to become equal, match, rival'; *šitnunum* Gt 'to equal one another, rival, compete with one another'.

[22] *gašārum* G (*i*) 'to become powerful, strong'; Verbal Adj. *gašrum* (*gašer-*) 'powerful, strong'.

25. *ša*(! BI-A)*-at i-ni-li a-ta-ar na-az-za-zu-uš*
26. *ka-ab-ta-at a-⸢ma⸣-as-sà el-šu-nu ḫa-ap-ta-at-ma*
27. *eš*$_4$*-tár i-ni-li a-ta-ar na-az-za-zu-uš*
28. *ka-ab-ta-at a-ma-as-sà el-šu-nu ḫa-ap-ta-at-ma*

[25] *šāt* see line 5.
nazzazum (*nazzaz*) 'station, position; attendant'.

[26] *ḫapātum* G (*i* and *u*) 'to become powerful, prevail'; Verbal Adj. *ḫaptum* (*ḫapit-*) 'powerful, triumphant'.

[28] *amātu(m)* for *awātum* (see §24.4(c)).

29. *šar-ra-as-su-un uš-ta-na-ad-da-nu si-iq-ri-i-ša*
30. *ku-ul-la-as-su-nu ša-aš ka-am-su-ú-ši*
31. *na-an-na-ri-i-ša i-la-qú-ú-ši-im*
32. *iš-šu-ú ù a-wi-lum pa-al-ḫu-ši-i-ma*

[29] Understand the first word as a sentence: *šarrassun (šī).*
uštanaddànū 'they discuss, deliberate' (see §36.1).

[30] *kullatum* (*kullat*) 'all, entirety, totality' (literary synonym of *kalûm*).
šâš for *ana šâšim.*

[31] *nannarum* (*nannar*) 'light' (literary word, usually — though not here — an epithet of Sîn or Ištar).

[32] *iššum* see line 4.

33. *pu-uḫ-ri-iš-šu-un e-te-el qá-bu-ú-ša šu-tu-úr*
34. *a-na* AN*-nim šar-ri-šu-nu ma-la-am aš-ba-as-su-nu*
35. *uz-na-am ne-me-qé-em ḫa-si-i-sa-am er-še-et*
36. *im-ta-al-li-i-ku ši-i ù ḫa-mu-uš*

[34] *malâm* (Adverb?) 'as an equal (*ana*: to)'[?].
aš-ba-as-su-nu for *wašbat-šunu*; *-šunu* is for expected *-šunūšim*, and means here 'with them'.

[35] *nēmequm* (*nēmeq*) 'knowledge, experience, skill, wisdom'; here apparently *nēmeqem* with *a* › *e* atypically in the acc. ending.
ḫasīsum (*ḫasīs*) 'understanding, wisdom'.
eršum (Adj., base *eriš-*) 'wise, clever, skillful'.

[36] *malākum* G (*i*) 'to give advice; to consider, deliberate, make a decision'; *mitlukum* Gt 'to deliberate, advise one another'; the reason for the extra vowel sign here is unclear.
ḫammum 'head of the family'.

37. *ra-mu-ú-ma iš-ti-ni-iš pa-ra-ak-ka-am*
38. *i-ge-e-gu-un-ni-im šu-ba-at ri-ša-tim*
39. *mu-ut-ti-iš-šu-un i-lu-ú na-zu-iz-zu-ú*
40. *ip-ši-iš pí-šu-nu ba-ši-à-a uz-na-šu-un*

[37] *ramûm* see line 11.
ištēniš (Adverb) 'together, as one' (cf. *ištēn*).

[38] *gigunnûm* (*-ā*; pl. *gigunnû*) a sacred building; temple tower.
rīštum (often pl. *rīšātum*) 'joy, rejoicing' (cf. *riāšum* in line 55).

[39] *muttum* (*mutti*) 'front'; *muttiš* 'in front of'.
nazuzzū (with a broken writing, *iz* for *uz*; see also lines 54, 55) 'they are standing' (see §37.2).

[40] *ipšum* (*ipiš*) 'work'; *ipiš nikkassī* 'rendering of accounts'; *ipiš pîm* 'utterance, command' (cf. *piam epēšum*).
The Verbal Adj. of *bašûm* appears in predicative construction, meaning 'is (present)', only in literary texts.

LESSON THIRTY-FIVE

35.1 The Dt Stem

(a) Form

(1) Sound Verbs

Infinitive:	*putarrusum*	Imperative:	*putarris*
Durative:	*uptarras*	Participle:	*muptarrisum*
Perfect:	*uptatarris*	Verbal Adj.:	*putarrusum*
Preterite:	*uptarris*	V. Adj. base:	*putarrus*

The Dt stem is based on the forms of the D, with the insertion between R_1 and R_2 of an infixed *-t-* or *-ta-*.

The prefixes of the finite forms are those of the D (and Š), i.e., *u-*, *tu-*, *nu-*.

As in the D (and Š), the Durative has *a* between R_2 and R_3, while the Preterite, Perfect, and Imperative have *i*. The Dt Preterite is formally the same as the D Perfect for all verb types. As usual, the Infinitive and Verbal Adjective have *u* between R_2 and R_3. The Infinitive, Verbal Adjective, and Imperative also have *u* between R_1 and R_2, differing in this respect from the corresponding forms of the Gtn, which have *i* between R_1 and R_2. The Dt Participle has the same form as the Gtn Participle (and the Dtn Participle; see below).

The *-ta-* infix undergoes the usual changes after sibilants, dentals, and *g*:

ûm ussannaq 'the grain will be inspected';
ligdammirū 'they (m) should be used'.

(2) Verbs I–*n*. As in the Gt and Gtn stems, the *n* of the root is assimilated in forms with prefixes, and lost entirely in the forms in which it would stand first (Infinitive, Verbal Adjective, Imperative); the latter resemble the corresponding forms of roots I–ʾ and roots I–*w*.

Infinitive:	*utakkurum*	Imperative:	[*utakker*]
Durative:	*uttakkar*	Participle:	*muttakkerum*
Perfect:	*uttatakker*	Verbal Adj.:	*utakkurum*
Preterite:	*uttakker*	V. Adj. base:	*utakkur*

(3) Verbs III–weak. Forms from roots other than III–*e* present no difficulties. In forms from roots III–*e*, *a*-vowels may either all remain *a* or all change to *e* (except for the usual endings), as in the D stem. Below are Dt forms of *malûm* and *redûm*.

Infinitive:	*mutallûm*	*rutaddûm / ruteddûm*
Durative:	*umtalla*	*urtadda / urtedde*
Perfect:	*umtatalli*	*urtataddi / urteteddi*
Preterite	*umtalli*	*urtaddi / urteddi*
Imperative:	*mutalli*	*rutaddi / ruteddi*
Participle	*mumtallûm*	*murtaddûm / murteddûm*
Verbal Adj.:	*mutallûm*	*rutaddûm / ruteddûm*
V. Adj. base:	*mutallu*	*rutaddu / ruteddu*

(4) Verbs I–ʾ. As expected, forms with prefixes have a lengthened vowel before the infix to compensate for the loss of the ʾ; the remaining forms lack any vestige of the initial consonant, and simply begin with *u*. In verbs I–*e*, as in verbs III–*e* (see 3, above), *a*-vowels either all remain *a* or all become *e* (except for the usual endings).

	I–*a*	I–*e*	I–*w*
Infinitive:	*utaḫḫuzum*	*utappušum / uteppušum*	*utaššurum*
Durative:	*ūtaḫḫaz*	*ūtappaš / ūteppeš*	*ūtaššar*
Perfect:	*ūtataḫḫiz*	*ūtatappiš / ūteteppiš*	*ūtataššer*
Preterite:	*ūtaḫḫiz*	*ūtappiš / ūteppiš*	*ūtaššer*
Imperative:	*utaḫḫiz*	*utappiš / uteppiš*	*utaššer*
Participle:	*mūtaḫḫizum*	*mūtappišum / mūteppišum*	*mūtaššerum*
Verbal Adj.:	*utaḫḫuzum*	*utappušum / uteppušum*	*utaššurum*
V. Adj. base:	*utaḫḫuz*	*utappuš / uteppuš*	*utaššur*

(5) Verbs I–*w*. In forms with prefixes, the *w* is lost before the *t* of the infix, and the vowel of the prefix is lengthened; in the remaining forms, the initial *w* is lost. All forms therefore have the same shape as the corresponding forms of roots I–ʾ, as the paradigm above shows.

(6) Verbs II–weak. These are patterned on the corresponding D forms (§29.1), with *-t-* inserted after the initial radical in forms with prefixes (*-ta-* in Perf.), and *-ut-* in the Infinitive, Verbal Adjective, and Imperative. As expected, the final radical is doubled whenever a vocalic ending appears.

Infinitive:	*kutunnum*		
Durative:	*uktān*	Imperative:	*kutīn*
Dur. 3mp:	*uktannū*	Imper. pl.:	*kutinnā*
Perfect:	*uktatīn*	Participle:	*muktinnum*
Perf. 3mp:	*uktatinnū*	Verbal Adj.:	*kutunnum*
Preterite:	*uktīn*	V.Adj. +3ms:	*kutūn*
Pret. 3mp:	*uktinnū*	+3fs:	*kutunnat*

(b) Meaning

The Dt stem is used as the passive of the D, less often as a reciprocal or reflexive of the D. Thus, the Dt serves with respect to the D as both the N and the Gt serve with respect to the G. Some examples:

uštallamū 'they (m) will be compensated' (*šalāmum*);
awâtūya lā uttakkarā 'my words may not be altered' (*nakārum*);
nišū ūtellilā 'the people became purified' (or, 'purified themselves'; *elēlum*).

Theoretically, Dt verbs may be formed from any root that occurs in the D stem; in fact, however, Dt verbs are relatively infrequent. There are, for example, very few Dt verbs attested for roots in which the D stem has the same meaning as the G (where the N is available for the passive and the Gt for the reciprocal).

The verb *šutaʾʾûm* (root *š*–ʾ–weak) 'to be idle' is unusual in that it occurs only in the Dt; it appears only in OB letters, where it is common.

35.2 The Dtn Stem

The Dtn is the iterative form of D verbs. The Durative of the Dtn is marked with the typical *-tan-* infix: *uptanarras*. In all other forms, however, the Dtn is **identical with the Dt** stem given above.

Infinitive:	*putarrusum*	Imperative:	*putarris*
Durative:	*uptanarras*	Participle:	*muptarrisum*
Perfect:	*uptatarris*	Verbal Adj.:	*putarrusum*
Preterite:	*uptarris*	V. Adj. Base:	*putarrus*

Apart from Durative forms, whether a given form is Dt or Dtn must be determined on the basis of the context. As a general rule, the Dtn occurs less frequently than the Dt (the Dtn is also relatively less common than the Gtn); further, Dtn forms normally will have a direct object, whereas Dt forms normally will not. Some examples:

awâtīya uktanallamakkim 'I will keep showing you (fs) my words'; *zīmīya uttakkerū* 'they (m) kept altering my features (*zīmū*)'; *uttanarrū* 'they (m) keep sending back'.

35.3 Interrogative Sentences

Sentence questions, in which no interrogative pronoun or adverb occurs (such as *mannum* 'who?', *mati* 'when?'), normally differ from assertions only in that the word that is the focus of the question (often the verb) receives additional stress. This extra stress is often, though not necessarily, indicated in the script by an extra vowel-sign, as in

LÚ.MEŠ *an-nu-tum* A.ŠÀ.MEŠ *i-ṣa-ab-ba-tu-ú ú-ul i-ṣa-ab-ba-tu-ú*, i.e., *awīlû annûtum eqlētim iṣabbatû ul iṣabbatû?* 'Should these men take possession of the fields (or) should they not take possession?';

i-na ki-ma i-na-an-na e-re-šum i-na qá-ba-al e-re-ši-i-im a-na KÁ.DINGIR.RA[ki] *ta-al-la-ka-nim*, i.e., *ina kīma inanna erēšum; ina qabal erēšîm ana Bābilim tallakānim?* 'Right now is the (time of) cultivating; will you (pl) come to Babylon in the middle of the cultivating?';

rēqet ekletum would mean 'Darkness is far away' (*rēqum* 'distant'); but the extra vowel sign in *re-qé-e-et ek-le-tum* (Gilgameš X 14) denotes a question: *rēqêt ekletum?* 'Is darkness far away?'.

Note in the first example that the negative is *ul*, as in main clause statements, whereas *lā* occurs after the interrogative words (§20.4).

EXERCISES

A. VOCABULARY 35.

Verbs:

batāqum G (*a–u*) 'to cut off, deduct; to cut through, pierce; to divide; to stop work'; *buttuqum* D = G; *butattuqum* Dt passive; *nabtuqum* N passive.

ḫaṭûm G (*i*) 'to make a mistake, fail, miss; to commit an offense, trespass' (cf. *ḫīṭum*).

mašûm G (*i*) 'to forget, neglect'; *mitaššûm* Gtn 'to forget constantly, be forgetful'; *šumšûm* Š causative; *namšûm* N passive.

naqûm G (*i*) 'to pour (out, as a libation), offer, sacrifice'; note *niqûm* (*niqi-*; also *nīqum*, bound form *nīq-*) 'offering, sacrifice'.
ṣamādum G (*i*) 'to tie, bind, attach; to yoke, harness; to make (something) ready'; *ṣummudum* D = G (cf. *ṣimdatum*).
šanûm a G (*i*) 'to do twice, double, again' (in hendiadys); *šunnûm* D 'to repeat, tell; to count'; *šutannûm* Dt passive of D.
šanûm b G (*i*) 'to change (intrans.), become different, strange'; *šunnûm* D 'to change, alter' (trans.); *šutannûm* Dt passive of D.
šebûm G (*e*) 'to become satisfied, sate oneself (with: acc.)'; *šubbûm* D 'to satisfy, please (someone with something: double acc.)'.
šutaʾʾûm Dt (only) 'to be idle, lazy (about: *ana*/dat.); to relax'.

Nouns:

gišimmarum (fem. and masc.; *gišimmar*; pl. *gišimmarātum*; log. ^{giš}GIŠIMMAR; Sum. lw.) 'date palm'.
ibrum (*ibir*; pl. *ibrū*) 'person of equal status, colleague, friend'.
kāsum (masc. and fem.; *kās*; pl. *kāsātum* and *kāsānū*) 'cup, goblet'.
napḫarum (*napḫar*) 'total, sum; totality, all' (cf. *paḫārum*).

Adverbs:

appūna, *appūnā-ma* 'moreover, besides, furthermore'.
kī maṣi (interrogative adverb and relative adverb) 'how much/many?; how(ever) much/many'.
mati (also *ina mati*) 'when?'; *matī-ma* 'when?; ever'; with negative: 'never'.
šattam 'this year'.

B. Learn the following sign:

OB Lapid.	OB Cursive	NA	values
	 		GIŠIMMAR= *gišimmarum*

C. Write the following words in cuneiform and in transliteration; use logograms where possible:

1. *zibbat iṣṣūrim*
2. *irat sukkallim*
3. *gišimmarāt Sippar*
4. *nūn almattim*
5. *wakil nāqidī*
6. *ereq šakkanakkim*

D. Write in normalized Akkadian:
1. the troop will purify itself
2. they (m) will be made well
3. you (ms) will keep bringing back to me.
4. the river that we were shown
5. live (ms) long (*labārum* Dt) and prosper!
6. you (ms) were lazy
7. they (m) will not be recognized
8. may he pay attention constantly
9. you (ms) will constantly encourage
10. may your (ms) face be changed (*šanûm* b)

E. Normalize and translate:
1. ᵈEN.LÍL *be-lum* ... *ša qí-bí-sú la ut-ta-ka-ru* (CH epilogue, r xxvi 53–56).
2. ᵍⁱˢGU.ZA KUG.SIG₁₇ *ú-ta-aḫ-ḫa-az*.
3. ᵍⁱˢTUKUL.MEŠ LÚ.KÚR.MEŠ-*ia li-iš-ta-ab-bi-ru*.
4. *na-di-na-nu-um ša bi-ša-am a-na* PN *id-di-nu ù* PN₂ *ub-ta-ar-ru iš-tu da-ba-ab-šu-nu i-na pu-úḫ-ri-im ub-ti-ir-ru a-na* É DINGIR *a-na bu-ur-ri* DINGIR *le-qé-šu-nu-ti*.
5. *a-di* PN *il-li-kam* 3 *ṣú-ḫa-ru-ú it-ti-ni wa-aš-bu i-na-an-na* 2 *ṣú-ḫa-ru-ú ša-nu-tum ur-ta-ad-du-ú*.
6. *ki-ma a-wi-lum šu-ú la ṣe-eḫ-ru-ú-ma ra-bu-ú ú-ul ti-de-e ki-ma a-wi-le-e aḫ-ḫi-šu* A.ŠÀ-*lam a-pu-ul-šu ki-ma la ša šu-ta-i-im šu-ú ú-ul ti-de-e la tu-uš-ta-ʾa₄-šum*.
7. *ša-at-ta-am bi-ti ù bi-ta-at ma-ri-ia us-sà-pa-ḫu*.
8. *šum-ma i-na ki-tim a-ḫi at-ta qí-bi-ma ši-ka-rum ša i-na bi-it ša-ar-ra-qí-im il-le-qú-ú ù* GUD *ša i-na qá-bé-e a-ḫi-ia a-na* SAG.ÌR *ut-te-er-ru a-na ṣú-ḫa-ri-ia li-ip-pa-aq-du*.
9. *mi-im-ma ša te-pu-ša-an-ni* ᵈIŠKUR *il-ka li-id-dam-mi-iq*.

F. CH:

§20 (For §§17–19 see lesson 31.) *šum-ma* ÌR *i-na qá-at ṣa-bi-ta-ni-šu iḫ-ta-li-iq a-wi-lum šu-ú a-na be-el* ÌR *ni-iš i-lim i-za-kar-ma ú-ta-aš-šar*.

§103 (For §102 see lesson 26.) *šum-ma ḫar-ra-nam i-na a-la-ki-šu na-ak-ru-um mi-im-ma ša na-šu-ú uš-ta-ad-di-šu šamallûm* (ŠAMAN₂.LÁ) *ni-iš i-lim i-za-kar-ma ú-ta-aš-šar*.

G. Omens from *YOS* 10:

1. *šum-ma na-ap-la-aš-tum ki-ma un-qí-im ma-a-tum ú-te-es-sé-er pi-i-ša a-na iš-te-en i-ta-ar.* (11 ii 7–9)
   unqum (fem.) 'ring'.
2. *šum-ma i-na šu-me-el ú-ba-nim ka-ak-kum is-ḫu-ur še-pu-um a-na ma-at na-ak-ri-im ú-ta-ša-ar.* (11 iii 27–30)
   šēpum here 'conveyance, transport', or the like.
3. MAŠ *re-eš* KÁ É.GAL *a-na ši-ni-šu pa-ṭe*$_4$*-er ... bu-tu-qá-*[*tum*] *ub-ta-ta-*[*qá*]. (26 iii 28-29)
   butuqtum (*butuqti*; pl. *butuqātum*) 'flood; sluice channel' (cf. *batāqum*).

H. Contract:

1. Lawsuit over property (*VAS* 7 16 = Schorr, *VAB* 5, no. 279).

^{1} ^{I}ÌR-^{d}EN.ZU DUMU ^{d}EN.ZU-*ga-mil* ^{2} *a-na ì-lí-a-wi-lim* DUMU *ì-lí-ú-ri* ^{3} *wa-ar-ki ì-lí-ú-ri* AD.DA.NI ^{4} *ù du-uš-šu-up-tum ummašu* (AMA.NI) *i-mu-tu* ^{5} *aš-šum* 1 SAR É KISLAḪ *ša du-uš-šu-up-tum* ^{6} KI ÌR-^{d}*Amurrim*(MAR.TU) *a-ḫi a-bi-šu i-*[*š*]*a-*⌜*mu*⌝ ^{7} *ù* $^{1}/_{2}$ SAR É *ša du-uš-šu-up-tum* ^{8} KI ÌR-^{d}EN.ZU *i-ša-mu* ^{9} ^{I}ÌR-^{d}EN.ZU *a-na ì-lí-a-‹wi›-lim ir-gu-um-ma* ^{10} *ki-a-am iq-bi um-ma šu-ma* ^{11} *i-nu-ma* É *du-uš-šu-up-tum umma*(AMA)*-ka i-pu-šu* ^{12} *a-na bi-ti-ia ...* ^{13} *... i-ru-ba-am* ^{14} *ù* $^{1}/_{2}$ SAR É *ša it-ti-ia i-ša-mu* ^{15} *bi-ti wa-tar ú-sà-na-aq!*(AN)*-ka iq-bi* ^{16} ^{I}*ì-lí-a-wi-lim* ^{17} LÚ.MEŠ DUMU.MEŠ *ba-ab-tim* ^{18} *mu-de-e-šu-nu ú-pa-ḫe-er-ma* ^{19} LÚ.MEŠ DUMU.MEŠ *ba-ab-ti-šu-nu* ^{20} *a-wa-ti-šu-nu i-mu-ru-ma* ^{21} *aš-šum* É *iš-tu* MU.20.KAM *ša-a-mu* ^{22} *a-na ma-la us-sà-na-qú-šu* ^{23} *ki-ma* [ÌR]-^{d}EN.ZU *iq-bu-ú* ^{24} *a-na wa-tar-ti bi-ti-šu* ^{25} 1 GÍN KUG.BABBAR *ša* 7 $^{1}/_{2}$ GÍN É ^{26} *ša e-li* 1 SAR *wa-at-ru* ^{27} *ù* 1 GÍN KUG.BABBAR *ša* 5 $^{1}/_{2}$ GÍN É ^{28} *ša e-li* $^{1}/_{2}$ SAR *i-na sú-un-nu-qí-im i-te-ru* ^{29} ^{I}*ì-lí-a-wi-lim ú-ša-am-gi-ru-ma* ^{30} 2 GÍN KUG.BABBAR *a-na* ÌR-^{d}EN.ZU *id-di-nu* ^{31} *ša wa-tar-ti* É*-šu a-pí-il* ŠÀ*-šu ṭà-ab* ^{32} *ana warkiāt ūmī* (UD.KÚR.ŠÈ) ÌR-^{d}EN.ZU *a-na ì-lí-a-wi-lim* ^{33} *a-na wa-‹ta›-ar-ti* 1 $^{1}/_{2}$ SAR É *ul iraggum*(INIM.NU.GÁ.GÁ) ^{34} MU ^{d}AMAR.UTU *ù sa-am-su-i-lu-na* LUGAL $^{35–43}$ Witnesses. $^{44–45}$ Date.

PNs: *Warad-Sîn*; *Sîn-gamil*; *Ili-awīlim*; *Ilī-ūrī*; *Duššuptum*; *Warad-Amurrim*.

^{5} SAR = *mūšarum* (*mūšar*) a surface measurement ('garden plot'; ca. 36 m.^{2}); É.KISLAḪ = KISLAḪ, here 'empty lot'; 1 SAR É.KISLAḪ = *ištēn mūšar maškanum* 'a one-*mūšar* lot'.

^{7} $^{1}/_{2}$ SAR É *mišil mūšar bītum* 'a half-*mūšar* house'.

$^{12–13}$ *ana bītīya ... īrubam* 'she went into my property (x distance)'.

I. Letters:

1. *TLB* 4, pl. 9 LB 1897 = Frankena, *AbB* 3 15.

^{1} *a-na ru-ut-tum qí-bí-ma* ^{2} *um-ma* ^{d}AMAR.UTU-*na-ṣi-ir-ma* ^{3} ^{d}UTU *ù* ^{d}AMAR.UTU *da-ri-iš* UD-*mi* ^{4} *li-ba-al-li-ṭú-ki* ^{5} ŠE-*um ša ib-ba-šu‹-ú› i-na* ^{giš}BÁN ^{d}UTU ^{6} *ma-aḫ-ri-ki li-iš-ta-an-ni-ma* ^{7} *li-ik-ka-ni-ik* ^{8} *aš-šum* ^{I}*ba-ba-tim ù ṣú-ḫa-ra-ti-ša* ^{9} *ṭa-ra*!(RI)-*di-im* ^{10} *ki-ma iš-ti-iš-šu e-eš-ri-šu* ^{11} *aš-tap-pa-ra-ak-k*[*i-i*]*m* ^{12} *ú-ul ta-pu-l*[*i-i*]*n-*[*n*]*i* ^{13} *i-bi-is-sà-ki tu-ub-ta-i-li* ^{14} *ap-pu-na-ma i-bi-is-sà-am* ^{15} *ša-ni-a-am ta-as-sà-na-ḫu-ri* ^{16} ^{I}*ba-ba-tim* ^{íd}*la-ga-bi-tum-ba-la-su* ^{17} *ù a-bi-li-ib-lu-uṭ* ^{18} *ṭú-ur-di-ši-na-a-ti-ma* ^{19} *lu-ud-di-iš* ^{20} *a-wa-tu-ia ma-ti i-in-ki* ^{21} *i-ma-ḫa-ra* ^{22} *i-na la mi-ta-gu-ri-ia* ^{23} [*i-bi-i*]*s-sà-a tu-ub-ta-na-ʾa₄-li* ^{24} *ša a-qá-ab-bu-ki-im* ^{25} *mu-ug-ri-in-ni-ma* ^{26} *a-wa-tum la iḫ-ḫa-aṭ-ṭi-a* ^{27} *šum-ma ḫa-ṭi-tam e-ep-pu-uš* ^{28} *la ta-ma-ga-ri-«ni»-in-ni.*

PNs: *Ruttum* (fem.); *Marduk-nāṣir*; *Babātum*; *Lagabītum-balāssu*; *Abī-liblut*.

^{5} *sūt Šamaš* 'the seah of (the) Shamash (temple)' (a seah of specific size).

^{10} *kīma ištīššu ešrīšu* 'ten times as often as once'.

^{13} *ibissûm* (*-ā*; Sum. lw.) 'financial loss'; *baʾālum* (*i*) G 'to be(come) (abnormally) large, important'; *buʾʾulum* D 'to enlarge, exaggerate'.

^{19} *uddušum* here 'to renew efforts'?

^{27} *ḫaṭītum* 'offense' (cf. *ḫaṭûm*).

2. *TLB* 4 pl. 9 and 10 LB 1771+1766 = Frankena, *AbB* 3 16+17.

^{1} *a-na ru-ut-tum* [*qí-bí-ma*] ^{2} *um-ma* ^{d}AMAR.UTU-[*na-ṣi-ir-ma*] ^{3} ^{d}UTU *ù* ^{d}AMAR.UTU [*da-ri-iš* UD-*mi*] ^{4} *li-ba-al-*[*li-ṭú-ki*] ^{5} *aš-šum* ŠE-*e-im ša ús-sà-an-na-qú* ^{6} *a-na mi-nim li-ib-ba-ki* ^{7} *im-ta-na-ar-ra-aṣ* ^{8} *ša-at-tam ku-um nu-um* ^{9} *ša a-na pa-ni-ki iš-ša-ak-nu* ^{10} *ta-am-ta-ši-i* ^{11} ŠE-*um ša ús-sà-an-na-qú* ^{12} *ú-ul a-na ka-ši-im* ^{13} *iš-tu ṣe-eḫ-ḫe-re-ku* ^{14} *a-wa-ti-ki aḫ-ḫi-ia* ^{15} *aḫ-ḫa-ti-ia* ^{16} *ù qé-er-bu-ti-ia* ^{17} *ú-ul ú-še-eš-mi* ^{18} *mi-nu-um ša a-na a-ḫa-ti-ki* ^{19} *ù aḫ-ḫi-ki i-na bu-bu-tim a-ma-at* ^{20} *ta-aš-pu-ri-im* ^{21} *ki ma-ṣí ḫi-ta-aṭ-ṭì-i* ^{22} ⌜^{I}*ba-ba*⌝*-tum ù ṣú-ḫa-ra-tim* ^{23} *ki-ma* [*aš*]-*pu-ra-am* ^{24} *ṭú-ur-di-*[*ši-na-ti*] ^{25} *la-ma al-l*[*i-ka-ak-ki-im*] ^{26} *lu-ud-di-iš* [......] ^{27} ⌜*a-wa*⌝*-ti la te-e*[*g*$^{?}$*-gi-i*$^{?}$].

PNs: *Ruttum* (fem.); *Marduk-nāṣir*; *Babātum*.

^{13} *ṣeḫḫerēku* = *ṣeḫrēku*.

^{16} *qerbum* here as a noun, 'relative'.

^{18} *mīnum ša* 'why is it that...?'.

^{19} *bubūtum* 'hunger'; the last three words of this line are a direct quote.

3. *TLB* 4 pl. 16 LB 1904 = Frankena, *AbB* 3 28.

^{1} *a-na šu-*^{d}*Amurrim*(MAR.TU) *ša* ^{d}[AMAR.UTU] ^{2} *ú-ba-al-la-ṭú-š*[*u*] ^{3} *qí-bí-ma* ^{4} *um-ma ì-lí-um-ma-ti-m*[*a*] ^{5} ^{d}UTU *ù* ^{d}AMAR.UTU *li-ba-al-li-ṭú-ka* ^{6} *me-e i-di-in-ma* ^{7} A.ŠÀ*-am ša pa-ni* GIŠ.GI ^{8} *li-iš-qú-ú* ^{9} *la tu-uš-ta-*$^{\supset}$*a*$_4$ ^{10} NUMUN*-šu-nu la i-ḫa-li-iq.*

PNs: *Šū-Amurrim; Ilī-ummatī.*

^{7} *apum* (pl. *apū*; log. GIŠ.GI) 'reed thicket, canebrake'.

^{8} *šaqûm* G (*i*) 'to cause/give to drink, to water' (used as the causative of *šatûm*).

4. *TCL* 7 64 = Kraus, *AbB* 4 64.

^{1} *a-na* ^{d}UTU*-ḫa-zìr* ^{2} *qí-bí-ma* ^{3} *um-ma* LÚ-^{d}NIN.URTA*-ma* ^{4} ^{d}UTU *li-ba-al-li-iṭ-ka* ^{5} ^{I}*pi-ir-ḫu-um* DUMU *mu-tum-*DINGIR ^{6} *ki-a-am ú-lam-mi-da-an-ni* ^{7} *um-ma* [*š*]*u-ú-ma* ^{8} *i-na bi-*[*it a*]*-bi-ia* ^{9} 1 KASKAL *i-na lāsimim*(LÚ.KAŠ$_4$.E) ^{10} 1 KASKAL *i-na kullizim*(ŠÀ.GUD) ^{11} *ni-il-la-ak* ^{12} A.ŠÀ *bi-it a-bi-ni* ^{13} *a-na kullizim*(ŠÀ.GUD)*-ma ug-da-me-er* ^{14} *i-ba-aš-ši-i a-ša-ar iš-te-en-ma* ^{15} *gu-um-mu-ru* ^{16} *wa-ar-ka-tam pu-ru-us-ma* ^{17} *šum-ma* 2 KASKAL*-šu-nu i-na bi-it a-bi-šu-nu* ^{18} *ba-ma-a zu-us-sú-nu-ši-im-ma* ^{19} É.GAL*-lam la ú-da-ba-ab.*

PNs: *Šamaš-ḫāzir; Lu-Ninurta; Pirḫum; Mutum-ilum.*

$^{9\text{-}11}$ *ḫarrānam alākum* 'to perform corvée service'; *lāsimum* (LÚ.KAŠ$_4$(.E)) 'courier, express messenger'; *kullizum* (ŠÀ.GUD) 'ox driver'.

^{14} *ibaššî* here, 'can it be, that ...?'.

^{18} *bāmâ* (adverb) 'in half'.

5. Thureau-Dangin, *TCL* 7 16 = Kraus, *AbB* 4 16.

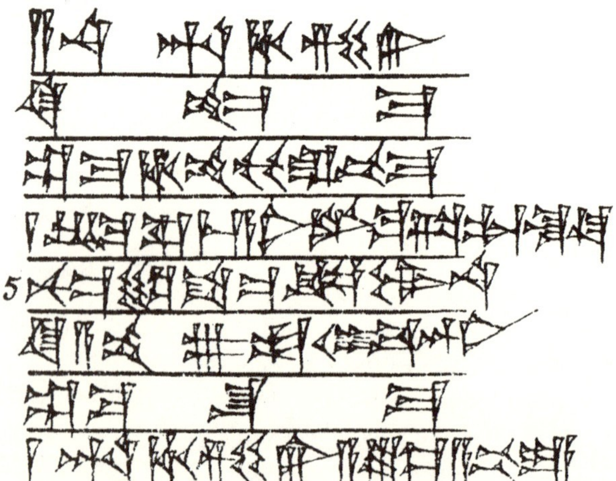

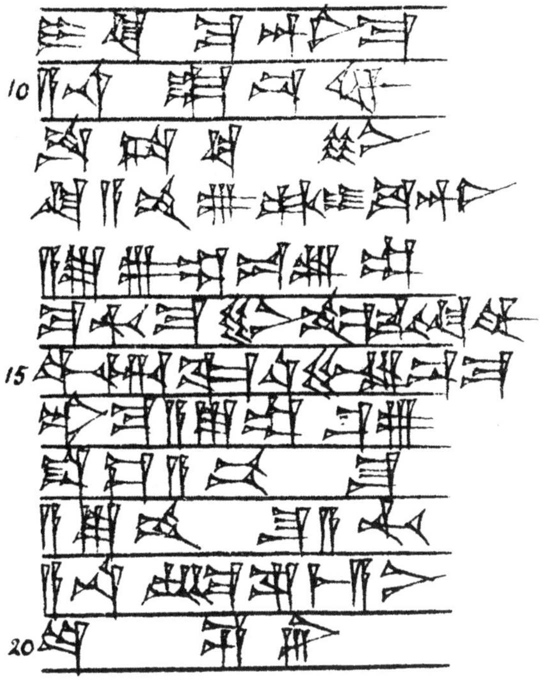

PNs: *Šamaš-ḫāzir*; *Sîn-išmeanni.*

4 *Kutalla* place name.

5 NU.^{giš}KIRI$_6$ = *nukaribbum* (*nukarib*) 'gardener'; after GIŠIMMAR read DILMUN.NA = *Dilmun(im)* 'of Dilmun' (place name).

13 *dūrum* b 'continuity; permanent status of property'; here in appostiton to *eqlum.*

J. Hymn to Ištar, stanzas 11–14 and prayer for King Ammī-ditāna (lines 41–60; see Lessons 33 and 34, exercises).

41. *šar-ru-um mi-ig-ra-šu-un na-ra-am li-ib-bi-šu-un*
42. *šar-ḫi-iš it-‹ta›-na-aq-qí-šu-nu-ut ni-qí-a-šu el-la-am*
43. *am-mi-di-ta-na el-la-am ni-qí-i qá-ti-šu*
44. *ma-aḫ-ri-i-šu-un ú-še-eb-bé li-i ù as*(!IA)*-li na-am-ra-i-i*

42 *šarḫiš* see line 11; *-šunūt* for expected *-šunūšim.* acc. *niqiašu* for prose *niqīšu*; cf. *narbiaš* in line 21.

43 *Ammī-ditāna* king of Babylon, 1683–47.

44 *lûm* (base *li-*; gen. *lîm,* acc. *liam*; pl. *lû*) 'bull' (cf. the fem. *lītum* / *littum* 'cow'); *aslum* (pl. *aslū*) 'young (male) sheep' (poetic word); *namrāʾū* (always pl.) 'fatlings'; the extra *-i* sign may be a scribal error.

45. *iš-ti* AN-*nim ḫa-we-ri-i-ša te-te-er-ša-aš-šu-um*
46. *da-ri-a-am ba-la-ṭa-am ar-ka-am*
47. *ma-da-a-tim ša-na-at ba-la-à-ṭi-im a-na am-mi-di-ta-na*
48. *tu-ša-at-li-im eš₄-tár ta-at-ta-di-in*

45 *išti* see line 13.
48 *šutlumum* Š (not in G) 'to give, bestow, confer, lend'.

49. *si-iq-ru-uš-ša tu-ša-ak-ni-ša-aš-šu-um*
50. *ki-ib-ra-at er-bé-e-em a-na še-pí-i-šu*
51. *ù na-ap-ḫa-ar ka-li-šu-nu da-ad-mi*
52. *ta-aṣ-ṣa-mi-su-nu-ti a-ni-ri-i-ši-ú*

51 *dadmū* (always pl.) 'habitations, settlements; the inhabited world'.
52 *nīrum* (*nīr(i)*) 'yoke'; *-ši-ú* for expected suffix *-šu* 'his'.

53. *bi-be-el li-ib-bi-i-ša za-ma-ar la-le-e-ša*
54. *na-ṭú-um-ma a-na pí-i-šu si-iq-ri é-a i-pu-is-si*
55. *ìš*(EŠ)*-me-e-ma ta-ni-it-ta-a-ša i-ri-us-su*
56. *li-ib-lu-uṭ-mi šar-ra-šu li-ra-am-šu ad-da-ri-iš*

53 *biblum* (*bibil*) 'marriage gift'; *bibil libbim* 'wish, desire' (cf. *babālum*).
lalûm (*lalā-*) 'desire, wish; wealth, happiness; luxury, luxuriance; attractiveness, charm'.
54 *naṭûm* G only in Verbal Adj. *naṭûm* (*naṭu-*) 'fitting, suitable, appropriate'.
Ea (usually written *é-a*) the god of fresh water, and of intelligence and cunning.
i-pu-is-si a broken writing, for expected *ippussi(m)* or *ippessim* (cf. *nazuzzū* in line 39).
55 The subject of *išme* and the following verb is Ea, who is also the speaker of line 56.
tanīttum (*tanītti*) 'praise, glory'.
riāšum G (*i*) 'to rejoice' (cf. *rīštum* in line 38); *i-ri-us-su* is another broken writing (see lines 39, 54) for expected *irīssu(m)*.

57. *eš₄-tár a-na am-mi-di-ta-na šar-ri ra-i-mi-i-ki*
58. *ar-ka-am da-ri-a-am ba-la-ṭa-am šu-úr-ki*
59. *li-ib-lu-uṭ*

60. giš.gi₄.gál.bi

60 This indented final line in Sumerian represents *meḫeršu* 'its (the hymn's) response', i.e. 'its antiphony'.

LESSON THIRTY-SIX

36.1 The Št Stems

There are two Št stems, with different meanings: the Št-passive and the Št-lexical (see below under (b)). Formally, the two stems differ only in the Durative, and are identical for all other forms.

(a) Form

The forms are, naturally, based on the corresponding Š stem. The infixed *-t-* (or *-ta-*) stands between the *š* and R_1. As in the Š (and D), the Durative forms have *a* as the theme-vowel, whereas the Preterite, Perfect, and Imperative have *i*. The Št Preterite is formally identical with the Š Perfect.

As noted above, the two Št stems are distinguished only in the Durative. The Durative of the Št-passive is patterned after that of the Š, and simply has *-t-* inserted after the *-š-*; the Durative of the Št-lexical has a doubled middle radical, like the G and Gt Durative (see under (b), on the meaning).

Given below are the Št paradigms of *parāsum*, of the I–*n* verb *nadānum*, and of the III–weak verb *malûm*. For verbs III–*e*, the change of *a*-vowels to *e* is optional (e.g., from *redûm*: Infinitive *šutardûm* or *šuterdûm*; Durative Št lex. *uštaradda* or *ušteredde*).

	Sound	**I–*n***	**III–weak**
Infinitive:	*šutaprusum*	*šutaddunum*	*šutamlûm*
Durative Št pass.:	*uštapras*	*uštaddan*	*uštamla*
Durative Št lex.:	*uštaparras*	*uštanaddan*	*uštamalla*
Perfect:	*uštatapris*	*uštataddin*	*uštatamli*
Preterite:	*uštapris*	*uštaddin*	*uštamli*
Imperative:	*šutapris*	*šutaddin*	*šutamli*
Participle:	*muštaprisum*	*muštaddinum*	*muštamlûm*
Verbal Adj.:	*šutaprusum*	*šutaddunum*	*šutamlûm*
V. Adj. base:	*šutaprus*	*šutaddun*	*šutamlu*

In verbs I–ʾ and I–*w*, the Durative forms of the two Št stems, like the rest of the paradigms, are identical. Št forms of verbs I-*w* have *a*- or *e*- vowels according to the corresponding Š forms. Below are the Št paradigms of *aḫāzum*, *ešērum*, *babālum*, and *waṣûm* (also III–weak).

	I–*a*	**I–*e***	**I–*w***	
Infinitive:	*šutāḫuzum*	*šutēšurum*	*šutābulum*	*šutēṣûm*
Durative:	*uštaḫḫaz*	*uštešše̱r*	*uštabbal*	*uštesṣe*
Perfect:	*uštatāḫiz*	*uštetēšer*	*uštatābil*	*uštetēṣi*
Preterite:	*uštāḫiz*	*uštēšer*	*uštābil*	*uštēṣi*
Imperative:	*šutāḫiz*	*šutēšer*	*šutābil*	*šutēṣi*
Participle:	*muštāḫizum*	*muštēšerum*	*muštābilum*	*muštēṣûm*
Verbal Adj.:	*šutāḫuzum*	*šutēšurum*	*šutābulum*	*šutēṣûm*
V. Adj. base:	*šutāḫuz*	*šutēšur*	*šutābul*	*šutēṣu*

Št forms of verbs **II–weak** are rare; the following forms are attested for a few roots:

Infinitive:	*šutakunnum*
Durative:	*uštakān*
3mp:	*uštakannū*
Preterite:	*uštakīn*
3mp:	*uštakinnū*
Participle:	*muštakinnum*

The few attested Št forms of verbs originally II–ʾ have strong ʾ.

(b) Meaning

(1) Št-passive

The Št stem with the shorter Durative, *uštapras*, serves as the passive of the Š stem and is therefore called the Št-passive (sometimes simply Št[1]). This is by far the less frequent of the two Št stems. Examples:

šutalputum 'to be destroyed';
šuterdûm 'to be conducted, caused to flow';
šutāpûm / *šutēpûm* (*wapûm*) 'to be made/become visible, famous; to be proclaimed; to shine forth';
šutēṣûm (*waṣûm*) 'to be brought out'.

(2) Št-lexical

The Št stem with the longer Durative form, *uštaparras*, has a wide range of uses and meanings. Because many of these are unpredictable, this form is termed the Št-lexical (or Št[2]).

One use of the Št-lexical is as the causative of the Gt stem, as in

šutamgurum 'to bring to agreement'; *mitgurum* Gt 'to come to an agreement';
šutamḫurum 'to cause to compare oneself with, compete with, rival'; *mitḫurum* Gt 'to face one another, be of equal size, correspond';
šutaṣbutum 'to collect, assemble, keep together, attach; to quarrel' (i.e., 'to cause to grasp one another'); *tiṣbutum* Gt 'to grasp one another';

The Št-lexical also functions as the reflexive of the Š, as in

šutēpušum (*epēšum*) 'to get busy, active' (cf. *šūpušum* Š 'to direct');
šutamruṣum 'to concern oneself, take trouble, labor' (cf. *šumruṣum* Š 'to make sick');
šutaddunum (*nadānum*) 'to intermingle, discuss' (cf. *šuddunum* Š 'to collect');
šuterdûm 'to continue, resume' (cf. *šurdûm* Š 'to conduct, lead');
šutēṣûm 'to escape' (cf. *šūṣûm* 'to let out'); also 'to fight with one another'.

Finally, the Št-lexical serves as a catch-all stem, the meanings of some forms having little obvious derivational relationship with the Š or the Gt of the roots in question. The meanings of these must be learned individually, since they are not readily classifiable.

šutāwûm 'to discuss, consider, ponder' (cf. *atwûm* Gt 'to speak, discuss');
šutēmudum (*emēdum*) 'to bring into contact, join, unite, add' (causative of *nenmudum* N);
šutēšurum (*ešērum*) 'to proceed; to thrive, prosper; to set right, put in order, provide justice; to guide properly; to send; to make prosper';
šutakunnum (*kânum*) 'to justify, examine' (Mari);
šutamlûm 'to assign, add, provide in full';
šutamṭûm 'to be in short supply';
šutassuqum (*nasāqum*) 'to put in order, prepare'; it may be that this verb derives from *nasākum* rather than *nasāqum* (all writings are ambiguous);
šutasḫurum 'to surround on all sides';
šutašnûm 'to double, give twice as much'; in hendiadys, 'to do again'.

Some verbs exhibit forms of both Št stems, as illustrated by *šuterdûm* and *šutēṣûm* above. Further, while the distinction between the Durative forms of the two Št stems is generally observed, there is occasionally some confusion of the forms; e.g.,

both *uštanaddanū* and *uštaddanū* for 'they (m) discuss'.

36.2 The Štn Stem

The Štn serves as the iterative stem of Š verbs.

In sound verbs, verbs I–*n*, and verbs III–weak, the forms of the Štn are identical to those of the Št listed above, with the important exception of the Durative (cf. the Dt and Dtn). The Štn Durative has the form *uštanapras*, with the characteristic *-tan-*. For verbs I–*n*, with the assimilation of the *n* of the root, the resulting form is identical to the Št-lexical Durative.

	Sound	**I–*n***	**III–weak**
Durative Štn:	*uštanapras*	*uštanaddan*	*uštanamla*

In verbs I–ʾ and verbs I–*w*, all Štn forms differ from the corresponding Št forms, in that R_2 is always doubled and preceded by a short vowel in the Štn, rather than single and preceded by a long vowel as in the Št.

	I–*a*	**I–*e***	**I–*w***	
Infinitive:	*šutaḫḫuzum*	*šuteššurum*	*šutabbulum*	*šuteṣṣûm*
Durative:	*uštanaḫḫaz*	*ušteneššer*	*uštanabbal*	*uštenesṣe*
Perfect:	*uštataḫḫiz*	*ušteteššer*	*uštatabbil*	*ušteteṣṣi*
Preterite:	*uštaḫḫiz*	*ušteššer*	*uštabbil*	*ušteṣṣi*
Imperative:	*šutaḫḫiz*	*šuteššer*	*šutabbil*	*šuteṣṣi*
Participle:	*muštaḫḫizum*	*mušteššerum*	*muštabbilum*	
	mušteṣṣûm			
Verbal Adj.:	*šutaḫḫuzum*	*šuteššurum*	*šutabbulum*	*šuteṣṣûm*
V. Adj. base:	*šutaḫḫuz*	*šuteššur*	*šutabbul*	*šuteṣṣu*

Štn forms of verbs **II–weak** occur too infrequently to present a paradigm.

36.3 Oaths

Statements made under oath in Akkadian exhibit a special grammar that sets them apart from ordinary statements. Two types of oath may be distinguished according to the time frame of the activity about which the oath is taken: assertory oaths refer to the past (or the present); promissory oaths refer to the future.

Assertory oaths (referring to the past) normally have as their predicate either a Preterite verb or a verbless clause (including a predicate Verbal Adjective). Promissory oaths (referring to the future) usually have a Durative verb as predicate.

Both assertory and promissory oaths may be positive (assertory 'I did do X', promissory 'I will do X') or negative (assertory 'I did not do X', promissory 'I will not do X').

Three means of expressing an oath occur in OB texts. In the most common, the predicate is a verb or predicate adjective with the subordination marker *-u* (on forms on which *-u* may appear); the absence of *ša* or any conjunction governing the verb marks this construction unambiguously as an oath. In negative oaths, the negative is *lā*. Predicates in this construction sometimes have a non-coordinating *-ma* for emphasis. Some examples:

Assertory:

umma šunū-ma: "kirûm pānûm burru; ina ilim telqû" 'thus they (m) (said): "the previous orchard was confirmed (*bârum* D V. Adj. *būr*); you (ms) took (it) under (an oath to) a god" ';

kiam lizkurū: "dāʾik PN *lā īdû; anāku lā ušāḫizu; u bašītam ša* PN *lā elqû, lā alputu"* 'they (m) must swear as follows: "I do not know the murderer of PN; I myself did not incite; further, I did not take (or even) touch PN's property" ';

Promissory:

ina maḫar awīlê annûtim kiam iqbû umma šunū-ma: "nīš šarrim ana dayyānī nillakū-ma" 'before these men they (m) said as follows: "by the life of the king we will go to the judges" ';

PN *itma: "ana* PN2 *lā araggamu"* 'PN swore, "I will not contest against PN2" '.

Another common construction, used only for positive oaths, has the asseverative particle *lū* (§29.3); predicates do not bear the subordination marker.

Assertory:

kaspam šuāti ana ummiānim abī lū utēr 'my father did return that silver to the lender';

bēl bītim nīš ilim izakkaršum-ma: "itti bušêka bušûya lū ḫalqū" 'the owner of the house will swear for him by the life of the god: "along with your goods, my goods were indeed (also) lost" ';

PN *ina bāb* DN *kiam izkur umma šū-ma: "lū mār* PN2 *anāku"* 'in the gate of DN, PN swore as follows: "I am indeed the son of PN2" ';

Promissory:

umma šū-ma: "šarram atma: 'ištu inanna adi ḫamšat ūmī kasapka lū anaddikkum' " 'he (said) as follows: "I swore by the king, 'in five days from now I will give you (ms) your silver' " '.

The third construction is the least common in OB texts, but becomes the sole means of expressing an oath in Akkadian dialects of the first millennium. It is essentially the protasis of a conditional sentence, without an apodosis expressed. The understood apodosis is 'may I be cursed, if ...'. The logic of the construction dictates that a positive oath must contain a negative (*lā*), while a negative oath must lack a negative: to express 'such-and-such shall happen', one writes 'if such-and-such does not happen(, may I be cursed)'; for 'such-and-such must not happen', one writes 'if such-and-such does happen(, may I be cursed)'.

> *ina šaptīšu kiam iššakin umma šū-ma: "šumma aḫī Purattim gulgullātim lā umalli"* 'the following was on his lips: "I will fill the banks of the Euphrates (*Purattum*) with skulls (*gulgullātum*)" ' (lit., "if I did not fill the banks of the Euphrates with skulls, ...");
>
> *šumma ṣibûtki lā ētepuš* 'I will carry out your (fs) wish (*ṣibûtum*)' (lit., 'if I have not carried out your wish, ...').

EXERCISES

A. VOCABULARY 36.

Verbs:

šasûm G (*i*; Preterite *išsi* or *issi*; Imperative *šisi* or *tisi*) 'to cry (out), shout, call (to), summon; to proclaim; to read (aloud)'; *šitassûm* Gtn 'to read, study'; *šussûm / šuššûm* Š causative; N passive.

watûm G (*a*; Dur. *utta*, Pret. *uta* [see §21.3(g)]) 'to find, discover'; *šutātûm* Št-lex. 'to meet (one another)'.

Learn the Št verbs given in §36.1.

Nouns:

eršum (fem.; *ereš*; pl. *eršētum*; log. ^{giš}NÁ) 'bed'.

igārum (*igār*; pl. *igārātum*; log. É.GAR$_8$; Sum. lw.) 'wall (of a building)'.

libittum (*libitti*; pl. *libnātum*; log. SIG$_4$) '(mud) brick'.

mīšarum (*mīšar*) 'justice, equity, redress' (cf. *ešērum*).

nēmelum (*nēmel*; pl. *nēmelētum*) 'benefit, gain, profit; surplus'; *nēmelam amārum* 'to make/gain a profit, to benefit'.

ṣibtum b (masc.; bound form *ṣibit*; pl. *ṣibtātum*) 'seizure; agricultural holding'; *ṣibit ṭēmim išûm / rašûm* 'to take action' (cf. *ṣabātum*).

šaplum (*šapal*) 'under part, side, bottom'; *šapal* (preposition; with suf. *šaplī-* or *šapal-*) and *ina šapal* (prepositional phrase; with suf. *ina šaplī-*) 'under, below, beneath'; *(ina) šapal šēp(ī)* 'at the feet of'.

tukultum (*tukulti*; pl. *tuklātum*) 'trust; object of trust' (cf. *takālum*).

Proper noun:

Purattum (log. ^{id}BURANUN [= UD.KIB.NUN]) the Euphrates.

B. Learn the following signs:

OB Lapid.	OB Cursive	NA	values
			UZU = *šīrum* determ. ^{uzu} before words denoting parts of the body
		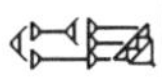	NÁ = *eršum*
	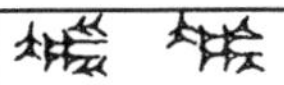	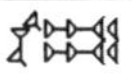	SIG_4 = *libittum* GAR_8 in É.GAR_8 = *igārum*

C. Write the following words in cuneiform and in transliteration; use logograms where possible:

1. *gišimmārātum ša aḫ Purattim*
2. *wakil bārî ina ereqqim irkab*
3. *sukkallum ina eršim inīl*
4. *libnāt igārim*
5. *ana šīr ilim iṭīb*

D. Write in normalized Akkadian, using Št and Štn forms:

1. you (ms) will collect
2. she will double
3. I assigned
4. they (m) will be destroyed
5. they (f) have resumed
6. get busy (pl)!
7. you (fs) will cause to enter repeatedly
8. it thrived
9. they (m) have brought into contact
10. they (f) will be brought out
11. surrounding on all sides (ms)
12. we will meet one another

E. Normalize and translate:

1. *sa-bi-tum a-na ša-a-šum is-sà-qar-am a-na* ^{d}GIŠ
   ^{d}GIŠ *e-eš ta-da-a-al*
   ba-la-ṭam ša ta-sa-aḫ-ḫu-ru la tu-ut-ta
   i-nu-ma DINGIR.MEŠ *ib-nu-ú a-wi-lu-tam*
   mu-tam iš-ku-nu a-na a-wi-lu-tim
   ba-la-ṭam i-na qá-ti-šu-nu iṣ-ṣa-ab-tu

   OB Gilgameš, X ii 14 – iii 5; *sābītum* 'innkeeper (fem.)'; ^{d}GIŠ = the OB writing for *Gilgameš; êš* (adv.) 'where, whither?'; *dâlum* G (*u*) 'to wander'; *awīlūtum* 'humanity'; *mūtum* 'death'.
2. *i-nu-ma* ^{d}AMAR.UTU *a-na šu-te-šu-ur ni-ši* KALAM *ú-si-im šu-ḫu-zi-im ú-wa-e-ra-an-ni ki-it-tam ù mi-ša-ra-am i-na* KA *ma-tim aš-ku-un ši-ir ni-ši ú-ṭi-ib*. (*usum* 'direction, guidance, custom'; CH prologue, v 14–24)
3. LUGAL *ša in* LUGAL-*rí šu-tu-ru a-na-ku a-wa-tu-ú-a na-ás-qá le-ú-ti ša-ni-nam* (*šāninum* 'rival') *ú-ul i-šu i-na qí-bí-it* ^{d}UTU *da-a-a-nim ra-bi-im ša* AN *ù* KI *mi-ša-ri i-na* KALAM *li-iš-te-pí*. (CH; epilogue, r xxiv 79–88)
4. *aš-šum* A.ŠÀ.MEŠ *ša* PN *a-na* PN$_2$ *še-e-em-ma ka-ma-si-im ù* É.GAL *a-pa-li-im lu-ú aš-pu-ra-aš-šu-um*.
5. *ki-a-am iq-bi-a-am um-ma šu-ma šar-ra-am at-ma iš-tu i-na-an-na a-di* UD.5.KAM KUG.BABBAR-*ka lu a-na-di-ku-um*.
6. *aš-šum* LÚ.KÚR *ú-še-ṣi-a-an-ni ak-li šu-ta-am-ṭú-ma ša a-ka-li-im ú-ul i-šu ù aš-šum a-wa-at* É.GAL *ša eš-mu-ú na-az-qá-ku ṭe*$_4$*-em-ki ar-ḫi-iš šu-up-ri-im-ma la a-na-az-zi-iq*.
7. *a-na* PN *aq-bi-i-ma a-na* KÁ.DINGIR.RA^{ki} SAG.ÌR *šu-a-ti ú-ul iṭ-ru-ud* PN KUG.BABBAR *i-ir-ri-iš* KUG.BABBAR *šu-bi-la-aš-šum-ma lu-uš-tam-gi-ir-šu-ú-ma* SAG.ÌR *šu-a-ti li-iṭ-ru-da-ak-kum*.
8. *at-ta ù šu-ú qá-qá-da-ti-ku-nu šu-te-mi-da-ma wa-ar-ka-tam šu-a-ti pu-ur-sa ša-ni-tam i-na-an-na pa-ṭa-ri qé-ru-ub ṣú-ḫa-ru-ú bi-tam a-na pa-ni-ia li-iš-ta-as-sí-qú ù* A.ŠÀ.MEŠ *lu-ú šu-ta-as-sú-qá*.
9. *i-nu-ma a-na-ku ù a-bi i-na* ZIMBIR^{ki} *nu-uš-ta-tu-ú ma-di-iš aḫ-du i-na-an-na mu-ša-ad-di-nu* KUG.BABBAR *uš-ta-na-ad-da-nu-ni-a-ti ù ma-di-iš nu-uš-ta-ma-ar-ra-aṣ*.
10. *šum-ma li-ib-ba-ka ṭe*$_4$*-em-ka ga-am-ra-am šu-up-ra-am-ma a-wi-lum šu-ú* KUG.BABBAR-*šu li-il-qé-ma li-il-li-ka-ak-kum* UDU. ḪI.A *i-di-iš-šum ù ṣú-ḫa-ru-um ša il-li-ka-ak-kum it-ti ṣa-bi-im šu-ta-aṣ-bi-ta-aš-šu*.

F. CH:

§101 *šum-ma a-šar (šamallûm,* from §100*) il-li-ku ne-me-lam la i-ta-mar* KUG.BABBAR *il-qú-ú uš-ta-ša-na-ma šamallûm*(ŠAMAN$_2$.LÁ) *a-na* DAM.GÀR *i-na-ad-di-in.*

§120 *šum-ma a-wi-lum* ŠE-*šu a-na na-aš-pa-ku-tim i-na* É *a-wi-lim*(! LUM) *iš-pu-uk-ma i-na qá-ri-tim i-ib-bu-ú-um it-tab-ši ù lu be-el* É *na-aš-pa-kam ip-te-ma* ŠE *il-qé ù lu* ŠE *ša i-na* É-*šu iš-ša-ap-ku a-na ga-am-ri-im it-ta-ki-ir be-el* ŠE *ma-ḫar i-lim* ŠE-*šu ú-ba-ar-ma be-el* É ŠE *ša il-qú-ú uš-ta-ša-na-ma a-na be-el* ŠE *i-na-ad-di-in.*

qarītum (*qarīt;* pl. *qariātum*) 'storeroom, granary'.
ibbûm (base *ibbā-;* Sum. lw.) 'loss, deficit'.

§126 *šum-ma a-wi-lum mi-im-mu-šu la ḫa-li-*[*iq*]*-ma mi-im-me-e ḫa-li-iq iq-ta-bi ba-ab-ta-šu ú-te-eb-bi-ir ki-ma mi-im-mu-šu la ḫal-qú ba-ab-ta-šu i-na ma-ḫar i-lim ú-ba-ar-šu-ma mi-im-ma ša ir-gu-mu uš-ta-ša-na-ma a-na ba-ab-ti-šu i-na-ad-di-in.*

ubburum D (G *abārum* rare) 'to accuse'.

§§145–147 §145 *šum-ma a-wi-lum* LUKUR *i-ḫu-uz-ma* DUMU.MEŠ *la ú-šar-ši-šu-ma a-na* ^{mí}*šu-gi*$_4$*-tim a-ḫa-zi-im pa-ni-šu iš-ta-ka-an a-wi-lum šu-ú* ^{mí}*šu-gi*$_4$*-tam i-iḫ-ḫa-az a-na* É-*šu ú-še-er-re-eb-ši* ^{mí}*šu-gi*$_4$*-tum ši-i it-ti* LUKUR *ú-ul uš-ta-ma-aḫ-ḫa-ar.* §146 *šum-ma a-wi-lum* LUKUR *i-ḫu-uz-ma* GEME$_2$ *a-na mu-ti-ša id-di-in-ma* DUMU. MEŠ *it-ta-la-ad wa-ar-ka-nu-um* GEME$_2$ *ši-i it-ti be-el-ti-ša uš-ta-tam-ḫi-ir aš-šum* DUMU.MEŠ *ul-du be-le-sà a-na* KUG.BABBAR *ú-ul i-na-ad-di-iš-ši ab-bu-ut-tam i-ša-ak-ka-an-ši-ma it-ti* GEME$_2$.ḪI.A *i-ma-an-nu-ši.* §147 *šum-ma* DUMU.MEŠ *la ú-li-id be-le-sà a-na* KUG.BABBAR *i-na-ad-di-iš-ši.*

šugītum (*šugīt;* log. ^{mí}ŠU.GI$_4$; Sum. lw.) a junior wife.
abbuttum (*abbutti*) the characteristic hair style of slaves.

§206 *šum-ma a-wi-lum a-wi-lam i-na ri-is-ba-tim im-ta-ḫa-aṣ-ma sí-im-ma-am iš-ta-ka-an-šu a-wi-lum šu-ú i-na i-du-ú la am-ḫa-ṣú i-tam-ma ù* A.ZU *i-ip-pa-al.*

risibtum (pl. *risbātum* [= sg.]) 'quarrel, fight'.
ina īdû see §26.2(a).

§227 *šum-ma a-wi-lum gallābam*(ŠU.I) *i-da-aṣ-ma ab-bu-ti* ÌR *la še-e-em ug-da-al-li-ib a-wi-lam šu-a-ti i-du-uk-ku-šu-ma i-na* KÁ-*šu i-ḫa-al-la-lu-šu gallābum*(ŠU.I) *i-na i-du-ú la ú-gal-li-bu i-tam-ma-ma ú-ta-aš-šar.*

gallābum (*gallāb*; log. ŠU.I) 'barber'; *gullubum* D (not in G) 'to shave'.
dâṣum G (*a*) 'to deceive'.
abbuttum (*abbutti*) the characteristic hair style of slaves.
ḫalālum G (*a–u*) 'to hang' (trans.).
ina īdû see §26.2(a).

§233 *šum-ma* ŠITIM É *a-na a-wi-lim i-pu-uš-ma ši-pí-ir-šu la uš-te-eṣ-bi-ma* É.GAR8 *iq-tu-up* ŠITIM *šu-ú i-na* KUG.BABBAR *ra-ma-ni-šu* É.GAR8 *šu-a-ti ú-dan-na-an*.

ṣubbûm D (not in G) 'to look at (something) from a distance; to carry out, execute properly, according to plan'; *šuteṣbûm* Št lex. 'to carry out, execute properly, according to plan'.
qâpum G (*u*) 'to buckle, cave in, collapse'.

§124:

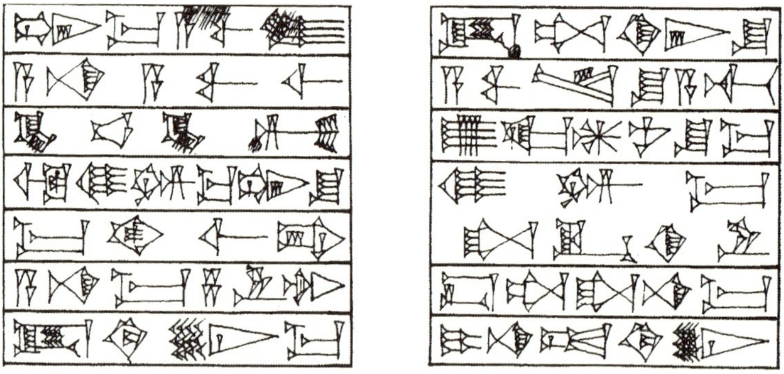

§§160–161:

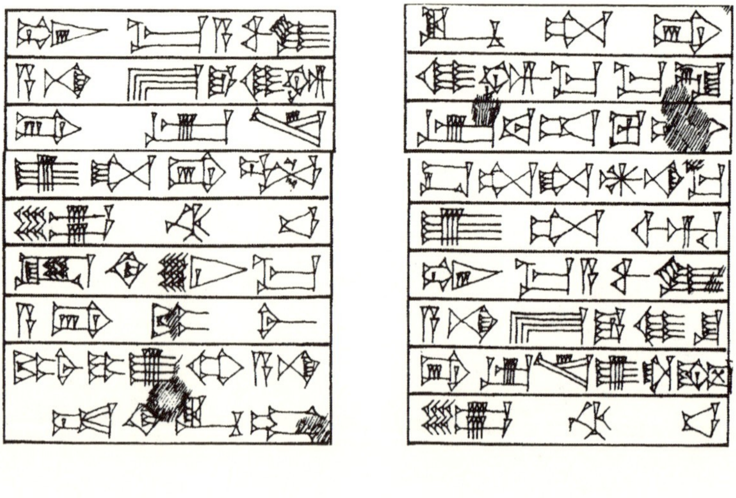

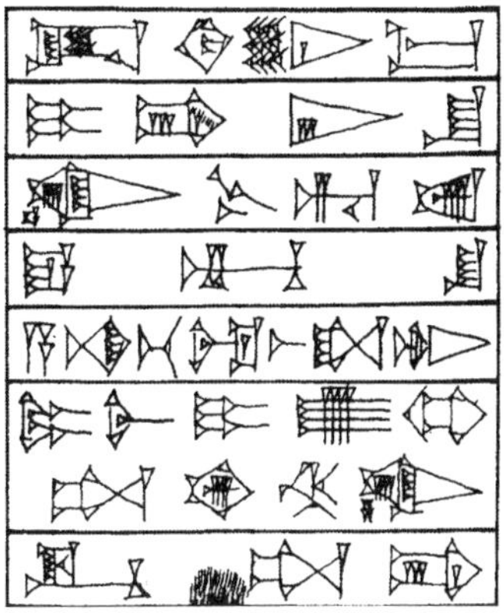

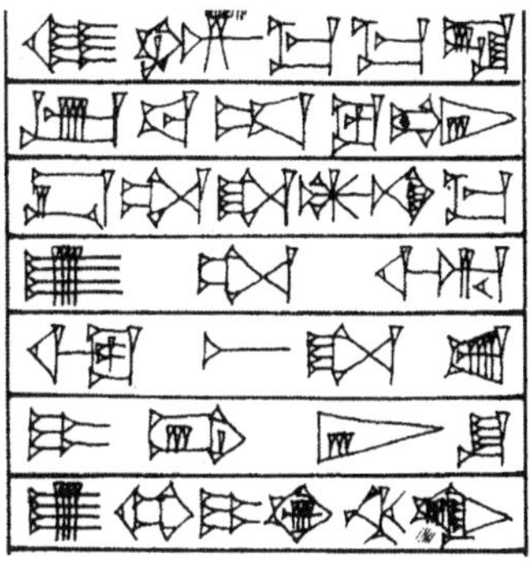

biblum (*bibil*) 'marriage-gift' (cf. *babālum*).
karāṣum G (*i*) 'to pinch, break off'; *kurruṣum* D = G; 'to slander'.

G. Omens from *YOS* 10:

1. [DIŠ *i-na* KÁ] É.GAL *qú-ú-um* ŠU.SI *iṭ-ṭù-ul wa-ši-ib maḫ-ri-ka pi-ri-iš-ta-ka uš-te-né-ṣe*. (25:72)

   qûm (*qā-*) 'filament, thread'.
   pirištum (*pirišti*) 'secret' (cf. *parāsum*).

2. [MAŠ *i-na*] *ṣe-er bi-ri-tim ka-ak-kum ši-na* [*it-ta*]*-aṭ-lu-ú-ma warki*(EGIR) *iš-di-i-šu* [ ]*-ú na-du-ú šar-ra-an* [*i-na pu-ú*]*ḫ-ri-im ú-ul uš-ta-da*$^{!}$*-nu*. (33 ii 35–38)

   birītum here 'border (area)' of the liver.
   Note *kakkum šinā* for 'two weapons'.

3. DIŠ *ma-as-ki-il-tum ša* ŠU.SI *ḫašîm*(UR$_5$) *ḫu-ur-ḫu-dam iṭ-ṭù-ul* MUNUS *a-wa-at pu-uḫ-ri-im uš-te-né-ṣe*. (36 iv 8-9)

   maskiltum part of the *ubānum*.
   ḫašûm (*ḫaši-*; log. UR$_5$ [the ḪAR sign]) 'lung'.
   ḫurḫudam / *urʾudum* 'throat, windpipe';
   awātam šūṣûm 'to betray a secret'.

4. DIŠ UDU *pi-i-šu ip-te-né-et-te-e ri-ig-mu-ú* DIŠ UDU *li-ša-an-šu uš-te-né-ṣe-a-am ni-ip-ru-ú* DIŠ UDU *li-ša-an-šu iš-ta-na-da-ad a-na* LUGAL *a-wa-tum da-mi-iq-tum i-ma-qú-ut*. (47:6–7)

   rigmum (*rigim*; pl. *rigmū*) 'call, shout, cry, noise, voice' (cf. *ragāmum*).
   niprum (pl. *niprū*) 'shoot, sprout; progeny'.

5. BE *i-na ki-ša-ad* MUŠEN *ki-ma ni-ri-im su-ma-am pa-ri-ik ì-lí* LÚ *šu-te-eq-ru-ba-am i-ri-iš*. (52 iii 1–3)

   iṣṣūrum here a part of the liver.

nīrum (*nīr(i)*) 'yoke'.
sūmum (*sūm(i)*; pl. *sūmū*) 'redness, red spot'.
parākum G (*i*) 'to lie across, crosswise; to obstruct, block'; Verbal Adj. *parkum* (*parik-*) 'lying crosswise (before: acc.)'.
šuqrubum Š (*qerēbum*) 'to petition' (rare).

H. Contract:

1. Lawsuit over an inheritance (*CT* 8 12b = Schorr, *VAB* 5, no. 260).

^{1} ^{I}GEME$_2$-^{d}UTU LUKUR ^{d}UTU *a-na um-m*[*i-a*]*-ra-aḫ-tum* ^{2} *a-na* IBILA *ir-gu-um-ma* ^{3} DI.KUD.MEŠ *di-nam ú-ša-ḫi-zu-ši-na-ti-ma* ^{4} *ši-bi-ši-na a-na* ^{d}UTU *ù* ^{d}IŠKUR ^{5} *a-na tu-ma-mi-tum*$^{!}$ ^{6} *i-di-nu-ma ma-ḫar* ^{d}UTU *ù* ^{d}IŠKUR ^{7} *ki-a-am um-ma šu-nu-*[*ma*] ^{8} *ša* ^{d}UTU-*ga-mil ù um-mi-*[*a-ra-aḫ-tum*] ^{9} *a-na* GEME$_2$-^{d}UTU *na-da-nam* ^{10} *la ni-du-ú* ^{11} *ù* DI.KUD.MEŠ *ši-bi* ^{12} *ú-ul im-gu-ru* ^{13} *um-ma* DI.KUD.MEŠ ^{14} *ki-ma ši-bu itmû*(IN.PÀD.DÈ.MEŠ) ^{15} *ù at-ti a-na eš*$_4$*-tár* ^{16} *ta-ta-mi-‹i›* ^{17} ^{I}*um-mi-a-ra-aḫ-tum* ^{18} *i-na* KÁ *eš*$_4$*-tár ki-a-am iq-*[*bi*]*«-ma»* ^{19} *um-ma ši-ma a-na-ku ù* ^{d}UTU-*ga-mil* ^{20} DUB-*pa-am la ni-iš-ṭú-ru* ^{21} *ù* IBILA-*ni la ni-di-nu* ^{22} MU ^{d}UTU ^{d}*a-a* ^{d}AMAR.UTU ^{23} *ù ḫa-am-mu-ra-pí itmû*(IN.PÀD.DÈ.MEŠ) $^{24\text{–}30}$ Witnesses.

PNs: *Amat-Šamaš; Ummī-Araḫtum; Šamaš-gamil.*
^{5} *tumāmītum* 'oath'; here incorrectly nom. for gen. (cf. *tamûm*).
$^{8\text{–}9}$ The syntax here is somewhat contorted; *ša* and all that follows it, up to *nadānam*, modifies *nadānam* (and would normally follow it rather than precede it; see §31.3(a3)): '(we do not know) the giving of Šamaš-gamil and Ummī-Araḫtum to Amat-Šamaš', i.e., '(we do not know) what Š. and U. gave to A.'.
^{15} *u* here 'also, likewise'.

I. Letters:

1. *CT* 43 13 = Kraus, *AbB* 1 13.

^{1} *a-na a-wi-lim qí-bí-ma* ^{2} *um-ma* ÌR-^{d}AMAR.UTU-*ma* ^{3} ^{d}UTU *ù* ^{d}AMAR.UTU *da-ri-iš* UD-*mi* ^{4} *li-ba-al-li-ṭú-ka* ^{5} [*lu ša*]*-al-ma-ta lu ba-al-ṭa-a-ta* ^{6} [DINGIR *na-ṣ*]*i-ir-ka re-eš-ka* ^{7} [*a-na da*]*-mi-iq-tim li-ki-il* ^{8} [*š*]*u-*[*lum-k*]*a ma-ḫar* ^{d}UTU *ù* ^{d}AMAR.UTU *lu da-ri* ^{9} *aš-šum di-ib-ba-tim ša* ^{d}EN.ZU-*še-mi a-ḫi-šu* ^{10} *ša i-na* É *abarakkim*(AGRIG) *ka-lu-ú* ^{11} ^{Id}AMAR.UTU-*mu-ba-lí-iṭ* DUMU UGULA DAM.GÀR‹.MEŠ› ^{12} *it-ti našparim*(NA.AŠ.BAR) *ša be-el-šu-nu* ^{13} *a-ḫi* ^{d}EN.ZU-*na-di-in-šu-mi-im* ^{14} *a-na* KÁ.DINGIR.RA^{ki} ^{15} *it-ta-al-kam* ^{16} *at-ta ù* DUMU *a-ḫi a-bi-ka* ^{17} *šu-ta-ti-a* ^{18} *ma-ḫar a-wi-lim be-el-šu-nu* ^{19} *pu-uṭ-ṭe*$_4$-

ra-a-šu-ma ^{20} *a-na* ZIMBIR^{ki} *li-it-ta-al-kam* ^{21} *ba-lu-šu la ta-al*!*-la*!*-kam*(written *ta-a-al-kam*) ^{22} [*a-na* UR]U BÀD-^{d}UTU *ṭú-ur-da-aš-šu* ^{23} [*i-na*] *an-ni-tam at-ḫu-tam* ^{24} *ku-ul-li-im.*

PNs: *Warad-Marduk; Sîn-šēmi; Marduk-muballiṭ; Bēlšunu; Sîn-nādin-šumim.*

^{9} *dibbatum* (*dibbat*; pl. *dibbātum*) 'agreement, discussion' (cf. *dabābum*).

$^{9–10}$ *aḫīšu ša ... kalû* 'the brother of him who is held'.

^{10} *abarakkum* (*abarak*; log. AGRIG [= IGI+DUB]) an official of temples and estates; 'steward'.

^{11} *našparum* (*našpar*; here written with pseudo-log. NA.AŠ.BAR) 'messenger, envoy' (cf. *šapārum*).

^{22} *Dūr-Šamaš* a town.

^{23} *atḫûtum* (*atḫût*) 'brotherly attitude, partnership' (cf. *aḫum*).

2. King, *LIH* 1 4 = Frankena, *AbB* 2 4, reverse (letter from Ḫammurapi to Sîn-iddinam).

$^{1'}$ [*a-d*]*i* [*ṭ*]*e₄-em-ka la aš-pur-am-*[*ma*] $^{2'}$ *ši-pi-ir* ÍD-*im ša iḫ-ḫe-ru-*[*ú*] $^{3'}$ *la i-mu-ru-nim* $^{4'}$ *mu-ú a-na ši-ip-ri-im ga-am-ri-im* $^{5'}$ *la uš-ta-ar-du-ú* $^{6'}$ *ù iš-tu ši-pi-ir* ÍD *ša i-na-an-na ṣa-ab-ta-ti* $^{7'}$ *i-na ḫe-re-e-em ta-ag-dam-ru* $^{8'}$ ^{íd}BURANUN *ša iš-tu* UD.UNUG^{ki} $^{9'}$ *a-di* URIM^{ki} $^{10'}$ *mi-iq-ti-ša ú-su-úḫ* $^{11'}$ *ḫa-mi-ša šu-ut-bi* $^{12'}$ *šu-te-še-er-ši.*

^{8} UD.UNUG^{ki} = *Larsa* a city.

^{9} URIM^{ki} = *Ur* a city.

^{10} *miqtum* (*miqit*) 'collapse, downfall; obstruction, debris' (cf. *maqātum*).

^{11} *ḫāmū* (pl.) 'litter (of leaves, etc.)'.

3. King, *LIH* 2 92 = Frankena, *AbB* 2 74.

^{1}*a-na* ^{d}⌜EN.ZU⌝-*i-din-nam* ^{2} KAR ZIMBIR^{ki} ^{3} *ù* DI.KUD.MEŠ ZIMBIR^{ki} ^{4} *qí-bí-ma* ^{5} [*um-ma a*]*-bi-e-šu-uḫ-ma* ^{6} ^{Id}*bu-*⌜*ne-ne*⌝*-na-ṣi-ir* ^{7} *ù ṣíl-lí-*^{d}UTU ^{8} DUMU.MEŠ *ri-i*[*š-*^{d}UTU] ^{9} *ki-a-am ú-lam-m*[*i-d*]*u-ni-in-n*[*i*] ^{10} *um-*[*m*]*a šu-nu-ma* ^{11} *ì-lí-i-din-nam a-ḫu-ni ra-bu-u*[*m*] ^{12} *ḫa-ab-la-an-ni-a-ti* ^{13} *iš-tu* MU.2.KAM ^{14} *ma-ḫar* KAR ZIMBIR^{ki} *ni-iš-ta-na-ak-ka-an-*[*m*]*a* ^{15} *ú-ul uš-te-eš-še-ru-ni-a-ti* ^{16} *ki-a-am ú-lam-mi-du-ni-in-ni* ^{17} DUB-*pí an-ni-a-a*[*m*] *i-na a-ma-r*[*i-im*] ^{18} ^{I}*ì-lí-i-din-nam šu-a-t*[*i*] ^{19} *ù ši-bi mu-de-e a-w*[*a-ti-šu*] ^{20} [*š*]*a* ^{d}*bu-ne-ne-na-ṣi-ir* ^{21} *ù ṣíl-lí-*^{d}UTU ^{22} DUMU.MEŠ *ri-iš-*^{d}[UT]U ^{23} *ú-ka-al-la-mu-ku-n*[*u-t*]*i* ^{24} *a-na* KÁ.DINGIR.RA$^{[ki]}$ ^{25} *ṭú-ur-da-ni*[*m-ma*] ^{26} *a-wa-a-tu-šu-n*[*u li-i*]*n-nam-ra.*

PNs: *Sîn-iddinam; Abī-ešuḫ* (king of Babylon, 1711–1684); *Bunene-nāṣir; Ṣillī-Šamaš; Rīš-Šamaš; Ilī-iddinam.*

4. *TLB* 4 pl. 31 LB 1886 = Frankena, *AbB* 3 55.

[1] *[a-n]a ša-pí-ri-ia qí-bí-ma* [2] *um-ma nu-ur-Amurrim* (^{d}MAR.TU)-*ma* [3] ^{d}UTU *ù* ^{d}AMAR.UTU *da-ri-iš* UD-*mi-im* [4] *li-ba-al-li-ṭú-ka* [5] ^{Id}AMAR.UTU-*na-ṣir ša aš-pu-ra-ak-kum* [6] *ú-úḫ-ḫi-ra-am-ma* ^{I}*ra-bu-ut-*^{d}EN.ZU *aṭ-ṭar-da-kum* [7] DUB-*pa-tum ša* DUMU É.DUB.BA.A 5 *it-ta-al-ka-nim* [8] *a-na* 24 IKU A.ŠÀ *ṣí-bi-it* DUMU-KI [9] *a-na sí-ka-tim ma-ḫa-ṣí-im* [10] *ki-a-am aš-pu-ur-šu-nu-ši-im* [11] *um-ma a-na-ku-ú-ma* [12] *a-na šukūs*(A.ŠÀ.ŠUKU) AGA.ÚS *šu-ta-am-li-im* [13] *iš-tu* ITU.1.KAM *wa-aš-ba-a-tu-nu* [14] DUB.SAR *ummānim*(UGNIM) *šukūs* (A.ŠÀ.ŠUKU)-*su-ú* [15] *šu-ta-am-li-a-at-ma-a* [16] *i-na* A.ŠÀ DUB.SAR *ummānim*(UGNIM) [17] *a-na* AGA.ÚS *sí-ka-tam ta-ma-ḫa-ṣa* [18] *a-na a-at-ta-a šassukkim*(SAG.DÙN) *iš-pu-ru-nim* [19] *qá-du-um aš-li-im ù* AGA.ÚS [20] *a-na* ^{uru}*lam-ma-a-a il-li-kam-ma* [21] *ni-iš šar-ri i-na pí-i-šu aš-ku-un-ma* [22] *aš-la-am a-na ta-ra-ṣí-im* [23] *ù sí-ka-tam a-na ma-ḫa-ṣí ú-ul ad-di-šum* [24] *iš-pu-ru-nim-ma a-na qá-ta-tim it-ta-ad-nu-ni-in-ni* [25] *um-ma-mi a-ša-al šar-ri ku-ub-bu-ra-at* [26] *a-wi-lu-ú ma-di-iš ṣú-ur-ru-mu* [27] DUB-*pa-tu-ka ú-ul i-ra-ḫa-nim-ma* [28] *ki-ma a-la-ki-šu-nu* [29] *sí-ik-ka-tam i-ma-ḫa-ṣú* [30] *a-na ì-lí-im-gur-an-ni* DUB-*pa-am ú-ša-bi-il-ma* [31] *me-ḫe-er* DUB-*pí u-ša-bi-lam-ma* [32] *uš-ta-bi-la-ak-kum* [33] [AG]À.ÚS *ša a-na* A.[Š]À-*im ṣa-ba-tim* [34] *[ir]-te-né-ed-du-ni-iš-šu* [35] *it-ti šu-ì-lí-šu i-il-la-ak* [36] DUB-*pa-ka a-na šu-ì-lí-šu li-il-li-kam* [37] *[i]-na* UD.29.KAM ^{d}AMAR.UTU-*na-ṣir aṭ-ru-da-kum* [38] *[i-]na* ITU.GUD.SI.SÁ UD.2.KAM *ra-bu-ut-Sîn*(30) *aṭ-ru-da-kum.*

PNs: *Nūr-Amurrum*: *Marduk-nāṣir; Rabût-Sîn; Mār-erṣetim; Attâ; Ilī-imguranni; Šū-ilīšu.*

[6] *aḫārum* G rare; *uḫḫurum* D 'to be delayed'.

[7] É.DUB.BA = *bīt ṭuppim* 'tablet house, school, archive'; DUMU.É.DUB.BA(.A) = *mār bīt ṭuppim* 'state scribe'; 5 probably goes with *ṭuppātum*.

[8] IKU = *ikûm* (*iku-*; Sum. lw.) measure of area (ca. 3600 m.^{2}); 24 IKU A.ŠÀ = *24 iku eqlim* (gen. here) 'a 24-*ikûm* field'.

[9] *sikkatum* (*sikkat*; pl. *sikkātum*) 'peg'; *sikkatam maḫāṣum* 'to drive in a peg' (to mark limits of ownership.).

[12] *šukūsum* (fem.; *šukūs*; log. A.ŠÀ.ŠUKU) 'subsistence plot/field'.

[14] *ṭupšar ummānim* 'military scribe'.

[18] *šassukkum* (log. SAG.DÙN; Sum. lw.) 'land-registry officer'.

[19] *ašlum* (fem.) 'rope' (here, surveyor's measuring rope).

[20] *Lammayya* a place name.

[23] *nadānum* here, 'to allow'.

[24] *qātātum* (pl. of *qātum*) 'security'; this clause unclear; *ummā-mi* = *umma šunū-ma*.

[25] *kabārum* G (*i*) 'to be(come) fat, heavy, thick'; *kubburum* D factitive.
[26] *ṣarāmum* G (*i*) 'to strive, exert oneself, be concerned'; *ṣurrumum* D=G.
[27] *arāḫum* (*a*) G 'to hasten, come quickly' (cf. *arḫiš*).
[37] UD.29.KAM 'the 29th (of the month)'.
[38] ITU.GUD.SI.SÁ = *(waraḫ) Ayyār(im)* the second month (April–May).

5. Dossin, *ARM* 10 129.

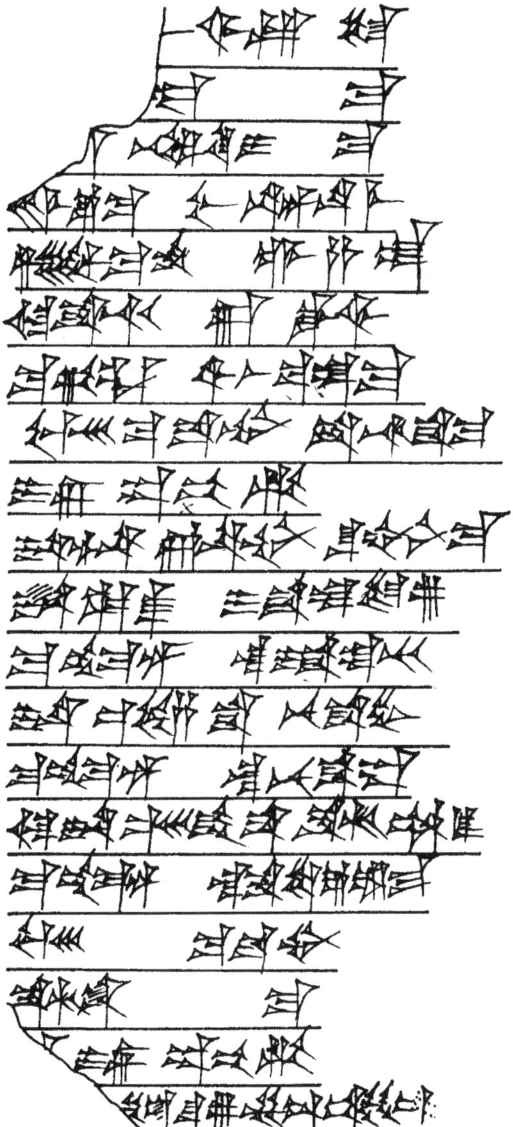

PNs: *Šibtu* (wife of Zimrī-Līm king of Mari); *Nanna*.

1 Restore [*a-na* ^{f}].

3 Restore [*um-m*]*a*.

4 Note that the clause following *šemûm* has the particle of direct speech *-mi* (here written ME = *mì*), as occasionally elsewhere in Mari letters (Durand 1983); see §15.4, end.

9 *sabākum* G (*i*) meaning uncert.; perhaps 'to gather, bring into contact'.

10 *dannātim šakānum* 'to give strong orders' (Mari).

13–14 The BAD sign here has the (relatively rare) value *úš*.

19 Restore [*l*]*a*.

20 Restore at the beginning [*sí-im-m*]*u-*; the last three signs are *-aḫ-ḫi-iz*.

J. Prayer in the form of a letter to the moon god Nanna, a petition for legal redress (*UET* 6/2 402; Gadd, *Iraq* 25 1963 177–80; see also Charpin 1986 326–29; Moran 1993; Foster 1996 1.156–57).

1 ^{d}NANNA LUGAL AN KI *at-ta* 2 *at-ka-al-ku-um-ma* 3 *e-la-lí* DUMU GÌR.NI-Ì.SÀ 4 *iḫ-ta-ab-la-an-ni di-ni di-in* 5 KUG.BABBAR-*am ú-la i-šu-ú-ma* 6 *iṭ-ḫe-a-am i-na ka-ás-pi-ia* 7 *ḫu-bu-li-šu ú-pi-il* 8 *a-na bi-it e-mi-im iš-si* 9 *ma-ra-am ù ma-ar-ta-am ir-ši* 10 *li-bi ú-la ú-ṭì-ib* 11 *ka-ás-pi ša-al-ma-am* 12 *ú-la ú-te-ra-am* 13 *ù na-aš* DUB(! LA)-*pa-ti-šu* 14 *iḫ-ta-ab-la-an-ni* 15 *a-na* ^{d}NANNA *at-ka-al-ma* 16 *i-na ki-ra-tim* 17 *me-eḫ-re-et* É.KIŠ.NU.GÁL 18 *la a-ḫa-ba-lu-ka-ma it-ma* 19 *i-na* KÁ.MAḪ *ša-pa-al* ^{giš}TUKUL 20 *ša ta-ra-mu it-ma* 21 ŠÀ KISAL.MAḪ *me-eḫ-re-et* É.KIŠ.NU.GÁL 22 *me-eḫ-re-et* ^{d}NIN.GAL *ša* É.GA.DI 23 IGI ^{d}NIN-ŠUBUR ŠUR KISAL.MAḪ 24 IGI ^{d}*a-la-mu-uš* 25 IGI ^{d}NANNA.IGI.DU *ù* ^{d}NANNA.Á.DAḪ *it-ma-a-am* 26 *ka-a-ti ù ma-ru-ka* 27 *la a-ḫa-ba-lu-ka-ma it-ma* 28 DINGIR.E.NE *an-nu-tum* 29 *lu ši-bu-ú-a-mi iq-bi* 30 *a-pu-na-ma i-na ki-ra-tim* 31 *me-eḫ-re-et* É.KIŠ.NU.GÁL 32 IGI ^{d}NANNA IGI ^{d}UTU *e-la-lí* 33 *ku-zu-la-am la a-ḫa-ba-lu-ma* 34 IGI ^{d}NANNA IGI ^{d}UTU 35 *a-pi*$_5$(NE)-*il e-la-lí a-a-ib-ši ki-a-am it-ma* 36 *ta-mi* ^{d}NANNA *ù* ^{d}UTU 37 *e-ep-qá-am i-ma-al-la* 38 *i-la-pi-in ù* IBILA *ú-la e-ra-aš-ši* 39 ^{d}NANNA *ù* ^{d}UTU *e-la-lí it-ma-ma* 40 *iḫ-ta-ab-la-an-ni* 41 ^{d}NIN-ŠUBUR LUGAL NÍG.GA *li-zi-iz-ma* 42 ^{d}NANNA *ù* ^{d}UTU *di-ni li-di-nu* 43 *ra-bu-ut* ^{d}NANNA *ù* ^{d}UTU *lu-mu-ur-ma*.

PNs: *Elali*; *Girni-isa*; *Kuzzulum*.

1 ^{d}NANNA (= ŠEŠ.KI) the Sumerian moon god.

7 *uppulum* D (rare) = *apālum* G.

8 *bīt emim* 'wedding, marriage'; *ana bīt emim šasûm* 'to summon to a wedding', i.e., 'to have a wedding'.

[13] *nāš ṭuppātim* 'creditor', in apposition to *-anni*.

[17] *meḫretum* (*meḫret*) 'opposite side'; bound form as preposition, 'in front of, before, opposite' (cf. *maḫārum*); *Ekišnugal* the temple of Nanna at Ur.

[18] The first two words are a direct quote; for *-ma* on the verb see p. 437.

[19] *Kamaḫ* (lit. 'august gate', Akk. *bābum ṣīrum*) one of the entrances to Ekišnugal.

[21] *kisalmaḫḫum* (*kisalmaḫ*; log. KISAL.MAḪ; Sum. lw.) 'main courtyard (of a temple)'.

[22–26] DNs: *Ningal*; *Nin-Šubur*; *Alammuš*; *Nanna-igidu*; *Nanna-adaḫ* (the last two are manifestations of Nanna).

[22] *Egadi* a temple.

[23] ŠUR is uncertain; perhaps for *maṣraḫum* (*maṣraḫ*) an emblem (rare).

[26] *ma-ru-ka* a mistake for *mārīka*.

[28] .E.NE, like MEŠ, marks plurals; it is found only with a small number of words, however.

[33] Kuzzulum is the plaintiff, the speaker of the text.

[37] *epqum* 'leprosy'; *epqam malûm* 'to become covered with leprosy'.

[38] *lapānum* G (*i*) 'to become poor'; Verbal Adj. *lapnum* (*lapun-*; fem. *laputtum*) 'poor'.

[41] *lizziz* 'may he stand forth' (see §37.2).

[43] *-ma* at the end of the text clearly does not function as a conjunction; its precise sense is elusive, but it may mark the end of its clause.

LESSON THIRTY-SEVEN

37.1 The Ntn Stem

Corresponding to the N is the iterative Ntn stem. As is true of the N, the personal prefixes of the Ntn are those of the G (*i-*, *ta-*, *a-*, *ni-*). The theme-vowel in all finite forms is that of the corresponding N Durative (see §31.1). The Ntn Preterite is identical to the N Perfect in form. For reasons that are unclear, some Ntn forms have the same meaning as (or, occur instead of) Gtn forms, i.e., are active rather than passive.

	Sound	**I–*n***	**III–weak**
Infinitive:	*itaprusum*	*itandunum*	*itabnûm*
Durative:	*ittanapras*	*ittanandin*	*ittanabni*
Perfect:	*ittatapras*	*ittatandin*	*ittatabni*
Preterite:	*ittapras*	*ittandin*	*ittabni*
Imperative:	*itapras*	*itandin*	*itabni*
Participle:	*muttaprisum*	*muttandinum*	*muttabnûm*
Verbal Adj.:	*itaprusum*	*itandunum*	*itabnûm*
V. Adj. base:	*itaprus*	*itandun*	*itabnu*

Note that in verbs I-*n*, the *n* of the root is not assimilated.

Verbs **I–ʾ**, as in the N (§32.1(a)), have forms in which the initial radical ʾ is replaced by *n*; in some forms this *n* is assimilated to R_2. Only Durative and Preterite forms of the Ntn stem are attested:

	I–*a*	**I–*e***
Durative:	*ittananḫaz* / *ittanaḫḫaz*	*ittenenpeš* / *itteneppeš*
Preterite:	*ittanḫaz* / *ittaḫḫaz*	*ittenpeš* / *itteppeš*

Ntn forms of verbs **I–*w*** and of verbs **II–weak** are not attested.

37.2 The Irregular Verb *izuzzum*

This verb, which means 'to stand, be standing', was originally a II–*w* verb, *zâzum b (*a*), that appeared primarily in the N stem, thus Durative *izzâz*, Preterite *izzīz* (see §32.1c). A number of the forms were reinterpreted by speakers, and a partly irregular paradigm resulted. In the standard modern grammars and dictionaries of Akkadian, the basic forms are listed as belonging to the G stem (rather than the original N), and vowel length is not indicated before the final radical (thus, Durative *izzaz* rather than *izzâz*, etc.). All forms, regardless of tense, have a doubled final *z* before a vocalic ending, except in the "G" Preterite, where it is optional (more common in later texts), and in the "G" Participle (which has a prefix *mu-*).

G	Infinitive:	*izuzzum* or *uzuzzum*
	Durative:	*izzaz, tazzaz,* 3mp *izzazzū,* etc.
	Perfect:	*ittaziz, tattaziz,* 3mp *ittazizzū,* etc.
	Preterite:	*izziz, tazziz,* 3mp *izziz(z)ū,* etc.
	Imperative:	*iziz,* pl *izizzā*
	Participle:	*muzzizum* or *muzzazum*
	Verbal Adj.:	with 3ms *nazuz,* 3mp *nazuzzū*

Note that *izuzzum* is an *a–i* verb, and that, contrary to expectation, the Perfect has the theme-vowel of the Preterite rather than that of the Durative (cf. D and Š verbs).

Note the byforms of the Participle and of the Infinitive. The G Verbal Adj. *nazuz* is rare, occurring only in the predicative construction and only in literary texts; in prose, the Durative is frequently found where the predicate Verbal Adj. might be expected (referred to in some Akkadian grammars as a "preformative Stative").

Gt	Durative:	*ittazzaz,* 3mp *ittaẓzazzū*
	Preterite:	*ittazaz,* 3mp *ittazazzū*

(Other forms are rare or unattested.)

Gtn	Durative:	*ittanazzaz,* 3mp *ittanazzazzū*
	Preterite:	*ittazzaz,* 3mp *ittazzazū*

(Other forms are rare or unattested.)

Š	Infinitive:	*šuzuzzum*
	Durative:	*ušzaz, tušzaz,* 3mp *ušzazzū*
	Perfect:	*uštaziz, tuštaziz,* 3mp *uštazizzū*
	Preterite:	*ušziz, tušziz,* 3mp *ušzizzū*
	Imperative:	*šuziz,* pl. *šuzizzā*
	Participle:	*mušzizzum*
	Verbal Adj.:	with 3ms *šuzuz,* 3mp *šuzuzzū*

Št Durative: *uštazzaz*
(Other forms are rare or unattested.)

Štn Durative: *uštanazzaz*, 3mp *uštanazzazzū*
(Other forms are rare or unattested.)

(A very rare Infinitive form, *nazzazum* / *nanzazum*, which looks like it belongs to a new **N** stem, also appears in a few OB literary texts.)

EXERCISES

A. VOCABULARY 37.

Verbs:

ḫiāṭum G (*i*) 'to watch over, take care of; to examine, explore, search'.

izuzzum (also *uzuzzum*; Dur. *izzaz*; Pret. *izziz*; see §37.2) 'to stand, be standing; to stand in service; to stand ready, be at (someone's) disposal; to stay'; *ana X izuzzum* 'to answer, be responsible for X; to help X'; *itti X* / *ina rēš X izuzzum* 'to serve X, be in the service of X'; *ana pānī X izuzzum* 'to oversee X, be in charge of X'; Participle *muzzazum* 'attendant' in various compounds, such as *muzzaz bābim* 'tax collector'; Gt (rare) = G; *šuzuzzum* Š 'to cause to stand/serve; to raise, erect, set (up), station'.

qiāpum G (*i*) 'to believe, trust; to entrust (someone with something: double acc.)'; Verbal Adj. *qīpum* (*qīp-*) 'trustworthy, reliable'; N 'to be believed; to be entrusted'.

zenûm G (*e*) 'to be(come) angry'; Verbal Adj. *zenûm* (*zeni-*) 'angry'; *zunnûm* D 'to anger'.

Nouns:

gerrum (masc. and fem.; *gerri*; pl. *gerrū* and *gerrētum*) 'road, path; journey, (business) trip, caravan; military campaign; expeditionary force; travel provisions'.

kurummatum (*kurummat*; log. ŠUKU) 'food (portion, allowance, ration)'.

niṭlum (*niṭil*) 'eyesight; look, gaze; opinion' (cf. *naṭālum*).
nukurtum (also *nikurtum*; bound form *nu / ikurti*; pl. *nukurātum*) 'war; hostility, enmity' (cf. *nakārum*).
ṭūbum (*ṭūb*) 'good(ness), kindness, happiness'; *ṭūb libbim* 'happiness'; pl. *ṭūbātum* 'friendliness; pleasure; voluntariness'; *ina ṭūbātim* 'voluntarily' (cf. *ṭiābum*).

B. Learn the following signs:

OB Lapid.	OB Cursive	NA	values
			PAD (lesson 24); ŠUKU = *kurummatum*

C. Write the following words in cuneiform and in transliteration; use logograms where possible:

1. *kurummat ṣāb Sippar*
2. *igār bīt šakkanakkim*
3. *nūnū ina Purattim imīdū*
4. *libitti bīt Anim*
5. *ina eršīya attīl*
6. *šīr iṣṣūrim*

D. Write in normalized Akkadian:

1. we saw each other (*amārum* N) again and again
2. keep looking (ms; *naplusum*)!
3. they (m) will join each other repeatedly
4. fire will keep breaking out
5. in order to see (*naplusum*) constantly
6. may they (m) turn themselves to me constantly
7. they (f) are standing
8. we have stood here
9. stand (pl)!
10. cause (ms) them (m) to stand!
11. I stood
12. he made it (f) stand

E. CH:

§§185–187 §185 *šum-ma a-wi-lum ṣe-eḫ-ra-am i-na me-e-šu a-na ma-ru-tim il-qé-ma úr-ta-ab-bi-šu tar-bi-tum ši-i ú-ul ib-ba-aq-qar.* §186 *šum-ma a-wi-lum ṣe-eḫ-ra-am a-na ma-ru-tim il-qé i-nu-ma il-qú-ú-šu a-ba-šu ù um-ma-šu i-ḫi-a-aṭ tar-bi-tum ši-i a-na* É *a-bi-šu i-ta-ar.* §187 DUMU *gerseqqêm*(GÌR.SÌ.GA) *mu-za-az* É.GAL *ù* DUMU [mí]ZI.IK.RU.UM *ú-ul ib-ba-aq-qar.*

ina mêšu 'at birth' (lit., 'with its (amniotic) fluid').
tarbītum (*tarbīt*) 'raising, upbringing; foster child, a child brought up' (cf. *rabûm*, D).
gerseqqûm (base *gerseqqā*; log. GÌR.SÌ.GA; Sum. lw.) 'an attendant, domestic (attached to the palace or a temple)'.
sekretum (*sekret*; pl. *sekrētum*; pseudo-log. [mí]ZI.IK.RUM/RU.UM) ' a (cloistered?) woman of high status'.

§253 *šum-ma a-wi-lum a-wi-lam a-na pa-ni* A.ŠÀ-*šu ú-zu-uz-zi-im i-gur-ma aldâm*(AL.DÙ.A-*am*) [*i*]-*qí-ip-šu* [ÁB].GUD.ḪI.A *ip-qí-súm* [*a-na*] A.ŠÀ *e-re-ši-im ú-ra-ak-ki-sú* [*šu*]*m-ma a-wi-lum šu-ú* ŠE. NUMUN *ù lu ukullâm*(ŠÀ.GAL) *iš-ri-iq-ma i-na qá-ti-šu it-ta-aṣ-ba-at ritta*(KIŠIB.LÁ)-*šu i-na-ak-ki-su.*

aldûm (base *aldu-*; log. AL.DÙ(.A); Sum. lw.) 'store of barley'.
ukullûm (*ukullā-*; log. ŠÀ.GAL) 'food allotment, food supply; fodder' (cf. *akālum*).

F. Omens from *YOS* 10:

1. *šum-ma i-na a-mu-tim* 4 *na-ap-la-sà-tum*(! TIM) *iš-te-ni-iš iz-za-az-za na-ak-rum a-na li-ib-bi a-li-i-ka i-te-bé-a-am-ma a-la-ni-i-ka i-ki-im-ma i-ta-ba-al.* (11 i 23–27)
2. [DIŠ ... *it*]-*ta-aṭ-lu i-lu ze-nu-tum a-na ma-t*[*im i*]-*tu-ru-nim.* (17:9)
3. DIŠ *naplaštum*(IGI.BAR) *a-na padānim*(ŠU.BAR) *iq-te-re-eb* DINGIR *ze-nu-um a-na a-wi-lim i-tu-ur-ra.* (17:38)
   For ŠU.BAR = *padānum* see Glassner 2000, Winitzer 2003.
4. *šum-ma mar-tum bu-da-ša da-ma-am bu-ul-la-am pa-aš-ša di-pa-ar ni-ku-ur-tim i-ša-tum i-na ma-tim it-ta-na-an-pa-aḫ.* (31 ix 45–53)
   būdum 'shoulder'.
   bullûm meaning uncertain.
   dipārum 'torch'.
5. DIŠ *warkat*(EGIR) *ḫašîm*(UR$_5$) *it-te-en$_6$*(IN)-*mi-id sa-li-mu-*[*um*] *iš-ša-ka-an.* (36 iii 28)
   ḫašûm (*ḫaši-*; log. UR$_5$ [the ḪAR sign]) 'lung'.
   salīmum (*salīm*) 'peace, concord'.
6. BE *i-na* SAG MUŠEN *i-na imittim*(Á.ZI) *su-mu«-um» iš-tu* 3 *a-di* 6 *it-ta-aš-ka-nu e-ri-iš-ti ni-qí-im ša bi-it ṣa-bi.* (52 i 3–5)
   iṣṣūrum here part of the liver.
   sūmum (*sūm(i)*; pl. *sūmū*) 'redness; red spot'.
   erištum (*erišti*) 'wish, desire, request' (cf. *erēšum*).

7. DIŠ *iz-bu-um pa-ni i-ṣú-ri-im le-mu-*[*tim*] *ša-ki-in ma-tum ši-i su-un-qá-am i-mar* LÚ.KÚR-*ša e-li-ša it-ta-za-az.* (56 i 28–30)
   sunqum 'famine'.

8. Text 1, complete; inscribed on a clay liver model.

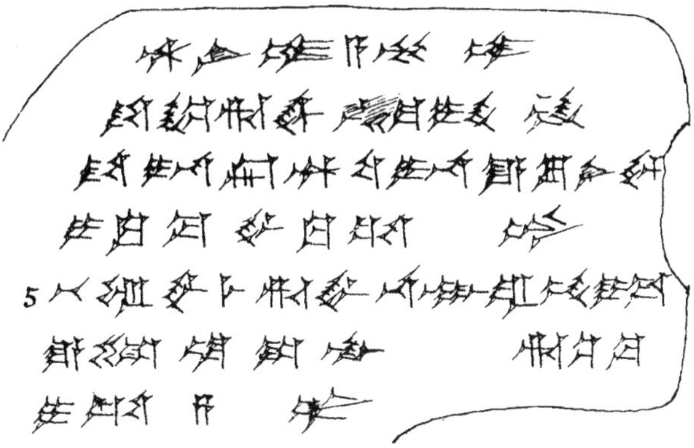

[2] *Sîn-iddinam* king of Larsa, 1849–43.

[3] *Elūnum*, also *Elūlum* (later *Ulūlu*) the sixth month (Aug.–Sept.).

[4] The first three signs are probably to be read I.DÍB.BA (with KU = DÍB) = *askuppum* or *askuppatum*, both '(stone) slab, doorsill, threshold'; another possibility is *i-qú-ma* (*naqûm*).

[5–6] The last three signs of line 6 follow the end of line 5; *darāsum* G (*i*) 'to trample upon, throw over, back'; *la ša-tim* see §25.3.

9. 31 xiii 36–41:

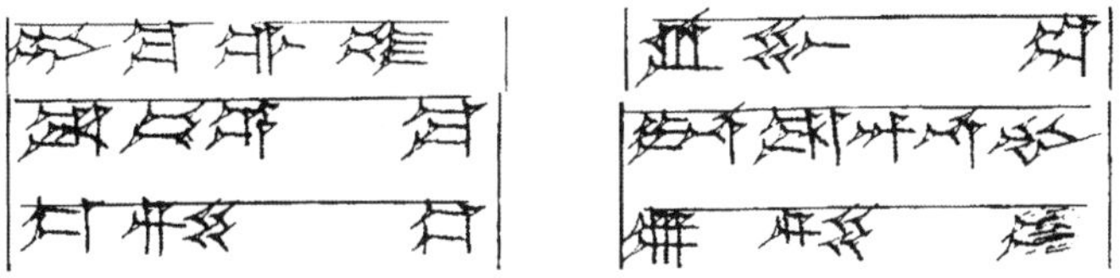

G. Contract:

1. Lease of sheep and goats (Szlechter, *Tablettes* 97 MAH 16.139).

[1–5] Numbers of various types of sheep and goats [6] *napḫarum*(ŠU.NIGIN) 36 U8.UDU.ḪI.A [7] *ša ib-ni-*^{d}URAŠ [8] *a-na a-ḫa-nir-ši* SIPAD [9] *pa*!*-aq-da* [10] *a-na pí-sà-tim* [11] *ù ḫa-li-iq-tim* [12] *i-za-az.* [13–15] Witnesses. [16–20] Date.

PNs: *Ibni-Uraš*; *Aḫa-niršī*.

[10] *pissûm* (or *pessûm*; base *pissa-*) 'lame?'.

H. Letters:

1. Waterman, *Business Documents of the Hammurapi Period* (1916) no. 32, p. 79 = Kraus, *AbB* 1 102.

(No salutation.) [1] *iš-tu* ITU.SIG$_4$.A [2] *aš-šum ṣe-eḫ-ḫe-ru-ti-ia i-ta-ap-lu-si-im* [3] *ú-na-á*ʾ*-*ʾ*ì-id-ka* [4] UD.4.KAM *a-di i-na-an-na* [5] *ṭe*$_4$*-em ši-ip-ra-tim ma-la i-pu-šu* [6] *ù* A.ŠÀ ŠE.GIŠ.Ì *ša i-pu-šu ú-ul ta-aš-pu-ra-am* [7] ^{I}*na-bi-*^{d}EN.ZU *a-na* KÁ.DINGIR.RA^{ki} *i-li-a-am-ma* [8] *ṭe*$_4$*-em-ka ri-qá-am ú-ul ta-aš-pu-ra-am* [9] *i-na-an-na na-bi-*^{d}EN.ZU [10] *a-na ma-aḫ-ri-ka aṭ-ṭar-dam* [11] *it-ti-šu a-na* A.ŠÀ *ri-id-ma* [12] A.ŠÀ *ši-ip-ra-tim ma-la i-pu-šu* [13] *ù* A.ŠÀ ŠE.GIŠ.Ì *ša i-pu-šu* [14] *i-ta-ap-la-ás-ma* [15] *i-na* DUB-*pí-ka pa-nam šu-ur-ši-a-am-ma* [16] *šu-up-ra-am* [17] *lu-uš-pu-ra-ak-kum-ma* [18] ŠE-*um a-na* ŠUKU *ṣe-eḫ-ḫe-ru-tim* [19] *ù* DUḪ DURU$_5$ *a-na* ŠÀ.GAL GUD.ḪI.A *li-in-na-di-in* [20] ^{I}*tak-la-ku-a-na-*^{d}AMAR.UTU [21] *it-ti na-bi-*^{d}EN.ZU *a-na* KÁ.DINGIR.RA^{ki} [22] *ṭú-ur-dam.*

PNs *Nabi-Sîn; Taklāku-ana-Marduk.*

[1] ITU.SIG$_4$.A = *Simānum* the third month (May-June).

[2] *ṣeḫḫerum* = *ṣeḫrum.*

[19] DUḪ = *ṭuḫḫum* (usu. pl. *tuḫḫū*) 'scraps, bran'; DURU$_5$ = *raṭbum* (*raṭub-*) 'moist'; ŠÀ.GAL = *ukkulûm* (*-ā*) 'food, fodder' (cf. *akālum*).

2. *TLB* 4 pl. 2 LB 1864 = Frankena, *AbB* 3 2.

[1] *a-na a-wi-il-*IŠTAR *qí-bí-ma* [2] *um-ma* ^{I}NIN.SI$_4$.AN.NA-MA.AN.SUM-*ma* [3] ^{d}UTU *ù* ^{d}AMAR.UTU *da-ri-iš* UD-*mi li-ba-al-li-ṭú-ka* [4] *aš-šum ṣú-ḫa-ri-ia ša qá-ti* ^{I}*be-ta-a* [5] ^{I}*be-ta-a ig-re-e aš-šum* GEME$_2$ *aš-šu-mi-ia-li-ib-lu-uṭ* [6] *di-ib-ba-tum ma-at-tum i-li-a-am-ma* [7] ^{I}*be-ta-a i-di* DUMU.MEŠ-*ša i-da-ab-bu-um-ma* [8] *pa-ni-ia ú-da-an-ni-in-ma pa-ni-ša ú-ul ú-bi-il* [9] *ki-ma ni-iṭ-li-ia it-ti-ša ad-bu-ub* [10] *ki-a-am aq-bi-ši-im um-ma a-na-ku-ú-ma* [11] *a-ḫu-ni ṣe-eḫ-rum aš-ša-tam ú-ul a-ḫi-iz-ma* [12] ^{I}*sag-gi-ia a-bu-ni aš-ša-tam ú-ša-ḫi-is-sú* [13] *i-na-an-na* DUMU.MEŠ-*šu ib-ta-aq-ru-ni-a-ti* [14] *šum-ma da-ba-bu-um an-nu-ú-um la ṭa-ba-ak-ki-im-ma* [15] DUMU.MEŠ-*ki i-na ta-*ʾ*i-iš-ti-ki la i-da-ab-bu-bu* [16] *at-ti-ma la ta-da-ab-bu-bi-ma* [17] *a-na pa-ni-ki la tu-uš-za-az-zi-ni-[a-t]i* [18] *ni-nu ù* DUMU.MEŠ-*ki a-na* DI.KUD.MEŠ *i ni-is-ni-iq* [19] *a-wa-ti-ni li-mu-ru-ma* [20] *šum-ma ša sag-gi-ia i-qí-ša-an-ni-a-ši-im* [21] DUMU.MEŠ-*šu le-qú-ú-um ka-ši-id* [22] DI.KUD.MEŠ *i-qá-ab-bu-ni-a-ši-im-ma* [23] GEME$_2$ *nu-ta-a-ar i-na a-wa-a-tim* [24] *ú-us-sí-ir-ši-ma* [25] *a-na la da-ba-bi-im a-an-nam uš-ta-as-sí-ši* [26] *mi-im-ma la ta-na-az-zi-iq* [27] *ki-ma la na-za-qí-ka e-ep-pu-uš* [28] *ù* ^{d}AMAR. UTU-*mu-ša-lim is-sà-an-qá-am* [29] *ṭe*$_4$*-ma-am an-ni-a-am ma-aḫ-ri-šu a-ša-ak-ka-an* [30] *ù at-ta ar-ḫi-iš at-la-kam-ma*

31 *la-ma* ^{d}AMAR. UTU-*mu-ša-lim a-ii-i-ša-am-ma iš-ta-ap-r*[*u*] 32 *i ni-ig-mu-ur-ši-na-ti* 33 *ki-ma ti-du-ú na-pí-iš-tam ú-ul i-šu* 34 *i-na ṭú-bi-ia uš-ta-ma-ar-ra-aṣ-ma* 35 4 IKU Ú.SAL *ša a-na i-di-ka e-ep-pé-eš* 36 *ki-ma ti-du-ú* A.ŠÀ-*um e-pé-ši* 37 *ù a-na* É.DURU$_5$ *ga-bi-ba*^{ki} *qé-re-bi* 38 *a-na ì-lí-šu-ul-li-ma-an-ni ú-ul ṭa-ab-ma* 39 *ú-še-pí-ša-an-ni-ma* 1 IKU A.ŠÀ 40 *a-na ip-qú-*^{d}*ša-la ad-di-in* 41 *i-na ṭú-ba-tim-ma* A.ŠÀ-*am šu-a-ti* 42 *la e-pé-ša-am* ^{I}*ip-qú-*^{d}*ša-la šu-ud-ki* 43 *ri-ip-qa-ti-šu šu-du-ud-ma* 44 *ša ma-na-ḫa-ti-šu a-na-ku a-ap-pa-al-šu* 45 *ki-ma a-na-ku e-ep-pé-šu qí-bi-šum* 46 *šum-ma ni-ṭì-il-šu qá-qá-dam* 47 *ša še-pi-it* Ú.SAL *ša te-pu-šu li-pu-uš* 48 4 IKU A.ŠÀ *šu-a-ti ú-ul tu-ša-ad-da* 49 *ú-ul tu-še-pé-ša-an-ni-ma* 50 *it-ti-ka e-ze-en-ne* 51 *šum-ma i-na ki-na-tim ta-ra-am-ma-an-ni la tu-uš-ta-ʾa*$_4$*-ma* 52 *li-ib-bi la i-ma-ar-ra-ṣa-ak-kum* 53 A.ŠÀ-*am šu-a-ti i-na qá-tim ki-il-la-aš-šu-ma* 54 *la a-na-az-zi-iq* 55 *ṭe*$_4$*-em-*{*x-*}*ka* 56 *šu-up-ra-am.*

PNs: *Awīl-Ištar; Ninsianna-mansum; Betâ* (fem.); *Aššumīya-libluṭ; Saggīya; Marduk-mušallim; Ilī-šullimanni; Ipqu-Šala.*

6 *dibbatum* 'dispute' (cf. *dabābum*).

15 *taʾis/štum* 'decrease, loss'.

20–21 'If it is fitting (*kašid*) for his sons to take what PN gave us ...'.

25 *annum* 'consent, approval; positive answer'; *annam* (adv. acc.) 'yes'.

31 *ayyīšam-ma* (adverb) 'somewhere, elsewhere'.

35 Ú.SAL = *ušallum* (Sum. lw.) 'shore-land, water-meadow'.

37 É.DURU$_5$ = *kaprum* 'village'; *Gabiba* a place name.

42 *šudkûm* (Š of *dekûm*) here 'to persuade' (rare).

43 *ripqum* 'dug-up land' (?).

44 *mānaḫtum* (*mānaḫti*; pl. *mānaḫātum*) 'toil, upkeep, repairs'.

47 *šēpītum* (*šēpīt*) 'lower part, end, foot' (cf. *šēpum*).

49–50 An unmarked conditional clause.

3. *UCP* 9/4 p. 329 no. 4 = Stol, *AbB* 11 168.

1 *a-na a-wi-lim* 2 *qí-bí-ma* 3 *um-ma zi-nu-ú-ma* 4 ^{d}UTU *ù* ^{d}NIN. ŠUBUR 5 *aš-šum-ia a-na da-ri-a-tim* 6 *li-ba-al-li-ṭú-ka* 7 *aš-šum* A.ŠÀ ŠE.GIŠ.Ì 8 *ša* AŠ.DUB.BA^{ki} 9 *ma-am-ma-an ú-ul ta-aš-ku-um-ma* 10 ŠE. GIŠ.Ì *im-ma-ša-a*ʾ 11 ^{Id}ŠUL.PA.È-*na-ṣir* 12 *ṭù-ur-dam-ma* 13 ŠE.GIŠ.Ì *li-iṣ-ṣú-ur-ma* 14 *la* [*i*]*-ḫa-li-*⌜*iq*?⌝ 15 *bi-tum ša-li-im* 16 *šu-lu*(! KU)*-um-ka šu-up-ra-am* 17 *li-ib-bi la it-te-né-eḫ-*[*p*]*e.*

PNs: *Zinû; Šulpae-nāṣir.*

4 *Nin-Šubur* DN.

8 *Ašdubba* a place name.

10 *mašāʾum* G (*a–u*; third radical ʾ atypically preserved) 'to take by force, rob, plunder'.

4. Schroeder, *VAS* 16 136 = Frankena, *AbB* 6 136.

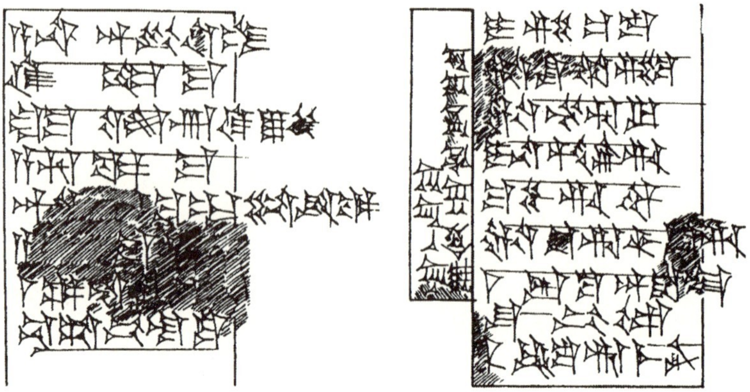

PNs: *Nannatum; Sippar-lūmur* PN; [...]*ḫulum; Ipqu-Šala; Sîn-rēmēnī.*

1 ^{d}ŠEŠ+KI = ^{d}NANNA (Sumerian moon god).

5 At the beginning, restore ^{d}U[TU *l*]*i-ba-* .

6 Read *a-*[*nu-um*]*-ma* [*x*]*-ḫu-lu-um*, the last three signs of the PN missed by the copyist.

7 Read 1 SAG.ÌR ^{l}[^{ú}TÚG]; ^{lú}TÚG (TÚG = KU) = *ašlākum* (*ašlāk*; pl. *ašlākū*) 'fuller, washerman'.

14 Last two signs: *ip-ri*.

18 *laššu* '(there) is/are not; is/are not here' (cf. *lā, išûm*).

I. A Royal Inscription of Ḫammurapi: commemoration of the digging of a canal called "Ḫammurapi-is-the-abundance-of-the-people" (King, *LIH* 1 95 = Frayne, *RIME* 4, p. 341–42).

1 *ḫa-am-mu-ra-pí* 2 LUGAL *da-núm* 3 LUGAL KÁ.DINGIR.RA^{ki} 4 LUGAL *mu-uš-te-eš-mi* 5 *ki-ib-ra-tim ar-ba-im* 6 *ka-ši-id ir-ni-ti* 7 ^{d}AMAR.UTU 8 SIPAD *mu-ṭi-ib* 9 *li-ib-bi-šu a-na-ku* 10 *ì-nu* AN *ù* ^{d}EN. LÍL 11 KALAM *šu-me-rí-im* 12 *ù ak-ka-di-im* 13 *a-na be-li-im id-di-nu-nim* 14 *ṣe-er-ra-sí-na* 15 *a-na qá-ti-ia* 16 *u-ma-al-lu-ú* 17 ÍD *ḫa-am-mu-ra-pí-nu-ḫu-uš-ni-ši* 18 *ba-bi-la-at me-e* ḪÉ.GÁL 19 *a-na* KALAM *šu-me-rí-im* 20 *ù ak-ka-di-im lu eḫ-re* 21 *ki-ša-di-ša ki-la-le-en* 22 *a-na me-re-šim lu u-te-er* 23 *ka-re-e áš-na-an* 24 *lu aš-tap-pa-ak* 25 *me-e da-ru-tim* 26 *a-na* KALAM *šu-me-rí-im* 27 *ù ak-ka-di-im lu aš-ku-un* 28 KALAM *šu-me-rí-im* 29 *ù ak-ka-di-im* 30 *ni-ši-šu-nu sa*$_{6}$*-ap-ḫa-tim* 31 *lu u-pa-aḫ-ḫe-er* 32 *mé-ri-tam ù ma-aš-qí-tam* 33 *lu aš-ku*(! LU)*-un-ši-na-ši-im* 34 *in nu-uḫ-šim ù* ḪÉ.GÁL 35 *lu e-re-ši-na-ti* 36 *šu-ba-at ne-eḫ-tim* 37 *lu u-še-ši-ib-ši-na-ti* 38 *ì-nu-mi-šu* 39 *ḫa-am-*

mu-ra-pí [40] LUGAL *da-núm* [41] *mi-gi-ir* DINGIR.GAL.GAL *a-na-ku* [42] *in e-mu-qé-en ga-aš-ra-tim* [43] *ša* ^{d}AMAR.UTU *id-di-nam* [44] BÀD *ṣi-ra-am* [45] *in e-pe-ri ra-bu-tim* [46] *ša* ⸢*re*⸣*-ša-šu-nu* [47] *ki-ma šadîm*(SA.DÚ-*im*) *e-li-a* [48] *in* KA ÍD *ḫa-am-mu-ra-pí-*⸢*nu-ḫu*⸣*-uš-ni-ši* [49] *lu* ⸢*e*⸣*-pu-uš* [50] BÀD ⸢*šu*⸣*-a-ti* [51] BÀD ⸢^{d}EN.ZU-*mu*⸣*-ba-lí-it*^{ki} [52] ⸢*a-bi*⸣*-im wa-li-di-ia* [53] ⸢*a-na*⸣ *šu-mi-im lu ab-bi* [54] ⸢*zi-kir*⸣ ^{d}⸢EN.ZU⸣*-mu-ba-lí-iṭ* [55] *a-bi-im wa-li-di-ia* [56] *in ki-ib-ra-tim* [57] *lu u-*⸢*še-pi*⸣.

6 *irnittum* (or *ernettum;* bound form *irnitti*) 'victory, triumph'.

10 *inu* poetic for *inūma.*

14 *ṣerretum* (*ṣerret;* pl. *ṣerrētum*) 'nose-rope, halter, lead-rope'.

17 *nuḫšum* (*nuḫuš*) 'abundance, plenty'; *Ḫammurapi-nuḫuš-nišī* is the name of the canal.

21 Here and in l. 42, *-ēn* for the dual gen.-acc. ending (or, read EN as in_4, a value not generally recognized for OB).

22 *mērešum* (*mēreš*) 'cultivated land, cultivation' (cf. *erēšum* b).

23 *karûm* (*karā-*; pl. *karû;* Sum. lw.) 'barley pile (for storage)'; *ašnan* (normally without a case-ending; fem.) 'grain, cereal'

32 *merītum* (or *mirītum*, also *merʾītum*) 'pasture(-land)' (cf. *reʾûm*); *mašqītum* (*mašqīt;* pl. *mašqiātum*) 'irrigation outlet, watering place'.

36 *nēḫtum* 'peace, security'; *šubat nēḫtim šūšubum* 'to let (someone) dwell in security'.

38 *inūmīšu* (adverb) 'at that time, then', used in royal inscriptions as a correlative of *inu*: 'when ..., at that time ...'.

42 For *emūqēn*, see on l. 21; *gašārum* G (*i*) 'to become powerful, strong'; Verbal Adj. *gašrum* (*gašer-*) 'powerful, strong'.

45 *eperum, eprum* (*eper;* often pl. *ep(e)rū*) 'dust, (loose) earth'.

51–52 These lines are the name of the wall.

53 *ana šumim nabûm* 'to name'.

LESSON THIRTY-EIGHT

38.1 Quadriradical Verbs

It was noted in §3.1 that a few roots have four radicals. With rare exception, these do not occur in the G stem, but have instead the N as their basic stem; causatives are formed with the Š stem, and the iterative Ntn and Štn stems are also attested. Most have either *l* or *r* as their second radical. A quadriradical of fairly high frequency is

nabalkutum N (*a*) 'to jump, to rebel'; *šubalkutum* Š causative.

Quadriradical roots in which the last radical is weak, i.e., verbs IV–weak, are also attested. As expected, in verbs IV–*e*, *a*-vowels become *e*. Examples:

naparkûm N (*u*) 'to cease, stop working';
neḫelṣûm N (*e*) 'to slip'; *šuḫelṣûm* Š causative.

N Stem	Sound	IV–*u*	IV–*e*
Infinitive:	*nabalkutum*	*naparkûm*	*neḫelṣûm*
Durative:	*ibbalakkat*	*ipparakku*	*iḫḫeleṣṣe*
Perfect:	*ittabalkat*	*ittaparku*	*itteḫelṣe*
Preterite:	*ibbalkit*	*ipparki*	*iḫḫelṣi*
Imperative:	*nabalkit*	*naparki*	*neḫelṣi*
Participle:	*mubbalkitum*	*mupparkûm*	*muḫḫelṣûm*
Verbal Adj.:	*nabalkutum*	*naparkûm*	*neḫelṣûm*
V. Adj. base:	*nabalkut*	*naparku*	*neḫelṣu*

Š Stem	Sound	IV–*u*	IV–*e*
Infinitive:	*šubalkutum*	*šuparkûm*	*šuḫelṣûm*
Durative:	*ušbalakkat*	*ušparakka*	*ušḫeleṣṣe*
Perfect:	*uštabalkit*	*uštaparki*	*ušteḫelṣi*
Preterite:	*ušbalkit*	*ušparki*	*ušḫelṣi*
Imperative:	*šubalkit*	*šuparki*	*šuḫelṣi*
Participle:	*mušbalkitum*	*mušparkûm*	*mušḫelṣûm*
Verbal Adj.:	*šubalkutum*	*šuparkûm*	*šuḫelṣûm*
V. Adj. base:	*šubalkut*	*šuparku*	*šuḫelṣu*

Ntn Stem

Infinitive:	*itablakkutum*		
Durative:	*ittanablakkat*	Imperative:	?
Perfect:	*ittatablakkat*	Participle:	*muttablakkitum*
Preterite:	*ittab(a)lakkat*		

Štn Stem

Infinitive:	*šutablakkutum*		
Durative:	*uštanablakkat*	Imperative:	?
Perfect:	*uštatablakkit*$^{?}$	Participle:	?
Preterite:	*uštablakkit*		

The irregular verb *mēlulum* 'to play' is derived from a quadriradical root II–weak (itself derived from a noun with prefix *ma-*, from a root ʾ$_3$–*l*–*l*, originally **ḫ*–*l*–*l*). Forms of this verb that have prefixes (Durative, Preterite, and Participle attested) are conjugated as though N stem forms of a verb **melēlum* (cf. the N as the basic form of other quadriradicals, above); forms without prefixes (Infinitive, Imperative), however, begin with the initial radical *m*:

Infinitive:	*mēlulum*		
Durative:	*immellel*, 3mp *immellelū*	Imperative:	*mēlil*
Perfect:	?	Participle:	*mummellum*
Preterite:	*immelil*, 3mp *immellū*	bound form:	*mummelil*

Note also the following iterative form:

Durative: *ittenemlel* (AbB 10 55:22).

38.2 Special Features of Geminate Verbs

Geminate verbs are those in which the second and third radicals are identical. The only unusual feature noted about such verbs thus far is the base of the Verbal Adjective of stative verbs: whereas the Verbal Adj. of an active verb such as *madādum* is regular, *madid-* 'measured', that of a stative verb, such as *danānum*, has no vowel between R_2 and R_3, *dann-* 'strong'.

Certain geminate roots in which the second and third radicals are *l* or *r* have N stem forms that differ from those of other verbs. In particular, the Infinitive and Verbal Adj. have the middle radical doubled, and all forms with prefixes (Durative, Perfect, Preterite, and Participle) have the third radical doubled before vocalic endings (cf. *izuzzum*, §37.2). Imperative forms of these verbs are not attested. Forms of *nagarrurum* N 'to roll around':

Infinitive:	*nagarrurum*	Imperative:	—
Durative:	*iggarrar*, 3mp *iggarrarrū*	Participle:	*muggarirrum*
Perfect:	*ittagrar*, 3mp *ittagrarrū*	bound form:	*muggarir*
Preterite:	*iggarir*, 3mp *iggarirrū*	Verbal Adj.:	*nagarrurum*

Iteratives of these verbs are conjugated like other Ntn verbs (§37.1).

Causatives of the roots described in the preceding paragraph may also have the middle radical doubled in the Infinitive and Verbal Adj. (*šugarrurum* 'to roll (trans.)'), but also in forms with prefixes, as in Pret. *ušgarrir* (for expected *ušagrir*); all such examples may be classified as ŠD forms, for which see the next section.

38.3 Rare Stems: ŠD; Nt; R; others

In addition to the G, D, Š, and N stems (and their *-t-* and *-tan-* forms) a number of other verbal stems are attested; each is of limited or rare occurrence.

(a) The ŠD Stem

In form the ŠD stem combines the features of both the Š and the D, namely, a prefixed *š* and doubled middle radical. For most roots the occurrence of the ŠD stem is restricted to literary texts, where it may replace either the D or the Š stem, apparently for poetic effect. Attested forms are the following:

Infinitive:	*šuparrusum*		
Durative:	*ušparras*	Imperative:	—
Perfect:	—	Participle:	*mušparrisum*
Preterite:	*ušparris*	Verbal Adj.:	—

As noted above under §38.2, causative forms of certain geminate roots in which the second and third radicals are *l* or *r* are conjugated like ŠD verbs; they are not restricted to literary texts, however. (The verbs *šugarrurum* 'to roll' and *šuparrurum* 'to spread out (trans.)' are listed as such separately in *AHw*.)

Two common verbs that may be noted here are *šukênum* 'to bow down, prostrate oneself' and *šupêlum* 'to change, exchange'. In dialects of Akkadian that are phonologically more conservative than OB, these verbs are conjugated as though ŠD forms of roots II–ʾ (Infin. *šukaʾʾunum* or *šukeʾʾunum*; Pret. *uškaʾʾin*; Participle *muškaʾʾinum*). In OB, however, the medial ʾ has been lost, and their conjugation is reminiscent of the simple Š stem of verbs II–ʾ (cf. §29.1(b)), except for the Infinitive. The verb *šupêlum* also occurs in a passive *-t-* stem.

Infinitive:	*šukênum*	*šupêlum*	[*šut(e)pêlum*?]
Durative:	*uškên*	*ušpêl*	*uštepêl*
3mp:	*uškennū*	*ušpellū*	*uštepellū*
Perfect:	—	*uštepēl* / *uštepīl*	—
3mp:	—	*uštep*ē/ī*lū*	—
Preterite:	*uškēn* / *uškīn*	*ušpēl* / *ušpīl*	[*uštepēl* / *uštepīl*]
3mp:	*uškēnū* / *uškīnū*	*ušpēlū* / *ušpīlū*	[*uštepēlū* / *uštepīlū*]
Imperative:	?	?	?
Participle:	*muškēnum* / *muškīnum*	*mušpēlum* / *mušpīlum*	
Verbal Adj.:	—	—	—

(b) The Nt Stem

An Nt stem probably occurs for a few verbs, mostly in later dialects; OB examples are rare. Attested forms of the Nt are identical to corresponding Ntn forms (Durative forms are not attested). The meaning is

reciprocal in some cases, such as the Nt of *emēdum* 'to join one another';

separative in the Nt of the N verb of motion *naprušum* 'to fly', Nt 'to fly away', Ntn 'to fly around' (cf. the separative Gt for G verbs of motion);

similar to the Gt in the Nt of *zakārum* (i.e., 'to speak').

(c) The R Stem

A few verbs occur in a stem in which the third radical is reduplicated, called the R stem (following Whiting 1981). As in the N, the prefixes of finite forms are those of the G verb (*i-*, *ta-*, *a-*, *ni-*). The following paradigm may be pieced together from attested forms of this stem:

Infinitive:	*parusisum* or *parususum*, as in *namušišum*, *šaḫururum* later *purassusum*, as in *šuḫarrurum*
Durative:	*iprassas*, as in *išḫarrar* (later *ušḫarrar*, 3mp *ušḫarrarrū*)
Perfect:	*iptarsas*, as in *ittamšaš* (root *n–m–š*; later *uštaqallil*)
Preterite:	*iprasis*, as in *išqalil* (later *ušqallil*, 3mp *ušqallil(l)ū*)
Imperative:	(later *šuqammim*)
Participle:	?
Verbal Adj.:	*parussum* (also *par*i/u*sisum*; later *purassusum*)
V.Adj.+3ms:	*parus* (also *parusis*, *parusus*; later *purassus*)
+ 3fs:	*parussat*

The R stem was no longer productive by the OB period; only the following verbs have finite forms in this stem in OB:

> *namušušum* R (lexical texts only) 'to die'; cf. *namāšum* G 'to move';
> *šaḫururum* R 'to be(come) completely inactive, paralyzed (with fear)';
> **šaqululum* R 'to become suspended, hang'; cf. *šaqālum* G 'to hang, weigh';
> **šaqumumum* R 'to become completely still, silent'.

Already in OB, and more commonly in later dialects, the last three of these were reanalyzed as ŠD forms of geminate roots (*ḫ–r–r*, *q–l–l*, *q–m–m*), and finite forms were provided with the *u-*, *tu-* set of prefixes. Unlike in other ŠD verbs, however, the final radical of these was doubled before a vocalic ending in the Durative and (probably) Preterite.

A few other roots exhibit the Verbal Adjective of this stem (not all occur in OB):

> *daʾummum* 'dark, gloomy' (cf. *daʾāmum* 'to become dark');
> *nawurrum* 'brilliant, bright' (cf. *nawārum* 'to shine, be bright');
> *rašubbum* 'glowing, fearsome' (cf. *rašābum* 'to glow');
> *šalummum* 'brilliantly radiant'.

As suggested by the examples cited here, the R stem connotes an intensification of the meaning of the root. Many of the forms express qualities of deities or other numinous qualities; **šaqululum*, however, appears to provide a passive or intransitive sense of the corresponding G verb.

(d) Forms with Reduplicated Middle Radicals

A very small number of verbs are written with an extra CV-sign that reduplicates the middle radical. Examples of G, D, and Š verbs, and of some of the *-t-* and *-tan-* stems of these, are attested. They all exhibit the insertion, before R_2 in the unaugmented form (G, Gtn, Dt, etc.), of -R_2*a*-; examples of G forms are:

> *i-ša-pa-ap-pa-ar-né-ti* (Mari) 'he will command us' (*šapārum*);
> *la ta-na-za-zi-iq* (Mari) 'do not worry (ms)' (*nazāqum*);

It is not clear whether these rare examples are to be interpreted as grammatically acceptable forms (if so, they may be labelled Gr, Gtnr, Dr, Dtr, Šr, etc., stems, although other grammars and *AHw* use other sigla, including simply R, which has been reserved here for the stem with reduplicated R_3; see under (c)), or whether most are scribal errors (in the first example above, the first *pa* erroneously written by a scribe who intended to indicate the doubling of the middle consonant, and so wrote *-ap-pa-*, but forgot to erase the first *pa*; in the second example, *za* for intended *az*, i.e., a CV sign for VC, a not-uncommon error).

A few "Dtr" forms, i.e., Dt verbs with reduplicated middle radicals, seem unlikely to be scribal errors. These occur in the Durative, Preterite, and Imperative; the contextual meanings of the forms indicate that the Dtr serves as a reflexive and reciprocal of the D.

Dur. *nuttamamma* 'we will adjure one another' (*tamûm*);
Pret. *ša ... nuktalallimu* 'which ... we showed to one another' (*kullumum*);
nīš ilī uzzakakkirū (Mari) 'they (m) adjured one another' (*zakārum*);
ūtelelli 'it raised itself' (*elûm*; in dictionaries under Infin. *utlellûm*);
Impv. *utlelli* 'be raised!' (*elûm*; in dictionaries under Infin. *utlellûm*).

38.4 OB Myths and Epics

Of the OB works of narrative literature, unfortunately much more remains lost than has been recovered. Fewer than a dozen myths and epics are attested, and none of these is complete. Most also exist in a later version or versions (in Standard Babylonian; see Appendix D), which allow a fuller understanding of the plot; most may also be related to earlier Sumerian literary works. The following is an incomplete list of attested OB myths and epics.

Anzû: The bird-god Anzû steals the 'tablets of destiny' (or 'decrees': *ṭuppāt šīmātim*) from Enlil, throwing the universe into disarray; a champion god — Ningirsu in the OB version (from Susa), Ninurta in the SB version — must defeat Anzû. (Pritchard, *ANET*³ 111ff., 514ff.)

Atraḫasīs, in OB *Atram-ḫasīs* (for *watram-ḫasīs* 'pre-eminent in understanding'; see §31.3, end): A three-tablet myth detailing the creation of humanity and the origin of various human customs, divine irritation at the noise created by the ever-increasing number of people, the sending of plagues and finally a great flood, and the rescue of Atra-ḫasīs by the god Ea. An exemplary edition, *Atra-Ḫasīs: the Babylonian Story of the Flood*, with introduction, transliteration, translation, notes, and a glossary, was published in 1969 by W. G. Lambert and A. R. Millard (Oxford).

Etana: Etana, a king who longs for a son (and dynasty), rides an eagle to heaven on a quest for the plant of birth. (Pritchard, *ANET*³ 114ff., 517ff.)

Gilgameš: The king of Uruk, Gilgameš, oppresses his people and in response to their cries the gods send an equal, Enkidu, as a companion to Gilgameš. The two share adventures until Enkidu falls ill and dies. Gilgameš mourns bitterly, and then begins a quest for eternal life. The second tablet of the OB version of Gilgameš appears as Supplementary Reading immediately following this Lesson.

Girra and Elamatum. Only the last of seven tablets is preserved, in a recently-published OB version. (Walker 1983.)

An underworld myth about *Ereškigal and Ningišzidda,* known only from one OB text from Ur. (Gadd, *UET* 6 no. 398.)

A fragmentary myth about the birth and youth of *Sîn.* (Römer 1966.)

EXERCISES

A. VOCABULARY 38.

Verbs:

garārum G (also *qarārum; u*) 'to roll, turn over; to twist, grow crooked'; *šugarrurum* irregular Š(D) (§§38.2, 38.3(a)) 'to roll' (trans.); *nagarrurum* irregular N (§38.2) 'to roll around, move'.

naʾarrurum N (*a*; see §38.2; the ʾ is usually strong, the *n* of the N stem is often not assimilated: Pret. *iʾʾarir* or *inʾarir*, pl. as described in §38.2 *inʾarirrū* or like other N verbs *inʾarrū* / *iʾʾarrū*) 'to come to help'.

nabalkutum N (*a*) 'to cross, pass (over); to slip out of place, change sides, allegiance; to rebel (against: acc.); to turn over, around'; *šubalkutum* Š causative; also, 'to overthrow'.

naparkûm N (IV–*u*) 'to stop, cease (doing: *ana* / *ina* + Infinitive); to fail, leave'.

neḫelṣûm N (IV–*e*) 'to slip, slide, glide'; *šuḫelṣûm* Š causative.

**šaqululum* (*šuqallulum*) R 'to hang, be suspended' (cf. *šaqālum* G).

šaqûm a G (*i*) 'to water, give water to, give (water) to drink (+ acc.: people, animals, fields, etc.)' (used as causative of *šatûm*).

šaqûm b G (*u*) 'to be(come) high, tall'; Verbal Adj. *šaqûm* (*šaqu-*; fem. *šaqūtum*) 'high, tall, elevated'; *šuqqûm* D 'to raise, elevate; to send upstream'.

šukênum Š(D) (§38.3(a)) 'to bow down, prostrate oneself'; Participle *muškēnum* see Vocab. 18.

šupêlum Š(D) (§38.3(a)) 'to change, exchange, substitute; turn (something) into'; *šut(e)pêlum* Š(D)t 'to interchange, be (ex)changed'.

zabālum G (*i*) 'to carry, transport, deliver'; *zubbulum* D 'to keep (someone) waiting'; *šuzbulum* Š causative; *nazbulum* N passive.

Noun:

awīltum (pl. *awīlātum*) '(free-)woman, lady' (cf. *awīlum*).

Adverb:

eliš 'above, up, upward, on top' (cf. *elûm*).

B. Write in normalized Akkadian:

1. they (f) will rebel
2. they (m) will roll around
3. she came to help
4. we stopped
5. they (m) will prostrate themselves
6. they (f) were exchanged
7. I caused them (f) to rebel
8. he will slip
9. it was suspended
10. they (m) will come to help

C. Normalize and translate:

1. *šum-ma šar-ru-um ša-nu-ú-um a-wa-ti-ia na-ás-qá-tim uš-te-pe-el ú-ṣú-ra-ti-ia* (*uṣurtum* 'plan') *ut-ta-ak-ke-er šu-mi ša-aṭ-ra-am ip-ši-iṭ* (*pašāṭum* G *i* 'to efface') *šum-šu iš-ta-ṭár* ^{d}UTU *da-a-a-nu-um ra-bi-um ša ša-me-e ù er-ṣe-tim mu-uš-te-še-er ša-ak-na-at na-pí-iš-tim be-lum tu-kúl-ti šar-ru-sú li-is-ki-ip* (*sakāpum* G *i* 'to overturn') *di-in-šu a-i-di-in i-ši-id um-ma-ni-šu li-iš-ḫe-el-ṣí i-na bi-ri-šu* (*bīrum* 'divination') UZU (here, 'omen') *lem-nam ša na-sa-aḫ i-ši-id šar-ru-ti-šu ù ḫa-la-aq ma-ti-šu li-iš-ku-un-šum* (cf. CH epilogue r xxvi 18 – xxvii 30).
2. PN ÌR KI PN$_2$ *be-li-šu i-gu-ur* ÌR *šu-ú i-ḫa-li-iq in-na-ab-bi-it ip-pa-ra-ak-ku-ma* PN$_2$ ÌR *i-ri-a-ab*.

D. CH:

§240 *šum-ma* $^{gi[š]}$MÁ *ša ma-ḫi-ir-tim* ^{giš}MÁ *ša mu-uq-qé-el-pí-tim im-ḫa-aṣ-ma uṭ-ṭe$_4$-eb-bi be-el* ^{giš}MÁ *ša* ^{giš}MÁ-*šu ṭe$_4$-bi-a-at mi-im-ma ša i-na* ^{giš}MÁ-*šu ḫal-qú i-na ma-ḫar i-lim ú-ba-ar-ma ša ma-ḫi-ir-tim ša* ^{giš}MÁ *ša mu-uq-qé-el-pí-tim ú-ṭe$_4$-eb-bu-ú* ^{giš}MÁ-*šu ù mi-im-ma-šu ḫal-qá-am i-ri-a-ab-šum*.

ša māḫirtim 'skipper of a boat going upstream'.

neqelpûm N (IV–*e*) 'to drift, glide, sail (downstream)'; Ptcpl. fem. *muqqelpītum* 'boat going downstream'; *ša muqqelpītim* 'skipper of a boat going downstream'; *šuqelpûm* Š 'to sail (a boat) downstream'.

ṭebûm G (*u*) 'to sink (intrans.)'; *ṭubbûm* D 'to sink (trans.)'.

E. Omens from *YOS* 10:

1. *šum-ma na-ap-la-aš-tim*! *e-li-iš iš-qú i-lu ša ma-tim i-ša-aq-qú-ú*. (11 ii 18–19)
2. *šum-ma i-na i-ši-id ma-at ú-ba-nim ka-ak-kum ša-ki-im-ma e-li-iš iṭ-ṭù-ul ṣi-bi-it-tum i-ba-la-ak-‹ka-›at*. (11 ii 27–30)
   mātum here, 'region'.
3. [DIŠ *pa-da*]*-nu i-mi-tam uḫ-ta-la-al ù i-na* ⌜ŠÀ⌝ *šu-me-lim šu-lum na-di i-na mu-úḫ-ḫe-el-ṣi-tim* GÌR LÚ *i-*⌜*ḫe*⌝*-le-ṣe*. (20:9)
   ḫalālum G (also *alālum*; *a–u*) 'to hang'; *ḫullulum* D=G; *ḫutallulum* Dt passive of D.
   šullum (*šulli*) 'wart'.
   muḫḫelṣītum 'slippery ground' (only here; cf. *neḫelṣûm*).
4. DIŠ KÁ É.GAL *ne-pe-el-ku-ú ḫu-ša-ḫu-um ib-ba-aš-ši-i*. (24:21)
   nepelkûm N (IV–*e*) 'to become wide (open), extended'.
   ḫušāḫum (*ḫušāḫ*) 'need, hunger'.
5. [DIŠ *qú*]*-ú-um iš-qá-la-al-ma ù li-bu-um* ⌜*ku*⌝*-ub-bu-ut-ma i-na ap-pi-šu ša-ki-in ni-šu bi-ša-ši-na a-na ma-ḫi-ri-im ú-še-ṣe-a*. (25:64)
   qûm (*qā-*) 'filament; thread'.
6. [DIŠ *ḫašûm*(UR$_5$)] *na-pa-ar-ku-d*[*a-a*]*t ma-as-sú ib-ba-la-ka-sú*. (36 i 21)
   ḫašûm (*ḫaši-*; log. UR$_5$) 'lung'.
   naparkudum N (*a*) 'to lie flat, against (something)'.
7. DIŠ *šēpum* (AŠ) *i-li-am-ma a-na re-eš mar-tim a-na wa-ar-ka-at a-mu-tim* [*na-di-at*] *a-al pa-ṭi-ka ša ib-ba-al-ki-tu-ka qá-at-ka i-ka-ša-ad*. (44:16–17)
8. Text 5, complete:

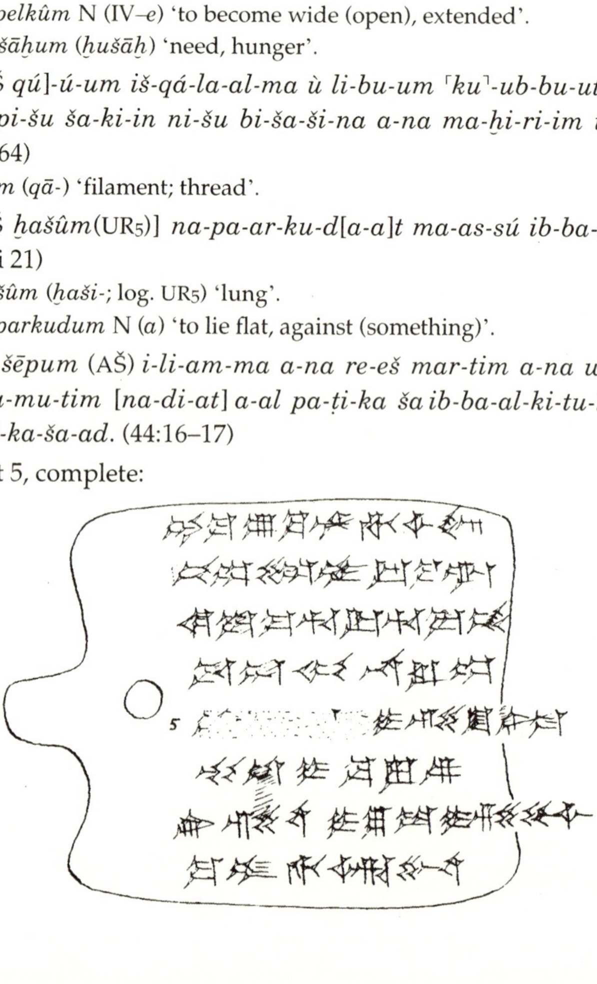

10 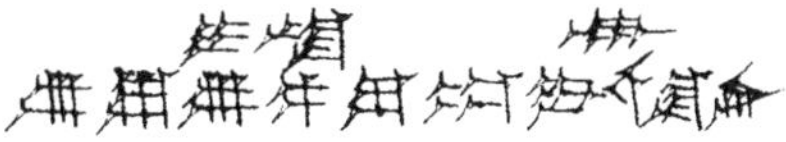

[1] *ḫašûm* (*ḫaši-*; log. UR$_5$) 'lung'.

[2] *qablûm* (*qablī-*; denom. adj.) 'mid, middle, median' (cf. *qablum*).

[2–3] Note the very unusual splitting of *ib-ba-al-ki-it-ma* over two lines.

[3] *ḫurḫudum* 'throat, windpipe'.

[5] The beginning of the line is probably an erasure, not to be restored; *sekērum* G (*e*) 'to shut, close, block'; *neskurum* N passive.

[6] *abālum* G (a) 'to dry up, out'.

[8] *ḫarbūtum* 'devastation'.

[10] *ú-lu-ú* for *ū lū*, often written as one word; *palûm* (*palā-*; Sum. lw.) 'reign'.

F. Contract:

1. Exchange of fields (*TCL* 1 74 = Schorr, *VAB* 5, no. 276).

[1] A.ŠÀ *ša ḫa-ra-ma-tum* [2] *i-ta* A.ŠÀ *la-ma-sí* DUMU.MUNUS ^{d}*še-rum-ì-lí* [3] *ki-ir-ba-nam a-na ḫa-ra-ma-tum is-sú-uk* [4] *ki-ir-ba-nam a-na* ^{id}BURANUN *is-sú-uk* [5] *ša ri-iš-*^{d}UTU ^{I}*ki-ma-a-ḫi-ia* [6] *ù za-ri-qum* DUMU.MEŠ ^{d}UTU-*a-bu-um* [7] KI GEME$_2$-^{d}UTU DUMU.MUNUS *bur-*^{d}EN.ZU [8] *ù la-ma-sí* DUMU.MUNUS ^{d}*še-rum-ì-lí* [9] *uš-pé-lu-ú-ma i-tu-ru-ú-ma* [10] ^{I}*ri-iš-*^{d}UTU ^{I}*ki-ma-a-ḫi-ia* [11] *ù za-ri-qum ib-qú-ru-ú-ma* [12] 5 GÍN KUG.BABBAR *ni-ip-la-at* A.ŠÀ-*im* [13] ^{I}GEME$_2$-^{d}UTU *ù la-ma-sí aš-šum* [*wa*]-*ta-ar-tim* [14] *iš-qú-la-a-ma ba-aq-ri-šu-nu* [15] *ù ru-gu-ma-ni-šu-nu* [16] *ša ri-iš-*^{d}UTU *ki-ma-a-ḫi-ia* [17] *ù za-ri-qum* [18] *is-sú-ḫa* [19] *ú-ul i-tu-ru-ú-ma* [20] ^{I}*ri-iš-*^{d}UTU ^{I}*ki-ma-a-ḫi-ia* [21] *ù za-ri-qum* [22] DUMU.MEŠ ^{d}UTU-*a-bu-um* [23] *a-na* GEME$_2$-^{d}UTU DUMU.MUNUS *bur-*^{d}EN.ZU [24] *ù la-ma-sí* DUMU.MUNUS ^{d}*še-rum-ì-lí* [25] *ú-ul i-ra-ga-mu* [26] MU ^{d}UTU ^{d}*a-a* MU ^{d}AMAR.UTU [27] *ù* ^{d}EN.ZU-*mu-ba-lí-iṭ* [28] *itmû* (IN.PÀD.DÈ.MEŠ). [29–37] Witnesses. [38] Date.

PNs: *Lamassī; Šērum-ilī; Rīš-Šamaš; Kīma-aḫīya; Zarriqum; Šamaš-abum; Amat-Šamaš; Būr-Sîn*

[1] *Ḫaramatum* a place name.

[3] *kirbānum* (*kirbān*) 'clod of earth'; *kirbānam nasākum* 'to throw a clod' = 'to become eroded' (*ana*: toward).

[5] *ša* begins a new predicate: 'The field of Ḫ. became eroded ... (and) is the one that R. ...'

[12] *nipiltum* (pl. *niplātum* = sg.) 'compensatory payment'.

[15] *rugummānû* irregular plural of *rugummûm*.

G. Letters:

1. *CT* 43 117 = Kraus, *AbB* 1 117.

^{1} *a-na ma-an-n[a-tum*$^{?}$*]* ^{2} *qí-bí[i-ma]* ^{3} *um-ma* NI-[...-*m*]*a* ^{4} *aš-šum ṭe*$_{4}$*-mi-ki i-[na-an-na*$^{?}$*]* ^{5} *ana* ^{uru}*za-mi-ri-i*^{ki} *a-[na ṭ]e*$_{4}$*-em a-wi-il-tim* ^{6} *šu-uk-bu-tim al-l[i-ik]* ^{7} *a-na* KÁ.DINGIR.RA^{ki} *a-al-la-ak* ^{8} *ù ab-ba-la-ka-tam* ^{9} *a-na* UD*-um ta-ša-ap-pa-ri-im* ^{10} *a-na a-wi-il-tim šu-up-ri-im-ma* ^{11} MÁ *a-na ra-ka-ab ṣú-ḫa-ar-tim* ^{12} *li-is-ki-pa-am* ^{13} *iš-tu-ma a-na šu-ba-al-ku-tim* ^{14} *la ta-am-gu-ri* ^{15} *e-bu-rum la i-ka-aš-ša-da-am* ^{16} *ṣú-ḫa-ar-tam ar-ḫi-iš* ^{17} *id-ni-im.*

PN: *Mannatum;* NI[...].

^{5} *Zamirū* place name; *awīltum* here, 'the (boss) lady'.

^{12} *sakāpum* G (*i*) 'to push away, overturn, reject; to repel, defeat; to dispatch (a boat), send (by boat)'.

^{13} *ištū-ma* 'if indeed'.

2. *CT* 4 35b = Frankena, *AbB* 2 100.

^{1} *a-na* ^{d}*na-bi-um-mu-ša-lim* ^{2} *qí-bí-ma* ^{3} *um-ma* ^{d}EN.ZU*-na-di-in-šu-mi-ma* ^{4} ^{d}UTU *ù* ^{d}AMAR.UTU *li-ba-al-li-ṭú-ka* ^{5} *[l]u ša-al-ma-ta* ^{6} *šu-lum-ka ma-ḫar* ^{d}UTU *ù* ^{d}AMAR.UTU *lu da-ri* ^{7} *aš-šum a-na pí-še-er-tim na-ga-ar-ru-ri* ^{8} *a-di eš-ri-šu aš-tap-ra-kum-ma* ^{9} *di-iʾ-tam ú-ul ta-ša-al-ma* ^{10} *ú-ul ta-li-a-am* ^{11} *ki-da-ma šu-ú iḫ-ta-li-iq* ^{12} *i-[n]a-a[n-n]a ṣe-e[ʾ]-pí* ^{13} *uš-ta-bi-la-ak-kum* ^{14} *šum-ma ta-al-li-a-am* ^{15} *ar-ḫi-iš [u]d-di-da-am-ma* ^{16} *a-li-a-am* ^{17} *šum-ma la ta-al-li-a-am* ^{18} *ar-ḫi-iš ṭe*$_{4}$*-ma-am ga-am-ra-am* ^{19} *šu-up-ra-am-ma ša pa-ni-ia* ^{20} *lu-up-pa-li-is-[m]a a-na-ku-ú-ma* ^{21} *lu-ug-ga-ri-ir* ^{22} *a-na* ^{f}*ḫu-un-na-tum qí-bi-ma* ^{23} *šum-ma i-il-li-a-am li-li-a-am* ^{24} *[k]i-ma pa-ni-ka* 2 *šu-ši* ^{giš}PISAN.ḪI.A ^{25} *le-qé-a-am* ^{26} *ù [x x x]-tim e-li-šu* ^{27} *ṣe-eʾ-[pí] uš-ta-bi-lam.*

PNs: *Nabium-mušallim; Sîn-nādin-šumī; Ḫunnatum.*

^{7} *pišertum* '(purchase of) surplus harvest$^{?}$'.

^{9} *diʾtum* (pl. *diʾātum*) 'notice, information' (cf. *edûm*).

^{11} *šū* refers to the grain.

^{12} *ṣeʾpum* 'sealed letter'.

^{15} *edēdum* G (*u*) 'to become pointed'; *uddudum* D factitive; also, in hendiadys, 'to act, do quickly'.

^{24} *kīma pānī-* with pron. sf. corresponding to sentence subject (here, 2ms), 'immediately'; *pišannum* (*pišan*; log. $^{(giš)}$PISAN; Sum. lw.) 'box'.

3. *TCL* 1 43 = Ungnad, *Babylonische Briefe* 117.

^{1} *a-na um-mi-i[a qí-bí-ma]* ^{2} *um-ma a-wi-i[l-*^{d}...] *ma-ru-ki-ma*

^{3} ^{d}UTU *ù* ^{d}[AMAR.UTU *da-ri-iš* UD-*m*]*i-im* ^{4} *li-ba-a*[*l-li-ṭú-ki*] ^{5} *iš-tu te-*[*x x x*] ^{6} *ki-ma ši-in-n*[*i-i*]*m* [*na-di-t*]*im* ^{7} *a-na pa-ni* ^{d}UTU *ta-ad-*[*di-i*]*n-ni* ^{8} *il-ku-um es-ra-an-ni-ma* ^{9} *na-pa-ar-ka-am ú-ul e-le-i* ^{10} *ù at-ti ma-ti-ma* ^{11} *ki-ma um-ma-tim* ^{12} *ú-ul ta-aš-pu-ri-im* ^{13} *li-ib-bi ú-ul tu-ba-li-ṭi* ^{14} *a-nu-um-ma ma-an-na-ši* ^{15} *aš-ta-ap-ra-ki-im* ^{16} 2 *qa*(SILA3) Ì.GIŠ *šu-bi-lim* ^{17} *mu-ur-ṣú-um iṣ-ba-ta-ni-ma* ^{18} *i-na na-pí-iš-tim an-na-di.*

PNs: *Awīl-...*; *Mannaši.*

$^{16-17}$ *qûm* (*qa*) unit of volume ('liter'); *murṣum* (*muruṣ*) 'pain, illness'.

4. Pinches, *CT* 4 32b = Frankena, *AbB* 2 98.

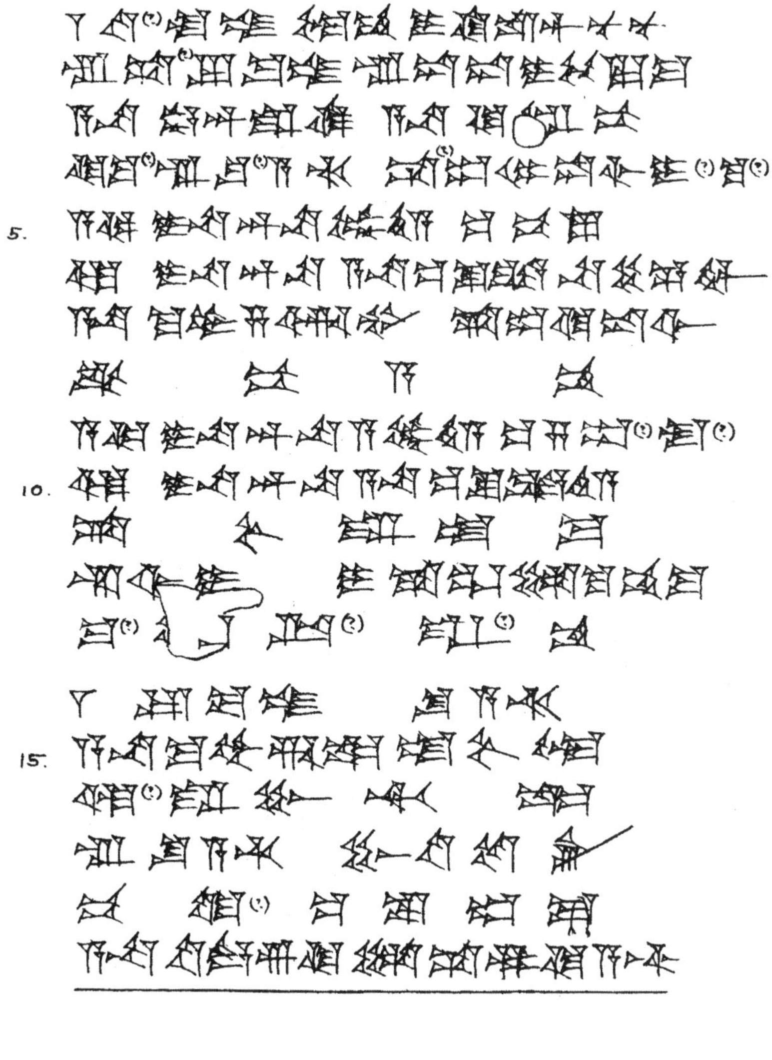

PNs: *Tamlatum; Qīš-Nūnu; Ibbatum.*

1 This letter lacks a salutation.

2 DU+DU = LAḪ$_5$; MÁ.LAḪ$_5$ = *malāḫum*.

3 At the end read *uš!*(A.NA)*-qé-el-pí;* for *šuqelpûm* see CH §240, above.

4–7 An indirect quote, all dependent on *kīma* 'that', which in turn is governed by *iqbiam* in line 8.

6 *ù* here resumes the *kīma* clause following the two relative clauses and may be rendered 'however' ('that that boat, which ... and ..., you however have now assigned ...'); the sign after GIŠ is ÙR; GIŠ.ÙR = *gušūrum* (Sum. lw.) 'beam, log'.

7 *maṣṣartum* here, 'safekeeping'.

10 GIŠ.ÙR GIŠIMMAR.ḪI.A the plural marker modifies GIŠ.ÙR.

12–13 These lines are probably a question; in 13, read *i*!-⸢*tu*⸣-*ur*!-*ra-am.*

16 For Ù at the beginning, read *ki!-ma!*.

H. A prayer of a diviner, to the gods of the night (von Soden, *ZA* 43 1936 306–7; English translations in Pritchard, *ANET* 391; Foster 2005 1.148–49; English versification in Ferry 1990).

1 *pu-ul-lu-sú*$^{?}$ / *lu*$^{?}$ *ru-bu-ú*
2 *wa-aš-ru-ú sí-ik-ku-ru ši-re-tum ša-ak-na-a*
3 *ḫa-ab-ra-tum ni-šu-ú ša-qú-um-ma-a*
4 *pe-tu-tum ud-du-lu-ú ba-a-bu*
5 *i-li ma-tim iš-ta-ra-at ma-a-tim*
6 ^{d}UTU ^{d}EN.ZU ^{d}IŠKUR ^{d}INANNA
7 *i-te-er-bu-ú a-na ú-tu-ul ša-me-e*
8 *ú-ul i-di-in-nu di-na-am ú-ul i-pa-ar-ra-sú a-wa-tim*

1 The reading of the fourth sign is uncertain. If *-sú*, note *palāsum* G (rare) 'to see', *pullusum* 'to occupy, divert' (cf. *naplusum*). If *-lu*, note *palālum* G (*i*) 'to watch over, guard', *pullulum* (otherwise unattested) = G$^{?}$ (Livingstone 1990).

2 *wašrum* a Verbal Adj., meaning uncertain; perhaps from a rare G stem of the root for *wuššurum*, hence 'released into place'; the word is replaced by *nadûm* 'situated' in parallel texts.
sikkūrum (*sikkūr*; pl. *sikkūrū*) 'bar, door-bolt'.
šērtum (pl. *šērētum*) 'ring' (Livingstone 1990).

3 *ḫabārum* G (*u*) 'to be noisy'; Verbal Adj. *ḫabrum* 'noisy'.
**šaqumumum* R 'to become completely still, silent'.

4 *edēlum* G (*i*) 'to lock'; *uddulum* D = G.
Note the unusual separation of the adjective *petûm* from the modified noun *bābum*.

5 *i-li* is an error for the expected nom. pl. (cf. line 14).
ištarum (pl. *ištarātum*) 'goddess' (cf. *Ištar*).

9 *pu-us-sú-ma-at mu-ši-i-tim*!
10 É.GAL-*lum ša-ḫu-ur ša-qú-um-mu ṣe-ru-ú*
11 *a-li-ik ur-ḫi-im* DINGIR-*lam i-ša-si ù ša di-nim uš-te-bé-er-re ši-it-ta-am*
12 [*da*]-*a-a-an ki-na-tim a-bi e-ki-a-tim*
13 ^{d}UTU *i-te-ru-ub a-na ku-um-mi-šu*
14 *ra-bu-tum i-li-i mu-ši-i-tim*
15 *na-wi-ru-um* ^{d}GIBIL
16 *qú-ra-du-um* ^{d}*èr-ra*
17 *qá-aš-tum ni-ru-um*
18 *ši-ta-ad-da-ru-um mu-uš-ḫu-uš-šu-um*
19 ^{giš}MAR.GÍD.DA *in-zu-um*
20 *ku-sa-ri-ik-ku-um ba-aš-mu-um*

9 *pasāmum* G (*i*) 'to veil, cover'; *pussumum* D = G.
mušītum (*mušīt*; pl. *mušiātum*) 'night, nighttime'; here incorrectly gen. for nom.

10 *šaḫururum* R 'to be(come) completely inactive, paralyzed (with fear)'.

11 *urḫum* (fem. and masc.; *uruḫ*; pl. *urḫātum*) 'way, road, path'
ša dīnim 'litigant'.
bitrûm Gt (rare; not in G) 'to last, be continuous'; *šutebrûm* Št-lex. 'to remain, continue; to make last'.
šittum 'sleep'; *šittam* here adverbial acc. 'asleep'.

12 *ekûm* (base *eku-*; usually fem. sg. *ekūtum*) 'homeless, orphan(ed)'; here fem. pl. *ekiātum* from a base *eki-*.

13 *kummum* (*kummi*) 'cella, private room'.

14 *i-li* as in line 5 an error for the expected nom. pl.

15 *nawārum* G (*i*; see §21.3(b)) 'to be(come) bright, light; to shine'; Verbal Adj. *nawirum* (*nawir-*) 'bright, shining'.
Gibil (log. GIBIL (= BIL+GI) the fire god.

16 *qurādum* (*qurād*; pl. *qurādū*) 'warrior' (synonym of *qarrādum*).
Erra the god of pestilence.

17 *qaštum* (pl. *qašātum*) 'bow'; here a constellation.
nīrum (*nīr(i)*) 'yoke'; here a constellation.

18 *šitaddarum* (Sum. lw.) 'Orion'.
mušḫuššum (Sum. lw.) great serpent, dragon; here a constellation.

19 *ereqqum* here a constellation.
enzum (also *ezzum*; here *inzum*; fem.; pl. *enzētum*) 'she-goat'; also the constellation Lyra.

20 *kusarikkum* 'bison'; also, a constellation.
bašmum a horned snake; the constellation Hydra.

21 *li-iz-zi-‹zu›-ú-ma*
22 *i-na te-er-ti e-ep-pu-šu*
23 *i-na pu-ḫa-ad a-ka-ar-ra-bu-ú*
24 *ki-it-ta-am šu-uk-na-an*
25 24 MU.BI *ik-‹ri›-ib mu-ši-tim*

23 *puḫādum* (*puḫād*) 'lamb'.
karābum G (*a–u*) 'to bless, invoke blessings; to praise; to dedicate an offering'.

24 *šu-uk-na-an* for expected *šuknā* or *šuknānim*; the final *-n* is obscure.

25 MU = *šumum*, here, 'line'.
ikribum (*ikrib*; pl. *ikribū*) 'blessing, benediction; prayer'.

SUPPLEMENTARY READING

Gilgameš

Old Babylonian version, Tablet II (Pennsylvania Tablet), based on George 2003, vol. 1, pp. 172–192 (copy vol. 2, plates 1–3).

Column i

it-bé-e-ma ^{d}GIŠ[1] *šu-na-tam*[2] *i-pa-aš-šar*
is-sà-qar-am a-na um-mi-šu
[u]m-mi i-na ša-a-at[3] *mu-ši-ti-ia*
⸢*ša*⸣*-am-ḫa-ku-ma*[4] *at-ta-na-al-la-ak*
[i-n]a bi-ri-it eṭ-lu-ti[m]
ip-⸢*zi-ru-nim*⸣*-ma*[5] *ka-ka-bu*[6] *ša-ma-i*
⸢*x-(x)*⸣*-rum ša a-nim im-qú-ut a-na ṣe-ri-ia*
aš-ši-šu-ma ik-ta-bi-it e-li-ia
*ú-ni-*IŠ*-su-ma*[7] *nu-uš-ša-šu ú-ul el-ti-ʾi*
UNUG^{ki}[8] *ma-[t]um pa-ḫe-er e-li-šu*
eṭ-lu-tum ú-na-ša-qú[9] *še*$_{20}$*-pi-šu*
ú-um-mi-id-ma pu-ti[10]
i-mi-du ia-ti

---

[1] ^{d}GIŠ is the OB writing for *Gilgameš*.

[2] *šunatum* an uncommon byform of *šuttum* (pl. *šunātum*) 'dream'.

[3] *šāt* frozen f. sg. of the determinative pronoun *ša* (which was originally declinable); *mūšum* and *mušītum* (pl. *mušiātum*) 'night(time)'; *ina šāt mušītīya* 'during that of my night', i.e., 'in my dream'.

[4] *šamāḫum* G (*u*) 'to grow thickly, thrive; to flourish; to attain great beauty or stature'; Verbal Adj. *šamḫum* (*šamuḫ-*) 'luxuriant; prosperous, majestic'.

[5] *pazārum* G (*i*) 'to hide oneself' (?; but this verb is otherwise unattested in the G; the D *puzzurum* means 'to hide (trans.)'). Another possible reading of this damaged form is *ib-*⸢*bi-ru-nim*⸣*-ma* from *ebērum* G (*i*) 'to cross, pass over'.

[6] *kakkabum* (pl. *kakkabū*) 'star'.

[7] *nâšum* G (*a–u*) 'to move, begin moving' (intrans.); *nuššum* D 'to move, set in motion' (trans.); it is possible to read the form here, *unīssu*, either as *ú-ni-iš-su* (a morphographemic writing, §18.4) or as *ú-ni-ís-su* (with IŠ = *ís*).

[8] UNUG^{ki} the city of *Uruk*.

[9] *našāqum* G (*i*) 'to kiss'; *nuššuqum* D = G.

[10] *pūtum* (*pūt(i)*) 'forehead, front'; *ina pūt* (prepositional phrase) 'opposite'.

aš-ši-a-šu-ma at-ba-la-aš-šu a-na ṣe-ri-ki
um-mi ^{d}GIŠ *mu-de-a-at ka-la-ma*[11]
is-sà-qar-am a-na ^{d}GIŠ
mi-in-de[12] ^{d}GIŠ *ša ki-ma ka-ti*
i-na ṣe-ri i-wa-li-id-ma
ú-ra-ab-bi-šu ša-du-ú
ta-mar-šu-ma ta-ḫa-du at-ta
eṭ-lu-tum ú-na-ša-qu še$_{20}$*-pi-šu*$^{!}$
te-ed-di-ra-⌜*aš*$^{!?}$-«*x*»-*šu*⌝-*ú-ma*[13]
⌜*ta*⌝*-tar-ra-aš-*⌜*šu*[14] *a-na*⌝ *ṣe-*⌜*ri-ia*⌝
[*i*]*t-ti-lam-ma i-ta-mar ša-ni-tam*
[*i*]*t-bé i-ta-wa-a-am a-na um-mi-šu*
[*um*]-⌜*mi a-ta*⌝*-mar ša-ni-tam*
[*x x x*] *me*$^{?}$*-e* UL.A[15] *i-na sú-qí-im*
[*ša* UNU]G^{ki} *re-bi-tim*[16]
⌜*ḫa-aṣ-ṣi*⌝*-nu*[17] *na-di-i-ma*
e-li-šu pa-aḫ-ru
ḫa-aṣ-ṣi-nu-um-ma ša-ni bu-nu-šu[18]
a-mur-šu-ma aḫ-ta-du a-na-ku
a-ra-am-šu-ma ki-ma aš-ša-tim
a-ḫa-ab-bu-ub[19] *el-šu*
el-qé-šu-ma aš-ta-ka-an-šu
a-na a-ḫi-ia
⌜*um-mi* ^{d}GIŠ *mu*⌝*-da-at* ⌜*ka-la*⌝*-ma*
[*is-sà-qar-am*] ⌜*a*⌝-[*na* ^{d}GIŠ]
[... 4 lines missing ...]

---

[11]*kalâmu* / *kalâma* 'everything'.

[12]*minde* (adverb) 'perhaps, possibly, who can say?'.

[13]*edērum* G (*i*) 'to hug, embrace'; *nendurum* N 'to embrace one another'.

[14]*tarûm* G (*u*) 'to bring, lead (forth)' (cf. *warûm*).

[15]Beginning of line unclear.

[16]*rebītum* '(city / town-)square, plaza'.

[17]*ḫaṣṣīnum* / *ḫaṣṣinnum* 'ax'.

[18]*būnum* (usually pl. *būnū*, but sg. here) 'features, face, appearance' (cf. *banûm*).

[19]*ḫabābum* G (*u*) 'to murmur, whisper; to caress'.

Column ii

aš-šum uš-[*ta*]*-ma-ḫa-ru it-ti-ka*
^{d}GIŠ *š*[*u-n*]*a-tam i-pa-šar*
^{d}EN.KI.[DU$_{10}$ *w*]*a-ši-ib ma-ḫar ḫa-ri-im-tim*[20]
úr-[*ta-ʾ*]*a*$_{4}$*-mu ki-la*$^{!}$*-al-lu-un*
⸢*ṣe*⸣*-*[*r*]*a-am im-ta-ši a-šar i-wa-al-du*
UD.⸢7⸣ *ù* 7 *mu-ši-a-tim*
^{d}EN.[KI.DU$_{10}$ *t*]*e-bi-i-ma*
ša-[*am-ka-ta*]*m*[21] *ir-ḫe*[22]
ḫa-r[*i-im-tum p*]*i-ša i-pu-ša-am-ma*
is-sà-qa[*r-am*] *a-na* ^{d}EN.KI.DU$_{10}$
a-na-ṭal-⸢*ka* ^{d}EN⸣.KI.DU$_{10}$ *ki-ma* DINGIR *ta-ba-aš-ši*
am-mi-nim [*i*]*t-ti na-ma-aš-te-e*[23]
ta-at-ta-[*n*]*a-la*$^{!}$*-ak ṣe-ra-am*
⸢*al*⸣*-kam lu-úr-de-ka*
a-na ŠÀ [UNU]G$^{⸢ki⸣}$ *re-bi-tim*
a-na É *e*[*l-l*]*im mu-ša-bi*[24] *ša a-nim*
^{d}EN.KI.DU$_{10}$ *ti-bé lu-ru-ka*
a-na É.[AN.N]A[25] *m*[*u-š*]*a-bi ša a-nim*
a-šar [*ši*]*-it-*⸢*ku-nu*[26] *né*⸣*-pe-še*$_{20}$*-tim*[27]
ù at-t[*a-m*]*a ki-*[*ma*] ⸢*a-wi-li-im-ma*$^{?}$
ta-aš-[*ta-ka*]*-a*[*n*$^{?}$] ⸢*ra*⸣*-ma-an-ka*[28]
⸢*al*⸣*-ka-ti-ma*[29] *i-*⸢*na*⸣ *qá-aq-qá-ri*[30]

---

[20]*ḫarīmtum* (pl. *ḫarīmātum;* log. KAR.KID) 'prostitute'.

[21]*šamḫatum / šamkatum* 'prostitute'.

[22]*reḫûm / raḫûm* G (*e / i*) 'to mate, copulate with; to procreate; to (over)flow (into, upon)'.

[23]*nammaštûm / nammaššûm* (*-ā*; collective sg.) 'animals'.

[24]*mūšabum* (*mūšab*) 'dwelling, domicile; seat' (cf. *wašābum*).

[25]*Eanna* (É.AN.NA; Sum. é . a n - a (k) 'house of heaven') Inanna's main temple in Uruk.

[26]*šitkunum* Gt appears mostly in literary texts and has meanings similar to the G *šakānum*; here: 'they (people) are engaged in (+ acc.)'.

[27]*nēpeštum* 'performance, execution, work, artifact' (cf. *epēšum*).

[28]George (2003: 175) translates, with reservation, 'you will [*make a place for*] yourself'.

[29]*alkatum* rare poetic variant of *alaktum* (pl. *alkātum*) 'behavior, custom(s), activity; road, way, passage; movement, traffic; caravan' (cf. *alākum*).

ma-a-al(!AG)[31] *re-i-im*
iš-me a-[*w*]*a-as-sà im-ta-gàr qá-ba-ša*
mi-il-[*k*]*um*[32] *ša* MUNUS
im-ta-[*q*]*ú-ut* ⸢*a*⸣*-na* ŠÀ-*šu*
iš-ḫu-uṭ[33] [*l*]*i-ib-ša-am*[34]
*iš-ti-nam ú-la-ab-bi-*IŠ*-su*[35]
li-ib-⸢*ša*⸣*-*[*a*]*m ša-ni-a-am*
ši-i ⸢*it*⸣*-ta-al-ba-aš*
ṣa-ab-⸢*ta*⸣*-at qá-as-sú*
ki-ma D[IN]GIR *i-re-*⸢*ed*⸣*-de-šu*
a-na ⸢*gu-ub-ri*⸣[36] *ša re-i-im*
a-š[*ar t*]*ar-ba-ṣi-im*
i-na [*ṣe*]*-*⸢*ri-šu*⸣ *i*[*p*]*-ḫu-ru re-iu-ú*
⸢*ki*⸣ [ ] *x x*
[... 4 lines missing ...]

Column iii

ši-iz-ba[37] *ša na-ma-aš-te-*⸢*e*⸣
i-te-en-ni-iq[38]
a-ka-lam iš-ku-nu ma-ḫar-šu
ip-te-eq-ma[39] *i-na-aṭ-ṭal*
ù ip-pa-al-la-as
ú-ul i-de ^{d}EN.KI.DU$_{10}$
NINDA[40] *a-na a-ka-lim*
KAŠ[41] *a-na ša-te-e-em*

---

[30]*qaqqarum* (*qaqqar*) 'ground, earth'.

[31]The meaning of *ma-a-ak* here is unknown (cf. *mākum* 'lack, absence'?); thus, read perhaps *ma-a-al*!, for *ma-a-a-al*: *mayyalum* (*mayyal*) 'bed, sleeping place' (cf. *niālum*).

[32]*milkum* (pl. *milkātum*) 'advice, instruction; intellectual capacity; mood; intent'.

[33]*šaḫāṭum* G (*a–u*) 'to tear off, away'; *šuḫḫuṭum* D = G; *našḫuṭum* N passive.

[34]*libšum* 'garment' (rare; cf. *labāšum*).

[35]Cf. note 6 above.

[36]*gubrum* 'shepherd's hut'.

[37]*šizbum* 'milk'.

[38]*enēqum* G (*i*) 'to suck'; *šūnuqum* Š 'to suckle'.

[39]*ip-te-eq* for *iptīq*; *piāqum* G (*a–i*) 'to become narrow', here, elliptically, 'to squint'?

[40]NINDA (= the NÍG sign) = *ak(a)lum*.

la-a lum-mu-ud
ḫa-ri-im-tum pi-ša i-pu-ša-am-ma
is-sà-qar-am a-na ᵈEN.KI.DU$_{10}$
a-ku-ul ak-lam ᵈEN.KI.DU$_{10}$
sí-ma-at[42] *ba-la-ṭi-im*
KAŠ *ši-ti ši-im-ti ma-ti*
i-ku-ul ak-lam ᵈEN.KI.DU$_{10}$
a-di še$_{20}$*-bé-e-šu*
KAŠ *iš-ti-a-am*
7 *as-sà-am-mi«-im»*[43]
it-tap-šar kab-ta-tum[44] *i-na-an-gu*[45]
i-li-iṣ[46] ŠÀ-*šu-ma*
pa-⸢nu-šu it⸣-tam-ru[47]
ul-tap-pi-⸢it⸣ ⸢ŠU⸣.I[48]
šu-ʾu$_{5}$*-ra-am*[49] *pa-ga-⸢ar-šu⸣*
ša-am-nam ip-ta-ša-aš-ma
a-wi-li-iš i-wi[50]
il-ba-aš li-ib-ša-am
ki-ma mu-ti i-ba-aš-ši
il-qé ka-ak-ka-šu
la-bi[51] *ú-ge-er*-RI
ís-sa-ak-pu[52] SIP[A.M]EŠ *mu-ši-a-tim*
ut-tap-pi-íṣ[53] *bar-ba-ri*[54]
la-bi uk-⸢ta⸣-ši-id

---

[41]KAŠ (= the BI sign) = *šikarum*.
[42]*simtum* (*simat*) 'what pertains, belongs, is appropriate to'.
[43]*assammum* 'jug'.
[44]*kabtatum* poetic variant of *kabattum* 'inside (of the body); emotions, mind'.
[45]*inangu* for *inaggu* (with nasalization); *nagûm* G (*u*) 'to sing happily'.
[46]*elēṣum* G (*i*) 'to rejoice'; *ulluṣum* D and *šūluṣum* Š 'to cause to rejoice'.
[47]*nawārum* (later *namāru*) G (*i*) 'to be(come) bright, light; to shine'; Verbal Adj. *nawirum* (later *namru*) 'bright, shining'; *nuwwurum* D 'to brighten (trans.)'; Š 'to cause to become bright'; ŠD = D
[48]ŠU.I = *gallābum* 'barber'.
[49]*šuʾʾurum* (D Verbal Adj.) 'hairy'.
[50]*ewûm* G (*i*; see §21.3(k)) 'to become, turn, change (*ana* / *-iš*: into)'.
[51]*lābum* (pl. *lābū*) 'lion'.
[52]*sakāpum* G (*u*) 'to lie down'.
[53]*napāṣum* G (*a–u*) 'to hurl; to kick, strike; to smash; to repel'; *nuppuṣum* D = G.
[54]*barbarum* (pl. *barbarū*) 'wolf'.

it-ti-lu na-qí-[d]u ra-bu-tum
^{d}EN.KI.DU$_{10}$ *ma-⸢aṣ⸣-ṣa-ar-šu-nu*
a-wi-lum ⸢e⸣-ru-um[55]
iš-[t]e-en eṭ-lum
a-na É *[e-m]i*$^{?}$[56] *ú[s*$^{?}$*]-sà-aq-qí-ir*[57]
⸢i-na⸣ [x]-⸢at-ta$^{?}$*-tim⸣ x x x x*
[... 5 lines missing ...]

Column iv (rev. i)

[... 7 lines missing ...]
⸢it-ti⸣ [ša-a]m-⸢ka-tim⸣
i-ip-pu-⸢uš⸣ [u]l-ṣa-am[58]
iš-ši-ma i-ni-i-šu
i-ta-mar ⸢a⸣-wi-lam
is-sà-qar$^{!}$*-am a-na* KAR.KID
ša-am-ka-at[59] *uk-ki-ši*[60] *a-wi-lam*
a-na mi-nim il-li-kam
zi-ki-ir-šu lu-⸢uš⸣-šu[61]
ḫa-ri-im-tum iš-ta-si a-⸢wi⸣-lam
*i-ku-*UŠ*-su-um-ma*[62] *i-ta-wa-aš-šu*
e-ṭe-él e-eš[63] *ta-ḫi-š[a-a]m*[64]
mi-nu a-la-ku ma-na-aḫ-t[i-k]a[65]
GURUŠ[66] *pi-šu i-pu-ša-am-[m]a*

---

[55]*êrum* (I–ʾ and II–*e*; Pret. *iʾēr*; see §21.3(d)) 'to become awake, alert'; Verbal Adj. *ērum* (*ēr*) 'awake, alert, watchful'.

[56]*bīt emim* is literally 'father-in-law's house', but here denotes 'wedding'.

[57]This reading suggested by George (2003: 1.186) would be *saqārum* Dt Pret., 'was summoned'.

[58]*ulṣum* (*uluṣ*) 'rejoicing, exultation'; *ulṣam epēšum* 'to make love' (cf. *elēṣum* in iii 20).

[59]Note the use of the absolute form as a vocative or PN.

[60]*akāšum* G (*u*) 'to go, move'; *ukkušum* D 'to drive away'.

[61]*lu-uš-šu* unclear; the following emendations have been suggested: *lu-uš-me, lu-uš-al; lu-uš-si-a(-am)*.

[62]Cf. n. 7 above.

[63]*êš* (adverb) 'whither, where to?'

[64]*ḫiāšum* G (*i*) 'to hasten, hurry'.

[65]*mānaḫtum* (*mānaḫti*; pl. *mānaḫātum*) 'toil, misery, weariness; maintenance, equipment'.

[66]GURUŠ (the KAL sign) *eṭlum*.

⸢*is-sà-qar*⸣*-am a-na* ^{d}E[N.KI.DU$_{10}$]
bi-ti-⸢*iš e-mu-tim*[67] *iq-ru-ni-ni*⸣[68]
ši-ma-a-at ni-ši-i-ma
ḫi-ia$^{!}$*-ar kal-lu-tim*[69]
a-na BANŠUR[70] *sak-ki-i*[71] *e-*⸢*ṣe*⸣*-en*[72]
uk-la-at[73] É *e-mi ṣa-a-a-ḫa-tim*[74]
a-na LUGAL *ša* UNUG^{ki} *re-bi-tim*
pe-ti pu-ug[75] *ni-ši a-na ḫa-a-a-ri*[76]
a-na ^{d}GIŠ LUGAL *ša* UNUG^{ki} *re-bi-tim*
pe-ti pu-ug ni-š[*i*]
a-na ḫa-a-a-⸢*ri*⸣
aš-ša-at ši-im-tim i-ra-aḫ-ḫ[*i*]
šu-ú pa-na-nu-um-ma[77]
mu-tum wa-ar-ka-nu[78]
i-na mi-il-ki ša AN *qá-bi-ma*
i-na bi-ti-iq[79] *a-bu-un-na-ti-šu*[80]
ši-ma-as-súm
a-na zi-ik-ri eṭ-li-im
i-ri-qú pa-nu-šu

---

[67]*emūtum* 'house (of the bride's family) in which a wedding takes place' (cf. *emum* and see n. 56 above).

[68]*qerûm* G (*i*) 'to call, summon, invite'.

[69]*kallūtum* status of *kallatum*.

[70]*paššūrum* (*paššūr*; log. BANŠUR; Sum. lw.) 'table'.

[71]Meaning uncert. here; note *sakkû* (pl.) '(cultic) rites'; *sagûm* / *sakkûm* 'shrine'.

[72]*ṣênum* G (*e*) 'to load, heap up'.

[73]*ukultum* (pl. *uklātum*) 'food(-supply), feeding, provisions'.

[74]*ṣayyaḫum* (adjective) 'delightful, fancy' (rare).

[75]*pūgum* (*pūg*) 'net' (rare; *AHw*: "zur Unterteilung von Räumen").

[76]*ḫa-a-a-ri* obscure.

[77]*pānānum* (adverb) 'earlier, formerly, firstly'.

[78]*warkānum* (adverb) 'later, afterward'.

[79]*bitqum* (*bitiq*) 'opening (of a canal); diverting (of water); cutting (rare); a measure/amount (of silver, flour)' (cf. *batāqum*).

[80]*abunnatum* 'navel; center, socket; umbilical cord$^{?}$'.

Column v (rev. ii)

[... 8 lines missing ...]
[ ] ⸢*su*$^{?}$ *lu*⸣ [ ]
i-il-la-ak ^{d}[EN.KI.DU$_{10}$]
ù ša-am-ka-t[*um*] ⸢*wa-ar*⸣-*ki-šu*
i-ru-ub-ma$^{!}$ *a*$^{!}$-*na*$^{!}$ ŠÀ UNUG^{ki} *re-bi-tim*
ip-ḫur um-ma-nu-⸢*um*⸣ *i-na ṣe-ri-*⸢*šu*⸣
iz-zi-za-am-ma ⸢*i*⸣-*na sú-qí-im*
ša UNUG^{ki} *re-bi-tim*
pa-aḫ-ra-a-ma ni-šu
i-ta-wa-a i-na ṣe-ri-šu
a-na-mi ^{d}GIŠ *ma-ši-il*[81] *pa-da*(!ID)-*tam*[82]
la-nam[83] [*š*]*a-pi-il*[84]
⸢*e-ṣe-em-tam*⸣ [*pu-u*]*k-ku-ul*[85]
m[*i-in-de ša*] ⸢*i-wa-al*⸣-*du*
i-n[*a š*]*a-di-i-*⸢*im*⸣
ši-iz-⸢*ba ša na-ma*⸣-*a*[*š-te*]-⸢*e*⸣
i-te-en-⸢*ni*⸣-*iq*
ka-a-a-na[86] *i-na* ⸢UNUG⸣^{ki} *ni-qí-a-tum*
eṭ-lu-tum ⸢*ú*⸣-*te-el-li-ṣú*[87]
ša-ki-in ur(!LU)-*ša-nu*[88]
a-na GURUŠ *ša i-ša-ru zi-mu-šu*[89]
a-na ^{d}GIŠ *ki-ma i-li-im*
ša-ki-iš-šum me-eḫ-rum
a-na ^{d}*iš-ḫa-ra*[90] *ma-a-a-lum*[91]

---

[81]*mašālum* G (*u*) 'to become similar, equal, half'; Verbal Adj. *mašlum* (*mašil-*) 'similar, equal, half'; *muššulum* D 'to make similar, equal; to copy'.

[82]*padattum* 'form, shape'.

[83]*lānum* 'body, appearance, stature, size, shape; person'.

[84]*šapālum* G (*i*) 'to become low, deep, small'; Verbal Adj. *šaplum* (*šapil-*) 'low, deep'; *šuppulum* D factitive.

[85]*pag/kālum* G 'to become strong' (rare); *puggulum/pukkulum* D 'to make strong'; Verbal Adj. 'very strong'.

[86]*kayyānum* (adjective) 'normal, regular; permanent, constant' (cf. *kânum*).

[87]*elēṣum* Dt 'to enjoy oneself'.

[88]*uršānum* 'hero, warrior'.

[89]*zīmum* (often pl. *zīmū*) 'appearance, looks, countenance'; *ana zīm(i)* (prep. phrase) 'corresponding to, according to, in view of'.

[90]*Išḫara* a goddess associated/equated with Eštar.

[91]*mayyalum* (*mayyal*) 'sleeping-place, bed' (cf. *niālum*).

na-⸢*di*⸣*-i-ma*
^{d}GIŠ *it-*⸢*ti*⸣ [*w*]*a-a*[*r-d*]*a-*[*t*]*im*[92]
i-na mu-ši ⸢*in*⸣*-né-*[*mi*]*-*⸢*id*⸣
i-ta-ak-⸢*ša*⸣*-am-ma*
it-ta-z[*i-iz*] ⸢*i*⸣*-na* SILA
ip-ta-ra-a[*s a-l*]*a-ak-tam*[93]
ša ^{d}GIŠ
[*x x (x) x uš-t*]*a-an-da-nu-ni-iš-šu*[94]
lacuna

Column vi (rev iii)

[... 3 lines missing ...]
⸢*i*⸣?*-ʾa*$_4$*-a*[*n-ni-ip*?[95] .....]
^{d}GIŠ *b*[*a*? ......]
i-na ṣe-⸢*ri*⸣*-š*[*u* ......]
i-ʾa$_4$*-an-ni-i*[*p x x x x*]
it-bé-ma ^{d}E[N.KI.DU$_{10}$]
a-na pa-ni-⸢*šu*⸣
it-tam-ḫa-ru i-na re-bi-tu ma-ti
^{d}EN.KI.DU$_{10}$ *ba-ba-am ip-ta-ri-ik*
⸢*i-na*⸣ *še*$_{20}$*-pi-šu*
^{d}GIŠ *e-re-ba-am ú-ul id-di-in*
iṣ-ṣa-ab-tu-ma ki-ma LI*-i-im*[96]
i-lu-du[97]
sí-ip-pa-am[98] *iʾ-bu-tu*[99]
⸢*i-ga*⸣*-rum ir-tu-ud*[100]

---

92 *wardatum* 'young woman'.

93 *alaktam parāsum* 'to cut off access, block the way'.

94 For *uštaddanū*; see §36.1 (b2), end.

95 *anāpum* / *ḫanāpum* G (*i*) 'to become angry' (only here).

96 *lûm* (from **līum*; masc. of *lītum* / *littum*; pl. *lû*) 'bull'; in *CAD le-i-im*, i.e., *lēʾîm* 'skilled', i.e., 'wrestler', is read.

97 *lâdum* G(*u*) 'to bend' (so *CAD* L 36b; *AHw* 527a "etwa 'in die Knie gehen'"; rare).

98 *sippum* 'door-post, door-frame'.

99 *abātum* (*a–u*; often with strong ʾ retained) 'to destroy'; *ubbutum* D = G; *utabbutum* Dt passive; *naʾbutum* N passive.

100 *râdum* G (*u*) 'to shake, quake'. Another possible reading is *ir-tu-ut*: *ratātum* G (*u*) 'to tremble, shake'. Neither verb is common.

^{d}GIŠ *ù* ⸢^{d}EN⸣.KI.DU$_{10}$
iṣ-ṣa-ab-tu-ú-ma
ki-ma LI-*i-im i-lu-du*
*sí-ip-pa-am i*ᵓ*-bu-tu*
i-⸢*ga*⸣*-rum ir-tu-ud*
ik-mi-is-ma ^{d}GIŠ
i-na qá-aq-qá-ri še$_{20}$*-ep-šu*
ip-ši-iḫ uz-za-šu-ma[101]
*i-né-e*ᵓ[102] *i-ra-as-sú*[103]
*iš-tu i-ra-sú i-né-*ᵓ*u*$_5$
^{d}EN.KI.DU$_{10}$ *a-na ša-ši-im*
iš-sà-qar-am a-na ^{d}GIŠ
ki-ma iš-te-en-ma um-ma-ka
ú-li-id-ka
ri-im-tum[104] *ša sú-pu-ri*[105]
^{d}NIN.SÚN.NA[106]
ul-lu e-li mu-ti re-eš-ka
⸢*šar*⸣*-ru-tam ša ni-ši*
i-ši-im-kum ^{d}EN.LÍL

DUB 2. ⸢KAM.MA⸣
⸢*šu*⸣*-tu-ur e-li š*[*ar-ri*][107]
edge 4 [*š*]*u-ši*[108]

---

[101]*uzzum* (*uzzi*; pl. *uzzātum*) 'anger, rage'.

[102]*nê*ᵓ*um* G (II–*e*, third radical ᵓ usually written; see §21.3(k)) 'to turn, turn away, loosen' (trans.).

[103]*irtum* (*irat*) 'chest, breast'; *irtam nê*ᵓ*um* 'to turn away, withdraw'.

[104]*rīmtum* 'wild cow' (cf. *rīmum* 'wild bull').

[105]*supūrum* 'sheep-fold, pen'.

[106]*Ninsunna* (Sum. n i n - s ú n . a (k) 'lady of the wild cow') the mother of Gilgameš.

[107]Akkadian literary texts did not have titles (such as "Gilgameš"); rather, they were known by their opening words (incipits). The three words *šūtur eli šarrī* began the OB text of Gilgameš (i.e., Tablet I, line 1). Lines 34'–35' here, which are written after a separation line, comprise a colophon, a notice to the reader that this is 'Tablet 2 of *Šūtur eli šarrī*'.

[108]*šūšum* (absolute form *šūš(i)*) '60'; i.e., 240 (lines on the tablet).

GLOSSARY OF AKKADIAN WORDS

Presented here are all words that appear above in the Lesson vocabularies, in examples, and in the Supplementary Reading.

Adjectives are listed under the masc. nom. sg., with the base given in parentheses. Verbal adjectives (including substantivized forms) and participles are listed under the infinitive of the verb.

For nouns, it should be assumed that forms with *t* before the case-ending are feminine, all others masculine, unless specifically indicated otherwise. The bound form, if known, is given in parentheses immediately following the main entry; the bound form before suffixes, if it differs from that before nouns, follows the latter after the siglum "sf." Plural forms are listed if known. Logographic writings are normally cited only if they have appeared in the lessons and readings above.

Verbs are listed under the G infinitive, unless the G stem is unattested, in which cases cross-references will direct the reader to the main entry. The theme-vowels of the G stem appear in parentheses. All stems in which a root commonly occurs are given, regardless of whether all such stems have been encountered in the lessons and readings above. The stems are listed in the following order: G, Gt, Gtn, D, Dt, Dtn, Š, Št (pass. or lex.), Štn, N, Ntn. The Gtn, Dtn, Štn, and Ntn stems are given only if they exhibit a meaning not easily predictable from their common iterative function.

Cross-references to forms appearing in this glossary that are derived from a common root are cited at the end of entries, as follows: the siglum "→" appears after entries of verbs or other basic forms, and directs the reader to all other derivatives of the root in the glossary; the siglum "cf." appears after all other entries, and directs the reader to the verb or other basic form of the root.

Words are listed alphabetically, as follows:

a, b, d, e, g, ḫ, i, y, k, l, m, n, p, q, r, s, ṣ, š, t, ṭ, u, w, z.

Note especially that *y* is counted alphabetically as *j*; ᵓ is ignored in alphabetization. The following hypothetical list will illustrate the order of entries differing only in vowel length: *babum, babūm, babûm, bābum, bābūm, bābûm, bâbum, bâbūm, bâbûm.*

A

abālum G (*a*) 'to dry up, out'.
abarakkum (*abarak*; log. AGRIG) an official of temples and estates; 'steward'.
abārum see *ubburum*.
abātum (*a–u*; often with strong ʾ retained) 'to destroy'; *ubbutum* D = G; *utabbutum* Dt passive; *naʾbutum* N passive.
abbuttum (*abbutti*; sf. *abbutta-*) the characteristic hair style of slaves.
abbūtum 'father's legal status; fatherly attitude' (cf. *abum*).
abnum (masc. and fem.; *aban*; pl. *abnū* and *abnātum*; log. NA$_4$) 'stone; rock, pebble; precious stone; stone weight'.
abšinnum (*abšin*; log. AB.SÍN; Sum. lw.) 'furrow; cultivated field'.
abullum (fem.; *abul*; sf. *abulla-*; pl. *abullātum*; log. ABUL [formerly read KÁ.GAL]) 'city gate, entrance gate'.
abum a (*abi*; sf. *abū-/abī-/abā-*; pl. *abbū*) 'father' (→ *abbūtum*).
Abum b (log. NE.NE.GAR) fifth OB month (July–August).
abunnatum (*abunnat*) 'navel; center, socket; umbilical cord$^{?}$'.
Adad (log. IŠKUR [the IM sign]) 'Adad' (storm god).
adānum (also *adannum*, *ḫadānum*; bnd. form *adān*, *adanni*; pl. *adānātum*, *adannātum*) 'appointed time; a specific date or period of time'.
adārum G (*a–u*) 'to fear'; *naʾdarum* N (*iʾʾaddar–iʾʾader*) 'to be feared'.
Addarum (log. ŠE.KIN.KUD) twelfth OB month (February–March).
adi (prep.; does not take sf.; log. A.RÁ) 'up to, as far as, until'; with numbers x-*īšu*: 'x times, x-fold' (e.g., *adi ḫamšīšu* 'five times, fivefold'); (conj.; rarely also *qadum*) 'until, as long as, while' (§26.2(a)); *adi* ... *lā* 'before' (§26.2(a)) (→ *adīni*).
adīni (adv.) 'until now'; usually with negative, '(not) yet' (cf. *adi*).
agārum G (*a–u*) 'to hire, rent'; vbl. adj. *agrum* (*agir-*) 'hired, rented', as noun (pl. *agrū*), 'hireling' (→ *igrum*).
agrum (vbl. adj.) see *agārum*.
agûm (*agā-*; log. AGA; Sum. lw.) 'crown, tiara'.
aḫārum G rare; *uḫḫurum* D 'to tarry, be delayed'.
aḫātum (*aḫāt*; pl. *aḫḫātum*; log. NIN) 'sister' (cf. *aḫum*).
aḫāzum G (*a–u*) 'to seize, hold, take; to take (a wife), marry; to learn'; *uḫḫuzum* D 'to mount, set, overlay (s.th.: acc.; in/with a precious material: acc.)'; *šūḫuzum* Š 'to cause to hold, cause to marry; to obtain (a wife for s.o.); to teach, instruct, to incite'; *dīnam šūḫuzum* 'to grant a legal case, hearing (to s.o.: acc.)' (→ *tāḫāzum*).
aḫḫūtum 'brotherhood, brotherliness; status of brother' (cf. *aḫum* a).
aḫītum see *aḫûm*.
aḫum a (*aḫi*; sf. *aḫū-/aḫī-/aḫā-*; pl. *aḫḫū*; log. ŠEŠ) 'brother'; *aḫum aḫam* 'one (subject) ... the other (object)' (e.g., *aḫum aḫam immar* 'one sees the other'; *aḫum ana aḫim* 'one (subject) ... to the other' (e.g., *aḫum ana aḫim ul iraggam* 'one will not lay claim against the other') (→ *aḫātum*, *aḫḫūtum*, *atḫûtum*).
aḫum b (*aḫ* [usually written *a-aḫ*] or *aḫi*; pl. rare) 'arm; side, flank; bank (of a river, canal), shore, edge; half, first half' (→ *aḫûm*).
aḫûm (denom. adj.; *aḫī-*; fem. *aḫītum*) 'strange, foreign; hostile; unusual, additional'; substantivized fem. *aḫītum* (*aḫīt*; pl. *aḫiātum*) 'additional payment'; ext. also 'misfortune, adverse feature; secrecy'; pl. also 'outskirts, outlying regions; dependents' (cf. *aḫum* b).
Ayya the consort of Šamaš.
ayyānum (adv.) 'where?' (cf. *ayyum*).
Ayyarum (log. GUD.SI.SÁ) second OB month (April–May).
ayyâšim see *anāku*.
ayyīkīam (adv.) 'where?' (cf. *ayyum*).
ayyīšamma (adv.) 'anywhere, somewhere; elsewhere' (cf. *ayyum*).

ayyum (interrog. pron., §14.2; *ayy-*; fs *ayyītum*; mp *ayyūtum*; fp *ayyātum*) 'which?' (→ *ayyānum, ayyīkīam, ayyīšamma, ayyumma, êš*).
ayyumma (adjectival indef. pron, §14.3; gen. *ayyimma*, acc. *ayyamma*; fem. *ayyītumma*) 'whichever, any, some'; substantivized 'someone, anyone'; with neg., 'no one' (cf. *ayyum*).
akalum, aklum (*akal*; log. NINDA) 'bread, food' (cf. *akālum*).
akālum G (*a–u*) 'to eat, consume; to use, have the use of (a field, etc.); to take for oneself'; *šūkulum* Š 'to cause, give to eat, to feed' (→ *akalum/aklum, ukullûm, ukultum*).
akāšum G (*u*) 'to go, move'; *ukkušum* D 'to drive away'.
Akkadûm (denom. adj.; *Akkadī-*) 'Akkadian'.
aklum see *akalum*.
alaktum (*alakti*; sf. *alakta-*; rare poetic biform *alkatum*, bnd. form *alkat*; pl. *alkātum* and *alkakātum*) 'behavior, custom(s); activity, movement; road, way, passage; caravan'; *alaktam parāsum* 'to cut off access, block the way' (cf. *alākum*).
alākum G (*illak–illik*; perf. *ittalak*) 'to go, walk, move, act'; *alākam epēšum* 'to travel'; *ḫarrānam alākum* 'to travel, undertake a military campaign; to do/perform corvée service' (see also *ālik ḫarrānim* below); *ilkam alākum* 'to perform *ilkum*-service, work *ilkum*-land'; *tappût X alākum* 'to assist X, lend X a hand, come to the aid of X' (e.g., *tappût aḫīya illikū* 'they assisted my brother'; *tappûssu allik* 'I assisted him'); ptcpl. *ālikum* (*ālik*) 'traveler, messenger'; *ālik ḫarrānim* 'expeditionary force'; *atlukum* Gt 'to go away, depart, move on, be off'; *atallukum* Gtn 'to be in motion, walk about, run around; to live, act'; *šūlukum* Š (rare) 'to cause to go; to fit' (→ *alaktum, ilkum*).
aldûm (*aldu-*; log. AL.DÙ(.A); Sum. lw.) 'store, reserve of barley'.
ali (adv.) 'where?'.
ālikum (ptcpl) see *alākum*.
alkatum see *alaktum*.
almattum (*almatti*; sf. *almatta-*; pl. *almanātum*; log. NU.MU.SU) 'widow'.
alpum (*alap*; log. GUD/GU$_4$) 'ox, bull'.
ālum (*āl(i)*; pl. *ālānū, ālānû*; log. URU) 'town, city'.
amārum G (*a–u*) 'to see, look at, observe; to find, discover, experience; to read (a tablet, etc.)'; *awātam/awâtim amārum* 'to investigate/look into a matter/case/situation'; vbl. adj. *amrum* (*amir-*) 'seen, checked'; *nanmurum* N 'to be seen, found, inspected; to appear, occur; to meet (see one another)'.
ammatum (abs./bound form *ammat*; pl. *ammātum*; log. KÙŠ) 'elbow'; a unit of length ('cubit') = ca. 50 cm. (see Appendix B.2).
Ammī-ditāna king of Babylon, 1683–47.
am-mīnim (or *ana mīnim*) 'why?'.
amrum (vbl. adj.) see *amārum*.
amtum (*amat*; pl. *amātum*; log. GEME$_2$) 'female slave, womanservant'.
Amurrûm (log. MAR.TU) 'Amorite'; *wakil Amurrîm* a high military officer.
amūtum (fem.; pl. rare) '(sheep's) liver; (liver) omen'.
-ān particularizing suffix; see §20.2.
ana (prep.; does not take sf.) 'to, toward, unto, for, as'; temporally, 'for, (with)in'; + inf. 'in order to'; *ana mīnim* 'why?'; *ana ša* (conj.; rare) 'because (of the fact that)' (§26.2(b)) (→ *anumma, aššum*).
anāku (pron.; gen.–acc. *yâti*; dat. *yâšim/ayyâšim*) 'I' (see §§2.4, 25.2).
anāpum/ḫanāpum G (*i*) 'to be(come) angry' (only one occurrence).
andurārum (*andurār*) 'freedom, manumission (of slaves); remission (of debts)'.
annam see *annum*.
annânum (adv.) 'here' (cf. *annûm*).
annīkiam (adv.) 'here' (cf. *annûm*).

annîš (adv.) 'hither' (cf. *annûm*).

annum (*anni*; sf. *anna-*) 'consent, approval; positive answer'; *annam* (adv. acc.) 'yes'.

annûm (*anni-*) 'this, these' (§6.3); *annûm* ... *annûm* 'one ... the other' (→ *annânum, annīkīam, annîš, inanna*).

Anum (log. AN, AN-*num*; Sum. lw.) the sky god, head of the pantheon.

anumma (adv.) 'now, hereby, herewith' (cf. *ana, ūmum*).

apālum G (*a–u*) 'to answer, respond; to satisfy a demand or claim; to pay (s.th.: acc.; to s.o.: acc. or *ana*)'; *atappulum* Gtn 'to answer, pay repeatedly; to be responsible for, answer for'; *uppulum* D (rare) = G.

apārum G (*i*) 'to cover the head, provide with a headdress'; vbl. adj. *aprum* (*apir-*) 'with covered head, wearing on the head'.

aplum (*apil*; log. IBILA [DUMU+UŠ]) 'heir, (oldest) son' (→ *aplūtum*).

aplūtum (*aplūt*; log. IBILA) 'position of heir; inheritance, estate'; *aplūtum ṣeḫertum u rabītum* institution of the younger and older heir (cf. *aplum*).

appārum (*appār*; pl. *appārātum*; log. AMBAR; Sum. lw.) 'reed marsh, reed bed'.

appum (*appi*; sf. *appa-*; dual *appān*; pl. *appātum*) 'nose; tip, end, edge'.

appūna, appūnā-ma (adv.) 'moreover, besides, furthermore'.

apputtum (adv.) 'please'.

aprum (vbl. adj.) see *apārum*.

apšitûm (*apšitā-*; Sum. lw.) 'agreed portion, number agreed upon.

apum (pl. *apū*; log. GIŠ.GI) 'reed thicket, canebrake'.

aqdamum presumably a Northwest Semitic word, meaning s.th. like 'ancient times'.

arāḫum G (*a*) 'to hasten, come quickly' (→ *arḫiš*).

arākum (log. GÍD(.DA)) G (*i*) 'to be (-come) long, last long; to be delayed'; vbl. adj. *arkum* (*arik-*) 'long'; *urrukum* D 'to lengthen, extend, prolong; to delay'; *šūrukum* Š (rare) 'to lengthen, prolong'.

arḫiš (adv.) 'quickly' (cf *arāḫum*).

arḫum (fem.; *araḫ*; pl. *arḫātum*; log. ÁB) 'cow'.

aribum see *erbum*.

arkum (vbl. adj.) see *arākum*.

arnum (*aran*; pl. *arnū*) 'crime, offense, wrongdoing, guilt; punishment'.

arûm G (also *erûm*; *i*; see §21.3 (e)) 'to conceive, become pregnant'; vbl. adj. *arītum* (also *erītum*) 'pregnant'.

askuppum or *askuppatum* '(stone) slab, doorsill, threshold'.

aslum (pl. *aslū*) 'young (male) sheep' (poetic word).

assammum (Sum. lw.) 'jug'.

asûm (gen. *asîm* or *asêm*, acc. *asâm* or *asiam*; bound form *asi*?; pl. *asû*; log. A.ZU; Sum. lw.) 'physician'.

ašar (conj.) 'where(ever)'; rarely 'when, what' (§26.2(b)) (cf. *ašrum*).

ašariš (adv.) 'there' (cf. *ašrum*).

ašāšum G (*u*) 'to be(come) disturbed, worried'; *uššušum* D 'to cause distress, mistreat'.

ašlākum (*ašlāk*; pl. *ašlākū*; log. [lú]TÚG) 'washerman, fuller'.

ašlum (fem.; *ašal*; pl. *ašlātum*; log. ÉŠ(E)) 'rope'; a unit of length = 120 *ammatum* = ca. 60 m. (see Appendix B.2).

ašnan (normally without a case-ending; fem.) 'grain, cereal'.

ašrum (*ašar*; pl. *ašrū* and *ašrātum*; log. KI) 'place, locale, setting'; *ašar ištēn* '(in) one place' (→ *ašar, ašariš, ašrānum*).

ašrānum (adv.) 'there' (cf. *ašrum*).

aššatum (*aššat*; pl. *aššātum*; log. DAM) 'wife' (→ *aššūtum*).

aššum (prep.; sf. *aššumīya, aššumīka*, etc.) 'concerning, because of, on account of, for the sake of'; (conj.) 'because'; rarely 'so that' (esp. Mari) (§26.2(b)) (cf. *ana, šumum*).

aššūtum (*aššūt*) 'marriage; status of wife' (cf. *aššatum*).

atappum (fem.) '(small) branch or offtake of a canal'.

atḫûtum (*atḫût*) 'brotherly attitude, relationship, partnership' (cf. *aḫum*).

atta (pron.; gen.–acc. *kâta / kâti*; dat. *kâšim / kâšum*) 'you' (ms) (see §§2.4, 25.2).

atti (pron.; gen.–acc. *kâti*; dat. *kâšim*) 'you' (fs) (see §§2.4, 25.2).

attina (pron.; gen.–acc. *kunūti*; dat. *kunūšim*) 'you' (fp) (see §§2.4, 25.2).

attunu (pron.) 'you' (mp) (§§2.4, 25.2).

atwûm Gt (G not used in OB) (*u*) 'to speak; to discuss'; *šutāwûm* Št-lex. 'to discuss, consider, ponder' (→ *awātum*).

awātum (*awāt*; pl. *awâtum* [‹ *awā* + *ātum*]; log. INIM) 'word, message, command; matter, affair, thing'; *awātam / awâtim amārum* 'to investigate/look into a matter/case/situation'; *awātam šūṣûm* to betray a secret (cf. *atwûm*).

awīltum (fem. of *awīlum;* pl. *awīlātum*) '(free-)woman, lady'; also, an epithet for *Bēlessunu*, a goddess.

awīlum (*awīl;* pl. *awīlû*, §20.3; log. LÚ) 'human being, person; grown man; free man; boss' (→ *awīltum, awīlūtum*).

awīlūtum 'humanity, human species, people; someone, anyone; soldier, worker; status of *awīlum*' (cf. *awīlum*).

awûm see *atwûm*.

B

ba'ālum G (*i*) 'to be(come) (abnormally) large, important'; *bu''ulum* D 'to enlarge, exaggerate'.

babālum G (for *wabālum;* dur. *ubbal* – pret. *ubil* [pl. *ublū* or *ubilū*]) 'to bear, carry, transport, convey'; vbl. adj. *bablum* (*babil-*) 'carried, transported' (rare); *itabbulum* Gtn 'to carry repeatedly'; also 'to manage, direct, organize'; *šūbulum* Š 'to cause to carry/bring; to send, dispatch (something)'. (→ *šībultum*).

Bābilim (log. KÁ.DINGIR.RA[ki]) 'Babylon'.

bablum (vbl. adj.) see *babālum*.

bābtum (*bābti;* sf. *bābta-* pl. *bābātum*) 'city quarter, neighborhood, district; goods/merchandise outstanding; loss, deficit' (cf. *bābum*).

bābum (*bāb;* pl. *bābū* and *bābātum;* log. KÁ) 'opening, door, gate; city quarter'; ext. *bāb ekallim* ('palace gate') the umbilical fissure (→ *bābtum*).

Bad-tibira (Tell Madā'in) a city in the south, near Uruk.

bā'erum (ptcpl.) see *bârum*.

balāṭum G (*u*) 'to live, be alive, be(-come) healthy; to get well, recover'; inf. used as a noun, 'life'; vbl. adj. *balṭum* (base *baliṭ-;* fem. *baliṭtum*) 'alive, healthy, safe'; *bulluṭum* D 'to keep (s.o.) alive, healthy, safe; to heal (tr.)' (→ *bulṭum*).

balṭum (vbl. adj.) see *balāṭum*.

balum (prep.; sf. *balukka, baluššu,* etc.) 'without, without the knowledge/consent of; apart from'; *ina balum* = *balum*.

bāmâ (adv.) 'in half'.

banûm a G (*i*) 'to build, rebuild, construct, create'; vbl. adj. *banûm* b (*bani-*) 'well-made, well-formed, fine, of good quality'; ptcpl. see *bānûm* (→ *būnum*).

banûm b (vbl. adj.) see *banûm* a.

banûm c G (*i*) 'to grow; to be(come) pleasant'; vbl. adj. *banûm* d (*bani-*) 'good, beautiful, friendly'; *bunnûm* D 'to treat kindly'.

banûm d (vbl. adj.) see *banûm* c.

bānûm (*bāni-*; fem. *bānītum;* ptcpl. of *banûm*) 'creator'.

baqārum G (*a–u*) 'to claim, lay claim to; to contest, bring suit (against s.o.: acc.; for s.th.: acc. or *aššum* or *ana*)'; substantivized vbl. adj. *baqrum*, usually pl. *baqrū* 'legal claims'; *baqrī rašûm* 'to incur legal claims'.

baqrū see *baqārum*.

barāmum G 'to be multicolored', only in vbl. adj. *barmum* (*barum-*) 'multicolored, speckled, variegated'; *bitrumum* Gt, only in vbl. adj. *bitrumum* = *barmum; burrumum* D 'to color, weave in colors' (→ *bitrāmum*).

barbarum (pl. *barbarū*; log. UR.BAR.RA) 'wolf'.
barmum (vbl. adj.) see *barāmum*.
Barsipa 'Borsippa', a city 25 km. s. of Babylon (modern Birs Nimrud).
barûm G (*i*) 'to look at, inspect, observe'; ptcpl. see *bārûm*.
bārûm (*bāri-*; ptcpl. of *barûm*; log. (lú)MÁŠ.ŠU.GÍD.GÍD) 'diviner, haruspex'.
bârum a G (*a*) 'to catch (fish, etc.)'; ptcpl. *bāʾerum* (*bāʾer*; log. (lú)ŠU.ḪA) 'fisherman'; also, a class of soldier.
bârum b G (*a–u*) 'to be firm, in good repair; to become proved' (rare in OB apart from PNs); *burrum* D 'to establish, ascertain (the true legal situation), prove, certify, explain, indicate'.
bašītum (*bašīt*; substantivized fem. vbl. adj. of *bašûm*), *bīšum* (*bīš(i)*), *bušûm* (*buši*; pl. *bušû*), *būšum* (*būš(i)*; pl. *būšū*) 'moveable property, valuables, goods; stock, what's on hand' (cf. *bašûm*).
bašmum a horned snake; the constellation Hydra.
bāštum (*bāšti*; sf. *bāšta-*) 'dignity, pride; good looks'.
bašûm a G (*i*) 'to exist; to be present, available; to happen'; dur. 3cs *ibašši* 'there is/are' may occur with pl. subjects; vbl. adj. *bašûm* b (*baši-*) 'on hand, available, present' (listed in the dictionaries as a ptcpl., *bāšûm*); see also substantivized fem. *bašītum* above; *šubšûm* Š 'to make appear, produce, create'; *nabšûm* N 'to come into existence, appear, become available (→ *bašītum*/*bīšum*/*bušûm*/*būšum*).
bašûm b (vbl. adj.) see *bašûm* a.
batāqum G (*a–u*) 'to cut off, deduct; to cut through, pierce; to divide; to stop work'; *buttuqum* D = G; *butattuqum* Dt passive; *nabtuqum* N passive (→ *bitiqtum*, *bitqum*, *butuqtum*).
bâʾum G (*a*; see §21.3(j)) 'to walk along'.
baz(a)ḫatum (Northwest Semitic word) 'military outpost'.
bēltum (*bēlet*; pl. *bēlētum*; log. NIN) 'lady; mistress, (female) owner' (cf. *bêlum*).
belûm G (*e*) 'to go out, be extinguished'; *bullûm* D 'to put out, extinguish (fire), destroy'.
bēlum (*bēl(i)*; pl. *bēlū*; log. EN) 'lord, master, owner'; *bēl dīnim* 'adversary (in court)'; *bēl ḫubullim* (sf. *bēl ḫubullī-*) 'creditor' (cf. *bêlum*).
bêlum G (*e*) 'to rule, have power over, exercise authority' (→ *bēl(t)um*, *bēlūtum*).
bēlūtum (*bēlūt*) 'lordship, dominion, rule; position of power; status of owner'; *bēlūtam epēšum* 'to rule, exercise authority' (cf. *bêlum*).
bennum (often pl. *bennū*) a type of epilepsy.
bērum (abs./bound form *bēr*; log. DANNA) a unit of length ('double-hour'; 'mile') = 21,600 *ammatum* = ca. 10.8 km. (see Appendix B.2).
bibbulum / *bubbulum* 'flood'; a month name (cf. *babālum*).
bibbum 'plague'.
biblum (*bibil*; pl. *biblātum*) '(marriage) gift'; *bibil libbim* 'wish, desire' (cf. *babālum*).
biltum (abs./bound form *bilat*; pl. *bilātum*; log. GUN/GÚ.UN) 'load, weight; tribute, rent'; a unit of weight ('talent') = 3,600 *šiqlum* = ca. 30 kg. (see Appendix B.1); *nāš(i) biltim* 'tenant (of a field owned by the state)' (cf. *babālum*).
birītum (*birīt*) 'interval, intervening space'; ext. also 'border (area)' of the liver; *ina birīt* (before suffix *ina bīrī-*) 'between, among'.
birtum (*birti*; pl. *bir(ān)ātum*) 'citadel, castle, fort'.
bīšum see *bašītum*.
bitiqtum (*bitiqti*; sf. *bitiqta-*) 'deficit, loss' (cf. *batāqum*).
bitqum (*bitiq*) 'opening (of a canal); diverting (of water); cutting (rare); a measure/amount (of silver, flour)' (cf. *batāqum*).
bitrāmum (adj.; *bitrām-*) 'brightly colored, multicolored' (cf. *barāmum*).

bitrûm Gt (rare; not in G) 'to last, be continuous'; *šutebrûm* Št-lex. 'to remain, continue; to make last'.
bitrumum (vbl. adj.) see *barāmum*.
bītum (masc.; *bīt(i)*; pl. *bītātum*; log. É) 'house, estate, household, temple'; *bīt abim* 'family; family/paternal estate, patrimony'; *bīt emim* (rare) 'wedding'; *bīt emūtim* 'house in which a wedding is held'; *bīt ṭuppim* (log. É.DUB.BA) 'tablet house, school, archive'; *mār bīt ṭuppim* (log. DUMU É.DUB.BA(.A)) 'state scribe'; *bītum epšum* 'built-on property'.
bu'ārum 'cheerfulness; prosperity'.
bubbulum see *bibbulum*.
bubūtum (*bubūt*; pl. *bubu'ātum*/*bubâtum*) 'hunger; famine; sustenance'.
būdum (fem.; *būd(i)*; du. *būdān*) 'shoulder'.
bullûm (adj.; *bullu-*) meaning unknown.
bulṭum (*buluṭ*) 'life, health' (cf. *balāṭum*).
būnum (usually pl. *būnū*) 'features, face, appearance' (cf. *banûm* a).
būrum (abs. *būr*; log. BÙR(iku); Sum. lw.) a unit of area = 18 *ikûm* = ca. 6.48 ha. (see Appendix B.3).
bussurtum (bound form irregularly *bussurat*) '(good) news, message'.
bušûm, *būšum* see *bašītum*.
butuqtum (*butuqti*; pl. *butuqātum*) 'flood; sluice channel' (cf. *batāqum*).

D

da'āmum G (*i* or *u*) 'to be(come) dark'; R vbl adj. *da'ummum* 'dark, gloomy'.
dabābum G (*u*) 'to speak, talk, tell; to discuss; to plead (in court); to complain, protest'; inf. as noun: 'speech, statement; plea, lawsuit; rumor'; *tuššam dabābum* 'to speak maliciously, calumniate'; *dubbubum* D 'to complain (to), entreat, bother' (→ *dibbatum*).
dagālum G (*a–u*) 'to look (at, upon)'; with *ana*, *(ina) pān*: 'to wait upon, attend to, belong to'.
dadmū (always pl.) 'habitations, settlements; the inhabited world'.
Dagan god of grain, an important deity in the Mari region.
dayyānum (*dayyān*; pl. *dayyānū*; log. DI.KUD/KU5) 'judge' (cf. *diānum*).
dâkum G (*a–u*) 'to kill, execute; to defeat'; *šudukkum* Š 'to have (s.o.) killed' (rare); N passive.
daltum (*dalat*; pl. *dalātum*) 'door, door-leaf'.
dâlum G (*a–u*) 'to wander'.
damāqum (*i*) 'to be(come) good, better, improve, prosper' vbl. adj. *damqum* (*damiq-*) 'good, of good quality; beautiful; favorable; expert'; substantivized fem. *damiqtum* (*damiqti*) 'good(ness), favor, luck; fame'; *dummuqum* D 'to make good, pleasing; to improve (tr.); to treat kindly (+ acc. or *ana*/dative)' (→ *damqiš*, *tadmiqtum*).
damiqtum see *damāqum*.
damqiš (adv.) 'well' (cf. *damāqum*).
damqum (vbl. adj.) see *damāqum*.
damum (*dam(i)*; pl. *damū*) 'blood'.
danānum a G (*i*) 'to be(come) strong'; vbl. adj. *dannum* (*dann-*) 'strong, solid; mighty, powerful; fortified; fierce, savage; severe, difficult; urgent'; substantivized fem. *dannatum* (*dannat*) 'famine, hard times; fortress; military service'; *dannātim šakānum* 'to give strong orders' (Mari); *dunnunum* D 'to strengthen, fortify, reinforce; to speak severely'; in hendiadys: 'to do s.th. forcefully' (→ *dannūtum*).
danānum b ext.: a part of the liver.
dannatum see *danānum*.
dannum (vbl. adj.) see *danānum*
dannūtum (*dannūt*) 'strength, power, violence'; late also: 'fortress' (cf. *danānum*).
darāsum G (*i*) 'to trample upon, throw over, back'.
dāriātum see *dārûm*.
dāriš (adv.), *dāriš ūmī* (adv. phrase) 'forever' (cf. *dārum*).

dārum (*dār(i)*) 'perpetuity', rare except in the adverb *dāriš* (→ *dārûm*).

dārûm (*dārī-*) 'perpetual, lasting, everlasting'; substantivized fem. pl. *dāriātum* 'perpetuity, eternity'; *ana dāriātim* 'forever' (cf. *dārum*).

dāṣtum 'deception' (cf. *dâṣtum*).

dâṣum G (*a*) 'to deceive' (→ *dāṣtum*).

daʾummum (vbl. adj.) see *daʾāmum*.

dekûm G (*e*) 'to move, remove; to arouse, raise, mobilize, call up (soldiers, officials)'; *šudkûm* Š 'to persuade' (rare).

diānum G (*a–i*) 'to judge, give a judgment (*dīnum*); to start a lawsuit, go to court' (cf. *dayyānum, dīnum*).

dibbatum (*dibbat*; pl. *dibbātum* = sg.) 'agreement' (cf. *dabābum*).

dikšum (*dikiš*; pl. *dikšū*) 'wound'; ext. aslo 'severed part'.

dimtum (*dimat*; pl. *dimātum;* log. AN. ZA.GÀR) 'tower; fortified area, settlement; district'.

dīnum (*dīn(i)*; pl. *dīnātum*) '(legal) decision, judgement, verdict; legal case, lawsuit'; *bēl dīnim* 'adversary (in court)'; *ša dīnim* 'litigant'; *dīnam šūḫuzum* 'to grant a legal case, hearing (to s.o.: acc.)' (cf. *diānum*).

dipārum (masc. and fem.; *dipār*; pl. *dipārātum*) 'torch'.

dirigûm (-*ā*; Sum. d i r i g (a)) 'intercalary month'; attested only once.

dīšum (*dīš(i)*; pl. *dīšū*) 'green grass, herbage, spring pasture; spring (-time)'.

diʾtum (pl. *diʾātum*) 'notice, information' (cf. *edûm*).

Dumuzi (log. ŠU.NUMUN.NA) fourth OB month (June–July).

duppurum D (not in G) 'to go away, absent oneself'.

dūrum a (*dūr(i)*; pl. *dūrānū*; log. BÀD) 'wall'.

dūrum b (*dūr(i)*) 'continuity; permanent status of property'.

duššupum (adj.; *duššup-*) 'sweet'.

E

Ea (usually written *é-a*) the god of fresh water, and of intelligence and cunning.

Eanna (Sum. é.an.na(k) 'house of heaven') Inanna's main temple in Uruk.

Ebabbar (log. É.BABBAR) the temple of Šamaš in the city of Sippar.

ebbum (vbl. adj.) see *ebēbum*.

ebēbum G (*i*) 'to be(come) clean'; vbl. adj. *ebbum* (*ebb-*; fem. *ebbetum*) 'clean, pure, holy; shining, polished; trustworthy'; *ubbubum* D 'to clean, purify; to clear (of claims), clear oneself'.

eblum (*ebel*; log. EŠE$_3$$^{(iku)}$) 'rope'; a unit of area = 6 *ikûm* = ca. 2.16 ha. (see Appendix B.3).

ebūrum (*ebūr*; log. BURU$_{14}$) 'harvest(-time); crop; summer'.

edēdum G (*u*) 'to be(come) pointed'; *uddudum* D factitive; also, in hendiadys, 'to act, do quickly'.

edēḫum G only in vbl. adj. *edḫum* (*ediḫ-*) 'covered with patches or a network'; *udduḫum* D 'to cover completely with (patches, etc.)'.

edēlum G (*i*) 'to close, lock' (tr.); *uddulum* D = G.

edērum G (*i*) 'to hug, embrace'; *nendurum* N 'to embrace one another'.

edēšum G (*i*) 'to be(come) new'; vbl. adj. *eššum* (‹ **edšum*; fem. *eššetum*, rarely *edištum*) 'new, fresh'; *uddušum* D 'to renew, restore'.

edḫum (vbl. adj.) see *edēḫum*.

edûm/*idûm* G (pret. *īde*; see §26.1) 'to know, be(come) experienced, familiar with'; *(w)uddûm* D 'to mark, assign; to make known, reveal, inform; to recognize, identify'; *šūdûm* Š (*edûm*) 'to make known, announce, proclaim (s.th.: acc.; to s.o.: acc. or *ana*/dat.)' (cf. *diʾtum*).

eʾēlum G (*i*; §21.3(d)) 'to bind (by an agreement, by magic)' (→ *eʾiltum*).

egûm G (*i* or *u*) 'to be(come) careless, negligent (concerning: *ana* or *aššum*)' (→ *ēgûtum*).

ēgûtum (*ēgût*) 'negligence' (cf. *egûm*).

eʾiltum (*eʾilti*; sf. *eʾilta-*) '(financial) liability, obligation' (cf. *eʾēlum*).

ekallum (fem.; *ekal*; sf. *ekalla-*; pl.

ekallātum; log. É.GAL; Sum. lw.) '(royal) palace'; ext.: *bāb ekallim* ('palace gate') the umbilical fissure.
ekallûm (denom. adj.; *ekallī-*) 'palace official'.
ekēmum G (*i*) 'to take away (s.th. from s.o.: double acc.), deprive (s.o. of s.th.: double acc.); to conquer, annex; to take away, snatch away; to absorb'; vbl. adj. *ekmum* (*ekim-*) 'taken away', etc.; ext. also 'stunted, atrophied'.
Ekišnugal the temple of Nanna at Ur.
ekmum (vbl. adj.) see *ekēmum*.
ekûm (base *eku-*; usually fem. sg. *ekūtum*) 'homeless, orphan(ed)'.
elēlum G (*i*) 'to be(come) pure, clean, free (of debt)'; vbl. adj. *ellum* (*ell-*; fem. *elletum*) 'clean, pure, holy, free'; *ullulum* D 'to purify, keep pure; to declare innocent, free (of debt); to consecrate (to a god)' (→ *tēliltum*).
elēnum (adv.) 'above, upstream; beyond, besides, in addition'; (prep.; sf. *elēnukka*, etc.) 'above; beside, in addition to, apart from' (cf. *elûm* a).
eleppum (fem.; *elep*; sf. *eleppa-*; pl. *eleppētum*; log. (giš)MÁ) 'ship, boat'.
elēṣum G (*i*) 'to rejoice'; *ulluṣum* D and *šūluṣum* Š 'to cause to rejoice' (→ *mēleṣum, ulṣum*).
eli (in literary texts also *el*; prep.; sf. *elī-*) 'on, upon, over, above, towards, against, beyond, more than' (cf. *elûm* a).
eliātum see *elûm* b under *elûm* a.
eliš (adv.) 'above, up(ward), on top' (cf. *elûm* a).
Ellil see *Enlil*.
ellum (vbl. adj.) see *elēlum*.
Elūlum see *Elūnum*.
elûm a G (*i*; see §21.3(e)) 'to go up, ascend'; with ventive, 'to come up, emerge, appear'; vbl. adj. *elûm* b (*eli-*; fem. *elītum*) 'high, tall, exalted'; substantivized fem. pl. *eliātum* 'additional sum'; *etlûm* Gt 'to move off, away'; *ina X etlûm* 'to forfeit X' (e.g., *ina X ītelli* 'he will forfeit X'); *ullûm* D 'to raise, elevate, extol'; *utlellûm* Dtr (§38.3(d)) 'to raise oneself'; *šūlûm* Š 'to cause to go up, send/lead/take/bring up; to raise, make emerge/appear; to summon/produce a witness (or document); to remove, oust' (→ *elēnum, eli, eliš, elûm* c).
elûm b (vbl. adj.) see *elûm* a.
elûm c (*elī-*; fem. *elītum*; rel. adj.) 'upper' (cf. *elûm* a).
Elūnum / *Elūlum* (later *Ulūlum*; log. KIN.dINANNA) sixth month OB (August–September).
ēma (rarely *ēm*; conj.) 'where(ever)' (§26.2(b)).
emēdum G (*i*) 'to lean against, touch, cling to; to reach, stand near/by; to place or lean (s.th. against s.th.: double acc.); to load, impose (taxes, punishment, etc.: acc.; on s.o.: acc.)'; *ummudum* D 'to lean, push, rest, set (s.th.) on, against (s.th.)'; *šutēmudum* Št-lex. 'to bring into contact, join, unite, add' (causative of *nenmudum* N); *nenmudum* N 'to be joined, come together, meet; to join forces' (→ *imittum* b).
Emeteursag temple of Zababa.
emum (sf. *emū-* / *emī-* / *emā-*) 'father-in-law (wife's father)'; *bīt emim* (rare) 'wedding'; *ana bīt emim šasûm* 'to summon to a wedding', i.e., 'to have a wedding' (→ *emūtum*).
emūqum (dual *emūqān*; pl. masc. *emūqū* and fem. *emūqātum*) 'strength, power, force, ability; armed forces; value'; also used in the dual and pl. with the same meanings.
Emutbalum a region east of the Tigris River.
emūtum 'wedding', in *bīt emūtim* house in which a wedding is held (cf. *emum*).
enēqum G (*i*) 'to suck'; *šūnuqum* Š 'to suckle'; ptcpl. fem. *mušēniqtum* 'wet-nurse' (→ *tēnīqum*).
enēšum G (*i*) 'to be(come) weak, impoverished'; vbl. adj. *enšum* (*eniš-*) 'weak, powerless'; *unnušum* D 'to make weak, weaken (tr.)'.

Enlil (or *Ellil*; log. ^{d}EN.LÍL) 'Enlil', one of the heads of the Mesopotamian pantheon.

enšum (vbl. adj.) see *enēšum*.

entum (log. NIN.DINGIR(.RA); Sum. lw.) 'high priestess'.

enûm G (*i*) 'to change, invert, revoke'.

enzum (also *ezzum, inzum*; fem.; pl. *enzētum*) 'she-goat'; also, the constellation Lyra.

eperum, eprum (*eper*; pl. *ep(e)rū* often = sg.) 'dust, (loose) earth'.

epēsum G 'to object'; *uppusum* D = G (both rare).

epēšum G (*e–u* or *u–u*) 'to do (s.th.: acc.; to s.o.: acc. or *ana*); to act (according to: *kīma*), be active; to make, build, construct; to treat (s.o.: acc.; like: *kīma*; for [e.g., a wound]: acc.)'; *alākam epēšum* 'to travel'; *ana šiprim epēšim* 'to do the work'; *bēlūtam epēšum* 'to rule, exercise authority'; *kakkī epēšum* 'to fight, do battle, make war'; *piam epēšum* 'to work/open one's mouth'; *simmam epēšum* 'to treat a disease'; *šarrūtam epēšum* 'to rule as king'; *šipram epēšum* 'to do (assigned) work; to work (s.th.: acc.; e.g., *eqlam šipram īpuš* he worked [i.e., plowed] the field)'; *tāḫāzam epēšum* 'to do battle, make war, fight'; *tappûtam epēšum* 'to do business together'; *têrtam epēšum* 'to perform extispicy'; *ulṣam epēšum* 'to rejoice; to make love'; vbl. adj. *epšum* (*epiš-*) 'built, cultivated, worked'; substantivized fem. *epištum* (*epišti*; pl. *epšētum*) 'work; construction; act, activity, achievement'; *epšēt qātim* 'handiwork'; *eqel epšētim* 'a field worked/prepared (for s.th.; lit., a field of [plowing, etc.] activities)'; *uppušum* D (not common in OB) = G; *šūpušum* Š 'to cause to do/make/build; to have (s.th.) built; to direct work'; *šutēpušum* Št-lex. 'to get busy, active' (→ *ipšum*).

epištum see *epēšum*.

epqum 'leprosy'; *epqam malûm* 'to become covered with leprosy'.

eprum see *eperum*.

epšum (vbl. adj.) see *epēšum*.

eqlum (*eqel*; pl. *eqlētum*; log. A.ŠÀ) 'plot of land, field; area, region'; *eqlam mayyarī maḫāṣum* 'to plow'; *eqel epšētim* 'a field worked/prepared' (for s.th.)'; *rēš eqlim* 'destination'.

erbe (also *erba, erbûm, arbaʾum*; with masc. nouns *erbet, erbetti, erbettum*) 'four' (→ *erbeā, erbîšu, rebiat, rebītum, rebûm*).

erbeā (also *erbâ*; indeclinable) 'forty' (cf. *erbe*).

erbîšu (adv.) 'four times, fourfold' (cf. *erbe*).

erebum, erebûm see *erbûm*.

erbûm (*erbi-*; (also *erbûm, erebu/ûm, aribu*; pl. *erebû*)) 'locust(s)'.

erēbum G (*u*) 'to enter, arrive, invade' (normally with *ana*: e.g., *ana bītim ērub* 'I entered the house'); *šūrubum* Š 'to cause to enter, send/lead/take/bring in'.

ereqqum (fem.; *ereq*, with suf. *ereqqa-*; pl. *ereqqētum*; log. $^{(giš)}$MAR.GÍD.DA) 'wagon, cart'; also, a constellation.

erēšum a G (*i*) 'to ask, request (s.th.: acc.; from s.o.: acc. or *itti*), desire, wish'; vbl. adj. *eršum* (*eriš-*) 'requested', esp. in substantivized fem. *erištum* (*erišti*) 'wish, desire, request'.

erēšum b G (*i*) 'to (plow and) seed, plant, cultivate (a field)' (→ *errēšum, mērešum*); *šūrušum* Š (rare) 'to cause to (be) cultivate(d), put under cultivation'.

erištum see *erēšum* a.

ernettum see *irnittum*.

Erra the god of pestilence.

errēšum (*errēš*; pl. *errēšū*) 'cultivator, tenant farmer' (cf. *erēšum*; → *errēšūtum*).

errēšūtum 'tenancy (of a field)' (cf. *errēšum*).

errū (pl.) 'intestines'.

erṣetum (*erṣet*; pl. *erṣētum*; log. KI) 'the earth; land, district, area; ground, earth; the nether world'.

eršum a (adj.; *eriš-*) 'wise, clever, skillful'.
eršum b (fem.; *ereš*; pl. *eršētum*; log. (giš)NÁ) 'bed'.
erûm see *werûm*.
ērum (vbl. adj.) see *êrum*.
êrum G (*e*; §21.3(d)) 'to awaken; to be(come) awake, alert'; vbl. adj. *ērum* (*ēr-*) 'awake, alert, watchful'.
Esagil (log. É.SAG.ÍL) the temple of Marduk in Babylon.
esēḫum G (*i*) 'to assign' (→ *isiḫtum*).
esēpum G (*i*) 'to collect, gather up'.
esērum a G (*i*) 'to enclose, shut in'; *ussurum* D 'to enclose, take captive'.
esērum b G (*i*) 'to press (s.o.: acc.; for payment, silver: acc.), put under pressure, collect'; *šērtam esērum* 'to impose a penalty, punishment'; *ussurum* D = G.
esiḫtum see *isiḫtum*.
eṣēdum G (*i*) 'to harvest, reap'; ptcpl. *ēṣidum* (*ēṣid*; pl. *ēṣidū*) 'harvester'.
eṣemtum (*eṣemti*; sf. *eṣemta-*; pl. *eṣmētum*; log. GÌR.PAD.DU) 'bone'.
ēṣidum (ptcpl.) see *eṣēdum*.
êš (‹ *ayyiš*; adv.) 'where, whither?' (cf. *ayyum*).
ešer (*ešrum* a; with masc. nouns *ešret*, *ešeret*, *ešertum*) 'ten' (→ *ešrā*, *ešret*, *ešrētum*, *ešrum* b, *ešrûm*, *šinšarûm*).
ešērum G (*i*) 'to be(come) straight; to move straight toward, charge (with *ana*); to prosper'; vbl. adj. irregularly *išarum* (base *išar-*) 'regular, normal; correct, fair, just; in good condition; prosperous'; *šūšurum* Š 'to move straight toward; to set straight, set on the proper course, make prosper'; *šutēšurum* Št-lex. 'to proceed; to thrive, prosper; to set right, put in order, provide justice; to guide properly; to send; to make prosper' (→ *mīšarum*).
Ešnunna (Tell Asmar) an important city east of the Tigris.
ešrā (gen.-acc. *ešrī*) 'twenty' (cf. *ešer*).
ešret (abs. of **eširtum*) 'one-tenth' (cf. *ešer*).
ešrētum (always pl.) 'tithe' (cf. *ešer*).
ešrum a see *ešer*.
ešrum b (adj.; fem. *ešurtum*) 'tenth' (cf. *ešer*).
ešrûm (fem. *ešrītum*) 'twentieth' (cf. *ešer*).
eššum (vbl. adj.) see *edēšum*.
etellum (adj.; *etel*; fem. *etelletum*) 'princely, sovereign, supreme'; substantivized masc. 'prince', fem. 'princess'.
etēqum G (*i*) 'to pass along, pass by, advance, elapse; to pass through, across; to exceed, transgress; to avoid'; *šūtuqum* Š 'to cause to move on/proceed/pass; to send on; to allow to elapse'.
eṭlum (pl. like an adjective, *eṭlūtum*; log. GURUŠ [the KAL sign]) 'young man, youth'.
ewûm G (*i*; see §21.3(k)) 'to become, turn, change (*ana* / *-iš*: into)'.
ezēbum G (*i*) 'to leave, leave behind, abandon; to neglect; to leave (s.th.: acc.; with s.o.: *ana*), entrust; to divorce; to make out (a legal document)'; *šūzubum* Š 'to cause to leave; to have (a document) made out; to save (persons, cities)' (→ *ezib* / *ezub*, *izbum*).
ezēḫum G (I–*y*; *i*) 'to gird'; *nēzuḫum* N 'to gird oneself, be girded'.
ezib and *ezub* (prep.; does not take sf.) 'apart from, besides' (cf. *ezēbum*).
Ezida (log. É.ZI.DA) the temple of Marduk in Borsippa.
ezub see *ezib*.
ezzum see *enzum*.

G

gagûm (base *gagi-*; Sum. lw.; log. GÁ.GI.A and GÁ.GI4.A) 'cloister'; part of the temple area, in which the *nadītum* women lived.
gallābum (*gallāb*; log. ŠU.I) 'barber' (cf. *gullubum*).
gamālum G (*i*) 'to treat kindly, please; to come to an agreement; to spare, save'.
gamartum 'totality; completion' (cf. *gamārum*).

gamārum G (*a–u*) 'to bring to an end; to annihilate; to use up; to settle; to encompass, control; to finish (doing: *ina* + inf.); to come to an end'; in hendiadys: 'to do s.th. completely'; vbl. adj. *gamrum* (*gamir-*) 'finished, settled; complete, entire, full (may follow another adj.: *šamnum ṭābum gamrum* 'the entire (amount of) fine oil')'; *ana gamrim* 'completely'; *gummurum* D = G; also, 'to pay in full' (→ *gamartum*).

gamrum (vbl. adj.) see *gamārum*.

gana (Sumerian g a n . a 'come!') 'come (on)!'.

garārum G (also *qarārum*; *u*) 'to roll, turn over; to twist, grow crooked'; vbl. adj. *garrum* (*garir-*) 'round, bulging'; *šugarrurum* irregular Š(D) (§§38.2, 38.3(a)) 'to roll' (tr.); *nagarrurum* irregular N (§38.2) 'to roll around, move'.

garrum (vbl. adj.) see *garārum*.

gašārum G (*i*) 'to be(come) powerful, strong'; vbl. adj. *gašrum* (*gašer-*) 'powerful, strong'.

gašīšum (*gašīš*) 'impaling stake'.

gašrum (vbl. adj.) see *gašārum*.

gerrum (masc. and fem.; *gerri*; pl. *gerrū* and *gerrētum*) 'road, path; journey, (business) trip, caravan; military campaign; expeditionary force; travel provisions'.

gerseqqûm (*gerseqqā-*; log. GÌR.SÌ.GA; Sum. lw.) 'an attendant, domestic (attached to the palace or a temple)'.

gerûm G (*e*) 'to be(come) hostile; to start a lawsuit (intr.), sue (tr.)'; *gitrûm* Gt 'to sue one another'; *gurrûm* D = G.

Gibil / *Girra* (log. GIBIL [written BIL + GI]) the fire god.

gigunnûm (*-ā*; pl. *gigunnû*) a sacred building; temple tower.

gilittum (*gilitti*; sf. *gilitta-*) 'fright, terror'.

gillatum (*gillat*) 'crime'.

gimlum 'reserve ox' (rare word).

Girra see *Gibil*.

gišimmarum (fem. and masc.; *gišimmar*; pl. *gišimmarātum*; log. [giš]GIŠIMMAR; Sum. lw.) 'date palm'.

gubrum (*gubur*) 'shepherd's hut'.

gulgullum, *gulgullatum* (*gulgul* / *gulgulat*; pl. *gulgullū*, *gulgullātum*) 'skull'.

gullubum D (not in G) 'to shave (off)' (→ *gallābum*).

gurgurrum (or *qurqurrum*; bound form *gurgur*; log. [lú]TIBIRA) 'wood- or metal-worker'.

gušūrum (*gušūr*; log. GIŠ.ÙR; Sum. lw.) 'beam, log'.

Ḫ

ḫabābum G (*u*) 'to murmur, whisper, chirp; to caress'.

ḫabālum G (*a–u*) 'to harm, wrong, oppress' (→ *ḫibiltum*).

ḫabārum G (*u*) 'to be noisy'; vbl. adj. *ḫabrum* (*ḫabur-*) 'noisy'.

ḫabātum G (*a–u*) 'to rob, plunder'; vbl. adj. *ḫabtum* (*ḫabit-*) 'robbed, plundered'; *naḫbutum* N passive (→ *ḫabbātum*, *ḫubtum*).

ḫabbātum (*ḫabbāt*) 'robber' (cf. *ḫabātum*).

ḫabrum (vbl. adj.) see *ḫabārum*.

ḫadîš (adv.) 'joyfully' (cf. *ḫadûm*).

ḫadûm a G (*u*) 'to rejoice, be(come) happy (at, in s.th.: *ina* or *ana*)'; vbl. adj. *ḫadûm* b (*ḫadi-*) 'happy, joyful, rejoicing'; *ḫuddûm* D 'to make happy' (→ *ḫadîš*, *ḫūdum*).

ḫadûm b (vbl. adj.) see *ḫadûm* a.

ḫāʾirum / *ḫāwirum* (ptcpl.) see *ḫiārum*.

ḫakûm G (Northwest Semitic word) 'to await' (only attested once).

ḫalālum G (also *alālum*; *a–u*) 'to hang, suspend' (tr.); *ḫullulum* D = G; *ḫutallulum* Dt passive of D.

ḫalāqum (*i*) 'to become missing, lost; to disappear, perish; to escape'; vbl. adj. *ḫalqum* (*ḫaliq-*) 'escaped; missing, lost'; *ḫulluqum* D 'to make disappear, let escape, destroy' (→ *ḫulqum*).

ḫalāṣum G (*a–u*) 'to press, squeeze out'.

ḫallum (*ḫalli*; sf. *ḫalla-*) 'crotch'; *ḫallān* (dual) 'hind legs'.

ḫalqum (vbl. adj.) see *ḫalāqum*.
ḫalṣum (pl. *ḫalṣū*) 'fortification; fortress'.
ḫamiš (*ḫamšum* a; with masc. nouns *ḫamšat*, *ḫamištum*) 'five' (→ *ḫamšā*, *ḫamšum* b).
ḫammû (pl.) 'rebels'; *šar ḫammê* 'usurper king'.
ḫammum 'head of the family'.
ḫamšā (indeclinable) 'fifty' (cf. *ḫamiš*).
ḫamšum a see *ḫamiš*.
ḫamšum b (adj.; fem. *ḫamuštum*) 'fifth; one-fifth' (cf. *ḫamiš*).
ḫāmū (pl.) 'litter (of leaves, etc.)'.
ḫanāmum G (*i*) 'to bloom' (rare).
ḫanāpum see *anāpum*.
ḫapārum G 'surround' (rare); *ḫuppurum* D = G.
ḫapātum G (*i* and *u*) 'to be(come) powerful, prevail'; vbl. adj. *ḫaptum* (*ḫapit-*) 'powerful, triumphant'.
ḫaptum (vbl. adj.) see *ḫapātum*.
ḫarbūtum (*ḫarbūt*) 'devastation'.
ḫarīmtum (*ḫarīmti*; pl. *ḫarīmātum*; log. (mí)KAR.KID) 'prostitute'.
ḫarrānum (fem.; pl. *ḫarrānātum*; log. KASKAL) 'road, path, way; journey; military expedition or campaign; caravan'; *ḫarrānam alākum* 'to perform corvée service'; *ḫarrānam ṣabātum* 'to take to the road, undertake a campaign'.
ḫasāsum G (*a–u*) 'to heed, think of, be mindful of, care for; to remember, refer to, mention; to plan; vbl adj. *ḫassum* (*ḫasis-*) 'intelligent'; *ḫissusum* Gt 'to consider' (rare); *ḫussusum* D 'to remind; to study' (→ *ḫasīsum*).
ḫasīsum (*ḫasīs*) 'understanding, wisdom' (cf. *ḫasāsum*).
ḫaṣṣīnum / *ḫaṣṣinnum* (pl. *ḫaṣṣīnū* / *ḫaṣṣinnū*) 'ax'.
ḫašāḫum G (*i*) 'to desire; to require, need'; *nuḫšuḫum* N passive (→ *ḫušāḫum*).
ḫašûm (*ḫaši-*; log. UR$_5$ [the ḪAR sign]) 'lung'.
ḫaṭītum 'offense' (cf. *ḫaṭûm*).
ḫaṭṭum (fem., rarely masc.; *ḫaṭṭi*; sf. *ḫaṭṭa-* pl. *ḫaṭṭātum*; log. GIDRI [the PA sign]) 'scepter, staff, stick, branch'; *ša ḫaṭṭātim* or *wakil ḫaṭṭim* (possible readings of PA.PA) 'captain'.
ḫaṭûm G (*i*) 'to make a mistake, fail, miss; to commit an offense, trespass' (→ *ḫaṭītum*; *ḫiṭītum*; *ḫīṭum*).
ḫāwirum (ptcpl.) see *ḫiārum*.
ḫegallum or *ḫengallum* (*ḫegal*; sf. *ḫegalla-*; log. ḪÉ.GÁL 'let there be'; Sum. lw.) 'abundance; abundant yield'.
ḫepûm a (*e*) 'to smash, destroy, wreck; to break, invalidate (a tablet, document); to split, divide'; vbl. adj. *ḫepûm* b (*ḫepi-*) 'smashed, broken, split'; *ḫuppûm* D = G.
ḫepûm b (vbl. adj.) see *ḫepûm*.
ḫerûm G (*e*) 'to dig'.
ḫiārum G (*a–i*) 'to choose a mate'; vbl. adj. *ḫīrum* (*ḫīr-*) 'chosen', in substantivized fem. *ḫīrtum* (*ḫīrti*; sf. *ḫīrta-*; pl. *ḫīrātum*) 'wife (of equal status with the husband)'; ptcpl. *ḫāʾirum* / *ḫāwirum* (*ḫāʾir* / *ḫāwir*) '(first) husband'.
ḫiāšum G (*a–i*) 'to hasten, hurry'.
ḫiāṭum G (*a–i*) 'to watch over, take care of; to examine, search, explore'.
ḫibiltum (*ḫibilti*; sf. *ḫibilta-*; pl. *ḫiblātum*) 'damage, wrong' (cf. *ḫabālum*).
ḫīrtum see *ḫiārum*.
ḫiṭītum (*ḫiṭīt*) 'damage, negligence, fault, crime' (cf. *ḫaṭûm*).
ḫīṭum (*ḫīṭ(i)*) 'fault, damage; offense, crime; negligence' (cf. *ḫaṭûm*).
ḫubtum (*ḫubut*) 'robbery' (cf. *ḫabātum*).
ḫubullum (*ḫubul*; with suff. *ḫubulla-*) 'obligation, debt with interest'; *bēl ḫubullim* (with suff. *bēl ḫubullī-*; pl. *bēlū ḫubullim* or *bēl ḫubullī*; see §12.4) 'creditor'.
ḫūdum (*ḫūd(i)*) 'joy' (cf. *ḫadûm*).
ḫulqum (*ḫuluq*) 'lost/missing property' (cf. *ḫalāqum*).
ḫumuṣṣīrum 'mouse'.
ḫuppudum D (not in G) 'to blind'.

ḫurāṣum (*ḫurāṣ-*; log. KUG.SIG17, also read GUŠKIN) 'gold'.
ḫurḫudam / *urʾudum* (*ḫurḫud* / *urʾud*) 'throat, windpipe'.
ḫušāḫum (*ḫušāḫ*) 'need, hunger' (cf. *ḫašāḫum*).

I

ibbûm (*ibbā-*; Sum. lw.) 'loss, deficit'.
ibissûm (*ibissā-*; Sum. lw.) 'financial loss'.
ibrum (*ibir*; pl. *ibrū*) 'person of equal status, colleague, friend'.
Id (log. dÍD) the river god.
idum (fem. and masc.; bound form *idi*, rarely *id*; dual *idān*; pl. *idū* and *idātum*; log. Á) 'arm; side, edge; strength; goal, purpose'; in sg. and in masc. pl. (log. Á or Á.BI): 'wages, hire, rent, payment'; *idi* (prep.; sf. *idī-*), *ina idi*, *ana idi* (prep. phrases) 'near, next to, beside, on the side of, with'.
idûm see *edûm*.
igārum (*igār*; pl. *igārātum*; log. É.GAR8; Sum. lw.) 'wall (of a building)'.
Igigi a name for the great gods.
igisûm (*igisā-*; IGI.SÁ; Sum. lw.) 'an annual tax (collected from merchants, priests); gift, offering'.
igrum (*igir*; pl. *igrū*) 'hire, rent; wages' (cf. *agārum*).
iyâšim see *yâšim*.
iyâti see *yâti*.
ikkarum (*ikkar*; pl. *ikkarū*; log. ENGAR; Sum. lw.) 'farmer, farm laborer, plowman' (→ *ikkarūtum*).
ikkarūtum 'agricultural work, plowing' (cf. *ikkarum*).
ikribum (*ikrib*; pl. *ikribū*) 'blessing, benediction; prayer' (cf. *karābum*).
ikûm (base *iku-*; log. IKU; Sum. lw.) a unit of area = 100 *mūšarum* = ca. 3,600 m.^{2} (see Appendix B.3).
ilkum (*ilik*; pl. *ilkū* and *ilkātum*) work or service performed, usually on a field or garden, for the state (king) by s.o. holding the land in tenure from the state; part of the yield of the land, i.e., payment; the land itself; the holder of the land; *ilkam alākum* to perform such service, work such land (cf. *alākum*).
iltum (*ilat*; pl. *ilātum*; fem. of *ilum*) 'goddess' (cf. *ilum*).
ilum (*il(i)*; sf. *il* or *ilū-* / *ilī-* / *ilā-*; pl. *ilū*, *ilānū*; log. DINGIR) 'god'; *kakkum ša ilim* a standard with a divine symbol (→ *iltum*, *ilūtum*).
ilūtum 'divinity, divine nature, divine power' (cf. *ilum*).
imērum (*imēr*; pl. *imērū*; log. ANŠE) '(male) donkey'; a unit of capacity ('homer') = 12 or 18 *sūtum* (in OB at Mari only).
imittum a (fem. and, often in omens, masc.; *imitti*; fem. of rare adj. *imnum* 'right'; log. ZAG) 'right (side), right hand'; *imittam* (adv.) 'on the right'.
imittum b (*imitti*; dual *imittān*; log. ZAG) 'shoulder of an animal' (cf. *emēdum*).
immerum (*immer*; pl. *immerū* or *immerātum*; log. UDU) 'sheep, ram'.
imṭû (always pl.) 'depletion, losses' (cf. *maṭûm*).
ina (in literary texts also *in*; prep.; does not take sf.) 'in, into, at, among; with (things), by means of, by; from, from within (a place, with verbs of motion and of taking, seizing; see §5.6)'; partitively, 'out of' (§34.2); temporally, 'in, on, at the time of'; (conj.) 'as long as, while' (see §26.2(a)); *ina kiam* 'therefore, thus'.
inanna (< **ina annâ*; adv.) 'now'; *(ina) kīma inanna* 'right now'.
inbum (*inib*; pl. *inbū* [often = sg.]) 'fruit, fruit tree; (sexual) attractiveness'.
inītum (*inīt*; pl. *iniātum*) 'services, rate of hire (of an ox or ox team)'.
inu poetic variant of *inūma*.
īnum (fem.; *īn*; dual *īnān*; log. IGI) 'eye; spring'; *īn X maḫārum* 'to please X'; *īnīn našûm* 'to look up'; *īnīn ana X našûm* 'to look at X, covet X'.
inūma (conj.; poetic/archaizing *inu*)

'when, as soon as, after, at the time that, while' (see §26.2(a)) (cf. *ina*, *ūmum*; → *inūmīšu*).

inūmīšu(-ma) (adv.) 'at that time, then', used in royal inscriptions as a correllative of *inu*: 'when ..., at that time ...' (cf. *inūma*).

iprum (*ipir*; pl. *iprū*; log. ŠE.BA) 'barley ration, food allowance'.

ipšum (*ipiš*) 'work' (cf. *epēšum*); *ipiš nikkassī* 'rendering of accounts'; *ipiš pîm* 'utterance, command' (cf. *piam epēšum* under *epēšum*).

ipṭerū (always pl.) 'ransom (price)' (cf. *paṭārum*).

irimmum (pl. *irimmū*) 'bead'.

īrimum/*irīmum* (pl. -*ū* [= sg.]) 'loveliness' (cf. *râmum*).

irnittum (or *ernettum*; bound form *irnitti*; sf. *irnitta*-) 'victory, triumph'.

irtum (bound form *irti* and *irat*; log. GABA) 'chest, breast'; *mār(at) irtim* (log. DUMU(.MUNUS) GABA) 'suckling baby'; *irtam nêʾum* 'to turn away, withdraw'.

isiḫtum (*isiḫti*)/*esiḫtum* 'assignment, task, duty; material assigned' (cf. *esēḫum*).

isinnum (*isin*; pl. *isinnū* and *isinnātum*; log. EZEN) 'religious festival'.

iṣṣūrum (masc. and fem.; *iṣṣūr*; pl. *iṣṣūrū* and *iṣṣūrātum*; log. MUŠEN) 'bird'; ext. also a part of the liver.

iṣum (*iṣi*; pl. *iṣṣū*; log. GIŠ) 'tree; wood, lumber, timber'.

īṣum (vbl. adj) see *wiāṣum*.

išarum (vbl. adj.) see *ešērum*.

išātum (*išāt*; log. IZI) 'fire'.

išdum (*išid*; dual *išdān* [often = sg.]; pl. *išdātum*) 'base, foundation, bottom; lower extremities; administration, organization (of a government)'.

Išḫara a goddess associated/equated with Eštar.

iškarum (*iškar*; pl. *iškarātum*) 'work assignment; supplies; delivery items; field on which assigned work is to be done'.

iškum (fem.; *išik*; dual *iškān*) 'testicle'.

iššiakkum (*iššiak*; log. ENSI$_2$; Sum. lw.) 'farmer; land agent'.

iššum (fem.; pl. *iššū*) 'woman' (rare word).

Ištar (log. EŠ$_4$.TÁR/IŠTAR; INANNA) an important Mesopotamian goddess (→ *ištarum*).

ištarum (pl. *ištarātum*) 'goddess' (cf. *Ištar*).

ištēn (fem. *išteat*) 'one'.

ištēniš (adv.) 'together, as one' (cf. *ištēn*).

išti (prep.; sf. *ištī*- or *ištā*-; in OB in literary texts only) 'with (a person, deity)' (synonym of *itti*).

ištīššu (adv.) 'once, one time' (cf. *ištēn*).

ištīʾum (fem. *ištītum*; rare; see §23.2(c)) 'first' (cf. *ištēn*).

ištu (prep.; does not take sf.) 'from, out of, away from (a place)'; temporally, 'since'; (conj.) 'after, as soon as, since' (§26.2(a)); rarely causal: 'because, since' (§26.2(b)); *ištū-ma* (conj.) 'if indeed'.

-*īšu* (adverbial ending; see §23.2(f)) 'x times, x-fold'.

išûm G (pret. *īšu*; see §26.1) 'to have, own'; *X Y eli Z īšu* 'Z owes Y to X' (e.g., *tamkārum šinā šiqil kaspam eli aḫīya īšu* 'my brother owes two shekels of silver to the merchant'); *ṣibit ṭēmim išûm* 'to take action'.

itā see *itûm*.

itinnum (log. ŠITIM; Sum. lw.?) 'house builder'.

itti (prep.; sf. *ittī*-; log. KI) 'with (persons, deities), in the company of, from (a person, with verbs of taking, receiving; see §5.6)'.

itʾudum see *naʾādum*.

itūlum see *niālum*.

itûm (*itā*-; bound form *itê* and *itā*; log. ÚS.SA.DU) 'border, neighbor, neighboring field, plot'; the bound form *itā* is used as a preposition (also with log. ÚS.SA.DU), 'bordering on, beside'.

iṭṭulum see *naṭālum*.

izbum (*izib*) 'malformed newborn human or animal' (cf. *ezēbum*).

izuzzum (also *uzuzzum*; dur. *izzaz*;

pret. *izziz*; see §37.2) 'to stand, be standing; to stand in service; to stand ready, be at (s.o.'s) disposal; to stay'; *ana X izuzzum* 'to answer, be responsible for X; to help X'; *itti X/ina rēš X izuzzum* 'to serve X, be in the service of X'; *ana pānī X izuzzum* 'to oversee X, be in charge of X'; ptcpl. *muzzazum* 'attendant' in various compounds, such as *muzzaz bābim* 'tax collector'; Gt (rare) = G; *šuzuzzum* Š 'to cause to stand/serve; to raise, erect, set (up), station' (*nazzazum*).

Y (J)

yâšim see *anāku*.
yâti see *anāku*.
yattum/n see *yûm*.
yâttun see *yûm*.
yāʾum see *yûm*.
yāʾūtun see *yûm*.
yûm (adj.; also *yāʾum*; fs *yattum/n*; mp *yûttun*, *yāʾūtun*; fp *yâttun*) 'my, mine' (§25.3).
yûttun see *yûm*.

K

kabālum G (rare); *kubbulum* D 'to hinder, immobilize'.
kabārum G (*i*) 'to be(come) fat, heavy, thick'; *kubburum* D factitive.
kabattum (*kabatti*; sf. *kabatta-*; poetic var. *kabtatum*) 'inside (of the body); emotions, mind' (cf. *kabātum*).
kabātum (*i*) 'to be(come) heavy, fat; to be(come) important, honored; to be(come) difficult, painful'; vbl. adj. *kabtum* (*kabit-*) 'heavy, fat; difficult, painful; important, serious, honored'; *kubbutum* D 'to honor, show respect to; to aggravate, make difficult' (→ *kabattum*).
kabtatum see *kabattum*.
kabtum (vbl. adj.) see *kabātum*.
kayyānum (adj.; *kayyān-*) 'normal'; *kayyānum kayyānum* 'completely normal' (cf. *kânum*).
kakkabum (*kakkab*; pl. *kakkabū*; log. MUL) 'star; meteor'.
kakkum (*kakki* or *kak*; sf. *kakka-*; pl. *kakkū*; log. (giš)TUKUL) 'weapon'; *kakkī epēšum* 'to fight, do battle, wage war'; ext. also a distinctive (and portentive) mark on the liver; *kakkum ša ilim* a standard with a divine symbol.
kalâmu, *kalâma* 'everything' (cf. *kalûm* b).
kalbum (*kalab*; pl. *kalbū*) 'dog'.
kallatum (*kallat*; pl. *kallātum*; log. É.GI4/GI.A) 'daughter-in-law, bride' (→ *kallūtum*).
kallūtum status of *kallatum*.
kalûm a G (*a*) 'to detain, delay, keep in custody; to prevent, hinder (s.o., s.th.: acc.; from doing: *ana* or *ina* + inf.); to refrain (from doing: *ana* + inf.); to withhold, hold back (s.th.: acc.; from s.o.: *ana*/dat. or *ina*)'.
kalûm b (*kala* [rarely *kali* or *kal*]; sf. *kalû/î/â-*) 'entirety, whole, all' (see §11.3) (→ *kalâmu/a*).
Kamaḫ (Sum., lit., 'august gate', Akk. *bābum ṣīrum*) one of the entrances to Ekišnugal.
kamārum G (*a–u*) 'to heap up, pile up'; *kummurum* D = G.
kamāsum a G (*i*) 'to gather, collect, assemble, bring in, complete'; *kummusum* D = G.
kamāsum b G (*i*) 'to squat, bend down, kneel'; *šukmusum* Š caus.
kanākum G (*a–u*) 'to seal; to place under seal'; in hendiadys, 'to give/take/send s.th. under seal'; vbl. adj. *kankum* (*kanik-*) 'sealed, under seal' (→ *kanīkum*, *kunukkum*).
kanāšum G (*u*) 'to bow down, submit'; vbl. adj. *kanšum* (*kaniš-*) 'submissive, subjected'; *kunnušum* D 'to bend, make submissive'; *šuknušum* Š 'to subjugate, make submissive'.
kanīkum (*kanīk*; pl. *kanīkātum*) 'sealed document' (cf. *kanākum*).
kankallum (*kankal*; log. KI.KAL; Sum. lw.) 'unbroken, hard soil'; *eqlum kankallum* 'unplowed field'.
kankum (vbl. adj.) see *kanākum*.

kannum (pl. *kannū*) 'fetter, band'.

kanšum (vbl. adj.) see *kanāšum*.

kânum G (*a–u*) 'to be(come) true, just, honest, correct; to be(come) firm, fixed, secure; to endure, last'; vbl. adj. *kīnum* (*kīn-*; fem. sg. *kīttum*) 'true, just; honest, loyal; normal, regular, correct; proper, legitimate; firm, fixed'; substantivized fem. *kīttum* ([given as *kittum* in the dictionaries] bound form *kītti*; pl. *kīnātum*) 'truth, justice; honesty, loyalty; normality, normal situation, correctness'; *kunnum* D 'to establish as true, confirm, convict (of doing: *ina* + inf.); to set (up), fix, establish, assign; to maintain'; *šutakunnum* Št-lex. 'to justify, examine' (Mari) (→ *kayyānum*, *kīniš*).

kapāṣum G (*i*) 'to bend, curl, droop'.

kaprum (pl. *kaprū* and *kaprātum*; log. É.DURU5) 'village'.

karābum G (*a–u*) 'to bless, invoke blessings; to praise; to dedicate an offering' (→ *ikribū*).

karānum (*karān*; log. GEŠTIN) 'grapes; grapevine; vineyard; wine'.

karāṣum G (*i*) 'to pinch, break off'; *kurruṣum* D = G; 'to slander' (→ *karṣum*).

karpatum (*karpat*; pl. *karpātum*; log. DUG) 'pot, container, vessel'.

karṣum (*karaṣ*; pl. *karṣū*) 'calumny'; *karṣī X akālum* 'to calumniate, denounce X' (cf. *karāṣum*).

karûm (*karā-*; pl. *karû*; Sum. lw.) 'barley pile (for storage)'.

kārum (*kār*; log. KAR; Sum. lw.) 'embankment, quay (wall); harbor district, harbor; merchant community'.

karzillum (*karzil*; log. GÍR.NI; Sum. lw.) 'physician's lancet'.

kaspum (*kasap*; log. KUG.BABBAR) 'silver'; *ana kaspim nadānum* 'to sell'.

kasûm G (*u* or *i*) 'to bind, arrest, imprison; to join, tie, bond together'; *kussûm* D = G.

kāsum (masc. and fem.; *kās*; pl. *kāsātum* and *kāsānū*) 'cup, goblet'.

kaṣārum G (*a–u*) 'to tie, bind, join (together), put together, form; to compile, collect; to organize, arrange'; vbl. adj. *kaṣrum* (*kaṣir-*) 'joined, organized' (→ *kiṣrum*, *makṣarum*).

kašādum G (*a–u*) 'to arrive (at a place: *ana* or acc.); to reach, achieve; to conquer, defeat'; vbl. adj. *kašdum* (*kašid-*; fem. sg. *kašittum*) 'successful, achieved; conquered; having arrived, available'; *tībum kašdum* 'successful attack'; *kuššudum* D 'to pursue, chase (away), exile; to approach; to conquer'.

kašāšum G (*a–u*) 'to exact services for a debt' (→ *kiššātum*).

kašdum (vbl. adj.) see *kašādum*.

kâšim, *kâšum* see *atta*, *atti*.

katāmum G (*a–u*) 'to cover'.

kâta, *kâti* see *atta*, *atti*.

kattum / *kattun* see *kûm*.

kâttun / *kâttun* see *kûm*.

kī (adv.) 'how?'; also, poetic for *kīma*, q.v.; *kī maṣi* (interrogative adv. and relative adv.) 'how much/many?; how(ever) much/many'.

kiam (adv.) 'thus, in this manner'.

kibrum (*kibir*; pl. *kibrātum*) 'edge, rim, bank, shore'; pl. *kibrātum* 'regions, edge, periphery'; *kibrātum arbaʾum* 'the four regions (of the world)' (with an archaic writing of 'four'), i.e., 'the whole world'.

kibsum (*kibis*; pl. *kibsū* and *kibsātum*) 'track, path; tracks, steps, traces; behavior'.

kīdum (*kīd(i)*; pl. *kīdū* and *kīdātum*) 'outside (region), open country'; *ana kīdim* '(to the) outside'; *ina kīdim* 'outside'.

kilallān (southern and Mari OB *kilallūn*; fem. *kilattān*) 'both' (see §23.2(a), end).

kīma (prep.; does not take sf.; in poetry also *kī*) 'like, as, according to, instead of'; (conj.) 'as soon as, when; that, the fact that; as, according as (also *ana kīma*, *ak-kīma*)', rarely also 'because; so that' (§26.2); *kīma inanna* (adv.) 'right now'; *kīma pānī-* (with pron. sf. corresponding to sentence subject) 'immediately';

kīma ša (conj.) 'as if' (cf. *kī*).
kīniš (adv.) 'truly' (cf. *kânum*).
kīnum (vbl. adj.) see *kânum*.
Kinūnum? (log. APIN.DU$_8$.A) eigth OB month (October–November).
kirbānum (*kirbān*) 'clod of earth'; *kirbānam nasākum* 'to throw a clod' = 'to become eroded' (*ana*: toward).
kirûm (base *kiri-*; pl. *kiriātum*; log. KIRI$_6$; Sum. lw.) 'garden, orchard'.
kisalmaḫḫum (*kisalmaḫ*; log. KISAL. MAḪ; Sum. lw.) 'main courtyard (of a temple)'.
Kislīmum (log. GAN.GAN.È) ninth OB month (November–December).
kiṣrum (*kiṣir*; pl. *kiṣrū*) 'knot; joint (of the body or a plant); constriction, concentration; lump; band, contingent (of soldiers); payment (for rent, services, etc.; often pl.); region, section'; *kiṣir libbim* 'anger'; *kiṣir šadîm* 'bedrock' (cf. *kaṣārum*).
Kiš (log. ^{uru}KIŠ^{ki}) an important and very ancient city some 10 km. to the east of Babylon (modern Tell Inharra/Tell Uhaymir).
kišādum (*kišād*; pl. *kišādātum*) 'neck, throat; bank (of a river, canal, etc.)'.
kišittum (*kišitti*; pl. *kišdātum*) 'conquest; booty; seizure'; pl. 'assets, acquisition' (cf. *kašādum*).
kišpū (always pl.) 'witchcraft, sorcery'.
kiššātum (always pl.) 'debt-servitude' (cf. *kašāšum*).
kīttum see *kânum*.
kubbulum see *kabālum*.
kullatum (*kullat*) 'all, entirety, totality' (literary synonym of *kalûm*).
kullizum (*kulliz*; pl. *kullizū*; log. ŠÀ. GUD) 'ox-driver'.
kullum D (root *k–w–l*; not in G) 'to hold, contain, have, maintain'; *rēšam kullum* 'to wait for, take care of, be ready for, at the disposal of' (e.g., *ṭuppaka rēšī likīl* 'let your (ms) tablet be ready for me, at my disposal'; *rēš awâtīša kīl* 'take (ms) care of her affairs'; note also, frequent in letters, DN *rēška ana damiqtim likīl* and DN *rēš damiqtīka likīl* 'may DN treat you (the addressee) well, provide you with good things'); ptcpl. *mukillum* (*mukīl*; fem. *mukiltum*) in *mukīl bābim* 'doorkeeper, guard'; *mukīl rēšim* 'attendant, spirit'; also a feature on the exta.
kullumum D (not in G) 'to show, reveal (s.th. to s.o.: double acc.); to produce (a person, document)'.
kûm (adj.; fs *kattum*; mp *kûttun*; fp *kâttun*) 'your(s) (sg.) (§25.3)'.
kummum (*kummi*; sf. *kumma-*) 'cella, private room'.
kunukkum (*kunuk*; pl. *kunukkū* and *kunukkātum*) 'seal, cylinder seal; seal impression; sealed tablet, document' (cf. *kanākum*).
kunûm (adj.) 'your(s) (pl.) (§25.3)'.
kunūšim see *attunu*.
kunūti see *attunu*.
kurrum (abs. *kur*; log. GUR; Sum. lw.) a unit of capacity ('kor') = 30 *sūtum* = 300 *qûm* = ca. 300 l. (see Appendix B.5).
kurummatum (*kurummat*; log. ŠUKU) 'food (portion, allowance, ration)'.
kusarikkum 'bison'; also, a constellation.
kussûm (fem.; *kussi-*; log. ^{giš}GU.ZA) 'chair, seat; throne'; *kussiam ṣabātum* 'to take the throne' (referring to both regular succession and usurpation).
kūṣum (also *kuṣṣum*; bound form *kūṣ(i)*, *kuṣṣi*) 'cold; winter'.
kušabkum (log. (A.)AB.BA) a thorn tree.
kûttum / *kûttun* see *kûm*.
kuzbum (*kuzub*) 'luxuriance, abundance; (sexual) attractiveness, sexual vigor'; also as euphemism for sexual parts.

L

lā (written *la-a* and *la*; adv.) 'not' (see §20.4); *ša lā* 'without'; *šumma(n) lā* 'except for'.
labārum G (*i*) 'to be(come) old, last, endure'; vbl. adj. *labirum* (*labir-*)

'old, ancient, remote (in time); original, traditional'; *lubburum* D 'to make last, prolong (the life of)'.

labāšum G (*a*) 'to put on clothing, clothe oneself, get dressed'; vbl. adj. *labšum* (*labiš-*) 'clothed (in), wearing'; *litbušum* Gt 'to put on, wear'; *lubbušum* D 'to clothe, provide with clothing' (→ *libšum, lubūšum*).

labiānum (*labiān*) 'tendon of the neck'.

labirum (vbl. adj.) see *labārum*.

labšum (vbl. adj.) see *labāšum*.

laʾbum 'a skin disease'.

lābum (pl. *lābū*) 'lion'.

lâdum G (*a–u*) 'to bend' (so *CAD* L 36b; *AHw* 527a "etwa 'in die Knie gehen'"; rare).

laḫmum (vbl. adj. of *laḫāmum*, no finite G forms attested) 'hairy'; *šārtam laḫim* 'is covered with hair'.

laḫrum (*laḫar*; pl. *laḫrātum*?; log. U8) 'ewe'.

lalûm (*lalā-*) 'desire, wish; wealth, happiness; luxury, luxuriance; attractiveness, charm'.

lāma (conj.) 'before' (§26.2(a)); (prep.) 'before (temporal)' (cf. *lā*).

lamādum G (*a*; impv. irreg. *limad*) 'to learn, study; to be(come) aware of, informed of; to understand; to know sexually'; *lummudum* D 'to inform, teach'.

lamassum (fem.; *lamassi*; sf. *lamassa-*; pl. *lamassātum*) 'protective spirit'; often occurs with *šēdum*, the two representing good fortune, health.

lānum (*lān(i)*) 'body, appearance, stature, size, shape; person'.

lapānum G (*i*) 'to be(come) poor'; vbl. adj. *lapnum* (*lapun-*; fem. *laputtum*) 'poor'.

lapātum G (*a–u*) 'to touch; to strike; to apply, smear (s.o. or s.th.); to assign (workers to a task)'; *lupputum* D 'to touch, smear; to tarry, delay'; *šulputum* Š 'to cause to touch (rare); to defeat, destroy; to desecrate, defile'; *šutalputum* Št-pass. 'to be destroyed' (→ *liptum*).

lapnum (vbl. adj.) see *lapānum*.

laputtûm (*laputtā-*; NU.BANDA5; Sum. lw.) 'lieutenant' (or the like).

Larsa (log. UD.UNUG[ki]) a city in southern Babylonia (modern Tell Senkereh).

larûm (*lari-*; pl. *larû*) 'branch, fork'.

lāsimum (pl. *lāsimū*; log. LÚ.KAŠ4(.E)) 'courier, express messenger'.

laššu (particle of non-existence) '(there) is/are not; is/are not here' (cf. *lā, išûm*).

lawûm a G (*i*; see §21.3(i)) 'to go around, circle, encircle; to surround, besiege'; vbl. adj. *lawûm* b (*lawi-*) 'encircled, surrounded'.

lawûm b (vbl. adj.) see *lawûm*.

lemēnum G (*i*) 'to be(come) evil; to come upon bad times'; with *libbum* as subject, 'to become angry' (e.g., *libbī ul ilemmin* 'I will not become angry'); vbl. adj. *lemnum* (*lemun-*; fem. *lemuttum*; fp *lemnētum*) 'evil, bad, malevolent'; substantivized fem. *lemuttum* (*lemutti*; sf. *lemutta-*) 'evil, wickedness; evil intentions; misfortune, danger'.

lemniš 'badly, wickedly' (*lemēnum*).

lemnum (vbl. adj.) see *lemēnum*.

lemuttum see *lemēnum*.

leqûm G (*e*) 'to take (in one's hand), accept, receive, obtain (from: *itti*), take along, take away; to take (a wife), marry'; *ana mārūtim leqûm* 'to adopt'; *nelqûm* N passive.

lētum (*lēt(i)*; pl. rare) 'cheek; side, vicinity, nearby region'; also, 'authority' .

leʾûm G (*i*; see §21.3(h)) 'to be able' (to do: + acc. Infin.; e.g., *epēš(am ša) bītim eleʾʾi* 'I am able to build the house'); 'to be(come) expert, a master; to overpower (s.o.), win (a legal case)'; ptcpl. *lēʾûm* (fem. *lēʾītum*) 'able, capable, expert'.

lēʾûm (ptcpl.) see *leʾûm*.

libbum (*libbi*; sf. *libba-*; log. ŠÀ) 'heart; mind, thought, wish; inside, center, midst'; *ana libbi* (prep. phrase; §12.3) 'to the center of, into'; *ina libbi* (prep. phrase; §12.3) 'in the midst of, inside, within, among, out of, from'; pl. *libbātum* 'anger'.

libittum (*libitti*; pl. *libnātum*; log. SIG4) '(mud) brick'.

libšum (*libiš*) 'garment' (rare; cf. *labāšum*).

līmum (absolute form *līm(i)*; log. LIM or LI) 'thousand' (see §23.2(a)).

liptum (*lipit*) 'handiwork' (cf. *lapātum*).

lipûm (*lipi-*) 'fat'.

Lismum month name ('footrace').

lišānum (fem., rarely masc.; *lišān*; pl. *lišānātum*, rarely *lišānū*; log. EME) 'tongue; language, speech'; *ša lišānim* 'informer'.

lītum (also *littum*; bound form *līt(i)*, *litti*; log. ÁB [but in OB, ÁB usually = *arḫum* 'cow']) 'cow'; pl. *liātum* (log. ÁB.GUD.ḪI.A) 'cattle, bovines (of both sexes)' (cf. masc. *lûm* 'bull').

līṭum (*līṭ(i)*; pl. *līṭū*) 'hostage, (person taken as a) pledge'.

lū '(either...) or' (§7.4(f); Vocab. 16); injunctive particle in verbless clauses (§22.2); asseverative particle, 'indeed, certainly, verily' (§29.3(c)).

lubūšum (*lubūš*; log. SÍG.BA) 'clothing, attire, wardrobe; clothing allowance' (cf. *labāšum*).

Luḫuššum a name of Nergal, the god of pestilence and disease.

lûm (base *li-*; gen. *lîm*, acc. *liam*; pl. *lû*) 'bull' (cf. fem. *lītum*/*littum* 'cow').

M

-ma enclitic conjunction, 'and (then)' (see §7.4); enclitic topicalizing particle (§29.2).

madādum G (*a–u*) 'to measure (out), pay (in a measured amount)'; *muddudum* D = G.

mādiš (adv.) 'much, greatly' (cf. *miādum*).

mādum (vbl. adj.) see *miādum*.

magal (adv.) 'very (much), greatly, exceedingly'.

magārum G (*a–u*) 'to be agreeable, agree (to do: *ana* + Infin.); to agree with, comply with, consent to (s.o. or s.th.: acc.); to grant, permit; to find acceptance'; *mitgurum* Gt 'to agree (with one another), come to an agreement'; *šutamgurum* Št-lex. 'to bring to agreement'; *namgurum* N 'to come to an agreement, agree' (→ *migrum*).

maḫārum G (*a–u*) 'to accept, receive (from s.o.: *itti* or *ina qāt*); to approach, meet, confront'; *īn X maḫārum* 'to please X' (e.g., *īn šarrim tamḫur* 'you (ms) pleased the king'); vbl. adj. *maḫrum* (*maḫir-*) 'received'; *mitḫurum* Gt 'to meet/face/confront/oppose one another; to correspond (to one another), be of equal size'; *muḫḫurum* D 'to approach; to make accept'; *šumḫurum* Š 'to make accept, to offer; to hand over'; *šutamḫurum* Št-lex. 'to cause to compare oneself with, compete with, rival' (→ *maḫīrum*, *maḫrum*, *maḫrûm*, *meḫretum*, *meḫrum*, *mitḫāriš*).

maḫāṣum G (*a*) 'to strike, hit, smite, wound, kill'; *eqlam mayyarī maḫāṣum* 'to plow'; *mitḫuṣum* Gt 'to fight, go to war' (i.e., 'to strike one another)'; *muḫḫuṣum* D = G.

maḫīrum (*maḫīr*; pl. *maḫīrū* and *maḫīrātum*) 'market place; business activity; rate, current price; purchase price' (cf. *maḫārum*).

maḫrum (*maḫar*; log. IGI) 'front (part, side)'; *(ina) maḫar* (prep. and prep. phrase, §12.3; with suff. *(ina) maḫrī-*) 'in front of, in the presence of, with (a person), (from) before, away from' (note *maḫar X šakānum* 'to inform X', as in *awâtīšu maḫrīni iškun* 'he informed us of his affairs'); *ana maḫar* (prep. phrase, §12.3; with suff. *ana maḫrī-* [northern OB; for southern and Mari, see *ṣērum*]) 'to, toward, into the presence of, before (a person)' (cf. *maḫārum*, *maḫrûm*).

maḫrûm (denom. adj.; *maḫrī-*) 'first (see §23.2(c)); former, earlier, previous' (cf. *maḫrum*).

mayyalum (*mayyal*) 'sleeping-place, bed' (cf. *niālum*).

mayyarum (*mayyar*) 'plow'; *eqlam*

mayyarī maḫāṣum 'to plow'.

makkūrum (*makkūr*; log. NÍG.GA) 'property, assets, valuables, goods' (cf. *namkūrum*).

makṣarum (*makṣar*; pl. *makṣarātum*) 'bundle' (cf. *kaṣārum*).

mala (also *mali*, *mal*; prep.) 'according to, as much as, as large as, to the same amount/degree as'; also a conjunction: 'as much/many as; everyone/everything that, whoever, whatever' (§19.3(f)); *mimma mala* (= *mimma ša*) 'anything that/which, whatever' (cf. *malûm* a).

malāḫum (*malāḫ*; log. MÁ.LAḪ5) 'sailor'.

malākum G (*i*) 'to give advice; to consider, deliberate, make a decision'; *mitlukum* Gt 'to deliberate, advise one another' (→ *milkum*).

malmališ / *mammališ* (adv.) 'likewise, to the same degree' (cf. *malûm* a).

malû (pl.) 'body hair'.

malûm a G (*a*) 'to be(come) full of, fill with (+ acc.; e.g., *eqlum mê imla* 'the field filled with water, became full of water'); to elapse (of periods of time)'; rarely: 'to fill' (s.th.: acc.; with s.th.: a second acc., as in *bēlum bītam šīpātim qatnātim imla* 'the owner filled the house with fine wool'); *epqam malûm* 'to become covered with leprosy'; vbl. adj. *malûm* b (*mali-*) 'filled, full'; *mullûm* D 'to fill (s.th.: acc.; with s.th.: acc.); to pay or deliver in full; to assign'; *šutamlûm* Št-lex. 'to assign, add, provide in full' (→ *mala*, *malmališ*, *mīlum*).

malûm b (vbl. adj.) see *malûm* a.

mamman (occasionally also *mamma*; indef. pron., §14.3) 'anyone, someone', with a negative 'no one' (cf. *mannum*).

mānaḫtum (*mānaḫti*; sf. *mānaḫta-*; pl. *mānaḫātum*) 'toil, weariness; upkeep, maintenance, improvements'.

manāma 'any(one), whoever', with negative 'no (one), none' (cf. *mannum*).

Maništū / *īšu* king of Akkad, ca. 2269–55 (son and second successor of Sargon).

mannum (interrog. pron., §14.2) 'who?' (→ *mamman*, *manāma*).

manûm a G (*u*) 'to count; to include; to hand over, deliver'; vbl. adj. *manûm* b (*mani-*) 'counted, included, delivered' (→ *manûm* c).

manûm b (vbl. adj.) see *manûm* a.

manûm c (base *manā-*; abs. *manā*; log. MA.NA) a unit of weight ('mina') = 60 *šiqlum* = ca. 500 g. (see Appendix B.1; cf. *manûm* a).

maqātum G (*u*) 'to fall, fall down, collapse; to arrive (said of news, people, etc.), happen; to fall upon, attack (with *ana*, *eli*)'; vbl. adj. *maqtum* (*maqit-*) 'fallen, collapsed, in ruins'; *šumqutum* Š 'to cause to fall, fell, strike down, overthrow, defeat'.

maqqarum (*maqqar*) 'chisel'.

maqtum (vbl. adj.) see *maqātum*.

marārum G (*a–u*) 'to hoe, break up soil'.

marāṣum G (*a*) 'to be(come) sick, fall ill; to be(come) painful; to be(come) troublesome, difficult (to, for s.o.: *eli*, *ana*)'; with *libbum* as subject: 'to be(come) annoyed' (e.g., *libbi šarrim imraṣ* 'the king became annoyed'); vbl. adj. *marṣum* (*maruṣ-*; fem. *maruštum* [see §5.4]) 'sick, ill; diseased, painful; difficult'; subtantivized fem. *maruštum* (*marušti*; pl. *marṣātum*) 'difficulty, hardship, trouble, duress'; *šumruṣum* Š 'to make sick, unhappy, worried; to cause trouble, difficulty'; *šutamruṣum* Št-lex. 'to concern oneself, take trouble, labor' (→ *murṣum*).

Marduk (log. dAMAR.UTU) 'Marduk', chief god of Babylon.

marṣum (vbl. adj.) see *marāṣum*.

martum (fem., rarely masc. in omens; pl. *marrātum*; log. ZÉ) 'gall bladder; bile, gall'.

mārtum (*mārat*; pl. *mārātum*; log. DUMU.MUNUS) 'daughter' (cf. *mārum*).

mārum (*mār(i)*; pl. *mārū*; log. DUMU)

'son'; *mār bīt ṭuppim* (log. DUMU É.DUB.BA.A) 'military, state scribe' (originally, 'student' or 'graduate'); *mār šiprim* (§12.4) 'messenger' (→ *mārtum, mārūtum*).

maruštum see *marāṣum*.

mārūtum (*mārūt*) 'sonship; status of son (natural or adopted)'; *ana mārūtim leqûm* 'to adopt' (cf. *mārum*).

maskiltum in ext., part of the *ubānum*.

masākum G only in infin. and in vbl. adj. *maskum* (*masik-*) 'bad'; *namsukum* N 'to become bad'.

maṣraḫum (*maṣraḫ*; log. ŠUR?) 'an emblem' (rare); ext. also 'cystic duct'?.

maṣṣartum (*maṣṣarti*; pl. *maṣṣarātum*) 'watch, guard, garrison; watchhouse; safekeeping, deposit' (cf. *naṣārum*).

maṣṣarum (*maṣṣar*; pl. *maṣṣarū*) 'watchman; watch; garrison' (cf. *naṣārum*).

maṣṣarūtum (*maṣṣarūt*) 'safe-keeping, custody' (cf. *naṣārum*).

maṣûm a G (*i*) 'to be(come) equal to; to amount to, be sufficient for'; *mala libbim maṣûm* 'to have full discretion, do what one wants' (e.g., *mala libbīšu imaṣṣi* 'he may do what he wants'); vbl. adj. *maṣûm* (*maṣi-*) 'sufficient, enough', in predicative use, *maṣi* 'is sufficient, enough; amounts to'; *kī maṣi* 'how much(?)'; *mala maṣû* 'as far as it extends, as much as there is'; *muṣṣûm* D 'to make reach, release'; *šumṣûm* Š 'to make suffice'; *mala libbi X šumṣûm* 'to give X full discretion'.

maṣûm b (vbl. adj.) see *maṣûm* a.

mašālum G (*u*) 'to be(come) similar, equal, half'; vbl. adj. *mašlum* (*mašil-*) 'similar, equal, half'; *muššulum* D 'to make similar, equal; to copy' (→ *mišlānū, mišlum*).

mašārum G (*a–u*) 'to drag (over the ground)'.

mašā'um G (*a–u*; third radical ' atypically preserved) 'to take by force, rob, plunder'.

maškanum (*maškan*; pl. *maškanū, maškanātum*; log. KISLAḪ) 'threshing floor; empty lot; location, site' (cf. *šakānum*).

maškum (*mašak*; pl. *maškū*; log. KUŠ [the SU sign]) 'skin; hide'.

mašqītum (*mašqīt*; pl. *mašqiātum*) 'irrigation outlet, watering place' (cf. *šaqûm*).

mašraḫū (alw. pl.) 'splendor' (rare).

mašûm G (*i*) 'to forget, neglect'; *mitaššûm* Gtn 'to forget constantly, be forgetful'; *šumšûm* Š causative; *namšûm* N passive.

mati (adv.; also *ina mati*) 'when?'; *matī-ma* 'when?; ever'; with negative: 'never'.

matīma see *mati*.

mātum (fem.; *māt(i)*; pl. *mātātum*; log. KALAM and KUR) 'country (political unit), native land; land, open country; region'.

mâtum G (*a–u*) 'to die'; vbl. adj. *mītum* (*mīt-*; fem. *mīttum*) 'dead'; *šumuttum* Š 'to put to death, to cause the death of' (→ *mūtānū, mūtum*).

maṭûm a G (*i*) 'to diminish (intr.), decrease, be(come) small, few, missing, poor (in size or quality)'; vbl. adj. *maṭûm* b (*maṭi-*) 'small, cheap, low, humble'; *piam maṭiam šakānum* 'to speak humbly'; *muṭṭûm* D 'to diminish (in quantity or quality; tr.), cause a decrease'; *šumṭûm* Š 'to diminish, belittle, treat badly'; *šutamṭûm* Št-lex. 'to be in short supply' (→ *imṭû*).

maṭûm b (vbl. adj.) see *maṭûm* a.

meatum (usually absolute form *meat*; pl. *meātum*; log. ME) 'hundred' (see §23.2(a)).

meḫretum (*meḫret*) 'opposite side'; bound form *meḫret* as preposition, 'in front of, before, opposite' (cf. *maḫārum*).

meḫrum (*meḫer*; pl. *meḫrū* and *meḫrētum*) 'copy (of a document), list; answer, reply; equivalent, fellow, person of the same rank; weir' (cf. *maḫārum*).

mēleṣum (*mēleṣ*) 'joy?' (rare) (cf. *elēṣum*).
mēlulum (irregular verb; see §38.1) 'to play'.
mēqûm (*mēqi-*) 'cosmetics' (rare).
mērešum (*mēreš*) 'cultivated land, cultivation' (cf. *erēšum* b).
merītum (or *mirītum*, also *merʾītum*; *merīt*) 'pasture(-land)' (cf. *reʾûm*).
mesûm G (*e* or *i*) 'to wash'.
-mi (enclitic particle) indicates that the clause of the word to which it is suffixed is part of a direct quotation; see §15.4.
miādum G (*a–i*) 'to increase, be(come) much, abundant, numerous, plentiful'; vbl. adj. *mādum* (fem. *māttum* [*mattum* in the dictionaries]; mp *mādūtum*, fp *mādātum*) 'much', pl.: 'many'; *šumuddum* Š 'to make much, increase, enlarge, make numerous'; in hendiadys, 'to do (s.th.) much, a lot' (→ *mādiš*).
migrum (*migir*; pl. *migrātum*) 'favorite, person endowed with favor (of the gods or the king)' (cf. *magārum*).
milkum (*milik*; pl. *milkātum*) 'counsel, advice, instruction; intelligence; mood, intent' (cf. *malākum*).
mīlum (*mīl(i)*) '(seasonal) flood (of rivers)' (cf. *malûm* a).
mimma (indef. pron., §14.3) 'anything, something, all', with a negative 'nothing'; *mimma šumšu* 'anything at all, everything' (cf. *mīnum*; → *mimmāmum*; *mimmû*).
mimmāmu(m) 'everything' (rare; cf. *mimma*).
mimmû (base *mimmā-*; no mimation; gen. *mimmê*, acc. *mimmâ*) 'something; all of; property' (cf. *mimma*).
minde (adv.) 'perhaps, possibly, who can say?'.
mīnum (interrog. pron., §14.2; base *mīn-*; also *minûm*, base *mina-*) 'what?'; *ana mīnim* and *am-mīnim* 'why?' (→ *mimma*).
miqittum (*miqitti*; sf. *miqitta-*) 'downfall' (cf. *maqātum*).
miqtum (*miqit*) 'collapse, downfall; obstruction, debris' (cf. *maqātum*).
mirītum see *merītum*.
mīšarum (*mīšar*) 'justice, equity, redress' (cf. *ešērum*).
mišlānū (pl.) 'half shares' (cf. *mašālum*).
mišlum (*mišil*; log. MAŠ) 'half; middle' (cf. *mašālum*).
mitḫāriš 'equally, to the same extent, each one; everywhere' (cf. *maḫārum*).
mû (always pl.; gen.-acc. *mê*; log. A(.MEŠ)) 'water, liquid'; *ina mêšu* 'at birth' (lit., 'with its (amniotic) fluid').
mūdûtum (*mūdût*) 'knowledge, information' (cf. *edûm*).
muḫḫelṣītum 'slippery ground' (only attested once) (cf. *neḫelṣûm*).
muḫḫum (*muḫḫi*; sf. *muḫḫa-*)) 'skull, top (part, side)'; *ina muḫḫi* (prep. phrase; §12.3) 'on, onto, upon, on top of, over; to the debit of'; *ana muḫḫi* (prep. phrase; §12.3; rare in OB) 'toward, into the care of'.
muʾirrum (D ptcpl.) see *wârum*.
mukillum (D ptcpl.) see *kullum*.
munaggerum (ptcpl.) see *nuggurum*.
muqqelpûm (N ptcpl.) see *neqelpûm*.
murṣum (*muruṣ*) 'disease, illness, sickness, pain' (cf. *marāṣum*).
mūṣûm (‹ **mawṣaʾum*; *mūṣā-*) 'exit, opening' (cf. *waṣûm*).
mūšabum (*mūšab*) 'dwelling, domicile; seat' (cf. *wašābum*).
mušaddinum (Š ptcpl.) see *nadānum*.
mūšarum (*mūšar*; log. SAR) a unit of area ('garden plot') = 1/100 *ikûm* = ca. 36 m.^{2} (see Appendix B.3).
mušēniqtum (Š ptcpl.) see *enēqum*.
mušḫuššum (Sum. lw.) 'great serpent, dragon'; also, a constellation.
muškēnum (ptcpl.) see *šukēnum*.
muštinnum 'urethra'.
mušītum (*mušīt*; pl. *mušiātum*) 'night, nighttime' (cf. *mūšum*).
mūšum (*mūš(i)*; pl. *mūšū*; log. GI$_6$) 'night' (→ *mušītum*).
mūtānū (always pl.) 'plague, epidemic' (cf. *mâtum*).
muttatum (*muttat*) 'half'.

muttum (*mutti*; sf. *mutta-*) 'front'; *muttiš* 'in front of'.
mutum (masc.; *mut(i)*; pl. *mutū*) 'husband, man' (→ *mutūtum*).
mūtum (*mūt(i)*) 'death' (cf. *mâtum*).
mutūtum (*mūtūt*) 'position of a husband' (cf. *mutum*).
muzzazum (ptcpl.) see *izuzzum*.

N

na'ādum G (*i*) 'to pay attention, heed (s.o.: *ana*/dat.); to be(come) concerned, worried (about: *ana*/dat.)'; in hendiadys: 'to do (something) carefully'; vbl. adj. *na'dum* (*na'id-*) and *nādum* (*nād-*) 'attentive, pious; careful'; *nu''udum* D 'to ask to pay attention, alert, instruct'.
na'arrurum N (*a*; see §38.2; the ' is usually strong, the *n* of the N stem is often not assimilated: pret. *i''arir* or *in'arir*, pl. as described in §38.2 *in'arirrū* or like other N verbs *in'arrū*/*i''arrū*) 'to come to help'.
nabalkattum (*nabalkatti*; sf. *nabalkatta-*; pl. *nabalkatātum*) 'crossing, scaling (of wall), burglary; retreat; rebellion, revolt' (cf. *nabalkutum*).
nabalkutum N (*a*) 'to cross, pass (over); to slip out of place, change sides, allegiance; to rebel (against: acc.); to turn over, around'; *šubalkutum* Š caus.; also, 'to overthrow' (→ *nabalkattum*).
nabrûm/*nabrû* (usually pl.) the name of a festival.
nabûm a G (*i*) 'to name; to invoke, call, summon, appoint; to decree, proclaim'; *ana šumim nabûm* 'to name'; vbl. adj. *nabûm* b (*nabi-*) 'called, named'.
nabûm b (vbl. adj.) see *nabûm* a.
na'butum N (not in G in OB; inf. also *nābutum*; dur. *innabbit*, pret. *innabit* or *innābit* [pl. *innabtū* or *innābitū*], perf. *ittabit* or *ittābit*) 'to flee'.
nadānum G (*i*) 'to give, grant; to hand over, deliver, transfer; to set, assign; to allow'; *ana kaspim nadānum* 'to sell'; *šuddunum* Š 'to cause to give, hand over, sell; to collect (taxes, etc.)'; ptcpl. *mušaddinum* 'collector (of taxes, etc.)'; *šutaddunum* Št-lex. 'to intermingle, discuss' (→ *niditum*, *nudunnûm*).
nadītum see *nadûm* b.
na'dum (vbl. adj.) see *na'ādum*.
nadûm a G (*i*) 'to throw (down), set (down), lay (down), pour (s.th. into s.th.); to neglect, abandon, ignore; to knock out (e.g., a tooth); to lay a criminal charge (against: *eli*)'; *aḫam nadûm* 'to be negligent (lit., to let down one's arm)'; *ša libbim nadûm* 'to have a miscarriage'; vbl. adj. *nadûm* b (*nadi-*; fem. *nadītum*) 'abandoned; fallow; laid, lying, situated'; substantivized fem. *nadītum* (*nadīt*; pl. *nadiātum*) 'fallow, bare land'; (log. LUKUR [MUNUS+ ME]) a woman dedicated to a god and not permitted to have children; *šuddûm* Š 'to cause to throw, drop, abandon; to let (a field) go fallow; to reduce to ruins' (→ *nidītum*, *nīdum*).
nadûm b (vbl. adj.) see *nadûm* a.
nādum (vbl. adj.) see *na'ādum*.
nagarrurum see *garārum*.
nagārum see *nuggurum*.
nāgirum (*nāgir*; log. NIMGIR) 'herald'.
nagûm G (*u*) 'to sing happily' (rare).
naḫālum G (*i*) 'to hand over (property)' (rare, Mari).
nâḫum G (*a–u*; see §21.3(b)) 'to rest, take a rest; to relent, be appeased, be(come) peaceful, abate, subside'; vbl. adj. *nēḫum* (*nēḫ-*) 'calm, quiet, secure, safe'; *nuḫḫum* D 'to pacify, calm, quiet, appease, put at rest (→ *nēḫtum*).
nakāpum G (*i*) 'to gore, butt'; *nukkupum* D = G (→ *nakkāpûm*).
nakarum (vbl. adj.) see *nakārum*.
nakārum G (*i*) 'to be(come) different, strange; to be(come) hostile, engage in hostilities; to change (intr.); to deny, dispute (s.th.: acc.; to/with s.o.: acc.)'; vbl. adj. *nakarum*, *nakirum*, *nakrum* (base *nakar-* or *nakir-*; log. KÚR) 'hostile, inimical; foreign';

substantivized (pl. *nak(a/i)rū*) 'enemy, foe'; *nukkurum* D 'to change, alter (tr.); to move, remove'; *šukkurum* Š 'to cause to rebel, cause enmity' (→ *nukurtum*).

nakāsum G (*i*) 'to cut off, cut down'; vbl. adj. *naksum* (*nakis-*) 'cut (off, down), felled'; *nukkusum* D = G.

nakirum (vbl. adj.) see *nakārum*.

nakkaptum (*nakkapti*; sf. *nakkapta-*; pl. *nakkapātum*) 'temple (of the head)'.

nakkāpûm (denominative adj.; base *nakkāpī-*) 'prone to goring' (cf. *nakāpum*).

nakrum (vbl. adj.) see *nakārum*.

nalbattum (*nalbatti*; sf. *nalbatta-*; pl. *nalbanātum*) 'brick-mold'.

nâlum see *niālum*.

namāru(m) see *nawārum*.

namāšum G (*u*) 'to move'; *namušušum* R (see §38.3(e); lexical texts only) 'to die' (→ *nammaštûm*).

namkūrum (*namkūr*; log. NÍG.GA) 'possession(s)'; *rēš namkūrim* (log. SAG NÍG.GA) 'available assets, stock' (cf. *makkūrum*).

nammaštûm / *nammaššûm* (*-ā*; collective sg.) 'animals' (cf. *namāšum*).

namrāʾū (always pl.) 'fattening'.

namrirrū (always pl.) 'divine luminosity' (cf. *nawārum*).

namru(m) (vbl. adj.) see *nawārum*.

Nanna (log. ᵈNANNA) the Sumerian moon god; *Nanna-igidu*, *Nanna-adaḫ* manifestations of Nanna.

nannarum (*nannar*) 'light' (lit. word).

napāḫum G (*a–u*) 'to blow, blow on (s.th.); to light (a fire, stove); to become visible, shine, light up'; vbl. adj. *napḫum* (*napiḫ-*) 'kindled, burning, shining; swollen, bloated'; *nanpuḫum* N 'to be kindled, break out' (of a fire).

naparkudum N (*a*) 'to lie flat, against (s.th.)'.

naparkûm N (IV–*u*) 'to stop, cease (doing: *ana* / *ina* + inf.); to fail, leave'.

napāṣum G (*a–u*) 'to hurl, dash down; to kick, strike; to smash, crush, demolish; to clear (accounts); to repel'; *nuppuṣum* D = G.

napāšum G (*u*) 'to breathe freely, to relax'.

napḫarum (*napḫar*) 'total, sum; totality, all' (cf. *paḫārum*).

napḫum (vbl. adj.) see *napāḫum*.

napištum (*napišti*, in lit. texts *napšat*; sf. *napišta-*; pl. *napšātum*) 'life, vigor, good health; person; personnel; self; throat; livelihood'.

naplasum (*naplas*) 'glance, look' (cf. *palāsum*).

naplaštum (*naplašti*; sf. *naplašta-*; pl. *naplasātum*) 'flap, lobe' (cf. *palāsum*).

naprušum N (not in G) 'to fly'; *šuprušum* Š 'to cause to fly, to rout'.

naqārum G (*a–u*) 'to tear down, destroy'.

nāqidum (*nāqid*; log. NA.GADA) 'shepherd'.

naqûm G (*i*) 'to pour (out, as a libation), offer, sacrifice' (→ *niqûm* / *nīqum*).

narāmum (*narām*) 'beloved one, favorite' (may be used in apposition after a noun: e.g., *ana šarrim narāmīša* 'for her beloved king', lit., 'for the king, her beloved one') (cf. *râmum*).

narbûm (*narbi-*) 'greatness' (cf. *rabûm* a).

narkabtum (*narkabti*; sf. *narkabta-*; pl. *narkabātum*) '(war-) chariot' (cf. *rakābum*).

narûm (base *naru-* / *narā-*; Sum. lw.) 'stela'.

nārum a (fem.; *nār(i)*; pl. *nārātum*; log. ÍD) 'river, canal'.

nārum b (*nār(i)*) 'musician'; *nārūtum* 'musician's craft'.

nasāḫum G (*a–u*) tr.: 'to remove, tear out, expel, reject, deport, transfer'; intr.: 'to move on, remove oneself; to pass (of time)'; *qātam ša X nasāḫum* 'to keep X away, keep the claim of X away' (e.g., *dayyānū qātam ša eṭlim issuḫū* 'the judges kept (the claim of) the youth away'); vbl. adj. *nasḫum* (*nasiḫ-*) 'uprooted, removed (from office)'; *nussuḫum* D

= G (→ *nisḫum*).

nasākum G (*u*) 'to throw (off, down), hurl, shoot (*ana*: to, into); to pile up (grain)'; *kirbānam nasākum* 'to throw a clod' = 'to become eroded' (*ana*: toward); *šussukum* Š 'to remove, reject, annul'.

nasāqum G (*a–u*) 'to choose, select'; vbl. adj. *nasqum* (*nasiq*-) 'selected, chosen, choice, precious'; *nussuqum* D=G; *šutassuqum* (or *šutassukum*?) Št-lex. 'to put in order, prepare'.

nasḫum (vbl. adj.) see *nasāḫum*.

nasqum (vbl. adj.) see *nasāqum*.

naṣārum G (*a–u*) 'to watch (over), protect, guard; to keep'; vbl. adj. *naṣrum naṣir*-) 'watched, protected, guarded, under guard'; *iṣṣurum* Gt 'to guard oneself' (→ *maṣṣartum*, *maṣṣarum*, *maṣṣarūtum*).

naṣraptum (*naṣrapti*) '(spatial) depression; crucible'; also part of a sheep's liver.

naṣrum (vbl. adj.) see *naṣārum*.

našāqum G (*i*) 'to kiss'; *nuššuqum* D = G (pluralic).

našpakum (*našpak*; pl. *našpakātum*; log. (É.)Ì.DUB) 'storage area for barley, dates, etc.; granary, silo'; also (with log. (giš)MÁ.Ì.DUB) 'cargo boat' (cf. *šapākum*; → *našpakūtum*).

našpakūtum 'storage' (cf. *šapākum*, *našpakum*).

našpartum (*našparti*; sf. *našparta*-) 'letter, message, instructions' (cf. *šapārum*).

našparum (*našpar*) 'messenger, envoy' (cf. *šapārum*).

našûm G (*i*) 'to lift (up), raise; to carry, bear, support; to transport, deliver; to take, accept, receive (from: *ina qāt*); to remove'; *īnīn našûm* 'to look up'; *īnīn ana X našûm* 'to look at X, covet X'; *rēšam našûm* 'to honor, exalt'; *nāši biltim* 'tenant (of a field owned by the state)'; *nāš ṭuppātim* 'creditor'; *itaššûm* Gtn 'to bear continuously'; also, 'to support, take care of, provide for (s.o.)'.

nâšum G (*a–u*) 'to move, begin moving (intr.)'; *nuššum* D 'to move (tr.), set in motion'.

naṭālum G (*a–u*) 'to see, look, look at, observe; to consider; to face'; *iṭṭulum* Gt 'to look at, face one another'; *nanṭulum* N passive of G (→ *niṭlum*).

naṭûm a G only in vbl. adj. *naṭûm* (*naṭu*-) 'fitting, suitable, appropriate'.

naṭûm b (*u*) 'to hit, beat'.

nawārum (later *namāru*) G (*i*; see §21.3(b)) 'to be(come) bright, light; to shine'; vbl. adj. *nawirum* (later *namru*; *nawir*- / *namir*-) 'bright, shining, brilliant'; *nuwwurum* D 'to brighten (tr.)'; Š 'to cause to become bright'; ŠD = D; R vbl. adj. *nawurrum* (§38.3(c)) 'brilliant, bright' (→ *namrirrū*).

nawirum (vbl. adj.) see *nawārum*.

nawûm a (*nawā*-) 'steppeland; area around a town'; denominative verb *nawûm* b G (*i*; see §21.3(k)) 'to be abandoned, in ruins'.

nawûm b (verb) see *nawûm* a.

nawurrum (R vbl. adj.) see *nawārum*.

nazāqum G (*i*) 'to worry, be(come) upset'; *šuzzuqum* Š 'to cause worry, upset'.

nazzazum (*nazzaz*) 'station, position; attendant' (cf. *izzuzum* / *uzzuzum*).

neḫelṣûm N (IV–*e*) 'to slip, slide, glide'; *šuḫelṣûm* Š causative.

nēḫtum 'peace, security'; *šubat nēḫtim šūšubum* 'to let (s.o.) dwell in security' (cf. *nâḫum*).

nēḫum (vbl. adj.) see *nâḫum*.

nēkemtum (*nēkemti*; sf. *nēkemta*-; pl. *nēkemētum*) 'loss; atrophied part of the exta' (cf. *ekēmum*).

nēmelum (*nēmel*; pl. *nēmelētum*) 'benefit, gain, profit; surplus'; *nēmelam amārum* 'to make/gain a profit, to benefit'.

nēmequm (*nēmeq*) 'knowledge, experience, skill, wisdom'.

nēmettum (*nēmetti*; sf. *nēmetta*-) 'tax, tribute; support, staff, crutch' (cf. *emēdum*).

nepelkûm N (IV–*e*) 'to be(come) wide (open), extended'.

nepûm G (*e*) 'to distrain, take as pledge, distress' (→ *nipûtum*).
neqelpûm N (IV–*e*) 'to drift, glide, sail (downstream)'; ptcpl. fem. *muqqelpītum* 'boat going downstream'; *ša muqqelpītim* 'skipper of a boat going downstream'; *šuqelpûm* Š 'to sail (a boat) downstream'.
nērebum (*nēreb*; pl. *nērebū*) 'entrance; mountain pass' (cf. *erēbum*).
Nergal the god of pestilence and disease.
nērtum 'murder' (cf. *nêrum*).
nērum (absolute form *nēr*; log. GÍŠ.U) 'six hundred' (see §23.2(a)).
nêrum G (*e*; also *nârum, a*) 'to slay, kill; to strike, destroy, defeat' (→ *nērtum*).
nesûm a G (*e*; see §21.3(c)) 'to be (-come) distant, recede, move away, depart'; vbl. adj. *nesûm* b (*nesi-*) 'distant, far away, remote'; *nussûm* D 'to remove, take far away'.
nesûm b (vbl. adj.) see *nesûm* a.
nēšum (pl. *nēšū*; log. UR.MAḪ) 'lion'.
nêʾum G (*e*; see §21.3(k)) 'to turn (around), turn away, loosen' (tr.); *irtam nêʾum* 'to turn away, withdraw'.
niālum G (*a–i*; also *nâlum, a*; see §21.3(b)) 'to lie down'; *itūlum* / *utūlum* Gt 'to lie down, lie (with s.o.: *itti*)'; *ina sūn(i) X niālum* / *itūlum* 'to have intercourse with X' (→ *mayyalum*).
niāšim see *nīnu*.
niāti see *nīnu*.
niattum / *niattun* see *nûm*.
nidittum (*niditti*; sf. *niditta-*; pl. *nidnātum*) 'gift, present' (cf. *nadānum*).
nidītum (*nidīt*) 'uncultivated plot/ land' (cf. *nadûm*).
nīdum (*nīd(i)*) 'lowering, dropping, base'; *nīdi aḫim* 'negligence, laxity, procrastination'; *nīdi aḫim rašûm* 'to procrastinate, be negligent, lax' (cf. *aḫam nadûm*); *nīdi kussîm* a part of the liver (cf. *nadûm*).
nikkas a unit of length = 3 *ammatum* = ca. 1.5 m.
nikkassum (*nikkas*; pl. *nikkassū* [often = sg.]; log. NÍG.KAS7; Sum. lw.) 'accounting, account (record)'.
nikurtum see *nukurtum*.
nindanum (log. NINDA) a unit of length ('rod') = 12 *ammatum* = ca. 6 m. (see Appendix B.2).
Ningal a god.
Ninmar a goddess.
Ninsunna (Sum. nin-sún.a(k) 'lady of the wild cow') the mother of Gilgameš.
Nin-Šubur a god.
nīnu (pron.; gen.–acc. *niāti*; dat. *niāšim*) 'we' (see §§2.4, 25.2).
nipiltum (pl. *niplātum* = sg.) 'compensatory payment'.
niprum (pl. *niprū*) 'shoot, sprout; progeny'.
nipûtum (*nipût*; pl. *nipâtum*) 'person or animal taken as pledge or distress' (cf. *nepûm*).
niqûm (*niqi-*; also *nīqum*, bound form *nīq-*; log. SISKUR) 'offering, sacrifice' (cf. *naqûm*).
nīrum (*nīr(i)*; pl. *nīrū* and *nīrātum*) 'yoke'; also, a constellation; ext: a part of the liver.
Nisānum (log. BARA2.ZAG.GAR) first OB month (March–April).
nisḫum (or *nisiḫtum*; pl. *nisḫātum*) 'removal'; *ṣāb nisḫātim rašûm* uncertain, 'to have deserters?' or 'to acquire conscripts?' (cf. *nasāḫum*).
nišū (fem. pl.) 'people' (→ *nišūtum*).
nīšum (*nīš(i)*; log. MU) 'life'; *nīš X tamûm* 'to swear by (the life of) X' (e.g., *nīš šarrim nitma* 'we swore by the life of the king').
nišūtum (*nišūt*) 'family, relatives' (cf. *nišū*).
niṭlum (*niṭil*) 'eyesight; look, gaze; opinion' (cf. *naṭālum*).
nudunnûm (base *nudunnā-*) 'gift, dowry' (cf. *nadānum*).
nuggurum D (not in G) 'to denounce', rare except for ptcpl. *munaggerum* (*munagger*) 'denouncer'.
nuḫatimmum (*nuḫatim*; pl. *nuḫatimmū*; Sum. lw.) 'cook'.
nuḫšum (*nuḫuš*) 'abundance, plenty, prosperity'.

nukaribbum (*nukarib*; pl. *nukaribbātum*; log. $^{(lú)}$NU.^{giš}KIRI$_6$; Sum. lw.) 'gardener'.

nukurtum (also *nikurtum*; bound form *nu / ikurti*; pl. *nukurātum*) 'war; hostility, enmity' (cf. *nakārum*).

nûm (adj.; fs *niattum / niattun*, mp *nûttum / nûttun*) 'our(s)' (§25.3).

numātum (*numāt*) 'household property, utensils, furnishings'.

nūnum (*nūn(i)*; pl. *nūnū*; log. KU$_6$) 'fish'.

nûttum / nûttun see *nûm*.

P

padānum (fem. and masc.; *padān*) 'path, road, way'; ext.: part of the liver near the *naplaštum*.

padattum 'form, shape'.

pagālum G (also *pakālum*) 'to become strong' (rare); D vbl. adj. *puggulum* (also *pukkulum*) 'very strong'.

pagrum (*pagar*; pl. *pagrū*) 'body, corpse; self' (often as a reflexive pronoun; e.g., *pagarka uṣur* 'guard yourself').

paḫārum G (*u*) 'to gather, assemble (intr.), come together'; *puḫḫurum* D 'to gather, collect, assemble (tr.)' (→ *napḫarum*, *puḫrum*).

pāḫatum see *pīḫatum*.

pakālum see *pagālum*.

palāḫum G (*a*; impv. irregular: *pilaḫ*) 'to fear, be afraid (of: acc.); to worship, respect, revere'; vbl. adj. *palḫum* (*paliḫ-*) 'feared, fearsome; timid, reverential' (→ *puluḫtum*).

palālum G (*i*) 'to watch over, guard'; *pullulum* D (rare) = G?.

palāsum G (*a–u*) 'to see' (rare); *pullusum* D 'to occupy, divert'; *naplusum* N 'to see, look at' (→ *naplasum*, *naplaštum*).

palāšum G (*a–u*) 'to pierce, break through, into' (→ *pilšum*).

palûm (*palā-*; log. BALA; Sum. lw.) 'reign'.

pāna (adv.) 'before, earlier, previously' (cf. *pānum* a).

pānānum (adv.) 'earlier, formerly, firstly' (cf. *pānum* a).

pānum a (*pān(i)*; pl. *pānū*; log. IGI) 'front (side, part)'; pl. *pānū* (occasionally also sg.) 'face'; *ana pān(i)* (prep. phrase; §12.3) 'at the disposal of, for the benefit of, for, on account of; opposite; before the arrival of, (rarely) toward'; *ina pān(i)* (prep. phrase; §12.3) 'in the presence of, in front of, before; in view of, because of; just before (temporal)'; *pānam rašûm* 'to be(come) clear, plain'; *pān(i) / pānī X ṣabātum* 'to lead X' (e.g., *pān ṣābīya aṣbat* 'I led my army'); *pānam / pānī šakānum* 'to proceed; to intend, decide' (to do: *ana* + infin.: *pānīšu ana epēš bītim iškun* 'he intended to build a house'); *pānī X babālum* 'to favor; to forgive X' (e.g., *šarrum pānīya ul ubil* 'the king did not favor/forgive me') (→ *pāna*, *pānānum*, *pānûm*).

pānum b (abs. *pān*; log. NIGIDA; Sum. lw.) a unit of capacity = 6 *sūtum* = 60 *qûm* = ca. 60 l. (see Appendix B.5; see *parsiktum*).

pānûm (denom. adj.; *pānī-*; fem. *pānītum*) 'earlier, former, previous; earliest, first (see §23.2(c))' (cf. *pānum* a).

paqādum G (*i*) 'to hand over, entrust, assign (s.th.: acc.; to s.o.: *ana*); to supply (s.o. with s.th.: double acc.), deliver; to take care of, look after; to inspect, muster'; vbl. adj. *paqdum* (*paqid-*; fem. *paqittum*) 'delivered, assigned'; *puqqudum* D = G (→ *piqittum*).

paqdum (vbl. adj.) see *paqādum*.

parakkum (*parak*; log. BARAG; Sum. lw.) 'throne-dais; sanctuary'.

parākum G (*i*; rarely *a–u*) 'to lie across, crosswise; to obstruct, block'; vbl. adj. *parkum* (*parik-*) 'lying crosswise (before: acc.)'; *purrukum* D = G; *šuprukum* Š caus.; *naprukum* N 'to get in the way; to be closed in'.

parasrab (log. KINGUSILA) 'five-sixths' (cf. *parāsum*; *rabûm* a).

parāsum G (*a–u*) 'to divide, separate (out), select; to decide (a legal case);

to keep away (enemy, demons, etc.)'; vbl. adj. *parsum* (*paris-*) 'divided, separated, separate'; *alaktam parāsum* 'to cut off access, block the way'; *purrusum* D = G (→ *pirištum*, *purussûm*).
parkum (vbl. adj.) see *parākum*.
parsiktum (log. NIGIDA) a unit of capacity = 6 *sūtum* = 60 *qûm* = ca. 60 l. (see Appendix B.5; cf. *parāsum*; see *pānum* b).
parsum (vbl. adj.) see *parāsum*.
parṣum (*paraṣ*; pl. *parṣū*) 'office; cultic custom, rite'.
paršīgum (*paršīg*; pl. *paršīgātum*; log. (túg)BAR.SI; Sum. lw.) 'headdress; cap'.
pasāmum G (*i*) 'to veil, cover'; *pussumum* D = G.
pašāḫum G (*a*; less often, *i*) 'to refresh oneself; to calm down, be(come) appeased, content'; *puššuḫum* D 'to pacify, soothe, calm'; *šupšuḫum* Š 'to quiet, calm, pacify, appease'.
pašārum G (*a–u*) 'to loosen, release, set free, dissolve; to sell; to explain, clarify; to report, reveal (a dream)'; *puššurum* D = G; *napšurum* N passive 'to become loose, relaxed'.
pašāšum G (*a–u*) 'to anoint, rub, smear (s.o.: acc.; with s.th.: acc. or *ina*)'; vbl. adj. *paššum* (*pašiš-*) 'anointed'; *piššušum* Gt 'to anoint oneself' (→ *piššatum*).
paššum (vbl. adj.) see *pašāšum*.
paššūrum (*paššūr*; log. (giš)BANŠUR; Sum. lw.) 'table'.
patāḫum G (*a–u*) 'to break through, break into'.
paṭārum G (*a–u*) tr.: 'to loosen, untie, remove, strip; to free, ransom, redeem; to end'; intr.: 'to break camp; to withdraw, go away, disperse, desert, avoid'; *puṭṭurum* D = G (→ *ipṭerū*, *piṭrum*).
pāṭum (*pāṭ(i)*; pl. *pāṭū*) 'boundary, border; district, territory'.
peḫûm G (*e*) 'to close, shut' (tr.).
petûm a G (*e*) 'to open' (transitive); vbl. adj. *petûm* b (*peti-*; fem. *petītum*) 'open'; *puttûm* D = G (→ *pītum*, *teptītum*).
petûm b (vbl. adj.) see *petûm* a.
piāqum G (*a–i*) 'to be(come) narrow; to squint(?) or squirm(?)' (→ *pīqat*).
pīḫatum (also *pāḫatum*; bound form *pīḫat*, *pāḫat*) 'responsibility, obligation, duty'; *ana pī/āḫatim šakānum* 'to assign to a task'; *bēl pī/āḫatim* 'deputy, delegate; commissioner'.
pilšum (*piliš*; pl. *pilšū*) 'breach, hole' (cf. *palāšum*).
pīqat (adv.) 'perhaps' (cf. *piāqum*).
piqittum (*piqitti*; pl. *piqdātum*) 'delivery; inspection' (cf. *paqādum*).
pirištum (*pirišti*; sf. *pirišta-*) 'secret' (cf. *parāsum*).
pissātum (*pissāt*) 'lameness?'.
pišannum (*pišan*; pl. *pišannū* and *pišannātum*; log. (gi)PISAN; Sum. lw.) 'basket, box'.
pišertum '(purchase of) surplus harvest?'.
piššatum (*piššat*; log. Ì.BA) 'oil ration' (cf. *pašāšum*).
pītum (masc.; *pīt(i)*) 'opening, breach' (cf. *petûm*).
piṭrum (*piṭir*; pl. *piṭrū*) 'fissure, cleft' (cf. *paṭārum*).
puggulum (D vbl. adj.) see *pagālum*.
puglum (*pugul*) 'radish'; ext.: a part of the liver.
pūgum (*pūg*) 'net' (rare).
puḫādum (*puḫād*; pl. *puḫādū*) 'lamb'.
puḫrum (*puḫur*; pl. *puḫrātum*) 'gathering, assembly, (council) meeting; totality' (cf. *paḫārum*).
pūḫum (*pūḫ(i)*; pl. *pūḫū* and *pūḫātum*) 'substitute, replacement'; often in apposition to a preceding noun (e.g., *eqlam pūḫam idnam* 'give me a replacement field, a field as replacement').
puluḫtum (*puluḫti*; sf. *puluḫta-*) 'fear' (cf. *palāḫum*).
pûm a (gen. *pîm*, acc. *piam* and *pâm*; bound form *pī*; with sf. *pī-* in all cases; pl. *pâtum*) 'mouth; word(s); utterance, speech, command; opening'; *piam epēšum* to work/open one's mouth'; *piam šakānum* 'to

issue commands'; *ana pī* and *ša pī* (prep. phrases; §12.3) 'according to, in accordance with'; *ana pîm* 'obediently'; *ina pîm* 'orally'; *ṣīt pîm* 'utterance, command'.

pûm b (often pl. *pû*; base *pā-*) 'chaff'; *ištu pê adi ḫurāṣim* 'from chaff to gold', i.e., 'everything'.

Purattum (log. idBURANUN) the Euphrates.

purussûm (base *purussā-*; pl. *purussû*) 'legal decision, case' (cf. *parāsum*).

pūṣum (*pūṣ(i)*) 'white; white fleck(s), spot(s)'.

pūtum (*pūt(i)*; pl. *pâtum*) 'forehead, front'; *ina pūt* (prep. phrase; cf. §12.3) 'opposite'.

Q

qablum a (*qabal*; dual *qablān* [often = sg.]; log. MURUB4) 'hip, waist; middle' (→ *qablûm*).

qablum b (fem. and masc.; *qabal*; pl. *qablātum* and *qablū*) 'battle, warfare'.

qablûm (denom. adj.; *qablī-*) 'mid, middle, median' (cf. *qablum*).

qabûm G (*i*) 'to say, tell, speak; to command, order; to give orders'; infin. as noun: 'utterance, saying, command, speech'; *qabâm šakānum* 'to promise, give a pledge'; *tuššam qabûm* 'to speak maliciously, calumniate' (→ *qibītum*).

qadum (prep.) 'together with; inclusive of, including' (also rarely a conj. = *adi*)

qalûm G (*i*) 'to burn (down), roast, refine'.

qâlum G (*a–u*) 'to heed, pay attention to' (→ *qūlum*).

qammatum a woman associated with the cult who wore a certain type of hair style (very rare word; Mari).

qanûm (base *qana-* / *qanu-*; pl. *qanû* and *qanâtum*; log. GI) 'reed; arrow'; a unit of length = 6 *ammatum* = ca. 3 m. (see Appendix B.2).

qâpum G (*a–u*) 'to buckle, cave in, collapse'.

qaqqadum (*qaqqad*; pl. *qaqqadātum*; log. SAG.DU) 'head, top; person; principal (amount), capital (financial)'; *ṣalmāt qaqqadim* 'the black-headed ones' (i.e., the people of Sumer and Akkad).

qaqqarum (*qaqqar*; pl. *qaqqarū* and *qaqqarātum*) 'ground, soil, earth; area, plot of land; terrain, region'.

qarābum see *qerēbum*.

qarārum see *garārum*.

qarītum (*qarīt*; pl. *qariātum*) 'storeroom, granary'.

qarnum (*qaran*; dual *qarnān*; pl. *qarnātum*) 'horn'.

qarrādum (*qarrād*; pl. *qarrādū*) 'warrior, hero' (→ *qarrādūtum*; cf. *qurādum*).

qarrādūtum (*qarrādūt*) 'ability in battle, heroism' (rare in OB) (cf. *qarrādum*).

qaṣārum G see *kaṣārum*.

qaštum (pl. *qašātum*) 'bow'; also, a constellation.

qatānum G (*i*) 'to be(come) thin, narrow, fine'; vbl. adj. *qatnum* (*qatan-*; fem. *qatattum*) 'thin, narrow; fine (said of wool, textiles)'.

qātātum (pl. of *qātum*) 'surety, guarantee, pledge'; *qātātim leqûm* 'to go surety, to guarantee'.

qatnum (vbl. adj.) see *qatānum*.

qātum (*qāt(i)*; dual *qātān*; pl. *qātātum*; log. ŠU) 'hand; care, charge, responsibility'; *ana qāt(i)* (prep. phrase; §12.3; rare in OB) 'into the possession, custody of'; *ana qātim* (also *qāta(q)qāti*; Mari) 'immediately'; *ina qāt(i)* (prep. phrase; §12.3) 'in the possession of, from (the possession of, with verbs of taking); in the care/custody of, in the jurisdiction of, by/under the authority of, through the agency of (a person)'; *qātam nasāḫum* 'to withdraw a claim'; *qātam ṣabātum* 'to help' (e.g., *qātam ša wardim aṣbat* 'I helped the slave'); *qātam šakānum* 'to begin' (+ *ana* + infin.: 'to do', as in *qātam ana šarāqim ša kaspim iškunū* 'they began to steal the silver'; + *ana* + noun: 'begin work on', as in *qātam ana bītim aškun* 'I began work on the house'); *ša qāt(i)* (prep. phrase; §12.3; log. NÍG.ŠU) 'in the charge of, under the authority of' (written syllabically before a pron. sf., NÍG.ŠU before PNs: *ṣābum ša qá-ti-ia* 'the work-force in my charge'; *awīlû* NÍG.ŠU [I]*gi-mil-lum* 'the men in G.'s charge'); for the plural form see *qātātum*.

qerbēnum (adv.) 'inside' (cf. *qerēbum*).

qerbiš 'in close combat(?)' (rare; cf. *qerēbum*).

qerbum (vbl. adj.) see *qerēbum*.

qerēbum G (*e* or *i*) 'to draw near, approach' (+ *ana*/dat.); vbl. adj. *qerbum* (*qerub-*) 'near, at hand, close by'; as noun: 'relative'; *qurrubum* D = G 'to bring/send near; to present, offer'; *šuqrubum* Š 'to petition' (rare; → *qerbēnum, qerbiš*).

qerûm G (*e*) 'to summon, invite, take along'; *ūm/ištu ilūšu iqterûšu* 'when/after his gods have summoned him' = 'when/after he has died'.

qiāpum G (*a–i*) 'to believe, trust; to entrust (s.o. with s.th.: double acc.)'; vbl. adj. *qīpum* (*qīp-*) 'trustworthy, reliable'; N 'to be believed; to be entrusted'.

qiāšum G (*a–i*) 'to give, bestow, grant'; vbl. adj. *qīšum* (*qīš-*) 'bestowed, granted'; substantivized fem. *qīštum*; (*qīšti*; sf. *qīšta-*; pl. *qīšātum*) 'gift; fee; votive offering'.

qibītum (*qibīt*; pl. *qibiātum*) 'speech, word, utterance, instruction, order, command' (cf. *qabûm*).

qinnatum (*qinnat*) 'anus, buttock(s).'

qinnāzum (*qinnāz*; log. $^{(kuš)}$USAN$_3$) '(ox-)tail, whip'.

qīpum (vbl. adj.) see *qiāpum*.

qištum (*qišti*; pl. *qišātum*; log. GIŠ.TIR) 'forest, grove'.

qīštum see *qiāšum*.

qīšum (vbl. adj.) see *qiāšum*.

q-l-p-weak see *neqelpûm*.

qūlum (*qūl(i)*) 'silence, stillness' (cf. *qâlum*).

qûm (base *qa-*; log. SILA$_3$) a unit of capacity = 1/10 *sūtum* = ca. 1 l. (see Appendix B.5).

qûm b (base *qā-*) 'thread, filament'.

qurādum (*qurād*; pl. *qurādū*) 'warrior' (synonym of *qarrādum*).

qurqurrum see *gurgurrum*.

R

rabât see *rebiat*.

rabbûm (adj.; *rabbi-*) 'very great; noble' (cf. *rabûm* a).

rabiānum (*rabiān*; pl. *rabiānū*) 'mayor' (cf. *rabûm* a).

rabiat see *rebiat*.

rabîš (adv.) 'greatly' (cf. *rabûm* a).

rabûm a G (*i*) 'to be(come) large, great; to grow (up), increase'; vbl. adj. *rabûm* b (*rabi-*; log. GAL) 'big, large; great, important; mature'; *ritabbûm* Gtn 'to grow ever greater, to grow greater and greater' (augmentative); *rubbûm* D 'to make large, great; to raise (offspring), raise (in rank)'; *šurbûm* Š 'to make great, increase'; vbl. adj. *šurbûm* (*šurbu-*) 'very great, greatest' (→ *narbûm, parasrab, rabbûm, rabiānum, rabîš, rabûtum, tarbītum*).

rabûm b (vbl. adj.) see *rabûm* a.

rabûtum (*rabût*) 'greatness, high status, high position' (cf. *rabûm* a).

rādum 'cloudburst, downpour'.

râdum G (*a–u*) 'to shake, quake' (intr.; rare).

ragāmum G (*u* and *a–u*) 'to shout; to call, summon, demand; to complain (against), sue (s.o.: *ana*; for/concerning: *ana* or *aššum*)' (→ *rigmum, rugummûm*).

raḫāṣum G (*i*) 'to flood (tr.), inundate'.

raḫûm see *reḫûm*.

rakābum G (*a*) 'to mount; to ride; to board'; *ritkubum* Gt 'to mate; to lie upon/against one another'; *rukkubum* D 'to pollinate'; *šurkubum* Š 'to cause to mount; to load (a ship, wagon, etc.)' (→ *narkabtum, tarkibtum*).

rakāsum G (*a–u*) 'to bind, tie (on),

wrap up; to put on, equip oneself with; to attack'; *rukkusum* D = G; 'to contract (with s.o.)'; *narkusum* N (*rakāsum*) passive; 'to conspire' (rare) (→ *riksum*).

ramānum (*ramān*) 'self, oneself; (one's) own; alone'; normally with a pron. sf., as a reflexive or intensive pronoun (e.g., *ramāššu ipaṭṭar* 'he will ransom himself'; *ramāššu illik* 'he himself went'); *ana ramānī-* 'for oneself'; *ina ramānī-* 'by oneself, of one's own accord, alone'; after a bound form: '(one's) own' (e.g., *ina ṭēm ramānīki* 'according to your (fs) own judgment').

ramûm G (*i*) 'to throw, cast, scatter; to live, reside'.

râmum G (*a*) 'to love, care for'; *ritūmum* Gt (rare) 'to love (= G?), love one another'; infin. in pl. 'mutual love'? (→ *īrimum*/*irīmum*, *narāmum*, *ruʾāmum*).

rapāšum G (*i*) 'to be(come) wide, broad'; vbl. adj. *rapšum* (*rapaš-*) 'wide, broad'; *uznum rapaštum* 'great intelligence, understanding'; *ruppušum* D 'to widen, broaden' (→ *rupšum*).

rapšum (vbl. adj.) see *rapāšum*.

rašābum G only in vbl. adj. *rašbum* (*rašub-*) 'commanding respect, awe-inspiring, imposing, awesome'; R vbl. adj. *rašubbum* (§38.3(c)) 'glowing, fearsome'.

rašbum (vbl. adj.) see *rašābum*.

rašubbum (R vbl. adj.) see *rašābum*.

rašûm G (*i*) 'to receive, obtain, get, acquire, gain'; *baqrī rašûm* 'to incur legal claims'; *pānam rašûm* 'to become clear, plain'; *šuršûm* Š 'to cause to acquire, provide (s.o. with s.th.: double acc.)'; note *pānam šuršûm* 'to make clear, explicit (a report, tablet, matter)'; *idam šuršûm* 'to raise objections'; *ṣibit ṭēmim rašûm* 'to take action'.

ratātum G (*u*) 'to tremble, shake' (intr.; rare).

raṭābum G rare except in vbl. adj. *raṭbum* (*raṭub-*; log. DURU$_5$) 'moist'.

raṭbum (vbl. adj.) see *raṭābum*.

rebiat (also *rabiat*, *rebât*, *rabât*) 'one-fourth' (cf. *erbe*).

rebītum (*rebīt*; pl. *rebiātum*) '(town) square, plaza' (cf. *erbe*).

rebûm (adj.; fem. *rebūtum*) 'fourth' (cf. *erbe*).

redûm G (*e*) 'to escort, conduct, lead, guide; to drive (animals, ships, wagons), follow; to lay claim to; to move along'; ptcpl. *rēdûm* (base *rēdi-*; pl. *rēdû*; log. AGA.ÚS) 'foot-soldier, attendant'; the fem. ptcpl. *rēdītum* (*rēdīt* or *rēdiet*) denotes '(legitimate) claimant, heir (fem.)'.; *ruddûm* D 'to add to, contribute to' (i.e., 'to make follow'); *šurdûm* Š 'to cause to bring, conduct, lead; to cause to flow'; *šuterdûm* Št-pass. 'to be conducted, caused to flow'; *šuterdûm* Št-lex. 'to continue, resume'.

rēdûm (ptcpl.) see *redûm*.

rēḫtum (bound form *rēḫet* or *rēḫti*; pl. *rēḫētum*; log. ÍB.TAG$_4$) 'rest, remainder'.

reḫûm G (*e*; also *raḫûm*, *i*) 'to copulate, mate, procreate, beget; to (over)flow (into, upon)'.

rēmum (*rēm(i)*) 'womb; pity'; *šilip rēmim*, lit., 's.th. pulled from the womb', probably refers to a child born through caesarian section.

rēqum (vbl. adj.) see *rêqum*.

rêqum G (*e*) 'to be(come) far, distant'; vbl. adj. *rēqum* (*rēq-*) 'far, distant'; *ūmam rēqam*, *ina ūmim rēqim* 'some time'; *ruqqum* D 'to make, keep distant'; *šuruqqum* Š 'to remove, move away'.

rēštum (*rēšti*, rarely *rēšet*; pl. *rēšētum*) 'beginning; peak; the best quality (of oil, dates, sheep); instalment (on a loan)' (cf. *rēšum*).

rēšum (*rēš(i)*; dual *rēšān* [often = sg.]; log. SAG) 'top; head; chief, principal; beginning; slave; front(age)'; *rēš eqlim* 'destination'; *rēš namkūrim* (log. SAG NÍG.GA) 'available assets, stock'; *šūt rēšim* 'court officials, commanders' (→ *rēštum*, *rēšūtum*).

rēšūtum 'slavery; service' (cf. *rēšum*).
re'ûm G (*i*; conjugated like *le'ûm*, see §21.3(h)) 'to tend, pasture (flocks); to graze (said of sheep)'; ptcpl. *rē'ûm* (base *rē'i-*; log. SIPA(D)) 'shepherd' (→ *merītum*).
rē'ûm (ptcpl.) see *re'ûm*.
riābum G (*a–i*) 'to replace, give back'.
riāqum G (*a–i*) 'to be(come) empty, unoccupied, idle, useless'; vbl. adj. *rīqum* (*rīq-*) 'empty; idle'; *ruqqum* D and *šuruqqum* Š 'to empty; to leave idle' (→ *rīqūtum*).
riāšum G (*a–i*) 'to rejoice' (→ *rīštum*).
rigmum (*rigim*; pl. *rigmū*) 'call, shout, cry, noise, voice' (cf. *ragāmum*).
riksum (*rikis*; pl. *riksātum* [often = sg.]) 'band; contract, agreement, treaty'; *riksam* / *riksātim šakānum* 'to establish an agreement, make out a contract' (cf. *rakāsum*).
rīmtum see *rīmum*.
rīmum (*rīm*; pl. *rīmū*; log. AM) 'wild bull'; fem. *rīmtum* (*rīmti*; pl. *rīmātum*; log. SÚN) 'wild cow'.
ripqum (pl. *ripqātum*) 'dug-up land?'.
rīqum (vbl. adj.) see *riāqum*.
rīqūtum (*rīqūt*) 'emptiness; idleness'; *rīqūt-* (with pron. sf.; adv. acc., see §18.3(d)) 'empty-handed' (e.g., *rīqūssu illak* 'he will go empty-handed') (cf. *riāqum*).
risibtum (pl. *risbātum* [= sg.]) 'quarrel, fight'.
rīštum (often pl. *rīšātum*) 'joy, rejoicing' (cf. *riāšum*).
rittum (*ritti*; sf. *ritta-*; dual *rittān*) 'hand; possibility'.
ru'āmum (*ru'ām*) 'charm, love' (cf. *râmum*).
rubātum (fem. of *rubûm*; pl. *rubâtum* [‹*rubā*+*ātum*]) 'princess' (cf.*rubûm*).
rubûm (*rubā-*; pl. *rubû*; log. NUN) 'prince, ruler' (→ *rubātum*,*rubûtum*).
rubûtum (*rubût*) 'principality; dominion' (cf. *rubûm*).
rugbum (*rugub*; pl. *rugbātum*) 'roof' (→ *ruggubum*).
ruggubum D 'to roof (over)' (cf. *rugbum*).
rugummûm (*rugummā-*; pl. *rugummû*, *rugummānû*) 'legal claim, lawsuit; penalty, fine awarded/assessed in a lawsuit' (cf. *ragāmum*).
rupšum (*rupuš*) 'width' (cf. *rapāšum*).

S

sābītum (ptcpl.) see *sabûm*.
sabûm G (*i*) 'to brew beer'; ptcpl. *sābûm*, fem. *sābītum* (log. LÚ/MÍ.KURUN.NA) 'innkeeper, beer merchant'.
sābûm (ptcpl.) see *sabûm*.
sadārum G (*a–u*) 'to arrange, put in order; to enter (s.th. into an account)'; in hendiadys: 'to occur/do regularly'; vbl. adj. *sadrum* (*sadir-*) 'in a row; regular, continual'; *suddurum* D = G.
sadrum (vbl. adj.) see *sadārum*.
sagûm (also *sakkûm*; Sum. lw.) 'shrine'.
saḫāpum G (*a–u*) 'to cover, spread over, overwhelm'; *suḫḫupum* D = G.
saḫārum G (*u*) 'to go/walk around, surround, circle, curve; to turn, turn around, turn back, rotate, twist (intr.); to seek, look for, turn to (s.o.)'; *suḫḫurum* D 'to turn around, aside, divert; to turn away, back, send away, back, repel, expel'; *šusḫurum* Š 'to cause to turn, cause to seek; to place around, surround (s.th. with s.th.: double acc.)'; *šutasḫurum* Št-lex. 'to surround on all sides'; *nasḫurum* N 'to turn (oneself)'.
sakālum G (*i*) 'to acquire illegally'; *sikiltam sakkālum* 'to appropriate s.th. fraudulently' (→ *sikiltum*).
sakāpum a G (*i*) 'to push away, overturn, depose, reject; to repel, defeat; to dispatch (a boat), send (by boat)'.
sakāpum b G (*u*) 'to lie down, rest'.
sakkû (only pl.; gen.-acc. *sakkî* / *sakkê*) '(cultic) rites, divine regulations'.
sakkûm see *sagûm*.
salīmātum (always pl.) 'ally; alliance, partnership' (cf. *salīmum*).
salīmum (*salīm*) 'peace, concord' (cf. *salīmātum*).

samāne (*samānûm*; with masc. nouns *samānūtum*) 'eight' (→ *samnat, samnum*).
samnat (a bound form) 'one-eighth' (cf. *samāne*).
samnum (adj.; fem. *samuntum*) 'eighth' (cf. *samāne*).
sāmum (adj.; *sām-*) 'red' (cf. *sūmum*).
sanāqum G (*i*) 'to arrive at, reach; to approach with a claim, proceed against (+ *ana*/dat.); to check, control, supervise; to question, to investigate'; *sunnuqum* D 'to check, inspect; to control; to question; to close' (→ *sunqum*).
sapāḫum G (*a–u*) 'to scatter, disperse, squander; to confound'; *suppuḫum* D = G; *naspuḫum* N passive.
saqārum see *zakārum*.
sarārum G (*a–u*) 'to be(come) false; to cheat'; vbl. adj. *sarrum* (*sarr-*; fs irregular *sartum*) 'false, criminal; liar'; substantivized fem. *sartum* (pl. *sarrātum*) 'lie, falsehood, treachery; misdeed, criminal act'; *surrurum* D 'to make false claims, claim falsely, contest'.
sarrum (vbl. adj.) see *sarārum*.
sartum see *sarārum*.
sebe (*sebûm*; with masc. nouns *sebet, sebetti, sebettum*) 'seven' (→ *sebītum, sebûm*).
sebītum (also *sebiatum; sebiat*) 'one-seventh' (cf. *sebe*).
sebûm (adj.; fem. *sebūtum*) 'seventh' (cf. *sebe*).
sekērum G (*e*) 'to shut, close, dam up, block'; ptcpl. *sēkirum* (log. $^{(lú)}$A.IGI. DU$_8$) 'canal worker'; *neskurum* N passive (→ *sekretum, sikkūrum*).
sēkirum (ptcpl.) see *sekērum*.
sekretum (*sekret*; pl. *sekrētum*; pseudo-log. ^{mí}ZI.IK.RUM/RU.UM) 'a (cloistered?) woman of high status' (cf. *sekērum*).
sepûm G (rare); *suppûm* D 'to abduct, remove by force' (rare).
sikiltum (*sikilti*; sf. *sikilta-*) 'aquisition, property'; *sikiltam sakālum* 'to appropriate s.th. fraudulenty' (cf. *sakālum*).
sikkatum (*sikkat*; pl. *sikkātum*) 'peg'; *sikkatam maḫāṣum* 'to drive in a peg' (to mark limits of ownership).
sikkūrum (*sikkūr*; pl. *sikkūrū*) 'bar, door-bolt' (cf. *sekērum*).
sikmū (always pl.) 'payment (for catching a fugitive)'.
Simānum (log. SIG$_4$.GA) third OB month (May–June).
simmum (*simmi*; sf. *simma-*; pl. *simmū*) 'wound; (skin) disease, carbuncle'; *simmam epēšum* 'to treat a disease'.
simtum (*simat*; pl. *simātum*) 'what pertains, belongs, is fitting, appropriate, suitable, worthy, necessary to (e.g., *bītum simat ilūtīšu* 'a temple befitting his divinity'); characteristic(s), features; proper appearance, behavior'.
Simānum (log. ITU.SIG$_4$.A) the third month (May-June).
Sîn (Sum. lw.; log. ^{d}EN.ZU read ^{d}ZUEN) 'Sin', the moon god.
sinništum (*sinništi*; sf. *sinništa-*; pl. *sinnišātum*; log. MUNUS/MÍ) 'woman; female'.
siparrum (log. ZABAR; Sum. lw.) 'bronze'.
Sippar (log. ZIMBIR^{ki}) an important city about 60 km. north of Babylon (modern Abu Habba).
sippum (*sippi*; pl. *sippū*) 'door-frame, door-jambs'; ext.: a part of the liver.
siqrum see *zikrum* b.
sirāšûm (*sirāši-*; log. ŠIM (also ŠIMĪGAR, ŠIM+GAR); Sum. lw.?) 'brewer'.
sukkallum or *šukkallum* (*s*/*šukkal*; log. SUKKAL; Sum. lw.) 'minister, vizier'.
sukkalmaḫḫum (log. SUKKAL.MAḪ) a high court official ('chief minister').
suluppum (pl. *suluppū*; log. ZÚ. LUM(.MA); Sum. lw.) 'date(s)'.
sūmum (*sūm(i)*; pl. *sūmū*) 'redness, red spot' (cf. *sāmum*).
sunqum 'famine' (cf. *sanāqum*).
sūnum (*sūn(i)*) 'lap, crotch'; *ina sūn(i) X niālum*/*itūlum* 'to have intercourse with X'.

supūrum (*supūr*; pl. *supūrū*) 'sheep-fold, pen'; an epithet of the city of Uruk.

sūqum (*sūq(i)*; pl. *sūqātum*, *sūqānū*; log. SILA) 'street'.

sūtum (*sūt*; absolute *sât*?; pl. *sâtum*; log. BÁN) a unit of capacity ('seah') = 10 *qûm* = ca. 10 l. (see Appendix B.5); *sūt Šamaš* 'the seah of (the) Shamash (temple)' (a seah of specific size).

Ṣ

ṣabātum G (*a*) 'to seize, take hold of, arrest, capture'; vbl. adj. *ṣabtum* (*ṣabit-*) 'seized; deposited; captive, prisoner'; *qātam ṣabātum* 'to help' (e.g., *qāssu aṣbat* 'I helped him'); *ḫarrānam ṣabātum* 'to take the road, undertake a campaign'; *ṭēmam ṣabātum* 'to take action (concerning: *ana*)'; *kussiam ṣabātum* 'to take the throne' (referring to both regular succession and usurpation); *pān(i) X ṣabātum* 'to lead X'; *tiṣbutum* a Gt 'to grasp one another, quarrel; to join/connect with one another; to be occupied, busy'; vbl. adj. *tiṣbutum* b 'connected, joined, engaged'; *ṣubbutum* D = G; *šutaṣbutum* Št-lex. 'to collect, assemble, keep together, attach; to quarrel' (lit., 'to cause to grasp one another'); *naṣbutum* N passive of G (→ *ṣibittum*, *ṣibtum* b).

ṣabtum (vbl. adj.) see *ṣabātum*.

ṣabûm (verb) see *ṣubbûm*.

ṣābum (*ṣāb(i)*; pl. *ṣābū*) 'worker, soldier'; coll. 'gang, army, troop(s)'.

ṣayyaḫum (adj.; *ṣayyaḫ-*) 'delightful, fancy' (rare).

ṣalāmum G (*i*) 'to be(come), turn black, dark'; vbl. adj. *ṣalmum* (*ṣalim-*) 'black, dark'; *ṣalmāt qaqqadim* 'the black-headed ones' (i.e., the people of Sumer and Akkad).

ṣalmum (vbl. adj.) see *ṣalāmum*.

ṣamādum G (*i*) 'to tie, bind, attach; to yoke, harness; to make (s.th.) ready'; *ṣummudum* D = G (→ *ṣimdatum*).

ṣarāmum G (*i*) 'to strive, exert oneself, be concerned'; *ṣurrumum* D=G.

ṣeḫērum G (*i*) 'to be(come) young, small, few, little; to decrease'; vbl. adj. *ṣeḫrum* (*ṣeḫer-*) 'small, young'; substantivized 'child'; *tiṣeḫḫerum* Gtn 'to become smaller and smaller' (augmentative); *ṣuḫḫurum* D 'to make small(er), reduce' (→ *ṣeḫḫerum*, *ṣuḫārtum*, *ṣuḫārum*).

ṣeḫḫerum (adj.; *ṣeḫḫer-*) '(very) small'; substantivized pl. 'retainers, servants' (cf. *ṣeḫrum*).

ṣeḫrum (vbl. adj.) see *ṣeḫērum*.

ṣēlum (less often *ṣellum*; pl. *ṣēlū*/ *ṣellū*) 'rib; side'.

ṣēnum (fem.), usu. pl. *ṣēnū* (fem.! pl.), both normally written with log. U₈.UDU.ḪI.A (all of which is also read USDUḪA) 'sheep; sheep and goats; flock (of sheep and goats)'.

ṣênum G (*e*) 'to load, heap up'.

ṣeʾpum (pl. *ṣeʾpētum*) 'sealed letter'.

ṣerretum (*ṣerret*; pl. *ṣerrētum*) 'nose-rope, halter, lead-rope'.

ṣērum (*ṣēr(i)*; log. EDIN) 'back (part, side); hinterland, back country; steppeland'; *ana ṣēr* (rarely with assimilation: *aṣ-ṣēr* [southern OB and Mari; for northern OB, see *maḫrum*]; prep. phrase; §12.3) 'in the direction of, to, toward, against; in addition to'; *ina ṣēr* (prep. phrase; §12.3; OB in poetry only) 'upon, on top of'.

ṣiārum G rare apart from vbl. adj. *ṣīrum* (*ṣīr-*; log. MAḪ) 'august, outstanding, first-rank, excellent'.

ṣibittum (*ṣibitti*; sf. *ṣibitta-*) 'prison, imprisonment' (cf. *ṣabātum*).

ṣibtum a (*ṣibat*; pl. *ṣibātum*; log. MÁŠ) 'interest' (cf. *waṣābum*).

ṣibtum b (masc.; bound form *ṣibit*; pl. *ṣibtātum*) 'seizure; agricultural holding'; *ṣibit ṭēmim išûm*/*rašûm* 'to take action' (cf. *ṣabātum*).

ṣibtum c ext: a part of the liver.

ṣibûtum (*ṣibût*) 'wish, need, request; purpose, enterprise'.

ṣīḫtum (*ṣīḫti*; sf. *ṣīḫta-*; pl. *ṣīḫātum*) 'smile, laughter'; *ṭuppum ṣīḫtum* 'fraud(ulent tablet)'.

ṣimdatum (*ṣimdat*; pl. *ṣimdātum*) 'royal decree; (specific) royal regulation' (also *ṣimdat šarrim*; cf. *ṣamādum*).

ṣīrum (vbl. adj.) see *ṣiārum*.

ṣītum (*ṣīt*; pl. *ṣiātum*) 'rise, rising (of sun), east; emergence, birth, origin; produce, product; lease; expenditure, loss; departure'; *ṣīt pîm* 'command, utterance'; pl. *ṣiātum* (also *ūm ṣiātim*) 'distant time (past or future)'; *ṣīt šamšim* 'sunrise, east' (cf. *waṣûm*).

ṣubātum (*ṣubāt*; pl. *ṣubātū*; log. TÚG) 'garment' (note also determinative túg before items of clothing).

ṣubbûm D (not in G) 'to look at (s.th.) from a distance; to carry out, execute properly, according to plan'; *šuteṣbûm* Št lex. 'to carry out, execute properly, according to plan'.

ṣuḫārtum (*ṣuḫārti*; sf. *ṣuḫārta-*; pl. *ṣuḫārātum*; log. MUNUS.TUR) '(female) child, young woman; female servant, employee' (cf. *ṣeḫērum*).

ṣuḫārum (*ṣuḫār*; pl. *ṣuḫārû*; log. TUR) '(male) child, adolescent; male servant, employee' (cf. *ṣeḫērum*).

ṣūmum (*ṣūm(i)*) 'thirst'.

ṣuppum a unit of length = 60 *ammatum* = ca. 30 m (see Appendix B.2).

Š

ša (determinative-relative pronoun) 'the one of; of'; *ša lā* (used as prep.) 'without' (e.g., *eqlum ša lā mê* 'a field without water'); *ša libbim* 'foetus'; *ša libbim nadûm* 'to have a miscarriage'; *ša qāt(i)* (log. NÍG.ŠU) 'in the charge of, under the authority of' (written syllabically before a pron. sf.; NÍG.ŠU before PN's: *ṣābum ša qá-ti-ia* 'the work-force in my charge'; *awīlû* NÍG.ŠU I*gi-mil-lum* 'the men in G.'s charge') (→ *šāt, šūt*).

šabārum see *šebērum*.

šabāsum G (*u*) 'to be(come) angry, annoyed' (with s.o.: *eli*); vbl. adj. *šabsum* (*šabus-*) 'angry, annoyed'.

Šabāṭum (log. ZÍZ.A.AN) eleventh OB month (January–February).

šabsum (vbl. adj.) see *šabāsum*.

šadādum G (*a–u*) 'to pull, draw, drag, tow, haul, convey; to bear; to stretch; to pull, tear out, off; to measure, survey (a field)'; vbl. adj. *šaddum* (*šadid-*) 'taut; elongated'; ptcpl. *šādidum* (*šādid*) 'boat-tower'.

šaddum (vbl. adj.) see *šadādum*.

šādidum (ptcpl.) see *šadādum*.

šadûm (base *šadu-*; pl. *šadû*; log. KUR and SA.TU) 'mountain, mountain region'; *kiṣir šadîm* 'bedrock'.

šaḫāṭum G (*a–u*) 'to tear off, away'; *šuḫḫuṭum* D = G; *našḫuṭum* N passive

šaḫûm (*šaḫa-*; log. ŠAḪ; Sum. lw.) 'pig'.

šaḫururum R (see §38.3(e)) 'to be(come) completely inactive, paralyzed (with fear)'.

šayyāmānum (*šayyāmān*) 'buyer' (cf. *šâmum*).

šakākum G (*a–u*) 'to harrow'.

šakānum G (*a–u*) 'to place, set, put; to establish, install, appoint, assign, impose'; vbl. adj. *šaknum* (*šakin-*) 'placed, lying, situated, located, present; established, appointed; endowed, provided'; substantivized, 'governor'; *dannātim šakānum* 'to give strong orders' (Mari); *maḫar ... šakānum* 'to inform ...' (e.g., *kīam maḫrīya iškun* 'thus he informed me', lit., 'placed before me'); *pānam / pānī šakānum* 'to proceed; to intend, decide' (to do: *ana* + infin.: *pānīšu ana epēš bītim iškun* 'he intended to build a house'); *piam šakānum* 'to issue commands'; *qabâm šakānum* 'to give a pledge'; *qātam šakānum* 'to begin' (+ *ana* + inf..: to do; + *ana* + noun: 'begin work on'); *riksam šakānum* 'to establish an agreement, make out a contract'; *šaknāt napištim* 'creatures (lit., those endowed with life)'; *ṭēmam šakānum* 'to give instructions, directions, information (to s.o.: *ana* / dat. or acc.)' (→ *maškanum, šakkanakkum, šukunnûm*).

šakkanakkum (*šakkanak*; log. GÌR.

NITA(Ḫ)2 [perhaps to be read ŠAKKANA6]; Sum. lw.?) '(military) governor' (cf. *šakānum*).
šaknum (vbl. adj.) see *šakānum*.
šalālum G (*a–u*) 'to plunder, loot; to take as booty; to take captive'; *našlulum* N 'to be plundered; to be taken captive, as booty'.
šalāmum G (*i*) 'to be(come) whole, sound, well, uninjured, safe; to recover; to arrive safely; to succeed, prosper; to be completed'; vbl. adj. *šalmum* (*šalim-*) 'whole, sound, well, safe, in good condition, intact, complete, favorable'; *šullumum* D 'to keep whole, well, safe; to heal (tr.); to preserve, take care of; to conduct or deliver safely; to make good, replace in full; to complete' (→ *šulmānum, šulmum*).
šalāpum G (*a–u*) 'to pull out, extricate' (→ *šilpum*).
šalāš (*šalāšum*; with masc. nouns *šalāšat, šalāštum*) 'three' (→ *šalāšā, šalāšīšu, šalšum* a, *šalšum* b).
šalāšā (indeclinable) 'thirty' (cf. *šalāš*).
šalāšīšu (adv.) 'thrice, three times, threefold' (cf. *šalāš*).
šallatum (*šallat*) 'plunder, booty, captives'.
šalmum (vbl. adj.) see *šalāmum*.
šalšum a (adj.; fem. *šaluštum*) 'third' (cf. *šalāš*).
šalšum b (*šaluš*; fem. *šaluštum*, bound *šalušti*) 'one-third' (cf. *šalāš*).
šalûm G (*i*) 'to dive, plunge into (+ acc.)'.
šâlum G (*a*) 'to ask, inquire, question' (s.o.: acc.; about: acc. or *aššum* or *ana*); *šitūlum* Gt 'to ponder, deliberate, reflect'; also reciprocal, 'to consult, take counsel; to question' (→ *šitūlum*).
šalummum (R vbl. adj.) 'brilliantly radiant'.
šaluštum see *šalšum* b.
šamāḫum G (*u*) 'to grow thickly, thrive, flourish; to attain great beauty or stature, be(come) majestic, proud, haughty'; vbl. adj. *šamḫum* (*šamuḫ-*) 'luxuriant; prosperous, thriving; majestic; proud, haughty' (→ *šamḫatum*).
šamallûm (base *šamallā-*; Sum. lw.) 'trading agent; assistant; apprentice'.
Šamaš (log. dUTU) 'Shamash', the sun god (cf. *šamšum*).
šamaššammum (ofen pl.; log. ŠE.GIŠ.Ì [also ŠE.Ì.GIŠ at Mari]) an oil-producing plant and its seed, probably 'sesame' (or, 'flax; linseed').
šamḫatum (also *šamkatum*; bound form and absolute form *šamḫat*) 'prostitute' (cf. *šamāḫum*).
šamḫum (vbl. adj.) see *šamāḫum*.
šamkatum see *šamḫatum*.
šammum (*šammi*; sf. *šamma-*; pl. *šammū* [often = sg.]; log. Ú) 'plant, grass; herb, drug; hay, fodder'.
šamnum (*šaman*; log. Ì, Ì.GIŠ) 'oil, fat'.
šamšum (*šamaš*; log. UTU) 'sun'; see also *Šamaš*.
šamû (alw. pl.; base *šamā-* [gen.–acc. *šamê*]; log. AN) 'sky, heaven'.
šāmum (vbl. adj.) see *šâmum*.
šâmum G (*a*) 'to buy, purchase' (from s.o.: *itti* or *ina qāt*); vbl. adj. *šāmum* (*šām-*) 'purchased, bought' (→ *šayyāmānum, šīmum* b).
šanānum G (*a–u*) 'to be(come) equal, match, rival'; *šitnunum* Gt 'to equal one another, rival, compete with one another'.
šandanakkum (*šandanak*; pl. *šandanakkātum*; Sum. lw.; log. ŠANDANA) 'administrator of date orchards'.
šangûm (*šangā-*; log. SANGA; Sum. lw.) 'temple administrator'.
šanītam (adv.) 'secondly, moreover' (cf. *šanûm* a).
šanûm a G (*i*) 'to do twice, double, again' (in hendiadys); vbl. adj. *šanûm* c (*šani-*; fem. *šanītum*) 'second; other, another; different'; substantivized 'another person, s.o. else'; *šunnûm* D 'to repeat, tell; to count'; *šutannûm* Dt passive of D; *šutašnûm* Št-lex. 'to double, give twice as much'; in hendiadys, 'to do again' (cf. *šinā, šanītam*).
šanûm b G (*i*) 'to change (intr.), be

(-come) different, strange'; *šunnûm* D 'to change, alter' (tr.); *šutannûm* Dt passive of D; *šušnûm* Š (Assyr. only) = D.
šanûm c (vbl. adj.) see *šanûm* a.
šapākum G (*a–u*) 'to heap up, pile up, store; to pour'; *našpukum* N passive (→ *našpakum, našpakūtum*).
šapal see *šaplum* b.
šapālum G (*i*) 'to be(come) low, deep, small'; vbl. adj. *šaplum* a (*šapil-*) 'low, deep'; *šuppulum* D 'to make low, deep, small' (→ *šapiltum, šaplānum, šapliš, šaplum* b, *šaplûm*).
šapārum G (*a–u*) 'to send (s.o., e.g., a messenger); to send word, send a message, report; to write; to command, give orders; to administer, oversee, govern'; rarely, 'to convey (goods)'; ptcpl. *šāpirum* (*šāpir*; pl. *šāpirū, šāpirūtum*) 'overseer; governor, prefect, commander, chief'; *šāpir mātim* 'governor' (cf. *našpartum, našparum, šiprum*).
šapiltum (*šapilti*; sf. *šapilta-*) 'remainder, amount outstanding' (cf. *šapālum*).
šāpirum (ptcpl.) see *šapārum*.
šaplānum (adv.) 'below, underneath'; (prep.; with sf. *šaplānukka*, etc.) 'below, under' (cf. *šapālum*).
šapliš (adv.) 'below' (cf. *šapālum*).
šaplum a (vbl. adj.) see *šapālum*.
šaplum b (*šapal*) 'under part, under side, bottom'; *šapal* (prep.; with sf. *šaplī-* or *šapal-*) and *ina šapal* (prep. phrase; with sf. *ina šaplī-*) 'under, below, beneath'; *(ina) šapal šēp(ī)* 'at the feet of' (cf. *šapālum*).
šaplûm (denom. adj.; *šaplī-*) 'lower' (cf. *šapālum*).
šaptum (*šapat*; dual *šaptān*; pl. *šapātum*) 'lip; utterance; edge, rim'.
šaqālum a G (*a–u*) 'to weigh out (silver, etc.), pay'; vbl. adj. *šaqlum* (*šaqil-*) 'weighed (out)'; *šaqululum* (*šuqallulum*) R (see §38.3(e)) 'to hang, be suspended' (→ *šiqlum*).
šaqālum b G (*a–u*) 'take (away), remove' (rare).
šaqlum (vbl. adj.) see *šaqālum* a.
šaqululum see *šaqālum* a.
šaqûm a G (*i*) 'to water, give water to, give (water) to drink (+ acc.: people, animals, fields, etc.)' (used as causative of *šatûm*) (→ *šaqītum*).
šaqûm b G (*u*) 'to be(come) high, tall'; vbl. adj. *šaqûm* c (*šaqu-*; fem. *šaqūtum*) 'high, tall, elevated'; *šuqqûm* D 'to raise, elevate; to send upstream'.
šaqûm c (vbl. adj.) see *šaqûm* b.
šaqumumum R (see §38.3(e)) 'to be (-come) completely still, silent'.
šarāḫum G only in vbl. adj. *šarḫum* (*šaruḫ-*) 'proud, splendid, magnificent'; *šurruḫum* D 'to make proud', etc.
šarākum G (*a–u*) 'to give, bestow' (→ *šeriktum*).
šarāmum G (*a–u*) 'to beat out, cut out'; *šurrumum* D 'to cut off, trim'.
šarāqum G (*i*) 'to steal'; vbl. adj. *šarqum* (*šariq-*) 'stolen' (→ *šarrāqum, šurqum*).
šarḫum (vbl. adj.) see *šarāḫum*.
šarqum (vbl. adj.) see *šarāqum*.
šarratum (*šarrat*; pl. *šarrātum*) 'queen' (cf. *šarrum*).
šarrum (*šar* or *šarri*; sf. *šarra-*; pl. *šarrū, šarrānū*; log. LUGAL) 'king' (→ *šarratum, šarrūtum*).
šarrāqum (*šarrāq*; pl. *šarrāqū*) 'thief' (cf. *šarāqum*).
šarrūtum (*šarrūt*; log. LUGAL*(-ru)-* [e.g., LUGAL*(-ru)-tam* = *šarrūtam*]) 'kingship; dominion; majesty'; *šarrūtam epēšum* 'to exercise kingship, rule as king' (cf. *šarrum*).
šārtam (*šārat*) 'hair'.
šārum (absolute form *šār*; log. SÁR; Sum. lw.) 'three thousand six hundred' (see §23.2(a)).
šassukkum (log. SAG.DÙN; Sum. lw.) 'land-registry officer'.
šasûm G (*i*; preterite *išsi* or *issi*; imperative *šisi* or *tisi*) 'to cry (out), shout, call (to), summon; to proclaim; to read (aloud)'; *šitassûm* Gtn 'to read, study'; *šušsûm*/*šussûm* Š causative; N passive.
šâšim, šâšum see *šī, šū*.

šāt archaic fem. sg. of det.-rel. *ša* 'the one of, the one who' (cf. the pl. *šūt* in *šūt-rēšim*); *ina šāt mušītīya* 'during that of my night', i.e., 'in my dream'.
šatammum (*šatam*; Sum. lw.) 'clerk, administrator'.
šâti, šâtu see *šī, šū*.
šattam see *šattum*.
šattum a (bound/abs. form *šanat*; pl. *šanātum*; log. MU) 'year'; *šattam* (adv.) 'this year'; *ana šattīšu* 'for one year'.
šattum b see *šûm*.
šâtu see *šuāti*.
šatûm G (*i*) 'to drink'.
šaṭārum G (*a–u*) 'to inscribe, write, write down, enter, register (s.th. in an account, list, etc.); to assign (s.th. to s.o., s.o. to a task, duty)'; vbl. adj. *šaṭrum* (*šaṭir-*) 'inscribed; registered; assigned'.
šaṭrum (vbl. adj.) see *šaṭārum*.
šebērum G (*e* or *i*) 'to break (tr.)'; vbl. adj. *šebrum* (*šebir-*) 'broken'; *šubburum* D = G (pluralic); *nešburum* N 'to break (intr.), be/get broken'.
šebrum (vbl. adj.) see *šebērum*.
šebûm G (*e*) 'to be(come) satisfied, sate oneself' (with: acc.); *šubbûm* D 'to satisfy, please' (s.o. with s.th.: double acc.); *šutebbûm* Dt passive of D.
šediš (*šeššum* a; with masc. nouns *šeššet, šedištum*) 'six' (→ *šeššum* b, *šuššum, šūšum*).
šēdum (*šēd*; pl. *šēdū*) a protective spirit; often occurs with *lamassum*; these represent good fortune, health.
šemûm a G (*e*) 'to hear; to listen; to listen to, obey'; vbl. adj. *šemûm* b (*šemi-*) 'heard; having heard, informed, aware; obedient'; *šušmûm* Š 'to cause (s.o.) to hear (s.th.), inform, cause to pay attention' (→ *tešmûm*).
šemûm b (vbl. adj.) see *šemûm* a.
šenā see *šinā*.
šēpītum (*šēpīt*; pl. *šēpiātum*) 'lower part, end, foot' (cf. *šēpum*).
šēpum (fem.; *šēp(i)*; dual *šēpān*) 'foot', also 'conveyance, transport'; *ubān šēpim* 'toe'; ext. (apparently masc.; log. AŠ) in protasis, a distinctive mark on the liver; in apodosis, '(military) expedition' (→ *šēpītum*).
šerʾānum (also *šerḫānum*; bound form *šerʾān*; pl. *šerʾānū*) 'band, strip; vein, artery, tendon, sinew'.
šeriktum, širiktum (*šerikti*; sf. *serikta-*) 'gift, dowry' (cf. *šarākum*).
šeršerrum (pl. *šeršerrū*) 'chain; ring'.
šērtum a (*šēret*) 'penalty, punishment'; *šērtam emēdum/esērum* 'to impose a penalty, punishment' (on s.o.: acc.).
šērtum b (*šēret*; pl. *šērētum*) 'ring'.
šerʾum (*šereʾ*; pl. *šerʾātum*; log. AB.SÍN) 'furrow; cultivated field'.
šeššet see *šediš*.
šeššum b (adj.; fem. *šeduštum*) 'sixth' (cf. *šediš*).
šētum (*šēt*; pl. *šētētum*) 'net'.
šeum see *ûm*.
šeʾûm G (*i* or *e*; conjugated like *leʾûm*, §21.3(h)) 'to seek, search, look for'; *šiteʾʾûm* Gtn often used instead of G.
šī (pron.; gen.–acc. *šuāti/šâti/šiāti*; dat. *šuāšim/šâšim/šiāšim*) 'she, it; that, the aforesaid' (§§2.4, 6.3, 25.2) (→ *šûm*).
šiābum G (*a–i*) 'to be(come)/grow old, gray'; vbl. adj. *šībum* (*šīb-*) 'gray, gray-haired, old'; as noun (*šīb(i)*; pl. *šībū* and *šībūtum*) 'old man, elder; witness' (→ *šībūtum*).
šiāḫum G (*a–i*) 'to grow tall, high' vbl. adj. *šīḫum* (*šīḫ-*) 'tall, high, full-grown'.
šiāmum G (*a–i*) 'to fix, set, establish, determine; to decree'; vbl. adj. *šīmum* a (*šīm-*) 'fixed'; substantivized fem. *šīmtum* (*šīmat* or *šīmti*; pl. *šīmātum*) 'what is established, fixed, decreed (by the gods), fate, destiny'; a euphemism for death, as in *ana šīmtim alākum* 'to die (of natural causes'; lit., 'to go to one's fate'); *ina šīmātim mâtum* 'to die of natural causes'; *šīmtam/šīmātim šiāmum* 'to decree/fix destiny, fate'.
šiāšim see *šī*.
šiāti see *šī*.
šībultum (*šībulti*) 'consignment, goods for transport' (cf. *babālum*).

šībum (vbl. adj.) see *šiābum*.
šībūtum (*šībūt*) '(old) age; testimony, witness' (cf. *šiābum*).
šīḫum (vbl. adj.) see *šiāḫum*
šikarum (*šikar*; log. KAŠ) 'beer, intoxicating liquid'.
šikrum (*šikir*; pl. *šikrātum/šikrētum*) 'handle'.
šilpum (*šilip*) 'a pulling out; s.th. pulled out'; *šilip rēmim*, lit., 's.th. pulled from the womb', probably refers to a child born through caesarian section (cf. *šalāpum*).
šīlum (pl. *šīlū*) 'hole'.
šimtum (*šimat* or *šimti*; dual *šimtān*; pl. *šimātum*) 'color(ing); mark, marking, brand'.
šīmtum see *šiāmum*.
šīmum a (vbl. adj.) see *šiāmum*.
šīmum b (*šīm(i)*; pl. *šīmū* and *šīmātum*; log. ŠÁM) 'purchase; price; article purchased' (cf. *šâmum*).
šina (pron.; gen.–acc. *šināti*; dat. *šināšim*) 'they (f.); those, the aforesaid' (§§2.4, 6.3, 25.2).
šinā (or *šenā*; fem. *šittā*) 'two' (→ *šinīšu, šinšarûm, šittān*; cf. *šanûm* a and c, *tašna*).
šināšim see *šina*.
šināti see *šina*.
šinip (also *šinipûm*, usually fem. *šinipiāt(um)*; log. ŠANABI) 'two-thirds'.
šinīšu (adv.) 'twice, two times, twofold' (cf. *šinā*).
šinnum (fem.; *šinni*; sf. *šinna-*; dual *šinnān*; log. ZÚ) 'tooth'; for 'teeth' the dual (i.e., two rows) is used.
šinšerûm (adj.; *šinšerī-*) 'one-twelfth' (cf. *šinā, ešer*).
šīpātum (always pl.; log. SÍG) 'wool'.
šiprum (*šipir*; pl. *šiprū, šiprānu*, and *šiprātum, šiprētum* [with an irregular shift of *ā* to *ē*]) 'sending, mission; message; work, labor, task; activity, action'; *mār šiprim* (with sf. *mār šiprīšu*, etc.; pl. *mārū šiprim* or *mār šiprī*) 'messenger'; *šipram epēšum* 'to do (assigned) work; to work' (s.th.: acc.; e.g., *eqlam šipram īpuš* 'he worked [i.e., plowed] the field') (cf. *šapārum*).
šiqlum (abs./bound form *šiqil*; pl. *šiqlū*; log. GÍN) a unit of weight ('shekel') = ca. 8.3 g.; a unit of area = 1/60 *mūšarum* = ca. .6 m.^{2} (see Appendix B.1,2) (cf. *šaqālum* a).
šiqqatum (*šiqqat*; pl. *šiqqātum*; log. $^{(dug)}$ŠAGAN) 'basin'.
šiqītum (*šiqīt*) 'watering; irrigation' (cf. *šaqûm*).
širiktum see *šeriktum*.
šīrum (*šīr(i)*; log. UZU) '(piece of) flesh, meat'; *ana šīr X ṭiābum* 'to be(come) pleasing to X' (e.g., *epištī ana šīr ilīya iṭīb* 'my deed pleased/ was pleasing to my god').
šišītum (*šišīt*; pl. *šišiātum*) 'membrane'.
šitaddarum (Sum. lw.) 'Orion'.
šitʾārum (adj.; *šitʾār-*) 'brilliant, iridescent (of eyes)' (*pitrās* adj. pattern connoting abundance of a quality).
šittān (gen.–acc. *šittīn* [i.e., dual]) 'two-thirds' (cf. *šinā*).
šittum 'sleep'; *šittam* adverbial acc. 'asleep' (cf. *šuttum*).
šitūltum (*šitūlti*) 'advice, counsel, consideration, deliberation' (cf. *šâlum*).
šizbum (*šizib*) 'milk'.
šīzum (also *šizûm*; log. ŠU.DÙ(.A)) a unit of length = 1/3 *ammatum* = ca. 16.7 cm. (see Appendix B.2).
šū (pron.; gen.–acc. *šuāti/šuātu/šâtu/šâti*; dat. *šuāšim/šâšum*) 'he, it; that, the aforesaid' (§§2.4, 6.3, 25.2) (→ *šûm*).
šuāšim see *šī, šū*.
šuāti, šuātu see *šī, šū*.
šubtum (*šubat*; pl. *šubātum*) 'dwelling, residence' (cf. *wašābum*).
šuduš see *šuššum*.
šugarrurum see *garārum*.
šuginûm (log.^{udu}ŠU.GI.NA; Sum. lw.) an offering consisting of sheep.
šugītum (*šugīt*; log. ^{mí}ŠU.GI$_4$; Sum. lw.) 'second wife (to a *nadītum*)'.
šukênum Š(D) (§38.3(a)) 'to bow down, prostrate oneself'; ptcpl. *muškēnum* (*muškēn*; pl. *muškēnū*; log. MAŠ.GAG.EN or MAŠ.EN.GAG) 'dependent, poor person, serf, commoner'.

šukkallum see *sukkallum*.
šuklulum Š (not in G) 'to complete, finish, accomplish, bring to an end'.
šukunnûm (*šukunnā-*) 'estimated yield'; *ana šukunnêm šakānum* 'to fix an estimate' (cf. *šakānum*).
šukūsum (fem.; *šukūs*; log. A.ŠÀ. ŠUKU) 'subsistence plot/field'.
šullum 'wart'.
šulmānum (*šulmān*; pl. *šulmānātum*) 'greeting; greeting-gift' (cf. *šalāmum*).
šulmum (*šulum*) 'well-being, health; wish for well-being, greeting' (cf. *šalāmum*).
šûm (adj.; fs *šattum*/*šattun*, mp *šûttum*/*šûttun*) 'his, her(s)' (§25.3).
šumēlum (*šumēl*; log. GÙB) 'left, left (side), left hand'.
Šumerûm (denom. Adj.; *Šumerī-*) 'Sumerian'.
šumma (conj.) 'if'; *šumma ... šumma* 'whether ... or'.
šumma(n) lā 'except for'.
šumum (*šum(i)*; pl. *šumū* and *šumātum*) 'name; fame, reputation; line (of a tablet or composition); meaning, interpretation (of an omen)'; *šanûm šumšu* 'another interpretation of it'; *mimma šumšu* 'anything at all, everything' (§14.3(b)); *ana šumim nabûm* 'to name' (→ *aššum*).
šunatum see *šuttum*.
šunu (pron.; gen.–acc. *šunūti*; dat. *šunūšim*) 'they (m.), those, the aforesaid' (§§2.4, 6.3, 25.2) (→ *šunûm*).
šunûm (adj.) 'their(s)' (§25.3).
šunūšim see *šunu*.
šunūti see *šunu*.
šuparrurum ŠD (§38.3(a)) 'to spread out (tr.)'.
šupêlum Š(D) (§38.3(a)) 'to change, exchange, substitute; turn (s.th.) into'; *šut(e)pêlum* Š(D)t 'to interchange, be (ex)changed'.
šūpûm b (Š vbl. adj.) see *wapûm*.
šuqallulum see *šaqālum* a.
šurbûm (Š vbl. adj.) see *rabûm* a.
šurqum (*šuruq*) 'theft, stolen property' (cf. *šarāqum*).
šūṣūtum (*šūṣūt*) 'leasehold estate' (cf. *waṣûm*).
šuššān see *šuššum*.
šuššum (*šuduš*; log. ŠUŠ) 'one-sixth'; dual *šuššān* (log. ŠUŠANA) 'one-third' (cf. *šediš*).
šūšum (absolute form *šūš(i)*; log. GÍŠ) 'sixty' (see §23.2(a)) (cf. *šediš*).
šūt archaic (frozen) pl. of det.-rel. *ša*, 'those of'; *awīlû šūt pīḫatim* 'the men responsible, the officials'; *šūt-rēšim* (with sf. *šūt-rēšīšu*) 'court officials, commanders' (lit., 'those at the head').
šutaʾʾûm Dt (root *š–ʾ*–weak; not in G) 'to be idle, lazy (about: *ana*/dat.); to relax' (only in OB letters, where common).
šutlumum Š (not in G) 'to give, bestow, confer, lend'.
šuttum (*šutti*; sf. *šutta-*; poetic biform *šunatum*, bound form *šunat*; pl. *šunātum*) 'dream' (cf. *šittum*).
šûttun see *šûm*.
šūturum b (vbl. adj.) see *watārum*.
šuʾʾurum (adj.; *šuʾʾur-*) 'hairy'.

T

tabālum G (*a*) 'to take, carry off, away; to take for oneself, take along' (cf. *babālum*).
tadmiqtum (*tadmiqti*; sf. *tadmiqta-*) 'interest-free advance (for a business trip)' (cf. *damāqum*).
tadnintum (*tadninti*; sf. *tadninta-*) 'strengthening' (cf. *danānum*).
tāḫāzum (*tāḫāz*; pl. *tāḫāzātum*) 'battle, combat'; *tāḫāzam epēšum* 'to do battle, make war, fight' (cf. *aḫāzum*).
taʾīṣtum (also *taʾīštum*) 'loss, deficit' (cf. *wiāṣum*).
tayyartum (*tayyarti*/*tayyarat*; sf. *tayyarta-*) 'return; pardon'; ext: 'coiling?' (cf. *târum*).
takālum G (*a*; impv. irregular: *tikal*) 'to trust (s.o./s.th.: + *ana*)'; vbl. adj. *taklum* (*takil-*) 'trustworthy, true, reliable'; *tukkulum* D 'to cause to trust; to encourage; to make trustworthy'; in hendiadys with *parāsum*: 'investigate carefully?' (→ *tukultum*).

takīttum (*takītti*) 'confirmation' (cf. *kânum*).
taklum (vbl. adj.) see *takālum*.
talmīdum (pl. *talmīdū*) 'student' (cf. *lamādum*).
tamāḫum G (*a–u*) 'to grasp, hold'.
tamḫārum (*tamḫār*) 'battle' (cf. *maḫārum*).
tamkārum (*tamkār*; pl. *tamkārū*; log. DAM.GÀR) 'merchant, trader' (cf. *makārum*, *makkūrum*).
tamûm G (*a*) 'to swear, take an oath (by s.o.: acc. or *ina*)'; *tummûm* D 'to make swear, adjure, bind by oath' (→ *tumāmītum*).
tanīttum (*tanītti*; sf. *tanītta-*) 'praise, glory'.
tappûm (base *tappā-*; pl. *tappû*; log. TAB.BA; Sum. lw.) 'business associate, partner' (→ *tappûtum*).
tappûtum (*tappût*) 'partnership, association; position of helper, partner'; *tappût X alākum* 'to assist X, lend X a hand, come to the aid of X' (e.g., *tappût aḫīya illikū* 'they assisted my brother'; *tappûssu allik* 'I assisted him'); *tappûtam epēšum* 'to do/enter into business together' (cf. *tappûm*).
taqtītum (*taqtīt*; pl. *taqtiātum*) 'end, ending'.
tarākum G (*a–u*) 'to hit, beat, pound'; vbl. adj. *tarkum* (*tarik-*) 'beaten, pounded; dark, black'.
tarāṣum G (*a–u*) 'to reach out, stretch out, extend, set up' (all tr.); *šutruṣum* Š = G.
tarbaṣum (*tarbaṣ*; pl. *tarbaṣātum*) 'cattle-pen, stable, fold'.
tarbītum (*tarbīt*) 'raising, upbringing; foster child, a child brought up' (cf. *rabûm* a).
tarkibtum 'date-palm pollination' (cf. *rakābum*).
tarkum (vbl. adj.) see *tarākum*.
tarûm G (*u*) 'to bring, lead (forth)' (cf. *warûm*).
târum G (*a–u*) 'to return (intr.), go/come back, turn back; to turn into, become (+ *ana*)'; in hendiadys, 'to do (s.th.) again' (§14.5); D *turrum* 'to return (tr.), restore, give/take/send/put/pay back; to turn (s.th.: acc.; into s.th. else: *ana*); to take captive in war' (→ *tayyartum*).
tašna (adv.) 'double, doubly' (cf. *šinā*).
Tašrītum (log. DU_6.KUG) seventh OB month (September–October).
tazkītum (*tazkīt*) 'purification, cleansing; release, dissolution' (cf. *zakûm* a).
tebûm a G (*e*) 'to arise, rise up, stand up; to occur, happen, appear on the scene; to set out'; vbl. adj. *tebûm* b (*tebi-*; fem. *tebītum*) 'standing, erect; under way; rebellious'; *šutbûm* 'to cause to arise; to set aside, remove' (→ *tībum*, *tibûtum*).
tebûm b (vbl. adj.) see *tebûm* a.
tēliltum 'purification' (cf. *elēlum*).
tēnīqum (*tēnīq*) 'suckling baby; wet-nursing expenses' (cf. *enēqum*).
teptītum (*teptīt*) 'opening; cultivation' (cf. *petûm*).
terḫatum (*terḫat*) 'bride-price'.
Terqa a city on the Euphrates up-river from Mari (modern Tell ᶜAšāra).
têrtum (‹ **tawʾertum*; *têrti*; sf. *têrta-*; pl. *têrētum*) 'direction, instruction, order, command, commission; extispicy (examination of entrails), extispicy omen, oracle, omen report/diagnosis'; *têrtam* / *têrētim epēšum* 'to perform extispicy' (cf. *wârum*).
tešât see *tešiat*.
tešiat (and *tešât*; bound forms) 'one-ninth' (cf. *tiše*).
tešûm (adj.; fem. *tešūtum*) 'ninth' (cf. *tiše*).
tešmûm (*tešmē-*; pl. *tešmû*) '(favorable) hearing; understanding; agreement' (cf. *šemûm*).
tibnum (*tibin*; log. IN.NU.DA) 'straw'.
tībum (*tīb(i)*; sf. *tīb(ū/ī/ā)-*) 'rise, uprising, attack, onslaught'; *tībum kašdum* 'successful attack' (cf. *tebûm*).
tibûtum (*tibût*; log. ZI(.GA)) 'rising, raising; muster, levy; attack' (cf. *tebûm*).
Tīrum an OB month name.

tiṣbutum b (Gt vbl. adj.) see *ṣabātum*..
tiše (*tišûm*; with masc. nouns *tišīt*, *tišītum*) 'nine' (→ *tešiat*, *tešûm*).
tuḫḫum (usually pl. *tuḫḫū*; log.DUḪ) 'scraps, bran'.
tukultum (*tukulti*; sf. *tukulta-*; pl. *tuklātum*) 'trust; object of trust' (cf. *takālum*).
tulûm (*tulā-*; log. UBUR) 'breast'.
tumāmītum 'oath' (cf. *tamûm*).
tupšikkum (*tupšik*; log. ^{gi}DUSU, ^{giš}DUSU) 'work, corvée duty'.
tuššum (pl. *tuššātum*) 'calumny, slander'; *tuššam nadûm* / *qabûm* / *dabābum* 'to slander, speak maliciously, calumniate'.

Ṭ

ṭābiš (adv.) 'well, pleasantly' (cf. *ṭiābum*).
ṭābtum see *ṭiābum*.
ṭābum (vbl. adj.) see *ṭiābum*.
ṭarādum G (*a–u*) 'to send, dispatch (person); to drive away'; vbl. adj. *ṭardum* (*ṭarid-*) 'expelled, banished, exile(d)'.
ṭardum (vbl. adj.) see *ṭarādum*.
Ṭebētum (log. ITI AB.È.A, also AB(.BA.È)) tenth OB month (December–January).
ṭebûm G (*u*) 'to sink, become submerged' (intr.); *ṭubbûm* D 'to sink' (tr.).
ṭeḫḫûm (*ṭeḫḫē-*) 'neighboring area or region' (cf. *ṭeḫûm*).
ṭeḫûm G (*e*) 'to go near, draw near, approach (+ *ana*/dat.)'; *ṭuḫḫûm* D 'to bring near' (→ *ṭeḫḫûm*, *ṭēḫum*).
ṭēḫum (*ṭēḫ(i)*; log. DA) 'proximity, what adjoins'; bound form as a preposition in OB contracts, DA É PN = *ṭēḫi bīt* PN 'adjoining the house of PN' (cf. *ṭeḫûm*).
ṭēmum (pl. *ṭēmū* and *ṭēmētum*) 'information, news, report; command; mind, attitude, intention, decision'; *ṭēmam ṣabātum* 'to take action (concerning: *ana*)'; *ṭēmam šakānum* 'to give a report, information' (to s.o.: *itti* or *maḫar*, see §12); *ṣibit ṭēmim išûm* / *rašûm* 'to take action'.
ṭēnum (vbl. adj.) see *ṭênum*.
ṭênum G (*e*) 'to grind (flour)'; vbl. adj. *ṭēnum* (*ṭēn-*) 'ground'.
ṭiābum G (*a–i*) 'to be(come) pleasant, pleasing (to: *eli*), sweet, good; to be(-come) satisfied'; *ana šīr X ṭiābum* 'to be(come) pleasing to X' (e.g., *epištī ana šīr ilīya iṭīb* 'my deed pleased/was pleasing to my god'); vbl. adj. *ṭābum* (*ṭāb-*; log. DÙG) 'pleasant, pleasing (to: *eli*), sweet, fine, good'; substantivized fem. *ṭābtum* (*ṭābti*) 'kindness'; *ṭubbum* D 'to make pleasant, sweet, good; to please, satisfy'; *šuṭubbum* Š = D (much less common than D) (→ *ṭābiš*, *ṭūbum*).
ṭūbātum see *ṭūbum*.
ṭūbum (*ṭūb(i)*; pl. *ṭūbū*, *ṭūbātum*) 'good(ness), kindness, happiness, satisfaction'; *ṭūb libbim* 'happiness'; fem. pl. *ṭūbātum* 'gladness, pleasure, voluntariness, friendliness, friendly relations'; *ina ṭūbātim* 'voluntarily' (cf. *ṭiābum*).
ṭulīmum (*ṭulīm*) 'spleen' (ext.).
ṭuppum (masc. and fem.; *ṭuppi*; sf. *ṭuppa-*; pl. *ṭuppū* and *ṭuppātum*; log. DUB; Sum. lw.) '(clay) tablet, document, letter'; *bīt ṭuppim* (log. É.DUB.BA) 'tablet house, school, archive'; *mār bīt ṭuppim* (log. DUMU É.DUB.BA(.A)) 'state scribe' (→ *ṭupšarrum*).
ṭupšarrum (*ṭupšar*; pl. *ṭupšarrū*; log. DUB.SAR; Sum. lw.) 'scribe'; *ṭupšar ummānim* 'military scribe' (cf. *ṭuppum*).

U

u (conj.) 'and'; in some contexts, also 'and also, likewise, moreover, furthermore, additionally, as well'.
ū, *lū*, *ū lū* (conj.; *ū* written *ù*, like *u* 'and') 'or, either ... or' (e.g., *X ū Y*; *X ū lū Y*; *(ū) lū X ū lū Y*; see §7.4(f)).
ubānum (fem.; abs./bound form *ubān*; pl. *ubānātum*; log. ŠU.SI) 'finger, toe'; a unit of length = 30 *ammatum*

= ca. 1.67 cm. (see Appendix B.2); ext.: part of the liver ('processus pyramidalis'); *ubān šēpim* 'toe'.

ubburum D (G *abārum* rare) 'to accuse'.

ugārum (*ugār*; pl. *ugārû*, *ugārātum*; log. A.GÀR; Sum. lw.?) 'open field, meadow, arable land'.

ukullûm (base *ukullā-*; log. ŠÀ.GAL) 'food allotment, food supply, fodder' (cf. *akālum*).

ukultum (*ukulti*; sf. *ukulta-*; pl. *uklātum*) 'food(-supply), provisions; feeding' (cf. *akālum*).

ul (adv.; less often *ula*, *uli*) 'not' (see §20.4).

ullânum (adv.) '(from) there'; (prep.; with sf. *ullânukka*, etc.) 'apart from, other than'; *ullânum-ma* (adv.) 'already'; also 'from there' (cf. *ullûm*).

ullīkiam (adv.) 'there' (cf. *ullûm*).

ullîšam (adv.) 'thither' (cf. *ullûm*).

ullītiš (adv.) 'the day after tomorrow' (cf. *ullûm*).

ullûm (*ulli-*) 'that, distant' (see §6.3, end) (→ *ullânum*, *ullīkiam*, *ullîšam*, *ullītiš*).

ulṣum (*uluṣ*) 'joy, rejoicing, exultation'; *ulṣam epēšum* 'to rejoice; to make love'; *uluṣ libbim* = *ulṣum* (cf. *elēṣum*).

Ulūlum see *Elūnum*.

ūm (conj.) see *ūmum*.

ûm (gen. *îm* or *êm*, acc. *âm*; bound form *ê*; with sf. nom. *û-*, gen. *î-*/*ê-*, acc. *â-*; with 1cs sf., nom.–acc. *ê*, gen. *êya*; Sum. lw.?; always written with log. ŠE, e.g., acc. ŠE-*am* or ŠE-*a-am* for *âm*; also written either ŠE.UM or ŠE.IM, regardless of case) 'barley, grain'. Note: until recently this word was always read in Akkadian as *šeum*, and it appears as such in both dictionaries and all text publications up through 1989, when it was proposed (Cavigneaux 1989) that the word was *ûm*, the reading adopted in the present book; many Assyriologists, however, continue to believe that *šeum* is the more correct (or more common) reading.

ūmam see *ūmum*.

ūmišam (adv.) 'daily' (cf. *ūmum*).

umma (adv.; particle introducing direct quotations) 'as follows' (§15.4); *ummāmi* = *umma* (common in Mari letters).

ummānum (fem.; *ummān*; pl. *ummānātum*; log. ERIN_2 and UGNIM) 'army, gang, crowd'.

ummiānum (*ummiān*; pl. *ummiānū*; log. UM.MI.A) 'artisan; scholar, expert; money lender'.

ummum a (fem.; *ummi*; sf. *umma-*; pl. *ummātum*; log. AMA) 'mother'.

ummum b (ext.) an unidentified part of the gall-bladder.

ummāmi see *umma*.

ūmum (*ūm(i)*; pl. *ūmū* and *ūmātum*; log. UD/U_4 [usually nom. UD-*mu-um*, gen. UD-*mi-im*, acc. UD-*ma-am*, bound form UD-*um*]) 'day, daytime'; *ūmam* (adv.) 'today, for a day'; *ina ūmim* 'in/on/during the day'; *ūm* (conj.; also *ina ūm*) 'when, while, at the time that, as soon as, after' (§26.2(a)) (→ *anumma*, *inūma*, *inūmīšūma*, *ūmišam*).

unqum (fem.; pl. *unqātum*) 'ring; stamp-seal'.

unūtum (*unūt*; pl. irreg. *uniātum*/*unêtum*) 'utensils, furnishings, property'.

uqnûm (base *uqni-*; log. $^{\text{na4}}$ZA.GÌN) 'lapis lazuli'.

Ur (log. URIM^{ki}; Sum. lw.) city in southern Mesopotamia (modern al-Muqayyar).

urḫum (fem. and masc.; *uruḫ*; pl. *urḫātum*) 'way, road, path'.

urram (adv.) 'tomorrow'.

uršānum (*uršān*; pl. *uršānū*; Sum. lw.) 'warrior, hero'.

urʾudum (also *ḫurḫudum*; bound form *urʾud*/*ḫurḫud*) 'throat, wind-pipe'.

Uruk (log. UNUG^{ki}; Sum. lw.) city in s. Mesopotamia (modern Warka).

ūsum (*ūs*; Sum. lw.) 'direction, guidance, (proper) custom'.

ušallum (*ušal*; sf. *ušalla-*; log. Ú.SAL; Sum. lw.) 'shore-land, water-

meadow, flood area'.
uššum (usually pl. *uššū*; Sum. lw.?) 'foundation'.
uššurum see *wuššurum*.
utlellûm see *elûm*.
utullum (*utul*; log. Ú.DÚL; Sum. lw.) 'chief shepherd'.
utūlum see *niālum* Gt.
uṭṭatum (also *uṭṭetum*; abs./bound form *uṭṭat*/*uṭṭet*; pl. *uṭṭātum*, *uṭṭētum*; log. ŠE) 'barley; grain'; a unit of weight ('grain') = 1/180 *šiqlum* = ca. 0.05 g.; a unit of length = 1/6 *ubānum* = ca. 2.8 mm.; a unit of area = 1/10,800 *mūšarum* = ca. 33 cm.^{2}; a unit of capacity = 1/180 *qûm* = ca. .005 l. (see Appendix B.1,2,3,5); a 'second' of time.
uṭṭetum see *uṭṭatum*.
ūṭum (abs. *ūṭ*; log. ZIPAḪ) a unit of length ('span') = 1/2 *ammatum* = ca. 25 mm (see Appendix B.2).
uznum (fem.; *uzun*; dual *uznān*; log. GEŠTUG) 'ear; wisdom, understanding, intelligence'; *uznum rapaštum* 'great intelligence, understanding'.
uzubbûm (base *uzubbā-*) 'divorce, divorce-payment' (cf. *ezēbum*).
uzuzzum see *izuzzum*.
uzzum (*uzzi*; sf. *uzza-*; pl. *uzzātum* = sg.) 'anger, rage'.

W

wabālum see *babālum*.
waklum (*wakil*; pl. *waklū*, *waklūtum*; log. UGULA) 'overseer, inspector, foreman'; *wakil ḫaṭṭim* (possible reading of log. PA.PA, as UGULA. GIDRI) 'captain'.
walādum G (*ullad–ulid*) 'to bear, give birth to, beget'; *(w)ulludum* D pluralic 'to bear, beget (many offspring)'; *šūludum* Š (rare; *a*–type, §28.1(b)) 'to cause to bear'.
wapûm G 'to appear, become visible' (rare); *šūpûm* a Š (*a*– or *e*–type, §28.1(b)) 'to proclaim (s.o.'s fame), announce, promulgate (a decree)'; vbl. adj. *šūpûm* b (*šūpu-*) 'proclaimed, illustrious, splendid'; *šutāpûm*/*šutēpûm* Št-pass. 'to be made/become visible, famous; to be proclaimed; to shine forth'.
waqārum G (*iqqer–īqer*) 'to be(come) precious'.
warādum G (*urrad–urid*) 'to descend, go/come down'; *šūrudum* Š (*e*–type, §28.1(b)) 'to send/bring down' (→ *wardatum*, *wardum*, *wardūtum*).
Waraḫsamnum ((giš)APIN.DU$_8$.A) the eighth month (Oct.–Nov.).
warāqum G (*irriq–īriq*) 'to be(come) yellow, green; to turn pale'; vbl. adj. *warqum* (*waruq-*) 'yellow, green; fresh (of plants)'; *(w)urruqum* D factitive.
wardatum (*wardat*; pl. *wardātum*) 'young woman' (cf. *warādum*).
wardum (*warad*; pl. *wardū*; log. ÌR/ARAD) 'male slave, man–servant' (cf. *warādum*).
wardūtum (*wardūt*) 'slavery; position of slave' (cf. *warādum*).
warḫišam (adv.) 'monthly' (cf. *warḫum*).
warḫum (*waraḫ*; pl. *warḫū*; log. ITI/ITU) 'month; new moon' (→ *warḫišam*).
warka a (adv.; also *ina warka*) 'afterwards; behind, in the rear' (*warka* b conj. see *warki*).
warkānum (adv.; also *warkānum-ma*) 'later, afterward' (cf. *warki*).
warkatum (*warkat*; pl. *warkātum*) 'rear, back (part, side; of a building, person, animal); estate, inheritance; circumstances (of a legal case)'; *warkatam parāsum* 'to investigate the circumstances of a case' (cf. *warki*).
warki (prep.; sf. *warkīšu*, etc.) locally, 'behind, in back of'; temporally, 'after, after the departure of, after the death of'; (conj.; also *warka* b) 'after' (in OB only in expressions involving death; §26.2(a)) (→ *warka* a, *warkānum*, *warkatum*, *warkûm*).
warkiātum, *warkītum* see *warkûm*.
warkûm (denom. adj.; *warkī-*; fem. *warkītum*) 'later, future'; substantivized fem. *warkītum* (*warkīt*; pl.

warkiātum often = sg.) 'future, later time, time afterward'; *ina warkītim / warkiātim* 'in (the) future, later on, afterward'; *ana / ina warkīt / warkiāt ūmim / ūmī* (log. UD.KÚR.ŠÈ) 'in future' (cf. *warki*).

warqum (vbl. adj.) see *warāqum*.

warûm G (*urru–uru*; see §21.3(g)) 'to lead, bring'; *itarrûm* Gtn 'to guide, steer; to rule'; *šūrûm* Š (*a*–type, §28.1(b)) 'to send, have brought' (→ *tarûm*).

wârum G (root originally *w–ʾ–r* [see D], but G dur. **iwīar / iwâr*, pl. *iwirrū*; pret. *iwīr*; see §21.3(f)) 'to advance against, attack'; *wuʾʾurum* D 'to send (a person, message); to command, order (to do: acc. infin. or *ana / aššum* + infin.)'; ptcpl. *muʾirrum* (*muʾīr*) 'director' (→ *têrtum*).

waṣābum G (*uṣṣab–uṣib*) 'to add (to), increase, enlarge; to pay as interest'; *(w)uṣṣubum* D = G (not common in OB) (→ *ṣibtum* a).

waṣûm a G (*uṣṣi–uṣi*; see §21.3(g)) 'to go out, go forth, depart, leave, escape; to protrude, grow'; with ventive: 'to come forth, out, emerge, appear'; vbl. adj. *waṣûm* b (*waṣi-*) 'gone (forth), outside; protruding'; *iṣṣûm* Gt 'to depart'; *šūṣûm* Š (*e*–type, rarely *a*–type, §28.1(b)) 'to cause to go/come out/forth, to send/lead/take/bring out; to make leave, send away, evict, expel; to remove (from a house, container), release; to let escape; to obtain, produce; to rent, hire'; *awātam šūṣûm* 'to betray a secret'; *šutēṣûm* Št-pass. 'to be brought out'; *šutēṣûm* Št-lex. 'to escape; to fight with one another' (→ *ṣītum, šūṣūtum*).

waṣûm b (vbl. adj.) see *waṣûm* a.

wašābum G (*uššab–ušib*) 'to sit down; to sit, be sitting, seated; to stay, remain (somewhere), reside, dwell'; vbl. adj. *wašbum* (*wašib-*) 'seated; resident, in residence'; *šūšubum* Š (*e*–type, §28.1(b)) 'to cause to sit down/stay/dwell; to install (officers, etc.), to garrison (soldiers); to settle, resettle (people)' (→ *mūšabum, šubtum*).

wašbum (vbl. adj.) see *wašābum*.

watartum see *watārum*.

watārum G (*itter–īter*) 'to be(come) exceeding, surpassing; to exceed, surpass'; vbl. adj. *watrum* (*watar-*) 'additional, in excess, superfluous; foremost, pre-eminent, excellent'; substantivized fem. *watartum* (*watarti*; sf. *watarta-*; pl. *watrātum*) 'excess, surplus, extra'; *(w)utturum* D 'to augment, increase (tr.)'; *šūturum* a Š (*a*–type, §28.1(b)) 'to cause to increase, cause to surpass, to enlarge'; vbl. adj. *šūturum* b (*šūtur-*) 'pre-eminent, surpassing'.

watrum (vbl. adj.) see *watārum*.

watûm G (*utta–uta*; see §21.3(g)) 'to find, discover'; *šutātûm* Št-lex. 'to meet (one another)'.

wēdum (adj.; *wēd-*) 'single, individual, solitary, alone' (→ *wēdûm*).

wēdûm (denom. adj.; *wēdī-*) 'unique; important, notable' (cf. *wēdum*).

werûm (also *erûm*; base *weri-*; log. URUDU) 'copper, bronze'.

wiāṣum G (*iwīaṣ–iwīṣ*; see §21.3(f)) 'to be(come) diminished, (too) small, (too) little, insufficient'; vbl. adj. *(w)īṣum* (*(w)īṣ-*; fem. *(w)īštum*, see §5.4) '(too) small, little, few' (→ *taʾīṣ / štum*).

(w)īṣum (vbl. adj.) see *wiāṣum*.

wuddûm see *edûm*.

(w)uššurum D (not in G) 'to release, set free'.

Z

zaʾānum G only in vbl. adj. *zaʾnum* (*zaʾin-*) 'overlaid, covered, decorated, endowed (with: acc.)'; *zuʾʾunum* D 'to overlay, cover, decorate'.

zabālum G (*i*) 'to carry, transport, deliver'; *zubbulum* D 'to keep (s.o.) waiting'; *šuzbulum* Š causative; *nazbulum* N passive.

zakārum (also *saqārum*) G (*a–u*) 'to declare, mention; to speak, address; to name, invoke'; *nīš X zakārum* 'to swear by X' (lit., 'to invoke the life of X'); *tizkurum* / *tisqurum* Gt 'to speak' (used as the G in literary texts); *nazkurum* N 'to be named, mentioned, said' (→ *zikrum* b).

zakûm a G (*u*) 'to be(come) clean, clear; to be(come) free (of claims, obligations)'; vbl. adj. *zakûm* b (*zaku-*) 'clear; clean(ed), pure; free (of claims)'; *zukkûm* D 'to cleanse, clear, winnow; to free, release' (→ *tazkītum*).

zakûm b (vbl. adj.) see *zakûm* a.

zamar (adv.) 'suddenly'.

zamārum G (*a–u*) 'to sing, sing of, about'.

zaʾnum (vbl. adj.) see *zaʾānum*.

zânum see *zaʾānum*.

zapārum G (*a*) rare apart from vbl. adj. *zaprum* (*zapur-*) 'malicious, false'; substantivized fem. *zapurtum* (*zapurti*; sf. *zapurta-*) 'malice, falsehood'.

zaprum (vbl. adj.) see *zapārum*.

zapurtum see *zapārum*.

zaqāpum G (*a–u*) 'to erect, set up; to plant (a garden), prepare (a garden, field) for planting'; *zuqqupum* D = G.

zâzum G (*a–u*) 'to divide, separate' (intr.); 'to divide, divide into shares (tr.), distribute (to/among: *ana*); to share, take a share (of: *ina*)'; vbl. adj. *zīzum* (*zīz-*) 'divided; sharing'; substantivized fem. *zīttum* (*zītti*; sf. *zītta-*; pl. *zīzātum*; with irregular assimilation in sg. [given as *zittum* in the dictionaries]; log. ḪA.LA) 'share (of an inheritance); inheritance'; *zuzzum* D 'to divide, distribute' (rare).

zenûm a G (*e*) 'to be(come) angry; to hate'; vbl. adj. *zenûm* b (*zeni-*) 'angry'; *zunnûm* D 'to anger'.

zenûm b (vbl. adj.) see *zenûm* a.

zērum (*zēr(i)*; pl. *zērū*; log. NUMUN and ŠE.NUMUN) 'seed; (male) descendents, progeny, offspring'.

zêrum G (*e*) 'to dislike, hate; to avoid'.

zibbatum (*zibbat*; dual *zibbān*; pl. *zibbātum*; log. KUN) 'tail; rear part'.

ziḫḫum (*ziḫḫi*; sf. *ziḫḫa-*; pl. *ziḫḫū*) 'cyst, scar'.

zikarum (also *zikrum* a; bound form *zikar*; pl. *zikarū*; log. NITA(Ḫ)$_2$) 'male; man'.

zikrum b / *siqrum* (*zikir* / *siqir*; pl. *zikrū* / *siqrū*) 'utterance, words; mention; (divine or royal) command, order; name, fame; oath' (cf. *zakārum* / *saqārum*).

zīmum (*zīm(i)*; sf. *zīm(ū / ī / ā)-*; pl. *zīmū* = sg.) 'appearance, looks; face, countenance; glow'; *ana zīm(ĭ)* (prep. phrase) 'corresponding to, according to; in view of'.

zinnum see *zunnum*.

zīttum see *zâzum*.

zumrum (*zumur*) 'body'.

zunnum (*zunni*; pl. *zunnū* [often = sg.]), also *zinnum* 'rain'.

LOGOGRAMS

A(.MEŠ) = *mû*; (A.)AB.BA = *kušabkum*; A.BA = *abum*; A.GÀR = *ugārum*; $^{(lú)}$A.IGI.DU$_8$ = *sēkirum*; A.NI = *-šu*/*-ša*; A.RÁ = *adi*; A.ŠÀ = *eqlum*; A.ŠÀ.ŠUKU = *šukūsum*; A.ZU = *asûm*; see also (ITU.)SIG$_4$.A; DURU$_5$

Á, Á.BI = *idum, idū*

AB in (A.)AB.BA = *kušabkum*; (ITU.) AB(.BA.È)/(ITU.)AB.È.A = *Ṭebētum*; AB.SÍN = *abšinnum, šerʾum*

ÁB = *arḫum, lītum*; ÁB.GUD.ḪI.A = *liātum*

ABUL (formerly read KÁ.GAL) = *abullum*

AD = *abum*

ÁG = *madādum*

AGA = *agûm*; AGA.ÚS = *rēdûm*

AGRIG (igi+dub) = *abarakkum*

AL.DÙ(.A) = *aldûm*

AM = *rīmum*

AMA = *ummum*

AMAR in ^{d}AMAR.UTU = *Marduk*

AMBAR = *appārum*

AN = *Anum, šamû*; AN.ZA.GÀR = *dimtum*; see also DINGIR

ANŠE = *imērum*

APIN in APIN.DU$_8$.A = *Kinūnum*$^{?}$; see also ENGAR (= apin)

ARAD/ÌR = *wardum*

AŠ = *šēpum* (in ext.)

ÀŠ = *šediš*

BA see (A.)AB.BA; A.BA; AB(.BA.È); Ì.BA; SÍG.BA; ŠE.BA

BABBAR (ud) see É.BABBAR; KUG.BABBAR; see also UD

BÀD = *dūrum* a

BALA = *palûm*

BÁN = *sūtum*

BANDA$_5$ (the dumu sign) see NU.BANDA$_5$

$^{(giš)}$BANŠUR = *paššūrum*

BAR in $^{(túg)}$BAR.SI = *paršīgum*; see also UR.BAR.RA; ZABAR (ud+ka+bar)

BARA$_2$ see BARAG

BARAG = *parakkum*; BARA$_2$ in BARA$_2$.ZAG.GAR = *Nisānum*

BE = *šumma*

BI = *-šu*/*-ša*

BU see GÍD

BÙR$^{(iku)}$ = *būrum*

^{íd}BURANUN(ud+kib+nun) = *Purattum*

BURU$_{14}$ = *ebūrum*

DA = *ṭēḫum*; see also IN.NU.DA

DAM = *aššatum*; DAM.GÀR = *tamkārum*

DANNA (kaskal+gíd) = *bērum*

DI in DI.KUD/KU$_5$ = *dayyānum*

DINGIR = *ilum*; see also AN; KÁ.DINGIR.RA^{ki}; NIN.DINGIR(.RA)

DIŠ = *ištēn, šumma*

DU see SAG.DU; LAḪ$_5$ (du+du)

DÙ = *banûm, epēšum*; see also AL.DÙ(.A); ŠU.DÙ(.A); GAG (= dù)

DU$_6$ in DU$_6$.KUG = *Tašrītum*

DU$_8$ see $^{(lú)}$A.IGI.DU$_8$; APIN.DU$_8$.A

DU$_{10}$ see DÙG

DUB = *ṭuppum*; DUB.SAR = *ṭupšarrum*; see also É.DUB.BA; (É.)Ì.DUB, $^{(giš)}$MÁ.Ì.DUB; igi+dub see AGRIG

DUG = *karpatum*

DÙG/DU$_{10}$ (the ḫi sign) = *ṭābum*

DÚL see Ú.DÚL

DUMU = *mārum*; DUMU É.DUB.BA(.A) = *mār bīt ṭuppim*; DUMU.MUNUS = *mārtum*; DUMU (.MUNUS) GABA = *mār(at) irtim*; ^{d}DUMU.ZI = *Dumuzi*; see also BANDA$_5$ (dumu) in NU.BANDA$_5$; IBILA (dumu+uš); TUR (dumu)

DÙN see SAG.DÙN

DURU$_5$ (the a sign) = *raṭbum*; see also É.DURU$_5$

^{gi}DUSU, ^{giš}DUSU = *tupšikkum*
É = *bītum*; É.BABBAR = *Ebabbar*; É.DUB.BA = *bīt ṭuppim*; É.DURU$_5$ = *kaprum*; É.GAL = *ekallum*; É.GAR$_8$ = *igārum*; É.GI$_4$/GI.A = *kallatum*; (É.)Ì.DUB = *našpakum*; É.SAG.ÍL = *Esagil*; É.ZI.DA = *Ezida*
È see GAN.GAN.È
EDIN = *ṣērum*
EME = *lišānum*
EN = *bēlum*; ^{d}EN.LÍL = *Enlil*; ^{d}EN.ZU read ^{d}ZUEN = *Sîn*; see also MAŠ.GAG.EN/MAŠ.EN.GAG
ENGAR = *ikkarum*; see also APIN
ENSI$_2$ (pa+te+si) = *iššiakkum*
ERIN$_2$ (or ERIM) = *ṣābum*, *ummānum*; ERIN$_2$.ŠE.KIN.KUD = *ēṣidum*
ÉŠ (or EŠE; the ku sign) = *ašlum*
EŠ$_4$.TÁR/IŠTAR = *Ištar*
EŠ$_5$ = *šalāš*
EŠE see ÉŠ
EŠE$_3$$^{(iku)}$ = *eblum*
EZEN = *isinnum*
GA see GÌR.SÌ.GA; NÍG.GA
GÁ in GÁ.GI.A and GÁ.GI$_4$.A = *gagûm*; see also INIM ... GÁ
GABA = *irtum*; see also DUMU (.MUNUS) GABA
GADA see NA.GADA
GAG see MAŠ.GAG.EN/MAŠ.EN. GAG; see also DÙ
GAL = *rabûm* b; GAL.UKKIN.NA = *muʾirrum*; see also ABUL (ká+gal); É.GAL; ŠANDANA (gal+ni)
GÁL see ḪÉ.GÁL; IGI.x.GÁL
GAN in GAN.GAN.È = *Kislīmum*
GAR see ŠIMxGAR, ŠIM+GAR
GÀR see A.GÀR; AN.ZA.GÀR; DAM. GÀR
GAR$_8$ see É.GAR$_8$
GEME$_2$ (also SAG.GEME$_2$) = *amtum*
GEŠTIN = *karānum*
GEŠTUG = *uznum*
GI = *qanûm*; see also É.GI/GI$_4$.A; GÁ.GI/GI$_4$.A; GIŠ.GI; ^{udu}ŠU.GI.NA; KUG.SIG$_{17}$ (SIG$_{17}$ = gi)
GI$_4$ see É.GI/GI$_4$.A; GÁ.GI/GI$_4$.A; ^{mí}ŠU.GI$_4$
GI$_6$ (the mi sign) = *mūšum*
GIBIL (written bil+gi) = *Gibil* / *Girra*
GÍD (the bu sign) in GÍD(.DA) = *arākum*; see also DANNA (kaskal+gíd); $^{(giš)}$MAR.GÍD.DA; $^{(lú)}$MÁŠ.ŠU. GÍD.GÍD
GIDRI (the pa sign) = *ḫaṭṭum*
GÍN = *šiqlum*
GÍR in GÍR.NI = *karzillum*
GÌR = *šēpum*; GÌR.NITA(Ḫ)$_2$ (perhaps to be read ŠAKKANA$_6$) = *šakkanakkum*; GÌR.PAD.DU = *eṣemtum*; GÌR.SÌ.GA = *gerseqqûm*
GIŠ = *iṣum*; GIŠ.GI = *apum*; GIŠ.TIR = *qištum*; GIŠ.ÙR = *gušūrum*; see also Ì.GIŠ; ŠE.GIŠ.Ì/ŠE.Ì.GIŠ
GÍŠ = *šūšum*; GÍŠ.U = *nērum*
^{giš}GIŠIMMAR = *gišimmarum*
GU in ^{giš}GU.ZA = *kussûm*
GÚ in GÚ.UN/GUN = *biltum*
GU$_4$ see GUD
GÙB (the kab sign) = *šumēlum*
GUD/GU$_4$ = *alpum*; (ITU.)GUD.SI.SÁ = *Ayyarum*; see also ÁB.GUD.ḪI.A
GUN/GÚ.UN = *biltum*
GUR = *kurrum*
GURUŠ (the kal sign) = *eṭlum*
GUŠKIN see KUG.SIG$_{17}$
ḪA in ḪA.LA = *zīttum*; KU$_6$ (= ḫa)
ḪÁ see ḪI.A
ḪAR see UR$_5$
ḪÉ in ḪÉ.GÁL = *ḫegallum* / *ḫengallum*
ḪI in ḪI.A (or ḪÁ) plural marker
ḪU see MUŠEN
ḪUN (the ku sign) in $^{(lú)}$ḪUN.GÁ = *agrum*
I see ŠU.I
Ì, Ì.GIŠ = *šamnum*; Ì.BA = *piššatum*; (É.)Ì.DUB, $^{(giš)}$MÁ.Ì.DUB = *našpakum*; see also ŠE.GIŠ.Ì/ŠE.Ì.GIŠ
I$_7$ see ÍD
IÁ = *ḫamiš*
ÍB in ÍB.TAG$_4$ = *rēḫtum*
IBILA (dumu+uš) = *aplum*, *aplūtum*
ÍD (or I$_7$) = *nārum*; ^{d}ÍD = *Id*
IGI = *īnum*, *maḫrum*, *maḫrûm*, *pā-*

num, pānū, pānûm, šībum; IGI.x. GÁL for fractions §23.2(e); see also $^{\text{(lú)}}$A.IGI.DU$_8$; igi+dub see AGRIG; see also LIM (= igi)
IKU = *ikûm*
ÍL see É.SAG.ÍL
ILIMMU = *tiše*
IM see IŠKUR
IMIN = *sebe*
IN in IN.NU.DA = *tibnum*
INANNA = *Ištar*
INIM (the ka sign) = *awātum*; INIM ... GÁ = *baqārum*
ÌR/ARAD (also SAG.ÌR/ARAD) = *wardum*; see also NITA(Ḫ)$_2$ (ìr)
IŠKUR (the im sign) = *Adad*
IŠTAR see EŠ$_4$.TÁR
ITI/ITU = *warḫum*
IZI (the ne sign) = *išātum*
KA = *pûm*; see also INIM (= ka); KIR(I)$_4$ (= ka); ZABAR (= ud+ka+bar); ZÚ (= ka)
KÁ = *bābum*; KÁ.DINGIR.RA^{ki} = *Bābilim*; for KÁ.GAL see ABUL
KAL see GURUŠ; KI.KAL
KALAM (the un sign) = *mātum*; see also UN
KAR = *kārum*; $^{\text{(mí)}}$KAR.KID = *ḫarīmtum*
KAS$_7$ see NÍG.KAS$_7$
KASKAL = *ḫarrānum*; see also DANNA (kaskal+gíd)
KAŠ (the bi sign) = *šikarum*
^{lú}KAŠ$_4$(.E) = *lāsimum*
KI = *ašrum, erṣetum, itti*; KI.KAL = *kankallum*; see also KISLAḪ (= ki+ud)
KIB see ^{íd}BURANUN (ud+kib+nun); ZIMBIR^{ki} (ud+kib+nun^{ki})
KID see $^{\text{(mí)}}$KAR.KID
KIN in KIN.^{d}INANNA = *Elūnum/Elūlum*; see also ERIN$_2$.ŠE.KIN.KUD
KINGUSILA = *parasrab*
KIR(I)$_4$ (the ka sign) = *appu*
KIRI$_6$ = *kirûm*; see also $^{\text{(lú)}}$NU.^{giš}KIRI$_6$
KISAL.MAḪ = *kisalmaḫḫum*
KISLAḪ (ki+ud) = *maškanum*
^{uru}KIŠ^{ki} = *Kiš*
KIŠIB in KIŠIB.LÁ = *rittum*
KU see ÉŠ; ḪUN; TÚG; TUKUL
KÙ see KUG
KU$_5$ see KUD
KU$_6$ (the ḫa sign) = *nūnum*; see also $^{\text{(lú)}}$ŠU.ḪA
KUD/KU$_5$ see DI.KUD/KU$_5$; ERIN$_2$.ŠE.KIN.KUD
KUG/KÙ = *ellum*; KUG.BABBAR = *kaspum*; KUG.SIG$_{17}$, also read GUŠKIN = *ḫurāṣum*; see also DU$_6$.KUG
KUN = *zibbatum*
KUR = *mātum, šadûm*
KÚR = *nakrum*
KURUN in LÚ/MÍ.KURUN.NA = *sābûm, sābītum*
KUŠ (the su sign) = *maškum*
KÙŠ = *ammatum*
LÁ see KIŠIB.LÁ; LAL (= lá); ŠAMAN$_2$.LÁ
LAḪ$_5$ (du+du) see MÁ.LAḪ$_5$
LAL/LÁ = *šaqālum*
LI = *līmum*
LÍL see ^{d}EN.LÍL
LIM = *līmum*; see also IGI
LIMMU = *erbe*
LÚ = *awīlum*
LUGAL = *šarrum*; LUGAL*(-ru)-* (e.g., LUGAL*(-ru)-tum*) = *šarrūtum*
LUKUR (munus+me) = *nadītum*
LUM see ZÚ.LUM(.MA)
MA in MA.NA = *manûm* c
$^{\text{(giš)}}$MÁ = *eleppum*; $^{\text{(giš)}}$MÁ.Ì.DUB = *našpakum*; MÁ.LAḪ$_5$ = *malāḫum*
MAḪ = *ṣīrum*; see also KISAL.MAḪ; SUKKAL.MAḪ; UR.MAḪ
MAR in MAR.TU = *Amurrûm*; $^{\text{(giš)}}$MAR.GÍD.DA = *ereqqum*
MAŠ = *mišlum, šumma*; MAŠ.GAG.EN/MAŠ.EN.GAG = *muškēnum*; see also ZIPAḪ (= maš)
MÁŠ = *ṣibtum* a; $^{\text{(lú)}}$MÁŠ.ŠU.GÍD.GÍD = *bārûm*
ME = *meat(um)*; see also LUKUR (munus+me)

MEŠ plural marker
MI = *ṣillum;* see also UM.MI.A; GI_6 (mi)
MÍ see MUNUS
MIN = *šinā*
MU = *nīšum, šattum* a, *šumum;* see also NU.MU.SU
MUL = *kakkabum*
MUNUS/MÍ = *sinništum;* MUNUS. TUR = *ṣuḫārtum;* see also DUMU. MUNUS; LUKUR (munus+me); Ú. SAL (munus = sal)
$MURUB_4$ = *qablum*
MUŠEN (the ḫu sign) = *iṣṣūrum*
NA in NA.GADA = *nāqidum;* see also ^{udu}ŠU.GI.NA
$^{(giš)}$NÁ = *eršum* b
NA_4 = *abnum*
NAGAR see ^{lú}TIBIRA (urudu+nagar)
^{d}NANNA = *Nanna*
NE in NE.NE.GAR = *Abum* b; see also IZI (= ne)
NI see A.NI; GÍR.NI; ŠANDANA (gal+ ni)
NÍG in NÍG.GA=*makkūrum, namkūrum;* NÍG.KAS_7= *nikkassum;* NÍG. ŠU =*ša qāt(i);* see also NINDA (níg)
NIGIDA = *pānum, parsiktum*
NIMGIR = *nāgirum*
NIMIN = *erbeā*
NIN = *aḫātum* (properly NIN_9), *bēltum, erištum;* NIN.DINGIR(.RA) = *entum*
NIN_9 = *aḫātum*
NINDA (the níg sign) = *ak(a)lum, nindanum*
NINNU = *ḫamšā*
NIŠ = *ešrā*
$NITA(Ḫ)_2$ (the ìr sign) = *zikarum;* see GÌR.$NITA(Ḫ)_2$
NU in NU.$BANDA_5$ = *laputtûm;* $^{(lú)}$NU.$^{giš}KIRI_6$ = *nukaribbu;* NU. MU.SU = *almattum;* see also IN. NU.DA
NUMUN and ŠE.NUMUN = *zērum*
NUN = *rubûm;* see also ^{íd}BURANUN (ud+kib+nun); ZIMBIR^{ki} (ud+kib+nun^{ki})
PA in PA.PA = *ša ḫaṭṭātim* or, as UGULA.GIDRI,*wakil ḫaṭṭim*(?);see also $ENSI_2$ (pa+te+si); GIDRI (pa)
PAD see GÌR.PAD.DU
PÀD = *tamûm*
$^{(gi)}$PISAN = *pišannum*
RÁ (the du sign) see A.RÁ
SA in SA.TU = *šadûm*
SÁ (the di sign) see (ITU.)GUD.SI.SÁ
SAG = *rēšum;* SAG NÍG.GA = *rēš namkūrim;* SAG.DU = *qaqqadum;* SAG.DÙN = *šassukkum;* SAG. $GEME_2$ = *amtum;* SAG.ÌR = *wardum;* see also É.SAG.ÍL; UR.SAG
SAL (munus) see Ú.SAL
SANGA = *šangûm*
SAR = *mūšarum;* see also DUB.SAR
SÁR = *šārum*
SI see (ITU.)GUD.SI.SÁ; ŠU.SI; $ENSI_2$ (pa+te+si)
SÌ see GÌR.SÌ.GA
SÍG = *šīpātum;* SÍG.BA = *lubūšum*
SIG_4 = *libittum;* SIG_4.GA = *Simānum*
SIG_{17} (the gi sign) see KUG.SIG_{17}
SILA (the tar sign) = *sūqum*
$SILA_3$ (the qa sign) = *qûm*
SIPA(D) = *rēʾûm*
SISKUR = *niqûm*
SU see KUŠ; NU.MU.SU
SUKKAL = *sukkallum;* SUKKAL. MAḪ = *sukkalmaḫḫum*
SÚN = *rīmtum*
ŠÀ (or $ŠAG_4$) = *libbum;* ŠÀ.GAL = *ukullûm;* ŠÀ.GUD = *kullizum;* see also A.ŠÀ; A.ŠÀ.ŠUKU
$^{(dug)}$ŠAGAN = *šiqqatum*
$ŠAG_4$ see ŠÀ
ŠAḪ = *šaḫûm*
$ŠAKKANA_6^?$ (GÌR.$NITA(Ḫ)_2$) = *šakkanakkum*
ŠÁM = *šīmum* b
$ŠAMAN_2$.LÁ = *šamallûm*
ŠANABI = *šinip; šittān*
ŠANDANA (gal+ni) = *šandanakkum*
ŠE (also ŠE.UM,ŠE.IM)=*ûm; uṭṭatum;* ŠE.BA = *iprum;* ŠE.GIŠ.Ì (also ŠE.Ì.

GIŠ at Mari) = *šamaššammū*; ŠE.KIN.KUD = *Addarum*; for ŠE.NUMUN see NUMUN; see also ERIN$_2$.ŠE.KIN.KUD
ŠEŠ = *aḫum*; see also URIM(šeš+ab)^{ki}
ŠIM (also ŠIMĪGAR, ŠIM+GAR) = *sirāšûm*
ŠITIM = *itinnum*
ŠU = *qātum*; ŠU.DÙ(.A) = *šīzum*; ^{udu}ŠU.GI.NA = *šuginûm*; ^{mí}ŠU.GI$_4$ = *šugītum*; $^{(lú)}$ŠU.ḪA (or ŠU.KU$_5$) = *bā'erum*; ŠU.I = *gallābum*; ŠU.NUMUN.NA = *Dumuzi*; ŠU.SI = *ubānum*; ŠU ... TI = *leqûm*; see also $^{(lú)}$MÁŠ.ŠU.GÍD.GÍD; NÍG.ŠU
ŠUKU = *kurummatum*
ŠUR$^?$ = *maṣraḫum*
ŠUŠ = *šeššat*; *šuduš*; *šuššum*
ŠUŠANA = *šuššān*
TAB in TAB.BA = *tappûm*
TAG$_4$ see ÍB.TAG$_4$
TÁR see EŠ$_4$.TÁR
^{lú}TIBIRA (urudu+nagar) = *gurgurrum*
TE see ENSI$_2$ (pa+te+si)
TI see ŠU ... TI
TIL = *gamārum*
TIR see GIŠ.TIR
TU see MAR.TU
TÚG (the ku sign) = *ṣubātum*; ^{lú}TÚG = *ašlākum*
$^{(giš)}$TUKUL (the ku sign) = *kakkum*
TUR (the dumu sign) = *ṣuḫārum*; see also DUMU; MUNUS.TUR
U = *ešer*; see also GÍŠ.U
Ú = *šammum*; Ú.DÚL = *utullum*; Ú.SAL = *ušallum*
U$_4$ see UD
U$_8$ = *laḫrum*; U$_8$.UDU.ḪI.A (also read USDUḪA) = *ṣēnū* / *ṣēnum*
UBUR = *tulûm*
UD/U$_4$ = *ūmum*; UD.KÚR.ŠÈ = *ana* / *ina warkīt* / *warkiāt ūmim* / *ūmī*; UD.UNUG^{ki} = *Larsa*; see also ^{íd}BURANUN (= ud+kib+nun); KISLAḪ (= ki+ud); BABBAR (ud); UTU (ud); ZABAR (ud+ka+bar); ZIMBIR^{ki} (ud+kib+nun^{ki})
UDU = *immerum*; see also U$_8$.UDU.ḪI.A
ÙG see UN
UGNIM = *ummānum*
UGULA (the pa sign) = *waklum*
UḪ = *tuḫḫum*
UKKIN = *puḫrum*; see also GAL.UKKIN.NA
UKU$_3$ see UN
UM in UM.MI.A = *ummiānum*
UN (or UKU$_3$ or ÙG) = *nišū*; see also KALAM (un)
UNUG^{ki} = *Uruk*; see also UD.UNUG^{ki}
UR in UR.BAR.RA = *barbarum*; UR.MAḪ = *nēšum*; UR.SAG = *qarrādum*
ÙR see GIŠ.ÙR
UR$_5$ (the ḫar sign) = *ḫašûm*; UR$_5$.RA = *ḫubullum*
URIM(šeš+ab)^{ki} = *Ur*
URU = *ālum*
URUDU = *werûm*; see also ^{lú}TIBIRA (urudu+nagar)
ÚS in ÚS.SA.DU = *itûm*, *itā*; see also AGA.ÚS
$^{(kuš)}$USAN$_3$ = *qinnāzum*
USDUḪA see U$_8$.UDU.ḪI.A
USSU = *samāne*
UŠU$_3$ = *šalāšā*
UTU = *šamšum*; ^{d}UTU = *Šamaš*; see also UD
UZU = *šīrum*
ZA in ^{na4}ZA.GÌN = *uqnûm*; see also AN.ZA.GÀR
ZABAR (ud+ka+bar) = *siparrum*
ZAG = *imittum* a and b; see BARA$_2$.ZAG.GAR
ZÉ = *martum*
ZI in ZI(.GA) = *tibûtum*; ^{mí}ZI.IK.RUM / RU.UM = *sekretum*; see also ^{d}DUMU.ZI; É.ZI.DA
ZIMBIR^{ki} (ud+kib+nun^{ki}) = *Sippar*
ZIPAḪ (the maš sign) = *ūṭum*
ZÍZ.A.AN = *Šabāṭum*
ZU see A.ZU; ^{d}EN.ZU
ZÚ (the ka sign) = *šinnum*; ZÚ.LUM(.MA) = *suluppum*

DETERMINATIVES

I/m	before (men's) names
d	(for ^{dingir}) before divine names
dug	before words for vessels
gi	before words for items made of reed
giš	before words for items made of wood
íd	before river names
iku	*after* words denoting surface measures
iti/itu	before month names
kam/kám	*after* numerical expressions
ki	*after* place names
ku_6	*after* words for fishes
kur	before words for countries and mountains
kuš	before words for items of leather
lú	before gentilics and words denoting men's occupations
mí/f	before women's names and words denoting women's occupations
mul	before names of stars and planets
mušen	*after* names of birds
na_4	before words for stones
síg	before words for varieties of wool
túg	before words for garments
ú	before words for plants
udu	before words denoting varieties of sheep and goats
uru	before names of cities and other place names
urudu	before words for metals
uzu	before words for parts of the body

ENGLISH – AKKADIAN WORD LIST

abandon, to *ezēbum*, *nadûm* a G,Š
abandoned *nadûm* b
abandoned, to be *nawûm*
abate, to *nâḫum*
abduct, to *sepûm*
ability in battle *qarrādūtum*
able *lēʾûm*
able, to be *leʾûm*
above *elēnum*, *eli*, *eliš*
absent oneself, to *duppurum* D
absorb, to *ekēmum*
abundance *ḫe(n)gallum*, *kuzbum*, *nuḫšum*
abundant, to be(come) *miādum*
accept, to *leqûm*, *maḫārum*, *našûm*
accomplish, to *šuklulum*
according as *kīma*
according to *ana pī*, *ana zīm(ī)*, *kīma*, *mala*, *ša pī*
account(record) *nikkassum*, (rendering of) *ipšum*
account of, on *aššum*
accounting *nikkassum*
accuse, to *ubburum*
achieve, to *kašādum*
achieved *kašdum*
achievement *epištum*
acquire, to *rašûm*, (conscripts) *ṣāb niḫātim rašûm*, (illegally) *sakālum*
acquisition *kišittum*
act *epištum*
act, to *alākum* G, Gtn, *epēšum*
act quickly, to *edēdum* D
action *šiprum*
active, to be *epēšum*
activity *alaktum*, *epištum*, *šiprum*
Adad *Adad*
add, to *emēdum* Št-lex, *malûm* a Št, *waṣābum*
add to, to *redûm* D, *waṣābum*
additional *aḫûm*, *watrum*
additional payment *aḫītum*
additional sum *eliātum*
additionally *u*
address, to *pānam rašûm*, *zakārum*
adjure, to *tamûm* D
administer, to *šapārum*
administration *išdum*
administrator *šatammum*, (of date orchards) *šandanakkum*
adolescent (male) *ṣuḫārum*
adopt, to *ana mārūtim leqûm*
advance, to *etēqum*
advance against, to *wârum*
adversary (in court) *bēl dīnim*
adverse feature *aḫītum*
advice *milkum*, *šitūltum*
advice, to give *malākum*
advise one another, to *malākum* Gt
affair *awātum*
afraid,to be(come) *palāḫum*
after *inūma*, *ištu*, *(ina) ūm*, *warki*
after the death/departure of *warki*
afterward *warka* a, *warkānum*, *ina warkītim*
again, to do *šanûm* a G, Št
against *ana ṣēr*, *eli*
age (old), *šībūtum*
aggravate, to *kabātum* D
agree, to *magārum* G, Gt
agreeable, to be *magārum*
agreed portion *apšitûm*
agreement *dibbatum*, *riksum*, *tešmûm*
agreement, to bring to *magārum* Št
agreement, to come to an *ga mālum* *magārum* Gt, N
agricultural holding *ṣibtum* b
agricultural work *ikkarūtum*
Akkadian *Akkadûm*
alert *ērum*
alert, to be(come) *êrum* G
alive *balṭum*
alive, to be *balāṭum*
alive, to keep (someone) *balāṭum* D
all *kalûm* b, *kullatum* ,*mim ma*, *mimmû*, *napḫarum*
alliance *salīmātum*
allow, to *nadānum*
allowance, food *kurummatum*
ally *salīmātum*
alone *ina ramānī-*, *ramānum*, *wēdum*
already *ullânum*
also *u*
alter, to *nakārum* D, *šanûm* D
among *ina*, *ina birīt*, *ina libbi*
Amorite *Amurrûm*
amount (of silver, flour) *bit qum*
amount outstanding *šapiltum*
amount to, to *maṣûm* a
ancient *labirum*
and (also) *u*
and (then) *-ma*
anger *kiṣir libbim*, *libbātum*, *uzzum*
anger, to *zenûm* a D
angry *šabsum*, *zenûm* b
angry,to be(come) *anāpum*, *lemēnum*, *šabāsum*, *zenûm* a
animals *nammaštûm*
annex, to *ekēmum*
annihilate, to *gamārum*

announce, to *edûm* Š, *wapûm* Š
annoyed *šabsum*
annoyed, to be(come) *marāṣum, šabāsum*
annual tax *igisûm*
anoint, to *pašāšum*
anoint oneself, to *pašāšum* Gt
anointed *paššum*
another *šanûm* c
answer *meḫrum*, (positive) *annum*
answer, to *apālum*, *ana X izuzzum*
answer for, to *apālum* Gtn
anus *qinnatum*
any *ayyumma*
anyone *awīlūtum*, *ayyumma*, *manāma, mamman*
anything *mimma*
anything at all *mimma šumšu*
anything that *mimma mala*
anywhere *ayyīšamma*
apart from *balum, ezib/ezub, ullânum*
appear, to *amārum* N, *elûm* a, *tebûm* a, *wapûm*, *waṣûm* a
appear, to make *elûm* a Š
appearance *būnum/būnū, lānum, zīmum*
appease, to *nâḫum* D, *pašāḫum* Š
appeased, to be(come) *nâḫum, pašāḫum*
apply, to *lapātum*
appoint, to *nabûm* a, *šakānum*
appointed *šaknum*
appointed time *adānum*
apprentice *šamallûm*
approach, to *kašādum* D, *maḫārum* G, D, *qerēbum*, *ṭeḫûm*
approach with a claim, to *sanāqum*
appropriate (adj.) *naṭûm* a
appropriate fraudulently, to *sikiltam sakālum*
approval *annum*
aquisition *sikiltum*
arable land *ugārum*
archive *bīt ṭuppim*
area *eqlum, erṣetum*
area around a town *nawûm* a
arise, to *tebûm* a
arm *aḫum, idum*
army *ṣābum*, *ummānum*
arouse, to *dekûm*
arrange, to *kaṣārum*, *sadārum*
arrest, to *kasûm*, *ṣabātum*
arrive, to *erēbum*, (at a place) *kašādum*, *sanāqum*, (of news, people, etc.) *maqātum*, (safely) *šalāmum*
arrow *qanûm*
artery *šerʾānum*
article purchased *šīmum*
artisan *ummiānum*
as *ana, kīma*
as far as *adi*
as far as it extends *mala maṣû*
as follows *umma*
as if *kīma ša*
as large as *mala*
as long as *adi*, *ina*
as much/many as *mala*
as much as there is *mala maṣû*
as one *ištēniš*
as soon as *inūma, ištu, (ina) ūm, kīma*
as well *u*
ascend, to *elûm* a
ascertain, to *burrum* D
ask, to *erēšum* a, *šâlum*
asleep *šittam*
assemble, to (intr.) *paḫārum* G, (tr.) D, *ṣabātum* Št-lex
assembly *puḫrum*
assets *kišittum*, *makkūrum*
assign, to *edûm* D, *esēḫum*, *kânum* D, *lapātum*, *malûm* a Št, *nadānum*, *paqādum*, *šakānum*, *šaṭārum*, (a task) *ana pī/āḫatim šakānim*
assigned *paqdum*, *šaṭrum*
assignment *isiḫtum*, *iškarum*
assist, to *tappût X alākum*
assistant *šamallûm*
association *tappûtum*
at *ina*
at birth *ina mêšu* (*mû*)
at hand *qerbum*
at that time *inūmīšu*
at the disposal of *ana pān(i)*
at the feet of *(ina) šapal*
at the time of *ina*
at the time that *inūma, (ina) ūm*
atrophied *ekmum*
attach, to *ṣabātum* Št-lex, *ṣamādum*
attack *tībum*, *tibûtum*, (successful) *tībum kašdum*
attack, to *maqātum*, *rakāsum*, *wârum*
attaingreat beauty/stature, to *šamāḫum*
attend to, to *dagālum*
attendant *gerseqqûm*, *mukīl rēšim* (*kullum*), *muzzazum, nazzazum*, *rēdûm*
attire *lubūšum*
attitude *ṭēmum*
attractiveness *lalûm*, (sexual) *inbum, kuzbum*
augment, to *watārum* D
august *ṣiārum*
authority *lētum*
available *bašûm* b, *kašdum*
available, to be *bašûm* a
available assets *namkūrum, rēš namkūrim*
avoid, to *etēqum*, *paṭārum*, *zêrum*
await, to *ḫakûm*
awake *ērum*
awake, to be *êrum*
awaken, to *êrum*
aware *šemûm* b
aware of, to be(come) *lamādum*
away (from) *ina maḫar, ištu*
awe-inspiring *rašbum*
awesome *rašbum*
ax *ḫaṣṣīnum/ḫaṣṣinnum*
baby, suckling *mār(at) irtim*
Babylon *Bābilim*
back (part, side) *ṣērum*, *warkatum*
back country *ṣērum*
bad *lemnun*, *maskum*
bad, to be(come) *masākum* N
badly *lemniš*

band *kannum, kiṣrum, rik-sum, šerʾānum*
banished *ṭardum*
bank (of river, canal) *aḫum, kibrum, kišādum*
bar *sikkūrum*
barber *gallābum*
bare land *nadītum*
barley *ûm, uṭṭatum*
barley pile (for storage) *karûm*
barley ration *iprum*
barley reserve *aldûm*
base *išdum, nīdum*
basin *šiqqatum*
basket *pišannum*
battle *qablûm* a, *tāḫāzum, tamḫārum*
battle, to do *kakkī epēšum, tāḫāzam epēšum*
bead *irimmum*
beam *gušūrum*
bear, to *babālum, našûm, šadādum*, (children) *walādum*
bear continuously, to *na-šûm* Gtn
beat, to *naṭûm* b, *tarākum*
beat out, to *šarāmum*
beaten *tarkum*
beautiful *banûm* d, *dam-qum*
because *aššum, ištu* (rare), *kīma*, (of the fact that) *ana ša*
because of *aššum, ina pān(i)*
become, to *ewûm, târum*
bed *eršum* b, *mayyalum*
bedrock *kiṣir šadîm*
beer *šikarum*
beer merchant *sābûm*
before *adi ... lā, ana maḫar, ina maḫar, ina pān(i), lāma, maḫar, pāna*
before the arrival of *ana pān(i)*
beget, to *walādum*
begin (work on), to *qātam šakānum*
begin moving, to *nâšum*
beginning *rēštum, rēšum*
behavior *alaktum, kibsum*
behind *warka* a, *warki*
believe, to *qiāpum*
believed, to be *qiāpum* N
belittle, to *maṭûm* Š
belong to, to *dagālum*
beloved one *narāmum*
below *šaplānum, šapliš, ina šapal*
bend, to *kanāšum* D, *kapā-ṣum, lâdum*
bend down, to *kamāsum* b
beneath *ina šapal*
benediction *ikribum*
benefit *nēmelum*
benefit, to *nēmelam rašûm*
beside *idi, itā*
besides *appūna, appūnā-ma, elēnum, ezib/ezub*
besiege, to *lawûm* a
best quality (oil, dates, sheep) *rēštum*
bestow, to *qiāšum, šarā-kum, šutlumum*
bestowed *qīšum*
betray a secret, to *awātam šūṣûm*
better, to be(come) *damā-qum*
between *ina birīt*
beyond *elēnum, eli*
big *rabûm* b
bile *martum*
bind, to *kasûm* G, D, *kaṣā-rum, rakāsum, ṣamādum*
bind by magic/agreement, to *eʾēlum*
bind by oath, to *tamûm* D
bird *iṣṣūrum*
birth *ṣītum*
bison *kusarikkum*
black *ṣalmum, tarkum*
black, to be(come) *ṣalā-mum*
black-headed ones *ṣalmāt qaqqadim*
bless, to *karābum*
blessing *ikribum*
blind, to *ḫuppudum*
bloated *napḫum*
block, to *parākum, sekērum*
block the way, to *alaktam parāsum*
blood *damum*
bloom, to *ḫanāmum*
blow (on), to *napāḫum*
board, to *rakābum*
boat *eleppum*,(going down-stream) *muqqelpītum*
boat-tower *šādidum*
body *lānum, pagrum, zum-rum*
body hair *malû*
bond *kannum*
bond together, to *kasûm*
bone *eṣemtum*
booty *kišittum, šallatum*
border *itûm, pātum*
border (area) of the liver *birītum*
bordering on *itā*
Borsippa *Barsipa*
boss *awīlum*
both *kilallān*
bother, to *dabābum* D
bottom *išdum, šaplum* b
bought *šāmum*
boundary *pāṭum*
bovines *liātum*
bow *qaštum*
bow down, to *kanāšum, šukênum*
box *pišannum*
bran *tuḫḫum*
branch *ḫaṭṭum, larûm*, (of a canal) *atappum*
brand *šimtum*
breach *pilšum, pītum*
bread *ak(a)lum*
break, to *ḫepûm* a, *šebērum* G (tr.), N (intr.)
break camp, to *paṭārum*
break into, to *palāšum, pa-tāḫum*
break off, to *karāṣum*
break out (of fire), to *napā-ḫum* N
break through, to *palāšum, patāḫum*
break up soil, to *marārum*
breast *irtum, tulûm*
breathe freely, to *napāšum*
brew beer, to *sabûm*
brewer *sirāšûm*
brick, mud *libittum*
brick-mold *nalbattum*
bride *kallatum*
bride-price *terḫatum*
bright *nawirum, nawurrum*
bright, to be(come) *nawā-rum*
brighten, to *nawārum* D, Š
brightly colored *bitrāmum*
brilliant *nawirum, nawur-rum, šitʾārum*

brilliantly radiant *šalummum*
bring, to *tarûm*, *warûm*
bring, to cause to *redûm* Š
bring down, to *warādum* Š
bring in, to *erēbum* Š, *kamāsum* a G, D
bring into contact, to *emēdum* Št-lex
bring near, to *qerēbum* D, *ṭeḫûm* D
bring out, to *waṣûm* a Š
bring suit, to *baqārum*
bring to an end, to *gamārum*, *šuklulum*
bring up, to *elûm* a Š
broken *ḫepûm* b, *šebrum*
broken, to be(come) *šebērum* N
bronze *siparrum*, *werûm*
brother *aḫum*
brother, status of *aḫḫūtum*
brotherhood, brotherliness *aḫḫūtum*
brotherly attitude/relationship *atḫûtum*
buckle, to *qâpum*
build, to *banûm* a, *epēšum*
builder (house) *itinnum*
building, sacred *gigunnûm*
built *epšum*
built-on property *bītum epšum*
bulging *garrum*
bull *alpum*, *lûm*
bundle *makṣarum*
burglary *nabalkattum*
burn (down), to *qalûm*
burning *napḫum*
business activity *maḫīrum*
business associate *tappûm*
busy, to be(come) *ṣabātum* Gt
butt, to *nakāpum*
buttock(s) *qinnatum*
buy, to *šâmum*
buyer *šayyāmānum*
by (means of) *ina*
by the authority of *ina qāti*

call *rigmum*
call, to *nabûm* a, *ragāmum*, *šasûm*
call up (soldiers, officials), to *dekûm*
called *ana šumim nabûm*
calm *nēḫum*
calm, to *nâḫum* D, *pašāḫum* D, Š
calm down, to *pašāḫum*
calumniate, to *karṣī akālum*, *qabâm šakānum*, *tuššam nadûm*/*qabûm*/*dabābum*
calumny *karṣum*, *tuššum*
campaign, military *gerrum*, *ḫarrānum*
campaign, to undertake *ḫarrānam ṣabātum*
canal *nārum* a, (branch) *atappum*
canal worker *sekērum*
canebrake *apum*
cap *paršīgum*
capable *lēʾûm*
capital (financial) *qaqqadum*
captain *ša ḫaṭṭātim* or *wakil ḫaṭṭim*
captive *ṣabtum*; captives *šal latum*
captive, to take *esērum* a D
capture, to *ṣabātum*
caravan *alaktum*, *gerrum*, *ḫarrānum*
carbuncle *simmum*
care *qātum*
care for, to *ḫasāsum*, *râmum*
careless, to be *egûm*
caress, to *ḫabābum*
cargo boat *našpakum*
carried *bablum*
carry, to *babālum*, *našûm*, *zabālum*
carry away/off, to *tabālum*
carry out, to *ṣubbûm*
cart *ereqqum*
case (legal) *dīnum*, *purussûm*
cast, to *ramûm*
castle *birtum*
catch (fish, etc.), to *bârum* a
cattle *liātum*
cattle-pen *tarbaṣum*
cave in, to *qâpum*
cease, to *naparkûm*
cella *kummum*
center *abunnatum*, *libbum*
center of, to the *ana libbi*
cereal *ašnan*
certainly *lū*
certify, to *burrum* D
chaff *pûm* b
chain *šeršerrum*
chair *kussûm*
change, to (intr.) *ewûm*, *nakārum* G, *šanûm* b G, (tr.) *enûm*, *nakārum* D, *šanûm* b D, *šupêlum*
change allegiance/sides, to *nabalkutum*
change into, to *ewûm*
channel, sluice *butuqtum*
characteristic(s) *simtum*
charge *qātum*
charge, to *ešērum*
chariot *narkabtum*
charm *lalûm*, *ruʾāmum*
chase (away), to *kašādum* D
cheap *maṭûm*
cheat, to *sarārum*
check, to *sanāqum* G, D
checked *amrum*
cheek *lētum*
cheerfulness *buʾārum*
chest *irtum*
chief *rēšum*, *šāpirum*
chief shepherd *utullum*
child *ṣeḫrum*, (female) *ṣuḫārtum*
chirp, to *ḫabābum*
chisel *maqqarum*
choice *nasqum*
choose, to *nasāqum*, (a mate) *ḫiārum*
chosen *ḫīrum*, *nasqum*
circle, to *lawûm* a, *saḫārum*
citadel *birtum*
city *ālum*
city gate *abullum*
city quarter *bābtum*, *bābum*
claim, to *baqārum*, (falsely) *sarārum* D
claimant *rēdītum*
clarify, to *pašārum*
clean *ebbum*, *ellum*, *zakûm* b
clean, to *ebēbum* D, *zakûm* a D
clean, to be(come) *ebēbum*, *elēlum*, *zakûm* a
cleanse, to *ebēbum* D, *zakûm* a D
cleansing *tazkītum*
clear *zakûm* b
clear, to *zakûm* a D, (ac-

counts) *napāṣum*, (of claims) *ebēbum* D, oneself *ebēbum* D
clear, to be(come) *pānam rašûm, zakûm* a
cleft *piṭrum*
clerk *šatammum*
clever *eršum* a
cling to, to *emēdum*
clod of earth *kirbānum*
cloister *gagûm*
close, to (tr.) *edēlum, peḫûm, sekērum*
close by *qerbum*
closed in, to be *parākum* N
clothe, to *labāšum* D, oneself *labāšum* G
clothed (in) *labšum*
clothing (allowance) *lubūšum*
cloudburst *rādum*
coiling *tayyartum*
cold *kūṣum*
collapse *miqtum*
collapse, to *maqātum, qâpum*
collapsed *maqtum*
colleague *ibrum*
collect, to *esēpum, esērum* b G,D, *kamāsum* a G, D, *kaṣārum, paḫārum* D, *ṣabātum* Št-lex, (taxes, etc.) *nadānum* Š
collector (of taxes, etc.) *mušaddinum, muzzaz bābim*
color, to *barāmum* Gt
colored brightly *bitrāmum*
coloring *šimtum*
combat *tāḫāzum*
come, to *alākum*
come (on)! *gana*
come back, to *târum*
come down, to *warādum*
come forth, to *waṣûm* a
come out, to *waṣûm* a
come quickly, to *arāḫum*
come to an agreement, to *gamālum*
come to an end, to *gamārum*
come to help, to *naʾarrum*
come to the aid of, to *tappût X alākum*
come together, to *emēdum* N, *paḫārum*
come up, to *elûm* a
come upon bad times, to *lemēnum*
command *awātum, ipiš pîm, pûm, qabûm, qibītum, ṣīt pîm, têrtum, ṭēmum, zikrum*
command, to *qabûm, šapārum, wârum* D
commander *šāpirum*, commanders *šūt-rēšim*
commanding respect *rašbum*
commission *têrtum*
commissioner *bēl pī/āḫatim*
commit an offense, to *ḫaṭûm*
commoner *šukênum*
compensatory payment *nipiltum*
compete with, to *maḫārum* Št
compete with one another, to *šanānum* Gt
compile, to *kaṣārum*
complain to, to *dabābum* G, D, *ragāmum*
complete *gamrum, šalmum*
complete, to *kamāsum* a G, D, *šalāmum* D, *šuklulum*
completed, to be(come) *šalāmum*
completely *ana gamrim*
completely, to do *gamārum*
completion *gamartum*
comply with, to *magārum*
conceive, to *arûm*
concentration *kiṣrum*
concern oneself to *marāṣum* Št
concerned, to be(come) *ṣarāmum*
concerning *aššum*
concord *salīmum*
conduct, to *redûm* G, Š, (safely) *šalāmum* D
confer, to *šutlumum*
confirm, to *kânum* D
confirmation *takīttum*
confound, to *sapāḫum*
confront, to *maḫārum* G, Gt
connect with one another, to *ṣabātum* Gt
connected *tiṣbutum*
conquer, to *ekēmum, kašādum* G,D
conquered *kašdum*
conquest *kišittum*
consecrate, to *elēlum* D
consent *annum*
consent to, to *magārum*
consider, to *awûm* Št, *ḫasāsum, malākum, naṭālum*
consideration *šitūltum*
consignment *šībultum*
constriction *kiṣrum*
construct, to *banûm* a, *epēšum*
construction *epištum*
consult, to *šâlum* Gt
consume, to *akālum*
contain, to *kullum*
container *karpatum*
content, to be(come) *pašāḫum*
contest, to *baqārum, sarārum* D
contingent (of soldiers) *kiṣrum*
continual *sadrum*
continue, to *bitrûm* Št-lex, *redûm* Št-lex
continuity *dūrum* b
continuous, to be *bitrûm* Gt
contract *riksum*
contract, to *rakāsum* D
contribute to, to *redûm* D
control, to *gamārum, sanāqum* G, D
convey, to *babālum, šadādum, šapārum*
conveyance *šēpum*
convict, to *kânum* D
cook *nuḫatimmum*
copper *werûm*
copulate, to *reḫûm*
copy *meḫrum*
copy, to *mašālum* D
corpse *pagrum*
correct *išarum, kīnum*
correct, to be(come) *kânum*
correctness *kīttum*
correspond, to *maḫārum* Gt
corresponding to *ana zīm(ī)*
corvée duty *tupšikkum*
corvée service, to perform *ḫarrānam alākum*
cosmetics *mēqûm*
counsel *milkum*
count, to *manûm* a, *šanûm*

D

counted *manûm*
countenance *zīmum*
country *mātum*, (open) *kīdum*
courier *lāsimum*
court, to go to *diānum*
court officials *šūt rēšim*
courtyard of a temple), main *kisalmaḫḫum*
cover, to *katāmum*, *pasāmum*, *saḫāpum*, *za'ānum* D, (completely) *edēḫum* D, (the head) *apārum*
covered *za'num*, (of head) *aprum*, (with patches/ network) *edḫum*
covet, to *īnīn ana X našûm*
cow *arḫum, lītum*
create, to *banûm* a, *bašûm* Š
creator *bānûm*
creatures *šaknāt napištim*
creditor *bēl ḫubullim, nāš ṭuppātim*
crime *arnum, gillatum, ḫīṭum*
criminal *sarrum*
criminal act *sartum*
crooked, to grow *garārum*
crop *ebūrum*
cross, to *nabalkutum*
crossing *nabalkattum*
crotch *ḫallum*, *sūnum*
crown *agûm, ummānum*
crucible *naṣraptum*
crush, to *napāṣum*
crutch *nēmettum*
cry *rigmum*
cry (out), to *šasûm*
cubit *ammatum*
cultic custom *parṣum*
cultivate, to *erēšum* b
cultivated *epšum*
cultivated field *abšinnum*, *šer'um*
cultivated land *mērešum*
cultivation *mērešum*, *teptītum*
cultivator *errēšum*
cup *kāsum*
curl, to *kapāṣum*
current price *maḫīrum*
curve, to *saḫārum*
custody *maṣṣarūtum*
custom *ūsum*, custom(s) *alaktum*
cut off, to *batāqum, nakāsum, šarāmum* G, D
cut off access, to *alaktam parāsum*
cut through, to *batāqum*
cutting (rare) *bitqum*
cylinder seal *kunukkum*
cyst *ziḫḫum*
cystic duct *maṣraḫum*

daily *ūmišam*
dam up *sekērum*
damage *ḫibiltum, ḫīṭum*
danger *lemuttum*
dark *da'ummum*, *ṣalmum, tarkum*
dark, to be(come) *da'āmum*, *ṣalāmum*
dash down, to *napāṣum*
date(s) *suluppum*
date palm *gišimmarum*
date palm pollination *tarkib tum*
daughter *mārtum*
daughter-in-law *kallatum*
day *ūmum*
day after tomorrow *ullītiš*
daytime *ūmum*
dead *mītum*
death *mūtum*
debris *miqtum*
debt with interest *ḫubullum*
debt-servitude *kiššātum*
deceive, to *dâṣum*
deception *dāṣtum*
decide, to *pānam/pānī šakānum*, *parāsum*
decision *ṭēmum*, (legal) *dīnum*
declare, to *zakārum*
declare innocent, to *elēlum* D
decorate, to *za'ānum* D
decorated *za'num*
decrease,to *maṭûm* ,*ṣeḫērum*
decree, to *nabûm* a, *šiāmum*
dedicate an offering, to *karābum*
deduct, to *batāqum*
deep, to be(come) *šapālum*
defeat, to *dâkum*, *kašādum*, *lapātum* Š, *maqātum* Š, *nêrum, sakāpum* a
deficit *bābtum*, *bitiqtum, ibbûm, ta'īṣtum*
defile, to *lapātum* Š
delay, to *arākum* D, *kalûm* a, *lapātum* D
delayed, to be *arākum*, *aḫārum* G, D
delegate *bēl pī/āḫatim*
deliberate, to *malākum*, *šâlum* Št
deliberation *šitūltum*
delightful *ṣayyaḫum*
deliver, to *manûm, nadānum, našûm, paqādum*, *zabālum*, (safely) *šalāmum* D
deliver in full,to *malûm* a D
delivered *manûm*, *paqdum*
delivery *piqittum*
delivery items *iškarum*
demand, to *ragāmum*
demolish, to *napāṣum*
denounce, to *karṣī X akālum, nuggurum*
denouncer *munaggerum*
deny, to *nakārum*
depart, to *alākum* Gt, *nesûm* a, *waṣûm* a G,Gt
departure *ṣītum*
dependent *šukênum*, dependents *aḫiātum*
depletion *imṭû*
deport *nasāḫum*
depose, to *sakāpum* a
deposit *maṣṣarum*
deposited *ṣabtum*
depression *naṣraptum*
deprive, to *ekēmum*
deputy *bēl pī/āḫatim*
descend, to *warādum*
descendents *zērum*
desecrate, to *lapātum* Š
desert, to *paṭārum*
desire *bibil libbim*, *erištum*, *lalûm*
desire, to *erēšum* a, *ḫašāḫum*
destination *rēš eqlim*
destiny *šīmtum*
destroy,to *abātum*, *belûm* D, *ḫalāqum* D, *ḫepûm* a, *lapā tum* Š, *naqārum* ,*nêrum*
destroyed, to be *lapātum* Št
detain, to *kalûm* a
determine, to *šiāmum*

devastation *ḫarbūtum*
diagnosis *têrtum*
die, to *mâtum*, *namāšum*, (of natural causes) *ina šīmātim mâtum*
different *šanûm* c
different, to be(come) *nakārum*, *šanûm* b
difficult *dannum*, *kabtum*, *marṣum*
difficult, to be(come) *kabātum*, *marāṣum*
difficulty *maruštum*
dig, to *ḫerûm*
dignity *bāštum*
diminish, to *maṭûm* G (intr.), Š (tr.)
diminished, to be(come) *wiāṣum*
direct, to *babālum* Gtn, (work) *epēšum* Š
direction *têrtum*, *ūsum*
directions, to give *ṭēmam šakānum*
director *mu'irrum*
disappear, to *ḫalāqum*
disappear, to make *ḫalāqum* D
discover,to *amārum*, *watûm*
discuss, to *awûm* Gt, Št, *dabābum*, *nadānum* Št
disease *murṣum*, (of skin) *simmum*
diseased *marṣum*
dislike, to *zêrum*
dispatch, to *ṭarādum*, (a boat) *sakāpum* a
disperse, to *paṭārum*, *sapāḫum*
disposal of, to be at the *izuzzum*, *rēšam kullum*
dispute, to *nakārum*
dissolution *tazkītum*
dissolve, to *pašārum*
distant *nesûm* b, *ullûm*
distant, to be(come) *nesûm* a, *rêqum*
distant time *ṣiātum*
distrain, to *nepûm*
distress, to cause *ašāšum* D
distress, to take as *nepûm*
distribute, to *zâzum* G,D
district *bābtum*, *dimtum*, *erṣetum*, *pātum*
disturbed, to be(come) *ašāšum*
dive, to *šalûm*
divert, to *palāsum*, *saḫārum* D
diverting (of water) *bitqum*
divide, to *batāqum*, *ḫepûm* a, *parāsum*, *zâzum* G,D
divided *parsum*, *zīzum*
divine luminosity *namrirrū*
divine nature/power *ilūtum*
divine regulations *sakkû*
divine symbol, standard with a *kakkum ša ilim*
diviner *bārûm*
divinity *ilūtum*
divorce *uzubbûm*
divorce, to *ezēbum*
divorce-payment *uzubbûm*
do, to *epēšum*, (assigned) work *šipram epēšum*
do again, to *šanûm* a G,Št, *târum*
do battle, to *kakkī epēšum*, *tāḫāzam epēšum*
do business together, to *tappûtam epēšum*
do forcefully, to *danānum* a
do much/a lot, to *miādum* Š
do quickly, to *edēdum* D
do regularly, to *sadārum*
do twice, to *šanûm* a
document *kunukkum*, *ṭuppum*, (sealed) *kanīkum*
dog *kalbum*
domestic (attached to the palace or a temple) *gerseqqûm*
domicile *mūṣarum*
dominion *bēlūtum*, *rubûtum*, *šarrūtum*
donkey, male *imērum*
door *bābum*, *daltum*
door-bolt *sikkūrum*
door-frame, -jambs *sippum*
doorkeeper *mukīl babim*
door-leaf *daltum*
door-sill *askupp(at)um*
double *tašna*
double, to *šanûm* a G, Št
double-hour *bērum*
doubly *tašna*
downfall *miqittum*, *miqtum*
downpour *rādum*
dowry *nudunnûm*, *šeriktum*
drag, to *mašārum*, *šadādum*
dragon *mušḫuššum*
draw, to *šadādum*
draw near, to *qerēbum*, *ṭeḫûm*
dream *šuttum*
dressed, to get *labāšum*
drift, to *neqelpûm* N
drink, to *šatûm*
drive, to *redûm*
drive away, to *akāšum* D, *ṭarādum*
droop, to *kapāṣum*
drop, to *nadûm* Š
dropping *nīdum*
drug *šammum*
dry up/out, to *abālum*
dug-up land *ripqum*
duress *maruštum*
dust *ep(e)rum*
duty *isiḫtum*, *pīḫatum*
dwell, to *wašābum*
dwelling *mūṣarum*, *šubtum*

each one *mitḫāriš*
ear *uznum*
earlier *maḫrûm*, *pāna*, *pānûm*, *pānānum*
earliest *pānûm*
earth *erṣetum*, *qaqqarum*, (loose) *ep(e)rum*
east *ṣītum*, *ṣīt šamšim*
eat, to *akālum*
edge *aḫum*, *appum*, *idum*, *kibrum*, *kibrātum*, *šaptum*
eight *samāne*
eighth *samnum*
either... or *ū* ... *ū*
elapse, to *etēqum*, *malûm* a
elbow *ammatum*
elder *šībum*
elevate, to *elûm* a D, *šaqûm* a D
elevated *šaqûm* c
elongated *šaddum*
elsewhere *ayyīšamma*
embankment *kārum*
emblem *maṣraḫum*
embrace, to *edērum*, (one another) *edērum* N
emerge, to *elûm* a, *waṣûm* a
emerge, to make *elûm* a Š

emergence *ṣītum*
emotions *kabattum*
employee, female *ṣuḫārtum*
emptiness *rīqūtum*
empty *rīqum*
empty, to *riāqum* D, Š
empty, to be(come) *riāqum*
empty-handed *rīqūt-*
empty lot *maškanum*
encircle, to *lawûm* a
encircled *lawûm* b
enclose, to *esērum* a G, D
encompass, to *gamārum*
encourage, to *takālum* D
end *appum* ,*šēpītum* ,*taqtītum*
end, to *gamārum* , *paṭārum*
ending *taqtītum*
endowed *šaknum* , *za'num*
endure, to *kânum* , *labārum*
enemy *nak(a/i)rum*
engage in hostilities, to *nakārum*
engaged *tiṣbutum*
enlarge, to *ba'ālum* D, *miādum* Š, *waṣābum* , *watārum* Š
enmity *nukurtum*
enough *maṣûm*
enter, to (intr.) *erēbum* , (tr.) *šaṭārum*, (into an account) *sadārum*
enter into business together, to *tappûtum epēšum*
enterprise *ṣibûtum*
entire *gamrum*
entirety *kalûm* b, *kullatum*
entrance *nērebum*
entrance gate *abullum*
entreat, to *dabābum* D
entrust, to *ezēbum* , *paqādum*, *qiāpum*
entrusted, to be *qiāpum* N
envoy *našparum*
epidemic *mūtānū*
epilepsy *bennum*
equal, to be(come) *maṣûm* , *mašālum* , *šanānum*
equal one another, to *šanānum* Gt
equal status, person of *ibrum*
equal to, to be *maṣûm* a
equally *mitḫāriš*
equip oneself with *rakāsum*
equity *mišarum*
equivalent *meḫrum*
erect *tebûm* b
erect, to *izuzzum* Š, *zaqāpum*
eroded, to be(come) *kirbānam nasākum*
escape, to *ḫalāqum*, *waṣûm* a G,Št
escaped *ḫalqum*
escort, to *redûm*
establish, to *burrum* D, *kânum* D,*šakānum* ,*šiāmum*, (an agreement) *riksam* / *riksātim šakānum*
established *šaknum*
estate *aplūtum*, *bītum*
estimated yield *šukunnûm*
eternity *dāriātum*
Euphrates *Purattum*
ever *matī-ma* (*mati*)
everlasting *dārûm*
everyone that *mala*
everything *kalâmu* , *mimma šumšu*, *mimmāmu(m)*
everything that *mala*
everywhere *mitḫāriš*
evict, to *waṣûm* a Š
evil *lemnun* , *lemuttum*
evil, to be(come) *lemēnum*
evil intentions *lemuttum*
ewe *laḫrum*
exact services for a debt, to *kašāšum*
exaggerate, to *ba'ālum* D
exalt, to *rēšam našûm*
exalted *elûm* b
examine, to *ḫiāṭum* , *kânum* Št
exceed, to *etēqum* , *watārum*
exceeding, to be(come) *watārum*
exceedingly *magal*
excellent *ṣīrum*, *watrum*
except for *šumma(n) lā*
excess *watartum*
exchange, to *šupêlum*
exchanged, to be *šupêlum* Š(D)t
execute, to *dâkum*
execute according to plan, to *ṣubbûm*
execute properly, to *ṣubbûm*
exercise authority,to *bêlum*, *bēlūtam epēšum*
exercise kingship, to *šarrūtam epēšum*
exert oneself, to *ṣarāmum*
exile(d) *ṭardum*
exile, to *kašādum* D
exist, to *bašûm* a
exit *mūṣûm*
expedition, military *ḫarrānum*
expeditionary force *ālik ḫarrānim*, *gerrum*
expel, to *nasāḫum* , *saḫārum* D, *waṣûm* a Š
expelled *ṭardum*
expenditure *ṣītum*
experience *nēmequm*
experience, to *amārum*
experienced, to be(come) *edûm*
expert *damqum*, *lē'ûm*, *ummiānum*
expert, to be(come) *le'ûm*
explain, to *burrum* D, *pašārum*
explore, to *ḫiāṭum*
express messenger *lāsimum*
extend, to *arākum* D, *tarāṣum*
extended, to be(come) *nepelkûm*
extinguish (fire), to *belûm* D
extinguished, to be *belûm*
extispicy (omen) *têrtum*
extol, to *elûm* a D
extra *watartum*
extremities, lower *išdum*
extricate, to *šalāpum*
exultation *ulṣum*
eye *īnum*
eyesight *niṭlum*

face *būnum* / *būnū*, *pānum* a, *zīmum*
face, to *maḫārum* Gt, *naṭālum*, (one another) *naṭālum* Gt
fact that, the *kīma*
fail, to *ḫaṭûm*, *naparkûm*
fair *išarum*
fall (down, upon), to *maqātum*
fall ill, to *marāṣum*
fallen *maqtum*
fallow *nadûm* b

false *sarrum*, *zaprum*
false, to be(come) *sarārum*
falsehood *sartum*, *zapurtum*
fame *damiqtum*, *šumum*, *zikrum*
familiar with, to be(come) *edûm*
family *bīt abim*, *nišūtum*
family estate *bīt abim*
family head *ḫammum*
famine *bubūtum*, *dannatum*, *sunqum*
fancy *ṣayyaḫum*
far (away) *nesûm* b
far, to be(come) *rêqum*
farmer *ikkarum*, *iššiakkum*
fat (adj.) *kabtum*, (n.) *lipûm*, *šamnum*
fat, to be(come) *kabārum*, *kabātum*
fate *šīmtum*
father *abum*
father's legal status *abbūtum*
father-in-law (wife's father) *emum*
fatherly attitude *abbūtum*
fattening *namrāʾū*
fault *ḫīṭum*
favor *damiqtum*
favor, to *pānī X babālum*
favorable *damqum*, *šalmum*
favorite *migrum*, *narāmum*
fear *puluḫtum*
fear, to *adārum*, *palāḫum*
feared *palḫum*
feared, to be *adārum* N
fearsome *palḫum*, *rašubbum*
features *būnum* / *būnū*, *simtum*
feed, to *akālum* Š
feeding *ukultum*
fell, to *maqātum* Š
felled *naksum*
fellow *meḫrum*
female *sinništum*
female servant/slave *amtum*, *ṣuḫārtum*
festival (religious) *isinnum*
fetter *kannum*
few *maṭûm*, *wīṣum*
few, to be(come) *ṣeḫērum*
field *eqlum*, (neighboring) *itûm*, (worked/prepared) *eqel epšētim*
fierce *dannum*
fifth, one- *ḫamšum* b
fifty *ḫamšā*
fight *risibtum*
fight, to *kakkī epēšum*, *maḫāṣum* Gt, *tāḫāzam epēšum*
fight with one another, to *waṣûm* a Št
filament *qûm* b
fill, to *malûm* a G,D
filled *malûm* b
financial loss *ibissûm*
find, to *amārum*, *watûm*
find acceptance, to *magārum*
fine (awarded in lawsuit) *rugummûm*
fine (adj.) *banûm* b, *ṭābum*, (wool, textiles) *qat num*
fine, to be(come) *qatānum*
finger *ubānum*
finish, to *gamārum*, *šuklulum*
finished *gamrum*
fire *išātum*
fire god *Gibil* / *Girra*
firm *kīnum*
firm, to be(come) *bârum* b, *kânum*
first *ištīʾum* (rare), *maḫrûm*, *pānûm*
first half *aḫum*
first husband *ḫāʾirum* / *ḫāwirum*
first-rank *ṣīrum*
firstly *pānānum*
fish *nūnum*
fish, to catch *bârum* a
fisherman *bāʾerum*
fissure *pitrum*
fit, to *alākum* Š
fitting *naṭûm* a
five *ḫamiš*
five-sixths *parasrab*
fix, to *kânum* D, *šiāmum*, (an estimate) *ana šukunnêm šakānum*
fixed *kīnum*, *šimum*
fixed, to be(come) *kânum*
flank *aḫum*
flap *naplasum*
flee, to *naʾbutum*
flesh *šīrum*
flock *ṣēnum*
flood *bibbulum* / *bubbulum*, *butuqtum*, *mīlum*
flood, to *raḫāṣum*
flood area *ušallum*
flourish, to *šamāḫum*
flow into/upon, to *reḫûm*
flow, to cause to *redum* Š
fly, to *naprušum*
fodder *šammum*, *ukullûm*
foe *nak(a/i)rum*
foetus *ša libbim*
fold (x-fold) *adi x-īšu*
fold (animal) *tarbaṣum*
follow, to *redûm*
food *ak(a)lum*, *ukultum*, (allotment, supply) *ukullûm*, (portion, allowance, ration) *iprum*, *kurumma tum*
foot *šēpītum*, *šēpum*
footsoldier *rēdûm*
for *ana*, *ana pān(i)*
for a day *ūmam*
for the benefit of *ana pān(i)*
for the sake of *aššum*
forcefully, to do *danānum* a
forehead *pūtum*
foreign *aḫûm*, *nak(a/i)rum*
foreman *waklum*
foremost *watrum*
forest *qištum*
forever *ana dāriātim*, *dāriš (ūmī)*
forfeit, to *ina X etlûm*
forget, to *mašûm*
forgetful, to be(come) *mašûm* Gtn
forgive, to *pānī X babālum*
fork *larûm*
form, to *kaṣārum* G
former *maḫrûm*, *pānûm*
formerly *pānānum*
fort *birtum*
fortification *ḫalṣum*
fortified *dannum*
fortified area *dimtum*
fortify, to *danānum* a D
fortress *dannatum*, *dannūtum*, *ḫalṣum*
forty *erbeā*
foster child *tarbītum*
found, to be *amārum* N
foundation *išdum*, *uššum*
four *erbe*

four regions (of the world) *kibrātum arba'um*
fourfold, four times *erbîšu*
fourth *rebûm*
fraud(ulent tablet) *ṭuppum ṣīḫtum*
free *ellum*, (of claims) *zakûm* b
free, to *paṭārum*, *zakûm* a D, (of debt) *elēlum* D
free, to be(come) *zakûm* a, (of debt) *elēlum*
free man *awīlum*
freedom *andurārum*
fresh *eššum*, (plants) *warqum*
friend *ibrum*
friendliness *ṭūbātum*
friendly *banûm* d
friendly relations *ṭūbātum*
fright *gilittum*
from *ina*, *ina libbi*, *ištu*, *itti*
from there *ullânum*
front *maḫrum*, *muttum*, *pānum* a, *pūtum*, *rēšum*
frontage *rēšum*
fruit, fruit tree *inbum*
full *gamrum*, *malûm* b
full (of), to be(come) *malûm* a
full, to pay in *gamārum*
full-grown *šīḫum*
fuller *ašlākum*
furnishings *numātum*, *unūtum*
furrow *abšinnum*, *šer'um*
furthermore *appūna*, *appūnā-ma*, *u*
future *warkītum*

gain *nēmelum*
gain, to *rašûm*
gall (bladder) *martum*
gang *ṣābum*, *ummānum*
garden *kirûm*
gardener *nukaribbum*
garment *libšum* (rare), *ṣubātum*
garrison *maṣṣartum*, *maṣṣarum*
garrison (soldiers), to *wašābum* Š
gate *bābum*, (city) *abullum*
gather, to (intr.) *paḫārum* G, (tr.) *kamāsum* a G, D, *paḫārum* D
gather up, to *esēpum*
gathering *puḫrum*
gaze *niṭlum*
get, to *rašûm*
gift *igisûm*, *nudunnûm*, *qīpum*, *qīštum*, *šeriktum*, (marriage) *biblum*
gird, to *ezēḫum*, oneself *ezēḫum* N
girded, to be *ezēḫum* N
give, to *nadānum*, *qiāšum*, *šarākum*, *šutlumum*
give a judgment, to *diānum*
give a pledge, to *qabâm šakā num*
give a report, to *ṭēmum šakā num*
give back, to *riābum*, *târum* D
give birth to, to *walādum*
give directions, to *ṭēmam šakānum*
give full discretion, to *mala libbi X šumṣûm*
give information/instructions, to *ṭēmam šakānum*
give orders, to *qabûm*, *šapārum*
give strong orders, to *dannātim šakānum*
give to drink, to *šaqûm* a
give to eat, to *akālum* Š
give twice as much, to *šanûm* Št-lex
give water to, to *šaqûm* a
gladness *ṭūbātum*
glance *naplasum*
glide, to *neqelpûm*, *neḫelṣûm*
gloomy *da'ummum*
glory *tanīttum*
glow *zīmum*
glowing *rašubbum*
go, to *alākum*
go around, to *lawûm* a, *saḫā rum*
go away, to *alākum* Gt, *duppurum* D, *paṭārum*
go back, to *târum*
go down, to *warādum*
go forth, to *waṣûm* a
go near, to *ṭeḫûm*
go out, to *belûm*, *waṣûm* a
go surety, to *qātātim leqûm*
go to court, to *diānum*
go to war, to *maḫāṣum* Gt
go up, to *elûm* a
goal *idum*
goats (sheep and) *ṣēnum*
goblet *kāsum*
god *ilum*, (of cunning, fresh water, intelligence) *Ea*, (fire) *Gibil* / *Girra*, (grain) *Dagan*, (pestilence) *Erra*, (river(s)) *Id*, (sky) *Anum*, (storm) *Adad*
goddess *iltum*, *ištarum*
gold *ḫurāṣum*
gone (forth) *waṣûm* b
good (adj.) *banûm* d, *damqum*, *ṭābum*, (n.) *damiqtum*, *ṭūbum*
good, to be(come) *damāqum*, *ṭiābum*
good condition, in *išarum*
good health *napištum*
good looks *bāštum*
good news *bussurtum*
good repair, to be in *bârum* b
goodness *damiqtum*, *ṭūbum*
goods *bašītum*, *makkūrum*, (for transport) *šībultum*
goods outstanding *bābtum*
gore, to *nakāpum*
govern, to *šapārum*
governor *šakkanakkum*, *šaknum*, *šāpirum*, *šāpir mātim*
grain *ašnan*, *ûm*, *uṭṭatum*
grain god *Dagan*
granary *qarītum*
granary silo *našpakum*
grant, to *magārum*, *nadānum*, *qiāšum*
grant a legal case/hearing, to *dīnam šūḫuzum*
granted *qīšum*
grapes, grapevine *karānum*
grasp, to *tamāḫum*, (one another) *ṣabātum* Gt
grass, green *dīšum*
gray(-haired) *šībum*
gray, to be(come) *šiābum*
graze, to (of sheep) *re'ûm*
great *rabûm* b, (very) *rabbûm*
great, to be(come) *rabûm* a
great gods *Igigi*
greatest *šurbûm*
greatly *mādiš*, *rabîš*
greatness *narbûm*, *rabûtum*
green *warqum*
green, to be(come) *warā-*

qum
green grass *dīšum*
greeting *šulmānum, šulmum*
greeting-gift *šulmānum*
grind (flour), to *ṭênum*
ground (adj.) *ṭēnum*
ground (n.) *erṣetum, qaqqarum*
grove *qištum*
grow, to *banûm* c, *rabûm* a, *waṣûm* a
grow crooked, to *garārum*
grow high, to *šiāḫum*
grow old, to *šiābum*
grow tall, to *šiāḫum*
grow thickly, to *šamāḫum*
grow up, to *rabûm* a
grown man *awīlum*
guarantee *qātātum*
guarantee, to *qātātim leqûm*
guard *maṣṣartum, mukīl bābim*
guard, to *naṣārum, palālum,* oneself *naṣārum* Gt
guarded *naṣrum*
guidance *ūsum*
guide, to *redûm, warûm* Gtn, (properly) *ešērum* Št
guilt *arnum*

habitations *dadmū*
hair *šārtam*
hair style characteristic of slaves *abbuttum*
hairy *laḫmum, šu''urum*
half *aḫum, mišlum, muttatum,* in half (adv.) *bāmâ*
half, to be(come) *mašālum*
half shares *mišlānū*
halter *ṣerretum*
hand *qātum, rittum,* left *šumēlum,* right *imittum*
hand over, to *manûm, maḫārum* Š, *nadānum, naḫālum, paqādum*
handiwork *epšēt qātim, liptum*
handle *šikrum*
hang, to *ḫalālum, šaqālum* a R
happen, to *bašûm* a, *maqātum, tebûm* a
happiness *lalûm, ṭūbum, ṭūb libbim*
happy *ḫadûm* b
happy, to be(come) *ḫadûm* a
happy, to make *hadûm* D
harbor (district) *kārum*
hard *dannum*
hard times *dannatum*
hard, unbroken soil *kankallum*
hardship *dannatum, maruštum*
harm, to *ḫabālum*
harness, to *ṣamādum*
harrow, to *šakākum*
haruspex *bārûm*
harvest(-time) *ebūrum*
harvest, to *eṣēdum* G
harvester *ēṣidum*
hasten, to *arāḫum, ḫiāšum*
hate, to *zenûm* a, *zêrum*
haughty *šamāḫum*
haul, to *šadādum*
have, to *išûm, kullum*
have a legal document made out, to *ezēbum* Š
have a miscarriage, to *ša libbim nadûm*
have full discretion, to *mala libbim maṣûm*
have intercourse with, to *ina sūn(i) X niālum / itūlum*
have power over, to *bêlum*
have the use of, to *akālum*
hay *šammum*
he *šū*
head *qaqqadum, rēšum,* (of the family) *ḫammum*
headdress *paršīgum*
headdress, to provide with *apārum*
heal, to (tr.) *balāṭum* D, *šalāmum* D
health *bulṭum, šulmum*
healthy *balṭum*
healthy, to be(come) *balāṭum*
healthy, to keep (someone) *balāṭum* D
heap up, to *kamārum* G, D, *ṣênum, šapākum*
hear, to *šemûm* a
heard *šemûm* b
hearing *tešmûm*
heart *libbum*
heaven *šamû*
heavy *kabtum*
heavy, to be(come) *kabārum, kabātum*
heed, to *ḫasāsum* G, *qâlum, šemûm*
heir *aplum,* (f) *rēdītum*
heir, position of *aplūtum*
help, to *ana X izuzzum, qātam ṣabātum*
helper, position of *tappûtum*
herald *nāgirum*
herb *šammum*
herbage *dīšum*
here *annânum, annīkiam*
hereby, herewith *anumma*
hero *qarrādum, uršānum*
heroism *qarrādūtum*
hide (n.) *maškum*
high *elûm* b, *šaqûm* c, *šīḫum*
high, to be(come) *šaqûm* b, *šiāḫum*
high position *rabûtum*
high priestess *entum*
high status *rabûtum*
hind legs *ḫallān*
hinder, to *kabālum* G, D, *kalûm* a
hinterland *ṣērum*
hip *qablum* a
hire *idum, igrum,* (rate of) *inītum*
hire, to *agārum, waṣûm* a Š
hired, hireling *agrum*
his, her(s) *šûm*
hit, to *maḫāṣum, naṭûm* b, *tarākum*
hither *annîš*
hoe, to *marārum*
hold, to *aḫāzum, kullum, tamāḫum*
hold back, to *kalûm* a
hole *pilšum, šīlum*
holy *ebbum, ellum*
homeless *ekûm*
honest *kīnum*
honest, to be(come) *kânum*
honesty *kīttum*
honor, to *kabātum* D, *rēšam našûm*
honored *kabtum*
honored, to be(come) *kabātum*
horn *qarītum*
horned snake *bašmum*
hostage *līṭum*
hostile *aḫûm, nak(a/i)rum*

hostile, to be(come) *gerûm*, *nakārum*
hostility *nukurtum*
house *bītum*
house builder *itinnum*
house of heaven *Eanna*
household *bītum*
household property *numātum*
how? *kī*
how many/much? *kī (maṣi)*
however many/much *kī (maṣi)*
hug, to *edērum*
human being *awīlum*
humanity *awīlūtum*
humble *maṭûm*
hundred *meatum*
hunger *bubūtum*, *ḫušāḫum*
hurl, to *napāṣum*
hurry, to *ḫiāšum*
husband *mutum*, (first) *ḫāʾirum*/*ḫāwirum*
husband, position of *mutūtum*
hut, shepherd's *gubrum*
Hydra (consellation) *bašmum*

I *anāku*
identify, to *edûm* D
idle, to be(come) *riāqum*, *šutaʾʾûm*
idleness *rīqūtum*
if *šumma*, if indeed *ištū-ma*
ignore, to *nadûm* a
ill *marṣum*
illness *murṣum*
illustrious *šūpûm*
immediately *ana qātim*, *kīma pānī*
immobilize, to *kabālum* G, D
impaling stake *gašīšum*
important *rabûm* b, *wēdûm*
important, to be(come) *baʾālum*, *kabātum*
impose, to *emēdum*, *šakānum*
impose a penalty/punishment, to *šērtam emēdum*/*esērum*
imposing *rašbum*
impoverished, to be(come) *enēšum*
impression, seal *kunukkum*
imprison, to *kasûm* G, D
imprisonment *ṣibittum*
improve, to (intr.) *damāqum*, (tr.) *damāqum* D
improvements *mānaḫtum*
in *ina*, (temporally) *ana*
in a row *sadrum*
in accordance with *ana pī*, *ša pī*
in addition *elēnum*, in addition to *ana ṣēr*
in back of *warki*
in close combat *qerbiš*
in excess *watrum*
in front of *ina pān(i)*, *maḫar*, *meḫret*, *muttiš*
in future *ina warkītim*, *ina*/*ana warkīt ūmim*
in good condition *šalmum*
in half (adv.) *bāmâ*
in order to *ana* + inf.
in residence *wašbum*
in ruins *maqtum*
in the care/charge/custody of *ina*/*ša qāti*
in the company of *itti*
in the direction of *ana ṣēr*
in the future *ina warkītim*, *ina*/*ana warkīt ūmim*
in the jurisdiction of *ina*/*ša qāti*
in the possession of *ina qāti*
in the presence of *ina pān(i)*, *maḫar*
in this manner *kiam*
in view of *ana zīm(ī)*, *ina pān(i)*
inactive, to be(come) *šaḫurūrum*
incite, to *aḫāzum* Š
include, to *manûm* a
included *manûm*
including, inclusive of *qadum*
increase, to (intr.) *miādum* G, *rabûm* a G, (tr.) *miādum* Š, *rabûm* a Š, *waṣābum*, *watārum* D
incur legal claims, to *baqrī rašûm*
indeed *lū*
indicate, to *burrum* D
individual *wēdum*
inform, to *edûm* D, *lamādum* D, *šemûm* a Š, *maḫar ... šakānum*
information *diʾtum*, *mūdûtum*, *ṭēmum*
information, to give *ṭēmam šakānum*
informed *šemûm* b
informed of, to be(come) *lamādum*
inhabited world, the *dadmū*
inheritance *aplūtum*, *zittum*
inimical *nak(a/i)rum*
innkeeper *sābûm*
innocent, to declare *elēlum* D
inquire, to *šâlum*
inscribe, to *šaṭārum*
inscribed *šaṭrum*
inside *ina libbi*, *libbum*, *qerbēnum*, (of the body) *kabattum*
inspect, to *barûm*, *paqādum*, *sanāqum* D
inspected, to be *amārum* N
inspection *piqittum*
inspector *waklum*
install, to *šakānum*, (officers) *wašābum* Š
installment (on loan) *rēštum*
instead of *kīma*
institution of the younger and older heir *aplūtum ṣeḫertum u rabītum*
instruct, to *aḫāzum* Š, *naʾādum*
instruction *milkum*, *qibītum*, *têrtum*, instructions *našpartum*
instructions, to give *ṭēmam šakānum*
insufficient, to be(come) *wiāṣum*
intact *šalmum*
intelligence *milkum*, *uznum*
intelligent *ḫasīsum*
intend, to *pānam*/*pānī šakānum*
intent(ion) *milkum*, *ṭēmum*
intentions, evil *lemuttum*
intercalary month *dirigûm*
interchange *šupêlum* Š(D)t
intercourse with, to have *ina sūn(i) X niālum*/*itūlum*
interest *ṣibtum* a

interest-free advance *ta-miqtum*
intermingle, to *nadānum* Št
interpretation (of omen) *šumum*
interval *birītum*
intervening space *birītum*
intestines *errū*
into *ana libbi*, *ina*
into the care/custody of *ana muḫḫi*, *ana qāt(i)*
into the possession of *ana qāt(i)*
into the presence of *ana maḫar*
intoxicating liquid *šikarum*
inundate, to *raḫāṣum*
invade, to *erēbum*
invalidate, to (a tablet, document) *ḫepûm*
invert, to *enûm*
investigate, to *awātam*/*awâtim amārum*, *sanāqum*, *warkatam parāsum*
invite, to *qerûm*
invoke, to *nabûm* a, *zakārum*, (blessings) *karābum*
iridescent (eyes) *šitʾārum*
irrigation *šiqītum*
irrigation outlet *mašqītum*
is/are not *laššu*
issue commands, to *piam šakānum*
it (f) *šī*, (m) *šū*

join, to *emēdum* Št-lex, *kasûm* G, (with one another) *ṣabātum* Gt, (together) *kasûm* G, D, *kaṣārum*
join forces, to *emēdum* N
joined *kaṣrum*, *tiṣbutum*
joined, to be *emēdum* N
joint (of body,plant) *kiṣrum*
journey *gerrum*, *ḫarrānum*
joy *ḫūdum*, *mēleṣum*, *rīštum*, *ulṣum*
joyful *ḫadûm* b
joyfully *ḫadîš*
judge *dayyānum*
judge, to *diānum*
judgment *dīnum*
judgment, to give a *diānum*
jug *assammum*
junior wife *šugītum*
just *išarum*, *kīnum*
just, to be(come) *kânum*
just before *ina pān(i)*
justice *kīttum*, *mīšarum*
justify, to *kânum* Št

keep, to *naṣārum*
keep away, to *parāsum*, *qātam nasāḫum*
keep distant, to *rêqum* D
keep in custody, to *kalûm* a
keep pure, to *elēlum* D
keep safe, to *šalāmum* D
keep together, to *ṣabātum* Št-lex
keep waiting, to *zabālum* D
keep well, to *šalāmum* D
keep whole, to *šalāmum* D
kick, to *napāṣum*
kill, to *dâkum*, *maḫāṣum*, *nêrum*
kindled *naphum*
kindled, to be *napāḫum* N
kindly, to treat *gamālum*
kindness *ṭābtum*, *ṭūbum*
king *šarrum*, (usurper) *šar ḫammê*
kingship *šarrūtum*
kiss, to *našāqum*
kneel, to *kamāsum* b
knock out, to *nadûm* a
knot *kiṣrum*
know, to *edûm*/*idum*, (sexually) *lamādum*
knowledge *mūdûtum*, *nēmequm*
known, to make *edûm* D

labor *šiprum*
laborer (farm) *ikkarum*
lady *awīltum*, *bēltum*
laid *nadûm* b
lame *pissûm*
land *erṣetum*, *mātum*, (plot) *eqlum*
land agent *iššiakkum*
land-registry officer *šassukkum*
lap *sūnum*
lapis lazuli *uqnûm*
large *rabûm* b
large, to be(come) *rabûm* a, (abnormally) *baʾālum*
last, to *arākum*, *bitrûm* Gt, *kânum*, *labārum*
last, to make *bitrûm* Št-lex
last long, to *arākum*
lasting *dārûm*
later *warkānum*, *warkûm*
later on *ina warkītim*
later time *warkītum*
laughter *ṣīḫtum*
lawsuit *dabābum*, *dīnum*, *rugummûm*
lawsuit, to start a *diānum*, *gerûm*
lax, to be(come) *nīdi aḫim rašûm*
laxity *nīdi aḫim*
lay (down), to *nadûm* a
lay claim to, to *baqārum*, *redûm*
lay criminal charge, to *nadûm* a
lazy, to be(come) *šutaʾʾûm*
lead, to *pān(i) X ṣabātum*, *redûm*G,Š, *tarûm*,*warûm*
lead forth, to *tarûm*
lead out, to *waṣûm* a Š
lead-rope *ṣerretum*
lean, to *emēdum* G, D
learn, to *aḫāzum*, *lamādum*
lease *ṣītum*
leasehold estate *šūṣûtum*
leave, to *ezēbum*, *naparkûm*, *waṣûm* a
leave behind, to *ezēbum*
leave idle, to *riāqum* D, Š
left (hand, side) *šumēlum*
legs, hind *ḫallān*
legal case *dīnum*
legal claim(s) *baqrum*/*baqrū*, *rugummûm*
legal claims, to incur *baqrī rašûm*
legal decision *dīnum*, *purussûm*
legitimate *kīnum*
lend, to *šutlumum*
lend a hand, to *tappût X alākum*
lengthen, to *arākum* D, Š
leprosy *epqum*, (to become covered with) *epqam malûm*
letter *našpartum*, *ṭuppum*
levy *tibûtum*
liability, financial *eʾiltum*
liar *sarrum*
lie (n.) *sartum*
lie, to *niālum*, G, Gt, *sakāpum* b

lie across, to *parākum*
lie against, to *naparkudum*
lie crosswise, to *parākum*
lie down, to *niālum* , G, Gt, *sakāpum* b
lie flat, to *naparkudum*
lie upon/against one another, to *rakābum* Gt
lieutenant *laputtûm*
life *balāṭum, bulṭum* , *napiš tum, nīšum*
lift (up), to *našûm*
light *nannarum*
light (a fire, stove), to *napāḫum*
light, to be(come) *nawārum*
like *kīma*
likewise *malmališ* , *u*
line (of tablet, composition) *šumum*
lion *lābum, nēšum*
lip *šaptum*
liquid *mû*
list *meḫrum*
listen, to *šemûm* a
litigant *ša dīnim*
litter (of leaves, etc.) *ḫāmū*
little *wīṣum*
little, to be(come) *ṣeḫērum*, *wiāṣum*
live, to *alākum* Gtn, *balāṭum, ramûm* , *wašābum*
livelihood *napištum*
liver, sheep's *amūtum*
liver omen *amūtum*
load *biltum*
load, to *emēdum, rakābum* Š, *ṣênum*
lobe *naplasum*
locale *ašrum*
located *šaknum*
location *maškanum*
lock, to *edēlum*
locust(s) *erbûm*
log *gušūrum*
long *arkum*
long, to be(come) *arākum*
look (n.) *naplasum* , *niṭlum*
look after, to *paqādum*
look at, to *amārum, barûm, dagālum, naṭālum* G, Gt, *īnīn ana X našûm*, (from a distance) *ṣubbûm*
look for, to *saḫārum, še*ʾ*ûm*
look into a matter/case/situation, to *awātam* / *awâ tim amārum*
look up, to *īnīn našûm*
look upon, to *dagālum*
looks *zīmum*
loose, to be(come) *pašārum* N
loose earth *ep(e)rum*
loosen, to *nê*ʾ*um, pašārum, paṭārum*
loot, to *šalālum*
lord *bēlum*
lordship *bēlutum*
loss *bābtum* , *bitiqtum, ibbûm, nēkemtum, ṣītum, ta*ʾ*īṣtum*, (financial) *ibissûm*, losses *imṭû*
lost *ḫalqum*
lost, to be(come) *ḫalāqum*
lost property *ḫulqum*
love *ru*ʾ*āmum*
love, to *râmum*
loveliness *īrimum*
low *maṭûm*
low, to be(come) *šapālum*
lower *šaplûm*
lower extremities *išdum*
lower part *šēpītum*
lowering *nīdum*
loyal *kīnum*
loyalty *kīttum*
luck *damiqtum*
lumber *iṣum*
lump *kiṣrum*
lung *ḫašûm*
luxuriance *kuzbum* , *lalûm*
luxury *lalûm*
lying *nadûm* b, *šaknum* , (crosswise) *parkum*
Lyra (constellation) *enzum*

magnificent *šarāḫum*
maintain, to *kânum* D, *kullum*
maintenance *mānaḫtum*
majestic, to be(come) *šamāḫum*
majesty *šarrūtum*
make, to *epēšum*
make a mistake, to *ḫaṭûm*
make appear, to *bašûm* Š
make difficult,to *kabātum* D
make disappear,to *ḫalāqum* D
make distant, to *rêqum* D
make emerge, to *elûm* a Š
make false claims, to *sarārum* D
make good, to *damāqum* D, *šalāmum* D, *ṭiābum* D
make great, to *rabûm* D, Š
make happy, to *hadûm* D
make known, to *edûm* D, Š
make large, to *rabûm* D
make last, to *bitrûm* Št-lex, *labārum* D
make love,to *ulṣam epēšum*
make much, to *miādum* Š
make numerous,to *miādum* Š
make out a contract, to *riksam* / *riksātim šakānum*
make out a legal document, to *ezēbum*
make pleasing,to *damāqum* D
make prosper, to *ešērum* Š
make ready, to *ṣamādum*
make sick, to *marāṣum* Š
make similar, to *mašālum* D
make suffice, to *maṣûm* Š
make unhappy, to *marāṣum* Š
make war,to *kakkī epēšum* , *tāḫāzam epēšum*
make weak, to *enēšum* D
make worried, to *marāṣum* Š
male *zikarum*
male donkey *imērum*
male servant *ṣuḫārum*, *wardum*
male slave *wardum*
malevolent *lemnun*
malformed newborn *izbum*
malice *zapurtum*
malicious *zaprum*
man *mutum* , *zikarum*, (free) *awīlum* , (grown) *awīlum* , (young) *eṭlum*
man-servant *wardum*
manage, to *babālum* Gtn
manumission (of slaves) *andurārum*
many *mādum*
Marduk *Marduk*
Marduk temple (Borsippa) *Ezida*
mark *šimtum*

mark, to *edûm* D
market place *maḫīrum*
marriage *aššūtum*
marriage gift *biblum*
marry, to *aḫāzum*, *leqûm*
master *bēlum*
master, to be(come) *leʾûm*
match, to *šanānum*
mate, to *rakābum* Gt, *reḫûm*
mate, to choose a *ḫiārum*
material assigned *isiḫtum*
matter *awātum*
mature *rabûm* b
mayor *rabiānum*
meadow *ugārum*
meaning *šumum*
means of, by *ina*
measure (of silver, flour) *bitqum*
measure, to *madādum*, *šadādum*
measure out, to *madādum*
meat *šīrum*
median *qablûm* a
meet, to *amārum* N, *emēdum* N, *maḫārum* G, Gt, (one another) *watûm* Št
meeting *puḫrum*
membrane *šīšītum*
mention *zikrum*
mention, to *ḫasāsum*, *zakārum*
merchandise outstanding *bābtum*
merchant *tamkārum*
merchant community *kārum*
message *awātum*, *bussurtum*, *našpartum*, *šiprum*
messenger *ālikum*, *mār šip rim*, *našparum*, (express) *lāsimum*
metal-worker *gurgurrum*
meteor *kakkabum*
mid *qablûm* a
middle/midst *libbum*, *mišlum*, *qablum* a
midst of, in the *ina libbi*
mighty *dannum*
mile *bērum*
military campaign *gerrum*, *ḫarrānum*
military campaign, to undertake a *ḫarranam alākum*
military officer *wakil Amurrîm*
military outpost *baz(a)ḫatum*
military scribe *ṭupšar ummānim*
military service *dannatum*
milk *šizbum*
mind *kabattum*, *libbum*, *ṭēmum*
mindful of, to be *ḫasāsum*
minister *s* / *šukallum*
miscarriage, to have a *ša lib bim nadûm*
misdeed *sartum*
misfortune *aḫītum*, *lemuttum*
miss, to *ḫaṭûm*
missing *ḫalqum*, *maṭûm*
missing, to be(come) *ḫalāqum*
missing property *ḫulqum*
mission *šiprum*
mistake, to make a *ḫaṭûm*
mistreat, to *ašāšum* D
mistress *bēltum*
mobilize, to *dekûm*
moist *raṭābum*
money lender *ummiānum*
month *warḫum*, (intercalary) *dirigûm*
monthly *warḫišam*
mood *milkum*
more than *eli*
moreover *appūna*, *appūnāma*, *šanītam*, *u*
mother *ummum* a
motion,to be in *alākum* Gtn
mount, to *rakābum*, (with a precious material) *aḫāzum* D
mountain (region) *šadûm*
mountain pass *nērebum*
mouse *ḫumuṣṣīrum*
mouth *pûm*
move, to *akāšum*, *alākum*, *dekûm*, *nagarrurum*, *namāšum*, *nâšum* G,D
move along, to *redûm*
move away, off, to *elûm* a Gt, *nesûm* a, *rêqum* Š
move on, to *alākum* Gt, *etēqum*, *nasāḫum*
move straight toward, to *ešērum* G, Š
moveable property *bašītum*
movement *alaktum*
much *mādiš*, *mādum*
much, to be(come) *miādum*
mud brick *libittum*
multicolored *barmum*, *bitrāmum*
multicolored, to be *barāmum*
murder *nērtum*
murmur, to *ḫabābum*
musician *nārum* b
musician's craft *nārūtum*
muster *tibûtum*
muster, to *paqādum*
my, mine *yûm*

name *šumum*, *zikrum*
name, to *nabûm* a, *ana šumim nabûm*, *zakārum*
named *ana šumim nabûm*
narrow *qatnum*
narrow, to be(come) *piāqum*, *qatānum*
native land *mātum*
navel *abunnatum*
near (adj.) *qerbum*, (prep.) *idi*
nearby region *lētum*
neck *kišādum*
need *ḫušāḫum*, *ṣibûtum*
need, to *ḫašāḫum*
neglect, to *ezēbum*, *mašûm*, *nadûm* a
negligence *ēgûtum*, *ḫīṭum*, *nīdi aḫim*
negligent, to be *aḫam nadûm*, *egûm*, *nīdi aḫim rašûm*
neighbor *itûm*
neighborhood *bābtum*
neighboring area/field/region *itûm*, *ṭeḫḫûm*
net *pūgum*, *šētum*
nether world *erṣetum*
network, covered with *edḫum*
never *matī-ma* (+ neg.)
new *eššum*
new, to be(come) *edēšum*
new moon *warḫum*
news *ṭēmum*, (good) *bussur tum*
next to *idi*
night *mušītum*, *mūšum*
nighttime *mušītum*
nine *tiše*
ninth *tešûm*

no one *ayyumma* (+ neg.), *mamman* (+ neg.), *ma-nāma* (+ neg.)
noble *rabbûm*
noise *rigmum*
noisy *ḫabrum*
noisy, to be *ḫabārum*
none *manāma* (+ neg.)
normal *išarum*, *kayyānum*, *kīnum*
normal situation *kīttum*
normality *kīttum*
nose *appum*
nose-rope *ṣerretum*
not *lā*, *ul*
not, (there) is/are *laššu*
not yet *adīni*
notable *wēdûm*
nothing *mimma* (+ neg.)
notice *di'tum*
now *anumma*, *inanna*
number agreed upon *ap-šitûm*
numerous, to be(come) *miādum*

oath *tumāmītum*, *zikrum*
obedient *šemûm* b
obediently *ana pîm*
obey, to *šemûm* a
object, to *epēsum* G, D
object of trust *tukultum*
obligation *ḫubullum*, *pīḫa-tum*, (financial) *e'iltum*
observe, to *amārum*, *barûm*, *naṭālum*
obstruct, to *parākum*
obstruction *miqtum*
obtain, to *leqûm*, *rašûm*, *waṣûm* a Š, (a wife for s.o.) *aḫāzum* Š
occupied, to be *ṣabātum* Gt
occupy, to *palāsum* D
occur, to *amārum* N, *tebûm* a
occur regularly, to *sadā-rum*
of *ša*
off, to be *alākum* Gt
offense *arnum*, *ḫatītum*, *ḫī-ṭum*
offense, to commit an *ḫa-ṭûm*
offer, to *maḫārum* Š, *na-qûm*, *qerēbum* D
offering *igisûm*, *niqûm*, (sheep) *šuginûm*
office *parṣum*
official (of temple or estate) *abarakkum*,
officials *awīlû šūt pīḫatim*
offshoot of a canal *atappum*
offspring *zērum*
oil *šamnum*
old *labirum*
old, to be(come) *labārum*, *šiābum*
old age *šībūtum*
old man *šībum*
oldest son *aplum*
omen (liver) *amūtum*, (ex-tispicy) *têrtum*
omen report *têrtum*
on *eli*, *ina*, *ina muḫḫi*
on account of *ana pān(i)*
on hand *bašûm* b
on hand, what is *bašītum*
on the side of *idi*
on top *eliš*
on top of *ina muḫḫi*, *ina ṣēr*
once *ištīššu*
one *ištēn*, as one *ištēniš*, one time *ištīššu*
one ... the other *aḫum aḫam*, *annûm* ... *annûm*
one-eighth *samnat*
one-fifth *ḫamšum* b
one-fourth *rebiat*
one-ninth *tešiat*
one-seventh *sebītum*
one-sixth *šuššum*
one-tenth *ešret*
one-third *šalšum* b, *šuššān*
one-twelfth *šinšerûm*
oneself *ramānum*
onslaught *tībum*
onto *ina muḫḫi*
open *petûm* b
open, to *petûm* a G,D, (one's mouth) *piam epēšum*
open country *kīdum*, *mā-tum*
open field *ugārum*
opening *bābum*, *mūṣûm*, *pītum*, *pûm*, *teptītum*, (ca nal) *bitqum*
opinion *niṭlum*
oppose one another, to *ma-ḫā rum* Gt
opposite (prep.) *ana pān(i)*, *ina pūt*
opposite (side) *meḫretum*
oppress, to *ḫabālum*
or *ū*
oracle *têrtum*
orally *ina pîm*
orchard *kirûm*
order *qibītum*, *têrtum*
order, to *qabûm*, *wârum* D
orders, to give strong *dan-nātim šakānum*
organize, to *babālum* Gtn, *kaṣārum*
organized *kaṣrum*
organization (of a govern-ment) *išdum*
origin *ṣītum*
original *labirum*
Orion *šitaddarum*
orphan(ed) *ekûm*
other *šanûm* c
other than *ullânum*
our(s) *nûm*
oust, to *elûm* a Š
out of *ina*, *ina libbi*, *ištu*
outlying regions *aḫiātum*
outside *ana kīdim*, *ina kī-dim*, *waṣûm* b
outside (region) *kīdum*
outskirts *aḫiātum*
outstanding *ṣīrum*
over *eli*, *ina muḫḫi*
overlaid *za'num*
overlay, to *za'ānum* D, (with a precious mate-rial) *aḫāzum* D
overpower (someone), to *le'ûm*
oversee, to *ana pānī izuz-zum*, *šapārum*
overseer *šāpirum*, *waklum*
overthrow, to *maqātum* Š, *nabalkutum*
overturn, to *sakāpum* a
overwhelm, to *saḫāpum*
owe, to (see *išûm*)
own (one's) *ramānum*
own, to *išûm*
owner (f) *bēltum*, (m) *bē-lum*
owner status *bēlūtum*
ox *alpum*, (reserve) *gimlum*
ox-driver *kullizum*
ox-tail *qinnāzum*

pacify, to *nâḫum* D, *pašā-*

ḫum D,Š
pain *murṣum*
painful *marṣum*
painful, to be(come) *kabātum, marāṣum*
palace (royal) *ekallum*
palace gate (ext.) *bāb ekallim*
palace official *ekallûm*
pale, to turn *warāqum*
paralyzed, to be(come) *šaḫururum*
pardon *tayyartum*
partner *tappûm*
partner, position of *tappûtum*
partnership *athûtum, salīmātum, tappûtum*
pass, to *etēqum, nabalkutum,* (of time) *nasāḫum*
pass across/along/by, to *etēqum*
pass over, to *nabalkutum*
pass through, to *etēqum*
passage *alaktum*
pasture (n.) *merītum,* (spring) *dīšum*
pasture, to *reʾûm*
pasture-land *merītum*
patches, covered with *edḫum*
paternal estate *bīt abim*
path *gerrum, ḫarrānum, kibsum, padānum, urḫum*
patrimony *bīt abim*
pay, to *apālum, madādum, šaqālum* a
pay as interest, to *waṣābum*
pay attention, to *naʾādum, qâlum*
pay back, to *târum* D
pay in full, to *malûm* a D
payment *idum,* (for catching a fugitive) *sikmū,* (for rent, services, etc.) *kiṣrum*
peace *nēḫtum, salīmum*
peaceful, to be(come) *nâḫum*
peak *rēštum*
pebble *abnum*
peg *sikkatum*
pen *supūrum*
penalty *rugummûm, šērtum* a

penalty, to impose a *šērtam esērum*
people *awīlūtum, nišū*
perform corvée service, to *ḫarrānam alākum*
perform extispicy, to *têrtam epēšum*
perform *ilkum*-service, to *ilkam alākum*
perhaps *minde, pīqat*
period of time *adānum*
periphery *kibrātum*
perish, to *ḫalāqum*
permanent status of property *dūrum* b
permit, to *magārum, nadānum*
perpetual *dārûm*
perpetuity *dāriātum, dārum*
person *awīlum, lānum, napištum, qaqqadum*
person endowed with favor *migrum*
person of equal status *ibrum*
person of same rank *meḫrum*
personnel *napištum*
persuade, to *dekûm* Š (rare)
pestilence, god of *Erra*
petition, to *qerēbum* Š
physician *asûm*
physician's lancet *karzillum*
pierce, to *batāqum, palāšum*
pig *šaḫûm*
pile up, to *kamārum* G, D, *nasākum, šapākum*
pinch, to *karāṣum*
pity *rēmum*
place *ašrum*
place, to *emēdum, šakānum*
place around, to *saḫārum* Š
place under seal, to *kanākum*
placed *šaknum*
plague *bibbum, mūtānū*
plain, to be(come) *pānam rašûm*
plan, to *ḫasāsum*
plant *šammum*
plant, to *erēšum* b, *zaqāpum*
play, to *mēleṣum*
plaza *rebītum*

plea *dabābum*
plead (in court), to *dabābum*
pleasant *ṭābum*
pleasant, to be(come) *banûm* c, *ṭiābum*
pleasantly *ṭābiš*
please *apputtum*
please, to *gamālum, īn X maḫārum, šebûm* D, *ṭiābum* D
pleasing *ṭābum*
pleasing, to be(come) *ṭiābum*
pleasure *ṭūbātum*
pledge *lītum, nipûtum, qātātum*
plentiful, to be(come) *miādum*
plenty *nuḫšum*
plot of land *eqlum, qaqqarum*
plow *mayyarum*
plow, to *erēšum* b, *maḫāṣum, eqlam mayyarī ma ḫāṣum*
plowing *ikkarūtum*
plowman *ikkarum*
plunder *šallatum*
plunder, to *ḫabātum, mašāʾum, šalālum*
plundered *ḫabtum*
plunge into, to *šalûm*
pointed, to be(come) *edēdum*
polished *ebbum*
pollinate, to *rakābum* D
ponder, to *awûm* Št, *šâlum* Gt
poor *lapnum, matûm*
poor, to be(come) *lapānum*
poor person *šukênum*
portion (agreed) *apšītûm,* (food) *kurummatum*
position *nazzazum,* (of heir) *aplūtum,* (of power) *bēlūtum,* (of slave) *wardūtum*
positive answer *annum*
possibility *rittum*
possibly *minde*
pot *karpatum*
pound, to *tarākum*
pounded *tarkum*
pour, to *nadûm* a, *naqûm, šapākum*
pour out, to *naqûm*

power *dannūtum*
power over, to have *bêlum*
power position *bēlūtum*
powerful *dannum, gašrum, ḫaptum*
powerful, to be(come) *gašārum, ḫapātum*
powerless *enšum*
praise *tanittum*
praise, to *karābum*
prayer *ikribum*
pre-eminent *šūturum, watrum*
precious *nasqum*
precious, to be(come) *waqārum*
precious stone *abnum*
prefect *šāpirum*
pregnant *arītum*
pregnant, to be(come) *arûm*
prepare for planting, to *zaqāpum*
present (adj.) *bašûm* b, *šaknum*
present, to *qerēbum* D
present, to be *bašûm* a
preserve, to *šalāmum* D
press, to *ḫalāṣum*, (for payment) *esērum* b G,D
pressure, to put under *esērum* b G,D
prevail, to *ḫapātum*
prevent, to *kalûm* a
previous *maḫrûm, pānûm*
previously *pāna*
price *šīmum*
pride *bāštum*
prince *etellum, rubûm*
princely *etellum*
princess *etelletum, rubātum*
principal (amount) *qaqqadum, rēšum*
principality *rubûtum*
prison *ṣibittum*
prisoner *ṣabtum*
private room *kummum*
proceed to *ešērum* Št, *etēqum, pānam / pānī šakānum*
proceed against, to *sanāqum*
proclaim, to *edûm* Š, *nabûm* a, *šasûm, wapûm* Š
proclaimed *šūpûm*
proclaimed, to be *wapûm* Št
procrastinate, to *nīdi aḫim rašûm*
procrastination *nīdi aḫim*
procreate, to *reḫûm*
produce (n.) *ṣītum*
produce,to *bašûm* Š, *waṣûm* a Š, (a person, document) *kullummum*, (a witness/ document) *elûm* a Š
product *ṣītum*
profit *nēmelum*
progeny *niprum, zērum*
prolong, to *arākum* D, Š, (the life of) *labārum* D
promise, to *qabâm šakānum*
promulgate, to *wapûm* Š
prone to goring *nakkaptum*
proper *kīnum*
proper appearance/behavior *simtum*
property *makkūrum, mimmû, siliktum, unūtum*, (built-on) *bītum epšum*, (lost/missing) *ḫulqum*, (permanent status of) *dūrum* b
prosper, to *damāqum, ešērum, šalāmum*
prosperity *buʾārum, nuḫšum*
prosperous *išarum*
prostitute *ḫarīmtum, šamḫatum*
prostrate oneself, to *šukênum*
protect, to *naṣārum*
protected *naṣrum*
protective spirit *lamassum, šēdum*
protest, to *dabābum*
protrude, to *waṣûm* a
protruding *waṣûm* b
proud *šamāḫum, šarāḫum*
proud, to make *šarāḫum* D
prove, to *bârum* b D
proved, to be(come) *bârum* b
provide (for), to *našûm* Gtn, (in full) *malûm* a Št, (justice0 *ešērum* Št, (with clothing) *labāšum* D
provided *šaknum*
provisions *ukultum*, (travel) *gerrum*
proximity *ṭēḫum*
pull, to *šadādum*
pull out, to *šalāpum*
punishment *arnum, šērtum* a
punishment, to impose *šērtam esērum*
purchase *šīmum*
purchase, to *šamum*
purchase price *maḫīrum*
purchased *šāmum*
pure *ebbum, ellum, zakûm* b
pure, to be(come) *elēlum*
pure, to keep *elēlum* D
purification *tazkītum, tēliltum*
purify, to *ebēbum* D, *elēlum* D
purpose *idum, ṣibûtum*
pursue, to *kašādum* D
push, to *emēdum* D
push away, to *sakāpum* a
put, to *šakānum*
put at rest, to *nâḫum* D
put back, to *târum* D
put in order, to *ešērum* Št, *sadārum*
put on (clothing), to *labāšum, labāšum* Gt, *rakāsum*
put out, to *belûm* D
put to death, to *mâtum* Š
put together,to *kaṣārum*
put under pressure, to *esērum* b G,D

quake, to *râdum*
quarrel *risibtum*
quarrel, to *ṣabātum* Gt,Št
quarter, city *bābtum*
quay (wall) *kārum*
queen *šarratum*
question, to *sanāqum* G,D, *šâlum* Gt
quickly *arḫis*
quickly, to act/do *edēdum* D
quiet *nēḫum*
quiet, to *pašāḫum* Š

radiant, brilliantly *šalummum*
rage *uzzum*
rain *zunnum*
raise, to *dekûm, elûm* a D,

Š, *izuzzum* Š, *našûm, rabûm* D, *šuqqûm* D, (oneself) *elûm* a Dtr
raise objections, to *pānam rašûm*
raising *tarbītum, tībûtum*
ram *immerum*
ransom (n.) *ipṭerū*
ransom, to *paṭārum*
rate *maḫīrum*, (of hire) *inītum*
ration (barley) *iprum*, (food) *kurummatum*
reach, to *emēdum, kašādum, sanāqum*
reach, to make *maṣûm* D
reach out, to *tarāṣum*
read, to *amārum, šasûm* G,Gtn
ready for, to be *rēšam kullum*
reap, to *eṣēdum* G
rear (part) *warkatum, zibbatum*
rear, in the *warka* a
rebel, to *nabalkutum*
rebellion *nabalkattum*
rebellious *tebûm* b
rebels *ḫammû*
rebuild, to *banûm* a
recede, to *nesûm* a
receive, to *leqûm, maḫārum, našûm, rašûm*
received *maḫrum*
recognize, to *edûm* D
recover, to *balāṭum, šalāmum*
red *sāmum*, red spot *sūmum*
redeem, to *paṭārum*
redness *sūmum*
redress *mīšarum*
reduce, to *ṣeḫērum* D
reduce to ruins, to *nadûm* Š
reed *qanûm*
reed bed, marsh *appārum*
reed thicket *apum*
refer to, to *ḫasāsum*
refine *qalûm*
reflect, to *šâlum* Gt
refrain, to *ana kalûm* a
refresh oneself, to *pašāḫum*
region *eqlum, kiṣrum, mātum, qaqqarum*, (nearby) *lētum*, (outside) *kīdum*, regions *kibrātum*
register, to *šaṭārum*
registered *šaṭrum*
regular *išarum, kīnum, sadrum*
regularly, to do/occur *sadārum*
reign *palûm*
reinforce, to *danānum* a D
reject, to *nasāḫum, sakāpum* a
rejoice, to *elēṣum, ḫadûm* a, *riāšum, ulṣam epēšum*
rejoicing *ḫadûm* b, *rīštum, ulṣum*
relative *qerbum*, relatives *nišūtum*
relax, to *napāšum, šutaʾʾûm*
relaxed, to be(come) *pašārum* N
release (n.) *tazkītum*
release, to *maṣûm* D, *pašārum, waṣûm* a Š, *(w)uššurum, zakûm* a D
relent, to *nâḫum*
reliable *qīpum, taklum*
religious festival *isinnum*
remain, to *bitrûm* Št-lex, *wašābum*
remainder *rēḫtum, šapiltum*
remember, to *ḫasāsum*
remind, to *ḫasāsum* D
remission (of debts) *andurārum*
remote *nesûm* b, (in time) *labirum*
removal *nisḫum*
remove, to *dekûm, elûm* a Š, *nakārum* D, *nasāḫum, našûm, nesûm* D, *paṭārum, rêqum* Š, *šaqālum* b, *tebûm* a Š, *waṣûm* a Š, (oneself) *nasāḫum*, (by force) *sepûm*
rendering (of accounts) *ipšum*
renew, to *edēšum* D
rent *biltum, idum, igrum*
rent, to *agārum, waṣûm* a Š
rented *agrum*
repair, to be in good *bârum* b
repeat, to *šanûm* D
repel, to *napāšum, saḫārum* D, *sakāpum* a
replace, to *riābum*, (in full) *šalāmum* D
replacement *pūḫum*
reply *meḫrum*
report *ṭēmum*
report, to *pašārum*
reputation *šumum*
request *erištum, ṣibûtum*
request, to *erēšum* a
requested *eršum*
require, to *ḫašāḫum*
reserve (of barley) *aldûm*
reserve ox *gimlum*
resettle (people), to *wašābum* Š
reside, to *ramûm, wašābum*
residence *šubtum*
resident *wašbum*
respect, to *palāḫum*
respond, to *apālum*
responsibility *pīḫatum, qātum*
responsible for, to be *ana X izuzzum, apālum* Gtn
rest *rēḫtum*
rest, to *emēdum* D, *nâḫum, sakāpum* b
restore, to *edēšum* D, *târum* D
resume, to *redûm* Št-lex
retainers *ṣeḫḫerum*
retreat *nabalkattum*
return (n.) *tayyartum*
return, to *târum* G (intr.), D (tr.)
reveal, to *edûm* D, *kullumum*, (a dream) *pašārum*
revere, to *palāḫum*
reverential *palḫum*
revoke, to *enûm*
revolt *nabalkattum*
rib *ṣēlum*
ride, to *rakābum*
right (side, hand) *imittum*
right, on the *imittam*
right now *kīma inanna*
rim *kibrum, šaptum*
ring *šeršerrum, šērtum* b, *unqum*
rise (n.) *ṣītum, tībum*
rise up, to *tebûm* a
rising *tībûtum*, (sun) *ṣītum*
rite *parṣum*, rites (cultic) *sakkû*
rival, to *maḫārum* Št, *ša-*

nānum G,Gt
river *nārum* a
river god, the *Id*
road *alaktum*, *gerrum*, *ḫarrānum*, *padānum*, *urḫum*
roast, to *qalûm*
rob, to *ḫabātum*, *mašāʾum*
robbed *ḫabtum*
robber *ḫabbātum*
robbery *ḫubtum*
rock *abnum*
roll, to *garārum*, *šugarrurum*, (around) *na garrurum*
roof *rugbum*
roof (over), to *ruggubum*
room, private *kummum*
rope *ašlum*, *eblum*
rotate, to *saḫārum*
round *garrum*
rout, to *naprušum* Š
royal decree *ṣimdatum*
rub, to *pašāšum*
ruins, in *nawûm*
rule as king, to *šarrūtam epēšum*
rule (n.) *bēlūtum*
rule, to *bêlum*, *bēlūtam epēšum*, *warûm* Gtn
ruler *rubûm*
rumor *dabābum*
run around, to *alākum* Gtn

sacred building *gigunnûm*
sacrifice *niqûm*
sacrifice, to *naqûm*
safe *balṭum*, *nēḫum*, *šalmum*
safe, to be(come) *šalāmum*
safe, to keep (someone) *balāṭum* D
safe-keeping *maṣṣar(ū)tum*
sail (downstream), to *neqelpûm*
sailor *malāḫum*
sake of, for the *aššum*
sanctuary *parakkum*
sate oneself, to *šebûm*
satisfaction *ṭūbātum*
satisfied, to be(come) *šebûm*, *ṭiābum*
satisfy, to *šebûm* D, *ṭiābum* D, (a claim/demand) *apālum*
savage *dannum*
save, to *gamālum*, (persons, cities) *ezēbum* Š
say, to *qabûm*
saying *qabûm*
scaling (of a wall) *nabalkattum*
scar *ziḫḫum*
scatter, to *ramûm*, *sapāḫum*
scepter *ḫaṭṭum*
scholar *ummiānum*
school *bīt ṭuppim*
scraps *tuḫḫum*
scribe *ṭupšarrum*, (state) *mār bīt ṭuppim*
seah *sūtum*
seal (cylinder) *kunukkum*
seal impression *kunukkum*
seal, to *kanākum*
sealed *kankum*
sealed document *kanīkum*
sealed letter *ṣeʾpum*
sealed tablet *kunukkum*
search, to *ḫiāṭum*, *šeʾûm*
seat *kussûm*, *mūṣarum*
seated *wašbum*
second (adj.) *šanûm* c, (n.; of time) *uṭṭatum*
secondly *šanītam*
secrecy *aḫītum*
section *kiṣrum*
secure *nēḫum*
secure, to be(come) *kânum*
security *nēḫtum*
see, to *amārum*, *naṭālum*, *palāsum* N, (one another) *amārum* N
seed *zērum*
seed, to *erēšum* b
seek, to *saḫārum*, *šeʾûm*
seen *amrum*
seen, to be *amārum* N
seize, to *aḫāzum*, *ṣabātum*
seized *ṣabtum*
seizure *kišittum*, *ṣibtum* b
select, to *nasāqum*
selected *nasqum*
self *napištum*, *pagrum*, *ramānum*
sell, to *pašārum*, *ana kaspim nadānum*
send, to *ešērum* Š, *ṭarādum*, *warûm* Š, *wârum* D, (by boat) *sakāpum* a, (a message/messenger, report) *šapārum*
send away, to *saḫārum* D, *waṣûm* a Š
send back, to *saḫārum* D, *târum* D
send down, to *warādum* Š
send near, to *qerēbum* D
send on, to *etēqum* Š
send out, to *waṣûm* a Š
send upstream, to *šaqûm* a D
send word, to *šapārum*
sending *šiprum*
separate (adj.) *parsum*
separate, to *parāsum*, *zâzum*
separated *parsum*
serf *šukênum*
serious *kabtum*
servant (female) *amtum*, *ṣuḫārtum*, (male) *ṣuḫārum*, *wardum*
serve, to (see *izuzzum*)
service *rēšūtum*, services *inītum*
sesame *šamaššammū*
set, to *emēdum* D, *izuzzum* Š, *kânum* D, *nadānum*, *nadûm* a, *šiāmum*, (with a precious material) *aḫāzum* D
set aside, to *tebûm* a Š
set down, to *nadûm* a
set free, to *pašārum*, *(w)uššurum*
set in motion, to *nâšum* D
set on the proper course, to *ešērum* Š
set out, to *tebûm* a
set right, to *ešērum* Št
set straight, to *ešērum* Š
set up, to *izuzzum* Š, *kânum* D, *tarāṣum*, *zaqāpum*
setting *ašrum*
settle, to *gamārum*, *wašābum* Š
settled *gamrum*
settlement *dimtum*, settlements *dadmū*
seven *sebe*
seventh *sebûm*
severe *dannum*
severed part (ext.) *dikšum*
sexual attractiveness *inbum*, *kuzbum*
sexual parts *kuzbum*
sexual vigor *kuzbum*
shake, to *ratātum*, *râdum*
Shamash *Šamaš*

shape *lānum*, (inheritance) *zīttum*
share, to *zâzum*
sharing *zīzum*
shave (off), to *gullubum*
she *šī*
she-goat *enzum*
sheep *immerum*, *ṣēnum*, (young male) *aslum*
sheep's liver *amūtum*
sheep offering *šuginûm*
sheepfold *supūrum*
shepherd *nāqidum*, *rēʾûm*, (chief) *utullum*
shepherd's hut *gubrum*
shine, to *napāḫum*, *nawārum*, (forth) *wapûm* Št
shining *ebbum*, *napḫum*, *nawirum*
ship *eleppum*
shoot (n.) *niprum*
shoot, to *nasākum*
shore *aḫum*, *kibrum*
shore-land *ušallum*
short supply, to be in *maṭûm* Š
shoulder *būdum*, (of animal) *imittum* b
shout (n.) *rigmum*
shout, to *ragāmum*, *šasûm*
show, to *kullumum*
show respect to, to *kabātum* D
shrine *sagûm*
shut, to *peḫûm*, *sekērum*
shut in, to *esērum* a
sick *marṣum*
sick, to be(come) *marāṣum*
sickness *murṣum*
side *aḫum*, *idum*, *lētum*, *ṣēlum*
silence *qūlum*
silent, to be(come) *šaqummumum*
silver *kaspum*
similar, to be(come) *mašālum*
sinew *šerʾānum*
since *ištu*
sing (of, about), to *zamārum*, (happily) *nagûm*
single *wēdum*
sink, to *ṭebûm* G (intr.), D (tr.)
sister *aḫātum*
sit (down), to *wašābum*
site *maškanum*
sitting, to be *wašābum*
situated *nadûm* b, *šaknum*
situation, normal *kīttum*
six *šediš*
six hundred *nērum*
sixth *šeššum* b
sixty *šūšum*
size *lānum*
size, to be of equal *maḫārum* Gt
skill *nēmequm*
skillful *eršum* a
skin *maškum*
skin disease *laʾbum*
skull *gulgull(at)um*, *muḫḫum*
sky *šamû*
sky god *Anum*
slab, stone *askupp(at)um*
slander (n.) *tuššum*
slander, to *karāṣum* D, *tuššam nadûm* / *qabûm* / *dabābum*
slave *rēšum*, (female) *amtum*, (male) *wardum*
slavery *rēšūtum*, *wardūtum*
slay, to *nêrum*
sleep *šittum*
sleeping-place *mayyalum*
slide, to *neḫelṣûm*
slip, to *neḫelṣûm*, (out of place) *nabalkutum*
slippery ground *muḫḫelṣītum*
sluice channel *butuqtum*
small *maṭûm*, *ṣeḫḫerum*, *ṣeḫrum*, *wīṣum*
small, to be(come) *maṭûm*, *ṣeḫērum*, *šapālum*, *wiāṣum*
smash, to *ḫepûm* a, *napāṣum*
smashed *ḫepûm* b
smear, to *lapātum* G, D, *pašāšum*
smile *ṣīḫtum*
smite, to *maḫāṣum*
snake, horned *bašmum*
snatch away, to *ekēmum*
so that *aššum*, *kīma*
socket *abunnatum*
soil *qaqqarum*, (unbroken and hard) *kankallum*
soldier *awīlūtum*, *bāʾerum*, *rēdûm*
solid *dannum*
solitary *wēdum*
some *ayyumma*
someone *ayyumma*, *awīlūtum*, *mamman*
someone else *šanûm* c
something *mimma*, *mimmû*
somewhere *ayyīšamma*
son *mārum*
son, oldest *aplum*
sonship *mārūtum*
soothe, to *pašāḫum* D
sorcery *kišpū*
sound (adj.) *šalmum*
sound, to be(come) *šalāmum*
sovereign *etellum*
span *ūṭum*
spare, to *gamālum*
speak, to *awûm* Gt, *dabābum*, *qabûm*, *zakārum*, (humbly) *piam maṭiam šakānum*, (maliciously) *qabâm šakānum*, *tuššam dabābum* / *nadûm* / *qabûm*, (severely) *danānum* a D
speckled *barmum*
speech *dabābum*, *pûm*, *qabûm*, *qibītum*
spirit *mukīl rēšim*, (protective) *lamassum*
spleen *ṭulīmum*
splendid *šarāḫum*, *šūpûm*
splendor *mašraḫū*
split *ḫepûm* b
split, to *ḫepûm* a
spread out, to *šuparrurum*
spread over, to *saḫāpum*
spring *īnum*
spring(-time, pasture) *dīšum*
sprout *niprum*
squander, to *sapāḫum*
square (town) *rebītum*
squat, to *kamāsum* b
squeeze out, to *ḫalāṣum*
squint, to *piāqum*
squirm, to *piāqum*
stable *tarbaṣum*
staff *ḫaṭṭum*, *nēmettum*
stake, impaling *gašīšum*
stamp-seal *unqum*
stand, to *izuzzum*, *tebûm* a
stand near/by, to *emēdum*
stand ready, to *izuzzum*
stand up, to *tebûm* a

standard with a divine symbol *kakkum ša ilim*
standing *tebûm* b
standing, to be *izuzzum*
star *kakkabum*
start a lawsuit, to *diānum*, *gerûm*
state scribe *mār bīt ṭuppim*
statement *dabābum*
station *nazzazum*
station, to *izuzzum* Š
stature *lānum*
status of *awīlum awīlūtum*
status of owner *bēlutum*
status of property, permanent *dūrum* b
status of son *mārūtum*
status of wife *aššūtum*
status, person of equal *ibrum*
stay, to *izuzzum*, *wašābum*
steal, to *šarāqum*
steer, to *warûm* Gtn
stela *narûm*
steppeland *nawûm* a, *ṣērum*
steps *kibsum*
steward *abarakkum*
stick *ḫaṭṭum*
still, to be(come) *šaqumumum*
stillness *qūlum*
stock *bašītum*, *namkurum*, *rēš namkūrim*
stolen *šarqum*
stolen property *šurqum*
stone *abnum*
stone slab *askupp(at)um*
stone weight *abnum*
stop, to *naparkûm*, (work) *batāqum*
storage *našpakūtum*
storage area for barley, dates *našpakum*
store (of barley) *aldûm*
store, to *šapākum*
store-room *qarītum*
storm god *Adad*
straight *išarum*
straight, to be(come) *ešērum*
strange *aḫûm*, *šanûm* b
strange, to be(come) *na kārum*
straw *tibnum*
street *sūqum*
strength *dannūtum*, *idum*
strengthen, to *danānum* a D
strengthening *tadnintum*
stretch, to *šadādum*
stretch out, to *tarāṣum*
strike, to *lapātum*, *maḫāṣum*, *napāṣum*, *nêrum*
strike down, to *maqātum* Š
strip *šer'ānum*
strip, to *paṭārum*
strive, to *ṣarāmum*
strong *dannum*, *gašrum*
strong, to be(come) *danānum* a, *gašārum*, *pagālum*
student *talmīdum*
study, to *ḫasāsum* D, *lamādum*, *šasûm* Gtn
stunted *ekmum*
subjected *kanšum*
subjugate, to *kanāšum* Š
submerged, to be(come) *ṭebûm*
submissive *kanšum*
submissive, to make *kanāšum* D, Š
submit, to *kanāšum*
subside, to *nâḫum*
subsistence field/plot *šukūsum*
substitute *pūḫum*
substitute, to *šupêlum*
succeed, to *šalāmum*
successful *kašdum*
suck, to *enēqum*
suckle, to *enēqum* Š
suckling baby *mār(at) irtim*, *tēnīqum*
suddenly *zamar*
sue, to *gerûm*, *ragāmum*, (one another) *gerûm* Gt
sufficient *maṣûm* b
sufficient for,to be *maṣûm* a
suitable *naṭûm*
sum *napḫarum*
summer *ebūrum*
summon, to *elûm* a Š, *nabûm* a, *qerûm*, *ragāmum*, *šasûm*
sun *šamšum*
sunrise *ṣīt šamšim*
superfluous *watrum*
supervise, to *sanāqum*
supplies *iškarum*
supply, to *paqādum*
support (n.) *nēmettum*
support, to *našûm* G,Gtn
supreme *etellum*
surety *qātātum*
surpass *watārum*
surpassing *šūturum*
surpassing,to be(come) *watārum*
surplus *nēmelum*, *watartum*
surplus harvest, purchase of *pišertum*
surround, to *ḫapārum*, *lawûm* a, *saḫārum* G, Š, (on all sides) *saḫārum* Št-lex
surrounded *lawûm* b
survey (a field), to *šadādum*
suspend, to *ḫalālum*
suspended, to be(come) *šaqālum* a N
sustenance *bubūtum*
swear, to *tamûm*, (by) *nīš X zakārum*, (by the life of) *nīš X tamûm*
sweet *duššupum*, *ṭābum*
sweet, to be(come) *ṭiābum*
swollen *napḫum*

table *paššūrum*
tablet (clay) *ṭuppum*, (sealed) *kunukkum*
tablet house *bīt ṭuppim*
tail *zibbatum*, (ox) *qinnāzum*
take, to *leqûm*, *našûm*, (action) *ṣibit ṭēmim išûm* / *rašûm*, *ṭēmam ṣabātum*, (counsel) *šâlum* Gt, (a wife) *aḫāzum*, *leqûm*, (a share) *zâzum*, (an oath) *tamûm*, (for oneself) *akālum*, *tabālum*, (the throne) *kussiam ṣabātum*, (to the road) *ḫarrānam ṣabātum*, (trouble) *marāṣum* Št, (as booty) *šalālum*, (as pledge) *nepûm*
take along, to *leqûm*, *qerûm*
take away, to *ekēmum*, *leqûm*,*šaqālum* b, *tabālum*
take back, to *târum* D
take by force, to *mašā'um*
take captive, to *esērum* a D, *šalālum*, *târum* D
take care of, to *ḫiāṭum*, *na-*

šûm Gtn, *paqādum*, *rēšam kullum*, *šalāmum* D
take far away, to *nesûm* D
take hold of, to *ṣabātum*
take off, to *tabālum*
take out, to *waṣûm* a Š
taken away *ekmum*
talent *biltum*
talk, to *dabābum*
tall *elûm* b, *šaqûm* c, *šīḫum*
tall, to be(come) *šaqûm* b, *šiāḫum*
tarry, to *aḫārum* G, D, *lapātum* D
task *isiḫtum*, *šiprum*
taut *šaddum*
tax *nēmettum*, (annual) *igisûm*
tax collector *mušaddinum*, *muzzaz bābim*
teach, to *lamādum* D, *aḫāzum* Š
tear away, to *šaḫāṭum*
tear down, to *naqārum*
tear off, to *šadādum*, *šaḫāṭum*
tear out, to *nasāḫum*
tear up, to *šadādum*
tell, to *dabābum*, *qabûm*, *šanûm* D
temple *bītum*, (of Marduk, in Borsippa) *Ezida*, (of Šamaš) *Ebabbar*
temple(of head) *nakkaptum*
temple administrator *šangûm*
temple official *abarakkum*
temple tower *gigunnûm*
ten *ešer*
tenancy (of a field) *errēšūtum*
tenant *nāš(i) biltim*
tenant farmer *errēšum*
tend, to *reʾûm*
tendon *šerʾānum*, (of the neck) *labiānum*
tenth (adj.) *ešrum* b
tenth, one- *ešret*
terrain *qaqqarum*
territory *pātum*
terror *gilittum*
testicle *iškum*
testimony *šībūtum*
that (adj.) *ullûm*
that (conj.) *kīma*
that (pron.) (f) *šī*, (m) *šū*
that of *šāt*
theft *šurqum*
their(s) *šunûm*
then *inūmīšu*
thence *ullânum*
there *ašariš*, *ašrānum*, *ullīkiam*
there is/are *ibašši*
there is/are not *laššu*
therefore *ina kiam*
they (f) *šina*, (m) *šunu*
thick, to be(come) *kabārum*
thicket, reed *apum*
thief *šarrāqum*
thin *qatnum*
thin, to be(come) *qatānum*
thing *awātum*
think of, to *ḫasāsum*
third *šalšum* a
thirst *ṣūmum*
thirty *šalāšā*
this *annûm*
this year *šattam*
thither *ullîšam*
thorn tree *kušabkum*
those (f) *šina*, (m) *šunu*
those of *šūt*
thought *libbum*
thousand *līmum*
thread *qûm* b
three *šalāš*
three-fold, three times *šalāšīšu*
three thousand six hundred *šārum*
threshing floor *maškanum*
threshold *askupp(at)um*
thrice *šalāšīšu*
thrive, to *ešērum* Št, *šamāḫum*
throat *ḫurḫudum*, *kišādum*, *napištum*, *urʾudum*
throne *kussûm*
throne, to take the *kussiam ṣabātum*
throne-dais *parakkum*
through the agency of (a person) *ina qāti*
throw, to *nadûm* a, *nasākum*, *ramûm*
throw back, to *darāsum*
throw down, to *nadûm* a
throw over, to *darāsum*
thus *kiam*, *ina kiam*
tiara *agûm*
tie, to *kasûm*, *kaṣārum*, *rakāsum*, *ṣamādum*
tie on, to *rakāsum*
tie together, to *kasûm* G, D
timber *iṣum*
time afterward *warkītum*
timid *palḫum*
tip *appum*
tithe *ešrētum*
to *ana*, *ana maḫar*, *ana ṣēr*
to the debit of *ina muḫḫi*
to the same amount/degree as *mala*, *malmališ*
to the same extent *mitḫāriš*
today *ūmam*
toe *ubān šēpim*
together *ištēniš*
together with *qadum*
toil *mānaḫtum*
tomorrow *urram*
tooth *šinnum*
top *muḫḫum*, *qaqqadum*, *rēšum*
top, on *eliš*
torch *dipārum*
total *napḫarum*
totality *gamartum*, *kullatum*, *napḫarum*, *puḫrum*
touch, to *emēdum*, *lapātum* G, D
tow, to *šadādum*
toward *ana*, *ana maḫar*, *ana muḫḫi*, *ana pān(i)*, *ana ṣēr*, *eli*
tower *dimtum*, (temple) *gigunnûm*
town *ālum*
town square *rebītum*
traces *kibsum*
track *kibsum*
trader *tamkārum*
trading agent *šamallûm*
traditional *labirum*
trample upon, to *darāsum*
transfer, to *nadānum*, *nasāḫum*
transgress, to *etēqum*
transport (n.) *šēpum*
transport, to *babālum*, *našûm*, *zabālum*
transported *bablum*
travel, to *alākam epēšum*, *ḫarrānam alākum*
travel provisions *gerrum*
traveler *ālikum*
treachery *sartum*
treat, to *epēšum*, (badly) *maṭûm* Š, (kindly) *damāqum* D, *banûm* D,

gamālum, (a disease) *simmam epēšum*
treaty *riksum*
tree *iṣum*
tremble, to *ratātum*
trespass, to *ḫaṭûm*
tribute *biltum, nēmettum*
trim, to *šarāmum* D
trip, business *gerrum*
triumph *irnittum*
triumphant *ḫaptum*
troops *ṣābum*
trouble *maruštum*
troublesome, to be(come) *marāṣum*
true *kīnum, taklum*
true, to be(come) *kânum*
truly *kīniš*
trust (n.) *tukultum*
trust, to *qiāpum* , *takālum*
trustworthy *ebbum, qīpum, taklum*
truth *kīttum*
turn, to *saḫārum* G, N, *târum*
turn around,t o *nabalkutum,nê'um,saḫārum* G,D
turn aside, to *saḫārum* D
turn away, to *nê'um, irtam nê'um, saḫārum* D
turn back,to(intr.) *saḫā rum* G, *târum* G,(tr.) *saḫārum* D, *târum* D
turn black/dark, to *ṣalāmum*
turn into, to (intr.) *ewûm, târum*, (tr.) *šupêlum, târum* D
turn over, to *garārum, nabalkutum*
turn pale, to *warāqum*
turn to, to *saḫārum*
twentieth *ešrûm*
twenty *ešrā*
twice *šinīšu*
twice, to do *šanûm* a
twist, to *garārum, saḫārum*
two *šinā*
two-thirds *šinip* , *šittān*
two times, twofold *šinīšu*

umbilical cord *abunnatum*
umbilical fissure *bāb ekallim*
unbroken, hard soil *kankal lum*
uncultivated plot/land *nidītum*
under *šaplānum* , *ina šapal*
under guard *naṣrum*
under part *šaplum* b
under seal *kankum*
under side *šaplum* b
under the authority of *ina qāti, ša qāt(i)*
under way *tebûm* b
underneath *šaplānum*
understand, to *lamādum*
understanding *ḫasīsum, teš mûm* , *uznum*
undertake a military campaign, to *ḫarranam alākum,ḫarrānam ṣabātum*
uninjured, to be(come) *šalāmum*
unique *wēdûm*
unite, to *emēdum* Št-lex
unoccupied,to be(come) *riāqum*
unplowed field *eqlum kankallum*
untie, to *paṭārum*
until *adi*, until now *adīni*
unto *ana*
unusual *aḫûm*
up *eliš*
up to *adi*
upbringing *tarbītum*
upkeep *mānaḫtum*
upon *eli* , *ina muḫḫi, ina ṣēr*
upper *elûm* c
uprising *tībum*
upset, to *nazāqum* Š
upset, to be(come) *nazāqum*
upstream *elēnum*
upward *eliš*
urethra *muštinnum*
urgent *dannum*
use, to *akālum*
use up, to *gamārum*
useless, to be(come) *riāqum*
usurper king *šar ḫammê*
utensils *numātum* , *unūtum*
utterance *ipiš pîm, pûm, qabûm* , *qibītum* , *ṣīt pîm* , *šaptum, zikrum*

valuables *bašītum, makkūrum*
variegated *barmum*
veil, to *pasāmum*
vein *šer'ānum*
verdict *dīnum*
verily *lū*
very *mādiš, magal*
very great *šurbûm*
very strong *puggulum*
vessel *karpatum*
vicinity *lētum*
victory *irnittum*
vigor *napištum* , (sexual) *kuzbum*
village *kaprum*
vineyard *karānum*
violence *dannūtum*
visible, to be(come) *napāḫum, wapûm* G,Št
vizier *s/šukallum*
voice *rigmum*
voluntarily *ina ṭūbātm*
voluntariness *ṭūbātum*

wage war, to *kakkī epēšum*
wages *idum* , *igrum*
wagon *ereqqum*
waist *qablum* a
wait for, to *rēšam kullum*
wait upon, to *dagālum*
walk about, to *alākum* Gtn
walk along, to *ba'ûm*
walk around, to *saḫārum*
wall *dūrum* a, *igārum*
wander, to *dâlum*
war *nukurtum*
wardrobe *lubūšum*
warrior *qarrādum* , *qurādum, uršānum*
wart *šullum*
wash, to *mesûm*
washerman *ašlākum*
watch (n.) *maṣṣartum, maṣṣarum*
watch (over), to *ḫiāṭum* , *naṣārum, palālum*
watched *naṣrum*
watchful *ērum*
watchman *maṣṣarum*
water *mû*
water, to *šaqûm* a
water-meadow *ušallum*
watering *šiqītum*
watering place *mašqītum*
way *alaktum, ḫarrānum* , *padānum* , *urḫum*
we *nīnu*
weak *enšum*
weak, to be(come) *enēšum*
weaken, to (tr.) *enēšum* D
wealth *lalûm*

weapon *kakkum*
wear, to *labāšum* Gt
weariness *mānaḫtum*
wearing *labšum*, (on the head) *aprum*
weave in colors, to *barāmum* D
wedding *emūtum*
wedding house *bīt emim*
weigh out, to *šaqālum* a
weighed (out), *šaqlum*
weight *biltum*, (stone) *abnum*
weir *meḫrum*
well (adv.) *damqiš*, *ṭābiš*
well, to be(come) *balāṭum*, *šalāmum*
well-being *šulmum*
well-formed, -made *banûm* b
wet-nurse *mušēniqtum*
wet-nursing expenses *tēnīqum*
what *ašar*, *ša*
what? *mīnum*, *minûm*
what adjoins *ṭēḫum*
what is decreed/established/fixed *šīmtum*
what pertains/belongs/is fitting *simtum*
whatever *mala*, *mimma mala*
when *ašar*, *ina*, *inūma*, *(ina) ūm*, *kīma*
when? *mati*
where (rel. adv.) *ēma*, *ašar*
where? *ali*, *ayyānum*, *ayyīkīam*, *êš*
wherever *ēma*, *ašar*
whether ... or *šumma* ... *šumma*
which? *ayyum*
whichever *ayyumma*
while *adi*, *ina*, *inūma*, *(ina) ūm*
whip *qinnāzum*
whisper, to *ḫabābum*
white *pūṣum*
whither? *êš*
who? *mannum*
who can say? *minde*
whoever *mala*, *manāma*
whole *kalûm* b, *šalmum*
whole, to be(come) *šalāmum*
why? *ana mīnim*, *ammīnim*
wickedly *lemniš*
wickedness *lemuttum*
wide (open), to be(come) *nepelkûm*
widow *almattum*
width *rupšum*
wife *aššatum*, (junior) *šugītum*, (of equal status with husband) *ḫīrtum*
wild bull *rīmum*
wild cow *rīmtum*
win (a legal case), to *leʾûm*
windpipe *ḫurḫudam*, *urʾudum*
wine *karānum*
winnow, to *zakûm* a D
winter *kūṣum*
wisdom *ḫasīsum*, *nēmequm*, *uznum*
wise *eršum* a
wish *bibil libbim*, *erištum*, *lalûm*, *libbum*, *ṣibûtum*, (for well-being) *šulmum*
wish, to *erēšum* a
witchcraft *kišpū*
with *idi*, *ina*, *ište*, *itti*
withdraw, to *paṭārum*, *irtam nêʾum*, (a claim) *qātam nasāḫum*
withhold, to *kalûm* a
within *ina libbi*, (temporally) *ana*
without *balum*, *ša lā*
witness *šībum*
witness, to produce a *elûm* a Š
wolf *barbarum*
woman *iššum* (rare), *sinništum*, (free-) *awīltum*, (of high status) *sekretum*, (young) *ṣuḫārtum*
woman-servant *amtum*
womb *rēmum*
wood *iṣum*
wood-worker *gurgurrum*
wool *šīpātum*
word *awātum*, *qibītum*, *pûm*, *zikrum*
work (n.) *epištum*, *šiprum*, *tupšikkum*
work, to *šipram epēšum*, (*ilkum*-land) *ilkam alākum*, (one's mouth) *piam epēšum*
work assignment *iškarum*
worked *epšum*
worker *awīlūtum*
worried, to be(come) *ašāšum*
worry, to *nazāqum*
worship, to *palāḫum*
wound *dikšum*, *simmum*
wound, to *maḫāṣum*
wrap up *rakāsum*
wreck, to *ḫepûm* a
write, to *šapārum*, *šaṭārum*
wrong *ḫibiltum*
wrong, to *ḫabālum*
wrongdoing *arnum*

year *šattum*, this year *šattam*
yellow *warqum*
yellow, to be(come) *warāqum*
yes *annam*
yet, not *adīni*
yield, abundant *ḫe(n)gallum*
yoke *nīrum*
yoke, to *ṣamādum*
you (fs) *atti*, (fp) *attina*, (ms) *atta*, (mp) *attunu*
young *ṣeḫrum*
young, to be(come) *ṣeḫērum*
young man *eṭlum*
young woman *ṣuḫārtum*
your(s) (sg.) *kûm*, (pl.) *kunûm*
youth *eṭlum*

SIGN LIST

Signs encountered in the lesson exercises are listed here as they are in the lessons, in their OB lapidary, OB cursive, and Neo-Assyrian forms. They are presented according to their forms in *OB cursive* script; as in some other lists of OB cursive signs, they are ordered by the following sequence of wedge types: 𒀸; 𒌋 or 𒌋; 𒁹. This sequence is applied successively to the whole sign. Thus, all signs beginning with one horizontal wedge appear before signs beginning with two horizontal wedges (one on top of the other), which in turn appear before signs beginning with three and then four horizontals. Thereafter come the signs beginning with an angled wedge or Winkelhaken, then signs beginning with two, then three, then four of these. And finally, signs beginning with one vertical wedge, then two, and so on, are listed. Within each of these groups, signs in which the first wedge or group of wedges is followed by a horizontal (and then two horizontals, etc.) precede signs in which the first wedge or group of wedges is followed by an angled wedge or Winkelhaken, etc. (For the most part, this list follows the order of the "List of Signs" in Hermann Ranke, *Babylonian Legal and Business Documents from the Time of the First Dynasty of Babylon, chiefly from Sippar*. BE 6/1. Philadelphia, 1906.)

An alphabetical cross-index of sign values immediately follows this list (pp. 575–76); the cross-index is keyed to the numbers in the left-hand column below.

	OB Lapid.	OB Cursive	NA	Values
001				*aš*, *rum*
002		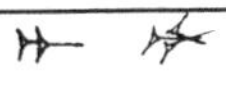		*ḫal*
003				*an*; AN = *šamû*; DINGIR = *ilum*; determinative ^{d} (for ^{dingir}) before divine names
003a				ligature of ^{d} and EN in divine names such as ^{d}EN.ZU
004			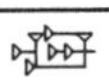	*ag*/*k*/*q*

	OB Lapid.	OB Cursive	NA	Values
005				*maḫ*
006				*la*
007				*be, bad/t/ṭ, til;* BE = *šumma*
008				NUMUN = *zērum;* ŠE.NUMUN also = *zērum*
009				*šu*
010	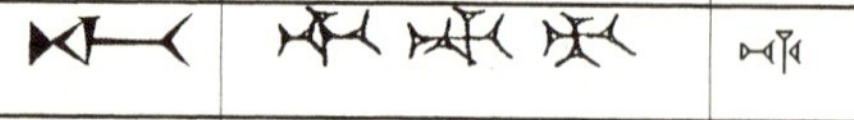			*ti, ṭì*
011	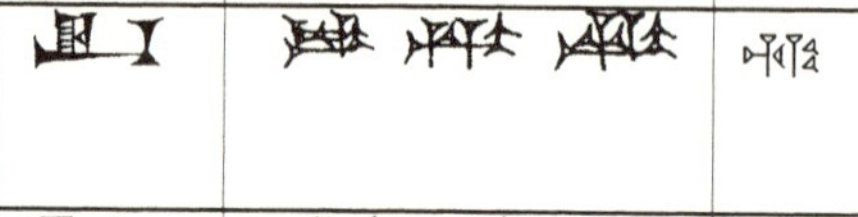			*ig/k/q, eg/k/q;* GÁL in ḪÉ.GÁL = *ḫegallum;* in fractions wr. IGI.x.GÁL (see §23.2(e))
012				*mu;* MU = *nīšum, šattum, šumum*
013				ŠEŠ = *aḫum*
014				*dim, tim, ṭim*
015	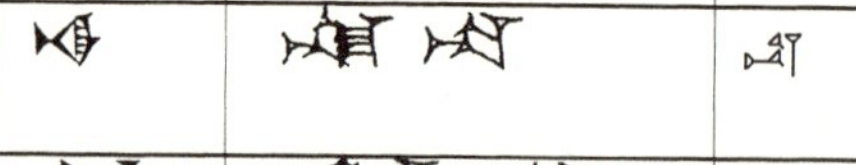			*na;* NA.GADA = *nāqidum;* NA.RU = *narûm*
016				ÌR (also read ARAD) = *wardum;* SAG.ÌR also = *wardum;* NITA(Ḫ)$_2$ = *zikarum;* GÌR.NITA(Ḫ)$_2$ = *šakkanakkum*
017				*nu*
018				BÁN = *sūtum*
019				*maš;* MAŠ = *mišlum;* MAŠ = *šumma;* MAŠ.GAG.EN or MAŠ.EN.GAG = *muškēnum*
019a				*bar, pár*
020				*ḫu*
021				MÁŠ = *ṣibtum;* MÁŠ.ŠU.GÍD.GÍD = *bārûm*
022	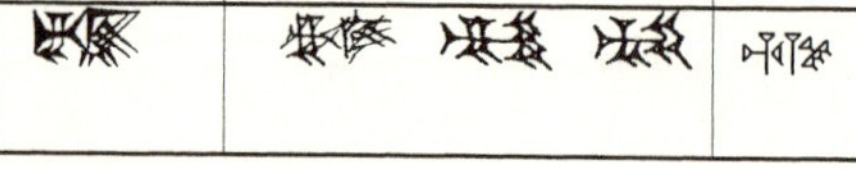			*nam*

	OB Lapid.	OB Cursive	NA	Values
023				*en*; EN = *bēlum*
024				*ri, re, tal, ṭal*
025				*zi, ze, sí, sé, ṣí, ṣé*
026				*gi, ge*; SIG_{17} in KUG.SIG_{17} (GUŠKIN) = *ḫurāṣum*
027				MÁ (also ^{giš}MÁ) = *eleppum*
028				INANNA = *Ištar*
029				NUN = *rubûm*; ud.kib.nun^{ki} = ZIMBIR^{ki} = *Sippar*
030				KUN = *zibbatum*
031				*kán*; IKU = *ikûm* a surface measure (ca. 3600 m.^{2}; see App. B.3)
032				*si, se*
033				KÚR (also ^{lú}KÚR or LÚ.KÚR) = *nakrum*
034				DÙ = *banûm, epēšum*; GAG in MAŠ.GAG.EN or MAŠ.EN.GAG = *muškēnum*
035				*ni, né, ì* (in *ì-lí* for *ilī*; rare otherwise); *lí* (only in *ì-lí* for *ilī*, *be-lí* for *bēlī*, and a few other archaic spellings); .NI denotes Sum. 'his', 'her', i.e., Akk. *-šu*, *-ša* (for personal/divine referent), e.g., DUMU.NI = *māršu* 'his son' or *märša* 'her son'; Ì (also Ì.GIŠ) = *šamnum*
036				NA_4 = *abnum*; det. ^{na_4} before words for stones, minerals
037				*ir, er*

	OB Lapid.	OB Cursive	NA	Values
038				LÚ = *awīlum*; determinative ^{lú} before men's occupations
039				*tab, tap*; TAB.BA = *tappûm*
040				*sa*
041				URU = *ālum*
042				*ab/p*
043	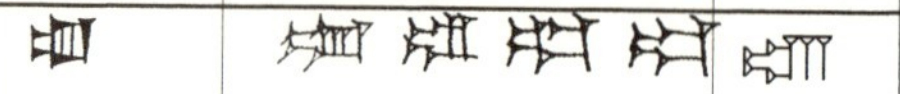			*um*
044				DUB = *ṭuppum*; DUB.SAR = *ṭupšarrum*
045				ḪÉ in ḪÉ.GÁL = *ḫegallum*; KÁM (alternative to KAM in expressions of time; §23.2(d))
046				*ad/t/ṭ*; AD = *abum*
047				*ṣi, ṣe, zí, zé*
048	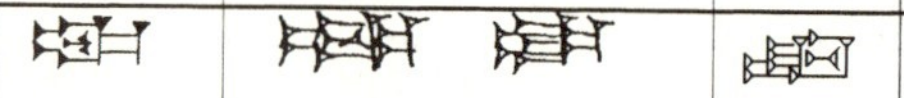			BÀD = *dūrum*
049				ŠÁM = *šīmum*
050	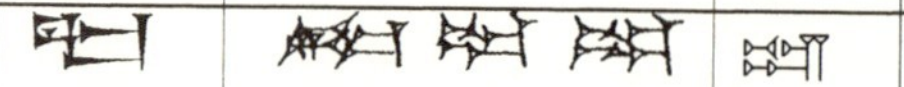			*úr*
051	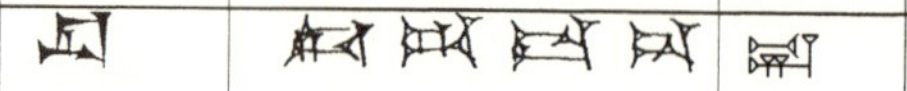			*uš, ús/ṣ/z*
052				*du, ṭù* ; RÁ in A.RÁ = *adi*
053				*iš, ís/ṣ/z, mil*
054	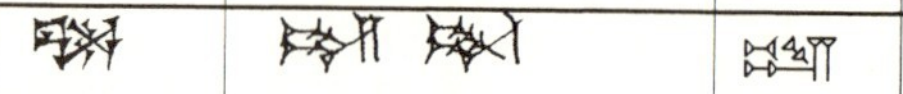			*il*
055	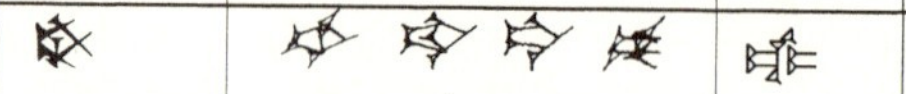			*ub/p*
056	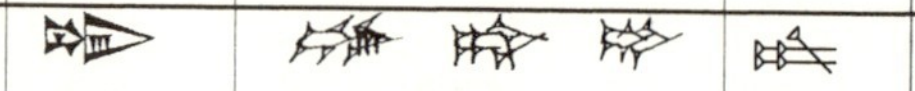			*šum*
057				*am*

	OB Lapid.	OB Cursive	NA	Values
058				*dur, ṭur, túr*
059				*ne, bí, bil, pil, ṭè*
060				*bíl, píl*
061				UZU = *šīrum*; determ. [uzu] before words denoting parts of the body
062				GÚ = *kišādum*; GUN (or GÚ.UN) = *biltum*
063				LUGAL = *šarrum*
064				*bi, bé, pí, pé*; .BI denotes Sum. 'its' (m. and f., non-personal referent), i.e., Akk. *-šu* and *-ša*, e.g., KÁ.BI = *bābša* 'its (the palace's [f.]) gate'; MÁŠ.BI = *ṣibassu* 'its (the grain's [m.]) interest'
065				*ga, qá*
066				*šim*
067				*kum*
068				*tum, dum, ṭum*
069				*ta, ṭá*
070				ŠITIM = *itinnum*
071				KÁ = *bābum*; KÁ.DINGIR.RA[ki] = *Bābilim*; ká+gal, read ABUL (or KÁ.GAL) = *abullum*
072				kib in ud.kib.nun[ki] = ZIMBIR[ki] = *Sippar*
073				GABA = *irtum*

	OB Lapid.	OB Cursive	NA	Values
074				KASKAL = *ḫarrānum*
075				*is/ṣ/z, es/ṣ/z*; GIŠ = *iṣum*; gìš before objects of wood and names of trees
076				GADA in NA.GADA = *nāqidum*
077	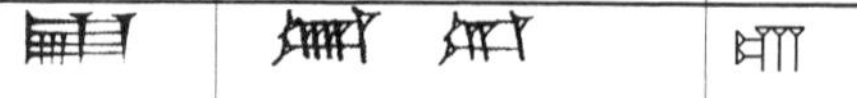			LÍL in dEN.LÍL = *Enlil*
078				É = *bītum*; É.GAL = *ekallum*; É.GAR$_8$ = *igārum*
079				*pa*; 2 BÁN (or BÁNMIN) = *2 sâtum*
080	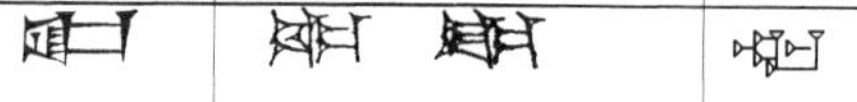			*ka*; KA = *pûm*
081	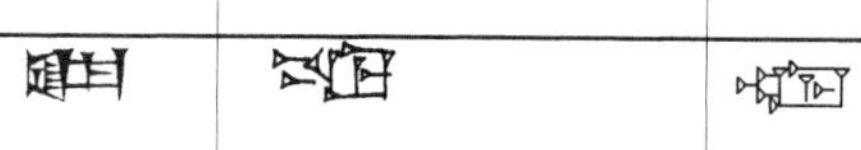			EME (ka ∞ me) = *lišānum*
082				SAG = *rēšum*; SAG.DU = *qaqqadum*; SAG.ÌR = *wardum* SAG. GEME$_2$ = *amtum*
083				SIPAD = *rēʾûm*
084	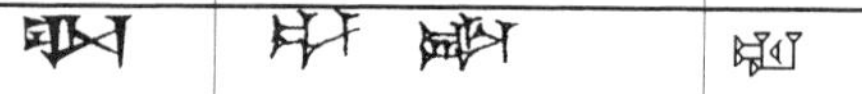			*al*
085	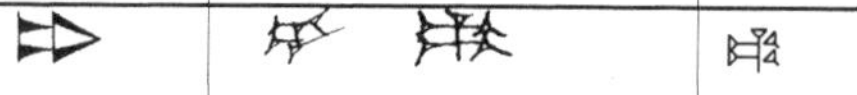			GUD (or GU$_4$) = *alpum*
086				*gur*
087				SANGA = *šangûm*; KAS$_7$ (or ŠID) in NÍG.KAS$_7$ (also read NÍG.ŠID) = *nikkassum*
088	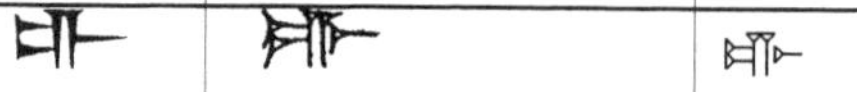			*mar*
089	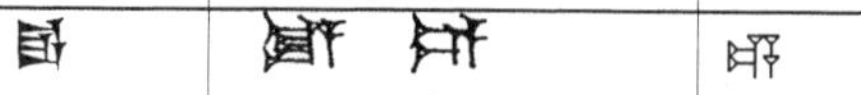			*e*
090				*nir*
091	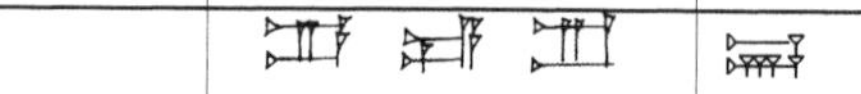			*dag/k/q, tág/k/q*

	OB Lapid.	OB Cursive	NA	Values
092				*ú*
093				*kal, dan, tan*
094	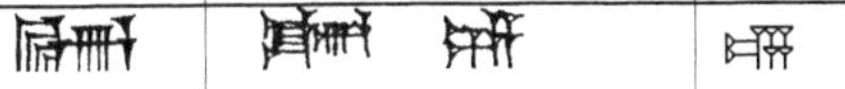			*un*; UN (also read UKU_3) = *nišū*; KALAM = *mātum*
095	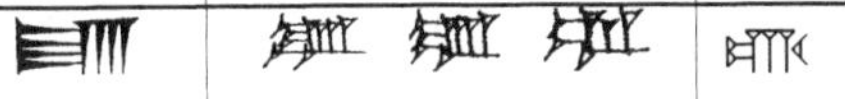			SUKKAL = *s/šukkallum*
096				ITI (or ITU) = *warḫum*
097				*i*
098				*ia, ie, ii, iu*
099				*ra*
100	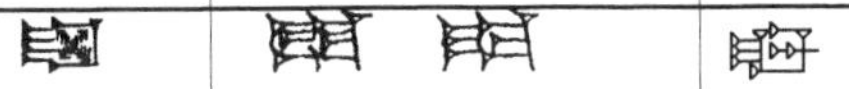			BARAG = *parakkum*
101				AGA = *agûm*; AGA.ÚS =*rēdûm*
102	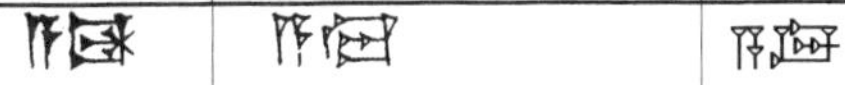			ÍD (also read I_7) = *nārum*; det. íd before names of rivers
103				*gàr, qar*
104				*ma*
105				*ba*
106				*ás/ṣ/z, áš*; 3 BÁN (BÁNEŠ) = *3 sâtum*; ZÍZ in the month name ZÍZ.A = *Šabāṭum*
106a				4 BÁN (BÁNLIMMU) = *4 sâtum*
106b				5 BÁN (or BÁNIA) = *5 sâtum*
107	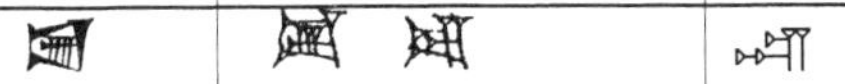			*zu, sú, ṣú*
108	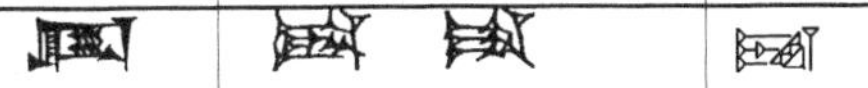			*id/t/ṭ, ed/t/ṭ*; Á = *idum* (also, Á.BI = *idum*)
109				*bur, pur*

	OB Lapid.	OB Cursive	NA	Values
110				*gir, kir, qir*
111				ZAG = *imittum* (a and b)
112	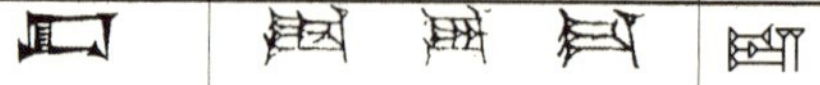			*da, ṭa*
113	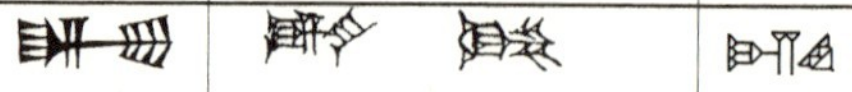			gi_4, ge_4
114	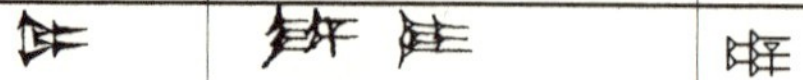			DUMU = *mārum*; DUMU. MUNUS = *mārtum*
115				*ša*
116	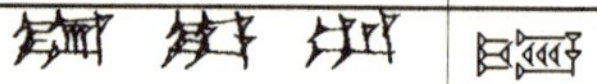			$MURUB_4$ = *qablum*
117				*gal, qal, kál*; GAL = *rabûm*; É.GAL =*ekal-lum*; ká+gal, read ABUL (or KÁ.GAL) = *abullum*
118	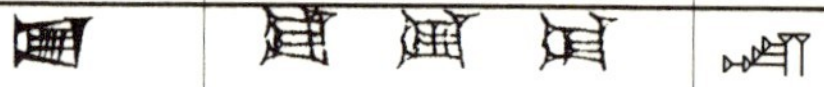			*su*
119				GÍN = *šiqlum*
120	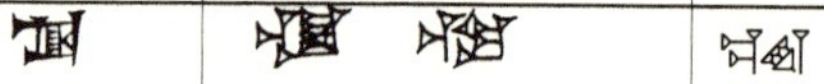			*dar, tár, ṭár*
121				KUG (also read KÙ) in KUG. BABBAR = *kaspum* and in KUG. SIG_{17} (SIG_{17} = GI; this log. is also read GUŠKIN) = *ḫurāṣum*
122				*u*
123				$eš_4$-*tár* or $EŠ_4$.TÁR or IŠTAR, the writing of the goddess *Ištar* (better, *Eštar*) in PNs
124	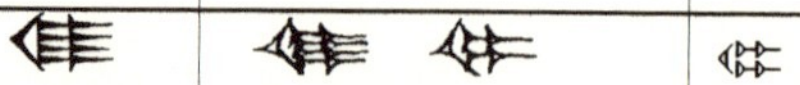			*mi, mé; ṣíl*
125				*gul* (not in OB), *kúl, qúl*
126				*ṣur*; AMAR, in ^{d}AMAR.UTU = *Marduk*
127	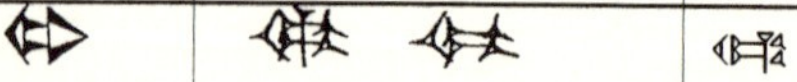			*ul*

	OB Lapid.	OB Cursive	NA	Values
128				ÁB = *lītum* (rarely); ÁB.GUD.ḪI.A = *liātum*
129				*nim, num*
130				*ši, še*$_{20}$, *lim*; IGI = *īnum*; *maḫrum* (and bound form *maḫar* 'before', before names of witnesses), *maḫrûm*; *pānum, pānū, pānûm*; *šībum*
131				*ar*
132				*ù*
133				*di, de, ṭi, ṭe*; DI = *dīnum*; DI.KUD = *dayyānum*
134				*ki, ke, qí, qé*; KI = *itti*; det. ^{ki} *after* geographical names
135				ŠUKU = *kurummatum*; PAD, in GÌR.PAD.DU = *eṣemtum*
136				NÁ = *eršum*
137				*eš, ìš*
138				*še*; ŠE = *ûm*; ŠE.NUMUN = *zē-rum*
139				*bu, pu*
140				*ṣir, zìr*
141				*us/ṣ/z*
142				*tir*
143				*li, le*
144				*kar*
145				*tu, ṭú*

	OB Lapid.	OB Cursive	NA	Values
146				*in*
147				*šar*; KIRI$_6$ (usually ^{giš}KIRI$_6$) = *kirûm*; SAR in DUB.SAR = *ṭupšarrum*
148				*kur, qúr, mad/t/ṭ*; KUR = *mātum, šadûm*; det. ^{kur} before names of countries, mountains
149				*ru*
150				*tar, ṭar*; KUD in DI.KUD = *dayyānum*
151	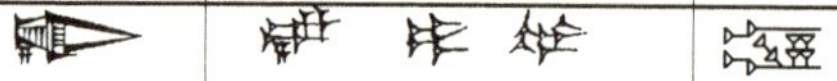			*as/ṣ/z*
152				*ug/k/q*
153				GÌR = *šēpum*; GÌR.PAD.DU = *eṣemtum*
154				*dam, ṭam*; DAM = *aššatum, mutum*; DAM.GÀR = *tamkārum*
155				*el, il$_5$*
156	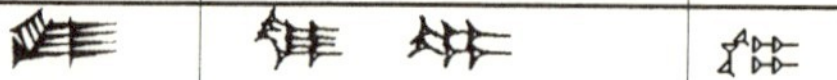			*lum, núm*
157	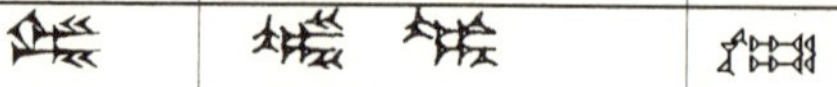			SIG$_4$ = *libittum*; GAR$_8$ in É.GAR$_8$ = *igārum*
158				*lam*
159	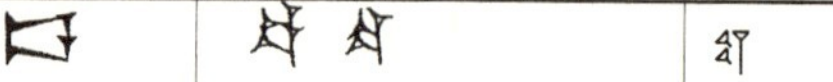			*ud/t/ṭ, tam*; UD (also read U$_4$) = *ūmum*; UTU = *šamšum*, ^{d}UTU = *Šamaš*; BABBAR in KUG.BABBAR = *kaspum*; ud.kib.nun^{ki} = ZIMBIR^{ki} = *Sippar*
160				*wa, we, wi, wu; pi, pe* (in southern OB texts)
161	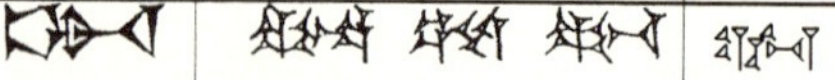			*úḫ*
162	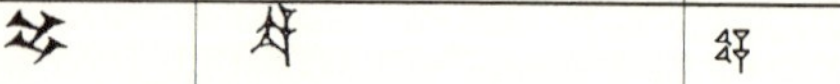			ERIN$_2$ (or ERIM) = *ṣābum*; *ummānum*

	OB Lapid.	OB Cursive	NA	Values
163				ŠÀ (or $ŠAG_4$) = *libbum;* A.ŠÀ = *eqlum*
164				*kam, qám;* KAM in logograhic expressions of time (§23.2(d))
165	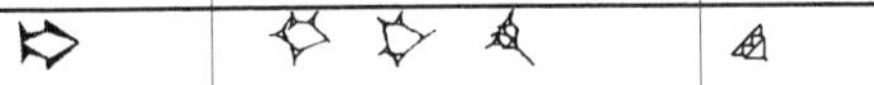			*ḫi, ḫe; ṭà;* DÙG (also read DU_{10}) = *ṭābum;* ḪI in ḪI.A (also read ḪÁ; or as a det. $^{ḫi.a}$ or ^{ḫá}) plural marker (not used with persons or deities; see p. 109)
166				*din*
167	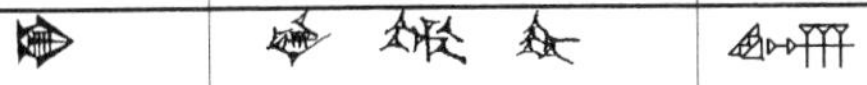			*aḫ, eḫ, iḫ, uḫ*
168				*ḫar, ḫur, mur*
169	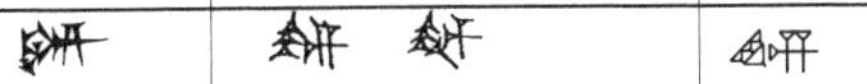			*im, em*
170	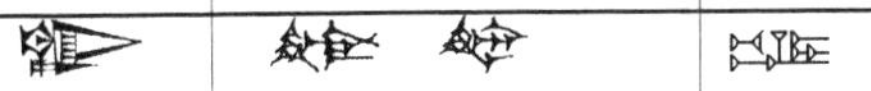			ANŠE = *imērum*
171	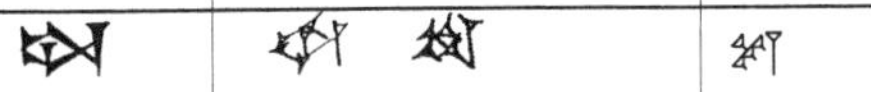			*te, ṭe*$_4$
172				'1' (see §23.2); det. ^{I} or ^{m} or ^{P} before PNs; DIŠ = *šumma*
173				*me, mì;* munus+me = LUKUR = *nadītum*
174				MEŠ or ^{meš} plural marker
175				*ib/p, eb/p*
176				SÍG = *šīpātum*
177	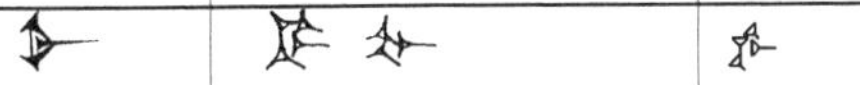			MUNUS (also read MÍ) = *sinništum;* DUMU.MUNUS = *mārtum;* det. ^{f} or ^{mí} (or ^{sal}) before women's names and occupations; munus+me = LUKUR = *nadītum*
178	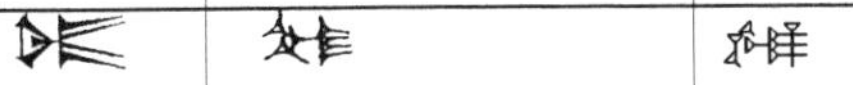			*zum, ṣum, súm; ṣu*

	OB Lapid.	OB Cursive	NA	Values
179	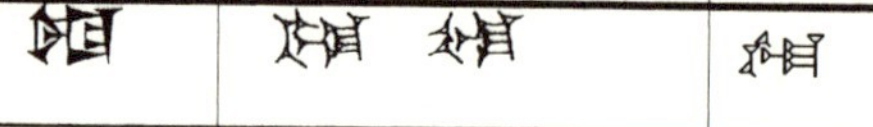			*nin*; NIN = *aḫātum, bēltum*
180				GEME$_2$ = *amtum*; SAG.GEME$_2$ also = *amtum*
181				*gu*; $^{\text{(giš)}}$GU.ZA = *kussûm*
182				*ku*, *qú*; TUKUL, ^{giš}TUKUL = *kakkum*
183	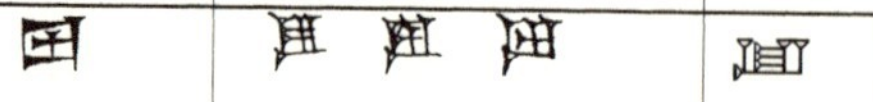			*lu*; UDU = *immerum*
184				LAL (or LÁ) = *šaqālum*, in Ì.LAL.E = *išaqqal*
185				U$_8$ (or US$_5$) in U$_8$.UDU.ḪI.A (also read USDUḪA) = *ṣēnū* (or, less often, *ṣēnum*)
186	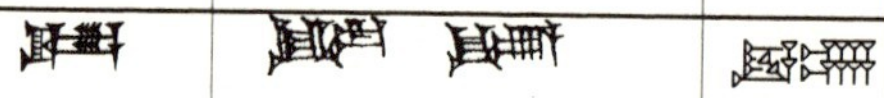			GIŠIMMAR= *gišimmarum*
187				*a*; A in A.MEŠ = *mû*; A.BA = *abum*; .A.NI = .NI (lesson 17); A.RÁ = *adi*; A.ŠÀ = *eqlum*; A.ZU = *asûm*
188				*ur*, *lig/k/q*, *taš*
189				*kab/p*; GÙB = *šumēlum*
190				*ṣa*, *za*, *sà*; $^{\text{(giš)}}$GU.ZA = *kussûm*
191				*ḫa*; ḪA.LA = *zīttum*
192	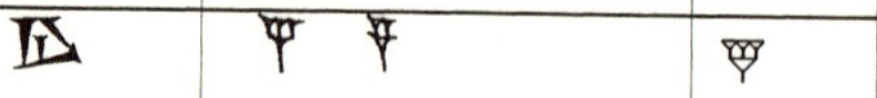			NÍG (or NÌ) (Sumerian for 'thing', frequent as a formative in compound words), in NÍG.GA = *makkūrum*; NÍG.KAS$_7$ (also read NÍG.ŠID) = *nikkassum*

ALPHABETICAL CROSS-INDEX OF SIGN VALUES

For most *Ce* values, see under the corresponding *Ci* value. *VC* and *CVC* signs in which the final *C* may be voiced, voiceless, or emphatic are listed only once, under the value with the final *C* voiced; thus, e.g., for *ut* one should look under *ud,* for *daq* one should look under *dag,* etc.

The numbers are keyed to the preceding Sign List.

a 187
Á 108
aʾ 167
ʾa$_4$ 191
ab/p 042
ÁB 128
ABUL 071
ad/t/ṭ 046
ag/k/q 004
AGA 101
aḫ 167
al 084
am 057
AMAR 126
an 003
ANŠE 170
ar 131
ARAD 016
as/ṣ/z 151
ás/ṣ/z 106
aš 001
áš 106
ba 105
BABBAR 159
bad/t/ṭ 007
BÀD 048
BÁN 018
bar 019a
BARAG 100
be 007
bé 064
bi 064
bí 059
bil 059
bíl 060
bu 139
bur 109
^{d} 003
da 112
dag/k/q 091
dam 154
dan 093
dar 120
di, de 133
dim 014
din 166
DINGIR 003
DIŠ 172
du 052
DÙ 034
DU$_{10}$ 165
DUB 044
DÙG 165
dum 068
DUMU 114
dur 058
e 089
eʾ 167
É 078
eb/p 175
ed/t/ṭ 108
eg/k/q 011
eḫ 167
el 155
em 169
EME 081
en 023
ERIN$_2$/ERIM 162
es/ṣ/z 075
eš 137
eš$_4$*-tár*/EŠ$_4$.TÁR 123
^{f} 177
ga 065
GABA 073
GADA 076
GAG 034
gal 117
GÁL 011
gàr 103
GAR$_8$ 157
GEME$_2$ 180
gi, ge 026
gi$_4$*, ge*$_4$ 113
GÍD 139
GÍN 119
gir 110
GÌR 153
GIŠ 075
GIŠIMMAR 186
gu 181
GÚ 062
GU$_4$ 085
GÙB 189
GUD 085
gul 125
GUN 062
gur 086
GUŠKIN 121
ḫa 191
ḪÁ 165
ḫal 002
ḫar 168
ḪÉ 045
ḫi, ḫe 165
ḫu 020
ḫur 168
i 097
ì 035
I$_7$ 102
iʾ 167
ʾì 165
ia, ie, ii, iu 098
ib/p 175
id/t/ṭ 108
ÍD 102
ig/k/q 011
IGI 130
iḫ 167
IKU 031
il 054
il$_5$ 155
im 169
in 146
INANNA 028
ir, er 037
ÌR 016
is/ṣ/z 075
ís/ṣ/z 053
iš 053
ìš 137
IŠTAR 123
ITI/ITU 096
ka 080
KÁ 071

kab/p 189
kal 093
kál 117
KALAM 094
kam 164
KÁM 045
kán 031
kar 144
KAS$_7$ 087
KASKAL 074
ki, ke 134
KIB 072
kir 110
KIRI$_6$ 147
ku 182
KÙ 121
KUD 150
KUG 121
kúl 125
kum 067
KUN 030
kur 148
KÚR 033
la 006
LÁ 184
LAL 184
lam 158
li, le 143
lí 035
lig/k/q 188
LÍL 077
lim 130
lu 183
LÚ 038
LUGAL 063
LUKUR 177
lum 156
^{m} 172
ma 104
MÁ 027
mad/t/ṭ 148
maḫ 005
mar 088
maš 019
MÁŠ 021
me 173
mé 124
MEŠ 174
mi 124
MÍ 177
mì 173
mil 053
mu 012
MUNUS 177
mur 168
MURUB$_4$ 116
na 015
NÁ 136
NA$_4$ 036
nam 022
ne 059
né 035
ni 035
NÌ 192
NÍG 192
nim 129
nin 179
nir 090
NITA(Ḫ)$_2$ 016
nu 017
num 129
núm 156
NUMUN 008
NUN 029
pa 079
PAD 135
pár 019a
pi, pe 160
pí, pé 064
pil 059
píl 060
pu 139
pur 109
qá 065
qal 117
qám 164
qar 103
qí, qé 134
qir 110
qú 182
qúl 125
qúr 148
ra 099
RÁ 052
ri, re 024
ru 149
rum 001
sa 040
sà 190
SAG 082
SANGA 087
SAR 047a
si, se 032
sí, sé 025
SÍG 176
SIG$_4$ 157
SIG$_{17}$ 026
SILA 150
SIPAD 083
su 118
sú 107
SUKKAL 095
súm 178
ṣa 190
ṣi, ṣe 047
ṣí, ṣé 025
ṣíl 124
ṣir 140
ṣu 178
ṣú 107
ṣum 178
ṣur 126
ša 115
ŠÀ 163
ŠAG$_4$ 163
ŠÁM 049
šar 147
še 138
še$_{20}$ 130
ŠEŠ 013
ši 130
ŠID 087
šim 066
ŠITIM 070
šu 009
ŠUKU 135
šum 056
ta 069
tab/p 039
tág/k/q 091
tal 024
tam 159
tan 093
tar 150
tár 120
taš 188
te 171
ti 010
til 007
tim 014
tir 142
tu 145
TUKUL 182
tum 068
túr 058
ṭa 112
ṭá 069
ṭà 165
ṭal 024
ṭam 154
ṭar 150
ṭár 120
ṭè 059
ṭe$_4$ 171
ṭi, ṭe 133
ṭì 010
ṭim 014
ṭú 145
ṭù 052
ṭum 068
ṭur 058
u 122
ú 092
ù 132
U$_8$ 185
uʾ 167
ʾu$_5$ 020
ub/p 055
ud/t/ṭ 159
UDU 183
ug/k/q 152
uḫ 167
úḫ 161
UKU$_3$ 094
ul 127
um 043
un 094
ur 188
úr 050
URU 041
us/ṣ/z 141
ús/ṣ/z 051
USDUḪA 185
uš 051
UTU 159
UZU 061
wa, we, wi, wu 160
za 190
ZAG 111
zi, ze 025
zí, zé 047
ZIMBIR 159
zìr 140
ZÍZ 106
zu 107
zum 178
1 172

APPENDIX A: SYSTEMS OF DATING

Many Mesopotamian texts, particularly contracts, bear the date on which they were written. In Old Babylonian texts, a complete date formula appears as

{ITI [Month-Name] + UD.[x].KAM + MU [Year-Name]}

as in:

> ITI *a-ia-ru-um* UD.3.KAM MU ^{giš}GU.ZA ^{d}*ṣar-pa-ni-tum* 'month (of) Ayyarum, day 3, year "the Ṣarpānītum throne (was installed)" ' (the date of *CT* 8 22b = Schorr, *VAB* 5, no. 77, a contract that appears in exercise H of Lesson 22).

In some dates only the month and year or only the year alone appeared. As the example above indicates, years were given names in the OB period. The modern reader must consult a list of year names to identify a given date-formula; the year name ^{giš}GU.ZA ^{d}*ṣar-pa-ni-tum*, for instance, is the twelfth year of Ḫammurapi. The year names may be quite lengthy, and are usually written in Sumerian. As other examples the date-formulae for Ḫammurapi years 1–4 may be given:

> MU *ḫa-am-mu-ra-pí* LUGAL.E 'year Ḫammurapi became king'
>
> MU NÍG.SI.SÁ KALAM.MA IN.GAR 'year he established justice in the land'
>
> MU ^{giš}GU.ZA BARAG MAḪ ^{d}NANNA KÁ.DINGIR.RA^{ki} MU.UN.NA.DÍM 'year he installed the throne and august dias of Nanna of Babylon'
>
> MU BÀD GÁ.GI.A BA.DÙ 'year the wall of the *gagûm* was built'

A convenient collection of year names may be found in the article "Datenlisten" in *RLA*. (In later periods in Babylonia, dates are identified by the regnal year of the king, as in MU.5.KAM RN 'year 5 of king RN'. In Assyria, years were named after important royal officials, in a fixed order; a given year was called 'the *limmum* (eponymy) of PN'.)

The names of the months of the year varied from one period to another and from region to region. Occasionally they are written syllabically, as in the example given above; usually, however, they are given logographically, or even in abbreviations (e.g., the first sign only) of the full logogram. Below are the most common month names for OB texts, with their modern equivalents.

OB Month Names

	logogram	Akkadian	modern equivalent
1.	$BARA_2$.ZAG.GAR	*Nisānum*	March–April
2.	GUD.SI.SÁ	*Ayyarum*	April–May
3.	SIG_4.GA	*Simānum*	May–June
4.	ŠU.NUMUN.NA	*Dumuzi*	June–July
5.	NE.NE.GAR	*Abum*	July–August
6.	KIN.^{d}INANNA(.NA)	*Elūnum* / *Elūlum* (later *Ulūlu*)	August–September
7.	DU_6.KUG	*Tašrītum*	September–October
8.	APIN.DU_8.A	*Kinūnum* (?) (later *Araḫsamna*)	October–November
9.	GAN.GAN.NA	*Kislīmum*	November–December
10.	AB.BA.È	*Ṭebētum*	December–January
11.	ZÍZ.A.AN	*Šabāṭum*	January–February
12.	ŠE.KIN.KUD	*Addarum*	February–March

APPENDIX B:
WEIGHTS AND MEASURES

Mesopotamian systems of weights and measures differed from one place to another and from one time to another. Below are presented the systems used in the OB period for expressing weight, distance, area, volume, and capacity. For more detail on these and on other systems, see the article by M. Powell in *RLA* vol. 7 (1987–90), pp. 457–517.

Measurements are almost invariably rendered logographically. Although many of the Akkadian terms for the units of measurement are known, and although the meaning of a given formulation is rarely in doubt, nevertheless the actual Akkadian pronunciation may usually not be determined with any certainty. Attempts at normalizing constructions involving measurements, therefore, are not generally recommended (except for simple expressions such as 5 GÍN KUG.BABBAR *im-ḫu-ur* for *ḫamšat šiqil kaspam imḫur* 'he received five shekels of silver'; see §23.2(b2)).

1. Weight Measures, p. 580.
2. Length Measures, p. 581.
3. Area (Surface) Measures, p. 582.
4. Volume Measures, p. 583.
5. Capacity Measures, pp. 584–85.

1. Weight Measures

sign	Sum.	Akk.	translation	= ŠE	= GÍN	= MA.NA	modern
𒊺	ŠE	*uṭṭatum*	'grain'				0.05 g.
𒂅	GÍN	*šiqlum*	'shekel'	180			8.3 g.
𒈠𒈾	MA.NA	*manûm*	'mina'	10,800	60		500 g.
𒄘(𒌦)	GÚ(.UN)	*biltum*	'talent'	648,000	3,600	60	30 kg.

Numbers of ŠE, GÍN, and MA.NA are written with regular signs: 𒁹, 𒈫, 𒐈;

Numbers of GÚ(.UN) are written with horizontal wedges: 𒀸, 𒐀, 𒐁.

2. Length Measures

sign	Sum.	Akk.	translation	= ŠU.SI	= KÙŠ	= GI	= NINDA	= ÉŠ(E)	= UŠ	modern
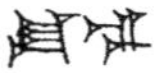	ŠU.SI	*ubānum*	‘finger’							1.67 cm.
	KÙŠ	*ammatum*	‘cubit’, ‘ell’	30						50 cm.
	GI	*qanûm*	‘reed’	180	6					3 m.
	NINDA	*nindanum*?	‘rod’, ‘pole’	360	12	2				6 m.
	ÉŠ(E)	*ašlum*	‘rope’, ‘cord’	3600	120	20	10			60 m.
	UŠ	?	‘sixty (NINDA)?’	21,600	720	120	60	6		360 m.
	DANNA	*bērum*	‘double-hour’	648,000	21,600	3,600	1,800	180	30	10.8 km.

Other linear measures:

	ŠE	*uṭṭatum*	‘grain’	= $^1/_6$ ŠU.SI	2.8 mm.
	ŠU.DÙ(.A)	*šīzum* / *šizûm*		= $^1/_3$ KÙŠ = 10 ŠU.SI	16.7 cm.
	ZIPAḪ (=MAŠ)	*ūṭum*	‘span’	= $^1/_2$ KÙŠ = 15 ŠU.SI	25 cm.
	—	*nikkas*		= 3 KÙŠ	1.5 m.
	—	*ṣuppum*		= $^1/_2$ ÉŠ(E) = 5 NINDA	30 m.

3. Area (Surface) Measures

sign	Sum.	Akk.	translation	= ŠE	= GÍN	= SAR	= IKU	= EŠE$_3$	= BÙR	= BÙR.U	= ŠÁR	modern
	ŠE	*uṭṭatum*	'grain'									33 cm.^{2}
	GÍN	*šiqlum*	'shekel'	180								.6 m.^{2}
	SAR	*mūšarum*	'garden plot'	10,800	60							36 m.^{2}
	IKU	*ikûm*	'field$^?$'		6000	100						3,600 m.^{2}
	EŠE$_3^{(iku)}$	*eblum*	'rope'			600	6					2.16 ha.
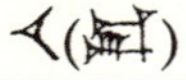	BÙR$^{(iku)}$	*būrum*				1,800	18	3				6.48 ha.
	BÙR.U					18,000	180	30	10			64.8 ha.
	ŠÁR$^{(iku)}$					108,000	1080	180	60	6		388.8 ha.
	ŠÁR.U					1,080,000	10,800	1,800	600	60	10	3888 ha.

The SAR is 1 NINDA^2 ; the IKU is 1 ÉŠ(E)^2 (for NINDA and ÉŠ(E) , see above, under length measures).

Numbers:

ŠE, GÍN, and SAR: with the regular numeral signs:  (60), .

IKU: with horizontal wedges: .

1 EŠE$_3$: ; 2 EŠE$_3$:  (i.e., BI).

BÙR: .

multiples of BÙR.U, ŠÁR, and ŠÁR.U are expressed by repeating the appropriate signs: 2 ŠÁR .

4. Volume Measures

Sum.	translation	dimensions	modern
ŠE	'grain'	2 ŠU.SI ∝ 6 ŠU.SI ∝ 1 KÙŠ	1.66 $dm.^3$
GÍN.TUR	'small shekel'	6 ŠU.SI ∝ 6 ŠU.SI ∝ 1 KÙŠ	5 $dm.^3$
MA.NA.TUR	'small mina'		100 $dm.^3$
GÍN	'shekel'		300 $dm.^3$
SAR	'garden plot'	1 surface SAR(= 1 NINDA ∝ 1 NINDA) ∝ 1 KÙŠ	18 $m.^3$
IKU	'field?'	1 surface IKU ∝ 1 KÙŠ	1,800 $m.^3$
$EŠE_3$	'rope'	1 surface $EŠE_3$ ∝ 1 KÙŠ	10,800 $m.^3$
BÙR		1 surface BÙR ∝ 1 KÙŠ	32,400 $m.^3$

1 ŠE of volume (1.66 $dm.^3$) = 1 $^2/_3$ $SILA_3$ of capacity (1.66 l.).

1 GÍN of volume (300 $dm.^3$) = 1 GUR of capacity (300 l.).

5. Capacity Measures

sign	Sum.	Akkadian	translation	= ŠE	= $SILA_3$	= BÁN	= "PI"	modern
	ŠE	*uṭṭatum*	'grain'					.005 l.
or	$SILA_3$	*qûm*	'liter'	180				1 l.
	BÁN	*sūtum*	'seah'	1,800	10			10 l.
	BÁNMIN	*2 sâtum*	'2 seahs'	3,600	20	2		20 l.
	BÁNEŠ	*3 sâtum*	'3 seahs'	5,400	30	3		30 l.
	BÁNLIMMU	*4 sâtum*	'4 seahs'	7,200	40	4		40 l.
	BÁNIA	*5 sâtum*	'5 seahs'	9,000	50	5		50 l.
	NIGIDA (PI)	*pānum* or *parsiktum*		10,800	60	6		60 l.
	$NIMIN_3$	*2 pānū*		21,600	120	12	2	120 l.
	NIEŠ	*3 pānū*		32,400	180	18	3	180 l.
	NILIMMU	*4 pānū*		43,200	240	24	4	240 l.
	GUR	*kurrum*	'kor'	54,000	300	30	5	300 l.

Construction:

(a) Larger units precede smaller units.
(b) GUR units '1' to '9' are written with horizontal wedges ("tens" with Winkelhaken), *without* the GUR sign. Note also, however, writings such as 5 ŠE GUR for (nom.) *ḫamšat kur ûm* '5 kor of barley'; cf. (f), below.
(c) *pānum / parsiktum* amounts are written with the signs given in the table above, *without* the PI sign.
(d) BÁN amounts are written as indicated in the table above.
(e) $SILA_3$ amounts are written with the regular number signs *with* the $SILA_3$ sign.
(f) The GUR sign is often added at the *end* of the expression, as a kind of determinative indicating that the preceding signs constitute an expression of capacity; see above, under (b), and below, the last example.
(g) A frequent convention for transliterating writings of this type is simply to write the relevant numbers, separated by commas, with '0' for missing units; see the examples.

Examples:

 4 (GUR) 3 ("PI") 2 BÁN 6 $SILA_3$; or 4 (GUR) NIEŠ BANMIN 6 $SILA_3$; or 4,3,2,6; = 1,406 *qûm*.

 3 (GUR) 4 BÁN 9 $SILA_3$; or 4 (GUR) BANLIMMU 9 $SILA_3$; or 3,0,4,9; = 949 *qûm*.

 1 (GUR) 2 ("PI"); or 1 (GUR) $NIMIN_3$; or 1,2,0,0 = 360 *qûm*.

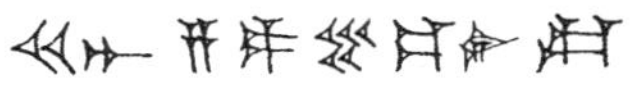 22 (GUR) 4 ("PI") 2 (BÁN) ŠE.GIŠ.Ì GUR ; or 22,4,2,0 ŠE.GIŠ.Ì GUR = 6,860 *qûm* of sesame.

APPENDIX C: HISTORICAL AKKADIAN PHONOLOGY

As noted in the Introduction, Akkadian is a member of the Semitic language family. Although it is the earliest attested, it has, by the OB period, undergone a more radical development in its phonological system than that exhibited by any other Semitic language until the modern period. Thus, for example, while Common Semitic may be reconstructed with thirty distinct consonants, OB has only twenty; while Common Semitic has three vowel qualities, OB has four. (At least some of these developments may be ascribed to the influence of Sumerian.) A knowledge of early Semitic phonology and of the historical development of Akkadian phonology is often helpful in understanding the processes observed in individual dialects like Old Babylonian.

1. Consonants

The Common Semitic complement of consonants may be represented as follows (vd = voiced; vl = voiceless; em = emphatic; approx. = approximants):

	stops			affricates			fricatives			approx.	nasals
	vd	vl	em	vd	vl	em	vd	vl	em	vd	vd
bilabial	*b*	*p*								*w*	*m*
interdental							*ð*	*θ*	*θ̣*		
dental	*d*	*t*	*ṭ*							*r*	*n*
alveolar				*z*	*s*	*ṣ*		*š*			
lateral						*ṣ́*		*ś*		*l*	
palatal										*y*	
velar	*g*	*k*	*q*				*ǵ*	*ḫ*	*x̣*		
pharyngeal							ʿ	*ḥ*			
glottal		ʾ						*h*			

The syllabary of Old Akkadian, the earliest attested period of the language, is unfortunately very ambiguous, and it is difficult to determine how many of these thirty consonantal phonemes had been lost to mergers and other changes by that period. (It is clear, however, that more consonants remained distinct than in OB [Hasselbach 2005]; see below.) In OB, the following developments have occurred:

(a) Common Semitic **ð* and **z* have merged to *z*:

**ðakārum* › *zakārum* 'to remember'; **ʾuðnum* › *uznum* 'ear';
**zamārum* › *zamārum* 'to make music'; **ʿazābum* › *ezēbum* 'to leave'.

(b) Common Semitic **ḫ* and **x̣* have merged to *ḫ*:

**ḫamišum* › *ḫamšum* 'five'; **šaḫānum* › *šaḫānum* 'to be warm';
**x̣apārum* › *ḫepērum* 'to dig'; **rax̣āṣum* › *raḫāṣum* 'to wash'.

(c) Common Semitic **ṣ*, **ṣ́*, and **θ̣* have merged to *ṣ*:

**ṣarāḫum* › *ṣarāḫum* 'to cry out'; **raṣāpum* › *raṣāpum* 'to pile up';
**ṣ́amādum* › *ṣamādum* 'to bind'; **ʾarṣ́atum* › *erṣetum* 'earth';
**θ̣iprum* › *ṣuprum* 'fingernail'; **naθ̣ārum* › *naṣārum* 'to watch'.

(d) Common Semitic **ś*, **š*, and **θ* have merged to *š*:

**śapatum* › *šaptum* 'lip'; **ʿaśarum* › *ešerum* 'ten';
**šakānum* › *šakānum* 'to place'; **našāqum* › *našāqum* 'to kiss';
**θalāθum* › *šalāšum* 'three'; **waθābum* › *wašābum* 'to dwell'.

In Old Akkadian, however, **θ* remained distinct from **ś / š*; **θ* was written with ŠA, ŠI, ŠU (as in *ú-ša-ab* for earlier **yuθθab* 'he dwells') while **ś / š* was written with SA, SI, SU (as in *sa-ap-ta-su* for earlier **śap(a)tā-šu* 'his lips (dual)'). (For Old Akkadian, von Soden in his *Grundriss*, *Syllabar*, and *AHw* writes Com. Sem. **θ* as *š* and Com. Sem. **ś / š* as *ś*.)

(e) Four of the Common Semitic "guttural" consonants, **ʾ*, **h*, **ḥ*, **ʿ* — i.e., the two glottal consonants and the two pharyngeals, respectively — gradually merged and were lost in most environments. These are referred to by Assyriologists as $ʾ_1$ through $ʾ_4$, respectively. Two of these consonants, **ḥ* and **ʿ* ($ʾ_{3-4}$), colored neighboring *a* vowels to *e* before they were lost. (See §6.1.)

**ʾamārum* › *amārum* 'to see';	**ḥarāθum* › *erēšum* 'to plow';
**halākum* › *alākum* 'to go';	**ʿazābum* › *ezēbum* 'to leave'.

It is likely that in at least some dialects of Old Akkadian these consonants had not yet merged or been lost completely.

Another "guttural" consonant, **ġ*, referred to as $ʾ_5$ by Assyriologists, was rare in early Semitic; its reflexes in Akkadian are varied: sometimes lost (occasionally with the change of _a_ › _e_, as with ʾ$_{3–4}$), sometimes retained as ʾ, and sometimes retained as _ḫ_ (Kogan 2001):

*_ǵaθāyum_ › _ešûm_ 'to confuse'; *_ṣaǵārum_ › _ṣeḫērum_ 'to be small'.
*_b-ǵ-y_ › _buʾʾûm_ D 'to search';

(f) Common Semitic *_w_ — sometimes referred to as ʾ$_6$ — was lost at the end of syllables (unless followed by another _w_, as in _nuwwurum_ 'to brighten'), with compensatory lengthening of the preceding vowel; the diphthong *_aw_ became _ū_ (probably _ō_ in some dialects of Babylonian for a time [Westenholz 1991]):

*_šuwrid_ › _šūrid_ 'send down (ms)!'; *_mawtum_ › _mūtum_ 'death'.

In late OB (§24.4) and later dialects, initial _w_ is also lost, as in _wašib_ › _ašib_ 'is seated (m)'.

(g) Common Semitic *_y_ — sometimes referred to as ʾ$_7$ — was also lost at the end of syllables (unless followed by another _y_, as in _dayyānum_ 'judge'), with compensatory lengthening of the preceding vowel; the diphthong *_ay_ became _ī_ in Babylonian (but _ē_ in Assyrian dialects: _bētum_ 'house'). Initial *_y_ was also lost by the OB period (perhaps not in Old Akkadian); initial *_ya-_ became _i-_:

*_rabiytum_ › _rabītum_ 'great (fs)'; *_baytum_ › _bītum_ 'house';
*_yupaḫḫar_ › _upaḫḫar_ 'he gathers'; *_yašarum_ › _išarum_ 'straight'.

(h) Initial _m_ (except for _mu-_) dissimilated to _n_ in forms with a labial radical (Barth's Law; §32.2):

*_markabtum_ ›_narkabtum_ 'chariot'; *_mapḫarum_ › _napḫarum_ 'total'.
*_mamṣarum_ › _namṣarum_ 'sword';

(i) In words and roots originally containing two Common Semitic emphatic consonants, one of the emphatics dissimilated to its non-emphatic voiceless counterpart (Geers' Law): _ṭ_ became _t_ in forms that also contained _q_ or _ṣ_ (from *_ṣ_, *_ṣ́_, or *_θ̣_); in forms with both _q_ and _ṣ_, the one that came first dissimilated, _q_ to _k_ and _ṣ_ to _s_:

*_ṣ́abāṭum_ › _ṣabātum_ 'to seize'; *_qaṣārum_ › _kaṣārum_ 'to tie';
*_qaṭārum_ › _qatārum_ 'to smoke'; *_ṣ́ayāqum_ › _siāqum_ 'to be narrow'.

(j) *_n_ assimilated to a following consonant, except in some instances when it was the second root consonant (§5.1):

*_ʾantī̆_ › _atti_ 'you (fs)'; _taddin-ma_ › _taddim-ma_ 'you (ms) gave and ...';
*_tanθ̣ur_ › _taṣṣur_ 'you (ms) guarded';
but _ʿanzum_ › _enzum_ 'she-goat'.

(k) Conversely, _n_, and sometimes _m_, may appear as the result of the nasalization of double consonants, usually voiced dentals; thus, e.g., expected *-dd-* appears as *-nd-* or *-md-*. This phenomenon is sporadically attested before the OB period, is occasionally found in some OB dialects, and becomes more common in latter phases of Babylonian. The most common examples are Durative forms of *nadānum*:

> *inaddin* may also appear as *i-na-an-di-in, i-na-am-di-in, i-nam-di-in*.

(l) Several consonants assimilated to the feminine ending *t* (§5.4); *d* and *ṭ* assimilated completely, while *s, ṣ,* and *z* became *š*:masc. *paqdum*, fem. *paqittum* ‹ **paqidtum* 'entrusted';

> masc. *balṭum*, fem. *balittum* ‹ **baliṭtum* 'alive';
> masc. *parsum*, fem. *parištum* ‹ **paristum* 'separated';
> masc. *marṣum*, fem. *maruštum* ‹ **maruṣtum* 'sick';
> *mazzaštum*, also written *mazzaztum* 'position' (from *izuzzum*).

(m) The the infix *-t-* of the Perfect and of the Gt and Dt stems assimilated completely when immediately before or after the consonants *d, s, ṣ, ṭ,* and *z* (§§17.1, 33.1) and when immediately before *š* (but not when after *š*). The infix *-t-* became *-d-* after *g*.

> *iddamiq* ‹ **idtamiq* 'it has improved'; *ḫiddulum* ‹ **ḫitdulum* 'to become knotted';
> *issaḫur* ‹ **istaḫur* 'she has turned'; *ḫissas* ‹ **ḫitsas* 'consider (ms)';
> *iṣṣabat* ‹ **iṣtabat* 'he has seized'; *iṣṣar* ‹ **(n)itṣar* 'guard yourself (ms)';
> *iṭṭarad* ‹ **iṭtarad* 'she has sent';
> *izzakar* ‹ **iztakar* 'he has mentioned';
> *ištakan* 'she has placed', but *piššušum* ‹ **pitšušum* 'to anoint oneself';
> *igdamar* ‹ **igtamar* 'he has finished'.

(n) The combination of a stem-final dental or sibilant (*d,t,ṭ,s,ṣ,z,š*) and *š* of the third person pronominal suffixes resulted in *-ss-* (§§11.1, 18.2):

> **qaqqad-ša* › *qaqqassa* 'her head';
> **imqut-šum* › *imqussum* 'it happened (fell) to him';
> **balāṭ-šina* › *balāssina* 'their (f) life';
> **ikkis-šu* › *ikkissu* 'he cut it (m) off';
> **ḫurāṣ-ša* › *ḫurāssa* 'her gold';
> **aḫḫaz-ši* › *aḫḫassi* 'I will marry her';
> **lūpuš-šināšim* › *lūpussināšim* 'let me act for them (f)'.

(o) Stem-final *b* and, less often, *p* assimilated to enclitic *-ma* (§7.4):

> *irkab-ma* › *irkam-ma* 'he rode and ...'.

(p) In late OB texts and in later dialects, mimation was lost when word-final (retained before *-ma* and pronominal suffixes; see §24.4(a)):

> *šarrum* › *šarru*;
> *eqlētum* › *eqlētu*;
> *išpuram* › *išpura*, but *išpuram-ma*;
> *ašpurakkum* › *ašpurakku*.

Akkadian	Proto-Semitic	Hebrew	Aramaic (Syriac)	Arabic	Ethiopic (Geᶜez)
ᵓ/ø	< *ᵓ =	ᵓ	ᵓ	ᵓ	ᵓ
	< *h =	h	h	h	h
	< *ḥ =	ḥ	ḥ	ḥ	ḥ
	< *ᶜ =	ᶜ	ᶜ	ᶜ	ᶜ
	< *ǵ =	ᶜ	ᶜ	ǵ	ᶜ
	(< *w =	w/y	w/y	w	w)
	(< *y =	y	y	y	y)
b	< *b =	b	b	b	b
d	< *d =	d	d	d	d
g	< *g =	g	g	ǧ	g
ḫ	(< *ǵ =	ᶜ	ᶜ	ǵ	ᶜ)
	< *ḫ =	ḥ	ḥ	ḫ	ḫ
	< *x̣ =	ḥ	ḥ	ḥ	ḥ
k	< *k =	k	k	k	k
l	< *l =	l	l	l	l
m	< *m =	m	m	m	m
n	< *n =	n	n	n	n
p	< *p =	p	p	f	f
q	< *q =	q	q	q	q
r	< *r =	r	r	r	r
s	< *s =	s	s	s	s
ṣ	< *ṣ =	ṣ	ṣ	ṣ	ṣ
	< *ṣ́ =	ṣ	ᶜ	ḍ	ḍ
	< *θ̣ =	ṣ	ṭ	ẓ	ṣ
š	< *ś =	ś	s	š	ś
	< *š =	š	š	s	s
	< *θ =	š	t	θ	s
t	< *t =	t	t	t	t
ṭ	< *ṭ =	ṭ	ṭ	ṭ	ṭ
w	< *w =	w/y	w/y	w	w
y	< *y =	y	y	y	y
z	< *ð =	z	d	ð	z
	< *z =	z	z	z	z

(q) For the benefit of individuals who have studied other Semitic languages, the chart on p. 590 presents the OB consonants along with their Proto-Semitic antecedents and the reflexes of the latter in the other major ancient languages.

2. Vowels

Common Semitic may be reconstructed with three vowel qualities, each occurring either long or short, as in classical Arabic: *a, ā, i, ī, u, ū*. A number of developments vis-à-vis Common Semitic are attested in all Akkadian dialects:

(a) Contraction of the diphthongs **aw* and **ay*; as noted above, **aw* became *ū* (probably *ō* in some early dialects of Babylonian) while **ay* became *ī* in Babylonian (also in Old Akkadian) and *ē* in Assyrian:

> **θawrum* › *šūrum* 'bull';
> **baytum* › Bab. *bītum*, Ass. *bētum* 'house'.
>
> (Note also forms such as **śayimum* › Bab. *šīmum*, Ass. *šēmum* 'decreed' and **kawinum* › **kayinum* › Bab. *kīnum*, Ass. *kēnum* 'true'; further, perhaps, **yiśayyam* › *išīam* 'he decrees' and **yitawwar* › Ass. *itūar* › Bab. *itâr* 'he returns'.)

(b) Initial **ya-* became *yi-*; subsequently (after the Old Akk. period), the initial *y* was lost:

> **yadum* › *yidum* › *idum* 'arm';
> **yašarum* › *yišarum* › *išarum* 'straight'.

(c) Short final **a* and **u* were lost; final **i* remained in the Old Akk. period, but was also lost thereafter:

> bound form sg. nom. **kalbu*, acc. **kalba* both › **kalb* (then › **kalab*), vs. gen. *kalbi* (in Old Akk.; later also › *kalab*) 'dog of';
> bound pl. nom. **ʾilātu* › *ilāt*, but gen.–acc. *(ʾ)ilāti* (in Old Akk.; later also › *ilāt*) 'goddesses of';
> dual nom. **ʿaynāna*, gen.–acc. **ʿaynayna* › *īnān*, *īnīn* (Ass. *ēnān*, *ēnēn*) 'eyes';
> predicative verbal adjective, 3ms **parisa* › *paris* 'is divided'.
>
> Apparent exceptions are the prepositions *ana* and *ina* (also *an*, *in* in Old Akk., later poetry) and the subordination marker *-u*.
>
> This rule means that, apart from the exceptions just mentioned, all final vowels in Akkadian originate as long vowels; see (k) below.

(d) Final consonant clusters created by the preceding change were resolved by the insertion of an anaptyctic vowel; in Bab. the inserted vowel echoed the preceding vowel, while in Ass. it was consistently *a*:

> **kalb* › *kalab* (Bab. and Ass.) 'dog of';
> **rigm* › Bab. *rigim*, Ass. *rigam* 'voice of';
> **puḫr* › Bab. *puḫur*, Ass. *puḫar* 'assembly of'.

(e) Syncope: the last of a sequence of two or more non-final short vowels in open syllables (except optionally before *l* and *r*) was deleted (§4.1):

> **rapašum* › *rapšum* 'wide (ms)', vs. *rapaš* (bound form/predicative);
> **rapašatum* › *rapaštum* 'wide (fs)';
>
> but *ʾ*akalum* › *akalum* / *aklum* 'food';
> **šikarum* › *šikarum* 'beer'.

(f) **a* was pronounced [e] before and after *ḥ* and ᶜ (and, occasionally, *ǵ*); in Bab., but not in Ass., *ā* was likewise pronounced [ē]. With the subsequent merging and loss of the gutturals (see 1 (d), above), *e* (and *ē*) achieved phonemic status:

> *ᶜ*azib* › ᶜ*ezib* › *ezib* 'he having left (ms)';
> **taḥpuš* › **teḥpuš* › *tēpuš* 'you (ms) did'.
>
> **a* also often became *e* in words containing PS *ʾ and a sonorant, especially **n* or **r*:
> *ʾ*arṣatum* › (ʾ)*erṣatum* › *erṣetum* 'earth';
> **raʾšum* › **reʾšum* › *rēšum* 'top'.
>
> The change **a* › *e* did not operate across certain morpheme boundaries, so that, e.g., in the accusative marker *-am*, in the plural marker -*ā*, and in the ventive marker *-am*, *a (ā)* remained unchanged:
> **qamḥam* › **qemḥam* › *qēmam* 'flour' (acc.);
> **yaptaḥā* › **yipteḥā* › *ipteā* 'they (f) opened';
> *ʾ*alqaḥam* › *ʾ*alqeḥam* › *elqeam* 'I brought hither'.

(g) **i* also had an allophone [e], which occurred before *r* and *ḫ* (§7.1); in some, but not all, instances, this merged with [e] from **a* (see (f), above).

> **ṣaḫir* › *ṣaḫer* (› *ṣeḫer*) 'it (m) is small';
> **taθabbir* › *tašabber* (› *tešebber*) 'you (ms) break'.

(h) Babylonian vowel harmony: **a (ā)* became *e (ē)* in words containing *e* or *ē* (§7.2):

> *ᶜ*azābum* › *ᶜ*ezābum* › *ezābum* (Ass.) › *ezēbum* 'to leave';
> **talqaḥ* › **talqeḥ* › *talqe* (Ass.) › *telqe* 'you (ms) took';
> **ṣaḫir* › *ṣaḫer* (Ass.) › *ṣeḫer* 'it (m) is small';
> **taθabbir* › *tašabber* (Ass.) › *tešebber* 'you (ms) break'.

This sound change was restricted by the same morpheme boundaries that prohibited *a › e in (f).

Not infrequently, forms in which no *e* appeared also underwent a change **a (ā)* › *e (ē)* as a result of the presence of *e* in other derivatives of the same root: e.g.,

**pātiḫum* → **pētiḫum* › *pētûm* 'opening' (ptcpl ms);
**šabārum* → *šebērum* 'to break'.

(i) Assyrian vowel harmony: unstressed short *a* in an open syllable was assimilated to a following vowel:

/šarrat-/: nom. *šarrutum*, gen. *šarritim*, acc. *šarratam* 'queen';
/taṣbat-/: *taṣbat(ā)* 'you (ms, -ā pl) seized', *taṣbutu* 'you (ms) seized' (subord.), *taṣbitī* 'you (fs) seized'.

(j) Vowel contraction (§6.1(c)): sequences of vowels — which arose with the loss of the guttural consonants, *w*, and *y* — generally contracted to ultralong versions of the original second vowel; exceptions are *ā* + *i* / *ī* › *ê* in all Bab. dialects, and the non-contraction of the sequences *ia* and *ea* (either vowel long or short) until late in the OB period. (In Old Akkadian and for most of the history of Assyrian, no vowel contraction took place.)

**yabniyū* › *ibniū* › *ibnû* 'they (m) built';
**tabniyī* › *tabnî* 'you (fs) built';
**tabniyā* › *tabniā* 'you (pl) built';
**banāyum* › **banāum* › *banûm* 'to build' (nom.);
**banāyim* › **banāim* › *banêm* 'to build' (gen.).

(k) As noted above under (c), original short final vowels were lost early in the history of Akkadian. Thus, with the exception of the prepositions *ana* and *ina* and the subordination marker *-u*, all final vowels that remain in dialects such as OB are originally **long** vowels. It is likely that all such vowels, except for contracted long vowels (*v̂*), were pronounced **short** when word-final. The various Assyriological reference works do not represent these vowels consistently in their transcriptions. Final long vowels may be classified into several groups, in addition to those that are long as the result of contraction:

(1) Morphologically long vowels inherited from Common Semitic. These are marked long (*v̄*) in the present textbook and in W. von Soden's standard grammar (*GAG*) and dictionary (*AHw*), but are unmarked in *CAD*; they include:

the markers of the masc. pl. on nouns (*-ū* / *-ī*) and the markers of the dual (*-ā* / *-ī*):

nom. *šarrū*, gen.–acc. *šarrī* 'kings' (probably pronounced [šarru], [šarri], but with suffixes, e.g., [šarrū-ni], [šarrī-šunu]);

nom. *īnā*, gen.–acc. *īnī* 'eyes of' (probably pronounced [īna], [īni], but with suffixes, e.g., [īnā-ka], [īnī-ša]);

the markers of the 2fs and of the second and third plural on finite verbs:

taprus-ī, iprus-ū, iprus-ā, taprus-ā (probably pronounced [taprusi], [iprusu], [iprusa], [taprusa], but with suffixes, e.g., [taprusī-šu], etc.).

(2) Common Semitic final vowels of variable length ("anceps vowels"), primarily in pronominal endings. These were usually retained in Akkadian, although some are omitted in certain dialects (especially in poetry). When word-final they are transcribed without a length mark by most Assyriologists; when not final they are transcribed variously unmarked (in *CAD*) or with a macron (elsewhere, including this textbook):

Com. Sem. *-šŭ̄* 'his'/'him' › Akk. *-šu* (but, e.g., *īmur-šū-ma*);

Com. Sem. *-šunŭ̄* 'their (m)' › Akk. *-šunu* (but, e.g., *ittī-šunū-ma* 'with *them*'; this appears as *-šun* in some dialects — see §30.2(e));

Com. Sem. *-ātă̄* 'you (ms)' › Akk. *-āta*, as in *damq-āta* (but *damqātā-ma*; this appears as *-āt* in some dialects).

(3) Vowels long from compensatory lengthening with the loss of a following consonant (guttural, *w*, *y*). When word-final they are transcribed without a length mark by most Assyriologists; when not final they are transcribed variously unmarked (in *CAD*) or with a macron (elsewhere, including this textbook):

**nimlaʾ* › *nimlā* = *nimla* 'we filled', but *nimlā-ma;*

**tukarrah* › *tukarrā* = *tukarra* 'you (ms) lessen', but *tukarrā-ma;*

**niptaḥ* › *niptē* = *nipte* 'we opened', but *niptē-ma;*

**tamnuw* › *tamnū* = *tamnu* 'you (ms) counted', but *tamnū-ma;*

**tabniy* › *tabnī* = *tabni* 'you (ms) built', but *tabnī-ma;*

**rabiya* › **rabiy* › *rabī* = *rabi* 'is great (3ms)', but *rabī-ma;*

**ʿadiy* › *adī* = *adi* 'up to', but *adīni* 'until now'.

APPENDIX D: STANDARD BABYLONIAN

As has already been mentioned in the Introduction to this textbook (p. xxiv), Standard Babylonian (SB) was a purely literary language, an artificial creation of scribes of the late second and the first millennium, in which they attempted to reproduce the grammatical forms of Old Babylonian poetry to write the great sacred and royal literature of the period. Although it is based on Old Babylonian, Standard Babylonian also exhibits forms that betray the influence of the scribes' colloquial dialects, Neo- and Late Babylonian. Assyrian scribes too used Standard Babylonian for literary and monumental texts, and their works show as well sporadic traces of Assyrian forms.

In German the term that corresponds to Standard Babylonian is *Jungbabylonisch* (abbr. *jB*), literally 'young Babylonian'. A thorough, linguistically-sophisticated description of SB grammar, especially of the morphology and syntax, is Brigitte Groneberg's *Syntax, Morphologie und Stil der jungbabylonischen "hymnischen" Literatur* (2 volumes; 1987).

In what follows only major differences from Old Babylonian grammar are presented.

1. Orthography

(a) Many more *CVC* signs are regularly used: e.g., 𒋃, with the values *lag / k / q* and *šid / t / ṭ*. Some OB *CV* and *VC* signs take on additional, *CVC* values: e.g., UD = *tam, par, pir, laḫ, liḫ, ḫiš*; ME = *šib / p*.

(b) (i) The U-sign (𒌋) is used often, although it does not replace Ú (𒌑) completely; one finds, e.g., both *ib-nu-u* and *ib-nu-ú*.

(ii) The PI-sign (𒉿), used for *wa / we / wi / wu* passim in OB texts and for *pi / pe* only in southern OB documents, is commonly used for *pi / pe* (and only rarely for *w*+vowel) in SB.

(iii) Two other frequent signs are *šú* () and *šá* (the NÍG-sign, ).

(c) A number of *CVm* signs take on *CV* values: e.g., TUM = tu_4, UD = *tam* and ta_5.

(d) There is a specific sign to represent *aleph* (ʾ): . Some Assyriologists transliterate this sign simply ʾ, while others assign it the values *ʾa, ʾe, ʾi, ʾu, aʾ, eʾ, iʾ, uʾ*: e.g., *ša-ʾ-a-lu* or *ša-ʾa-a-lu* for *šaʾālu* 'to ask'; *šá-ʾ-il* or *šá-ʾi-il* for *šaʾil* 'is asked (m)'; *na-ʾ-du* or *na-aʾ-du* for *naʾdu* 'pious (ms)'.

(e) There are a number of specific signs for the emphatic consonants: e.g.,  KIN, also *qi/qe*; further, KUM is used with the value *qu*; GÍN is used with the value *ṭu*.

2. Phonology

(a) The loss of mimation noted for late OB texts in §24.4(a) is reflected more regularly: *šarru/šarri/šarra; iddina* 'she gave to me'; *-ku* 'to you (ms)'. Although *CVm* signs often still appear word-finally, *-Vm* signs usually do not: e.g., *šar-ru* or *šar-rum* (which may also be read *šar-rù*) for nom. sg. *šarru* (OB *šarrum*); *šar-ra-tu* or *šar-ra-tú* (*tú* = UD) or *šar-ra-tum* (= *šar-ra-*tu_4) for nom. sg. *šarratu* (OB *šarratum*). When not the final consonant, i.e., before *-ma* or pronominal suffixes, mimation is not lost: *iddinam-ma; iddinakkum-ma*.

(b) The contraction of the vowel sequences *ia, ea*, attested already in late OB (§24.4(b)), is normal: *qibiam* › *qibâ* 'say (ms) to me'; *išmeā* › *išmâ* 'they (f) heard'.

(c) *š* usually appears as *l* before the dentals *d, t, ṭ*: e.g.,

OB *iktašdam* › SB *iktalda* 'she arrived here';
OB *taštakan* › SB *taltakan* 'you (ms) have placed';
OB *ašṭur* › SB *alṭur* 'I inscribed'.

It was noted in §5.4 that in OB *s, ṣ*, and *z* normally become *š* before the feminine ending *-t*, as in *maruštum*, the fem. of *marṣum* 'sick'. In SB this *š* usually appears as *l*:

SB *marṣu*, fem. *marultu* 'sick';
OB *rikistum* 'agreement' › SB *rikiltu*;
OB *mazzaštum* (also *mazzaztum*, from *izuzzum*) 'position' › *manzaltu*.

OB *išsi/issi* '(s)he called' appears in SB as either *issi* or *ilsi*.

(d) Initial *w* is lost (also rarely in late OB texts; see §24.4(c)):

OB *wardum* › SB *ardu* 'male slave';
OB *walādum* › SB *alādu* 'to give birth'.

Within a word, i.e., between vowels, OB *w* is written as *m*:

OB *awīlum* › SB *amīlu* 'man';
OB *uwaššar* › SB *umaššar* 'he releases'.

The existence of *umaššar* gives rise to forms such as the Infinitive *muššuru*, with an initial *m*- rather than the expected simple loss of the OB initial *w*- (OB *wuššurum*).

(e) Double consonants, especially the voiced dentals -*dd*- and -*zz*-, are often nasalized, i.e., › -*nd*-, -*nz*- (see Appendix C 1 (j)):

inaddin › *inandin* 'she gives';
mazzaštum › *manzaltu* 'position';
abbi › *ambi* 'I named'.

(f) In the D and Š Preterite, Perfect, and Precative, the *a* of the second syllable sometimes undergoes partial assimilation to the *i* or *e* of the following syllable, appearing as *e*:

ušaknis › *ušeknis* 'he subjugated';
uptaḫḫer › *upteḫḫer* 'I have gathered';
lilabbiš › *lilebbiš* 'let him clothe'.

(g) *m* plus the infix -*t*- usually become -*nd*-:

as OB *wuššurum* is replaced by SB *muššuru* (see d, above), the OB Perfect *ūtaššer* is replaced by *umtaššer*, which appears as *undaššer* (or, with (f), above, as *undeššer*).

(h) In verbs II–ʾ, the aleph often appears as a strong consonant:

OB *šâlum* but SB *šaʾālu* 'to ask';
OB *išāl* (written *i-ša-al*) but SB *išʾal* (written *iš-al*) 'she asked'.

(i) Many Assyrian vocalisms occur; see Appendix E, below.

3. Morphology

(a) The case endings on nouns are no longer strictly adhered to; in particular:

(i) The accusative is often replaced by the nominative; the genitive is also occasionally replaced by the nominative:

OB *awātam iqbiam* = SB *amātu iqbâ* 'she said a word to me'.

(ii) Sometimes no case-ending at all appears:

tukallam nūr 'you (ms) show the light' (*nūru(m)* 'light').

(iii) The ending for nouns in the plural is often the oblique *-ī* or *-ē* (the latter from Assyrian; see App. E, 2 (b2)), even when the noun is nominative; this is especially true for the bound form:

šarrē mātāti illikūni 'the kings of the lands came'.

(iv) The ending for nouns in the dual is often the nominative *ā*, even when the noun is oblique; the dual also appears on words for parts of the body that are not paired:

oblique *šēpāšu* 'his feet';
kišādāšu 'his neck'.

(b) As in OB literary texts (see §30.2(f)), a number of feminine nouns exhibit different bound forms than they do in OB prose; e.g.,

napištu 'life', bound form *napišti* (as in OB) or *napšat.*

(c) (i) The plural demonstrative pronouns *šunūti* and *šināti* (§6.3) are replaced by *šuātunu* (or *šâtunu*) and *šuātina* (*šâtina*), respectively.

(ii) As in OB literary texts (§30.2(e)), the genitive pronominal suffixes may appear without their final vowels:

šalamtaš for *šalamtaša* 'her corpse';
niṭilšun for *niṭilšunu* 'their (m) glance'.

(iii) *-šu* and *-ša* are sometimes not distinguished.

(d) The regular plurals of *ilu* 'god' and *šarru* 'king' appear as *ilānū* / *ilānī* and *šarrānū* / *šarrānī* (see §20.2).

(e) The terminative-adverbial ending *-iš* (§28.2) takes on a comparative nuance (equivalent to *kīma* with the genitive) in addition to its OB uses:

iliš 'like a god'.

(f) Verbs III–weak all tend to become III–*i*:

imnu or *imni* 'she counted'; *ikla* or *ikli* 'he prevented'.

(g) The ventive occurs frequently, but often without a clear function.

(h) The predicative form of the adjective with 3fs subject *-at* may take the subordinate marker *-u*:

OB *ša wašbat* but SB *ša ašbatu* 'who (f) is resident'.

(i) Many Assyrian forms occur; see Appendix E, below.

APPENDIX E: ASSYRIAN PHONOLOGY AND MORPHOLOGY

See the Introduction (p. xxiv) for a review of the Assyrian dialects. Only major features that contrast with their Babylonian counterparts are listed here. A detailed treatment of Old Assyrian is K. Hecker, *Grammatik der Kültepe-Texte* (1968); for Middle Assyrian see W. Mayer, *Untersuchungen zur Grammatik des Mittelassyrischen* (1971); and for Neo-Assyrian, see J. Hämeen-Anttilla, *A Sketch of Neo-Assyrian Grammar* (2000).

1. Phonology

(a) There are no vowel contractions until Neo-Assyrian, thus, e.g.,

Bab.	*dâku(m)*	=	Ass.	*duāku(m)*	'to slay';
	rubû(m)			*rubāu(m)*	'prince';
	rabû(m)			*rabiu(m)*	'large'.

(b) *a* and *e* are compatible in the same word; thus there is no change of *a* (*ā*) to *e* (*ē*) because of the presence of an *e*-vowel elsewhere in the word:

Bab.	*erēbu(m)*	=	Ass.	*erābu(m)*	'to enter';
	tešemme / *tašamme*			*tašamme* (never *tešemme*)	'you (ms) hear';
	bēlētu(m)			*bēlātu(m)*	'ladies'.

(c) There is, however, a different rule of vowel harmony in effect in Assyrian dialects: short *a* in an open, unaccented syllable assimilates to the vowel in the following syllable; thus, e.g., the declension of 'queen' is:

nom.	*šarrutu(m)*
gen.	*šarritim* / *šarrete* (see d, below)
acc.	*šarrata(m)*

while the Preterite of *ṣabātu(m)* 'to seize' has the following forms:

	3ms	*iṣbat* (as in Bab.)
but	2fs	*taṣbitī* (vs. Bab. *taṣbatī*)
	3mp	*iṣbutū* (vs. Bab. *iṣbatū*)

(d) Assyrian loses mimation at about the same time as Babylonian; i.e., OA has mimation, later dialects, MA and NA, do not. With the loss of mimation, the word-final sequence *-im* becomes *-e* (viz., in the genitive singular, the oblique plural of fem. nouns and all adjectives, the ventive for the plural, and the 3fs and 2fs dative suffixes):

OB	*šarratim*	OA	*šarritim*	MA	*šarrete*
	rabûtim		*rabiūtim*		*rabiūte*
	illikūnim		*illikūnim*		*illikūne*
	išpuršim		*išpuršim*		*išpurše*
	išpurakkim		*išpurakkim*		*išpurakke*

(e) The Common Semitic diphthong **ay* becomes *ē* in Assyrian, not *ī* as in Babylonian; e.g.,

Bab. *bītu(m)*, but Ass. *bētu(m)* 'house'.

(f) From MA on, the infix *-t-* tends to become *-ṭ-* after *q*:

OB	*iqtabi*	OA	*iqtibi*	MA	*iqṭibi*

(g) From MA on, initial *wa-* becomes *u-* (rather than *a-* as in Bab.):

OB/OA	*wardum*	SB	*ardu*	MA	*urdu*
	wašābum		*ašābu*		*ušābu*

2. Morphology

(a) Pronouns

(1) Many Assyrian pronouns differ from their Babylonian counterparts; among the most important are:

		Babylonian	**Assyrian**
independent subject:	1cs	*nīnu*	*nēnu*
	3ms	*šū*	*šūt*
	3fs	*šī*	*šīt*
enclitic subject:	1cp	*-ānu*	*-āni* (*marṣāni* 'we are sick')
accus. suffix:	2mp	*-kunūti*	*-kunu*
	2fp	*-kināti*	*-kina*
	3mp	*-šunūti*	*-šunu*
	3fp	*-šināti*	*-šina*

dative suffix:	2mp	*-kunūšim*	*-kunūti*
	2fp	*-kināšim*	*-kināti*
	3mp	*-šunūšim*	*-šunūti*
	3fp	*-šināšim*	*-šināti*

(b) Nouns

(1) The bound forms of nouns of the *pirs* and *purs* type have an anaptyctic *a*-vowel:

uznu(m) 'ear': Bab. *uzun*, but Ass. *uzan*;
šipru(m) 'message': Bab. *šipir*, but Ass. *šipar*.
(For *kalbu(m)* 'dog', both Bab. and Ass. have *kalab*.)

(2) The oblique plural of masculine nouns ends in *-ē* (vs. Bab. *-ī*):

Bab. *ana bēlī* 'to the lords', but Ass. *ana bēlē*.

(3) The nominal abstract ending, *-ūt* in Bab. (§14.4), is *-utt* in Ass.:

Bab. *šarrūtu(m)* = Ass. *šarruttu(m)* 'kingship'.

(c) Numbers

(1) The base of the ordinal numbers, *parus-* in Bab. (§23.2(c)), is *paris-* in Assyrian.

(d) Verbs

(1) The 3fs prefix of verbs is *ta-* rather than *i-* as in Bab. (except, in Old Assyrian only, when the subject is inanimate, in which case the prefix is *i-* as in Bab.); thus, the 3fs and the 2ms have the same form:

tallik 'she went' or 'you (ms) went'.

(2) The Precative in Assyrian always takes the form of the Preterite, plus a prefixed *l-*. The 1cp has *lū* rather than *i*. Thus:

		Babylonian	**Assyrian**
3ms	*parāsu(m)*	*liprus*	*liprus*
	bulluṭu(m)	*liballiṭ*	*luballiṭ*
	(w)abālu(m)	*libil*	*lubil*
1cs	*parāsu(m)*	*luprus*	*laprus*
	bulluṭu(m)	*luballiṭ*	*luballiṭ*
	(w)abālu(m)	*lubil*	*lubil*
1cp	*parāsu(m)*	*i niprus*	*lū niprus*
3fs	*parāsu(m)*	*liprus*	*lū taprus*

(3) There is a special ending for subordinate forms, *-ni*, in addition to the ending *-u*. In Old Assyrian, *-ni* is attached to any form that, because it has another ending already, cannot take the ending *-u* (these are the forms that remain unmarked for the subordinative in Babylonian). From MA on, *-ni* is added even to forms that are already marked with *-u*. *-ni* is added at the end of the form, following even pronominal suffixes (but not the particle *-ma*).

	main clause	**subordinate clause**		
	OB/OA	**OB**	**OA**	**M/NA**
Pret. 3ms	*iprus*	*ša iprusu*	*ša iprusu*	*ša iprusū-ni*
+ Vent.	*iprusam*	*ša iprusam*	*ša iprusan-ni*	*ša iprusan-ni*
+ 3ms sf.	*iprussu*	*ša iprusūšu*	*ša iprusūšu*	*ša iprusūšū-ni*
+ Vent. + sf.	*iprusaššu*	*ša iprusaššu*	*ša iprusaššū-ni*	*ša iprusaššū-ni*
Vbl.Adj.+3fs	*parsat*	*ša parsat*	*ša parsat-ni*	*ša parsutū-ni*

(4) A number of verbs exhibit different theme-vowels in Assyrian than they do in Bab.; e.g.,

> *balāṭum* 'to live' is (*u*) in Bab. (*iballuṭ–ibluṭ*) but (*a*) in Ass. (*iballaṭ–iblaṭ*); *emādum* 'to impose', *epāšum* 'to do', and *erābum* 'to enter' are all (*a–u*) verbs (see under (6) below for *epāšum*).

(5) The Gt Infinitive and Verbal Adjective have the form *pitarsum*, vs. Babylonian *pitrusum*.

(6) In the D and Š Imperative, Infinitive, and Verbal Adjective, where Babylonian has *u* in the first syllable, Assyrian has *a*:

			Babylonian	**Assyrian**
D	*parāsu(m)*	Imperative:	*purris*	*parris*
		Infin./Vbl.Adj.:	*purrus*	*parrus*
	aḫāzu(m)	Imperative:	*uḫḫiz*	*aḫḫiz*
		Infin./Vbl.Adj.:	*uḫḫuz*	*aḫḫuz*
Š	*parāsu(m)*	Imperative:	*šupris*	*šapris*
		Infin./Vbl.Adj.:	*šuprus*	*šaprus*
	aḫāzu(m)	Imperative:	*šūḫiz*	*šāḫiz*
		Infin./Vbl.Adj.:	*šūḫuz*	*šāḫuz*

(7) In verbs I–ʾ (both *a* and *e* types), wherever a form in Babylonian begins with *i-* (or *ī-*), in Assyrian the form begins with *e-* (or *ē-*): e.g.,

			Babylonian	**Assyrian**
I–*a*	G Pret.	3ms	*īkul*	*ēkul*
	G Dur.	3ms	*ikkal*	*ekkal*
		3mp	*ikkalū*	*ekkulū*
I–*e*	G Pret.	3ms	*īpuš*	*ēpuš*
		(1cs	*ēpuš*	*ēpuš*)
	G Dur.	3ms	*ippeš*	*eppaš*
		(1cs	*eppeš*	*eppaš*)
		3mp	*ippešū*	*eppušū*
	Gtn Dur.	3ms	*īteneppeš*	*ētanappaš*

(8) The verb 'to give' differs in a number of forms from the Bab.:

	Babylonian	Assyrian
Infinitive	*nadānu(m)*	*tadānu(m)*
Durative	*inaddin*	*iddan*
(3mp	*inaddinū*	*iddunū*)
Perfect	*ittadin*	*ittidin*
(3mp	*ittadnū*	*ittadnū*)
Preterite	*iddin*	*iddin*
Imperative	*idin*	*din*
Verbal Adj.	*nadin-*	*tadin-*

(9) In verbs II–*w* and II–*y* several forms differ from the Bab.:

		Babylonian	Assyrian
G	Durative	*ikân*	*ikūan*
	(3mp	*ikunnū*	*ikunnū*)
	Perfect	*iktūn*	*iktūan*
	(3mp	*iktūnū*	*iktūnū*)
	Infinitive	*kânu(m)*	*kuānu(m)*
	Verbal Adj.	*kīn*	*kēn*
D	Durative	*ukān*	*ukân*
	Perfect	*uktīn*	*ukta*ʾʾ*in*
	Preterite	*ukīn*	*uka*ʾʾ*in*
	Imperative	*kīn*	*ka*ʾʾ*in*
	Infinitive	*kunnu(m)*	*ka*ʾʾ*unu(m)*
	Verbal Adj.	*kunn-*	*ka*ʾʾ*un-*

PARADIGMS

1. Personal Pronouns: Independent Forms (§§2.4, 25.2)

	NOM.	GEN.-ACC.	DATIVE
1cs	*anāku*	*yâti*	*yâšim, ayyâšim*
2ms	*atta*	*kâta, (kâti)*	*kâšim, kâšum*
2fs	*atti*	*kâti*	*kâšim*
3ms	*šū*	*šuāti, šuātu, šâti, šâtu*	*šuāšim, šâšim, šâšum*
3fs	*šī*	*šuāti, šâti, (šiāti)*	*šuāšim, šâšim, (šiāšim)*
1cp	*nīnu*	*niāti*	*niāšim*
2mp	*attunu*	*kunūti*	*kunūšim*
2fp	*attina*	[*kināti*]	[*kināšim*]
3mp	*šunu*	*šunūti*	*šunūšim*
3fp	*šina*	*šināti*	*šināšim*

2. Pronominal Suffixes on Nouns, Prepositions, Verbs (§§10.3, 11.1, §18.2)

	POSSESSIVE (on nouns, prepositions)	ACCUSATIVE (on verbs)	DATIVE (on verbs)
1cs	*-ī, -ya*	*-anni/-nni/-ninni*	*-am/-m/-nim*
2ms	*-ka*	*-ka*	*-kum*
2fs	*-ki*	*-ki*	*-kim*
3ms	*-šu*	*-šu*	*-šum*
3fs	*-ša*	*-ši*	*-šim*
1cp	*-ni*	*-niāti*	*-niāšim*
2mp	*-kunu*	*-kunūti*	*-kunūšim*
2fp	*-kina*	*-kināti*	*-kināšim*
3mp	*-šunu*	*-šunūti*	*-šunūšim*
3fp	*-šina*	*-šināti*	*-šināšim*

3. Independent Possessive Adjectives (§25.3)

	MASC. SG.	FEM. SG.	MASC. PL.	FEM. PL.
1s	*yûm(yaʾum)/yêm/yâm*	*yattu*^{m}/$_n$	*yaʾūt(t)u*^{m}/$_n$, *yût(t)u*^{m}/$_n$	*yât(t)u*^{m}/$_n$
2s	*kûm/kêm/kâm*	*kattu*^{m}/$_n$	*kûttu*^{m}/$_n$	*kâttu*^{m}/$_n$
3s	*šûm/šêm/šuʾam(šâm)*	*šattu*^{m}/$_n$	*šûttu*^{m}/$_n$	—
1p	*nûm/nîm/nâm(niam)*	*niattu*^{m}/$_n$	*nûttu*^{m}/$_n$	—
2p	*kunûm*	—	—	—
3p	*šunûm/šunîm/šuniam*	—	—	—

4. Nouns: Free Forms (§§2.1, 6.1)

a. Basic Declension

		MASCULINE		FEMININE			
SINGULAR	nom.	*ilum*	*šarrum*	*iltum*	*šarratum*	*nārum*	*bēltum*
	gen.	*ilim*	*šarrim*	*iltim*	*šarratim*	*nārim*	*bēltim*
	acc.	*ilam*	*šarram*	*iltam*	*šarratam*	*nāram*	*bēltam*
DUAL	nom.	*ilān*	*šarrān*	*iltān*	*šarratān*	*nārān*	*bēltān*
	g.–a.	*ilīn*	*šarrīn*	*iltīn*	*šarratīn*	*nārīn*	*bēltīn*
PLURAL	nom.	*ilū*	*šarrū*	*ilātum*	*šarrātum*	*nārātum*	*bēlētum*
	g.–a.	*ilī*	*šarrī*	*ilātim*	*šarrātim*	*nārātim*	*bēlētim*

b. Final-weak Nouns

		IN *-a*	IN *-ā*	IN *-i/ī*	IN *-u/ū*
SINGULAR	nom.	*šadûm*	*rubûm*	*bārûm*	*ikûm*
	gen.	*šadîm*	*rubêm*	*bārîm*	*ikîm*
	acc.	*šadâm*	*rubâm*	*bāriam*	*ikâm*
DUAL	nom.	*šadân*	*rubân*	*bārân*	*ikân*
	g.–a.	*šadîn*	*rubên*	*bārîn*	*ikîn*
PLURAL	nom.	*šadû*	*rubû*	*bārû*	*ikû*
	g.–a.	*šadî*	*rubê*	*bārî*	*ikî*

5. Adjectives: Free Attributive Forms (§§4.2, 6.1)

	BASE:	*ṭāb-*	*dann-*	*ell-*	*damiq-*	*rabi-*
MASC. SG.	nom.	*ṭābum*	*dannum*	*ellum*	*damqum*	*rabûm*
	gen.	*ṭābim*	*dannim*	*ellim*	*damqim*	*rabîm*
	acc.	*ṭābam*	*dannam*	*ellam*	*damqam*	*rabiam*
PL.	nom.	*ṭābūtum*	*dannūtum*	*ellūtum*	*damqūtum*	*rabûtum*
	g.-a.	*ṭābūtim*	*dannūtim*	*ellūtim*	*damqūtim*	*rabûtim*
FEM. SG.	nom.	*ṭābtum*	*dannatum*	*elletum*	*damiqtum*	*rabītum*
	gen.	*ṭābtim*	*dannatim*	*elletim*	*damiqtim*	*rabītim*
	acc.	*ṭābtam*	*dannatam*	*elletam*	*damiqtam*	*rabītam*
PL.	nom.	*ṭābātum*	*dannātum*	*ellētum*	*damqātum*	*rabiātum*
	g.-a.	*ṭābātim*	*dannātim*	*ellētim*	*damqātim*	*rabiātim*

6. **Nouns and Adjectives: Bound and Suffixal Forms (§§8.3, 11.1)**

A. PLURAL

		FREE FORM	BOUND	SUFFIXAL
Masc. Pl. Nouns	nom.	*mārū*	*mārū*	*mārūka*
	gen.-acc.	*mārī*	*mārī*	*mārīka*
Fem. Pl. Nouns/Adj.s	nom.	*mārātum*	*mārāt*	*mārātūka*
	gen.-acc.	*mārātim*		*mārātīka*
Masc. Pl. Adj.s	nom.	*damqūtum*	*damqūt*	*damqūtūka*
	gen.-acc.	*damqūtim*		*damqūtīka*

B. DUAL

		FREE FORM	BOUND	SUFFIXAL
	nom.	*uznān*	*uznā*	*uznāka*
	gen.-acc.	*uznīn*	*uznī*	*uznīka*

C. SINGULAR

1. base in -*VC*

		FREE FORM	BOUND	SUFFIXAL
a. 2-syllable	nom.	*awīlum*		*awīlka*
	acc.	*awīlam*	*awīl*	
	gen.	*awīlim*		*awīlīki*
	nom.	*nakrum*		*nakerka*
	acc.	*nakram*	*naker*	
	gen.	*nakrim*		*nakrīka*
b. 1-syllable	nom.	*bēlum*		*bēl(ū)ka*
	acc.	*bēlam*	*bēl(i)*	*bēl(ā)ka*
	gen.	*bēlim*		*bēlīka*
c. *abum, aḫum*	nom.	*abum*		*abūka*
	acc.	*abam*	*abi*	*abāka*
	gen.	*abim*		*abīka*

2. base in -C_1C_1

		FREE FORM	BOUND	SUFFIXAL
a. 1-syllable	nom.	*libbum*		*libbaka*
	acc.	*libbam*	*libbi*	
	gen.	*libbim*		*libbīka*
b. 2-syllable, *-tt*	nom.	*ṣibittum*		*ṣibittaka*
	acc.	*ṣibittam*	*ṣibitti*	
	gen.	*ṣibittim*		*ṣibittīka*
c. 2-syllable,other	nom.	*ekallum*		*ekallaka*
	acc.	*ekallam*	*ekal*	
	gen.	*ekallim*		*ekallīka*

(C. SINGULAR, CONTINUED)

3. base in -C_1C_2, $C_2 \neq t$, i.e., $pVrs$

		FREE FORM	BOUND	SUFFIXAL
a. pars	nom. acc. gen.	kalbum kalbam kalbim	kalab	kalabka kalbīka
b. pers	nom. acc. gen.	eqlum eqlam eqlim	eqel	eqelka eqlīka
c. pirs	nom. acc. gen.	šiprum šipram šiprim	šipir	šipirka šiprīka
d. purs	nom. acc. gen.	puḫrum puḫram puḫrim	puḫur	puḫurka puḫrīka

4. base in -Ct (fem.)

   a. 2-syllable

i. most	nom. acc. gen.	napištum napištam napištim	napišti	napištaka napištīka
ii. fem. Ptcpl.	nom. acc. gen.	māḫirtum māḫirtam māḫirtim	māḫirat	māḫirtaka māḫirtīka

   b. 1-syllable

i.	nom. acc. gen.	qīštum qīštam qīštim	qīšti	qīštaka qīštīka
ii.	nom. acc. gen.	mārtum mārtam mārtim	mārat	māratka mārtīka

5. base in -V

a. -CCi	nom. acc. gen.	kussûm kussiam kussîm	kussi	kussīka
b. -Ci	nom. acc. gen.	rabûm rabiam rabîm	rab(i)	rabīka
c. -$ā$	nom. acc. gen.	rubûm rubâm rubêm	rubê / rubi / rubā	rubûka rubâka rubêka
d. other vowels	nom. acc. gen.	šadûm šadâm šadîm	šada / šadi / šad	šadûka šadâka šadîka

Verbs: Sigla for the Derived Stems in the Main Dictionaries

AHw	*CAD*
G	I/1
Gt	I/2
Gtn	I/3
D	II/1
Dt	II/2
Dtn	II/3
Š	III/1
Št	III/2
Štn	III/3
ŠD	II/III
N	IV/1
Ntn	IV/3

7a. Sound Verbs: Stem Forms

Stem	Infinitive	Durative	Perfect	Preterite	Imperative	Participle	Vbl. Adj.	
G	(*a–u*)	*parāsum*	*iparras*	*iptaras*[1]	*iprus*	*purus*[1]	*pāris-*	*paris-*[1]
	(*a*)	*ṣabātum*	*iṣabbat*	*iṣṣabat*[1,2]	*iṣbat*	*ṣabat*[1]	*ṣābit-*	*ṣabit-*[1]
	(*i*)	*šarāqum*	*išarriq*	*ištariq*[1]	*išriq*	*širiq*[1]	*šāriq-*	*šariq-*[1]
	(*u*)	*maqātum*	*imaqqut*	*imtaqut*[1]	*imqut*	*muqut*[1]	*māqit-*	*maqit-*[1]
Gt	(*a–u*)	*pitrusum*	*iptarras*	*iptatras*	*iptaras*[1]	*pitras*	*muptaris-*[1]	*pitrus-*
	(*a*)	*tiṣbutum*[2]	*iṣṣabbat*[2]	*iṣṣatbat*[2]	*iṣṣabat*[1,2]	*tiṣbat*[2]	*muṣṣabit-*[1,2]	*tiṣbut-*[2]
	(*i*)	*šitruqum*	*ištarriq*	*ištatriq*	*ištariq*[1]	*šitriq*	*muštariq-*[1]	*šitruq-*
	(*u*)	*mitqutum*	*imtaqqut*	*imtatqut*	*imtaqut*[1]	*mitqut*	*mumtaqit-*[1]	*mitqut-*
Gtn	(*a–u*)	*pitarrusum*	*iptanarras*	*iptatarras*	*iptarras*	*pitarras*	*muptarris-*	*pitarrus-*
	(*a*)	*tiṣabbutum*[2]	*iṣṣanabbat*[2]	*iṣṣatabbat*[2]	*iṣṣabbat*[2]	*tiṣabbat*[2]	*muṣṣabbit-*[2]	*tiṣabbut-*[2]
	(*i*)	*šitarruqum*	*ištanarriq*	*ištatarriq*	*ištarriq*	*šitarriq*	*muštarriq-*	*šitarruq-*
	(*u*)	*mitaqqutum*	*imtanaqqut*	*imtataqqut*	*imtaqqut*	*mitaqqut*	*mumtaqqit-*	*mitaqqut-*
N	(*a–u,a,u*)	*naprusum*	*ipparras*	*ittapras*	*ipparis*[1]	*napris*	*mupparis-*[1]	*naprus-*
	(*i*)	*našruqum*	*iššarriq*	*ittašriq*	*iššariq*[1]	*našriq*	*muššariq-*[1]	*našruq-*
Ntn	(*a–u,a,u*)	*itaprusum*	*ittanapras*	*ittatapras*	*ittapras*	*itapras*	*muttapris-*	*itaprus-*
	(*i*)	*itašruqum*	*ittanašriq*	*ittatašriq*	*ittašriq*	*itašriq*	*muttašriq-*	*itašruq-*
D		*purrusum*	*uparras*	*uptarris*	*uparris*	*purris*	*muparris-*	*purrus-*
Dt		*putarrusum*	*uptarras*	*uptatarris*	*uptarris*	*putarris*	*muptarris-*	*putarrus-*
Dtn		*putarrusum*	*uptanarras*	*uptatarris*	*uptarris*	*putarris*	*muptarris-*	*putarrus-*
Š		*šuprusum*	*ušapras*	*uštapris*	*ušapris*	*šupris*	*mušapris-*	*šuprus-*
Št passive		*šutaprusum*	*uštapras*	*uštatapris*	*uštapris*	*šutapris*	*muštapris-*	*šutaprus-*
Št lexical		*šutaprusum*	*uštaparras*	*uštatapris*	*uštapris*	*šutapris*	*muštapris-*	*šutaprus-*
Štn		*šutaprusum*	*uštanapras*	*uštatapris*	*uštapris*	*šutapris*	*muštapris-*	*šutaprus-*

[1]Loss of vowel before final radical with addition of vocalic ending: G perf. *iptarsū*, impv. *pursā*, vbl. adj. *parsum*; Gt pret. *iptarsū*, ptcpl. *muptarsum*; N pret. *ipparsū*, ptcpl. *mupparsum*.

[2]Metathesis/assimilation of initial root sibilant and infix *-t-*.

7b. Sound Verbs: Finite Forms (G, N, D, Š)

		Durative	Perfect	Preterite	Imp'v.	Precative	Vetitive
G (*a–u*)	3cs	*iparras*	*iptaras*	*iprus*		*liprus*	*ayy-iprus*
	2ms	*taparras*	*taptaras*	*taprus*	*purus*		*ē-taprus*
	2fs	*taparrasī*	*taptarsī*	*taprusī*	*pursī*		*ē-taprusī*
	1cs	*aparras*	*aptaras*	*aprus*		*luprus*	*ayy-aprus*
	3mp	*iparrasū*	*iptarsū*	*iprusū*		*liprusū*	*ayy-iprusū*
	3fp	*iparrasā*	*iptarsā*	*iprusā*		*liprusā*	*ayy-iprusā*
	2cp	*taparrasā*	*taptarsā*	*taprusā*	*pursā*		*ē-taprusā*
	1cp	*niparras*	*niptaras*	*niprus*		*i niprus*	*ē-niprus*
G (*i*)	3cs	*išarriq*	*ištariq*	*išriq*		*lišriq*	*ayy-išriq*
	2ms	*tašarriq*	*taštariq*	*tašriq*	*širiq*		*ē-tašriq*
	2fs	*tašarriqī*	*taštarqī*	*tašriqī*	*širqī*		*ē-tašriqī*
	1cs	*ašarriq*	*aštariq*	*ašriq*		*lušriq*	*ayy-ašriq*
	3mp	*išarriqū*	*ištarqū*	*išriqū*		*lišriqū*	*ayy-išriqū*
	3fp	*išarriqā*	*ištarqā*	*išriqā*		*lišriqā*	*ayy-išriqā*
	2cp	*tašarriqā*	*taštarqā*	*tašriqā*	*širqā*		*ē-tašriqā*
	1cp	*nišarriq*	*ništariq*	*nišriq*		*i nišriq*	*ē-nišriq*
G (*a*)	3cs	*iṣabbat*	*iṣṣabat*	*iṣbat*		*liṣbat*	*ayy-iṣbat*
	2ms	*taṣabbat*	*taṣṣabat*	*taṣbat*	*ṣabat*		*ē-taṣbat*
	2fs	*taṣabbatī*	*taṣṣabtī*	*taṣbatī*	*ṣabtī*		*ē-taṣbatī*
	1cs	*aṣabbat*	*aṣṣabat*	*aṣbat*		*luṣbat*	*ayy-aṣbat*
	3mp	*iṣabbatū*	*iṣṣabtū*	*iṣbatū*		*liṣbatū*	*ayy-iṣbatū*
	3fp	*iṣabbatā*	*iṣṣabtā*	*iṣbatā*		*liṣbatā*	*ayy-iṣbatā*
	2cp	*taṣabbatā*	*taṣṣabtā*	*taṣbatā*	*ṣabtā*		*ē-taṣbatā*
	1cp	*niṣabbat*	*niṣṣabat*	*niṣbat*		*i niṣbat*	*ē-niṣbat*
G (*u*)	3cs	*imaqqut*	*imtaqut*	*imqut*		*limqut*	*ayy-imqut*
	2ms	*tamaqqut*	*tamtaqut*	*tamqut*	*muqut*		*ē-tamqut*
	2fs	*tamaqqutī*	*tamtaqtī*	*tamqutī*	*muqtī*		*ē-tamqutī*
	1cs	*amaqqut*	*amtaqut*	*amqut*		*lumqut*	*ayy-amqut*

		Durative	Perfect	Preterite	Imp'v.	Precative	Vetitive
	3mp	*imaqqutū*	*imtaqtū*	*imqutū*		*limqutū*	*ayy-imqutū*
	3fp	*imaqqutā*	*imtaqtā*	*imqutā*		*limqutā*	*ayy-imqutā*
	2cp	*tamaqqutā*	*tamtaqtā*	*tamqutā*	*muqtā*		*ē-tamqutā*
	1cp	*nimaqqut*	*nimtaqut*	*nimqut*		*i nimqut*	*ē-nimqut*
N (*a–u, a, u*)	3cs	*ipparras*	*ittapras*	*ipparis*		*lipparis*	*ayy-ipparis*
	2ms	*tapparras*	*tattapras*	*tapparis*	*napris*		*ē-tapparis*
	2fs	*tapparrasī*	*tattaprasī*	*tapparsī*	*naprisī*		*ē-tapparsī*
	1cs	*apparras*	*attapras*	*apparis*		*lupparis*	*ayy-apparis*
	3mp	*ipparrasū*	*ittaprasū*	*ipparsū*		*lipparsū*	*ayy-ipparsū*
	3fp	*ipparrasā*	*ittaprasā*	*ipparsā*		*lipparsā*	*ayy-ipparsā*
	2cp	*tapparrasā*	*tattaprasā*	*tapparsā*	*naprisā*		*ē-tapparsā*
	1cp	*nipparras*	*nittapras*	*nipparis*		*i nipparis*	*ē-nipparis*
D	3cs	*uparras*	*uptarris*	*uparris*		*liparris*	*ayy-uparris*
	2ms	*tuparras*	*tuptarris*	*tuparris*	*purris*		*ē-tuparris*
	2fs	*tuparrasī*	*tuptarrisī*	*tuparrisī*	*purrisī*		*ē-tuparrisī*
	1cs	*uparras*	*uptarris*	*uparris*		*luparris*	*ayy-uparris*
	3mp	*uparrasū*	*uptarrisū*	*uparrisū*		*liparrisū*	*ayy-uparrisū*
	3fp	*uparrasā*	*uptarrisā*	*uparrisā*		*liparrisā*	*ayy-uparrisā*
	2cp	*tuparrasā*	*tuptarrisā*	*tuparrisā*	*purrisā*		*ē-tuparrisā*
	1cp	*nuparras*	*nuptarris*	*nuparris*		*i nuparris*	*ē-nuparris*
Š	3cs	*ušapras*	*uštapris*	*ušapris*		*lišapris*	*ayy-ušapris*
	2ms	*tušapras*	*tuštapris*	*tušapris*	*šupris*		*ē-tušapris*
	2fs	*tušaprasī*	*tuštaprisī*	*tušaprisī*	*šuprisī*		*ē-tušaprisī*
	1cs	*ušapras*	*uštapris*	*ušapris*		*lušapris*	*ayy-ušapris*
	3mp	*ušaprasū*	*uštaprisū*	*ušaprisū*		*lišaprisū*	*ayy-ušaprisū*
	3fp	*ušaprasā*	*uštaprisā*	*ušaprisā*		*lišaprisā*	*ayy-ušaprisā*
	2cp	*tušaprasā*	*tuštaprisā*	*tušaprisā*	*šuprisā*		*ē-tušaprisā*
	1cp	*nušapras*	*nuštapris*	*nušapris*		*i nušapris*	*ē-nušapris*

7c. Sound Verbs: Non-Finite Forms (G, N, D, Š)

	Infinitive		Active Participle			Verbal Adj., Attributive			Vbl. Adj.+Pron. Subj.	
G	nom.	*parāsum*	ms	nom.	*pārisum*	ms	nom.	*parsum*	1cs	*parsāku*
	gen.	*parāsim*		gen.	*pārisim*		gen.	*parsim*	2ms	*parsāta*
	acc.	*parāsam*		acc.	*pārisam*		acc.	*parsam*	2fs	*parsāti*
									3ms	*paris*[1]
			fs	nom.	*pārištum*	fs	nom.	*parištum*[1]	3fs	*parsat*
				gen.	*pārištim*		gen.	*parištim*		
				acc.	*pārištam*		acc.	*parištam*	1cp	*parsānu*
									2mp	*parsātunu*
			mp	nom.	*pārisūtum*	mp	nom.	*parsūtum*	2fp	*parsātina*
				gen.-acc.	*pārisūtim*		gen.-acc.	*parsūtim*	3mp	*parsū*
									3fp	*parsā*
			fp	nom.	*pārisātum*	fp	nom.	*parsātum*		
				gen.-acc.	*pārisātim*		gen.-acc.	*parsātim*		

[1]Note also *rapšum* with attributive fs *rapaštum* and predicative 3ms *rapaš*; *marṣum* with attributive fs *maruštum* and predicative 3ms *maruṣ*.

	Infinitive		Active Participle			Verbal Adj., Attributive			Vbl. Adj.+Pron. Subj.	
N	nom.	*naprusum*	ms	nom.	*mupparsum*	ms	nom.	*naprusum*	1cs	*naprusāku*
	gen.	*naprusim*		*gen.*	*mupparsim*		gen.	*naprusim*	2ms	*naprusāta*
	acc.	*naprusam*		acc.	*mupparsam*		acc.	*naprusam*	2fs	*naprusāti*
									3ms	*naprus*
			fs	nom.	*mupparištum*	fs	nom.	*napruštum*	3fs	*naprusat*
				gen.	*mupparištim*		gen.	*napruštim*		
				acc.	*mupparištam*		acc.	*napruštam*	1cp	*naprusānu*
									2mp	*naprusātunu*
			mp	nom.	*mupparsūtum*	mp	nom.	*naprusūtum*	2fp	*naprusātina*
				gen.-acc.	*mupparsūtim*		gen.-acc.	*naprusūtim*	3mp	*naprusū*
									3fp	*naprusā*
			fp	nom.	*mupparsātum*	fp	nom.	*naprusātum*		
				gen.-acc.	*mupparsātim*		gen.-acc.	*naprusātim*		

	Infinitive		Active Participle			Verbal Adj., Attributive			Vbl. Adj.+Pron. Subj.	
D	nom.	*purrusum*	ms	nom.	*muparrisum*	ms	nom.	*purrusum*	1cs	*purrusāku*
	gen.	*purrusim*		*gen.*	*muparrisim*		gen.	*purrusim*	2ms	*purrusāta*
	acc.	*purrusam*		acc.	*muparrisam*		acc.	*purrusam*	2fs	*purrusāti*
									3ms	*purrus*
			fs	nom.	*muparrištum*	fs	nom.	*purruštum*	3fs	*purrusat*
				gen.	*muparrištim*		gen.	*purruštim*		
				acc.	*muparrištam*		acc.	*purruštam*	1cp	*purrusānu*
			mp	nom.	*muparrisūtum*	mp	nom.	*purrusūtum*	2mp	*purrusātunu*
				gen.-acc.	*muparrisūtim*		gen.-acc.	*purrusūtim*	2fp	*purrusātina*
									3mp	*purrusū*
			fp	nom.	*muparrisātum*	fp	nom.	*purrusātum*	3fp	*purrusā*
				gen.-acc.	*muparrisātim*		gen.-acc.	*purrusātim*		
Š	nom.	*šuprusum*	ms	nom.	*mušaprisum*	ms	nom.	*šuprusum*	1cs	*šuprusāku*
	gen.	*šuprusim*		*gen.*	*mušaprisim*		gen.	*šuprusim*	2ms	*šuprusāta*
	acc.	*šuprusam*		acc.	*mušaprisam*		acc.	*šuprusam*	2fs	*šuprusāti*
									3ms	*šuprus*
			fs	nom.	*mušapristum*	fs	nom.	*šupruštum*	3fs	*šuprusat*
				gen.	*mušaprištim*		gen.	*šupruštim*		
				acc.	*mušaprištam*		acc.	*šupruštam*	1cp	*šuprusānu*
			mp	nom.	*mušaprisūtum*	mp	nom.	*šuprusūtum*	2mp	*šuprusātunu*
				gen.-acc.	*mušaprisūtim*		gen.-acc.	*šuprusūtim*	2fp	*šuprusātina*
									3mp	*šuprusū*
			fp	nom.	*mušaprisātum*	fp	nom.	*šuprusātum*	3fp	*šuprusā*
				gen.-acc.	*mušaprisātim*		gen.-acc.	*šuprusātim*		

8a. Verbs I–*a* (I–ʾ$_{1-2}$) including *alākum*: Stem Forms

Stem	Infinitive	Durative	Perfect	Preterite	Imperative	Participle	Vbl. Adj.	
G	(*a–u*)	*aḫāzum*	*iḫḫaz*	*ītaḫaz*[1]	*īḫuz*	*aḫuz*	*āḫiz-*	*aḫiz-*[1]
	(*i*)	*arākum*	*irrik*	*ītarik*[1]	*īrik*	*arik*	*ārik-*	*arik-*[1]
	(*u*)	*akāšum*	*ikkuš*	*ītakuš*[1]	*īkuš*	*akuš*	*ākiš-*	*akiš-*[1]
	alākum (*a–i*)	*alākum*	*illak*	*ittalak*[1]	*illik*	*alik*	*ālik-*	*alik-*[1]
Gt	(*a–u*)	*atḫuzum*	*ītaḫḫaz*	*ītatḫaz*	*ītaḫaz*[1]	*atḫaz*	*mūtaḫiz-*[1]	*atḫuz-*
	alākum	*atlukum*	*ittallak*	*ittatlak*	*ittalak*[1]	*atlak*	*muttalik-*[1]	*atluk-*
Gtn	(*a–u*)	*ataḫḫuzum*	*ītanaḫḫaz*	*ītataḫḫaz*	*ītaḫḫaz*	*ataḫḫaz*	*mūtaḫḫiz-*	*ataḫḫuz-*
	(*i*)	*atarrukum*	*ītanarrik*	*ītatarrik*	*ītarrik*	*atarrik*	*mūtarrik-*	*atarruk-*
	(*u*)	*atakkušum*	*ītanakkuš*	*ītatakkuš*	*ītakkuš*	*atakkuš*	*mūtakkiš-*	*atakkuš-*
	alākum	*atallukum*	*ittanallak*	*ittatallak*	*ittallak*	*atallak*	*muttallik-*	*atalluk-*
N[2]	(*a–u,a,u*)	*nanḫuzum*	*innaḫḫaz*	*ittanḫaz*	*innaḫiz*[1]	*nanḫiz*	*munnaḫiz-*[1]	*nanḫuz-*
Ntn	(*a–u*)	?	*ittananḫaz* / *ittanaḫḫaz*	?	*ittanḫaz* / *ittaḫḫaz*	?	?	?
D		*uḫḫuzum*	*uḫḫaz*	*ūtaḫḫiz*	*uḫḫiz*	*uḫḫiz*	*muḫḫiz-*	*uḫḫuz-*
Dt		*utaḫḫuzum*	*ūtaḫḫaz*	*ūtataḫḫiz*	*ūtaḫḫiz*	*utaḫḫiz*	*mūtaḫḫiz-*	*utaḫḫuz-*
Dtn		*utaḫḫuzum*	*ūtanaḫḫaz*	*ūtataḫḫiz*	*ūtaḫḫiz*	*utaḫḫiz*	*mūtaḫḫiz-*	*utaḫḫuz-*
Š		*šūḫuzum*	*ušaḫḫaz*	*uštāḫiz*	*ušāḫiz*	*šūḫiz*	*mušāḫiz-*	*šūḫuz-*
Št[3]		*šutāḫuzum*	*uštaḫḫaz*	*uštatāḫiz*	*uštāḫiz*	*šutāḫiz*	*muštāḫiz-*	*šutāḫuz-*
Štn		*šutaḫḫuzum*	*uštanaḫḫaz*	*uštataḫḫiz*	*uštaḫḫiz*	*šutaḫḫiz*	*muštaḫḫiz-*	*šutaḫḫuz-*

[1]Loss of vowel before final radical with addition of vocalic ending: G perf. *ītaḫzū*, impv. *aḫzā*, vbl. adj. *aḫzum*; Gt pret. *ītaḫzū*, ptcpl. *mūtaḫzum*; N pret. *innaḫzū*, ptcpl. *munnaḫzum*. [2]A small number of verbs exhibit strong ʾ: Infin. *naʾdurum*, dur. *iʾʾaddar*, pf. *itaʾdar*, pret. *iʾʾader*. [3] Št-passive and Št-lexical forms are the same in verbs I–ʾ.

8b. Verbs I–*a* (I–ʾ$_{1-2}$) including *alākum*: Finite Forms (G)

	a–u **class: *amārum***				***i*** **class: *arākum***			
	Durative	Perfect	Preterite	Imp'v.	Durative	Perfect	Preterite	Imp'v.
3cs	*immar*	*ītamar*	*īmur*		*irrik*	*ītarik*	*īrik*	
2ms	*tammar*	*tātamar*	*tāmur*	*amur*	*tarrik*	*tātarik*	*tārik*	*arik*
2fs	*tammarī*	*tātamrī*	*tāmurī*	*amrī*	*tarrikī*	*tātarkī*	*tārikī*	*arkī*
1cs	*ammar*	*ātamar*	*āmur*		*arrik*	*ātarik*	*ārik*	
3mp	*immarū*	*ītamrū*	*īmurū*		*irrikū*	*ītarkū*	*īrikū*	
3fp	*immarā*	*ītamrā*	*īmurā*		*irrikā*	*ītarkā*	*īrikā*	
2cp	*tammarā*	*tātamrā*	*tāmurā*	*amrā*	*tarrikā*	*tātarkā*	*tārikā*	*arkā*
1cp	*nimmar*	*nītamar*	*nīmur*		*nirrik*	*nītarik*	*nīrik*	

	u **class: *akāšum***				***alākum***			
	Durative	Perfect	Preterite	Imp'v.	Durative	Perfect	Preterite	Imp'v.
3cs	*ikkuš*	*ītakuš*	*īkuš*		*illak*	*ittalak*	*illik*	
2ms	*takkuš*	*tātakuš*	*tākuš*	*akuš*	*tallak*	*tattalak*	*tallik*	*alik*
2fs	*takkušī*	*tātakšī*	*tākušī*	*akšī*	*tallakī*	*tattalkī*	*tallikī*	*alkī*
1cs	*akkuš*	*ātakuš*	*ākuš*		*allak*	*attalak*	*allik*	
3mp	*ikkušū*	*ītakšū*	*īkušū*		*illakū*	*ittalkū*	*illikū*	
3fp	*ikkušā*	*ītakšā*	*īkušā*		*illakā*	*ittalkā*	*illikā*	
2cp	*takkušā*	*tātakšā*	*tākušā*	*akšā*	*tallakā*	*tattalkā*	*tallikā*	*alkā*
1cp	*nikkuš*	*nītakuš*	*nīkuš*		*nillak*	*nittalak*	*nillik*	

9a. Verbs I–*e* (I–ʾ$_{3–4}$ and I–*y*): Stem Forms

Stem		Infinitive	Durative	Perfect	Preterite	Imperative	Participle	Vbl. Adj.
G	(*e–u*)	*epēšum*	*ippeš / ippuš*	*ītepeš / ītepuš*[1]	*īpuš*	*epuš*[1]	*ēpiš-*	*epiš-*[1]
	(*i*)	*ezēbum*	*izzib*	*ītezib*	*īzib*	*ezib*[1]	*ēzib-*	*ezib-*[1]
	(*u*)	*erēbum*	*irrub*	*īterub*	*īrub*	*erub*[1]	*ērib-*	*erib-*[1]
Gt	(*u*)	*etrubum*	*īterrub*	*ītetrub*	*īterub*[1]	*etrub*	*mūterib-*[1]	*etrub-*
Gtn	(*e–u*)	*eteppušum*	*īteneppeš*	*īteteppeš*	*īteppeš*	*eteppeš*	*mūteppiš-*	*eteppuš-*
	(*i*)	*etezzubum*	*ītenezzib*	*ītetezzib*	*ītezzib*	*etezzib*	*mūtezzib-*	*etezzub-*
	(*u*)	*eterrubum*	*ītenerrub*	*īteterrub*	*īterrub*	*eterrub*	*mūterrib-*	*eterrub-*
N	(*e–u,e,u*)	*nenpušum*[2]	*inneppeš*[3]	*ittenpeš*[3]	*innepiš*[1,3]	*nenpiš*[2,3]	*munnepiš-*[1]	*nenpuš-*[2]
	(*i*)	*nenzubum*[2]	*innezzib*	*ittenzib*	*innezib*	*nenzib*[2]	*munnezib-*[1]	*nenzub-*[2]
Ntn	(*e–u*)	?	*ittenenpeš / itteneppeš*	?	*ittenpeš / itteppeš*	?	?	?
	(*i*)	?	*ittenenzib / ittenezzib*	?	*ittenzib / ittezzib*	?	?	?
D		*uppušum*	*uppaš*	*ūtappiš*	*uppiš*	*uppiš*	*muppiš-*	*uppuš-*
Dt		*uteppušum*	*ūteppeš*	*ūteteppiš*	*ūteppiš*	*uteppiš*	*mūteppiš-*	*uteppuš-*
Dtn		*uteppušum*	*ūteneppeš*	*ūteteppiš*	*ūteppiš*	*uteppiš*	*mūteppiš-*	*uteppuš-*
Š		*šūpušum*	*ušeppeš*	*uštēpiš*	*ušēpiš*	*šūpiš*	*mušēpiš-*	*šūpuš-*
Št[4]		*šutēpušum*	*ušteppeš*	*uštetēpiš*	*uštēpiš*	*šutēpiš*	*muštēpiš-*	*šutēpuš-*
Štn		*šuteppušum*	*ušteneppeš*	*ušteteppiš*	*ušteppiš*	*šuteppiš*	*mušteppiš-*	*šuteppuš-*

[1]Loss of vowel before final radical with addition of vocalic ending: G perf. *ītepšū*, impv. *epšā*, vbl. adj. *epšum*; Gt pret. *ītepšū*, ptcpl. *mūtepšum*; N pret. *innepšū*, ptcpl. *munnepšum*.

[2]Verbs originally I–*y* have long *ē* rather than *n* before R_2 in forms without prefixes: infin./vbl. adj. *nēzuḫum*, impv. *nēziḫ*.

[3]The N of *epēšum* also exhibits finite forms with theme-vowel *-u-*: dur. *inneppuš*, pf. *ittenpuš*, pret. *innepuš*, impv. *nenpuš*.

[4]Št-passive and Št-lexical forms are the same in verbs I–ʾ.

9b. Verbs I–*e* (I–$ʾ_{3–4}$ and I–*y*): Finite Forms (G)

e–u class: ***epēšum***

	Durative	Perfect	Preterite	Imp'v.
3cs	*ippeš / ippuš*	*ītepeš / ītepuš*	*īpuš*	
2ms	*teppeš / teppuš*	*tētepeš / tētepuš*	*tēpuš*	*epuš*
2fs	*teppešī / teppušī*	*tētepšī*	*tēpušī*	*epšī*
1cs	*eppeš / eppuš*	*ētepeš / ētepuš*	*ēpuš*	
3mp	*ippešū / ippušū*	*ītepšū*	*īpušū*	
3fp	*ippešā / ippušā*	*ītepšā*	*īpušā*	
2cp	*teppešā / teppušā*	*tētepšā*	*tēpušā*	*epšā*
1cp	*nippeš / ippuš*	*nītepeš / nītepuš*	*nīpuš*	

i class: ***ezēbum***

	Durative	Perfect	Preterite	Imp'v.
3cs	*izzib*	*ītezib*	*īzib*	
2ms	*tezzib*	*tētezib*	*tēzib*	*ezib*
2fs	*tezzibī*	*tētezbī*	*tēzibī*	*ezbī*
1cs	*ezzib*	*ētezib*	*ēzib*	
3mp	*izzibū*	*ītezbū*	*īzibū*	
3fp	*izzibā*	*ītezbā*	*īzibā*	
2cp	*tezzibā*	*tētezbā*	*tēzibā*	*ezbā*
1cp	*nizzib*	*nītezib*	*nīzib*	

u class: ***erēbum***

	Durative	Perfect	Preterite	Imp'v.
3cs	*irrub*	*īterub*	*īrub*	
2ms	*terrub*	*tēterub*	*tērub*	*erub*
2fs	*terrubī*	*tēterbī*	*tērubī*	*erbī*
1cs	*errub*	*ēterub*	*ērub*	
3mp	*irrubū*	*īterbū*	*īrubū*	
3fp	*irrubā*	*īterbā*	*īrubā*	
2cp	*terrubā*	*tēterbā*	*tērubā*	*erbā*
1cp	*nirrub*	*nīterub*	*nīrub*	

10a. Verbs I–*n*: Stem Forms

Stem		Infinitive	Durative	Perfect	Preterite	Imperative	Participle	Vbl. Adj.
G	(*a–u*)	*naqārum*	*inaqqar*	*ittaqar*[1]	*iqqur*	*uqur*[1]	*nāqer-*	*naqer-*[1]
	(*i*)	*nakāsum*	*inakkis*	*ittakis*[1]	*ikkis*	*ikis*[1]	*nākis-*	*nakis-*[1]
	(*u*)	*nasākum*	*inassuk*	*ittasuk*[1]	*issuk*	*usuk*[1]	*nāsik-*	*nasik-*[1]
Gt	(*a–u*)	*itqurum*	*ittaqqar*	*ittatqar*	*ittaqar*[1]	*itqar*	*muttaqer-*[1]	*itqur-*
	(*i*)	*itkusum*	*ittakkis*	*ittatkis*	*ittakis*[1]	*itkis*	*muttakis-*[1]	*itkis-*
	(*u*)	*issukum*[2]	*ittassuk*	*ittassuk*[2]	*ittasuk*[1]	*issuk*[2]	*muttasik-*[1]	*issuk-*[2]
Gtn	(*a–u*)	*itaqqurum*	*ittanaqqar*	*ittataqqar*	*ittaqqar*	*itaqqar*	*muttaqqer-*	*itaqqur-*
	(*i*)	*itakkusum*	*ittanakkis*	*ittatakkis*	*ittakkis*	*itakkis*	*muttakkis-*	*itakkus-*
	(*u*)	*itassukum*	*ittanassuk*	*ittatassuk*	*ittassuk*	*itassuk*	*muttassuk-*	*itassuk-*
N	(*a–u,a,u*)	*nanqurum* / *naqqurum*	*innaqqar*	*ittanqar*	*innaqer*[1]	*nanqer* / *naqqer*	*munnaqer-*[1]	*nanqur-* / *naqqur-*
	(*i*)	*nankusum* / *nakkusum*	*innakkis*	*ittankis*	*innakis*[1]	*nankis* / *nakkis*	*munnakis-*[1]	*nankus-* / *nakkus-*
Ntn	(*a–u,a,u*)	*itanqurum*	*ittananqar*	*ittatanqar*	*ittanqar*	*itanqar*	*muttanqer-*	*itanqur-*
	(*i*)	*itankusum*	*ittanankis*	*ittatankis*	*ittankis*	*itankis*	*muttankis-*	*itankus-*
D		*nuqqurum*	*unaqqar*	*uttaqqer*	*unaqqer*	*nuqqer*	*munaqqer-*	*nuqqur-*
Dt		*utaqqurum*	*uttaqqar*	*uttataqqer*	*uttaqqer*	*utaqqer*	*muttaqqer-*	*utaqqur-*
Dtn		*utaqqurum*	*uttanaqqar*	*uttataqqer*	*uttaqqer*	*utaqqer*	*muttaqqer-*	*utaqqur-*
Š		*šuqqurum*	*ušaqqar*	*uštaqqer*	*ušaqqer*	*šuqqer*	*mušaqqer-*	*šuqqur-*
Št passive		*šutaqqurum*	*uštaqqar*	*uštataqqer*	*uštaqqer*	*šutaqqer*	*muštaqqer-*	*šutaqqur-*
Št lexical		*šutaqqurum*	*uštanaqqar*	*uštataqqer*	*uštaqqer*	*šutaqqer*	*muštaqqer-*	*šutaqqur-*
Štn		*šutaqqurum*	*uštanaqqar*	*uštataqqer*	*uštaqqer*	*šutaqqer*	*muštaqqer-*	*šutaqqur-*

[1]Loss of vowel before final radical with addition of vocalic ending: G perf. *ittaqrū*, impv. *uqrā*, vbl. adj. *naqrum*; Gt pret. *ittaqrū*, ptcpl. *muttaqrum*; N pret. *innaqrū*, ptcpl. *munnaqrum*. [2]Assimilation of infix *-t-* to medial root sibilant.

10b. Verbs I–*n*: Finite Forms (G)

a–u class: ***naqārum***

	Durative	Perfect	Preterite	Imp'v.
3cs	*inaqqar*	*ittaqar*	*iqqur*	
2ms	*tanaqqar*	*tattaqar*	*taqqur*	*uqur*
2fs	*tanaqqarī*	*tattaqrī*	*taqqurī*	*uqrī*
1cs	*anaqqar*	*attaqar*	*aqqur*	
3mp	*inaqqarū*	*ittaqrū*	*iqqurū*	
3fp	*inaqqarā*	*ittaqrā*	*iqqurā*	
2cp	*tanaqqarā*	*tattaqrā*	*taqqurā*	*uqrā*
1cp	*ninaqqar*	*nittaqar*	*niqqur*	

i class: ***nakāsum***

	Durative	Perfect	Preterite	Imp'v.
3cs	*inakkis*	*ittakis*	*ikkis*	
2ms	*tanakkis*	*tattakis*	*takkis*	*ikis*
2fs	*tanakkisī*	*tattaksī*	*takkisī*	*iksī*
1cs	*anakkis*	*attakis*	*akkis*	
3mp	*inakkisū*	*ittaksū*	*ikkisū*	
3fp	*inakkisā*	*ittaksā*	*ikkisā*	
2cp	*tanakkisā*	*tattaksā*	*takkisā*	*iksā*
1cp	*ninakkis*	*nittakis*	*nikkis*	

u class: ***nasākum***

	Durative	Perfect	Preterite	Imp'v.
3cs	*inassuk*	*ittasuk*	*issuk*	
2ms	*tanassuk*	*tattasuk*	*tassuk*	*usuk*
2fs	*tanassukī*	*tattaskī*	*tassukī*	*uskī*
1cs	*anassuk*	*attasuk*	*assuk*	
3mp	*inassukū*	*ittaskū*	*issukū*	
3fp	*inassukā*	*ittaskā*	*issukā*	
2cp	*tanassukā*	*tattaskā*	*tassukā*	*uskā*
1cp	*ninassuk*	*nittasuk*	*nissuk*	

11a. Verbs I–*w*: Stem Forms

Stem		Infinitive	Durative	Perfect	Preterite	Imperative	Participle	Vbl. Adj.
G	active (*a–i*)	*warādum*	*urrad*	*ittarad*[1]	*urid*[1]	*rid*	*wārid-*	*warid-*[1]
G	stative (*i*)	*watārum*	*ittir*	*ītetir* / *ītatir*[1]	*ītir*	—	—	*watir-*[1]
Gt	(*a–i*)	*itrudum*	*ittarrad*	*ittatrad*	*ittarad*[1]	*tarad*[?]	*muttarid-*[1]	*itrud-*[1]
Gtn	(*a–i*)	*itarrudum*	*ittanarrad*	*ittatarrad*	*ittarrad*	*itarrad*	*muttarrid-*	*itarrud-*
N	(*a–i*)	?	*iwwallad*[2]	?	*iwwalid*[1,2]	?	*muwwalid-*	?
D		*(w)uššurum*	*uwaššar*	*ūtaššir*	*uwaššir*	*(w)uššir*	*muwaššir-*	*(w)uššur-*
Dt		*utaššurum*	*ūtaššar*	*ūtataššir*	*ūtaššir*	*utaššir*	*mūtaššir-*	*utaššur-*
Dtn		*utaššurum*	*ūtanaššar*	*ūtataššir*	*ūtaššir*	*utaššir*	*mūtaššir-*	*utaššur-*
Š	*a*-type	*šūbulum*	*ušabbal*	*uštābil*	*ušābil*	*šūbil*	*mušābil-*	*šūbul-*
	e-type	*šūrudum*	*ušerred*	*uštērid*	*ušērid*	*šūrid*	*mušērid-*	*šūrud-*
Št[3]	*a*-type	*šutābulum*	*uštabbal*	*uštatābil*	*uštābil*	*šutābil*	*muštābil-*	*šutābul-*
Št[3]	*e*-type	*šutērudum*	*ušterred*	*uštetērid*	*uštērid*	*šutērid*	*muštērid-*	*šutērud-*
Štn	*a*-type	*šutabbulum*	*uštanabbal*	*uštatabbil*	*uštabbil*	*šutabbil*	*muštabbil-*	*šutabbul-*
	e-type	*šuterrudum*	*uštenerred*	*ušteterrid*	*ušterrid*	*šuterrid*	*mušterrid-*	*šuterrud-*

[1]Loss of vowel before final radical with addition of vocalic ending: G perf. *ittardū, ītatrū*, pret. *urdū*, vbl. adj. *wardum, watrum*; Gt pret. *ittardū*, ptcpl. *muttardum*; N pret. *iwwaldū*. [2]Sometimes with -ʾʾ- rather than -*ww*-: dur. *iʾʾallad*, pret. *iʾʾalid*. [3]Št-passive and Št-lexical forms are the same in verbs I–*w*.

11b. Verbs I–*w*: Finite Forms (G)

	Active ***a–i*** class: ***warādum***				Stative ***i*** class: ***watārum***			
	Durative	Perfect	Preterite	Imp'v.	Durative	Perfect	Preterite	Imp'v.
3cs	*urrad*	*ittarad*	*urid*		*ittir*	*ītetir / ītatir*	*ītir*	
2ms	*turrad*	*tattarad*	*turid*	*rid*	*tettir*	*tētetir / tātatir*	*tētir*	—
2fs	*turradī*	*tattardī*	*turdī*	*ridī*	*tettirī*	*tētetrī / tātatrī*	*tētirī*	—
1cs	*urrad*	*attarad*	*urid*		*ettir*	*ētetir / ātatir*	*ētir*	
3mp	*urradū*	*ittardū*	*urdū*		*ittirū*	*ītetrū / ītatrū*	*ītirū*	
3fp	*urradā*	*ittardā*	*urdā*		*ittirā*	*ītetrā / ītatrā*	*ītirā*	
2cp	*turradā*	*tattardā*	*turdā*	*ridā*	*tettirā*	*tētetrā / tātatrā*	*tētirā*	—
1cp	*nurrad*	*nittarad*	*nurid*		*nittir*	*nītetir / nītatir*	*nītir*	

12a. Verbs II–weak: Stem Forms

Stem		Infinitive	Durative sg/pl	Perfect sg/pl	Preterite sg/pl	Imp'v sg/pl	Participle	Vbl. Adj.
G	(*a–u*)	*kânum*	*ikân / ikunnū*	*iktūn / iktūnū*	*ikūn / ikūnū*	*kūn / kūnā*	*dāʾik- / mudīk-*	*kīn-*
	(*a–i*)	*qiāšum*	*iqīaš / iqiššū*	*iqtīš / iqtīšū*	*iqīš / iqīšū*	*qīš / qīšā*	*qāʾiš- / muqīš-*	*qīš-*[1]
	(*a*)	*šâlum*	*išâl / išallū*	*ištāl / ištālū*	*išāl / išālū*	*šāl / šālā*	*šāʾil-*	*šāl-*
	(*e*)	*nêrum*[2]	*inêr / inerrū*[2]	*ittēr / ittērū*[2]	*inēr / inērū*[2]	*nēr / nērā*[2]	*nēʾir-*[2]	*nēr-*[2]
Gt	(*a–u*)	*kitūnum*	*iktân / iktunnū*	*iktatūn / iktatūnū*	*iktūn / iktūnū*	*kitūn / kitūnā*	*muktīn-*	*kitūn-*
	(*a–i*)	*itūlum*[3]	*ittīal / ittillū*	*ittatīl / ittatīlū*	*ittīl / ittīlū*	*itīl / itīlā*	*muttīl-*	*itūl-*
	(*a*)	*šitūlum*	*ištâl / ištallū*	*ištatāl / ištatālū*	*ištāl / ištālū*	*šitāl / šitālā*	*muštāl-*	*šitūl-*
Gtn	(*a–u*)	*kitayyunum*	*iktanân / iktanunnū*	?	*iktūn / iktunnū*	?	?	*kitayyun-*
	(*a–i*)	*qitayyušum*	*iqtanīaš / iqtaniššū*	?	*iqtīš / iqtiššū*	?	?	*qitayyuš-*
	(*a*)	*šitaʾʾulum*	*ištanaʾʾal / ištanaʾʾalū* *ištanâl / ištanallū*	?	*ištaʾʾal / ištaʾʾalū*	*šitaʾʾal*	*muštaʾʾil-*	*šitaʾʾul-*
N	(*a–u*)	?	*iddâk / iddukkū*	?	*iddīk? / iddīkū?* *iddūk? / iddūkū?*	?	?	?
	(*a–i*)	?	*iqqīaš / iqqiššū*	?	*iqqīš / iqqīšū*	?	?	?
	(*a*)	?	*iššâm / iššammū*	?	*iššām / iššāmū*	?	?	?
	(*e*)	?	*innêr / innerrū*	?	*innēr / innērū*	?	?	?
D		*kunnum*	*ukān / ukannū*	*uktīn / uktinnū*	*ukīn / ukinnū*	*kīn / kinnā*	*mukīn / mukinn-*	*kūn / kunn-*
Dt		*kutunnum*	*uktān / uktannū*	*uktatīn / uktatinnū*	*uktīn / uktinnū*	*kutīn / kutinnā*	*muktīn / muktinn-*	*kutunn-*
Dtn		*kutunnum*	*uktanān / uktanannū*	*uktatīn / uktatinnū*	*uktīn / uktinnū*	*kutīn / kutinnā*	*muktīn / muktinn-*	*kutunn-*
Š		*šumuttum*	*ušmāt / ušmattū*	*uštamīt / uštamittū*	*ušmīt / ušmittū*	*šumīt / šumittā*	*mušmīt / mušmitt-*	*šumūt / šumutt-*
Št[4]		*šutamuttum*	*uštamāt / uštamattū*	?	*uštamīt / uštamittū*	?	*muštamitt-*	*šutamutt-*

[1]Note also the stative vbl. adj. base *ṭāb-*, from *ṭiābum*. [2] Less often with *a*--vowels rather than *e* throughout. [3]Root *n-y-l* (G *niālum*). [4]Št-passive and Št-lexical forms are the same in verbs II-weak; Štn forms are not attested.

12b. Verbs II–weak: Finite Forms (G, D)

	G, *a–u* class: ***kânum***				G, *a–i* class: ***qiāšum***				G, *a* class: ***šâlum***			
	Durative	Perfect	Pret.	Imp'v.	Durat.	Perfect	Pret.	Imp'v.	Durat.	Perfect	Pret.	Imp'v.
3cs	*ikân*	*iktūn*	*ikūn*		*iqīaš*	*iqtīš*	*iqīš*		*išâl*	*ištāl*	*išāl*	
2ms	*takân*	*taktūn*	*takūn*	*kūn*	*taqīaš*	*taqtīš*	*taqīš*	*qīš*	*tašâl*	*taštāl*	*tašāl*	*šāl*
2fs	*takunnī*	*taktūnī*	*takūnī*	*kūnī*	*taqiššī*	*taqtīšī*	*taqīšī*	*qīšī*	*tašallī*	*taštālī*	*tašālī*	*šālī*
1cs	*akân*	*aktūn*	*akūn*		*aqīaš*	*aqtīš*	*aqīš*		*ašâl*	*aštāl*	*ašāl*	
3mp	*ikunnū*	*iktūnū*	*ikūnū*		*iqiššū*	*iqtīšū*	*iqīšū*		*išallū*	*ištālū*	*išālū*	
3fp	*ikunnā*	*iktūnā*	*ikūnā*		*iqiššā*	*iqtīšā*	*iqīšā*		*išallā*	*ištālā*	*išālā*	
2cp	*takunnā*	*taktūnā*	*takūnā*	*kūnā*	*taqiššā*	*taqtīšā*	*taqīšā*	*qīšā*	*tašallā*	*taštālā*	*tašālā*	*šālā*
1cp	*nikân*	*niktūn*	*nikūn*		*niqīaš*	*niqtīš*	*niqīš*		*nišâl*	*ništāl*	*nišāl*	

	G, *e* class: ***nêrum***				D[1] of ***kânum***[2]			
	Durative	Perfect	Preterite	Imperative	Durative	Perfect	Preterite	Imp'v.
3cs	*inêr / inâr*	*ittēr / ittār*	*inēr / inār*		*ukān*	*uktīn*	*ukīn*	
2ms	*tenêr / tanâr*	*tettēr / tattār*	*tenēr / tanār*	*nēr / nār*	*tukān*	*tuktīn*	*tukīn*	*kīn*
2fs	*tenerrī / tanarrī*	*tettērī / tattārī*	*tenērī / tanārī*	*nērī / nārī*	*tukannī*	*tuktunnī*	*tukinnī*	*kinnī*
1cs	*enêr / anâr*	*ettēr / attār*	*enēr / anār*		*ukān*	*uktīn*	*ukīn*	
3mp	*inerrū / inarrū*	*ittērū / ittārū*	*inērū / inārū*		*ukannū*	*uktinnū*	*ukinnū*	
3fp	*inerrā / inarrā*	*ittērā / ittārā*	*inērā / inārā*		*ukannā*	*uktinnā*	*ukinnā*	
2cp	*tenerrā / tanarrā*	*tettērā / tattārā*	*tenērā / tanārā*	*nērā / nārā*	*tukannā*	*tuktinnā*	*tukinnā*	*kinnā*
1cp	*ninêr / ninâr*	*nittēr / nittār*	*ninēr / ninār*		*nukān*	*nuktīn*	*nukīn*	

[1]Similarly in the Š of verbs originally II–*w* and II–*y*, as in dur. 3ms *ušmāt*, 3mp *ušmattū*; pf. 3ms *uštamīt*, 3mp *uštamittū*; pret. 3ms *ušmīt*, 3mp *ušmittū*; impv. ms *šumīt*, pl *šumittā*. [2]For verbs originally II–ʾ, note, e.g., dur. 3ms *ušaʾʾal / ušâl*, 3mp *ušaʾʾalū / ušallū*; pf. 3ms *uštaʾʾil*, 3mp *uštaʾʾilū*; pret. 3ms *ušaʾʾil*, 3mp *ušaʾʾilū*; impv. *šuʾʾil*.

13a. Verbs III–weak: Stem Forms

Stem		Infinitive	Durative	Perfect	Preterite	Imperative	Participle	Vbl. Adj.
G	(*a*)	*malûm*	*imalla*	*imtala*	*imla*	*mila*	*māli-*	*mali-*
	(*i*)	*banûm*	*ibanni*	*ibtani*	*ibni*	*bini*	*bāni-*	*bani-*
	(*u*)	*manûm*	*imannu*	*imtanu*	*imnu*	*munu*	*māni-*	*mani-*
	(*e*)	*leqûm*	*ileqqe / ilaqqe*	*ilteqe*	*ilqe*	*leqe / liqe*	*lēqi-*	*leqi- / laqi-*
Gt	(*a*)	*mitlûm*	*imtalla*	*imtatla*	*imtala*	*mitla*	*mumtali-*	*mitlu-*
	(*i*)	*bitnûm*	*ibtanni*	*ibtatni*	*ibtani*	*bitni*	*mubtani-*	*bitnu-*
	(*u*)	*mitnûm*	*imtannu*	*imtatnu*	*imtanu*	*mitnu*	*mumtani-*	*mitnu-*
	(*e*)	*litqûm*	*ilteqqe*	*iltetqe*	*ilteqe*	*litqe*	*multeqi-*	*litqu-*
Gtn	(*a*)	*mitallûm*	*imtanalla*	*imtatalla*	*imtalla*	*mitalla*	*mumtalli-*	*mitallu-*
	(*i*)	*bitannûm*	*ibtananni*	*ibtatanni*	*ibtanni*	*bitanni*	*mubtanni-*	*bitannu-*
	(*u*)	*mitannûm*	*imtanannu*	*imtatannu*	*imtannu*	*mitannu*	*mumtanni-*	*mitannu-*
	(*e*)	*liteqqûm*	*ilteneqqe*	*ilteteqqe*	*ilteqqe*	*liteqqe*	*multeqqi-*	*liteqqu-*
N	(*a*)	*namlûm*	*immalla*	*ittamla*	*immali*	*namli*	*mummali-*	*namli-(?)*
	(*i*)	*nabnûm*	*ibbanni*	*ittabni*	*ibbani*	*nabni*	*mubbani-*	*nabni-*
	(*u*)	*namnûm*	*immannu*	*ittamnu*	*immani*	*namni*	*mummani-*	*namnu*
	(*e*)	*nelqûm / nalqûm*	*illeqqe / illaqqe*	*ittelqe / ittalqe*	*illeqi / illaqi*	*nelqi / nalqi*	*mull*^{e}/$_a$*qi-*	*n*^{e}/$_a$*lqi-(?)*
Ntn	(*a*)	*itamlûm*	*ittanamla*	*ittatamla*	*ittamla*	*itamla*	*muttamli-*	*itamlu-*
	(*i*)	*itabnûm*	*ittanabni*	*ittatabni*	*ittabni*	*itabni*	*muttabni-*	*itabnu-*
	(*u*)	*itamnûm*	*ittanamnu*	*ittatamnu*	*ittamnu*	*itamnu*	*muttamni-*	*itamnu-*
	(*e*)	*itelqûm*	*ittenelqe*	*ittetelqe*	*ittelqe*	*itelqe*	*muttelqi-*	*itelqu-*
D		*mullûm*	*umalla*	*umtalli*	*umalli*	*mulli*	*mumalli-*	*mullu-*
		luqqûm	*uleqqe / ulaqqa*	*ulteqqi / ultaqqi*	*uleqqi / ulaqqi*	*luqqi*	*mul*^{e}/$_a$*qqi-*	*luqqu-*
Dt		*mutallûm*	*umtalla*	*umtatalli*	*umtalli*	*mutalli*	*mumtalli-*	*mutallu-*
		lut^e/$_a$*qqûm*	*ult*^{e}/$_a$*qq*^{e}/$_a$	*ult*^{e}/$_a$*t*^{e}/$_a$*qqi*	*ult*^{e}/$_a$*qqi*	*lut*^{e}/$_a$*qqi*	*mult*^{e}/$_a$*qqi-*	*lut*^{e}/$_a$*qqu-*
Dtn		*mutallûm*	*umtanalla*	*umtatalli*	*umtalli*	*mutalli*	*mumtalli-*	*mutallu-*
		lut^e/$_a$*qqûm*	*ult*^{e}/$_a$*n*^{e}/$_a$*qq*^{e}/$_a$	*ult*^{e}/$_a$*t*^{e}/$_a$*qqi*	*ult*^{e}/$_a$*qqi*	*lut*^{e}/$_a$*qqi*	*mult*^{e}/$_a$*qqi-*	*lut*^{e}/$_a$*qqu-*

Stem	Infinitive	Durative	Perfect	Preterite	Imperative	Participle	Vbl. Adj.
Š	*šumlûm*	*ušamla*	*uštamli*	*ušamli*	*šumli*	*mušamli-*	*šumlu-*
	šulqûm	*ušelqe*	*uštelqi*	*ušelqi*	*šulqi*	*mušelqi-*	*šulqu-*
Št passive	*šutamlûm*	*uštamla*	*uštatamli*	*uštamli*	*šutamli*	*muštamli-*	*šutamlu-*
	šutelqûm	*uštelqe*	*uštetelqi*	*uštelqi*	*šutelqi*	*muštelqi-*	*šutelqu-*
Št lexical	*šutamlûm*	*uštamalla*	*uštatamli*	*uštamli*	*šutamli*	*muštamli-*	*šutamlu-*
	šutelqûm	*ušteleqqe*	*uštetelqi*	*uštelqi*	*šutelqi*	*muštelqi-*	*šutelqu-*
Štn	*šutamlûm*	*uštanamla*	*uštatamli*	*uštamli*	*šutamli*	*muštamli-*	*šutamlu-*
	šutelqûm	*uštenelqe*	*uštetelqi*	*uštelqi*	*šutelqi*	*muštelqi-*	*šutelqu-*

13b. Verbs III–weak: Finite Forms (G)

Verbs III–*i*

	Durative	Perfect	Preterite	Imp'v.
3cs	*ibanni*	*ibtani*	*ibni*	
2ms	*tabanni*	*tabtani*	*tabni*	*bini*
2fs	*tabannî*	*tabtanî*	*tabnî*	*binî*
1cs	*abanni*	*abtani*	*abni*	
3mp	*ibannû*	*ibtanû*	*ibnû*	
3fp	*ibanniā*	*ibtaniā*	*ibniā*	
2cp	*tabanniā*	*tabtaniā*	*tabniā*	*biniā*
1cp	*nibanni*	*nibtani*	*nibni*	

Verbs III–*u*

	Durative	Perfect	Preterite	Imp'v.
3cs	*iḫaddu*	*iḫtadu*	*iḫdu*	
2ms	*taḫaddu*	*taḫtadu*	*taḫdu*	*ḫudu*
2fs	*taḫaddî*	*taḫtadî*	*taḫdî*	*ḫudî*
1cs	*aḫaddu*	*aḫtadu*	*aḫdu*	
3mp	*iḫaddû*	*iḫtadû*	*iḫdû*	
3fp	*iḫaddâ*	*iḫtadâ*	*iḫdâ*	
2cp	*taḫaddâ*	*taḫtadâ*	*taḫdâ*	*ḫudâ*
1cp	*niḫaddu*	*niḫtadu*	*niḫdu*	

Verbs III–*a*

	Durative	Perfect	Preterite	Imp'v.
3cs	*imalla*	*imtala*	*imla*	
2ms	*tamalla*	*tamtala*	*tamla*	*mila*
2fs	*tamallî*	*tamtalî*	*tamlî*	*milî*
1cs	*amalla*	*amtala*	*amla*	
3mp	*imallû*	*imtalû*	*imlû*	
3fp	*imallâ*	*imtalâ*	*imlâ*	
2cp	*tamallâ*	*tamtalâ*	*tamlâ*	*milâ*
1cp	*nimalla*	*nimtala*	*nimla*	

Verbs III–*e*

	Durative	Perfect	Preterite	Imp'v.
3cs	*ileqqe / ilaqqe*	*ilteqe*	*ilqe*	
2ms	*teleqqe / talaqqe*	*telteqe*	*telqe / talqe*	*leqe / liqe*
2fs	*teleqqî / talaqqî*	*telteqî*	*telqî / talqî*	*leqî / liqî*
1cs	*eleqqe / alaqqe*	*elteqe*	*elqe / alqe*	
3mp	*ileqqû / ilaqqû*	*ilteqû*	*ilqû*	
3fp	*ileqqeā / ilaqqeā*	*ilteqeā*	*ilqeā*	
2cp	*teleqqeā / talaqqeā*	*telteqeā*	*telqeā / talqeā*	*leqeā / liqeā*
1cp	*nileqqe / nilaqqe*	*nilteqe*	*nilqe*	

13c. Verbs III–weak: Non-Finite Forms (G)

	Infinitive			Active Participle			Verbal Adj., Attributive			Verbal Adj. + Pron. Subj.		
		III–*i*/*a*/*u*	III–*e*		III–*i*/*a*/*u*	III–*e*		in -*i*	in -*u*		in -*i*	in -*u*
G	nom.	*banûm*	*leqûm*	ms nom.	*bānûm*	*lēqûm*	ms nom.	*banûm*[1]	*zakûm*	1cs	*baniāku*[2]	*zakâku*
	gen.	*banêm*	*leqêm*	gen.	*bānîm*	*lēqîm*	gen.	*banîm*	*zakîm*	2ms	*baniāta*	*zakâta*
	acc.	*banâm*	*leqēam*	acc.	*bāniam*	*lēqiam*	acc.	*baniam*	*zakâm*	2fs	*baniāti*	*zakâti*
										3ms	*bani*[1]	*zaku*
				fs nom.	*bānītum*	*lēqītum*	fs nom.	*banītum*	*zakūtum*	3fs	*baniat*	*zakât*
				gen.	*bānītim*	*lēqītim*	gen.	*banītim*	*zakūtim*			
				acc.	*bānītam*	*lēqītam*	acc.	*banītam*	*zakūtam*	1cp	*baniānu*	*zakânu*
										2mp	*baniātunu*	*zakâtunu*
				mp nom.	*bānûtum*	*lēqûtum*	mp nom.	*banûtum*	*zakûtum*	2fp	*baniātina*	*zakâtina*
				g.-a.	*bānûtim*	*lēqûtim*	g.-a.	*banûtim*	*zakûtim*	3mp	*banû*	*zakû*
										3fp	*baniā*	*zakâ*
				fp nom.	*bāniātum*	*lēqiātum*	fp nom.	*baniātum*	*zakâtum*			
				g.-a.	*bāniātim*	*lēqiātim*	g.-a.	*baniātim*	*zakâtim*			

[1]Similarly in verbs III-*e* ms *leqûm*/*leqîm*/*leqiam*, fs *leqītum*, mp *leqûtum*, fp *leqiātum*. [2]Similarly in verbs III-*e* 1cs *leqiāku*, 2ms *leqiāta*, etc.

13d. Verbs III–weak: Finite Forms (N)

Verbs III–*i*

	Durative	Perfect	Preterite	Imp'v.
3cs	*ibbanni*	*ittabni*	*ibbani*	
2ms	*tabbanni*	*tattabni*	*tabbani*	*nabni*
2fs	*tabbannî*	*tattabnî*	*tabbanî*	*nabnî*
1cs	*abbanni*	*attabni*	*abbani*	
3mp	*ibbannû*	*ittabnû*	*ibbanû*	
3fp	*ibbanniā*	*ittabniā*	*ibbaniā*	
2cp	*tabbanniā*	*tattabniā*	*tabbaniā*	*nabniā*
1cp	*nibbanni*	*nittabni*	*nibbani*	

Verbs III–*u*

	Durative	Perfect	Preterite	Imp'v.
3cs	*immannu*	*ittamnu*	*immani*	
2ms	*tammannu*	*tattamnu*	*tammani*	*namni*
2fs	*tammannu*	*tattamnu*	*tammani*	*namnî*
1cs	*ammannu*	*attamnu*	*ammani*	
3mp	*immannû*	*ittamnû*	*immanû*	
3fp	*immannâ*	*ittamnâ*	*immaniā*	
2cp	*tammannâ*	*tattamnâ*	*tammaniā*	*namniā*
1cp	*nimmannu*	*nittamnu*	*nimmani*	

Verbs III–*a*

	Durative	Perfect	Preterite	Imp'v.
3cs	*ikkalla*	*ittakla*	*ikkali*	
2ms	*takkalla*	*tattakla*	*takkali*	*nakli*
2fs	*takkallî*	*tattaklî*	*takkalî*	*naklî*
1cs	*akkalla*	*attakla*	*akkali*	
3mp	*ikkallû*	*ittaklû*	*ikkalû*	
3fp	*ikkallâ*	*ittaklâ*	*ikkaliā*	
2cp	*takkallâ*	*tattaklâ*	*takkaliā*	*nakliā*
1cp	*nikkalla*	*nittakla*	*nikkali*	

Verbs III–*e*

	Durative	Perfect	Preterite	Imp'v.
3cs	*illeqqe/illaqqe*	$itt^{e}/{}_{a}qle$	*illeqi/illaqi*	
2ms	*telleqqe/tallaqqe*	$t^{e}/{}_{a}tt^{e}/{}_{a}qle$	*telleqi/tallaqi*	*nelqi/nalqi*
2fs	*telleqqî/tallaqqî*	$t^{e}/{}_{a}tt^{e}/{}_{a}qle$	*talleqî/tallaqî*	*nelqî/nalqî*
1cs	*elleqqe/allaqqe*	${}^{e}/{}_{a}tt^{e}/{}_{a}qle$	*elleqi/allaqi*	
3mp	*illeqqû/illaqqû*	$itt^{e}/{}_{a}ql\hat{u}$	*illeqû/illaqû*	
3fp	*illeqqeā/illaqqeā*	$itt^{e}/{}_{a}qle\bar{a}$	*illeqiā/illaqiā*	
2cp	*telleqqeā/tallaqqeā*	$t^{e}/{}_{a}tt^{e}/{}_{a}qle\bar{a}$	*telleqiā/tallaqiā*	*nelqiā/nalqiā*
1cp	*nilleqqe/nillaqqe*	$nitt^{e}/{}_{a}qle$	*nilleqi/nillaqi*	

13e. Verbs III–weak: Non-Finite Forms (N)

Subj.	Infinitive		Active Participle			Verbal Adj., Attributive			Vbl. Adj. + Pron.	
N[1]	nom.	*nabnûm*	ms	nom.	*mubbanûm*	ms	nom.	*nabnûm*	1cs	*nabniāku*
	gen.	*nabnîm*		gen.	*mubbanîm*		gen.	*nabnîm*	2ms	*nabniāta*
	acc.	*nabnâm*		acc.	*mubbaniam*		acc.	*nabniam*	2fs	*nabniāti*
									3ms	*nabni*
			fs	nom.	*mubbanītum*	fs	nom.	*nabnītum*	3fs	*nabniat*
				gen.	*mubbanītim*		gen.	*nabnītim*		
				acc.	*mubbanītam*		acc.	*nabnītam*	1cp	*nabniānu*
									2mp	*nabniātunu*
			mp	nom.	*mubbanûtum*	mp	nom.	*nabnûtum*	2fp	*nabniātina*
				gen.-acc.	*mubbanûtim*		gen.-acc.	*nabnûtim*	3mp	*nabnû*
									3fp	*nabniā*
			fp	nom.	*mubbaniātum*	fp	nom.	*nabniātum*		
				gen.-acc.	*mubbaniātim*		gen.-acc.	*nabniātim*		

[1]In verbs III–*e*, *a* before or after first radical may appear as *e*: infin. *nelqûm / nalqûm*, ptcpl. *mulleqûm / mullaqûm*, v. adj. base *nelqi- / nalqi-(?)*.

13f. Verbs III–weak: Finite Forms (D, Š)

	D				Š			
	Durative	Perfect	Preterite	Imp'v.	Durative	Perfect	Preterite	Imp'v.
3cs	*ubanna*	*ubtanni*	*ubanni*		*ušabna*	*uštabni*	*ušabni*	
2ms	*tubanna*	*tubtanni*	*tubanni*	*bunni*	*tušabna*	*tuštabni*	*tušabni*	*šubni*
2fs	*tubannâ*	*tubtannî*	*tubannî*	*bunnî*	*tušabnî*	*tuštabnî*	*tušabnî*	*šubnî*
1cs	*ubanna*	*ubtanni*	*ubanni*		*ušabna*	*uštabni*	*ušabni*	
3mp	*ubannû*	*ubtannû*	*ubannû*		*ušabnû*	*uštabnû*	*ušabnû*	
3fp	*ubannâ*	*ubtanniā*	*ubanniā*		*ušabnâ*	*uštabniā*	*ušabniā*	
2cp	*tubannâ*	*tubtanniā*	*tubanniā*	*bunniā*	*tušabnâ*	*tuštabniā*	*tušabniā*	*šubniā*
1cp	*nubanna*	*nubtanni*	*nubanni*		*nušabna*	*nuštabni*	*nušabni*	

13g. Verbs III–weak: Non-Finite Forms (D,Š)

	Infinitive		Active Participle[1]			Verbal Adj., Attributive			Vbl. Adj. + Pron. Subj.	
D	nom.	*bunnûm*	ms	nom.	*mubannûm*	ms	nom.	*bunnûm*	1cs	*bunnâku*
	gen.	*bunnîm*		gen.	*mubannîm*		gen.	*bunnîm*	2ms	*bunnâta*
	acc.	*bunnâm*		acc.	*mubanniam*		acc.	*bunnâm*	2fs	*bunnâti*
									3ms	*bunnu*
			fs	nom.	*mubannītum*	fs	nom.	*bunnūtum*	3fs	*bunnât*
				gen.	*mubannītim*		gen.	*bunnūtim*		
				acc.	*mubannītam*		acc.	*bunnūtam*	1cp	*bunnânu*
									2mp	*bunnâtunu*
			mp	nom.	*mubannûtum*	mp	nom.	*bunnûtum*	2fp	*bunnâtina*
				gen.-acc.	*mubannûtim*		gen.-acc.	*bunnûtim*	3mp	*bunnû*
									3fp	*bunnâ*
			fp	nom.	*mubanniātum*	fp	nom.	*bunnâtum*		
				gen.-acc.	*mubanniātim*		gen.-acc.	*bunnâtim*		
Š	nom.	*šubnûm*	ms	nom.	*mušabnûm*	ms	nom.	*šubnûm*	1cs	*šubnâku*
	gen.	*šubnîm*		gen.	*mušabnîm*		gen.	*šubnîm*	2ms	*šubnâta*
	acc.	*šubnâm*		acc.	*mušabniam*		acc.	*šubnâm*	2fs	*šubnâti*
									3ms	*šubnu*
			fs	nom.	*mušabnītum*	fs	nom.	*šubnūtum*	3fs	*šubnât*
				gen.	*mušabnītim*		gen.	*šubnūtim*		
				acc.	*mušabnītam*		acc.	*šubnūtam*	1cp	*šubnânu*
									2mp	*šubnâtunu*
			mp	nom.	*mušabnûtum*	mp	nom.	*šubnûtum*	2fp	*šubnâtina*
				gen.-acc.	*mušabnûtim*		gen.-acc.	*šubnûtim*	3mp	*šubnû*
									3fp	*šubnâ*
			fp	nom.	*mušabniātum*	fp	nom.	*šubnâtum*		
				gen.-acc.	*mušabniātim*		gen.-acc.	*šubnâtim*		

[1] In verbs III–*e*, *a* before or after first radical may appear as *e*: D *muṭeḫḫi-*/*muṭaḫḫi*, Š *mušešmi-*/*mušašmi-*.

14. Doubly Weak Verbs: Stem Forms

	Stem	Infinitive	Durative	Perfect	Preterite	Imperative	Participle	Vbl. Adj.
(a) I–*n* and II–ʾ: *naʾādum* ‘to heed’								
	G	*naʾādum*	*inaʾʾid*	*ittaʾid*	*iʾʾid*	*iʾid*	*nāʾid-*	*naʾid-*
	Gt	*itʾudum*	*ittaʾʾid*	?	*ittaʾid*	*itʾid*	*muttaʾid-*	*itʾud-*
	D	*nuʾʾudum*	*unaʾʾad*	*uttaʾʾid*	*unaʾʾid*	*nuʾʾid*	*munaʾʾid-*	*nuʾʾud-*
(b) I–*n* and II–*w* or II–*y*: *nawārum* ‘to shine’; *nâḫum* ‘to rest’; *niālum* ‘to lie down’								
a	G	*nawārum*	*inawwir*	*ittawir*	*iwwir*	**iwir*	**nāwir-*	*nawir-*
	D	*nuwwurum*	*unawwar*	*uttawwir*	*unawwir*	*nuwwir*	*munawwir-*	*nuwwur-*
b	G	*nâḫum*	*inâḫ* / *inuḫḫū*	*ittūḫ*	*inūḫ*	**nūḫ*	—	*nīḫ-*
	D	*nuḫḫum*	*unāḫ*	*uttīḫ*	*unīḫ*	*nīḫ*	*muniḫḫ-*	*nuḫḫ-*
c	G	*niālum*	*inīal* / *inillū*	*ittīl*	*inīl*	*nīl*	—	*nīl*
	Gt	*itūlum* / *utūlum*	*ittīal* / *ittillū*	*ittatīl*	*ittīl*	*itīl*	*muttīl-*	*itūl-* / *utūl-*
	Š	*šunullum*	*ušnāl* / *ušnallū*	*uštanīl* / ..*nillū*	*ušnīl* / *ušnillū*	*šunīl* / *šunillā*	—	*šunull-*
(c) I–*n* and III–weak: *nadûm* ‘to put down’								
	G	*nadûm*	*inaddi*	*ittadi*	*iddi*	*idi*	*nādi-*	*nadi-*
	Gtn	*itaddûm*	*ittanaddi*	*ittataddi*	*ittaddi*	*itaddi*	*muttaddi-*	*itaddu-*
	N	*naddûm* / *nandûm*	*innaddi*	*ittaddi* / *ittandi*	*innadi*	*naddi* / *nandi*	*munnadi-*	*na*^{n}/$_{d}$*du-*
	Š	*šuddûm*	*ušadda*	*uštaddi*	*ušaddi*	*šuddi*	*mušaddi-*	*šuddu-*
(d) I–ʾ and II–weak: *eʾēlum* ‘to bind’; *êrum* ‘to awaken’								
a	G	*eʾēlum*	*iʾʾil*	?	*īʾil*$^{?}$	*eʾil*	—	*eʾil-*
b	G	*êrum*	*iʾêr*$^{?}$	?	*iʾēr*	*ēr*$^{?}$	—	*ēr-*
(e) I–ʾ and III–weak: *arûm* ‘to become pregnant’; *elûm* ‘to go up’								
a	G	*arûm* / *erûm*	*irri*	*ītari* / *īteri*	*īri*	—	—	*ari-* / *eri-*
b	G	*elûm*	*illi*	*īteli* / *ītali*	*īli*	*eli* / *ali*	*ēli-*	*eli-*
	D	*ullûm*	*ulla*	*ūtelli*	*ulli*	*ulli*	*mulli-*	*ullu-*
	Š	*šūlûm*	*ušelle* / *ušalla*	*uštēli*	*ušēli*	*šūli*	*mušēli-*	*šūlu-*

	Stem	Infinitive	Durative	Perfect	Preterite	Imperative	Participle	Vbl. Adj.
(f)	I–*w* and II–weak: *wiārum* / *wârum* ‘to advance’; *wiāṣum* ‘to become (too) little’							
	G	*wârum* / **wiārum*	**iwīar* / *i(w)âr* pl. *i(w)irrū*	?	*iwīr* pl. *iwīrū*	*iʾir*	—	*(w)īṣ-*
	D	*wuʾʾurum* / *wûrum*	*uwaʾʾar* / *uwâr* pl. *uwaʾʾarū* / *uwarrū*	*ūtaʾʾer*	*uwaʾʾer*(/*uwêr*) pl. *uwaʾʾerū*(/*uwerrū*)	*wuʾʾer*	*muwaʾʾer-*	*wuʾʾur-* / *wûr-*
(g)	I–*w* and III–weak: *waṣûm* ‘to go out’; *watûm* ‘to find’; *warûm* ‘to lead’							
a	G	*waṣûm*	*uṣṣi*	*ittaṣi*	*uṣi*	*ṣi*	*wāṣi-*	*waṣi-*
b		*watûm*	*utta*	*ittata*	*uta*	*ta*	*wāti-*	*wati-*
c		*warûm*	*urru*	*ittaru*	*uru*	*ru*	*wāri-*	*wari-*
	Š	*šūṣûm*	*ušeṣṣe* / *ušaṣṣa*	*uštēṣi* / *uštāṣi*	*ušēṣi* / *ušāṣi*	*šūṣi*	*mušēṣi-* / *mušāṣi-*	*šūṣu-*
(h)	II–ʾ and III–weak: *leʾûm* ‘to be able’; *buʾʾûm* ‘to look for’							
	G	*leʾûm* / *leyûm*	*ileʾʾi* / *ilê* / *ilî*	*ilteʾi* / *iltê*	*ilʾe* / *ilē*	?	*lēʾi-* / *lēyi-*	*leʾi-*
	D	*buʾʾûm*	*ubʾʾa* / *ubâ*	*ubtaʾʾi*	*ubaʾʾi*	*buʾʾi*	*mubaʾʾi-*	*buʾʾu-*
(i)	II–*w* and III–weak							
	G	*lawûm*	*ilawwi*	*iltawi*	*ilwi*	*liwi*	*lāwi-*	*lawi-*
	Š	*šulwûm*	*ušalwa*	*uštalwi*	*ušalwi*	*šulwi*	*mušalwi-*	*šulwu-*

15. Quadriradical Verbs: Stem Forms

Stem		Infinitive	Durative	Perfect	Preterite	Imperative	Participle	Vbl. Adj.
N	Sound	*nabalkutum*	*ibbalakkat*	*ittabalkat*	*ibbalkit*	*nabalkit*	*mubbalkit-*	*nabalkut-*
	IV–*u*	*naparkûm*	*ipparakku*	*ittaparku*	*ipparki*	*naparki*	*mupparki-*	*naparku-*
	IV–*e*	*neḫelṣûm*	*iḫḫeleṣṣe*	*itteḫelṣe*	*iḫḫelṣi*	*neḫelṣi*	*muḫḫelṣi-*	*neḫelṣu-*
Ntn		*itablakkutum*	*ittanablakkat*	*ittatablakkat*	*ittab(a)lakkat*	?	*muttablakkit-*	—
Š	Sound	*šubalkutum*	*ušbalakkat*	*uštabalkit*	*ušbalkit*	*šubalkit*	*mušbalkit-*	*šubalkut-*
	IV–*u*	*šuparkûm*	*ušparakka*	*uštaparki*	*ušparki*	*šuparki*	*mušparki-*	*šuparku-*
	IV–*e*	*šuḫelṣûm*	*ušḫeleṣṣe*	*ušteḫelṣi*	*ušḫelṣi*	*šuḫelṣi*	*mušḫelṣi-*	*šuḫelṣu-*
Štn		*šutablakkutum*	*uštanablakkat*	*uštatablakkit*?	*uštablakkit*	?	?	—

16. The Verb with the Ventive (§15.2)

	Durative	Perfect	Preterite	Precative/Imperative
3cs	*išapparam*	*ištapram*	*išpuram*	*lišpuram*
2ms	*tašapparam*	*taštapram*	*tašpuram*	*šupram*
2fs	*tašapparīm*	*taštaprīm*	*tašpurīm*	*šuprīm*
1cs	*ašapparam*	*aštapram*	*ašpuram*	*lušpuram*
3mp	*išapparūnim*	*ištaprūnim*	*išpurūnim*	*lišpurūnim*
3fp	*išapparānim*	*ištaprānim*	*išpurānim*	*lišpurānim*
2cp	*tašapparānim*	*taštaprānim*	*tašpurānim*	*šuprānim*
1cp	*nišapparam*	*ništapram*	*nišpuram*	*i nišpuram*

17. The Verb with Object Suffixes (§18.2)

(a) The Verb with Accusative (Direct Object) Suffixes

suffix	3cs verb	2fs verb	3mp verb	
no sf.	*iṣṣur*	*taṣṣurī*	*iṣṣurū*	'(s)he/you/they protected ...
1cs	*iṣṣuranni*	*taṣṣurīnni*	*iṣṣurūninni*	... me'
2ms	*iṣṣurka*		*iṣṣurūka*	... you'
2fs	*iṣṣurki*		*iṣṣurūki*	... you'
3ms	*iṣṣuršu*	*taṣṣurīšu*	*iṣṣurūšu*	... him'
3fs	*iṣṣurši*	*taṣṣurīši*	*iṣṣurūši*	... her'
1cp	*iṣṣurniāti*	*taṣṣurīniāti*	*iṣṣurūniāti*	... us'
2mp	*iṣṣurkunūti*		*iṣṣurūkunūti*	... you'
2fp	*iṣṣurkināti*		*iṣṣurūkināti*	... you'
3mp	*iṣṣuršunūti*	*taṣṣurīšunūti*	*iṣṣurūšunūti*	... them'
3fp	*iṣṣuršināti*	*taṣṣurīšināti*	*iṣṣurūšināti*	... them'

(b) The Verb with Dative (Indirect Object) Suffixes

suffix	3cs verb	2fs verb	3mp verb	
no sf.	*išpur*	*tašpurī*	*išpurū*	'(s)he/you/they sent ...
1cs	*išpuram*	*tašpurīm*	*išpurūnim*	... to me'
2ms	*išpur(ak)kum*		*išpurū(nik)kum*	... to you'
2fs	*išpur(ak)kim*		*išpurū(nik)kim*	... to you'
3ms	*išpur(aš)šum*	*tašpurī(š)šum*	*išpurū(niš)šum*	... to him'
3fs	*išpur(aš)šim*	*tašpurī(š)šim*	*išpurū(niš)šim*	... to her'
1cp	*išpur(an)niāšim*	*tašpurī(n)niāšim*	*išpurū(nin)niāšim*	... to us'
2mp	*išpur(ak)kunūšim*		*išpurū(nik)kunūšim*	... to you'
2fp	*išpur(ak)kināšim*		*išpurū(nik)kināšim*	... to you'
3mp	*išpur(aš)šunūšim*	*tašpurī(š)šunūšim*	*išpurū(niš)šunūšim*	... to them'
3fp	*išpur(aš)šināšim*	*tašpurī(š)šināšim*	*išpurū(niš)šināšim*	... to them'

The dative suffixes are optionally preceded by the Ventive (in parentheses).

INDEX OF TEXTS

Below are listed the texts reproduced in whole or in part in the Lesson Exercises. *Italics* refer to Lesson numbers.

AbB
- 1 13 *36*
- 1 14 *28*
- 1 76 *25*
- 1 92 *33*
- 1 96 *27*
- 1 102 *37*
- 1 117 *38*
- 2 2 *24*
- 2 4 *36*
- 2 14 *31*
- 2 24 *34*
- 2 54 *31*
- 2 56 *29*
- 2 62 *34*
- 2 74 *36*
- 2 98 *38*
- 2 100 *38*
- 2 129 *30*
- 2 131 *32*
- 3 2 *37*
- 3 15 *35*
- 3 16+17 *35*
- 3 28 *35*
- 3 55 *36*
- 4 13 *27*
- 4 16 *35*
- 4 19 *28*
- 4 26 *32*
- 4 30 *28*
- 4 64 *35*
- 4 79 *34*
- 4 113 *26*
- 4 132 *33*
- 5 135 *26*
- 5 136 *28*
- 5 225 *24*
- 6 9 *33*
- 6 136 *37*
- 6 213 *25*
- 7 30 *24*
- 8 11 *24*
- 11 99 *30*
- 11 168 *37*
- 12 10 *24*
- 12 84 *26*
- 12 128 *24*

ARM(T)
- 2 105 *30*
- 4 22 *33*
- 10 80 *29*
- 10 90 *29*
- 10 129 *36*
- 26/1 197 *29*

BE
- 6/1 96 *34*

CH
- v 14–24 *36*
- r xxiv 79–88 *36*
- r xxvi 53–56 *35*
- §1 *25*
- §2 *25*
- §3 *21*
- §4 *34*
- §5 *32*
- §6 *19*
- §7 *22*
- §8 *30*
- §§9–12 *32*
- §13 *34*
- §14 *17*
- §15 *28*
- §§17–19 *31*
- §20 *35*
- §21 *18*
- §§22–24 *31*
- §25 *31*
- §26 *22*
- §§27–29 *29*
- §§30–31 *29*
- §32 *31*

CH (continued)
§33 *22*
§§35–37 *33*
§42 *30*
§44 *29*
§45 *29*
§47 *25*
§49 *31*
§52 *27*
§§53–54 *31*
§§55–56 *28*
§57 *33*
§58 *32*
§59 *23*
§60 *18*
§§61–62 *32*
§64 *33*
§66 *31*
§75e/R *29*
§101 *36*
§102 *26*
§103 *35*
§104 *19*
§105 *31*
§106 *21*
§109 *31*
§112 *28*
§113 *30*
§§114–115 *26*
§116 *33*
§§117–118 *31*
§119 *19*
§120 *36*
§121 *25*
§122 *24*
§124 *36*
§125 *34*
§126 *36*
§127 *27*
§128 *22*
§§129–132 *33*
§§133–133b *23*
§§134–136 *32*
§137 *32*
§138 *24*
§141 *31*
§§142–143 *33*
§144 *30*
§§145–147 *36*
§§148–149 *34*
§150 *19*
§§151–152 *28*
§153 *29*
§154 *28*
§§155–157 *33*
§159 *32*
§§160–161 *36*
§§162–163 *29*
§§165–166 *33*
§167 *18*
§168 *30*
§§170–171 *26*
§§173–174 *29*
§175 *20*
§176 *32*
§177 *30*
§179 *27*
§180 *26*
§§182–184 *26*
§183 *18*
§§185–187 *37*
§§188–189 *32*
§190 *24*
§191 *34*
§192 *24*
§193 *26*
§194 *27*
§195 *17*
§§196–199 *24*
§200 *21*
§201 *23*
§202 *31*
§204 *23*
§205 *17*
§206 *36*
§§207–208 *30*
§§215–217 *24*
§§218–220 *18*
§221 *24*
§§224–225 *29*
§226 *25*
§227 *36*
§§228–229 *29*
§233 *36*
§240 *38*
§245 *29*
§246 *18*
§247 *17*
§249 *19*
§250 *30*
§251 *28*
§253 *37*
§254 *25*
§§255–256 *34*
§261 *30*
§265 *31*
§267 *27*
§§268–269 *23*
§271 *34*
§273 *23*
§277 *23*
§278 *20*
§279 *20*
§280 *26*
§282 *26*
§R/75e *29*

CT
2 28 *13*
2 35 *24*
2 41a *20*
2 44 *21*
2 50 *14*
4 31b *23*
4 32b *38*
4 35b *38*
6 37a *34*
6 40c *13*
6 42a *13*
8 5a *29*
8 12b *36*
8 22b *22*
8 24b *14*
8 36a *19*
8 37d *20*
8 42b *16*
8 48a *26*
29 6a *30*
29 7a *32*
43 13 *36*
43 14 *28*
43 76 *25*
43 92 *33*
43 96 *27*
43 117 *38*
52 30 *24*

Edzard, *Tell ed-Dēr*
4 *19*
15 *28*
23 *15*
32 *28*

Gilgamesh
II *Supp. Rdg.*
X ii 14 – iii 5 *36*

Iraq
25 177–80 *36*

Jeyes, *OB Extisp.*
no. 14:31 *33*

LIH
1 2 *24*
1 4 *36*
1 14 *31*
1 24 *34*
1 45 *26*
1 56 *31*
2 72 *29*
2 77 *28*
2 80 *34*
2 92 *36*
2 94 *30*
2 95 *37*

Meissner, *BAP*
43 *18*
78 *25*
90 *17*

OECT
3 1 *34*
3 35 *26*
3 54 *33*

PBS
7 99 *30*
7 133 *32*
8/2 186 *21*
8/2 188 *18*
8/2 196 *33*
8/2 252 *33*

RA
22 169–77 *35*
44 23ff.:5–6 *30*

RIME
4 334–36 *32*
4 341–42 *37*
4 354–55 *30*

Scheil, *SFS*
p. 131 *24*

Schorr, *VAB* 5
2 *17*
4 *21*
8 *15*
9 *16*
12 *20*
13A *24*
18 *29*
19 *20*
27 *26*
29 *34*
32 *18*
34 *34*
41 *16*
52 *13*
54 *19*
64 *27*
66 *23*
70 *14*
77 *22*
130 *22*
171 *25*
172 *13*
205 *32*
239 *32*
259 *18*
260 *36*
267 *14*
274 *13*
276 *38*
279 *35*
290 *14*

Szlechter, *Tablettes*
3–4 MAH 15951 *34*
64 MAH 15.958 *30*
68 MAH 16.643 *16*
82 MAH 15.880 *23*
97 MAH 16.139 *37*
110 MAH 16.148 *17*
121–22 MAH 16.482 *30*
125 MAH 16.351 *14*

Szlechter, *TJA*
20-21 UMM H42 *29*
26 UMM H10 *19*
41 UMM G4 *15*
42 UMM H32 *21*
53f. UMM H57 *31*
102f. FM 31 *31*
151 UMM G40 *30*

TCL
1 43 *38*
1 74 *38*
7 13 *27*
7 16 *35*
7 19 *28*
7 26 *32*
7 30 *28*
7 64 *35*

TIM
2 11 *24*
7 4 *19*
7 15 *28*
7 23 *15*
7 32 *28*

TLB
4 pl. 2 LB 1864 *37*
4 pl. 9 and 10 LB 1771+1766 *35*
4 pl. 9 LB 1897 *35*
4 pl. 16 LB 1904 *35*
4 pl. 31 LB 1886 *36*

UCP
9/4 p. 329 no. 4 *37*

UET
6/2 402 *36*

Ungnad, *Babylonische Briefe*
116 *31*
117 *38*
258 *32*
259 *29*

VAS
7 16 *35*
7 196 *25*
7 201 *32*
7 202 *29*
8 4–5 *18*
8 15 *32*
8 26 *27*
8 37 *32*
8 62 *22*
8 73 *16*
8 123–24 *14*
8 127 *15*
16 9 *33*
16 32 *31*
16 136 *37*

Waterman, *Bus.Doc.*
no. 32 *37*

YOS 10
1 *37*
4:1–8 *26*
5 *38*
6:3–6 *28*
9:4–6 *31*
9:13–14 *22*
9:21–23 *22*
11 i 1–2 *28*
11 i 3–4 *24*
11 i 14–17 *24*
11 i 23–27 *37*
11 ii 1–2 *31*
11 ii 3–6 *23*
11 ii 7–9 *35*
11 ii 14–17 *23*
11 ii 18–19 *38*
11 ii 20–23 *25*
11 ii 24–26 *25*
11 ii 27–30 *38*
11 ii 33 – iii 2 *28*
11 iii 3–12 *28*
11 iii 25–26 *34*
11 iii 27–30 *35*
11 iv 16–18 *23*
11 iv 21–23 *32*
11 v 1–2 *24*
11 v 12–13 *26*
12:4–5 *32*
14:8–9 *30*
15:17–19 *33*
17:9 *37*
17:27 *30*
17:38 *37*
20:9 *38*
21:4 *30*
23:5–7 *30*
23:8 *33*
23:9 *30*
24:2 *34*
24:21 *38*
24:29 *25*
24:30 *30*
25:25 *29*

YOS 10 (continued)
25:28 *33*
25:64 *38*
25:72 *36*
26 i 8 *27*
26 iii 28–29 *35*
31 i 1–4 *23*
31 i 12–17 *32*
31 i 32–40 *28*
31 ii 1–12 *22*
31 ii 13–15 *23*
31 ii 24–30 *23*
31 ii 31–37 *23*
31 ii 42–47 *23*
31 ii 48–55 *24*
31 iii 6–12 *26*
31 iii 45–54 *32*
31 iv 7–11 *26*
31 iv 19–24 *23*
31 iv 39–44 *34*
31 iv 45–50 *23*
31 v 13–17 *29*
31 v 37–39 *22*
31 viii 7–10 *33*
31 viii 17–17 *31*
31 viii 30–37 *23*
31 ix 28–35 *23*
31 ix 45–53 *37*
31 x 21–25 *22*
31 x 34–39 *28*
31 x 41–44 *33*
31 xi 22–25 *22*
31 xi 30–36 *28*
31 xi 43–47 *23*
31 xii 14–19 *31*
31 xii 27–35 *30*
31 xiii 36–41 *37*
33 ii 28–30 *33*
33 ii 35–38 *36*
36 i 21 *38*
36 iii 28 *37*
36 iv 8–9 *36*
36 iv 10–11 *34*
41:30 *30*
41:55–56 *34*
42 i 54–55 *22*
42 iv 21–23 *30*
44:16–17 *38*
44:19 *27*
44:69 *30*
46 iv 19–22 *33*
46 iv 30–31 *29*
47:6–7 *36*
47:9 *25*
50:8 *33*
51 ii 27–28 *29*
51 iv 15–18 *34*
52 i 3–5 *37*
52 iii 1–3 *36*
53:8 *32*
56 i 6–7 *32*
56 i 10–11 *28*
56 i 18–20 *27*
56 i 23–25 *31*
56 i 28–30 *37*
56 i 31–33 *23*
56 i 34–35 *25*
56 ii 1–4 *31*
56 ii 11–13 *24*
56 ii 23–24 *23*
56 ii 31–34 *33*
56 ii 35–39 *23*
56 iii 3–5 *31*
56 iii 21–23 *27*

ZA
43 306–7 *38*

INDEX OF GRAMMATICAL FORMS AND SUBJECTS

Numbers refer to sections in the Lessons, unless otherwise specified.

ʾ, Writing of *21.4*
Absolute Form of the Noun *23.1*
Abstract Suffix *-ūt* *14.4*
Accent *1.3*
Accusative(s):
  Adverbial Use of *18.3*
  Double-Duty Objects *10.4*
  Verbs with Two *5.5*
"Active Stative" *33.2*
Adjective(s):
  Attributive Declension and Agreement *4.2*, *Paradigm 5*
  Demonstrative *6.3*
  Denominative *6.2*
  Indefinite *14.3*
  Independent Possessive *25.3*, *Paradigm 3*
  Substantivization *4.4*
  Verbal (G) *4.3*
Adverbial Use of the Accusative *18.3*
Adverbs *28.4*
Agreement in Verbal Clauses *3.6*
Akkadian dialects *Introduction*
Akkadian Language *Introduction*
Akkadian Poetry *33.3*
aleph, Writing of *21.4*
alākum, G *8.1* (Infin., Pret., Vbl. Adj.); *13.1* (Dur.); *18.1* (Perf.)
-ān (Particularizing Suffix) *20.2*
Apposition *11.2*
Assimilation of *n* *5.1*
Assyrian Grammar, Major Features *Appendix E*
Asyndeton *7.5*
Attributive Form of Adjective *Paradigm 5*

b › *m* before *-ma* *7.4*
babālum *10.2*
Bound Form of the Noun *8.3*, *Paradigm 6*

Casus Pendens *21.5*
Clauses:
  Asyndeton *7.5*
  Conditional Sentences *17.3*
  Coordination *7.4, 7.5*
  Interrogative Sentences *35.3*
  Negation *20.4*
  Relative *19.3*
  Subordinate *26.2*
  Topicalization by Preposing 21.5
  Verbal Hendiadys *14.5*
  Verbal: Agreement *3.6*
  Verbal: Word Order *3.6*
  Verbless *2.5*
  Verbless, Injunctions in *22.2*
Commands and Wishes, Negative *16.3*
Comparative and Superlative, Expression of *27.3*
Compound Noun Phrases *12.4*
Conditional Sentences *17.3*
Consonant Loss, Vowel Changes due to *6.1*
Contracts *13.5*
Coordination *7.4, 7.5*
Coordinators (*-ma, u, ū (lū)*) *7.4*

D Stem: Meaning *24.3*
Dating, Systems of *Appendix A*
Declension of Nouns *2.1*, *Paradigm 4a*
Demonstrative Adjectives and Pronouns *6.3*
Denominative Adjectives *6.2*
Derived Stems, Sigla in the Main Dictionaries *Before Paradigm 7*
Derived Verbs *24.1*
Determinative Pronoun *ša* *2.3*
Determinatives *13.3*
Dialects of Akkadian *Introduction*
Dictionaries *Introduction*
Direct Speech *15.4*

Double-Duty Objects *10.4*
Doubly Weak Verbs *21.3, Parad. 14*
Dt Stem *35.1*
Dtn Stem *35.2*
Durative, Meaning of *12.2*

E–type Verbs *21.2*
edûm *26.1*
Epics *38.4*

Feminine Marker *t*, Sound Changes before *5.4*
Final-weak Nouns *Paradigm 4b*

G Stem: Summary of *21.1*
Geminate Verbs, Special Features *38.2*
Genitive *8.2*
Genitive: Constructions and Functions *31.3*
Genres *Introduction*
  Contracts *13.5*
  Epics *38.4*
  Laws *17.4*
  Letters *24.5*
  Mari Letters *29.4*
  Myths *38.4*
  Omens *22.3*
  Royal Inscriptions *30.3*
Gt Stem *33.1*
Gtn Stem *34.1*

Ḫammurapi, Laws of *17.4*
Hendiadys, Verbal *14.5*
Hymns and Prayers *33.4*

Imperative, G *16.1*
ina, Partitive Use of *34.2*
Indefinite or Unspecified Subject *15.3*
Indefinite Pronouns and Indefinite Adjective *14.3*
Independent Personal Pronouns *2.4, 25.2*
Independent Possessive Adjectives *25.3, Paradigm 3*
Infinitive, Syntax of *30.1*
Infinitive: Form (G) and Meaning *3.3*
Injunctions in Verbless Clauses *22.2*
Injunctive Forms, Use of to Express
  Purpose *16.4*
Interrogative Sentences *35.3*
Interrogative Words *14.2*
Irregular Masculine Plurals *20.3*
-iš (Terminative-adverbial Ending) *28.2*
išûm *26.1*
izuzzum *37.2*

kalûm *11.3*

Late OB Texts, Features of *24.4*
Laws of Ḫammurapi *17.4*
Letters *24.5*
Letters from Mari *29.4*
Literary Diction *30.2*
Loanwords, Sumerian *32.3*
Locative-adverbial Ending *-um* *28.3*
Logograms *13.2*
lū *29.3*

-ma *7.4, 29.2*
Mari, Letters from *29.4*
Measures *Appendix B*
Morphographemic Writings *18.4*
Myths and Epics *38.4*

N Stem, Meaning of *31.2*
Negation *20.4*
Negative Adverb *ul(a)* *4.5*
Negative Commands/Wishes *16.3*
Non-coordinating *-ma* *29.2*
Noun(s):
  Absolute Form *23.1*
  Basic Declension *Paradigm 4a*
  Bound Form *8.3, Paradigm 6*
  Declension *2.1, Paradigm 4a*
  Final-weak Forms *Paradigm 4b*
  Irregular Masculine Plurals *20.3*
  Locative-adverbial Ending *-um* *28.3*
  Particularizing Suffix *-ān* *20.2*
  Patterns *32.2*
  Phrases, Compound *12.4*
  Suffixal Form *11.1, Paradigm 6*
  Terminative-adverbial Ending *-iš* *28.2*
Nt Stem *38.3*
Ntn Stem *37.1*
Numbers *23.2*

Oaths *36.3*
Object Pronominal Suffixes on the Verb *18.2, Paradigm 17*
Objects, Double-Duty *10.4*
Old Babylonian *Introduction*
Omen Texts *22.3*

parsāku, Transitive *33.2*
Participle (G) *20.1*
Particularizing Suffix -*ān* *20.2*
Partitive Use of *ina* *34.2*
Patterns of Nouns *32.2*
Perfect: Meaning of *17.2*
Personal Names *13.4*
Personal Pronouns, Independent *2.4, 25.2, Paradigm 1*
Personal Pronouns, Suffixes on Nouns, Prepositions, Verbs *Paradigm 1*
Phonology:
- *a* › *e* *7.2*
- Assimilation of *n* *5.1*
- Assimilation of -*t*- infix *17.1(a)*
- *b* › *m* before -*ma* *7.4*
- dental/sibilant + pron. -*š*- › -*ss*- *11.1(c)*
- Feminine Marker *t*, Sound Changes before *5.4*
- Historical *Appendix C*
- *i* › *e* *7.1*
- Syncope *4.1*
- Vowel Changes due to Consonant Loss *6.1*
- Vowel Harmony (*a* › *e*) *7.2*

Plurals, Irregular Masculine *20.3*
Poetry, Akkadian *33.3*
Possessive Adjectives, Independent *25.3, Paradigm 3*
Prayers *33.4*
Precative *16.2*
Predicative Construction *22.1*
Preposing, Topicalization by *21.5*
Prepositional Phrases *12.3*
Prepositions *2.2*
Prepositions with Verbs *5.6*
Prepositions, Pronominal Suffixes on *10.3*
Prepositions: Partitive Use of *ina* *34.2*
Preterite (G): Form and Meaning *3.5*
Prohibitive *16.3*
Pronominal Suffixes:
- on Nouns *11.1, Paradigm 2*
- on Prepositions *10.3, Paradigm 2*
- on Verbs *18.2, Paradigms 2, 17*

Pronoun(s):
- Determinative (*ša*) *2.3*
- Demonstrative *6.3*
- Indefinite *14.3*
- Independent Personal *2.4, 25.2*

Purpose Clauses: Injunctive Forms Used for *16.4*

Quadriradical Verbs *38.1, Paradigm 15*
Quantifier *kalûm* *11.3*

R Stem *38.3*
Rare Stems (ŠD; Nt; R; others) *38.3*
Relative Clauses *19.3*
Research Tools *Introduction*
Root, Semantic *3.1*
Royal Inscriptions *30.3*

Semantic Root *3.1*
Semantics of Verbs *3.4*
Sentences: *see Clauses*
Signs *9.2, 13.2, Sign List*
Sound Change *i* › *e* *7.1*
Sound Changes before the Feminine Marker *t* *5.4*
Sounds of Akkadian *1.1*
Speech, Direct *15.4*
Standard Babylonian Grammar *Appendix D*
"Stative, Active" *33.2*
"Stative" Construction *22.1*
Stress (Accent) *1.3*
Subject, Indefinite *15.3*
Subject, Unspecified *15.3*
Subjunctive Marker (-*u*) *19.2*
Subordinate Clauses *26.2*
Subordination Marker (-*u*) *19.2*
Substantivization (of Adjectives) *4.4*
Suffixal Form of Noun *Paradigm 6*
Suffixes, Pronominal *10.3* (on Prepositions), *11.1* (on Nouns), *18.2* (on Verbs), *Paradigm 2* (all)
Sumerian, Akkadian and *Introduction*

Sumerian Loanwords *32.3*
Superlative, Expression of *27.3*
Syllabification *1.2*
Syncope *4.1*
Š Stem, Meaning of *27.2*
ŠD Stem *38.3*
Št Stems *36.1*
Štn Stem *36.2*

Terminative-adverbial *-iš* *28.2*
Text Genres *see Genres*
Topicalization by Preposing *21.5*
Transitive *parsāku* Construction *33.2*

u *7.4*
ū (lū) *7.4*
ul(a) *4.5*
-um (Locative-adverbial) *28.3*
Unspecified Subject *15.3*
-ūt (Abstract Suffix) *14.4*

Ventive *15.2, Paradigm 16*
Verb(s):
- Adjective, Verbal *4.3*
- Derived *24.1*
- Durative, Meaning *12.2*
- *E*–type *21.2*
- Imperative *16.1*
- Infinitive, Meaning and Syntax *30.1*
- Morphology: Introductory Considerations *3.2*
- *Paradigms 7–15*

Verb(s) (continued):
- Participle *20.1*
- Perfect, Meaning *17.2*
- Precative *16.2*
- Prepositions with *5.6*
- Preterite, Meaning *3.5*
- Prohibitive *16.3*
- Pronominal Suffixes on *18.2, Paradigm 17*
- Semantics *3.4*
- Stems:
  - G *3.2, 21.1*
  - Gt *33.1*
  - Gtn *34.1*
  - D *24.2,3*
  - Dt *35.1*
  - Dtn *35.2*
  - N *31.1,2*
  - Š *27.1,2*
  - Št *36.1*
  - Štn *36.2*
  - ŠD *38.3*
  - rare stems *38.3*
- Two Accusatives *5.5*
- Verbal Adjective *4.3*
- Verbal Hendiadys *14.5*
- Vetitive *16.3*
- Weak *5.2*

Sound Verbs:
- Stem Forms *Paradigm 7a*
- Finite Forms *Paradigm 7b*
- Non-Finite Forms *Parad. 7c*
- G Preterite *3.5*
- G Durative *12.1*
- G Perfect *17.1*
- Gt Stem *33.1*
- Gtn Stem *34.1*
- D Stem *24.2*
- Dt Stem *35.1*
- Dtn Stem *35.2*
- N Stem *31.1*
- Š Stem *27.1*
- Št Stems *36.1*
- Štn Stem *36.2*
- ŠD Stem *38.3*

Verbs I–ʾ (I–*a* and I–*e*; *alākum*):
- *Paradigms 8a, 8b, 9a, 9b*
- G Durative *13.1*
- G Infinitive, Preterite, Verbal Adjective *8.1*
- G Perfect *18.1*
- D Stem *25.1*
- N Stem *32.1*
- Š Stem *28.1*

Verbs I–*n*:
- *Paradigms 10a, 10b*
- G Durative 12.1
- G Infinitive, Preterite, Verbal Adjective *5.3*
- G Perfect *17.1*
- D Stem *24.2*
- N Stem *31.1*
- Š Stem *27.1*

Verbs I–*w*:
- *Paradigms 11a, 11b*
- G Durative *15.1*
- G Infinitive, Preterite, Verbal Adjective *10.1*
- G Perfect *19.1*
- D Stem *25.1*

N Stem *32.1*
Š Stem *28.1*
Verbs II–weak:
Paradigms 12a, 12b
G Durative *14.1*
G Infinitive, Preterite, Verbal Adjective *9.1*
G Perfect *19.1*
D and Š Stems *29.1*
N Stem *32.1*
Verbs III–weak:
Paradigms 13a–13g
G Stem *Paradigms 13b, 13c*
G Durative *12.1*
G Infinitive, Preterite, Verbal Adjective *7.3*
G Perfect *17.1*
Stem Forms *Paradigm 13a*
D Stem *24.2, Parad. 13f, 13g*
Š Stem *27.1, Parad. 13f, 13g*
N Stem *31.1, Parad. 13d, 13e*
Verbs Doubly Weak *21.3*
Verbless Clauses, Injunctions in *22.2*
Verbless Sentences *2.5*
Vetitive *16.3*
Vocative *23.3*
Vowel Changes due to Consonant Loss *6.1*
Vowel Harmony (*a* › *e*) *7.2*
Vowel Harmony, Assyrian *Appendix E, 1c*
Vowel Syncope *4.1*

Weak Verbs *5.2*
Weak Verbs: Doubly Weak *21.3*
Word Order in Verbal Clauses *3.6*
Writing of ᵓ *21.4*
Writing System:
Determinatives *13.3*
General *9.2*
Logograms *13.2*
Morphographemic Writings *18.4*
Writing of ᵓ *21.4*
see also *Sign List*

Corrections to Huehnergard, *Grammar of Akkadian*, 2nd ed. (2005)

49 §7.4: (a) *-ma* normally connects clauses with verbs of the same mood (i.e., indicative or injunctive), whereas *u* has no such restriction.

67 §9.1, introductory paragraph:

Verbs II–weak originally had as their second radical *w*, *y*, or one of the Proto-Semitic *aleph*s that were lost in Akkadian (§6.1).

89 §11.1(d)(ii), seventh pair of examples:

rabûtūya 'my nobles (i.e., great ones)' (nom.); *rabûtīya* 'my nobles (i.e., great ones)' (gen.-acc.);

143 §16.1(b) line "ms":

ms *bini (biniam)* *ḫudu (ḫudâm)* *mila (milâm)* *šeme (šemeam)*

209 §21.4, third line: insert the sign .

261 Vocabulary 24, Nouns, *appum*: insert log. KIR(I)$_4$ (the KA sign).

284 §26.2(a), chart:

	Main Clause Action in **Past**; Tense of Temporal Clause:	Main Clause Action in **Present or Future** Tense of Temporal Clause:
(1) *inūma, ūm, ištu, kīma, warki, adi*	Preterite	Perfect: explicit anteriority Durative: unmarked
(2) *adi ... lā*	—	Preterite: explicit anteriority Durative: unmarked
(3) *lāma*	Durative	Preterite: real, immediate Durative: potential, indefinite

384, first line: §176 (For §175 see lesson 20): *ù šum-ma* ÌR É.GAL *ù lu* ÌR

607, b, 2nd last column, Dual g.–a.: for *bārân* read *bāriān*.

611, 616: The headers "Infinitive, Durative, ... , Vbl. Adj." should be moved one column to the right.

624: The header "Infinitive" should be moved one column to the right.

In the row "D" the forms *kūn*/*kunn-* should appear under "Vbl.Adj."